THE LETTERS OF THEODORE ROOSEVELT

VOLUME VI

The Big Stick

1907—1909

THE LETTERS OF
Theodore Roosevelt

SELECTED AND EDITED BY
ELTING E. MORISON

JOHN M. BLUM
Associate Editor

ALFRED D. CHANDLER, JR.
Assistant Editor

SYLVIA RICE
Copy Editor

Harvard University Press
Cambridge, Massachusetts
1952

Contents

Illustrations and Charts

"To Restore Confidence,"
continued
December 1907–January 1908

SYMBOLS

⟨ ⟩   Single angle brackets indicate material crossed out but decipherable.

« »   French quotation marks indicate editorial interpretations of illegible words.

[ ]   Square brackets indicate editorial interpolations.

. . .   Three dots indicate a missing word.

. . . .   Four dots indicate two or more missing words.

0   A superior zero placed after the manuscript source indicates that the entire letter is in Roosevelt's handwriting.

A, B, C, . . .   A small capital, A, B, C, etc., placed after a letter number indicates that that letter was acquired and inserted after the original manuscript had gone to press.

Washington, December 13, 1907

My dear Mr. Cortelyou: I regard it as most fortunate that you are going to be able to send a complete and full statement to the Senate Committee as to your actions in meeting the panic. It is a matter of such importance that I should much like to look over your statement before you transmit it to the Senate.[1] *Sincerely yours*

4528 · TO FRANCIS EMROY WARREN   *Roosevelt Mss.*

Private   Washington, December 15, 1907

My dear Senator Warren: After our conversation of yesterday I saw General Crozier and have gone over the letter and enclosures which he submitted to the Acting Secretary of War on December 7th, and which I suppose you have. These enclosures completely knock the bottom out of this antimony business.[1] Whatever the analysis of the Union Metallic Company bullets which are available may show, we now have positive knowledge contained in the report of Colonel Frank Heath of the Ordnance Department, commanding the Frankfort Arsenal (see his report dated February 7, 1906). This shows that the Union Metallic Cartridge Company did use antimony in some of the bullets sampled in their model of 1903 cartridges furnished on their contract of 1905, these being therefore in some of the cartridges which were used by the troops of the army at the time of the Brownsville incident. The test of these bullets which showed antimony therein was on January 26, 1906. The official report says that these union metallic cartridges had from one and a half to three per cent of antimony in the bullets. It therefore appears from the official papers of the Department that analysis of the union metallic bullets made January, 1906, only seven months before the shooting at Brownsville occurred, the bullets being some of those issued to all the army during those seven months, contained antimony. The majority of the cartridges picked up at Brownsville were of the date of December, 1905, that is they were of the date just one month prior to the making of this analysis in January, 1906, and they were of the same manufacture, the Union Metallic Cartridge Company. In other words, it is clearly established that some, and

---

[1] This report, submitted on January 29, 1908, remains one of the most cogent summaries of the panic.

---

[1] Two of seven bullets picked out of the walls of houses at the scene of the Brownsville riot had contained antimony. Maintaining that the ammunition issued the Negro troops was composed of one part tin, thirty-six parts lead, and no antimony, Foraker argued that the composition of the two bullets demonstrated the innocence of the troops. Roosevelt's rebuttal helped Warren present the case of the majority of the Senate investigating committee which concluded that the President's policy had been justified.

it is perfectly possible that all, of the bullets of the Union Metallic Cartridge Company used by the army at the time of this occurrence contained antimony, just as the analysis showed to be the case with respect to these bullets.

There is not a shred left of the argument that Senator Foraker predicated on the finding of antimony in these bullets. *Sincerely yours*

4529 · TO JOHN SPARKS   *Roosevelt Mss.*

Telegram   Washington, December 17, 1907

I sent the troops at your request because from the tenor of your telegrams and from the representations made me by the two Senators from Nevada and the member of the Lower House of Congress from Nevada it appeared that an insurrection was imminent against which the State authorities would be powerless. The troops have now been in Goldfield ten days and no insurrection has occurred, and seemingly no circumstances exist to justify your now calling on me for action by the troops under the provision of the Constitution. The troops were sent to Goldfield to be ready to meet a grave emergency which seemed likely at once to arise, and not to provide a substitute for the exercise by the State of its police function. I do not feel at liberty to leave them indefinitely under such circumstances that they will in effect be performing on the part of the United States those ordinary duties of maintaining public order in the State of Nevada which rest upon the State Government. As the legislature of Nevada has not been convened I am bound to assume that the powers already vested in the peace officers of the State are adequate and that if they choose to do so they can maintain order themselves. Under these circumstances, unless there be forthwith further cause shown to justify keeping the troops at Goldfield, I shall direct that they return to their former stations.

4530 · TO FREDERIC HARRISON   *Roosevelt Mss.*

Washington, December 18, 1907

My dear Mr. Harrison: I am sure that any President would be pleased to receive such a letter as you have written, coming from so distinguished a man of letters who is also a man of the moralities — to use a sentence that seems about a century and a quarter out of date. My dear sir, you touch upon something that has puzzled me not a little. On the one hand I freely confess that I hate for personal reasons to get out of the fight here and that I have the uncomfortable feeling that I may possibly be shirking a duty. On the other hand, it is the business of every practical statesman to reckon with the temper of the people to whom he owes his position, and he can accomplish nothing worth accomplishing if he does not retain their confidence in his integrity and disinterestedness. Now there are some peoples who have grown, by training, to accept the position that the longer a man remains at the head of public affairs the more useful he is, and who do not feel the fear — very possibly the vain fear — that he will intrench himself in power against their wishes as a sequence to staying in power in accordance with their wishes. But there are other peoples who do not accept this point of view; who fear lest a President too long kept in power might do as has been done in more than one Spanish-American Republic, as was done in France at the close of the second Republic, and gradually establish what is in fact a dictatorship under the form of popular government. No matter whether these fears are just or not, no matter whether the beliefs of these peoples on this point are with or without warrant, a man who tries to serve them can do so only by frankly reckoning with this mental attitude.

Moreover, in my case remember that I had embarked on a course of action which has peculiar attractions for the demagog, for the man who hopes to raise himself to high political position by posing as the incorruptible foe of the great and the wealthy. The man who in public life consciously or unconsciously panders to the great and the wealthy when they are wrong receives his reward in ways wholly alien to popular favor, and this man is under no temptations to follow a course such as I followed. But the demagog — and by demagog I mean not demagog in the old Greek sense, but in the modern and sinister sense, the man who panders to the prejudices of, and excites what is base and evil in, the people, just as the typical courtier does in dealing with a monarch — foregoes all possible advantage to be obtained by the first type of evil public servant and counts for his reward for the evil which he does on popular favor and the offices which result from popular favor. Now, I believe that if I have rendered or can render any service at all to the American people it is because of their belief in my disinterestedness and sincerity. This sounds as if I were talking like a prig, or at least with an unpleasantly priggish self-consciousness; and perhaps I am; but I do not know how else to express my meaning, which is that whatever of value in the way of service I can render my country is conditioned upon their believing that it is not rendered with an eye to my personal well-being. I think that to show them that they are justified in this belief as to my character is probably as important a service as I can render; in other words, whether or not I think that I have certain peculiar advantages of position and temperament which would enable me to continue to render service to the people, it yet remains true that taking into account their inherited mental attitude on the subject of the long continuance of a President in place, I can render them the best service by showing that in what I have done I have been actuated, not by self-interest, but by devotion to a high ideal together with the firm purpose to try measurably to realize that ideal in practical fashion.

Do you recollect my once speaking to you about the Mongol conquest of eastern Europe, anent your essay on the 13th century? I wish you would look at Curtin's book on the Mongols which is just out.[1] I know your studies have dealt chiefly with Latin Europe; but that world outburst of the Mongols was so phenomenal that it is worth your while glancing at the first readable book in English which has told the story.

Again thanking you, my dear sir, I am, *Sincerely yours*

P.S. One of the chief things I have tried to preach to the American politician, and the American businessman, is not to grasp at money, place, power, or enjoyment in any form, simply because he can probably get it, without regard to considerations of morality and national interest — which means the interest of the neighbor, for the nation is simply all of our neighbors combined. Now, when I am preaching this and striving to lead the forces of decency in a sane but resolute effort to put a stop to greed, selfishness, arrogance and hatred, I am bound in honor so to conduct myself as not to give good people cause to doubt whether I am not myself actuated by the same kind of self-interested motives and disregard of the higher and finer ethical considerations which I denounce in others.

4531 · TO JOHN SPARKS   *Roosevelt Mss.*

Telegram   Washington, December 20, 1907

I have received no answer from you to my telegram of December seventeenth in which I said that unless there was forthwith further cause shown to justify keeping the troops at Goldfield I should direct their return to their former stations. I am informed by the three representatives of the Department of Commerce and Labor who are in Goldfield by my order that you have stated to them in writing that you will not convene the legislature to consider call for troops nor take the necessary steps to form a State military force. Their report further satisfies me that there is no disturbance threatened which the Government of Nevada ought not to be able to control if it starts to work with a serious purpose to do so, but that no effort is being made by the Government of Nevada to take the steps necessary in the matter. I stand ready to see that the national Government does its full constitutional duty in the matter of preserving order, but this readiness on the part of the National Government does not excuse the State Government for failure to perform its full duty in the first place. Federal aid should not be sought for by the State as an ⟨excuse⟩ method of relieving itself from the performance of this duty, and the state should not be permitted to substitute the Government of the United States for the government of the State in the ordinary duties of maintaining order within the State. For the reasons given in this and my former telegram I have accordingly directed the troops to return to their former stations on Monday, December thirtieth next.

[1] Roosevelt had written an introduction to Jeremiah Curtin's *The Mongols; A History*. Curtin died before the book was published.

Washington, December 21, 1907

Dear Cecil: As usual Mrs. Roosevelt and I were equally pleased and interested with your letter. You speak as if you were to have a little holiday from official life. Cannot you take advantage of it to bring your wife over and spend a few days with us at The White House? Not so very much time remains now, and I do wish we could see you both here. Do not leave the diplomatic service unless you have to. You have worked thru the years of mere drudgery. You have made your reputation. You are at the very time of life when your training and experience will enable you to do your best; and even if the harness galls a little, you will be happier doing steady trace-and-collar work. If you have to get out, well and good. You have done honorably; you have won your spurs, and it is all right. But if you can go on, by all means go on. My own case is peculiar, for I am not very clear that there will be anything possible for me to do after a year from the next fourth of March. But we are all on the knees of the Gods and must await events; tho when the opportunity comes we can improve it, and, indeed, can to a certain extent make it.

I do very much wish to talk with you over some of the questions which you raise which I can hardly discuss at length in a letter. Fundamentally my philosophy is yours, tho not so pessimistic. I do not think we know enough about the future to be able to say with certainty how great any given danger is. The things we dread do not occur, and evils which no human being had foreseen or could have foreseen loom portentous. We may have a race conflict such as you dread in the Pacific, but I hope not; and therefore I hope that the ten-year limit that you set is altogether too short. I very much wish that Australia would either encourage European immigration or would see a higher birth rate among its own citizens. It is not pleasant to realize how slowly the scanty population of that island continent increases. But as long as Great Britain retains her naval superiority and Australia is part of the British Empire Australia is safe. On our own Pacific coast British Columbia feels exactly as our Pacific Coast States feel. Both the United States and Canada are increasing so much in population that it is hard to imagine an ethnic conquest by a yellow race here on the mainland; but of course national folly on the part of the United States, both in permitting outrages against the Japanese and in declining to keep the navy up to the highest point of efficiency, might result in a bitterly humiliating and disastrous war which would turn over not only the Philippines but Hawaii to Japan. I do not anticipate any such war, and I think I am taking the best possible measures to prevent it and to get the two races or nations on a footing which will permit a policy of permanent friendliness or at least mutual toleration. Here again all we can say is that the future is dim before our eyes. With the voyages of Columbus and Vasco da Gama, the invention of printing, and the Reformation, began the great modern movement of spreading European civilization and its influences over the whole world, just as at one time the Greek civilization spread so largely over the Mediterranean world. Tho checked here and there, and while one European race after another has fallen back, the movement as a whole has gone on for four centuries, with as one side of it the spread of the European peoples and their influence over Asia, Africa, America and Australia, with as the other side, the development within their own limits of a highly complex, highly efficient, but luxurious and in some respects enervating and demoralizing, industrial civilization. There is as yet no sign of the movement as a whole being arrested. Industrial inventiveness of all kinds and the exploitation of the world's resources go on with increasing rapidity. Our children and our children's children will see the mechanical agents of this civilization working with an ever increasing strength and effectiveness. Gyroscope trains may cross these continents in a day; we may see airships; we may see all kinds of things; on the other hand the century that has opened may in all probability see something like a timber famine and also the approaching exhaustion of the iron fields. Even the coal itself cannot last for many centuries. What will come after? Will substitutes be found? Will a simpler and saner civilization, really better, succeed our own; or will it be overwhelmed by barbarism from within or without? No one can tell. It matters very little whether we are optimists or pessimists. Our duty is to do our work well and abide the event.

As regards myself, I am at the moment having rather more than my usual share of difficulties. The panic is bad and it has produced great depression in business, with, as a consequence, laborers thrown out of employment, farmers suffering, and an unhealthy stagnation everywhere. Inevitably and naturally ignorant good men, under the lead of men who are neither ignorant nor good, tend to hold me responsible for this condition. As a matter of fact, it is in part the kind of reaction that comes under any circumstances; it is in part due to unhealthy and dishonest methods in the field of speculative high finance; and my own share is limited to having exposed abuses and therefore to bringing on the crisis a little quicker than it otherwise would have come, but making it less severe. In large part, however, the movement is world-wide. You have with great acuteness stated in your letter the exact fact about the newspapers and any movement on behalf of the fundamental rights of the people as a whole, such as that in which I think I may fairly say I have taken a considerable part. The movement itself will in the end succeed, but the man who leads it must necessarily fail or seem to fail for the time being. All I am fighting for, in the last analysis, is honest methods in business and in politics, and justice alike for (and on to) capitalist and working man. I have never hesitated to oppose labor unions when I thought them wrong, any more than to oppose corporations when I thought them wrong. I am certain that if our Republic is to endure on a healthy basis, it must proceed along the course I have outlined. But the thing that astonishes me is not that I should now be attacked, but that I should have been triumphant for so long a period, for I have awakened the bitter antagonism of very powerful men and very powerful interests whose memory is as long as the memory of the public at large is short, and their attacks on me thru the papers which they subsidize (and these are the big papers of the biggest industrial centers) never cease for a moment. They misrepresent everything I say or do; the wonder is that anyone should have any belief in me at all. But it is all in the day's work. I have had an uncommonly good run for my money; I have been treated mighty well and favored by fortune above my deserts; and whatever comes in the future, I am ahead of the game.

It certainly is curious how the great racial questions are looming up. I was glad to see your agreement with Russia; but of course we are all perfectly ignorant of what Russia's future will be. As for the governing class in England having no real foreign policy, of course our people tend to have even less, and the melancholy fact is that the capitalist and educated classes are those least to be trusted in this matter. It is, as you say, a melancholy fact that the countries which are most humanitarian, which are most interested in internal improvement, tend to grow weaker compared with the other countries which possess a less altruistic civilization. The great countries with strong central government and military instincts do tend to be the dominant ones; and I have fought, not very successfully, to make our people understand that unless freedom shows itself compatible with military strength, with national efficiency, it will ultimately have to go to the wall. For your sins I send you a copy of my message and ask you to look at what I say about the army and navy, pages 45 to 55. It is astounding to see how short-sighted many people in your country and mine and even in France are where war is concerned. Carnegie represents the most objectionable class of these peace advocates. He represents those people who in crude and foolish fashion have imbibed Tolstoi's foolish theory that good men should never make war because, forsooth, when bad men are stronger than good men they make war in evil fashion, and who add a peculiar baseness to this view by championing an industrialism which wrecks far more lives than any ordinary war. The country that loses the capacity to hold its own in actual warfare with other nations, will ultimately show that it has lost everything. I abhor and despise that pseudo-humanitarianism which treats advance in civilization as necessarily and rightfully implying a weakening of the fighting spirit and which therefore invites destruction of the advanced civilization by some less-advanced type.

Good-by, Springy; and do bring Mrs. Springy over to see us sometime this year. *Ever yours*

Washington, December 21, 1907

My dear Mr. Watson: Your letter deeply touches me, and the concluding paragraph gave me grave concern. It is of very little consequence what becomes of me or of any other one man, but it is of very great consequence that the people — the plain people — in the country and city shall be relieved from suffering, from financial panic, and yet that this relief shall in no wise represent any backing down from our principles in the matter of corporation controls. I have more difficulty about dealing with the currency than with anything else, for I feel less sure of my ground in the matter, and at the moment I cannot answer you save by again expressing how touched I am, my dear sir, by your good opinion. I hope I shall not forfeit it. I shall certainly try not to deserve to forfeit it. *Sincerely yours*

P.S. It seems to me that the trouble about issuing greenbacks as you suggest is that it is like a man temporarily relieving himself by issuing notes of indebtedness. He can do it with safety if he exercises severe self-control; but a government will not permanently exercise such self-control. I have no doubt that $50,000,000 of greenbacks, if it was absolutely certain that no more would be issued, would achieve something of the purpose that you have in mind; but I also believe that most people would think that it foretold an indefinite issuance of greenbacks and that in consequence it would have a frightening effect.[1]

Personal   Washington, December 22, 1907

My dear Governor Kibbey: The enclosed explains itself. Mr. Sturges was not present at the last meeting of the National Committee, and I am informed that he sent his proxy to Senator Dick, who has joined Senator Foraker in his assault on the administration, one feature of this assault being the reduction of the number of delegates allowed each Territory.[1] I think Mr. Sturges'

[1] By authorizing the issue of $150,000,000 worth of government bonds, Roosevelt had made possible an increase of circulation three times as large as the one Watson was suggesting.

[1] W. S. Sturges, Republican national committeeman from Arizona, had given his proxy for the December meeting to Senator Dick, who, alone at that meeting, represented Foraker's interests. Because Taft had the votes of most territorial delegates, Dick, with the other opponents of Taft, voted to reduce the territorial representation at the national convention. The senator, however, not without whimsey joined the Taft men in voting for Kansas City as the convention site in 1908. Doubtless he expected that Chicago would, as it did, win that honor handily. For giving Dick his proxy Sturges offered no explanation, received no patronage.

position should be explained before I accept any of his recommendations. What do you think of Mr. Nichols?

With regard, believe me, *Sincerely yours*

4535 · TO CHARLES EDWARD MAGOON   *Roosevelt Mss.*

Washington, December 23, 1907

My dear Governor: I feel like an awful reprobate to grab what was to have been your Christmas present to Mrs. Roosevelt! But the fact is, my dear Governor, that the pitcher and basin are so very beautiful that I simply cannot bear not to give them to her myself; and after all, altho I shall have to make you permit me to pay for them (so please send me the amount I owe you), the major part of the gift, that is, the trouble in finding it and the taste in choosing it, cannot but be yours, and so you have simply put us *both* under an obligation. If I had not written you first I should not have the heart to take this course; but as I did write you first, and felt very proud of myself for having found out something that Mrs. Roosevelt really wanted, I shall ask you to let it remain on this basis. Remember that our obligation is as great to you as if I had followed the other course.

I thank you heartily for the cigars.

Wishing you a merry Christmas and many happy New Years, I am, *Faithfully yours*

4536 · TO CHARLES JOSEPH BONAPARTE   *Roosevelt Mss.*

Washington, December 23, 1907

My dear Mr. Attorney General: Is there no way by which the Government could interfere in regard to an injunction or contempt proceeding by a court which it regarded as being improper? Would it not be possible for us to get such a case before the Court of Appeals? It seems to me that if we thus acted on behalf of one or two labor organizations where we regarded the injunction as wrong, it would strengthen us when we regarded the injunction as right. I have in view Judge Gould's decision here in the District and Judge Dayton's decision in West Virginia.[1] *Sincerely yours*

[1] These decisions enjoined labor unions from using boycotts, which in the view of the courts constituted conspiracies in restraint of trade. This basis for an injunction was clearly one which Roosevelt had had in mind when in his annual message he had urged that "some way . . . be devised which will limit the abuse of injunctions and protect those rights which from time to time it unwarrantably invades" (*State Papers*, Nat. Ed. XV, 432). Before the Sundry Civil Act of June 1913, however, the abuse was not limited. See No. 4859.

Washington, December 24, 1907

To the Secretary of State: The enclosed letter of Colonel Goethals explains itself. As I understand it the State Department has already assumed what is obviously the only position we could assume, namely, that Panama has no jurisdiction whatever of any kind, sort or description over the waters thru which ships pass in entering the canal, and that we will not even discuss any proposition which does not concede that the ten-mile strip gives access to the great ocean highway, open to all nations, thru waters only under the control of the American Government.[1]

4538 · TO ARTHUR HAMILTON LEE   *Roosevelt Mss.*

Washington, December 26, 1907

My dear Lee: It was a great pleasure to receive your long and interesting letter, but I do wish you could come over here and give me a glimpse of you in person.

I do not need a rest and do not want one, and there is nothing I should like so well as to stay in the fight; but every public man if he is to do good work must understand the temper and convictions of the people for whom he works. Our people feel very strongly about a third term, and in dealing with them my chief asset of value is their belief in my disinterestedness and honesty. I would not for anything give them cause to alter this belief. Here in the United States, and I suppose in many other countries as well, there are always the twin opposite dangers to be feared — the Scylla of mob rule, and the Charybdis of subjection to a plutocracy. It does not help one to have avoided the reef on the right if shipwreck follows from striking on the reef to the left. Again and again in my public career I have had to make head against mob spirit, against the tendency of poor, ignorant and turbulent people who feel a rancorous jealousy and hatred of those who are better off. But during the last few years it has been the wealthy corruptionists of enormous fortune, and of enormous influence thru their agents of the press, pulpit, colleges and public life, with whom I have had to wage bitter war. In consequence, I find myself on many points at one with some of the demagogs, and

[1] Panama, challenging the right of the Central and South American Telegraph Company to lay a cable in Manzanillo Bay, had interpreted Article II of the Hay–Bunau–Varilla Treaty "in such a way as to deprive the United States of jurisdiction over the waters of Manzanillo Bay and over the waters affording entrance to the canal." Stating Roosevelt's view, and in accordance with Adee's official message to Panama of August 14, Bacon in January advised the Panamanian government that the United States considered that Panama had "no jurisdiction whatever, of any kind, over the waters through which ships must pass in entering the Panama Canal." For the exchange of messages on this issue, see *Foreign Relations*, 1908, pp. 677–680.

I feel it all the more important that I should make it evident that I am not following this course, so congenial to the demagogic temperament, from any unworthy motives. But as I say, I hate to get out of the fight, and I am fully awake to the fact that there is always something very real to be said against the leader who, from whatever motives, does leave the fight before it is finished. In this case I am certain that the arguments on one side are far outweighed by the arguments in favor of the course I have followed, however.

That the course which I have taken in dealing with the big corporations is the only course compatible with the real welfare of the Republic, I am certain. It has not caused the panic, but it may have brought it on a little sooner than otherwise and have accentuated it for the moment; but it was simply impossible to permit such wild speculation and gross corruption as existed to go on unchecked. At the worst it was an operation for appendicitis. The patient's life may depend upon the surgeon acting at once, but it is certain that the patient will have to stay in bed a few days no matter how successful the operation is. The *Sun, Harper's Weekly, Times, Evening Post*, and so forth, are owned or controlled by Wall Street. I do most seriously feel that this reactionary crowd may succeed in convincing the plain people that they had better go to Hearst or Bryan as long as the businessmen won't accept me or a man like me. To use the terminology of Continental politics, I am trying to keep the left center together.

I like the correspondents of the London *Times*. Of course if Taft succeeds me our foreign policy will go on absolutely unchanged. Indeed, I think this will be the case with almost any Republican. I do not think there will be any real outburst against Great Britain, even under a Democrat. Then the danger would be with Japan, and would come from the possibility of some foolish doctrinaire declining to control mob action against the Japanese, and at the same time declining to keep the navy in such shape that we could resist if attacked. In the Japanese matter our Pacific States and Australia and British Columbia feel exactly alike, and fundamentally their attitude is proper; but its manifestations are often exceedingly improper.

I am greatly interested in what you say of your own politics.

Now about your friend the great Hungarian portrait painter, Laszló.[1] It seems very churlish for me not to say "yes" out of hand, but you have no conception of the pressure there is upon me to have my picture painted and of the small amount of time at my disposal. Nevertheless, my dear fellow, I am very much touched at your wanting my picture for yourself and at your wanting to have it painted by a real genius. Will you let me see Laszló when he comes and find out just how long he will need? Give him a note of introduction to me.

With warm regards to Mrs. Lee, believe me, *Always your friend*

[1] Philip Alexius Laszló de Lombos, the painter of Edward VII, Wilhelm II, Roosevelt, Harding, and Mussolini.

En route to North Garden, Virginia, December 26, 1907

To the Editor of the Tribune,[1] Simply for the information of the paper and *not* for publication I wish to call your attention to your Editorial about Admiral Brownson headed "Honorable Retirement." I do not wonder that it is difficult to do good work in the navy when it is possible for a good paper to contain such an editorial as this. It is inexcusable for the writer, or for any sensible man, to condone Admiral Brownson's conduct; and really it is hard to use language in which to characterize the statement that it is safe to say that "the President respects Admiral Brownson's candor and courage." The facts are that Admiral Brownson has subordinated the interests of the service to a mental attitude which would discredit a spiteful school girl. The incident is not very important, but it is deeply discreditable to the Admiral; and it is simply incomprehensible to me how the *Tribune* could take the view it has taken about it, and could thereby put a premium upon a very silly but a possibly damaging act of bad temper and insubordination.[2]

Remember that the rightfulness or wrongfulness of the regulation against which the Admiral protested has nothing whatever to do with the case. Arguments can be made on both sides of the matter, altho, in my judgment, the weight of them is overwhelmingly on the side of the position of the Surgeon General; but if the Surgeon General, (had the decision been against him), had resigned, he would have been guilty; and Admiral Brownson is actually

[1] Hart Lyman, editor-in-chief of the New York *Tribune*, 1905–1912.

[2] Roosevelt's surprisingly heated references to the *Tribune's* mild and perfunctory editorial on Brownson's retirement probably reflect an anxiety as to the damaging effect the incident might have on his naval program; see No. 4549. They may also indicate an appreciation of the uncertainty of his position in protesting against the resignation of a top-ranking officer over matters of administrative policy rather than military command; see No. 4570.

Brownson, voicing the general view of the line officer, on December 24 had resigned from his post as Chief of the Bureau of Navigation rather than carry out a policy of placing a medical officer in command of a hospital ship. The controversy over this policy was an old one. A joint board of army and navy officers convened by Roosevelt in February 1906 to settle the question recommended that a hospital ship should be commanded by a medical officer with a civilian shipping master in charge of her navigation. When the Bureau of Navigation refused to accept this decision, the President and the Secretary of the Navy reviewed the case. Roosevelt in December 1906 approved Bonaparte's order embodying the board's recommendations. He agreed that in view of naval and military precedents and the noncombatant status of such ships, hospital ships should be treated as floating hospitals and that the medical officers who were responsible for carrying out their functions as hospitals must have complete command; see No. 4550.

The commissioning of the hospital ship *Relief*, which was to accompany the Great White Fleet, once again raised the question. Brownson, for reasons not made public, urged Roosevelt to rescind the earlier order. When Roosevelt refused, he resigned on the grounds that he no longer had the confidence either of the officers and men of the Navy or of his commander in chief. The controversy, besides bringing to public view a serious conflict within the service, so delayed the commissioning of the *Relief* that the fleet sailed for the Pacific without a hospital ship. Today, as in years past, line officers of the navy are in command of hospital ships.

guilty, not merely of a well-nigh inconceivable smallness and pettiness, but of a disloyalty to the navy and the Nation which it is unpardonable to excuse or condone. *Sincerely yours*

4540 · TO JOHN SPARKS   *Roosevelt Mss.*

Telegram   Charlottesville, Virginia, December 28, 1907

Your telegram December 26 is received. It, in effect, declares that you have failed to call the Legislature together because, in your judgment, the Legislature would not call upon the Government of the United States for the use of troops, altho in your opinion it ought to do so. The Constitution of the United States imposes, not upon you, but upon the Legislature if it can be convened, the duty of calling upon the Government of the United States to protect the State of Nevada against domestic violence. You now request me to use the armed forces of the United States in violation of the Constitution because in your judgment the Legislature would fail to perform its duty under the Constitution. The State Government certainly does not appear to have made any serious effort to do its duty by the effective enforcement of its police functions. I repeat again what I have already said to you several times, that under the circumstances now existing in the State of Nevada as made known to me, an application from the Legislature of the State is an essential condition to the indefinite continuance of the troops at Goldfield. Circumstances may change and if they do I will take whatever action the needs of the situation require so far as my constitutional powers permit. But the first need is that the State authorities should do their duty, and the first step towards this is the assembling of the Legislature. It is apparent from your telegram that the Legislature of Nevada can readily be convened. You have fixed the period of three weeks as the time necessary to convene and organize a special session. If within five days from the receipt of this telegram you shall have issued the necessary notice to convene the Legislature of Nevada, I shall continue the station of the troops at Goldfield during such period of three weeks.[1] If within the term of five days such notice has not been issued, the troops will be immediately returned to their former stations.

4541 · TO JOHN CRAWFORD ANDERSON   *Roosevelt Mss.*

Washington, December 30, 1907

My dear Judge Anderson:[1] If you will allow me to say so, you are a judge after my own heart! Of course the only effective action to regulate corporate abuses of the kind of which you speak must come from the Federal Government. But the obstacles are two-fold. In the first place, the railroads and

[1] The governor, after some delay, issued the order.

[1] John C. Anderson, Associate Justice of the Supreme Court of Alabama, 1904–1916.

the big corporations generally seek to prolong their period of imperfectly checked domination — until within the last few years there was practically no check at all. In the next place, a great many well-meaning but foolish people, in the North and West quite as much as in the South, play the game of the very beneficiaries of and actors in the corporate abuses which they are trying to regulate, because in their eagerness to get radical action and their belief that it can be more radical in certain States than the Nation will permit, they resent the Nation's doing anything, and spend their energies in getting on the statute books State laws which will be declared unconstitutional or else will amount to nothing, instead of helping to get national laws which really would amount to something.[2]

With great regard, *Sincerely yours*

4542 · TO WILLIAM HOWARD TAFT   *Roosevelt Mss.*

Confidential   Washington, December 31, 1907

Dear Will: The letter you enclose from Charlie does not call for any action as regards Capers, but as regards Bettmann.[1] I turned down the man Foraker asked for and I appointed the man Charlie and Vorys chose. If they cannot hold their own man, whom I appointed against Foraker's and Dick's protest, not a thing will be gained by any action against Capers. There never was a clearer-cut case than this. Neither Capers nor any other Washington official has anything to do with it. Bettmann is a Taft man, appointed at the request of the Taft managers, and I turned down the man recommended by both the Senators to appoint him. Now surely the Taft people must be able to control him, or else you and I are helpless in accepting any recommendation from them. What does Charlie mean when he says "We cannot allow Foraker to walk away with the federal offices in Cincinnati"? And how in the name of all that is sacred does Charlie propose to "let Foraker know that he is to keep his hands off of the federal officeholders," and how would this be a notice of the attitude of the Treasury Department, as Charlie supposes? Everything was done that by any possibility could be done, so far as the federal people here at Washington are concerned, when Bettmann was appointed on Charlie's

[2] At a special session held in November, the Alabama Legislature had passed a series of drastic laws intended to control the railroads and to make it as difficult as possible for them to obtain injunctions against state officials. Despite the wording of the laws, Judge Jones early in December issued injunctions restraining the state from enforcing nine of the new statutes. By the end of the year, the railroads, the state, and the federal court had returned to the impasse of the previous summer. The conflict was resolved when the Supreme Court, as Roosevelt had predicted, declared such laws unconstitutional. See *Outlook*, 87:834–835 (December 21, 1907), 88:802–803 (April 11, 1908); and Ripley, *Railroads, Rates and Regulation*, pp. 632–633.

[1] Roosevelt had nominated Bernhard Bettmann for collector of internal revenue at Cincinnati. Unconfirmed during the first session of the Sixtieth Congress, the nomination was renewed and confirmed at the following session. Bettmann, an influential Cincinnati Jew, was later a director of the First National Bank of that city and a minor essayist and poet.

suggestion. If he recommends a man who cannot be trusted, why that is all there is about it; but it is idle to propose to make the error good by suggesting impossible schemes of action against Foraker or vague and unreliable plans about the Treasury Department. As to Capers, let them get me some definite statements and not rumors.[2]

I thought your speech admirable. The *Sun* editorial this morning shows that in no way could you ever gain the support of that crowd. The hardest and most aggressive hitting is the way to reach them. *Ever yours*

4543 · TO LEO STANTON ROWE *Roosevelt Mss.*

Washington, December 31, 1907

My dear Dr. Rowe:[1] I have been deeply interested in going over with you the results of your trip thru South America, and the various plans which you have in mind for fostering closer intellectual relations between the northern and the southern sections of the continent. I deem it most important that in addition to the friendly relations existing between the governments of the American republics, close personal ties should be formed between the leaders of thought in these republics. Such personal relations strongly tend to destroy the foolish prejudices and misconceptions that arise out of lack of knowledge of one another. In this Western Hemisphere, each of our republics can both learn and teach when brought into touch with her sister republics.

I know of no agencies better adapted to the accomplishment of this great purpose than the universities of the American Continent. There are many economic, social and industrial problems — not to speak of others more purely scientific — that are distinctively American in character and continental in scope. Thru the co-operation of the students and investigators of our different nations the accumulated experience of this hemisphere can be brought to bear on these problems and their successful solution thereby rendered more probable. The community of thought and action thus aroused will also serve a larger patriotic service in binding together more and more closely all the peoples of this Western Hemisphere.

I heartily wish all success to this movement. *Sincerely yours*

[2] Rumor, particularly newspaper stories, had Capers working to line up Southern Republicans, now for a third term for Roosevelt, now for Cortelyou, now for Fairbanks, but never for Taft. Charles Taft, therefore, with other Taft supporters, attempted without success to persuade Roosevelt not to renew Capers' appointment. By convention time, Capers, secure in office, had become a useful Taft adherent.

[1] Leo S. Rowe, professor of political science at the University of Pennsylvania, authority on Latin American government, in 1901–1902 member of the Commission to Revise and Compile the Laws of Porto Rico, in 1906 United States delegate to the third International Conference of American States, in 1908–1909 chairman of the United States delegation to the first Pan-American Scientific Congress.

Washington, December 31, 1907

Dear Dan: I had read your article in abbreviated shape. I hail the chance of reading it at length. I need hardly say how cordially I agree with you, and how admirable it is, in my judgment, that you should say just this kind of thing. There are one or two minor points in which my judgment would not be yours; for instance, I would put Lounsbury beside Henry C. Lea; I do not feel that Sumner and Wilson have any real place in the study of economics and government; and I feel that Hart Merriam is the greatest living mammalogist. These are trivial and indeed utterly unimportant minor points of difference. You preached the kind of lesson that should be preached to our people.[1] Do let me see you soon. *Faithfully yours*

Washington, January 1, 1908

Dear Sir George: The loving cup[1] has at last gone and I hope will reach you. It represents, my dear sir, a very genuine affection and admiration in three of your many American friends.

I look forward eagerly to your next volume. With one of the smaller fights with which you will have to deal, that of King's Mountain, I am fairly well acquainted. I made rather a study of it, as well as of the western campaigns of George Rogers Clark during the Revolution, in a book I wrote called *The Winning of the West.* I look forward to seeing what you say of Tarleton. My admiration for that dashing, even tho somewhat ruthless, cavalryman has steadily grown. In my library his volume stands side by side with the memoirs of Lighthorse Harry Lee — where it belongs. As you so well say, men are very apt to consider as cruel any form of killing to which they are unaccustomed. The British thought the sharpshooters who picked off their officers were nothing short of murderers; and the Americans stigmatized as a massacre any fight that was won by unsparing use of saber or bayonet, whether under Tarleton or Grey. It seems to me you have been eminently just to Burgoyne, Howe and Clinton. It is nonsense to attack them as so many British historians, and with still less excuse so many American historians, have done. They were not military men of the first rank; but very few such are produced in any war; and many far less deserving men to whom the fates were kind now hold respectable positions as victors in the histories

---

[1] Addressing the meeting for the award of academic distinctions at Harvard, Wister had reviewed American contributions to scholarship. "No American University," he concluded, "possesses one single teacher of undisputed pre-eminence." The challenge of this deficiency, he suggested, should spur Americans to provide greater honor and support for the scholar; see *Outlook,* 88:67–69 (January 11, 1908).

---

[1] A Christmas present inscribed: "To the Historian of the American Revolution from his friends — Theodore Roosevelt, Henry Cabot Lodge, and Elihu Root."

of commonplace campaigns against mediocrities. I shall be interested in seeing what you say of Rawdon. His name always possesses for me an attraction which I suppose is due to a subconscious feeling that he *must* be connected in some way with his namesake, that fundamentally good fellow, Captain Crawley. I look forward especially to your account of Cornwallis. Green and Cornwallis were the two commanders who stood next to Washington; Wayne got his growth after the Revolutionary War had ended. It seems to me that there has never been a more satisfactory summing up of Washington as a soldier than is contained in your pages 284 to 286. How well you have done Benedict Arnold! How will you deal with his fall; with the money-paid treason of the rider of the war storm? What a base web was shot thru the woof of his wild daring! He was at heart a Lucifer, that child of thunder and lover of the battle's hottest heat; and dreadful it is to think that when he fell his fall should have been, not that of the lightning-blasted Son of the Morning, but that of a mere Mammon or Belial. Your etching of Morgan's riflemen is fine. The victors of King's Mountain were just such men, but without a Morgan to train them. Now, for a bit of brag. My Rough Riders, hunters of the mountains and horsemen of the plains, could not, taken as a whole, have walked quite as well as Morgan's men, nor yet have starved as well, tho they were good enough at both. But they rode without thought horses that Morgan's men would not have ventured so much as to try to get on, and I firmly believe that they were fully as formidable in battle. Mine was a volunteer regiment, and at least half of the officers at the outset were very bad, so that in a long campaign I should have had to make a complete change among them — a change that was already well begun when the regiment was disbanded. But as compared with any volunteer regiment of the Revolution or the Civil War during a like short period of service — four months — I think its record stood well. It was raised, drilled — so far as it was drilled — armed and equipped, kept two weeks on transports, and put thru two victorious aggressive (not defensive) fights, in which it lost over a third of its officers and nearly a fourth of its men, and this within sixty days. The men already knew how to ride, shoot, and live in the open; and they had the fighting edge.

You speak of the Indians just as they should be spoken of; altho I am not sure that from your account men will realize what formidable and terrible foes they usually were on their own ground.

I was especially delighted with your account of Franklin abroad, and of the unfortunate diplomats whom Congress first sent to Europe. You have, it seems to me, done justice as regards the civilian agents of the Revolution.

Now, poor André! His tragedy was like that of Nathan Hale; and the tragedy was the same in the case of the brilliant young patrician, gallant, fearless, devoted, and the plain, straightforward yeoman who just as bravely gave up his life in performing the same kind of duty. It was not a pleasant kind of duty; and the penalty was rightly the same in each case; and the countrymen of each man are also right to hold him in honor and to commemorate his memory by a monument. Among our monstrosities in the statue line in New York we have one really beautiful statue by a master; it is Nathan Hale's. By the way, it is one of the sad ironies of history that a difference in the outcome of a war should necessarily in so many cases utterly change the way the descendants of the two sides look at one another's heroes. In Canada, for instance, Wolfe and Montcalm are equally national heroes, now, because the English conquered the French and yet live in the country on terms of absolute equality with them; so that of necessity, if they are to have a common national tie, they must have as common heroes for both peoples the heroes of each people. So in a very striking fashion it is with us and the memories of the Civil War. My father's people were all Union men. My mother's brothers fought in the Confederate navy, one being an admiral therein, and the other firing the last gun fired by the *Alabama* before she sank. When I recently visited Vicksburg in Mississippi, the state of Jefferson Davis, I was greeted with just as much enthusiasm as if it had been Massachusetts or Ohio. I went out to the national park which commemorates the battle and siege and was shown around it by Stephen Lee, the present head of the Confederate veterans' organization, and had as a guard of honor both ex-Confederate and ex-Union soldiers. After for many years talking about the fact that the deeds of valor shown by the men in gray and the men in blue are now the common heritage of all our people, those who talked and those who listened have now gradually grown, first to believe with their minds, and then to feel with their hearts, the truth of what they have spoken. But where such results flow from battles as flowed from Bannockburn and Yorktown, centuries must pass before the wound not only scars over but becomes completely forgotten, and the memory becomes a bond of union and not a cause of division. It is our business to shorten the time as much as possible; and no one has done better work toward this end than you yourself.

This Christmas I was given an original proclamation issued in 1776 by my great-great-grandfather, the first governor (or, as he was called, President) of the Revolutionary State of Georgia. Two among my forbears were soldiers who fought under Marion and Sumter, one was in the Continental army of the North, and one a member of the Continental Congress. They were plain people, farmers or merchants, for the most part, tho I suppose one or two would have been ranked among the gentry. In 1693 one of them was "Landgrave" of South Carolina under Locke's absurd constitution.

I should like to write you of my troubles here, but I forbear. I am engaged in the difficult business of trying to keep together the men who are equally bent on reform and resolute not to go into anything vindictive or visionary. A government like ours must equally dread the Scylla of mob rule and the Charybdis of the reign of a mere plutocracy. I have often had to take measures against the mob spirit in its various forms; but during the last six years my chief fight has been to prevent the upgrowth in this country of the least attractive and most sordid of all aristocracies, as unattractive now as in the days of Carthage, a plutocracy, a caste which regards power as exprest only in its basest and most brutal form, that of mere money. The typical American multimillionaire is an unlovely being, and scant is his share of heirship in Washington and Lincoln, in the deeds of the men who in successive generations founded this Government, conquered this continent, and fought to a finish the great war for union and for liberty. *Faithfully yours*

[*Handwritten*] P.S This morning I shook hands with six thousand people at the White House reception. This afternoon I took a two hours good hard ride with four of my children and a dozen of their cousins and friends; jumping fences, scrambling over the wooded hills, gallopping on the level; and it was the kind of fun to fit a public man for work.

4546 · TO GEORGE BRUCE CORTELYOU   *Roosevelt Mss.*

Washington, January 2, 1908

Dear Mr. Cortelyou: Don't you think we ought to have our currency plan formulated as soon as possible and make a strike to get it thru?[1]

Won't you send me around the nomination of Wanmaker?[2] I would like to have it announced now and his name sent to the Senate as soon as Congress reconvenes. *Sincerely yours*

4547 · TO CHARLES JOSEPH BONAPARTE   *Roosevelt Mss.*

Washington, January 2, 1908

My dear Bonaparte: I must congratulate you on your admirable speech at Chicago.[1] You said the very things it was good to say at this time. What

---

[1] In his annual message, Roosevelt, repeating a request earlier made in many of his 1906 messages, had asked Congress for an emergency currency which "must be based on adequate securities approved by the government, and must be issued under a heavy tax." The Administration's plan was embodied in a bill introduced by Senator Aldrich on January 7. This bill provided for a possible emergency issue of $500,000,-000 by permitting, in time of financial stringency, national banks whose outstanding issues met certain requirements to issue additional notes, based on specified state, municipal, and railroad bonds. A tax of one half of one per cent a month or six per cent a year was placed on the emergency notes to assure their rapid retirement once the stringency was past. In May after much debate the bill was enacted with the addition of several significant amendments; see Numbers 4560, 4566. Stephenson, *Aldrich,* pp. 326–331, emphasizes the bill's political significance and Henry P. Willis, *The Federal Reserve System* (New York, 1923), pp. 44–68, discusses its economic aspects.
[2] George W. Wanmaker was appointed appraiser of the port of New York. His was one of several offices in the customs service at New York that changed hands after the voluntary resignation of Collector Nevada N. Stranahan. Colonel E. S. Fowler, Cortelyou's choice, replaced Stranahan as collector.

---

[1] On December 21 Bonaparte had delivered a variation on Roosevelt's theme of a square deal before the law for rich and poor alike. The President on December 23

you said bore especial weight because it represented what you had done. You have shown by what you have actually accomplished that the law is enforced against the wealthiest corporation, and the richest and most powerful manager or manipulator of that corporation, just as resolutely and fearlessly as against the humblest citizen. The Department of Justice is now in very fact the Department of Justice, and justice is meted out with an even hand to great and small, rich and poor, weak and strong. Those who have denounced you and the action of the Department of Justice are either misled, or else are the very wrongdoers, and the agents of the very wrongdoers, who have for so many years gone scot-free and flouted the laws with impunity. Above all, you are to be congratulated upon the bitterness felt and exprest towards you by the representatives and agents of the great law-defying corporations of immense wealth, who, until within the last half dozen years, have treated themselves and have expected others to treat them as being beyond and above all possible check from law.

It was time to say something, for the representatives of predatory wealth, of wealth accumulated on a giant scale by iniquity, by wrongdoing in many forms, by plain swindling, by oppressing wageworkers, by manipulating securities, by unfair and unwholesome competition, and by stockjobbing, in short by conduct abhorrent to every man of ordinarily decent conscience, have during the last few months made it evident that they are banded together to work for a reaction, to endeavor to overthrow and discredit all who honestly administer the law, and to secure a return to the days when every unscrupulous wrongdoer could do what he wisht unchecked, provided he had enough money. They attack you because they know your honesty and fearlessness, and dread them. The enormous sums of money these men have at their control enable them to carry on an effective campaign. They find their tools in a portion of the public press including especially certain of the great New York newspapers. They find their agents in some men in public life — now and then occupying, or having occupied, positions as high as Senator or Governor[2] — in some men in the pulpit, and most melancholy of all, in a few men on the bench. By gifts to colleges and universities they are occasionally able to subsidize in their own interest some head of an educational body,[3] who, save only a judge, should of all men be most careful to keep his skirts clear from the taint of such corruption. There are ample material rewards for those who serve with fidelity the Mammon

---

drafted a long letter congratulating Bonaparte on the speech. It is quoted in part in Bishop, *Bonaparte*, p. 150. A second draft of this letter, dated January 2, is reproduced here. From this draft Roosevelt quoted in his *Autobiography*, Nat. Ed. XX, 442–451.

[2] Former Governor Frank S. Black of New York had joined the critics of the President. Describing himself as a reactionary, Black on December 12 expressed "astonishment and dismay" at Roosevelt's "wild and undigested proposals."

[3] Chancellor James Roscoe Day had continued and intensified his attacks on Roosevelt in *The Raid on Prosperity* (New York, 1907).

of unrighteousness, but they are dearly paid for by that institution of learning whose head, by example and precept, teaches the scholars who sit under him that there is one law for the rich and another for the poor. The amount of money the representatives of the great monied interests are willing to spend can be gauged by their recent publication broadcast thruout the papers of the country from the Atlantic to the Pacific of huge advertisements, attacking with envenomed bitterness the Administration's policy of warring against successful dishonesty, advertisements that must have cost enormous sums of money. This advertisement, as also a pamphlet called "The Roosevelt Panic," and one or two similar books and pamphlets, are written especially in the interest of the Standard Oil and Harriman combinations, but also defend all the individuals and corporations of great wealth that have been guilty of wrongdoing. From the railroad rate law to the pure food law, every measure for honesty in business that has been pressed during the last six years, has been opposed by these men, on its passage and in its administration, with every resource that bitter and unscrupulous craft could suggest, and the command of almost unlimited money secure. These men do not themselves speak or write; they hire others to do their bidding. Their spirit and purpose are made clear alike by the editorials of the papers owned in, or whose policy is dictated by, Wall Street, and by the speeches of the public men who, as Senators, Governors, or Mayors, have served these their masters to the cost of the plain people. At one time one of their writers or speakers attacks the rate law as the cause of the panic; he is, whether in public life or not, usually a clever corporation lawyer, and he is not so foolish a being as to believe in the truth of what he says; he has too closely represented the railroads not to know well that the Hepburn Rate Bill has helped every honest railroad, and has hurt only the railroads that regarded themselves as above the law. At another time, one of them assails the Administration for not imprisoning people under the Sherman Antitrust Law; for declining to make what he well knows, in view of the actual attitude of juries (as shown in the Tobacco Trust cases and in San Francisco in one or two of the cases brought against corrupt businessmen) would have been the futile endeavor to imprison defendants, whom we are actually able to fine. He raises the usual clamor, raised by all who object to the enforcement of the law, that we are fining corporations instead of putting the heads of the corporations in jail; and he states that this does not really harm the chief offenders. Were this statement true he himself would not be found attacking us. The extraordinary violence of the assault upon our policy contained in speeches like these, in the articles in the subsidized press, in such huge advertisements and pamphlets as those above referred to, and the enormous sums of money spent in these various ways, give a fairly accurate measure of the anger and terror which our actions have caused the corrupt men of vast wealth to feel in the very marrow of their being.

The man thus attacking us is usually, like so many of his fellows, either a great lawyer, or a paid editor who takes his commands from the financiers and his arguments from their attorneys. If the former, he has defended many malefactors and he knows well that, thanks to the advice of lawyers like himself, a certain kind of modern corporation has been turned into an admirable instrument by which to render it well-nigh impossible to get at the really guilty man, so that in most cases the only way of punishing the wrong is by fining the corporation or by proceeding personally against some of the minor agents. These lawyers and their employers are the men mainly responsible for this state of things, and their responsibility is shared with the legislators who ingeniously oppose the passing of just and effective laws, and with those judges whose one aim seems to be to construe such laws so that they cannot be executed. Nothing is sillier than this outcry on behalf of the "innocent stockholders" in the corporations. We are besought to pity the Standard Oil Company for a fine relatively far less great than the fines every day inflicted in the police courts upon multitudes of pushcart peddlers and other petty offenders, whose woes never extort one word from the men whose withers are wrung by the woes of the mighty. The stockholders have the control of the corporation in their own hands. The corporation officials are elected by those holding the majority of the stock and can keep office only by having behind them the good will of these majority stockholders. They are not entitled to the slightest pity if they deliberately choose to resign into the hands of great wrongdoers the control of the corporations in which they own the stock. Of course innocent people have become involved in these big corporations and suffer because of the misdeeds of their criminal associates. Let these innocent people be careful not to invest in corporations where those in control are not men of probity, men who respect the laws; above all let them avoid the men who make it their one effort to evade or defy the laws. But if these honest innocent people are in the majority in any corporation they can immediately resume control and throw out of the directory the men who misrepresent them. Does any man for a moment suppose that the majority stockholders of the Standard Oil are others than Mr. Rockefeller and his associates themselves and the beneficiaries of their wrongdoing? When the stock is watered so that the innocent investors suffer, a grave wrong is indeed done to these innocent investors as well as to the public; but the public men, lawyers and editors, to whom I refer, do not under these circumstances express sympathy for the innocent; on the contrary they are the first to protest with frantic vehemence against our efforts by law to put a stop to overcapitalization and stock-watering. The apologists of successful dishonesty always declaim against any effort to punish or prevent it on the ground that such effort will "unsettle business." It is they who by their acts have unsettled business; and the very men raising this cry spend hundreds of thousands of dollars in securing, by speech, editorial, book or pamphlet, the defense by misstatement of what they have done; and yet when we correct their misstatements by telling the truth, they declaim gainst us for breaking silence, lest "values be unsettled"! They have hurt honest businessmen, honest workingmen, honest farmers; and now they clamor against the truth being told.

The keynote of all these attacks upon the effort to secure honesty in business and in politics, is exprest in a recent speech in which the speaker stated that prosperity had been checked by the effort for the "moral regeneration of the business world," an effort which he denounced as "unnatural, unwarranted and injurious" and for which he stated the panic was the penalty. The morality of such a plea is precisely as great as if made on behalf of the men caught in a gambling establishment when that gambling establishment is raided by the police. If such words mean anything they mean that those sentiments they represent stand against the effort to bring about a moral regeneration of business which will prevent a repetition of the insurance, banking and street railroad scandals in New York; repetition of the Chicago and Alton deal; a repetition of the combination between certain professional politicians, certain professional labor leaders and certain big financiers from the disgrace of which San Francisco has just been rescued; a repetition of the successful efforts by the Standard Oil people to crush out every competitor, to overawe the common carriers, and to establish a monopoly which treats the public with the contempt which the public deserves so long as it permits men like the public men of whom I speak to represent it in politics, men like the heads of colleges to whom I refer to educate its youth. The outcry against stopping dishonest practices among the very wealthy is precisely similar to the outcry raised against every effort for cleanliness and decency in city government because, forsooth, it will "hurt business." The same outcry is made against the Department of Justice for prosecuting the heads of colossal corporations that is made against the men who in San Francisco are prosecuting with impartial severity the wrongdoers among businessmen, public officials, and labor leaders alike. The principle is the same in the two cases. Just as the blackmailer and the bribe-giver stand on the same evil eminence of infamy, so the man who makes an enormous fortune by corrupting Legislatures and municipalities and fleecing his stockholders and the public stands on a level with the creature who fattens on the blood money of the gambling house, the saloon and the brothel. Moreover both kinds of corruption in the last analysis are far more intimately connected than would at first sight appear; the wrongdoing is at bottom the same. Corrupt business and corrupt politics act and react, with ever increasing debasement, one on the other; the rebate-taker, the franchise-trafficker, the manipulator of securities, the purveyor and protector of vice, the blackmailing ward boss, the ballot-box-stuffer, the demagogue, the mob leader, the hired bully and man-killer, all alike work at the same web of corruption, and all alike should be abhorred by honest men.

The "business" which is hurt by the movement for honesty is the kind of business which, in the long run, it pays the country to have hurt. It is the kind of business which has tended to make the very name "high finance" a term of scandal to which all honest American men of business should join in putting an end. One of the special pleaders for business dishonesty, in a recent speech, in denouncing the Administration for enforcing the law against the huge and corrupt corporations which have defied the law, also denounced it for endeavoring to secure a far-reaching law making employers liable for injuries to their employees.[4] It is meet and fit that the apologists for corrupt wealth should oppose every effort to relieve weak and helpless people from crushing misfortune brought upon them by injury in the business from which they gain a bare livelihood and their employers fortunes. It is hypocritical baseness to speak of a girl who works in a factory where the dangerous machinery is unprotected as having the "right" freely to contract to expose herself to dangers to life and limb. She has no alternative but to suffer want or else to expose herself to such dangers, and when she loses a hand or is otherwise maimed or disfigured for life it is a moral wrong that the burden of the risk necessarily incidental to the business should be placed with crushing weight upon her weak shoulders and the man who has profited by her work escape scot-free. This is what our opponents advocate, and it is proper that they should advocate it, for it rounds out their advocacy of those most dangerous members of the criminal class, the criminals of vast wealth, the men who can afford best to pay for such championship in the press and on the stump.

It is difficult to speak about the judges, for it behooves us all to treat with the utmost respect the high office of judge; and our judges as a whole are brave and upright men. But there is need that those who go wrong should not be allowed to feel that there is no condemnation of their wrongdoing. A judge who on the bench either truckles to the mob or bows down before a corporation; or who, having left the bench to become a corporation lawyer, seeks to aid his clients by denouncing as enemies of property all those who seek to stop the abuses of the criminal rich; such a man performs an even worse service to the body politic than the Legislator or Executive who goes wrong. In no way can respect for the courts be so quickly undermined as by teaching the public thru the action of a judge himself that there is reason for the loss of such respect. The judge who by word or deed makes it plain that the corrupt corporation, the law-defying corporation, the law-defying rich man, has in him a sure and trustworthy ally, the judge who by misuse of the process of injunction makes it plain that in him the wageworker has a de-

---

[4] The Supreme Court was then considering two cases involving the constitutionality of the federal law of 1906 making common carriers in interstate commerce liable for injuries sustained by their employees. By a five to four decision the court on January 6 declared that law unconstitutional. Justice White, speaking for the majority, described it as an overextension of the power of Congress over commerce. Against this view both Moody and Holmes wrote strong dissents.

termined and unscrupulous enemy, the judge who when he decides in an employer's liability or a tenement house factory case shows that he has neither sympathy for nor understanding of those fellow citizens of his who most need his sympathy and understanding; these judges work as much evil as if they pandered to the mob, as if they shrank from sternly repressing violence and disorder. The judge who does his full duty well stands higher, and renders a better service to the people, than any other public servant; he is entitled to greater respect; and if he is a true servant of the people, if he is upright, wise and fearless he will unhesitatingly disregard even the wishes of the people if they conflict with the eternal principles of right as against wrong. He must serve the people; but he must serve his conscience first. All honor to such a judge; and all honor cannot be rendered him if it is rendered equally to his brethren who fall immeasurably below the high ideals for which he stands. There should be a sharp discrimination against such judges. They claim immunity from criticism, and the claim is heatedly advanced by men and newspapers like those of whom I speak. Most certainly they can claim immunity from untruthful criticism; and their champions, the newspapers and the public men I have mentioned, exquisitely illustrate by their own actions mendacious criticism in its most flagrant and iniquitous form.

But no servant of the people has a right to expect to be free from just and honest criticism. It is the newspapers and the public men whose thoughts and deeds show them to be most alien to honesty and truth who themselves loudly object to truthful and honest criticism of their fellow servants of the great monied interests.

We have no quarrel with the individuals, whether public men, lawyers or editors, to whom I refer. These men derive their sole power from the great, sinister offenders who stand behind them. They are but puppets who move as the strings are pulled by those who control the enormous masses of corporate wealth which if itself left uncontrolled threatens dire evil to the Republic. It is not the puppets, but the strong, cunning men and the mighty forces working for evil behind, and to a certain extent thru, the puppets, with whom we have to deal. We seek to control law-defying wealth, in the first place to prevent its doing evil, and in the next place to avoid the vindictive and dreadful radicalism which if left uncontrolled it is certain in the end to arouse. Sweeping attacks upon all property, upon all men of means, without regard to whether they do well or ill, would sound the death knell of the Republic; and such attacks become inevitable if decent citizens permit rich men whose lives are corrupt and evil to domineer in swollen pride, unchecked and unhindered, over the destinies of this country. We act in no vindictive spirit, and we are no respecters of persons. If a labor union does what is wrong we oppose it as fearlessly as we oppose a corporation that does wrong; and we stand with equal stoutness for the rights of the man of wealth and for the rights of the wageworkers; just as much so for one as for the other. We seek to stop wrongdoing; and we desire to punish the wrongdoer only so far as is necessary in order to achieve this end. We are the staunch upholders of every honest man, whether businessman or wageworker.

I do not for a moment believe that our actions have brought on business distress; so far as this is due to local and not world-wide causes, and to the actions of any particular individuals, it is due to the speculative folly and flagrant dishonesty of a few men of great wealth, who now seek to shield themselves from the effects of their own wrongdoings by ascribing its results to the actions of those who have sought to put a stop to the wrong-doing. But if it were true that to cut out rottenness from the body politic meant a momentary check to an unhealthy-seeming prosperity, I should not for one moment hesitate to put the knife to the cancer. On behalf of all our people, on behalf no less of the honest man of means than of the honest man who earns each day's livelihood by that day's sweat of his brow, it is necessary to insist upon honesty in business and politics alike, in all walks of life, in big things and in little things; upon just and fair dealing as between man and man. We are striving for the right in the spirit of Abraham Lincoln when he said:

Fondly do we hope — fervently do we pray — that this mighty scourge [of war] may speedily pass away. Yet, if God wills that it continue until all the wealth piled by the bondsmen's two hundred and fifty years of unrequited toil shall be sunk, and until every drop of blood drawn with the lash shall be paid by another drawn with the sword, as was said three thousand years ago, so still it must be said, "The judgments of the Lord are true and righteous altogether."

With malice toward none; with charity for all; with firmness in the right, as God gives us to see the right, let us strive on to finish the work we are in.

Sincerely yours

4548 · TO ARCHIBALD BULLOCH ROOSEVELT   *Roosevelt Mss.*

Washington, January 2, 1908

Dear Archie: Friday night Quentin had three friends, including the little Taft boy, to spend the night with him. They past an evening and night of delirious rapture, it being a continuous roughhouse, save when they would fall asleep for an hour or two from sheer exhaustion. I interfered but once, and that was to stop an exquisite jest of Quentin's, which consisted in procuring sulphurated hydrogen to be used on the other boys when they got into bed. They played hard, and it made me realize how old I had grown and how very busy I had been these last few years to find that they had grown so that I was not needed in the play. Do you recollect how we all of us used to play hide-and-go-seek in the White House, and have obstacle races down the hall when you brought in your friends?

Mother continues much attached to Scamp, who is certainly a cunning little dog. He is very affectionate, but so exceedingly busy when we are out on the grounds that we only catch glimpses of him zigzagging at full speed from one end of the place to the other. The kitchen cat and he have strained relations but have not yet come to open hostility.

Miss Young and Mademoiselle are just as nice as they can be. I thoroly enjoy them. Mother is as pretty and cunning as ever. Last night she had a headache and came down to dinner in a pink dressing gown, feeling very woebegone, but she quite waked up in her delight at my having misunderstood some story and then trying to find out about it by questions, which, she said to Aunt Emily, with pitying glances, made her understand how Kermit inherited *his* habit of asking questions! This seemed to be the turning point in her evening and she brightened up and got over her headache, every now and then making a sudden little assault upon me, just as I have seen a bird ruffle up its little feathers and give a sudden peck; then she would feel heartsmitten lest she had been too severe, and pet me to make up.

I have been very busy, of course, but that I have to expect. *Your loving father*

4549 · TO VICTOR HOWARD METCALF   *Roosevelt Mss.*

Washington, January 2, 1908

To the Secretary of the Navy: In accordance with our conversation of today, Captain Pillsbury will be appointed Chief of the Bureau of Navigation.

The action of the late chief of the Bureau, Admiral Brownson, in tendering his resignation because he did not agree with the President and the Department regarding an order, issued before he came into the Bureau, by the Secretary of the Navy, as to the control of the hospital ships, was unseemly and improper, and, coupled with the various controversies among the officers of the navy and their adherents as to details of naval construction and methods of training, has undoubtedly been prejudicial to the interests of the navy and may seriously impair the confidence in the navy which is essential to securing the legislation so sorely needed by the navy.[1] The way

[1] Roosevelt was justifiably concerned by controversies within the service. The Brownson resignation, coming as it did over matters of bureau jurisdiction and line and staff prerogatives, seemed to document perfectly the contention of a provocative article that had been published in *McClure's Magazine*. This article, written by Henry Reuterdahl at the suggestion and with the advice of Sims, Key, and other younger naval officers working for naval reform, had asserted that the navy's antiquated administrative organization of isolated independent bureaus was injuring the efficiency and morale of its personnel and the fighting qualities of its ships. Reuterdahl described grave defects in ship design which, though thoroughly discussed in naval circles, had not been revealed to the general public. His main charges were that even the newer ships had insufficient freeboard, badly placed armor plate, and dangerous open-shaft ammunition hoists. "No human being is responsible," he stressed. "It is done by a system — an organization so constituted that its very nature compels it to perpetuate mistakes." Until the bureau system was reorganized, Reuterdahl concluded, the navy would remain completely unprepared for war.

Reuterdahl's charges and Brownson's resignation jeopardized Roosevelt's naval program. In his annual message to Congress, the President, departing from the policy

in which these controversies have been carried out is highly injurious to the service, whether the communications are made openly over the signatures of the naval officers, or by civilians who have evidently gained their information from naval officers. There always are and always will be defects to correct both in the construction of ships and in the organization of the Department and in the actual drill of the fleet. It is well that these defects should be pointed out, but it is also well that they should be pointed out without hysterical exaggeration or malicious untruthfulness; while it is of course reprehensible in the highest degree to exploit them in grossly exaggerated form in the fancied interest of an individual or clique of individuals, or for the sake of supplying sensational material to some service or non-service newspaper. The officers of the navy who are guilty of such conduct deserve grave rebuke. They cast discredit upon the service and their conduct is deeply mortifying to every American who believes in the navy and is anxious to uphold its interest and honor. There has been so much misrepresentation and exaggeration that I desire you to make me a statement as to the exact facts concerning which there has been dispute. In particular I desire you to get the opinion of Admiral Converse, who, until last spring, was Chief of the Bureau of Navigation, and whose high professional standard of conduct and duty, and high professional knowledge and attainments, render him peculiarly fit to give judgment.

I would willingly pass over the conduct of Admiral Brownson because of his fine service in the past if it were not that at a time when a new chief is chosen to succeed him it becomes imperative to stamp with disapproval the behavior which, if followed thruout the navy generally, would literally ruin the navy's efficiency. The question as to which Admiral Brownson took issue with the Department I will deal with in a separate letter. It is one as to which there can be entirely legitimate differences of opinion, altho in my judgment the considerations in favor of the course decided upon are overwhelming. But there is no room for difference of opinion as to the gross impropriety of the Admiral's conduct in resigning sooner than carry out the orders of his superior officers in such a matter. The officers of the navy must

---

announced in December 1905 of building one ship a year, asked for four battleships, "plenty" of destroyers and torpedo boats, and bases and shore facilities in the Pacific. In Roosevelt's opinion, the Japanese crisis and the plans of Germany and Japan to build several revolutionary dreadnought-type battleships made necessary such an expanded building program (see Numbers 4699, 4700). The majority of Congressmen, however, disagreed with these contentions. Therefore, in the committees and debates of an unsympathetic Congress, such opponents of naval expansion as Hale, Burton, Cannon, Foss, and Tawney were able to make effective use of the ammunition provided by Reuterdahl and Brownson in their efforts to defeat the President's program. Their task was made easier by Roosevelt's intemperate criticism of Brownson which tended to identify the President in the public mind as an active participant in the Navy's factional controversies. For the general background of the 1908 building program, see Harold and Margaret Sprout, *The Rise of American Naval Power* (Princeton, 1946), pp. 264–268. For its passage through Congress see Numbers 4635, note 1, 4647, 4648, 4687.

remember that it is not merely childish but in the highest degree reprehensible to permit either personal pique, wounded vanity, or factional feeling on behalf of some particular bureau or organization, to render them disloyal to the interests of the navy and therefore of the country as a whole. The question whether one officer or another shall command a ship is of little consequence compared with the weakening of all command and discipline which would result if officers were to refuse to serve whenever their tempers are ruffled by adverse decisions on the part of their superiors. Their sole concern should be the good of the service, and save only courage in actual warfare, obedience and loyalty are the most essential qualities in keeping the service up to the highest standard. The different bureaus of the Department, the different branches of the service, must act in co-ordination, and the questions that arise between them must be settled by the authority of the Secretary of the Navy and of the President, under and in accordance with the law enacted by Congress; and the first duty of every officer, whether of the line, of the pay department, of the medical department, or of the construction department, whether in one bureau or in another, is to give immediate and loyal obedience to every lawful command of a superior, and of course above all to the law itself. This duty is incumbent upon all, but it is most incumbent upon those highest in rank, whose example may be of far-reaching effect.

4550 · TO VICTOR HOWARD METCALF   *Roosevelt Mss.*

Washington, January 4, 1908

To the Secretary of the Navy: Your predecessor in the Navy Department on December 12, 1906, directed that hospital ships should be treated as floating hospitals and that each such ship should therefore be placed under the command of a medical officer, the navigation being controlled by a competent sailing master. This order was issued after the most careful consideration, by the Secretary of the Navy and by the President, of all the reasons that could be adduced for and against it. The case has now been reopened and the Secretary of the Navy and the President have again listened to and considered all the reasons that could be adduced against putting the order into effect. After the fullest consideration I have determined that the order is right, and it is hereby confirmed.[1]

The hospital ships of the navy will hereafter, unless otherwise directed by Congress, be placed under the control and command of medical officers of the navy, their navigation being exclusively controlled by a competent sailing master and civilian crew, the sailing master having the complete responsibility for everything connected with the navigation of the ship. Such a ship is merely a floating hospital. The hospital ship now in question, the *Relief*, has already been used by the United States Army as such. It was then commanded by a medical officer, with a sailing master under him. This

[1] See No. 4539, note 1.

893

arrangement worked well, and it is preposterous to suppose that it will not work as well under a medical officer of the navy as under a medical officer of the army.

Certain hospital ships in the British, German, Japanese and Italian navies have already been commanded by medical officers — sometimes fleet surgeons, sometimes Red Cross surgeons. In these navies the only ships of which I have been been able to get record were thus commanded; save that in the Japanese navy the hospital ships at the beginning of the late war were commanded by line officers, but were then put under the command of medical officers to avoid all question of possible breach of neutrality. In our own service, at the close of the Civil War, by general order of February 6, 1865, hospital transports and hospital boats were placed exclusively under the control of the medical department; the hospital ship on the Mississippi being under the command of a fleet surgeon with an acting master under him as navigating officer. In the Spanish-American War the hospital ships *Vigilancia, Relief, Missouri, Bay State* and *Olivette* were by various orders (Nos. 103, 122, 188, 212, 273, &c.) placed under the charge of, or the command of, various army surgeons, the order sometimes reading that the surgeon will "take charge of" the hospital ship, sometimes that he will "assume command of" the hospital ship, this last being the form of words used in connection with the ship *Relief*, the one that we are now considering. The manual of the medical department of the United States Army for 1906 provides that hospital boats shall be exclusively under the control of the medical department; and the order of the Secretary of the Navy of December 12, 1906, puts hospital ships under the command of naval surgeons. At present two pay officers are serving in naval hospitals under the command of medical officers of the navy, and the present Paymaster General of the Navy served under the command of a medical officer of the Navy in 1879.

Military surgeons, including naval surgeons, have special knowledge of hospital ships, and they have in addition certain military duties of command, organization, drills and discipline, just as do officers of the line, awarding punishments, and being guided and governed in these military duties by the same regulations that guide and govern officers of the line. The command of a hospital ship should unquestionably be vested in a medical officer, and no line officer should be aboard it. The medical officer in such case is simply the responsible head of a large hospital plant, which by reason of his training he is peculiarly fitted to command. It is not his province to navigate the vessel; this should be left to a civilian sailing master; but he, and he alone, is best qualified to respect and guard the neutrality of the ship. The absurdity of permitting a line officer to command a hospital ship was shown in the case of the United States Hospital Ship *Solace* during the war with Spain, when the line officer in command actually attempted to put in a claim for prize money for the part the *Solace* took in the capture of the *Adula*, while the *Solace* was flying the Red Cross flag and professing neutrality. On another occasion the *Solace* interfered with the progress of a schooner in the old Bahama channel, so that the United States torpedo boats nearby could board and investigate her. On yet another occasion, but for the vigilance of the medical officer aboard her, the *Solace* would have carried armed men from New York to Cuba. Her senior medical officer reported the violation of neutrality to the Navy Department, and the ship was recalled after passing thru the Narrows and the armed men removed. In the Russo-Japanese War a Russian hospital ship violated her neutrality and was captured and confiscated by the Japanese. In time of war the presence of combatants — that is, of line officers or crew — would certainly cast a suspicion upon the neutrality of the ship; and no line officer worth his salt would wish to be on such a ship, while it seems incredible that any line officer should desire to have another line officer on board such a ship. Hospitals, afloat or ashore, should no more be under the command of line officers than regiments or warships should be under the command of surgeons; one kind of appointment is quite as inappropriate as the other. Hospital ships should be maintained in time of peace exactly under the same conditions as in time of war. The system has been tried in the army, and tried in foreign navies, and has worked without a hitch. It is the only system that should be tolerated; and if it fails to work well, this failure can only be due to lack of desire to have it work well on the part of those concerned.

I direct that unless Congress provides otherwise the practice in the navy be assimilated to that now obtaining in the army. In the army the hospital ship is treated as a general hospital; and article 1467 reads as follows: "General Hospitals will be under the exclusive control of the Surgeon General, and will be governed by such regulations as the Secretary of War may prescribe. The senior surgeon will command the same."

4551 · TO JOHN SPARKS *Roosevelt Mss.*

Washington, January 4, 1908

Sir: I have received the copy of your proclamation, dated December 30, 1907, summoning the legislature. As I have notified you, the troops will stay for three weeks from the date of this call, so that the legislature can meet and opportunity be given the State authorities to take efficient action for the preservation of the public peace in the exercise of the police powers of the State. I call your especial attention to the telegram sent to you on December 14th by the Secretary of State. This sets out what must be shown as a matter of actual fact to exist in order to warrant the President in acting on the request of the State authorities. The action must be either to suppress an insurrection which the State authorities are unable to suppress, or to secure to some portion or class of the people of the State the equal protection of the laws to which they are entitled under the Constitution of the United States, and which is denied them. Action under this or any other section requires the production of evidence sufficient to sustain a judgment by the President, that the condition described in the statute exists. A mere statement of domestic disturbance, still less a mere statement of apprehension of domestic disturbance, is not sufficient, even tho it comes from as high and unimpeachable a source as the Governor of a State. Such a communication from the Governor or from the legislature warrants the President in taking immediate steps to put himself in readiness to act, in view of the probability of conditions arising which will require his action. I accordingly sent the troops to Nevada on your request, and I have now directed that they be kept there pending the assembling of the legislature. Meanwhile, I sent out Assistant Secretary of Commerce and Labor Lawrence O. Murray, Commissioner of Corporations Herbert Knox Smith, and Commissioner of Labor Charles P. Neill to investigate and report to me the actual condition of affairs in Goldfield. I have just received a report from these three gentlemen, which sets forth in the most emphatic language their belief, after a careful investigation on the ground, that there was no warrant whatever for calling upon the President for troops, and that the troops should not be kept indefinitely at Goldfield. The report further states that there was no insurrection against the power of the State at the time the troops were called for, that nobody supposed that there was such an insurrection, and that none of the conditions described in sections 5297–8–9 of the Revised Statutes as warranting interference by the Federal Government existed, and that the effort was and is plainly an effort by the State of Nevada to secure the performance by the United States of the ordinary police duties which should, as a matter of course, be performed by Nevada herself. The report further says:

There is absolutely no question that if the State of Nevada and the County of Esmeralda exercise the powers at their disposal they can maintain satisfactory order in Goldfield; that so far, these authorities have done nothing but are relying upon Federal aid, and their attitude now is expressly that of refusing to do anything and desiring to throw their own burdens upon the Federal Government for the maintenance of those elementary conditions of order for which they, and they only, are responsible.

The signers of the report express their conviction that the troops should remain in Nevada until the assembling of the legislature, so as to preserve the *status quo* in order that the legislature may deal with the situation as it exists; but that shortly thereafter the troops should be removed.

I agree with the recommendations of this report, of which I enclose a copy, and shall act accordingly. Unless it can be shown that the statements of the report are not in accordance with the facts, it will be incumbent upon the legislature of Nevada, when it convenes, itself to provide for enforcing the laws of the State. The State of Nevada must itself make a resolute effort in good faith to perform the police duties incident to the existence of a State. *Sincerely yours*

The Art Critic

Theodore Roosevelt and Robley D. Evans

The Cruise Around the World

Washington, January 4, 1908

Sir: I transmit herewith a report from the Chief of Staff, which is self-explanatory.[1]

The field officers of our army cannot be held exclusively responsible for the poor riding which has been frequently observed among them. The quality of our horses does not equal that of mounts used in foreign armies. Furthermore, tho all infantry captains in European armies are mounted, an infantry officer in our service has little opportunity to practice riding until he becomes a field officer.

The only practicable way in which we can improve our military mounts is to pursue the method adopted in foreign armies in obtaining remounts. They purchase young horses, send them to remount stations, where they are trained for about a year and finally assigned to the service, well broken and trained for military use. This has proven to be cheaper in the end, by making the horses last much longer in the service.

I have instructed the Secretary of War to take such steps as may be necessary to bring to the attention of your Committee the desirability of legislation for mounting infantry captains and for the establishment of remount depots. It is hoped that the Military Committees of both Houses of Congress may give favorable consideration to these two measures which are essential in improving horsemanship in our army, and in raising the standard of efficiency thruout the service. *Sincerely yours*

Washington, January 6, 1908

Dear Matt: I enclose you copies of my message about Panama. Now, you say it was hard to meet the statement that the whole revolution was planned at Washington with the connivance of the administration, and you add "This, of course, I said I did not believe, but I did not have any positive proof." Point out to your questioner that it is the man making such an assertion, and not the man denying it, who has to bring the positive proof. If for instance he asserted that you had killed your grandmother it is *he*, not *you*, who would have to bring the positive proof. His "specific assertion" about the date of my message was a lie, which you can tell him from me in that exact language. As a matter of fact, I had prepared a message advocating our taking possession of the Isthmus openly under the exercise of the undoubted ethical right of international domain, which would have had ultimately to obtain in such a case. But the revolution which everyone knew was seething on the

[1] General Bell's report on horsemanship in foreign armies further convinced Roosevelt of the need for higher standards of riding in the American army. Unable to obtain legislation from Congress to improve the Army's horsemanship, he had to be satisfied with his orders raising the riding requirements for all field officers.

Isthmus broke out, and I rewrote entirely my message, to meet the completely altered conditions. Long after the event I gained information which led me to believe that certain Americans had been among the crowd of people who had been fomenting the revolution, (everyone on the Isthmus had been, in fact); to some, but by no means all, of these I suspected the fact at the time; but all that I *knew* is set forth in the messages I enclose you. *Sincerely yours*

"Nominated Solely on My Assurances"

January 1908–June 1908

Roosevelt Mss.

Washington, January 6, 1908

Dear Will: Do you want any action about those Federal officials? I will break their necks with the utmost cheerfulness if you say the word! [1] *Ever yours*

4555 · TO GEORGE MEREDITH *Roosevelt Mss.*

Washington, January 9, 1908

My dear Mr. Meredith: Will you permit a stranger to join in very hearty greetings to you on your eightieth birthday? After a writer's work reaches a certain height, he can no longer be claimed only by the people of his own nation; and there are now as many in America as in England who owe you a debt of honorable obligation. I hardly venture to suppose that you will come to America; if you could, your greeting would be warm; and not the least warm from those of us who do not put your poems second to your prose writings. It is good to hear the sound of trumpet and horn, whether in verse or prose; in Attila or Brann, or when the Goshawk fights the marauder Baron; and as each man necessarily thinks especially of the problems of his own trade, it is natural for me to feel that what was written to Colonel Charles should appeal to the public men of every free country.[1]

With high regard and all good wishes, believe me, *Sincerely yours*

4556 · TO DOUGLAS ROBINSON *Roosevelt Mss.*

Washington, January 10, 1908

Dear Douglas: I have your letter of the 9th instant. Naturally I was extremely pleased with the accounts. Apparently I have saved up more last year than I ever have before, and I am mighty glad of it, for next year Ted will go out into the big world, and from that time right along the little birds will hop off one after another out of the nest. I can never sufficiently thank you, old man.

Indeed, Douglas, I understand to the full that your work is just as trying

---

[1] "I am not asking that the federal officials shall help me," Taft had concluded, "but I do not think it is unfair that they shall keep their fingers out. . . . It may be necessary to remove Capers at once" (Pringle, *Taft*, I, 322). It proved unnecessary either to remove Capers or to break his neck.

---

[1] George Meredith, better known for his prose than for his verse, for a time the son-in-law of Thomas Love Peacock, was the author of *The Ordeal of Richard Feverel, Diana of the Crossways* and *The Egoist*, novels dear to the hearts of a fanatically loyal, but exceedingly small, band of admirers. The sound of trumpet and horn — clearer perhaps in his verse — is frequently lost in the long and winding lanes of his prose.

in its way as mine is in its.[1] That was a mighty nice announcement of Judge Lacombe. I wish you would give him my regards when you see him.

I am eager to see you and learn about the condition of things, or rather the details of the conditions as you found them. What a hideous business it was! Am looking forward to seeing you and Corinne. *Ever yours*

4557 · TO LIGON JOHNSON   *Roosevelt Mss.*

Washington, January 11, 1908

My dear Mr. Johnson: [1] The Appalachian National Forest Association stands for a movement in which my interest is very keen. In Raleigh, on October 19, 1905, I said:

> If the Eastern States are wise, then from the Bay of Fundy to the Gulf we will see, within the next few years, a policy set on foot similar to that so fortunately carried out in the high Sierras of the West by the National Government. All the higher Appalachians should be reserved, either by the States or by the Nation. I much prefer that they should be put under national control, but it is a mere truism to say that they will not be reserved either by the States or by the Nation unless you people of the South show a strong interest therein.
>
> Such reserves would be a paying investment, not only in protection to many interests, but in dollars and cents to the Government. The importance to the southern people of protecting the southern mountain forests is obvious. These forests are the best defense against the floods which in the recent past have during a single twelvemonth destroyed property officially valued at nearly twice what it would cost to buy the Southern Appalachian Reserve. The maintenance of your southern water powers is not less important than the prevention of floods, because if they are injured your manufacturing interests will suffer with them. The perpetuation of your forests, which have done so much for the South, should be one of the first objects of your public men.

We know also that these forests are of the utmost importance to navigation on the streams to which they give rise. All the water which falls in the southern Appalachians goes to the sea thru navigable channels which it has cost the Government over $30,000,000 to keep clear from sand, silt, and gravel. This detritus is increasing every year as the mountains are denuded of their cover. The task of cleaning out the southern streams and harbors grows heavier each year. Until we remove the cause by protecting these mountain forests from fire and reckless cutting, we shall inevitably expend increasing sums without permanent result.

Eight years ago the movement for the purchase of these forests took definite shape. While it has grown and is stronger now than ever, its merits

[1] Robinson, as one of the two receivers appointed by Judge Emile H. Lacombe for the New York Railway Company, a subsidiary of the Interborough Transit Company, was unraveling one of the most complicated financial tangles in American corporate history.

[1] Ligon Johnson, at this time president of the Appalachian National Forest Association.

should make it far stronger than it is. Therefore I am pleased at the organization of your association with the definite purpose of getting these forests established. As I said in my last message to Congress, "We should acquire in the Appalachian and White Mountain regions all the forest lands that it is possible to acquire for the use of the Nation." [2] *Sincerely yours*

4558 · TO WILLIAM HOWARD TAFT   *Roosevelt Mss.*

Washington, January 11, 1908

To the Secretary of War: It seems to me a very great misfortune to lay so much stress upon mathematics in the curriculum at West Point and fail to have languages taught in accordance with the best modern conversational methods. I should like to have this matter taken up seriously. I have several times called attention to it, but nothing has been done.[1] Mathematical training is a necessary thing for an engineer or an artilleryman, doubtless; but I esteem it of literally no importance for the cavalryman or infantryman. If tomorrow I had to choose officers from the regular army for important positions in the event of war, I should care no more for their mathematical training than for their knowledge of whist or chess. A man who learns a language by studying a book but cannot speak it, loses at least half the benefit obtainable. I would like a full report on this matter.

Also, is there not danger of too much mere book learning being required in the Fort Riley school? We need soldiers, not mere students; or, rather, we need students only so far as study helps toward soldiership. A man with an eye to the country, who can take care of men and of horses, and whose administrative capacity is developed, is more valuable than a closet student, to the army.

4559 · TO WILLIAM RUFUS DAY   *Roosevelt Mss.*

Washington, January 11, 1908

My dear Judge Day: I send you herewith *Moral Overstrain*. I want you to look at the last two chapters.[1]

I am very much puzzled sometimes to know just how far I ought to go

[2] Federal legislation to this end was passed during Taft's administration.

[1] The War Department took no action on Roosevelt's suggestions; the Navy, about this time, made half-hearted efforts to modify the curriculum as the President proposed. In general, however, the excessive emphasis on mathematics continued at both service schools, and both continued to teach French, German, and Spanish, in accordance with the hallowed tradition established by all American institutions of higher learning, as a series of archaeological expeditions into the remains of dead languages.

[1] In the last two chapters of his *Moral Overstrain* (Boston, 1906), George W. Alger had stated a strong case for employers' liability laws. Roosevelt, however, assigned this reading too late. Day had already concurred in White's majority opinion declaring unconstitutional the federal employers' liability law.

in the fight for what I conceive to be the fundamental rights of the people of small means, of the wageworkers, the farmers, and the plain people generally. I am at liberty to attack the acts of executives and legislators as freely as I wish, provided I speak truthfully; and this liberty I have always exercised and shall continue to exercise. But I wish I could get from some of you judges, whom I respect more than I do any other public men, some satisfactory scheme, which would permit of the necessary protest against the few unrighteous, and the less few unwise decisions, without impairment of that respect for the law which must go hand in hand with respect for the courts, and which it should be a prime object of every statesman carefully to conserve. Look at what is said in the last article but one of the little book I enclose as to the decision of the Supreme Court in the New York bakery law; as to the decision of the New York Court of Appeals in the tenement house act. If the spirit which lies behind these two decisions obtained in all the actions of the Federal and State courts, we should not only have a revolution, but it would be absolutely necessary to have a revolution, because the condition of the worker would become intolerable. Now, what I am puzzling over is how to work for a condition of feeling which shall minimize the number of such decisions, and at the same time not do damage by discrediting the courts. I enclose you a copy of a telegram I sent Judge Willard Bartlett, of New York, last fall.[2] He is an old personal friend, a man of means, whom both the Republicans and the Democrats renominated. He wrote asking me for my support, and I did not think I could give it because I had in view just such decisions as that of the court to which he belonged in this tenement house cigar factory case.

With great regard, *Sincerely yours*

4560 · TO GEORGE BRUCE CORTELYOU   *Roosevelt Mss.*

Washington, January 12, 1908

Dear Mr. Cortelyou: Will you glance at the enclosed? I do not know quite how to answer it, and I should like a little information which would enable me to do so. As far as I can make out, the chief objection (outside of New York) to our course is the allegation that money is loaned to bankers without interest which they loan for speculative purposes to the stock brokers at a high rate of interest.[1] I do wish we could tax stock speculation out of exist-

[2] Willard Bartlett, associate judge of the New York Court of Appeals, Democrat, before and after his long career on the bench a legal associate of Elihu Root.

[1] To meet this objection, the Aldrich Bill was amended so that the tax on emergency note issues was raised from one half of one per cent a month to five per cent on issuance increasing one per cent monthly until the rate reached ten per cent. The strongest objection to the bill was not, however, that it encouraged speculative call loan operations but that it would unjustly enhance the value of railroad securities. Led by La Follette, Southern and Western senators forced the withdrawal of the railroad bond provision shortly before the bill passed the Senate on March 27, 1908.

ence. The purchase and sale of stocks on a margin is gambling, pure and simple. I know how difficult it is to do anything effective to stop such practices, but I do wish that it were possible to devise some scheme to effect the object. *Sincerely yours*

[*Handwritten*] Will you go over the enclosed papers from Root; and return them with your comments and suggestions?

4561 · TO ALBERT BUSHNELL HART   *Roosevelt Mss.*

Washington, January 13, 1908

Dear Hart: Your letter is of real importance. I have sent it at once to Bonaparte. I have been very uneasy about Mrs. Quackenboss. She comes in the large class of people who to a genuine desire to eradicate wrong add an unsoundness of judgment which is both hysterical and sentimental. She has done some good work, and I think she has done a great deal more bad work. The fact is that on those southern plantations we are faced with a condition of things that is very puzzling. Infamous outrages are perpetrated — outrages that would warrant radical action if they took place in Oyster Bay or Cambridge; but when they actually do occur the surroundings, the habits of life, the sentiments of the people, are so absolutely different that we are in reality living in a different age, and we simply have to take this into account in endeavoring to enforce laws which cannot be enforced save by juries — that is, in the long run by the neighborhood sentiment. It is like trying to enforce a prohibition law in New York City.

Cannot you and Mrs. Hart come down for the Congressional reception and supper on February 6th? Then I will have a chance to talk with you more at length about this matter. *Ever yours*

4562 · TO JAMES FRANKLIN BELL   *Roosevelt Mss.*

Washington, January 13, 1908

My dear General: Judging from the knowledge gained by our experience with the navy it seems to me important not to permit any officer to pass from one detail to another without serving with troops.[1] As you and I have often said in our conversations, our object should be to put service with troops above service on any detail. No officer is indispensable in any position, any more than any civilian is indispensable in any position — from the President down. Will you give me a list of the officers on details away from their regiments, battalions, companies or corps who have been more than four years away from them, and who had not then served, during the time immediately preceding the detail, a period of two years with such regiment, battalion, company or corps?

[1] The Navy had increased the sea duty requirements for prospective commanders of its larger ships.

What do you think of my issuing some such order as this? —

I hereby direct that hereafter no officer be detailed on the General Staff of the Army, or in any of the staff corps or departments, or on any other duty or duties away from his company, battalion, regiment or corps, who has not served on duty with such company, battalion, regiment or corps for a period of two years immediately preceding such detail.

All officers now serving on such details whose records do not conform to the above order will be relieved from such details and ordered to join their respective commands.

Service as aides to general officers, at service schools whether as assistants or instructors, and on recruiting duty or at recruiting depots will not be considered as service with troops within the meaning of this order.[2]

Sincerely yours

4563 · TO GEORGE CABOT LEE, JUNIOR   *Roosevelt Mss.*

Washington, January 13, 1908

Dear George: [1] I have your letter of the 11th with the accompanying magazine. I had already read the article. It has some very good points in it. The trouble is that it does not take account of facts as we have to face them. For instance, it says that we should punish the officials and not the stockholders, and says that to fine the corporation is an act of great injustice and outrage. This simply is not so. In the case of the Standard Oil Company, for instance, five sixths of the stock is held by the Rockefellers and their associates. In every corporation it is the stockholders who are responsible for the acts of the officials, and if they choose not to make their officials do right they have nobody but themselves to blame if a crime is committed. The form of corporate organization has so many advantages that it is a necessity in modern business; but among its disadvantages is the fact that it too often shields from punishment for his misdeeds the real offender unless he is punished thru the corporation itself. The man who can be imprisoned or personally fined is too often merely the agent, and the alternative is to let the big scoundrel go scotfree or punish him by fining the corporation, which is really he himself, or which he controls, or which could if it wisht prevent him from wrongdoing. I have no patience with this cry about "the innocent stockholder."

Next, as for "letting bygones be bygones." How far back is this meant to apply? The statute of limitations applies to everything that happened more than two or three years ago; (always provided it is not also happening now). Surely during those two or three years the people have had ample warning. As a matter of fact I have let up in every case where I have had any possible excuse for so doing. The only prosecution that we are even thinking of in

---

[2] This order was not issued. The shortage of officers made impractical a rigid plan for the rotation of officers on detached duty; see No. 4683.

[1] George Cabot Lee, Jr., Alice Hathaway Lee Roosevelt's brother, a partner in the Boston firm of Lee, Higginson and Company.

New England, so far as I know, is that of Mellen and his road, where I went, if anything, beyond the verge of propriety in condoning offenses; and, as I have generally found to be the case with these great "captains of industry," the minute I showed a disposition to treat the corporation as well as possible, the head of that corporation promptly proceeded to perpetrate new forms of iniquity, relying upon my purpose to treat him decently as a protection.

If you are coming on here I will make some of these statements to you more in detail. *Ever yours*

4564 · TO HENRY SMITH PRITCHETT   *Roosevelt Mss.*

Washington, January 13, 1908

My dear Sir: I regret that I am not able to accept the invitation to be present at the first annual meeting of the Society for the Promotion of Industrial Education.[1]

My interest in this cause arises not only out of the important results to be achieved by Industrial Education both for the wage earner and the manufacturer, but more than all else out of the desire to see the American boy have his best opportunity for development. Today the boy of fourteen who leaves the public school finds the door to industrial efficiency closed. The apprenticeship system has practically disappeared. Unless he is given an opportunity for industrial training by a combination of school and shop instruction his chance for such training is small, and he is likely to continue to spend, as he does today, the years between fourteen and eighteen in minor occupations of an unfruitful character — occupations which neither minister to his intellectual nor his moral betterment. In the interest, therefore, of the American boy I welcome the efforts of any society like this to focus public attention upon the question and to suggest practical methods for solving it. *Very truly yours*

4565 · TO WILLIAM HOWARD TAFT   *Roosevelt Mss.*

Washington, January 13, 1908

My dear Mr. Secretary: I approve the report of Governor Magoon and your letter thereon, and they will be transmitted to Congress together with a copy of this letter. I direct that the installation of the President and Congress of Cuba, who will be elected next December, and the turning over of the island to them, take place not later than February 1, 1909. If it can be turned over earlier I shall be glad; but under no circumstances and for no reason will the date be later than February 1, 1909.[1] *Sincerely yours*

[1] The meeting, held in Chicago on January 23, was made conspicuous by an absence of trade-union men and the attendance of many strongly anti-union businessmen.

[1] The transfer of the government of Cuba to Cuban authorities took place January 28, 1909.

Washington, January 15, 1908

Dear Kohlsaat: I have your letter and the enclosed clipping. It has seemed to me very doubtful whether Fowler's bill would not make our situation worse instead of better.[1] It provides for extension, but not for contraction. In other words, it seems to me to be merely an inflation measure. This financial business is very puzzling.

I wish many happy new years to you and yours. _Faithfully yours_

4567 · TO IRA REMSEN _Roosevelt Mss._

Washington, January 16, 1908

Dear President Remsen: [1] We have reached a point in the enforcement of the Pure Food and Drugs Act where it has become necessary that some scientific

[1] Fowler, as chairman of the House Banking and Currency Committee, had introduced a measure calling for far-reaching currency reform. This bill, anticipating much of the later federal reserve legislation, called for the replacement of bond-secured currency by an asset currency, the formation of regional associations of national banks, the establishment of compulsory mutual deposit and note insurance funds, and the endowment of national banks with trust company functions. The provisions, purposes, and limitations of the bill can be found in _House Report,_ 60 Cong., 1 sess., No. 1126.

Like Roosevelt, most congressmen in both parties thought Fowler's bill both impractical and inflationary. The Administration forces, therefore, had little difficulty in substituting the milder Vreeland Bill, which, like the Aldrich Bill, provided for emergency currency rather than currency reform. The most important section of the Vreeland Bill incorporated the demands of the West and South for a broader-based currency by providing for the use of "any securities, including commercial paper" by national banks as security for emergency currency. Such collateral, however, had to be secured by the indorsement of the "national currency association" to which the issuing bank belonged. These were to be voluntary associations including at least ten banks having an aggregate capital and surplus of over five million dollars. After prolonged conferences the Senate substantially accepted the House provisions and on May 30, 1908, the Aldrich-Vreeland Bill became law.

Much less controversial was the House provision for a national monetary commission to investigate the currency problem and suggest permanent reform. This provision, recommended by Roosevelt and strongly supported by a large majority of Congress and the press, was approved by the Senate without debate. The commission under the chairmanship of Aldrich began work in the summer of 1908 and submitted in 1912 its well-known report.

[1] Ira Remsen, Gilman's successor as president of The Johns Hopkins University and one of the great chemists of his time, served as chairman of the board which was appointed to settle certain issues that arose under the Pure Food and Drugs Law. The President appointed the board in part because he did not trust, for reasons not altogether clear, the judgment of Dr. Harvey W. Wiley, the chief chemist of the Department of Agriculture. Before selecting the personnel and defining the duties of the body, Roosevelt consulted Presidents Alderman of Virginia, Hadley of Yale, Harris of Northwestern, and Wheeler of California. The board is interesting as an early example of the employment of academic experts on technical problems involving the relation of government and industry. Remsen did an excellent job as presiding officer, but he shrank from the attendant publicity and disliked the personal

questions shall be settled. For this purpose, I have decided that we shall have a Referee Board, of five members, eminent medical men or physiological chemists. The Secretary of Agriculture will certify to this Board each question upon which he desires a final determination. Only those questions will be referred to the Board concerning which there exists a serious difference of opinion among eminent authorities. It is proposed that members of the Board will devote only a portion of their time to Government work, and that they will be paid liberally for the time employed. The Board will have full authority to make all experiments necessary to reach a decision upon the questions submitted. A Secretary for the Board and other clerical help will be provided, and the expenses incident to investigations will be paid.

It is my desire to secure men of such high character and attainments that when the Referee Board speaks, it will be the final word on the subject so far as the United States is concerned. The questions now pressing for solution which will probably be referred to the Board immediately, are, whether sulphur dioxide and benzoate of soda are harmful in foods. The Board will enjoy the greatest independence. The Government will certify the questions and the Board will work out the answers in its own way, free from hampering influence of any kind.

Perhaps you know one or two men who are available. If so, I ask that you will write me fully about them; also that you will ascertain if their services may be secured, all, of course, in a confidential and tentative way. Prompt action is necessary in this matter, as the Board will be appointed within a very short time.

With expressions of regard and esteem, believe me, *Sincerely yours*

4568 · TO PHILIP BATHELL STEWART   *Roosevelt Mss.*

Private   Washington, January 17, 1908

Dear Phil: For your private consideration only and not for communication to anyone else, I send you the enclosed letter which I have just received from Garfield. I think I told you once that I did not believe that there was anything against Hagerman's personal honesty, but I am obliged to state now that the evidence seems to show that he has been a prominent factor in what really amounts to a swindle upon the Government; and what has been shown in the case set forth in Garfield's letter makes me seriously doubt whether his action as regards the Pennsylvania Land Company at the time he was Governor was not influenced by worse motives than I had supposed.[1]

Is there any chance of seeing you here this winter? *Always yours*

altercations in which, inevitably, the members of such a body became involved. His colleagues included Russell H. Chittenden, Christian A. Herter, John H. Long, and Alonzo E. Taylor.

[1] See No. 4302.

Private   Washington, January 17, 1908

My dear Mr. Post: [1] Apropos of Madame Versäy,[2] you may possibly be amused to know my experience in connection with the decision of the United States Supreme Court that Confederate notes were not counterfeit. While Knox was Attorney General there came before me the case of two criminals who had passed these notes. The lower court held that the notes were counterfeit and both men were imprisoned. One of the men took an appeal and the other did not. After some time the superior court declared that Confederate notes were not counterfeits and thereupon the man was released. Knox then brought around to me a formal order for the release of the other. This I promptly refused to issue, and Knox and I then had an argument, he standing for the law and I for rude and primitive justice. The argument reminded me a little of the famous discussion between the King, the Queen and the Headsman in *Alice in Wonderland*. Knox's position was that as the act committed by the man had been declared by the court not to be criminal, I could not keep him in prison. My position was that as he was undoubtedly a scoundrel and a swindler and morally a criminal, I certainly would not let him out of prison; and that as for saying that I could not keep him in, why, he *was* in, and that was all there was about it. I think Knox had the best of the argument as regards the law, but I had the final say-so as to the facts and the man stayed in for nearly a year longer. I was sorry I could not punish both scoundrels, but at least I was able to punish one.[3] *Sincerely yours*

---

[1] Melville Davisson Post, West Virginia lawyer; a successful manipulator with his law partner, John T. McGraw, of the Democratic party in his state in the 1890's. In the intervals between political trafficking and the practice of his profession he constructed short stories of crime and mystery. His great character was Randolph Mason, a sharp-witted, evil man whose knowledge of the interstices in the body of the law enabled him to circumvent the claims of justice and the state. There was a technical perfection in the organization of his stories that offset his hopelessly conventional understanding of personality.

[2] "A certain variety actress," "a bad one," key figure in a Randolph Mason adventure, the plot of which hinged on the passing of Confederate currency.

[3] When Theodore Roosevelt once spent the night in the home of the president of Harvard he arrived with a revolver, presumably to defend himself against a raid by Charles W. Eliot or Bishop Lawrence, with whom Roosevelt was to have breakfast. Since carrying a revolver without a permit was against the laws of the Commonwealth of Massachusetts, Mr. Eliot concluded that the President of the United States was a "lawless man." This letter is delightful evidence in support of Eliot's humorless but discerning conclusion. Roosevelt's feeling for the perfection of his own moral code as a basis for the ordering of civilization was, perhaps like any conservative's, above his feeling for the inhibitions of the law as it existed at any given moment.

Washington, January 17, 1908

My dear Dr. Abbott: [1] I am somewhat puzzled whether to write to you about the opening editorials in the present issue of the *Outlook;* because I suppose you will think that I am writing to defend myself or from my own interest.[2] As a matter of fact, I am writing only because I feel that it is a grave and serious wrong to the navy to condone and approve mutinous and insubordinate conduct such as that of Admiral Brownson's. I do not know how extensive the circulation of the *Outlook* is in naval circles; but apart from its effect there, it is a real and serious wrong to encourage such views in the community. I received the following letter on the subject from General Grenville M. Dodge:

January 7, 1908.

My dear Mr. President:

I have read your letter to the Secretary of the Navy in relation to the command of the hospital ships, also Admiral Brownson's letter in which he declines to obey the order of his superior officer, and resigning his position.

If you will pardon me, I wish to say I think you made a mistake in accepting Admiral Brownson's resignation. In my opinion, you should have insisted upon his obeying the order, and in case of refusal he would have been court-martialed. One of the cardinal principles of discipline is to obey an order from the proper authority. If one does not desire to remain in the service under the officer who issues the order, then *after* obeying it is the time to resign. This setting up of one's individual wishes against the rules, regulations and orders of an organization is becoming altogether too frequent, and in case of the army and navy is becoming an absolute detriment to the service. The influence upon young officers of the service is demoralizing. They would naturally assume that if they did not like an order all they have to do is not to obey it and resign. I have heard some criticisms because you did not publish Admiral Brownson's letter, but I think any person who has at heart the interest of the service would say that it would have been a great favor to Admiral Brownson if his letter had never seen the light.[3]

Respectively and sincerely,
Your obedient servant,
GRENVILLE M. DODGE.

[1] The letter was not sent to Abbott. Roosevelt, however, had Loeb forward it to J. T. Williams, Washington correspondent for the Boston *Evening Transcript*, with the request that Williams see the President about it on the following day.

[2] The *Outlook* had admonished Roosevelt for his castigation of Brownson; see No. 4549. It reasoned that Brownson was justified in resigning and leaving a policy which he felt injurious to the well-being of the Navy to be carried out by officers who approved of it. The editorial also stressed that Brownson "ought not to be publicly rebuked for such resignation without being heard in his own defense, and that unworthy motives ought not to be imputed to him without evidence to sustain the imputation."

[3] Although Dodge, like Roosevelt, did not differentiate between obedience to an order of military command and a decision of administrative policy, he did make a distinction that Roosevelt failed to appreciate or at least to state publicly. If the President had pointed out that Brownson's fault was not in the act of resigning but rather in resigning before rather than after carrying out an order, he might have been less vulnerable to criticism. Possibly the realization that Dodge's opinions did

My chief reason for not following the course that General Dodge advised (which in the abstract, as a mere matter of justice, would have been the best course) was that it would have entailed severe measures being taken as regards Admiral Brownson, and I knew that both the ignorance and the sentimentality of many good people would make them condone his conduct. I will frankly say that it never occurred to me, however, that the *Outlook* would be capable of assuming a position so mischievous to the service. If Brownson was right in resigning rather than carry out my orders, then any of his subordinates would be right in resigning rather than carry out his orders, and this would be true afloat just as much as ashore. If Brownson was right, then any naval captain at Rio who thinks that Admiral Evans ought to go around the Horn instead of thru the Strait of Magellan ought to resign instead of continuing with the fleet. Literally the position is too absurd for discussion, if there is to be any order or discipline in the navy. I spoke as leniently as I possibly could of Brownson. To let his conduct go unrebuked would have been gravely culpable. Remember too that this did not cloud the real issue, for the real issue is not: who shall command the hospital ship. That issue is absolutely unimportant compared to the issue as to whether or not the highest officer in the navy shall do his duty and obey orders, or whether he shall set an example of insubordination which would ruin the service at once and irretrievably if it were generally followed. I do not regard this as a small matter; and it is difficult to regard it as a matter as to which there are two sides. *Sincerely yours*

4571 · TO FRANCIS EMROY WARREN   *Roosevelt Mss.*

Washington, January 17, 1908

My dear Sir: I set before you for the confidential consideration of your committee the following facts regarding the imperative need of fitting Pearl Harbor, in Hawaii, as a fortified naval station.[1]

The proper defense of the territorial possessions of the United States in the Pacific Ocean requires imperatively that this country shall possess at one or more points in that ocean a naval base or bases capable of being maintained against strong attack during war, which shall afford stations for the supply and repair of naval vessels and transports en route between the United States and our possessions in the Far East. Above all, such a station should exist in the Hawaiian Islands where, besides serving the purpose just

---

not fully support his position was the reason Roosevelt did not send this letter to Abbott.

---

[1] Roosevelt regarded the base at Pearl Harbor as one of the essential items of the naval program he had presented Congress in December. During the early part of the session he concentrated successfully on winning support for the development of the base. Congress gave him substantially all he requested, including funds for dredging the channel, for construction of a dry dock, and for fortifications. See Numbers 4593, 4608.

referred to as one of a chain of bases connecting our Pacific possessions, it would prevent the occupation of the islands in question by any enemy that might otherwise be in a position to operate therefrom against our continental coast; and it would still further afford a base for a force of our own which, by placing itself upon the flank of any enemy seeking to attack our Pacific coast from north, west or south, would afford far greater security to California, Oregon and Washington than could be obtained by a like expenditure for fortifications within the limits of those States themselves.

Pearl Harbor in the Hawaiian Islands has long been favorably reported upon as the one place in those islands suited for a naval station. It is naturally well protected, has sufficient depth of water, and is capable of being strongly fortified. Its one defect is its tortuous channel of approach, which, trending around coral reefs, presents dangers which render navigation by large vessels impracticable. The establishment at this place of a naval base of a character which the military interests of the Nation require would therefore comprehend:

(1) A sufficient amount of dredging to straighten the entrance channel so as to insure safety in ingress and egress for all classes of naval vessels.

(2) The construction of a dry dock to accommodate naval vessels, with accompanying facilities for repair work for vessels visiting the station for docking or other purposes.

(3) The erection of permanent land defenses to protect the stations from attack by sea, with such other works as may be needed for defense against attack by land from a force disembarked elsewhere upon the coast.

Regarding the requirement for straightening the channel, estimates based upon a naval hydrographic survey indicate that the amount to be removed in order to secure a practicable channel would be in the neighborhood of 2,000,-000 cubic yards; equally reliable testimony further indicates that the material to be removed is of a nature that lends itself to comparatively easy dredging. This feature will thus be seen to be a work of no great magnitude.

Since the various works involved in the creation of a naval station are all such as to require a considerable time for their execution, the necessity will be apparent for authorizing an immediate and simultaneous beginning with all; it would, for example, be most ill-advised to defer the start on the dry dock to await the completion of the dredging, or the start on the dredging to await the completion of the fortifications. All should proceed at once, so that within the shortest possible time we may have a base of the nature recommended.

If it were needed to offer other arguments for the work than considerations of the national defense, it might be pointed out that the proposed development of Pearl Harbor would result in great advantage to the commercial interests of the islands. The harbor of Honolulu is inadequate to the demands being put upon it by the increased size and number of merchant vessels that now make the Hawaiian Islands a place of call. Pearl Harbor is near enough to Honolulu to render the development of the former of the same importance to the capital city as the otherwise impossible extension of its own harbor facilities.

I suppose that this matter relates to what must go before more than one committee of your body. Will you tell me to which other committees I should send copies of this letter? *Very truly yours*

4572 · TO WILLIAM DUDLEY FOULKE   *Roosevelt Mss.*

Washington, January 19, 1908

My dear Foulke: Indeed I will take any letter kindly, from such an old and dear friend as yourself, but, my dear fellow, you must pardon my also feeling a certain amount of good-humored amusement over your letter. You enclose me an editorial from the Indianapolis *Star.* This editorial says that Mr. Cortelyou has been trying to rehabilitate the Knickerbocker Trust Company because there is $55,000 of mine deposited there, and it also says that I am trying to use the officeholders to nominate Taft. The first statement is an unqualified lie as I have not one cent on deposit in the Knickerbocker Trust Company; but it is no more a lie than the second. You ought to know this from your own observation. How are the officeholders behaving in your own State of Indiana? As far as I know the District Attorney in Indiana is the chief worker on behalf of the Fairbanks canvass,[1] and I do not know a single Taft supporter among the federal officials in Indiana. If any office-holder under me has been perniciously active in politics it has been this District Attorney who has been active on behalf of the *Star's* candidate for the Presidency, Mr. Fairbanks. In Ohio four fifths of the officeholders are actively against Mr. Taft and for Foraker. Literally all I have done is to try to make it understood that in order for a man to hold my commission it shall not be an indispensable prerequisite that he shall be against my policies and a violent opponent of the man who of all the candidates among the people comes nearest to recognizing those policies. In New Hampshire I nominated one man at the suggestion of Winston Churchill when the two Senators disagreed.[2] As far as I know all the other officeholders of the state are working in accordance with the dictates of the Boston and Maine Railroad machine against Taft. Will any human being less disinterested than the New York *Evening Post* maintain that this is using patronage to advance anyone's candidacy? Remember that two months ago all these papers that now accuse me of using the patronage to nominate Taft were accusing me of using Taft as a blind and of being really treacherous to him and resolute to nominate myself.

[1] Joseph B. Kealing, prominent Indianapolis Republican, then United States Attorney for the District of Indiana and manager of the Fairbanks campaign, later resigned his office rather than prosecute Roosevelt's libel charge against the Indianapolis *News;* see Bowers, *Beveridge,* pp. 296–297.
[2] Churchill's candidate for pension agent at Concord, C. Fairbanks, was rejected by the Senate.

You say "there is a violation of two provisions of the Civil Service Law; first, that no official is under any obligation to render any political service and will not be prejudiced for refusing to do so, and second, that no person in the service has any right to use his authority or influence to coerce the action of any person or body." It is possible that I have offended against these two positions on just one occasion, and that is when I issued my directions to the officeholders generally that they were not to support me for a third term. If any man wishes to maintain that in doing this I was using my authority to coerce the action of these officeholders he is quite welcome to do so. But it is the only charge that can be sustained.

Now, my dear fellow, will you produce the name of a single man whom I have coerced or influenced? Will you give me the name (in the "direction" to which you object) of the official in New York, or elsewhere, whom you speak of as having been controlled by threat of dismissal, or implied threat of dismissal, or from whom I have demanded support for Taft — in short will you give me one particle of justification for the fears that you express? Name the man whom I have appointed because he was for Taft or whom I have removed because he was not for Taft, or threatened to remove because he was not for Taft. You cannot do so, and as you cannot, why do you not repeat this challenge to the *Star*, assert that their words are absolutely false, and challenge them to make good? Ask them about the activity of District Attorney Kealing in Indiana and ask them if they can give the case of any official who is supporting Taft in similar fashion. Doubtless some of the appointees I have nominated during the past few months are for Taft, but I know that the most prominent appointment I have made in New York, that of Collector of Customs, is a man actually hostile to Taft. I know that some of the men I have appointed are favorable to Knox and Cannon. In short the whole statement in the *Star* is a lie pure and simple, and what is needed is not any action on my part but a prompt assertion that this statement is a lie and a demand upon the man or men making it to submit something in the way of proof thereof.[3] *Faithfully yours*

[*Handwritten*] I have consulted Taft in Ohio exactly as I have consulted Bonaparte in Maryland. If you will write to Bonaparte he can give you with exact nicety just how I have "used" the offices in Maryland; and I have used them there precisely as elsewhere.

4573 · TO ARCHIBALD BULLOCH ROOSEVELT *Roosevelt Mss.*

Washington, January 20, 1908

Dear Archie: Mrs. Peabody wrote Mother a very dear and very funny letter about you. She said you had a cold and had gone to the infirmary, and that in addition the Rector had fallen on you while skating, but that this had not

[3] This was the first of several letters Roosevelt wrote Foulke on the subject of patronage and the nomination of Taft; see also Numbers 4587, 4633.

damaged you; but that if I felt that reparation was owing, she would send down Betsey for me to fall upon!

Quentin is just as funny as ever, and just as much of a philosopher. The other day at breakfast he said — "Well, Father, I just saw a puzzle card with a picture of you whacking the trusts, and the motto 'We're for Teddy because Teddy protects the poor man'; but I suppose next year all the enthusiasm will be for Mr. Taft!" The Y.M.C.A. seems to be a good deal of comfort to Quentin, and he practices much in the gymnasium and uses the swimming bath. *Your loving father*

4574 · TO KERMIT ROOSEVELT

Roosevelt Mss.

Washington, January 27, 1908

Dear Kermit: The campaign for Taft seems to be getting along well. Of course the statements that I am trying to dictate his nomination are ludicrous falsehoods, and the statements that I am using the offices to force his nomination are wicked falsehoods. But I believe with all my soul that Taft, far more than any other public man of prominence, represents the principles for which I stand; and, furthermore, I believe in these principles with all my soul; and I should hold myself false to my duty if I sat supine and let the men who have taken such joy in my refusal to run again select some candidate whose success would mean the undoing of what I have sought to achieve. The men most hostile to me show a tendency to gather around Hughes. Hughes is a fairly good man (but not a big man) and an inordinately conceited one. He is therefore jealous of me, and the men who are backing him believe that they could count upon his jealousy of me to make him take action which would amount in effect to undoing what I had done, altho that might not be Hughes' conscious purpose. Hughes is not knee-high to Taft in any way, but he has the kind of quality which is apt to win out in conventions as against a man of bold, generous type like Taft, who looks out too little for his own interests. But this year I believe we shall be able to awaken people to what the real situation is. I am confident that if the convention was held at once Taft would be nominated. It is always unsafe to prophesy in politics, and all that can be said is that if we can hold things as they are we shall be all right. Whether we can so hold them I cannot tell, and nobody can.

We are at the height of the social season, and as formal social entertainments are rather a nightmare to me, I look forward eagerly to its ending. I am worked up to my limit, having just been carefully preparing a message to Congress in which I intend to draw the issue as sharply as I well can between the men of predatory wealth and the administration. As I also try to get some exercise riding or walking every day this means that going to entertainments in the evening makes a serious tax upon me. *Your loving father*

Washington, January 28, 1908

My dear Mr. Thompson: [1] That is an exceedingly interesting volume on the old illuminated manuscripts. Naturally, I was particularly interested in the hunting adventures of that exceedingly capable Fourteenth-century princess, and it is perfectly delightful that they should have been contained in her prayer book! To think of her, in a riding habit not unlike that she would have worn today, killing a wild boar with a spear! I do not quite understand why you called her a Scotch princess. Evidently the prayer book had been in the possession of some Scotch person or persons; but she hunted, not the stag, but the fallow buck, and I supposed the fallow buck and the boar were characteristic of English rather than of Scotch sport. This may be all a mistake on my part, however, and of course there must have been plenty of fallow deer along the Border.

It was delightful catching a glimpse of you last year. I still remain a heretic about Spenser. *Faithfully yours*

4576 · TO EMILY TUCKERMAN *Roosevelt Mss.*

Washington, January 31, 1908

Dear Emily: Both of those editorials are certainly amusing. Oh heavens! Why doesn't righteousness more often go with the capacity to be entertaining? *Ever yours*

4577 · TO WILFRID LAURIER *Roosevelt Mss.*

Washington, February 1, 1908

My dear Sir Wilfrid: Mr. Mackenzie King[1] arrived yesterday with the very important message from you.[2] After seeing him I had him see Mr. Root. He then called on Ambassador Bryce, and today I had the Ambassador and Mr. King at lunch with me and went over the matter with them afterwards. The Ambassador was as interested as I had previously been in Mr. King's statement of the feeling in Western Canada, and especially in British Columbia, and in the fact that this feeling is at least as strong as that which obtains on the same subject in California, Oregon and Washington. He cordially agreed that it would be a good thing to have Mr. King go to the other side to explain

---

[1] Henry Yates Thompson, world traveler and bibliophile, won his place in the *Dictionary of National Biography* for bringing together an unexcelled collection of illuminated manuscripts.

---

[1] William Lyon Mackenzie King, the great Canadian political figure, was then Commissioner of Labor and Immigration.

[2] For the purport of this message and Roosevelt's reaction to it, see No. 4578, and Bailey, *Roosevelt and the Japanese-American Crises*, pp. 270–272; see also Jessup, *Root*, II, 31–32.

matters fully to the Imperial Government, which Mr. King tells me is what you propose to have him do. It seems to me that this course is eminently wise. I have spoken with entire freedom and frankness to Mr. King and at the Ambassador's request Mr. Bacon showed Mr. King the documents concerning our own negotiations, so that he will be able to speak with full knowledge to the Imperial authorities. I think it altogether admirable that this step should have been taken and that there should now be a fair likelihood of both nations working cordially together for their own interest, while at the same time being scrupulously careful to behave in the most honorable manner to Japan and to safeguard her interests.

Mr. King also handed me a memorandum about wood pulp and lumber which I gave to Bacon after the conversation which he will repeat to you.

Believe me, my dear Sir Wilfrid, that it was a particular pleasure to hear from you and to meet Mr. King and that I feel that the directness, simplicity and good faith of such a communication is a happy omen for the future, and as an admirer of you personally and of the great and wonderful country at the head of whose government you stand, I am exceedingly pleased at the steps that have been taken to bring our several peoples into closer and more friendly connection.

With assurances of my hearty regard, believe me, *Very sincerely yours*

4578 · TO ARTHUR HAMILTON LEE   *Roosevelt Mss.*

Private   Washington, February 2, 1908

Dear Lee: That is an awfully nice letter of yours, my dear fellow, and the enclosures also really interested me. Maurice Low is a circumcised skunk.[1] A couple of years ago, when he was blackballed in the Metropolitan Club here, someone came to me complaining about my receiving him and told me that he had been circulating very outrageous slanders in an English monthly magazine for which he had been writing during the Presidential campaign. I had not seen them at the time, but lookt them up and found that they were really bad — in other words, that Low had characteristically refrained from making accusations against me on his own authority, but had repeated campaign slanders about my having practically blackmailed big corporations into paying money for my campaign expenses. They were accusations that only the yellowest of the yellow papers made here, and they were

[1] Maurice Low, in the London *Morning Post* of December 26, 1907, reported that "many people were fully convinced that Mr. Roosevelt was endeavoring to manipulate public sentiment so as to force his nomination." Low also asserted that Roosevelt had failed in almost everything he had undertaken. On January 4, 1908, Strachey in an editorial in *Spectator*, and on January 11, Lee in a private letter to the same journal, defended Roosevelt, particularly against Low's "insidious and indirect" charge that the President sought a third term.

put forward in a particularly mean way. I had Low in, showed him what he had said, and told him that in view of his mendacity and malice he would not thereafter be allowed at the White House or at any of the Departments. He never has been allowed in since, and has revenged himself by writing as he did in this instance. It is no case of his being mistaken as to the facts. He deliberately invents his stories. I am surprised that Ware[2] should keep him, for he is a thoroly disreputable little creature. However, I do not think he is of any earthly importance. Do tell Strachey for me that I really appreciate his two editorials on the subject.

All right, László shall paint that picture, and that is all there is about it.

Now for a matter of importance. The other day Mackenzie King, the Canadian Commissioner of Labor and Immigration, was down here. It was evident that he had been sent down in an informal way by Sir Wilfrid Laurier to sound me because the Canadians had become very seriously disturbed over the situation affecting Japanese immigration. King struck me as a very capable, resolute fellow, and his decision of character, coupled with his official position, had enabled him to get hold of a number of Japanese documents such as we on this side of the line had never seen. These documents he said fully bore out what he had suspected but could not prove, namely, that the Japanese Government had deliberately overissued two or three times the number of passports which they said they were issuing; and he asserted that they showed that the immigration was really completely under the control of their Government. The papers he seized were in the possession of an agent of the Japanese Immigration people, who had formerly been the Japanese Consul. They contained many official papers from the Japanese Government which as he stated showed its thoro understanding of all the crooked work that was going on. Among other things, he told me that in the first ten months of last year they received some 35000 Japanese who had passports to the United States — the Japanese having arranged with us that the only Japanese who should come here were those who had passports direct to the United States and who were shipped direct to our shores. After the investigations were completed King states that a very curious touch was given to the proceeding by the fact that the Japanese ex-Consul and other Japanese gave him a dinner in Japanese style, and that at this dinner the ex-Consul made a speech the intent of which, inasmuch as he was an Oriental, I cannot follow, but which in an Occidental would have been insolence; for he got up and to the intense and evident excitement of his countrymen repeated a dream that he had had to the effect that Japan had taken the mastery of the Pacific and pocketed the Island of Vancouver, and then had swallowed all America west of the Rocky Mountains. King, who is a gentleman and made a very favorable impression upon me, went on to state that the western portions of Canada, that is, British Columbia and Alberta, were prepared to make the exclusion of the Japanese their cardinal political tenet, and if the central Government of

[2] Sir Fabian Ware.

Canada or the Empire should object, would secede and set up, together with our Pacific States, a new and separate Republic. To be sure that I understood him aright, I got King to repeat this and he did so saying that under such circumstances — that is, assuming that Washington, London and Ottawa all declined to take measures to restrict Japanese immigration — the people of the Pacific Slope north and south of the forty-ninth parallel would form a new republic of their own. I laughed and said there would be no such new republic formed. He said that he agreed with me, but that he did very much wish that the London Government — and for the matter of that, the people in Eastern Canada as well as the people in the Eastern United States — could be awakened to the feeling. He thanked me very earnestly for having sent our fleet to the Pacific. I told him that in my view the thing to be done was to have the Imperial and the American authorities in London and Washington work together; explain to Japan our hearty friendship (the friendship in one case of an ally and in the other of an old friend) but point out that in the present stage of the world's development it was highly inadvisable for any people to send its laboring class into another land where they were not wanted; that Japan would certainly not tolerate having forty or fifty thousand American and Canadian miners turn up in Sakhalin or Formosa, and that similarly there must be a complete cessation of the emigration of Japanese laborers to the English-speaking countries surrounding the Pacific. I also told him that the Japanese had given us at last the most positive and unequivocal assurance that the flood of emigration to America would be stopt, and that we had informed them plainly that we could no longer accept excuses, and that if as the result of their measures we did not see a very great diminution in the immigration it would be but a short while before Congress passed laws restricting this immigration. You probably know that under our treaty with Japan we have a perfect right to pass such laws, and that Japan has already exercised her right to do so, and by Imperial edict has forbidden laborers from foreign countries from settling in Japan outside of two or three places. This restriction is aimed at the Chinese, but in its terms applies to all nationalities.

After a very full and pleasant talk King left, but I received a telegram from him almost as soon as he reached Ottawa, asking me if he could see me again. Of course I telegraphed in the affirmative, and day before yesterday he turned up. He informed me that he had been requested to come down by Sir Wilfrid Laurier to speak to me as to the advisability of his going at once to England so as to inform the Imperial Government in detail as to the actual condition of sentiment in British Columbia and in western Canada generally, and of the identity of this sentiment with that obtaining in our western, and especially the Pacific, States, and of the great desirability that the United States and the British Empire should work together in this matter, for the interest of one as much as of the other. I answered that I cordially agreed with this view; that I felt that the mere fact that there was cordial understanding and agreement between the two nations as to what was to be done, always provided that there was a real purpose to prevent any humiliation to Japan, would be of immense importance from every standpoint, and would be a guarantee of peace. Canadian diplomacy, like much of the diplomacy of my own native land, is evidently much on the *sans gêne* order, which has its advantages in getting work quickly done, but which can be carried to an extreme. I was much amused (this of course you must not repeat) that King had no idea that he was to call on Ambassador Bryce. I of course told him that he must do so at once, and also exprest my emphatic approval of Sir Wilfrid's suggestion that Earl Grey should be informed of the matter. I also had King see Root. Yesterday Bryce and King and Bacon lunched with me, and Bryce exprest his approval of King's going over to explain the facts to your Government. I asked him if he would not also cable Sir Edward Grey expressing the hope that certain leaders of the opposition might be likewise fully informed of the facts. I told King that I should write you, in absolute confidence, of our interview, and asked him to call on you when he reaches London. For fear there is some miscue I should be much obliged if you would look him up. Do not show this letter to anyone, except that in strict confidence you can show it to Grey, Balfour, and Strachey, if, as I assume to be the case, you feel sure that they will understand my writing you. You can also speak to Carter, our First Secretary, about it, as I shall tell him that I have written you, (altho I shall tell him very little of the subject matter.)

I believe we have now got our negotiations with Japan in good shape, which, together with Japan's agreement with Canada,[3] will probably bring about a peaceable and satisfactory solution. But of course everything depends upon the good faith and effectiveness with which Japan carries out her agreements. What British Columbia and the Pacific States will insist upon is that there shall be a great falling off actually visible in Japanese immigration, and that the immigrants shall not be laborers of any kind. No mere nominal compliance with regulations will satisfy them, and if they are not satisfied trouble is inevitable both for the Empire of Great Britain and for the United States. Under such circumstances I think it greatly to the interest of both peoples that they should work with a cordial understanding of one another's position and should convince the Japanese that in the first place our peoples have nothing but the friendliest and most respectful feeling for Japan, but that in the second place, in the interest of lasting peace and good will between Japan and the English-speaking peoples, it is imperative that all immigrants of the working class from Japan should be kept out of English-speaking countries and those of the same class from English-speaking countries should be kept out of Japan.

With warm regards to Mrs. Lee, believe me, *Faithfully yours*

[3] Japan had agreed to limit the passports to Canada to one hundred fifty a year.

Washington, February 2, 1908

Dear Kermit: On January 31st everything was frozen hard and this put the tennis court in fair condition, so the Tennis Cabinet had what I think will really be its last session until spring. Gifford Pinchot and I played six sets against the French Ambassador and Alford Cooley, breaking even. It was bitterly cold but we thoroly enjoyed it. I had been riding with mother the two or three previous days, but February opened with a snowstorm and then freezing weather, and I think walking will be good enough as a form of exercise for some little time to come.

On Friday I sent in my message on the trusts and labor, and incidentally on corporations. I am well satisfied with the message and I think it was time to send it in. Of course it caused a great flutter in the dovecote. As we approach nearer the convention more and more people will pay heed to what the candidates will say rather than to what the President may say, and this is well-nigh the last occasion I shall have to speak when all men, however unwilling, must listen, and I wanted to put my deep and earnest convictions into the message. All of my advisers were naturally enough against my sending it in, for councils of war never fight; but Mother really likes the message, and I am sure that it is on the right track and that it says what ought to be said and that the ultimate effect will be good.[1] *Your loving father*

[*Handwritten*] 7.30 now I have just come in from a brisk three hours walk over the frozen snow out to Chevy Chase and back by Rock Creek. Meyer and Winthrop went with me.

[1] To the Congress which in large part had ignored the recommendations in his annual message, Roosevelt in a special message on January 31 stated with vigorous conviction the mature progressiveness that characterized his thought for the next five years. The two messages, furthermore, taken together, proposed in some detail the basic national reforms achieved under Taft and Wilson. To the conservative public of 1908, the special message seemed particularly dangerous. While Bryan applauded (see No. 4582), Nicholas Murray Butler was shocked (see No. 4584).

The special message, a long, discursive, and aggressive document (published in full as Appendix III), called for a new employers' liability act, for an act compensating government employees for injuries sustained in service, for restrictions on the use of injunctions in labor cases, for increased government control over railways and industrial corporations, and for federal control of securities issues. Congress granted only the first two requests. The rest of the message Roosevelt repeated with indignant emphasis in his campaign of 1910–1912. Clearly, in January 1908, long before he read Herbert Croly or fought with Taft, Roosevelt had come, in policy though not in politics, to the great divide.

Characteristically, however, Roosevelt used the message not only to bludgeon Congress and inform public opinion but also for political manipulation. He timed it so that it reached the newspapers on the day they were to publish Hughes' statement of his national principles. The President's message got the headlines; Hughes' program the secondary space.

Telegram   Washington, February 4, 1908

Telegram received. It seems to me that it is quite unnecessary to delay sixty days. Surely with reasonable expedition the police force can be organized, armed and equipped in a tenth of that time. Certainly to allow a quarter of the time is ample. If there are any reasons why troops should remain beyond the fifteenth of this month I should like to hear them at once.

4581 · TO MILTON DWIGHT PURDY   *Roosevelt Mss.*

Washington, February 4, 1908

My dear Mr. Purdy: I would be very much obliged if you would get in touch with Senator Dolliver. He is engaged in the preparation of a bill which will go into the question of a better supervision over the issue of stock and securities of the great interstate carriers.[1] Would you see him, give him such aid as you properly can, and, if it is out of your bailiwick, tell him who in the Department of Justice or in the Interstate Commerce Commission or in the Bureau of Corporations can help him? *Sincerely yours*

4582 · TO WILLIAM JENNINGS BRYAN   *Roosevelt Mss.*

Washington, February 4, 1908

My dear Mr. Bryan: I thank you heartily for your note of congratulation on my message. I most earnestly hope that Congress will as speedily as may be act on the lines I therein recommend. It seems to me that the decision just handed down from the Supreme Court further emphasizes the need of such action.[1]

Again thanking you for your kindness, believe me, *Sincerely yours*

4583 · TO CHARLES BEARY LANDIS   *Roosevelt Mss.*

Washington, February 5, 1908

My dear Mr. Landis:[1] The information you have given me this morning

[1] Dolliver did not introduce such a bill. Of the five bills proposed at the first session of the Sixtieth Congress to provide for supervision of the stock issues of interstate carriers, none emerged from committee.

[1] In *Adair v. United States*, 208 U. S. 161 (1908), the Supreme Court declared unconstitutional a federal statute penalizing common carriers for discharging any employee because of membership in a labor union. Speaking for an unexpectedly unanimous court, Justice Harlan declared the law an "arbitrary interference with the liberty of contract" amounting to a denial of due process of law, and an "unwarranted extension of the commerce power." Roosevelt in his special message had urged the need for a new statute to accomplish the same end without violating the court's interpretation of the Constitution.

[1] Charles Beary Landis, brother of Judge Kenesaw Mountain Landis; Republican congressman from Indiana, 1897–1909; in 1908 chairman of the House Committee on Printing.

is so important that I deem it best that there should be a written record thereof. I had already begun some weeks ago an investigation into the Government Printing Office under Mr. Stillings; this investigation originating because of information which reached me as to the increased cost of the printing to the Departments. I accordingly directed Mr. Havenner, of the Department of Commerce and Labor, to investigate and report upon this matter. His report on its face was severely condemnatory of Mr. Stillings. I furnished Mr. Stillings with a copy and requested an answer from him, which I have not yet received.

I enclose you a copy of Mr. Havenner's report and as soon as I receive the answer I shall also forward that to you for your information, and will let you know what action I have taken on the report.

You now inform me that your Committee has discovered circumstances in connection with the Printing Office, notably in connection with expenditures for furniture in the Printing Office and the purchase of supplies, which makes you feel that there is great irregularity therein. You also inform me that you believe that the present audit system of the Printing Bureau serves to shield these irregularities and that the persons in charge of this audit system exert an undue and improper influence, not only in the purchase of supplies for the Government Printing Office, but in the management of the office itself. You also say that your Subcommittee feels that it cannot make a satisfactory investigation of the office while Mr. Stillings and the persons in charge of the audit system are in the office, and request that I suspend Mr. Stillings pending investigation and also suspend the execution of the contract made under the audit system.

I have accordingly temporarily suspended Mr. Stillings and shall put Mr. Rossiter in his place, directing him to co-operate in every way with your Committee, and furthermore to make an exhaustive report to me on conditions in the office.[2] *Sincerely yours*

4584 · TO NICHOLAS MURRAY BUTLER   *Roosevelt Mss.*

Washington, February 6, 1908

Dear Murray: Your letter of the 4th does not surprise me, for I had heard thru Jimmy Speyer how you felt, and of course I have been aware that for the last year or two you have been steadily growing out of sympathy with my purposes and policies.

Really, my dear fellow, there is very little I can answer to your letter. You think that my last message is like Andrew Johnson's speeches and messages. I think you might just as well have said that it is like Jefferson Davis'; but that is a mere difference of opinion. You say that it has left a very

[2] Rossiter's report as well as further investigations demonstrated that Stillings, while honest and well-intentioned, had permitted gross inefficiencies in procedures and audits in the printing office. At Roosevelt's request, Stillings resigned. In April, John S. Leech was appointed to succeed him.

924

painful impression upon the public mind and that everywhere the loyal supporters of my administration, east and west, speak of the message with grief and sorrow, and that only my critics and enemies are delighted. Of course I may be utterly mistaken, but my experience has been that whereas my critics and enemies have foamed at the mouth over it, and whereas my lukewarm friends and the men who have been preparing to turn, have been upset by it, yet my real supporters — those whose deep convictions I most nearly represent — have hailed it as they have no other speech or action of mine for a long time. In the mail with your letter, for example, comes one from General Horatio C. King, a copy of which I enclose. This is typical of the hundreds of letters I have received, and I have received more from judges, relatively, than from any other body of men. But they have not been corporation judges, or the judges who, tho honest, are susceptible to corporation influences. Of course, as I have said, I am well aware that I may be entirely mistaken, but I will add that the events of the last three months have made me for the first time sincerely regret that this is not my first term, and that I cannot have a showdown with my foes both without and within the party. In my judgment, there would not be even a fight west of the Alleghenies; and if I were a betting man I should like to bet heavily on the fight in New York.

But this feeling represents in me only the old Adam, which is not wholly eradicated from any man, and does not at all represent my deepest feelings. I care not at all that the fight must now be carried on by somebody else, provided only that it is carried on. You regret what I have done. To me your regret is incomprehensible. You blame me for what I have done. To me it seems that I have the right to the fullest and heartiest support of every good man whose eyes are not blinded by unhappy surroundings, and who has in him a single trace of the fervor for righteousnes and decency without which goodness tends to be an empty sham. If your soul does not rise up against corruption in politics and corruption in business, against the unspeakable degradation and baseness of a community which will accept Rockefeller and Harriman, Foraker and Black, and Chancellor Day, as its leaders in the business world and in political thought, and which will tolerate the vileness of the New York *Sun* and kindred newspapers in its family — why, then naturally you are out of sympathy with me. If you felt, as I do, that the interests which these men and papers represent tell for unspeakable degradation in the Nation, and if left unchecked and unoffset would work a ruin such as was worked in the last days of the Roman Republic by similar forces — why, then you would naturally support my action. *Sincerely yours*

4585 · TO SETH LOW   *Roosevelt Mss.*

Personal   Washington, February 6, 1908

Dear Seth: That is a very nice speech of yours and I was glad to read it. Personally, I feel that the Governor should now be consulted as to whom he would like to have for delegates at large and his wishes followed; provided of course that the names are those of men like yourself and Andrew D. White — in short, men of high character, and not the corrupt and disgruntled politicians who have been pushing forward the Hughes boom without any regard for him and simply to ensure their own return to power.[1]

On March 6th I shall of course see your committee, and am mighty glad you are taking the matter up.[2] *Ever yours*

[1] Roosevelt had, rather complacently, done nothing to interfere with the developing Hughes boom in New York. This movement was organized and directed by the Hughes League, which contained both calloused manipulators like Brackett, Lauterbach, and Aldridge and independents like Seth Low. After pretending for many weeks that the organization did not really exist, the governor on January 21 announced that he would not seek but that he would accept the Republican Presidential nomination.

Two days later Taft wrote Herbert Parsons that he would "greatly deprecate a contest that might imperil Republican victory in New York in November." Thus directed, Taft's friends let the New York delegation to the Republican nominating convention go by default to Hughes.

This policy of noninterference was made possible by the fact that at all stages — in the county committee, in the state committee, and in the convention itself — Roosevelt and his allies were actually in control of the general political situation. So obvious was this that Seth Low — a delegate-at-large — implored Hughes to release the New York delegation before the balloting began in the nominating convention. Hughes refused and was, on the initial ballot, a poor third.

When, after this reverse, Hughes refused the Vice-Presidency offered by the Taft forces, his New York supporters rallied behind James S. Sherman for the office. Hughes was thus, as the convention ended, standing alone in the Republican party.

[2] Low, then president of the National Civic Federation, was the head of a committee preparing an amendment to the Sherman Act designed to implement the decisions of the 1907 Conference on Trusts. The first proposals of this committee, although largely ignored by Congress, were significant precursors both of the Supreme Court's "rule of reason" decision and of the Progressive platform of 1912. The committee's bill, introduced in modified form as H.R. 19745 by William P. Hepburn, provided that corporations or labor unions might register with either the Interstate Commerce Commission or the Bureau of Corporations, presenting, on registration, full information on charters, membership, financial condition, and the like. Those organizations that had registered could then submit for government approval contracts or agreements that seemed to them to constitute only reasonable restraints of trade. If the government at that time did not find the submitted agreements unreasonable, it surrendered its right to combat the proposals in the future. This method in effect would have established a kind of permanent consent decree system for most business arrangements then prevented by the judicial interpretation that the Sherman Act forbade every combination in restraint of trade. Corporations that did not choose to register remained under the operation of the unamended law. Labor unions, whether registered or unregistered, profited from a provision explicitly legalizing the right to strike. The bill did not, however, mention organized boycotts or the black list, leaving the question of the legality of those instruments to the courts. For Roosevelt's strongest dissent from the recommendations of the federation, see No. 4660; for Hepburn's version of the bill, see No. 4686.

Telegram   Washington, February 7, 1908

In accordance with your telegram of this date I have issued an order that the troops return to their permanent stations thirty days from February sixth, that is, on March seventh. I am sure you will understand that it is impossible for me again to defer the date of their return.

4587 · TO WILLIAM DUDLEY FOULKE   *Roosevelt Mss.*

Washington, February 7, 1908

My dear Mr. Foulke: The statement that I have used the offices in the effort to nominate any presidential candidate is both false and malicious. It is the usual imaginative invention which flows from a desire to say something injurious. Remember that those now making this accusation were busily engaged two months ago in asserting that I was using the offices to secure my own renomination. It is the kind of accusation which for the next few months will be rife. This particular slander will be used until exploded, and when exploded those who have used it will promptly invent another. Such being the case, I almost question whether it is worth while answering; but as it is you who ask, why, the answer you shall have.

Since the present Congress assembled two months ago, I have sent to the Senate the names of all the officials I have appointed for the entire period since Congress adjourned on the 4th of March last, that is, for eleven months. Excluding army and navy officers, scientific experts, health officers, and those of the revenue-cutter service, I have made during this period about thirteen hundred and fifty-two appointments subject to confirmation by the Senate, eleven hundred and sixty-four being postmasters. Of these, appointments in the diplomatic and consular services and in the Indian service have been made without regard to politics; in the diplomatic and consular services, more Democrats than Republicans having been appointed, as we are trying to even up the quotas of the Southern States. In nominating judges I have treated politics as a wholly secondary consideration, and instead of relying solely upon the recommendations of either Senators or Congressmen, have always conducted independent inquiries myself, personally thru members of the bench or the bar whom I happen to know, or thru Attorney General Bonaparte, Secretary Taft, who was himself a judge, Secretary Root, because of his great experience at the bar, or Senator Knox, who was formerly my Attorney General. In a number of the other offices, chiefly assistant secretaries or heads of bureaus here at Washington, but also Governors of Territories or men holding peculiar positions — such, for instance, as that of Commissioner of Education in Porto Rico — and also in a few other cases, notably those of marshals in certain of the Western States, but including various offices also here and there thruout the Union, I have either felt that the position was of such a character that the initiative in the choice could only with propriety come from me or from one of the Cabinet officers, or else I have happened personally to know or to know of a man of such peculiar qualifications that I desired to appoint him on my own initiative.

There remain the great bulk of the offices, including almost all of the post offices, the collectorships of customs, the appraiserships, the land officers, and the like, numbering some twelve hundred and fifty or thereabouts. It is of course out of the question for me personally to examine or have knowledge of such a multitude of appointments, and therefore as regards them I normally accept the suggestions of Senators and Congressmen, the elected representatives of the people in the localities concerned, always reserving to myself the right to insist upon the man's coming up to the required standard of character and capacity, and also reserving the right to nominate whomever I choose if for any reason I am satisfied that I am not receiving from Senator or Congressman good advice, or if I happen personally to know some peculiarly fit man. Where the man has done well in office I prefer to reappoint him, and do so when I can get the consent of the Senators from his locality; but if they refuse, the reappointment cannot be made. Ordinarily, as a matter of convenience, the appointment can best be settled by consultation beforehand, the advice of the Senator or Congressman, who is elected and has peculiar means of knowing the wishes of his constituents being taken. But where a Senator treats this not as a matter of consultation or mutual agreement, not as a matter of convenience and expediency, but as a matter of right on his part to nominate whomever he chooses, the custom is necessarily discontinued.

In the South Atlantic and Gulf States, which have contained neither Senators nor Congressmen of my own party, I have been obliged to seek my advice from various sources. In these States I have appointed large numbers of Democrats, in certain States the Democrats appointed outnumbering the Republicans. For advice in appointing the Republicans I have relied wherever possible not upon officeholders at all, but upon men of standing and position who would not take office and on whose integrity I could depend. As instances merely, I will refer to Colonel Cecil A. Lyon, of Texas, commanding one of the Texas National Guard regiments and a man of independent means, engaged in active business; and to Mr. Pearl Wight, of Louisiana, and to Mr. Coombs,[1] of Florida, also men of independent means and of large business affairs; all of them being among the most respected men in their several States. These men, and most of the others upon whom I rely, could not be persuaded to take any office in my gift; and I could no more coerce

[1] James N. Coombs of Apalachicola, Florida, Republican national committeeman, leader of the pro-Taft delegation from Florida which was seated at the national convention. The anti-Taft Republicans of Florida had bolted Coombs's leadership and, at a separate state convention, elected an uninstructed delegation to the national convention.

Teddy in Timberland

Old Dr. Roosevelt

or control their political action than I could, for instance, that of presidents of chambers of commerce or colonels of national guard regiments in similar States in the North. In all of these States I have done my best, when I came to appointing Republicans, to put the best men in office — those whom the people of the locality accepted as such and regarded as leading citizens; and I have every reason to believe that the average of my appointees is very high. At present various efforts are being made to get up bolting delegations from the Southern States, and the meetings at which these so-called delegates are chosen are usually announced as "non-officeholders' " conventions. As a rule, this means only, so far as it means anything, that they are held under the lead of persons who wish to be put in office, but whose character and capacity are such that they have not been regarded as fit to be appointed under this administration. In these cases, be it remembered that the failure to secure office is not the result of the political action of the men in question; on the contrary, their political action is due to their failure to secure office.

You quote a newspaper saying:

We are now getting daily lessons in civil service reform from the White House, which ought to attract national attention. The appointment of Taft workers to post offices in Ohio,[2] and of the totally unfit George W. Wanmaker as appraiser of this port, is now followed by the President's refusal to reappoint a good Hughes man as collector of customs at Plattsburg.

This article is a good example of the accusations made by those of our opponents whose partisanship renders them especially unscrupulous and untruthful. Mr. Wanmaker's appointment was recommended by the three Congressmen from New York County and by the two Senators, the appointment being made precisely as the hundreds of similar appointments of postmasters, appraisers, internal revenue collectors and the like, which are confirmed by the Senate, are made, and in conformance with the custom which has obtained thruout my term of service, and thruout the terms of service of Mr. McKinley, Mr. Cleveland, and my other predecessors. In this particular case, as it happens, Mr. Wanmaker is peculiarly fit for the position, being already an assistant appraiser who has rendered good service in that place, and his appointment is the promotion of a proper man; he was appointed assistant appraiser by President McKinley twelve years ago, has served as acting appraiser several times, and has a very good record. "The refusal to reappoint a good Hughes man as collector of customs at Plattsburg" refers to the case of Mr. Walter Witherbee, and the accusation in this case is particularly comic, because Mr. Witherbee was an open and avowed Taft man, the classmate of Secretary Taft's brother at Yale, and both Secretary Taft and his brother requested his reappointment — the only New York officeholder for

[2] Foraker had prevented the confirmation by the Senate of four pro-Taft Ohioans whom Roosevelt had nominated for vacant postmasterships.

whom they made such a request. The Congressman from his district and the Senators have not agreed about his successor, and he is still in office. These facts were either known to the editors of the paper in question, or could have been found out by the slightest inquiry. There remains the allegations as to the appointment of "Taft workers" to post offices in Ohio. In Ohio I have made fifty-eight post-office appointments; twenty-seven of these were reappointments, thirty-one were new appointments, the last including the cases where the incumbent had died, had been removed for cause, or had resigned. Generally the appointment was made exactly as in other States, upon the recommendation of the Congressman from the district. In various cases, however, as at Maumee, Strasburg, Bluffton, Greenville, and Leipsic, the nominations were made upon the recommendation of both Senators Foraker and Dick, or of one or the other. In four cases, the nominations were rejected by the Senate. In two of these, Dennison and Uhrichsville, the nominations of the new men were made on the recommendation of the then Congressman, Mr. Smyser; in each case the previous incumbent had not been giving very satisfactory service, in one instance he having failed to give sufficient personal attention to the office, as reported by the inspector, and in the other case the postmaster being also the publisher and editor of a newspaper and various irregularities having been noticed, some resulting in violation of law in the interest of the postmaster's paper. The course followed was precisely similar to that followed in the case of the various other post offices in Ohio in the districts represented by Congressmen Keifer, Kennedy, Cole, and others, and precisely similar to the course followed as regards the recommendations of this same Congressman Smyser in other offices. At Spencerville investigation by the inspector showed that it was inadvisable to reappoint the incumbent, and that Mr. Wetherill, who had been originally recommended for the position by Senator Dick, should be appointed. Senator Dick afterwards withdrew his recommendation, but the inspector reported that Mr. Wetherill had by that time already been appointed, and that to withhold his commission would be a great injury to him and would defeat the ends of justice. The nomination was accordingly sent in. At Wapakoneta the incumbent did his work well, but the post-office inspector reported that the feeling was almost unanimous among his fellow townsmen that there should be a change, and a Mr. Moser appointed, it appearing that the postmaster was not popular with the people, while the man suggested for the nomination was unquestionably the choice of the patrons of the office, being regarded by them as a most progressive and public-spirited young businessman, possest of more than ordinary ability, "extremely popular with the people of his native city, irrespective of party affiliations." I call your attention to the fact that the Senate withdrew its opposition to one of these four men and confirmed him, so that the charge relates to only three out of the whole number, eleven hundred and sixty-four post offices; that of these three, two were nominated in the usual fashion on the recommendation of the outgoing

Congressman; and that the third nomination was made on the report of the inspector and would have been made without the slightest regard to whether there was a presidential canvass on hand or not.

The statements in the editorial in question are therefore untrue in every particular.

As for your quotation from another newspaper, running as follows:

> Federal officeholders may be commanded to use their influence and their authority in behalf of a candidate. Such a command has been issued and the President should know of it. * * * Somebody has instructed postmasters that they must obtain from their subordinates either their resignations or their pledges of support for Taft delegates to the convention. * * *
> Even in Massachusetts efforts of this kind have recently been made, but happily they have been stopped, partly because the postmasters on whom the attempts were made had the courage to resist, and partly from other causes.

there is really nothing to say except that it does not contain the slightest particle of truth, and that the misstatement is so gross that it is difficult to believe it other than a deliberate invention. There is not the slightest foundation for it, and no successful effort can be made to show that there is the slightest foundation for it. As regards the Massachusetts post offices, in all except five cases my appointments were reappointments; that is, the incumbent was renominated, with the consent of the Senators or Congressmen, at the expiration of the regular term. Of these five cases, new men were put in three times because of death and twice because of the resignation of the incumbent. In each case, whether of appointment or reappointment, I followed the ordinary custom, accepting the suggestion either of the Senators or of the Congressmen, or both, as in each case the men suggested were eminently fit. Not a particle of difference has been made in this respect between those Congressmen who were for one presidential candidate and those Congressmen who were for another; and so far as I know, in every case the appointment has fully satisfied the local people. In other words, the appointments have been made not to control, but to recognize, the sentiment of the locality.

If such assertions as those of these papers are made in good faith, on knowledge of facts, and with any other purpose than to produce a political effect by false pretense, or by reckless statement without knowledge, let those making them produce the specific cases to which they refer. If in any such case the accusation is found true, it will have occurred without my knowledge, and I shall deal with it in the precise spirit of my instructions to the Civil Service Commission hereinafter referred to.

So far as I know the only other accusations that have been made as to the use of patronage have been in connection with the pension agent in New Hampshire and a collector of internal revenue in Ohio. In the case of the pension officer, the Senators and Congressmen could not agree on a nominee, two recommending one man and two another. I decided to send in a man recommended to me by outsiders, whom I believed to be better than either. The Senate rejected him. His name would have been sent in if there had been no presidential canvass at all at this time. As regards collectors of internal revenue, some are appointed upon the recommendations of Senators, and some on the recommendations of Congressmen. In Ohio the collector of internal revenue whom I nominated in the First District was recommended by the Congressman of the district. In the Tenth District I followed the recommendation of the two Senators. In other words, I followed the same course in Ohio as in other States as regards all these nominations, the only difference being that Ohio is the single State where the bulk of the Federal employees have been inclined to be against the presidential candidate from the State. In New York, Pennsylvania, Illinois, Indiana, and Wisconsin, so far as I know, the enormous majority of appointees are in each case for the presidential candidate from the State. This has not been true in Ohio; and my interference with patronage matters in Ohio has been limited to insisting, as I should insist anywhere else, that opposition to the purposes, policies, and friends of the administration shall not be considered as a necessary prerequisite to holding the commission of the President.

In my letter to the Civil Service Commission of June 12, 1902, which now holds good, and will be enforced, officers are warned not to use their places to control political movements, nor to coerce their subordinates, nor to neglect their public duties for political work, nor to cause any public scandal by their political activity; but outside of the classified service they are not otherwise limited in political activity. No officer will be permitted to violate the above injunction, with my knowledge, no matter for what candidate he may be working; and I may add that the only officers as to whom any question of violation of this injunction has hitherto arisen, have been men who are not working for Mr. Taft.

The above is a full statement of the facts. Not an appointment has been made that would not have been made if there had been no presidential contest impending, and in no case has there been a deviation from the course that I would have pursued had none of those who actually are candidates for the nomination been candidates; nor has a single officeholder been removed or threatened with removal, or coerced in any way to secure his support for any presidential candidate. In fact, the only coercion that I have attempted to exercise was to forbid the officeholders from pushing my own renomination, this being done in the following letter sent to the members of my Cabinet on November 19, 1907:

I have been informed that certain officeholders in your Department are proposing to go to the national convention as delegates in favor of renominating me for the Presidency, or are proposing to procure my endorsement for such renomination by State conventions. This must not be. I wish you to inform such officers as you may find it advisable or necessary to inform in order to carry out the spirit of this instruction, that such advocacy of my renomination, or acceptance of an election as delegate for that purpose, will be regarded as a serious violation of official propriety, and will be dealt with accordingly.[3]

Yours truly

4588 · TO WALTER FRANCIS FREAR   *Roosevelt Mss.*

Telegram   Washington, February 7, 1908

Your action in communicating with the Japanese Consul as stated in your letter to Secretary of Interior is disapproved and you will immediately communicate with him stating that it is disapproved. You will keep in mind hereafter that it is a violation of law for you to enter upon negotiations with the representative of any foreign government. Moreover your whole attitude on the matter in question is against the policy and purposes of the administration. A letter on the matter will be sent you.[1]

4589 · TO THOMAS JEFFERSON COOLIDGE, JUNIOR   *Roosevelt Mss.*

Personal   Washington, February 8, 1908

My dear Coolidge:[1] I have just heard that you feel that Taft should be nominated. You know how thoroly I believe in Taft and how strongly I feel that the country would indeed be fortunate to have him for President. Naturally, I am overjoyed to learn that a man of your standing and influence should be for him.

I am sorry to say that I think the forces banded together to beat Taft will stop at no means, from bribery down, to accomplish their purpose, and they especially intend to control those among the Southern delegates who are

---

[3] Roosevelt's letter, particularly the final quotation, was published in full or in part by newspapers throughout the country.

---

[1] Federal immigration policies impeded the attempts by Hawaiian planters to procure a continuing, cheap labor supply. For the Japanese who had left the islands for the Pacific Coast there were available no adequate replacements. Chinese immigration had long been forbidden. The immigration of Japanese laborers, no longer permitted to enter the United States via Hawaii, had already begun to fall off. Congress would not sanction the importation of contract labor from Europe. In their efforts to remedy this situation the planters had a champion in Walter Francis Frear, lawyer, Republican, Chief Justice of the Hawaiian Supreme Court, 1900–1907, Territorial Governor, 1907–1913. Frear, by marriage a member of the influential Dillingham family, perhaps the wealthiest of the planter group, had apparently communicated with the Japanese consul in Honolulu about accelerating the immigration of coolie labor. Roosevelt's cable terminated those negotiations. The letter the President promised is not in the Roosevelt Mss.

---

[1] Thomas Jefferson Coolidge, Jr., great-great-grandson of Thomas Jefferson; son of the Bostonian merchant, financier, and diplomat of the same name. His family was active and effective throughout the nineteenth century in the financial, textile, transport, and utility interests that provided the substance of so many great Massachusetts families. He himself founded the Old Colony Trust Company. He was a Democrat.

venal; to try to organize bolting conventions; to get at members of the National Committee; and so forth, and so forth. The first thing they count upon doing is to try to control the National Committee, so as to put in the convention these bolting delegates from the South, who will be for the most part utterly venal men, and who have not the slightest claim to admission to a Republican convention. Such a course would mean far more than detriment to Mr. Taft, for it would mean the kind of triumph of bribery and corruption that would lastingly damage the Republican party. I am therefore very anxious to see that the National Committeemen, whatever may be their individual preferences for presidential candidate, shall stand right on this proposition;[2] that is, shall stand for decency and honesty. Now, the National Committeeman from Georgia, Judson Lyons, is a colored man. Foraker and the men whom Foraker represents, whose primary purpose is to secure immunity and favoritism for great law-defying corporations, have used the Brownsville incident and the appeal to the worst passions of the colored people as one method of achieving their purpose. I think they have made a very strong appeal to Judson Lyons in the hope that he can be induced to vote to seat the purchased delegations to which I refer.[3] I am informed that thru your influence it may be possible to get men who are genuine friends of Judson Lyons to ask him simply to stand on these questions as an honest man should stand. More than that I would not ask, and if you can see your way to doing this I should be very greatly obliged.

With great regard, believe me, *Sincerely yours*

4590 · TO RICHARD WATSON GILDER   *Roosevelt Mss.*

Washington, February 8, 1908

Dear Gilder: I don't think I can undertake reminiscences; and I don't want to go around the world; and I won't be Mayor or Senator! There! that looks like a mild negative confession of faith, but it about sums up all I have to think of at the moment. I have a year more of work and tho I do not suppose it will be very active after June, when the candidates are nominated,

[2] To this end Roosevelt was then conferring with members of the National Committee; see No. 4592.
[3] Roosevelt apparently hoped that Coolidge, whose family had long been active in philanthropic work for the Southern Negroes, could influence Lyons' political decisions. Lyons was not only a potential ally of Foraker, but also already an opponent of the President, who in 1906 had not reappointed him Register of the Treasury. It developed, however, that Coolidge's influence, whatever it may have been, was unnecessary. Because of the clear superiority of the Taft forces in Chicago, the anti-Taft delegation from Georgia made no effort to have itself seated in place of the pro-Taft forces. Within Georgia, no pro-Taft group had wrested control of the party machinery from Lyons. Although he was a delegate-at-large to the convention, Lyons, in June 1908, lost his seat on the National Committee to Henry Blun, a preconvention supporter of the nominee.

still there will be something to do even then. I wish I could see you. *Sincerely yours*

Washington, February 10, 1908

This memorandum is drawn up after reading a memorandum of Senator Lodge's relating certain circumstances in connection with George Lyman and his attitude toward Senator Lodge and myself. The memorandum of Senator Lodge, so far as it relates to me, is entirely correct; but I should like to add a few lines in connection with it.

Altho I had met Cabot Lodge once or twice in the Porcellian Club, I never really knew him until the spring of 1884 when we came together in connection with the effort to prevent Blaine's nomination for President. We both took the same view, namely: that if possible Blaine should not be nominated, but that if nominated we would support him. From that time on he was my closest friend, personally, politically, and in every other way, and occupied toward me a relation that no other man has ever occupied or ever will occupy. We have not always agreed, but our subjects of disagreement have been of but little weight compared to the matters upon which we did agree. For the past twenty-four years I have discust almost every move I have made in politics with him, provided he was at hand and it was possible for me to discuss it; and as regards many matters of policy and appointment, it would be quite impossible for me now to say whether it was he or I who first suggested the appointment I made or the course that I followed. Thus I have quite forgotten whether it was I who first suggested that Moody should come into the Cabinet or whether it was Lodge who made the suggestion. We had both agreed that Moody and Meyer were peculiarly fit to do good work in high positions.

George Lyman I met once or twice while I was still at college. I took no great fancy to him as he seemed to have a harsh and vindictive temper; and (what would perhaps seem a little comic) I also distrusted him because I became convinced that he did not tell the truth in his hunting stories. But he was a man of power, and after 1884, when he was one of the comparatively few men among those I knew socially who felt as I did about Blaine, I saw rather more of him. When I went to Boston I usually stayed with Lodge, if he was in Boston. If he was not in Boston I was apt to stay with Frank Lowell. Lyman would often ask me to stay with him; and as I became prominent — that is, when I became Governor and Vice-President — I found that Lyman, whose temper was bad but whose friendship was quite genuine, had his feelings hurt because I did not stay with him. I accordingly went once or twice to his house instead of Lowell's, but always with an uncomfortable feeling, because I hate to accept courtesies and attentions from people who I fear will expect in return some acknowledgment which it may not be in my power to give; and I always had this feeling about Lyman. When I was Vice-President I on one occasion stayed at his house and he had Murray Crane (then Governor of Massachusetts) and one or two others at dinner, this being on commencement day, 1901; and Murray Crane and he then of their own accord took up the question of my candidacy for the Presidency and announced themselves as heartily favoring it and as intending to do everything they could to see that I was nominated. I afterwards offered Crane the Secretaryship of the Treasury, which he could not take — this being, I think, the following year. As soon as I became President, Lyman communicated with me, as did two or three others, in a way which really made me uncomfortable, for I was sure that he (like these others) believed I would offer them positions which I did not feel able to offer them. Frank Lowell, for instance, represented the exactly opposite type; he never expected me to offer him anything, and I was overjoyed when I could give him a promotion as judge; he was quite incapable of thinking that the fact that I had been at his house and he at mine established a right on his part to my giving him an office. But with George Lyman the exact reverse was true. Lodge asked me to invite him to Washington. I objected because I was sure he would think that my doing so was tantamount to offering him a place; but I yielded and asked him here. His infirmities of temper and judgment had evidently become accentuated by the excitement of having me President and of believing that I was going to put him in some high position. I was as friendly and pleasant as possible with him and showed him every social attention; but when he spoke to me, as he did on different occasions, about being Ambassador and Cabinet officer — the Secretaryship of the Navy being the particular place he mentioned — I had to explain that it was impossible for me to appoint him; that I was delighted to continue him as Collector of Customs as long as he wisht to remain in that office, but that there were various men, mentioning Moody and Meyer, whom I would have to consider ahead of him for the higher positions. This decision on my part had nothing whatever to do with Lodge, but was arrived at before I had spoken to Lodge on the matter. I would never have made Lyman a Cabinet officer or Ambassador, no matter if all my best friends and warmest political supporters had besought me to do so. He was entirely unfit for either place; altho he has some strong and good qualities.

4592 · TO AUGUSTUS PEABODY GARDNER   *Roosevelt Mss.*

Washington, February 10, 1908

Dear Gussie: We have had positive assurances from the following men: Scott of Alabama, Clayton, Brooker, Coombs, Hart, Mulvane, Wight, Williams, Blodgett (who, however, I think ought to be lookt up; perhaps Newberry can tell something about him), Kellogg, Moseley, Akins, Waite, Streeter, Duncan, Herrick, Capers, Greene, Lyon, Loose, Martin, Pexton, Luna, Cade,

Robertson, McCoy. We have also received assurances from Ankeny, Babcock and Morrill, but I am not willing to speak personally about them. I have been given the positive promises of McKenzie and Heid, but I should be very anxious to have you see both gentlemen yourself. Ward comes to lunch with me Thursday. I have every reason to believe he will be all right. I shall see Reyburn myself, and also New. As soon as possible I shall get Hitchcock[1] to go west to see Knight, Flanigan (who states he is thoroly loyal to me), Stevenson (who has promised to be with us, but whom I would like to have Hitchcock see again), and Sturges of Arizona (who Hitchcock is sure will be with us, but about whom I have felt doubtful). If you can get at Babcock I think you ought to. You say that Lyons is all right; I have not put him down on my list as being so. Lowden I see tomorrow. He will of course be for Cannon; but he is an honest man and he ought to agree to go straight when it comes to admitting the delegations from the South; for we can be beaten only by downright brazen corruption. *Sincerely yours*

4593 · TO VICTOR HOWARD METCALF   *Roosevelt Mss.*

Washington, February 11, 1908

To the Secretary of the Navy: I desire to have from the Joint Board at the earliest possible moment a well thought out plan as to what should be the fortifications provided in Hawaii and what should be done with Pearl Harbor. What I wish to know is whether we should have fortifications at Pearl Harbor, have the harbor dredged and a dry dock provided, or whether we should have fortifications at Honolulu, or whether we should have both. I wish this problem considered not as something merely academic but as something practical; that is, from the standpoint of our need of a naval station at Hawaii and our need for naval stations elsewhere, due consideration being paid to our probable military and naval resources and policies. I wish the question of having fortifications at Honolulu and Pearl Harbor, both or only one, to be considered from the same common-sense standpoint.

I call the attention of the Joint Board to the grave harm done to army and navy by such vacillation and one-sided consideration as has been shown in the treatment of the army and navy experts of the Philippine problem; that is, of the question as to whether Manila Bay or Subig Bay should be fortified.[1] For a long time I was informed by almost every naval officer and by many army officers that Subig Bay was the one all-important post to

---

[1] Frank H. Hitchcock in February left the Post-Office Department to devote his full energy to managing the Taft campaign.

---

[1] On January 31, 1908, the Army and Navy Joint Board headed by Admiral Dewey recommended Manila rather than Subig Bay as the site for the major naval station in the Philippines. The board, which had been ordered by Roosevelt in October 1907 to study Philippine defense, made this proposal in spite of the fact that Congress, by virtue of earlier recommendations by this and other boards, had already appropriated $2,750,000 for a dry dock, coaling plant, and buildings at Subig Bay.

fortify and defend, and that it alone could be made impregnable to attack. Of course when assertions like this are made to a layman, whether he be President or a member of Congress, the layman assumes and has a right to assume that those making them are to be supposed to recommend what is best under actual conditions. I am now informed that the recommendations made to me by naval and army officers for so many years and upon which recommendations I have repeatedly acted in the way of advising Congress, are all wrong, because Subig Bay could not possibly be defended from a land attack; and by way of explanation I am further informed that it is not the province of the navy to advise upon anything but naval matters. I have had just such experiences with army officers. Now, I have the very highest regard for the officers of the army and navy. I think them on the whole about the best citizens we have, and I want to back them in every way; but they justify their most trenchant critics when they act in such manner. No naval officer has a right to advise the fortification of Subig Bay without putting in the most careful proviso that the advice is only to be considered in case the military authorities report the scheme as satisfactory. This year a great many Senators and Congressmen have said to me that they disbelieved in the general staff for either the army or navy because of the curious attitude of the Joint Board in this Philippine defense matter. I now wish careful consideration given to all the elements of the defense of Hawaii by both army and navy and a report made to me thereon.[2]

I direct that the Secretaries of War and the Navy make a full inquiry and report to me upon the action of the previous board; since October, 1900, in recommending Subig Bay, including particularly the action of the Joint Board in December, 1903. In November, 1903, the Secretary of the Navy in his annual report stated that the two boards and all others concerned were unanimous in their views on this Subig Bay matter and that he knew of no other military question on which such unanimity existed. I ask that a report be made with especial reference to the question as to what study was given to the subject, what methods were employed in coming to the conclusion, and what circumstances occurred to bring about not merely the change in, but the absolute reversal of, what appeared at one time to be the unanimous conclusion. Congress has a right to complain of the Executive Department for its action in this matter, and of course this action was based solely upon the strongly exprest and reiterated opinions thru a number of years of the army and navy advisors of the Government.

Was this ever made a general staff study? If so, I desire to see the reports. I desire to know whether the successive and widely varying conclusions

[2] The Joint Board after a thorough investigation recommended that Pearl Harbor should be developed as the main naval base in the Pacific. It further advised that only one comparatively small unfortified repair station should be maintained in the Philippines at Subig Bay. The President approved of the board's fundamental decision on American naval defense in the Pacific. By the spring of 1909 the work at Pearl Harbor had begun.

reached are due to original and careful study by the members of the general boards and joint boards, or whether they have resulted from the perfunctory ratification of the views of some subordinate officer in any case. It is quite evident that there is some defect in method which ought to be removed. I desire that in the Hawaiian matter, which is of course much more simple, there shall be no possibility of repetition of our humiliating experience in regard to Subig and Manila bays.

4594 · TO PHILANDER CHASE KNOX   *Roosevelt Mss.*

Washington, February 11, 1908

My dear Senator: I have both of your speeches and I hardly know which pleases me most.[1] The Kalamazoo speech is a masterly portrayal of what has been done in exercising in the interest of the people the national authority over the railroads; the chief steps in making this control effective having been begun during your great administration of the Department of Justice, and you having, as Senator, been among those most instrumental in carrying on the work in its later stages. Your address to the Chamber of Commerce of Pittsburgh puts the waterway question and the general question of the conservation of our natural resources into a singularly graphic form and is one of the most effective appeals that I have seen in the matter. I have sent it to Gifford Pinchot, for I feel that this speech marks a long stride in getting the project before the serious consideration of the country.

With hearty congratulations and all good wishes, believe me, *Sincerely yours*

4595 · TO GEORGE WALBRIDGE PERKINS   *Roosevelt Mss.*

Washington, February 11, 1908

My dear Perkins: I have received your letters of the 6th and 8th instant. That is a very interesting speech of yours and it is needless to say that I am in substantial agreement with most of the propositions that it contains, altho there are one or two of what I may call side propositions which I would

[1] Reporting Knox's Kalamazoo and Pittsburgh speeches, the *Outlook* concluded that they demonstrated that Knox was "a believer both in the philosophy and the practice of the New Federalism." At Kalamazoo, speaking on the railroad problem, Knox pointed out that the American people had gradually realized that "they were living substantially under railroad domination so far as their business interests were concerned." The laws sponsored by the Roosevelt Administration had rectified this condition, he asserted, concluding that "it would be difficult to overstate the enormous value of this legislation to the public." At Pittsburgh he supported Roosevelt's program for waterways development, partly in order to remedy the congestion on the railroads. The senator had doubtless spoken the convictions he then held. Doubtless also as an active Presidential candidate he had hoped for such praise as the *Outlook* gave him. Whatever his convictions or motives, the *Outlook's* assessment was, as the next decade showed, premature; *Outlook*, 88:377–379 (February 22, 1908).

like to think over before committing myself about. I thank you for your reference to me.[1]

With all good wishes, believe me, *Sincerely yours*

4596 · TO EDWARD VII

Royal Archives, Windsor Castle°

Washington, February 12, 1908

My dear King Edward; The beautiful Sévres Porcelain book has come, and I send this note of thanks by the Ambassador. The book is a delight to the eye — it is almost like seeing the porcelain.

I am much interested in the trip of our fleet to the Pacific; the ships have just come out of the Straits. I feel very strongly that the real interests of the English-speaking peoples are one, alike in the Atlantic and Pacific; and that, while scrupulously careful neither to insult nor to injure others we should yet make it evident that we are ready and able to hold our own. In no country where the population is of our stock, and where the wageworkers, the laborers, are of the same blood as the employing classes, will it be possible to introduce a large number of workmen of an utterly alien race without the certainty of dangerous friction. The only sure way to avoid such friction, with it's possible consequences of incalculable disaster, is by friendly agreement in advance to prevent the coming together in mass of the wageworkers of the two races, in either country.[1]

[1] In this speech, delivered at Columbia University, Perkins extolled the advantage of combination over competition. Business combination in the form of the modern corporation had, according to Perkins, evolved naturally and inevitably from the chaotic and destructive competition of an earlier day. Since the new form of business organization offered innumerable benefits to all classes of the community, the citizen, he maintained, should concentrate his energy rather upon devising methods for its regulation and control than upon discovering means for its extermination. Perkins assured his listeners that President Roosevelt wholeheartedly concurred with this view. "In spite of what apparently has been an almost persistent determination to misunderstand or ignore his real purpose," he asserted, "the fact is that President Roosevelt, from the time he was Governor of New York down to his message to Congress last week, has repeatedly proclaimed his belief that modern industrial conditions are such that combination is not only necessary but inevitable; that corporations have come to stay, and that, if properly managed, they are the source of good and not evil."

[1] To this paragraph King Edward replied:
"We have watched with the greatest interest the cruise of your fine Fleet in the Pacific and have admired the successful manner in which your Admirals have so far carried out this great undertaking. As you are no doubt aware my Australian Colonies have conveyed through my Government an invitation to your Fleet to visit their principal ports, and if it be possible for your Government to authorise the acceptance of this invitation, I feel sure that it will be warmly appreciated both here and in Australia.
"I entirely agree with you that the interests of the English speaking peoples are alike in the Atlantic and the Pacific, and I look forward with confidence to the co-operation of the English speaking races becoming the most powerful civilizing factor in the policy of the World.

But for the moment our internal problems here are far more pressing than our external ones. With us it is not as it is with you; our men of vast wealth do not fully realize that great responsibility must always go hand in hand with great privilege.

Again thanking you, and with very high regard, believe me *very sincerely yours*[2]

4597 · TO CHARLEMAGNE TOWER   *Roosevelt Mss.*

Washington, February 12, 1908

My dear Mr. Ambassador: Will you personally express to the Emperor my cordial appreciation of the message sent thru you? The presence of the Japanese in Mexico I have already known.[1] A large number of them do not stay in Mexico but in one way or the other get over our line. More, however, have come down from Canada, but this has now been pretty well stopt by the action of the Dominion Government. A large number of these immigrants are undoubtedly soldiers, but I am not sure as to how far this means some ulterior design by the Japanese Government and how far it merely means that many of the soldiers who returned from Manchuria found the bee-like or ant-like conditions of normal Japanese life intolerable and sought to go elsewhere. Thus the Emperor may remember that over a year ago a number of Japanese seal poachers tried to land on our seal islands in Bering Sea and that our people attacked them, killed a half-dozen or so, and captured ten or fifteen others who were tried and imprisoned. Among those whom we thus killed or captured there were several ex-soldiers and one ex-officer of the Japanese army or navy, chiefly if I remember aright of the army.

I am much imprest by the information in reference to Teneriffe.[2]

Tell the Emperor how pleased I am that he approves of what I did about

---

"The question of the immigration and competition of coloured races in other Countries is one which presents many difficulties, and especially to me, who have so many coloured subjects in my Empire. It is one, however, which has, so far, proved capable of adjustment by friendly negotiation, and I rely upon the recent agreement, at which my Government have arrived with that of Japan, being loyally carried out in all its details by the Japanese Government." — Edward VII to Roosevelt, March 5, 1908, Royal Archives, Windsor Castle.

[2] We have to acknowledge His Majesty's gracious permission to publish letters preserved in the Royal Archives, Windsor Castle.

---

[1] German diplomats, the Kaiser told Tower, had reported that the Japanese had thousands of potential troops in Mexico, Peru, and Chile. The Kaiser was sure that Japan, expecting war with the United States, was planning to attack Panama; see Bailey, *Roosevelt and the Japanese-American Crises*, pp. 268–269.

[2] Teneriffe, largest of the Canaries. Britain, France, Spain, and Germany, by the Pact of Cartagena of May 1907, had agreed to preserve the *status quo* in the Mediterranean and that part of the Atlantic near the shores of Europe and Africa. The agreement was directed largely at alleged German designs on the Balearic and Canary islands, but the designs, in spite of the agreement, were widely supposed to persist.

the fleet. I do not believe it is possible to keep the fleet in the Pacific, but it is of very real importance to have had it go there, and it will make it comparatively easy to send it back.

Pray thank the Emperor most warmly for the information, which I very sincerely appreciate. *Sincerely yours*

4598 · TO FLORENCE LOCKWOOD LA FARGE   *Roosevelt Mss.*

Washington, February 13, 1908

Dear Florence: I have read Miss Addams' book[1] and I am greatly disappointed in it. Hull House has done admirable work which means that Miss Addams has done admirable work; just as Dr. Rainsford in his parish did admirable work which I am not sure was not even better in its ultimate results upon the people affected. But evidently Miss Addams is one of those confused thinkers whose thought cannot be accepted for the guidance of others. In certain of the chapters of her book she states facts and conditions that are interesting and once or twice develops theories which have in them an element of good. But there is always in what she says an element both of the fantastic and of the obscure; «and» this is absolutely inevitable when the book is written with an *idée fixe* — the theory that antimilitarism is the solvent for all troubles. Of course she might just as well say that vegetarianism or antivaccination would solve our industrial problems as to say that militarism has «anything» of the kind, sort or description to do with any of either the social or industrial troubles with which this country is confronted. «Her idea» on militarism is itself preposterous; but granting that it were right the fact would remain that militarism has no more to do with the «crisis» of American society than, say, eating horseflesh in honor of Thor. The benefits and abuses of militarism are very real in the social and industrial life of the nations of continental Europe; but militarism has been a practically imponderable element in producing the social and industrial conditions of England during the last ninety years, and has not been any element at all in the United States for the past forty years.

The trouble evidently is that Miss Addams is a striking example of the mischievous effect produced by the teachings of a man like Tolstoi upon a mind without the strength, training and natural ability to withstand «them.» Tolstoi is a great novelist, and his novels like *Anna Karenina, War and Peace, The Cossacks,* and *Sevastopol* can be read with advantage if we read them just as we read the novels of medieval Poland by Sienkiewicz; but the minute that Tolstoi is accepted as a moral teacher he can benefit only the very small fraction of mankind which can differentiate the good he teaches from the

[1] Jane Addams, *Newer Ideals of Peace* (New York, 1907). To the criticisms of her book by Roosevelt, Miss Addams had in effect replied: "At the present moment the war spirit attempts to justify its noisy demonstrations by quoting its great achievements in the past and by drawing attention to the courageous life which it has evoked and fostered." — p. 210.

mass of fantastic and unhealthy absurdity in which it is embodied. As it happens, I have never yet met any human being who had been morally benefited by Tolstoi; but I have met hundreds of well-meaning, crude creatures who have been seriously damaged by him. He preaches against war, for instance, just as «he preaches» against marriage. His *Kreutzer Sonata* is treated by his admirers as if it were a melancholy and unnatural production of his. It is melancholy, but it is not unnatural in the least. The same law of action and reaction which tended under the old regime in France to make the debauchee and the devotee alternate in the same family and sometimes in the same individual, makes it natural that a filthy and repulsive book like the *Kreutzer Sonata* should be written by a man in whom a fantastic theory of race annihilation by abstention from marriage is fitly and inevitably supplemented by gross and criminal aberrations of the sexual passion. No really good pure-minded and healthy man or woman could have written or approved of the *Kreutzer Sonata;* and just as little would any such man or woman be capable of approving either the unnatural asceticism which Tolstoi preaches or the gross and unnatural debauchery which such asceticism in its turn inevitably breeds.

Now all this applies in principle just as much to his assault on all war — which foolish Jane Addams, like still more foolish Justice Brewer, enthusiastically applauds. Of course Tolstoi himself is logical in his folly. He is against all industrialism just as he is against all war; and he wants the whole race to die out immediately. Industrialism under any circumstances means the loss of thousands of lives. Industrialism in the United States has to its credit probably a hundred times the number of men and women killed and crippled that have been killed and crippled since the foundation of the Republic in all our wars. We must make every effort to lighten the suffering that this killing and crippling entails; but to declare that because lives are lost in mines, on railways and in factories, we should abandon all work in or on them, would be not one bit better and not one bit worse than declaring that righteous people must not be prepared to defend their rights because scoundrels often do wrong by violence. There is no possible theory by which the existence of a policeman can be justified that does not also justify the existence of a soldier. Russia, Tolstoi's own country, suffers primarily because for two centuries and a half she was under the hideous Tartar yoke, and she endured this slavery because her people could not fight successfully. If the Russians of the 13th, 14th and 15th centuries had been able to fight as the Swiss fought at the same period, I very firmly believe that Russia would today be as prosperous and progressive as Switzerland. There is misery and suffering in Switzerland, but nothing like what there is in Russia. The doctrine of nonresistance is old, and its results have always been evil. The same fantastic morality on this point which Tolstoi now develops was rife in the later ages of Byzantium, and that decadent people disbelieved in militarism as heartily as Miss Jane Addams. Up to the very last, with the Turk at their gates, there were plenty of priests and laymen in Constantinople who declared it unlawful to shed blood, even that of an enemy; and such an attitude had no small part in producing the condition which has subjected southwestern Europe for four centuries to the unspeakable horror of Turkish rule. In our own country the most sordid political corruption has, as Owen Wister recently pointed out, existed in the regions where the English and German nonresistant and antimilitary sects had supreme control. What the distant future holds in store, no man can tell; but today it is just as wicked to preach unrighteous peace as to preach unrighteous war, and it is even more foolish.

With love to Grant, *Ever yours*

4599 · TO THEODORE ROOSEVELT, JUNIOR   *Roosevelt Mss.*

Washington, February 14, 1908

Dear Ted: I just received your letter and I am extremely pleased with your success in the midyear's. You have admirable marks. Now, do not repeat a feat of your father's. I think it was in my senior year (but it may have been my junior year) when I got remarkable marks for the first half of the course under William James and was sure I was going to do wonderfully in it, so sure that I loafed and did not study and trusted to natural smartness to give a specious appearance of familiarity with the subject; and as a result got left and stood low in the course on account of shortcomings in my finals.

Frank Witherbee was here yesterday and mentioned that if his boy had lived he had intended sending him up under John Greenway, because he thought in that particular locality and under that particular man the chance of success was better than anywhere else. Witherbee has extensive mines in northern New York. His wife and daughter were with him, and Agnes Landon, too, by the way.

Gymnasium work is certainly dull. About all that can be said of it is that it is better than endeavoring to take hygienic exercises in one's own room. *Your loving father*

4600 · TO THORNTON HOWARD SIMMONS   *Roosevelt Mss.*

Personal   Washington, February 14, 1908

Dear Joe: [1] I do not know anything about that matter now. I do not recall the letter I am said to have written twenty-four years ago; but about six years ago, after some similar business, I took up the matter, examining the records, and found that I never had been lightweight champion. At that time — six or eight years ago — I had got it in my mind that I had defeated a man named Cushing or Coolidge for the lightweight championship, and had been on a subsequent occasion beaten by Hanks; but on looking up the records I

---

[1] Thornton Howard Simmons, a Harvard classmate of Roosevelt, in 1908 a clothing merchant in Boston and an active amateur oarsman.

found that Hanks' victory was at the same time and I had merely won my trial heat. The letter in question was written twenty-four years ago. I remember nothing about it and would be wholly unable to say whether my statement was a mere slip of the pen, or whether at that time, as on this subsequent occasion six or eight years ago, I had forgotten that my victory over Cushing or Coolidge was merely a trial heat. Of course I do not remember very distinctly the details of these boxing matches. It seems to me I was once beaten by Sharon of our class, and that I beat a man named Thompson. I also remember wrestling with Jack Tebbetts and beating him in a series of three bouts, and being beaten by Charley Davis and I think by Gaston. I am also inclined to think that Gaston beat me in boxing on one occasion; but that could not have been at the championship meetings because if I remember aright he was a middleweight and I was a lightweight. I was often beaten of the big men.

Let me emphatically say in closing that I do not claim ever to have won the lightweight championship; that I do not remember ever having made such a claim; but of course I cannot be certain I did not, because I do remember very clearly six or eight years ago a correspondence in which I assumed that I had been champion, this correspondence originating from a description given by Hanks of his contest with me, in which he stated that he won by knocking off my spectacles. I was quite sure that this could not have happened, and that it was impossible that I could have worn spectacles in boxing; and it was in looking up this matter that I found out that my memory had been in error as to my victory over Cushing being in a final, and that it was only in a trial the same year that I fought Hanks. At this length of time it is quite impossible for me to remember which of the various bouts I fought with different men at different times were in the regular annual meetings, and which were at private or semipublic matches. You are welcome to show this letter to Mr. Underwood; but I do not wish it published or any statement from me made in the matter. I have much too serious work on hand to want to go into a preposterous discussion of this nature. *Sincerely yours*

4601 · TO ELIHU ROOT   *Roosevelt Mss.*

Personal   Washington, February 15, 1908

Dear Root: Please go over this memorandum, submitted to me by Sims, about those Brazilian battleships.[1] It certainly looks as if there was an even chance that these ships might not go to Brazil. If so, we ought to be exceedingly careful that they do not go to Japan. Would it not be possible to make some arrangement with the Brazilians on the subject? *Faithfully yours*

[1] In reply to a verbal request from Roosevelt, Sims had submitted a report on three ships building in England for Brazil. Since their design was identical with that of ships under construction there for Japan, Sims seriously doubted whether they were actually intended for Brazil. The suspected transfer did not occur; and the three ships were delivered to Brazil between 1909 and 1912.

Personal   Washington, February 15, 1908

Dear Phil: You are certainly a friend worth having. The Hagermans ought to be proud of having a man like you as a friend, and it is almost enough to shake my faith in the conclusions of the Department of the Interior. As for Mr. Hitchcock,[1] it is simply impossible for me to believe that he was not a straight man, altho his judgment and his temper were so bad that I finally lost all confidence in his actions.

Now give my regards to Mrs. Stewart, and do get on here and let me see you as soon as possible. *Ever yours*

Private   Washington, February 17, 1908

My dear Judge Dunklin:[1] I thank you heartily for your letter, both for its personal allusions to myself and for its excellent recommendations. The evil you speak of I have been very keenly aware of, and curiously enough I had thought of the very remedy you had suggested, namely, when a trust does as trusts so frequently do, that is, freezes out a competitor by selling at an abnormally low price, to fix that price as a maximum. I will take the matter up with the Interstate Commerce Commission. *Sincerely yours*

Personal   Washington, February 17, 1908

Dear Elihu: The enclosed memorandum from Sternberg explains itself. In addition, Sternberg told me that the German Military Attaché in Peking had reported that he was convinced that Japan did not at this time meditate war on the United States, but, on the contrary, its preparations were for trouble with or in China. This corresponds not only with what is set forth in the enclosed memorandum but with the information our people have given us from China as to the Chinese growing steadily more suspicious and distrustful of the Japanese. It helps to correct the imperial pipe dream forwarded thru Ambassador Tower. *Faithfully yours*

Washington, February 18, 1908

To the Interstate Commerce Commission: I am informed that a number of railroad companies have served notice of a proposed reduction of wages on their employees. One of them, the Louisville and Nashville, in announcing

---

[1] Ethan Allen Hitchcock.

[1] Irby Dunklin, Texas district judge at Fort Worth.

the reduction, stated that "the drastic laws inimical to the interests of the railroads that have in the past year or two been enacted by Congress and the State Legislatures" are largely or chiefly responsible for the conditions requiring the reduction.

Under such circumstances it is possible that the public may soon be confronted by serious industrial disputes, and the law provides that in such case either party may demand the services of your Chairman and of the Commissioner of Labor as a Board of Mediation and Conciliation.[1] These reductions in wages may be warranted, or they may not. As to this the public, which is a vitally interested party, can form no judgment without a more complete knowledge of the essential facts and real merits of the case than it now has or than it can possibly obtain from the special pleadings certain to be put forth by each side in case their dispute should bring about serious interruption to traffic. If the reduction in wages is due to natural causes, the loss of business being such that the burden should be, and is, equitably distributed between capitalist and wageworker, the public should know it. If it is caused by legislation, the public, and Congress, should know it; and if it is caused by misconduct in the past financial or other operations of any railroad, then everybody should know it, especially if the excuse of unfriendly legislation is advanced as a method of covering up past business misconduct by the railroad managers, or as a justification for failure to treat fairly the wage-earning employees of the Company.

Moreover, an industrial conflict between a railroad corporation and its employees offers peculiar opportunities to any small number of evil-disposed persons to destroy life and property and foment public disorder. Of course, if life, property and public order are endangered, prompt and drastic measures for their protection become the first plain duty. All other issues then become subordinate to the preservation of the public peace, and the real merits of the original controversy are necessarily lost from view. This vital consideration should be ever kept in mind by all law-abiding and farsighted members of labor organizations.

It is sincerely to be hoped, therefore, that any wage controversy that may arise between the railroads and their employees may find a peaceful solution thru the methods of conciliation and arbitration already provided by Congress, which have proven so effective during the past year. To this end the Commission should be in a position to have available for any board of conciliation or arbitration relevant data pertaining to such carriers as may become involved in industrial disputes. Should conciliation fail to effect a settlement and arbitration be rejected, accurate information should be available in order to develop a properly informed public opinion.

I therefore ask you to make such investigation, both of your records and by any other means at your command, as will enable you to furnish data concerning such conditions obtaining on the Louisville and Nashville and

[1] The Erdman Act of 1898.

any other roads, as may relate, directly or indirectly, to the real merits of the possibly impending controversy.[2]

4606 · TO HENRY LEE HIGGINSON   *Roosevelt Mss.*

Washington, February 19, 1908

My dear Major Higginson: Indeed I feel that you are right in the propositions that you advance. The trouble that I have comes from the fact that the big corporations that are working to discredit the laws and prevent proper laws being passed continually force me into action which is unavoidable, unless I am content to see the policies in which I believe overthrown, and yet which I very sincerely regret having to take. The Louisville and Nashville Railroad, for instance, in its endeavor to discredit the law, announces a reduction of wages, which it says is due to our unwise legislation. Such a challenge as that must at once be accepted by the Government to the extent of ordering an immediate investigation to ascertain its truth. So it is with my message to Congress. The outrageous fabrications and falsehoods of the Standard Oil and Harriman people, the Santa Fe people and others, were producing an effect that had to be counteracted. These corporations have probably spent a million dollars in their enormous advertisements and books, and insertion of matter in "patent insides" for the country papers, and the like — prominent newspapermen having told me that they reckoned that a million dollars was an underestimate of the amount they must have spent — and this is an earnest of how much more they are willing to spend for a

[2] Roosevelt's vigorous threat of publicity probably helped prevent serious wage controversies. Within less than a week after this letter had been made public the managers of the major Eastern and transcontinental roads promised the railroad brotherhoods that there would be no wage reductions. In the Southeast, where the most severe wage reductions had been contemplated, the letter hastened the use of government mediation. On February 25 the Southern Railroad, invoking the provisions of the Erdman Act, asked Neill, the Commissioner of Labor, and Knapp, the chairman of the Interstate Commerce Commission, to mediate a wage dispute. Two days later union representatives from the Louisville and Nashville and nine other Southeastern roads requested similar mediation. The mediators then reached an understanding with these roads that the agreement arrived at in the Southern case would set the regional wage pattern. The Southern and other Southeastern roads, accepting the mediators' recommendations that wage reductions were not warranted by current business conditions, made no cuts.

In using the facilities of the Interstate Commerce Commission to strengthen the provisions of the Erdman Act, Roosevelt, whatever his motives may have been, won the commendation of organized labor. Gompers and other union leaders gave him credit for preventing wage reductions. Roosevelt had also strengthened the precedent of government mediation. The provisions of the Erdman Act, which until the previous year had never been used, were for the next four years constantly invoked. By permitting satisfactory agreement without resort to strike, government mediation soon became the accepted method both by the railroads and by the union for handling labor disputes; see Charles P. Neill, "Mediation and Arbitration of Railway Labor Disputes in the United States," *Bulletin of Bureau of Labor,* No. 98 (January 1912). In describing the operation of the Erdman Act, Neill also gives a concise summary of the wage reduction controversies of 1908.

reaction. Now it is simply out of the question for me to submit, on behalf of the great mass of our people, to the success of such a movement, so engineered, and for such purposes. It is they who force the fighting, and not I.

Take another instance — that of legislation I am advocating. I am advocating just the legislation the necessity for which you have again and again pointed out — that is, amendments to the antitrust and interstate commerce laws in order to make legal proper combinations. But the very corporations that have been loudly insisting that those laws are bad, take not the slightest interest in their amendment. They do not want them changed and they do not care to have them removed from the statute books, but they expect to have them administered crookedly. Of course, as far as I am concerned such expectation is vain.

Now about the banking and currency system: I agree with you in your main contention. I would like to see a thoroly good system of banking and currency; but apparently you think little of the Aldrich bill, and yet this is the only measure that has been proposed that we can seriously consider. The trouble is that the minute I try to get action all the financiers and businessmen differ so that nobody can advise me, nobody can give me any aid; and only Senator Aldrich has prepared a bill. I have taken the liberty of sending to Senator Aldrich what you say about the banking and currency measure, together with a communication from Andrew Carnegie.[1] *Sincerely yours*

4607 · TO JAMES MONROE MILLER   *Roosevelt Mss.*

Washington, February 19, 1908

My dear Mr. Miller: [1] In my recent message I spoke of the hard case of P. B. Banton, who was crippled for life while doing his duty on the Panama Canal and is now helpless with a wife and three little children. I cannot too strongly say how earnestly I feel that this man's claim should be acted on by the Government. If we had the proper kind of employers' liability law such a claim would be paid as a matter of course. As we have no such law and as it would not be retroactive such claims should be provided for in a special bill. I understand that before your Committee there are many other claims of deserving claimants. If they are deserving I feel most strongly that they should have relief. Will it not be possible to have a general bill past to remedy the injustice

[1] In this communication, a copy of an address delivered before the Economic Club of New York, Carnegie urged Congress to lay the foundation for a "perfect" banking system by separating the banks from the government, requiring them to keep ample gold reserves and permitting them to issue notes based on assets.

[1] James Monroe Miller, Republican congressman from Kansas, 1899–1911, in 1908 chairman of the House Committee on Claims.

under which Banton and those like him are suffering? No more righteous act could be past by Congress.[2] *Sincerely yours*

4608 · TO CHARLES WARREN FAIRBANKS   *Roosevelt Mss.*

Confidential   Washington, February 21, 1908

Sir:[1] From its nature this letter must be treated as confidential; I beg that you will read it yourself and lay it before the committee or committees having to deal with the subject matter; these being I suppose the appropriations, the military, and the naval committees.

The present military and naval needs in the Pacific are so urgent as to force me to ask that consideration be given by the Congress to the necessity of completing as promptly and expeditiously as possible the defensive works on our Pacific coasts, in our insular possessions in the Pacific, and the providing of docks and other utilities which will permit of the maintenance of our battle fleet in those waters.

All of these works are being prosecuted on approved plans prepared by the National Defense Board and the Navy Department, and work upon them has progressed as rapidly as the appropriations made by Congress would permit; but the time seems to have arrived when the recognition of a special necessity for pushing them to completion must be considered the best and safest policy for the Government; for our fleet can never be diverted from its proper and legitimate function of seeking out and defeating the main fleet of the enemy and relegated to the passive and illegitimate function of coast and harbor guard.

As to the conditions of the defenses in the Philippine Islands, they are in such a state that any enemy can enter Manila Bay and occupy the city of Manila with little or no risk; the defenses of Subig Bay are still so far from completion that it has been deemed necessary to improvise a defense for that harbor from attack from the sea, by emplacing, temporarily and until the permanent defenses are completed, such spare guns as the army and navy possess in that region, and to prepare plans for the concentration of all our resources in those Islands for the defense from attack, capture or destruction by a land force, of the naval dry dock and coal supply there located, which would be of vital importance to our navy, if operating in those waters. In fact we would, in case of war, be compelled, in the present state of the defenses of Manila Bay, to abandon the capital of those Islands and make a desperate effort to hold the necessary utilities for naval operations in that

[2] Congress passed neither a general relief bill nor the special measure to relieve Pembroke B. Banton. For the future, such cases as his were covered by the liability act that did pass. This law referred to all government employees, including those in the Canal Zone, engaged in hazardous work.

[1] An identical letter was sent to the Speaker of the House. For Cannon's reactions to the letter see No. 4615.

region with a very small force, hastily concentrated behind improvised defenses at Subig Bay.

As to the condition of the defenses of Pearl Harbor, Hawaiian Islands, not a single gun is mounted to defend the harbor, and the only progress made consists of excavations for the emplacements for eight 12″ mortars, and the only garrison we have there to hold the harbor and Islands, — in the face of a foreign population of seventy or eighty thousand, which would probably become hostile in case of war, — is one infantry battalion of between 200 and 300 men. Moreover, the entrance channel must be straightened by dredging and a dry dock and accessories constructed before it will satisfy the naval requirements. Pearl Harbor is considered by naval and military experts as the key to the Pacific Ocean; its position off our coasts and in relation to the Panama Canal and the coasts of Alaska, as well as its position in relation to the Philippine Islands, indicates that it is not only of vital importance that the United States should develop it as a naval base and hold it, but that it is of still greater importance that, when so developed, it should not fall into the hands of an enemy based on the Pacific, to be used as a naval base from which to threaten not only our Pacific Coast States and Alaska, but the Pacific exit of the Panama Canal as well.

As to the condition of the defenses of the Pacific Coast States; the defenses of those States consist of seacoast forts at Puget Sound, Washington; Columbia River, Oregon; San Francisco and San Diego, California, with submarine mine defenses in such of the harbor waters as will permit of their use.

The defenses of Puget Sound are planned for the purpose of guarding the principal cities of Washington and Oregon, as well as the navy yard at Bremerton, at which yard is located the only naval dry dock suitable for large ships of the battleship and cruiser class. These defenses are in a very backward state and in their present condition cannot be depended upon to close the Sound against an enterprising enemy, even tho nothing more serious than raiding operations are to be expected on that coast until the United States has lost control of the sea.

The defenses of Columbia River, San Francisco and San Diego, are in much better condition than those of Puget Sound, but they lack a number of elements to be effective, which should be supplied.

Attention should also be given to the defenses of the naval base at Guantánamo, Cuba. They are very far from completion, only four 6″ guns and four 3″ guns of the total armament being mounted at the present time. Guantánamo will be the main naval base of the United States in the Caribbean Sea and the principal guard of the Atlantic entrance of the Panama Canal. The period of time which will be needed to complete the defensive works, as well as the naval utilities at this place, indicates that they should be undertaken now if the base is to be available on the completion of the Canal.

Nearly all of the deficiencies in the coast defenses and naval utilities referred to above are covered by the estimates of the War and Navy Departments now before Congress; they are based upon matured plans and must eventually be provided for, and as it is evident that the expense involved will not be decreased by delay, I deem that existing conditions warrant provision being made by Congress at once for the completion of all these works. In my judgment complete provision for the defense of Hawaii and Manila is of most pressing and immediate importance, while provision for the defense of Guantánamo will not become pressing until the Panama Canal nears completion.[2] But as to Hawaii and Manila, and above all as to Hawaii, there should be no delay; for it is impossible to foresee when the matter may become vital. With the fortifications herein advocated, and with the navy increased as it should be in battleships and torpedo-boat destroyers we will be able practically to guarantee peace to the country. *Very truly yours*

4609 · TO VICTOR HOWARD METCALF   *Roosevelt Mss.*

Washington, February 21, 1908

My dear Secretary Metcalf: In view of the statements of the Joint Board made thru Admiral Dewey it may well be that we should keep our fleet in the Pacific a longer time than I had supposed. Will you, after consulting all the proper officers, report to me in detail as to how long the fleet can be kept in a first-class state of efficiency on the Pacific coast?

Moreover, for reasons which Secretary Root will explain to you I particularly desire the fleet to visit Australia. Is this feasible? Will you have the matter worked out and have a tentative plan reported to me?[1] *Sincerely yours*

4610 · TO HOKE SMITH   *Roosevelt Mss.*

Washington, February 22, 1908

My dear Governor Smith:[1] I am of course greatly pleased with your letter. I shall bring it before the Interstate Commerce Commission. It seems to me

---

[2] The Sixtieth Congress substantially fulfilled Roosevelt's requests as modified by the recommendations of the Joint Board. It provided the desired funds for the Pearl Harbor base, adequate money for the Philippine station, and practically nothing for Guantánamo.

---

[1] The Australian government had suggested to the State Department that the fleet visit the Antipodes. This invitation precipitated Roosevelt's decision, announced March 14, the day after the fleet reached Magdalena Bay, to send the fleet around the world. Five days later the Japanese ambassador invited the fleet to visit Japan. The background and the events of the cruise to Australia and Japan are covered in detail by Bailey, *Roosevelt and the Japanese-American Crises,* pp. 274-293.

---

[1] Hoke Smith, Governor of Georgia, 1907-1909.

at the first blush that we should get at the facts before we decide on a policy in connection with legislation in the matter of control over wages. It is curious how we have both been working along the same lines in this matter — that you should have been engaged in a conference with your State Railroad Commission with a view to taking the very action that at the same time I was conferring with the National Commission about taking.[2] *Sincerely yours*

4611 · TO KERMIT ROOSEVELT   *Roosevelt Mss.*

Washington, February 23, 1908

Dearest Kermit: I quite agree with you about Tom Pinch. He is a despicable kind of character; just the kind of character that Dickens liked, because he had himself a thick streak of maudlin sentimentality of the kind that, as somebody phrased it, "made him wallow naked in the pathetic." It always interests me about Dickens to think how much first-class work he did and how almost all of it was mixt up with every form of cheap, second-rate matter. I am very fond of him. There are innumerable characters that he has created which symbolize vices, virtues, follies and the like almost as well as the characters in Bunyan; and therefore I think the wise thing to do is simply to skip the bosh and twaddle and vulgarity and untruth and get the benefit out of the rest. Of course one fundamental difference between Thackeray and Dickens is that Thackeray was a gentleman and Dickens was not. But a man may do some mighty good work and not be a gentleman in any sense.

Yes, it was Phil Roosevelt who wrote that poem.[1] I do not wonder that you were astonished at it. His own family have been quite as much surprised; I saw Cousin Emlen and Christine at lunch yesterday with the Frank Lowells. I really think the poem is very good; and, as Ted pointed out, the simile of the sagebrush and the puma is not only excellent but altogether new. How in the world Phil did it I do not know. They say that he has shown remarkable ability as a debater, and I should not wonder if he was cut out for a lawyer.

Last night I dined with the Jusserands, the only other guest being Justice Moody, and we had a thoroly enjoyable evening. You and I, if we get the chance, must surely call on him and look at his books the next time you are here. *Your loving father*

---

[2] See No. 4605.

[1] The poem, by Philip J. Roosevelt, a cousin of the President, then a student at St. Mark's School, was about the "barren plains country." "Your poem," the President wrote the boy, "gives the feeling that I had when I lived out in those lands as no other poem that I ever remember reading does give it." — Roosevelt to Philip J. Roosevelt, February 17, 1908, Roosevelt Mss.

Washington, February 27, 1908

Dear Cushing: [1] With the exception of one letter, from Samuel Crothers, I am tempted to say that of all the letters that have been written me, yours is the one that has touched me most; and without exception, yours is the letter that most clearly sets forth just what I have felt and have tried to do — with what failure to achieve complete success I am only too well aware.

I feel just exactly as you do. Most of the men of our little world do not see beyond their own circle. They know nothing of the lives and desires of their fellow countrymen. They do not realize the fervor of intensity with which these countrymen are demanding a change in the old order of things in politics and in the world of great business. The evils against which they rise in revolt are very real, and moreover are very base; and if the men in revolt are not well led, and if a substantial measure of victory is not achieved under sane and moderate leadership, there is danger that we shall embark on that evil course of oscillation between extremes that permanently lowered the French character during the years between 1789 and 1871. The abuses of the old regime, the folly of the reactionaries, and the folly of the demagogs, combined to bring about the Red Terror. The reaction against the Red Terror brought about Napoleonism. Then came the White Terror, and the reaction against this also found vent in revolution. The July monarchy really marked the victory of the moderates; but partly thru their own fault and partly thru the folly and wickedness of the extremists on both sides, the legitimists and the radicals, this monarchy was overthrown. The Second Republic came in under the nominal lead of the moderates; but the extreme radicals, the men who would correspond to some of the Bryanites and some of the Debsites of today, got control and adopted every kind of impossible policy, including the famous national workshops for the unemployed; and the moderates and radicals grew so distrustful of one another, the moderates showed such inefficiency and the radicals such wicked folly, while the extreme reactionaries conspired against both and welcomed disaster provided only that it hurt their foes for the moment, that in the end Louis Napoleon's pinchbeck empire of intrigue was the inevitable result. This could exist only when based on force, corruption and repression. When it fell the Red Commune rose on its ruins.

Now, what we ought all to strive for here is a steady and orderly development along the lines of fair dealing between man and man, and of honesty demanded from all men in business and politics alike. Ours must neither be a movement of the rich nor of the poor. If it can be kept, as I believe it can and will be kept, along these lines, the future of the nation is secure; and such an issue is well worth fighting for in spite of any temporary discouragement.

[1] Grafton Dulany Cushing, Boston lawyer, man of affairs, active Republican, in 1908 a member of the Massachusetts House of Representatives.

Of course, both the foolish and sinister radical and the foolish and sinister reactionary will take advantage, as it was inevitable that they would take advantage, of this year of depression, and temporarily the outcome may be bad in one direction or the other; but I think we have made substantial gain, lookt at from the larger viewpoint, and that some of the gain will be permanent.

I wish you could get down here this spring to visit us for a day or two. Is this possible? If you can, I will have you meet a number of the men who are really carrying out the policies of this administration. *Faithfully yours*

P.S. As you so well put it, our aim must be the supremacy of justice, a more satisfactory distribution of wealth — so far as this is attainable — with a view to a more real equality of opportunity, and in sum a higher social system. In international affairs we have in the past six years measurably realized our ideal; we have shown our ability to hold our own against the strong; while no nation has ever behaved towards the weak with quite the disinterestedness and sanity combined which we have shown as regards Cuba and the Philippines.

4613 · TO VICTOR HOWARD METCALF   *Roosevelt Mss.*

Washington, February 28, 1908

To the Secretary of the Navy: It is directed that a Board shall be formed composed of two officers of the Engineer Corps of the United States Army and one member from the Civil Engineer of the Corps of the Navy as members, and a Civil Engineer of the Navy as Recorder of the Board, to thoroly investigate the question of the hydraulics of the Mare Island Straits and approaches, having in view the construction of works for the permanent improvement of the approaches and the Straits so that ships of deepest draft can go up to the Mare Island Navy Yard.[1]

4614 · TO JONATHAN BOURNE, JUNIOR   *Roosevelt Mss.*

Washington, February 28, 1908

My dear Senator Bourne: Those letters were most interesting. I am proud of my countrywoman's prowess. Curiously enough, this very morning I received a letter from the English Colonel Patterson with whom she has been out, and he speaks of her and says "She was delightful in every way and is plucky enough to tackle a trust king." I laughed immensely over this phrase, in view of the fact that she is Archbold's daughter. His letter described the

[1] The Navy Department, anxious to have its only completed dry dock on the Pacific Coast available to all ships, acted quickly. The board, appointed at once, made its report in June. As soon as Congress provided the necessary appropriations, work was begun in Mare Island Strait.

Christmas day which she described in one of her letters to her father.
Sincerely yours

4615 · TO JOSEPH GURNEY CANNON   *Roosevelt Mss.*

Confidential   Washington, February 29, 1908

My dear Mr. Speaker: In reference to our conversation of this morning and to your statement that my recent letter to you and the Vice-President said either too much or too little, do let me repeat to you, so that you may repeat it to others (say to Mr. Foss) if necessary, that in such a letter as this it is not possible for me with wisdom to put on paper all that I feel.[1] I am not acting with a view to an emergency of the next year or two. I am acting with a view to the emergencies that there is a reasonable chance may arise within the next decade or two. At this session every provision should be made for the fortification of Hawaii and the establishment of a naval station at Pearl Harbor, and we ought to provide four battleships and a reasonable number of torpedo destroyers — the submarines are well enough, but the need for them is not nearly as great; just as the need for the Chicago station is less. I do not think that in this case, as regards Hawaii and the navy, considerations as to the need of economy should be allowed to offset the far greater need of guaranteeing the preservation both of peace and of the national honor and interest. *Sincerely yours*

4616 · TO THE WAR DEPARTMENT   *Roosevelt Mss.*

Washington, February 29, 1908

To the War Department: Senator Newlands' bill in reference to the Waterways Commission will doubtless be sent to the War Department for a report. In the regular routine this would go to General Mackenzie.[1] This is undesirable. The bill should not go to any of the engineers. It represents in a general sense the policy of the Commission, which policy is mine, but which policy is not the one approved by General Mackenzie and the engineers. Therefore I desire that the bill be sent direct to me, and I will, after confer-

[1] Cannon later claimed that, unimpressed by the President's arguments for the need of a stronger navy, he continued to combat successfully the President's naval program (Busbey, *Cannon*, pp. 224–226). Nevertheless, the appropriations bill for the base at Pearl Harbor, the primary objective of Roosevelt's first letter to Cannon (No. 4608, note 1), passed the House by a vote of 246 to 1.

[1] Brigadier General Alexander Mackenzie, since 1904 Chief of the Army Engineers, opposed the Newlands Bill and other measures giving congressional sanction to and appropriating funds for an inland waterways commission. Such a commission, Mackenzie maintained, would duplicate the work and perhaps even arrogate the functions of the army engineers. His opinion provided a rationalization for Cannon and other congressmen who opposed the bill for reasons of economy. In spite of Roosevelt's strong and continuing support, the Newlands Bill, later combined with one of Congressman Burton's, failed to pass.

ence with the Secretary of War, direct what answer shall be sent in reference thereto.

4617 · TO ELIHU ROOT   *Roosevelt Mss.*

Washington, February 29, 1908

To the Secretary of State: What is the present status of the Venezuela affair? We have suffered a great deal of wrongdoing at the hands of Venezuela. Has the time come when we ought to take action, or not? [1]

4618 · TO WILLIAM HOWARD TAFT   *Roosevelt Mss.*

Washington, March 1, 1908

Dear Will: I have your letter of February 28th. Oh Lord! I can assure you from bitter experience that if you were President and began making exceptions in such a case as that of Mrs. Sanderson you would get yourself into a greater variety of scrapes and do more miscellaneous damage to the service than you can well imagine! *I*'ve been there! It is a pure sympathy case, and as Mrs. Sanderson has been out of the service over thirty years the odds are a hundred to one that she is not fit for any position. A couple of years ago I undertook to make an occasional exception on grounds of sympathy. I began very gradually and where the cause was far better than in this of Mrs. Sanderson. I think my first half dozen exceptions were probably all right: but they served as precedents to open the gate. Last year I found I had made seventy or eighty and not all of them good cases; and I have had to shut down absolutely short. If I let in Mrs. Sanderson there would not be any reason for not letting in a thousand other worthy ladies for whom one feels great sympathy and who are, in all probability, entirely incompetent for the positions they seek. I speak as a reformed culprit and beg that when in the White House you will profit by my awful example! *Ever yours*

4619 · TO G. H. DAVIS   *Roosevelt Mss.*

Washington, March 2, 1908

Sir: [1] I have received your protest against the enactment of child labor legislation by the Congress. I heartily favor the enactment by Congress of any

[1] Root was then attempting with more patience than success to persuade Venezuela either to grant redress to American citizens injured by Castro's policies, or to submit the American claims to arbitration. "Although he found Venezuela 'intensely irritating' and Castro a 'crazy brute,'" the Secretary of State advised Roosevelt that the time for action had not yet arrived. Venezuela's continuing intransigence within four months changed Root's views. He arranged in June to break off diplomatic relations. Until Castro was overthrown, Brazil represented American interests at Caracas; see Jessup, *Root,* I, 497–499; *Foreign Relations of the United States,* 1908 (Washington, 1912), pp. 774–830.

[1] G. H. Davis, secretary, Manufacturers' Bureau, Indianapolis.

legislation which it has the power to enact which will prevent the gross abuses of child labor, just as I heartily favor the passage of an employers' liability law. I am certain that under the interstate commerce clause of the Constitution an employers' liability bill can be enacted into law. I feel that we should enact a child labor law for the District of Columbia and the Territories at the earliest possible date; and, unless the States act in a thorogoing and drastic way in the matter, I shall favor the enactment of a law under the interstate commerce clause of the Constitution to prohibit child labor. *Very truly yours*

4620 · TO WILLIAM HOWARD TAFT *Roosevelt Mss.*

Washington, March 4, 1908

My dear Mr. Secretary: Is it not possible that we have too difficult examinations for army chaplains? We cannot be too careful in getting the right kind of chaplain, but I am very doubtful whether the scholastic examination is not given altogether too much weight. For instance, I cannot imagine any necessity for a chaplain to know anything whatever about mathematics. The best clergymen and priests I know have no knowledge of mathematics. You are very busy, but could you not ask Oliver or someone to take up this matter and bring the examination papers over to me? We want to see that the chaplain is a man of practical sense, of genuine morality, of deep religious feeling, with the attainments of a gentleman. But scholastic development per se accounts for but very little in the matter. *Sincerely yours*

4621 · TO KERMIT ROOSEVELT *Roosevelt Mss.*

Washington, March 4, 1908

Dearest Kermit: Recently President Pardo, of Peru, sent me a florid South American telegram about our navy visiting Peru. I never saw it. Adee, in the State Department, prepared one of the usual fatuous answers, into which he unwarily put the statement that I extended to him all good wishes from "me and my people." Jaded, overworked Root did not have his attention attracted by the phrase, and as it was a routine telegram signed my name to it and sent it off. Thereupon all the New York papers had hysteria over this as showing marked imperialistic and megalomaniac tendencies on my part, and all kinds of cartoons and editorials appeared on the subject. I send you one amusing cartoon and another amusing poem. Of course I could not possibly explain, because to do so meant that poor President Pardo would have had his feelings deeply hurt by learning that I had never seen his telegram or my answer! But I gave orders that hereafter nobody was to sign my name but me myself.

You have recently been writing me about Dickens. Senator Lodge gave me the following first-class quotation from a piece by Dickens about "Proposals for Amusing Posterity":

And I would suggest that if a body of gentlemen possessing their full phreno-logical share of the combative and antagonistic organs, could only be induced to form themselves into a Society for Declaiming about Peace, with a very considerable war-whoop against all nondeclaimers; and if they could only be prevailed upon to sum up eloquently the many unspeakable miseries and horrors of War, and to present them to their own country as a conclusive reason for its being undefended against War, and becoming a prey of the first despot who might choose to inflict those miseries and horrors — why then I really believe we should have got to the very best joke we could hope to have in our whole Complete Jest-Book for Posterity and might fold our arms and rest convinced that we had done enough for that discerning Patriarch's amusement.

This ought to be read before all the tomfool peace societies and anti-imperialist societies of the present day. *Your loving father*

4622 · TO CHARLES E. KNOBLAUCH   *Roosevelt Mss.*

Washington, March 5, 1908

My dear Knoblauch: [1] I know nothing of the Hepburn bill, and of course never told you there would be no legislation, for the simple reason that, as you must know, I cannot control what the members of Congress choose to do. The only bill that I have been backing was the bucket shop bill, and I do not even know that that has been introduced. *Sincerely yours*

4623 · TO ARTHUR JAMES BALFOUR   *Roosevelt Mss.*

Washington, March 5, 1908

My dear Mr. Balfour: Thru Arthur Lee I have just received the copy of *Decadence,*[1] and thank you for it. I confess I began to read it with some apprehension lest it might have something to do with some phase of French literary thought. Naturally, therefore, I was glad when the first few lines showed that my fears were groundless.

It seems to me that you are eminently right in seeing that it is good to give a name to something of vital consequence, even tho in a sense the name

---

[1] Charles E. Knoblauch, a Rough Rider and member of the New York Stock Exchange, had written Roosevelt protesting against various proposed bills, including one of Hepburn, imposing prohibitive taxes or other restrictions on stock transactions. Intended to prevent gambling in stocks, these measures failed properly to discriminate between legitimate and illegitimate trading. None emerged from committee. Knoblauch's unauthorized revelation of Roosevelt's opinion provoked a brief bullish spurt noteworthy only because the President had for so long been the symbol of the bears.

---

[1] *Decadence* (Cambridge, England, 1908), the Henry Sidgwick memorial lecture, one of those searching, sensitive essays that through the years created uncertainty in so many minds, including perhaps his own, as to whether Arthur James Balfour belonged more properly in the halls of Westminster or in the towers of Oxford.

959

only expresses our ignorance. It is a curious thing in mankind, but undoubtedly true, that if we do not give such a name to our ignorance, most of us gradually feel that there is nothing to be ignorant about. Most emphatically there is such a thing as "decadence" of a nation, a race, a type; and it is no less true that we cannot give any adequate explanation of the phenomenon. Of course there are many partial explanations, and in some cases, as with the decay of the Mongol or Turkish monarchies, the sum of these partial explanations may represent the whole. But there are other cases, notably of course that of Rome in the ancient world, and, as I believe, that of Spain in the modern world, on a much smaller scale, where the sum of all the explanations is that they do not wholly explain. Something seems to have gone out of the people or peoples affected, and what it is no one can say. In the case of Rome, one can say that the stocks were completely changed, tho I do not believe that this in the least represents even the major part of the truth. But in the case of Spain, the people remain the same. The expulsion of Moor and heretic, the loss of the anarchistic and much-misused individual liberties of the provinces and towns, the economic and social changes wrought by the inflow of American gold — all of them put together do not explain the military decadence of the Spaniard; do not explain why he grew so rigid that, at first on sea and then on land, he could not adapt himself to new tactics; and above all, what subtle transformation it was that came over the fighting edge of the soldiers themselves. For nearly a century and a half following the beginning of Gonsalvo's campaigns, the Spanish infantry showed itself superior in sheer fighting ability to any other infantry of Europe. Toward the end of the sixteenth century, neither the Hollanders, fighting with despair for their own firesides, nor the Scotch and English volunteers, actuated by love of fighting and zeal for their faith, were able on anything like equal terms to hold their own against the Spanish armies, who walked at will to and fro thru the Netherlands, save where strong city walls or burst dikes held them at bay. Yet the Hollander, the Englishman and the Scotchman were trained soldiers, and they were spurred by every hope and feeling which we ordinarily accept as making men formidable in fight. A century passed; and these same Spaniards had become contemptible creatures in war compared with the Dutch and Scotch, the English and French, whom they had once surpassed. Many partial explanations can be given for the change, but none that wholly or mainly explains it.

What is true of military prowess is even more true of national life as a whole. I do not see how any thinking man can fail to feel now and then ugly doubts as to what may befall our modern civilization — the civilization of the white races, who have spread their influence over the entire world — and the culture they have inherited or acquired in extreme western Asia and in Europe during the last three or four thousand years. There are unpleasant analogies between the twentieth century and Hellenistic antiquity in the first period of the post-Alexandrian monarchies; and of course the resemblance is even closer with the orderly, peace-loving, cultivated Roman world from Trajan to Marcus Aurelius. The resemblances are in the way of analogy rather than homology it is true, and there are deep fundamental differences. But the resemblances are there. Why the creative literary spirit should practically have vanished from Roman lands after the time of Trajan, we do not know. We can see better why the citizens lost the traits which make good individual soldiers; but we cannot see why the very time of the astounding urban growth of North Africa, Gaul and Spain should have been coincident with the growth of utter inability to organize on a sufficiently large scale either in peace or war, until everything grew to depend upon the ability of one or two men on top. Much of the fall of the Roman Republic we can account for. For one thing, I do not think historians have ever laid sufficient emphasis on the fact that the widening of the franchise in Italy and the provinces meant so little from the governmental standpoint because citizens could only vote in one city, Rome; I should hate at this day to see the United States governed by votes cast in the city of New York, even tho Texas, Oregon and Maine could in theory send their people thither to vote if they chose. But the reasons for the change in military and governmental ability under the empire between, say, the days of Hadrian and of Valens are hardly even to be guessed at.

I have always been greatly interested in what you point out as to the inability of the people of that strip of Western Asia which is geographically North Africa ever to recover themselves after the downfall of the Roman Empire. It is a rather irritating delusion — the delusion that somehow or other we are all necessarily going to move forward in the long run no matter what the temporary checks may be. I have a very firm faith in this general forward movement, considering only men of our own race for the past score or two centuries, and I hope and believe that the movement will continue for an indefinite period to come; but no one can be sure; there is certainly nothing inevitable or necessary about the movement. For a thousand years, from the days of Alexander to the days of Mahomet, in spite of fluctuations, the civilization of Asia west of the Euphrates was that of Greeks and of Asiatics profoundly affected by Greek influences. Then it disappeared from the land; just as the extraordinary Roman civilization disappeared from North Africa, and left not a vestige behind save the ruins of cities and the masonry around the springs that have dried up under the destructive impotence of the rule that succeeded it.

It is hopeful of course to think how peoples do revive now and then; peoples doubtless partly the same in blood as those that fell, and at least with the ancestral inheritance of language, of culture. You have pointed out the greatest instance of this in Italy. A totally different and much smaller example is furnished by modern Switzerland.

The intrusion of an alien race into another civilization, its growth and supremacy and dying away, is of course curiously paralleled by what we see in the animal world, and the parallel is complete in at least one point — that is, in the fact that in each case the causes may be shrouded in absolute darkness. South America, until the middle of the Tertiary period, had a mammalian fauna almost as unique as that of Australia, composed chiefly of small marsupials, and of what we loosely call edentates, also of small size. Then there occurred physical union with the great arctogeal continent by the Isthmus of Panama. There followed an inrush of northern fauna and an extraordinarily powerful and abundant faunal life sprang up. The dominant forms were those of the intruders — saber-tooth tigers, bear, deer, elephants, swine, camels, tapirs, horses, all of great abundance in species, and many of the species of giant size. Under the pressure most of the old forms disappeared; but some of the so-called edentates developed into ground sloths and giant armadillos as large as elephants; and some of these forms when thus developed proved not only able to hold their own in South America, but gradually in their turn made their way north across the Isthmus and spread into North America in the teeth of the competition of the descendants of the forms that had anciently overrun South America. Thus there grew up in South America a faunal life as gigantic, as fierce, as varied, as that of Central Africa at this moment, and on the whole more like that of Central Africa than like the life of South America today, and infinitely more so than like the old eocene life of South America. Then there came a change, we know not why. In North America the glacial period may have had much to do with it, but surely this cannot have been true of South America; yet all of these huge formidable creatures died out, alike the monsters of alien type from the North, and the monsters developed from ancient autochthonous types. A few weak representatives were left, of both types; but the old magnificent fauna completely vanished; and why we cannot say, any more than we can explain why the Roman so completely failed permanently to leave North Africa to his descendants.

Of course there is a small side trouble, due to our terminology. All species of animals of course ultimately disappear, some because their kind entirely dies out, and some because the species is transformed into a wholly different species, degenerate or not; but in our nomenclature we make no distinction between the two utterly different kinds of "disappearance." So it is, of course, with nations. I really believe that people sometimes think of "new" nations as being suddenly created out of nothing; they certainly speak as if they were not aware that the newest and the oldest nations and races must of course have identically the same length of racial pedigree. They talk, moreover, of the "destruction" of the inhabitants of Mexico, and of the "destruction" of the inhabitants of Tasmania, as if the processes were alike. In Tasmania the people were absolutely destroyed; none of their blood is left. But the bulk of the blood of Mexico, and a part of the blood of the governing classes of Mexico (including Diaz), is that of the Mexicans whom Cortez and his successors conquered. In the same way Australia and Canada and the United States are "new" commonwealths only in the sense that Syracuse and Cyrene were new compared with Athens and Corinth.

Another thing that makes one feel irritated is the way that people insist on speaking as if what has occurred during the last three or four hundred years represented part of the immutable law of nature. The military supremacy of the whites is an instance in point. From the rise of the Empire of Genghis Khan to the days of Selim, the Mongol and Turkish tribes were unquestionably the military superiors of the peoples of the Occident, and when they came into conflict it was the former who almost always appeared as invaders and usually as victors. Yet people speak of the Japanese victories over the Russians as if they had been without precedent thruout the ages.

One practical problem of statesmanship, by the way, must be to keep on good terms with these same Japanese and their kinsmen on the mainland of Asia, and yet to keep the white man in America and Australia out of home contact with them. It is equally to the interest of the British Empire and of the United States that there should be no immigration in mass from Asia to Australia or to North America. It can be prevented, and an entirely friendly feeling between Japan and the English-speaking peoples preserved, if we act with sufficient courtesy and at the same time with sufficient resolution. But this is leaving speculative history for present politics.

With regard, *Sincerely yours*

4624 · TO HARRY STEWART NEW   *Roosevelt Mss.*

Personal   Washington, March 6, 1908

My dear New: Don't you think it would be a good thing to have Beveridge temporary chairman of the Convention? It seems to me that he has earned it from the party. What are your views? Of course do not understand me as desiring in any way to dictate, and if I have no excuse for making the suggestion, consider it withdrawn.[1] *Sincerely yours*

4625 · TO JAMES CREELMAN   *Roosevelt Mss.*

Private   Washington, March 7, 1908

My dear Mr. Creelman:[1] Let me congratulate you and thank you for your admirable article on President Diaz. I quite agree with you that President

---

[1] New, since December the chairman of the National Committee, considered the suggestion withdrawn. Increasingly hostile to progressive ideas, he was already quietly but effectively opposing Beveridge in the intraparty struggles in Indiana. He joined the standpatters on the National Committee who selected as temporary chairman a safe, unimaginative spokesman of their position — Senator Julius Caesar Burrows of Michigan. This selection and Burrows' keynote speech, contrasting as they did with the party's overwhelming acceptance of Roosevelt's choice for the Presidency, suggested even as Taft was nominated the division that was to be his undoing.

[1] James Creelman, former editorial writer for the New York *World,* in 1908 associate editor of *Pearson's Magazine.*

Diaz is the greatest statesman now living, and he has done for his country what no other living man has done for any other country — which is the supreme test of the value of statesmanship. I think you gave our people in this article the best and most vivid picture that has yet been given of this great President of our sister Republic, and I thank you for doing so. *Sincerely yours*

4626 · TO AUGUSTUS PEABODY GARDNER   *Roosevelt Mss.*

Washington, March 7, 1908

Dear Mr. Gardner: Referring to our conversation yesterday respecting the Tokyo Exposition and your varied and interesting inquiries concerning it, I enclose for your further information a revised memorandum from the Department of State which comprises many excellent suggestions and a draft bill containing proposed amendments of an eminently practical nature, which I am sure will be of use during the consideration of the bill providing for participation by this Government in the Exposition at Tokyo in 1912.[1]

There is abundant and emphatic reason for accepting and accepting at once the cordial invitation of the Japanese Government to take part in the proposed exposition. This exposition at Tokyo will be the first great international fair to be held in the Orient, and it will offer opportunities of rare and unique value to manufacturers, farmers and exporters of the United States, who are seeking to enlarge the markets for their products in the far East. The Tokyo Exposition will bring together in a friendly and instructive way the peoples of the Occident and of the Orient. It will be an important promoter of peace, of amity and of international trade. No international exposition in which this Government has taken part has seemed to offer such rich possibilities for the increase of the foreign commerce of the United States as does the one which is to be held at Tokyo four years hence.

There are many sound reasons, both of a diplomatic and commercial character, why we should accept Japan's invitation and arrange promptly, generously and effectively for participation in the Tokyo Exposition. We are under a heavy debt of obligation to Japan. She has responded many times generously and handsomely to the invitation of this Government to participate in our great fairs, and she has contributed largely and brilliantly to their success, so that we are bound, both in duty and honor, to give heed to her invitation and to see to it that we participate in her Exposition of 1912 in a manner wholly worthy of the intelligence, the wealth, the progress, the resources, and the civilization of the American people. This can only be adequately done by setting to work earnestly and at once. By commencing

[1] Roosevelt's suggestions for United States participation in the Tokyo exposition, endorsed by Augustus P. Gardner, the chairman of the House Committee on Industrial Arts and Expositions, and by his committee and its counterpart in the Senate, were accepted by Congress. A bill passed in May appropriated $1,500,000, established a commission on arrangements, and authorized military transportation for an American exhibit. This letter was also sent to Baron Kaneko.

our preparations now a great deal of money will in the end be saved and there will be ample time for producing an artistic, varied and highly creditable exhibit. The American exhibits at foreign expositions have too often lost in effectiveness by reason of the enforced haste with which they were assembled.

I very earnestly hope you will consider, either at this time, in connection with the pending bill, or certainly not later than next December, the feasibility of providing for taking the salient part of the American industrial exhibit at Tokyo at the close of the exposition on Government transports to some of the principal seaports of the Orient for exhibition. Such cities as Shanghai, Hong Kong, Canton, Singapore and Sydney, Australia, might be visited by this "floating exposition" with profit, and a superb opportunity given to our exhibitors to display their wares at small additional cost in the great marts of the Orient.

I also invite your attention to the amendment providing salaries for the officers of the American commission. If we are to have a successful and impressive exhibit at Tokyo, we must give adequate compensation to the men who are responsible for it.

I also call attention to article 3 of the draft bill, which seems admirably to cover the matter of appropriation. *Sincerely yours*

4627 · TO ARTHUR HAMILTON LEE   *Roosevelt Mss.*

Personal   Washington, March 7, 1908

My dear Lee: I enclose a letter to Balfour in acknowledgment of his book. Will you hand it to him?

Since writing you I received a letter from Sir Wilfrid Laurier, one paragraph of which runs as follows:

Unfortunately we know, from experience, that wherever on this continent, as well as in other lands, labourers of Asiatic races come in competition with labourers of the Caucasian races, serious troubles immediately arise, and that for many years and perhaps many generations the only way of preventing those troubles is to restrict, to the narrowest limits possible, the contact of those races in the labour market of our continent.

I think this expresses the view which, with all possible courtesy and consideration for Japan, those responsible for the welfare of Canada, Australia and the United States should take. In other words, there should be no immigration in mass of Orientals to the countries where the English-speaking peoples now form and will form the population of the future. For Japan's own sake it would not do to have masses of Englishmen or Americans come into her possessions; and as a matter of fact the Japanese have, wisely and properly, always gotten rid of all foreigners who have come over to teach them how to manage any of their industries, as soon as the lesson had been taught. Japan has been quite right in taking this attitude; and in the same way, we are quite right in protecting our working classes, our wageworkers, farmers, and small traders, from an influx that would mean the submergence of our own people. When I say "we," in this instance, I mean all the English-speaking people of America and Australia.

We had an invitation from Deakin[1] that the fleet should visit Australia, and accordingly the fleet will be sent there.

I suppose by this time you have seen Commissioner King. He came down to visit me again, carrying the letter from Sir Wilfrid, shortly after I last wrote you. *Sincerely yours*

4628 · TO CORINNE ROOSEVELT ROBINSON   *Robinson Mss.*[0]

Washington, March 7, 1908

Darling sister, We have grieved greatly over the tragedy in the life of dearest little Corinne; you know how fond we are of her; I love her as if she were my own daughter; and I hate to think of her suffering, and of yours.

I think the Doctor is quite right in wishing her to be away, and not with you. The one and only thing for her to do now is to treat the past as past, the event as finished and out of her life; to dwell on it, and above all to keep talking of it, with you or anyone else, would be both weak and morbid. Let her try not to think of it; this she can not wholly avoid; but she can wholly avoid speaking of it. Let her show a brave and cheerful front to the world, whatever she feels; and let her never speak one word of the matter, henceforth, to you or to anyone else. In the long future, when the memory is too dead to throb, she may if she wishes again speak of it; but if she is wise and brave she will not speak of it now. *Ever lovingly your brother*

4629 · TO FRANCIS EMROY WARREN   *Roosevelt Mss.*

Washington, March 9, 1908

My dear Senator Warren: I am entirely in accord with the bill you showed to me as expressing the sentiments of yourself and Senators Lodge and Warner.[1]

---

[1] Alfred Deakin, in 1908 Prime Minister of the commonwealth.

[1] This bill, representing the majority opinion of the Senate Military Affairs Committee on Brownsville, Roosevelt explicitly supported in his special message to Congress of March 11. It extended for a year the time limit within which the President could reinstate any man who in his judgment appeared "not to be within the class whose discharge was deemed necessary in order to maintain the discipline and morale of the Army" (*Senate Document*, 60 Cong., 1 sess., no. 377). Opposing this bill and supporting his own, Foraker delivered his celebrated speech of April 14 on behalf of the Negro companies (see Foraker, *Notes of a Busy Life*, II, 261-298). This carefully reasoned brief, skillfully presented, convinced many neutral observers that the President and the majority of the Senate committee were wrong. Taft ordered still another investigation of the Brownsville affair, this time by a journalist and a private detective. While these men worked, the puzzled Congress delayed action on the proposed bills. Not until the next session was the issue revived.

I have also seen the bill submitted from your Committee to the Secretary of War as having been introduced by Senator Foraker in reference to the restoration to the army of all soldiers of the three companies — B, C, and D — of the 25th Infantry who were discharged because of their implication in the murderous assault on Brownsville, or because of having guilty knowledge thereof. This bill provides that all these soldiers shall, on taking oath of their innocence, be reappointed. The investigation of your Committee as disclosed by its report has conclusively shown that the murderous assault in question was committed by various soldiers, probably ten to twenty in number, of those mustered out of the service. An additional number must have had guilty knowledge before or after the event of the assault and have declined to make this knowledge known to the proper authorities. This conclusion of your Committee had already been reached by the military authorities, and in my judgment it is the only conclusion that can justly be reached in the matter. Senator Foraker's bill therefore amounts simply to a proposal to condone murder and perjury in the past and put a premium upon perjury in the future by permitting any murderer or perjurer, who will again perjure himself, to be restored to the United States army, and again wear the uniform which he has already disgraced, and again take oath to obey the laws which he has already violated, and again to assume the duty of protecting the lives and property of the fellow citizens of those whom he has already murdered or attempted to murder. The bill therefore, even if effective, would be in the highest degree objectionable. But discussion of it is really academic, because the bill would not be effective even tho it ultimately received a two-thirds vote in both Houses and was therefore past over my veto and put upon the statute books. It proposes to usurp the appointing power of the President, which under the Constitution cannot be done. If the inconceivable should happen and the bill be enacted in its present form it would simply be null, for no reappointment would be made under it by me. *Sincerely yours*

4630 · TO VICTOR HOWARD METCALF   *Roosevelt Mss.*

Personal   Washington, March 9, 1908

My dear Mr. Secretary: I am not satisfied with our present organization of the Navy Department. It does not seem to me that those responsible for our building program have done as well, for instance, as the Japanese. In the present Japanese fleet there are four battleships superior to any four of ours. There are four armored cruisers superior to any armored cruisers of ours and probably equal to our average battleship. There are two battleships and one armored cruiser building better than any battleships or armored cruisers we have building.[1] Now it seems to me we should be taking steps to keep in

[1] Roosevelt exaggerated the deficiency in American ship design. Nevertheless the newer Japanese ships were in several respects superior to comparable American vessels.

advance of other nations rather than behind them in matters of construction. I realize, of course, that under the naval committees of the Senate and House respectively, we have very much to contend with; but at least we should put ourselves on record in most emphatic shape in communications of the Department (and of the President as well) to the two Houses and to the two naval committees.[2] *Sincerely yours*

4631 · TO HENRY ADAMS *Roosevelt Mss.*

Washington, March 9, 1908

Dear Adams: Of course I have read your grandfather's diary; but I have at once sent for another copy to reread in part about those years. There was just two years' interval, then, between his Presidency and his nominal appearance in Congress. Oh Lord! I wish I did not sympathize with him and the rest of his family about being bored! The capacity to be bored whether treated as a sin or a misfortune is an awful handicap. *Always yours*

4632 · TO ERNEST HAMLIN ABBOTT *Roosevelt Mss.*

Personal Washington, March 12, 1908

My dear Abbott: You have seen my last message to Congress on the Brownsville incident. I enclose you for your private information a copy of a private letter I had sent at the same time to Senator Warren, Chairman of the Senate Military Committee, to be used or not in his discretion. The Foraker bill I should refuse to sign, and should refuse to obey if it were passed over my veto. The Warren bill is entirely proper. As my message sets forth, I was engaged in an investigation to see whether there were any soldiers who could clear themselves at the time that Foraker began his investigation in the Senate. Of course I could not continue it while the Senate was carrying on its investigation without appearing to enter into ridiculous rivalry. Now, as by the Senate's own action, thanks to the resolution of Foraker, the time has gone by within which it was possible for me to reinstate any man, I asked for an extension of the time so as to be able to do what I actually was doing when the Senate interrupted the work.

From the information I have, there are probably five or six men who, because of being on pass or being in barracks out of the way, can be legitimately reinstated. If Congress does not pass the bill I asked for, my present intention is to have the investigation made anyhow, and next year to recommend to Congress the passage of the bill to permit the reinstatement of the specific soldiers I will name. *Sincerely yours*

[2] The communications of the department to the congressional committees and a Presidential message to Congress urging authorization and appropriation for four dreadnoughts had little effect. Congress passed the House committee's bill providing for two battleships.

Roosevelt Mss.

Washington, March 12, 1908

Dear Foulke: Many thanks for your letter of the 7th and the clippings. I think your speech is admirable, and naturally, my dear fellow, I was very much touched by what you said.

As to that item from the Indianapolis *News*, I did my level best to have Porter, who was a hearty Taft man, appointed. The Senate refused to confirm him, because, I think, of an intrigue in which the supporters of Fairbanks and Cannon in Oklahoma took the leading part. I then, on the recommendation of the two national committeemen, the Chairman of the State Committee, the Congressman, and all the men whose recommendations I have been following in such matters (whenever I thought them good), nominated a new man whom I did not personally know.[1] I had not the slightest idea, as a matter of fact, whom he favored,* but the editorial of the *News* is delicious if you take into account these two considerations:

1. The *News* asserts that the rejection of Porter enabled me to appoint a man who turned over the delegation to Taft.

2. Porter was my nominee, whom I did my level best to have confirmed, who was a strong Taft man, and who was beaten, as I have said, primarily because of the intrigues of the Fairbanks and Cannon men, all the Taft men being for him, and he being an excellent man whom it was an outrage to have beaten.

It therefore appears, according to the *News* editorial, that the Cannon and Fairbanks supporters succeeded, much against my earnest efforts, in causing a situation which turned out for the benefit of Taft! *Ever yours*

* It appears now that he has always been a Taft man.

Roosevelt Mss.

Personal

Washington, March 13, 1908

My dear Abbott: That is a capital sketch[1] and I return it herewith. I have not a suggestion to make, except to say that as regards the proposed alliance between Taft and Foraker there is more than you set forth. Taft's view is that Foraker is a thoroly corrupt man, who has made his money by improper work for corporations while Senator. He did not regard it as his province to attack Foraker. It is out of the question for any public man to go on with his own work if he makes miscellaneous efforts to reform *all* abuses. He did not propose himself to try to make a fight against Foraker for the Senate. All he

---

[1] Samuel Grant Victor, former chairman of the Republican Committee of Indian Territory, was nominated and confirmed as United States Marshal for the Eastern District of Oklahoma, the office for which G. A. Porter had been rejected.

---

[1] Roosevelt had read Lyman Abbott's "William H. Taft," published in the April 4, 1908, *Outlook.*

did was to refuse to make a bargain or deal by which he should agree actively to support Foraker for the Senate in return for Foraker's support for the Presidency. He would not have done this for Foraker any more than he would have made a similar deal to use his influence to make Cox mayor of Cincinnati. The Washington *Star*, the *Evening Post*, the Boston *Herald*, and similar papers, which are usually loud in denouncing "deals," have been either openly attacking Taft or covertly sneering at him for not going into this one. *Sincerely yours*

4635 · TO VICTOR HOWARD METCALF   *Roosevelt Mss.*

Personal   Washington, March 14, 1908

My dear Mr. Secretary: I have your letter of the 14th, with enclosures, in reference to the American and Japanese building programs. I do not agree with the Chief Constructor's view of those battleships.[1] The weight of metal thrown at a discharge is an utterly misleading method of comparison. The ten-inch guns are more formidable than double their number of 8-inch guns as against battleships. Moreover, no account is taken of the all 12-inch gun battleships which are being built for the Japanese; according to Clowes' Pocketbook they were being built before ours were being built.

As regards armored cruisers, I think the *Ikoma*, on account of her 12-inch guns, should really go under the head of battleships rather than armored cruisers. Certainly this is true of the *Kurama*, which has the 8-inch guns.

To say that in battery power the American vessels of the *Vermont* type "are equal if not superior to" the *Katori* type is, to my mind, ⟨. . . misleading⟩ mistaken. The *Satsuma* and *Aki* are not "in course of construction" in

[1] While there was much to be said on both sides, Roosevelt's contentions appear more correct than those of Chief Constructor Washington L. Capps. If the greater weight of metal thrown by the *Vermont's* batteries of four twelve-inch, eight eight-inch, and twelve seven-inch guns gave her an advantage at the shorter ranges, the more numerous "great guns" in the *Katori's* batteries of four twelve-inch, four ten-inch, and twelve six-inch guns gave her the edge at the more critical longer ranges. The Japanese were, as the Clowes' pocketbook stated, building two more dreadnoughts, the *Settsu* and the *Kawachi*. The *Ikoma* and the *Kurama*, carrying twelve-inch guns, were more heavily armed than any American cruiser and several American battleships. Finally, most naval authorities agreed that construction on the *Satsuma* and the *Aki*, both of which were scheduled for completion in 1908, was well ahead of that on the four American ships. Actually the two Japanese ships and the *Michigan* and the *South Carolina* were finished within a few months of each other in late 1909 and early 1910.

These assertions on the superiority of the recently built Japanese ships and the advanced stage of Japan's building program became a major argument for the congressional defenders of Roosevelt's naval program. In committee and in the debates on the navy bill they contended that four battleships were essential if the United States were to retain her naval supremacy over Japan. Their opponents, insisting that this supremacy was not challenged, countered with Capps' statement before the Senate naval committee that American ships were as effective as any comparable ships built or being built by the Japanese.

the same sense that the *Delaware, North Dakota, South Carolina* and *Michigan* are; for the first two are practically or nearly finished. Certainly one of them is; while our four are nowhere near completion. *Sincerely yours*

4636 · TO JOHN ST. LOE STRACHEY   *Roosevelt Mss.*

Washington, March 14, 1908

My dear Mr. Strachey: Indeed, I shall be greatly pleased to have you dedicate that book to me.[1] I congratulate you on the defeat of the socialists, which I read of this morning, in the vote on the "work for the unemployed" bill. How people can support that type of legislation I am wholly unable to understand. I wish they would read just what happened when the Republic of France went into a similar experiment.

    With great regard, believe me, *Sincerely yours*

4637 · TO CLINTON HART MERRIAM   *Roosevelt Mss.*

Personal   Washington, March 15, 1908

Dear Merriam: Is there any kind of air gun which you would recommend which I could use for killing English sparrows around my Long Island place? I would like to do as little damage as possible to our other birds, and so I suppose the less noise I make the better. *Faithfully yours*

4638 · TO KERMIT ROOSEVELT   *Roosevelt Mss.*

Washington, March 15, 1908

Dearest Kermit: Alas for Pendennis Ted! Sometimes he is almost too much like Pendennis. Now he is on probation again and for conduct so utterly silly that it is very hard to keep my patience with him. Since January 1st he has cut thirty-eight lectures without sufficient excuse, and so he has been put on probation, as the Dean writes me. I am really at a loss to understand how Ted could have been so silly. He is over 20; he is a junior, and hopes to graduate this year; and I cannot treat him as if he were Quentin. Quentin, for instance, thanks I believe to his excitement over baseball, did not do his lessons well this week and Miss Dulin complained to his Mother. Of course we will discipline Quentin; but in Ted's case it is impossible for us — when he assures us that his absences from recitations are all right; that everything is smooth — to write ourselves to the Dean and inquire, as if Ted were merely

[1] Strachey dedicated his *Problems and Perils of Socialism* (London, 1908), a volume in Macmillan's sixpenny series, to "Theodore Roosevelt . . . . one of the most convinced and powerful opponents of Socialism living." The dedication, from which Roosevelt could scarcely have dissented, read in part: "You have kept that just mean which Tennyson ascribes to the spirit of English freedom . . . . While opposing Socialism . . . . , you have never failed to insist that a lawless Capitalism is as great a foe to the nation as a lawless Communism."

a schoolboy. He does not seem to have any head in such matters. Now I assume he won't be able to go on the Mississippi trip and this will be a bitter disappointment to him. Yet he has gone fatuously ahead cutting these recitations, for no earthly purpose, and has put himself in this preposterous position. I get uneasy about him, too, because he does not seem to understand the folly of getting beaten owing to neglect of what the slightest effort would enable him to accomplish. In this life, no matter how much energy and ability and foresight we show, we are often certain to be trampled upon by men and events. We are often defeated under circumstances where all our courage and ability do not enable us to cope, either with some adversary who is naturally more formidable than we are, or with a combination of events from which it is not humanly possible to wrest success. Therefore we are sure to have a sufficient number of defeats anyhow. The only way to come out ahead is not wantonly to court defeat where by the exercise of ordinary prudence and forethought and skill and resolution it is possible to be sure of victory. If Archie, thru sheer inability, failed in mathematics, I should be very sorry but I should not in the least hold it against him; but where Ted gets on probation because he has been such an utter goose as pointlessly to cut his recitations I am not only much irritated but I also become apprehensive as to how Ted will do in after life. All I can hope is that when he leaves college he will put away boyish things and turn in seriously, to work as he worked, and to show the character that he showed, during the year before he went to college.

Mother goes off to New York with Aunt Emily today, and Aunt Emily soon sails for Italy. I presume Mother will return the end of the week. *Your loving father*

4639 · TO WILLIAM BOURKE COCKRAN   *Roosevelt Mss.*

Washington, March 16, 1908

My dear Mr. Cockran: I return, with thanks for your courtesy, the letter of the Most Reverend D. Falconio, the Apostolic Delegate, together with the telegram sent by Mr. Anthony Matre to him on the 11th of March, saying that he had received and given to the Associated Press a telegram as follows:

Shanghai Catholics, through Reverend Kennelly, repudiate charge of Roosevelt and Root classifying them vicious people, as reported in American telegram, and renew petition for Wilfley's removal.

The Apostolic Delegate is of course right in the belief which he expresses that neither the President nor Mr. Root ever used such language as appears to have been reported. The Secretary of State examined and reported upon certain charges against Judge Wilfley, which has been filed with me. I made a decision dismissing the matter. Neither the charges, nor Mr. Root's opinion, nor my decision, mentioned or referred to Catholics in Shanghai, or to persons of any religious faith there or anywhere. It is evident, as the Apostolic Delegate says, that some interested person has sent a cablegram to Shanghai for the purpose of exciting the Catholic population there.[1]

It seems to me, however, that there is a serious side to this correspondence which ought not to be overlooked. Mr. Anthony Matre, who is described by the Apostolic Delegate as Secretary of the American Federation of Catholic Societies, appears to have received and without verification or inquiry to have made himself responsible for the publication of a false and defamatory telegram regarding the President of the United States and the head of the Department charged with the conduct of the relations between the United States and foreign nations. The telegram is of a character well adapted to create religious dissension in the United States, to create animosity on the part of the Roman Catholic citizens of the United States against the

[1] Lebbeus R. Wilfley, Attorney General of the Philippine Islands, 1901–1906; judge of the United States Court for China, 1906–1909; perhaps the "most hated American in China," had been charged with "mal and corrupt conduct and . . . high crimes and misdemeanors" by several members of the Shanghai bar. Articles of impeachment filed against Wilfley in the House of Representatives dwelt principally with his alleged favoritism for his friends and his discrimination against their competitors. He was accused also of participating in the management of a lottery and, in order to gain for himself a reputation as a great reformer, of falsely declaring "that the American community in Shanghai . . . . is corrupt, depraved, and . . . in the hands and control of depraved, corrupt, and criminal persons." Certain Catholics in Shanghai, particularly those who had had power within the American community and those who had been denied permission to practice before the judge, were emphatic in the last of the accusations.

As the House Committee on the Judiciary reported, there was no basis for any of the charges. Wilfley had raised the standards of the legal profession by forcing applicants for permission to appear in his court to take an examination. Those who failed sponsored the charge of discrimination. He had been associated with no lottery. Concerning the last charge against him, Root reported before the House committee. Wilfley had indeed described the American community in Shanghai as depraved, but his description, Root found, had been accurate. So bad was the reputation of that community that prostitutes in Shanghai and elsewhere in China were commonly called "American girls." Wilfley properly set about to clean up the American section of the city. For this, Root concluded, the judge was entitled to "high credit." Roosevelt endorsed Root's report. "It is clear," the President stated, "that Judge Wilfley has been attacked not because he has done evil, but because he has done good. The assault on him is simply an impeachment of decency . . . . If the attacks were to succeed, the beneficiaries would be every keeper of a house of prostitution, every swindling lawyer, every man who lives by . . . corruption in the cities of the Far East . . . . It is not too much to say that this assault on Judge Wilfley in the interest of the vicious and criminal classes is a public scandal." — *Outlook*, 88:572–573 (March 14, 1908).

Doubtless Roosevelt's statement was not too strong, but to those who, while dissatisfied with Wilfley, were not themselves corrupt, it was open to possible misconstruction. Clearly Reverend Kennelly and Mr. Matre misconstrued it. They may also have hoped to influence the decision of the Judiciary Committee. If that was their intent, they failed, for in May the committee recommended that no action be taken on the articles of impeachment. The judge was vindicated, but still unpopular, and in the end he found he had won a Pyrrhic victory. Perhaps uneasy over the unpopularity of the judge's zeal, Roosevelt in 1909 decided not to renew his appointment.

constituted authorities of the country, and to create unfriendly feeling on the part of foreign countries whose people are of the Roman Catholic faith against the United States. Such was the manifest purpose of the cable dispatch and of this purpose Mr. Matre has made himself the willing instrument, bringing to the accomplishment of the design the authority and influence which he doubtless possesses as Secretary of a Federation of American Catholic Societies. It seems to me that such action by a person having such official relations with the Roman Catholics of the United States ought not to be overlooked, but should be dealt with in such a manner as to preclude a probability of any similar conduct in the future. *Sincerely yours*

4640 · TO JAMES MONROE MILLER   *Roosevelt Mss.*

Washington, March 17, 1908

My dear Mr. Miller: In connection with my letter to you of March 11th, I have received the enclosed report from Messrs. Garfield, Newell and Walcott.[1] If action must be had at once I should suggest that a rough estimate proportioning to the United States 20 per cent of the amount expended to reimburse the Southern Pacific Railroad for the actual repairing of the break in Mexico would probably represent as near justice as we can come with our present knowledge. But evidently, from this letter, it would be well to have a thoroly trained man investigate the entire subject matter. Cannot an appropriation be made which will enable the Department of the Interior to procure such an expert for this purpose? *Sincerely yours*

4641 · TO WILLIAM HUTCHINSON COWLES   *Roosevelt Mss.*

Private   Washington, March 18, 1908

My dear Mr. Cowles:[1] I have received your recent letter. As for the Spokane case, I do not know just what to say to you about it, except that I believe that there is in the Interstate Commerce Commission a strong feeling — and I think, fundamentally a sound feeling — of caution about taking action just at this moment that will serve as an excuse for a reduction of wages.[2] I do not know whether this applies to their feeling in your case. I know it applies to their feeling in the Southeastern cases.

[1] Roosevelt had written Miller that the United States should pay "as a matter of moral and equitable obligation" a share of the cost of repairing the Colorado River break of December 1906 (see Numbers 4169, 4177). He further informed the chairman of the House Committee on Claims that he had asked Garfield, Walcott and Newell to recommend what the government should pay. The committee took no action. A bill to reimburse the railroad did not come to a vote until 1911 when it was defeated.

[1] William Hutchinson Cowles, owner and publisher of the Spokane *Spokesman Review*.
[2] No wage reduction disputes on roads passing through Spokane reached the stage where mediation was requested under the Erdman Act or where strikes were called.

As for Senator Bourne, I think him a sincere fanatic. I have every reason to believe in the sincerity of his friendship for me, but he is the only one of my friends who adopts the third term attitude. All the others are strong for Taft, save in two or three States where they have to give perfunctory support to local candidates. *Sincerely yours*

4642 · TO WILLIAM PIERCE FRYE   *Roosevelt Mss.*

Washington, March 18, 1908

Sir: Numerous bills granting water rights in conformity with the General Act of June 21, 1906, have been introduced during the present session of Congress, and some of these have already past. While the General Act authorizes the limitation and retention of water rights in the public interest, and would seem to warrant making a reasonable charge for the benefits conferred, those bills which have come to my attention do not seem to guard the public interests adequately in these respects. The effect of granting privileges such as are conferred by these bills, as I said in a recent message, "taken together with rights already acquired under State laws, would be to give away properties of enormous value. Through lack of foresight we have formed the habit of granting without compensation extremely valuable rights amounting to monopolies on navigable streams and on the public domain. The repurchase at great expense of water rights thus carelessly given away without return has already begun in the East, and before long will be necessary in the West also. No rights involving water power should be granted to any corporation in perpetuity, but only for a length of time sufficient to allow them to conduct their business profitably. A reasonable charge should of course be made for valuable rights and privileges which they obtain from the National Government. The values for which this charge is made will ultimately, thru the natural growth and orderly development of our population and industries, reach enormous amounts. A fair share of the increase should be safeguarded for the benefit of the people, from whose labor it springs. The proceeds thus secured, after the cost of administration and improvement has been met, should naturally be devoted to the development of our inland waterways." Accordingly I have decided to sign no bills hereafter which do not provide specifically for the right to fix and make a charge and for a definite limitation in time of the rights conferred.[1] *Sincerely yours*

[1] This statement of policy on water power sites, sent also to Congressman Burton and Secretary of War Taft, supported the work already begun by Gifford Pinchot. Disturbed by the reckless alienation of sites by the Eastern states, determined to protect the great proportion of national sites which lay in the still unalienated areas of the West, Pinchot had resisted impatient Western demands for commercial water power developments. In 1905, by an agreement between the Interior and Agricultural departments, the authority to issue permits for water power development within the forest preserves was given to the Chief Forester. The next year he withdrew 2,565 sites on the pretext that they were to be used as ranger stations. Then and later he urged the President to restrain Congress from granting special

Washington, March 18, 1908

My dear Mr. Philbin: I have your letter of the 17th instant. Of course I value your speaking frankly. All I can say is that I do not believe, and have found not the slightest justification for the belief, that there is any policy pursued by those in authority in the Philippines which excludes that recognition which every citizen is entitled to in the preservation of his rights. After the last careful inquiry I have become more and more convinced that from the beginning every effort has been made in the Philippines to secure just this recognition and preservation of rights of the individual citizen. Every time I have laboriously hunted down a complaint I have found that there was no justification, or else the justification was so small that it could be classed under the head of those incidental troubles that are bound to occur under any and every administration of any governmental entity. My belief is, my dear Mr. Philbin, that this Government has been peculiarly careful, has been most scrupulous, to preserve the rights of the people of your faith. General Weston, a Catholic, will soon be at the head of the military forces of the Island; Governor Smith, a Catholic, is at the head of the civil forces; Judge Tracey, a Catholic, is on the bench, and of all those on the bench is the man with whom I have been in the closest touch and in constant correspondence. Captain McIntyre, one of the best men in the army, a Catholic, reports to me that there is not a thing in Bishop Hendrick's complaints which would warrant an investigation. As for Father Rawlinson, I shall ask you to consider as confidential what I told you about him, unless Secretary Taft gives permission to the contrary.[1]

What I am about to say now is for your personal information and naturally not for repetition, because I do not wish to hurt the memory of a good man, and still less to hurt the feelings of a good man that is living. I think that Bishop Rooker did real damage to the Catholic cause in the Islands. I went very carefully into his case and came to the conclusion that he was entirely wrong and that there was no justification for his attitude. Bishop Hendrick has been one of the dearest and best-intentioned and kindly men I have ever known. He was a most admirable parish priest. Out in the

---

hydroelectric privileges. Following his advice in deed as well as word, Roosevelt vetoed two measures, one in 1908 and one in 1909, which contravened the principles defined in the above letter. His veto messages insisted that Congress grant water power privileges only in accordance with a carefully constructed, long-range policy which would ensure maximum public benefits and prevent monopolistic hydroelectric combinations. For a full account of the more important of these vetoes, that of 1909, see No. 5156, note 2. For discussions of the water power policy of the Roosevelt Administration, see Robbins, *Our Landed Heritage*, pp. 333–335, 345–346, 366; Pinchot, *Breaking New Ground*, pp. 333–339.

---

[1] Father Rawlinson, Bishop Hendrick's private secretary, had told Taft that the bishop, pitifully senile, was making charges against the Philippine government that were without foundation. — Roosevelt to Philbin, March 13, 1908, Roosevelt Mss.

Philippines I fear that he has not been able to do good service because his powers have failed. I am very fond of Father Tom, and I would not say anything that would hurt his feelings; but I think that fact is patent. Let me repeat that from the beginning of our administration in the Philippines thruout the term of my Presidency I believe that the attitude of the Government toward the Catholic Church in the Philippines has been admirable; that every investigation of every complaint made to me during these six and a half years has tended to show more strongly than before how admirable the general action of the governmental authorities in the Philippines was; and that while occasional acts of unwisdom or wrongdoing had been shown, they had been instantly corrected and were merely such as were inevitable under the circumstances and in no way reflected upon the general attitude of the administration. Just at present not any of these minor acts of wrongdoing or of folly have been shown so far as I am aware.

With regard, believe me, *Sincerely yours*

4644 · TO THE DEPARTMENT OF JUSTICE   *Roosevelt Mss.*

Washington, March 20, 1908

To the Department of Justice: By my direction the Postmaster General is to exclude *La Questione Sociale,* of Paterson, New Jersey, from the mails, and it will not be admitted to the mails unless by order of the court, or unless you advise me that it must be admitted. Please see if it is not possible to prosecute criminally under any section of the law that is available the men that are interested in sending out this anarchistic and murderous publication. They are of course the enemies of mankind and every effort should be strained to hold them accountable for an offense far more infamous than that of any ordinary murderer.

This matter has been brought to my attention by the Mayor of the city of Paterson. I wish every effort made to get at the criminals under the Federal law. It may be found impossible to do this. I shall also, thru the Secretary of State, call the attention of the Governor of New Jersey to the circumstances, so that he may proceed under the State law, his attention being further drawn to the fact that the newspaper is circulated in other States. After you have concluded your investigation I wish a report from you to serve as a basis for a recommendation by me for action by Congress. Under section 3893 of the Revised Statutes lewd, obscene, and lascivious books and letters, publications for indecent and immoral uses or of an indecent and immoral nature, and postal cards upon which indecent and scurrilous epithets are written or printed, are all excluded from the mail, and provision is made for the fine and imprisonment of those guilty. The newspaper article in question advocates murder by dynamite. It specifically advocates the murder of enlisted men of the United States army and the officers of the police force, and the burning of houses of private citizens. The preaching of mur-

der and arson is certainly as immoral as the circulation of obscene and lascivious literature, and if the practice is not already forbidden by the law it
should be forbidden. The immigration law now prohibits the entry into the
United States of any person who entertains or advocates the views exprest
in this newspaper article. It is of course inexcusable to permit those already
here to promulgate such views. Those who write, publish and circulate those
articles stand on a level with those who use the mails for distributing poisons
for the purpose of murder; and convictions have been obtained when the
mails have thus been used for the distribution of poisons. No law should
require the Postmaster General to become an accessory to murder by circulating literature of this kind.[1]

4645 · TO JOHN HENRY PATTERSON   *Roosevelt Mss.*

Private   Washington, March 20, 1908

My dear Colonel Patterson: [1] A year hence I shall leave the Presidency, and,
while I cannot now decide what I shall do, it is possible that I might be able
to make a trip to Africa. Would you be willing to give me some advice about
it? I shall be fifty years old, and for ten years I have led a busy, sedentary
life, and so it is unnecessary to say that I shall be in no trim for the hardest
kind of explorers' work. But I am fairly healthy, and willing to work in order
to get into a game country where I could do some shooting. I should suppose
I could be absent a year on the trip. Now, is it imposing too much on your

---

[1] Replying to this letter on March 31, Bonaparte examined in detail the legal status
of the Italian-language newspaper, *La Questione Sociale*. Without doubt the paper
had preached revolution, urging in one issue that "we must get into the armory;
and in case we can not, then we will blow it down with dynamite. Then . . . . we
must set fire to three or four houses . . . . Then we will start a fire in the center of
the city." The Postmaster General, Bonaparte concluded, would be justified in excluding from the mails any issue of this or any other periodical, otherwise entitled
to the privilege of second-class mail matter, which contained any article constituting
a seditious libel and counseling such crimes as murder, arson, riot, and treason.
Bonaparte observed, however, that while the printing and circulation of such a
paper was clearly an offense at common law, it was not an offense against the United
States in the absence of a federal statute making it one. There was no such statute;
but Congress, Bonaparte declared, had full power to pass a law excluding publications like *La Questione Sociale* from the mail and making the use of the mails for
the transmission of such a publication a crime against the United States. Acting
on this opinion, the Postmaster General denied to *La Questione Sociale* the
privilege of second-class mail matter. Roosevelt on April 9 sent a message to Congress submitting Bonaparte's opinion and requesting legislation for the suppression of
anarchy. Congress, however, did not act. For the complete texts of the President's
message and Bonaparte's opinion see *Senate Document*, 60 Cong., 1 sess., no. 426.

---

[1] John Henry Patterson, British lieutenant colonel, veteran of Boer and Indian campaigns, explorer, hunter, railroad engineer, and biographer of the man-eating lions of
Tsavo. Along with Selous, Leigh S. J. Hunt, and others, Patterson honored Roosevelt's continual requests, of which this letter is an early and typical example, for
advice on planning the African trip. Only a small selection of Roosevelt's volumi-
nous correspondence on this subject is printed in the remainder of this volume.

good nature to tell me when and where I ought to go to get some really good shooting, such as you and your friends had last Christmas day, for instance. Would it be possible for me to go in from Mozambique or some such place and come out down the Nile? How much time should I allow in order to give ample opportunity for hunting? Would it be possible for you to give me any idea of the expense, and to tell me how I should make my preparations; whom to write to in advance, etc.? Is there anyone who outfits for a trip like that to whom I could turn to know what I was to take?

I trust you will excuse me if I am trespassing too much on your good nature. It may be that I shall not be able to go at all; but I should like mightily to see the great African fauna, and to kill one or two rhino or buffalo and some of the big antelopes, with the chance of a shot at a lion. *Sincerely yours*

[*Handwritten*] I suppose that in a year's trip I could get into a really good game country; I am no butcher, but I would like to *see* plenty of game, and kill a few head.

4646 · TO CHARLES STILLMAN SPERRY   *Roosevelt Mss.*

Washington, March 21, 1908

My dear Admiral Sperry:[1] You are to take the fleet back, and it will be an even more responsible voyage than the outward one, for you are to visit Australia and Japan, as well as coming home thru Suez. I need not tell you that you should exercise the most careful watch thruout the time that you are in Oriental waters — for you will naturally exercise the most careful watch at all times both before and after you leave the Orient. I wish to impress upon you, what I do not suppose is necessary, to see to it that none of our men does anything out of the way while in Japan. If you give the enlisted men leave while at Tokyo or anywhere else in Japan be careful to choose only those upon whom you can absolutely depend. There must be no suspicion of insolence or rudeness on our part. Of course the most important thing is to guard our ships against possible attack by fanatics; but next to this in importance is to prevent there being any kind of action by any one of our men which would give an excuse for the feeling that we had been in any way guilty of misconduct. Aside from the loss of a ship I had far rather that we were insulted than that we insult anybody under these peculiar conditions. I firmly believe that the Japanese Government will use every effort to see that the highest consideration and courtesy are accorded to our people, and you of course will do everything in your power to show the utmost consideration and courtesy to the Japanese with whom you are brought in contact, not only in Japan but elsewhere. We want to take peculiar care in this matter.

I am delighted with your letter to Secretary Metcalf; so much so that I

[1] Charles Stillman Sperry had been promoted to rear admiral in 1906.

want parts of it published. I have just seen your letter to Pillsbury. We will try to get you a proper ship.

With regard, believe me, *Sincerely yours*

4647 · TO VICTOR HOWARD METCALF   *Roosevelt Mss.*

Washington, March 23, 1908

My dear Mr. Secretary: It seems to me that the armor belt ought to be higher. Will you let me know just where it is planned to be on the new ships? We now have, as I understand it, the two-hoist turrets. Are the old turrets to be changed?

Don't you think it would be well to have a line officer as Second Assistant Secretary of the Navy? [1] *Sincerely yours*

4648 · TO JOSEPH GURNEY CANNON   *Roosevelt Mss.*

Washington, March 23, 1908

Dear Mr. Speaker: Will it be possible to get a rule that will allow the Pearl Harbor matter to come up in connection with the naval bill? I earnestly hope

[1] Roosevelt had been impressed by the arguments of the naval reformers. Sims, Key, Cameron Winslow, and the other insurgents had effectively supported, before the Senate Naval Committee, the criticisms presented in the Reuterdahl article, "The Needs of Our Navy" (see No. 4549). They had shown that the armor plate was placed too low to afford proper protection and that the unbroken ammunition hoist, from handling room to turret, had been the source of several serious accidents. Though prevented by Senator Hale, chairman of the committee, from saying very much about naval administrative organization, the insurgent witnesses succeeded in making their point that the errors in ship construction were produced by the statutory independence of bureau chiefs from each other and from the seagoing officers. Their remedy, as defined by Key, was the appointment of a line officer as a chief of staff, accountable to the Secretary of the Navy, to co-ordinate and direct the activities of the several bureaus.

While basically agreeing with the insurgents on the need for reform, Roosevelt was reluctant to accept their remedy. There were, apparently, several considerations that prevented him from introducing into the Navy the general staff principle of control which he and Root had successfully imposed upon the Army. To begin with, Evans, Cowles, and other senior officers whose opinions he respected argued that no drastic change in the Navy Department was necessary. Far more important, congressmen were sure to protest against the loss of control over the Navy which they believed was entailed in dealing with one officer rather than directly with the several bureaus. Moreover, many congressmen, like many of their constituents, distrusted centralized military authority within the naval establishment. There was in 1908, as there always has been up to recent times, for reasons that are interesting to speculate upon, a feeling in this country that the dangers of irresponsible militarism were more likely to be generated in the Navy than in the Army.

Roosevelt was anxious not to arouse this sensitive public opinion. He believed the first need of the Navy was more battleships. He did not wish to place this primary objective — his building program — in jeopardy by disturbing the Congress unduly on what he took to be a secondary issue — the creation of a chief of staff. Therefore he did little to support the recommendation of Key and his insurgents, though he did enough to hold the threat of naval administrative reform over the heads of congressmen who were uncertain about supporting the construction program.

this can be done. We ought to have four battleships. If not, we ought to have three; and beyond all question we ought at this session to provide for the proper fortification of Hawaii, the building of a dock, and so forth.[1]

If you knew the stormy time I have been having on your behalf with all kinds of people in connection with the tariff commission,[2] I think you would look favorably on this Pearl Harbor request! *Sincerely yours*

4649 · TO ROBLEY DUNGLISON EVANS   *Roosevelt Mss.*

Washington, March 23, 1908

My dear Admiral: It is with very great regret that at your own request I relieve you from command.[1] You have now practically finished your active service in the United States navy; and you have brought your long and honorable career, identified to a peculiar degree with the whole history of the navy, to a close by an achievement which marks the entrance of the United States into the rank of naval powers of the first class. In your early youth, as a young officer, you won a reputation for signal gallantry in the Civil War. You have closed your career by conducting a great battle fleet from the North Atlantic to the North Pacific in a manner which has shown you to be a master of your profession. The fleet comes to San Francisco in better shape than when it left Hampton Roads; better fit for service in every way; and the officers and men owe no small part of their improvement in their profession to the mastery of your profession which your handling of the fleet has shown.

With thanks, congratulations and good wishes, believe me, *Sincerely yours*

4650 · TO CHARLES JOSEPH BONAPARTE   *Roosevelt Mss.*

Washington, March 25, 1908

My dear Mr. Attorney General: I enclose copy of a letter from Rev. Dr. Wallace Radcliffe in reference to Sunday work in the different Departments. At the Cabinet meeting yesterday it was unanimously agreed that there should be no Sunday work done unless it was imperatively necessary. I know that this is your feeling and that of your colleagues. I ask that you make an investigation in your Department and see that no work is done on Sunday

---

[1] Cannon did not comply. The Pearl Harbor bill was passed almost unanimously before the naval appropriations bill was reported out of committee.
[2] Beveridge and H. E. Miles were then imploring the President to support a bill to create a tariff commission. Roosevelt heard but resisted their demands; see Bowers, *Beveridge*, pp. 275–277.

---

[1] Evans had requested his retirement because of failing health. Throughout his long career he had been troubled by a leg wound suffered during the Civil War. He had been a useful if overpublicized officer.

that can, with due regard to the interests of the public, be avoided.[1] *Sincerely yours*

4651 · TO ALBERT LENOIR KEY   *Roosevelt Mss.*

Personal   Washington, March 26, 1908

My dear Key: I have read your reports with interest. I think that you and Sims and Winslow[1] have rendered real service by fearlessly calling attention to defects in our naval administration. But I think you sometimes exaggerate the defects, and I do not think the remedies you propose would work as well as you think. For instance, I have just seen Admiral Evans' letter on the armor belts. His actual experience on this trip has made him very doubtful whether in any seaway our armor belt is not too high instead of too low; that is, whether, where there is enough rolling, it is not possible for shots to strike under the armor belt, which would of course be infinitely more disastrous than above it; and tho he is inclined to think that the armor belt is a little too low, he regards it as but a matter of a few inches. In other words, if there is enough sea to make the low afterturrets on some of the ships of any consequence, there will be enough sea to expose the ship below the armor belt at certain times; and under such circumstances, with the present width of armor belt, it would be far more dangerous to have it higher than at present than to have it lower.[2] I think the discussion is more or less academic as regards our new vessels, which are well protected in either event.

Next, as to the proposed general scheme. In a nutshell, this is that the line shall have more complete responsibility and greater power than at present, so that the admiral in charge of the fleet and the line officer who should be the responsible military head ashore, ⟨should⟩ could be the two men chiefly consulted. This is precisely the case now. Converse, a line officer of much experience and very highly thought of thruout the service, has been filling practically the precise position which Fox filled in the Civil War, or which he (Converse or Pillsbury) would fill if we had a line officer as second assistant secretary. Moreover, the charge about the lack of battle maneuvers is simply a charge against Evans, the most distinguished line officer on our list at present. If this charge is well founded, then Evans has been derelict in his duty, and there is no change in system needed, merely a change in the line officer who serves as admiral of the fleet. So with the Naval Board. This

---

[1] Roosevelt sent an identical letter to each of the Cabinet officers.

[1] Cameron McRea Winslow, who like his fellow insurgents, Sims and Key, had served as Roosevelt's naval aide.

[2] Roosevelt, however, did not present Evans' major assertion that the standard width of eight feet for the armor plate on American battleships was too narrow to afford adequate protection and that the question of its location, therefore, "becomes an academic discussion; with certain arguments on each side."

comes near being a general staff.[3] It has done great good; but it committed a capital mistake on the Subig Bay proposition.

In short, while I think there can be some improvement in the system, and tho I think the criticisms have done good, I also think that the changes suggested would make no radical revolution; and that if adopted during the last year and a half, they would have accomplished very little indeed; they would have resulted in but a small improvement. Mind you, I approve of them as a whole; but I don't expect too much of them.

With great regard, believe me, *Sincerely yours*

4652 · TO CHARLES JOSEPH BONAPARTE   *Roosevelt Mss.*

Personal   Washington, March 26, 1908

To the Attorney General: Is it clearly understood that in the new indictment in Idaho, the indictment shall not repeat the charge of conspiracy of these men *together with Borah?* That is, is it clearly understood that under no circumstances is Borah's name to be mentioned in the indictment? Of course Borah's acquittal would prevent his reindictment, but we want to avoid any chance of a smirching of his name.[1]

4653 · TO SETH LOW   *Roosevelt Mss.*

Washington, March 28, 1908

Dear Seth: I have your letter of the 27th. I myself wish that the labor clause could have been more in line with the recommendation in my message.[1]

As for the businessmen's proposal which you recite, as you know, my desire is to strengthen the hand of the executive in dealing with these matters,

---

[3] Roosevelt was, perhaps, expediently disingenuous in this whole paragraph for reasons cited in No. 5106, note 1. Admiral Converse, in 1908 already past the retirement age, had been retained as Chief of the Board on Construction while Pillsbury, as Chief of the Bureau of Navigation, had no legal control of any kind over any other bureau chief. Nor was the General Board in any sense a general staff. It existed at the will of the Secretary of the Navy, serving, in theory, as a sort of reservoir of naval wisdom on which the Secretary could draw if the thought occurred to him. Thus in its early years the board's influence on the Navy was negligible. As time passed and the board entered an institutional phase, it became a preserve for two kinds of officers — those who were relieved of active duty before retirement because their energy and imagination threatened to disrupt the even tenor of the service and those who had been relieved of active duty before retirement for other reasons. In old age the board won, what general staffs can rarely obtain, the affection of the service. The feelings of purely sentimental regret at its passing, set forth with understanding by Hanson Baldwin in the New York *Times,* were shared by many.

---

[1] Borah was not reindicted.

---

[1] Roosevelt's reference was to the absence of any provision regulating the use of injunctions in the National Civic Federation's proposed amendment to the Sherman Act.

and not to turn them over to what I regard as the chaos and inefficiency necessarily produced by an effort to use the courts as the prime instrument for administering such a law. Whatever they may say, I think we have what is in substance a very good bill. You have done admirable work for the public, my dear fellow — as usual. *Faithfully yours*

4654 · TO ELIHU ROOT   *Roosevelt Mss.*

Washington, March 28, 1908

To the Secretary of State: The enclosed figures are interesting. Again it appears that over 150 Japanese laborers came here during February. It is certainly to be regretted that as large a number come in. Even without them, there are more Japanese coming to America than I like to see, having in view the future good relations between Japan and the United States.

4655 · TO ELIHU ROOT   *Roosevelt Mss.*

Washington, March 29, 1908

To the Secretary of State: This cable of Russell to my mind makes it evident that we have got to act about Venezuela. I think it would be well to have several ships at once sent there and arrangements made to send a transport with Marines to land. Also I think the Joint Board should be at once requested to have plans formulated for action in case we have to take it. We can at least seize the customs houses.[1]

4656 · TO JOHN CARTER ROSE   *Roosevelt Mss.*

Washington, March 30, 1908

My dear Rose: Many thanks for your letter of the 28th. I do not think I am for that compromise. I want full power given to the *Executive* officers in the matter of the Sherman Antitrust Law. I do not think the present law is wise, but I think it would be much more unwise to amend it by leaving the matter to be fought out after the event before the courts, or by giving the courts any original power in the matter. My notion is to keep the bill [1] in that respect just as it is. *Sincerely yours*

[1] Russell had reported that Venezuela was unwilling to consider arbitration. Again Root restrained Roosevelt, but on March 31 the President instructed the nation in the details of American-Venezuelan negotiations by submitting the relevant diplomatic correspondence to the Senate. While that body contemplated placing a prohibitive tariff on Venezuelan products, the American reaction to Castro's position prepared the way for the rupture of diplomatic relations.

[1] The amendment to the Sherman Act proposed by the National Civic Federation; see No. 4585, note 2.

Personal   Washington, March 30, 1908

My dear Mr. Ambassador: Again I thank you for your interesting note. I am glad you set the English people clear on the point that Mackenzie King came from the Canadian authorities on their own initiative. You have a copy of my letter to Sir Wilfrid. I wrote it especially because I wanted a written record of the fact that Mackenzie King had come down here from Laurier without my knowing anything whatever about the circumstances; that he saw me without any suggestion on my part, and that I was informed he was to go to London before I entered into any correspondence with Laurier in the matter. Personally I do not care a rap about their saying I took the initiative in the matter for I think it the sign of a small mind to be meticulous on such points. But it is just as well that the facts should be on record. My object simply is, as you know, to see whether, in the interest of permanent peace and of a permanent good understanding between the English-speaking peoples and Japan, we cannot quietly insure unity of action between the Republic and the Empire with a view to securing the exclusion of all Japanese laborers; that is, of all Japanese who work with their hands, of retail traders or of agriculturists, from North America and Australia, and yet to secure such exclusion in a manner that will avoid causing any soreness of feeling in Japan. *Sincerely yours*

[*Handwritten*] The fleet wo'n't be able to stop anywhere after leaving the orient, not in England or anywhere.

Washington, March 30, 1908

My dear Senator Beveridge: I very earnestly hope that you will not offer your general child labor bill as an amendment to any measure that may come up affecting child labor in the District of Columbia. I find that some people feel that the failure to have a good child labor law for the District of Columbia is due, as they claim, to your announced intention last year and this year of insisting on offering your measure as an amendment to the District child labor bill. I have told my informants that I was sure this was a mistake, but that in any event I would write you and say that I very earnestly hoped you would not do anything that would mix up the two measures. There is no question whatever that we should have a model child labor law for the District, whereas many excellent people, whether misguided or not, did not favor as yet the proposed Federal law — I mean the one to get at the products of child labor everywhere thruout the Union. Under such circumstances the wise thing is to get what is imperatively needed and can be had, and not to throw it away in making what is certain to be an unsuccessful effort to get something else in addition.

I am confident that this is your own view, but my informants were so positive that I write you anyhow.[1] *Sincerely yours*

4659 · TO TRUMAN HANDY NEWBERRY   *Roosevelt Mss.*

Washington, April 1, 1908

Dear Newberry: I do not at all like the way the men are being discharged at the navy yard while at the same time at the Firth-Sterling plant[1] it is reported that they are working two shifts a day entirely on Government work. It has a very bad look to see the Government employees turned adrift at the same time complaint is made to me that the employees of the contractor who is doing Government work are kept busy night and day and on Sundays. We cannot afford to be put in the position of seeming to try to break down our own Government plants. This is bad from the standpoint of public policy, and of course it is peculiarly damaging at the present moment, when there is industrial depression, and when at the outset of the Presidential campaign our opponents are on the watch to misconstrue everything that is done. Please see Commissioner Neill this afternoon or tomorrow and report to me Saturday morning what has been done. *Sincerely yours*

4660 · TO SETH LOW   *Roosevelt Mss.*

Washington, April 1, 1908

Dear Seth: I am in receipt of your letter of the 30th ultimo with accompanying letter from Mr. Morawetz. I am sorry to say that I regard that provision as vital. I will not ⟨at present⟩ say that I would veto a measure inserting the word "reasonable," [1] but my present impression is that I should do so; and certainly before any such measure passed I should be obliged to send a message to Congress pointing out its utter ⟨inaccuracy⟩ inadequacy and emphasizing the fact that while it would accomplish certain good results, it would

[1] Honoring the President's repeated requests, Beveridge joined Lodge and Dolliver as a floor leader for the Administration's successful bill prohibiting child labor in the District of Columbia. Beveridge saw fit, however, to clarify his own opinion for the Senate. "My very earnest gratification at the passage of this bill," he observed, "is not because I think it will greatly remedy anything. As has been pointed out by several Senators, this is not a great industrial center . . . . There are no factories here; there are no mines here; there are no sweat shops here . . . . Neither do I think it will be particularly effective as an example, because . . . . examples already exist . . . . in as many as seven States . . . . Nevertheless this bill is a step, a brief one, a short one, in the right direction. It is at least an affirmative moral action upon the part of the National Legislature . . . ." — *Congressional Record*, XLII, 5801.

[1] The Firth-Sterling Company plant at Washington, D. C., manufacturing armor-piercing shells for the Navy, was operating at full capacity in order to complete on schedule its government contract. The Navy Yard, on the other hand, trying to stretch its meager appropriation from Congress, as was customary at the beginning of the last quarter of the fiscal year, was reducing its costs to a minimum.

[1] See No. 4585, note 2.

undoubtedly do a great deal of mischief. I am afraid that the Congressmen with whom Mr. Morawetz talked are more or less covertly against every form of proper control of the great corporations and simply represent the reactionary feeling. My own position, as you know, has never varied. I believe that we should not forbid all combinations, good or bad; but I emphatically believe that the power should be put in the hands of some branch of the Executive to take the initial action in deciding whether the great combinations are or are not contrary to the interests of the country, and that this power should be greater than merely to obtain publicity. Let the Congressmen whom Mr. Morawetz has met come out openly and give their names and make their arguments, and meet openly what I shall say in my message as to their proposals.

The legislation which these Congressmen apparently seek might represent a benefit in some ways, but I think would represent an evil in other ways. At the best, I should think the benefit hardly worth while achieving. At the worst, I might be forced to veto the bill on the ground that it did more harm than good. I am unalterably opposed to the folly of trying to leave a measure like this to be determined in the first instance by the courts. It is possible that some such scheme of mere control by the courts could be devised which, tho clumsy and foolish, would yet be a small improvement on the present system, ⟨this scheme providing for original action by the courts;⟩ but the proper way, and the only proper way, to meet the matter is by lodging supervisory power in some branch of the Executive. There isn't the slightest warrant for the objections raised against this course. The Interstate Commerce Commission has done excellent work, and it would have been fatal to have adopted the plan of putting their work on the courts instead of on an administrative body. *Sincerely yours*

[*Handwritten*] Your second letter has just come. Come in to breakfast at 8.30 Friday morning. My views agree with Lawrence Abbott's. I could not advise about Stetson or Morawetz.

4661 · TO THE DEPARTMENT OF JUSTICE   *Roosevelt Mss.*

Washington, April 2, 1908

To the Department of Justice: I forward herewith the report of the Interstate Commerce Commission containing its order of June 27, 1907, and the report of the failure of the railroad company to obey this order, under date of March 26, 1908, together with a letter of the Commission of April 1, 1908. It appears that the Nashville, Chattanooga & St. Louis Railway Company has not complied with the order of the Commission to furnish the same facilities to colored passengers paying first-class fare that are furnished to white passengers paying first-class fare.[1] From time to time various complaints have

[1] The railroad complied with the commission's order on April 10, two days after this letter was printed in the newspapers.

been made to me by reputable colored people to the effect that the accommodations furnished to colored persons on certain railways are filthy and inadequate compared to the same accommodations furnished to white passengers paying the same fare. The Commission has taken what is unquestionably the right ground: that where separate accommodations are provided for white and colored passengers the accommodations for colored passengers shall be as good as those furnished to white passengers for the same money. In other words, while there is nothing in the law which forbids separate accommodations, these accommodations must be equal. This principle of equality of accommodation is set out explicitly in various State laws. For instance, the code of the State of Alabama provides that there shall be "equal, but separate accommodations for the white and colored races, by providing two or more passenger cars for each passenger train, or by dividing the passenger cars by partitions." The action of the Commission has simply been to insist that the accommodations be equal in convenience and comfort, for the same money, wherever the separation is made. In this particular case where the railway has neglected to comply with the order of the Commission it is important that compliance with this order be immediately obtained. I suggest that you proceed to enforce the order by injunction proceedings, unless in your judgment some other course is preferable.

4662 · TO BOOKER TALIAFERRO WASHINGTON   *Roosevelt Mss.*

Washington, April 2, 1908

My dear Mr. Washington: Pending our correspondence the Commission forwarded to me a statement that the Nashville and Chattanooga Railway had declined to comply with its order of June 27th last. Accordingly it seemed best not to write to the Commission, but to write to the Attorney General requesting that immediate steps be taken by the Department of Justice for the purpose of enforcing the order. I enclose a copy of my communication to the Attorney General.[1] I have adopted substantially the changes you suggested, except that I did not add the paragraph about freight and human beings, because I thought it would look a little bit *ad captandum;* and there was also one sentence where I think you confused my allusion to the Federal law with your allusion to the State law.

I was delighted that we were able to appoint Williams. Yes, I recall that we now have got in office all the men whom you and I discust when I first came into the Presidency; and I wish to thank you now, not so much on my own account as on behalf of the people of this country, and especially the colored people, for the high character of the men whom you have suggested.

I look forward to seeing you on April 7th or 8th, as you indicate in your letter to Mr. Loeb. *Sincerely yours*

[1] See No. 4661.

4663 · TO TRUMAN HANDY NEWBERRY *Roosevelt Mss.*

Washington, April 2, 1908

My dear Mr. Newberry: That is first-rate about the work in the navy yards.

Now in reference to your letter of March 30th, I do not think it is advantageous that any government such as is suggested in the report of the Secretary of the Navy under the caption of "Tutuila and Guam" should be given ⟨them⟩ the former, at least. Do not urge any action on Congress. Things are going on well there at present.[1] *Sincerely yours*

4664 · TO CECIL ANDREW LYON *Roosevelt Mss.*

Washington, April 2, 1908

My dear Colonel: I am in receipt of your letter, enclosing your draft of proposed plan for the Texas State Convention. When friends in other States have asked my opinion as to similar forms of resolutions I have urged them as strongly as I now urge you not to favor my renomination. I have advised them and I now advise you, inasmuch as you ask my advice, to have your delegates instructed for Taft. In view of your close relations with me, as well as with Hitchcock, I fear any other course would be misunderstood.[1]

With all good wishes, believe me, *Faithfully yours*

4665 · TO CHARLEMAGNE TOWER *Roosevelt Mss.*

Confidential Washington, April 3, 1908

My dear Mr. Tower: Your letter of March 16th has just come. Between the date when you posted it and the date of its reception the widest publicity had been given to the information it contained, and official and definite action has been had by cable in reference to the subject.[1]

As to the publicity, this is due in some form or manner to information given out from your embassy in Berlin. The fact that you had cabled the

---

[1] The Navy Department had repeatedly asked Congress to provide a permanent form of government for these dependencies. After receiving the President's letter it stopped pressing for such legislation and continued to govern, as it had done in Guam since 1898 and Tutuila in the Samoan Islands since 1900, under the authority of an executive order; see Julius W. Pratt, *America's Colonial Experiment* (New York, 1950), pp. 221–233.

---

[1] Lyon had persisted in advocating Roosevelt's nomination. This letter finally persuaded him to swing Texas for Taft, which he accomplished in spite of the strong Fairbanks organization there.

---

[1] Tower's office had divulged the story, widely published in the United States, that the Kaiser opposed the appointment of David J. Hill as ambassador to Germany. Officially this was not the case (see Numbers 4667, 4678). Privately, however, William II, like Tower himself, considered Hill an unhappy choice, because this capable man lacked the financial means to entertain the court and the diplomatic corps in Berlin in the baroque style to which they had long been comfortably accustomed. Nevertheless, Hill received the appointment.

State Department and sent me a letter was known here by cable from Berlin before I received my cable from you. The details of your conversation were in substantially, altho not wholly, accurate form, sent here by cable from Berlin before I received them myself. For instance, the fact of Griscom's connection with the unfortunate affair was stated in the cable from Berlin before I received your cable giving me the information. It is therefore evident that there was some leak in your office at Berlin.

In a personal message to me the Emperor flatly contradicts your account of the conversation. Your account is as follows:

During the course of this conversation the Emperor touched also upon the subject of an American Ambassador in Berlin, and expressed with much earnestness the hope that you will not appoint Mr. David J. Hill to this post when it becomes vacant; to which I replied that I know nothing officially of your intention, nor have I been otherwise informed in the least as to that, beyond the fact that I have seen Mr. Hill's name published in the newspapers as that of the future Ambassador. The Emperor declared then: "But he is not the kind of man we ought to have here, and I do not want him! I think something ought to be done, and that the President ought to know this!"

I inquired whether the Emperor wished me to make this an official communication to you as coming from him, in which case I should, of course, not fail to do so immediately. Whereupon he answered that whilst he did not wish to proceed to a formal official declaration, he felt sure that you would meet his wishes if they were presented to you personally, which is what he would prefer to have done. He said: "My brother, Prince Henry, knew this Mr. Hill in America, and he tells me that he will not do at all for Germany. Admiral von Tirpitz and Admiral von Müller, who know him, have said the same thing; — and all my reports from The Hague are unfavorable."

I did not conceal from the Emperor the embarrassment that I found myself in or the extreme delicacy that I felt in treating personally a question of this nature, which relates to my own post and to my own immediate successor; which, indeed, he admitted at once that he understood fully.

It happened, however, that just at this time, Lloyd Griscom had come up from Rome for a few days to make me a visit and it occurred to the Emperor that he might make this personal communication to you through him. He asked me what Mr. Griscom's relations are with you, to which I replied that you are a personal friend of his; whereupon the Emperor said: "Very well, then I shall make a clean breast of it to Griscom!"

He talked with him for a long time afterward, and sent you a message which I think Mr. Griscom, who is leaving Rome, will write to you from there within a few days.

The Emperor's message to me is as follows:

I have talked about Mr. Hill with Mr. Tower and Mr. Griscom and found that both were of the opinion that Mr. Hill was not a suitable man for this post. Mr. Griscom was the first to point out to me that during the visit of Prince Henry Mr. Hill had made an unfavorable impression. This induced me to suggest to Mr. Griscom to furnish the President with a hint, but as his (Griscom's) personal opinion. Mr. Tower did not feel inclined to touch the matter and this I found explicable. Hence I clearly pointed out that Mr. Tower should in no way interfere with it. I think there must be a misunderstanding on the part of Mr. Tower.

Without any question as to whose memory is most accurate, or as to how the evident misunderstanding between you and the Emperor arose, it is enough for me to point out the grave indiscretion, and, indeed, I fear I must add, impropriety, of your communicating with me on such a subject, and especially of your so managing the communication that the information became public. You should at once have explained that it was not a matter that you could touch or interfere with in any way, both because Dr. Hill was to be your successor and because the announcement of his appointment had been made four months before and had been acquiesced in — for this was a matter of common notoriety. I may add that information from Berlin had reached me to the effect that very unfavorable comment was caused by your not having Dr. Hill at the dinner to meet the Emperor when he (Dr. Hill) was at the time in Berlin.

I need hardly point out to you the exceedingly embarrassing position in which you placed yourself, and to that extent (altho to no other extent) placed your Government, by what has occurred. Information was confidentially furnished the Secretary of State and me today to the effect that under the circumstances it would be more agreeable to the German Government if you would leave Berlin as speedily as possible. I think it is better that you should do so, from every standpoint. I do not desire that any further publicity of any kind should be given to this unfortunate affair, or any talk aroused. I therefore request that you leave of your own initiative, arranging on receipt of this letter to ask for a leave of absence, and within a few days to take your departure.[2] *Very truly yours*

P.S. No letter at all has been received from Mr. Griscom.

4666 · TO CHARLEMAGNE TOWER   *Roosevelt Mss.*

Confidential   Washington, April 4, 1908

My dear Mr. Tower: Your letter of March 16th has just come. The matter of which it treats is now obsolete, and no further action thereon is required by me. Between the date when you posted your letter, and the date of its reception, the widest publicity had been given to the information it contained. Seemingly, the press obtained its information from the Embassy at Berlin. At any rate we received by cable from Berlin, thru the press, knowledge of the fact that you had cabled the State Department and sent me a letter, before I received my cable from you; and the details of your second cable were, in substantially, altho not wholly, accurate form, sent here by cable from Berlin before I received the message itself.

I have also received a cable message from the Emperor himself, giving a very different account of the conversation. Griscom also has written me. From Griscom's letter it would appear at least doubtful whether you were called upon to write me at all. Certainly in such a very delicate matter, where

[2] For this letter, which he decided not to send, Roosevelt substituted No. 4666.

it was so obviously desirable to avoid all publicity, you should have confined yourself to writing personally to me and not have cabled the State Department. Mischief has been caused by the publicity given to the affair.

I need hardly add that in a case of this kind, where there is conflict of memory between the Emperor and an Ambassador as to a conversation which the Emperor has not made public, the only course to follow is not to say one word about the matter; until you leave Berlin, which of course will be no later than June 1st, and earlier if you desire a leave of absence, be exceedingly discreet, and under no circumstances discuss this unfortunate affair with anyone. *Very truly yours*

4667 · TO WILLIAM II

Roosevelt Mss.

Washington, April 4, 1908

My dear Emperor William: Sternberg gave me your message. Shortly afterwards, letters came from Tower and Griscom. Tower also cabled twice; and from Berlin (whether or not from the American Embassy I cannot be sure) the substance of his communications to me was unfortunately made public.

In the first place I wish to assure Your Majesty how deeply, as President of the American people, I feel and appreciate the admirable work you have done in promoting friendship between Germany and the United States. I know well how the natural prejudices of an old, conservative nation would tend to make it indifferent to the friendship of a nation of the New World; would tend to make it think that Europe was the world. I attribute the constantly growing feeling of good will between the two nations more to your own influence than to anything else. Your Majesty's Ambassador to the United States has been peculiarly fortunate in the impression that he has had upon our people; and I very deeply appreciate the evident personal courtesy to me, and the thoughtfulness, shown by you in appointing him. I should have sent you any man you wished, had I known in time that you were interested for or against anyone. I hope, by the way, that Your Majesty has personally seen Sternberg's letter of November last, reciting Hill's career, which letter resulted in the statement from your foreign office that Hill's appointment would be acceptable. Embarrassing though it would have been to change at so late a day, after Hill's appointment had been announced, nevertheless if I had only been notified privately that you preferred someone else, I should have at once made the change; but Tower's first cable was not to me but to our Department of State, and was answered accordingly; and following this the unfortunate publicity of the affair resulted in a condition of public sentiment which made me feel that you were wise in having your Government state that there was no objection to Hill's appointment.

Let me again express to Your Majesty my appreciation, not only of the way you have treated this incident, but of your constant friendliness toward the United States. It has been a very real pleasure to me to be able so often to co-operate with you and to second your efforts. This reminds me to say that the Chinese Minister, although he has been here for some little time, has made no motion nor given any hint in reference to action upon the territorial integrity of, or the open door in, China.

I trust you have noticed that the American battleship fleet has completed its tour of South America on schedule time, and is now having its target practice off the Mexican coast. After visiting San Francisco and Puget Sound, it will start on its return voyage via Australia, Japan, China, the Philippines, and the Suez Canal. When it leaves the Orient it will have to hurry home without stopping. I saw the ships leave Hampton Roads, and if possible I shall go thither again to see them rise over the world's sea rim as they steam homewards into harbor after their long voyage.

Their target practice has been excellent.

With high regard, believe me, *Very faithfully your friend*

4668 · TO CHARLES EDWARD MAGOON　　　　　　　*Roosevelt Mss.*

Washington, April 4, 1908

My dear Governor Magoon: The time is rapidly coming when we must formulate just the kind of government which we wish to leave in Cuba on February 1st. next, when we abandon the Island, and also the terms and conditions, if any, which we shall make before leaving. Baron Sternberg, a very intelligent observer, has sent me the following remarks as to what he thinks we should do in leaving:

1. Leave the rural guards under an adviser of the quality of Dougherty.[1] Raise their number from the present number, 5000, to 7500, thus creating a necessary reserve of 2500. Without your adviser they will soon fall into the hands of the cursed politician and your present system of promotion, solely by merit, will cease quickly, bringing back the old evils.

2. Place the department of justice under an equally strong adviser. The curse of the old Spanish system of administering law is still paramount in Cuba. There seem to be special laws for the politician and official and such for the rich and for the poor.

3. Place the treasury under an adviser to prevent the respreading of corruption. Otherwise the old Spanish system seems sure to spread quickly, especially in the customs.

Sir W. C. Van Horne[2] in writing to Baron Sternberg states as follows:

I am much pleased at what you said to the President concerning the Cuban situation. I am sure your diagnosis is the correct one. Instead of two political parties Cuba now has half a dozen or more factions and the jealousies and hatreds which have grown up in the last two years make a successful Cuban gov-

[1] Brigadier General William Edgeworth Dougherty, veteran of Civil War, Indian, Cuban, and Philippine campaigns.
[2] Sir William C. Van Horne, American-born Canadian railway promoter and executive, "responsible perhaps more than any other individual for Cuban railroad development."

ernment impossible for a considerable time to come unless controlled and upheld by the U. S. through a protectorate or something of the kind. One danger I see is that a third intervention may be resisted and that would mean a guerilla warfare and the loss of many lives — not, perhaps, by bullets, but by fevers — a repetition to some extent of the experience of Spain.

To set up a Cuban Government and leave U. S. troops to support it for a time, as has been suggested would be absurd for a government so started would not stand a week after the withdrawal of the military support.

I think no time should be lost in getting up a tentative scheme for discussion. I am myself very doubtful about leaving a temporary military force. I do not know whether it would be feasible or advisable to have a military force left permanently somewhere in the neighborhood of Havana. At any rate will you now as speedily as may be submit to me your views, obtained after consultation with any people, Cubans or others, whom you desire to consult? Throw these views as nearly as possible into a rough scheme so that I shall be able to go over it with Root and Taft.[3] *Sincerely yours*

4669 · TO EDWARD S. CURTIS   *Roosevelt Mss.*

Washington, April 8, 1908

My dear Mr. Curtis:[1] I have read those papers thru with great interest, and after reading them I am uncertain as to what is the best course to advise. I never heard of the three Crow scouts that you mention, and did not know that they were with Custer. I need not say to you that writing over thirty years after the event it is necessary to be exceedingly cautious about relying upon the memory of any man, Indian or white. Such a space of time is a great breeder of myths. Apparently you are inclined to the theory that Custer lookt on but a short distance away at the butchery of Reno's men, and let it take place, hoping to gain great glory for himself afterward. Such a theory is wildly improbable. Of course, human nature is so queer that it is hard to say that anything is impossible; but this theory makes Custer out both a traitor and a fool. He would have gained just as much glory by galloping down to snatch victory from defeat after Reno was thoroly routed as in any

[3] In keeping with "Root's policy of the soft hand," which Roosevelt had long endorsed, the United States government withdrew from Cuba completely in 1909. An advisory committee under the Magoon administration had framed laws to provide the island with a stable form of government, but with the departure of United States officials and troops these laws were disregarded. The judiciary fell again under the domination of the executive and the treasury lay open to the raids of Cuban politicians. In the Taft administration the United States developed a policy of "preventive interference," military and financial, in the island. For a detailed account of American reforms in Cuba during the second occupation see Fitzgibbon, *Cuba*, pp. 135–141; and Jessup, *Root*, I, 538–540.

[1] Edward S. Curtis, the official photographer for the Harriman expedition to Alaska. In 1906 he persuaded J. P. Morgan to help him organize the North American Indian Incorporated. This organization published a history of the Indian in eleven volumes in which the theory about Custer's behavior here propounded was not set forth.

other way; and with Reno routed, he must have been obsessed not to see that he was almost insuring his own death. Odd things happen in a battle, and the human heart has strange and gruesome depths and the human brain still stranger shallows; but the facts should be clearly brought out indeed, and the proof overwhelming, before at so late a day a man of high repute deliberately publishes a theory such as the above.

As to the citizens who you say are to publish this theory anyway, that is not your affair or mine. Unless they are very responsible people no attention whatever will be paid to anything that they write; any more than, for instance, to such a pamphlet as I saw the other day proving that Grant's Vicksburg campaign was nothing but a succession of blunders and that he should have been court-martialed for these blunders, that his success was a matter of pure luck, and that the only general in this campaign that deserved any praise was McClernand. *Sincerely yours*

P.S. I return the enclosures herewith.

4670 · TO ARTHUR HAMILTON LEE   *Roosevelt Mss.*

Personal   Washington, April 8, 1908

My dear Lee: That was a very nice editorial in the *Times.* I had not seen it, and am obliged to you for sending it to me. Indeed, my dear fellow, the obligation is altogether mine as regards the Laszlós, for I like the picture he has made of me better than any other, and so does Mrs. Roosevelt. I took a great fancy to Laszló himself, and it is the only picture which I really enjoyed having painted; for he wanted me to have in people to talk to me, and I accordingly usually had in two or three interesting visitors, especially Mrs. Lodge, and if there weren't any visitors I would get Mrs. Laszló, who is a trump, to play the violin on the other side of the screen. So I did not mind being painted at all; and I was delighted with the sketch of Mrs. Roosevelt's head.

I want to thank you heartily for all you have done in connection with Mackenzie King. The visit has achieved just what I hoped. There isn't anything more to do just at the moment; but no one can tell when the situation will grow acute. For instance, the Japanese immigrants are still coming here at the rate of about five hundred a month, and more than half of these are really laborers. Now such immigration is relatively insignificant, yet it is large enough to keep alive the ill-feeling; and if, in a period of depression, when white men are starving they suddenly see some thousands of yellow men taking their places at needed employment, there is a big chance that bricks may begin to fly. Moreover, every nation is always peculiarly susceptible to horror over forms of wickedness which it, tho equally wicked, happens not to possess; and I never can tell when race animosity will be called into exercise by some sexual misconduct on the part of a Japanese. But the trip of our fleet has had a most beneficial effect. The Japanese Government has asked us to Tokyo, where of course we shall go. Great good, by the way, has come to the fleet from its cruise so far, and the target practice is excellent. Wiseacres kept saying that just to jog a few thousand miles at a ten-knot gait would do no good; but in actual practice it has done great good.

I enclose a letter from Admiral Sperry which may interest you.

Give my warm regards to Mrs. Lee.

With renewed thanks, believe me, *Sincerely yours*

4671 · TO HENRY FOOTE HODGES $\qquad$ *Roosevelt Mss.*

Washington, April 9, 1908

My dear Colonel Hodges: In view of the renewed recommendation of Colonel Goethals in his reply of April 8th, and of your accompanying memorandum, I do not feel at liberty to refuse to follow the course recommended by Colonel Goethals. Accordingly, let the readvertising for both kinds take place as he recommends.[1]

I desire Colonel Goethals advised of the great embarrassment caused when the specifications are so drawn that, after bidding has been entered into in good faith, bids are rejected, for causes which should have been known at the time the specifications were drawn. Moreover, such rejection not only causes justifiable chagrin and disappointment to bidders, and therefore tends to keep responsible men from bidding for Government contracts, but it must be remembered that it is the very method that has been pursued from time to time in the past when special contractors were improperly favored. In work improperly conducted it has not infrequently happened that the rejection of the first bids either discouraged the first bidders and prevented them from applying, leaving the field free for those whom it was desired to favor, or else permitted the favored bidder to profit by the knowledge of what his competitors had done.

It is unnecessary to say that no suspicion of any such motive can attach to the management of the Panama Canal Commission; but it is very necessary that the Commission should keep such considerations in mind «and should» be exceedingly careful not to take action which shall arouse . . . unjustifiable suspicion or which shall dishearten honest contractors «or» make them reluctant to bid for Government work. Unquestionably, . . . will sometimes arise where it is necessary to reject all bids, and . . . . that this is one of them and direct that action be taken accordingly but these cases should be rare and in each case the necessity «of» rejecting all the bids should be made clearly manifest. *Sincerely yours*

[1] Bids on 4,500,000 barrels of cement for the construction of the locks were to have been submitted on April 13. The readvertised bids were opened on June 1.

Personal   Washington, April 9, 1908

Dear Seth: I have your letter of the 7th. The more I think over it the more I believe that to pass the bill on the Stetson-Morawetz line would be worse than passing nothing. Incidentally, I do not believe there would be the slightest chance of passing it, and I believe it would be ruinous politically. By this bill in substantially the present form we offer the big corporations engaged in interstate business what they have profest to want; that is, the chance to go into proper combinations without molestation. If they choose to back and fill; if they won't recognize the need of action; then the blame for the continuance of the present system will rest upon them and upon no one else. So it is with the labor men. Of course it may be that the only measure that could be passed is one which shall grant improper favors to the corporations on one side and improper favors to the labor men on the other; and it may even be that such action would result well at the moment. But as I have said before, I believe it would be in the end ruinous politically; and, what is more important, it would represent a very grave setback in the movement for corporation control — a movement which I believe essential to the well-being of the country. Both the big corporations and the labor unions would find such a victory as they desire a costly one in the end.

Bonaparte does not really favor the bill, his reasons being the direct reverse of those that make Stetson and Morawetz lukewarm; for his chief objection is to the insertion of the word "reasonable." I know few of the big New York lawyers. I very firmly believe that if you could get Frank B. Kellogg, of Saint Paul, Minnesota, he would fight hard for the bill, altho of course I have no authority to say this. *Faithfully yours*

4673 · TO VICTOR HOWARD METCALF   *Roosevelt Mss.*

Washington, April 9, 1908

To the Secretary of the Navy: I am concerned at the fact that on all sides I hear that the engine-room force is difficult to recruit and that the members desert at the earliest opportunity.[1] I should like a report upon this. It seems to me that either more pay should be given them or a different arrangement made so as to make this service other than one of mere drudgery.

4674 · TO HENRY CABOT LODGE   *Roosevelt Mss.*

Washington, April 9, 1908

Dear Cabot: Almost simultaneously with your telephone message I received two telegrams from Gussie. Your memorandum ran as follows:

[1] In 1908, 5036 men or 9 per cent of the total enlisted personnel deserted. Army desertions for the same period were only 5.6 per cent of its total complement.

Senator Lodge telephones from Boston that he has carried out the program as discust with the President on Sunday. The other side has agreed to a division of the delegates-at-large on the understanding that no resolution will be passed. He says that if the Taft resolution is now introduced it will be beaten and the effect will be bad. If anyone from Massachusetts should speak to the President and try to get the President to advise any other course the President should say that he sustains the position Senator Lodge has taken.

Gussie's two telegrams are as follows:

Boston, Massachusetts,
April 8, 1908. 6 P.M.

William Loeb, Jr.,
   Washington.
   Lodge says to Taft people that his attitude against preference resolutions has approval of President. I did not understand the President that way. Please wire me to Touraine Hotel, Boston. Shall not publish your telegram.

A. P. GARDNER.

Boston, Massachusetts,
April 8, 1908. 8:56 P.M.

William Loeb, Jr.
   Washington.
   Believe chances of passing resolutions of preference excellent; think O'Brien, of Boston *Transcript*, judges situation wrongly.

A. P. GARDNER.

I sent the following telegram to Gussie:

April 8, 1908.

Hon. A. P. Gardner,
   Touraine Hotel,
      Boston, Massachusetts.
   Lodge wires me that he said merely that he had discust the program with me. But I have thought much of the matter since you spoke to me yesterday, and I very strongly feel that no matter what may be thought of the advisability of Lodge's action yet, as it has been taken, it would be most unwise to bring in the resolution. If beaten, the effect would be very bad on Taft, whereas now he has certainly two of the four delegates. Whether beaten or not, the introduction of the resolution would now have as a chief effect the damaging of Lodge, which is most undesirable from every standpoint, personal and public, State and National. I therefore urge that the resolution be abandoned, and if you desire you can quote me as so advising.

I look forward to seeing you and going over the whole situation.[1] *Ever yours*

P.S. I have shown Hitchcock copy of my telegram to Gussie.

[1] The situation developed according to Roosevelt's desires. By previous arrangement the Massachusetts Republican Convention, which met on April 10, considered no resolution endorsing Taft. The pro- and anti-Administration forces divided the four delegates-at-large, electing Lodge and Sidney O. Bigney, both Taft supporters, and Murray Crane and John D. Long, both "uninstructed" opponents of Taft. The Taft men, without dividing the party, won a decisive victory when the convention resolved that the majority of delegates desired Taft's nomination. Other resolutions endorsed Roosevelt's policies and the principle of protection.

Personal   Washington, April 10, 1908

Dear Parsons: Fassett will tell you that I object strongly to the proposal to put in the platform the plan about cutting down Southern representation because of the suppression of the negro vote.[1] The best colored men I know, like Booker Washington for instance, say that no good can come from such a movement. My own feeling is that no good comes from any movement which is insincere, and that nothing but evil comes of a threat which irritates and yet which is not followed by any action. Now, this proposal, as you yourself know as well as anyone, would result in absolutely nothing. It would be an empty threat and no measure whatever would be taken to follow it up. If the resolution is introduced by some cheap and noisome agitator like Milholland, or Humphrey, or Gilchrist Stewart,[2] or any one of the creatures, black or white, who have been doing so much to the detriment of both negro and white man by their wicked and silly agitation of the Brownsville matter, the proper course to follow is to vote it down. These creatures have no place in the Republican party and are entitled to the scorn and abhorrence of every patriotic citizen. Foraker's desire is simply to scuttle the ship. He wants to do all the damage he can to the Republican party, and in order to achieve his purpose is willing to strike hands with Tillman or anyone else in order to do everything he possibly can to damage and discredit the nation and to impair the future well-being of decent colored men and decent white men alike. No particle of encouragement should be given to such a movement. The way to meet any entirely sinister movement of this kind is by grasping the nettle firmly. Tell the negro or white agitator who declaims about Brownsville that he is standing up for murder and occupies a position in its essentials like that occupied by the defenders of the bomb-throwers in Chicago or New York or Paterson, and hound him out of companionship with decent men. *Sincerely yours*

4676 · TO ALBERT LENOIR KEY   *Roosevelt Mss.*

Washington, April 10, 1908

My dear Key: I have read thru your letter very carefully, and seen Captain Helm.[1] I think that in your last letter you have come down to the real cause

[1] The New York Republican Convention, meeting on April 11, passed a resolution calling for the adjustment of representation in Congress and the electoral college to accord with "the letter and spirit of the Fourteenth and Fifteenth Amendments." Another resolution favored the reinstatement of all innocent members of the Brownsville battalions. These resolutions were not, however, incorporated in the platform the convention adopted.

[2] Of these reform Republicans, one, John E. Milholland, had assisted Roosevelt in the battles of his police commissionership, and another, Andrew B. Humphrey, had helped Governor Roosevelt resist Lou Payn.

[1] James Meredith Helm as captain of the newly commissioned *Idaho* had probably verified some of Key's arguments about the errors made by the Bureau of Construction in battleship design; see No. 4647.

of complaint; for the men whom you specifically hold accountable, either in their own persons or as representing classes, for the shortcoming of the Navy, are most of them line officers, including Admirals Evans, Brownson, Converse and Pillsbury. The bureaus *are* as a whole under the control of the «men who fight» and serve in the ships. Your complaint is that the old officers, as a class, are not so fit to perform the duties of their positions as would be the case with the young officers.[2] Merely putting in a line officer as Assistant Secretary would accomplish little or nothing. The right kind of Secretary, with the right kind of Chief of the Bureau of Navigation and the right kind of members of the General Board, can do all now that could be done under the proposed change. When one of the most distinguished of our Admirals, Admiral Porter, was head of the Navy Department, affairs went very badly; and in the Civil War, Fox could have been as much use as Chief of the Bureau of Navigation as he was as Assistant Secretary. I do not think any material good would come from a change in the system. Your letter makes it clear, for instance, that it is not accurate to say that the Navy is all right but the administration at Washington all wrong, for your criticism is quite as severe of Admirals Evans and Sperry, in command of the fleet, as of the men at the head of the department. In other words, your complaint really is that the present old men are not as good as younger men would be. From my own knowledge, I am sure that none of the older men would be better than those who actually are or have been in control of the department and of the fleet; so that it is not a matter of shifting among the old men, but a matter of shifting younger ones for them. Here, in the main, I am inclined to agree with you. I very strongly feel that our men come altogether too old to the advanced grades; that we should have both vice-admirals and admirals, for instance, and that the average rear admiral should begin to serve as such when he is fifty. But this means to introduce a change of policy which I believe it would be impossible to persuade the country to sanction. My belief is based upon my experience in the Army. My best major generals are Wood and Bell. But no one incident of my administration has caused me more criticism, more difficulty, more trouble of every kind, than getting Wood made major general. The Army was against it, Congress was against it, and the people at large were overwhelmingly against it. Yet his services have been so striking as to make it evident that if people would resent his promotion they would resent anyone's. In the same way, such grave discontent was caused by my promotion of younger men to be brigadier generals (altho, as

[2] Key, in repeating his earlier suggestions, had urged a change in personnel policies as well as administrative organization. Reform was impossible, he maintained, if Roosevelt continued to permit older and often retired officers to serve as bureau chiefs and on the important naval boards.

The reformers chose an inopportune time to push their demands. The debate on the naval appropriations bill had just begun in the House where the opponents of expansion were in control. Roosevelt was preparing his special message to Congress asking for four battleships. At the moment he could hardly be expected to support recommendations for changes which would disrupt the Navy Department.

a matter of fact, these younger men have proved to be by far the most efficient among the brigadier generals) that the Senate finally declined positively to ratify the nomination of any man hereafter for the position of brigadier general unless he was already a colonel. Fight as hard as I could I was finally obliged to recognize the fact that the people at large, the Senate, and even the Army itself, were against my passing by the older men; and tho I have been able occasionally to get in a younger man, I have usually had to promote the older ones, whose value to the service was not great. There ought not to be such an attitude of mind in the public at large or in the Army; but unfortunately there is. The same would be true as regards the Navy. We have to continue fighting, as I have been fighting, to create a popular belief in promotion by merit, and in getting men who are not too old into the advanced grades. Until we have accomplished this, it is a simple impossibility to avoid the employment of the older men in the responsible positions in time of peace.

Evans has again written saying that the actual experience of this trip has convinced him that it would be a great mistake to raise the lower edge of the armor belt. *Sincerely yours*

[*Handwritten*] All that you propose would be achieved by putting younger men in the present positions, such as at the head of the bureau of navigation, in command of the fleet; and to this in time of peace, and with our people as educated . . . , would cause a perfect explosion in the Congress, among the people, *and in the navy*.

4677 · TO VICTOR HOWARD METCALF   *Roosevelt Mss.*

Washington, April 10, 1908

My dear Mr. Metcalf: I am informed by the Washington Congressional delegation that they have been told at the Navy Department that it will take six to eight years to complete the dry dock at the Puget Sound navy yard. This seems to me nonsense. We should have a dry dock there within two or three years.[1] In other words, we should arrange to have the new dry dock ready even before the battleships provided for in this year's bill. I would like a full report on this matter of the dry docks on the Pacific slope, including Hawaii; as to how many we need; as to how long it will take to provide them, if Congress gives us the money; or as to any reason why the time should not be short. *Sincerely yours*

[1] Although two to three years was the normal construction time for dry docks built for private concerns, those built for the Navy usually took a much longer time to complete. The completion dates, for example, of the four docks authorized in 1898 were 1904, 1905, 1907, and 1909. The Navy in contracting for docks suffered from two handicaps. First, it had to accept the lowest bid even when made by an unreliable contractor. Second, as the Department constantly reiterated, the Navy could not at the salaries it was able to offer obtain competent designers and draftsmen. This meant that the designs which the contractor followed were occasionally faulty.

Washington, April 11, 1908

Dear Cecil: I was delighted with the Mazzini, and with no part of it quite so much as with the poem on the title page. How I wish that you and Mrs. Springy were to be here! There is such an infinity of things to talk over and I cannot begin to write about them all. Mrs. Roosevelt and I were thinking just the other day, in connection with the recent fuss over the American Ambassador to Berlin, about a remark in your last letter in which you spoke of the growing materialism of the Germans. The ambassadorial incident emphasized this. Tower is a good fellow, of great wealth, & of rather cultivated tastes. Hill is a somewhat better man — in fact I think a decidedly better man — but without the wealth. In consequence, to my surprise, I found that not only the American sojourners abroad who belong to the class of the vulgar rich, but all of the vulgar rich in Berlin, and especially those who are connected with the court circle, were violently against the change. Not a few both in the court circle and among the traveling Americans stated with obvious sincerity that under Tower the American Embassy stood easily foremost in Berlin as compared with all the other Embassies, and it evidently never entered their heads that in the question of standing foremost there was anything to be considered save wealth combined with social aptitude. As a matter of fact I am anxious to have it understood that it is not necessary to be a multimillionaire in order to reach the highest positions in the American diplomatic service. The trouble was entirely unexpected to me. I am simply unable to understand the value placed by so many people upon great wealth. I very thoroly understand the need of sufficient means to enable the man or woman to be comfortable; I also entirely understand the pleasure of having enough more than this so as to add certain luxuries, and above all, that greatest of all luxuries, the escape from the need of considering at every turn whether it is possible to spend a dollar or two extra; but when the last limit has been reached, then increase in wealth means but little, certainly as compared with all kinds of other things. In consequence, I am simply unable to make myself take the attitude of respect toward the very wealthy men which such an enormous multitude of people evidently really feel. I am delighted to show any courtesy to Pierpont Morgan or Andrew Carnegie or James J. Hill; but as for regarding any one of them as, for instance, I regard Professor Bury, or Peary, the Arctic explorer, or Admiral Evans, or Rhodes, the historian, or Selous, the big game hunter (to mention at random guests who have been at the White House not long ago) — why, I could not force myself to do it even if I wanted to, which I do not. The very luxurious, grossly material life of the average multimillionaire whom I know, does not appeal to me in the least, and nothing would hire me to lead it. It is an exceedingly nice thing to have enough money to be able to take a hunting trip in Africa after big game (if you are not able to make it pay for itself in some other way). It is an exceedingly nice thing, if you are young, to have one or two good jumping horses and to be able to occasionally hunt — altho Heaven forfend that anyone for whom I care should treat riding to hounds as the serious business of life! It is an exceedingly nice thing to have a good house and to be able to purchase good books and good pictures, and especially to have that house isolated from others. But I wholly fail to see where any real enjoyment comes from a dozen automobiles, a couple of hundred horses, and a good many different homes luxuriously upholstered. From the standpoint of real pleasure I should selfishly prefer my old-time ranch on the Little Missouri to anything in Newport.

There! I did not intend to go into a statement of my own views. I merely got interested in trying to explain why it is that I have been quite unable either to get on with the typical multimillionaire, or to understand the attitude of admiration toward him assumed by a good many different persons, from sovereigns down.

Give my love to Mrs. Springy. *Faithfully yours*

4679 · TO WILLIAM JONATHAN NORTHEN *Roosevelt Mss.*

Washington, April 11, 1908

My dear Governor Northen: [1] I am in receipt of your letter of the 9th instant, with enclosures. If you will simply read the interstate commerce law, read the decisions of the courts, and read the opinion of the Interstate Commerce Commission itself — one of the members, by the way, being a Georgian — you will see that your letter is completely answered.[2] What you say about the separation of races has no bearing whatever upon anything that I have said of any kind or sort. I am almost inclined to think that you did not read what I wrote before writing your letter or you would have seen that I quoted the law of Alabama, which contains the same provisions as the Georgia law in reference to equal accommodations for the same money. You ask me if "it did not occur" to me that the initiative should be taken before your State Commission or your State courts. A little reflection, my dear Governor, would show you that your question should be asked of someone whose duty it was to take the initiative, and not of me. I did not take the initiative. If you or someone else had taken the initiative before your own Commission or in your own court, then very possibly no one would have felt it necessary to take the initiative in appealing to me or to the Interstate Commerce Commission. But inasmuch as no one did take the initiative of which you speak, before the State authorities, it was certain that it would be taken by someone else in the way of an appeal to me or to the Federal courts. The railroads dealing in interstate commerce whether carrying passengers or freight are *not* engaged in a "purely local matter." Not only is this recognized

[1] William Jonathan Northen, Governor of Georgia, 1890–1894.
[2] See No. 4661.

by the courts, but I do not believe that any court has ever hesitated so to recognize it.

Now, my dear Governor, I do not think it well that this correspondence should be made public, because I think you have been singularly misled as to the facts in writing your letter. You enclose me statements made by you as to the "Supremacy of the law as seen in two counties," and as to the "Right and wrong way to deal with crime." I am most heartily in accord with the position you take in these sketches, and I applaud you for it. I am most heartily in accord with what you say as to your hope that you would have my "personal and official support in the efforts of good men in the South to solve this most difficult problem." I am simply endeavoring to stand behind the good men of the South. In this particular instance I am upholding the hands, among others, of an Interstate Commerce Commissioner, Judge Clements, a Democrat from Georgia, an ex-Congressman. It is just as foolish, altho not as wicked, for well-meaning Southerners to protest against the administration for taking notice of a complaint made as to nonobedience to a great Federal statute like the interstate commerce law, as it is for well-meaning Northerners to protest because in the Brownsville case I had visited upon Negro soldiers, who had been guilty of misconduct, the same punishment that I would have inflicted had the offenders been white. *Sincerely yours*

4680 · TO ARCHIBALD BULLOCH ROOSEVELT   *Roosevelt Mss.*

Washington, April 11, 1908

Dearest Archie: Ethel has bought on trial an eight-months' bulldog pup. He is very cunning, very friendly, and wriggles all over in a frantic desire to be petted.

Quentin really seems to be getting on pretty well with his baseball. In each of the last two games he made a base hit and a run. I have just had to give him and three of his associates a dressing down — one of the three being Charlie Taft. Yesterday afternoon was rainy, and the four of them played five hours inside the White House. They were very boisterous and were all the time on the verge of mischief, and finally they made spitballs and deliberately put them on the portraits. I did not discover it until after dinner, and then pulled Quentin out of bed and had him take them all off the portraits, and this morning required him to bring in the three other culprits before me. I explained to them that they had acted like boors; that it would have been a disgrace to have behaved so in any gentleman's house, but that it was a double disgrace in the house of the Nation; that Quentin could have no friend to see him, and the other three could not come inside the White House, until I felt that a sufficient time had elapsed to serve as a punishment. They were four very sheepish small boys when I got thru with them! *Your loving father*

Washington, April 11, 1908

Dearest Kermit: Enclosed find the ballad of Taillefer The Trouvère. I have marked the four lines that I really like.

Poor "Dr. Birch's young gentlemen"! I hope the younger of the pair does not feel as sad as the elder. But it won't be long now before you are out for good.

I have begun my correspondence about the African trip, altho it is not possible yet to say whether or not I can make it. Mr. Selous thinks that we ought to go in by Mombasa, because the Uganda-Nile regions are not healthy, and we will get acclimated in the healthy regions; moreover, we would then have some hunting to the good anyway, even if we did not get out well from the Nile trip.

I think the results in Massachusetts and New York have settled the nomination for Taft.[1] The Hughes boom has collapsed. Personally, I should be anything but surprised if Taft's name was the only name brought before the convention.

Fitz has been putting Roswell in harness, and Ethel and he drove Roswell up in the cart to the south portico of the White House today so that I could see him. Apparently he is going very well. Mother perfectly loves Nicoletta, and evidently it has made an enormous difference in her enjoyment of riding, and I never was better pleased than at having got the little horse for her.

It is beautiful spring weather here, with everything in bloom. My work is hard, but in a sense not as hard as I would like to have it, because Congress is refusing to do what it ought to do. It is taking refuge in a policy of mere inaction. It is of course part of the penalty that must be paid for giving up power; they feel it safe to disregard me as they would not if I were to be their candidate for President. *Your loving father*

Washington, April 13, 1908

My dear Congressman Humphrey: The enclosed memoranda explain themselves. You will see that the dock can be completed within three years. It can certainly be so completed if you secure the insertion of the clause permitting us to construct the dry dock by contract or otherwise, as may be necessary.[1]

[1] In New York, Roosevelt was most pleased by the defeat of Edgar T. Brackett's resolution suggesting that the district delegates support Hughes and declaring that the people would not be satisfied with "perfunctory or spiritless support." The rejection of this resolution by the convention permitted Taft to win many district delegates and forecast the lack of enthusiasm of the Hughes group.

[1] William E. Humphrey, Republican congressman from Washington, 1903–1917, introduced such a clause as an amendment to the naval bill. He also asked for an

Let me say again what I said to you and your colleagues from the State of Washington, that it is urgently necessary to authorize these dry docks for Puget Sound and Hawaii and provide for their early completion; and that it is no less necessary to provide for four battleships. I am unable to understand objection to building these four battleships by any good American, who loves the peace of justice, who loves the honor of his land, and who looks into the future. *Yours sincerely*

4683 · TO JAMES FRANKLIN BELL   *Roosevelt Mss.*

Washington, April 13, 1908

My dear General Bell: I thank you for your memorandum of April 11th. I agree with you that at present the proposed law would not be desirable, as in a number of cases its operation might be contrary to the best interests of the service. But a list should be published, as suggested by General Oliver, periodically, showing the amount of time spent by officers on different classes of duty, foreign and field service, regimental and detached, in staff corps, as aides, etc. This list should also show who is eligible for detached service and who is not, so that all commanders may be able to comply with the regulations in detaching officers. I see by the list you furnish that a number of aides have been detached beyond four years. I understand that officers are limited to a tour of four years as regimental staff officers. I see no reason why the four-year rule should be departed from in the case of aides. I should like you to go over this list with the Secretary of War, with a view of having such officers relieved as can be relieved without injury to the service. Please then report to me the names of the officers who are to be relieved and the names of those who are not to be relieved, with, in the case of the latter, the reasons in detail for each case. *Sincerely yours*

4684 · TO HERBERT PARSONS   *Roosevelt Mss.*

Personal   Washington, April 14, 1908

My dear Parsons: Can't you help to make E. H. Butler chairman of the New York delegation to Chicago? [1] He is a man who by his services to the party

increase in current appropriations for the dry dock from $100,000 to $1,000,000. This sum, said Humphrey, would enable the government to take over the construction of the dry dock whenever it became apparent that private contractors were failing to meet the specifications required to complete the dock in three years. He withdrew the amendment when Foss assured him that the Secretary of the Navy could let the contracts covering the whole cost even though only a small sum had been appropriated.

[1] The New York delegates-at-large, elected April 11, were Stewart L. Woodford, the national Hughes manager, Seth Low, Frederick R. Hazard, and Edward H. Butler, founder and proprietor of the Buffalo *News*. Woodford was made chairman of the delegation.

and his standing generally is entitled to it. More than that, he knows the game and he can give the New York delegation a standing that no one else can in Chicago. Every newspaperman in the United States knows him. I hope you can help in this. *Sincerely yours*

4685 · TO KNUTE NELSON   *Roosevelt Mss.*

Washington, April 14, 1908

My dear Senator: Your letter causes me much concern. Most certainly I should never dream of discriminating against you in any way, and I do not see how you can suppose that I would. But surely, my dear Senator, you must know that in the matter of the election of judges I exercise both an initiative and a scrutiny which I would not dream of trying to exercise with most other appointments. I have several times in the past appointed judges over 60, in each case for special and unusual reasons, where I knew the man personally and where the feeling of the bar was not only practically unanimous for him but very urgently and insistently for him; and where the men were far more distinguished than Mr. Hale. Mr. Justice Holmes, for instance, whom you mention, was one of the most distinguished men of the whole country; Quarles was a Senator.[1] In each case I acted on my own initiative; in no one of the cases would I have appointed a man of that age of whom I had never heard until his appointment was recommended. Yet even in these cases — all of them by the way happened to be veterans of the Civil War — I feel the practice was an error. I feel very strongly that the judges should retire at 70. Individuals who do good work on the bench beyond that age are much outnumbered by those whose good work has ceased at that age. It is therefore on every account desirable that the man shall have ahead of him ten years' service before he is 70, so that he can retire on a pension.

I do not feel that I can appoint the man whom you have recommended. I am exceedingly sorry. In a somewhat similar case at the moment I am refusing to appoint an old and valued friend.[2]

With great regret and high regard, believe me, *Sincerely yours*

4686 · TO HERBERT KNOX SMITH   *Roosevelt Mss.*

Washington, April 14, 1908

Dear Smith: The enclosed protest of the New York Board of Trade and Transportation is interesting. This protest is primarily aimed at the Hepburn bill because it practically licenses interstate commerce corporations, thus submitting them to the control of the Federal Government. In other words the chief objection of the New York Board of Trade and Transportation to the

[1] Joseph V. Quarles had been appointed a United States district judge.
[2] Judge John Allison of Tennessee had been recommended for a federal judgeship by John Wesley Gaines.

bill is to that measure which it is of most consequence to have enacted into law; our «aim» is to secure . . . Federal control of these corporations. The second objection is as to the legalization of the black list and the boycott. Here I agree with them, and would favor a modification of the bill along the lines of my message. *Sincerely yours*

4687 · TO RICHMOND PEARSON HOBSON $\qquad$ *Roosevelt Mss.*

Personal $\qquad$ Washington, April 16, 1908

My dear Congressman: [1] Yesterday the House seemed to possess an infinite capacity to go wrong, except, praise Heaven! in beating the scandalously unpatriotic proposal to cut down the increase of the navy to one battleship.[2]

[1] Richmond Pearson Hobson, Democratic congressman from Alabama, 1907–1915; leader of the naval expansionists in the House. An Annapolis graduate, for twelve years a naval constructor, he achieved extraordinary fame for his futile attempt to bottle up Cervera's fleet by sinking a hulk in the channel of Santiago harbor. This fame he first capitalized upon as a writer and lecturer, and then extended by his willingness to accept the kisses of the young ladies who flocked to see and hear him in his public appearances.

[2] On April 15, a spectacular debate over battleship appropriations climaxed the fight in the House over the Navy bill. On the afternoon of the 14th, Roosevelt sent a strong message to Congress urging the authorization of four battleships. He had already threatened to veto a favorite pork-barrel measure, the public buildings appropriation bill, if Congress failed to provide for these ships.

The following morning, shortly after the House approved the appropriations for the Subig Bay station, Foss presented the naval committee's recommendation for two battleships. Hobson immediately proposed an amendment authorizing four. Tawney then countered with an amendment reducing the number to one. The ensuing debate summarized the arguments which had been made for and against naval expansion during the previous week's discussions on the bill.

The Administration forces led by Hobson, Humphrey, and Longworth emphasized the need for an effective navy. Only a strong fleet, they maintained, could give force to such vital American policies as the Monroe Doctrine and the Open Door, or could adequately protect the nation from aggression. By discouraging attempts by foreign nations to challenge our policies or to threaten our coasts, such a fleet, they argued, was the best insurance against war. However, to be effective the Navy must have new battleships of the dreadnought type. Britain, Germany, and Japan had all launched extensive dreadnought programs, and unless the United States carried out a similar program she would soon become a fourth-rate naval power. The greatest danger, as Hobson especially stressed, came from Japan, whose growing navy not only threatened American commercial interests in the Far East but also white supremacy in all parts of the Pacific area.

The opponents of naval expansion, including Tawney, Foss, Bartholdt, and Burton, insisted that a big navy was an expensive and dangerous luxury. The United States, isolated as it was by two great oceans, was, they contended, immune from foreign aggression. A big navy, therefore, implied preparation for an overseas attack by this country. As such it could only increase distrust and fear of the United States abroad and thus intensify international tensions. The small-navy men especially censured the Administration for increasing such tensions by exploiting the Japanese danger to win votes. Finally, these congressmen made much of Roosevelt's earlier statements of 1906 that naval expansion had been completed and that one new battleship a year would be sufficient to keep the fleet up to full strength.

The debate closed when Hobson called for a division on his amendment, which was soundly beaten by a vote of 83 to 199. Tawney's amendment for one ship was

Among the things it did wrong was to keep the naval station at Subig Bay. I went carefully into that, and it is obviously impossible to defend that naval station from land attack without an army as large as the entire regular army of the United States at its maximum, including coast artillery. Such being the case, it is to my mind evident that Manila and not Subig Bay should be the point we should select to defend and at which all the troops should be concentrated, in the event of war, until the American navy definitely established control of the seas. This does not mean that Subig Bay should not be so fortified as to prevent its being used as a harbor of refuge by the enemy. You were mistaken yesterday in supposing that I had not approved the report of the joint board, signed by Admiral Dewey, in favor of Manila as against Subig Bay.[3] *Sincerely yours*

4688 · TO GEORGE WASHINGTON GOETHALS   *Roosevelt Mss.*

Personal   Washington, April 16, 1908

My dear Colonel Goethals: I have seen Balfe and I am sorry to say that his information merely corroborates what I have been learning from other sources and what has made me extremely uncomfortable. On every hand I hear the greatest praise of the engineering work, the actual work of construction and digging. But I think we are on the verge of an ugly scandal in connection with the subsistence and commissary, including such details as cleanliness of beds, cleanliness of water closets, and the like.[1] I am also uncomfortable over the things I hear about Jackson Smith. I feel that the measures outlined by Secretary Taft should be adopted forthwith; but I am by no means certain that Jackson Smith ought to be kept. Of course in this matter I must rely on you; but if you are dissatisfied with him, then ask for his resignation and let him leave at once.

The subsistence and commissary ought to be separated from labor and

---

then even more decisively defeated, 65 to 199. On the following day Congress passed, with only minor changes, the committee's original bill authorizing two battleships, ten destroyers and eight submarines. No provision of funds to construct the authorized ships was made, however. The Senate, quite reluctantly, made up this deficiency (see Numbers 4698, 4699, 4700). There is an excellent brief summary of this legislative struggle in Harold and Margaret Sprout, *American Naval Power*, pp. 264–270.

[3] See No. 4593, notes 1, 2.

[1] To forestall criticism, Roosevelt appointed a commission composed of James Bronson Reynolds, Samuel B. Donnelly, union leader, and Henry Beach Needham, magazine writer, to investigate living conditions on the Isthmus. The commission reported in August that these conditions were excellent (see No. 4856).

By the time the commission made its report, Goethals had carried out Roosevelt's suggestions by asking Jackson Smith to resign and by abolishing the department of labor, quarters, and subsistence. Most of Smith's duties were transferred to the newly created quartermaster's department under Major Carroll Devol. Others were divided between a second new agency, the subsistence department, and the personnel division of the chairman's office.

quarters. It is too much for any one man to supervise. Major Devol is the man of all others, in my judgment as well as that of Secretary Taft, who is best fitted to take charge of labor and quarters. The situation is sufficiently grave to justify your cabling on receipt of this letter. *Sincerely yours*

4689 · TO ELIHU ROOT   *Roosevelt Mss.*

Washington, April 17, 1908

Dear Elihu: These enclosures from Speck are most interesting. Note the divergence of view in the report of the German Consul and the German Military Attaché. Also note the matter-of-course way in which the Japanese accept the view that in the event of war they will obtain the naval supremacy of the Pacific. The views of their military men offer a bitter commentary on the folly of the lower House of Congress yesterday in refusing to vote for the four battleships. Indeed, it is the kind of folly which can only be called wicked. You will also see that this statement of the German Military Attaché corroborates the information we have had both ⟨from⟩ through the Austrian Embassy at Tokyo and the French Embassy at St. Petersburg, to the effect that many of the Japanese generals and of the military party generally accept as a matter of course the view that they would land a strong army on the Pacific Slope; and you may remember that this was the view that Mackenzie King found to obtain among some of the Japanese in British Columbia. You will also see that the German Consul takes exactly your view, that the Japanese can restrict immigration hither if they wish to. It is an act of the most one-sided folly for this country not to make the military preparations, and especially naval preparations, sufficient to put a stop to all thoughts of an aggressive war on the part of Japan. I think that the probabilities are that that war will not take place; but there is a sufficient likelihood to make it inexcusable for us not to take such measures as will surely prevent it. If we have adequate coast defenses and a really large navy, the war cannot take place. *Ever yours*

4690 · TO CHARLES JOSEPH BONAPARTE   *Roosevelt Mss.*

Personal   Washington, April 17, 1908

My dear Bonaparte: I have called in Neill about that employers' liability bill. We may have to make Congress recall it. We do not want another unconstitutional law.[1]

[1] The report of the House Committee on the Judiciary on the employers' liability bill, H.R. 20310, was in large part devoted to the question of the constitutionality of the measure (see *House Report*, 60 Cong., 1 sess., no. 1386). The majority of the committee considered the bill constitutional. The minority wrote a vigorous dissent which, repeated in substance by opponents of the bill in both houses, apparently raised doubts in the President's mind. These doubts must have been resolved, for on April 24 Roosevelt signed the bill. It was never declared unconstitutional.

I thought that suit was to be brought against Mellen for the trolley line business. What is the status thereof? It seemed to me that it was a clear case of violation of the law, so far as those trolley lines were concerned, and if so, of course we should take action.[2] *Sincerely yours*

4691 · TO FRANCIS EMROY WARREN   *Roosevelt Mss.*

Washington, April 18, 1908

My dear Senator: The enclosed explains itself. I am afraid the promise about Utah was definite; but, my dear Senator, for reasons which I will give you in full, I feel that every real friend of this country — every real patriot — is bound to make the fight for the four battleships. If we get the four, Wyoming shall be the name of one.

Can't you see that the law is amended by taking out the four ridiculous monitors from the list of those war vessels which have to be named after States? They are utterly worthless ships, and were put in against the protest of the Navy Department by Senator Hale, at the time when he was howling for a warship to protect Portland against a Spanish attack. *Sincerely yours*

4692 · TO WHITELAW REID   *Roosevelt Mss.*

Personal   Washington, April 18, 1908

My dear Mr. Ambassador: Your letter, with the interesting clippings, has come. I am glad to see Asquith at the head of affairs. I have a favorable opinion of him. I thank you for telling me about that Pilgrims' Club business. What a set of notoriety hunters they are! I shall have Hill cabled not to go to the dinner.

The other day three heads of Irish societies called on me to protest — of all things in the world! — against the arbitration treaty with Great Britain. I received them with the utmost good humor, and read them that part of Washington's farewell address in which he warned his countrymen above all things not to give way to national antipathies, because to do so was evil for the nation and made a slave of the individual.

It was delightful catching a glimpse of dear Mrs. Reid.

With warm regards, *Faithfully yours*

4693 · TO FRANK ANDREW MUNSEY   *Roosevelt Mss.*

Private   Washington, April 18, 1908

My dear Mr. Munsey: I wish to thank you not only for your personal and repeatedly shown friendship for me, but far more for the able and effective

[2] Bonaparte on May 22 brought suit under the Sherman Act to restrain the New Haven "from the equipment and use of the stock and franchise of interstate trolley lines which it indirectly held and of the Boston and Maine Railroad." There the matter rested for the rest of Roosevelt's term.

fight you have made for the policies in which I so deeply believe and which I regard as so essential for the welfare of this Nation. I have read your March and April articles on the business situation and I feel that they will do real good. The people of this country will not be deluded by certain big speculators in Wall Street and their representatives in politics and the press into abandoning the effort for the betterment of social and business conditions in which we are engaged.

Again thanking you and congratulating you, I am, *Sincerely yours*

4694 · TO PEARL WIGHT *Roosevelt Mss.*

Washington, April 18, 1908

My dear Mr. Wight: I have your letter of the 16th instant. Of course it is not in my province in any way to dictate, but I am *very* sorry that it is not possible for you to send any colored man from Louisiana. I did my best to get New York State to send a colored man as a delegate-at-large, and succeeded in having him sent as an alternate-at-large. The very considerations which make me set my face like flint against white and black demagogs who attack me for my action in the Brownsville matter, make me feel that we should be scrupulously careful to do justice to the decent colored man.

I have asked the Attorney General to report to me about the marshal.

With regard, believe me, *Sincerely yours*

4695 · TO KERMIT ROOSEVELT *Roosevelt Mss.*

Washington, April 19, 1908

Dearest Kermit: Ted turned up Thursday morning with a very sore throat, the doctor having sent him home. Being home with Mother and Ethel, and the rest and good food, speedily set him all right, and by Friday afternoon he was able to play tennis with great vigor, and Saturday he and Fitz went out riding. Mother and I also rode, going up the new bridle trail beside Rock Creek just beyond the other end of the Park. It is in low ground, and the flowers were too beautiful for anything, especially the Virginia cowslips and the dogtooth violets.

I made a hard fight to get Congress to give me four battleships, but they wouldn't do it. Most of them mean well enough, but do not know much, and the leaders are narrow-minded and selfish, and some of them, like Senator Hale, profoundly unpatriotic, and others, like McCall and Burton, if not unpatriotic, at least utterly indifferent to the honor and interest of the country when compared with their own advancement. I cannot give in public my reasons for being apprehensive about Japan, for of course to do so might bring on grave trouble; but I said enough to put Congress thoroly on its guard, if it cared to be on its guard. I do not believe there will be war with Japan, but I do believe that there is enough chance of war to make it eminently wise to insure against it by building such a navy as to forbid Japan's hoping for success. I happen to know that the Japanese military party is inclined for war with us and is not only confident of success, but confident that they could land a large expeditionary force in California and conquer all of the United States west of the Rockies. I fully believe that they would in the end pay dearly for this, but meantime we would have been set back at least a generation by the loss of life, the humiliation, and the material damage. *Your loving father*

[*Handwritten*] I enclose another poem of Phil's; good, but not as good, or as original, as the first.

4696 · TO GEORGE BRUCE CORTELYOU   *Roosevelt Mss.*

Washington, April 19, 1908

My dear Mr. Cortelyou: I do not at all like having so much gold in San Francisco. Have you yet shipped much of it to Denver? If not please take steps to get at least the bulk of it there during the next six months. San Francisco is on every account an undesirable place in which to leave it; a fatal place should there ever be a war.[1] *Sincerely yours*

4697 · TO ANDREW LINTNER HARRIS   *Roosevelt Mss.*

Washington, April 22, 1908

My dear Governor:[1] I have your letter of the 20th instant with enclosures. I do not agree with the views of my good friends in the matter of which you write. It is a matter on which arguments can be made on both sides. My own feeling is very strong that the National Government under no circumstances should abandon its right to lay inheritance taxes, but that it should only lay them in the case of large inheritances — inheritances so large that if the proper kind of progressive tax was placed thereon it would make it a matter of importance to have the action National rather than State, because, among other reasons, of the extreme improbability of getting uniform action by all the States, and the premium that would be put upon fraud if the action were not Federal. *Sincerely yours*

[1] The Secretary of the Treasury was perhaps less worried than was the President about the imminence of a Pacific war. In any case, his annual reports mention no movement of gold from San Francisco.

[1] Andrew Lintner Harris, Republican Governor of Ohio, 1906–1909.

Washington, April 22, 1908

My dear Senator Piles: [1] I am delighted that you are to introduce the amendment to give us four battleships. From every standpoint of farsighted patriotism it will be a damage and a discredit to us as a nation if we fail at this session to get these four battleships. I am wholly unable to understand the shortsightedness of those who fail heartily to back up this proposal. *Sincerely yours*

4699 · TO HENRY CABOT LODGE *Roosevelt Mss.*

Washington, April 22, 1908

Dear Cabot: From two or three Senators I hear that you are either lukewarm or hostile to the proposition to try to get four battleships. Piles is to introduce the amendment tomorrow, but of course he feels that with your known attitude toward me, if you take an attitude that is lukewarm, it will be understood as meaning that I take it. As you know, I feel that there is nothing before the Congress as important as to get these four battleships. I do not think that any patriotic man can afford not to fight for it as hard as he knows how. I am sure that these Senators simply misunderstand your attitude; but I wish you would tell Piles that of course you are heartily for the proposition. [1] It is a simple outrage from the national standpoint not to provide for these four battleships. *Ever yours*

4700 · TO HENRY CABOT LODGE *Roosevelt Mss.*

Washington, April 22, 1908

My dear Senator Lodge: The enclosed letter of Secretary Metcalf explains itself. From it you will see that in 1906 in reality no provision was made for a battleship at all. As the battleship nominally provided for was of a new type and as the act required that the plans should be submitted to Congress before they were approved by the Secretary of the Navy, and therefore whether money was provided for a battleship or not was of little consequence. This nominal provision for a battleship in that year was in effect merely a promise to provide for it the following year. The promise was kept and in 1907 provision for this battleship and for another similar battleship was made. A

[1] Samuel Henry Piles, Republican senator from Washington, 1905–1911, with Beveridge led the fight for four battleships. After a three-day debate in which the arguments closely followed those previously made in the House, the Piles amendment was defeated, 23 to 50. Although Roosevelt failed to get his four battleships, the navy bill as finally passed set a precedent for two ships a year, and was in fact a significant victory for the Administration.

[1] Lodge complied. During the debate he supported, though unenthusiastically, Piles's amendment for four battleships.

very liberal provision had already been made in the navy estimates for the battleship nominally authorized the preceding year, so that it was not absolutely necessary to make specific appropriation for the last authorized battleship in view of the balances then carried in the general appropriation "Increase of the Navy." In other words, the act of 1907 provided for two battleships, and the appropriation for 1907 was for two battleships, and it was made in such manner that work upon the two battleships could be immediately begun, and as a matter of fact was immediately begun. The contracts for both ships were let at practically the same time. No distinction was made between these two ships thus authorized in letting the contracts, and the work upon them is already from twenty to thirty per cent completed.

It appears therefore that the provision made for the two battleships in 1907 was a bona fide provision, made in such terms that the work upon them could be actually begun at once; the work was actually begun, and the contracts let; and under these contracts the two ships are completed to the extent of over twenty per cent — indeed one of them to the extent of nearly thirty per cent; this all being under the act of 1907.

Under the present bill as it now stands no provision whatever is made for the two battleships and ten torpedo destroyers authorized. In other words, the bill is a sham in so far as these two battleships and ten destroyers are concerned. There is not the slightest necessity for delay. The Navy Department is ready to act upon these vessels now. The plans and specifications are already prepared, and if the ships are provided for in bona fide fashion, that is, if provision is made in good faith, bids will be advertised for at once, and the contracts will be let and construction begun by July 1st, the beginning of the new fiscal year, as soon as the money becomes available. The Secretary indicates in his letter the amendments necessary if the act is to be effective. If it is the intention of Congress to increase the navy at all, that is, to provide for two more battleships and ten more destroyers, then the money will have to be provided as suggested by the Secretary of the Navy. If it is not the intention of Congress to provide for any additional battleships or torpedo boats, then they should not be nominally, but not really, put into the bill. Literally no useful purpose whatever will be achieved by keeping the bill in its present form as regards these two battleships and ten torpedo destroyers. If in its present form the bill should become a law the Department cannot take a single step that it is not now able and ready to take under the existing law. No useful purpose of any kind can possibly be served by making a pretense of providing for these two ships, and yet not really making such provision. If it is the desire of Congress to provide for the very moderate increase in the navy of two battleships and ten torpedo destroyers — and I greatly regret that there is not a provision for four battleships — then money both for hulls and machinery and armor and armament and equipment should be appropriated, so that the work can be begun at once. If the appropriation is not made for armor and armament the work in our gun factory here at

Washington will have to cease and two thousand men be discharged in the course of a few months. If it is not the intention of Congress to provide any increase in the navy, but on the contrary to allow it to remain not only stationary, but relatively to other nations steadily to go backward, then I trust the intention will be plainly exprest and that the deceptive form of the present bill will not be preserved; for the present bill does *not* provide for the increase of the navy as regards the two battleships and ten torpedo boats, and we could not spend a dollar for their construction, while all the plans for them are already in existence. So that in its present form as regards these two battleships and ten torpedo destroyers the bill is simply a sham and pretends to do what it does not really do.

I enclose you a copy of a letter already sent by the Secretary of the Navy to the Chairman of the Committee on Naval Affairs.[1] *Sincerely yours*

4701 · TO FRANK PUTNAM FLINT　　　　　　　　*Roosevelt Mss.*

Washington, April 23, 1908

My dear Senator Flint: I trust you will do everything you can to get those four battleships. Until yesterday the bill was a simple sham and I should have been obliged to veto it if it had been passed in that form, for it nominally authorized two battleships but really appropriated for none. It is unpatriotic not to authorize four battleships and to appropriate for them. *Sincerely yours*

4702 · TO WILLIAM ALDEN SMITH　　　　　　　*Roosevelt Mss.*

Washington, April 24, 1908

My dear Senator:[1] The quotation you give me, if it refers to any speech of mine, of which I am not sure, is certainly garbled. It does not mention the day or the place where I spoke. Of course I cannot discuss an alleged statement when there is not the slightest pretense of stating with precision when and where it is alleged to have been made. It is possible it is a twisted quotation of some statement I made, not as to an enlisted man, but as to a commissioned officer. You are of course aware that the contract of employment of a commissioned officer has no resemblance at all to that of an enlisted man, and that enlisted men can be and are discharged by the hundreds, precisely as in the case of these Brownsville soldiers, in accordance with the judgment and will of the Executive; whereas the Executive has no such power over the

---

[1] The chairman of the committee had already acceded to the demands of the department and the President. On the morning of the 22nd, Hale announced to the Senate that the committee with reluctance had prepared the amendment providing for the funds for the ships authorized by the House bill.

---

[1] William Alden Smith, Republican congressman from Michigan, 1895–1907; senator, 1907–1919.

commissioned officers, no matter how much he may wish he could exercise it. I am not discussing what the law ought to be, but what the law is.[2]

Let me repeat, about the Brownsville matter, that the Foraker bill is a purely academic measure, and that pressing it has merely been a means of preventing the possibility of restoring such colored troops, if any, as can show that they were not implicated in murder and in shielding murderers. I say "academic," because even if it got a two-thirds vote in each House (which is not possible) and could therefore be passed over by veto, it would be clearly unconstitutional and I should pay not the slightest heed to it. No law can take away my power of appointment or force me to make appointments, any more than I could by Executive order decree that I had the power to make appropriations. The Legislature cannot usurp the functions of the Executive any more than the Executive can usurp the functions of the Legislature.

As regards the Brownsville matter I wish to reiterate with all possible emphasis that an exhaustive investigation has proved beyond all possible doubt, beyond all intelligent and honest opposition, that the murderous assault was committed by from ten to twenty of the negro soldiers, and that a large number of their comrades had guilty knowledge either before or after the event. There is no more question about it than there is that Czolgosz shot McKinley, or that Guiteau shot Garfield and the move on behalf of these murderers is as essentially vicious as a move on behalf of Guiteau or Czolgosz would have been. Mr. Foraker's proposal is simply to replace murderers in the public armed forces of the United States on the sole condition that to the crime of murder in the past they add the crime of perjury in the future. *Sincerely yours*

4703 · TO HENRY WHITE   *Roosevelt Mss.*

Washington, April 27, 1908

My dear White: Your letter was very interesting. Personally, I admire Asquith a good deal more than Campbell-Bannerman,[1] but like you I am not at all certain how he will handle his followers.

What a delightful man Trevelyan is. I wish I could see him.

Congress will not stand for the four battleships. To be frank, I did not suppose that they would; but I knew I would not get thru two and have those

[2] Roosevelt was discussing what he thought the law was. His thought was wrong. Officers serve at the pleasure of the President; they may be retired or honorably discharged at his will; they may be dishonorably discharged only for cause and after trial. Enlisted men, contracting to serve for a specific number of years, may be discharged during that term of years only for cause and after trial. At the termination of a contract, the service may, of course, decline to renew it.

---

[1] Sir Henry Campbell-Bannerman, Asquith's predecessor as Prime Minister, a wise liberal and fastidious Victorian, who fought with Elizabethan boldness for his party and his convictions. He died in April 1908.

two hurried up unless I made a violent fight for four. Moreover they have now, as a result of the fight, announced as a steady policy that of building two ships a year — a great gain.[2]

I think your reading of the Kaiser-Tower-Hill case was absolutely accurate.

With love to Mrs. White, believe me, *Faithfully yours*

4704 · TO ELIHU ROOT

Roosevelt Mss.

Washington, April 27, 1908

Dear Elihu: I send you Magoon's letter. Taft has been over it. If Magoon is correct there is nothing for us to do save to try to leave Crowder as legal adviser,[1] so to speak, and some man to help with the troops, together with what is most important of all, a very strong Minister. If this proves to be all that we can with wisdom do the problem is simple, and I will merely ask you to select the very best man for Minister.[2] Would not Magoon be the best man? Of course I do not know whether he would accept it — one can never tell when any individual will feel aggrieved because what seems to be a valuable offer to do service is not accepted by him as quite up to his merit.

Taft feels that there is not much to do now, in view of this report, until the Cubans elect their President, which will be some months before we evacuate on the 1st of February. He is inclined to think that the President who is elected will himself desire our troops to stay there. Unless he does so desire, I think the case is clear as made out by Magoon, that our troops should leave. *Faithfully yours*

[2] The announcement did mark a significant gain. On April 27, before the vote defeating Piles's amendment was taken, Allison and Hale had agreed that it should be "generally understood in this Chamber and in the other House and in the country that we have now entered upon the construction of two battleships per annum instead of one." At the same time they both went on record as accepting the policy begun in the previous session of appropriating funds for the ships in the same bill that authorized them. By asking for four ships, by insisting on two to the extent of threatening a veto, Roosevelt had forced Congress into approving an expanded and accelerated building program.

With precedent established in 1908, the President was able in the following year to obtain two more battleships from a still more intransigent Congress. Thus by getting funds for six dreadnoughts between 1907 and 1909, he was able, in the face of the German and Japanese dreadnought construction program, to maintain his basic naval policy of having a navy second in strength only to England's. Roosevelt further increased American naval strength relative to that of Japan during the 1908 session by winning congressional approval for the construction of a major base at Pearl Harbor. For the total naval construction authorized during Roosevelt's term of office, see No. 5163.

[1] Colonel Enoch H. Crowder of the judge advocate general's office was the able chairman of the advisory law commission in Cuba. He left the island at the end of the occupation but returned a decade later to revise the nation's electoral code.

[2] Edwin V. Morgan remained in that post.

Washington, April 29, 1908

My dear Mr. Speaker: There are two provisions in the sundry civil bill to which I think I ought to call your attention. The War Department informs me that no opportunity was given those most conversant with the needs at Panama to protest against the provision in the sundry civil bill limiting the excess of wages paid in Panama over corresponding employment in the United States to twenty-five per cent. Mr. Taft and Colonel Edwards both inform me that it is possible that this provision would utterly demoralize the whole service at Panama, and that the gravest results might follow. The work there is being done so admirably, such extraordinary results are being accomplished, the spirit of the force is so excellent, that I should suppose we ought to exercise great care in doing anything that might work real harm. Of course no saving which resulted in the arrest of the work would be of ultimate benefit, and it does not seem to me wise that action of this kind should be taken save after the fullest opportunity is given for investigation by those responsible for the work, and until they have been heard.[1]

In the matter of the prohibition against the use by other departments than the Treasury of the secret-service men, I feel that I ought to point out that it is the belief of the heads of the departments that this will materially interfere with the administration of justice and will benefit only one class of people — and that is the criminal class. The Secretary of State, for instance, reports to me that this provision will hamper him seriously in dealing with anarchists when he receives notice that such are in the country; that, for instance, it would have hampered him in the past in giving protection to foreign visitors when he learned anarchists meditated outrages upon them. The Department of Justice reports that its work would be very seriously hampered; that it would have to try to organize a corps of its own, which under existing legislation it could do but imperfectly. Of course the outcry against "spies" is an outcry of a peculiarly cheap sort. It is one with which I was very familiar while Police Commissioner in New York. By "spies" are meant detectives or secret-service men — that is, the agents thru whom alone it is possible to get at four fifths of the criminals whom we ought to punish.[2]

One more matter. The child labor bill for the District has appeared in two forms, one in the Senate and one in the House. The Senate bill, I am informed, is all right; but those most interested in the matter say they would prefer

[1] On May 7, by a vote of 101 to 10, the House removed the limitation on wages paid in Panama.

[2] The restrictions on the employment of the secret service remained. The majority of the House, led by Cannon and Tawney, objected particularly to the use of an "army of spies" by the Justice Department to investigate business arrangements. Rejecting Roosevelt's increasingly strong demands, these congressmen continued at this and the following session to confine the activities of the secret service to Treasury Department affairs. Before the President left office the issue had provoked hostilities perhaps larger than its importance merited; see Busbey, *Cannon*, pp. 230–242.

to have no legislation at all rather than the bill now in the House, which bill legalizes the labor of children above twelve, or, in other words, legalizes the very abuse against which we have been trying to make the hardest fight; for of recent years the men who contend for child labor usually make their especial fight on permitting it in the case of children between the ages of twelve and fourteen.[3] *Sincerely yours*

4706 · TO JOSEPH GURNEY CANNON   *Roosevelt Mss.*

Washington, April 30, 1908

My dear Mr. Speaker: There is one matter connected with the sundry civil bill to which I should call your special attention, and that is the cutting down of the appropriation asked for by the Interstate Commerce Commission to carry into effect the twentieth section of the Hepburn law to only $50,000. In accordance with the request of the Committee on Appropriations in carrying out the desire of the leaders of the House, the Interstate Commerce Commission, instead of asking as they originally asked for $500,000, which was the amount necessary in order to do the best work in carrying out the twentieth section, cut down the request to $350,000, the very minimum under which the work can be done effectively at all. To provide only $50,000 really amounts to making a sham appropriation. It would be better to repeal the twentieth section or suspend its operation for a year, for such a course would have the merit of frankness. I regard this twentieth section as containing one of the most important provisions of the Hepburn Act, and to refuse to provide means for carrying it on is equivalent to repealing for this year that section, and it would undoubtedly be so understood by the country at large. I feel that the Hepburn Act was one of the great pieces of legislation for which Congress, under your direction and guidance, has been responsible, and for which it has received such deserved credit. It would be from every standpoint a very real misfortune now to nullify one of the important provisions of that act. The only people benefited would be the very worst of the big railroad men whose misdeeds we are trying to prevent or correct. The Commission has been at work with the railroads for two years preparing to put this section into execution thru the means of a board of examiners. To refuse to give them $350,000 (for to appropriate $50,000 serves no purpose whatever) is to nullify completely these two years' work.[1] *Very sincerely yours*

[3] The House accepted the Senate's view on this matter. Much of the rest of the bill reflected the sentiment of the House.

---

[1] The twentieth section of the Hepburn Act provided for uniform bookkeeping procedures throughout the railroad industry. The reduction of the appropriation for this section was sponsored by the same congressmen who wished to restrict the activities of the secret service. These representatives, to defeat one of the purposes of the act, sought to have section twenty apply only to the records of known violators of the law. After a long debate, the House, following the President's recommendation, appropriated the full $350,000.

[Handwritten] I may also add that if carried into effect the proposal in the bill «limiting» the wages on the Panama Canal may completely upset the admirable work now being done thereon; and of course the provision about the employment of the secret service men will work very great damage to the Government in its endeavor to prevent and punish crime. There is no more foolish outcry than this against "spies"; only criminals *need fear our* «detectives».

4707 · TO JAMES FRANKLIN BELL   *Roosevelt Mss.*

Personal   Washington, May 2, 1908

My dear General Bell: I have seen the German Ambassador, who says that the Emperor will undoubtedly be very glad to see General Wood come unofficially to the maneuvers, but that of course in such case the General cannot go officially to any other maneuvers; so notify him that under such circumstances not only could we not ask for any official invitation from the French, but he could not accept any. If he goes to any maneuvers he must go on the same terms to each.[1] The Ambassador, who is himself an old soldier, also said something in which I am inclined to agree, namely, that the real advantage does not come from attending these big maneuvers, which are largely mere spectacles, but from seeing the smaller units of the army hard at work in their actual practice. I think this might be mentioned to General Wood. *Sincerely yours*

4708 · TO CHARLES EDGAR LITTLEFIELD   *Roosevelt Mss.*

                                                 Washington, May 2, 1908

Dear Sir: An official communication of the specific names and cases which you call for would entitle the persons named to be heard, and would in effect commit the President to a prosecution of certain judges before the Judiciary Committee of the House.[1] It ought not to be necessary to point out the ob-

---

[1] Wood, in an unofficial capacity, attended both the German and the French maneuvers held during the summer of 1908.

---

[1] Littlefield sharply dissented from Roosevelt's contention that "instances of abuse in the granting of injunctions" continued to occur. On March 11 the congressman had written Bonaparte for the names of cases showing such abuses. Bonaparte replied that he could not comply with this request because the Department of Justice was not informed "regarding the incidence of suits between private parties." Littlefield then twice wrote Roosevelt asking him what cases he had in mind. When Roosevelt in this reply did not cite any case, Littlefield suggested that the President was less reluctant than misinformed. In fact, Littlefield argued in a long address opposing any legislation on injunctions, the courts had not discriminated against labor. The length of his analysis was greater than its depth, for many of the cases he cited documented the argument Roosevelt had refused to defend. For Littlefield's speech, which included his correspondence with Bonaparte and Roosevelt, see *Congressional Record,* XLII, Appendix, pp. 512–564.

vious impropriety of such a course. It would be on a par with a communication by the President giving the names of the senior officers of the army and navy alluded to in the statement in the President's messages to the effect that the lack of a system of selection for promotions in the army and navy tended to bring to the highest rank as many men of mediocre as of first-class ability.

If the Committee cannot itself perceive that there have been instances of abuse in the granting of injunctions it must give to the statement in the message that such instances exist whatever weight the Committee deems proper, without calling upon the President for proof. *Yours truly*

4709 · TO ELIHU ROOT

Roosevelt Mss.

Washington, May 4, 1908

Dear Elihu: This dispatch from O'Brien shows that over a thousand steerage passengers left Japan for the United States and Hawaii in April. The Japanese might as well be given to understand that if this thing goes on an exclusion law will be past.[1] *Faithfully yours*

4710 · TO EMERSON HOUGH

Roosevelt Mss.

Washington, May 4, 1908

My dear Mr. Hough: [1] By George! I should like to have your letter to the "militant socialist" published. It is one of the best things I have seen on the subject. You and I are individualists; but because we are against a brutal and lawless and uncontrolled individualism which would itself produce two thirds of the evils of socialism among the great mass of the people, we are therefore often misunderstood as being "socialistic" in tendency ourselves. They might as well say that because we believe in the free public schools and compulsory attendance of children at schools (both of which are of course, in a sense, socialistic) we are therefore committed to all of Karl Marx's theories.

When next you come on here, let me know in advance. I want to talk to you about a good many other things besides the men of the border. By George! it is good to have known the old-style frontier existence, isn't it? *Faithfully yours*

---

[1] There was no official action at this time, but gradually during the remaining months of Roosevelt's term the immigration from Japan was reduced.

---

[1] Emerson Hough, journalist, novelist, historian of the West and its ways, devotee of outdoor life, had published his first best seller, *The Mississippi Bubble*, in 1902. He later wrote *The Passing of the Frontier* (1918), a volume in the Chronicles of America series, and *The Covered Wagon* (1922), the basis for a popular motion picture.

Roosevelt Mss.

Washington, May 6, 1908

My dear Emperor William: I have asked your Majesty's Ambassador to present this to you personally. I hope you can see your way clear to have your Government enter into a treaty of arbitration with the United States. In the form in which the treaty now is I freely admit that it is not as effective as I could wish.[1] Nevertheless good would result from the expression of good will implied in the treaty; and it would have a certain binding effect upon the Senate, making it morally obligatory to accept any reasonable agreement which might subsequently be made. Moreover it would confer a real benefit in the event of any sudden flurry both by providing the executives of the two countries with an excellent reason for demanding cool consideration of any question by their respective peoples, and also by enabling them to make a strong appeal under the sanction of a solemn treaty to both the peoples and their legislatures to accept an honorable arbitration. It seems to me that these advantages are in themselves not to be overlooked; and furthermore the effect of such a treaty between Germany and the United States will be to furnish another evidence of the friendship between the two countries, while not to have the treaty, when such treaties have already been made with France, England, Japan, Italy, Spain, and various other powers, would I think invite comment. Merely to exchange notes of good will between the Governments would be no adequate substitute. On the contrary, it would invite attention to the fact that there is no treaty with Germany whereas there are treaties with the various powers above named; and indeed might be construed by our people as meaning that Germany did not believe any treaty should be made with us in view of our form of government.

With great regard and earnest good wishes for your continued success in your great career, believe me, *Sincerely yours*

4712 · TO CLINTON HART MERRIAM *Roosevelt Mss.*

Washington, May 6, 1908

My dear Merriam: Many thanks for the pamphlets on Mendel's Law, which I read with a good deal of interest. I return most of them, and the others will follow in a day or two.

Oh Heavens! how I wish I could make you really appreciate what I said the other day, and sit down in good faith and all solemnity and write that great faunal natural history of the mammals of North America, life histories and all, which you alone can write, and which, if you would only write it, would add so substantially to the sum of American achievement in science and letters. It would be worth at least fifty thousand little pamphlets, and papers,

[1] The form of the arbitration treaties had been altered to meet the objections of the Senate in 1904–1905 (see No. 3420). No treaty was negotiated with Germany.

and special studies of osteology, and disquisitions on new series of shrew mice, and preliminary reviews of the genera of pocket mice, and the like![1] *Always yours*

Roosevelt Mss.

Washington, May 7, 1908

My dear Senator:[1] Judging from your question yesterday I do not think you entirely appreciate my position as to my rights and duties in the army. The proposal of Senator Foraker is that Congress shall take away from the President the power of discipline and control over the army, and shall itself exercise the appointing power without regard to the President. At the same time Senator Rayner intimates that Congress may take away the power of the President to deal with worthless and inefficient officers by depriving them of command and saying where they shall or shall not be assigned to duty. My position is that Congress wholly lacks the power to take either motion. I enclose you copies of letters I have sent to Senator Rayner and Senator William Alden Smith. I will no more entertain the proposition as regards enlisted men who are black than I will as to the colonel who is white. Not only do I feel that both in the case of Colonel Stewart[2] and of the colored troops at Brownsville I am absolutely right; but I feel even more intensely that the proposed action by Congress in each case would be ineffective, because absolutely without warrant under the Constitution (as well as, to the last degree pernicious). We might literally as well disband the army as permit it to be commanded by some . . . of Congress as Senator Foraker proposes; that is, permit murderers to be reinstated, under fancied party exigencies or to gratify political and personal spite; or on the other hand, to permit a colonel unfit for command to be restored to command partly because he has influential social backing which appeals particularly to the Senators from

---

[1] Merriam apparently disagreed, for the "great faunal natural history of the mammals" remained unwritten while he published *The Dawn of the World* (1910), *The Acorn, a Neglected Source of Food* (1918), and *The Buffalo in Northern California* (1926).

---

[1] John Wolcott Stewart, Vermont Republican governor, 1870–1872; congressman, 1883–1891; United States Senator (briefly replacing Redfield Proctor who had died), 1908.

[2] Colonel William F. Stewart and Senator Stewart were related only in their distaste for President Roosevelt. The colonel, an officer of the regular Army, had been for years, as Roosevelt observed, a vexation to his superiors and an irritant to civilians. Stewart considered his assignment to an obscure post in Arizona and his failure to receive a promotion unjust punishments. This view was championed by a coterie of anti-Administration senators led by Senator Isidor Rayner of Maryland. Rayner, likening the Stewart case to the Dreyfus case, introduced a resolution directing the President to hold a court of inquiry. Properly described by Roosevelt as a usurpation of executive authority, this resolution did not pass. In October, on the recommendation of the retiring board, the President placed Stewart, permanently a colonel, on the inactive list.

Maryland, and partly because this also offers an opportunity for attack upon the Administration. Of course in each case the large class of maudlin sentimentalists gathers around the wrongdoers, exactly as similar people always petition for the pardon of murderers and other criminals — as, for instance, they championed the cause of Thaw.[3] Moreover, a few excellent men sincerely believe that Colonel Stewart or the colored soldiers did no wrong; just as General Gordon for instance, who was an able man, believed that by consulting the Prophet Isaiah he could get practical advice in dealing with the political exigencies of today; just as otherwise well-behaved, tho humble, fellow citizens of ours believe in the efficacy of the left hind foot of a graveyard rabbit. There is nothing so foolish that some otherwise intelligent men cannot be found to believe in it. But the great point to consider is that under the Constitution the President alone has power to appoint, just as the Legislature alone has power to pass laws and appropriate money. The Legislature may think that the Executive ought to make a particular appointment, just as the Executive may think that the Legislature ought to pass a particular law; but neither side can make the other perform the act which that other is alone competent to perform, without a complete, and I may add, an exceedingly inadvisable, change in the Constitution. I am often accused of violating the Constitution (the accusation being usually made with especial vehemence when I am carrying on a lawsuit, which the courts themselves decide); but no action of which I have been even accused is so clearly a violation of the Constitution as the attempted usurpation by one branch of the Government of the power of another branch of the Government; such would be the effort (and, I may add, the futile effort) to deprive me of my power of appointment. *Sincerely yours*

4714 · TO LYMAN ABBOTT

Confidential

Roosevelt Mss.

Washington, May 10, 1908

My dear Dr. Abbott: I am much pleased to get your letter. I send you herewith, confidentially, copies of my letters to Senators Warren, Smith, Rayner and Stewart. The first three were *in answer* to letters from the senators. With every inclination in the world to avoid trouble with the Senate or trouble with my own party, I cannot possibly give way on this question of the army. Have you seen the *Tribune* of today? If so, look at the account it gives of the Harrison veto of a bill which tried to take away from him

[3] On the evening of June 25, 1906, Harry Thaw shot three times and killed Stanford White, the architect, who was sitting alone at a table in the crowded Madison Square Garden roof. Thaw's celebrated trials for this murder provided yellow hues for headlines. The motive was revenge, for the killer believed that his wife, Evelyn Nesbit, a former chorus girl, was White's paramour. The first trial resulted in a hung jury; the second in the commitment of Thaw to an insane asylum from which he later escaped.

the power of appointment. Arthur vetoed a similar bill. It would be a bad thing to have the control of any part of the executive service taken from the President; but it would be ruinous to have the army thus taken from his control; and no better proof could be given than that of the two incidents of which Senators Foraker and Rayner are for the moment heroes. In one case we have the proposal to put murderers and perjurers back in the army simply because there is a genuine fear among Republican Senators and Congressmen as to the effect of alienating the negro vote. When I say simply because of this fact, I am not overlooking the sentimentalists who stand up for these negro soldiers just as other sentimentalists stand up for Thaw and for every variety of noxious murderer and criminal when this murderer or criminal is punished. Nor am I overlooking the fact that with many men and newspapers, as in the case of Foraker, as in the case of the New York Sun, and as in the case of a number of other public men and newspapers, the real and underlying reason for attacking me about the Brownsville incident has nothing whatever to do with the negro, but represents simply the purpose of the great capitalistic reactionaries to do damage to the policies for which I stand. But these considerations by themselves would not influence enough of the Senators to make the fight formidable. The fact is, as is perfectly freely admitted to me by great numbers of Senators and Congressmen, that they are uneasy at the threatened black bolt, many of them because of their fear that it will hurt the Republican party in the presidential election; others, as Hemenway of Indiana, because they fear it will hurt them personally in impending senatorial and congressional elections. I not only hope, but believe, that I have stood as valiantly for the rights of the negro as any President since Lincoln; and I should be a traitor to the negro as well as to the white man and to the country if I now sanctioned a crime in order to placate the negro vote. The one hope of the negro in the South is to be treated each man individually on his worth as a man, and not as a member of a race which will be judged collectively; and his greatest danger comes from the white man in the South thus treating each negro primarily as a negro and not individually as a man. The great argument which the white man makes in favor of this course is that the negroes as a race always stand by their own criminals, and this Brownsville matter has given the greatest possible impetus to this argument. In hundreds of cases where the Brownsville matter has been up and where arguments have been made, the negro has simply fallen back on the statement, "I am not going to go back on my own color." In other words, Foraker and the New York Sun and their allies are engaged in a most dangerous effort to put a premium on murder and perjury among the enlisted men of the army by restoring murderers and perjurers because the race to which they belong declines to consider the question of their guilt or innocence and says that they must be restored to duty.

Similarly, in the case of Colonel Stewart. I have never known him and know nothing about him excepting what the records show, and excepting that as his wife was a Pinckney, he has great social influence behind him, so that much social and much political influence has been brought to bear in his behalf. Here we have a man whom five generals under whom he has served during the last two years, not to speak of his own second in command and of the officers of his own staff, report to be so tyrannical and so grossly abusive toward enlisted men, so insolent with civilians, so oppressive in dealing with junior commissioned officers, that he is unfit to exercise any command. They also report that in their judgment he has not committed any offense for which he could be court-martialed and put out of the army, and that to punish him without putting him out of the army would not benefit the army, because the only way to benefit the army would be to deprive him of command. I send him to a post where he has no one to command. He need not stay there a day longer than he wishes, because he can at any time retire, having served forty years. It is at his own volition that he stays, and he only stays because he is trying to bargain for a brigadier generalship, which I shall not give him, and which I should regard myself as infamous if I did give him. Every contentious and litigious officer always asks for a court of inquiry. To have such a court in this case would accomplish no essential purpose, for I should certainly not believe a court if it found adversely to the various generals and other officers whose statements have been enumerated in my letter to Senator Rayner. My present impression is that I shall not grant it and that Congress cannot make me grant it. If Congress can make me grant it, then it ought not to be able to. If granted to Stewart, it should by right be granted to scores of other officers, and the whole army ought to resolve into endless courts of inquiry.

These cases afford extraordinary instances of the illogical habit of the human mind. At this very moment I am engaged in the process of removing a district attorney, a number of postmasters, two or three land agents, and other public officials; nor is this unusual, for during the time I have been President I have removed several hundred officials personally or by direction to the heads of the different departments. Congress has never questioned my right to do this, and of course would not assert that it could force me to reappoint the men whom I have removed. I am at this moment transferring to a less desirable post the Superintendent of Mails of the San Francisco post office, because I do not think he ought to be removed, but do not think that he ought to stay where he is, in consequence of some conduct of his in the past — conduct by no means as bad as Colonel Stewart's. Yet there is no thought of demanding that I shall hold courts of inquiry in these various cases where I am exercising disciplinary powers. Of course discipline could not be maintained, under such circumstances, in the army.

With great regard, *Faithfully yours*

Washington, May 10, 1908

My dear Chapman: John Burroughs and I had a very pleasant time during our three days at Pine Knot. I was much pleased to be able to show him all the birds I had said I would, including the Bewick's wren, the blue grosbeak, the gnatcatcher, the summer redbird, etc. The one bird about which we were doubtful was the Henslow's bunting. I think he found the place almost too primitive, for a family of flying squirrels had made their abode inside the house. This tended to keep *him* awake at nights, whereas *we* have become rather attached to them. In one plowed field I found a nighthawk sitting. If I had chosen to knock it down with my hat I could have done so, but I wanted not to hurt it; and as I endeavored softly to seize it, it got away just as my fingers touched it. It did not go far, but sat lengthwise along the limb of a small tree and let me come up within two feet of it before flying. When I see you again I am going to point out one or two minor matters in connection with the song of the Bewick's wren and the looks of the blue grosbeak, where we were a little puzzled by your accounts. I suppose that there is a good deal of individual variation among the birds themselves as well as among the observers.

I now feel as tho I wonder how I ever got on without your "Birds of the Eastern United States" and your book on warblers. It was a great pleasure having you at lunch the other day. *Sincerely yours*

Telegram   Washington, May 11, 1908

Your cable of May tenth received. You are authorized to say to President Amador that the Government of the United States will consider any attempt at the election of a successor by fraudulent methods or methods which deny to a large part of the people opportunity to vote constitutes a disturbance of public order which under Panama's constitution requires intervention and this government will not permit the Government of Panama to pass into the hands of anyone so elected. The failure which you describe to comply with the laws assuring to the people of Panama the opportunity to have their names entered in the registry of voters appears in advance to be sufficient to invalidate the election and if the facts are as they have been represented to you the wrong already done must be redressed and fair registry lists made up. In case we find occasion for intervention it will be necessary for this government to consider what steps it will take for redress of the wrong done and to prevent repetition in future. This may be followed by suggestions contained in your supplemental dispatch of May eleventh.[1] Your proposed course about Jackson Smith is approved.[2]

4717 · TO TRUMAN HANDY NEWBERRY   *Roosevelt Mss.*

Washington, May 12, 1908

My dear Newberry: What do you think of my issuing the enclosed memorandum? I want to get at the captains and commanders. They are the people who ought to be retired, and not the junior officers.[1] Will you report to me about this? *Sincerely yours*

[1] Taft was worried by the intensity of the political campaign then taking place in Panama. It occurred to him that the tensions of the canvass might be reduced if Panama could be persuaded to request the United States to supervise the election. Roosevelt's support for this maneuver insured its success, but President Amador deeply resented this reversal of Root's hands-off policy. American observers prevented abuses at the polls, while Amador and his followers, bitter and humiliated, refused to vote. His opponent, José Domingo de Obaldía, was easily elected. For good accounts of the intervention see Jessup, *Root*, I, 524–526; McCain, *United States and Panama*, pp. 71–72.
[2] See No. 4688, note 1.

[1] In his annual message of 1907, Roosevelt had again stressed the need for a reform in the Navy's promotional system. Ability, not seniority, he insisted, must be the criterion for advancement to command rank. Under the existing system, American naval officers, unlike those of other nations, rarely attained positions of responsibility until they had almost reached retirement age (see chart below). "Those who object to promotion otherwise than by mere seniority," the President told Congress, "should reflect upon the elementary fact that no business in private life could be successfully managed if those who enter at the lowest rungs of the ladder should each in turn, if he lived, become the head of the firm, its active director, and retire after he had held the position a few months. On its face such a scheme is an absurdity."

During the congressional session, Roosevelt, concentrating on his battleship program, did not work actively to reform promotion methods. However, he did what he could under the existing law to put his views into practice. In 1908, the naval retirements included 14 rear admirals, 10 captains, and 5 commanders, but no lieutenant commanders and only 3 lieutenants. By the end of the year there were the following senior officers on the naval list: 27 admirals, 80 captains, 120 commanders, 213 lieutenant commanders and 313 lieutenants.

COMPARATIVE AVERAGE AGE OF NAVAL OFFICERS

	United States Yrs. Mo.		Germany Yrs. Mo.		Japan Yrs. Mo.		England Yrs. Mo.		France Yrs. Mo.		
Rear Admiral	60	8	53	0	53	6	53	1	58	3	
Captain	55	5	47	0	43	9	53	6	60	0	oldest
							36	5	40	1	youngest
Commander	47	1	42	0	40	0	50	0	57	10	oldest
							32	0	42	2	youngest

Washington, May 12, 1908

Dear Ted: It was good to hear from you. I quite agree with you about Rabelais. I have no doubt that he has a certain merit of his own, but after vain effort I find that I no more care to read him than I would to examine a gold chain encrusted in the filth of a pigpen. What is more, among those who do read him, where there is one who reads him for his merits there are ten who read him for his demerits; just as with the *Decameron*, the *Heptameron*, and a lot of other books of the same kind. Our medieval ancestors may have been better than we are on some points, altho I cannot recall them; but there is no use in telling me that we have not made an enormous advance, taking it as a whole, from the days of the "Ages of Faith" and the Renaissance.

I should have given much to have seen you reading the Ballad of the Revenge to the by no means wholly sober Brothers. I am sending you copies of some of my books for the club library.

Yesterday I played Gifford Pinchot singles, and he beat me just about as you did last summer. At your best, you and he ought to play nearly alike.

I do not think James' match is a very fortunate one. His wife must be ten or fifteen years older than he is. He has been working so well and has shown such good qualities that I do hope he will be happy.

Under the tuition of James, the butler, Quentin is really beginning to know a little about baseball, and he is certainly devoted to it. His nine absorbs a large part of his thoughts. At the moment he is captain of it. It has been christened the Invincibles, because of the number of its victories!

Kermit writes me that poor Archie lost his head in the Groton race against the substitute freshman crew and steered into them. I am awfully sorry.

Mother and I had a beautiful time at Pine Knot with Oom John.

I am now ending my experience with Congress for the year; giving and taking heavy blows! *Your loving father*

Washington, May 13, 1908

My dear Mr. Speaker: Apropos of our talk last evening, there is one matter that I think we must have passed at this session, and that is a simple bill, such as the enclosed, to continue the Inland Waterways Commission, with an appropriation of say $20,000. In view of the extraordinary meeting of the Governors of the States which is now taking place, it would be unpardonable in my view if we did not make this provision.[1] Of course, in any event

[1] The Inland Waterways Commission, like the other special commissions on conservation appointed by Roosevelt, worked without an appropriation or a special staff. By May 1908 the commission had demonstrated its value. Its splendid report of February, a landmark in the history of conservation, presented with discernment the

I would continue the present Commission, but for me to do so when Congress had failed to recognize it would serve to emphasize an omission by Congress as to a matter in which I think the country is very deeply interested. *Sincerely yours*

4720 · TO DE ALVA STANWOOD ALEXANDER   *Roosevelt Mss.*

Washington, May 18, 1908

Dear Mr. Alexander: I do hope you will succeed in getting the compensation act for government employees amended in the Senate along more liberal lines than were followed in the House.

The compensation in case of death, at the best, will ordinarily be very small, and in the event that an injured man died after ten or eleven months, the amount that would be paid to his wife and children would be so pitifully small as to be almost a mockery.

There ought certainly to be some provision for permanent disability. Where a man is not killed but his earning power is entirely and permanently destroyed, his family is really in a more pitiable condition economically than if it had actually lost its breadwinner thru death, for it has not only lost his earning power, but has to carry the burden of an invalid member.

We are probably the richest nation in the world, yet we are doing less, far less, for those injured or killed in the service of the Government than even the poorest of the European countries have done.

On the other hand, I think very careful consideration should be given to the suggestion that some time should elapse between the injury and the payment of benefits. We do not want to put a premium upon malingering nor to destroy the spirit of self-reliance or self-help. It seems to me that the bill in its present form goes too far in relieving cases where the burden upon the injured man and his family would be slight, and leaves without adequate relief cases where the burden would be severe and crushing.

I think, too, the bill ought to be extended to cover any civilian employee who is injured or killed while protecting the property of the United States or while enforcing its laws.

---

need for the systematic improvement of waterways, the development of water power, the control of floods, and the reclamation of land. The conference of governors, which Roosevelt had called at the commission's suggestion, applauded the work. The President's trip down the Mississippi had popularized that work (see Pinchot, *Breaking New Ground*, pp. 326-333). Yet Roosevelt, even with the assistance of Burton and Newlands, both members of the commission, could not persuade Congress to prevent the "unpardonable." Strongly opposed by the majority of the Old Guard, the bill to continue the commission, debated but not brought to a vote, lay over until the next session. In the interim, the commission, at Roosevelt's request, continued to serve voluntarily (see No. 4741). Following one of its recommendations, the Rivers and Harbors Act of March 1909 created a national waterways commission which, with Burton as its chairman, ably continued the work of its predecessor.

I hope that before the bill is reported by the Senate Committee you will go over it with Mr. Neill, as I have before suggested, and see if we cannot secure a little more satisfactory bill than the present one.[1] *Sincerely yours*

4721 · TO ELBERT FRANCIS BALDWIN   *Roosevelt Mss.*

Personal   Washington, May 19, 1908

My dear Mr. Baldwin: I have your letter of the 18th and the enclosed clipping. The statements contain rather less than the ordinary proportion of usual *Sun* falsehoods. I was consulted as to the temporary chairmanship and found that the chairman of the committee, New, desired Beveridge, it being customary for the chairman to make the appointment. I heartily approved of the choice — just as when consulted four years ago I heartily approved of the choice of Root. I was not in any sense hostile to Dolliver, however, and explained to those who backed him that altho I had already exprest a favorable opinion of Beveridge, I felt that Senator Dolliver also stood for the progressive principles of the party. I said I cared for the *kind* of man, not the *particular* man. I exprest an earnest hope that as the speech of the temporary chairman is usually expected to set the keynote of the convention, they would not choose a reactionary, but would choose someone who would do what he could to have the convention state its hearty sympathy with the purposes and policies which have been the administration purposes and policies, and therefore the Republican purposes and policies, for the last six years. Senator

[1] De Alva S. Alexander had introduced the compensation bill which, with few changes, the House passed on May 18. This measure, substantially unamended, the Senate later accepted after Roosevelt had persuaded Beveridge to forsake an alternative proposal that would have accomplished what this letter requested (see Numbers 4726, 4727, and *Congressional Record*, XLII, 6674–6675).

  Neither bill provided as generous compensation as that stipulated in the laws of the twenty-one nations which had already passed similar legislation. Alexander's bill covered all artisans and laborers employed by the United States in its manufacturing establishments, in navy yards, and in hazardous occupations under the Isthmian Canal Commission — about 55,000 employees in all. An injured employee was entitled to receive his full pay for the period of his incapacity up to one year. If an injured employee died, his dependents were to receive and divide his annual wage. No compensation was to be granted, however, if the injury were "due to the negligence or misconduct" of the employee.

  Beveridge and Representative Sterling advocated a more liberal measure. It covered all those affected by the Alexander Bill and also all other employees of the Isthmian Canal Commission and certain other employees in the United States — about 350,000 in all. If, because of injury, an employee were incapacitated, he was to receive only sixty per cent of his monthly wage, but not more than $50.00 a month. However, if the incapacity proved permanent, he was to receive a lump-sum payment equal to ten times his annual wage. If an injured employee died, his dependents were to receive and divide five times his annual wage, or at least $2,000 but no more than $10,000. The Sterling-Beveridge Bill, moreover, provided that the compensation be paid unless the injury were "due to serious and willful misconduct." This phrase, copied from British legislation, unlike the negligence clause of the successful Alexander Bill, eliminated the traditional legal interpretation of contributory negligence which had so often prevented workmen from receiving compensation.

Burrows has always been an opponent of these policies, taking a leading part against reciprocity with Cuba, against a more liberal tariff for the Philippines, against the regulation of corporations, against an increase of the powers of the Interstate Commerce Commission, and so forth and so forth. In short, his selection in part represents the effort to put the soft pedal on the policies of the administration.

As for Senator Foraker's services, I think you will find that it is the reactionaries who regard them as essential to the success of the Republican ticket. For the last year Senator Foraker, from the standpoint of Republicanism, has simply been engaged in an effort to scuttle the ship.

Of course this is a purely private letter for your own guidance. *Faithfully yours*

4722 · TO ALBERT SHAW   *Roosevelt Mss.*

Personal   Washington, May 22, 1908

Dear Shaw: I absolutely agree with you. The ruling clique in the Senate, the House, and the National Committee, seem to regard every concession to decency as merely a matter of bargain and sale with *me*, which *I* must pay for in some way or fashion. I most earnestly wish to avoid being impracticable, and to avoid a break; and I think I can get to the end of my term without a break; but that does not mean that I will abandon my principles; and I absolutely agree with you that the Republican National Convention should not accept a program made out for it by the National Committee unless the program is entirely satisfactory to the Convention itself. If in my power, I should upset such a program, whether of personnel or policy, without a moment's hesitation, if I were myself in the convention — as I shall not be!

Are you to be in Washington any time within a week or two of the adjournment of Congress? I should like to go over all that has been done, and perhaps more especially a good deal that has *not* been done. *Faithfully yours*

4723 · TO EDWARD NORTH BUXTON   *Roosevelt Mss.*

Washington, May 23, 1908

My dear Buxton: [1] You are giving me precisely the information that I wish, and I shall expect to follow out almost the itinerary you propose. It has been suggested to me that I ought to get into German East Africa for a short trip, especially if I want to get elephants, and I may do this. Of course I should be immensely pleased if I made such a bag as you made in the two African trips which you describe in your last volume. But I don't expect to! I sup-

---

[1] Edward North Buxton, British sportsman; veteran of the hunt in three continents; author of *Two African Trips, with Notes and Suggestions on Big Game Preservation in Africa* (London, 1902).

pose that there is so much chance in connection with lions that it is out of the question to count on getting one, but I should like to try, and I should also like to try for one bull elephant apiece for both Kermit and myself. I suppose I will be able to get a special license, will I not? If I get a chance I should *like* to kill one giraffe, one eland, one gnu, one buffalo. I know I need not tell you that I shall do nothing in the nature of butchery, and unless they are actually needed for food shall shoot simply one head of each species; Kermit doing the same. I am glad you know Leigh Hunt. When I write him I will give him your message. Have you any idea how late in the winter we could start down the Nile? I want to take time enough for the whole trip so as to be sure I can get into a game country. I should be very glad to get back into civilization after a few months in the wilds, of course; but still, I would far rather stay in them than not get my game! But I suppose that in a year (and of course I would like it better if it was within nine months) I *can* get my game. *Always yours*

4724 · TO THEODORE ROOSEVELT, JUNIOR *Roosevelt Mss.*

Washington, May 23, 1908

Dear Ted: It gave me quite a pang to receive your letter and feel that you are really making up your mind to what you are going to do next fall. Of course I feel sad to think of the little bear going out into the world at last with a good many troubles and hard times before him. But you will be twenty-one, Ted; you want to make your own way, and I have the utmost confidence and belief in you, and indeed, am very proud of you; and I am sure you will succeed. It will be hard at first; especially when you are working your utmost, while Kermit and I, eaten alive with ticks, horseflies, jiggers, and the like, are enjoying ourselves in Africa. The only thing will be to remember that you have had first-rate fun as a boy up to the time you were twenty-one; and that the man who is to succeed must buckle to real work during the early and most important years of his manhood.

Yes, that is an interesting book of Winston Churchill's about his father; but I can't help feeling about both of them that the older one *was* a rather cheap character, and the younger one *is* a rather cheap character.[1] Recently I have been reading my usual odd variety of books, including for the last three

[1] This comment is interesting primarily because it conforms so closely to the conventional attitude of that day toward Winston Churchill. Randolph Churchill with his dramatic resignation and Winston Churchill with his caustic restlessness revealed to Roosevelt, and to his contemporaries, the difficulties under which men of brilliance, insight, vigor, and independence must labor within the party lines when they have come to distrust the party responses to prevailing conditions. Possessing the Churchillian talents, although perhaps in lesser degree, and the Churchillian defects, although perhaps to a greater extent, Roosevelt may in 1908 have come more naturally by his skepticism of the Churchillian personality than he would have four years or thirty-two years later.

or four nights Creasy's *History of the Ottoman Turks*,[2] which gave me much comfort. I had a very nice note from the Brothers in acknowledgment of the volumes I sent on.

David Gray[3] was here this week. Both Roswell and Audrey are laid up, much to my disappointment; but good Bob Bacon gave David Gray a horse, and good George Meyer gave me another, and the four of us had a first-class ride. I was on George Meyer's crack jumper, and really I think he is the best heavyweight carrier I have ever been on, unless, perhaps, it was one horse of Austin Wadsworth's up in the Geneseo Valley. Sagamore, in the old days, did not have to carry my present weight. This horse is a good deal better than Roswell, being both a more powerful and more willing jumper. Still Roswell is a mighty good horse. *Your loving father*

4725 · TO WHITELAW REID   *Roosevelt Mss.*

Washington, May 25, 1908

My dear Mr. Ambassador: First let me extend my very earnest good wishes for Miss Jean.[1] Mrs. Roosevelt found an old book dealing with New York which we hoped that she, as a New Yorker, might accept as a trifling token of our regard for her, no less than for you and Mrs. Reid.

I was immensely amused and somewhat irritated at the recital of your experiences with that Virginia young lady as to whom I wrote you in connection with a presentation at court. I was fairly caught in the matter, for it was asked for by her aunt, a dear old Virginia gentlewoman, with of course not the slightest idea of what she was asking, who showed us certain courtesies and upon whom we were calling while at Pine Knot. But since then I have adopted the plan of never under any circumstances making a request that anyone be presented at court or presented to a sovereign unless on urgent public business. I am exceedingly glad that you failed to find the foolish young lady in question, and that owing to her own fault she has missed the presentation; and now I ask that you be careful not to present her if she should again turn up. I have grown to have a constantly increasing horror of the Americans who go abroad desiring to be presented at court or to meet sovereigns. In very young people it is excusable folly; in older people it is mere snobbishness. I am exceedingly sorry I ever asked you to present the Shontses; but officially he was entitled to it, and until I made my present rule of never asking a presentation, his was just a case which it was impossible to refuse. I cannot be too sincerely grateful that when Mrs. Roosevelt and I were abroad before I was President, we refused to be presented. I have a hearty

[2] Sir Edward Shepherd Creasy, *History of the Ottoman Turks* (London, 1877).
[3] David Gray, Buffalo, New York, journalist and lawyer; author of light essays, novels, and plays, including *The Recantation of an Anti-Imperialist, Gallops,* and *Ensign Russell;* thrice-decorated liaison officer to the French during World War I.

[1] Jean Reid, the ambassador's daughter, was about to be married.

respect for the right kind of a king and for the right kind of aristocracy, and for the right kind of Englishman who wishes to be presented or have his wife or daughter presented; but it is the business of an American to be a Republican, a Democrat, to behave in a simple and straightforward manner, and, without anything cheap or blatant about it, to be just what he is, and that is, a plain citizen of the American Republic, an intensely Democratic Republic; and he is thoroly out of place, loses his dignity in the eyes of others, and loses his own self-respect, when he tries to play a role for which he is not suited, and which personally I think is less exalted than his own natural role. I have been immensely amused, and not a little astonished, to find how many people, some of them pretty good people, believe that when I am thru here I shall visit the courts of Europe. It would take ten strong yoke of oxen to drag me thither; and my present intention is not to go to Europe at all until the memory of my Presidency has faded, so as not to make the wretched sovereigns and statesmen feel obliged to see me or entertain me. Then, if I can go just as I went before I was President, sometime I should like to take Mrs. Roosevelt; to see the picture galleries, the quaint cities, the scenery; but not otherwise. When I stop being President I stop being President. I become an ordinary citizen, entirely contented to be such; and as I am not a man of large means I neither wish myself to be put into the position of the earthen pot driven downstream with the brazen pots, nor to see my children so placed. If, for instance, I could meet the German Emperor now, when each is head of a big State and there are plenty of things on which we could naturally talk from an equal standpoint, why, I should be delighted to do so. But I haven't the slightest desire to meet him when my hand is no longer on the lever. I hope to get a holiday next spring and go for nine months or a year to Africa, to see the big game, and shoot a very moderate number of head, taking my second boy, Kermit, with me; and if the British and German officers of the territories in which I go will then show me whatever consideration they show to other fairly well-known people of good character who behave themselves — why, that is all I shall ask, and quite as much as I have any right to expect.

Congress is ending, by no means in a blaze of glory. The leaders in the house and Senate felt a relief that they did not try to conceal at the fact that I was not to remain as President, and need not be too implicitly followed; and they forgot that the discipline they have been able to keep for the last six years over their followers was primarily due to the fact that we had a compact and aggressive organization, kept together by my leadership, due to my hold, and the hold the policies I championed had, upon the people. Accordingly they have seen their own power crumble away under their hands and both the House and Senate are now in chaos. All opposition to Taft has died down and he will be nominated easily. But in electing him we shall have no help from the record of the present Congress. The election must be won upon his own personality; upon the general Republican achievement of the past twelve years; and, by no means least, upon the rather absurd attitude of the Democracy.

I hope you have seen Laszló's picture and like it. *Faithfully yours*

4726 · TO ALBERT JEREMIAH BEVERIDGE   *Roosevelt Mss.*

Washington, May 25, 1908

My dear Senator: I have seen the bill in its present form and gone over it with Commissioner Neill. Senator McLaurin's amendment is all wrong.[1] Otherwise the bill will represent a real and marked advance and it will be a fine thing to pass it. I find there is a very strong feeling among some of the labor people not only that the bill ought to be past, but that its failure now will be charged to your opposition last week. I greatly regret that you felt obliged to offer the substitute.[2] McLaurin's amendment ought to be defeated. Otherwise, in my judgment, the duty of the friends of the policies which we have tried to put thru during the last six years is to turn in heartily and try to enact this bill, and not try to kill it by the effort to substitute any other for it. I would have preferred a better bill, a more radical bill, such as I understand was the one that you preferred when you held up this bill last week; but to kill a good bill because we cannot get thru a better one would be a very grave mistake. You spoke of this bill this morning as a sham. It is not a sham. On the contrary it is a good bill, which does not go far enough, but which does achieve something substantial so far as it goes. We should in the future have far better chance of getting what we want as an amendment to this bill than if we now defeat this bill. The position is analogous to that of the Hepburn railway rate bill a couple of years ago when certain people very unwisely wisht to defeat the bill because they thought it did not go far enough. If they had had their way we should have had no legislation at all; whereas in actual fact we got a most excellent measure. I sincerely hope that all you can do to help Depew in getting thru this bill (knocking out the McLaurin amendment) will be done. If the bill does not go thru the Senate it will look like bad faith, and I do not believe that the labor people will discriminate as to whether the opposition took the form of insisting on an impossible better bill, or of simply beating any bill offered. *Sincerely yours*

P.S. Soon after Congress adjourns I will arrange to see you, when we can have a chance for a full talk.

[1] McLaurin's amendment to the compensation act would have transferred the power to pass on the question of contributory negligence from the Secretary of Commerce and Labor to the judge of the district in which a federal employee was injured. The amendment was voted down.
[2] See No. 4720, note 1.

Washington, May 26, 1908

My dear Senator: I have your letter of the 25th, with enclosure, which I return herewith. Mr. Neill came to me and told me how the labor men felt and showed me a statement in a newspaper asking that the bill be passed now in its present form. Senator Depew told me that he was trying to get the bill up but that they could do nothing if you insisted upon your substitute, and the men who have been most anxious to get the bill thru were those who felt that last week it would have gone thru if it had not been for the fact that the impression was conveyed to the Senate, as I find it was conveyed, that you would force a fight on your substitute. I entirely agree with what you say about the attitude of Senators Hale and Aldrich in attempting to kill this bill. My effort has been to prevent the possibility of the friends of the legislation, and notably of you, being put in the position of being responsible for the defeat of the bill — just as it was my desire that no excuse should be given the people who were against the child labor bill for the District (in the shape of a statement) to say that they dared not bring it up because you would try to substitute the national child labor legislation for it. A very long experience has taught me that the wisest and most cunning foes of reform legislation of this kind hail with peculiar delight the overradical movement of some fervent friend who thereby puts them in the attitude of being able to say that he shares with them the responsibility for the defeat of the movement.

Moreover, when you speak about my being misinformed as to your attitude I must remind you that my knowledge was gained from you yourself here the other morning in your conversation with me in the presence of Taft. You vigorously denounced the bill as a sham; stated that you had tried to get a better bill substituted for it; that we ought to beat the present bill and substitute the bill for which you were fighting in its place. So that when I spoke of your killing the bill I was simply speaking of the attitude you took with the utmost possible emphasis and in entirely unmistakable language in this interview with me yesterday morning. You did not utter one word in that interview to give me the impression that you were fighting for the bill; but you again and again said with all possible emphasis and in many different forms of expression that the bill was a sham, a pretense, an insult; that it ought to be beaten; and that you were going to fight to substitute another bill in its place. If I have been in error as to your attitude the error was due to your own words in this interview.[1] *Sincerely yours*

[1] In the debate on the compensation bill, Beveridge had been a restrained advocate of his own substitute measure (see No. 4720, note 1). Nevertheless, even before Roosevelt interceded, the senator had worked "to get the bill up for consideration and to advance it" on the calendar. Roosevelt's letters persuaded him to abandon the proposed substitute.

Roosevelt Mss.

Personal Washington, May 28, 1908

My dear Judge: [1] One word additional, which I know I can write you be-cause of our past relations. I see that two of the West Virginia delegates who were elected under instructions for Taft have announced that they will go for me, and I have seen a letter from Governor Dawson[2] in which he states that he has first-hand information that they have done this in response to pressure from the Standard Oil Company. I should doubt the trustworthiness of the last, because all the information I have, public and private, is that the first thing the Standard Oil Company wishes is to have *anybody* else nomi-nated to succeed me in the Presidency,[3] and they are trying to defer all liti-gation simply to have it past over the fourth of March next. But the rumor is of importance because it shows the kind of thing that will be said, and will inevitably be said, of any man who, having been instructed for Taft, changes and goes for me ⟨(especially if as in this case the change is made even before the convention meets, even before the first ballot is held)⟩. Can you not quietly inform the gentlemen in question how strongly I feel (and I trust how strongly you also feel) that they ought to abide by their instructions? I think this is important from their own standpoint, from my standpoint, and what is of infinitely more consequence, from the standpoint of the party and the country. *Faithfully yours*

4729 · TO JOHN ALBERT TIFFIN HULL *Roosevelt Mss.*

Washington, May 28, 1908

My dear Chairman Hull: I enclose a letter which Secretary Taft has just sent me. He informs me that he has submitted to the Military Affairs Committees of the House and Senate a bill for the elimination of dead material in the army among the officers which will facilitate promotions.[1] Of course, I know that probably nothing can be done at this session, but I sincerely trust a bill will be past at the next session. *Sincerely yours*

[1] Alston Gordon Dayton, Republican congressman from West Virginia, 1895-1905; since 1905 United States district judge for the northern district of his state.
[2] William Mercer Owens Dawson, chairman of the West Virginia Republican State Committee, 1891-1904; Governor of West Virginia, 1905-1909.
[3] Roosevelt's doubts were legitimate; there is no evidence that the rumor had any basis in fact. If for any reason the West Virginia delegation in May wavered from the true course, by June it had returned. All fourteen of the state's votes were cast for Taft.

[1] The elimination bill revised the army promotion system by automatically retiring at regular intervals a fixed number of officers who were "not necessarily unfit, but the least fitted to remain in the service." Congress, with its characteristic lack of interest in administrative or military reforms, took no action.

Washington, May 28, 1908

Dear Cabot: I am surprised at what you say about Harriman. Did you notice that his stocks fell off five points, much more markedly than any other stocks on the market, when the news of what we had done in this merger suit was made public? Of course I am a good deal more skeptical as to what Mellen and even Byrnes may say about this matter since the experience I had with them at the time of the steamboat merger. You remember that they at that time used Morse as the bugbear just as they are now using Harriman. They told me they did not want to dispose of the steamboats then because to do so would give Morse a monopoly of all steamboat traffic to Boston. I think that what they said had an element of truth in it, but the result of my declining to interfere, which was all they asked, was that they then proceeded themselves to obtain the exact monopoly which they had warned me that Morse would obtain.[1]

Your letter is so private in its character that I hardly like to put it before Bonaparte; but if you or any of those for whom you are speaking will write to me a letter that can be kept on the files of the Department of Justice, for them to consider in reference to any future action, please send it to me.

With love to dear Nannie, *Ever yours*

[*Handwritten*] We think of you and your poor sister all the time; with the deepest tenderness and concern for you, the deepest concern and sympathy for her; we know how dark are the days through which you are passing.

4731 · TO ALSTON GORDON DAYTON   *Roosevelt Mss.*

Personal   Washington, May 29, 1908

My dear Judge: A line in addition to what I wrote you yesterday, as I fear I did not express quite as plainly as I should my feeling on one point. I most strenuously object to any friend of mine going for me on *any* ballot. But what I wanted to convey was that as regards the first ballot the only honorable course, in my judgment, which an instructed delegate can follow is to vote in accordance with his instructions. To do otherwise would necessarily give rise to very unpleasant comment, not only as regards the delegate him-

[1] As Roosevelt explained, the Administration had permitted the New Haven to retain its steamboat holdings after Mellen and Timothy E. Byrnes argued that the disposition of those holdings would permit Charles W. Morse and his associates to monopolize Atlantic coastal shipping. This preventive cure, the President now realized, was no better than the disease would have been. That Roosevelt cited the episode in this letter suggests that Lodge, the persistent advocate of the New Haven, had maintained that Bonaparte's petition against that railroad benefited the Harriman interests. Such an argument was a characteristic device of the defenders of the New Haven, who had throughout the long controversy over the road's holdings continually accused Brandeis of persecuting Morgan in order to aggrandize Kuhn, Loeb and Company and Harriman.

self but as regards the man for whom he voted. As a matter of fact, we will nominate Taft on the first ballot by about 700 votes; so we do not really have to concern ourselves with what comes after the first ballot, and my object is to keep men square on this ballot. But I need hardly add that even if there should have to be another ballot, my friends are *not* to go for me. *Sincerely yours*

4732 · TO LYMAN ABBOTT   *Roosevelt Mss.*

Washington, May 29, 1908

My dear Dr. Abbott: As to the matter of my renomination, it seems to me that the proper ground to take is that any man who supposes that I have been scheming for it, is not merely a fool, but shows himself to be a man of low morality. He reflects upon himself, not upon me. There has never been a moment when I could not have had the Republican nomination with practical unanimity by simply raising one finger. At this moment I am still actively engaged in getting delegates for Taft — as in Texas, for instance, to mention something that occurred a week ago; or in preventing delegates who have been instructed for Taft from declaring that they would go for me anyhow — to cite action which I took yesterday as regards two delegates in West Virginia. Any man competent to express any opinion whatever knows this perfectly well. He knows that not merely the far West but that, for instance, the conventions of New York, New Jersey, Massachusetts and Vermont would have gone for me with the wildest enthusiasm if I had merely said I was willing to abide by the judgment of the party as to whether or not it was expedient that I should run.[1] Under such circumstances, when I could without the slightest difficulty have made each State convention declare for me with infinitely greater enthusiasm than any State convention has shown about anything yet, it is simply silly to suppose that I would go into some intrigue even more futile than tortuous — an intrigue that would have to be kept secret from all my best friends, including, for instance, Senator Lodge, and Loeb, and all my family — an intrigue which would be entirely pointless, and almost certainly of no avail. Moreover, be it remembered that the same people who speak of this as my secret intention are at other times the ones who are loudest in denouncing me for trying to bring about Taft's nomination. The real fact is, as most of them know perfectly well, that noth-

[1] This was also the view of Seth Bullock, who on May 31 wrote Loeb: "As you know the Western States in my bailiwick have all had their roundups and selected delegates to the Chicago Convention each delegate being branded with a circle T, the Secretary's brand; they would only stand for a hair brand, however, and it will be necessary to have them counted quickly at the Convention on the 16th of June, for if they 'mill around' much [of] the hair will shed off and disclose the Maltese Cross brand burned into their hides by the people and there will be trouble about the ownership. The people want and will insist on the President holding his position for another term so you may expect many bad half hours at Chicago." — Roosevelt Mss.

ing could have prevented my renomination excepting the most resolute effort on my part to get someone else accepted as representing me and nominated in my place; and I had this object partly in view in endeavoring to get Taft nominated, altho I was of course mainly actuated by the fact that I think that of all men in this country Taft is the best fitted at this time to be President and to carry on the work upon which we have entered during the past six years.

The facts about the third-term agitation are that it does not come from any men high in public life, but from plain people who take no very great part in politics, and who seem to have been puzzled at my attitude in declining to run. The politicians, like the big-business men, all cordially agree with me that I ought not to run again. A few weeks ago there was an article published in *Success* which you ought to see if you have any desire to know where the third-term talk comes from; it isn't "inspired" from above at all. Yesterday, for instance, Vorys, Taft's campaign manager in Ohio, suddenly told me that he had difficulty in Ohio in preventing the ordinary voters, the men whom he would meet at the drugstores or in the cars, or in similar places, from insisting upon my being renominated. Under such circumstances I would be exasperated, if I were not amused, at so much as anybody talking about the supposition that I was engaged in an effort to have the renomination forced upon me. As a matter of fact I doubt if Taft himself could be more anxious than I am that Taft be nominated, and that any stampede to me be prevented. I wish it on every account, personal and public, and I am bending every energy now to prevent the possibility of such a stampede; because if the convention were stampeded and I were nominated an exceedingly ugly situation would be created, a situation very difficult to meet at all, and ⟨probably difficult⟩ impossible to meet satisfactorily; whereas, if as I have every reason to believe, Taft is nominated almost by acclamation, certainly on the first ballot, everything is as it should be.

Do tell your Mr. Steiner how I like his articles on the immigrant.[2] I grow extremely indignant at the attitude of coarse hostility to the immigrant taken by so many natives of the type he describes. I have never had much chance to deal with the Slav, Magyar, or Italian; but wherever I have had the chance I have tried to do with them as with the German and the Irishman, the Catholic and the Jew, and that is, treat them so as to appeal to their self-respect and make it easy for them to become enthusiastically loyal Americans as well as good citizens. I have one Catholic in my Cabinet and have had another, and I now have a Jew in the Cabinet; and part of my object in each appointment was to implant in the minds of our fellow-Americans of Catholic or of Jewish faith, or of foreign ancestry or birth, the knowledge that they have in

[2] Edward Alfred Steiner, European-born and educated American sociologist; professor of applied Christianity at Grinnell College, Iowa; author of several books on the immigrant, had just published in the May 30, 1908, *Outlook* his essay, "From the Lovczin to Guinea Hill."

this country just the same rights and opportunities as everyone else, just the same chance of reward for doing the highest kind of service; and therefore just the same ideals as a standard toward which to strive. I want the Jewish young man who is born in this country to feel that Straus stands for his ideal of the successful man rather than some crooked Jew money-maker. I want the young Catholic of Irish or French descent to feel that if he acts as a good American should, he can become a Cabinet minister like Bonaparte or Wynne; a Governor of the Philippines, like Smith; a judge, like Tracey; in short, that the right chance is open to him and the right ideals before him. In my Cabinet there sit together Meyer, whose granduncle was a colonel under Blucher at Waterloo; and Bonaparte, whose great grandfather was Napoleon's brother and a king whom Meyer's granduncle helped to over-throw. That they are both good Americans and nothing else is all that we think of; ⟨and it is not considered⟩ nobody asks whether any member of my Cabinet is of English, or Scotch, or Dutch, or German, or Irish descent; whether he is Protestant, Catholic or Jew. In short, we have acted on prin-ciples of straight Americanism; and I am glad that before I end my term I shall have in my Cabinet Luke Wright, a representative of the South, a man who fought in the Confederate service, and who is just as loyal an American today as the best veterans of the Grand Army. It was the one thing which I felt was wanted to ⟨point out⟩ emphasize the entire Americanism of the Cab-inet, to give it from the national standpoint an absolutely representative char-acter.

So give my regards to Steiner. I wish I could help in some striking fashion to do justice to, and get justice for, the Slav! ⟨just as I hope I have succeeded in doing any good for representatives of other races⟩ — and our other recent immigrants just as has finally been done for the sons of those who came here a generation ago. *Faithfully yours*

4733 · TO KERMIT ROOSEVELT   *Roosevelt Mss.*

Washington, May 30, 1908

Dearest Kermit: This week has been real summer weather. The grounds are too beautiful for anything. After lunch Mother and I often sit on the seat by the fountain under the apple tree. Every evening we have had dinner together out on the East terrace, screened by the bay trees from the view of any passersby, and after dinner we have usually sat for an hour on the south portico — the air heavy with the fragrance of the honeysuckle and jasmine. We have had two or three good rides, I on old Achilles as neither Roswell nor Audrey is yet well; and I have never seen the laurel lovelier than this season; but the woods are lovely all through. I am so glad that our last spring at the White House has been so beautiful.

I don't mind a bit your having been turned off the first eight, and I am very glad you have continued, going on the second. I am very much concerned over what you have written about Archie, but I shall say nothing to him at present. I know the little fellow has worked as hard as he knew how, and I quite agree with you that he ought to be allowed to try to stay with his form. Personally I would a great deal rather that he kept on after a fashion with his form for three years and then left Groton, instead of now being dropped into another form. But I will have to wait before I make any decision.

Congress is ending with a pointless and stupid filibuster by La Follette,[1] who is an entirely worthless Senator; it is sheer idiocy for the Senate to permit such silly rules as will allow this kind of filibuster. Congress has not given me nearly all the legislation I should have had; but there has been some advance, after all. In foreign matters and as regards the navy and the army Congress has really done well. A number of treaties have been ratified, the upbuilding of the fleet continued, the army and navy better paid, the Tokyo exposition has been provided for, the Chinese indemnity returned.[2] Then in home matters we have past a good employers' liability bill and a child labor bill for the District of Columbia. We have handled the Alaska coal fields as they ought to be handled.[3] So that, altho I am chagrined that more has not been done, I am glad that we have gone a little ahead and not a little behind.

I have two first-rate maps of the part of Africa we are to go to. As soon as I see you we will begin to try to crystallize our plans for the trip. *Your loving father*

4734 · TO THEODORE ROOSEVELT, JUNIOR   *Roosevelt Mss.*

Washington, May 30, 1908

Dearest Ted: Of course you shall buy a dingo pup if you want it. We can stand it if you can! But what in the world started you to want to get it? I should think it would be about as sociable as a hyena. But if you wish it, *of course* get it.

Mother and Ethel have just gone down the river for a three days' trip with several other people, including brothers honorary Winthrop and Phillips. I am very busy as Congress is just closing. Today old Captain Bill Mc-

[1] La Follette, in a preliminary test of his own strength before his later, more celebrated, filibusters, had condemned the Aldrich-Vreeland Bill (See No. 4566) for eighteen hours. He had, along the way, touched also upon the failure of Congress to pass more comprehensive labor and antitrust legislation. Assisting him were Democratic Senators William J. Stone of Missouri and Thomas P. Gore of Oklahoma. Capitalizing on Gore's blindness, Gallinger on May 30 moved a roll call just in time to save the currency measure; see Stephenson, *Aldrich*, pp. 330–331.
[2] The United States returned $10,785,286 of the Boxer indemnity. This money the Chinese government placed in a trust fund for the education of Chinese youths in America.
[3] Following the recommendation of the President and the Secretary of the Interior, Congress had passed a law enabling coal locators in Alaska to consolidate their holdings so as to facilitate the development of coal fields in the territory; see *House Report*, 60 Cong., 1 sess., no. 1728.

Donald, the Texas ranger, who was with me on my wolf hunt turned up and took lunch with me. I said to him "By the way, Captain, since I saw you you have killed a man," to which he responded coyly, "Why, Colonel, — I have killed a bunch!" Until Quentin goes to bed the house is entirely lively; after that the rooms seem big and lonely and full of echoes. The carpets and curtains are all away, as the heat of summer has begun. You are now hard at work at your examinations. Well, in three weeks I shall see you, and we are looking forward eagerly to it and to talking everything over with you. *Your loving father*

[*Handwritten*] I went out to Arlington with nice old Major Loeffler to put flowers on the graves.

4735 · TO HENRY CABOT LODGE   *Roosevelt Mss.*

Private   Washington, June 1, 1908

Dear Cabot: I enclose a letter of which Hitchcock has a copy.[1] It is to be shown quietly to any of the Taft delegates who show the slightest symptoms of going for me, for you will see that it is written for use with the two Taft delegates from West Virginia. Just this morning I have spoken to Hopkins, of Illinois, and Campbell, of Kansas, telling them that they were to join with you and Hitchcock to see that no stampede for me was to gather headway for a moment. I am exceedingly anxious on every account, my own no less than Taft's, to avoid the necessity of another public utterance, which I think would do real damage and make us both look rather ridiculous. So I hope that you and Hitchcock can use the letter I enclose with any delegates who seem at all doubtful, and I should think it would straighten them out. I think the best plan to follow would be not to show this letter to any person unless both you and Hitchcock agree that it is really necessary. Be extremely careful that it is regarded as absolutely secret, and under no circumstances is reference to it to be made in the press. I fear that if it does get out I will be put in the position of protesting too much.

I thought that Knox made a tomfool Memorial Day address at Gettysburg. Imagine a Republican Senator saying that if necessary we ought to resort to civil war in order to prevent the Union from destroying the States![2] There is no such danger; and Knox makes La Follette look a miracle of self-

[1] The enclosed was No. 4728. Roosevelt on June 1 sent a copy to Frank H. Hitchcock with instructions similar to those in this letter to Lodge.
[2] Knox's tomfoolery had been less dangerous politically than one of Taft's ineptitudes. Speaking at Grant's Tomb on Memorial Day to an audience consisting largely of Union veterans, Taft described Grant's amazing recovery from that time when the hero of the G.A.R. had "resigned from the army because he had to. He had yielded to the weakness of a taste for strong drink." Although Taft told the truth, although he praised Grant's achievements, the veterans deeply resented what they considered an unnecessary and irrelevant discussion of their commander's youthful indiscretions; see Pringle, *Taft*, I, 348–349.

restraint and unselfish wisdom by comparison when he indulges in such chatter. *Ever yours*

4736 · TO ELMER HASKELL YOUNGMAN *Roosevelt Mss.*

Washington, June 2, 1908

My dear Sir: [1] I am in receipt of your letter of the 1st instant. You say that the currency measure "was passed against the protest of some of the best-informed monetary authorities of the country." The distressing feature of the situation was that every measure that was mentioned of every kind, sort or description was protested against, not merely by some but by the majority of those whom we had a right to regard as the best-informed monetary authorities of the country. These same best-informed monetary authorities were wholly unable to agree upon anything substantive or constructive. They could not even agree upon any measure that would help us to a temporary solution. The effort in Congress was only to do just precisely what you describe — that is, accomplish something in the interest of producers, wage earners, and merchants. I am confident that this was done; but I am ⟨confident⟩ well aware that it was only a makeshift, an emergency measure, and that the commission provided for ought to be able to adopt some permanent plan. The course that has been adopted is "square and honest," and the course that will be adopted for the future will be square and honest. I very earnestly hope that in the future we will receive more assistance than we have yet received from the well-informed monetary authorities to enable us to have a law past, not in any way in the interest of stock speculators and bond syndicates, but in the interest of the businessmen, farmers and wageworkers. *Sincerely yours*

4737 · TO RAY STANNARD BAKER *Roosevelt Mss.*

Personal Washington, June 3, 1908

Dear Baker: I have your letter of the 5th instant. I read your article[1] with interest, but on some points with much less agreement than I have felt with most of your articles. I have been obliged to study the careers of Tillman, Vardaman, and Jefferson Davis of Arkansas, simply in connection with my

[1] Elmer Haskell Youngman, editor of the *Bankers' Magazine*, journal of the American Bankers' Association, which had vigorously opposed the Aldrich-Vreeland Bill (see No. 4566). In an attack oddly parallel to that of La Follette, Youngman denounced the bill, passed on May 30, as the work of "certain financial interests" who were seeking a market for their "indigestible securities." He urged Roosevelt to veto "this bond-syndicate and stock speculators' currency law." Youngman and the American Bankers' Association, almost as strongly opposed to the radical Fowler Bill, advocated a third plan providing for modified asset currency.

[1] Ray Stannard Baker, "Negro in Politics," *American Magazine*, 66:169–180 (June 1908). This was the last of a series of five articles by Baker on various aspects of the Negro problem.

work. I am satisfied that they have had a deeply debasing effect upon our young men. I have no question that Tillman has some good points — the other two may have good points because they are human beings, but I have not discovered them. They have trained all the young men who have come under their influence to believe that yelling, foul-mouthed vulgarity; coarse abuse in the most violent terms of all opponents; crass and brutal class selfishness, equally hostile to the class above or the class below; blatant contempt for the ordinary decencies of civilization, including common courtesy and physical cleanliness; and readiness violently to champion everything from murder down if the slightest political advantage is to be gained therefrom — they have taught the young men that to indulge in all this is the way to achieve success. It seems to me a great pity that you and the *American Magazine* should in the name of reform and civic betterment add to this impression. Yet I think that this is precisely the impression that you strengthened; for from what I have seen the deepest mark left on the average man from the South who does not consider well is that you are standing by Tillman and Vardaman and Jefferson Davis. Of course those who read carefully will see far more in your article, but there are a great multitude who do not read carefully.

Personally I think you lay altogether too much stress, or rather a twisted stress, upon your theory that everywhere and at all times political thought divides itself into two opposing forces, two great parties or points of view "representing the fundamental social conflict between the few and the many." I think the facts of history directly disprove your statement that slavery in the South was abolished, as an incident to this struggle, "because it was undemocratic." On the contrary the mob of the North, and most of the politicians who howlingly demanded the rule of mere numbers, were violently pro-slavery. This was as true in the country districts of Indiana as in the crowded city of New York. The restriction of slavery was due to the growth of the ethical resentment against it. Its abolition was due to the firm belief which finally grew up in the minds of men that it was inconsistent with national union. A greater proportion of the Few than of the Many went into the final movement for its destruction. Tillman, Jefferson Davis, and Vardaman do not represent in the least championship for the Many on principle; but championship either of the Many or of the Few by accident. There are in every community some men who are natural champions of privilege; and others, of the Lincoln type, who are natural opponents of privilege and champions of equal rights. There are in addition a great many men of good instincts who do not think clearly on the subject; and finally there are a considerable number of men who are actuated by their self-interest or by the accidents of their position. The coarsest and most violent demagogs are often at bottom of precisely the same nature and actuated by the same motives as the coarsest and most violent despots. The man is either despot or demagog as the accidents of his position determine. The three men you mention exactly illustrate what I mean. It has been to their interest to champion the cause of the poor white, the ignorant white, who lives in poverty, as against the white man who has more money and has enjoyed greater advantages. To the superficial view, therefore, they appear as the representatives of the great principle of democracy as against aristocracy. How ridiculous this view is, is shown by the fact that each man stands, not passively or moderately, but with a fury which amounts to mania and frequently turns into homicidal mania, against the majority where the majority happens to be black. This is partly because neither of the men is a genuine democrat at all but is simply an intolerant advocate of privilege for his own caste — for the poor whites as against the well-to-do whites, for the poor whites as against the blacks. It is even more an expression of a fundamental fact far deeper than that which you think is fundamental; the fact of the conflict between race and race, which, with the average man, goes immeasurably farther down in his soul than any conflict between the Few and the Many. If you treat the trouble that we have with the Negro, the trouble as regards misconduct on the part of the white man and misconduct on the part of the black man, as merely an incident to a democratic struggle, you will fall into the most far-reaching error. The question is one of race. This is not a matter of theory at all. All you have to do is to study the history of Haiti when it yielded to the influence of the French Revolution, and see what became of the Jacobite or ultrademocratic movement after it had been tried for a year or two in that island. The condition of Haiti today and the condition of Liberia today is something with which I am obliged practically to deal as President; just as I have to deal now and then with race prejudice both in the South and in the North. To say that any trouble or any conflict in connection with the fearful deterioration of either Haiti or Liberia has anything whatever to do with the conflict between the Few and the Many is, my dear Mr. Baker, pure nonsense. In exactly the same way no progress whatever will be made toward solving the Negro problem if we apply to it a wholly inapplicable simile.

I have so greatly enjoyed your articles and have profited so much from them that I am really sorry to see you show symptoms of being misled by this prevalent habit of hasty and exceedingly unwise generalization. Here in America, taken as a whole our salvation lies in applying the democracy of Abraham Lincoln. I have a thoro and hearty distrust, a distrust which has grown steadily ever since I left college and took part in the practical affairs of men, both of the very well-to-do people who would like to give our Government and our social system a plutocratic caste, and of the other people, who find their chief exponents in papers like the New York *Nation* and New York *Evening Post*, who believe that an arid and cloistered culture produces a class worthy of special consideration; I am a democrat of the democrats; my friends and supporters, the people in whom I believe, are the plain people who work with their hands, on the farm, in the factory, on the railroads. But I no more believe in a mob than I believe in a plutocracy;

and I am no more to be misled by a foolish appeal on behalf of the Many than by a foolish appeal on behalf of the Few. As regards many races, and as regards some populations of the remaining races, notably some European populations, the whole effort to translate the terms of the real struggle for righteousness into the terms of a fanciful struggle between the Many and the Few is an effort which does not represent real facts and which can only result in confusion and damage. Most of our fighting for betterment has to do not at all with a conflict between the Few and the Many, but with the improvement of the man as a man, whether he comes in one category or the other. At the moment I am engaged in a savage fight with the big financier caste, the big Wall Street crowd, because I am fighting privilege; but I have fought the Western Federation of Miners, the whole mob spirit, just as hard; and I believe with all my soul that irreparable harm is done by teaching men to substitute hatred of evil in one class only for hatred of all evil as it shows itself in any man in any class. Marat and Robespierre did not improve on the morality of the worst nobles of the Old Regime; they merely damaged freedom as their predecessors had damaged order. I fight against privilege; I fight for the control of great wealth; I fight against mob rule; I fight for equal opportunities for all; but more ardently still I desire to see the growth of a morality which will make each man self-respecting, will make him ashamed of either supporting or opposing another because that one belongs to either the Few or the Many, or to any other artificial aggregation of human beings, will make him just as intolerant of little graft as of big graft (otherwise both will flourish), will make him judge his neighbor, rich or poor, on that neighbor's worth, will make him try to be hardworking, energetic, thrifty, a good husband and father, a man concerned with his rights but concerned still more with his duties.

As for what you say about the colored man I have profited much by it; but I should like to put before you some considerations you have not emphasized.

If you can come on here I will explain what I mean more at length. *Sincerely yours*

4738 · TO CHAUNCEY MITCHELL DEPEW   *Roosevelt Mss.*

Washington, June 3, 1908

My dear Senator Depew: Congressman Malby[1] has written me as follows:

Late Friday afternoon, I found both Senators, Platt and Depew, in their seats in the Senate. I explained to both of them that I was obliged to leave that evening for New York, and would not return if Congress adjourned on Saturday; that I believe that public and political interests positively demanded a settlement of the situation at Plattsburg; and that there was but one way to settle it; and that the doing of anything else would be a gross mistake.

[1] George Roland Malby, a New York state senator while Roosevelt was governor, had been elected to Congress in 1906.

Senator Platt, whom I addressed first, wanted to know how Senator Depew felt about it. I told him that we would ascertain, and then requested Senator Depew to sit up close; I being between the two of them. Senator Platt said that he would do whatever Senator Depew would agree to. I then turned to Senator Depew and said: "Senator, it is up to you." He said: "All right, I will agree with Senator Platt." Then, I said: "You both, then, agree with me, first, that the President shall appoint Mr. John F. O'Brien collector of the Port of Champlain at Plattsburg, and that you will confirm before the present Senate adjourns, if you have an opportunity; and second, if you do not have an opportunity before adjournment, that you have no objections to the President's making the appointment during the recess, and that upon the reconvening of Congress that you will see to it that he is confirmed."

Both said "Yes, that is our agreement. If the President will make the appointment we will have no objections."

There was much more talk before we arrived at this definite conclusion, but this was the result.

In accordance therewith I shall appoint O'Brien. *Sincerely yours*

4739 · TO JOHN FRANKLIN JAMESON   *Roosevelt Mss.*

Washington, June 4, 1908

My dear Mr. Jameson:[1] I thank you for your letter. I realized that Mr. Adams[2] spoke humorously but I thought it just as well to emphasize the fact that we do not in the least need an addition of tons of printed matter to the hundreds of tons of printed matter for which the government is already responsible. The art of selection and rejection is almost as important as the arts needed by the modern historical investigator. *Sincerely yours*

4740 · TO JOSEPH LINCOLN STEFFENS   *Roosevelt Mss.*

Private and Personal   Washington, June 5, 1908

My dear Steffens: In view of Mr. Cosgrave's statement that I had read the proof of your very interesting article,[1] I think I ought to leave it on record

[1] John Franklin Jameson, professor of history at Brown, 1888-1901; Chicago, 1901-1905; director of the department of historical research of the Carnegie Institution, 1905-1928; chief of the division of manuscripts, Library of Congress, 1928-1937; managing editor of the *American Historical Review*, 1895-1901, 1905-1928; president of the American Historical Association, 1906-1907; author and editor of many informative volumes on American history.

[2] Charles Francis Adams was then a member of the subcommittee, appointed by Roosevelt, of the Committee on Departmental Methods, which was reviewing the government's policy on the publication of documentary materials. The other members of this subcommittee, leaders of the historical profession at that time, were Jameson, Worthington C. Ford, Albert Bushnell Hart, Alfred T. Mahan, Charles M. Andrews, William A. Dunning, Andrew C. McLaughlin, and Frederick Jackson Turner.

[1] Lincoln Steffens, "Roosevelt–Taft–La Follette on what the matter is in America and what to do about it," *Everybody's Magazine*, 18:723-736 (June 1908).

that I had not read the proof. I do this simply because the ordinary man would gather the impression — which I fear Cosgrave intended to convey — that as I had read the proof I endorsed all that you say. Now, as regards myself I am often interested in what you say; I sometimes agree with it and sometimes not; but I am always a hundred times more interested in some idea that you develop in the course of what you say about me than I am in what you thus say about me. You have an entire right to your opinion; and while I may or may not be interested in this opinion, I am a hundred-fold more interested in some idea which you apparently consider as incidental. Indeed, often I have been so wholly uninterested in your view of me, and so genuinely interested in your view of something else which you have developed in connection with the former, that I have simply forgot that you were expressing any view of me, and concentrated my attention on the other matter. It is a little difficult for me to express myself clearly without seeming to be slightly uncomplimentary. I know you will acquit me of any such intention. I merely wish to make it clear that I am not to be held as acquiescing in what you say because I do not express dissent from it. To me, for instance, it seems simply nonsense — a nonsense not much above the average spiritualistic seance type, or, to use another simile, not much above the average long-haired and wild-eyed violent socialist type, or the silly, self-advertising parlor socialist of the Robert Hunter type,[2] — to say that I am not interested in fighting *the* Evil or do not see the great underlying cause of it; whereas others, by which I suppose you mean La Follette, do see it. When you express this view either in conversation or writing I do not contradict you or comment upon it because it seems to me a mere foolish vagary on your part, and I pass it by to deal with the points where you really do express needed truths that have not been exprest as well. For instance, in this article, if I gather aright what you mean, you contend that Taft and I are good people of limited vision who fight against specific evils with no idea of fighting against the fundamental evil; whereas La Follette is engaged in a fight against *the* "fundamental" evil. Now, I am really flattered by your having as good an opinion of me as you have. I am pleased at it; and it would never enter my head to point out where I think it is erroneous, if it were not that apparently I am considered as having endorsed your views. Not only I do not endorse them, but I think them on this point childish. Your attitude is to my mind precisely the attitude of the man who patronizes a good country doctor because the latter admits that he cannot cure *all* diseases nor give a specific remedy against all "Disease"; whereas when you prefer La Follette as a type, I feel just as if you held up as better than this country doctor the man who blazons out that he has a particular kind of vegetable pill which will cure old age, consumption, broken legs, and every other ill to which flesh is heir. You

[2] Wiles Robert Hunter, sociologist; organizing secretary of the Chicago Bureau of Charities, 1896–1902; head worker, University Settlement of New York, 1902–1903; author of *Poverty* (1904), *Socialists at Work* (1908), and *The Crisis* (1909).

can say quite truthfully that the country doctor is fighting evils, not "*the Evil*"; you can also say that the other individual is showing real "leadership" and is going to put a stop not only to "evils" but to *all* "Evil"; but if you said this you would be saying something that was foolish. The same is absolutely as true of political life as of medical life. It is only the quack who will tell you that he has a cure for everything, whether in the world of medicine and surgery, in the world of politics, or in the world of social and industrial endeavor. For instance, you speak of La Follette as standing for the great principle of really representative government, and you seem to imply that the application of this principle would put a stop to all evils. It will do nothing of the kind, and if you proceed upon the assumption that it will, you will yourself work far-reaching harm and will work it in a foolish manner. I have made a pretty careful study of communities in which the initiative and referendum exist, as compared with communities which live under representative institutions, and the difference between them in point of average welfare is so small that I am unable to get up any special enthusiasm for one side or the other. The system of direct primaries under the law works a *slight* betterment over existing conditions. That is, it works, I think, on the whole a very slight improvement over the other system, but it is very slight and consists, on the whole, of a preponderance of slight betterments over slight hurts. An absolutely representative government in the Yazoo would bring about the condition of Haiti. You must have a pretty robust faith in names and theories if you think the conditions of Haiti satisfactory. Absolutely representative government in the city of New York would mean the very most trifling improvement over present conditions unless with it went hand in hand the uplifting of the conscience of the average man. I am trying, however feebly, to make men better, as well as to get better laws, better administration of the laws; and the first is by far the most important. Graft obtains in little things as well as in big; the little grafter is morally as bad as, and no worse than, the big grafter; and I wish to fight against graft, as such, and not let the issue be twisted into an attack on a class, which attack can never result in any real betterment. I am fighting evil in the mass, in the only way in which it is possible to fight it, when I fight different evils in the concrete. When you speak of "the system" you use a word that has a certain convenience and that appeals more or less to the imagination; but when you begin practically to speak of fighting "the system," as if it meant anything else than doing a man's duty according to the old standards, you simply lapse back into the condition of those religious enthusiasts of the days of Cromwell who announced that they wisht to fight "principalities and powers" and that they were for the "fifth monarchy, the monarchy of Jesus," and that it was useless to try to improve humanity unless by a radical change and the installation of the "fifth monarchy." This kind of talk did not indicate advanced morality nearly as much as it indicated an unsound mind, and the same statement applies exactly to those who use large phrases to cover up utter vagueness of thought when they come to deal with the political and social evils of today. La Follette has been three years in the Senate. His "plan" which you quote in the article referred to consists so far as it is good of a string of platitudes, and, practically, to adopt it wouldn't mean anything. He talks about the railroads; but as far as action goes, he has not helped at all, since he came to the Senate, in the great work we have actually done towards getting control over the railroads. He has rather hindered this work. Like Tillman he has made great personal gains by what he has done as Senator, because he has advertised himself so that both he and Tillman are very popular in chautauquas, where the people listen to them both, sometimes getting ideas that are right, more often getting ideas that are wrong, and on the whole not getting any ideas at all and simply feeling the kind of pleasurable excitement that they would at the sight of a two-headed calf, or of a trick performed on a spotted circus horse. I tried faithfully to work with La Follette, just as I tried faithfully to work with Aldrich. Neither has been of much use in public life during the last three years, each has often worked detriment. Now and then I have been able to work a little with one, and now and then to work with the other; but the deification of one is just as absurd as the deification of the other — I might add just as absurd as the diabolization of one or the other. The men who have done good in the twenty-five years I have been in politics are those who have had ideals but who have tried to realize them in plain, practical fashion, and who have tried to do each his duty as the day came, and to fight each evil as they found it arise without bothering their heads as to the "ultimate" evil. I believe in the men who take the next step; not those who theorize about the 200th step. Again my experience has been that mighty little good comes from the individual who is fighting "the system" in the abstract; just as mighty little good comes from the church member who is fighting Beelzebub in the abstract. I care nothing either for the reformer or the church member who does not try to do good in the concrete, and who is not ashamed to cover his deficiencies in particular concrete cases by vague mouthings about general abstract principles which are as nebulous in his mind as in the minds of others. It was Lincoln and Oliver P. Morton and the men like them who really saved the Union and abolished slavery, and relatively thereto the part was insignificant which was played by the Wendell Phillips and the Garrisons and the others who liked to think of themselves as "leaders," and to construct an imaginary plan for the perfection of everything which could not even be defined, and which could not have worked in one smallest part if there had been any attempt to realize it.

If you will come down to see me I will go over all this more at length with you, and for once, instead of passing by or brushing aside what you say about me or about anyone else with which I disagree, I will tell you just what I *do* disagree with. *Sincerely yours*

Washington, June 5, 1908

My dear Sir: The Inland Waterways Commission was appointed on March 14, 1907. It was appointed to meet the strongly expressed and reasonable demands of the people. Commercial organizations throughout the Mississippi Valley and elsewhere demanded then and still demand such improvement of waterways and development of navigation as will prevent traffic congestion and develop commerce.[1] It is an unpleasant fact that although the Federal Government has in the last half century spent more than a third of a billion dollars in waterways improvement, and although the demand for transportation has steadily increased, navigation on our rivers has not only not increased, but has actually greatly diminished. The method hitherto pursued has been thoroughly ineffective; money has been spent freely for improving navigation, but river navigation at least has not been improved; and there is a just and reasonable demand on the part of the people for the improvement of navigation in our rivers in some way which will yield practical results. It was for such reasons as these that the Commission of which you are Chairman was requested to consider and recommend a general plan of waterway improvement giving reasonable promise of effectiveness.

The preliminary report of the Inland Waterways Commission was excellent in every way. It outlines a general plan of waterway improvement which when adopted will give assurance that the improvements will yield practical results in the way of increased navigation and water transportation. In every essential feature the plan recommended by the Commission is new. In the principle of co-ordinating all uses of the water and treating each waterway system as a unit; in the principle of correlating water traffic with rail and other land traffic; in the principle of expert initiation of projects in accordance with commercial foresight and the needs of a growing country; and in the principle of co-operation between the States and the Federal

---

[1] The influence of "commercial organizations" on the development of Roosevelt's policies and the progressive movement deserves more attention. Along the Ohio, Missouri, and upper Mississippi rivers local manufacturers, merchants, and real-estate men formed committees to agitate for the improvement of inland waterways long before Roosevelt appointed a commission for this purpose. Earlier, associations of Midwestern grain dealers and national hardware producers and retailers had, before the introduction of the Hepburn Bill, demanded the expansion of the authority of the I.C.C. Typical of the groups whose membership supplied one source of recruits for the Bull Moose party was the United States Express Conference, an organization of Eastern shippers interested in the reduction of freight rates.

Roosevelt in his autobiography, making no reference to commercial organizations, attributed to Gifford Pinchot credit for inspiring the appointment of commissions on inland waterways, national conservation, and country life (*Autobiography,* Nat. Ed. XX, 359, and Numbers 4750, 4841). These commissions, concerned as they were with the problems of the American West, advanced and popularized the President's views on resources. Yet Roosevelt's motive in appointing them in 1908 was doubtless not entirely altruistic, for their work had immediate appeal for the voters in the most doubtful political region in the Presidential campaign.

Government in the administration and use of waterways, etc.: the general plan proposed by the Commission is new, and at the same time sane and simple. The plan deserves unqualified support. I regret that it has not yet been adopted by Congress,[2] but I am confident that ultimately it will be adopted.

Pending further opportunity for action by Congress, the work of the Commission should be continued with the view of still further perfecting the general plan by additional investigations and by ascertaining definitely and specifically why the methods hitherto pursued have failed. To this end I ask that the present members of the Waterways Commission continue their most commendable public service. I am asking three others to join them, namely: Senator William B. Allison, of Iowa; Hon. Joseph E. Ransdell, of Louisiana, a member of the Rivers and Harbors Committee of the House of Representatives and President of the National Rivers and Harbors Congress; and Professor George F. Swain, of the Massachusetts Institute of Technology, a recognized authority on water power. When a Chief of Engineers is appointed to succeed General Alexander MacKenzie, retired, I shall also designate him a member, in lieu of General MacKenzie, whose retirement relieves him of further duty on the Commission. The Commission will thus be increased from nine members to twelve.

In order to facilitate the work of the Commission, I shall shortly issue an Executive order along the lines suggested by your findings and recommendations, directing the Executive Departments to give the Commission access to their records and all necessary and practicable assistance in securing information for submission to the President and to Congress.

An indirect but useful result of the work of the Commission was the recent Conference of Governors on the Conservation of our Natural Resources, held in the White House May 13–15. I take great pleasure in repeating my public expression of indebtedness and my congratulations to the Commission for their signal public service in connection with this great Conference; it was an event which is likely to exert a profound and lasting influence on the development and history of our country.

Copies of this letter are being sent to each of the twelve members of the Inland Waterways Commission. *Sincerely yours*

4742 · TO WILLIAM BOYD ALLISON   *Roosevelt Mss.*

Washington, June 5, 1908

My dear Senator Allison: The work of the Inland Waterways Commission is of such importance to the people of the United States and especially to those of the Mississippi Valley that I am very anxious it should have the benefit of your assistance and advice, as well as the prestige of your name as one of its members. You have acted so thoroly with me in endeavoring to carry out the

[2] See No. 4719, note 1.

policies for which this Administration stands, your services to the country as a Senator have been so great and your co-operation would be so valuable that I sincerely hope you will find it possible to accept. Were it not that Mr. Burton is already Chairman of the Commission, and that the position entails an amount of work which you might find it difficult to give, I should ask you to take the Chairmanship and direct the work of the Commission. As it is, I hope you will give me the real pleasure of counting you among its members. *Sincerely yours*

4743 · TO JOHN LANCASTER SPALDING, EARL CRANSTON, EDWARD EVERETT HALE, AND OTHERS *Roosevelt Mss.*

Washington, June 6, 1908

Gentlemen: [1] In answer to your communication I can do little except express my cordial approval of what you say and my earnest hope that it may find practical realization. It is the merest truism to say that the power exercised by and thru the newspapers upon thought is far greater than ever before, and that therefore it is pre-eminently desirable that thru the newspapers there should systematically be brought to the minds of our people quickening and vital truths, and wise and timely counsel so exprest that it may be absorbed into the intellectual and spiritual life of the people. You who have signed this call occupy positions and possess qualifications which ought to enable you to appeal with peculiar effect to our people. I wish you Godspeed in your work. The list of signers includes the names of clergymen, of laymen, of educators, lawyers, men of capital, leaders of labor organizations. You should be able to cover well-nigh the whole broad field of our social, govern-mental and inner life. Of one thing I am certain, and this certainty makes me peculiarly glad to wish you well. You will speak not merely to men of one class, of one creed, of one occupation, but to all Americans, in the name of the great fundamental truths of righteousness which are alike dear to, and necessary to, each one of us. It would indeed be a sad and evil thing for America if the day should ever arrive when the great body of our people would feel their first loyalty to some caste or class rather than to the Nation as a whole, when they would treat any man primarily as an individual in, or representative of, a certain class, rather than on his worth as a man. To illustrate what I mean let me point out what has recently occurred in San Francisco. In an issue of the *Mining and Scientific Press* of last May appears the following statement:

[1]Spalding, Hale, Earl Cranston, Methodist Bishop of Washington, and other eminent clergymen of their views were, as usual, seeking to make the church a more effective force for good in American life. In this project their managing director was Earl C. Stinespring.

San Francisco's troubles began with the dominance of the labor union. The men who labor had to combine to protect themselves, for only by the force of combined action could they exact their share of industrial prosperity. Having discovered the power of combination, the labor unions went into politics. They made one of their own men Mayor of the city and obtained control of the municipal government. The nominees of the labor party proved to be crooks. An exposure followed. On the top of a wave of reformation an honest Mayor and a reputable Board of Aldermen were elected. An effort was made to punish those who had enriched themselves by bribery and other ways of corruption almost unspeakable. It was found that the merchants of the city and the captains of industry were accessories to the crime already partly investigated and exposed. All the power of the men in control of State politics, a large part of the financial power of the banks, a preponderance of the social power of the rich and fashionable people of the city, united in an effort to stifle the prosecution of the offenders against civic integrity, as soon as their own friends and associates were implicated. The crooks of the labor party went into offensive and defensive alliance with the crooks of the corporation party. The better kind of laboring man saw that if his leaders were crooked, the leaders of the capitalist class were no better and if money were to be made crookedly his own leaders might as well have it. The labor unions began the undermining of civic decency in this community; the corporations completed it. Thus the professional man, the average honest laborer, the average honest merchant, the average honest citizen, found himself between the upper millstone of the corrupting corporations and the nether millstone of the corrupted labor unions. That is the plight of San Francisco today.

One incident will suffice to indicate the true conditions of affairs. A Mr. A., the vice-president and general manager of a telephone company, was indicted, tried, and convicted of bribing the supervisors or board of aldermen. It was proved that $55,000 of the telephone company's money had been used for bribery and that $7500 was returned by some supervisors who accepted bribes from a rival telephone company anxious to get permission to do business in the city. In the code of thievery, a man who takes bribes from both sides is not honest, but one who stays bought is a real gentleman! The official who took the money from the telephone company's treasury and handed it to the go-between who paid it to the supervisors, gave evidence before the Grand Jury but refused to testify in the trial of his superior officer, and was sentenced to jail. This effort to shield crime was hailed as loyalty. Not long afterward, while A was still in jail, unable to attend to any business and unlikely to be able to take part in any of the affairs of the company, the directors of the telephone company met and re-elected him second vice-president and the other man third vice-president of their company. The directors of this company include some of the "best citizens" of San Francisco. By their action they set the seal of their approval on crime, they honored a man duly and properly convicted of a felony, and they asserted their rights to flout justice.

Now there are many lessons to be learned from the condition of affairs above set forth, but the first and most important lesson is the idle folly, the wicked folly, of attempting to substitute for the rule of right and wrong, the rule of adherence to some class, whether to labor or a labor union, or to capital or a corporation. The class consciousness shown by the businessmen of high social standing who shield a crook because not to do so will hurt business is on an exact level with the conduct of the labor people who stand by a crook because he is supposed to favor labor. Honest businessmen, honest capitalists, honest wageworkers should join to express their abhorrence of the crooked labor leader, of the corrupt or vicious or disorderly wageworker, and if possible their even greater abhorrence of the corrupt or brutally selfish capitalist or employer, and especially of the crooked political or business leader of great wealth and high social position. There are interests which particularly affect farmers as a class, or wageworkers as a class, or businessmen as a class. It is right that there should be special heed paid in legislation to these special interests. But the great fundamental interests are those affecting good citizenship, affecting all good citizens no matter what their occupations or their social prominence. The bonds that unite all decent men who think clearly and work hard, who perform their duties as good citizens toward their families, toward their neighbors, toward the state, are of immeasurably greater consequence than the bonds which merely unite the men who happen all to belong to a given profession or all to follow a given occupation. I hope you will preach the great doctrine that the tie which connects one laboring man with another, one capitalist with another, one businessman with another, is of indeed little consequence compared with the ties that should unite together all men who lead hardworking, useful, upright lives, without the slightest regard as to whether they are men who work with their heads or their hands, men who work for wages or who employ wageworkers, without the slightest regard to what creed they may profess or as to whether or not they are socially prominent. Of course those who have much should be judged more severely when they go wrong, than those of less opportunity, to whom temptation would naturally be greater. In such a case as that quoted above, the conduct of business and social leaders who commit crime should awaken an even greater abhorrence than the like conduct of labor men, of men of small means. But let us not forget that we cannot afford to condone little graft any more than big graft. If we attack crookedness, not because it is crookedness, but because it is shown by a certain class of men, we really play into the hands of those who are crooked; for they are only too delighted to substitute class consciousness, class feeling, for the elementary rules of morality. The scoundrel is always helped when he is attacked, not as a scoundrel, but as a member of a class; he is the one who really benefits by the substitution of class consciousness, class loyalty, for loyalty to the cause of fine and sound manhood. If we are to do our duty we must stand for good citizenship and for good citizens wherever they are found, and must condemn without stint, and try so far as may be to secure the punishment of, the evil doer, simply because he *is* an evil doer, and without the slightest regard to whether he is rich or poor, to whether his crime is one of cunning or one of violence. *Very truly yours*

Washington, June 6, 1908

My dear Mr. Bonaparte: Will you look at what Grosscup has done?[1] It seems to me at least doubtful whether we ought not to present articles of impeachment of him to Congress. At any rate will you not have the matter lookt into?

In theory Grosscup has always been an ultra anticorporation man, and for quite a time he took me in. I believed him, and believed that his trouble was chiefly that he was too radical.[2] I gradually became convinced that his radical views were exprest only in outside speeches and that his decisions were often improperly favorable to the corporations. I had, however, no idea that there was any such condition as, to judge by this publication, really existed. I think we should look up the matter to see whether or not we should not present him for impeachment to Congress. *Sincerely yours*

Washington, June 6, 1908

Dearest Kermit: Here summer is fully under way. During the past week the laurels have been in full bloom and as lovely as possible; in fact I have never seen a lovelier spring here in Washington than this one. Of course all of the spring blossoms have now gone — the iris flowers have vanished from round the north fountain. But the masses of honeysuckle everywhere in the country make the air fragrant, as they do the south portico after nightfall. I have never seen anything lovelier than the wealth of red, white and pink roses, mixt with purple and lilac clematis, on the iron railings that border the garden and on the trellis near the tennis court. The gardens are lovely too. After breakfast, and usually again after lunch, Mother and I walk round the grounds. Mother is very well and too dainty and pretty for anything.

[1] According to newspaper clippings which H. H. Kohlsaat had sent Roosevelt, United States Circuit Judge Grosscup had requested passes from railroad companies (see No. 4955). These charges reflected a strong antagonism which had grown up in Chicago against Grosscup, primarily because his recent decisions in the Chicago Union Traction Company cases favored the company. This hostility, however, may have had its origins in the Pullman strike of 1894 when Grosscup with Judge William A. Woods issued the injunction against Debs and the other officials of the American Railway Union and then with the district attorney wired Cleveland for troops.
[2] Although Grosscup favored regulation of corporations, he was certainly not a radical. In these years the judge was advocating in speeches and writings "with the constancy of a crusader" the need for industrial combination. Consolidation, he argued, was inevitable and promised great benefits to American society. As such, within proper bounds of government regulation, it was "the surest method of combatting socialism." Such an economic philosophy made him, despite his conflict with Roosevelt, a strong Progressive in 1912.

I enclose you letters from Buxton and Selous, and maps, together with an envelope in which please place them, after you have looked at them, and send them back to me. I shall not answer them until I have consulted with you. The time is near enough now for us to make our plans pretty definitely. I think I shall get a double-barrelled 450 cordite, but shall expect to use almost all the time my Springfield and my 45–70 Winchester. I shall want you to have a first-class rifle, perhaps one of the powerful new model 40 or 45 caliber Winchesters. Then it may be that it would be a good thing to have a 12-bore shotgun that could be used with solid ball. Perhaps you should also have a spare rifle. I am afraid the 30–30 is too light for African game. In any event we would thus have four rifles and the shotgun between us so as to allow for accidents. It is no child's play going after lion, elephant, rhino and buffalo. We must be very cautious; we must be always ready to back one another up, and probably we ought each to have a spare rifle when we move in to the attack. I shall have to consult with you as to the time to go, whether about the middle of April, or about the first of July.

The Rector has sent me what I am bound to say is a very convincing statement about Archie. I am tempted to let him drop back a class with the intention of having him then stay two years at Groton to get thoroly grounded in the rudiments, and then come up for two years' study of simply the things necessary to pass the Annapolis examination. But I shall wait until I see him and see you and talk things over. Your views impress me.

I enclose you an interesting note from Seth Bullock to Mr. Loeb.[1] It will be a hair-trigger convention at Chicago. If anything like a mass meeting of Republicans were assembled I do not deem it would be possible for me or anyone else to prevent my nomination. But we have as a matter of fact more than half the delegates elected under solemn pledges to Taft, and if we can prevent, as I am confident we can prevent, any break on the first ballot we shall in my judgment nominate him without any difficulty. In this case everything will go off quietly and well, for I don't see how there can be even an effort made to stampede the convention for me until after the first ballot. But if Taft's foolish opponents, who are even more my opponents, are able to hold up the nomination until after the first ballot there is a chance of a stampede for me, and if it really gets under way nothing that I could do would stop it. I don't think the chance is great; in fact, I think it very small, not more than one in a hundred; but I shall be heartily glad when the convention is over. All my close friends will do their best to stop a stampede of course, and I think they will succeed; for, as I have explained to them, if they allow the stampede to take place, nothing would ever persuade a certain number of people that it had not been with my connivance. I send you copies of letters I have put in the hands of Lodge and Hitchcock for use at the convention. *Your loving father*

[1] See No. 4732, note 1.

Washington, June 7, 1908

My dear Mr. Chapman: That is a most attractive invitation, but I am afraid at Oyster Bay we have no means of arranging to see the photographs. We have no electric light and no suitable rooms. Could you not come down to Washington next fall when we have returned here, and give us a chance to see the pictures in the White House? Then we could have in a number of people who ought to see them also. When you come I shall go over the question of what we should do about photographic matters on my African trip. My son Kermit, who is going with me has always been much interested in photography.

As regards the blue grosbeak, your description of the habits was exactly borne out by the conduct of the individuals we saw. They did not behave at all like indigo buntings or rosebreasted grosbeaks, but stayed by preference along the bushy sides of a ditch in the middle of an open pasture, frequently going out into the open grass. Both males and females would sit solemnly on the tops of some thick stalk or small twig a couple of feet high beside the ditch. The Bewick's wrens were very tame and confiding. To our ears not only their song but their subdued conversational chirping had a marked ventriloqual effect, seeming to be much farther away than it was. It had no resemblance to the song of the house wren, and none whatever to that of the Carolina wren.

I do not understand the principles upon which the sparrows are generically divided. The swamp sparrow seems to me in color scheme and even in voice to be more like a spizella than a zonotrichia. *Sincerely yours*

Telegram
Washington, June 7, 1908

I heartily agree with Taft's telegram to Hitchcock. No single contest should be settled except on its actual merits. In each case the man entitled to his seat should receive it, wholly without regard to whether he is for Taft or for any other candidate. It therefore follows that no compromise should even be considered, for failure to act on the simple principle of doing what is right in each case would amount to putting a premium upon wrong-doing. The great majority of the contests in the Southern States have been sheer fake contests, where, as I happen to know personally was the case in Florida, the so-called anti-Taft contestants were not in any proper sense of the word contestants at all, having literally no particle of claim to consideration and representing nothing whatever but the grossest and most barefaced fraud, and often fraud induced by money sent into the Districts from the North. It would be gravely hurtful to the future of honest politics to give the slightest consideration to claims so flimsy and so corrupt. It is no case for compromise.

Treat each contest absolutely on its merits. If the Taft delegate is entitled to his seat give it to him; if he is not so entitled, then give it to his opponent, no matter how distasteful or offensive this opponent may personally be.[1]

Roosevelt Mss.

Washington, June 8, 1908

My dear Mr. Spreckels: Now and then you, Mr. Langdon and Mr. Heney and the others who are associated with you must feel downhearted when you see men guilty of atrocious crimes who from some cause or other succeed in escaping punishment, and especially when you see men of wealth, of high business, and in a sense of high social, standing, banded together against you.[1] My dear sir, I want you to feel that your experience is simply the experience of all of us who are engaged in this fight. There is no form of slander and wicked falsehood which will not as a matter of course be employed against all men engaged in such a struggle, and this not only on the part of men and papers representing the lowest type of demagogy, but, I am sorry to say, also on the part of men and papers representing the interests that call themselves pre-eminently conservative, pre-eminently cultured. In such a struggle it is too often true that the feeling against those engaged in it becomes peculiarly bitter, not merely in the business houses of the great financiers who directly profit by the wrongdoing, but also in the clubs, in certain newspaper offices where business interests exercise an unhealthy control and, I regret to add, in other newspaper offices which like to be considered as to a marked degree the representatives of the cultivation and high social standing of the country. Now, I do hope that you and your colleagues will treat all this bitterness with entire disregard. It is of small consequence to you, or to any of us who are engaged in this work, whether men think well or ill of us personally; but it is of very great consequence that we should do the work without flinching, on the one hand, and, on the other hand, without losing our good-humored common sense, without becoming angered and irritated to a degree that will in any way cause us to lose our heads.

Therefore, I hope that you, Langdon, and Heney, and your associates, will

[1] The National Committee was then ruling on the claims of contesting delegations to the National Convention. To preserve harmony, various Taft and anti-Taft leaders had proposed the compromise solution of seating some delegates from each faction. Although such an arrangement would not have prevented Taft's nomination, it might have permitted the opponents of the President to exercise more control over the new National Committee whose members were to be chosen by the state delegations. Perhaps to prevent this, Roosevelt and Taft refused to condone compromise. Of the contests at issue, all involving Southern delegations, only one, that of Louisiana, was compromised; see Lodge, II, 299, and No. 4589.

[1] Rudolph Spreckels, the most aggressive and versatile member of his family, after succeeding in the management of the Hawaiian Commercial and Sugar Company and of the San Francisco Gas Company, divided his energies between banking and civic reform. In the latter capacity, he organized and financed the San Francisco graft prosecution of 1906.

keep reasonably good-natured; but that above all things you will not lose heart. You must battle on valiantly, no matter what the biggest businessmen may say, no matter what the mob may say, no matter what may be said by that element which may be regarded as socially the highest element. You must steadfastly oppose those foolish or wicked men who would substitute class consciousness and loyalty to class interest, for loyalty to American citizenship as a whole, for loyalty to the immutable laws of righteousness, of just and fair dealing as between man and man. It is just as bad to be ruled by a plutocracy as by a mob. It is profoundly un-American, and, in a social sense, profoundly immoral, to stand for or against a given man, not because he is or is not a brave, upright and able man, but because he does or does not belong to a labor union or does or does not represent the big business interests. In their essence, down at the foundation of things, the ties that are all important are those that knit honest men, brave men, square-dealing men, together, and it is a mighty poor substitute if we replace these ties by those that bind men together, whether they are good or bad, simply because they follow a particular business, have a given social standing, or belong to a particular organization. It is an evil and a dreadful thing for laboring men to endeavor to secure the political dominance of labor unions by conniving at crooked-ness or violence, by being "loyal" to crooked labor leaders; for to be "loyal" to the fancied interests of the unions, when they are against the laws of morality and the interests of the whole people, means ultimately the destruction of the unions themselves, as an incident to the destruction of all good citizenship. But it is if anything an even more evil and dreadful thing to have the merchants, the businessmen, the captains of industry accessories to crime and shielders and supporters of criminals; it is an even more dreadful thing to see the power of men high in State politics, high in finance, high in the social life of the rich and fashionable, united to stifle the prosecution of offenders against civic integrity if these offenders happen to be their friends and associates; and most evil of all is it when we see the crooks of a labor party in offensive and defensive alliance with the crooks of a corporation party. Labor unions and corporations alike should be heartily supported when they do good work, and fearlessly opposed when they stand for what is evil. The best kind of wageworker, the best kind of laboring man, must stand shoulder to shoulder with the best kind of professional man, with the best kind of businessman, in putting a stop to the undermining of civic decency, and this without any regard to whether it is a labor union or a corporation which is undermining it, without any regard to whether the offender is a rich man or a poor man. Indeed, if there can be any degrees in the contemptuous abhorrence with which right-thinking citizens should regard corruption, it must be felt in its most extreme form for the so-called "best citizens," the men high in social and business life, who by backing up, or by preventing the punishment of, wealthy criminals, set the seal of their approval on crime, and give honor to rich felons. The most powerful ally of lawlessness and mob violence is the man, whoever he may be, politician or business-man, judge or lawyer, capitalist or editor, who in any way or shape works so as to shield wealthy and powerful wrongdoers from the consequences of their misconduct.

You have heartbreaking difficulties with which to contend. You have to fight not only the banded powers of evil, but, alas that it should be said, the supineness and indifference of many good men upon whose zealous sup-port you had a right to feel that you could rely. Do not be discouraged; do not flinch. You are in a fight for plain decency, for the plain democracy of the plain people, who believe in honesty and in fair dealing as between man and man. Do not become disheartened. Keep up the fight.[2] *Very sincerely yours*

4749 · TO HENRY CABOT LODGE   *Roosevelt Mss.*

Washington, June 8, 1908

Dear Cabot: Taft called on me yesterday morning with messages from Hitch-cock about the proposal for a compromise made to him by Crane and others, and after consultation together he sent a telegram to Hitchcock and I sent one to you.[1] We both of us felt strongly that it was an outrage to compromise these cases. If any man claiming to be for Taft also claims a seat to which he is not entitled, turn him out at once—in other words, treat each contest absolutely on its merits. But it is not merely wicked, but foolish to the last degree, to propose to compromise as Murray Crane does, and such compro-mise merely means giving to a man like Bradley,[2] of Kentucky, delegates to which he is not entitled and taking them away from supporters of ours who have honestly and fairly won them. Do you know that Murray Crane and Aldrich have approached Taft, as Taft informs me, to tell him that they wanted you permanent chairman of the Convention, but that they particu-larly did not want you to take part in the work of the National Committee? These people admit that Taft's nomination is inevitable, but they are re-actionaries down at heart, just as much as ever, and they are in a cabal to try

[2] The District Court of Appeals in San Francisco had in January reversed the con-viction of ex-Mayor Eugene Schmitz. Although there were substantial legal reasons for this reversal, the decision was received with much popular disappointment and some resentment. Most people failed to understand the technical errors in the intro-duction of evidence and cross-examination which invalidated the conviction, but they very well understood the family connections of four of the judges with those who had been identified with the graft in the city. "Among the wealthier classes" who had opposed the prosecution the reversal was popular. Roosevelt wrote there-fore to buttress the morale of the men who had conducted the prosecution. Before the letter was published, he inserted, at Heney's suggestion, references to William Henry Langdon, district attorney of San Francisco, who had been as active as Heney, Spreckels, and Hiram Johnson in forcing the removal from office of Schmitz and his city supervisors.

[1] See No. 4747.

[2] William O'C. Bradley led an anti-Taft delegation. It was not seated.

to keep their power to try to control the National Committee and the organization, to turn down all delegates they do not like, and to write the platform to suit themselves; and as a sequel to control the organization of the Senate and the House, so as to make them as ineffective and as reactionary, as they have shown themselves thruout the last six months, until they were afflicted with panic in the concluding fortnight of the session. They are *against you*. I hope you will not yield to them one inch. Not only do they deserve no consideration, but it would be a detriment to Taft to show them consideration. I hope that in the platform you will refuse to allow them to shape it in any way, and that you will put in a straight, thoro-going platform as free from the Hale type of reactionary policy as from the La Follette type of fool radicalism. It would not be at all a bad thing for Taft to have the platform put thru as the sequel of a victory over the reactionary forces.

As to my accident, it might have been bad, but it turned out that I was not hurt at all; tho I felt the effects of the shaking for a couple of days. The horse was young and nervous and I tried to force him to cross the ford. He got into an utter panic and sprang up the bank rearing. I leant way forward, letting the reins hang loose. At the top of the bank he fell over backward into the stream, the bottom of which is there covered with boulders. Fortunately I fell clear of him on the side away from his heels, and the water was deep enough to prevent there being much shock from the boulders. He went right on his back in the water, and I went practically under water. He behaved perfectly well for the rest of the ride, which lasted about an hour after our ducking. *Ever yours*

P.S. Nothing could be more disheartening for our friends who have fought valiantly for us than to have us now go back on them in the matter of these contests and give the victory away to our bitter opponents.

[*Handwritten*] Murray Butler, and his associates, who have sent you a memorial about the courts,[3] are our bitter opponents; the Sun is behind them; to do what they wish would be interpreted as a slap at me. Take *no* plank from Butler & his crowd. If you say anything about the courts, do have it carefully thought over, & let it come from our side, and not from our reactionary opponents.

4750 · TO THEODORE ELIJAH BURTON   *Roosevelt Mss.*

Washington, June 8, 1908

My dear Mr. Burton: The recent Conference of Governors in the White House confirmed and strengthened in the minds of our people the conviction that our natural resources are being consumed, wasted, and destroyed at a

[3] Butler, Joseph Choate, Cornelius N. Bliss, and other distinguished New Yorkers had circulated a memorial asserting confidence in the general integrity of the federal courts. They objected particularly to the attitude the President had expressed about injunctions, the subject which provoked more controversy than did any other in the framing of the Republican platform; see Numbers 4760, 4761, 4762.

rate which threatens them with exhaustion. It was demonstrated that the inevitable result of our present course toward these resources, if we should persist in following it, would ultimately be the impoverishment of our people. The Governors present adopted unanimously a Declaration reciting the necessity for a more careful conservation of the foundations of our national prosperity, and recommending a more effective co-operation to this end among the States and between the States and the Nation. A copy of this Declaration is enclosed.

One of the most useful among the many useful recommendations in the admirable Declaration of the Governors relates to the creation of State commissions on the conservation of resources, to co-operate with a Federal Commission. This action of the Governors cannot be disregarded. It is obviously the duty of the Federal Government to accept this invitation to co-operate with the States in order to conserve the natural resources of our whole country. It is no less clearly the duty of the President to lay before the Federal Congress information as to the state of the Union in relation to the natural resources, and to recommend to their consideration such measures as he shall judge necessary and expedient. In order to make such recommendations the President must procure the necessary information. Accordingly, I have decided to appoint a Commission to inquire into and advise me as to the condition of our natural resources, and to co-operate with other bodies created for a similar purpose by the States.

The Inland Waterways Commission, appointed March 14, 1907, which suggested the Conference of Governors, was asked to consider the other natural resources related to our inland waterways, and it has done so. But the two subjects together have grown too large to be dealt with by the original body. The creation of a Commission on the Conservation of Natural Resources will thus promote the special work for which the Inland Waterways Commission was created, and for which it has just been continued and enlarged, by enabling it to concentrate on its principal task.

The Commission on the Conservation of Natural Resources will be organized in four sections to consider the four great classes of water resources, forest resources, resources of the land, and mineral resources. I am asking the members of the Inland Waterways Commission to form the Section of Waters of the National Conservation Commission. In view of the lateness of the season and the difficulty of assembling the members of the Sections at this time, a Chairman and a Secretary for each Section have been designated, and the Chairmen and Secretaries of the Sections will act as the Executive Committee, with a Chairman who will also be Chairman of the entire Commission. I earnestly hope that you will consent to act as a member of the Commission, in common with the following gentlemen:

Waters.

Hon. Theodore E. Burton, Ohio, Chairman
Senator William B. Allison, Iowa

Senator Francis G. Newlands, Nevada
Senator William Warner, Missouri
Senator John H. Bankhead, Alabama
Mr. W. J. McGee, Bureau of Soils, Secretary
Mr. F. H. Newell, Reclamation Service
Mr. Gifford Pinchot, Forest Service
Mr. Herbert Knox Smith, Bureau of Corporations
Hon. Joseph E. Ransdell, Louisiana
Prof. George F. Swain, Institute of Technology, Massachusetts
The Chief of Engineers, U. S. Army

Forests.

Senator Reed Smoot, Utah, Chairman
Senator Albert J. Beveridge, Indiana
Senator Charles A. Culberson, Texas
Hon. Charles F. Scott, Kansas
Hon. Champ Clark, Missouri
Dr. I. C. White, W. Va.
Prof. Henry S. Graves, Yale Forest School, Conn.
Mr. William Irvine, Wisconsin
Ex-Governor Newton C. Blanchard, Louisiana
Mr. Charles L. Pack, New Jersey
Mr. Gustav H. Schwab, National Council of Commerce, New York
Mr. Overton W. Price, Forest Service, Secretary
Mr. J. B. White, Missouri

Lands.

Senator Knute Nelson, Minnesota, Chairman
Senator Francis E. Warren, Wyoming
Hon. John Sharp Williams, Mississippi
Hon. Swagar Sherley, Kentucky
Hon. Herbert Parsons, New York
Ex-Governor N. B. Broward, Florida
Mr. James J. Hill, Minnesota
Ex-Governor George C. Pardee, California
Mr. Charles McDonald, Am. Society of Civil Engineers, New York
Mr. Murdo Mackenzie, Colorado
Mr. Frank C. Goudy, Colorado
Mr. George W. Woodruff, Interior Department, Secretary
Prof. C. J. Chamberlain, Univ. of Chicago

Minerals.

Hon. John Dalzell, Pennsylvania, Chairman
Senator Joseph M. Dixon, Montana
Senator Frank P. Flint, California

Senator Lee S. Overman, North Carolina
Hon. Philo Hall, South Dakota
Hon. James L. Slayden, Texas
Mr. Andrew Carnegie, New York
Prof. Charles R. Van Hise, Wisconsin
Mr. John Mitchell, Illinois
Mr. John Hays Hammond, Massachusetts
Dr. Irving Fisher, Yale University, Conn.
Mr. Joseph A. Holmes, Geological Survey, Secretary

Executive Committee

Mr. Gifford Pinchot, Chairman
Hon. Theodore E. Burton
Senator Reed Smoot
Senator Knute Nelson
Hon. John Dalzell
Mr. W. J. McGee
Mr. Overton W. Price
Mr. G. W. Woodruff
Mr. Joseph A. Holmes.

One of the principal objects of the Federal Commission on the Conservation of Natural Resources will be to co-operate with corresponding commissions or other agencies appointed on behalf of the States, and it is hoped that the Governors and their appointees will join with the Federal Commission in working out and developing a plan whereby the needs of the Nation as a whole and of each State and Territory may be equitably met.

The work of the Commission should be conditioned upon keeping ever in mind the great fact that the life of the Nation depends absolutely on the material resources, which have already made the Nation great. Our object is to conserve the foundations of our prosperity. We intend to use these resources; but to so use them as to conserve them. No effort should be made to limit the wise and proper development and application of these resources; every effort should be made to prevent destruction, to reduce waste, and to distribute the enjoyment of our natural wealth in such a way as to promote the greatest good of the greatest number for the longest time.

The Commission must keep in mind the further fact that all the natural resources are so related that their use may be, and should be, co-ordinated. Thus, the development of water transportation, which requires less iron and less coal than rail transportation, will reduce the draft on mineral resources; the judicious development of forests will not only supply fuel and structural material but increase the navigability of streams, and so promote water transportation; and the control of streams will reduce soil erosion, and permit American farms to increase in fertility and productiveness and so continue to feed the country and maintain a healthy and beneficial foreign commerce. The proper co-ordination of the use of our resources is a prime requisite for continued National prosperity.

The recent Conference of the Governors, of the men who are the direct sponsors for the well-being of the States, was notable in many respects; in none more than in this, that the dignity, the autonomy, and yet the interdependence and mutual dependence of the several States were all emphasized and brought into clear relief, as rarely before in our history. There is no break between the interests of State and Nation, these interests are essentially one. Hearty co-operation between the state and the national agencies is essential to the permanent welfare of the people. You, on behalf of the Federal Government, will do your part to bring about this co-operation.

In order to make available to the National Conservation Commission all the information and assistance which it may desire from the Federal Departments, I shall issue an Executive Order directing them to give such help as the Commission may need.

The next session of Congress will end on March 4, 1909. Accordingly, I should be glad to have at least a preliminary report from the Commission not later than January 1st of next year.[1] *Sincerely yours*

4751 · TO WILLIAM HOWARD TAFT   *Roosevelt Mss.*

Washington, June 9, 1908

To the Secretary of War: It is beginning to look to me as if Colonel Symons'[1] conduct had not been quite such as would make me willing to have him head of the Engineer Corps. While doing the work as Government engineer in the district covering Coos Bay he purchased property in Coos Bay. The value of this property could not but be affected by his action as Government expert. Altho not liking this, I was inclined to pass it by in view of the public commitment to the appointment of Colonel Symons and of the fact that the then head of the War Department knew of the transac-

[1] The complete, three-volume report of the National Conservation Commission, submitted in January 1909, formed "the most exhaustive inventory of our natural resources" that had ever been made. Observing that most of the public domain had been disposed of and that natural resources of all kinds were being depleted at a dangerous rate, the commission urged the government to classify carefully and control systematically what remained. It recommended the repeal of the Timber and Stone Act, the commutation clause of the Homestead Act, and the Desert Land Act, legislation which had permitted fraudulent and wasteful possession of mineral and agricultural lands. It also recommended large-scale reforestation, an increase in the number and size of forest reserves, government control of grazing lands to prevent the excessive grazing that fostered erosion, protection of agricultural lands from wash, the leasing of coal lands, and the substitution where possible of more plentiful minerals in the current uses of the dwindling oil and natural gas supplies. For a detailed discussion of these recommendations presented too late for action during the Roosevelt administration, see Robbins, *Our Landed Heritage*, pp. 356–362.

[1] Thomas W. Symons.

tion over fourteen years ago, and tho he privately exprest to a third person his disapproval thereof, no official action in reference thereto was ever taken and no adverse expression of opinion or censure was ever conveyed to Colonel Symons. It now appears, however, that at about the same time, while he was engineer in charge of the district in question, which included Seattle, he accepted employment as consulting engineer from a company desiring to build the so-called South canal by or thru Seattle between Puget Sound and Lakes Union and Washington; the Government having already been committed to the so-called North canal or Government canal. It appears by the papers you have transmitted that great stress was put by the then Major Symons' opinion to the company, as giving standing to the South canal project. The Government authorities have, however, even since then (as well as before) declared that this project is impracticable, or at best inadvisable, and that the old North canal, or Government canal, project should be persevered with. It seems to me very questionable whether the Government expert committed to carrying out one Government canal should permit himself for hire to give the weight of his name and authority to another canal project at the same time, this being in a sense a rival canal project, and apparently regarded as undesirable by the other Government officers. I do not think that either of these transactions was of a nature that would warrant more than a reprimand of Colonel Symons and a warning not to take similar action again. But they do seem to me to show the lack of a nice sense of propriety on Colonel Symons' part. In view of this fact I am not willing to make him head of the Corps.

Will you find out if Colonel Marshall [2] has ever been in any way connected with similar transactions or with transactions which bear any kind of similarity whatsoever to these in which Colonel Symons has participated.

4752 · TO FRANK HARRIS HITCHCOCK   *Roosevelt Mss.*

Telegram   Washington, June 9, 1908

I hope the Louisiana case like every other case will be settled exactly on its merits. I urged Pearl Wight, than whom there is no man in public life for whom I have a higher regard, to see that colored men were put on the delegation, both because I thought this was right as a matter of equity and because I was certain that the failure to do so would inevitably greatly jeopardize his case and prevent his case being judged absolutely on its merits. I trust that our friends will insist so far as they have power to do so upon the case being thus judged on its merits pure and simple. I hope Mr. Wight will abide by the decision of the committee and accept your judgment as to what his action should then be. Explain to Mr. Wight that neither Mr. Lodge nor anyone else is my representative or has authority to speak for me and that I

[2] On July 2, 1908, Roosevelt appointed William Louis Marshall Chief of Engineers.

am to be judged by my own utterances as in this telegram to you and my previous letter to you.[1]

4753 · TO GEORGE WALBRIDGE PERKINS   *Roosevelt Mss.*

Private   Washington, June 11, 1908

My dear Mr. Perkins: I have received your letter and the report,[1] and will take time to look it over. It seems to me that the precedent set, that of giving the public complete information at the same time the securities of the corporation are offered to the public, ought to be of the most widespread usefulness. With thanks and congratulations, *Sincerely yours*

4754 · TO JOHN SHARP WILLIAMS   *Roosevelt Mss.*

Personal   Washington, June 12, 1908

My dear Mr. Williams: I thank you for your kind letter. I am sorry you cannot serve. You have written me so frankly I know you will pardon my writing you equally frankly and I trust in an equally kindly spirit when I say that the theory on which you decline,[1] if carried out logically, would mean that the President ought not to listen to the advice of anybody — including Mr. John Sharp Williams himself — unless there was a law past by Congress allowing him to do so in the case of that particular person. In short, my dear Mr. Williams, your theory, if carried out to its natural consequences, would probably mean that we have not a government at all and that the great statesmen who founded the Constitution were elaborately engaged in a solemn piece of tomfoolery designed to look like a government,

[1] Pearl Wight supported the white delegation from Louisiana which was headed by Henry C. Warmoth. The opposing delegation, led by Walter L. Cohen, included Negroes. Both delegations supported Taft; both had been elected by unlovely methods. Recognizing that there was no "merit" in this situation, the National Committee worked out a solution which in effect repudiated both factions: both delegations were seated, each was assigned half a vote, and Wight's re-election as national committeeman was prearranged. Roosevelt endorsed this solution; see Roosevelt to Hitchcock, June 10, 1908, Roosevelt Mss.

[1] Perkins had sent Roosevelt the first published annual report of the International Harvester Company. Like the recent report of the United States Steel Corporation, the fifty-seven page document not only set forth in detail the corporation's financial structure, but also described with photographs and maps its extensive properties and numerous products. Industrial corporations, unlike railroads, were not legally required to make annual statements, but Gary and Perkins, realizing the value of full, clear, and attractively presented reports for improving public relations and advertising securities and products, set a new standard of voluntary publicity.

[1] Williams maintained that the President had no right to appoint commissions such as that on conservation without the express approval of Congress, a theory which appealed also to the Republican opponents of Roosevelt's policies; see No. 4841, note 6.

but designed most carefully to see that there was no government. *Sincerely yours*

P.S. If your theory is correct, my dear Mr. Williams, I ought not to have organized that Waterways Commission last year; I ought not to have asked the Governors to come here to advise and consult with me; and it was highly unconstitutional for these same Governors, including the Governor of Mississippi, to come!

4755 · TO JOSEPH LINCOLN STEFFENS   *Roosevelt Mss.*

Personal   Washington, June 12, 1908

Dear Steffens: That is a nice letter of yours. If I am not in Washington come out to Oyster Bay, and I will go over the matter with you. But come, come, friend Steffens, if your theory is correct the Government has got to own the saloons, refuse to collect customs duties, own every public service corporation, and own every possible thing there can possibly be bribery in; including Life Insurance Companies, by the way. When I was Police Commissioner I found that the dry goods merchants and the small Jew shopkeepers were blackmailed just as much as anybody else. They were given certain privileges designedly for the purpose of levying blackmail upon them. I think you are in error about Europe. The European governments do not as a rule own the saloons. They almost all have protective tariffs. They all without exception have ship subsidies. Many of them own the public service franchises; that is, for instance, the railroads; but England does not own the railroads and her management of them is just as free from corruption as is the case in Germany and France where the government does own them. I do not believe that you have struck the right cause, nor come near striking the right cause of our corruption, and I think you are trying to cure a symptom and not a cause. I am heartily with you in the campaign for the abolition of privilege. Curiously enough, events have forced me to make my chief fights in public life against privilege, but I know from actual experience — from experience of the most intimate kind in the little village of Oyster Bay and out in the West at Medora, when there was not a special privilege of any kind in either place — that what is needed is the *fundamental fight for morality*. However, I won't go into this until I see you personally. *Sincerely yours*

[*Handwritten*] For the Government to own everything, from saloons and Insurance companies to steamship lines and railroads, as to which there can even be a question of privilege or blackmail, would of course mean socialism; incidentally, it would'n't work and would mean bankruptcy; but aside from this, my knowledge of the postal service, & of Tammany Hall, shows me that under government ownership corruption can flourish just as rankly as under private ownership.

Personal   Washington, June 13, 1908

My dear Mr. Ambassador: Your letter of the 1st, as usual, is most interesting. I am happy to say that it now looks as if Taft would surely be nominated on the first ballot, by a three to one vote. There are still a great many people bound to try to force a third term. As I have tried to explain to them, and as I have succeeded in convincing most of them, my value as an asset to the American people consists chiefly in a belief in my disinterestedness and trustworthiness, in the belief that I mean what I say, and that my concern is for the good of the country; and if they should now nominate me, even under circumstances that would force me to take the nomination, I could only take it as the least of two evils, and with the bitter knowledge that many good people would have their faith in me shaken, and that therefore my influence for good would be measurably, and perhaps greatly, diminished.

By the way, when I get a little gloomy over the more preposterous variety of mugwump, the individual who writes for the New York *Evening Post*, the *Nation*, or *Atlantic Monthly*, and is treated with great solemnity as a "thinker" by his fellows, it does me good to read such an article by a British analogue or variant of the same type, as Edward Dicey's solemn effusion on the trip of the fleet to the Pacific. It was in the January number of the *Empire Review*, and Mahan sent it to me the other day, apparently treating Dicey as someone whom I had heard of. I do not remember ever hearing of him; but somebody told me that he was a constitutional lawyer or lecturer or something of that kind, and was regarded as a man of exalted intelligence and information in England. If so, Heaven help those who thus regard him. Not Gamaliel Bradford,[1] of Boston, not Rollo Ogden, or Oswald Villard, can be a more fully fledged jack.

A year hence, by this time, I shall hope to be either in British or German East Africa, and if fortune favors me I shall spend a year there.

With warm regards to your family, believe me, *Faithfuly yours*

4757 · TO KENTARO KANEKO   *Roosevelt Mss.*

Washington, June 13, 1908

My dear Baron Kaneko: I thank you now for the various telegrams and letters you have written me. I enclose you a copy of the bill which was finally enacted into law as regards our commission to your exposition. From it you will see that we have been able to meet the wishes you exprest, and I think I may say that we have met them exactly in the spirit that you desired they

---

[1] Gamaliel Bradford, Boston banker, perennial Mugwump, author of *The Lesson of Popular Government* (1899), contributor of several thousand letters on political reform to the Boston press, and father of the prose impressionist, Gamaliel Bradford, Jr.

should be. Never before for any exposition have we made such an appropriation or made such provision so far in advance as in this case. Secretary Root and I devoted hours this winter in getting the bill thru in just such form that you, speaking for your Government and your countrymen, desired that it should be done; for I felt, as did Mr. Root, that from every standpoint it was important that America should take the lead, should set the pace, as regards this exposition, and should in the heartiest manner co-operate with your people to make the exposition one of the highest international importance — one that will reflect the utmost credit upon Japan. We have nominated the three best men in the country for commissioners, two of them, Skiff,[1] the Director of the Columbian Exposition at Chicago, and Frank D. Millet, the artist, being personal friends of ours and having had great experience in similar expositions; while the third, Loomis, was formerly Assistant Secretary of State, has held high diplomatic position, has shown excellent executive ability, and has occupied peculiarly close and trusted relations with the State Department, both under John Hay and since. I wish to have these commissioners, or some of them, go to Tokyo just as soon as their visit would be useful to you or to us. I of course desire that at the earliest practicable moment they shall be able to secure such location, and provisions regarding space and the like, as will enable us to utilize to the best advantage the appropriation which Congress has made and to justify in the eyes of Congress and our people the expenditure which we have persuaded them to authorize. I must trust largely to your judgment as to the time when it will be advisable and expedient for these commissioners, or some of them, to visit Tokyo.

You know how genuine my regard and liking for Japan are. I very earnestly desire to see Japan make a great success of this, the first international exposition ever held in the Orient. Whatever I can do to contribute toward that success will be done. Messrs. Skiff and Millet have had great experience not only with our own expositions here but as American representatives at the Paris Exposition. It is possible that if they should soon go to Japan your people might derive some benefit from consultation with them.

With regard to the Baroness and best wishes to all your children, believe me, *Sincerely yours*

4758 · TO WILLIAM BOYD ALLISON   *Roosevelt Mss.*

Washington, June 15, 1908

My dear Senator: There is no reason why you should not make public my letter to you of June 5th. I did not deem it well for me to write you for publication before the result of the primaries was announced. I have felt

[1] Frederick James Volney Skiff, museum director and exposition manager, director-in-chief of the United States exhibits at the Paris Exposition, 1898–1901; St. Louis Exposition, 1901–1905; and Japanese Exposition, 1917.

grave concern over the division in Iowa, and a strong desire that it should not proceed to disastrous lengths. My relations with you and Senator Dolliver have been uniformly close and pleasant. I have been able to work with both of you for a common end — the betterment of our political, industrial and civic conditions. But I have also been on excellent terms with Governor Cummins, and I have felt that fundamentally, so far as I could judge from his public expressions, he and I believed in much the same policies and that there was no possible reason why we should not work together.[1]

With all good wishes, believe me, *Sincerely yours*

P.S. Will you make this letter public at the same time you publish my letter to you of June 5th?

4759 · TO JOEL CHANDLER HARRIS   *Roosevelt Mss.*

Washington, June 15, 1908

Dear Uncle Remus: Here is something in which I would like to get the assistance of Mr. Billy Sanders, the sage of Shady Dale, and of all the readers of the *Home Magazine* and of all who think as the editors of the *Home Magazine* evidently do think.

Last Saturday, in the late afternoon, when it had grown a little cool, I was riding with two of my aides, Captain Fitzhugh Lee, and Captain Archie Butt[1] of your own State and my Mother's State of Georgia. The mare I was on by the way was named Georgia, and a good mare she is, too, well-behaved, and a good jumper. We were taking our horses out to exercise them over some jumps. We had just been listening to the really superb singing of

[1] Allison had just defeated Cummins in a fiercely contested preferential primary for the Republican senatorial nomination in Iowa. Both the senator and the President feared that the liberal Cummins faction might desert the party in the autumn elections. The publication of this letter and of Roosevelt's letter of June 5 (No. 4742), which had praised Allison for "endeavoring to carry out the policies for which this Administration stands" probably did something to mollify the liberals. In any case Cummins neither after the primary nor after liberal defeats at the National Convention contemplated a bolt. There was a chance, however, that simply through inaction he might place the Republican fortunes in jeopardy. This contingency never presented itself; Allison died in August, and Cummins, after bitter struggles, was elected to fill his unexpired term.

[1] Archibald Willingham Butt served with pleasure as a military aide (1908–1912) to two Presidents. Of his years in the White House he left two full reports, *The Letters of Archie Butt, Personal Aide to President Roosevelt* (New York, 1924), and *Taft and Roosevelt, the Intimate Letters of Archie Butt* (New York, 1930). Like all really great gossips he had a highly developed feeling for the purely conventional. Though scarcely sharing, as Lawrence Abbott once tried to maintain, in the spirit of Herodotus, Erasmus, and Emerson, he did possess attractive and wholly innocent high spirits of his own that fill his correspondence. Lacking either the coarseness or the real curiosity that rounds out the work of Boswell or Pepys, he had the accurate ear, the sharp eye, and the retentive memory of the good diarist. Like the sundial, however, he contented himself with recording only the sunny hours. In 1912 he went down with the *Titanic*.

the men's chorus of the Arion Singing Society, an organization of citizens of German birth or parentage, who were about to go abroad to appear at certain courts and elsewhere in Europe, and who had wisht to sing in the White House as a farewell before starting on their foreign journey. Among other things they had, at my request, sung "Dixie" (as well as the Old Kentucky Home and the Suwanee River). While riding we were talking over the fact that "Dixie" was far and away the best tune (and the best military tune, that we knew, not even excepting Garry Owen), and that it had won its way until it was the tune which would bring everybody to his feet with a yell in any audience in any part of the country; and we were bemoaning the fact that there never had been any words which were in any way adequate to the tune, and dwelling on the further fact that it was such a fine battle tune — the best battle tune of our army. Captain Butt then added that just as "Dixie" stood alone among tunes, so we had in Julia Ward Howe's great "Battle Hymn of the Republic" the very finest and noblest battle hymn possest by any Nation of the world, a hymn that in loftiness of thought and expression, in both words and tune, lent itself to choral singing as no other battle hymn did in any country; and he added that there was not a sectional line in the hymn, not a word that could awaken a single unpleasant thought in the mind of any American, no matter where he lived and no matter on which side he or his father had fought in the great war. I told him I entirely agreed with him, and that, just as "Dixie" was becoming the tune which when played excited most enthusiasm among Americans everywhere, so I hoped that sooner or later all Americans would grow to realize that in this "Battle Hymn of the Republic" we had what really ought to be a great National treasure, something that all Americans would grow to know intimately, so that in any audience anywhere in the land when the tune was started most of the audience should be able to join in singing the words. We then grew to wondering if this good result would ever be achieved, and we thought it would be worth while to write to you. We know that any such movement can come, if at all, only because of a genuine popular feeling, and with small regard to the opinion of any one man or any particular set of men; and it can only come slowly in any event; but we thought it might be helped on a little if what we had to say was published in your magazine.[2] I append a copy of the Battle Hymn. *Faithfully yours*

4760 · TO HENRY CABOT LODGE   *Roosevelt Mss.*

Telegram   Washington, June 15, 1908

What are rumors that Burrows has ordered reference to postal savings banks struck from his speech and that the leaders are against the injunction plank?

[2] This letter was published in the August issue of *Uncle Remus's Home Magazine* by Julian Harris (see No. 4794). Uncle Remus died July 3, 1908.

It seems to me they should realize that it will be very damaging not to insert these two planks.[1] Taft is committed to them over and over again and it would simply mean that he would have to stand for them in his letter of acceptance and then put us in the damaging position of an incongruity between the platform and the candidate. Please telegraph me the facts.

Strong protests were made to ⟨us⟩ Taft against Sherman as Vice-Presidential candidate for the very reason that it was believed we could not afford to put on any member of the House who would be held in any way responsible for failure to act at this last session on these very matters among others. Taft thinks, and it seems to me he is right, that all discussion about Vice-Presidency might well be postponed until after platform is adopted and President nominated. I am not committed for or against any candidate.[2]

[1] Roosevelt obtained half a loaf. Burrows' keynote speech and the Republican platform favored the establishment of a postal savings-bank system. Of the influential politicians at Chicago only Cannon opposed that plank. But a majority of the delegates rejected Roosevelt's views on injunctions. Neither the President nor Taft favored as strong a statement as Gompers wanted, but both had requested legislation limiting the use of injunctions in labor cases. This the National Association of Manufacturers and the conservative Republicans strongly resisted. Burrows in his keynote made no mention of injunctions. Lodge, replying to Roosevelt's telegram, stated that "an anti-injunction plank that would satisfy Gompers I for one should oppose. A colorless plank I cannot see the use of." Yet only a "colorless plank" had a chance of adoption. Bowing to the opinion of their party, Taft and Roosevelt modified their original request and accepted a compromise that read: "The Republican party will uphold at all times the authority and integrity of the courts. . . . We believe, however, that the rules of procedure in the Federal Courts with respect to the issuance of the writ of injunction should be more accurately defined by statute, and that no injunction . . . . should be issued without notice, except where irreparable injury would result from delay. . . ."

As Lodge had predicted, this "colorless plank" was of little use. The National Association of Manufacturers considered it dangerously radical. Gompers declared that labor had been "thrown down, repudiated and relegated to the discard by the Republican party." He had supported a plank pledging "the enactment of a law to prohibit the issuance of injunctions in cases arising out of labor disputes, when such injunctions would not apply when no labor disputes existed, and providing that in no case shall an injunction be issued when there exists a remedy by the ordinary process of law." When the Democrats accepted a like proposal, Gompers declared for Bryan. This broke the precedent under which the head of the American Federation of Labor had remained neutral in Presidential campaigns.

The injunction issue is well treated in Pringle, *Taft*, I, 350–351; Gompers, *Seventy Years of Life and Labor*, II, 262–266, 271–272. See also Numbers 4761, 4762; Roosevelt Scrapbooks; and *Official Report of the Proceedings of the Fourteenth Republican National Convention* (Columbus, Ohio, 1908), especially pp. 119–120, 129.

[2] The postponement of discussion of the Vice-Presidency, the inactivity of Roosevelt and Taft, the refusals of Hughes, Hadley, and Beveridge to consider taking second place on the ticket, and the factionalism in Iowa that impeded the nomination of Cummins or Dolliver permitted the Old Guard to arrange the nomination of James S. Sherman as Taft's running mate. Sherman, Pringle has aptly observed, was "distinguished chiefly for his nickname, 'Sunny Jim.'" He contributed neither strength nor dignity to the ticket or to the office he won.

Telegram　　　　　　　　　　　　Washington, June 16, 1908

I hope you will be utterly unmoved by the artificial and worked-up clamor about the injunction plank. It is engineered by the Manufacturers' Association just as they engineered during the last session an attack upon all child labor legislation and an attack upon the employers' liability bill. It does not represent a particle of real feeling except where it is based upon complete misunderstanding. We are not advocating an anti-injunction plank at all, but a singularly moderate and reasonable provision which in its essence merely asks that judges shall think before they act, but which does not in any way hamper their action when once they have thought. In other words the plank's chief value is that it shows our willingness to be just and our purpose to call the attention of the courts to a bad habit into which some judges have fallen. We have no more expectation of satisfying the extreme labor agitator than of satisfying the equally extreme representatives of the Manufacturers' Association, but we wish to be right and to make it so evident that we are right as to enable honest and fair-minded labor men and honest and fair-minded employers and property owners heartily to join with us on the basis of justice to all American citizens.[1]

Telegram　　　　　　　　　　　　Washington, June 16, 1908

Telegram received. I not merely would oppose but have in most open and efficient fashion opposed the Gompers injunction plank, but I think it very necessary that we should have not a colorless but a moderate plank, and that is what the plank is as published. Certainly Taft has shown in actual work on the bench his entire fearlessness in using injunctions when necessary. For the last two years, including his speech at Bath, which everyone so heartily approved, Taft has been taking the very positions he now takes on this injunction matter. I have not the slightest expectation of placating or gaining the ultraviolent labor men, but I do want in the first place to put in a plank which will enable the labor men who would naturally be with us to feel that they have a justification for staying with us; and in the next place on the highest ethical grounds I hope that the Republican Party will take the position which is right, and that in my judgment is the position which Taft has taken in this matter. It is just as weak and unwise to yield to the demands of the Manufacturers' Association when they are wrong as to yield to the demands of Gompers when he is wrong. Our action would not satisfy the extremists on either side and I should be exceedingly sorry if it did. The

[1] Roosevelt sent an identical telegram to Albert J. Hopkins.

Manufacturers' Association has been just as violent against child labor and employers' liability legislation as against this plank.

4763 · TO LYMAN ABBOTT

Roosevelt Mss.

Washington, June 17, 1908

My dear Dr. Abbott: May I venture a suggestion in connection with what you say of the meeting of Christian socialists[1] — those clergymen, or whoever they were? The longer I have lived the more indifferent I have become to any effort to frighten me by calling a given doctrine socialistic, and the less attention I have paid to what I cannot help regarding as mere fetishism, of holding up as a bogey either "individualism," or "socialism," treated *in vacuo,* so to speak, and apart from all surroundings. But the longer I have lived the more profoundly I have grown to distrust and disbelieve in the men and the doctrines who and which in a special and peculiar sense are considered as embodying socialism.

Have you read a little book on *English Socialism of To-day* by Arnold-Forster?[2] It is not quite right on all points, but I am bound to say that it is much more nearly right than any socialist publication that I have come across. Now, what especially impresses me in this book of Forster's is his exposure both of the utter looseness of thought of the average agitator who calls himself a socialist, and of the mischief he does. This is exactly what I should feel in connection with the gathering of which you spoke. I am perfectly willing to admit that most of the people who attended the meeting were well-meaning, and that so far as they were not well-meaning they were simply seeking after the notoriety or prominence which men of feeble character can only get by taking part in a movement like this — just as a man like Robert Hunter, for instance, who is both weak and untruthful, cannot possibly get recognition anywhere except by doing as he has done. But these men as a whole, as far as I can see, do only a little good, and do some real harm. In so far as these socialists wake up serious people who are shortsighted and force them to think of the evils of modern life, they do good. But most of what they do is merely to add to the mass of aimless discontent; and to give it a wrong aim; and to hold up men and principles to admiration, whereas these men are really of bad character and their principles mischievous.

For instance, this special body of clergymen did but one thing that attracted popular attention, and that was to welcome Debs and make him their

[1] The Third National Conference of the Christian Socialist Fellowship met in New York City, May 28–31, 1908. "The Conference," the *Outlook* reported, "was plain proof of the growth and the grip that Socialist or Socialistic principles have already gained in the churches. . . . The term Christian Socialist is a loose one; but it is not large enough to include all who believe in human brotherhood." — *Outlook,* 89:319 (June 1908).

[2] Hugh Oakeley Arnold-Forster, British author and politician, grandson of Arnold of Rugby, long-time advocate of military and naval expansion and reform, Secretary of State for War, 1903–1905; author of *English Socialism of To-day* (1908).

idol. What the different individuals said made little impression, and what they meant, still less. The lasting impression was conveyed by their action. Have you ever seen Debs' paper, *The Appeal to Reason?* On its merits it should be kept out of the mails,* for it is an appeal, not to reason but to hatred and malice; and again and again it contains open incitement to murder, while it always justifies murder. I enclose you a letter I wrote to the Attorney General at the time that Debs was championing Moyer and Haywood, and I show therein that in his paper he chuckled over and approved of the murder of Steunenberg. To praise and champion Debs, to condone his faults, is precisely like praising and championing Tweed and condoning Tweed's faults. Civilization can no more get along permanently with one type of man at the head than with the other type. The well-meaning, or ill-meaning clergymen and others who now champion Debs stand on a par with the New York voters of one of the tenement house districts who after Tweed was exposed sent him to the State Senate. They sent him to the Senate on the ground that he had stolen from the rich men, but was the poor man's friend. It is among them, and their successors, and those like them, among whom you will find support for Debs on the ground that, tho he advocates murder, that tho he does preach envy and hatred and malice, and incites to violence, he is yet entitled to the support of all kinds of people of mushy morality because he is for the opprest and against the oppressor. What these parlor socialists, these clerical socialists, need is a little clear-cut morality and clear-cut common sense. They are not helping what is good; they are helping what is bad. They are obstacles and not helps to those who really are, in honest and common sense fashion, endeavoring to do away with privilege, with inequality and injustice, and to work for the betterment of our people and especially for the betterment of those who are least fortunate. A high-sounding platform, on which Debs is nominated, means no more than the moral platitudes of the platform on which Tweed was nominated. The unspeakably wicked Jacobins delighted in the loftiest sentiments.

Hand in hand with this socialistic movement — or, to speak more accurately, as part of it — there goes an only partially concealed crusade against domestic morality. One of the allies of Hunter and these clergymen is a man named John Russell Coryell.[3] He has recently been lecturing under their auspices, as, for instance, in an address to the "liberty congregation" at Lyric Hall. The front page of the publication containing this address (which is itself called "Making a Revolution," and is a companion-piece to others entitled "The Rent Strike," etc.) contains advertisements of other pamphlets by the same speaker which embrace titles like "Love and Passion," "Sex-Union and Parenthood," "What is Seduction?" and "A Child of Love." I

[3] It is not clear what man Roosevelt had in mind, but John Russell Coryell achieved his measure of eminence not as a socialistic clergyman but as the creator for Street and Smith of Nick Carter, detective.

got these pamphlets, which are published by a publishing company which calls itself the publishers of "liberal literature in general." Under the thin disguise of standing for a movement for social reform, these different pamphlets and others like them are largely mere pieces of pornographic literature; just as Debs' paper and speeches are largely mere pieces of the literature of criminal violence. One of these parlor socialists the other day, in addressing a girls' college, told them that "motherhood was the curse of women." Miss Jane Addams, in her recent book, shows lamentably by her own utterances the effects of belief in the socialism which bases itself upon Tolstoi (himself a sexual degenerate, whose *Kreutzer Sonata* is a fit supplement to his "My Religion," for erotic perversion very frequently goes hand in hand with a wild and fantastic mysticism).

It seems to me that those of us who are most interested in the campaign against privilege, most interested in securing genuine liberty, genuine justice and fair-dealing, and at least a measurable approach to equality of opportunity, are the very men of all others upon whom it is most incumbent to stand with robust and fearless sanity against the socialistic hysteria of these clergymen, and of the party which has Debs at its head, the party of Robert Hunter, and Moyer, and Haywood, and Jack London; and incidentally of almost all of the anarchists, for you may notice that the socialists and anarchists, altho in theory and on academic grounds not in accord, have in practice adopted the red flag as a common symbol and cheerfully work together. We must not allow ourselves to be put into the position of the New York *Sun* and *Evening Post*, and of excellent men like Nicholas Murray Butler who have unfortunately grown to adopt this position; we must never take the position of defending, or refraining from fighting, the grave and real abuses of the social and industrial system of today; but we must also set our faces like flint against the preachings, the practices, and the leadership which would merely lead to trying on a vaster scale the experiment of the Paris Commune — an experiment which would not only be hideous in itself, but which would, in the reaction, perpetuate all the worst abuses which it was nominally supposed to remedy.

Nine tenths of my fighting has been against the men of enormous wealth, and their henchmen in the world of business, of politics, of the lawyers, of the newspapers, who do their bidding; I am fighting privilege, whether in law, or erected in business or social life thru lack of law; at this moment I am trying my best to get the Republican convention to put in a moderate injunction plank, so as to make it evident that we mean to do justice to the workman, and to prevent a sense of wrong driving him into the ranks of envious discontent; but the Debs type of socialist points the way to national ruin as surely as any swindling financier or corrupt politician. *Sincerely yours*

* We have not kept it out, because to do so would I think work more mischief than the paper itself does.

Washington, June 17, 1908

To Assistant Secretary Newberry: Please confer with Secretary Taft and have on the Isthmus as near as may be twelve hundred marines in connection with the approaching elections. Ask the commander of the force to confer with both Secretaries Root and Taft, so as to secure his instructions from them. I do not believe there will be the least need of using these men; but as there is an apparent purpose among the Panama factions, on the part of one side to carry the election by fraud, and on the part of the other to attempt a revolution if it is so carried, we should have a sufficiency of force to enable us to act as may be necessary; and of course the larger the force is the less chance there is of bloodshed.

Incidentally, will you please ask the commander of marines on the Isthmus to report to me in full about the liquor sold on the Isthmus to the men and as to its effect on the men?

Washington, June 17, 1908

Dear Kohlsaat: Taft is reading the letter of yours now and chuckling over it heartily. We are going to elect him with a swoop; but we must all work on the assumption that it is a very hard contest! *Faithfully yours*

Personal and Confidential   Washington, June 17, 1908

My dear President Wheeler: What a wise letter yours of the 15th is! That is an adjective that cannot often be used with propriety, but it exactly fits your judgment on this convention. You have summed up admirably the situation as regards Taft's strength as a candidate, and the wrong estimate thereof. I am myself a little surprised at the conservative temper of the delegates — what you well call the "old commercial conservatism" of that Republicanism which dominated the party for many years and culminated in Hanna, and which was as totally unlike the Lincoln Republicanism of the party's first decade as the latter was unlike Tammany Democracy or socialistic populism. I think that the cause is to be found in the fact that there was no fight, *on a principle,* made in choosing the delegates. Before they were chosen the reactionaries had made up their minds that I could be beaten only by their accepting Taft, and accordingly they put all their strength into getting men of their stamp who would nevertheless be avowedly for Taft, and as of course this prevented any fight, they naturally got a rather ultraconservative set of delegates.

Hughes' selfish indifference to all considerations excepting his own welfare have, I suppose, prevented New York getting her nominee as Vice-President. Really it seems to me as tho Dolliver or Cummins would be the most available of all the *possible* men who have been suggested, as conditions really are. But I have carefully avoided taking sides for or against anyone, and this statement is for you personally.

With warm regards, believe me, *Faithfully yours*

4767 · TO HENRY CABOT LODGE *Roosevelt Mss.*

Telegram Washington, June 18, 1908

I am proud of and deeply touched by your really noble speech. It seems to me to cover the whole situation. Of course publish my telegram to you and the letter to Judge Dayton at any moment when or if you think it necessary. I think you have stated my personal relation to the matter in the best possible shape.[1] Taft is with me as I am dictating this telegram.

4768 · TO ANNA CABOT MILLS LODGE *Roosevelt Mss.*

Washington, June 19, 1908

Dearest Nannie: Sturgis Bigelow wrote us the other day giving us all the news and telling us all about you. We were so glad to hear from him. Now I wish to send you just a line, primarily to say how admirably I think Cabot handled the peculiarly delicate and difficult work at Chicago. In point of judgment, taste and power it would be literally impossible to better either his words or his actions. He was in a peculiar sense the guardian not only of the national interests but of my own personal honor; and to do his full duty as guardian it was necessary for him effectively to thwart the movements not merely of my foes but of the multitude of my well-meaning friends who did not think deeply or who were not of very sensitive fibre. It was absolutely necessary that any stampede for me should be prevented, and that I should not be nominated; for now that it is over we can confess to one another that it would have been well-nigh impossible for me to refuse the nomination, and perhaps ruin the party thereby, if the nomination had ac-

---

[1] In his speech as permanent chairman of the Republican convention, Lodge began with the usual political platitudes, continued by praising the party's achievements in regulating "enormous combinations of capital," then paid a tribute to Roosevelt, "the best abused and the most popular man in the United States today." His reference to the President set off a demonstration that lasted forty-nine minutes. The gallery began a chant that the delegates took up: "Four — four — four years more!" For a time some thought the convention would be stampeded. But Lodge stilled the tumult: "His refusal of a renomination, dictated by the loftiest motives and by a noble loyalty to American traditions, is final and irrevocable." The delegates applauded. "Any one, who attempts to use his name as a candidate for the presidency impugns both his sincerity and his good faith, two of the President's greatest and most conspicuous qualities, upon which no shadow has ever been cast." The delegates cheered. The crisis was past. Lodge continued with more platitudes. Those in the Taft wagon, hitched as it was to the star of Roosevelt, prepared to strike up the band.

tually been made; and yet if I had accepted, my power for useful service would have forever been lessened, because nothing could have prevented the wide diffusion of the suspicion that I had not really meant what I had said, that my actions did not really square with the highest and finest code of ethics — and if there is any value whatever in my career, as far as my countrymen are concerned, it consists in their belief that I have been both an efficient public man, and at the same time, a disinterested public servant.

We loved having all of you with us at dinner, and sitting out on the portico afterwards in the summer evening, the last night you were in Washington. The weather has been beautiful this spring. In fact, I think it has been the most beautiful spring and early summer we have seen in Washington, and Edith and I have enjoyed it to the full. We have ridden a great deal together, and on the afternoons I did not ride I have played tennis and Edith has usually come around afterwards to superintend the cold tea for the players. I have never known the grounds to be more beautiful, nor the flowers and the flower-bearing trees more lovely. Massachusetts Avenue is now fragrant with the scent of the lindens. Edith and I breakfast and lunch on the south portico and dine on the west terrace; and after breakfast and lunch we usually stroll around the grounds. I do not believe anyone else has ever enjoyed the White House as we have enjoyed it, and now we are ready to leave it without a pang with plenty of interest and pleasure ahead of us.*

Have you read Murray's book on the History of the Greek Epic? If not, it is well worth your while reading. You probably know some of his poetic translations of the old Greek dramatists.

Goodbye, dear Nannie. *Ever lovingly yours*

* Of all persons, that cheerful small pagan Quentin remarked thoughtfully today "there is a little hole in my «stomach» when I think of leaving the White House"!

4769 · TO HARRIS DICKSON   *Roosevelt Mss.*

Washington, June 19, 1908

My dear Mr. Dickson: [1] I have your letter of the 17th. Do come right to Oyster Bay with that stinging snake. I would be more pleased to have it than any beast or reptile in Africa! For Heaven's sake don't let any accident happen to it! Come out and take lunch with me at Oyster Bay next Tuesday at 1:30 o'clock, and then tell me about the Metcalfs and Major Helm, and all the rest.

Now take extra care of that snake and bring it out. If we actually get possession of a snake which has a genuine sting in the tail — a genuine sting

---

[1] Harris Dickson, lawyer and writer, judge of the municipal court at Vicksburg, 1905–1907; creator of "sunlover Sam"; *Collier's* correspondent during the First World War; author of such novels as *The Black Wolf's Breed* (1899), *She That Hesitates* (1903), and *Duke of Devil-May-Care* (1905).

which can be worked in and out — we have made a tremendous advance in the knowledge of natural history.[2] *Sincerely yours*

Washington, June 19, 1908

My dear Trevelyan: Well, the convention is over and Taft is nominated on a platform which I heartily approve. No one can prophesy in politics, and so I cannot be sure that we shall elect him, but the chances I believe favor it, and most certainly it will show . . . in the country if he is not elected. For, always excepting Washington and Lincoln, I believe that Taft as President will rank with any other man who has ever been in the White House.[1]

It has been a curious contest, for I have had to fight tooth and nail against being nominated myself, and in the last three weeks it has needed very resolute effort on my part to prevent a break among the delegations, which would have meant a stampede for me and my nomination. I could not have prevented it at all unless I had thrown myself heart and soul into the business of nominating Taft and had shown to the country that he stood for exactly the same principles and policies that I did, and that I believed with all my heart and soul that under him we should progress steadily along the road this administration has traveled. He and I view public questions exactly alike. In fact, I think it has been very rare that two public men have ever been so much at one in all the essentials of their beliefs and practices.

When I made my announcement three years ago last November, just after the election, that I would under no circumstances again be a candidate, I of course acted on a carefully thought-out and considered theory. Having made it and having given my word to the people at large as to what I would do, and other men, including Taft, having entered the field on the strength of this statement of mine, I never felt the slightest hesitancy, the slightest wavering, as to the proper course to follow. But the developments of the last year or two have been so out of the common that at times I have felt a little uncomfortable as to whether my announced decision had been wise. But I think it was wise; and now I want to give you my reasons in full.

In the first place, I will freely admit what there is to say against it. I have a good deal of contempt for the type which Mirabeau condemned in Lafayette as the "Cromwell-Grandison" type, for those who, like Dante's Pope,

---

[2] Unhappily the snake "proved to have no sting whatever." "It does seem curious," Roosevelt later observed, apparently forgetting his initial excitement, "that they should not have thought of looking into so self-evident a matter before they sent him on."

---

[1] Roosevelt had already made public a similar assessment. Congratulating the country immediately after Taft was nominated, the President declared that Taft "would be as emphatically a President of the plain people as Lincoln, yet not Lincoln himself would be freer from the least taint of demagogy. . . . He has a peculiar and intimate knowledge of and sympathy with the needs of all our people — of the farmer, of the wage worker, the business man, the property owner."

are guilty of "il gran refuito" (I am a trifle uncertain as to the correctness of the Italian.) I do not like any man who flinches from work, and I like him none the better if he covers his flinching under the title of self-abnegation or renunciation or any other phrase, which may mean merely weakness, or else that he is willing to subordinate great and real public interests to a meticulous and fantastic morality in which he is concerned chiefly for the sake of his own shriveled soul. There is very much to be said in favor of the theory that the public has a right to demand as long service from any man who is doing good service as it thinks will be useful; and during the last year or two I have been rendered extremely uncomfortable both by the exultation of my foes over my announced intention to retire, and by the real uneasiness and chagrin felt by many good men because, as they believed, they were losing quite needlessly the leader in whom they trusted, and who they believed could bring to a successful conclusion certain struggles which they regarded as of vital concern to the national welfare. Moreover, it was of course impossible to foresee, and I did not foresee, when I made my public announcement of my intention, that the then leadership I possest would continue (as far as I am able to tell) unbroken, as has actually been the case; and that the people who believed in me and trusted me and followed me would three or four years later still feel that I was the man of all others whom they wisht to see President. Yet such I think has been the case; and therefore, when I felt obliged to insist on retiring and abandoning the leadership, now and then I felt ugly qualms as to whether I was not refusing to do what I ought to do, and abandoning great work on a mere fantastic point of honor.

These are strong reasons why my course should be condemned; yet I think that the countervailing reasons are still stronger. Of course when I spoke I had in view the precedent set by Washington and continued ever since, the precedent which recognizes the fact that, as there inheres in the Presidency more power than in any other office in any great republic or constitutional monarchy of modern times, it can only be saved from abuse by having the people as a whole accept as axiomatic the position that one man can hold it for no more than a limited time. I don't think that any harm comes from the concentration of powers in one man's hands, provided the holder does not keep it for more than a certain, definite time, and then returns to the people from whom he sprang. In the great days of the Roman Republic no harm whatever came from the dictatorship, because great tho the power of the dictator was, after a comparatively short period he surrendered it back to those from whom he gained it. On the other hand, the history of the first and second French Republics, not to speak of the Spanish-American Republics, not to speak of the Commonwealth, in Seventeenth-Century England, has shown that the strong man, and even the strong man who is good, may very readily subvert free institutions if he and the people at large grow to accept his continued possession of vast power as being necessary to good government. It is a very unhealthy thing that any man should be considered necessary to the people as a whole, save in the way of meeting some given crisis. Moreover, in a republic like ours the vital need is that there shall be a general recognition of the moral law, of the law which, as regards public men, means belief in efficient and disinterested service for the public rendered without thought of personal gain, and above all without the thought of self-perpetuation in office. I regard the memories of Washington and Lincoln as priceless heritages for our people, just because they are the memories of strong men, of men who cannot be accused of weakness or timidity, of men who I believe were quite as strong for instance as Cromwell or Bismarck, and very much stronger than the Louis Napoleon type, who, nevertheless, led careers marked by disinterestedness just as much as by strength; who, like Timoleon and Hampden, in very deed, and not as a mere matter of oratory or fine writing, put the public good, the good of the people as a whole, as the first of all considerations.

Now, my ambition is that, in however small a way, the work I do shall be along the Washington and Lincoln Lines. While President I have *been* President, emphatically; I have used every ounce of power there was in the office and I have not cared a rap for the criticisms of those who spoke of my "usurpation of power"; for I knew that the talk was all nonsense and that there was no usurpation. I believe that the efficiency of this Government depends upon its possessing a strong central executive, and wherever I could establish a precedent for strength in the executive, as I did for instance as regards external affairs in the case of sending the fleet around the world, taking Panama, settling affairs of Santo Domingo and Cuba; or as I did in internal affairs in settling the anthracite coal strike, in keeping order in Nevada this year when the Federation of Miners threatened anarchy, or as I have done in bringing the big corporations to book — why, in all these cases I have felt not merely that my action was right in itself, but that in showing the strength of, or in giving strength to, the executive, I was establishing a precedent of value. I believe in a strong executive; I believe in power; but I believe that responsibility should go with power, and that it is not well that the strong executive should be a perpetual executive. Above all and beyond all I believe as I have said before that the salvation of this country depends upon Washington and Lincoln representing the type of leader to which we are true. I hope that in my acts I have been a good President, a President who has deserved well of the Republic; but most of all, I believe that whatever value my service may have comes even more from what I *am* than from what I *do*. I may be mistaken, but it is my belief that the bulk of my countrymen, the men whom Abraham Lincoln called "the plain people" — the farmers, mechanics, small tradesmen, hard-working professional men — feel that I am in a peculiar sense their President, that I represent the democracy in somewhat the fashion that Lincoln did, that is, not in any demagogic way but with the sincere effort to stand for a government by the people and for the people. Now the chief service I can render these plain people who believe in me is, not to destroy their ideal of me. They have followed me for the past six or seven years, indeed for some years previously, because they thought they recognized in me certain qualities in which they believed, because they regarded me as honest and disinterested, as having courage and common sense. Now I wouldn't for anything in the world shatter this belief of theirs in me, unless it were necessary to do so because they had embarked on a wrong course, and I could only be really true to them by forfeiting their good will. For instance, if they made up their minds that they would repudiate their debts, or under a gust of emotion decided to follow any course that was wrong, I could show loyalty to them only by opposing them tooth and nail, without the slightest regard to any amount of unpopularity or obloquy. But this of course isn't what I mean when I say I do not want to shatter their belief in me. What I mean is that I do not want to make them think that after all I am actuated by selfish motives, by motives of self-interest, that my championship of their cause, that my opposition to the plutocracy, is simply due to the usual demagog's desire to pander to the mob, or to the no more dangerous, but even more sinister, desire to secure self-advancement under the cloak of championship of popular rights. Of course I may be wrong in my belief, but my belief is that a great many honest people in this country who lead hard lives are helped in their efforts to keep straight and avoid envy and hatred and despair by their faith in me and in the principles I preach and in my practice of these principles. I would not for anything do the moral damage to these people that might come from shattering their faith in my personal disinterestedness. A few months ago three old back-country farmers turned up in Washington and after a while managed to get in to see me. They were rugged old fellows, as hairy as Boers and a good deal of the Boer type. They hadn't a black coat among them, and two of them wore no cravats; that is, they just had on their working clothes, but all cleaned and brushed. When they finally got to see me they explained that they hadn't anything whatever to ask, but that they believed in me, believed that I stood for what they regarded as the American ideal, and as one rugged old fellow put it, "We want to shake that honest hand." Now this anecdote seems rather sentimental as I tell it, and I do not know that I can convey to you the effect that incident produced on me; but it was one of the very many incidents which have occurred, and they have made me feel that I am under a big debt of obligation to the good people of this country, and that I am bound not by any unnecessary action of mine to forfeit their respect, not to hurt them by taking away any part of what they have built up as their ideal of me. It is just as I would not be willing to hurt my soldiers, to destroy my influence among men who look up to me as leader, by needlessly doing anything in battle which would give the idea that I was not personally brave; even tho some given risk might seem a little unnecessary to an outsider. However certain I might be that in seeking or accepting a third term I was actuated by a sincere desire to serve my fellow countrymen, I am very much afraid that multitudes of thoroly honest men who have believed deeply in me, (and some of whom, by the way, until I consented to run might think that they wisht me to run) would nevertheless have a feeling of disappointment if I did try to occupy the Presidency for three consecutive terms, to hold it longer than it was deemed wise that Washington should hold it.

I would have felt very differently, and very much more doubtful about what to do, if my leaving the Presidency had meant that there was no chance to continue the work in which I am engaged and which I deem vital to the welfare of the people. But in Taft there was ready to hand a man whose theory of public and private duty is my own, and whose practice of this theory is what I hope mine is; and if we can elect him President we achieve all that could be achieved by continuing me in the office, and yet we avoid all the objections, all the risk of creating a bad precedent.

There, my dear Sir George! I am afraid there is a good deal of ego in this letter, but I wanted you to feel just what it was that actuated me in the course I have followed, and I think you will understand me.

When I get thru the Presidency next year I am going for ten months or a year to Africa, and I am already in consultation with Edward North Buxton and Selous about the details of my trip. As I wrote to Selous, my aim is to visit the Pleistocene and the world "as it lay in sunshine unworn of the plow"; to see the great beasts whose like our forefathers saw when they lived in caves and smote one another with stone-headed axes. I do not want to do any butchering, but I would like to get a few trophies. Probably all to be put in the National Museum here at Washington. My second son will go with me, and if I come out by the Nile the following spring I shall hope to meet Mrs. Roosevelt and my younger daughter there. I should then greatly like to spend a few weeks in North Italy, France and England; but I shall not try to if I find I have to be presented at the various courts, & meet the sovereigns, prime ministers, and others. When I am thru with the Presidency I am thru with it, definitely and once and for all. The second my successor takes the oath of office I become a private citizen, and then I wish to go downstream among the earthen pots and not among the brazen pots. For instance, I should be delighted to meet the Kaiser if I could meet him now and talk with him and consult with him as the head of one great country can and ought to talk and consult with the head of another, but I have not the slightest desire to meet him when I am thru with the Presidency. On the contrary I should very much object to doing so. I should think it would bore him, and I know it would bore me. In fact, I should go nearly crazy if I were obliged to make numbers of formal visits to people of merely titular interest; and I should mind even more the fact that they, poor creatures, were suffering because from a mistaken sense of duty they thought they ought to see me. If I can visit England without having my own ambassador or anyone else call on me, without being expected to see anybody I didn't already know, I should love to come. I should love to meet you and Selous and Buxton and Arthur Lee, and to see the English lanes in spring, and stop at English country inns, and see a cathedral here and there; and if just before, provided it were not too hot, I could have seen some of the hill towns of Italy and seen some Provençal towns and some of the French cathedrals, and have gotten to Paris for a day in the Louvre — why this is what I should like most of all to do. But if all this is impossible, and I have to go thru the dreary farce of unspeakably foolish formal entertainment at the cost of people in whom I take not the slightest real interest, why I shall come straight back from Africa to the United States. *Faithfully yours*

"*Taft Will Carry on the Work*"

June 1908–November 1908

Oyster Bay, June 20, 1908

My dear Dr. Walcott: [1] About the 1st of April next I intend to start for Africa. My plans are of course indefinite, but at present I hope they will be something on the following order:

By May 1st I shall land at Mombasa and spend the next few months hunting and traveling in British and German East Africa; probably going thence to or toward Uganda, with the expectation of striking the Nile about the beginning of the new year, and then working down it, with side trips after animals and birds, so as to come out at tidewater, say, about March 1st. This would give me ten months in Africa. As you know, I am not in the least a game butcher. I like to do a certain amount of hunting, but my real and main interest is the interest of a faunal naturalist. Now, it seems to me that this opens the best chance for the National Museum to get a fine collection not only of the big game beasts, but of the smaller mammals and birds of Africa; and looking at it dispassionately, it seems to me that the chance ought not to be neglected. I will make arrangements in connection with publishing a book which will enable me to pay for the expenses of myself and my son. But what I would like to do would be to get one or two professional field taxidermists, field naturalists, to go with us, who should prepare and send back the specimens we collect. The collection which would thus go to the National Museum would be of unique value. It would, I hope, include rhinoceros, giraffe, hippopotamus, many of the big antelope, possibly elephant, buffalo, and lion, together with the rare smaller animals and birds. I have not the means that would enable me to pay for the one or two taxidermists and their kit, and the curing and transport of the specimens for the National Museum. But as I say, I doubt if the National Museum would ever again have the chance to get a collection which would be from every standpoint as interesting. Of course the actual hunting of the big game I would want to do myself, or have my son do; but the specimens would all go to the National Museum, save a very few personal trophies of little scientific value which for some reason I might like to keep. Now, can the National Museum arrange, in view of getting these specimens, for the services of one or two field taxidermists, and for the care and transport of the specimens? Could the money be provided without Congressional action? If not, I would try to get Congress to act by authorizing the expenditure of the comparatively small sum necessary; or it may be that I would be able to get the Carnegie Institute to help. I shall send a copy of this letter to Mr. Root, because of his connection with the Carnegie Institute. If the National Museum won't do anything in the matter, I may communicate with the American Museum of Natural

---

[1] Since 1907 Walcott had been secretary of the Smithsonian Institution. With genuine personal enthusiasm he made the arrangements requested by Roosevelt in this letter.

History of New York; but of course, as ex-President, I should feel that the National Museum is the museum to which my collection should go.

With high regard, *Sincerely yours*

4772 · TO RAY STANNARD BAKER   *Roosevelt Mss.*

Personal   Oyster Bay, June 22, 1908

My dear Mr. Baker: I have your letter of the 20th. I knew David Grayson already, but I had no idea that he was you. I value the book and thank you for sending it to me. I shall read it with real interest; I have already read much of it.[1] *Sincerely yours*

4773 · TO BENJAMIN IDE WHEELER   *Roosevelt Mss.*

Private   Oyster Bay, June 22, 1908

My dear President Wheeler: I feel precisely as you do about the nomination of Sherman, he is a good man, but not known in the west. My own idea was strongly to get Dolliver or Cummins,[1] as long as we could not get Hadley of Missouri,[2] because I expect ⟨us⟩ Taft to carry the East anyhow, whereas I am doubtful about the country west of the Mississippi — indeed, about some of the States just east of the Mississippi, where the radicals feel exceedingly suspicious of anything that looks like reaction.

Thanking you for your letters, which were very interesting, I am, *Sincerely yours*

4774 · TO HENRY LEWIS STIMSON   *Roosevelt Mss.*

                                                 Oyster Bay, June 23, 1908

Dear Harry: I am more amused than I can say at getting your letter and finding out who it was. Now do remember hereafter that when I haven't my spectacles on I can see no human being. I can't tell a white man from an Indian. I would not recognize my own sons ten feet off. And I don't wear

[1] Relieving the tension of muckraking for the *American Magazine*, Ray Stannard Baker, under the pen name of David Grayson, had written the first of his delightful essays to "express the joy . . . and the sense of beauty and of peace, in country life and country ways." The appropriate title of the initial volume of these essays, published in 1907, was *Adventures in Contentment*.

[1] Iowa conservatives opposed the nomination of either Cummins or Dolliver. They did not want Cummins on the ticket and they feared that if Dolliver were nominated, Cummins would inherit his seat in the Senate.
[2] Herbert Spencer Hadley, while attorney general of Missouri, 1904–1909, won national attention for his successful prosecution of cases against various railroads, the International Harvester Company, and the Standard Oil Company. A liberal Republican, Hadley was elected Governor of Missouri in 1908, the first of his party to win that office. He led the Roosevelt forces at the Republican National Convention of 1912 but would not bolt to the Bull Moose.

spectacles in bathing! We are driven nearly frantic by parties of picnickers who, if they happen along when we are in swimming together, come up with wild enthusiasm, certain that Mrs. Roosevelt and I and the children, while swimming or standing on the beach in drenched bathing clothes, will be glad to hold an impromptu levee. I have found that with these ardent picnickers, the time I was swimming was just the one time that I had to be absolutely firm in refusing to shake hands or spend the time in genial conversation. I hadn't the vaguest idea who you were, nor had Mrs. Roosevelt. I simply took it for granted that you were one of the ordinary picnickers or holiday makers with whom we have exactly such experiences. . . . Hereafter, if you see me without my spectacles, be sure to proclaim your identity.

Now won't Mrs. Stimson and you come over to lunch with us Saturday next at 1:30? I expect Taft and Luke Wright.[1] *Sincerely yours*

4775 · TO HENRY CABOT LODGE   *Roosevelt Mss.*

Oyster Bay, June 24, 1908

Dear Cabot: Yes, I shall have to wait for that talk until you come back; but I was mighty glad to get your letter. I shall take up the ship business with Luke Wright on Saturday, altho you did not enclose the memorandum you mention.[1]

On every side I hear of the great success you made as Chairman. Loeb tells me that various people returning from the convention told him how well your voice carried; whereas on the contrary Burrows was not heard at all. I am very much pleased to learn how well Crane did. Certainly he contrasted with Gallinger and John Kean.[2] I saw the incident of your twirling the young man with the megaphone. (Here Loeb interjects that he wishes you had broken his neck. It appears he knows the gentleman and is prejudiced against him.) In short, you rendered a great public service, and you also rendered me a personal service.

I think we are in good shape, but of course I wish I knew more of the extent of the radical movement west of the Alleghenies. I believe the Pacific Coast is all right, and the Rocky Mountain States, barring, perhaps, Montana and Nevada. But I await with some concern further information about the States in the upper Mississippi Valley. Sherman's nomination I think helps us in New York by interesting the organization; but in the upper Mississippi Valley he is considered identified with Cannon and I have been disturbed by the extent of the hostility to and the revolt against Cannon. Whether

[1] Luke Wright had been appointed Secretary of War to succeed Taft, who resigned to conduct his campaign.

[1] Roosevelt referred to a proposed sale of ships to the Isthmian Canal Commission; see Numbers 4882, 5017, 5018.
[2] Murray Crane, unlike most other conservative senators, had co-operated with Lodge on the seating of contesting delegations and the framing of the platform.

there is any chance of our carrying Kentucky, Tennessee, or North Carolina, I do not know. If Bryan is nominated, as I suppose is sure,[3] we shall carry Maryland, I think, without a doubt, and then of course there is a small chance in Virginia. But what I am looking forward to getting information about is the district in the upper Mississippi River Valley, from Indiana to Nebraska and Minnesota.

Meanwhile, I am developing my African trip along satisfactory lines. I hope to be able to make it a scientific expedition on behalf of the National Museum; that is, I will pay absolutely for the expenses of Kermit and myself, but I will get the National Museum to send a couple of field taxidermists with us. They will collect specimens under my direction. They will skin and cure the big game we shoot, and the Museum will pay for them, their equipment and attendants, and for the transport of the trophies home. Everything I shoot will then go to the National Museum. I would a great deal rather have this a scientific trip, which would give it a purpose and character, than simply a prolonged holiday of mine. I am no longer fit to do arduous exploring work, and this will probably be about the last time that I shall be fit even for the moderate kind of trip I have planned. But it seems to me that there is something worth doing to be done along the lines I have laid out — something that is still the work of a man of action; and I should like to remain a man of action as long as possible. Of course everything I can do for Taft's success will be done; but after all, most of what I can thus do has already been done, and I do not wish to become officious or a busybody. Taft and his chosen friends must run the campaign, and I will help so far as the President properly can help. Barring a cataclysm, I am pretty well thru the great stress of my work as President, or at least the hardest work and most intense worry.

With love to dear Nannie, and a pleasant voyage, *Ever yours*

4776 · TO PRESCOTT FARNSWORTH HALL   *Roosevelt Mss.*

Oyster Bay, June 24, 1908

My dear Mr. Hall: Would you object to my showing your letter to Senator Lodge?[1] I have a very high regard for Secretary Straus and it is exceedingly difficult for me to believe that there has been the slightest conscious failure on his part to enforce the immigration law. Lodge is very anxious that it

---

[3] Bryan easily carried the Democratic convention. John W. Kern of Indiana was nominated for Vice-President.

---

[1] Hall's letter was forwarded to Lodge. The senator wrote Roosevelt that, on making an "unheralded" inspection of immigration offices in Baltimore, Philadelphia, New York, and Boston, he "could detect no evidence of what Mr. Hall alleges." Although believing that "Mr. Straus is adverse to the laws which affect the entry of poor Jews, and especially to the poor physique clause," Lodge assured the President that the immigration law was carefully enforced (Lodge, II, 306). Roosevelt was completely satisfied by Lodge's answer to Hall's charges; see No. 4836.

should be enforced with the utmost strictness, and if the Immigration Commission under him cannot make the investigation that you desire, then I shall have to think very seriously as to how it should be made. *Sincerely yours*

4777 · TO CHARLES JOSEPH BONAPARTE *Roosevelt Mss.*

Oyster Bay, June 26, 1908

My dear Bonaparte: To take up first the last part of your letter of the 24th, you rather paralyze me by what you say of Bourne's going to Oregon, for he has arranged to bring his client, Mr. Archbold, out to see me next Monday.[1] I send you his letter, as it may amuse you. But he has ceased to be amusing to me. On the "second elective term" he can at least no longer interview me. But I think I shall have to explain to both him and Archbold, what I have tried to explain to both of them two or three times already — indeed, to Bourne a dozen times — that it is absolutely useless to see me, and that Bourne can be of no possible service to Archbold or us in the matter; that Archbold's attorneys, the Standard Oil attorneys, must see you and Kellogg; and that after that, if they and you come to an agreement, then and not till then it will be time enough to lay the matter before me. I am anxious to show every Senator all possible courtesy; but there are limits!

In the Lingenfelter matter,[2] how would it do to forward the papers to Cooley and tell him on his way back from Alaska to stop and make a thoro investigation of the whole business? On the one hand, I am prepared to have any exposure made about anyone in Idaho; on the other hand, I am entirely convinced that Ruick and the ex-Marshal were in an exceedingly dirty conspiracy, and I expect charges from them against their successors as a matter of course. *Faithfully yours*

P.S. I never heard of Mr. Lovely, of course. I am glad you have written Meyer about it.

By George! I am so obliged to you for thinking of Rose. It is the appointment of all others that I would like to make. It is an ideal appointment. How in the name of Heaven I never happened to think of him myself, I don't know. Do make both announcements at once. It is true, Rose is a personal friend of yours and mine; but nobody except perhaps the *Evening Post* would have the right to think that this serves as a disqualification for office under us.[3]

[1] Senator Bourne and John D. Archbold, vice-president of the Standard Oil Company of New Jersey, visited Oyster Bay on Monday, the twenty-ninth. Oil company officials, troubled by Kellogg's effective presentation before Federal Examiner Franklin Ferriss of the government's case against the parent company, hoped as they had the previous December to arrange a settlement out of court (see No. 4522). Roosevelt, as he indicated to Bonaparte, quickly ended their hopes; see No. 4791.
[2] C. H. Lingenfelter, successor to Ruick as United States district attorney for Idaho.
[3] Rose refused the post of assistant to the Attorney General which was ultimately given to Wade H. Ellis, attorney general of Ohio and author of the 1908 Republican platform.

Oyster Bay, June 29, 1908

My dear Mr. Twitchell: [1] To the Irrigation Congress which is to assemble at Albuquerque in September for the sixteenth time I send greetings and congratulations upon the well-deserved and widespread public interest in the meetings of this Congress, and in the cause which it represents. Irrigation, as one of the lines of conservation and development of the natural resources of the Nation, is more and more appreciated by the people of the whole country. There has been a notable change in public sentiment regarding irrigation and its place in the National economy since the beginning of your work. I attribute much of this to the discussions at your meetings.

My attention has been given especially to the irrigation of Government lands under the terms of the Reclamation Act. At the same time I appreciate the great progress which has been made through private and corporate efforts in the reclamation of our arid and semiarid lands, and in the making of homes. Praise is due to the men who have been pioneers in this great work.

All roads to success in the creation of homes upon the arid lands should be made easy. Ultimately every possible drop of water should be conserved and every acre of land that can be irrigated should be put under the most productive system of cultivation. There is no line of effort more helpful to the public welfare than the conservation of the waste waters, bringing them out upon the waste lands, and creating small prosperous farms owned and tilled by self-respecting, independent citizens.

I am glad to call your attention to the fact that the Reclamation Service, under the direction of Secretary Garfield and Mr. Newell, has effectively continued its work during the past year and is now taking water to 250,000 acres of land. The larger works nearing completion will soon bring water to an additional area of 1,000,000 acres. Not only has much land been irrigated, but the works built or being finished are of the most permanent nature.

The landowners who have settled on the reclaimed areas are already returning to the Treasury, in small amounts, a part of the investment by the Government. The success already attained shows that with continued good administration it will be possible to replace in the Treasury the entire investment, and to use it again in the building of other works. The gloomy predictions which were made at the outset that the cost of the works could not or would not be repaid by the people will fail. We have already advanced to a point where I think it is perfectly safe to assert that the people of the West will repay the Reclamation Fund in full, and will be able to do it out of the profits from the crops on the reclaimed land. *Sincerely yours*

---

[1] Ralph Emerson Twitchell, New Mexico Republican, railroad attorney, and conservationist; first vice-president of the National Irrigation Congress.

Personal   Oyster Bay, June 29, 1908

Dear Will: The more I think over that the more sure I am that while Hitchcock would be an entirely satisfactory man to run the campaign, and infinitely better than any of his critics and rivals, yet the best man would be
Frank Kellogg.[1] It would be a very serious sacrifice for him to take it, but I
think he would take it. I believe, however, that before you ask him you
ought to see Bonaparte and find out just what provision could be made for
a substitute for him. We owe this to the Government; tho as a matter of fact,
if, as you intend, you put him in as Attorney General, he would be carrying
on the suit ultimately himself anyhow. As I say, I had an absolutely satisfactory talk with him after you left.

It was delightful seeing you. I think we made no mistake in Luke Wright.
Give my love to Mrs. Taft, and believe me, *Faithfully yours*

4780 · TO CHARLES JOSEPH BONAPARTE *Roosevelt Mss.*

Telegram   Oyster Bay, June 29, 1908

Please communicate at once with the State and War Departments in reference
to the action as to infringement of neutrality laws on the border of Mexico,
and wire district attorneys and marshals of Texas immediately to take steps
effectively to co-operate with the military and stop all violations of the
neutrality laws and to make searching investigation in Del Rio, El Paso and
elsewhere to find out and apprehend guilty parties. Every possible effort
is to be made to bring to justice every man directly or indirectly connected
with the offense.[1]

[1] In choosing a chairman for the National Committee, Taft had to consider the conflicting claims of the men who had managed his prenomination campaign. Frank H.
Hitchcock, the ablest and best-known nationally of these managers, was the logical
choice, but Vorys in particular was jealous of Hitchcock. The selection of Kellogg,
who had not been identified with the prenomination campaign, might have reduced
the tensions within the Taft camp. Moreover, Kellogg, then Minnesota national committeeman, had for long been a practicing lawyer and a successful government
attorney with desirable political and business connections; he was also acceptable to
progressives as well as to conservatives. More than any of the Taft managers, his
stature approximated that of a Hanna or Cortelyou. But Kellogg was reluctant to
serve; Bonaparte did not feel he could spare him from the Justice Department; and
Taft had obligations to those who had performed so well. Hitchcock was chosen as
chairman.

[1] On June 26 a group of Mexican revolutionists began an abortive insurrection by
raiding the town of Las Vacas, which was across the Rio Grande from Del Rio,
Texas. During the skirmish at Las Vacas, Mexican troops fired across the border at
those raiders who were attempting to return to their bases in the United States. For
several days the insurrectionists, working partly from American bases, made sporadic
raids on towns and garrisons in northern Mexico. Mexican authorities promptly
dispatched cavalry to the troubled area and by July 1 had captured most of the

Oyster Bay, June 29, 1908

My dear Bishop: Your letter touched me. Indeed I realize to the full the great problems of the Orient; but do you not think that sometimes a man has a certain freshness if he turns to new problems?[1] I cannot tell you how much it would have been to me, for instance, during the past seven years if there had been someone in Washington who would have lookt at the problems afforded by the slums, by the poor districts in Washington, with the intense zeal of a missionary, and yet with the practical judgment of a cool-headed reformer. There are very few such people. You are one. It may be that the next President will not feel as I do in such matters. (This is quite compatible with his being a far better man, as I need hardly say.) But my work with the police force depended, as far as real good was concerned, very largely upon my having Jacob Riis to advise me; and so I believe if you had been Bishop of Washington thruout my term of service, that you and I and certain other men, like Gifford Pinchot and Jim Garfield, could have accomplished an astonishing amount in connection with the city. But of course this particular work was only an infinitesimal part of my task, and there was no one who made it his first consideration in exactly the spirit that you would have done; and so this particular work was left unaccomplished. I loved and admired Bishop Satterlee, but he of course was of a different type from the type necessary for such a job.

With all good wishes, believe me, *Faithfully yours*

---

leaders of the revolt. At Mexico's request, the United States acted to enforce the neutrality laws which forbade filibusters of the type that had begun the insurrection. The Governor of Texas, on Adee's instructions, sent Texas forces to patrol the border. Even before Roosevelt intervened, the Justice Department had alerted United States marshals and their deputies. Finally, on June 30, Brigadier General A. L. Myer, in command of the Department of Texas, sent four troops of cavalry to the border. These measures cut off the escape of the insurrectionists and prevented further raids from Texas. By July 2 quiet had been restored. President Diaz in September publicly thanked the United States for its prompt and effective action. Not serious in itself, the episode and the occasional outbreaks that followed it, like the unsuccessful revolution of September 1906, revealed the increasing discontent with the Diaz regime and foreshadowed the successful revolution of 1910.

---

[1] Brent had declined the bishopric of Washington, vacated in February 1908, when Henry Yates Satterlee died. Satterlee had spent his most constructive energy in planning the Washington Cathedral. Roosevelt had hoped Brent, later Satterlee's biographer, would give new direction to the work of the church in the District of Columbia.

Oyster Bay, June 30, 1908

To the Secretary of the Navy: Will you please submit Commander Key's letter of June 9th[1] (an official copy of which is on file in the Navy Department) to the General Board and the Naval War College, with orders that these two bodies make a joint report on the subjects referred to therein, and on the design of the *North Dakota* class, including an opinion as to the defects, if any, in the designs of these vessels; an opinion as to whether any or all of these defects can be wholly or partially remedied, and particularly a recommendation as to all of the military characteristics which should be required in the battleships to be built in the immediate future, this recommendation to include specific reference to the question of armor protection for hull and battery, the number, calibre, and location of the guns of the main battery, the number, calibre, special design, and location of the torpedo-defense guns, and the number and location of the torpedo tubes.

Also ask them as to whether it would be well to have all commanders in chief directed to require the commanding officer of each ship in the navy to appoint a board to determine what is to be the draft under the conditions prescribed by the Walker board — that is, what the draft would be when fully equipped for service, and with two thirds of the full allowance of stores, ammunition and coal on board; and whether it would not be well to have the commanding officers of our ships furnish stability statements containing information corresponding to that furnished in the British naval stability statements — that is, the actual weight carried at normal draft, deep-load draft, and light draft, and the exact draft of the ships when carrying each of these loads.[2]

[1] Key's letter, written June 9, had described defects in design of the *North Dakota*. While on duty at the Fore River Yard where the *North Dakota* was building, Key had carefully studied the navy's newest battleship. He concluded that the guns of the torpedo battery were too close to the water and were improperly protected; the twelve-inch guns were less powerful than similar guns of foreign navies; the location of the turrets and one of the powder magazines hampered the fighting qualities of the ship; and finally, as was true of all recent American ships, the main armor belt was too low to afford adequate protection. Such defects seemed, in Key's opinion, to verify the contentions that he, Sims, and other younger seagoing officers had made at the Senate naval committee's hearings in February 1908 about the deficiencies of the Bureau of Construction and the bureau system of administration which permitted such errors of design to occur; see Numbers 4549, 4647, 4651.

Realizing that his letter would be pigeonholed by the Bureau of Construction, Key took the precaution of sending a copy to Sims. Sims forwarded it to Roosevelt with a communication of his own in which he urged the President to call a conference to study Key's charges. Roosevelt, approving his naval aide's suggestion, followed almost exactly the wording of Sims's letter in writing the above letter to Metcalf. At the conference which met at Newport during late July and August, Sims, Key, and other younger officers fought strenuously but unsuccessfully to remedy the present and prevent future errors in ship design; see Numbers 4839, 4847, and Morison, *Sims,* ch. xiii.

[2] The *North Dakota's* armor belt was too low, Key charged, because the Bureau of Construction failed to follow the draft measurements prescribed by the Walker

Oyster Bay, July 1, 1908

My dear Newberry: I have your letter of the 29th ultimo. In addition to the reports of Capps and the Bureau of Construction, I want reports from sea-going officers about those battleships.[1] Last year, while I became convinced that Sims, Key, Winslow, and the other junior officers had greatly exaggerated the defects of which they complained, I was left with the very uncomfortable feeling that there might be some real defects, and I want if possible to avoid any slip-up.[2] *Sincerely yours*

4784 · TO GEORGE VON LENGERKE MEYER *Roosevelt Mss.*

Personal Oyster Bay, July 1, 1908

Dear George: What do you think about my showing your letter to Taft, or at least to the Chairman of the National Committee when he is nominated? It strikes me as very important.[1] As for Frick, I am a little surprised.[2] I have had him again and again at the White House and have shown him far more consideration than Carnegie. He asked me to appoint a man for Interstate Commerce Commissioner who, in the first place, I did not think ought to be appointed, and who, in the next place, could not be appointed for geographical reasons. It does not make the slightest difference whether we have two judges of the Supreme Court from Massachusetts; but it would make a great deal of difference if we left the country west of the Mississippi or south of Mason and Dixon's line without a judge; and this would have been analogous to what Frick wanted me to do. *Ever yours*

[*Handwritten*] I have treated Frick just as, for example, I have treated Gary; I gave each all consideration, listened to what each had to say with the hope I could do what was asked; but in each case acting finally on my own judgement of what was best. But I judged them to possess good faith, as certain other such men do not; therefore on their representations, I allowed their corporation to purchase the Tennessee Coal & Iron Co., in the panic; but where they asked something wrong, as when Frick asked me to appoint Hyde as Ambassador at Paris — . . . .

Board of 1896. As a result Key was certain that the *North Dakota*, like all the recently built battleships, would have an excessive and dangerous overdraft. He not only recommended a return to the specification of the Walker Board, but also urged the adoption of the more careful and accurate methods of draft determination used by the British.

---

[1] The *North Dakota* and *Delaware;* see No. 4782.
[2] See Numbers 4549, 4647.

---

[1] The letter dealt with the potential importance of the postal savings-bank plan as an issue in the election; see No. 4811.
[2] Frick was "feeling sore"; see No. 4786.

Oyster Bay, July 1, 1908

My dear Admiral: I am pleased with your letter, of course.[1] I think the assault at San Juan was a good bit of work, but it always reminded me a little of Corbett's victory over Sullivan. Corbett deserved great credit for the nerve he showed in going against Sullivan, whose reputation and ferocity of aspect in the ring tried the courage of any man, and Corbett needed to keep his nerve for three or four rounds; but after that he must have seen that he had the fight in hand. So at San Juan, we made a good attack on a formidable position which we believed at the time was ⟨slenderly⟩ . . . held; but as a matter of fact it was held by so few Spaniards that, tho they inflicted a heavy loss upon us, we were able to go right thru their lines; then when the Spaniards made a very halfhearted attempt in full force to retake the hill, there was no possible difficulty in repulsing them.

I take the liberty of sending you the last edition of the *Rough Riders* to ask your attention to the notes of Captain Barber and letter of General Sumner in the last appendices.

It seemed to me that Cervera acted with great courage, and yet here again I do not know that I put the deed quite as high as you do; for it is one of the queer facts about that queer animal, man, that he can sometimes make up his mind to take the chance of death when he can't quite screw up his nerves to the point of making a punishing fight against the adversary. If, instead of running, Cervera had gone straight for our fleet and had tried to sink just one vessel before his own fleet was lost, I would have thought more of his feat.

With warm regards to Mrs. Chadwick, *Sincerely yours*

4786 · TO GEORGE VON LENGERKE MEYER *Roosevelt Mss.*

Personal Oyster Bay, July 2, 1908

My dear George: Curiously enough, immediately after writing you I discovered the reason for Frick's discontent. Naturally, what I have to write must be treated as confidential; but Frank Kellogg came in and I told him what you had reported Frick as saying, and my guess as to why Frick was ⟨put out⟩ feeling sore. He simply told me he thought he had a far better explanation, because last winter Frick came to him and asked him as a personal favor to put off for several months the trial of the Harriman suit, and was greatly irritated when he (Kellogg) answered that of course it was not possible for him to consider such a proposition, and that he (Frick) had no right to make such a request. Kellogg added that in his judgment there was no question that Frick intended to use the time for certain operations on the stock market. *Faithfully yours*

[1] Chadwick, then working on his history of the Spanish-American War, had written Roosevelt about the battle at the San Juan ridge.

Personal   Oyster Bay, July 2, 1908

Dear Elihu: This paper which sends me the enclosed protest is a very ardent supporter of mine, and it offers one of the amusing complications of the present political situation. My idea is that we might with advantage have the acceptance of that gift deferred until Mrs. Roosevelt and Mrs. Longworth are back in Washington, which will not be the case as regards both of them until about December 1st next. That will give us time to decide what ought to be done. Of course if people were rational they would understand that it is a very delicate matter to have the wife of the President refuse a decoration from a foreign potentate;[1] but people are not reasonable. However, we can settle it later on. There is just one redeeming feature about all these nationalities, and that is that the entrance of all these new nationalities has diminished what used to be the one feeling of hostility, that against England. The Irish always want to embroil us with England, and therefore feel friendly to Russia. The Jews always want to embroil us with Russia, and therefore feel friendly with England. They also feel friendly with Turkey; but the Greeks feel very hostile to Turkey, as do the Armenians. The Germans would like to see us hostile to both France and England; but the Poles, Danes, and Norwegians wish us to be hostile to Germany, and the Swedes, to Russia. The Italians have a hostile feeling to both the Germans and French, and like the English, as do also the Danes and Scandinavians generally. The result of this mixture of ethnic prejudice is that in a measurable degree each acts as an antiscorbutic to the others. In other words, it is a good thing from the standpoint of the Americans of this country that we have many different race elements coming, instead of simply one. The French-English-German feeling shifts so completely from decade to decade that it is difficult to keep track of it. The English now hate the Germans and like the French; and the French, who are mostly French Canadians, approve of the English and do not like any other foreigners, including the Irish, who cordially reciprocate the feeling. *Ever yours*

Personal   Oyster Bay, July 2, 1908

Dear Will: I think you are absolutely right. I saw Kellogg and Ward, and it has been a good thing our speaking of Kellogg, because it has brought Ward around red-hot for Hitchcock, and as you have ironed out the Ohio trouble[1] it leaves Hitchcock the one pre-eminently desirable man. Down

---

[1] Mrs. Roosevelt accepted the Grand Cordon of the Order of the Nichan-I-Chefakat, conferred only upon women by the Sultan of Turkey.

---

[1] "The Ohio trouble" was Vorys, whose disappointment over the selection of Hitchcock as Taft's campaign manager was assuaged when he was left in charge of the campaign in Ohio.

at bottom I have always felt that if I were in your place I should take Hitchcock right out of hand, but knowing the way Charley and Harry[2] felt about it I was very loath to advise this, and my horseback judgment was that Kellogg would fill the bill; but for the reasons you give I have come to your conclusion, that it would be unwise from every standpoint, especially from Kellogg's own standpoint. Kellogg came here yesterday to explain, what he said he had already explained to you, why he could not regard it as anything but unwise for him to take the position. Hitchcock has everything in hand. He has extraordinary executive capacity and he will be able to begin the campaign practically as soon as Bryan is nominated.

As to what you have written about Steinhart I entirely agree with you. The only change I would have suggested, and this simply from the standpoint of recognizing how knaves can mislead fools — I would not have put into the letter the statement that the conferences[3] should be as free from public observation as possible. Of course the purpose of this is to prevent people from getting the idea that Steinhart has influence with Magoon, and therefore to prevent the possibility of any trading on such influence; and every honest and intelligent man will realize that this is what he meant, but if this letter is published pending the campaign dishonest men will try to persuade unintelligent men that in accordance with our well-known natures we are advising Magoon to do something furtive!

As for the telephone business, I will take no final action until I hear from Luke Wright and Magoon. I do not like that crowd, and I think we should be extremely careful in our dealings with them. They are entitled to justice, but they are not entitled to a particle more.[4]

I return the letter of Browne. It is possible, altho not probable, that we shall get something important out of this investigation.[5] Will you let me know any way you desire it handled?

Best luck, and love to dear Mrs. Taft. *Ever yours*

4789 · TO ROBERT BRIDGES   *Roosevelt Mss.*

Confidential   Oyster Bay, July 2, 1908

Dear Bridges: I have been really puzzled about the African trip articles.[1] For the purely confidential information of you and Mr. Charles Scribner and

[2] Charley Taft and Harry New.
[3] About arrangements for the American evacuation of Cuba.
[4] Scrymser and his associates were having their recurrent difficulties over cable rights of way. This problem, concerning both the Cuban government and the United States, which had jurisdiction over Guantánamo harbor, was resolved to the mutual satisfaction of all those involved.
[5] Herbert J. Browne and W. G. Baldwin had been hired by Taft to investigate again the Brownsville affair. Although they used a "large force of detectives" and spent "about $15,000," they found nothing new.

[1] Of the many letters on Roosevelt's negotiations for the publication of articles about his African trip, this is a representative example. Ultimately he rejected an offer from

nobody else I send you a letter I have just received from McClure, which please return. I will say frankly I had no idea that anyone would regard my African articles as worth as much as McClure and Collier apparently consider them. Now, I have given no answer to either. I prefer to do this for Scribner's. If you cared to offer me $50,000 and then 20 per cent on the book, I should accept; $50,000 being for all the serial rights of my African trip, it being understood that I would give you twelve articles if I could, but of course I might not be able to give you as many. On this point I refer you to my former letter as to what I said to Collier's.

Now, it may very well be that you think such a sum altogether out of proportion, as I certainly should have thought it before McClure, Collier and Caspar Whitney came to me, each with a proposal and the minimum proposal being Collier's. If you do think it out of proportion, say so, of course, and tell me whether you want the book at 20 per cent. I would rather deal with you than with anyone else. I would regard this preference as being well worth the $10,000 less which I should get from you than from McClure, and the slightly less favorable terms I would have for the book from you than from McClure; because I know you; I know you have got the same standards of propriety that I have; that, for instance, you would make no advertisement of the articles and book until I had left the presidency or at least until within two or three weeks of my leaving. But for the reasons given in my previous letter, I do not feel that I could treat this as warranting me in overlooking the difference between $25,000 and $50,000 or $60,000. If, as I suppose will be the case, you do not want the articles, my preference would be to give them to Collier's for $50,000 and let you take the book if you wisht it. I would be more inclined to do this because McClure knew that Collier had offered me $50,000, and under such circumstances I would not like to accept simply a small advance. Whitney's offer was far more, but it was for a syndicate story for the newspapers and involved my trying to write something every week, or if not that every month, and of course I could not be sure that this would be a possibility.

My present intention is not to go around the world or do anything excepting these African articles on hunting and natural history, with the incidental traveling and other observations; but of course it is possible, however improbable, that I should decide in addition to go elsewhere on a different kind of a trip, and if so the arrangements for such a trip would stand by itself and would be an entirely different matter. *Sincerely yours*

Robert J. Collier of $100,000 for his work and accepted one of $50,000 from Scribner's. He also, in July, arranged with the *Outlook* for a series of articles on social and political questions and, in the same month, informed Putnam that he would not complete *The Winning of the West*. From the large number of letters on this subject, the following have been selected: Numbers 4799, 4803, 4815, 4822.

Personal   Oyster Bay, July 3, 1908

My dear Mr. Newberry: I have your letters of the 2d instant. You had better send the plans of the *North Dakota* type to the fleet officers to consider during the cruise from Melbourne to Manila; but we may not be able to wait until January 1st to use them. About that I will determine later. Meanwhile, I think your suggestion of sending the seagoing officers who have had battle-ship experience for temporary duty at the War College, is excellent. They can be consulted by the General Board and War College, and I can talk over the report with any of them, if necessary. I particularly want the benefit of Winslow's experience in the matter. *Sincerely yours*

[*Handwritten*] How soon can the seagoing officers be at Newport?[1] I think I should like to meet them . . . .

4791 · TO JONATHAN BOURNE, JUNIOR   *Roosevelt Mss.*

Oyster Bay, July 3, 1908

My dear Senator: Mr. Loeb has transmitted to me your telephone message as to Mr. Kellogg submitting a written memorandum. My dear Senator, let me repeat in writing what I have said again and again to Mr. Archbold and you, and what I stated at such length in our interview of last Monday.[1] In my judgment it is not only a waste of time but inadvisable to try to carry on the negotiations thru you as intermediary. Let the Standard Oil lawyers, any or all of them as Mr. Archbold or Mr. Rockefeller or anyone else may choose, decide as to the course they wish to follow, and then communicate direct with Mr. Kellogg or the Attorney General. I read you what Mr. Bonaparte wrote me, which I had previously read to Mr. Kellogg, and I furnished you with a copy of it. You now inform Mr. Loeb that this is not specific enough. It was not meant to be specific. It was not meant to show you. It was meant by Mr. Bonaparte to advise me as to what he and Mr. Kellogg thought was the proper course to follow. I read it to you so that you might understand what the attitude of the Department of Justice was; and when I read it to you I explained explicitly to Mr. Archbold and yourself what I have now put into writing above, namely, that it was undesirable to attempt to carry on negoti-ations thru you, and that the proper person for you to communicate with was not me but Mr. Bonaparte or Mr. Kellogg. Then an appeal can always be made to me; but obviously the first thing to do is to have the counsel of the Standard Oil communicate with the counsel of the Department of Justice, Mr. Kellogg, or with Mr. Bonaparte himself. *Sincerely yours*

---

[1] The seagoing officers were at Newport before the President's visit to the War College on July 22. Their arrival strengthened the reform element at the Newport conference.

---

[1] See No. 4777.

Personal   Oyster Bay, July 6, 1908

My dear Admiral: [1] Your letter of the 2d instant has been received. I shall be very glad to arrange to come. I could make but a very brief address, for in my judgment all that a layman can do is to insist upon four or five vital principles which even a layman can understand to be vital, and which, unfortunately, highly trained professional men often in actual practice ignore.[2] I want when I come down to see not only the War College but the General Board, to talk over the plans of our battleships. Have you any idea when the General Board will be at the college? I should like some leeway given me in choosing; I think between the 20th and 30th of this month. *Sincerely yours*

Oyster Bay, July 6, 1908

My dear Mr. Harris: Your sad prescience has been verified, and your most touching and interesting letter has reached me only after the death of your dear father. As soon as I met you I took a great fancy to you, for I felt that I could not only like you but believe in you; and if anything were needed to make this impression definite and ineffaceable, it would be your letter.

I absolutely agree with your father about the monument. It is *Uncle Remus's Magazine* that can do most to perpetuate his memory, and can do it by rendering just the service he so loved to render. Now, I would like to help. Of course I am under real limitations. The chance of my even writing . . . . something, for instance, is remote, because I am pledged far in advance to old friends like those of the *Scribner's*, the *Century*, and the *Outlook*, for the only things I have now in mind. But do you know, I think that if you are willing, I could help your magazine if you would allow me to publish the letter you have just sent me, together with a brief letter of mine commenting upon it,[1] and asking that the monument which your father desired be raised in the way he desired it — that is, by standing in support of the magazine,

---

[1] Admiral John Porter Merrell was then president of the Naval War College.

[2] Roosevelt delivered two addresses at Newport during his brief visit on July 22. In the first, a public address, he made a stirring appeal for a big navy. Stressing that "diplomacy rests on the substantial basis of potential force," the President declared that "the Monroe Doctrine unbacked by a navy is an empty boast." "If we have a coast defense navy only," he continued, "we had better at once turn over the Panama Canal to some stronger and broader nation . . . . give up Hawaii, give up Porto Rico, give up Alaska."

The second talk, addressed to the officers attending the conference on battleship plans, was confidential. According to one report Roosevelt demanded that defects be remedied immediately and prevented in the future. He further insisted that seagoing officers should have a substantial voice in the designing of new ships and that their suggestions "must not hereafter suffer from pigeonholing in desks of bureau chiefs."

---

[1] See No. 4794.

which really does give the South recognition thru a medium broad and un-biased enough to reflect a national sentiment; for of course I regard your magazine as not merely a Southern but an American magazine. I do not know whether this will be agreeable to you, and I am a little puzzled as to how to publish the letter. I should really think it could be done best in the magazine itself. This number, if you do not change your plan, will contain the letters I have already written, and perhaps this might in a way pave the path for the printing of your letter to me and of my letter in the next issue.[2] But, my dear sir, I want your absolutely unbiased judgment on this suggestion, and if you do not think it wise we won't dream of adopting it. All I want is to try to help in whatever way you think best.

With deep sympathy and regard, believe me, *Faithfully yours*

4794 · TO JULIAN HARRIS   *Roosevelt Mss.*

Oyster Bay, July 6, 1908

My dear Mr. Harris: Your letter of July 2d has come; and while it was on its way your father died. I mourn his loss. I mourn it for your sake; I mourn it for my own; I mourn it for the sake of our country; for he was one of the best of all good citizens. He represented part of the sum of American achieve-ment which should make Americans proud of their country. I very firmly believe that his writings will last; that they will be read as long as anything written in our language during his time is read. To very few writers indeed is it given to create one of the undying characters of story, and this was given to Joel Chandler Harris in the creation of Uncle Remus. But his Uncle Remus stories are but a small part of that mass of his writings which have great and permanent value. I *know* that they appeal deeply to all of our fellow countrymen, and I *believe* that they appeal deeply to all of the English-speaking peoples; and not the least of the good services they rendered was to give to the rest of the country a feeling of affectionate admiration and respect for the strong, kindly, manly people about whom he especially wrote, the people of my mother's State of Georgia. I don't know whether the purely literary critics would object to what I am about to say; but from the standpoint of our common American citizenship it seems to me that the ethical quality of your father's writings was quite as important as their purely literary value. I have never subscribed and I never shall subscribe to the doctrine that a man of genius is to be admired when he so uses his genius as to do evil and not good to his fellow men; on the contrary, the greater the artist, the more heartily he is to be condemned if he uses his power for mischief, and this for the very reason that the man of the pen or the brush has at least as much effect upon national character as the man whose profes-sion is statecraft. Now your father was a genius; and furthermore he was a

[2] These two letters were printed in the September issue of *Uncle Remus's Home Magazine*.

man who in his private life, in its modesty, its simplicity, its kindliness and refinement, illustrated the very quality which we must all of us like to see typical of the homes of the nation; and, finally, he never wrote anything which did not make the man or woman reading it feel a little better, feel that his or her impulses for good had been strengthened, feel a more resolute purpose to do with cheerfulness and courage with good sense and charity, whatever duty was next to be done. No writer was ever less didactic; but, quite unconsciously, every reader of his writings, learned to set a new and higher value upon courage, upon honesty, upon truth, upon kindly generosity, upon all of those qualities that make a man a good man in his family, a good neighbor, a good citizen in peace or war. The whole country is the debtor of your Father.

How can we best pay this debt? It seems to me that we can best pay it by supporting the magazine which he founded, and which he ardently wished to perpetuate so that it might spread abroad the principles for which his whole life stood. He sought in this magazine to give to the South the greatest opportunity the South has yet had to secure recognition thru what you have well characterized as a "medium broad and unbiased enough to reflect a national sentiment." We ourselves must correct our own faults. It does no good to have them pointed out by an enemy, or even by an outsider who is not sympathetic, for such action merely stirs resentment; and one good feature of a magazine like *Uncle Remus's* lies in the fact that it does not hesitate in kindly and friendly fashion to be severe with all of us or any of us when an honest desire to serve us requires such severity. There are plenty of faults in our American life, in each and every section, and we should be thankful to the friend, to the man of our own household, who, in no snarling or captious spirit, with no ill will or insincerity, but with a kindly and honest purpose to help us, points out these faults and indicates the remedy.

Surely all of us must be deeply touched by what your father said as you quote it in your letter. "The magazine must succeed. If this illness takes me off and they try to start any monument business, don't let them do it. A statue will stand out in the rain and the cold, or dust-covered, useless and disfiguring, and be soon forgotten except by the sparrows in nesting time. If what little I have done is found worthy of commendation, tell the people of the South to let the magazine succeed — to stand back of it with their subscriptions. And if it is not too much trouble, run a little line somewhere 'Founded by Joel Chandler Harris.' "

This is the way our dead friend, the man who was the friend of all of us, South and North, East and West, wished to be remembered; and I earnestly hope that all of us, South and North, East and West, will show our respect and affection for his memory, and our appreciation of his wisdom, by doing as he desired and heartily backing up the magazine he founded; a magazine notable in many ways; a magazine standing on so high a plane, not merely of purpose, but of literary achievement, that it would be a very grave reflection upon our national good taste if it failed to receive the abundant and encouraging and ungrudging support to which it is entitled.[1]

With all good wishes, *Sincerely yours*

Oyster Bay, July 6, 1908

Dear George: Your letter of the 2d with enclosures has been received. The First Assistant Postmaster General committed one of those hideous blunders which can never be entirely retrieved.[1] How such a form of wording could ever have been used I do not understand. You will have to give him a severe wigging, and look carefully over any language used by him hereafter in any letter you are asked to sign. I am inclined to think that it would be well to write to Culberson stating frankly what had occurred — that is, that you had signed the letters hastily without reading them; that you were genuinely obliged to him for calling your attention to a practice of which you were ignorant and which you would forthwith stop. Of course it is not defensible to offer questions of establishing post offices to any outsider; and the trouble with the letters prepared by the First Assistant is that they do not state the whole case, but on the contrary put you in the position of doing just what you do not do. The letters would undoubtedly be taken as implying that you turned over not only the patronage but questions of the utmost importance to all the people, like the establishment of a post office, to the dictation of the head of a minority political organization. Of course all that you do is, as a matter of convenience, and as it is necessary to take the advice of someone, to take the advice of Colonel Lyon, accepting this as prima facie to be followed. But, as I happen to know, you have repeatedly refused to follow it; and really you are not following his personal advice, save in a very few instances, but the advice of a number of men, and you will accept information from any source which would cause you to reject the advice in question. Now, nothing of this is exprest in those letters which were presented for your signature. On the contrary, those letters put you in the position of having abdicated your function and made Lyon an irresponsible autocrat. I strongly advise you to go over the forms used by the First Assistant and the other assistants under

---

[1] Roosevelt's appeal was not enough. After a courageous struggle against a declining subscription list young Harris was forced to abandon the magazine in 1913.

[1] Charles P. Grandfield, promoted from chief clerk to First Assistant Postmaster General after Hitchcock resigned, had in one candid letter offended the local pride that lurks deep in the heart of Texas and violated the political tradition that in matters of patronage the best is silence. The daughter of General Sam Houston, hero of San Jacinto, had been removed from her office as postmistress at Abileen, Texas. The old lady's inefficiency was reason enough for the removal. But Grandfield, drafting a letter for Meyer to send Senator Culberson, who had protested against the action, explained the episode in terms of Republican politics. Colonel Lyon, he pointed out, had chosen a deserving successor for the office. The damage done could not be repaired even by the President's less candid explanation; see No. 4812.

you, and see that under no circumstances do they ever again prepare letters even remotely resembling these particular letters; for it is a bad blunder to send out letters which, unless accompanied by long, elaborate explanations, give the ordinary citizen a totally false idea of what has been done, and give this false idea not to the advantage but to the detriment of the Department.

You can show this letter of mine to the First Assistant Postmaster General; and I hope you will give him clearly to understand that no excuse should be accepted for a second blunder of this kind on the part of a man occupying as responsible a position as he occupies. Advise with referees about appointments, but about nothing else; and even in the matter of advising with them about appointments I would be cautious how in the official records I gave the advice improper prominence, for it is simply establishing a prima facie case for your individual guidance.

Any time you are able, come over and see me here. *Ever yours*

[*Handwritten*] I don't think the letter will . . . .

4796 · TO WILLIAM HOWARD TAFT   *Roosevelt Mss.*

Oyster Bay, July 7, 1908

Dear Will: I have your letters of the 3d and 4th instant. Of course you are having a hard time; but, you old trump, surely you know by this time how rare it is to find men who will give you both disinterested and efficient service. There are a number of such entirely disinterested men under me, whom I have appointed to office; you are the chief of them, and there are others more or less like you. There are certain men outside who have helped me, as I believe, with entire disinterestedness, not so much, of course, out of regard for me as out of the belief in the policies I represent. That is one of the reasons why I stand by men like Reynolds and Needham, even tho I sometimes get exasperated by them. But with the enormous majority of men you have to remember that there must necessarily be a large alloy of self-interest in their work. It does not follow by any means that there is no element of disinterestedness; but both qualities have to be taken into account; while there is in yet others only that element of disinterestedness which would be represented by what chemists call a "trace." But these, too, have their uses, and must on occasions be employed even tho it is well known that in some shape or way they expect to be paid.

The same objections that are made to Hitchcock with you were made to Cortelyou with me, altho of course by the time my nomination was reached objections had lost much of their force. Men told me I had no business to put forward a devoted adherent of McKinley, a close friend of Mark Hanna, and to slight my own devoted adherents. For example, when I first continued Cortelyou as Secretary plenty of my friends in New York not only dwelt upon my unwisdom, but insinuated that I was ungrateful to Loeb, who was my secretary as Vice-President, in passing him by for Cortelyou. Loeb never took this view, and therefore he is Secretary now. I think your decision about Hitchcock wise, and I am struck by your telling me that Crane has reached, as Ward had already reached, the conclusion that no other appointment was now possible. Both Crane and Ward were against the appointment originally, and their decision may be accepted as representing simply the recognition by sensible men of the best course to be pursued under the actual circumstances. I am sorry that Hitchcock should not have behaved with more consideration than by your letter he seems to have shown, and I am a little surprised. I am less surprised in Vorys' case, simply because I have had some rough experiences with Vorys in the past. He — assisted, however, I am bound to say, by others, including so admirable a man as Colonel Nelson — unwittingly last fall did all he could to shake my resolution; and he made one curious remark about you of which I will tell you when we meet. He has been a devoted worker for you, but he is not a big man.

I will take up the Balfe matter at once; but if his bid is not the lowest I don't see how we can take it. *Ever yours*

P. S. The enclosed letter and paper explain themselves. Pringle[1] represents the very best type of labor people, altho he must be used cautiously because the radicals are against him, assert that he is paid by the employers, etc. I think it would be well worth your while to see him personally, and to have you arrange to have the new Chairman of the National Committee see him.

4797 · TO FRENCH ENSOR CHADWICK   *Roosevelt Mss.*

Oyster Bay, July 8, 1908

My dear Admiral: I have your letter of the 6th instant. I think you have defined the Spaniards in capital shape. The Spaniards — and, for the matter of that, the southern Italians — are much more like the Berbers than like the tall, long-headed, blond races of North Europe, or the round-headed, comparatively tall, and comparatively blond people of Middle Europe. I am bound to say however that I think that the Spaniards on shore have showed themselves formidable fighters for the century and a half following Gonsalvo, the Great Captain. It certainly seems to me that thruout the Sixteenth Century the French, Germans, English, Scotch and Dutch were as a rule greatly inferior to the Spanish infantry on stricken fields. But taking their history thruout, I agree with you absolutely that their courage is primarily that of passive endurance, not of active and aggressive daring. Moreover, I am delighted at what you say about Nelson at Trafalgar and the English navy at the period of its greatest glory. It is a curious commentary upon the inability of mankind

---

[1] John D. Pringle, editor of the *Labor World* of Pittsburgh, was rewarded for supporting Taft with an appointment from Roosevelt as appraiser of merchandise at Pittsburgh.

to appreciate the achievement at its true worth that everyone, even Mahan himself, should ignore the fact that the English navy at that great culminating period of its achievement and glory should have won its tremendous victories against foes of utter military inefficiency. At Copenhagen the Danes had only hulks. They had not been engaged in a war for eighty years, and the hulks were manned for the most part by volunteers. The Russian fleet in the Baltic, as had been shown in its previous conflict with the Swedes, was manned by landsmen and could barely maneuver. The Spanish warships were such in name only; it was physically impossible for them to win against an antagonist who could fight at all. The Dutch navy suffered from precisely the trouble of the French, as it was a revolutionary navy, disorganized by a revolution which also in part took the form of a foreign invasion. The French navy, the chief foe, was during the earlier years of the republic officered and manned in a fashion which made it ludicrous to think of its opposing any respectable opponent, and it was saved from utter annihilation only because of the wooden formalism of the elderly officers who commanded the English fleets of that period, and of the further fact that, as always then after a peace, the English navy had itself been allowed to sink into a condition of great inefficiency. Then these initial successes of the English put the French at such a disadvantage that they were never able to dispute the English supremacy with anything like equal chances. Trafalgar and the Nile were great victories; but in according to the great sea captain who won them all the praise to which he is entitled, it yet remains true that his opponents were of so poor an order as to offer him every possible advantage and to make his victory as nearly certain as such a thing can be. Contrast all this with the feats of that greatest of all soldiers, Hannibal, who led a mercenary army upon an expedition as daring as that of Alexander, into the heart of the most formidable fighting nation of antiquity, and with his Sepoys again and again defeated the superior numbers of the most formidable troops that the world then held. Nelson won crushing and decisive victories over a foe whom all his fellow admirals also invariably, tho much less decisively, beat. But Hannibal defeated a foe against whom no army not commanded by himself could make head, and for a space nearly equaling the lifetime of half a generation, marched to and fro at will thru that foe's own country.

With regard, believe me, *Sincerely yours*

4798 · TO JONATHAN BOURNE, JUNIOR   *Roosevelt Mss.*

Personal   Oyster Bay, July 8, 1908

My dear Senator: Your letter of the 7th instant has been received. I very earnestly hope that at the next session a resolute effort will be made to pass a federal incorporation bill of the kind I have so repeatedly advocated in my messages.[1] As a matter of tactics I feel that it is most important that the bill

---

[1] No such effort was made; see No. 5013, note 1.

should be prepared by or come either from the Government or from an organization like the Civic Federation. Personally I need hardly say that I have not the slightest patience with the foolish creatures who oppose a good measure because big corporations are wise enough to see that it is a good measure and to advocate it; but I need hardly point out to a man of your experiences that the chance of passing any such measure would be greatly diminished if it was supposed to be prepared by, and introduced primarily in the interest of, big corporations. There is no hurry about preparing the bill. I should want to have the advice both of Herbert Knox Smith and of Garfield about it, as well as the advice of the Attorney General; for I found myself rather closer to the two former than to the latter when we were discussing the details of the bill introduced by the Civic Federation last winter.

Give my warm regards to Mrs. Bourne, and with all good wishes for a pleasant summer, believe me, *Faithfully yours*

4799 · TO ROBERT JOSEPH COLLIER   *Roosevelt Mss.*

Oyster Bay, July 9, 1908

Dear Collier: Your letter really makes me feel badly. I never connected this hunting trip with your offer of eighteen months ago at all; indeed there *isn't* any connection! Scribner's have handled my hunting stories for years, and I told them that they should have first call for my subsequent ones. I told them also that if there was too marked a difference between what they offered and what some other reputable firm should offer I could not accept it. I shall say frankly that I am glad you did not make the offer you now make to me when you came out here, because the offer that Scribner's actually did make was one which I felt that I was warranted in taking, the difference being a little in favor of Scribner's, on the whole, as compared with the offer you actually made me. This present offer, however, is of course much more advantageous to me and I should have been in great doubt about it; in doubt because I should have liked for pecuniary reasons to have accepted it, and yet I should have felt very doubtful about doing so because I do not see how you could with advantage pay as much. When I saw you I did not suppose that Scribner's were going to make such an offer as they actually made (altho I may mention that Mr. Loeb did!). I do not see how a hundred thousand dollars for those articles would repay you, and if you had offered it, and I had accepted it as I doubtless should have done, I would always have felt thoroly uncomfortable as to my capacity for giving you the money's worth.

I had a very nice talk with Mark Sullivan yesterday and I gathered from what he said that you thoroly understood the situation.

Now, you have been so very nice to me that I have somewhat the same feeling of loyalty to you that I have toward Scribner's. Do not forget, my dear sir, that the very fact that I do show loyalty to Scribner's means that under similar circumstances I would show loyalty to you. Now, cannot I have a talk with you and Sullivan, and possibly Hapgood? Are you to be in this neighborhood next week; if so won't you and Sullivan motor over here to lunch on Wednesday, bringing, I hope, Mrs. Collier and Mrs. Sullivan, and also Hapgood? If this is inconvenient, are you going to be here the first week in August? If not, I shall try for Sullivan and Mrs. Sullivan anyhow. *Very sincerely yours*

[*Handwritten*] If I had gone on that world tour, or on anything like it, I should have accepted your offer; but it never occurred to me that you would care for a hunting tour. So I have told the Outlook that I would do certain politico-social work for them; but I should never have consulted them about either the world tour or my hunting book.

4800 · TO RICHMOND PEARSON HOBSON   *Roosevelt Mss.*

Oyster Bay, July 9, 1908

My dear Congressman: I assume of course that you were misquoted when you were reported to have made the statement in your speech at Denver that you heard the President call war a "probability." [1] I never made any such statement, and do not believe it, either as regards Japan or any other nation. On the contrary, as I have repeatedly told you and as you have agreed with me, all that we need to do is to build a sufficient navy, and we shall make war a practical impossibility. In addition, my dear Mr. Hobson, I know you realize that if I found that you tried to quote in public our private conversations, it would mean that I could hold no private conversation with you whatever. The obligation of not quoting private conversations between gentlemen is tenfold stronger when they occupy official positions, and when one of them is President. My experience has always been that if anyone so far forgot himself as to try to quote what I had said to him in private, it usually turned out that his memory was too defective to enable him to quote it correctly. I am of course sure that you did not attempt to quote me; and of course I made no such statement as that attributed to your «speech» but it is well not to use language that will make people mistakenly believe that you are trying to quote me. *Very truly yours*

[*Handwritten*] In addition, I feel that harm comes from any public man of note speaking in a way that will tend to cause bitterness between us and *any* other power.

[1] Hobson's statement at the Democratic convention was quoted correctly; see No. 4820.

Roosevelt Mss.

Oyster Bay, July 10, 1908

Dear Will: I think the enclosed editorial from the New York *Times* of today is very good.[1] It is not altogether complimentary of me! But it seems to me that it is the kind of editorial that will do good. Look at it and see if at any rate parts of it cannot be circulated.

I think Sheldon is the best selection that could be made.[2] He was the treasurer of the Hughes campaign. He assisted Mr. Bliss in my campaign. The fact that Bliss recommended him was strongly in his favor. It would have been a great mistake to have taken certain of the men with whom Wall Street would have been especially satisfied. It is no mistake to have taken Sheldon. I think your statement about the publicity of the contributions admirable in every way. *Ever yours*

4802 · TO CHARLES WILLIAM ELIOT

Roosevelt Mss.

Oyster Bay, July 10, 1908

My dear President Eliot: I had of course no idea that the telegram Bacon and I sent you would be made public. But in view of its publication, together with your response, I feel I ought to write you so that if the matter should come up in the future there can be no chance to misunderstand my position. I telegraphed freely because I took it for granted that the matter would be kept confidential; and therefore put in none of the qualifications and explanations that I would have put in had I supposed the correspondence would be made public, with the accompanying certainty of wilful misconstruction by certain outsiders. The telegram we sent ran as follows:

Is it not possible, and would it not be more fitting and just, to substitute another punishment for Fish and Morgan, if, as is stated, they merely took away a book which they were permitted to use in the library? It seems to us, and we feel sure to the great body of graduates, it is unfair and unnecessary to make all of us suffer for an offense of this kind for which some other punishment might surely be found.

---

[1] This read in part: "We know that public policies, the old and the new alike, will be executed by Mr. Taft reasonably, with calmness, with sanity. He is less impulsive than Mr. Roosevelt, not given to disturbing utterance, averse to spectacular and ill-judged display. We know nothing of the kind of Mr. Bryan, for he has not been tried. We do know that his mind is unsteady, his principles unsafe. If he at all believes what he says, ... his election to the presidency . . . . would be an immeasurable calamity. The difference between the two candidates is so marked and distinct . . . . and it is a difference so vital to the public welfare that the rejection of Mr. Taft and the election of Mr. Bryan would be an appalling evidence of popular delusion." The *Times's* view was representative of that of the conservative press of both parties.
[2] George R. Sheldon had been appointed treasurer of the Republican National Committee.

I take the above from what has appeared in print in the newspapers, which is substantially correct. The newspapers, as by the attached, put on, falsely, an Oyster Bay date. I have no copy of the telegram, and never have had one. It was written by Bacon, who submitted it to me. I approved and signed it, and he took it away with him. It is therefore absolutely impossible that this telegram could have gotten out from my office. Bacon says that when he sent it he gave the original to his private secretary, and that it is absolutely impossible it could have gotten out from his office. I do not know who in your office had access to it; but if it did not get out from there, it must have been taken from the files of the telegraph company, which I should regard as well-nigh impossible. Whoever put on, or procured the putting on, of the Oyster Bay date and headline, committed a hundredfold worse offense than that of Fish and Morgan.

Your telegram in answer read as follows:

Each man did a dishonorable thing. One violated in his private interest and in a crooked way a rule made in the common interest. The other gave a false name and did not take a subsequent opportunity to give his own. The least possible punishment was put on probation, but even that drops from the crews. A keen and sure sense of honor being the finest result of college life, I think the college and the graduates should condemn effectively dishonorable conduct. The college should also teach that one must not do scurvy things in the supposed interest or for the pleasure of others.

There then followed the telegrams between Mr. Greene and Mr. Loeb:

Cambridge, Mass., June 23, 1908.
Wm. Loeb, Jr.,
Oyster Bay.
President Eliot is much concerned at publication of telegrams in New York paper with Boston date. Careful inquiry has excluded possibility of their having come from his office.
J. D. Greene.

Oyster Bay, N.Y., June 24, 1908.
J. D. Greene,
Harvard University,
Cambridge, Mass.
Your telegram received. The telegrams were certainly not published from this office. As a matter of fact we have no copy of message sent by the President and Mr. Bacon, which was sent by Mr. Bacon from Washington after having been submitted to the President and approved by him. In view of their publication the President is making certain inquiries and will write President Eliot himself.
Wm. Loeb, Jr., Secretary.

The publication of the telegrams of course left the impression that you regarded what Bacon and I did as an effort to secure the pardoning of "dishonorable" and "scurvy" conduct. Now, one reason why I regretted the publication was because I did condemn the conduct of the two boys. I think it deserved punishment of some kind, and I do not wish the boys to feel that such conduct should not be condemned. But I must also add that I think the punishment was ill-judged, and so excessive that I am convinced the effect has been the exact reverse of what you believe, and of what you and the faculty undoubtedly sought to obtain. The publication of your telegram, stigmatizing the conduct as "crooked," "scurvy," and "dishonorable," was an added punishment; a severe, and as I believe, an unwarranted and improper punishment. Other publications in the press, seemingly emanating from the college, have denounced the act as a "theft." To speak of the act as a "theft," in any but a purely technical sense, is nonsense. Morgan's act had nothing whatever in common with that of the student or graduate who some years ago did actually steal certain books and keep them for months in his room, removing the college bookplate, etc. Fish and Morgan, on the two crews, were emphatically engaged in doing work that was of benefit to the whole college, and according to my view, it would be eminently desirable to make them feel that they were doing work for the benefit of the whole college. They had to go down to Red Top just about the time of the examinations, and the college authorities, as a matter of honorable obligation, should have endeavored to give them every facility to study at Red Top to just as much advantage as if they were not at Red Top. There was a book in the library in question which Morgan needed to study in connection with his thesis. He was entitled to study it. It is unfortunate if the rules are such that under these circumstances he was unable to take it with him to Red Top; but apparently they are such, and therefore by obeying the rule he would be put at a disadvantage compared with his fellow students, who were not rowing, and who were therefore, according to my way of looking at it, not entitled to quite the consideration that he was entitled to. From conversation with a number of Harvard undergraduates during the last fortnight, I find that taking these books out has been by no means an uncommon thing, and that in several instances where men have been discovered, the man discovering them has simply given them a sharp dressing down, or has prohibited them from using the library for a month. The action of the faculty has convinced the students that it was because a member of the crew committed the misdeed that the punishment was made heavy. Morgan took out a book intending to read it on the way down in the train to Red Top, and then to send it back. There is no suggestion that he intended to keep it, and he was getting no unfair advantage over any fellow student. He of course had no business to take the book, as it was forbidden, and he deserved punishment; but in my view his offense was venial compared with the offense of the college authorities in the method and therefore degree of punishment they allotted. Fish's offense had both a less serious and a more serious side. He had no interest whatever in the book, was simply trying to help his rowing mate, and therefore received it when it was passed out of the window. He had nothing to gain at all from the transaction. But when caught and asked his name, he gave a false name. Immediately afterwards, when his interlocutor lookt up the name, found that there was a Harvard student of that name, and asked him if he was the man, he responded that he was not; I do not know whether he merely said he was not the Harvard student of that name, altho he admitted that he was a Harvard student, or that he said that it was not his name — not a difference which I regard as very important, as it is perfectly clear that he was admitted to be a Harvard student, that he gave a false name, and that as soon as it was found that there was another and only one other man in the college who bore that name, he promptly repudiated it. He had on his crew hat ribbon; his offense was on the order of, altho more serious than, the offense of the man who is caught driving an automobile beyond the speed limit and gives a false name when paying his fine. I reprobate the action in each case; but in neither case does the action really amount to a lie; there is no real intent to deceive; it is simply an improper way of refusing to give the man's real name. I think that Fish was much to blame and should have been punished; but I do not think that the punishment should have taken such form as to take him off the crew. People tell me that no other form of punishment could be provided; my answer must be that when it comes to purely administrative acts, it is almost always possible to avoid serious injustice.

My concern was somewhat for the crew, because, like most sane and healthy Harvard graduates, I am always anxious to see the eleven, or the nine, or the crew, or the track team, win. I abhor dishonorable conduct. But I reprobate also the false perspective and confusion of ideas which are implied in improperly heavy punishment for an offense which should be condemned and punished, but which it is absurd to treat as a crime. However, I am far more concerned with the effect upon the college morals than upon the crew; for I entirely agree with you that the matter of first importance is to have the proper standard of character, the proper standard of morality, for the college. Now, I have spoken to scores of undergraduates, and to a number of graduates, since this matter occurred, and without exception the former, and almost without exception the latter, condemned unstintedly the action of the faculty, and felt so much more indignant at the faculty than at the two offenders that they were in the very dangerous attitude of not regarding the latter as having been guilty of misconduct at all. I cordially agree with what you say as to the need of the college inculcating a keen and sure standard of honor. But I also sincerely believe that by the action taken in this case you have tended, not to preserve, but to blunt that sense of honor. Yesterday at lunch there were present certain Harvard graduates and undergraduates, and three or four editors of leading periodicals, and I was interested to find that they all of them attributed the action of the faculty, attributed your action, simply to your hostility to athletics; that is, they all accepted as a matter of course the view that no such disproportionate punishment would have been inflicted, excepting for the fact that this gave an opportunity for the Harvard College authorities to strike a blow at Harvard athletics. I of course am sure that their view was wrong, and told them so; but it is in my judgment exceedingly unfortunate to have taken action which makes such a view accepted as natural and proper, and most certainly such action defeats its own end if the end is to establish a higher sense of honor among the students. The general expression among the undergraduates was, "Well, this year we have been able to beat both Yale and the faculty. Whether we can do it another year or not, we don't know." And those who thought much on the matter — which, I am bound to say, most of them did not — evidently simply felt that the action showed that the faculty was thoroly out of sympathy with the students and with their purposes and ambitions, and that their own attitude in the future must be to prevent any chance of the faculty's being able to strike another blow at the crew or at athletics. They have not profited by "raising their standard of honor"; they feel that the use of such words as "scurvy" and the like was worse than the original offense; and what might have been their condemnation of this original offense has been diverted by the unfortunate action of the faculty into mere bitter resentment against the faculty. I believe the crew themselves, if properly approached, would have joined with the faculty in taking steps which really would have made it a matter of honor never to permit the repetition of such an offense.

I may add that the only thorogoing defense of the faculty's position which I happen to have heard was from a very large trust magnate, of the kind who thinks that the refusal to have wine on his table offsets sharp practice in business on the largest scale; and I thought it eminently natural that this particular man should take such a purely technical view of the offense, and decline to look at the offense and punishment combined in their larger aspect.

If the telegrams had not been made public, and had been kept purely private, with the rest of the correspondence, unknown to the boys, I should not have felt it necessary to write you; but as things are, it may come up in the future, and if so I want my position to be perfectly clear. I do not want to be misunderstood as failing to condemn the conduct of the two boys, or as failing to see that it should be punished; but I do wish it to be understood that I think the punishment was so ill-judged and excessive as to turn the current of sympathy toward the offenders, and to make many undergraduates, and many graduates and outsiders, believe that the faculty was influenced not so much by the desire to punish wrongdoing as by the desire to interfere with athletics; and that the net result of the unfortunate incident has been to do harm rather than good from the standpoint of the inculcation of a proper sense of honor. Perhaps I can make the last point clearer when I say that without exception every man I have spoken to has felt that the conduct of these two boys did not really show that they lacked a fine sense of honor, or would be unfit to trust in business or profession, in private life or in public life; and that at any rate their offense was venial as compared to the offense of their punishment. I believe that many good people, who have little knowledge of college boys of the more vigorous type, approve your action;

but I believe it has on the whole done damage to the college boys themselves. I believe the faculty could with much advantage read *Verdant Green;* in that book — not an immoral or criminal book — (and indeed in much higher books, like *Tom Brown at Oxford*) they would find the hero and his friends doing deeds much like those of Fish and Morgan, and yet the author would treat with healthy amusement the idea that the doers were really "scurvy," "dishonorable," and "crooked." Such deeds should be punished; but the punishment defeats its own end if it is of a character that ought to be reserved for offenses that really do show the man to be "scurvy" and "dishonorable." I am continually being confronted with acts of all degrees of wrongdoing; I see, and condemn, and have to punish acts of homicide, of protection of criminals, of theft, of betrayal of trust, and I also have brought before me numbers of offenses about on a level with driving an auto beyond the speed limit and then giving a false name when arrested. I condemn and punish the latter type of offense; but if I punished it, or extravagantly denounced it, as if it came in the former class, I should merely tend to blunt the fine sense of honor so necessary in our life, because such punishment or extravagance of denunciation is itself an offense against the nicest sense of honor — as any man who deals with either army or navy would speedily find out.

Several of the boys have made mention to me of an incident which occurred a few years ago. A Harvard professor — a professor I think of ethics and a doctor of divinity who had formerly been a member of The Pudding, had on The Pudding files a poem or something of the kind, written while he was an undergraduate, and which as a Harvard professor and doctor of divinity he wished he had not written. The Pudding records were kept in a safe deposit company, and they were of course the property of The Pudding. The professor in question obtained access to the records in the safe deposit company and cut out or destroyed the poem or writing in question. Immediately afterwards he went abroad. Now, this was not a defensible act, and in my judgment it was a more serious offense than the action for which Fish and Morgan have been held up before the country in terms of opprobrium, which would not have been much more severe if they had been boodle aldermen or wreckers of an insurance company. Yet, as far as I am aware, no public action whatever was taken by the Harvard authorities in this case. I doubt very much whether it called for any action; certainly, if the professor's course had been publicly stigmatized as "dishonorable," "crooked," and "scurvy," or as "theft," then whatever technical justification there might have been for the terms, and however much men of meticulous minds and other thoroly good men who in this particular matter had lost their sense of proportion, might have applauded the action, I should have strongly censured it, and should have felt that the original wrong was far more than offset by the action taken; especially if the punishment had been so inflicted as to bring into disrepute the whole body of professors, and for the time being at least to remove the professor in question in spite of his otherwise excellent character and record from all connection with the college. As a matter of justice a similar course should have been pursued in one case as that pursued in the other, and the same reasons which have made me feel that it would have been unjust and improper to go to extremes in denouncing and punishing the improper act of the Harvard professor makes me feel that it is unjust, unwise, improper, and harmful to the student body to have gone to extremes in denouncing and punishing the admittedly improper act of the two Harvard students. *Very sincerely yours*

4803 · TO GEORGE HAVEN PUTNAM *Roosevelt Mss.*

Oyster Bay, July 10, 1908

Dear Haven: My attention has been called to the enclosed letter in the New York *Times* this morning in which you speak of my being under contract to finish *The Winning of the West* for you. I thought that was finished.[1] It may be that I shall be able to go on with it, as there is one particular volume, that on the Republic of Texas, which I should like to write; but it may also be that it will be impossible to go on with it. What are the sentences in the contract to which you refer? I do not distinctly remember the wording, but I do remember very clearly that we brought out the book in such shape as to make it complete with the first two volumes if we found it inadvisable to go on; complete with the third volume if that was to be the end, and complete with the fourth volume, the number we actually issued. I certainly did not understand that there was any obligation on my part to go on and write additional volumes irrespective of whether or not I thought it advisable and whether the plan developed itself so that the work could be done. *Faithfully yours*

4804 · TO WILLIAM HOWARD TAFT *Roosevelt Mss.*

Personal Oyster Bay, July 11, 1908

Dear Will: I have your letter of the 9th. I have already written you about the Sheldon matter. It was eminently all right. I cannot understand Perkins' objection to him. There was a great fuss made to me that a Wall Street man

[1] Ten years had altered Roosevelt's thinking. In February 1898, he had told William Peterfield Trent that he was unwilling to "surrender . . . the purpose of going on with *The Winning of the West*" (see No. 932). After Roosevelt declined to go on with the study, Putnam arranged to have Robert M. McElroy write *The Winning of the Far West,* published in 1914 in the same format as the Roosevelt volumes.

was to be taken, which being interpreted I now find means that some Wall Street men objected to Sheldon being taken. Now, my dear fellow, I need hardly say how thoroly I agree with you in the course of conduct you have followed and propose to follow in the matter of contributions. It is characteristic of you in every way. It shows the qualities of entire fearlessness and entire disinterestedness and sound judgment which I believe our people will more and more grow to recognize as your great and salient characteristics.

I have been looking over the Bryan platform and in a day or two will begin to make memoranda for a letter on the subject of you in the campaign. Lyman Abbott writes me a letter which he is very anxious I should use as the excuse for the letter about you. I enclose Dr. Abbott's letter. We can discuss exactly what my letter shall be and the occasion for its production, after I get the rough draft out.[1] I will then send it on to you. There is plenty of time, for of course it should not come out until well after your letter — at least that is my idea. What do you think of it? Please think whether you would like anything from me following a few weeks after your speech, or whether you think it would be better for me to say nothing until after your letter, which I suppose will come out some time early in September. You will want to consult your managers, and simply use my letter or letters in the way in which they will do the most good.

I entirely agree with your decision in the Hemenway matter, and I think the reasons you give are controlling. The prime purpose of whoever manages the western end of your campaign should be the election of President.[2] It is evident from the composition of the Bryan ticket and the platform that they intend to make their main fight in the Mississippi Valley, so as to carry the States between Ohio and the Rocky Mountains. This was why I so cordially agreed with you as to where we should choose our Vice-presidential nominee. It is now incumbent upon us to make our main fight in that region, and the very utmost care should be taken in choosing the personnel of those who are specially to direct this part of the battle.

With love to Mrs. Taft. *Ever yours*

[1] Roosevelt waited until September to write his first important public letter in behalf of Taft's candidacy, sending it at that time to Conrad Kohrs of Montana; see No. 4880.
[2] To the western vote Taft managers gave their continuing careful attention. In August Frank H. Hitchcock and Elmer Dover moved the headquarters of the national committee to Chicago in order to be in close touch with the campaign in the Midwest and Far West. Before this move, Senators Hemenway and Dolliver had been the committee's agents in Chicago. The selection of Hemenway for that task was the product of nice political calculation. An undeviating spokesman of old-line conservatism, he had consistently opposed Roosevelt's policies and at Chicago had directed the Fairbanks forces. Just such a man was needed to assure the active allegiance of anti-Administration Midwestern organizations and the financial assistance of anti-Administration men of wealth. Furthermore, Hemenway's personal strength in Indiana served as a useful counterpoise to that of the Democratic Vice-Presidential nominee, John W. Kern. If Republican progressives, particularly Beveridge, were distressed by Hemenway's prominence, they were nevertheless not alienated. For the Old Guard his prominence was a welcome concession.

Oyster Bay, July 11, 1908

My dear Sir Harry: I was greatly interested in your letter and it makes me very sincerely desirous that you should come to the United States while I am President.[1] If you do, I hope it will be after September 25th, and that you will give me the pleasure of spending a night at The White House. Your conscience can be reasonably free in the matter of my hunting; altho not entirely so, for tho emphatically against game butchery, or any other kind of butchery of wild things, and emphatically in favor of the preservation of all wild life that can be preserved without detriment to mankind, I still do feel, not only that there is no objection to a reasonable amount of hunting, but that the encouragement of a proper hunting spirit, a proper love of sport, instead of being incompatible with a love of nature and wild things, offers the best guaranty for the preservation of wild things. Even here on Long Island, which has been settled for three centuries and is no wilder than the least wild districts of England, we can preserve deer, for example, only thru the efforts of sportsmen. If they were never shot at all they would increase so that the farmers would kill them completely out. They have to be kept down somehow, and it is best to have them kept down thru legitimate hunting.

But all this is not serious. What I am seriously concerned with is the great problem which you discuss; the problem, or rather the group of many complex problems, which we mean when we speak of the Negro question. I do wish I could hear from you at length, of course best of all in personal conversation, about Liberia; and I very earnestly hope that if you get over here you will visit the other Negro Republic — Haiti. I should like a more sympathetic interpretation of Haiti than that of St. John's book.[2] It may be that he tells fundamentally the truth, but yet that he does not give this truth its proper relative value. That Haiti stands behind the ordinary tropical American re-

---

[1] Johnston had written about his plans to visit the United States to study "the transplanted African." Few men had a broader knowledge and better understanding of the African Negro than this distinguished explorer and administrator. Johnston, after opening up much of Central Africa to British trade, served in numerous consular and colonial posts in that area. Between 1899 and 1901 he rendered his most notable service when as special commissioner for Uganda he succeeded in transforming that distracted and turbulent region into one of Britain's most progressive African provinces. Owing to this success, he was asked in 1904 by the President of Liberia to reorganize "the financial, judicial, and defensive administration" of the Negro republic. As part of his work he made careful historical, ethnological, and economic studies which were summarized in his books, *The Uganda Protectorate* (1902) and *Liberia* (1906).

Johnston arrived in the United States in the fall of 1908. After a short stay at the White House and an extended tour of the South, he visited the West Indies, Central, and South America. In 1910 he published a penetrating analysis of the American race problem entitled *The Negro in the New World.*

[2] Spenser Buckingham St. John, *Hayti; or, The Black Republic* (London, 1884). St. John, a British diplomat, had spent more than a decade in Haiti and Santo Domingo before writing this book.

public, low tho some of these tropical American republics are, is, I believe, beyond question. But what I would like to know is, whether the falling back has literally been to the old West African level. It seems to me that if St. John had compared Haiti, not with its pretensions, not with civilized or semicivilized states, but with the savage states or low-grade barbaric states from which the ancestors of most of the Haitian Negroes originally came, we would have had better material on which to base judgment. I know no one who by experience, training, temperament and ability is better able to make such a comparison than you are. I will of course help you in every way to look into the Negro problem here, and I think I could tell you a good deal about it and put you in the way of learning much for yourself . . . . I do not know whether you are familiar with South Africa or not. In connection therewith, I am struck by how little this problem has to do, after all, with the question of the black — just as little as «the existence of» anti-Japanese feeling, for instance, has to do with whether its location is Vancouver or San Francisco. Thus the information I have would certainly go to show that Negroes are better treated in Jamaica than in most of the black-belt districts of the United States. On the other hand, at Johannesburg and Kimberly the Negroes are certainly treated worse. I never had a complaint from an American Negro who goes to Jamaica. On the contrary, we commonly hear from such Negro that the British treat his people better than the Americans. But the American Negroes who go to South Africa write volumes of complaints about such indignities, for instance, as being forced to walk in the middle of the street and not on the sidewalk; or being herded in with savage kaffirs in the . . . , and so forth, and so forth.

On the one hand I very firmly believe in granting to Negroes and to all other races the largest amount of self-government which they can exercise. On the other hand, I have the impatient contempt that I suppose all practical men must have for the ridiculous theorists who decline to face facts and who wish to give even to the most utterly undeveloped races of mankind a degree of self-government which only the very highest races have been able to exercise with any advantage. An even more noxious type, by the way, is the man who panders to these theorists so far as advocating treatment of races that are far away, but promptly repudiates their theories when the application is sought nearer home. Usually such sentimentalists play into the hands of the excessively unsentimental individuals who are occupied in nothing whatever but in exploiting inferior races for their own benefit.

Indeed, if you are kind enough to send me your new book on the Congo you may feel sure that among all its readers there will be none more interested than I am. I do hope that you will get over here. *Sincerely yours*

[*Handwritten*] A book on the negro as he really is «on» the islands and coasts of the Caribean sea, by the historian of Uganda on that would indeed «be» worth reading. The mulatto and «zombie» (I . . . .) . . . . study;

especially by one who «has» studied the effect of the crossing of ". . ." types «of» the negroes of . . . , Northern and Central Africa.

4806 · TO WILLIAM HOWARD TAFT   *Roosevelt Mss.*

Oyster Bay, July 13, 1908

Dear Will: DeBell's letter is of course a simple piece of blackmail.[1] I have sent it to Leupp saying if DeBell is on an Indian reservation he is to be put off at once on the ground that he is trying to commit blackmail.

Root has been here, as wise and amusing as ever. He thinks that no letter of mine should be published until late in the campaign; certainly not until after not only your speech of acceptance but your letter of acceptance. Four years ago my letter of acceptance was issued September 12th, and if you issue yours somewhere about that date it will give plenty of time for any letter of mine; and perhaps the campaign will have developed to such an extent as to enable me to put what I have to say in most effective fashion. Loeb's view is essentially that of Root. I have great respect for the judgment of both, but the final say-so is yours, of course, and I will do or leave undone anything, just as you think it wise.

We ought to be able to score on that trial by jury business in their platform.[2] Moreover, we ought to be able to make a telling point, a point that should really count, upon their advocacy of a policy which will invite trouble and refuse to prepare for it. They desire to insult Japan by excluding all Japanese immigration, and at the same time recommend cutting down the navy so that it could only be used for coast defense. They might as well say that they advocate provoking Japan to go to war with us, and at the same time abandoning the Philippines, Hawaii and Alaska to her, not to speak of the Canal.

I think you have handled the National Committee matters in fine shape. Certainly everything seems to be starting out well. Of course we have got to make up our minds to fight hard, but we are going to win. *Ever yours*

[1] E. J. DeBell, an Indian post trader from South Dakota, threatened to disclose some dreadful corruption of Loeb, Cortelyou, and Leupp unless his license to trade, which had been revoked, were restored. His threat resulted neither in restoration nor disclosure.

[2] Taft scored. In his speech of acceptance he attacked the Democratic plank "providing that in prosecutions for contempt in Federal courts, where the violation of the order constituting the contempt charge is indirect, i.e., outside of the presence of the court there shall be a jury trial." "This provision," Taft asserted, was "a most dangerous attack upon the power of the courts to enforce their orders and decrees," for it permitted "a recalcitrant witness who refuses to obey a subpoena" to "insist on a jury trial before the court can determine that he received the subpoena." Such a potential delay in judicial procedure, Taft observed, would inure not to the benefit of "the poor workingman" but to the advantage of "the wealthy and unscrupulous defendant, able to employ astute and cunning counsel and anxious to avoid justice"; see *Republican Campaign Text-Book*, 1908 (Philadelphia, 1908), pp. 16–17.

It was very nice getting your letter of the 12th and to find out how well you are. I was interested in what you say about the Democratic platform. We will be able to riddle it.[3] Take the point you make as to smashing the trusts by abolishing the tariff wherever they exist. This might do, and probably would do, damage here and there to the trusts; but it would absolutely kill the small competitors of the trusts. It may be perfectly proper to cut down the tariff on steel, but to deliberately alter it so as to damage the steel trust would mean ruin to all the small competitors of the steel trust. Of course your speech hangs over you like a nightmare, but that and your letter will be the two great utterances of the campaign. You cannot work too carefully over it.

About Bannon,[4] I entirely agree with you. I have already upset one change made on his recommendation, by ordering the reinstatement of Dr. Frizell, a pension examiner, whose removal he had secured. I will now see that Meyer acts on the suggestion in your letter about the post offices.

Now, I enclose you what the *Herald* says about Major Ray.[5] I know you have always felt as I have, that we might be causing ourselves serious trouble by permitting Ray to go into this campaign. Charley has been red-hot for it. I think that much more damage may come thru the scandal of having Ray here than would be offset by the good that would be gained thru his efforts. Will you look over the matter and tell me how you feel? We had him ordered back to the Philippines. Luke Wright is no politician, and it is a matter you will have to decide for yourself. Go over this with Hitchcock.

Also look at the clipping about Stadler.[6] He is a Tammany Democrat, and a German who takes the German view about beer. His action will be influential with the Germans. I think it will more than offset Ridder, for you may remember that Ridder was wild against me four years ago.

For your information I send you a copy of my letter to Leupp about DeBell.

[3] Beyond the issues discussed in this letter, the Democrats and Republicans differed in 1908 primarily on the questions of federal guarantee of bank deposits, a federal limitation on the size of corporations engaged in interstate commerce, a constitutional amendment legalizing the income tax, and an immediate declaration in favor of Philippine independence, all of which the Democrats favored and the Republicans opposed.

[4] Henry Towne Bannon, Republican congressman from Ohio, 1905–1909, was associated in politics with Foraker and in his legal work with the railroads. He was not a candidate for re-election in 1908.

[5] Beecher B. Ray, a major in the paymasters corps, who had allegedly received preferential treatment in his duty assignments, was campaigning for Taft.

[6] Charles A. Stadler, president of the American Malting Company, sympathizing with Taft's view on prohibition (see No. 4810) and disturbed by Bryan's radical reputation, had announced his support of the Republican candidate.

Personal　　　　　　　　　　　　　　Oyster Bay, July 14, 1908

My dear Mr. McCormick: Your letter dated July 3d was not received until the 13th. Of course the Democrats will adopt a plank satisfactory to the Newspaper Publishers' Association, because they will adopt any plank that will promise anything, without the slightest regard to whether it can be put thru or not.[1] I do not think the Association should stand back of Ridder in his publications, when you know that he is a strong Bryan man and a bitter opponent of Republican policies, and anxious only to discredit us. You also know that he utterly failed to make good in the promises he made as to what could be shown to the Department of Justice. I will take the matter up again with the Department, but I am convinced that the only effective action must be by legislation, and this in two ways: in the first place, in greatly increasing the Federal control over all combinations engaged in interstate commerce, instead of relying upon the foolish antitrust law; or Mr. Bryan's still more foolish proposed . . . . ;[2] and in the second place, thru putting wood pulp and all the like substances on the free list. This simply expresses my personal opinion, and is for you privately and not for quotation. *Sincerely yours*

Oyster Bay, July 15, 1908

My dear Mr. Hitchcock: I enclose you a letter forwarded to me thru Jim Sherman. Will you see John Williams, the Labor Commissioner of New York? With most of what he says in this letter I entirely agree. Money spent on fake labor leaders and on sending around what is known as political literature, represents at least 98 per cent sheer waste of money. What we need is organization in all the industrial States, such as we have been trying to get here in New York; and above all, we want to treat the workingmen whom we are trying to influence as shrewd, intelligent, well-meaning, but often suspicious, men, whom above all else we wish to convince that we are acting in good faith. I hope you can speedily see Mr. Williams, and go carefully over the matter with him. *Sincerely yours*

[1] "Existing duties," the Democratic platform stated, "have given to the manufacturers of paper a shelter behind which they have organized combinations to raise the price of pulp and of paper, thus imposing a tax upon the spread of knowledge. We demand the immediate repeal of the tariff on wood pulp, print paper, lumber, timber and logs, and that these articles be placed upon the free list."

[2] Bryan had compelled the Democratic convention to adopt a plank calling for legislation to prohibit any corporation from controlling more than 50 per cent of the production of any product consumed in the United States.

Oyster Bay, July 16, 1908

My dear Gray: That was a mighty nice letter of yours to me, my dear fellow, and I appreciate almost more your letter to Kermit. Yes, Kermit had told me all about his mortifying experience on the day in question and he has already begun to profit by it and by your teaching. He has shortened his stirrups and is practicing just along the lines you mention. I wish I had been with him when the thing happened, for I think I could have given him advice out of my own experience. I tend to ride with too long stirrups myself because of my western experience (and the whole trouble with Kermit's riding is that he practically learned to ride out in the West and then has had only the teaching of one or two cavalrymen, who also usually ride with their stirrups too long). Up at Geneseo once I was given a very big and hard-jumping horse, the name of which I at the moment forget. It was one of the best jumpers I have ever been on; would take anything; never refused and never came down; but over the first few jumps I think I left the saddle at least two feet. I found finally, as I told Kermit, that instead of paying no heed to my seat but to adapting myself unconsciously to the horse's movement, I was obliged in this case to make a conscious effort and to remember at each jump that immediately after the horse rose I had to bend backwards from the hips. So far did I bend backwards that once the horse actually touched the brim of my soft hat with his haunches as he gave a great twist in going over a fence. I kept my seat all right after I had once learned what I had to do. I saw the Tommy Hitchcocks[1] the other day over at Meadowbrook, and we talked much of you. That is an extremely interesting photograph of the jump as they both took it. Good gracious, it makes me shiver merely to look at it!

Do let me repeat how genuinely obliged I am to you for your interest in Kermit. You have taught him a great deal and your kindness and friendship have meant much to him. I am also naturally very glad you like my action about the Presidency . . . . as you do. I quite agree with you that most men expected me to repudiate the promise I had made and would not have felt the worse of me if I had done it; but this made it all the more incumbent upon me, if I were going to live up to my professions, to do nothing that could legitimately be accepted as shady. If you are to be in this neighborhood this summer do be sure to let me know so that I may have you here at lunch or dinner, and if to dinner to spend the night. Give me warning in advance, so that in the unlikely event of all the rooms being taken I can wire to you to say so. *Faithfully yours*

---

[1] They were Mr. and Mrs. Thomas Hitchcock, Jr., members of a large family devoted to the horse and all his works, parents of Tommy Hitchcock, 3rd, one of the greatest and most fearless polo players of his, or any, time.

Oyster Bay, July 16, 1908

Dear Will: I have your note of the 14th, enclosing copy of your second letter to D. D. Thompson.[1] Of course your position is absolutely sound. If ever there was a wicked attitude it is that of those fantastic extremists who advocate a law so drastic that it cannot be enforced, knowing perfectly well that lawlessness and contempt of the law follow. But as a mere matter of precaution I would be careful to put in your hearty sympathy with every effort to do away with the drink evil. You will hardly suspect me of being a prohibitionist crank; but such hideous misery does come from drink that I cordially sympathize with any successful effort to do away with it or minimize its effects. I think there are plenty of country districts where prohibition has worked well. I would accordingly favor the local option plan, which permits any district where the sentiment demands it to refuse to allow liquor to be sold. But to pass prohibitory laws to govern localities where the sentiment does not sustain them is simply equivalent to allowing free liquor, plus lawlessness, and is the very worst possible way of solving the problem. My experience with prohibitionists, however, is that the best way to deal with them is to ignore them. I would not get drawn into any discussion with them under any circumstances. I would explain to Thompson for his private information the nonsense that the prohibitionists are talking; but also explain to him that you are not to be quoted in any way, as you do not wish to be drawn into any controversy, direct or indirect, in the matter. *Ever yours*

Oyster Bay, July 17, 1908

Dear Will: I have your letter of the 15th. If there are new things which Bryan has put into his platform which you do not feel like discussing, then do not refer to them at all. My advice is very strongly that you do not "say that they are new propositions not considered by the Republican Party, and upon which, without further consideration, you do not feel justified in expressing an opinion." There will be a great number of well-meaning but thoughtless persons who will not understand such a statement, and will say that from a Presidential candidate they expect an opinion upon everything that is raised as an issue.

I think you will have to speak on the Government guaranty of deposit business. After the discussion in the Cabinet when you and Root, and indeed

---

[1] To Reverend D. D. Thompson, an advocate of mandatory prohibition, Taft had explained that he regarded prohibition as "not a national, but . . . necessarily a state and local issue, and . . . one upon which Republicans differ as do Democrats." Taft had earlier declared that he favored local option; see Pringle, *Taft*, I, 375.

all the members except George Meyer, seemed to feel so strongly in opposition to Government guaranty, I thought that you had very clear convictions on the matter. You exprest them not only forcefully, but, as I thought, in admirable form, on that occasion. Of course it is very difficult for one man to advise another just how to go at a thing. My own voice is always for aggressive warfare, and in your position I should go hard at Bryan and the Bryanites, on this as on other matters. The reason I felt as strongly as I exprest myself on that occasion at the Cabinet meeting, was because I was convinced that this guaranty of bank deposits would be an issue and that it would have to be met fairly and squarely, for it has attracted a great deal of attention. I wish you could get hold of George Meyer, who would be able, I think, to furnish you the exact facts which would permit you to slash savagely at the Bryanite platform and its half-hearted endorsement of postal savings banks, and show that the postal savings bank is the real way to protect the small depositor.[1] As a very rough bit of advice, I would suggest that you point out that your chief care is for the small depositor; that the small depositor is the one who should be protected in every possible way, and that the only way to give this absolute guaranty to him is thru the postal savings bank, and that it is completely given by the establishment of the postal savings bank as we have proposed. Point out that the Bryanite platform in this respect shows no real purpose to benefit the small man, but an effort to gain party capital at the cost of the small man by attacking the only possible measure for the postal savings banks under the false pretense that it is designed to help Wall Street; whereas those who drew up the platform, if they possest any intelligence, must know that the entire opposition to the postal savings banks came from the very people who they falsely assert were interested in having it passed. So that the Bryanite position in this, as in so many other matters, is while nominally advocating a policy, really to oppose any method which is actually suggested in order to carry that policy into effect. Furthermore, say that having thus cared for the needs of the small depositors by the postal savings banks, you are delighted to consider any

[1] The Democratic platform pledged the party to pass "legislation under which the national banks shall be required to establish a guarantee fund for the prompt payment of the depositors of any insolvent national bank, under an equitable system which shall be available to all State banking institutions wishing to use it." The party also favored "a postal savings bank if the guaranteed bank can not be secured" and if the postal savings bank were "constituted so as to keep the deposited money in the communities where it is established." The platform condemned "the policy of the Republican party in providing postal savings banks under a plan . . . . by which they will aggregate the deposits of the rural communities and redeposit the same while under Government charge in the banks of Wall street, thus depleting the circulating medium of the producing regions and unjustly favoring the speculative markets."

Roosevelt's letter spelled out the standard Republican rebuttal which Taft used in his acceptance speech and the Republicans incorporated in their campaign textbook. For both the Democratic argument and the complete Republican reply, see *Republican Campaign Text-Book*, 1908, pp. 471-472, 307-317.

plan for protecting the large depositors, who are the only ones that will be materially benefited by Mr. Bryan's proposals; but point out that these proposals in their present shape are absolutely meaningless, because they are impracticable unless there is a complete change in our banking system. It is mere wind to talk of a system of guaranteeing deposits in national banks which would also be available to all State banking institutions. Ask what is meant by this. It is either utterly meaningless, or else Mr. Bryan intends that all the State banking institutions shall be put under national control, which is a step in centralization of an inadvisable kind, and going much further than anyone had dreamed of suggesting on our side. Point out further that exactly as a Government guaranty could not be given unless the Government possest absolute and complete control over the business and practically went into the business itself, so it is impossible to make the national banks establish on a large scale and in permanent form this national guaranty fund without giving to the association of banks vastly more control over the individual banks than is now the case; that is, the responsible banks must be permitted to establish and enforce regulations of a drastic kind which will prevent the wildest banks coming in at all, or else they would find themselves wholly unable to go into the establishment of a guaranty fund. In other words, there must be a radical change in our Government system as regards banks; a far closer supervision and control over each bank, and a great extension of the power of the safe banks over the unsafe banks, before any such scheme as that which Mr. Bryan proposes is debatable.

As you know, I felt, and, altho to a less extent, Meyer felt, that this securing of a guaranty for depositors by the action of the Government, or by the action of the banks, was something that ought ultimately to come, and so I am a little puzzled how to furnish you a complete and slashing answer to Bryan's proposal. But it is a foolish and meaningless proposal as he has made it, for he and his followers have not been willing to look ahead and face all the consequences of the change, and I believe you can riddle his proposals, either along the lines indicated above or along others.

If there are some of these matters that you do not feel able to develop in satisfactory shape prior to your little speech of acceptance, I should not touch upon them at all beyond saying that you will discuss them in your letter of acceptance later. I suppose (for your sins) you have copies of my speech and letter of acceptance before you. You will notice that I made my speech comparatively short, but made it as aggressive as possible, and that the more elaborate discussion I reserved for my letter.

I am afraid I have not been very helpful, but this is about all I am able to suggest at the moment. *Ever yours*

[*Handwritten*] I believe you will be elected *if we can keep things as they are;* so be *very* careful to say nothing, not one sentence, that can be misconstrued, and that can give a handle for effective attacks. I have always had to exercise lynxeyed care over my own utterances!

Oyster Bay, July 18, 1908

My dear Senator Culberson: I have your letter of the 19th instant. I do not believe that you yourself can be more anxious than I am to do honor to the memory of General Sam Houston. Purely on my own initiative I appointed one of his sons United States Marshal, and I took particular pride in appointing and reappointing Mrs. Morrow, his daughter, as postmaster at Abilene. Many complaints have been made to me of her misconduct, and an investigation of the office last fall showed such gross irregularities that her removal was recommended by the inspector making the investigation. Under ordinary circumstances she would have been removed forthwith on this showing, but because she was the daughter of Sam Houston I personally took an interest in the case and asked that she be given another trial. This June, after eight months of additional trial, there was a reinspection, and this reinspection showed not only that there was no improvement, but that Mrs. Morrow had been guilty of misconduct so gross that it was evident that I could not longer extend clemency. The case was submitted to me because of my personal interest in Mrs. Morrow and my very earnest desire that no injustice should be done her. It appears that she was guilty of deceitful conduct, in addition to the grossest inefficiency.

I can assure you, my dear Senator, that I acted with the greatest reluctance in this case. In my own State of New York, for instance, I do not believe I have ever permitted a postmaster to be given a second chance, as Mrs. Morrow was, if the postmaster had been guilty of such misconduct as Mrs. Morrow has been guilty of. After the second showing I did not feel that I could any longer interfere with the action of the Department, without creating a precedent that would make it impossible for me ever to hold the Department to account if it tolerated inefficiency in the other post offices under it.

With regret, believe me, *Sincerely yours*

Oyster Bay, July 19, 1908

Dear Cabot: It was a great pleasure to receive your letter. Indeed, I cannot too strongly say how high I put your success as presiding officer of the convention. Speaking quite dispassionately, and simply as a historian, I do not believe that any other speech ever made before a national convention will rank with yours. Very, very few such speeches will go down in history; but yours certainly will, even tho not one other should. I think very little of mere oratory. I feel an impatient contempt for the man of words if he is merely a man of words. The great speech must always be the speech of a man with a great soul, who has a thought worth putting into words, and whose acts bear out the words he utters, and the occasion must demand the speech. Judged by this criterion your speech measures up to any standard.

So much for the public side of your speech. Personally, it was of course to me a matter of very great importance that it should be my closest friend, the man whom everybody recognized as speaking for me, who required the convention to guard my honor, to respect my good faith. It would have been a great mistake had you made any extended allusion to me, and indeed no extended allusion, no matter if you had spoken for hours, could have conveyed higher praise, could have been better worth cherishing, than the one you actually made. You said exactly what was right, neither too little nor too much, and you said it exactly as I should have wisht to have it said; I do not recall any speech at any nominating convention which is either so sure of permanence as yours, or which at the very moment attracted such widespread and practically unanimous approval. As for the *Sun's* attack upon it, and upon you and me, I should as soon pay attention to an attack in *Town Topics,* or in Debs' *Appeal to Reason.* There are many occasions when the highest praise one can receive is the attack of some given scoundrel.

As for my own action, there was never any room for doubt. Whatever my service has been, small or great, and for however brief a period it may be remembered, its usefulness has been predicated upon the belief of the plain people that it was sincere and disinterested, as well as courageous, and that when I had given my word, my word was good. The ordinary plain man, the man who has stood behind me in what I have done or have striven to do, and who has accepted me as his special representative, is not given to hair-splitting or to making fine distinctions. Even when he did not approve of my having said that I would not run, and wisht that I could be nominated again, his final verdict was certain to be "Well, he said he would not run, and he never goes back on his word, and that is all there is tó it." I should have damaged this man morally if I had made him feel that after all I was vacillating or insincere; and even tho he had voted for me, as I think he would have done, he would thereafter have put me on a lower plane, and his own character would thereby have been somewhat hurt, while my ability to do good work would have been immeasurably decreased.

Of course there have been uncomfortable moments when I have felt very doubtful as to whether I had not by my action deserved a place beside your Dante's Pope, «he» who was guilty of the great renunciation; whether I had not put myself in the class of those whom Mirabeau jeered at as Grandison-Cromwells. But these doubts as to whether I ought to have taken the position (which never for a moment affected my purpose to adhere to the position inasmuch as it had been taken) were always evanescent. I am sure I was right. I believe in the perpetuity of the American Republic, partly because we as a people give our heartiest admiration and respect, not to the mere strong man, regardless of whether he is good or bad, nor yet to the weakling of good purposes, but to the strong man who uses his strength disinterestedly for the public good; and our greatest national asset is that, of this type, the Timoleon and Hampden type, as have produced the greatest examples that the world has ever seen in Washington and Lincoln. These were the greatest good men and the best great men that the world has ever seen; and the lesser men can best serve their country by keeping to these men's standards of purpose and achievement. I have a perfectly definite philosophy about the Presidency. I think it should be a very powerful office, and I think the President should be a very strong man who uses without hesitation every power that the position yields; but because of this very fact I believe that he should be sharply watched by the people, held to a strict accountability by them, and that he should not keep the office too long.

I am lucky enough to have strong tastes in more than one direction, and in addition, when I am thru with anything I am thru with it, and am under no temptation to snatch at the fringes of departing glory. When I stop being President I will stop completely; and by great good fortune I have gradually developed the very plan which of all others would have most attractions for me, and is best for me to follow out. I am going to Africa for the National Museum at Washington. I shall be absent about a year. Most of the time I shall expect to be in British, or possibly in German, East Africa, and then to come out northward by the Nile, or possibly southward to the Zambesi. I shall hunt, but, excepting for food, my hunting will be merely for specimens of big game for the National Museum. They will send two field naturalists and taxidermists with me, they paying for these taxidermists and for the transport of the specimens home. Scribner's is to give me $50,000 for the serial rights of my trip. Collier's offered me $100,000, but I thought it much more dignified and appropriate that the series should appear in *Scribner's;* and moreover, I think there is such a thing as making too much money out of a given feat, even tho the money be made with entire honesty. Kermit is now hard at work getting up his photography, as he will be the photographer of the trip. Bar accidents, whether from fever or wild beasts, the trip ought to be a success, and I am already looking forward to it with most eager interest and pleasure.

I felt exactly as you did about Curtin's work, and I was disappointed to find that he did not cover the history of the Mongols in Europe, and especially in Russia. I am immensely amused to think that I forgot that it was you who recommended Murray's History of the Greek Epic to me.

As yet the campaign has not begun. Taft is bearing himself well, and unless he makes some hopeless break, or unless there is some entirely unforeseen cataclysm, I do not see how he can be beaten. But we need to keep our eyes on the Middle West. If there is any trouble, it will come there.

With warm love to dear Nannie, *Ever yours*

Oyster Bay, July 20, 1908

Dear Elihu: In a few days Bob[1] will go up to see you to talk about Cuban matters. I am sorry to say that the reports on file about Bahía Honda seem to be conclusive against our making any attempt to turn the place into a naval station or put any troops there.[2] I don't understand why we ever got such a reservation. The Bay is a poor one for ships, and as regards troops, it is forty miles from any railroad, the roads are extremely bad, and there are no provisions in the country to draw on. Moreover, the reservation itself contains literally no drinking water, and but one small hillock, sufficient for encampment of about fifty men, where it would be possible to put any men at all. Most of it is mangrove swamp and the mosquitoes literally make life insupportable, and they include both yellow fever and malarial varieties.

I think the time has come when we should settle definitely as to our course in Cuba. Magoon gets on beautifully with the Cuban; he has done his work well, but he is not a man of masterful type or, indeed, of great force, and he shrinks from following any course to which he thinks any considerable number of Cubans would object, whether rightly or wrongly. I believe that when we provide for the election of the president and Congress under whom the Island is to resume its independence we should state explicitly that the election is held on the understanding that all the acts of the Provisional Government are to be considered as in full force when the new government takes effect, precisely as if they were adopted by this new government, and that any official who takes his seat will be held as subscribing to this condition. I want to have it understood that without any action by the new government all that we have done is ratified and stands on the statute books as law until specifically overturned. The inertia and governmental incapacity of the new Cuban Congress, if it is like the preceding Cuban Congresses, may very possibly be such as to prevent their re-enacting these laws even if they really intended to do so; and I want to have the laws continued in effect automatically as it were. I don't care in the least what scheme is adopted to bring about this purpose, and I have very much more confidence in your judgment as to the kind of scheme to adopt than I have in my own. Then, when the Congress and the President are elected, I think we ought to communicate to them with great seriousness and in a manner that will impress them, our earnest desire that the new government shall be perpetual; that Cuba shall indeed remain free and independent, and therefore our hope that they will themselves ask us to make such arrangements, probably by leaving certain assistants in the Island as will secure permanence of govern-

[1] Robert Bacon.
[2] The American government made no attempt to establish a base at Bahía Honda. In 1908 the State Department, at the request of the Navy Department, was attempting to obtain Cuba's permission to enlarge the Guantánamo reservation in exchange for the Bahía Honda lease. These negotiations failed; see Fitzgibbon, *Cuba*, pp. 106–107.

ment. This can be secured only by providing that the finances be kept straight; that order be maintained; and that fair elections be guaranteed. We must try to make them understand that our purpose is not to interfere with the design of limiting their independence, but to interfere so as to enable them to retain their independence. We must try to make them understand, what is the exact truth, that we would object to having to take charge of the Island quite as much as they would object to our doing so, and that our sole and genuine purpose is to help them so to manage their affairs that there won't be the slightest need of further interference on our part.

I need not have you down here to see Luke Wright; but if Taft comes on I shall probably wire you at once, as that will be something of genuine importance.

With love to Mrs. Root, *Faithfully yours*

4815 · TO GEORGE HAVEN PUTNAM   *Roosevelt Mss.*

Oyster Bay, July 21, 1908

Dear Haven: How would it do for you to take lunch with me on Friday, August 21st? But, my dear Haven, I do not believe it will be possible for you to make any announcement next year. I appreciate all that you urge in favor of finishing *The Winning of the West,* but I do not know that I can go into any historical work needing exhaustive ⟨discussion⟩ research, for some time to come; and there are reasons, some of which I will discuss with you when I see you, why it is possible I should prefer some other type of historical work, if I ever do find myself, as I suppose will ultimately be the case, able to take up history again. I simply *can't* bind myself now. *Sincerely yours*

4816 · TO CECIL ARTHUR SPRING RICE   *Roosevelt Mss.*

Oyster Bay, July 21, 1908

Dear Cecil: As usual, we enjoyed your letter much. You deal with the subjects that must appeal to every thoughtful man. With most of what you say I entirely agree. The love of pleasure, the love of ease, and the growth of extravagance and luxury among the upper classes, and a certain frivolous habit of mind and failure to fix the relative values of things, all of these are very dangerous and very marked among the English-speaking peoples, as well as in France. It is idle to say that such growth does not contain the possibility of national disaster, for it does. Moreover, I agree with you that Germany alone among the modern nations of high civilization has been able thoroly to organize her powers, has been able successfully to combat the more dangerous tendencies that have been at work among other peoples for the last half century — being careful to include among these dangerous tendencies those of the silly people who call themselves beyond all others humanitarians, just as much as the tendencies to vice, luxury and levity. But the

Germans themselves are beginning to be infested by the vices of industrialism, just as is the case with those formidable creatures, the Japanese; and moreover, we ought to draw some comfort from Germany's example, for it must teach us how easy, after all, it is for a nation to revive and recover when it has sunk pretty low. There was nothing in Germany's history for the century succeeding the close of the Seven-Years' War to make us anticipate the extraordinary growth in power and efficiency, alike in military and in industrial affairs, on land and on sea, which has marked her career for the last forty-five years. Of course the Slavs may have the future as theirs; but remember that for two centuries everyone has been prophesying of Russia a growth of power that has never come to pass, and has believed that she held a menace to the rest of the world which has never been made good save in the case of Sweden alone — for Poland had sunk so low that it is quite impossible for me to regard the Russians as having made it sink much lower. It may be, and I hope it will be, that Russia will steer the middle course and slowly rise, avoiding the gulf of absolutism and bureaucracy on the one side, and the gulf of anarchy, ranging from nihilism to Tolstoyism, on the other side. But if this does come, her rise then would not be fraught with danger to the rest of the world. Moreover, Springy, I think you sometimes idealize the past. The dangers of the present are very real, and there are plenty of evil tendencies at work now that were not at work in the past. But on the other hand, we have overcome many of the evil tendencies of the past; and while I do not wish to be a foolish optimist, I cannot help thinking that on the whole things, tho bad enough, are better and not worse than they were a half century, or one century, or two, or three, or four centuries ago. It may be that we have reached the condition of the Greek world after Alexander, of the Roman world after Trajan; but frankly, I don't think so. Moreover, it is rather a comfort to know that the prophets of dire evil are generally as much mistaken as the prophets of the Millennium.

At any rate, come good or come evil, our duty is the same. It is our business to do everything we can individually, and collectively, nationally, to be both decent and efficient under conditions as we actually find them.

I do wish you could get over here. Isn't it possible before we leave the White House for you and your wife to visit us there? I'd like to show you Sagamore Hill again, too. *Ever yours*

4817 · TO WILLIAM HOWARD TAFT   *Roosevelt Mss.*

Telegram   Oyster Bay, July 21, 1908

Both of the first two paragraphs should certainly be omitted. The rest of the speech is I think admirable, with two or three corrections. On pages thirty-seven and thirty-eight reference to bank deposits is weak and most of it should be omitted. It is apologetic and hesitating and would give advantage to opponents. The last two thirds of page forty-six should be omitted and supplanted by something else, or at least entirely changed. In present shape, there are phases which would not please the negro and would displease the white. I do not like the stray pages about injunction and am doubtful about the page concerning the identity of interest of employer and employees. I think that the number of times my name is used should be cut down. You are now the leader, and there must be nothing that looks like self-depreciation or undue subordination of yourself. My name should be used only enough thoroly to convince people of the identity and continuity of our policies. The first two paragraphs should for different reasons certainly come out.[1]

4818 · TO GEORGE WALBRIDGE PERKINS   *Roosevelt Mss.*

Oyster Bay, July 23, 1908

My dear Mr. Perkins: You spoke to me of raises in railway rates at the time of our last interview. Since then I have seen newspaper statements to the effect that there were going to be general raises in railway rates. I earnestly hope that these reports are erroneous, as I suppose to be the case.[1] It may well be that given rates should be raised; just as it may be that given rates should be lowered. But anything in the nature of a general raise is simply an invitation to an attack, because most people do not believe that the conditions are the same as regards all shipments or in all portions of the country, and I am sure that the general feeling would be not that such a raise was

---

[1] Taft accepted part of Roosevelt's advice. The candidate's speech of acceptance, delivered July 28, began with two paragraphs to which there could have been no objections from a Republican and was firm on the bank deposits issue. It did, however, include many laudatory references to Roosevelt; see *Republican Campaign Text-Book*, 1908, pp. 1–28.

[1] These reports were correct. Deterred from cutting wages, in part by Roosevelt's vigorous statements in February 1908 (see No. 4605), many railroads contended that profit could be stabilized during the current business recession only through raising rates. By the middle of July the roads in the Trunk Line Association, the Southeastern Freight Association, and the "Southwestern Territory" had already announced substantial raises which were to become effective after August 1. Shippers and manufacturers immediately protested and through their local associations, of which the manufacturers' associations of New York and Illinois were the most vocal, gave widespread publicity to the proposed measures.

Roosevelt, more troubled immediately by the political implications than by harmful effects on the shippers, hoped to avoid any sizable rate rise, at least until after the election. He asked the Interstate Commerce Commission "to let it unofficially be known that if there is such a general raise the Commission would be obliged at once to make an investigation. . . ." (Roosevelt to the Interstate Commerce Commission, July 23, 1908, Roosevelt Mss.).

Besides writing Perkins, Roosevelt also saw William C. Brown, senior vice-president of the New York Central, who, by published letters to and speeches before associations of manufacturers and shippers, had been presenting the railroads' arguments for the proposed rates (see No. 4832). Owing to pressures from Washington and the shippers, the eastern roads delayed their plans. However, the southern roads, characteristically refusing to be deterred by outside agencies, put the new rates into effect; see No. 4848.

warranted or demanded by business needs, but that it was made simply with a purpose of enabling some railroads to gain an improper advantage, while others were gaining a needed relief. The information that has come to me has been very clear that on certain railroads no raise should be permitted; that on certain ones reductions in rates, at least on certain articles, should be made. But of course there are others where it may well be that the rates, at least on certain articles, should be raised. I do not know whether you have firsthand information on this matter or not, but I think if you are in touch with any railroad people you ought to inform them in the matter and put them in touch with the Interstate Commerce Commission before they act. I believe I am expressing the views of the Commission as gathered from conversations I had last spring with members thereof.

With regard, believe me, *Sincerely yours*

4819 · TO CHARLES JOSEPH BONAPARTE   *Roosevelt Mss.*

Oyster Bay, July 23, 1908

My dear Mr. Bonaparte: I have your letter of the 20th. Offhand, my judgment would be against such a suit, but it is not necessary to make a final decision until the question arises. I send you a copy of a letter I have sent to the Interstate Commerce Commission.[1]

I have had the enclosed statement made public.[2] Will you not consult Mr. Kellogg in the matter? Every effort should be made to bring these peo-

[1] See No. 4818, note 1.

[2] Roosevelt's statement, made public by Loeb, directed the Attorney General to take immediate steps for the retrial of the case against the Standard Oil Company of Indiana. On July 22 the circuit court of appeals with Judge Grosscup presiding had reversed Judge Landis' decision fining the company $29,240,000 for violating the Elkins Act. Grosscup held that the government had failed to prove that the defendant had knowingly accepted rates below those on the published schedules. Furthermore, the circuit court contended that Landis had not followed the meaning of the law when he calculated the fine on the number of carloadings instead of the number of shipments. Finally Grosscup characterized the fine as an "abuse of judicial discretion" because its amount was equivalent to the total assets of the Indiana company.

Roosevelt's indignation at the circuit court's action was fully expressed in Loeb's statement to the press. "The reversal of the decision of the lower court," it read, "does not in any shape or way touch the merits of the case, except so far as the size of the fine is concerned. There is absolutely no question of the guilt of the defendants or of the exceptionally grave character of the offenses. The President would regard it as a gross miscarriage of justice if, through any technicality of any kind, the defendants escaped punishment which would have been meted out to any weaker defendant who had been guilty of such offenses."

Bonaparte immediately began to make arrangements for a retrial. At the new hearings held before District Judge Anderson in Indianapolis, Kellogg and the other government attorneys disputed Grosscup's interpretation of the Elkins Act. They hoped to show that the necessity to prove absolutely that a shipper knowingly received concessions would nullify the usefulness of the law in preventing rebates. Anderson, however, in March 1909, upholding Grosscup's decision, acquitted the company.

ple to justice. I have always felt that Landis hurt the case by the excessive size of the fine which he imposed; but I think these three judges have hurt the cause of civilization and property by, instead of reducing the fine, bringing in technicalities which enabled them to throw the whole case open again with the evident purpose of shielding the corporation from all punishment. Grosscup I believe to be a scoundrel.[3] The other two judges[4] are merely the ordinary type produced by improper subserviency to corporations.

It was a great pleasure seeing you the other day.

With warm regards to Mrs. Bonaparte, believe me, *Faithfully yours*

4820 · TO RICHMOND PEARSON HOBSON   *Roosevelt Mss.*

Oyster Bay, July 24, 1908

My dear Mr. Hobson: I have your letter of the 21st instant.[1] I have not forgotten the conversation to which you refer. So far from saying that there was the "greatest probability of trouble with Japan," I told you explicitly, in answer to your statement that you were certain we would have war with Japan, that I did not think so, and that one reason I wisht a big navy was because it would avert the probability of war with any power, whereas if we had an insufficient navy we should at any time be apt to have trouble with any power with which we might at any moment be embroiled.

But whether you were right or I am right as to the probability of war, two things are equally clear. One is that it is the duty of this Nation to make every effort to make such efficient preparation as to guarantee us against trouble. The other thing, I am sorry to say, is that to make what you call "raw, brutal statements," to be "brutally frank," is the surest way to bring about trouble and is an exceedingly poor way of preparing for it. I regret that I must add that it is literally unpardonable when in addition to showing these qualities of "raw brutality" and of "brutal frankness" you deliberately quote the President of the United States in a way that would cause grave mischief if the quotation were correct; and, as a matter of fact, you misquote him. You say that you "took the responsibility of violating the confidence of our private conversation," and that you expected me to deny the statement officially, but that it is in the nature of a surprise to receive a private denial. I wish you would think over just what this statement of yours means in all its bearings. When a man is guilty of such a breach of honorable confidence, he cannot expect to be trusted to repeat accurately what he has heard. You in effect state that having determined to violate the confidence necessary to intercourse among gentlemen if such intercourse is to continue, you expected me to tell an untruth in public, and apparently would

[3] Even before this decision Roosevelt considered Grosscup, because of his requests for railroad passes, a corrupt judge.

[4] Francis Elisha Baker and William Henry Seaman.

[1] In reply to No. 4800.

have approved of it so long as I did not confirm my public statement by a private statement.[2] Surely such an extraordinary proposition calls for no comment; but it does make it necessary for me to protect myself in the future by not placing similar confidence in you again; that is, by not again having a private conversation with you. *Very truly yours*

4821 · TO CHARLES JOSEPH BONAPARTE   *Roosevelt Mss.*

Oyster Bay, July 25, 1908

Dear Bonaparte: I have your letter of the 23d with enclosures. That is an important matter.[1] Don't you think you and Kellogg could come down here and let me talk over the whole matter with you? So far I think there has been only one possible mistake, and even that a possible one. Our advantage consists in being morally exactly right, and I have always felt that Landis' fine was excessive. If it would have been proper for the Government to have stated that it thought the fine excessive and would acquiesce in any modification that the upper court desired, I think this would have been from the standpoint of justice a good thing to do. No doubt, however, the same men who are attacking us for punishing the Standard Oil would have then attacked us for favoring it. *Sincerely yours*

P.S. I have your letter of the «20th» instant. I take exactly the view you do about the Standard Oil case. I heartily approve of your giving out the interview and trying to have a rehearing. I rather feel like making a savage fight on this Grosscup outcry in my next message. I shall certainly do it when I get thru with the Presidency. More power to your elbow!

I send you a clipping about the Standard Oil case, which please return to me when you are thru with it.

P.P.S. Your letter of the 25th has just come. I agree with you absolutely that Archbold must have known in advance what the Grosscup decision was to be. I feel pretty ugly over that decision. The reduction of the fine could have been all right, but the action of the court amounts precisely and exactly to saying that the biggest criminals in this country should be shielded and the law of Congress nullified, and that it should be done in the most adroit and keenest of ways; that is, that it should be done by so deciding that the law become really ineffective instead of declaring it unconstitutional.

[2] There is an interesting story bearing on this expression of outrage to Hobson. It still circulates among the older members of the working press and is vouched for by one wholly reliable man who claims to have been present, on one occasion, when Roosevelt spoke the words traditionally attributed to him in the story. It was his habit, it is said, when giving newspapermen what is now called "off the record" material, to preface his remarks with some such words as "I will now tell you this for your own information. If you print it, I can assure you I will deny that I said it." An interview with the press and a private discussion with the ineffable Hobson are of course not analogous.

[1] The retrial of the Standard Oil case, see No. 4819.

In the railroad matter I quite agree with you that the railroads ought not to raise their rates until December.[2] I have not much sympathy with most of the shippers, however, as the men who are making the most talk in this matter are those wealthy concerns, many of them by no means of impeccable character in their own private business.

4822 · TO WILLIAM BAILEY HOWLAND

Roosevelt Mss.

Personal

Oyster Bay, July 30, 1908

My dear Mr. Howland: I have your letter of the 28th, and enclosures. The editorial announcement is all right and I return it herewith, having retained a copy. I assume of course that when it says that *The Outlook* "will be the exclusive channel for the expression of his views on political, industrial, and social topics" it does not mean that I shall not make addresses on such subjects, but that I shall not write for other publications on such subjects; and my speeches are at least in part on such «subjects.»

As regards the letter of Mr. Abbott to you of July 23d, it expresses the situation precisely as I see it. I will very gladly give a signed letter to *The Outlook* for the 5th of March. I shall try, as I told you and Lawrence the other day, to get some articles, say on socialism, ready for you before I leave, but as the editorial announcement itself says, of course until I return from my trip I cannot expect to give you anything like the number of articles I will then; so if you had not made the proposition that I should join on March 5th next, I should not have made it myself, as I should have been doubtful as to giving you the full equivalent of what you gave me.

It was a great pleasure to see you both the other day. *Faithfully yours*

4823 · TO WILLIAM HOWARD TAFT

Roosevelt Mss.

Oyster Bay, July 30, 1908

Dear Will: I congratulate you most heartily. As far as I can see from here the speech is a great success and has achieved exactly the purposes you sought to obtain. Of course the *Sun, Times,* and *Evening Post* are dreadfully pained at your having praised me, or rather, as they phrase it, having submitted to my insistence that you should praise me. I am glad they did not see your speech before I got at it. But we can afford entirely to disregard what these gentry say. Neither they nor their supporters will go for Bryan; whereas if they were able to show or to seem to show that you had turned about, the result might easily be disastrous.

I hope that your representatives will carefully refrain from giving any expression about the Hughes business in New York. I have never seen anything like the bitterness on the two sides. Any number of good people say

---

[2] The railroads, excepting those in the South, postponed changing their rates until after the election; see No. 4818.

that they will not vote for anybody else but Hughes, and any number of good people say they won't under any circumstances vote for Hughes. I think the wise thing to do is to take no part in the contest whatever, and to let it be fought out fairly in the primaries. Of course a change may come that may necessitate action, but at present this is the way things look.[1]

With love to Mrs. Taft, believe me, *Faithfully yours*

P.S. I have written Bonaparte to have the Standard Oil Company suits go right on regardless of the campaign and that I would suggest to you the advisability of announcing that you would not permit your campaign managers to accept one dollar of contribution from the Standard Oil Company or anyone connected with it.

4824 · TO CHARLES SPRAGUE SMITH *Roosevelt Mss.*

Oyster Bay, July 31, 1908

My dear Mr. Smith: I am in receipt of your letter of the 29th. That is an interesting and important statement of yours. I have received many letters for and against Mr. Hughes' nomination. Among those whose judgment I most trust, including men like yourself, the Editor of the *Rural New Yorker*,[1] etc., I believe the majority are for Governor Hughes' nomination; but a very large minority of these men are at present against the renomination. I have never known such a combination of bitterness toward a candidate and enthusiasm for him being shown to the same degree. There was, for instance, even more bitterness against me in small circles, but the circles were so small that whenever we have had a showdown they were not able to get as much as a delegate against me. Here, however, the whole party seems to be at this moment almost equally divided. I do not believe it will be necessary for me to take any part in the contest whatever. At present I am inclined to think that if we could get an absolutely fair expression of opinion in the primaries, without any possible attempt at dictation, the result would be best.

Of course it may ultimately be necessary for me to interfere, but I shall

[1] The battle in New York over the renomination of Hughes for governor continued for over a month. To this issue Roosevelt in that period gave more attention than to any other. His many letters on the Hughes renomination adequately define the issue and the political alignments. Yet they leave a false impression of Hughes. He was incontrovertibly an aloof, often difficult man whose insensitivity to the traditionally legitimate obligations of party politics alienated not only callous district leaders but also such sincere and purposeful politicians as Herbert Parsons. This very characteristic, however, while endangering his control of legislation as well as of election processes, enhanced his deserved reputation with the electorate for dogged honesty. That quality, too rare in politics, Hughes combined with a genuine and thoughtful progressivism. Contrary to Roosevelt's frequent accusation, Hughes was not the tool or the spokesman of any interest but the public welfare as he interpreted it. He fought ably for the regulation of corporations, the democratization of primary and election devices, and the elimination of gambling influences in politics.

[1] H. W Collingwood.

do it with the utmost reluctance. At present it looks to me as tho what might be called the "upper ten thousand" among the Republicans — that is, the men of leisure and cultivation, the men who are my social friends — are very strongly for Hughes and would resent in the bitterest way the failure to renominate him; and a great many others feel that he stands as identified with the cause of antibossism and independence in politics and should be heartily supported. On the other hand, a great many workingmen, mechanics, and the like, are against him; why, it is sometimes difficult to find out, except that they regard him as being narrow and not sufficiently favorable to the just demands of labor, and not having sympathy with the small people. I am gravely concerned over the situation and I wish I saw my way clear to know what to do. Perhaps in a few weeks it may clear, so that we can see which way the popular feeling really is.

With regard, believe me, *Sincerely yours*

4825 · TO EDGAR ALEXANDER MEARNS   *Roosevelt Mss.*

Oyster Bay, August 1, 1908

My dear Doctor: [1] Three cheers! It is delightful to be in official communication with the "naturalist and medical adviser of the African expedition." I hereby authorize and request you to take up the whole matter of medical equipment, and make requisition for everything necessary from the medical supply department of the army, and have the material stored ready for transportation in the United States National Museum. I am already taking steps for the equipment of Kermit and myself. This practically means, however, only our clothes, guns, and personal necessaries, as undoubtedly we can get at Nairobi or Mombasa everything else. You and your assistant, whether Mr. Palmer or anyone else whom you choose,[2] will, I suppose, follow the same course; that is, will take your weapons, clothes, personal kit, &c., from here, but outfit at Nairobi. When we meet at Washington in the fall I can send word to Nairobi to get everything ready for all of us.

I shall sail on March 23d on the *Hamburg*, of the Hamburg-American Line, and have got a stateroom for Kermit and myself. Wouldn't it be well for you to write the people telling them you and your assistant will want a stateroom on the same boat, and also asking them to engage a stateroom for you and your assistant in company with myself on the German boat for

[1] Edgar Alexander Mearns, a retired lieutenant colonel of the Army Medical Corps, author of *Mammals of the Mexican Boundary of the United States* (1907), was chief naturalist and physician for the Roosevelt expedition to Africa. "Doctor Mearns," Roosevelt reported, "in addition to birds and plants, never let pass the opportunity to collect anything else from reptiles and fishes to land-shells. Moreover, he was the best shot in our party." — *African Game Trails* (New York, 1910), Nat. Ed. IV, 118.

[2] The other naturalists who accompanied Roosevelt were Edmund Heller of California and J. Alden Loring of New York. A Scot, R. J. Cuninghame, and an Australian, Leslie Tarlton, met the party in Africa.

Mombasa, with which we connect at Naples. I suppose that you and your assistant will both have shotguns. In that case the ammunition should be shipped well in advance to Mombasa, care Smith, Mackenzie & Co. Do go down to Burroughs, «Walicomb» & Co., as you suggest.

I am looking forward greatly to the trip. Surely we ought to make it a success. *Faithfully yours*

4826 · TO JAMES BRYCE   *Roosevelt Mss.*

Confidential   Oyster Bay, August 3, 1908

My dear Mr. Bryce: I do not know whether your Foreign Office, in view of the relations between Tibet and India, would or would not take the slightest interest in the letter[1] a copy of which I enclose. From its nature, it must of course be treated as entirely confidential, so that I would rather that it was only shown to the Foreign Office people unless there is someone else who you think really ought to know it — it may be that your Indian Office ought to see it instead of the Foreign Office; of course I am entirely willing that any of the Government should see it.

Things here seem to be going along in commonplace fashion. I think we shall elect Taft, but it is as yet a little early to be positive. I am absorbed in my African trip, and I hear you have been very kind about it. I am going for the National Museum, and the only shooting I shall do, except for food, will be to obtain one or two specimens of each kind of big game for the National Museum. I shall have two field naturalists who are good taxidermists with me.

With warm regards to Mrs. Bryce, *Faithfully yours*

4827 · TO JEAN JULES JUSSERAND   · *Roosevelt Mss.*

Personal   Oyster Bay, August 3, 1908

My dear M. Jusserand: The two books have come, and I am certain I shall greatly enjoy both. It was most kind of you to send them.

It is always well that the past should be past. As you know, I have always been frank in saying that I should have particularly liked to have remained as President if I had felt it was proper for me to do so but looking at things from the purely personal standpoint, it seems to me that instead of being melancholy because I cannot remain as President, I ought to be exceedingly grateful that I have such an alternative as a trip to Africa. I am already absorbed in it. I shall go on behalf of the National Museum at Washington, and my hunting, aside from getting food, will merely be so much as will allow

[1] The letter, from Rockhill, described the declining status of the Dalai Lama. The British welcomed this and later observations of the American minister whose discerning reports on Tibetan matters (see, for example, No. 5077, note 1), helped set the stage for his later, significant collaborations with Hippisley on the direction of Anglo-American policy in the Orient.

me to get specimens of each of the large game animals for the National Museum. I will take with me a couple of field naturalists and taxidermists sent by the Museum.

I have been reading the French translation of Ferrero's last volumes, and as I know you so well I shall venture on the rather priggish statement that it is a real satisfaction to me to feel that so far as my action is of any consequence at all, it is a help and not a hurt to the principles of orderly freedom; in other words, that I certainly have no place in the swarm of conscienceless revolutionaries or reactionaries such as those who — quite as much the reactionaries as the revolutionaries — brought about the downfall of the Roman Republic. We cannot any of us tell whither civilization is tending, or what may be the strength or even the direction of the great blind forces working all around us. But I very cordially agree with Lord Acton that we are in honor bound # to do right *because* it is right. Moreover I believe that it is a leader's duty to lead efficiently, as well as in the right direction. I think that the President should be a strong man, and that he should make the Presidency the strongest kind of office; but because of this very belief, I feel that he should also make it evident that he has not the slightest intention to grasp at permanent power. Our public men must be . . . if they are to be of use.

By the way, I have been much imprest by a rather imaginative but genuinely valuable and instructive work on *La Production, le Travail et le Problème Social* [1] of today by Léon Poinsard. Do you know who he is? He has, what so few students outside of France have, the power to combine thought and erudition with ease and charm of expression.

I am particularly pleased to hear what you say of White. He is a thoroly good fellow.

Yes, Turkey is an infinitely worse problem than Venezuela. How I wish I could get the American people to take the least interest in Castro. It is literally true that if I started to deal with him as he deserves, the enormous majority of my countrymen would be so absolutely amazed and so absolutely out of sympathy with me as if I undertook personally to run down and chastise some small street urchin who yelled some epithet of derision at me while I was driving. As for the Moorish business, I wish to Heaven, not in your interest but in the interest of all civilized mankind, that France could take all Morocco under its exclusive charge.

Mrs. Roosevelt and I both laughed over the clippings you had pasted into your letter. She sends both of you her love, in which I join. *Very faithfully your friend*

Don't you like Acton's essays on Liberty and kindred subjects just published? [2]

[1] *La Production, le Travail et le Problème Social dans Tous les Pays au Début du XXme Siècle* (Paris, 1907), by Léon Poinsard, French economist and sociologist.
[2] Sir John Emerich Edward Dalberg Acton, Baron Acton, *The History of Freedom and Other Essays* (London, 1907), edited with an introduction by John N. Figgis and Reginald V. Laurence.

Oyster Bay, August 3, 1908

Dear Will: I hope you will discipline Hitchcock without the slightest hesitation and with all needful severity. He is a man who needs to have a strong hand kept on him.[1]

It is evident that your reception in Cincinnati was a great success. Judging from the quotations, the papers in the West are very much pleased with your speech. I am mighty glad that Root is to speak at the State convention here in New York,[2] tho I am at my wits' end as to whether it is absolutely necessary to nominate Hughes, or whether it would be suicidal to do so, as I have a great volume of correspondence about equally, with frantic vehemence, divided on this point.

Yes, that was a good letter in the *Sun*. I suppose it will be some little time yet before you will have any idea as to the line you will want me to take in my letter. In fact, I should think it would be well, until we see what fire your letter draws, and just where, if at all, we need any strengthening. At the moment it looks to me as if we should do substantially what we did four years ago, except that we shall probably carry Maryland and probably lose Missouri. There is, however, a chance for Missouri, Oklahoma, Kentucky and Tennessee, and on the other hand our opponents have a chance in Nevada, Nebraska and Indiana. But this is all in the air at present, because it is too far in advance to make any definite forecast.

Hitchcock is coming out here to lunch on Friday.

I enclose a letter from Foulke. *Faithfully yours*

Oyster Bay, August 3, 1908

Dear Elihu: I was just sending you a letter begging you to preside when I received your letter saying that you would. The second page of the letter was missing, by the way. I gather from the last line of the first page that it was occupied chiefly with remarks of a highly unpleasant character concern-

---

[1] Speaking to the Ohio Republican central and executive committees in Cincinnati on July 27, Taft stated that "it is a great comfort to me to know that in the strenuous times that are to follow from now on, I shall have the close personal, and most useful assistance and aid of our friend . . . 'Jake' Vorys." Because Hitchcock was openly antagonistic to Vorys, this statement reassured those in Ohio to whom Vorys had made preconvention promises. Vorys himself "beamed with delight." Taft also observed that "organization" in the campaign would be "absolutely necessary" to "bring out the vote." The following day the smooth organization of Vorys and Brown mustered enthusiastic marching clubs to welcome Taft officially to his home city, to demonstrate Republican preparedness, and to provide the traditional background for the candidate's notification and acceptance speech.

[2] Root was to be temporary chairman of the New York Republican Convention, where his keynote speech, devoted largely to the national campaign, was a useful contribution to the party's September propaganda.

ing my great and good friends, the Presidents of the various Central American Republics, and the excessively free and independent peoples over whom they preside.

I have written to Hitchcock at once to send you any literature that he has. I have also asked him to send you the two platforms. Your speech will be one of the great assets of our campaign, and this will be a peculiarly good place in which to make it. While you must have all the literature, still, you know Taft, you know the situation, you know the issues, and it will be on this knowledge that your speech will primarily be built. I wish I knew what to advise about the nomination for Governor. Fortunately, we have a month ahead before we need definitely make up our minds. There is the bitterest feeling against Hughes, not only among the machine people proper, but among a great many others, and this bitterness goes so far that I fear it will show itself in the vote. On the other hand, he has the strongest support among, I think, the majority of the more or less independent Republicans — that is, of those not actively engaged in politics — and these would resent a failure to nominate him quite as bitterly as the others would resent his nomination; and moreover, he would undoubtedly draw a great many Democrats. But I do not know how far there is hostility to him among working people, and how far there is a general discontent with his alleged narrowness among people who are good and straight citizens, but who like to go to baseball matches and the like. As at present advised, I should be inclined to say that he ought to be nominated, (though his strength may be as unreal as Jerome's two years ago). But I don't feel like insisting to the organization that he should be nominated, because I did that two years ago, and he has treated them with such wanton and foolish insolence, and has shown such entire selfishness and disregard of anybody's interests but his own, that it is very difficult to get the organization people to support him. So far, I have simply declined to take any part one way or the other in the business. It may be that during this month the situation will clarify, and we can see our way clear as to what action should be taken. *Always yours*

[*Handwritten*] I send you copies of letters I have just received about Hughes.

I entirely agree with what you say in the Japanese matter.

4830 · TO HENRY FAIRFIELD OSBORN   *Roosevelt Mss.*

Oyster Bay, August 5, 1908

Dear Fair: If you can send me the Royal Natural History I shall greatly appreciate it. But do tell me if I am asking too much. I do not want to overdo the thing when you are being so particularly kind to me.[1] *Faithfully yours*

[1] This is a typical letter — one of perhaps thirty — that Roosevelt wrote to Fairfield Osborn while preparing his reading list for the African trip.

Oyster Bay, August 5, 1908

Dear Egan: [1] I send you that speech. I very much wish I could study the socialistic movement in Denmark. It also exists in Sweden. Whether it does in Norway or not I am ignorant. Of course, socialism may mean almost anything. The socialism that nominates Debs is a well-nigh unmixed evil, and the ultrasocialism which has for one of its necessary tenets free love would, if applied, bring men back to the unpolished stone age and to living as scattered hordes of savages; were it not for the fact that long before this event could happen, it would have produced by simple reaction the rule of absolutism and despotism everywhere, in order to save civilization. But there are plenty of people who call themselves socialists, many of whose tenets are not only worthy of respect but represent real advances.

Is Rennell Rodd a colleague of yours? Do tell him that Mrs. Roosevelt and I always read whatever he writes that we can get hold of.

Taft seems to be doing very well. I cannot believe the country will fail to elect him. *Always yours*

Oyster Bay, August 6, 1908

My dear Mr. Brown: I thank you for your letter and the extremely interesting enclosures, which I find in a high degree instructive.

Let me at the outset, however, in view of the final sentences of your letter repeat what I already said in our interview. I did not ask to see you because I know you were favorable to the election of Mr. Taft; for this matter is of such vital importance that I should have seen you and have had precisely the same conversation with you if you had been the staunchest supporter of Mr. Bryan. It is a simple recognition of facts patent to everybody to say that the three months immediately preceding a Presidential election offer a very poor time in which to expect to get fair and reasonable consideration of such a matter as an advance or readjustment of freight rates; because it is always highly probable that partisan politicians will see in the agitation of any such question at such a time the chance for them by championing one side or the other to gain a party advantage without regard to the ultimate interest of the whole people. A complicated and very important question such as this should be settled purely on its merits and therefore not at a time when a good

---

[1] Maurice Francis Egan, sometime professor of English at Notre Dame and Catholic University; author of mellowed essays, sonnets, and novels; United States Minister to Denmark, 1907–1918; at Copenhagen the "Prince Charming" of the diplomatic corps; at home or abroad, a gifted and versatile man whose aptly titled *Recollections of a Happy Life* (1924) reflect a felicitous marriage of personality and situation.

many ordinarily sober-minded people become so excited as to be unable to look at questions of this nature as coolly as they at other times would.

Let me repeat that your letters have been of great interest and I believe of great profit to me. *Faithfully yours*

P.S. After having dictated this letter, the volume of your speeches[1] has come, and, my dear Sir, I want you to understand how genuinely touched I am by your inscription. You have said what I would most like to feel would be the verdict upon my work. I know perfectly well that I have both erred and stumbled from time to time as I have felt my way along, but I have done my best to war for decency and fair dealing as between man and man.

4833 · TO LYMAN ABBOTT   *Roosevelt Mss.*

Oyster Bay, August 6, 1908

To the Editor of The Outlook: A friend has just called my attention to a clipping from the New York *Sun* seemingly of about a fortnight ago, containing what purports to be an extract from a private letter of the late Mr. Henry Loomis Nelson to Mr. George Harvey, written in April, 1906, and printed in *Harper's Weekly* on the day of the issue of the *Sun*. This clipping runs in part as follows:

The truth about the letter of Mr. Cleveland accepting a place on Mr. Roosevelt's commission has never appeared. When in 1904 Mr. Cleveland was spoken of as a possible candidate, certain Republican leaders, especially one editor, announced that there existed a letter from Mr. Cleveland, intimating that it was an acceptance of an appointment on the coal arbitration committee, which would be published if Mr. Cleveland were nominated by the Democrats. The truth is that Mr. Cleveland was never offered a position on this commission, and therefore never accepted it. There seems to have been some confusion in Mr. Roosevelt's own mind about it, and the idea that Mr. Cleveland had consented to be a member of the commission was studiously encouraged and spread abroad by interested Republicans.

Mr. Cleveland gave me an account of the whole affair, so far as his own connection with it was concerned. Moved by the suffering, especially of people of moderate means, who were living about him in Princeton, he wrote to Mr. Roosevelt a letter which apparently he regrets now to have sent him. In this letter Mr.

[1] The volume entitled *Freight Rates and Railway Conditions* included speeches and correspondence in which Brown presented the railroads' case for a rate raise. The railroads, maintained the senior vice-president of the New York Central, were caught between rising costs and falling receipts. Freight traffic and hence net earnings had declined appreciably since the financial panic of the previous October. Meanwhile the roads were paying an estimated $100,000,000 more a year to meet the wage increases granted early in 1907. Legislation restricting hours of labor had, Brown believed, added $25,000,000 to operating expenses; while the recently passed Employers Liability Act would, he feared, "add enormously to the expenses of the roads." Stressing that he favored such social legislation and opposed wage reductions, Brown contended that the new financial burdens should not be shouldered entirely by the railroad stockholders, but should be shared by the whole community through rate increases.

Cleveland told the President that he thought that the two opposing bodies should be asked, in the interest of the public, to agree to a truce, and that during this truce some investigation should be made of the situation. It was a letter that he wrote under the strong feeling that the suffering of the people about him had aroused. Shortly afterward, when Mr. Roosevelt determined to take some action, he wrote to Mr. Cleveland asking him to be a member of a commission to investigate conditions. As Mr. Cleveland had written the first letter he felt that he had put himself in the power of the President, or had given the President a right to call upon him, and, saying so, told Mr. Roosevelt that he would accept. His letter had hardly reached Washington when he received a telegram from Mr. Roosevelt saying that it would not be necessary to call upon him. This pleased Mr. Cleveland very much.

Then Mr. Roosevelt decided upon another course, and upon the appointment of a committee of arbitration — the composition of which and the purpose of which and the result of the deliberation of which we are all familiar with — it appeared to have got into Mr. Roosevelt's mind that he had offered Mr. Cleveland a place on this commission. Subsequently, when the two met at some function, Mr. Roosevelt said to Mr. Cleveland that he had tried very hard to have him appointed one of the commissioners, but that the labor unions or the coal operators, one or the other or both, desired representatives of certain professions or branches of government appointed. Upon hearing this Mr. Cleveland said to Mr. Roosevelt that he had never accepted a position on such a commission; he added that he would never have taken such a place, and that under no circumstances would he have consented to be a member of such a commission. Not long afterward the two met somewhere else and Mr. Roosevelt repeated his remark about his desiring to appoint Mr. Cleveland a member of the arbitration commission. Then Mr. Cleveland said to him, "Why, Roosevelt, I have already told you that I never would have accepted a place on such a commission; it was an entirely different commission that you proposed to me, and it was on that different commission that I reluctantly consented to act, but I never could have been induced to be one of the arbitrators." [1]

Mr. Cleveland was offered a position on the commission as I originally intended to form it, and accepted it, and he never had any such conversation with me as those quoted in the latter part of the article, and never said to me anything remotely resembling what he is there alleged to have said. As a matter of fact I do not for a moment believe that there is any truth in the allegation that he told Mr. Nelson that he had made such statements. The facts of the case are as follows:

On October 3, 1902, I held a meeting in Washington between the coal operators and the strikers to endeavor to get them to come to an agreement or to submit their differences to some outside body of men. The strikers were willing to do as I suggested, provided the operators would also consent; but the operators refused to consent, and on the whole showed much more violence in the interview with me than the strikers did; and these facts were

[1] Following Cleveland's death on June 24, 1908, American newspapers and magazines printed too many articles and reminiscences mobilizing the spirit of the late President in behalf of the candidates in the current campaign. Roosevelt's rebuttal to Nelson's letter was published in the *Outlook*, 89:881–884 (August 22, 1908). It rests on the correspondence published in Volume III, this work, on the development of the anthracite strike.

made public in the papers next day, by some of the operators themselves. Immediately on seeing them Mr. Cleveland wrote me the following letter:

Princeton, Oct. 4, 1902

My dear Mr. President:

I read in the paper this morning on my way home from Buzzards Bay, the newspaper account of what took place yesterday between you and the parties directly concerned in the coal strike.

I am so surprised and "stirred up" by the position taken by the contestants, that I cannot refrain from making a suggestion which perhaps I would not presume to make if I gave the subject more thought. I am especially disturbed and vexed by the tone and substance of the operators' deliverances.

It cannot be that either side, after your admonition to them, cares to stand in their present plight, if any sort of an avenue, even for temporary escape, is suggested to them.

Has it ever been proposed to them that the indignation and dangerous condemnation now being cannonaded against both their houses, might be allayed by the production of coal in an amount, or for a length of time, sufficient to serve the purposes of consumers, leaving the parties to the quarrel, after such necessities are met, to take up the fight again where they left off "without prejudice" if they desire?

This would eliminate the troublesome consumer and public; and perhaps both operators and miners would see enough advantage in that, to induce them to listen to such a proposition as I have suggested.

I know there would be nothing philosophical or consistent in all this; but my observation leads me to think that when quarreling parties are both in the wrong, and are assailed with blame so nearly universal, they will do strange things to save their faces.

If you pardon my presumption in thus writing you, I promise never to do it again. At any rate it may serve as an indication of the anxiety felt by millions of our citizens on the subject.

I have been quite impressed by a pamphlet I have lately read, by a Mr. Champlin of Boston, entitled I believe "The Coal Mines and the People." I suppose you have seen it.*

Very respectfully,
Your obedient servant,
Grover Cleveland.

To the President.

* This was a pamphlet recommending exceedingly radical action against the operators; far more radical action than I took.

I immediately answered him describing among other things the attitude of the operators at the conference and their refusal to consider what I regarded as Mr. Mitchell's entirely fair proposition, and continued,

I think I shall now tell Mitchell that if the miners will go back to work I will appoint a commission to investigate the whole situation, and will do whatever in my power lies to have the findings of such commission favorably acted upon. This seems to be . . . the best step at the moment to take. I feel the gravest apprehension concerning the misery pending over so many people this winter and the consequent rioting which may, and probably will, ensue.

Immediately afterwards Mr. Cleveland wrote me asking me to be his guest when I came on to Princeton, which I was then intending to do. I answered on October 10th explaining that because of an injury from which I had not recovered I would not be able to go to Princeton; and I then continued stating that I was about to ask him to render a service which I knew he would be reluctant to undertake, and which I only asked because I felt we were in the midst of so serious a crisis and one so deeply affecting the welfare of the people. I continued,

My efforts to get the operators and miners to agree failed, chiefly through the fault of the operators. I then asked the miners to go back to work so that the pressing necessities of the public might be met, promising at once to appoint such a commission as Mr. Mitchell had suggested, and stating that I would do all in my power to have the recommendations of that commission adopted, of course meaning that I should do all in my power to have whatever legislation they advocated enacted, as well as backing up their recommendations in all other ways. But Mitchell refused on behalf of the miners to entertain this proposition. * * * I shall now direct Carroll D. Wright to make a full and careful investigation. * * * I wish to join with him two eminent men — men of such character that save in a crisis like this I would not dream of appealing to them to render any Government service. In all the country there is no man whose name would add such weight to this inquiry as would yours. I earnestly beg you to say that you will accept.

To this, Mr. Cleveland wrote on October 12th as follows:

Princeton, Oct. 12, 1902

My dear Mr. President:

Since the receipt of your letter yesterday, I have given its subject matter serious consideration.

You rightly appreciate my reluctance to assume any public service. I am also quite certain that if my advice was asked as to the expediency of naming me in the connection you mention, I should as a matter of judgment, not favor it.

I cannot however, with proper deference to your opinion, consider this phase of the question as open to discussion. I have therefore felt that I had only to determine whether your request involved a duty which I ought not to avoid, and whether my engagements and the present demands upon my time would permit me to undertake it.

So far as the latter are concerned, this is my situation: I am to take part and say something, at President Wilson's inauguration on the 25th inst; and I have agreed to do the same at the opening of the new building of the Chamber of Commerce in New York, on the 11th of November. My preparation for the inaugural exercises is complete; but for the other occasion it is hardly begun. I am absurdly slow in such work.

I have no idea of the time which would be exacted by a compliance with your request, nor how early you would expect a result from the Commission.

I feel so deeply the gravity of the situation, and I so fully sympathize with you in your efforts to remedy present sad conditions, that I believe it is my duty to undertake the service, if I can do so and keep the engagements I have already made.

This I will leave for your decision — only suggesting that I ought to have the next week at least for preparation to keep my New York engagement.

If after reading this you shall notify me that you still think I can undertake the duty you suggest, will you deem it amiss if I hint that I should be glad to know who the third member of the Commission will be?

Your obedient servant,
Grover Cleveland

The President,
  Washington, D. C.

In this letter I call attention to the fact that he expressly alludes to the body on which he was to serve as a "Commission," which does away with any quibble as to the terminology. I received this letter on the 13th. I immediately wrote to a certain Federal judge asking him to be the third member of the commission; but during the next two days I finally got both the operators and the miners to consent to the appointment of the commission, which relieved me from the necessity of appointing it without their consent. The operators, however, wisht the commission to be of five men instead of three, and each side insisted upon having certain types of men represented on the commission; and in order to get all these types on I finally had to increase the commission to a membership of seven; and even then my efforts to get both sides to agree to abide by the decision of the commission and meanwhile to resume work, nearly failed, for the strikers insisted upon having a labor man on the commission, and the operators positively refused to consent to such an appointment. After hours of patient negotiation I finally found that the operators really objected to the labor man being appointed *as such;* and as they wished someone of the commission to be what they called a "sociologist," I finally appointed a labor man and called him a sociologist, which, rather to my amusement, and greatly to my relief gave entire satisfaction to both sides. I endeavored to get the consent of both sides to appoint Mr. Cleveland in place of one of the men who actually was appointed, but as he did not come under any of the categories which they had named, and as they declined to permit me to appoint him in place of one of the men included in these categories, I had to abandon the effort. Of course it would have been not merely silly, but wicked, for me to have insisted upon the appointment of any one man, at the risk of jeopardizing the agreement of the two sides to resume work and to submit the whole question to the judgment of the commission which I was about to appoint. I therefore appointed the commission, and telegraphed and wrote to Mr. Cleveland as follows:

THE WHITE HOUSE,
Washington, October 16, 1902.

Hon. Grover Cleveland,
  Princeton, N. J.   Strictly Personal

Deeply grateful for your letter. Propositions that have been made since have totally changed situation so that I will not have to make the demand upon you which three days ago it seemed I would have to for the interest of the nation. I thank you most deeply and shall write you at length.

Theodore Roosevelt.

Washington, October 16, 1902.

Personal

My dear Mr. Cleveland:

I appreciated so deeply your being willing to accept that it was very hard for me to forego the chance of putting you on the commission. But in order to get the vitally necessary agreement between the operators and miners I found I had to consult their wishes as to the types of men. Of course I knew that it was the greatest relief to you not to be obliged to serve, but I did wish to have you on, in the first place, because of the weight your name would have lent the commission, and in the next place, because of the effect upon our people, and especially upon our young men, of such an example of genuine self-denying patriotism — for, my dear sir, your service would have meant all this. I do not know whether you understand how heartily I thank you and appreciate what you have done.

Faithfully yours,

Theodore Roosevelt.

Hon. Grover Cleveland,
Princeton, N. J.

The above correspondence shows not only that Mr. Cleveland accepted my offer to put him on the commission, but that he actually accepted it at a time when the appointment of this commission was not acquiesced in by either operators or miners, and when therefore every argument made by ultraconservatives against the appointment of the commission, applied with a hundredfold greater force than when the commission was actually appointed.

4834 · TO WILLIAM HOWARD TAFT   *Roosevelt Mss.*

Oyster Bay, August 7, 1908

Dear Will: You blessed old trump, I have always said you would be the greatest President, bar only Washington and Lincoln, and I feel mighty inclined to strike out the exceptions! My affection and respect for you are increased by your attitude about contributions. But really I think you are altogether oversensitive. If I were in your place I should accept that contribution of Cromwell's with real gratitude. He has put it in such a way that I regard it indeed as your duty to accept it. I must say it has greatly raised my estimate of him and entirely justifies all you have ever said of him. He gives in the ideal spirit with which a man should give for a campaign like this, and he does it in a way which, as I have said above, in my opinion makes it your duty to accept. Moreover, personally I should not in the least feel that your accepting the contribution "ended the possibility" of your "appointing Cromwell." [1] I know you have now no intention of appointing him

---

[1] William Nelson Cromwell, besides contributing to Taft's campaign fund, had been a conspicuous and influential member of the candidate's political council throughout July and had successfully championed the selection of Sheldon as treasurer of the national committee. Taft found no occasion during his presidency, however, to appoint Cromwell to public office.

to any office, but if hereafter there was some office to which you thought he ought to be appointed, I should really think less of you if you hesitated to appoint him to it. Root contributed to my campaign four years ago. I don't suppose he contributed as heavily as Cromwell, and I don't know what the sum was; but as a guess I should suppose it was five or ten thousand dollars, which, probably, with Root's means and the calls made upon him, would represent about as much relatively as in Cromwell's case. Furthermore, Root collected money from several different sources for me. But when a year later John Hay died, the above facts did not make me hesitate for a moment in trying to get him to accept the Secretaryship of State, the biggest office in my gift; his taking it represented a great monetary sacrifice on his part. As for Cromwell's being mixt up in corporations, Root was the greatest corporation lawyer in the country, but neither he nor I ever gave this fact a thought when it came to appointing him. I see no objection at all to Cromwell's going on the advisory committee as suggested. Indeed, I look on this contribution of his as rather a fine thing. The difficulty about a law requiring publicity of contributions comes in the fact that a great many men who want nothing whatever from a candidate and would like to contribute to his election, are afraid to do so if their names and the amount of the contribution are to be made public, because they are thin-skinned and know they will be attacked in certain newspapers for making the contribution, while the attention of the entire begging fraternity will be called to them if the contribution is of any size. Several people have spoken to me this year with great uneasiness, saying that they wanted to contribute to your campaign, but that they were not willing to do it if their contributions were to be made public, giving the reasons as above. Now, it requires some boldness to bell the cat in a case like this, and Cromwell has belled it. There will be plenty of people willing to follow his lead who would not have taken the lead themselves. I think it is a mighty fine thing on his part. I strongly advise your accepting it and having him put on the advisory committee.

I shall see Hitchcock today at lunch. *Ever yours*

4835 · TO ARTHUR HAMILTON LEE   *Roosevelt Mss.*

Oyster Bay, August 7, 1908

My dear Lee: Really, my dear fellow, I am overwhelmed. I do not know whether to be most touched by your generous kindness, or most surprised at the way in which you have read my inmost thoughts. Upon my word, I feel almost uncomfortable, for I feel as if my admiration of that picture must have been really too open. Ever since I first saw it in your house it has appealed to me as very, very few pictures ever have appealed, and I have really lookt forward to seeing it again when I should go to London and could see you. Therefore you can imagine how I prize the gift.[1] But, my

¹ See No. 3004.

dear fellow, great tho the value of the gift is, I prize infinitely more the spirit that lay behind it. Your letter also made me feel almost uncomfortable, for it said the things that of all others I would like to have said of me, and yet which I realize in the fullest manner I do not deserve to have said of me in the way in which you have put them. But I prize them none the less for that; and even if you are mistaken, I am glad you should feel as you do. I am especially pleased at your feeling that I "made good" at Chicago. Many of my English friends have been unable to see why I acted as I did, but it seemed to me all-important that when once I had given my word, even "without a consideration," so to speak, that word should be made good.

Cowles went up as Admiral to the celebration at Quebec, to which I also sent the Vice-President. My sister was there and has given me most interesting accounts of everything. The Vice-President wrote me that two things were made very evident by the English representatives.[2] One was the closeness of the tie between the home government and Canada; and the other, their hearty friendship for the United States. I trust that our representatives made equally plain the hearty friendship of the United States for England. Do you know, I think I have become almost as anxious as you are to have the British fleet kept up to the highest point of efficiency. It is a great guaranty for the peace of the world. I should like, if it were feasible, to put a limitation upon armaments, including one on the size of ships; but as that does not seem feasible, I am almost as interested as you are in seeing the British fleet kept in the present position of relative power. I suppose I shall hear from our people a good deal about their reception in Australia, and I will let you know all about it. You did a real service to both countries in connection with Mackenzie King.

Give my love to Mrs. Lee. Mrs. Roosevelt joins me therein, and she is just as much touched as I am by your thoughtful kindness. Indeed, I never remember to have received such a gift. It will always be one of my most cherished possessions.

Next March I start for Africa, where I shall spend about a year. If things favor me I shall then take a short trip thru Italy and France, going home via England. But I don't want to make this trip if it means that I have to spend my time in wearisome and fantastic ceremonies. I should like if I could be treated as traveling incog. and see no one but my old friends. But if this would seem churlish, I would of course pay my respects to the sovereigns and big public men in the different countries. But if more than this is expected, if there is going to be a tendency to entertain me in all kinds of ways so that I cannot see my friends, and cannot for instance spend a few days among the hill towns of Italy, or visit certain parts of southern France, and in London see the Turners in the National Academy at my leisure, and go to one or two places in the English country districts — why, if my going

[2] Quebec's tercentenary celebration was distinguished by the presence of the Prince of Wales, the Duke of Norfolk, the Earl of Dudley, and other English notables.

abroad means that I cannot do any of these things, nor have really satisfactory talks with you and two or three other old friends, I should give up the effort and come straight back home from Naples. *Ever yours*

[*Handwritten*] The "Seats of the Mighty" now hangs in the North Room; I go hither to see it the whole time; I can't tell you what a living pleasure it is, and always will be, to me; there just ar'n't words that will express all I feel about such a gift coming in such a way

4836 · TO HENRY CABOT LODGE   *Roosevelt Mss.*

Personal   Oyster Bay, August 8, 1908

Dear Cabot: Your letter about the immigration matter was just what I expected and is conclusive.[1] I can't do anything more about it.

Both Edith and I were delighted to hear that the trip had already done you and Nannie good. I was sure that such would be the case. I ordered the Maeterlinck essays and told Edith about it, but she only remarked that she had read them already and liked them, and that naturally you would like them; but she did not think *I* would care for them. When I heatedly resented the imputation that as they were good literature they were probably beyond my powers of appreciation, she exprest a pained surprise at my having so totally misunderstood her, and explained that she was merely stating what she supposed to be a fact. I now feel that it is incumbent upon me to like the essays, if necessary by main force of will. Edith is really well; she and I have delightful rides, and we row on the Sound.

When you come back I will of course have many things political and otherwise to talk over with you. The puzzling feature of the campaign at the moment is the governorship here in New York. Hughes represents ⟨the most⟩ an objectionable type of public man, and the exact type peculiarly dear to the *Evening Post* style of dishonest mugwump. He is as much under the domination of a machine as any bread-and-butter politician, but the machine which he fears and truckles to is the newspaper press, and especially the mugwump press. Now, the press, (vile though it is in New York) even including the mugwump press, frequently demands things that ought to be done and which the ordinary politician is very loath to do. Accordingly a man like Hughes does some things that are good, and is violently antagonized because of them by the machine politicians; and this gives him the very earnest support of a number of good people. But he also needlessly insults and wrongs a number of other good people, and he especially irritates the honest party men who have elected him and who want nothing in return except that he shall treat them decently and stand for the party principles to which he has been committed during the campaign. Hughes has the fanatical support of the reformers of all grades, from fantastic visionaries and sour, dishonest creatures, to perfectly genuine men like Lyman Abbott and Jake

[1] See No. 4776.

Riis, and all the intermediate classes, such as Charles Sprague Smith, of the People's Institute. He also has the very ardent support of a large number of people who are not fanatical reformers, but who feel that he has done, or at least attempted, certain excellent things in the teeth of bitter and vindictive political opposition. This support includes a great many clergymen and religious men, some independent editors, some thinking men, and good citizens in every walk of life. The aggregate of this makes a very formidable body of public opinion, which is intensely in earnest, and which may be so indignant if Hughes is not nominated as to jeopardize Republican success. On the other hand, most of the men who go to primaries and conventions, who want nothing for themselves but who are good party men and who bitterly resent pharisaism and feel a natural indignation at a man who ardently desires their support prior to election, and is afraid even to associate with them after election, are intensely against Hughes' nomination. There is a strong feeling against him among the laboring people, and there is also a good deal of contempt for him among people who think he is hypocritical, selfish and cold; while finally, the sporting crowd is bitterly down on him, and many of the businessmen feel that his insurance and similar legislation has been much worse than a failure and has worked far-reaching harm. Among these people there is I think as large a body of men who will leave the party if Hughes is nominated as there is among the other crowd of those who will leave the party if he is not nominated. The situation is very puzzling. At the moment, if I had to decide, I am inclined to think I should say that we ought to nominate him, simply because I don't see who else there is to nominate, with whom we would not be even worse off. But it may be that the feeling in the organization is so bitter that we simply can't nominate him, and it also may be that when the time comes the feeling in his favor will collapse, just as was the case with Jerome two years ago. But it is a very ugly situation, caused by Hughes' utter selfishness and coldness, and his desire to pander to the mugwump crowd. If Hughes a year ago had thrown himself heartily behind me, had acted as a good Republican, and identified himself thoroly with our wing of the party, in my judgment it would have been impossible to prevent his nomination as President. But he was misled by the mugwump outfit, and in consequence he has himself failed and he has hurt everybody else.

My African trip is all decided, and I am more and more convinced, as you always have been convinced, that it is the wisest thing I could possibly do. On March 23d I leave New York, and, going by Naples, reach Mombasa about a month later. Probably about December I shall reach the headwaters of the Nile, via the Nyanza lakes, and will leave Cairo somewhere about the last of March. I shall travel for the National Museum at Washington, they giving me two taxidermists and paying for the expense of these taxidermists and for the transport of the specimens home. In other words I shall be able to make it a scientific instead of merely a hunting trip, and all my trophies will go to the National Museum — a great relief to Edith, who, I think, felt she would have to move out of the house if I began to fill it full of queer antelopes, stuffed elephants, and the like. As a matter of fact I don't want any more trophies. I closed with Scribner's offer of fifty thousand dollars for the serial rights and twenty per cent on the book. Collier's offered me one hundred thousand dollars, but for various reasons, including especially the kind of advertisement that would be inevitable under the circumstances, I did not feel it wise to accept this offer. It is very hard to strike the happy middle between being quixotic in such a matter, on the one hand, and, on the other, following a course which is not quite proper for an ex-President whose reputation is what I hope mine is. I want to make money, but I cannot afford to make it in any way that is not exactly in accordance with my ideas; and while I am very sincere in saying that I want to make money, there are a good many other things that I want even more. But my own view of such matters, coupled with what I felt I ought to do, and did, about a third term, makes me at times feel very uncomfortable lest I really may be playing . . . a Quixotic part.

Edith will meet me at Khartoum. I should like then to spend a couple of months on a trip thru the hill towns of Italy, thru certain parts of Southern France, and finally a week or two in England. Whether or not I can make this tour depends upon what I shall have to do if I go to these countries. If it means that I have to make a kind of mock triumphal progress and spend my time at dismal and expensive entertainments which I shall loathe even more than the wretched creatures who feel obliged to give them, why I won't go, and shall simply come straight home. If I can travel purely as a private citizen of small means without seeing anybody but my old friends, why that I should prefer. I am inclined to think that if necessary I would compromise, and to avoid seeming churlish would be entirely willing to be presented privately at court, or call on the leading public men in the different countries, if this did not involve foolish and elaborate functions, and did give me time to see the sights I want to see and to call on the friends I want to call on. But all this can be settled later.

I am glad to say that I have also made provision for some work to do after leaving the Presidency. I have accepted an offer to be connected with the *Outlook* as editorial correspondent, so to speak. Whatever I write on social, political or economic subjects is to appear in the *Outlook*. It can be little or much, but will probably represent a dozen articles a year of from one to five thousand words each. They would be signed by me, and the *Outlook* would not be responsible for my opinion nor I for the *Outlook's* opinion. In return I get twelve thousand dollars a year, beginning on March 5th next — and this in spite of the fact that for the first year I shall be away. Here again I was puzzled how to avoid being quixotic by refusing large monetary offers, while at the same time I could not make up my mind to accept money for doing something which I did not quite care to do. Two or three times the sum was offered me by other publications, but the *Outlook* is of all the publications the one that comes nearest to representing my convictions, and its editors, altho I do not always agree with them by any means, are sincere, patriotic, painstaking men, who always try to practice what they preach. Moreover, accepting this offer gives me a certainty of just the kind of occupation I desire, with a salary which was of real importance to me, while at the same time the work is of such a kind as to leave me free to do any other work of any kind I desire — even traveling in Africa.

All this is only for Nannie and you, of course. *Ever yours*

4837 · TO JOHN HAYS HAMMOND   *Roosevelt Mss.*

Oyster Bay, August 8, 1908

My dear Mr. Hammond: [1] I was glad to get your telegram; but really it never occurred to me that the matter needed any courage.[2] In the first place I had always supposed that everyone ⟨thought⟩ knew that the whole Brownsville business had been carried on under my personal supervision; and in the next place, when I get angry my impulse always is to move up as close to my antagonist as possible; and if there was the slightest doubt on the subject I was exceedingly anxious that everybody concerned should know that I not only accepted but claimed the entire responsibility for the affair. *Faithfully yours*

4838 · TO ELIHU ROOT   *Roosevelt Mss.*

Personal   Oyster Bay, August 8, 1908

Dear Elihu: Oscar King Davis, of the New York *Times,* a thoroly trustworthy fellow, was in to see me today from that paper to show me two extraordinary letters which had just been sent to them by their man Hale,[1] who has gone abroad especially to interview the Kaiser. He succeeded in

[1] John Hays Hammond, Massachusetts Republican and mining engineer; in 1908 briefly an aspirant for the Vice-Presidential nomination; earlier, 1895–1896, an associate of Cecil Rhodes and a leader of the reform movement in the Transvaal; later, 1911, American representative at the coronation of George V.
[2] With Roosevelt's approval, Lieutenant General Henry C. Corbin, who was devoting the new freedom of his retirement from the army to the Taft campaign, had explained to the press that "any credit or blame" in the Brownsville affair "cannot in any way be laid to Mr. Taft." Roosevelt, Corbin pointed out, issued the order to dismiss the troops and sustained that order in spite of Taft's request that it be suspended. To document his explanation, Corbin released the President's cable to Taft of November 21, 1906 (see No. 4141). "Of course," Corbin declared, "the Brownsville affair is going to be paraded in the campaign," but, he maintained, "the colored vote . . . will be for Taft." Roosevelt on August 7 announced that Corbin's statement was "absolutely correct."

[1] William B. Hale.

getting an interview, and in his first letter described it. The Kaiser had spent two hours talking to this unknown newspaperman in language which would invite an international explosion if made public. He stated among other things that he had arranged with the United States to back up China against Japan and thereby keep the equilibrium in the East, and that a Chinese statesman was at this moment on the way to Washington to arrange the details, which he admitted had not yet been put into form. He exprest himself with intense bitterness about England and said that very shortly Germany would have to go to war with her, and that he believed the time had nearly come, and that England was a traitor to the white race, as had been shown by her alliance with Japan. With fine consistency he added that he was helping the Mohammedans in every way in giving them rifles and officers because he thought they would be a barrier against the yellow peril, about which he discoursed at length. He said that now everybody recognized that Russia had been fighting for the entire white race, but that she had fought very badly and that if German battalions had had to do the fighting, the Japanese would have been worsted. He stated that within a year or two we, the Americans, would certainly have to fight the Japanese; that he was glad we were preparing for it. He exprest himself most bitterly against the Catholics, and said that Archbishop Ireland was a Jesuit and in reality an enemy of the United States, and that he had fooled Taft at Rome, and added that he did not like Taft because he was under Catholic influence. He stated that Australia would welcome our fleet to show that she repudiated England's Japanese policy.

These are the salient points of an interview which really sounds as wild as one of Hobson's speeches. Of course the Emperor, whatever his other faults, is a gentleman, whereas Hobson is a blackguard, and is a cad, but upon my word one seems about as wild as the other.

The second letter from Hale to the *Times* was written in a gloomy vein, for he had shown his interview to the German Foreign office and to Hill, and while Hill stated he had no doubt the Emperor was willing to be quoted, he yet also added that it would be most unwise and improper to quote him, while the Foreign Office very naturally had a spasm at the very thought of such a conversation being quoted, and said it would do the most widespread damage. I told Davis that I should reprobate in the strongest manner such a conversation being made public; that it could do no possible good and might do a great deal of harm; and that the Emperor was certain to repudiate it, so that I did not see what could be gained by giving publicity to the affair.

It was such an extraordinary incident that I thought I would let you know about it.[2]

[2] Roosevelt later communicated the substance of the Kaiser's views to Arthur Lee; see No. 4953. Shortly thereafter the substance of another interview of similar tone was published in England; see No. 4952, note 1.

I saw Hitchcock today and I am happy to say that he is taking steps to have a quiet canvass made in a dozen different and representative districts thruout the State to find out what the real feeling is as to the renomination of Hughes. He is as much puzzled as I am by the utterly contradictory reports that come to him by shoals. Every day I receive letters, often from people whose judgment and convictions are entitled to respectful consideration, to the effect that the failure to nominate Hughes will be a fatal mistake, and I receive just as positive and emphatic letters, altho perhaps scarcely as many, to the effect that if he is nominated we are overwhelmingly beaten. I don't know that we could persuade the organization to nominate him anyhow; but of course circumstances might easily arise which would make it our duty to try; and I should like information that I could trust as to what the real feeling among Republicans was as to his nomination. If Hitchcock can get an honest expression of opinion in various representative quarters, the results may be invaluable. It may be that the feeling is now as hollow as the feeling for Jerome two years ago.

With love to Mrs. Root. *Ever yours*

4839 · TO TRUMAN HANDY NEWBERRY   *Roosevelt Mss.*

Oyster Bay, August 10, 1908

Dear Mr. Newberry: I am puzzled in this case of Lieutenant Walker. I do not attach weight to the board's finding that he is not professionally qualified for advancement. It seems to me that the testimony as to his conduct is such as clearly to show that his professional record is above the average. I believe that his professional record bears out the statements of Lieutenant Commander Laws in his letter of August 6, 1908 that "Lieutenant Walker is an efficient and able officer, quick in emergency, of excellent judgment, having good command of men; such an officer as would be naturally selected for any unusual duties that might arise requiring intelligence, self-reliance, firmness, and professional skill." Lieutenant Walker has repeatedly shown in the face of the enemy qualities which we should be glad to have all officers show in the face of the enemy.

There remains the question of his drinking. It seems to me that it is clearly shown that he does drink, and if he were a worthless or inefficient type of officer I should be delighted to turn him out; but I am inclined to think that he is a good type of officer, and if he would swear off drinking, we could well afford to give him another chance.

Will you look over these papers and tell me your views when you come to see me Monday evening?[1] *Sincerely yours*

[1] James Erling Walker was promoted to lieutenant commander and then resigned in May 1909.

P.S. Bring with you the full report of the conference. This is a matter in which I am personally interested. I want the *Florida* and *Utah* to be immeasurably more powerful ships than the *North Dakota;* that is, unless convincing reasons can be shown me to the contrary, I want to have them mount fourteen-inch guns and to have heavier armor, altho preserving the same general measurements and tactical properties, so that they can maneuver as units with the *North Dakota.*[2] We have been following and not leading, as we ought to be, in battleship construction, and I want now to step ahead of all other nations. This we can do. I suppose there will be certain delays in the preparation of the plans, but I am certain there will be no delay with the guns or armor. All that will have to be done is to let the bureaus know that there *must* be no delay, and it will have to be understood that any delay for changing the plans must be limited at the outside to sixty days or so.

4840 · TO WILLIAM ALLEN WHITE

Roosevelt Mss.

Personal

Oyster Bay, August 10, 1908

Dear White: That is mighty interesting and mighty instructive. I am not in the least in danger of shooting the pianist, and there is only one thing you say in your letter to which I would like to take exception, and that is where you speak of the people being behind Burton in Ohio.[1] Burton has certain points of usefulness, but he is not a really valuable man. Last year not only was he bitterly against us as regards the navy and everything pertaining to it, but he is bitterly and foolishly against every wise step as regards a foreign policy, and he has hampered us greatly in our fight for the conservation of natural resources because he really does not believe in the policy, and does not want anyone to have anything to do with it excepting just as he says.

I think you have struck it just right about the third term. The people are a great deal better off if they fight and fail, and make mistakes and profit by them, and fight again, and work it out themselves, rather than if they sit by and cheer and get someone else to do the job for them. Down at the bottom my main reason for wishing to go to Africa for a year is so that I can get where no one can accuse me of running, nor do Taft the injustice of accusing him of permitting me to run, the job.

Is Kansas safe for Taft? *Faithfully yours*

[2] Sims had written Roosevelt that conservative officers at the Newport conference were opposing an increase in the size of the guns and the weight of armor for the *Utah* and *Florida;* see No. 4847.

[1] Burton aspired to succeed Foraker in the Senate. This ambition seemed remote in early August, but Hearst's revelations in September of Foraker's connections with Standard Oil (see No. 4906, note 2) and Roosevelt's intercession in Ohio politics in December (see No. 5104, note 1) assured Burton of his goal.

Oyster Bay, August 10, 1908

My dear Professor Bailey: [1] No nation has ever achieved permanent greatness unless this greatness was based on the well-being of the great farmer class, the men who live on the soil; for it is upon their welfare, material and moral, that the welfare of the rest of the nation ultimately rests. In the United States, disregarding certain sections and taking the nation as a whole, I believe it to be true that the farmers in general are better off today than they ever were before. We Americans are making great progress in the development of our agricultural resources. But it is equally true that the social and economic institutions of the open country are not keeping pace with the development of the nation as a whole. The farmer is, as a rule, better off than his forebears; but his increase in well-being has not kept pace with that of the country as a whole. While the condition of the farmers in some of our best farming regions leaves little to be desired, we are far from having reached so high a level in all parts of the country. In portions of the South, for example, where the Department of Agriculture thru the Farmers' Co-operative Demonstration work of Doctor Knapp,[2] is directly instructing more than thirty thousand farmers in better methods of farming, there is nevertheless much unnecessary suffering and needless loss of efficiency on the farm. A physician, who is also a careful student of farm life in the South, writing to me recently about the enormous percentage of preventable deaths of children due to the unsanitary condition of certain southern farms, said:

Personally, from the health point of view, I would prefer to see my own daughter, nine years old, at work in a cotton mill, than have her live as tenant on the average southern tenant one-horse farm. This apparently extreme statement is based upon actual life among both classes of people.

I doubt if any other nation can bear comparison with our own in the amount of attention given by the Government, both Federal and State, to agricultural matters. But practically the whole of this effort has hitherto been directed toward increasing the production of crops. Our attention has been concentrated almost exclusively on getting better farming. In the beginning this was unquestionably the right thing to do. The farmer must first of all grow good crops in order to support himself and his family. But when this

[1] Liberty Hyde Bailey, botanist and horticulturist, assistant to Asa Gray, 1882–1883, director of the College of Agriculture at Cornell, 1903–1913, author and editor of many volumes on agriculture including *The State and the Farmer* and *The Country-Life Movement*, at first declined but on reconsideration accepted the chairmanship of the President's Commission on Country Life.

[2] Seaman Asahel Knapp, since 1902 in charge of farmers' co-operative demonstration work in the South; earlier the author of the first bill providing for agricultural experiment stations (1882), president of Iowa State College, 1883–1884, and special investigator for his friend, James Wilson, of agricultural conditions in Porto Rico and the Orient, 1898–1902.

has been secured, the effort for better farming should cease to stand alone, and should be accompanied by the effort for better business and better living on the farm. It is at least as important that the farmer should get the largest possible return in money, comfort, and social advantages from the crops he grows, as that he should get the largest possible return in crops from the land he farms. Agriculture is not the whole of country life. The great rural interests are human interests, and good crops are of little value to the farmer unless they open the door to a good kind of life on the farm.

This problem of country life is in the truest sense a national problem. In an address delivered at the Semicentennial of the Founding of Agricultural Colleges in the United States a year ago last May, I said:

There is but one person whose welfare is as vital to the welfare of the whole country as is that of the wageworker who does manual labor; and that is the tiller of the soil — the farmer. If there is one lesson taught by history it is that the permanent greatness of any State must ultimately depend more upon the character of its country population than upon anything else. No growth of cities, no growth of wealth, can make up for a loss in either the number or the character of the farming population.

*　　　　*　　　　*　　　　*

The farm grows the raw material for the food and clothing of all our citizens; it supports directly almost half of them; and nearly half the children of the United States are born and brought up on farms. How can the life of the farm family be made less solitary, fuller of opportunity, freer from drudgery, more comfortable, happier, and more attractive? Such a result is most earnestly to be desired. How can life on the farm be kept on the highest level, and where it is not already on that level, be so improved, dignified, and brightened as to awaken and keep alive the pride and loyalty of the farmer's boys and girls, of the farmer's wife, and of the farmer himself? How can a compelling desire to live on the farm be aroused in the children that are born on the farm? All these questions are of vital importance not only to the farmer, but to the whole nation.

*　　　　*　　　　*　　　　*

We hope ultimately to double the average yield of wheat and corn per acre; it will be a great achievement; but it is even more important to double the desirability, comfort, and standing of the farmer's life.

It is especially important that whatever will serve to prepare country children for life on the farm, and whatever will brighten home life in the country and make it richer and more attractive for the mothers, wives, and daughters of farmers, should be done promptly, thoroly, and gladly. There is no more important person, measured in influence upon the life of the nation, than the farmer's wife, no more important home than the country home, and it is of national importance to do the best we can for both.

The farmers have hitherto had less than their full share of public attention along the lines of business and social life. There is too much belief among all our people that the prizes of life lie away from the farm. I am therefore anxious to bring before the people of the United States the question of securing better business and better living on the farm, whether by co-operation between farmers for buying, selling, and borrowing; by promoting social advantages and opportunities in the country; or by any other legitimate means that will help to make country life more gainful, more attractive, and fuller of opportunities, pleasures, and rewards for the men, women, and children of the farms.

I shall be very glad indeed if you will consent to serve upon a Commission on Country Life, upon which I am asking the following gentlemen to act:

Professor L. H. Bailey, New York State College of Agriculture, Ithaca, N.Y., Chairman.

Mr. Henry Wallace,[3] *Wallace's Farmer*, Des Moines, Iowa.

President Kenyon L. Butterfield,[4] Massachusetts Agricultural College, Amherst, Massachusetts.

Mr. Gifford Pinchot, United States Forest Service.

Mr. Walter H. Page,[5] editor of *The World's Work*, New York.

My immediate purpose in appointing this Commission is to secure from it such information and advice as will enable me to make recommendations to Congress upon this extremely important matter. I shall be glad if the Commission will report to me upon the present condition of country life, upon what means are now available for supplying the deficiencies which exist, and upon the best methods of organized permanent effort in investigation and actual work along the lines I have indicated. You will doubtless also find it necessary to suggest means for bringing about the redirection or better adaptation of rural schools to the training of children for life on the farm. The National and State Agricultural Departments must ultimately join with the various farmers' and agricultural organizations in the effort to secure greater efficiency and attractiveness in country life.

In view of the pressing importance of this subject, I should be glad to have your report before the end of next December.[6] For that reason the

---

[3] "Uncle Henry" Wallace, beloved farmer-editor of Iowa, father of Henry C. Wallace, Secretary of Agriculture for Harding and Coolidge, and grandfather of Henry A. Wallace who as Secretary of Agriculture and in other offices served the second Roosevelt.

[4] Kenyon Leech Butterfield, president of Rhode Island State College, 1903–1906; of Massachusetts Agricultural College, 1906–1924; and of Michigan State College, 1924–1928.

[5] Walter Hines Page, usually remembered as an editor and diplomat, was also, surprisingly, an agricultural expert. He frequently devoted the columns of his *World's Work* to the encouragement of agricultural improvement, especially in the South. This experience, and that which he had on the Country Life Commission, made him in 1912 Wilson's most informed adviser on agricultural policy.

[6] The report, based on information compiled from thousands of questionnaires and extensive field work, revealed the difficulties and frustrations, economic and social, of the farm population of the United States. Transmitted by the President to Congress on February 9, 1909, it "laid before . . . . the country," Roosevelt recalled, "a mass of information so accurate and so vitally important as to disturb the serenity of the advocates of things as they are" (*Autobiography*, Nat. Ed. XX, 407). Congress, dominated by those advocates, refused to appropriate funds for the publication and circulation of the report and pondered forbidding the President to appoint any further commissions without specific Congressional authorization.

Commission will doubtless find it impracticable to undertake extensive investigations, but will rather confine itself to a summary of what is already known, a statement of the problem, and the recommendation of measures tending towards its solution. With the single exception of the conversation of our natural resources, which underlies the problem of rural life, there is no other material question of greater importance now before the American people. I shall look forward with the keenest interest to your report. *Sincerely yours*

4842 · TO WILLIAM HOWARD TAFT   *Roosevelt Mss.*

Personal   Oyster Bay, August 12, 1908

Dear Will: Tell Charley I am with him on the contribution question! Don't be in the least nervous about what Bryan says.[1] Whatever he does, we will beat him all right. If he attacks you about the use of postmasters and Government patronage, my strong feeling would be that the answer should be made not by you but by me, and I will make it in good shape if you wish.

I had a pleasant talk with Hitchcock and was very favorably imprest by him. I told him I did not like putting du Pont on the committee,[2] but that I did not regard it as a vital matter.

I am inclined to come to the same conclusion that you are about Hughes, but the situation is not at all an easy one. There are any number of thoroly good people who violently object to his nomination, and we may get beaten out of our boots with him. *Ever yours*

4843 · TO JAMES BRONSON REYNOLDS   *Roosevelt Mss.*

Oyster Bay, August 12, 1908

My dear Reynolds: I am delighted with both your reports and with the accompanying paper.[1] By the way, I do not see anything reflecting upon the

[1] Both Taft and Bryan in 1908 took firm positions on the subject of campaign contributions. At the end of the first session of the 60th Congress a law had been passed forbidding contributions by corporations. Going beyond that law, both candidates refused contributions from individuals whose corporate affiliations seemed to identify them as potential seekers of privilege. Bryan in May had also suggested that Taft join him in supporting a law providing for compulsory publication before election day of all contributions. This Taft refused to do, but he did announce in May that he favored a law for compulsory publicity after the campaign; after his campaign in fact he voluntarily publicized the contributions he had received.

[2] Thomas Coleman du Pont, from 1902 president of E. I. du Pont de Nemours Powder Company, in 1908 the new Republican national committeeman from Delaware and the chairman of the Republican speakers' committee, had been fighting the government's suit against the powder trust. Initiated under Roosevelt, this suit, resulting in the trifurcation of the du Pont gunpowder interests, reached its successful conclusion under Taft.

[1] Reynolds, as chairman of the special commission to investigate labor and housing conditions in Panama, had sent the report of the investigation to Roosevelt; see No. 4688.

steel corporation at all in these reports. Is there any such part I may have skipped over?

Now, exactly what disposition do you recommend my making of these reports? Shall I make them public now and send them in to Congress when it meets, meanwhile sending them down to Colonel Goethals and asking him to put into effect the recommendations as far as possible, and where he deems this impossible or impracticable, to report the fact to me with his reasons?[2]

I hope you will have a delightful holiday. *Faithfully yours*

4844 · TO WILLIAM SOWDEN SIMS   *Roosevelt Mss.*

Oyster Bay, August 13, 1908

My dear Commander Sims: All right, but are you sure of the personnel of that commission?[1] We cannot afford to slip up. Would it not be well to have ex-Secretary Herbert on it among the civilians? He is a Democrat, and the ones you have named are all Republicans. There is no use having the commission if after it has reported there is reason to believe that its report is not what we ought to have. I enclose a draft of a letter that I shall send when I appoint the commission.[2] *Sincerely yours*

---

[2] This was the way in which Roosevelt disposed of the reports.

[1] Sims had written Roosevelt recommending the appointment of a commission to study the reorganization of the Navy. He had done so at the suggestion of Rear Admiral Stephen B. Luce. Although retired, Admiral Luce, on all naval matters in which the intelligence was as important as the conditioned reflex, remained the ablest man on the Navy list. Despite his immediate approval of Luce's project, Roosevelt did not appoint such a commission until January 1909; see Numbers 5106, 5140.

[2] The enclosed draft read:

"I have appointed you as a member of a commission to consider certain needs of the navy. The organization of the Department is now not such as to bring the best results, and there is a failure to co-ordinate the work of the Bureaus and to make the Department serve the one end for which it was created, that is, the development and handling of a first-class fighting fleet. With this proposition in view I will ask you to consider:

"1. All defects in the law under which the Navy Department is now organized, including especially the defects by which the authority of Chiefs of Bureaus is made in certain respects practically equal to that of the Secretary or the President.

"2. The division of responsibility and consequent lack of co-ordination in the preparations for war and conduct of war.

"3. The functions of certain Bureaus, so as to see whether it is not possible to consolidate them.

"4. The necessity of providing the Secretary of the Navy with military advisers, who are responsible to him for co-ordinating the work of the Bureaus and for preparation for war.

"5. The necessity for economical allotment and disbursement of appropriations and for a system which will secure strict accountability.

"6. Finally, I want your views as to how best to recognize and emphasize the strictly military character of the navy, so that preparation for war shall be controlled under the Secretary by the military branch of the navy, which bears the responsibility for the successful conduct of war operations."

Oyster Bay, August 14, 1908

Dear Bridges: I have put the statement on the back of the advertisement, as you request; but I would rather you did not specify where I am going. If you say I am to hunt in British and German East Africa, you run the risk of having enterprising newspapers arrange to have correspondents meet me there. I have tried to keep the exact localities where I am to hunt very vague in the public mind, and the times also, because otherwise there is always the chance that we may have trouble with enterprising apostles of sensationalism. If you thought it well I would be pleased to have you emphasize a little more my connection with the National Museum, and the fact that my trip will be undertaken, as far as the collection of specimens is concerned, in its behalf.

Now, about *The Outlook.* Its articles will have no reference whatever to anything connected with my African trip or my trip abroad. I shall try, for instance, to leave with it two or three articles on socialism and kindred matters, which can be published while I am abroad. My connection with *The Outlook* will begin as soon as I leave the Presidency, but will have no kind of relation to this trip, no kind of relation to you, and can by no possibility conflict with you. Do you understand that what pieces I write for *The Outlook* will relate to political, social, and economic questions? I supposed you did understand this; and surely if you do you will see that they have no connection whatever, and cannot possibly conflict with my articles for you. You might just as well feel that if I delivered the Romanes lecture at Oxford, while abroad, I was in some way interfering with my articles for you. Even in Africa I shall sometimes think of other subjects than big game; I shall write nothing about my hunting trip except for you; and nothing else about any trip, if at all, until after your articles have appeared — and in all human probability not then. *Faithfully yours*

Personal   Oyster Bay, August 14, 1908

Dear Will: It is all right that it should be known that you personally favor Hughes, but it will be all wrong for you to make any statement about him. I have had a number of the leaders in, the men who are your friends, and they would feel very bitterly if you tried to force their hands; they would feel that you were traveling in the path of Hughes himself, and if they ever got that idea firmly fixt in their heads, the campaign would be over so far as New York State is concerned. I am not at all sure that even if I decide to try to make them nominate Hughes I could succeed; and I am not at all sure but that if I did succeed we might be worse off than we undoubtedly shall be if we do not nominate him. He is a thoroly selfish and cold-blooded creature, and if we interfere the effect will be merely that he will feel a sense of triumph over us and a desire to do us an injury as soon as the occasion arises. I have had one experience with him when I strove to help him and he started the entire mugwump press cackling with glee about the way in which he had repudiated my help and did not care for it, and relied purely upon the people.[1] He would be quite capable of doing the same thing now — of letting me nominate him and then solemnly saying that he regretted my interference which was entirely gratuitous, and that it was to the people alone that he owed his nomination.

I still feel that on the whole the wisest thing to do will be to nominate him; but I do not see my way clear to interfere as yet, and I am bound to say that most of the leaders feel that it would be suicidal to nominate him and that there are plenty of thoroly good men not active in politics who feel the same way. The railway brotherhoods are bitterly antagonistic to him. *Ever yours*

[*Handwritten*] I hear we shall have to nominate Hughes but I am not yet sure and as yet I do not believe I am called upon to act it will be a bad business either way.

P.S. Donovan has just turned up with your letter about the St. Joseph business. Great Heavens, Will, I hope that the next time you will let me know privately and in advance if there is anything like this on foot. Of course if I am to speak at all (which I think extremely doubtful) it must only be after the most careful thought and consideration, and after carefully going over where I am to speak. My own view is that it would be preposterous for me to go to this tournament or to any similar tournament. Indeed I do not see how I could possibly do it in view of the places I have already refused. I do not believe it would do you the slightest good to have me go there. I quite understand that it might do you good if you yourself went, always providing it did not cause you more harm by your failure to go elsewhere. But for me to go out to St. Joseph to a military tournament when I have declined at least two similar military tournaments, would simply cause heartburning and mischief. If I did not make political speeches, the effect of my visit would be nil. If I were myself a candidate I could see where it might do me good, just as the trip down the Mississippi would have done me good if I had been a candidate last year; but it would not help the ticket the least bit in the world. If, on the other hand, I were to make political speeches, I think there are plenty of places very much more important than St. Joseph in which to make them, and my present impression is against making political speeches at all on my part. Most certainly we should not even consider the question of my making them at any one place, or going to any one place, until after the most careful consideration as to whether I should go at all, and then the most careful consideration as to where I should go. I do not think I ought to go at all, and certainly not to St. Joseph.[2]

[1] See No. 4482, note 1.
[2] Roosevelt spoke neither at St. Joseph nor at any other military tournament.

Telegram   Oyster Bay, August 15, 1908

I desire Newport Conference to submit to me as a whole their recommendations concerning the *Utah* and *Florida*, these recommendations covering
plans to remove all defects found in the *North Dakota* and *Delaware*, without
regard to delay and without regard to any existing plans or arrangements
relative to the *Utah* or *Florida*, their armor or armament; also to state how
much delay there will be if the recommendations for the changes are
adopted; also submit recommendations with reference to those two ships that
will involve practically no delay in their plans.[1] I desire to have the whole
matter before me for judgment.

4848 · TO CHARLES JOSEPH BONAPARTE   *Roosevelt Mss.*

Personal   Oyster Bay, August 15, 1908

Dear Bonaparte: From Taft's letter I should not suppose that you would
desire Ellis. Go ahead and follow your own judgment in the whole matter.
Now, as to those southern railroads.[1] I do not want to go into a suit or an

---

[1] Roosevelt sent these special instructions to the Newport conference in response to
a telegram from Sims. Sims had wired the President in an effort to prevent the
conference from approving the perpetuation of the defects of the *North Dakota* in
the plans for the *Utah* and *Florida*. Although by the first week in August the conference had officially admitted that Key's charges were correct, the conservative
members succeeded in passing a resolution which declared that these defects were
only "minor" and that to remedy them would invoke too great a waste of time
and money to be borne.

These same conservatives, led by Philip Alger, an ordnance expert, and Admiral
Capps of the Bureau of Construction, then advocated that the design of the *Utah* and
Florida should with only nominal alterations conform to that of the *North Dakota*.
They were especially adamant against increasing the caliber of the main battery guns
from twelve to fourteen inches. Sweeping changes, they claimed, meant prolonged
and costly delay. Had the conservatives countenanced such changes, they would
have in effect admitted that the deficiencies in the *North Dakota* design were not
"minor," that the Bureaus of Construction and Ordnance had been negligent in
their duty, and that the bureau system was responsible for the building of inefficient
ships; see No. 4782.

When Sims was certain the conference would accept the conservative view he
telegraphed Roosevelt "to have an order issued to the conference to have both
plans, the conservatives' without delay and ours with delay, placed in your hands for
decision." Roosevelt's reply served Sims's purpose. Instead of making a final decision
on designs, the conference drew up two plans for the President's approval. The
majority's plan modified only slightly the *North Dakota* design. Its adoption would
delay construction only two months. The minority's, backed by Sims, Key, and the
younger seagoing officers, provided for heavier armor and a main battery of eight
fourteen-inch guns. It would have caused a delay in construction of fifteen months.
After careful study of both plans, Roosevelt with great reluctance accepted that
favored by the conservatives; see No. 4865.

---

[1] The southern roads, untroubled by shippers' protests (see No. 4818), had instituted
a general rate raise. The shippers at once began legal proceedings against the roads.
In Georgia, District Judge Emory Speer issued an injunction which was dissolved

action which will temporarily harass business if we do not know the facts and if we do not feel reasonably confident that we can win. Now it seems to me that the Grosscup decision is the vital matter on which to fight. It deals with the Sherman antitrust law.[2] If that decision is upheld in all its bearings it does not seem to me that there will be the ghost of a chance of our doing anything with those southern railroads. It is a question with me whether we ought not to fight that decision thru first, and then see just where we stand. But I will wait until you have seen Comer's representatives, and until you have decided just the form in which you are going to act about the reargument of the Standard Oil case. I think your telegram very strong.

When are you going back to Washington? Perhaps you could stop and go over these matters with me then, if they could wait until then. *Faithfully yours*

P.S. I did not like the selection of du Pont and told Hitchcock so. As for the interference of Ward and others, or as to the indiscreet talk of Noble and Jackson,[3] I feel much as I did about our friend Senator Bourne and the Standard Oil. Inasmuch as we were absolutely straight on the Standard Oil business, I knew they could not successfully make any point against us. And so in this case. Our record will be perfectly clear anyhow; but I will warn Ward.

I am much amused at what you tell me about the republication of your address of twelve or fourteen years ago. Last winter a leather-lunged ex-Congressman of violent reform proclivities published a letter of mine resigning from the Reform Club of New York on the ground that I was a Republican first and a tariff reformer second.[4] The letter attracted much attention at the moment, but was forgotten before it came to my notice. As a matter of fact the letter had been sent in just twenty-two years previously; but reformers seem to think the date of no particular consequence.

---

a week later, restraining the roads of the Southeastern Freight Association from putting the new rates into effect until the Interstate Commerce Commission had decided upon their reasonableness. Speer took this opportunity to deliver a strong attack on the roads that "control the price of everything on which the comfort and very life of the people depend." Shortly after Speer's statement, Governor Comer of Alabama and Senator Culberson of Texas appealed to the federal government for immediate action against the southern roads. At the suggestion of the Interstate Commerce Commission, the railroad commissions of Alabama and Georgia filed complaints against the roads of the Southeastern Association for their "unreasonable advance in rates" and the Texas commission began a similar suit against the southwestern roads. Because the Interstate Commerce Commission had taken jurisdiction of the southern rate case, the Justice Department made no attempt to bring suit against the roads for conspiracy to maintain prices in violation of the Sherman Antitrust Act.

[2] Roosevelt was confused. The Grosscup decision did not deal with the Sherman Law but was concerned with violations by the Standard Oil Company of Indiana of rebate provisions of the Elkins Act.

[3] William Purnell Jackson, Maryland Republican; son of the incumbent Republican congressman, William H. Jackson; in 1908 a member of the national committee; United States Senator, 1912–1914.

[4] Roosevelt was probably referring to No. 91.

I have written you about what I think should be done in connection with the railroads. Of course Culberson and his people are merely trying a political dodge; and probably that is true of the Alabama men, from what I now hear. They think any action would hurt us because they think they could twist any action to suit themselves. I dare say they are right, and therefore before taking any action I want to go over the matter very carefully with you. What Speer has said comes in under this whole matter.

That is a first-class suggestion of yours about Cooley. I think it would be well for you to have the advance sent to him.

I am immensely amused at the interview of Noble with you. You handled it exactly right; and I should rather like to send what you told Noble to Ward, with the statement that it meets my hearty approval. But I won't do this unless you think proper.

4849 · TO ROBERT MEANS THOMPSON   *Roosevelt Mss.*

Oyster Bay, August 15, 1908

My dear Colonel Thompson:[1] In reference to your letter of August 3d in behalf of Mr. Curtis, and the enclosed petition from eighty-seven presidents, vice-presidents and other officers of banks, trust companies, and the like, including the President of the Chamber of Commerce, I have to enclose you copies of letters from the Attorney General and the District Attorney.[2]

Now, my dear Colonel Thompson, you will see on reading this letter that Curtis is guilty, and that he has been given an opportunity to become a witness for the Government against Morse and has declined. You say that Mr. Curtis was deceived by Morse, but if so, he should have no hesitancy in helping the Government authorities to bring Morse to justice, yet he refused. You also enclose a petition of the executive council of the American Bankers'

[1] Robert Means Thompson was a New York lawyer and financier.
[2] Alfred H. Curtis and Charles W. Morse, president and vice-president respectively of the National Bank of North America, had been indicted for misuse of their bank's funds. At the hearings in October 1908, Henry L. Stimson argued that, although Curtis was the responsible head of the bank, Morse had dominated its affairs. It was Morse, Stimson pointed out, who used the bank's monies to finance the extensive speculations that had been one of the causes of the panic of 1907; see No. 4473. The court found both men guilty but gave Curtis merely a suspended sentence while condemning Morse to fifteen years in prison.
  Morse served only a small part of his term. After persistent efforts by friends and relatives to obtain his pardon from President Taft had failed, Morse contracted with Harry M. Daugherty to secure his release. Daugherty soon arranged for a commission of army doctors to verify a rumor that Morse was suffering severely from Bright's disease. The commission examined the banker and reported to Taft that Morse was, indeed, a dying man. Taft then signed the pardon and Morse left for Europe for medical treatment. Sometime later Daugherty, unable to collect his fee, informed the Attorney General's office that Morse's condition had been caused by drinking a concoction of soapsuds and chemicals just before the medical examination. The whole case, Taft later told newspapermen, "shakes one's faith in expert examination."

Association in favor of Curtis, these men representing the banks in many different cities thruout the Union. Now, my dear Colonel, this gives a good idea of the difficulty that we have in getting justice in cases of this kind. The business associates, or professional or other associates, of the men concerned are too apt to try to shield the man to whom they are bound by professional or social ties. Fundamentally, this is of course the same feeling whether shown in the case of the labor men who tried to shield the officers of the Western Federation of Miners, or in the case of bank presidents and businessmen who try to shield a man who has incurred some of the responsibility for one of those outrageous business transactions which not only helped precipitate the last panic, but pre-eminently worked such mischief by convincing the average plain citizen that men of wealth tend to acquire their wealth in dishonest and improper fashion.

With regret that I cannot do what you desire, I am, *Sincerely yours*

4850 · TO GEORGE NATHANIEL CURZON *Roosevelt Mss.*

Oyster Bay, August 18, 1908

My dear Lord Curzon: [1] It was good to hear from you; and I can think of few things which I would rather do than to deliver the Romanes lecture. I accept with pleasure, and if Oxford desires to give me a degree I shall be much pleased to receive it. [2] Indeed, your letter relieves me from rather a quandary. Next March, immediately after leaving the Presidency, I shall go to Africa, starting in at Mombasa, working to and fro in British and perhaps in German, East Africa, and coming out via the Nyanzas and the Nile at Cairo about the first of April following. Now there are many friends whom I have in England whom I should really like to see; but I have rather a horror of ex-Presidents traveling around with no real business, and thereby putting unfortunate potentates who think they ought to show courtesy to the United States in a position where they feel obliged to entertain the said ex-Presidents, no matter how great a bore it may be. If I could make the sovereigns and leading men of each country understand that I did not expect any attention and would be only too glad to be left to my own resources and be permitted to call upon the people I already knew and a very few others whom I would like to know, why that would be all right; but to make a kind of mock triumphal procession would offer about as unattractive an outlook to me as

[1] George Nathaniel Curzon, eminent British conservative statesman, former viceroy of India, after 1907 chancellor of Oxford University, later an able but erratic member of the Inner War Cabinet during World War I.
[2] Roosevelt later accepted invitations to speak at the Sorbonne and the University of Berlin. These invitations, while flattering, were surely less so than that from Oxford, for the Romanes lecture, founded in 1891 by George John Romanes, eminent British physiologist, was offered annually to naturalists of great reputation. Roosevelt delivered his lecture, fittingly entitled "Biological Analogies in History" (*Literary Essays*, Nat. Ed. XII, 25–60), on June 7, 1910, at which time he received an honorary LL.D.

could be imagined. On the other hand as Mrs. Roosevelt and my daughter will meet me in Khartoum (one of my sons accompanying me on the trip itself) I really wanted to make a short trip with them thru some of the hill towns of Italy, to Nîmes and Arles and a few other places in France, and then to finish in England. Now this invitation gives me exactly the justification I require! Of course I know all about the Romanes lecture, and to be asked to deliver it is an honor that I sincerely appreciate; and it will give me the excuse I desire to spend a fortnight in England and see certain of my friends.

Now as to the time. I do not know what the Oxford arrangements are, but from your letter I gather that it would be all right for me to speak about the 15th of May or the first of June 1910. The fact that you would introduce me and be reponsible for me adds much to my desire to accept.

I look forward to seeing you. I sincerely appreciate what you say of my work as President. In your public career you have shown the great and unusual power of dealing successfully with some of the most difficult problems that any public man of today can have to solve. I much desire to talk over with you certain matters connected with both India and the Empire; and certain dangers which your people and our people alike have to face and which I believe we have the power to overcome if only we choose to exercise reasonable forethought, reasonable care, for the national honor in the future.

I suppose I can wait some months before telling you what the title of the lecture will be.

Again thanking you, and with great regard, believe me, *Sincerely yours*

4851 · TO WILLIAM HOWARD TAFT   *Roosevelt Mss.*

Oyster Bay, August 18, 1908

Dear Will: Will you return me this letter of White's after you have read it?

I am inclined to feel your way about Hughes — that is, that he ought to be renominated. But I am not certain that I can do anything in the matter, and the situation is anything but clear. I enclose you a copy of a letter from a strong supporter of yours, a Catholic Democrat named Harvier, who, I think, gives a very clear estimate of most of the forces that work one way or the other in the matter.

As to my making a speech, my judgment is that it would do harm rather than good. I cannot see that Bryan's speech has made any effect.[1] In fact I don't think anybody has read it. Of course I have one difficulty to contend with and that is my real inability to understand how any decent man of intel-

[1] Bryan formally accepted the Democratic nomination on August 12 at Lincoln, Nebraska. In his speech the Great Commoner dwelt particularly on the tariff, anti-trust legislation, publicity for campaign contributions, Cannonism, and, in general, his own promise "to consecrate whatever ability I have to the one purpose of making this, in fact, a government in which the people rule."

ligence can hesitate for a moment how he will vote. I will see Hitchcock this week and talk with him about my letter.

Bryan has been playing strong in chautauqua circles and elsewhere for the church vote, and among narrow churchmen he may have made some headway; but I think that is a very dangerous kind of game to play when it takes the form of an attack upon another man because of his religious views. Your letter to Hill is admirable. Go over every word of it before you make it public, and if possible submit it to that ever present help in time of trouble — the beloved Root.[2] *Ever yours*

P.S. I should not under any circumstances answer Littlefield.[3] He is simply striving to make trouble, and he is as dishonest as the New York *Sun* or the *Evening Post*. It is a mistake for you, in my judgment, to advertise him by giving him a letter. Above all, it is a mistake for you to seem to be explaining your position.

I enclose a letter from Lawrence Murray which gives me real satisfaction.

4852 · TO HENRY CABOT LODGE   *Roosevelt Mss.*

Oyster Bay, August 18, 1908

Dear Cabot: To my immense delight, which I know you will share, the New York *Herald* last Sunday contained the following item:

Fort Worth, Texas, Saturday. — Word reached here today from Brownfield, in Terry county, Western Texas, that residents there on Thursday erected a life-size statue of President Roosevelt after a street fight in which fifty shots were fired. One person was killed and nine others were wounded. The statue represents Mr. Roosevelt in hunting costume and stands in the town square.

Brownfield is one hundred miles from the nearest railroad, the Texas Pacific. Its population is 1,500, composed largely of cattlemen, cowboys and planters. The erection of the statue was vigorously opposed by democrats and some republicans, but it had already been ordered from Denver by a citizens' committee, which refused to turn from its plans. The unveiling was opposed because it was pointed out that Roosevelt was still President and because the democrats wanted a Bryan statue on the opposite of the square and the town could not afford both statues.

Efforts were made to steal the statue and it was buried for a week. When the

[2] Bryan was attempting to make political capital of Taft's Unitarianism. To the Democratic candidate, as to many of the fundamentalists of the Middle West, a Unitarian was little better than an avowed pagan. Curiously, while the Unitarian issue was troubling, it was perhaps less troubling than the charges that Taft was in reality a Roman Catholic and therefore a minion of the Pope. This idea Taft's enemies documented by references to the Philippine friar land problem. Wisely Taft refrained both from a direct reply to his critics and from theological debate. For a discussion of his religious views and of his letter to J. W. Hill defining them, see Pringle, *Taft*, I, 373–374; see also No. 4866.

[3] The Maine congressman, who was, as usual, expounding the view of the National Association of Manufacturers on injunctions, had asked Taft for an explanation of his position on that controversial problem.

ceremonies took place on Thursday a band of cowboys made a rush and met a determined crowd. Revolvers, clubs and fists were freely used, but the statue was not disturbed.

After the riot a mass meeting was held, at which a compromise was effected whereby it was agreed that should Bryan be elected, his statue should be placed near that of Roosevelt.

I never heard of the statue and indeed I never heard of Brownfield before and I think there is something delightful beyond words in the idea of this sudden erection of a statue of me in hunting costume at the cost of a riot in which one man was killed and nine wounded; and the final compromise by which it was agreed to put up another statue of Bryan in case he was elected. I wonder what that statue looks like. Who with a sense of humor and a real zest for life would not be glad to be prominent in American politics at the outset of the 20th Century?

Curzon, who is Chancellor of Oxford, has just asked me to go there to get a degree and to deliver the Romanes lecture in the spring of 1910 on my way back from Africa. This I am really glad to do. The lecture has been delivered in the past by men like Gladstone, Huxley, John Morley, and Bryce, and I regard it as an honor to be asked and moreover, as something right in my line. Then it gives me a legitimate reason for visiting England. I felt I would really like, when I left Africa, to spend a couple of months in Italy, France, and Holland and to end with a couple of weeks in England; but I rather hated to go there without a genuine object, because, when, if I finally came to the conclusion that I would have to be presented to the King and call on various public men, it would look as if I were simply traveling about for that purpose. Now this puts the matter right.

The Hughes situation grows worse and worse. If only he were not Governor, and had never been made Governor, Taft would be certain of carrying New York by a very heavy vote. But Hughes has put us in a position where we shall lose heavily if we nominate him, and I am afraid even more heavily if we do not. The Republican workers have such just cause for hatred of him, and loathe him so, that I am by no means sure that I could get them to nominate him anyhow, and if I did interfere by forcing his nomination they would probably treat the whole ticket with sullen apathy, while many of the workingmen would cut it entirely. On the other hand, the church element, and the silk-stocking reformers of every degree, will be equally bitter if Hughes is not renominated. I enclose you a very sensible article on the subject by the editor of an independent Democratic newspaper who has always supported me and is now supporting Taft.

Have you read Lord Acton's *History of Freedom and Other Essays*, and Frederic Harrison's *National and Social Problems*? They are both worth your reading. I have a letter from the former head of the Uganda Protectorate, Sir Harry Johnston, to show you when you come back. I think it will amuse you as much as it did me. Dearest love to Nannie. *Always yours*

Private   Oyster Bay, August 18, 1908

My dear Mr. Buell: I have received your letter and the enclosures in reference
to the winners in the Olympic games. You say that it seems to you "that before congratulations are extended to the team by me the public should know
the truth in reference to the running of Carpenter in the 400 meters race,"
and you state that you have seen that he has said that he has "no recollection
of having touched Lieutenant Halswelle at all," and that you feel that the
American sportsmen should not be given praise where praise is not due.[1]

I entirely agree with you as to the desirability of the public's knowing
the truth and of no praise being given where praise is not due; but it seems to
me that you do not fully understand the bearing of the extract from the
American in London which your letter contains nor the clippings from
English papers which you enclose. You apparently accept without question
the statement of your correspondent as to the disgraceful conduct of the
Americans and endorse her remark that the English people are justified in
thinking Americans unprincipled, dishonest and unsportsmanlike. Your correspondent speaks of a photograph of the footmarks which show how one
man was crowded from the track. You enclose a print from a sporting English
paper called *The Daily Mirror* which contains what I suppose is this photograph. Immediately above it is the print of the same race with Carpenter
finishing, and if you would simply glance at the two prints you would see
that the footmarks in the lower have been put in in the engraving, or in some
way altered in the engraving, for there are no such footprints which appear
in the upper one; and if you have ever taken photos of footprints on the
track you would know that it would be in the highest degree unlikely for
them to appear as they appear in this picture. Your correspondent states how
at dinner an English lady told her that no American barristers were honest,
and she also states that at the finish of the Marathon race there was very bitter
feeling and no enthusiasm that the American won. It seems to me that these
two statements of hers offer conclusive proof of a bitterness of hostile feeling
on the part of English people of her acquaintance that would render them
utterly unfit to pass judgment upon whether or not Carpenter had been
guilty of fouling, a bitterness so discreditable to them that it deprives them of
all right to criticize others.

You enclose me a paper called *The Sportsman* containing an account of
this fouling which apparently you wish accepted as the truth. This paper
opens by saying that in advance of the race it had announced that it believed
there would be foul tactics on the part of the three Americans, and, in a tone

[1] Cornell's Carpenter in the 400-meter dash arranged a neat "box" of his British
rival, thus eliminating that competitor's perhaps slim opportunity to pass the field and
win the race. Carpenter was duly disqualified. This decision of the judges, so repel-
lent to Roosevelt, seemed to the editors of the *Outlook* to have been eminently fair,
perhaps even necessary.

which is even more hysterically foolish than offensive, the paper continues that what occurred in this race casts a slur upon American sportsmanship in the eyes of all Europe which can never be eradicated, and it uses language which, even if the offense ⟨was true⟩ really occurred as alleged, nevertheless shows that this British sporting paper was guilty of a far more serious offense itself. I am astonished that you or whoever sent you this paper should not perceive this fact. Let me repeat that if Carpenter was guilty of the offense the comments of this British paper itself deliberately inviting attention the day before to the probability of what it now says actually happened (and thereby of course giving the excuse to everybody who so desired, and who wisht to make believe that it happened, to pretend that it did actually happen) make its offense worse than that which it condemns. This is so evident that it ought not to be necessary to point it out. There are papers in this country whose utterances make one feel heartily ashamed, but I have yet to see an American paper writing on this Olympic matter whose utterances should be condemned as unstintedly as those of this paper, *The Sportsman,* which you enclose and apparently approve.*

This unmeasured vituperation by the English press, and above all this fact that English sporting authorities, apparently considered in England as reputable, deliberately invited the trouble by saying in advance that they expected the foul, thus taking exactly the attitude that would have been taken by anyone who intended to claim a foul in any event if his candidate did not win, shows so unworthy a spirit as inevitably to cast doubt upon the justice of the decision. Moreover, you seemingly completely fail to understand what is shown by the article from the *Morning Post* which you enclose. This states that when the Italian came on the track at the Stadium he fell; that he was stimulated by the cheers of the spectators and officials *and by other forms of encouragement,* and proceeded. This British paper which you send me as an authority evidently lacks the honesty to state that the other forms of encouragement were stimulants administered to the Italian in utter disregard of every principle of fair play, and because of which, if the officials who were then cheering him had themselves possest the slightest sense of their duty, they would have ordered him removed from the track. The paper then goes on to say that after going a little further the Italian then fell, but was helped to his feet again, and fell once more. This English paper thus shows that for the second time he was illegally and improperly helped and that the English officials took no notice and did not order him from the track. It then goes on to say that after fifty yards more he "falls once more and with much difficulty is got to his feet." But again the British officials decline to take the action which they are bound to take, their conduct being in scandalous contrast to the way in which the day before they broke the tape and crowded onto the track in advance of any decision as to the fouling by Carpenter. This paper, the paper you quote as authority, goes on to say that the Italian once more falls but that by vigorous chafing of his limbs and in other ways he is got to his feet and helped onwards. It seems literally incredible that even at this time the British officials did not order him off the track but permitted him to finish and to have his name go up as winner. The judges, who had waited for no protest to permit the people to rush on the track the day before and to declare Carpenter's race no race, now with all this happening before their eyes, refused to take any action until the Americans on behalf of the man who had really won entered a protest. This showing from this British paper which you enclose is such as to make it evident that the judges four times declined to do their duty; that they again and again connived at improper assistance being rendered to the one man on the track who they thought might beat the American champion, and that they showed a scandalous partiality which ought to cause you very grave doubts before accepting their verdict in the case of Carpenter.

I re-enclose you these papers as you request.

Carpenter is a Cornell man. He has contested again and again in intercollegiate and other contests here. A young cousin of mine, George Roosevelt, who won his "H" for Harvard in the high jumping contest, once in the intercollegiates and in another year in the dual games with Yale, has repeatedly been on teams where Carpenter has been on the opposing team, and he says that he is a good, straight fellow and that there has never been a suspicion of crookedness about him. In all his contests here there has never been so much as a hint raised by any of his competitors to the effect that he has misbehaved himself. Now it is of course possible that he did misbehave himself; but the extraordinary misconduct of the English officials at the close of the Marathon race as set forth in the papers you send me, and the outrageous attitude of certain other sporting papers and of certain high social people as portrayed by the papers you send me and by your correspondent, show a bitterness of prejudice on their part and a willingness to believe evil in advance and to announce possible fouls in advance which puts their conduct under the gravest suspicion. If *The Sportsman*, for instance, copy of which you enclose, had been deliberately preparing for a successful conspiracy to steal the victory away from the American if he won, by claiming foul play, it would have acted precisely as it did in announcing in advance that it believed there would be foul play and that precautions were being taken to prevent it. If under similar circumstances here any American paper so behaved it would be accepted everywhere in England as proof positive of such a conspiracy. Moreover, it is very difficult to understand the conduct of the British officials in refusing to hear Carpenter or his side, deciding the case without permitting any statement to be made on that side, and in permitting officials and others to swarm in over the track when the American was ahead and before any official decision had been rendered in the matter. When with such overzealousness against the American one day coupled such blind indifference to misconduct of the grossest kind when practiced against the American the next day at the close of the Marathon race, it is hard not to draw an uncharitable conclusion.

Now, I never should have stated my views at all, even privately, except in answer to a letter such as yours, and I state them to you for your private information merely. Fouls continually occur in races, both rowing and running, where there is no intentional misconduct at all. Thirty years ago I was in a foot race in which I was beaten, where my antagonist and I touched, and each of us firmly believed that the other had fouled him. Neither of us made the claim and neither for a moment supposed that the other had fouled him intentionally. When the Groton eight (with one son of mine rowing, and another cox) rowed the Harvard freshmen this year it fouled them, but nobody for a moment dreamed that the foul was intentional. Carpenter is a gentleman of good character. The judges, who were not of his nationality but of the nationality of his opponent, held him guilty of fouling. The wise thing to do was to accept their decision as being honestly given on the one hand, and on the other not to attack Carpenter as having been guilty of disgraceful conduct. The action of the judges and the crowd, however, seems to have shown a very violent and malignant spirit. On the other hand, I think that the Americans by the protest they made in the papers and by their bitter complaints of English unfairness behaved as badly themselves. Carpenter alone behaved well, for he has never said anything excepting that he does not remember having touched his competitor and that he thinks that there ought to be no more talk about it. When the next day the British competitor, who had thus been handed the race as a gift, ran over the course alone and tried to make record time, he failed to come up to Carpenter's time. But it is well to remember that the conduct of the British judges at the end of the Marathon race, on the statement of the English authorities themselves, showed impropriety at least as gross as that of which Carpenter is alleged by his most malignant critics to have been guilty; and whereas, altho it may have been entirely proper to rule Carpenter out, there is no sufficient proof that he was guilty of turpitude, the misconduct of the British officials in this instance is perfectly clear. Now, it would be improper, ungenerous, unwise and tend to no good purpose to make any such statement as this in public. Entirely honorable men when prejudiced and under great excitement are capable of doing deeds which seem very improper to others, and which indeed are improper. I should deprecate in the strongest way any kind of public criticism of the British judges for the Marathon race, any criticism of or impugning of the motives of the judges who decided against Carpenter in his race; but it is nonsense to talk about "the public knowing the truth about the running of Carpenter," by which you apparently mean that the public should accept as gospel the blackguardly article of that English paper, *The Sportsman;* and as for "not giving American sportsmen praise where praise is not due," I think that man is a mighty poor American and a mighty poor sportsman who fails in the heartiest way to give praise to our men who went abroad and won out so gallantly in those Olympic contests. I do not suppose that if I have anything to do with it there will be any effort to discriminate among the members of the team, save perhaps in bringing before me the victors; and as Carpenter was not adjudged a victor he, of course, won't come before me in any such special class — that is, if the team comes to see me at all, of which I know nothing.

Understand me. If I am convinced of the moral turpitude of any American and I have any duty in the matter I will condemn him unhesitatingly. But to condemn him on such clippings as you enclose would be even more silly than wicked, especially where these same clippings conclusively prove that the British judges, the officials who above all others should be held to the highest standard of rectitude, had been culpably remiss in the matter of the Marathon race.

My idea is to refrain from every statement which will tend to cause international bitterness, and simply to congratulate the American team, which, as your correspondent shows, before an unfriendly audience and with unfriendly surroundings nevertheless scored so signal a triumph. *Yours truly*

* Remember also that the conduct of the judges in the Carpenter race in breaking the tape, crowding on the track and declaring the race off on a foul, before any investigation could possibly have been held, was itself in the highest degree improper and unsportsmanlike.

P.S. Your correspondent and the papers you enclose omit all mention of the fact that after requiring our team in the tug of war to wear only ordinary shoes, the British officials permitted their team to appear with hobnails and steel plates. They permitted this upon the ground that they were policemen and that these were ordinary policemen's shoes. Here is a case where there is far greater justification than in the Carpenter case for the accusation of bad faith; nevertheless I should not for one moment make it. It is perfectly possible that our men understood the prohibition in one way and lived up to it strictly, whereas the British did not desire that it should be so strictly lived up to, and that therefore it was an honest misunderstanding. But papers like *The Sportsman* and people such as those with whom your correspondent comes in contact would have exhausted their vocabulary of vituperation in screaming against Yankee trickery and foul play and lack of good sportsmanship if it had been the American team that wore those shoes when the British team did not; and you might just as well protest against the Englishmen giving any credit to any of their people in view of this tug of war incident as to protest, as you seemingly do, against the American team receiving credit for its remarkable aggregate of victories because, forsooth, in one case possibly prejudiced judges alleged a foul.

1185

Confidential Oyster Bay, August 20, 1908

Dear Mr. Ambassador: Your long and exceedingly interesting letter has just come. First, as to my African trip, I am mighty glad that you think that Lord Crewe[1] will "give us whatever we want." Will you explain to him clearly that I am not going on a game-butchering trip, but on a scientific trip, and that all of the specimens that I shoot, excepting of course whatever I kill for meat, under the terms of my license, will be sent to the National Museum at Washington? This would mean, I suppose, a male and female of each species if I were able to get them. As I think I told you, outside of these specimens I would not want a half-dozen trophies all told for myself, for I have no room for them in my house. Of course if, under the terms of my license, I could kill, say one extra elephant and I were able to do so, I would, so as to keep the tusks as a trophy. Under the terms of the license I could kill an extra rhinoceros and an extra lion if I had the luck to get one. Then if I could kill an extra buffalo I should have all the trophies that I would care to keep personally. Now, if I could be allowed in the reserves I would shoot none of the more common animals, and of the bigger or rarer kinds only such as were absolutely needed in order to get specimens of each for the National Museum. This would enable me, if the reserves were near a railway, or near a river, to transport the specimens with far less difficulty than would otherwise be the case; and, moreover, as Kermit has a first-class photographic machine which he will take it will give us the chance to get photographs of the commoner kinds of game, which I am very anxious to do. There is no hurry about getting the permission to enter these reserves, excepting, of course, that I should like to have it sometime before the New Year, so as to be able to make my plans definitely. I have written to the Sirdar. What you say about Churchill's talking to you is interesting; and whatever my present opinion of him, I suppose it will have to be altered if he does give me any useful suggestions!

Now, as to what you say about my course in the spring of 1910 when I come out from my African trip at Cairo. Since I wrote you I have received from Curzon a request on behalf of Oxford to go there in order to get the same kind of degree they gave to the Emperor last year and, what I prize far more, to deliver the Romanes lecture. This last is a compliment which I genuinely appreciate, and I wrote my acceptance, saying that I would go there sometime between May 15th and June 1st, 1910. This makes matters easy for me, because it gives me a genuine reason for going to England. I suppose you are right and that even tho I am a private individual it would look boorish for me not to pay my respects to the sovereigns or heads of

[1] Robert Offley Ashburton Crewe-Milnes, Marquess of Crewe, in 1908 Secretary of State for the Colonies.

governments of the countries thru which I pass. Very possibly my plan will be to leave Cairo about the first of April, spend a fortnight in Italy, and then a fortnight in France. In each case I suppose I shall have to make up my mind to call, in Rome on the King and the Pope, in Paris on the President and the Prime Minister. Then I am afraid that the German Kaiser would have his feelings deeply injured if I did not call on him. At least this is George Meyer's opinion, as well as that of those who have recently been in Germany. My idea would be simply to go straight from Paris to Berlin, then from Berlin to Holland to spend two or three days, and from thence to cross over to England, where I would spend a fortnight or three weeks. Now, while I thus entirely recognize that I shall have to be presented to the sovereigns, I most earnestly hope, and after my talk with George Meyer I believe, that I can arrange to be presented informally. That is, as Meyer tells me, compatible with my going simply in a frock coat and top hat; and Mrs. Roosevelt in whatever is the corresponding feminine garb. I want to avoid the frightful nuisance of big banquets or other formal entertainments. My idea, if it meets with your approval, is that I should take with me the dress uniform of a colonel of United States cavalry (which I am entitled to wear as an ex-Colonel of the Spanish war — not a paper colonel, either, but one who saw service). Then if I have to appear at some function I could wear this, and if it was felt that in a military country like Germany or Italy they would like to see me in uniform when I called on the sovereign I could wear it. But I should hope to avoid wearing it and that I could go in civilian costume as above.[2] In each country I shall want to spend some days looking at picture galleries or cathedrals or little old cities which may for some reason seem peculiarly attractive either to Mrs. Roosevelt or to me. In addition I shall want in England to see various people, especially the half-dozen personal friends I already have, but of course certain public men, ranging from Grey and Asquith to John Burns. I should like to see Lord Rosebery and talk to him about his life of Pitt; and Oman[3] and talk to him about his *Art of War*. Now, if I have to go to formal functions it would mean just so much loss of time to see the men and the places that I really wish to see. The fact that I am to deliver the Romanes lecture will, I suppose, put me naturally in the way of seeing the very people I would like to see, and will give a point to my visit. Finally, if I went to see the sovereigns and chief men informally I could really talk with them, which I could not do if I went to big functions.

[2] Roosevelt made his appearance in "civilian costume."

[3] Charles W. C. Oman, Chichele Professor of Modern History at Oxford, where, as an undergraduate, he had won two firsts; Fellow of the British Academy; later president of the Royal Historical Society, 1917–1921; K.B.E., 1920; author of graceful and perceptive histories of Greece, the Byzantine Empire, Europe, and England; a thoughtful specialist in military histories including *A History of the Art of War, The Middle Ages from the Fourth to the Fourteenth Century* (1898); *A History of the Peninsular War* (1902–1930); *Wellington's Army, 1809–1814* (1912); and *Studies in the Napoleonic Wars* (1929).

The big functions would, of course, have a spectacular interest which might very well appeal to young people, but for me they would not have any very great interest.

The Australians and New Zealanders are sending me cables of the utmost enthusiasm about our fleet.

I was greatly interested in what you told me about Komura and his messages to me. If you think proper pray write and tell him how much I appreciate what he has said. I am confident that he says what is true as to the feeling of the Government and the responsible classes in Japan. As corroborating this I have received the following letter and enclosure from Takahira:

Imperial Japanese Embassy
Washington,
Buena Vista Springs, Pa.
August 19, 1908

Mr. President.

I am instructed to present to Your Excellency the explanation of the Imperial Government in the sense of the statement herewith enclosed, in regard to the proposed postponement of a grand exposition now in contemplation from 1912 to 1917.

In making a communication of this nature to Your Excellency, I am fully sensitive of the importance of the subject which might lead you to desire for further information before you are prepared to express your views, but in view of the question regarding an immediate action while I am not certain when you would find it convenient to favor me with an audience if I request it, I beg leave to take the liberty of making representation in this manner and to request that you would be pleased to inform me of your views thereon at your convenience.

I need not say that I shall always be ready to place myself at your disposal and to come to Oyster Bay if you desire to see me personally on the subject.

I have the honor to be
Your Excellency's very humble servant
K. TAKAHIRA

The Ministry since entering upon its duties, has found it necessary to submit the project of a grand exposition in Tokyo in 1912 to a new and careful analysis and examination. The plan as originally devised, was of moderate dimension and it was believed confidently that the country would be able and ready at the time indicated to deal successfully with the undertakings, but gradually the scheme was permitted to expand far beyond the original design and unfortunately investigations on the subject of ways and means did not keep with such expansion. It has moreover been found that to carry out the project on the scale now contemplated, it would be necessary for the Imperial Government to appropriate very large additional amount of money. It has been also made abundantly clear that making due allowance for unforeseen but inevitable delays there is not sufficient time before 1912 to prepare properly for the exhibits or to complete those numerous preparations, which are essential to the success of such an undertaking. Under these circumstances, the Imperial Government have been obliged to consider, whether they should endeavor to carry out the enterprise at the appointed time and in the appointed manner regardless of the final issue, or postpone the undertaking until all necessary arrangements which serve as guarantees of success can be perfected and put into operation. The cordial and sympathetic encouragement which the President has uniformly extended to the proposed exposition and the exceptionally generous support which the Congress upon his recommendation gave the project, has induced the Imperial Government before finally and formally deciding between the alternatives above presented, and in advance of making known elsewhere their conviction, to explain the situation frankly and fully to the President, in the hope that he will see in the proposed resolution of postponement the wiser course. It should be added that in 1917 will be celebrated the fiftieth anniversary of the accession of his Imperial Majesty, and it is proposed to take advantage of that happy occasion to inaugurate the exposition. The administrative organization shall be maintained and the work of preparation continued.

To this I answered as follows:

The White House
Washington

Oyster Bay, N. Y.
August 20, 1908

My dear Mr. Ambassador:

I very deeply appreciate the courtesy of your Government in informally notifying me of its project as regards the exposition in Japan, and I still more deeply appreciate the friendly confidence in me shown by a desire to have my views. I am perfectly clear that the wise action of the Ministry, in view of the statements contained in the memorandum accompanying your letter, is that which they so strongly incline to adopt when they say that they hope I will "see in the proposed resolution of postponement the wise course to follow." It seems to me as the Ministry suggests that the year 1917, the fiftieth anniversary of the accession of His Imperial Majesty, will be a peculiarly fit time for the inauguration of the exposition.

Now, my dear Mr. Ambassador, is there any way in which I can help to put this matter before our countrymen, or before the world, in the proper light? I feel that your Government is showing great wisdom. Our own experience with expositions has been that they almost invariably cost more than is expected and that they are very rarely ready on time. I think that your Nation is acting in a spirit of the most admirable common sense in deferring until a more appropriate season a plan which it now appears would cost so much money as to make it inexpedient to carry it thru, especially in view of the likelihood of its proving impossible in any event to get ready in time. When Japan celebrates her first great international exposition I earnestly desire that it shall be done in a way which will make all the world feel that there is no other exposition that has ever been given by any nation with which the Japanese exposition need fear comparison. I will be glad to make any announcement that may be fitting and appropriate in the matter if you so desire. Would you care to have me recommend to Congress, and announce in advance that I will so recommend, that our appropriation be continued to take effect when your exposition is held? Any desire that your Government has that is in my power to meet I shall be very glad to meet.

I am writing you thus at once so that your Government may be immediately assured not only of my approval of its proposed action, but of my desire to do anything which they may feel will make it more easy for them to announce their intention. To me personally their proposed action, in view of the conditions they set forth, affords an additional proof of the wisdom and good judgment which have been so conspicuous in the management of the Empire of Nippon during the past forty years and furnishes another instance of what it would be wise for our people to copy. I shall communicate a copy of this letter to Mr. Root, and before you make public anything that I say it might be well for you to come on here and see me. If, therefore, when you have informed your Government what I have said and have heard from them in response it shall appear to you desirable that I take any action or make any utterance will you not come down here to see me? Meanwhile I shall have heard from Mr. Root.

Sincerely yours,
THEODORE ROOSEVELT.

Baron Kogoro Takahira,
    The Japanese Ambassador,
        Buena Vista Springs, Pennsylvania.

I thought it rather touching of the Japanese to write me in this way, and of course I want in any way I can to help them and to make their position more easy; for much tho I admire their common sense in not going into the exposition when it will evidently be such a drain on an already straightened treasury, I can understand that they may feel sensitive at having to make the public avowal that they are not in shape to carry thru the matter as they had hoped, and if I can help them put a good face on it I am delighted to do so.

I was particularly pleased to get your full and convincing statement as to just what had occurred at the Olympic games. I agree with every word of opinion that you express, and my knowledge of the men makes me sure that you have seen the facts just as they occurred. I do not believe in these international matches. Where the feeling is so intense it is almost impossible that there should not be misunderstandings. I think your criticisms of both sides eminently just. Even between such colleges as Harvard and Yale frightful rows now and then occur, each side being convinced that the other has acted with black infamy, and all athletic relations between the universities being suspended in consequence. Now, where this occurs between American universities it is idle to expect that similar trouble won't occur when heterogeneous masses of men representing the two nations and drawn from every class of life are put into competition. I must say I thought the conduct of the judges and of the British public in connection with the Marathon race very bad indeed. As regards the 400-meter event Carpenter is well known in intercollegiate athletics here and I don't for a moment believe that he intended to commit a foul; and here again the conduct of the English judges was so bad that we on this side will never be sure that Carpenter committed a foul even unwittingly. But my idea is that in public there shall nothing whatever be said about the matter that will not be entirely pleasant and agreeable and that the talk shall be permitted to die down. Desborough[4] must be a very

[4] William Henry Grenfell Desborough, First Baron of Taplow, veteran and hero of the playing fields of Harrow and Oxford; ascender of the Alps, Rockies, and Himalayas; twice swimmer of the Niagara; champion épéeist; stroke of a transchannel eight; later captain of the Yeoman of the Guard; author of articles on the Rocky Mountains, the House of Lords, and bimetallism.

good fellow. Years ago I met him while on a hunting trip in the Big Horn Mountains.

With hearty thanks, *Sincerely yours*

4855 · TO EDGAR ALEXANDER MEARNS   *Roosevelt Mss.*

Oyster Bay, August 20, 1908

My dear Major Mearns: The enclosed letter explains itself. What do you want me to do?

Wood wrote me very nicely and is enthusiastic about your going with me. By the way, how much whisky ought we to take? I never drink anything for what might be called convivial reasons on trips of this kind, and we merely wish to take whisky or brandy, whichever you think best, sufficient for medicinal purposes. In the West I used very little whisky or brandy indeed; a single flask would do me for any trip however long; and I generally took brandy instead of whisky.

I suppose you will have small mammal traps and the like. *Sincerely yours*

[*Handwritten*] I ought to see you in October to make definite arrangements.

4856 · TO JAMES BRONSON REYNOLDS, SAMUEL BRATTON DONNELLY,
AND HENRY BEACH NEEDHAM   *Roosevelt Mss.*

Oyster Bay, August 21, 1908

Gentlemen: I have received your admirable report upon conditions at Panama.[1] I am greatly impressed with it, and shall submit it to Congress with appropriate recommendations as soon as that body convenes. Meanwhile, I shall send your recommendations to Col. Goethals, and ask him to put them into effect so far as possible, and where he deems this impossible or impracticable to report the fact to me with his reasons. I am naturally extremely pleased at the very satisfactory showing that your report makes of conditions under Col. Goethals and his associates. I doubt if there is any piece of work undertaken on behalf of the American people of recent years of which the American people have more reason to be proud than of the work hitherto done on the Panama Canal. The success has literally been astounding. Five years ago when we undertook the task, no sane man would have dared to hope for the results which have already been achieved. The work itself has been advanced more expeditiously than we had ventured to think possible,

---

[1] The Reynolds commission (see Numbers 4688, 4843) reported that labor and housing conditions at Panama were on the whole excellent. It made only a few recommendations: a simplification of the wage schedules, an increase in the pay of skilled labor (then only 10 per cent above construction wages in New York City), adequate compensation for permanent disability received on canal work, and the appointment of a "labor secretary" to investigate complaints about employment, food and housing. The report is given in full in *Senate Document*, 60 Cong., 2 sess., no. 539.

and the rapidity of the rate of progress has steadily increased. Meanwhile the treatment of hygienic conditions on the Isthmus has been such as to make it literally the model for all work of the kind in tropical countries. Five years ago the Isthmus of Panama was a byword for unhealthiness of the most deadly kind. At present the Canal Zone is one of the healthiest places on the globe, and the work which is being prosecuted with such tremendous energy is being prosecuted under conditions so favorable to the health and well-being of the workers that the mortality among them is abnormally small.

Finally, in addition to the extreme efficiency of the work under Col. Goethals and his associates, and the extraordinary hygienic success achieved under Dr. Gorgas, there is the further and exceedingly gratifying fact that on the Isthmus the United States Government has been able to show itself a model employer. There are matters to correct of course, as your report shows, but on the whole it is true that the United States Government is looking after the welfare, health, and comfort of those working for it as no other Government has ever done in work of like character.

Again thanking you for your report, I am, *Sincerely yours*

4857 · TO LYMAN ABBOTT   *Roosevelt Mss.*

Personal   Oyster Bay, August 21, 1908

My dear Dr. Abbott: I have had to throw up my hands — it is really perfectly comic to see how the theory that a man in public office should not try to do anything but fulfill the duties of his public office breaks down in practice. When Hughes was nominated you may remember how the *Sun* and *Evening Post* exulted in his statement that he did not believe that the Governor should have anything to do with legislation, and pointed out how all this contrasted with my shameless activity. Yet the reason Hughes is now a candidate for the renomination and must be accepted by the Republican party is that he abandoned and reversed this attitude and deliberately fought thru the legislature an anti-race-gambling bill.

So with myself and party leadership. I have sincerely endeavored to avoid being thrust into the position of a New York party leader who, because of the curious condition of our politics, inevitably tends to develop a little bit on the lines of a boss. I equally carefully endeavored to avoid seeming to usurp too much leadership in the Nation at large, for I thought it would cause jealousy, and give a handle to my opponents. But two years ago I found that the only way to defeat Hearst was myself to take the leadership and to insist on the nomination of Hughes, which I did. So last fall I found that unless I was prepared to take the nomination myself I had to turn in actively and nominate Taft for President. And now it is perfectly evident I shall have to try to see that Hughes is nominated. It is just as you say about this State. The leaders do not lead (excepting one or two men like Barnes, who, altho very influential and powerful in the organization, and able to do much therein, fail to reckon with many vital outside elements). I had a number of leaders here yesterday, all of them anti-Hughes people, excepting two who kept quiet until I had spoken. I told them that I had gone carefully over the State situation; that I had endeavored to sound public opinion wherever I could; that I realized to the full that Hughes had treated them improperly and had shown the peculiarly unpleasant trait of greedy anxiety to avail himself of their services and selfish haste to repudiate any obligation in return on his part once he had received the benefit of this service; that I realized also that there were various elements in the community whom, by his own fault and needlessly, he had alienated in addition to those elements which it was creditable to him to have alienated, and that I was well aware of the possibility that he might prove a weak candidate at the polls, or, if successful, a well-nigh intolerable person to get on with at the head of the party in the State; but that I was convinced that the best elements in the community, those who would give most strength to the party and to whose wishes we should pay most heed, sincerely and earnestly favored Mr. Hughes and that under such circumstances, and as the feeling for him outside the State was even stronger than within it, I felt that from the highest standpoint of the public interest, and therefore of the party interest, it behooved us to renominate Mr. Hughes; that I did not intend to try to dragoon anybody into voting for him, but that the delegates from my own district would, I believed, take this view, and that I should state frankly that as a private citizen it was my view. Immensely to my amusement, a look of relief came over their faces and they said all right, if I was willing to take the responsibility they would act on my suggestions, and that they would notify Parsons, Woodruff, Raines, Barnes, Fassett and Hendricks what I had said. I believe that some of these men will accept my view; that others will not; but I now think that we shall be able to nominate Hughes.

I return the letters you enclosed. *Sincerely yours*

4858 · TO WILLIAM BARNES, JUNIOR   *Roosevelt Mss.*

Personal   Oyster Bay, August 21, 1908

My dear Mr. Barnes: Yesterday I saw Sherman, Bennet, George Smith,[1] Mike Dady,[2] Cocks,[3] and Hitchcock, Chairman of the National Committee, here. I have been carefully going into the Hughes matter since I saw you. I appreciate to the full the force of the arguments you urged against his renomination. It is not pleasant for me to support a man who has wantonly behaved badly to the very men who did most in securing his election — I would ⟨not in the least object to his behaving badly to them when that was necessary in the⟩ approve his turning them down in the public interest, but I do object

[1] George Joseph Smith, New York businessman, Republican congressman, 1903–1905.
[2] Michael J. Dady, Brooklyn Republican, for long an associate of T. C. Platt.
[3] William W. Cocks, New York Republican congressman since 1905.

to its being done wantonly. Moreover I appreciate that he has alienated quite needlessly very many voters, and if we had the right man to put in his place (the right man from the standpoint of getting votes) I should say that it was certainly wise to nominate such a man. But no such man is in sight, and there does not seem to be the slightest chance of his arising. Under the conditions it seems to me that while it will do damage to renominate Hughes, it will do more damage not to renominate him and that this damage will extend outside of the State. While, therefore, I want most emphatically to disclaim any intention of seeming to dictate the nomination I think I ought to tell you that my judgment is that the convention ought to renominate him. I am sure that the delegates from this district will be for him. Bennet, Sherman, and Dady insist that there is no alternative to his renomination. Hitchcock says that not to renominate him would be a harm to the canvass outside of New York as well as, in his judgment, in New York. Even Smith finally announced that he was inclined to take the same view. I may add that everyone present agreed to keep absolutely quiet in this matter and to consult with you, among others, before any kind of conclusion was announced; but from the papers I should judge someone had talked. It was not I, for no newspaperman communicated with me directly or indirectly, and I was as much surprised as anyone when I saw the statements in the papers. *Sincerely yours*

4859 · TO WILLIAM HOWARD TAFT   *Roosevelt Mss.*

Oyster Bay, August 24, 1908

Dear Will: If I gave an interview to the Baltimore *Sun*,[1] I think it would convert the Baltimore *American* and other Republican and Independent papers into ardent advocates of Mr. Bryan! Seriously, I could not do that for one paper without bringing a perfect hornets' nest around my ears. I have had the same kind of proposition made to me again and again in my own interest, and always gave them the same answer.

I quite agree with all you say about Sherman's speech of acceptance and Root's little speech on Sherman.[2] They were both admirable. Here in New York I think things are coming out better. After the most careful weighing of all considerations, and taking into account the National as well as the local needs, I have come to the conclusion that Hughes ought to be renominated and have so informed the leaders. Of course I cannot be sure that they will pay heed to me, but I think that they will. Hughes is not a man I care for; he is not a man whose actions have really tended to the uplifting of

[1] The Baltimore *Sun*, normally a Democratic paper, had announced its support of Taft, explaining that he was "safer" than Bryan. The influence of the newspaper, Republicans hoped, would put Maryland, a doubtful state, in the Taft column.
[2] Sherman on August 18 formally accepted the vice-presidential nomination at Utica, New York. His short address, consonant in tone with Taft's, is published in the *Republican Campaign Text-Book*, 1908, pp. 537-539.

political life; but he is financially an entirely honest man and one of much ability, and I am convinced that while to nominate him will do harm, not to nominate him will do more harm, because I am convinced that the bulk of the Republicans including the best men in the party outside of the active organization men, are for him.

I regard your support by the Baltimore *Sun* as ten times as important as the support of Bryan by the *World* and the *Herald*. Remember that both of these papers were far more enthusiastic supporters of Parker against me than they can possibly be of Bryan against you. The *Herald's* news columns will not hurt you at all in my judgment. They have never hurt me. It was a long time before I ever knew which way the *Herald* felt about me; and I never cared. In 1900 before the Republican convention it went perfectly crazy in demanding that I should be nominated for President instead of McKinley. If it could ever have embarrassed me at all, it would have embarrassed me by that action, but it is such a prize jackass that even that did not annoy me. In 1904 I never even discovered which way it was going except by an accident. Neither have I ever attributed any weight to the *World*. Nevertheless I should very strongly object to anything like overconfidence. You have exactly the right attitude of mind in the matter. In 1904 I never permitted myself to regard the election as anything but doubtful. White's letter is of importance, and from Jake Riis and Cal O'Laughlin I find that there is great apathy in the West among the farmers. I am coming to believe more and more that you are right and that you should make one speech each in all the States you mention; *and one at Denver*. Foraker need have no heed from us. I liked your last utterance, and I think it essential that your personality should be put with all possible force into the campaign.

I regard Van Cleave[3] as one of Bryan's most effective helps. Every particle of notoriety given to Van Cleave means just so much more strength to Bryan. If there is any way, thru Cromwell or otherwise, to get him to hold up that contempt case which is to take place in September before Judge Gould in Washington, it should be done.[4] Gompers, as I happen to know, is anxious

---

[3] James Wallace Van Cleave served, when only thirteen, with Morgan's raiders in the Confederate Army. Always precocious and always able, he started a business at eighteen and continued as president of the Bucks Stove and Range Company until his death. A Republican, a Presbyterian, a president of the National Association of Manufacturers, he believed that things in American life should change very little and very, very slowly.

[4] Judge Gould in December 1907 had, in the case of the Bucks Stove and Range Company, issued an injunction forbidding the A.F. of L. to boycott the company's products (see No. 4536). Gould then held, as did the Supreme Court in a later decision, that a labor boycott violated the Sherman Act. Gompers, Morrison, and other A.F. of L. officials, before the injunction was to take effect, mailed literature to federation members which virtually perpetuated the boycott. Some of that literature was delivered after the effective date of Gould's ruling. Also after that date, John Mitchell at a U.M.W. convention exhorted his union members not to buy the products of the Bucks company. For these actions, Gompers, Morrison, and Mitchell were charged with contempt of court. Their case was pending in August 1908. The case was

for the case to proceed and hopes to be sent to jail. If he were, and especially if Mitchell were sent with him, I think a well-nigh fatal blow would have been struck us in the election. That injunction contempt case ought under no circumstances be tried until after the election. It really begins to look to me as if Van Cleave wanted you defeated.

Don't get one particle discouraged. Of course, you have moments when you feel downhearted. We have a hard fight, and we want to put in every ounce of strength we have, but in my judgment your electoral majority will be as big as McKinley got in 1900 or as I got in 1904. If, as I hope, you gain Maryland and Kentucky, it will offset many small losses. *Ever yours*

4860 · TO WILLIAM BARNES, JUNIOR   *Roosevelt Mss.*

Personal   Oyster Bay, August 24, 1908

My dear Barnes: Most emphatically whatever my friends do up in Albany I shall stand by them. I have given them, including you, my best judgment. It is not a judgment based on newspapers; it is a judgment based on what Congressman Bennet has found from his personal canvass; what Sol Strassburger finds on the East Side of New York; what Prendergast and Mike Dady find in Brooklyn; what Cocks finds here in my own District; what Jim Sherman finds to be the overwhelming sentiment right near you in central New York; what Hitchcock said as to the effect outside. Now, if you and those like you ⟨feel that it is⟩ fear that I shall asking you to cut your throats ⟨I am not going to do it⟩ your fear is groundless. But my judgment is that the convention will nominate Hughes, and that it would hurt very much more not to nominate him than to nominate him; altho it will undoubtedly hurt us also to nominate him. *Sincerely yours*

4861 · TO HERMANN VON HATZFELDT-WILDENBURG   *Roosevelt Mss.*

Telegram   Oyster Bay, August 24, 1908

Am shocked and grieved at the news of the death of the Ambassador.[1] He was not only my intimate personal friend and one of the most fearless, sin-

---

ultimately decided not by Judge Gould but by his colleague Judge Wright, who in December found the labor leaders in contempt. His decision rested first on the prevailing legal interpretation of boycotts and secondly on more controversial findings as to the actual violations of Gould's injunction. Particularly with respect to Gompers and Morrison it seemed harsh to insist that the delivery date rather than the posting date of the literature they had mailed constituted an offense. Wright's decision came too late to affect the campaign. Had it been rendered in September, Gompers might have made much of the fact that Gould in 1907 cited as his authority a definition of boycott made by Taft while he was a circuit judge in 1893. For Roosevelt's reaction to Wright's decision see No. 5093.

[1] Baron von Sternberg, long afflicted with cancer, had died in Germany during an operation. Temporarily his official duties were assumed by the German chargé, the addressee of this telegram.

cere and loyal men I ever met, but also a diplomat of signal ability who
served Germany with fervent patriotism and yet who showed such intelligent good will for America that it would be difficult to overestimate the
value of what he did in strengthening and bringing closer the ties of friendship and good will between the two countries. I mourn his loss for my own
sake, and I deeply regret it for the sake of the people of the United States.

4862 · TO FRANK HARRIS HITCHCOCK   *Roosevelt Mss.*

Oyster Bay, August 25, 1908

My dear Mr. Hitchcock: I want you to see Mr. D. L. Cease,[1] of Cleveland,
Ohio, and go over with him the question of Taft's labor decisions. It is useless to expect the labor people to read all the decisions; but Mr. Cease can
point you out some extracts from them which make his position as clear as
a bell. Mr. Cease is one of the most valuable men in the country to get in, and
to keep in, the closest touch with. *Sincerely yours*

4863 · TO WILLIAM SHEFFIELD COWLES   *Roosevelt Mss.*

Oyster Bay, August 25, 1908

Dear Will: That is most interesting and important. Of course I am not competent to express an opinion on the subject, but it seems to me that this comes
mighty near to revolutionizing naval warfare so far as torpedoes are concerned.[1] I wish you would talk it over with Winslow in connection with
the plans for the new battleships.[2] What a good fellow Winslow is! *Faithfully yours*

4864 · TO HERBERT PARSONS   *Roosevelt Mss.*

Oyster Bay, August 27, 1908

My dear Parsons: I have far too many necessary encounters with men I do
not like, to permit myself to feel even a passing irritation at sharp words
from men whom I not only like but thoroly respect, as I do you. Now, my
dear fellow, when you ask if you are "to understand that I am opposed to
having the Republicans of New York County express their wishes in this

[1] D. L. Cease, editor of the *Railway Trainmen's Journal.*

[1] Cowles had written about the trials of the Davis torpedo. Lieutenant Commander
Cleland Davis was developing from the standard Whitehead torpedo a warhead that
would not detonate until it had penetrated the hull of its target. For a full account of
this significant advance in torpedo design, see Frederick A. Talbot, *Submarines, Their
Mechanism and Operation* (Philadelphia, 1915), pp. 141–144.
[2] See No. 4937.

matter on primary day." [1] I think you must be giving vent to a very natural irritation rather than asking a serious question. You know, of course, that I am not in the least opposed, and cannot be opposed, to having the Republicans of any county express their wishes on primary day. On the contrary, when you were out here with Barnes, Hendricks and the others, what I kept saying to you was that I earnestly hoped we could get just such ⟨an opinion⟩ a free expression of the voters' wishes. You are entirely right in saying that you understood that I was unwilling, in view of Hughes' conduct toward you, Hendricks and Barnes, to ask any of you to support him. I am very unwilling to do so, and when I saw you I hoped that no necessity would ever arise for me to do it; but we also agreed at that time that the situation might change at any time and that we could not tell what would have to be done when the time came — unless the situation cleared. You were very strong in your statements of what the men under you said as to Hughes' unpopularity, and I certainly understood you to say that Bennet felt exactly as you did (as an unimportant incident I may mention that Amos Pinchot[2] notified me that you had entirely mistaken him and that he favored the nomination of Hughes). When Bennet tells me, as the local leaders like Strassburger tell me, that the sentiment is very strong for the renomination of Hughes I have got to take notice of it. I entirely agree with all you say as to your just reasons for complaint against Governor Hughes, and furthermore with all you say as to the fact that many of those who desire his renomination desire it chiefly for the purpose of hurting the Republican party. Moreover, my dear Parsons, you can hardly seriously suppose that, to quote your own words, I am trying to "treat you as a puppet" — that is, if you mean *me* when you say "those in charge of the national campaign," which of course I am not. On the contrary, I have written again and again to Taft and to Hitchcock not to make any open statement, and I haven't the slightest intention of "telling you what to do" and never will "tell the newspapers that you will be told what to do" and never have thought of so telling them. You wrote me requesting to see me, and asking that I say nothing until I had seen you. I saw you. We went over the situation. I afterwards saw Bennet and various others, including Sherman, and the situation as they related it was so totally different that I felt I ought to tell you that this, with other knowledge brought to me, had made me alter my mind as to what was the wise thing to do. But surely my letter most explicitly disclaims any intention to dictate to you.

Those canvasses that you mention are very instructive, but it is difficult to reconcile them with Strassburger's, is it not? Still I absolutely agree with you that there are many cross currents; that there are many currents against

[1] After an unofficial primary in New York City, Parsons reluctantly announced on September 10 that in his opinion a large majority of the delegates to the nominating convention from New York County would favor Hughes.
[2] Amos Pinchot, younger brother of Gifford, in 1908 a New York lawyer and social worker; later as one of the first Progressives the spirited, sometimes irresponsible leader of the opponents of George W. Perkins.

Hughes; but I don't see whom you are going to put in his place who won't be weaker. *Sincerely yours*

[*Handwritten*] Let me repeat, that of course I want the fullest and most open expression of preference at the primaries; that I'll stand heartily for whatever you, Fassett and the rest of the leaders finally do, and have no intention of "forcing the nomination," or of trying to; but that, unless you object, I should like, as a good Republican and party man and a staunch believer in you, to tell you my judgment for whatever it is worth

4865 · TO TRUMAN HANDY NEWBERRY   *Roosevelt Mss.*

Oyster Bay, August 28, 1908

My dear Mr. Newberry: After careful investigation I have reluctantly come to the conclusion that the only course now open is that recommended in your letter of the 26th, and I accordingly direct that the course you therein outline be followed.[1] At the same time I cannot but feel that if the officials responsible for the plans had been willing, not merely to listen to, but to try to get the opinions of, the younger officers of the type represented at the Newport Conference, the *Utah* and *Florida* would be much more formidable vessels than will actually be the case. I do not for a moment accept the view that under the act of Congress it was necessary that they should not be improvements upon the two vessels already partially built. It would be a simple absurdity to suppose that any such wording as that you quote would prevent us from making ships the best of their kind. But the officials responsible for these ships seem to have limited themselves to the desire not to lag far behind other nations instead of doing what they of course ought to have done; that is, tried to lead other nations. I do not think that this is to their credit. I think that the present organization of the Department, no matter how excellent may be the individual officers at the head of the bureaus, tends to a certain woodenness of administration, to a lack of initiative and flexibility, which is not advantageous. Moreover, I feel that the unfortunate habit of promotion only by seniority and that at a late age results in making our naval officers of and above the grade of captain usually inferior relatively to those of junior rank, and I regard it as a mistake not to consult at length the best of the younger officers.[2] Of course there are plenty of exceptions to

[1] Newberry had recommended that Roosevelt accept the Newport conference's majority plan for the design of the *Utah* and *Florida* (see No. 4847, note 1). For an analysis of Roosevelt's reasoning in reaching this distasteful conclusion see Morison, *Sims*, pp. 210–211. The President was determined, however, that plans for the ships which he expected Congress to authorize at its next session should include the changes urged by the younger officers at Newport (see Numbers 4900, 5022). Nevertheless the *Wyoming* and the *Arkansas*, authorized early in 1909, were built with main batteries of twelve-inch rifles.
[2] For Roosevelt's efforts to change the Navy's promotion system, see No. 4717.

this statement both ways — for instance, there is no man whose advice I would value more than that of Captain Winslow.

Captain Winslow, by the way, submitted to me a paper from a friend of his dealing with the necessity of a greater amount of armor protection which, whether right or wrong, deserves consideration, as does the new development in torpedo practice. I take it for granted that in the plans for the four- or five-turret battleships with fourteen-inch guns and heavier armor such considerations as these will receive careful attention. I look forward to seeing these plans in January. *Sincerely yours*

4866 · TO WILLIAM HOWARD TAFT *Roosevelt Mss.*

Oyster Bay, August 28, 1908

Dear Will: I think Root is right. I think yours was an excellent answer to the editor of the *Home Herald.* The irritating thing of such nonsensical attacks as this made upon you in this matter is that they tend to put a premium upon hypocrisy. If there arises any real need I think that we can make up a smashing answer, partly on the line of yours, which Root very wisely advises you not now to publish, and partly on the line of the answer of the editor of the *Home Herald* to that Judge who wrote him. I would simply say that you decline to permit any such gross violation of the first principles of our Government as an effort to make you subscribe to any given principles of dogmatic theology before counting you as eligible to receive votes; that opposition had been made to you on the ground that you are a Unitarian; that the Chaplain of the Senate at this moment was a clergyman of your faith, the Rev. Edward Everett Hale, and that there was not in all the United States a man more revered by the clergymen of every denomination, a man with whom every true Christian must feel eager to be associated in Christian brotherhood; that the people had now forgotten that the same attack was made upon Lincoln as being a nonorthodox Christian as upon you, and far severer attacks upon Jefferson; and that this effort to proscribe you because you believed in Christianity, in religion, as Abraham Lincoln believed and practiced both, will fail as it did fail when Lincoln was the object and when Jefferson and John Adams and John Quincy Adams were the objects. Then quote the end of the first chapter and the beginning of the second chapter of the Epistle of James. I am mighty weak on the Lutheran and Calvinistic doctrines of salvation by faith, myself, and tho I have no patience with much of the Roman Catholic theory of church government, including the infallibility of the Pope, the confessional, and a celibate clergy, I do believe in the gospel of works as put down in the Epistle of James.

I have taken up with Wade Ellis the matter of the railways and I think have arranged it. *Faithfully yours*

Oyster Bay, August 29, 1908

My dear Dr. Abbott: It is mighty good of you to have seen Richards. I think your second suggestion is an excellent one. He has told me that he will come out to see me, and if he does, and will give me some data on which to go,[1] I will gladly write an article for the *Outlook* based exactly on the considerations you mention in your second paragraph.

That is a great quotation from Woodrow Wilson. I had not read the book[2] because I have felt rather impatient with his recent attitude on certain matters, notably the effort to control corporations; but this is a really first-class paragraph.

Now, about the letter from your son's brother-in-law. He raises a very important point. It was once before raised in connection with the Colorado River, but Congress decided that under the conditions in that case the Federal Government had no power to act. I will see if I have power to act in this case. *Faithfully yours*

[*Handwritten*] Who is William Garrott Brown? Somebody has sent me a piece of his in the Evening Post which is a really scandalous perversion of the truth.[3]

Oyster Bay, August 29, 1908

Dear Will: From Loudenslager and McKinley I hear that you approve of my letter taking the form of a letter to them.[1] I shall accordingly send it to you when I have finished the rough draft, so as to see if it meets the situation.

[1] Howard Richards, Jr., an Episcopal missionary returned from Wuchang, gave Roosevelt an impressive account of the educational work of various Christian denominations in China. This the President used in his article, "The Awakening of China," *Outlook*, 90:665–667 (November 28, 1908).

[2] *Constitutional Government in the United States.*

[3] Republican Presidents, particularly Roosevelt, this article asserted, had prevented the development of the party in the South by manipulating patronage for their personal advantage. William Garrott Brown, the author of the article, in 1908 an editorial writer for *Harper's Weekly*, predicted that Southern conservatives would become Republican if they were permitted to build locally controlled organizations. The South would then he felt become a two-party area. Brown, a Gold Democrat, the biographer of Andrew Jackson, Stephen A. Douglas, and Oliver Ellsworth, and in 1901–1902 a lecturer in history at Harvard, simply dismissed race as an issue. This unrealistic analysis reflected the hope of unreconstructed anti-Bryan Democrats that they might soon find a sanctuary in a reconstructed Republican party.

[1] William Brown McKinley, Republican congressman from Illinois, 1905–1913, 1915–1921, was chairman and Henry Clay Loudenslager, Republican congressman from New Jersey, 1893–1911, was secretary of the Republican Congressional Campaign Committee in 1908. For Roosevelt's public letter in behalf of the Republican congressional campaign, see No. 4881. For the President's longer contributions to campaign literature in 1908, see Numbers 4880, 4915, 4921, 4956, 4959.

Have you seen the admirable article about you as a Judge in the last *McClure's Magazine*?[2] It was written by young Alger, whom you may remember I wisht to appoint Judge in New York when you and Root and Moody memorialized me in a round robin not to do so! It is such a good article that I think it ought to be widely circulated. I am more and more inclined to think that you ought to make a certain number of big speeches, just as you suggest; say one in each of a number of States from New York to Colorado. Your recent speeches have taken well. I earnestly want your personality put into this campaign, and I want us to choose our ground and make the fight aggressively. If things keep as they are now I am confident we shall win; but there is no question but that Bryan is stronger than before, and all kinds of local fights, not to speak of the liquor question, hurt us here and there. In this State, for instance, there is an absolute revolt among the leaders about nominating Hughes and whether I can get him nominated or not I do not know. I am extremely reluctant to seem to dictate in the matter, for it is very easy to get people sullenly hostile by dictation. Even as it is I have spoken to the leaders far more emphatically as to the wisdom of nominating him than ever I spoke to them as to the wisdom of nominating you — a fact of which the lying blackguards in the *Sun* and the lying hypocrites in the *Evening Post* affect to be, but probably are not, ignorant. I still think we shall get him nominated when the time comes, but I cannot be sure.

The enclosed letter from Landis[3] explains itself. Loeb was entirely right last winter when he prophesied the trouble that we should have over this guaranty of bank deposits business. I myself felt that we were going to have trouble, and that we ought to be able in some way to beat it; but I know very little about finance, and those who ought to know were so strongly against the plan that I did not feel I could insist upon any action. It is very difficult for me now to advise, just because I wasn't in sympathy with the attitude our people took. Of course Bryan's proposal is preposterous, because he doesn't take into account the need for a complete remodeling of our currency laws if any such plan is to be adopted. Those who are wiser than I must advise you in this matter, and I think that the men in the States affected by the movement should tell you whether it is best to thresh the thing fairly out, stating exactly your position, or whether it is best not to make the fight on this issue, but to force it aggressively on the general policies. If the former course is decided upon it will be well to consider whether you should not say that you frankly recognize both the extreme difficulty of providing for the safety of the depositors and the extreme desirability of doing so as far as possible; that postal savings banks will reach the very smallest men, the men

[2] George William Alger, "Taft and Labor," *McClure's*, 31:597–602 (September 1908).
[3] Charles B. Landis was in 1908 the member from Indiana on the Republican Congressional Campaign Committee.

whose deposits do not go into sums of any size; and that as regards the other men, we now have a currency commission which you shall urge to study this question and to see if it is possible by a reshaping of our banking system to render it practicable to get the guaranty desired. I cannot speak as definitely as I would like on this matter, because I am not sure of my ground. I do not practically know how the Oklahoma system has in actual politic worked, for instance. *Ever yours*

4869 · TO CHARLES MITCHELL HARVEY   *Roosevelt Mss.*

Personal   Oyster Bay, August 29, 1908

My dear Mr. Harvey:[1] I have not seen that article of Mr. Creelman's and doubtless the exact language is not mine; but there is no question that I on more than one occasion last spring said something substantially to that effect. That is, I stated that I had just as much difficulty with Mr. Van Cleave, Mr. Parry,[2] and their association on one hand as with Mr. Gompers and his association on the other; and indeed my present impression is that Mr. Van Cleave and Mr. Parry went further the wrong way last winter than Mr. Gompers did — and Mr. Gompers went a good distance also. The opposition of the National Association of Manufacturers to every rational and moderate measure for benefiting workingmen — for instance, to the measures abolishing child labor, and to secure employers' liability legislation — caused me real and grave concern. I felt that it was ominous of evil for the whole country to have men who should stand high in wisdom and in guiding force take a course and use language which directly incited to revolution; for if Messrs. Van Cleave and Parry and their followers were able to commit this government to their viewpoint, we would be certain to see the most extreme Socialist or Populist party come into power on the reaction. Mr. Van Cleave's personal utterances condemning and attacking me have been more extreme than anything Mr. Gompers has said about me. *Sincerely yours*

4870 · TO WILLIAM HOWARD TAFT   *Roosevelt Mss.*

Oyster Bay, September 1, 1908

Dear Will: Here is that letter. It is of course sent to you for the purpose of slashing corrections. I have sent copies of it to Sherman, McKinley, Hitchcock and Root, asking them to return the letter to me as soon as possible with any comments that they desired to make. In addition, I feel very strongly that you ought to consult some of the western radicals about it.

[1] Charles Mitchell Harvey, leading political editorial writer of the St. Louis *Globe-Democrat*, author of *History of the Republican Party*.
[2] David Maclean Parry, hardware and automobile manufacturer, past president of the N.A.M.

Why not have in some such man as Governor Cummins, or perhaps some labor man, and go over it with him? I do not think that La Follette would give you anything worth having, but it is possible that Cummins might. If you object to this, how about a man like Burkett or Dolliver? Dolliver's judgment is pretty sound. I thought it best to take the aggressive and fighting attitude thruout. *Ever yours*

[*Handwritten*] Vermont is all right;[1] and the country will be all right in November. But I agree that you ought to be on the stump, but only speak once or twice in each State you visit. Do not *answer* Bryan; attack him! Don't let *him* make the issues, and never *define* your religious belief! I do not believe you had best say a word about it. Can't you make one speech in South?

Do ask McBee to come and see you. Also Thompson of the N. W. Christian Advocate.

4871 · TO WILLIAM SOWDEN SIMS   *Roosevelt Mss.*

Oyster Bay, September 2, 1908

My dear Commander Sims: I have your letter of the 30th. Nothing that the *Herald* says should receive any attention from us. I see it has given publication to a statement that the Newport conference was stacked.[1] This is of course a gross falsehood merely designed to do harm, just as the statement you quote is so designed. *Sincerely yours*

4872 · TO ARTHUR HAMILTON LEE   *Roosevelt Mss.*

Oyster Bay, September 2, 1908

Dear Arthur: Somewhere in one of the old *Punches* there is a description of Maudle being given a picture by his friend Postlethwaite and fervently expressing his purpose to live up to it. Ever since "The Seats of the Mighty" arrived this family has been convulsed in a by no means entirely successful effort to get the house fixt so as to live up to it!

Seriously, that picture has not only been the source of greater delight to me than any present I ever remember receiving, but it has been a real anxiety because we have not been able to devise just the right place for it, a place really worthy of it. Did we build the north room since you were here, or was

---

[1] The Republican state ticket carried Vermont by 29,000 votes, 4,000 more than the 25,000 generally considered by forecasters to be the measure of safety for the November elections. The returns were particularly satisfactory because Hearst's Independence party, tested in Vermont for the first time, received negligible support.

---

[1] The Navy Department, the *Herald* reported with surprising accuracy, "had stacked the cards" against the reform element at the Newport conference. Therefore, it predicted, no radical changes would be made in ship design. The paper further maintained that the department was planning to muffle criticism by ordering Commander Sims and other troublesome insurgents to Samoa or some equally isolated duty.

it built at the time of your last visit? We have another Simons, a very beautiful and striking picture, altho not to me quite as wonderful a picture as "The Seats of the Mighty," for which we practically in part built the north room, building the picture into the wall over the mantelpiece, it being a long instead of an upright picture like "The Seats of the Mighty." Now we have not been able to get quite as good a place for "The Seats of the Mighty." I should like to have put it in a room by itself, but the only other room that was suitable was the hall, over the fireplace, and that was too dark. I could put it in the library, but the library isn't nearly as handsome a room as the north room; and moreover, we would be brought up very close to the picture. Accordingly we have kept it in the north room, putting it in a big panel to the left of the door as you enter from the hall; we shall inlay it in the panel. This is all right in one way, but if the picture is seen from full in front there is a curtain which has to be pulled down so as to avoid a reflection from the glass; and then it really isn't quite as distinguished a position as the picture ought to have. I don't suppose I shall ever build another addition to the house, but if I do it shall be built primarily with a view to this picture. Meanwhile, it is where I see it whenever I sit in the north room, and the north room is my favorite and special room.

The other day Curzon wrote me an awfully nice letter as Chancellor of Oxford, asking me to deliver the Romanes lecture there, and I have accepted for May, 1910. I shall be returning from my African hunt. Then I shall have the chance of seeing you and dear Mrs. Lee, and I need hardly say how I look forward to it. Your people are being awfully nice with me about the trip.

Here, politically, things I think are going well. Taft I believe will be elected, perhaps not by quite such a popular majority as mine, but by substantially the same electoral vote. He may lose Missouri and Nevada and possibly one or two other western States of the second rank; but he will gain Maryland, and perhaps Kentucky, and he may not lose anything at all.

When I see you I shall have one or two extraordinary things to tell you which I don't think I ought to put on paper. *Ever yours*

4873 · TO WHITELAW REID   *Roosevelt Mss.*

Oyster Bay, September 3, 1908

My dear Reid: As usual, your letter is exceedingly interesting. Naturally I was especially pleased with the inside light you gave me as to the Newfoundland business,[1] which inside light made the editorial from the *Morning Post* particularly good reading.

[1] The continuing negotiations for the submission of the fisheries matter to the Hague Court for arbitration were then concerned with reserving from consideration the problem of the Bay of Fundy. Before the final exchange of notes in January and March 1909 settling this issue, Newfoundland representatives persisted in their efforts

I am very glad your son, the stag shooter, is to be back here during the campaign. It shows a thoroly good spirit on his part to wish to cast his vote. I am very pleased that he and Mrs. Reid were able to get to Ireland, tho I wish you could have done so, too.

I am also much interested in what Morley said to you about India. Sometime or other, if the opportunity favors me, I should like to visit both the Philippines and India, stopping perhaps at the Dutch colonies on the way. The problem of the control of thickly peopled tropical regions by self-governing northern democracies is very intricate. A legislative body most of the members of which are elected by constituencies that in the nature of things can know nothing whatever of the totally different conditions of India, or the Philippines, or Egypt, or Cuba, does not offer the best material for making a success of such government. Moreover we have passed the period when a nation with even an imperfectly developed conscience is content simply to exploit for its own benefit a country that it has conquered; and the effort to govern such a country in its own interest without falling into mawkish sentimentality implies some mighty difficult steering. The Indian Babu, who is educated in English methods, receives what is in many ways a peculiarly bad training. He is fitted by his education only to hold public office or to practice as a lawyer in the courts under English control. But a limited proportion can hold public office, and the remainder including almost all of the lawyers, find the path of agitation against the government almost the only one open to them, and it is rendered congenial by the bitterness they feel because of the aspirations which their education has kindled and which cannot be gratified. In some ways the case of the Indian noble educated in England is even worse, because as soon as he gets back to India he has to suffer the well-nigh intolerable humiliation of discovering that he is not regarded as an Englishman but as an inferior, while his education has made him feel that the one thing to be desired is to be accepted by Englishmen as an equal, as substantially one of themselves.

I wrote you, did I not, that Curzon had requested me to deliver the Romanes lecture at Oxford, and I have accepted for the spring of 1910, when I shall be on my way back from Africa? Then I shall hope to see Morley, among others, and to talk over these Indian matters.

That is fine about the Sirdar. He is doing for me just exactly what I wisht in giving me a small steamer, which will give me a better chance to get good sport off the beaten tracks, and in opening the reserves. Now, when you see Lord Crewe I wish you would ask him if it is not possible to have the British East African and Uganda people give me the same privileges to shoot in the reserves, if they deem it advisable limiting my privilege to shoot-

---

to persuade the British government to concede less than had already been granted to American fishermen by the effective *modus operandi* and in the arbitration convention. On October 9 the Newfoundlanders, impatient with the Crown's policy, revoked all concessions that had been granted to Americans.

ing one specimen (or perhaps two specimens, one of each sex) of each of the rarer kinds of game, and these simply for the National Museum. Most of my hunting will be done in British East Africa, and it is even more important for me to get the privilege of shooting on the British East African reserves than it is of shooting on the reserves of the Sudan. This is especially true as regards killing the rhinoceros and elephant, where it would be of great consequence to kill them near enough to a railway to make their transportation as easy as possible. Also, we could do better photographic work on the reserves.

The Vermont election has come off uncommonly well and seems to indicate that in the East we shall fall but little short of the majorities of the last two presidential elections. In the West the situation is not quite as clear, but I don't believe we shall fall very much below the electoral vote of 1904. I am doing all I can to persuade the Republican politicians to renominate Hughes, but he has been very unwise in the needless way he has antagonized them. *Faithfully yours*

4874 · TO ELIHU ROOT   *Roosevelt Mss.*

Oyster Bay, September 5, 1908

Dear Elihu: I wish you would give your personal attention to the extradition for the Russian Government of certain alleged political offenders in this country.[1] Herbert Parsons brought the matter up. The *Outlook* and all kinds of philanthropic bodies, not to speak of socialists and others, are very much interested over the cases. It is not a matter that should be handled by Adee or others in the Department in a perfunctory way. You should go over it carefully yourself. I asked that special reports should be sent to me before action was taken by the Department, but this was only to forestall action being taken without you or me knowing anything about it.

At the moment I am not pleased with what I hear about the campaign. I greatly fear that the revival of the liquor agitation, which is always damaging to the Republican party, and usually damaging to temperance, may have as its first results a Democratic victory in Maine. I do not think that the National Committee is being handled by any means as well as it was handled under Cortelyou, and for reasons which I am absolutely unable to fathom Taft does not arouse the enthusiasm which his record and personality warranted us in believing he ought to arouse.

[1] Roosevelt was concerned by the possible political effect of the Russian extradition cases on the New York Jewish vote. On August 14, Extradition Commissioner Shields decided to accept the Russian demand to return Jan Janov Pouren, a revolutionary who had been accused by the Russian government of arson, burglary, and attempted murder. Pouren's American sympathizers protested that Pouren's crimes were of a political nature. Since the extradition treaty with Russia provided that fugitives should not be surrendered for political offenses, they claimed that Shields had erred. For Root's handling of the case see No. 4934.

As for the nomination for Governor of New York, I am convinced that Hughes ought to be renominated. But the people outside of the organization, except in distinct categories like volunteer firemen, railroad men, &c., want him renominated, and not to renominate him would be to jeopardize in this State even the National ticket. But to renominate him is only less bad. He has wantonly and needlessly insulted the party workers, so that in my own county of Nassau I am having great difficulty in getting them to endorse him and I can only obtain it as a personal favor to me. The fact is that Hughes is a thoroly unhealthy element in public life, for just the same reason that the professional prohibitionist is an unhealthy element in public life; but exactly as it is not wise because of indignation against a professional prohibitionist to offend honest temperance sentiment, so it is not wise because of indignation with Hughes to offend the religious and moral sentiment of the men who make up the backbone of the Republican party.

I received your notes on my letter and shall doubtless adopt them. I shall split the letter in two parts, sending one to McKinley and one to a private citizen in the West, because I think this will be the most effective way both for Congress and for the National ticket.[2]

It may be that you will want to write me a letter on the Hughes business which I shall answer, and which you can use or not at the convention just as the exigencies demand.[3] *Ever yours*

[*Handwritten*] I enclose copy of a letter from Bryce.

4875 · TO JAMES SCHOOLCRAFT SHERMAN   *Roosevelt Mss.*

Oyster Bay, September 5, 1908

My dear Mr. Sherman: I enclose you Clark's answer to the communication from the railroad man addrest to Congressman Samuel W. Smith.[1]

I wish you would undertake some oversight to the management of the National Committee. It seems to me that there is something radically wrong, as I hear complaints from everybody. Such an interview as that Clark refers to by Mr. Upham is of course as damaging as anything could be.[2] I quote from a letter received from a prominent Republican this morning:

[2] See Numbers 4880, 4881.
[3] Roosevelt had already made public his position on the New York governorship. The morning papers on September 2 carried his statement to William Ward: "I have no intention of trying to dictate the action of the Republican State Convention. But I am a citizen of New York State, and am therefore entitled to express my judgment on such an issue as the nomination for Governor, and my judgment is that it is absolutely necessary to nominate Mr. Hughes." This message Roosevelt repeated in his telegram to Root of September 14, No. 4897. In his official capacity the President had already supported his judgment by forbidding federal officeholders in the upstate regions from working for the nomination of Hughes's opponents.

[1] Samuel William Smith, Republican congressman from Michigan, 1897–1915.
[2] Frederic William Upham, Chicago businessman, president of the Illinois Manufacturers' Association, in 1908 western treasurer of the Republican National Committee,

I enclose a synopsis of opinion received from men identified with the League. Their views are emphatically an endorsement of the President's mind as regards Hughes. It would simply be fatuous for the Republican organization to force the nomination of any machine man in the face of Hughes' active candidacy.

Every person that has come in to see me since I returned from Montreal has expressed a longing for some of the enthusiasm of four years ago. There is a mystery and solemnity about headquarters that has been very disconcerting to almost everybody who has visited the place. Incidentally, a friend of mine took a very prominent businessman there last week whose only purpose was to express an opinion as to certain matters, and to hand in a check for $10,000 as a contribution to the campaign fund. After waiting around for several hours and getting no farther into the presence than the third assistant doorkeeper, these gentlemen left, and on the following day the New York merchant sailed for Europe taking his $10,000 check with him.

The campaign is being conducted in such a blankety business-like way that all the sentiment which is the very foundation of political enthusiasm and activity has been squeezed out of the canvass. If it were possible to inject the fire and enthusiasm of just two weeks of four years ago into this campaign and melt some of the political icicles that make headquarters a political refrigerating plant, it would do more for the ticket than anything possible.

Sincerely yours

4876 · TO WILLIAM HOWARD TAFT   *Roosevelt Mss.*

Strictly private   Oyster Bay, September 5, 1908

Dear Will: I do not want this letter to be seen by anyone but you and Mrs. Taft. It does not seem to me that the National Committee is accomplishing quite as much as it should. Du Pont's connection with the speakers' committee has done far-reaching harm, especially in the West.[1] It may be that it is too late to do anything about this, but if he should retire now I cannot help feeling that some of the damage would be undone.

I believe you are entirely right about the wisdom of making a few speeches on just the terms you mention. You should put yourself prominently and emphatically into this campaign. Also I hope to see everything done henceforth to give the impression that you are working steadily in the campaign. It seems absurd, but I am convinced that the prominence that has been given to your golf playing has not been wise, and from now on I hope your people will do everything they can to prevent one word being sent out about either your fishing or your playing golf. The American people regard

---

held views on labor policies closer to those of the N.A.M. than to those of Roosevelt or Taft. Upham's interview, characteristic of many expressions by leading Republicans, disturbed such other Republicans as E. E. Clark who, close to labor, recognized the damage Upham did to Taft's campaign.

[1] Referring specifically to du Pont, Bryan and other Democratic speakers had insisted that it would be impossible for the Republicans to enforce the laws against trusts because officials representing trusts were "intimately connected" with the party in the campaign. The effect of this argument and of Roosevelt's prodding led to du Pont's resignation as chairman of the speakers' committee; see No. 4920.

the campaign as a very serious business, and we want to be careful that your opponents do not get the chance to misrepresent you as not taking it with sufficient seriousness. I wish you could keep your hand on Hitchcock a little. I don't want to see him travel around the country, but I think he ought now and then to visit you and that you should impress upon him the desirability of prompt access to him by the people of importance. I know that complaints are always made of the manager of any campaign, and many of the complaints of Hitchcock simply represent this general tendency; but there is a pretty widespread feeling that things are not quite as lively as they should be at headquarters. Brooker and Ward, for instance, have mentioned the fact that they do not know what their duties are or what is expected of them.[2]

I am doing everything I can to force the nomination of Hughes, but it is a much more difficult job than I anticipated. Hughes has succeeded in arousing a very bitter feeling against him. Here in my own county I am having difficulty in forcing his endorsement. The workers are bitter against him. *Ever yours*

4877 · TO JAMES BRYCE   *Roosevelt Mss.*

Oyster Bay, September 7, 1908

My dear Bryce: I have sent your letter to Rockhill, calling his especial attention to Morley's statement as to how useful it would be to know anything that passes between the Lama and the Chinese at Peking,[1] and have asked Rockhill to let me know if he can find out anything on the subject. If he does I shall forward it to you.

Yes, the fleet has had a wonderful reception in Australia, and I quite agree with you that one of the real and great benefits of the voyage is getting us a little in touch with your people in the South Seas. Poor Speck! Every word you say of him is true.

With warm regards to Mrs. Bryce, *Faithfully yours*

4878 · TO WILLIAM WOODVILLE ROCKHILL   *Roosevelt Mss.*

Oyster Bay, September 7, 1908

My dear Rockhill: Your letter containing the account of your extraordinary interview with the Dalai Lama struck me as so important from the standpoint of the British Government that I let Bryce show it to certain of the highest officials. I enclose you copy of his letter, from which you will see how much

[2] Charles F. Brooker and William L. Ward, both members of the Republican National Executive Committee, in late September received enlarged powers in the conduct of the campaign in the East by a reallocation of authority impelled in part by Roosevelt's intercession.

[1] This information was important to Viscount Morley in his capacity as Secretary of State for India.

it imprest them. If we can do a good turn to England in this matter I shall be glad; and if you find out anything as to what passes between the Lama and the Chinese at Peking, pray let me know about it in full.

Give my warm regards to Mrs. Rockhill and let me congratulate you again on your interview with the Dalai Lama.

With hearty thanks, *Sincerely yours*

4879 · TO CHARLES FREDERICK WELLER   *Roosevelt Mss.*

Oyster Bay, September 8, 1908

My dear Mr. Weller: [1] The National Capital should be a model city. It is so already in certain respects; and even in its less favored neighborhoods and among the "Neglected Neighbors" whom you describe, the problems, as you suggest, can be much more readily solved than in other great cities. The situation in Washington is such that it may readily be mastered if the people and the authorities will only set themselves at the task. I believe that your study will be helpful both in pointing out the evils which block the way and in suggesting remedial measures.

We of this country are just beginning to appreciate the social problems which have developed while our cities have been growing so marvelously and while our people have been overabsorbed in their industrial and commercial tasks. We are now becoming conscious of some of the unevenness which has naturally resulted from the rapidity of material growth, this overabsorption in material things; we are beginning to think of the neighbors and neighborhoods which have been neglected. In a democracy like ours, it is an ill thing for all of us, if any of us suffer from unwholesome surroundings or from lack of opportunity for good home life, good citizenship and useful industry.

It seems to me that your suggestions for the improvement of housing conditions in American cities are wise. Washington is not worse than other cities, but simply like them, in the fact that the living conditions of its less resourceful citizens need to be studied and improved. In appointing the Homes Commission I sought to begin for the National Capital such work as was accomplished for New York City by the several tenement house committees organized there at various times. Doubtless the work which has been inaugurated in Washington by the Homes Commission will need to be continued and extended, as you suggest, by a special philanthropic organization or by subsequent commissions officially appointed.

[1] Charles Frederick Weller, expert social service worker; active during his long career in positions of responsibility for the administration of charity and the formulation of social service policies in Chicago, Washington, Pittsburgh and New York; in 1908 executive secretary of the President's Homes Commission. Author of *Neglected Neighbors* (1909); later a founder of the Fellowship of Faiths and, by his own description, a lecturer on "Foreigners, Democracy, Peace and Brotherhood through Neighborliness."

I think that your stories of specific families and typical incidents will be more effective with general readers than the statistics and formal statements which usually characterize reports as to housing conditions. As Mr. James Bronson Reynolds has said, your book may well be considered "a study of a people." It will afford to anyone who reads it a larger and more sympathetic understanding of the problems and difficulties which beset those who live in "the alleys, tenements, and shanties" of the National Capital.

I know that you desire for your work no other return than the consciousness that it has been of service in improving the home life and enlarging the opportunities of these "Neglected Neighbors." To that end, I hope the book will receive the careful consideration of those persons, both in Washington and elsewhere, who may be able to help in the improvement of living conditions among the less-favored dwellers in our cities. *Very truly yours*

4880 · TO CONRAD KOHRS   *Roosevelt Mss.*

Oyster Bay, September 9, 1908

My dear Mr. Kohrs: [1] I have received your letter about the candidacy of Mr. Taft, the man who I feel is in an especial sense the representative of all that in which I most believe in political life.

Every good citizen should desire to see both prosperity and justice, prosperity and fair and righteous dealing as between man and man, obtain permanently in this great republic. As a people we are justly proud of our business industry, of our energy and intelligence in our work; and it is entirely right that we should ask ourselves as to any given course of conduct, "Will it be profitable?" But it is also no less emphatically true that the bulk of our people, the plain people who found in Abraham Lincoln their especial champion and spokesman, regard the question, "Is this morally right?" as even more important than the question, "Is this profitable?", when applied to any given course of conduct. Indeed, in the long run our people are sure to find that in all dealings, alike in the business and the political world, what is really profitable is that which is morally right. The last few years have seen a great awakening of the public conscience and the growth of a stern determination to do away with corruption and unfair dealing, political, economic, social. It is urgently necessary that this great reform movement should go on. But no reform movement is healthy if it goes on by spasms; if it is marked by periods of frenzied advance, followed, as such periods of frenzied advance must always be followed, by equally violent periods of reaction. The revolutionary and the reactionary really play into one another's hands, to the extent that each by his excesses necessarily tends to arouse such

[1] Conrad Kohrs had first known Roosevelt when they were both members of the Montana Stock Growers' Association. Since that time Kohrs had become a successful cattleman and locally prominent Republican. This long letter to him was released for publication in the morning papers of September 14.

disgust, such a feeling of revolt, in the minds of quiet people, as temporarily to restore the other to power. To permit the direction of our public affairs to fall alternately into the hands of revolutionaries and reactionaries, of the extreme radicals of unrest and of the bigoted conservatives who recognize no wrongs to remedy, would merely mean that the Nation had embarked on a feverish course of violent oscillation which would be fraught with great temporary trouble, and would produce no adequate good in the end. The true friend of reform, the true foe of abuses, is the man who steadily perseveres in righting wrongs, in warring against abuses, but whose character and training are such that he never promises what he cannot perform, that he always a little more than makes good what he does promise, and that, while steadily advancing, he never permits himself to be led into foolish excesses which would damage the very cause he champions. In Mr. Taft we have a man who combines all of these qualities to a degree which no other man in our public life since the Civil War has surpassed. To a flaming hatred of injustice, to a scorn of all that is base and mean, to a hearty sympathy with the opprest, he unites entire disinterestedness, courage both moral and physical of the very highest type, and a kindly generosity of nature which makes him feel that all of his fellow countrymen are in very truth his friends and brothers, that their interests are his, and that all his great qualities are to be spent with lavish freedom in their service. The honest man of means, the honest and law-abiding businessman, can feel safe in his hands because of the very fact that the dishonest man of great wealth, the man who swindles or robs his fellows, would not so much as dare to defend his evil-doing in Mr. Taft's presence. The honest wageworker, the honest laboring man, the honest farmer, the honest mechanic or small trader, or man of small means, can feel that in a peculiar sense Mr. Taft will be his representative because of the very fact that he has the same scorn for the demagog that he has for the corruptionist, and that he would front threats of personal violence from a mob with the unquailing and lofty indifference with which he would front the bitter anger of the wealthiest and most powerful corporations. Broad tho his sympathies are, there is in him not the slightest tinge of weakness. No consideration of personal interest, any more than of fear for his personal safety, could make him swerve a hair's breadth from the course which he regards as right and in the interest of the whole people.

I have naturally a peculiar interest in the success of Mr. Taft, and in seeing him backed by a majority in both houses of Congress which will heartily support his policies. For the last ten years, while I have been Governor of New York and President, I have been thrown into the closest intimacy with him, and he and I have on every essential point stood in heartiest agreement, shoulder to shoulder. We have the same views as to what is demanded by the National interest and honor, both within our own borders, and as regards the relations of this Nation with other Nations. There is no fight for decency and fair dealing which I have waged, in which I have not had his heartiest and most effective sympathy and support, and the policies for which I stand are his policies as much as mine.

It is not possible in the space of this letter to discuss all the many and infinitely varied questions of moment with which Mr. Taft as President would have to deal; let him be judged by what he has himself done, and by what the administration, in which he has played so conspicuous a part, has done. But to illustrate just what his attitude is, let me touch on two matters now prominent in the public mind.

Mr. Taft can be trusted to exact justice from the railroads for the very reason that he can be trusted to do justice to the railroads. The railroads are the chief instruments of interstate commerce in the country, and they can neither be held to a proper accountability on the one hand nor given proper protection on the other, save by the affirmative action of the Federal Government. The law as laid down by the Federal courts clearly shows that the States have not and cannot devise laws adequate to meet the problems caused by the great growth of the railroads doing an interstate commerce business, for more than four fifths of the business of the railroads is interstate, and under the constitution of the United States only the Federal Government can exercise control thereover. It is absolutely necessary that this control should be affirmative and thorogoing. All interstate business carried on by the great corporations should, in the interest of the whole people, be far more closely supervised than at present by the National Government; but this is especially true of the railroads, which cannot exist at all save by the exercise of powers granted them on behalf of the people, and which, therefore, should be held to a peculiar accountability to the people. It is in the interest of the people that they should not be permitted to do injustice; and it is no less to the interest of the people that they should not suffer injustice. Their prime purpose is to carry the commodities of the farmers and the businessmen; they could not be built save for the money contributed to them by their shareholders; they could not be run at all save for the money paid out in wages to the railroad employees; and, finally, they could not be run judiciously, or profitably to anyone, were it not for the employment by them of some masterful guiding intelligence, whether of one man or of a group of men. There are therefore several sets of interests to be considered. Each must receive proper consideration, and when any one of them selfishly demands exclusive consideration the demand must be refused. Along certain lines all of these groups have the same interests. It is to the interest of shipper, farmer, wageworker, businessman, honest shareholder, and honest manager alike that there should be economy, honesty, intelligence, and fair treatment of all. To put an effective stop to stock watering would be a benefit to everybody except the swindlers who profit by stock watering; it would benefit the honest shareholder because honest investments would not be brought into competition with mere paper; it would benefit the wageworker because when the money earned does not have to go in paying interest on watered capital, more of it is left, out of which to pay wages; it would benefit the shipper because when only honest stockholders have to be paid interest, rates need not be improperly raised; it would benefit the public because there would be ample money with which to give efficient service. Similarly, the prevention of favoritism as among shippers does no damage to anyone who is honest, and confers great good upon the smaller businessman and the farmer, whom it relieves of oppression. Again, such supervision of accounts and management as will prevent crookedness and oppression works good, directly or indirectly, to all honest people. Therefore everything that can be done along all these lines should be done; and no man's legitimate interest would thereby be hurt. But after this point has been reached great care must be exercised not to work injustice to one class in the effort to show favor to another class; and each class naturally tends to remember only its own needs. The stockholders must receive an ample return on their investments, or the railroads cannot be built and successfully maintained; and the rates to shippers and the wages to employees, from the highest to the lowest, must all be conditioned upon this fact. On the other hand, in a public service corporation we have no right to allow such excessive profits as will necessitate rates being unduly high and wages unduly low. Again, while in all proper ways rates must be kept low, we must always remember that we have no right and no justification to reduce them when the result is the reduction of the wages of the great army of railroad men. A fair working arrangement must be devised according to the needs of the several cases, so that profits, wages, and rates shall each be reasonable with reference to the other two — and in wages I include the properly large amounts which should always be paid to those whose masterful ability is required for the successful direction of great enterprises. Combinations which favor such an equitable arrangement should themselves be favored and not forbidden by law; altho they should be strictly supervised by the Government thru the Interstate Commerce Commission, which should have the power of passing summarily upon not only the question of the reduction but the raising of rates.

This railroad problem is itself one of the phases of one of the greatest and most intricate problems of our civilization; for its proper solution we need not merely honesty and courage, but judgment, good sense, and entire fairmindedness. Demagogy in such a matter is as certain to work evil as corruption itself. The man who promises to raise the wages of railroad employees to the highest point and at the same time to reduce rates to the lowest point is promising what neither he nor anyone else can perform; and if the effort to perform it were attempted disaster would result to both shipper and wageworker, and ruin to the business interests of the country. The man to trust in such a matter as this is the man who, like Judge Taft, does not promise too much, but who could not be swayed from the path of duty by any argument, by any consideration; who will wage relentless war on the successful wrongdoer among railroad men as among all other men; who will do all that can be done to secure legitimately low rates to shippers and absolute evenness among the rates thus secured; but who will neither promise nor attempt to secure rates so low that the wage-earner would lose his earnings and the shareholder, whose money built the road, his profits. He will not favor a ruinous experiment like government ownership of railways; he will stand against any kind of confiscation of honestly acquired property; but he will work effectively for the most efficient type of government supervision and control of railways, so as to secure just and fair treatment of the people as a whole.

What is here said as to his attitude on the railway question applies to the whole question of the trusts. He will promise nothing on this subject unless he firmly believes he can make his promise good. He will go into no chimerical movement to destroy all great business combinations; for this can only be done by destroying all modern business; but he will in practical fashion do everything possible to secure such efficient control, on behalf of the people as a whole, over these great combinations as will deprive them of the power to work evil. Mr. Taft's decision in the Addystone Pipe Line case while on the bench is proof, by deeds not by words, of the farsighted wisdom with which he serves the interests of the whole people even when those of the most powerful corporations are hostile thereto.

If there is one body of men more than another whose support I feel I have a right to challenge on behalf of Secretary Taft it is the body of wageworkers of the country. A stauncher friend, a fairer and truer representative, they cannot find within the borders of the United States. He will do everything in his power for them except to do that which is wrong; he will do wrong for no man, and therefore can be trusted by all men. During the ten years of my intimate acquaintance with him, since I have myself, as Governor and President, been obliged to deal practically with labor problems, he has been one of the men upon whose judgment and aid I could always rely in doing everything possible for the cause of the wageworker, of the man who works with his hands, or with both hands and head.

Mr. Taft has been attacked because of the injunctions he delivered while on the bench. I am content to rest his case on these very injunctions; I maintain that they show why all our people should be grateful to him and should feel it safe to entrust their dearest interests to him. Most assuredly he never has yielded and never will yield to threat or pressure of any sort, as little if it comes from labor as if it comes from capital; he will no more tolerate the violence of a mob than the corruption and oppression and arrogance of a corporation or of a wealthy man. He will not consent to limit the power of the courts to put a stop to wrongdoing wherever found. This very fact should make the labor people feel a peculiar confidence in him. He has incurred the bitter hostility of foolish and bigoted reactionaries by his frank criticism of the abuse of the power of injunction in labor disputes, and he is pledged to do all he can to put a stop to the abuses in the exercise of the power of injunction. He will never promise anything that he will not do all in his power to perform. He can always be trusted to do a little better than his word, and the fact that before election he will not promise the impossible is in itself a guaranty that after election all that is possible will be done.

His record as a judge makes the whole country his debtor. His actions and decisions are part of the great traditions of the bench. They guaranteed and set forth in striking fashion the rights of the general public as against the selfish interests of any class, whether of capitalists or of laborers. They set forth and stand by the rights of the wageworkers to organize and to strike, as unequivocally as they set forth and stand by the doctrine that no conduct will be tolerated that would spell destruction to the Nation as a whole. As for the attack upon his injunctions in labor disputes, made while he was on the bench, I ask that the injunctions be carefully examined. I ask that every responsible and fair-minded labor leader, every responsible and fair-minded member of a labor organization, read these injunctions for himself. If he will do so, instead of condemning them he will heartily approve of them and will recognize this further astonishing fact, that the principles laid down by Judge Taft in these very injunctions, which laboring people are asked to condemn, are themselves the very principles which are now embodied in the laws or practices of every responsible labor organization. No responsible organization would now hesitate to condemn the abuses against which Judge Taft's injunctions were aimed. The principles which he therein so wisely and fearlessly laid down serve as a charter of liberty for all of us, for wageworkers, for employers, for the general public; for they rest on the principle of fair dealing for all, of evenhanded justice for all. They mark the judge who rendered them as standing for the rights of the whole people; as far as daylight is from darkness, so far is such a judge from the time-server, the truckler to the mob, or the cringing tool of great, corrupt and corrupting corporations. Judge Taft on the bench — as since, in the Philippines, in Panama, in Cuba, in the War Department — showed himself to be a wise, a fearless, and an upright servant of the whole people, whose services to the whole people were beyond all price. Moreover, let all good citizens remember that he rendered these services, not when it was easy to do so, but when lawless violence was threatened, when malice domestic and civic disturbance threatened the whole fabric of our government and of civilization; his actions showed not only the highest kind of moral courage but of physical courage as well, for his life was freely and violently threatened.

Let all fair-minded men, wageworkers and capitalists alike, consider yet another fact. In one of his decisions upon the bench Judge Taft upheld in the strongest fashion, and for the first time gave full vitality to, the principle of the employers' liability for injuries done workmen. This was before any national law on the subject was enacted. Judge Taft's sense of right, his indignation against oppression in any form, against any attitude that is not fair and just, drove him to take a position which was violently condemned by shortsighted capitalists and employers of labor, which was so far in advance of the time that it was not generally upheld by the State courts, but which we are now embodying in the law of the land. Judge Taft was a leader, a pioneer, while on the bench, in the effort to get justice for the wageworker, in a jealous championship of his rights; and all upright and far-sighted laboring men should hold it to his credit that at the same time he fearlessly stood against the abuses of labor, just as he fearlessly stood against the abuses of capital. If elected, he has shown by his deeds that he will be President of no class, but of the people as a whole; he can be trusted to stand stoutly against the two real enemies of our democracy — against the man who to please one class would undermine the whole foundation of orderly liberty, and against the man who in the interest of another class would secure business prosperity by sacrificing every right of the working people.

I have striven as President to champion in every proper way the interests of the wageworker; for I regard the wageworker, excepting only the farmer, the tiller of the soil, as the man whose well-being is most essential to the healthy growth of this great nation. I would for no consideration advise the wageworker to do what I thought was against his interest. I ask his support for Mr. Taft exactly as I ask such support from every farsighted and right-thinking American citizen; because I believe with all my heart that nowhere within the borders of our great country can there be found another man who will as vigilantly and efficiently as Mr. Taft support the rights of the working man, as he will the rights of every man who in good faith strives to do his duty as an American citizen. He will protect the just rights of both rich and poor, and he will war relentlessly against lawlessness and injustice whether exercised on behalf of property or of labor.

On the bench Judge Taft showed the two qualities which make a great judge; wisdom and moral courage. They are also the two qualities which make a great President. *Sincerely yours*

4881 · TO WILLIAM BROWN MC KINLEY   *Roosevelt Mss.*

Oyster Bay, September 9, 1908

My dear Sir: I have received your letter of August 28th. I agree with all that you say as to the amount of affirmative and constructive legislation for the social and economic benefit of our people which has been accomplished by the Congress during the last seven years. The law establishing a national system of irrigation was of vital importance, and stands in its line as second only to the homestead law. The interstate commerce law has been amended so as to make it a new law, with three-fold the efficiency of the old law. The enactment of the pure food law was of almost or quite equal importance. The creation of the Department of Commerce and Labor, together with the creation of a Bureau of Corporations, which marks the beginning of Federal control over the huge corporations doing an interstate business, the employers' liability law, the safety appliance law, the law limiting the working hours of railway employees, the meat inspection law, the denatured alcohol law, the antirebate law, the laws increasing the powers of the Department of Justice in dealing with criminals of great wealth and power, the law making the Government liable for injuries to its employees, the laws under which the Panama Canal was acquired and is being built, the Philippines administered, and the navy developed, the laws creating a permanent Census Bureau and reforming the consular service and the system of naturalization, the law forbidding child labor in the District of Columbia, the law providing a commission under which our currency system can be put on a thoroly satisfactory basis, the laws for the proper administration of the forest service, the laws for the admission of Oklahoma and the development of Alaska, the great appropriations for the development of agriculture, the legal prohibition of campaign contributions from corporations — all these represent but a portion of what has been done by Congress, and form a record of substantial legislative achievement in harmony with the best and most progressive thought of our people. It is urgently necessary, from the standpoint of the public interest, to elect Mr. Taft, and a Republican Congress which will support him; and they seek election on a platform which specifically pledges the party, alike in its executive and legislative branches, to continue and develop the policies which have been not merely profest but acted upon during these seven years. These policies can be successfully carried thru only by the hearty co-operation of the President and the Congress in both its branches, and it is therefore peculiarly important that there should obtain such harmony between them. To fail to elect Mr. Taft would be a calamity to the country; and it would be folly while electing him, yet at the same time to elect a Congress hostile to him, a Congress which under the influence of partisan leadership would be certain to thwart and baffle him on every possible occasion. To elect Mr. Taft, and at the same time to elect a Congress pledged to support him, is the only way in which to perpetuate the policy of the Government as now carried on. I feel that all the aid that can be given to this policy by every good citizen should be given; for this is far more than a merely partisan matter.

Both your Committee, and the National Committee, of which Mr. Hitchcock is Chairman, are endeavoring to secure the active co-operation on the stump of Senators and Congressmen, party leaders and independent citizens generally. I most heartily join in urging the importance of such co-operation. I hope that every disinterested public servant, that every disinterested private citizen whose sole concern in politics is to have the right kind of man carry out the right kind of policy will join in backing up your Committee as well as the National Committee in this movement. No service is as effective, as valuable, as the disinterested service given in such manner by men whose one concern is for the triumph of the principles in which they believe; and I

appeal with all the strength there is in me to such men to give such support.[1]
Sincerely yours

4882 · TO HENRY CABOT LODGE   *Roosevelt Mss.*

Oyster Bay, September 9, 1908

Dear Cabot: You don't know how much I have had those ships with me this
summer![1] I have eaten and drunk and slept with them, so to speak. I originally gave the exact order which you now ask me to give, but I found that
in the law there were certain matters that had to be complied with. For
instance, there had to be a report by the Navy Department and by the people
at Panama. I went to the length of having Newberry down here in person,
so as to explain the whole situation to him. I found him most reasonable. I
will now write to Wright. I suppose the third survey of which you speak
is as to their value. We cannot of course pay an excessive amount — you
would not want us to pay it; we must (and ought to) obey the law. I think
we will get the thing thru all right, and you must rest assured that I have
kept my eye sharply upon it all summer. All I can with propriety do I will
do. *Faithfully yours*

4883 · TO MARK SULLIVAN   *Roosevelt Mss.*

Personal and Private   Oyster Bay, September 9, 1908

My dear Sullivan: I have been looking over the last number of *Collier's*, and
sometime or other I wish you and Hapgood could either come out here to
lunch or take lunch with me at the White House, for I would like to say one
or two things in connection with Hapgood's political articles[1] in that num-

---

[1] This letter was released for publication on September 21.

---

[1] Lodge had asked Roosevelt to hasten the purchase of two ships by the War Department from the Boston Steamship Company for the Isthmian Canal Commission.
In the previous session of Congress the senator had introduced an amendment to the
Sundry Civil Appropriations Bill authorizing the purchase of two ships of American
registry to carry cement, lumber, and other bulky materials. On the completion of
the canal they were to be transferred to the Navy to be used as colliers. The amendment, by stating that the ships should not be less than 9000 gross tons and yet
not exceed $1,550,000 in cost, limited the purchase to the *Shawmut* and *Tremont*,
two old ships which had been recently laid up by the Boston Steamship Company.
Goethals protested against the purchase, maintaining that the Canal Commission did
not need such ships and that in any case they were unfit for transporting heavy
materials. Newberry seconded Goethals' opposition. Nevertheless, Taft wrote Lodge
and Hale his emphatic approval of Lodge's amendment. Owing to Taft's commitment
in favor of the sale and Lodge's persistence in pushing through the transaction, the
Canal Commission became saddled with two comparatively useless ships; see Numbers 5017, 5018, 5035, 5036; Lodge, II, 315–316, 328; *Canal Record*, 2:121–122 (December 16, 1908).

---

[1] *Collier's* editorials, balanced rather than partisan, recognized some merits in Bryan's
views on labor, banking, and the regulation of trusts.

ber. But in the present letter I want to discuss the article you published by Jack London,[2] and especially the headlines of the article — my position being that of the South Carolina lawyer who, in the dark days shortly after the Civil War, finally protested to a reconstruction judge that he could live under bad law but that he could not live under bad Latin. In the headlines (to this article by Jack London) for which I suppose *Collier's* itself is responsible, he is described as "locating the President in the Ananias Club." Now neither you nor I regard falsehood as a jest, and therefore we neither of us regard an accusation of falsehood as a jest. If that headline were correct, *Collier's* would not be justified in making the effort it did to get me to write for it. Moreover, there is, as far as I am able to see, in Jack London's article not a line in which London says anything on which such a headline could be based. If there is I should be glad to have you point it out to me.

Now as for Jack London himself; and here again I want to speak to *Collier's* rather than to Jack London, altho of course you are perfectly welcome to show him this letter, with the distinct understanding, however, that I am not entering into a controversy with him but with *Collier's*; and that of a purely private, not public, nature. In my Presidential speeches and messages which Collier published, in Volume VI on pages 1333 to 1345, you will find what I said on nature faking and nature fakers, including London, and my concluding words were that my quarrel was not with these nature fakers "but with those who give them their chance" — "who, holding a position which entitles them to respect, yet condone and encourage such untruth." In the first place, read thru this article of mine and anything else that I have written and you will see at once that when London says that I state that animals do not reason, that all animals below man are automatons and perform actions only of two sorts, mechanical and reflex, and that in such actions no reasoning enters at all, and that man is the only animal that is capable of reasoning or ever does reason — when London says this he deliberately invents statements which I have never made and in which I do not believe. As a matter of fact, on this point I disagree with John Burroughs, my points of agreement with John Burroughs being my admiration for his accuracy of observation, and the way he can report his observations, and for his abhorrence of untruth. As a matter of fact, I believe that the higher mammals and birds have reasoning powers, which differ in degree rather than in kind from the lower reasoning powers of, for instance, the lower savages. London's statement as to my attitude on this point — a statement to which you give currency — is wholly without basis; and he cannot find, and nobody else can find, anything that I have written which forms a basis for it.

But this is not his only invention or misstatement. In my article I stated and proved (see page 1325) that London knew nothing whatever about wolves or lynxes; that his story *White Fang* would be excellent if it was avowedly put forth as a fable, but as realism it was nonsense, and mischie-

[2] Jack London, "The Other Animals," *Collier's*, 41:10–11, 25–26 (September 5, 1908).

vous nonsense to boot. I attributed his making misstatements simply to ignorance; but in this article in *Collier's* his misstatements are deliberate. They are not due to ignorance at all. Get his book *White Fang* to which I am about to refer, and open it at the pages I shall mention, comparing them with my article on the page I have given you, and with his article in *Collier's*. In the first place he says that I tried and condemned him because a big fighting bulldog whipped a wolf dog. I did not. I condemned him because his wolf (for the amount of dog in it, or indeed in its mother, is so small that Jack London continually alludes to both as wolves and not wolf dogs) and his bulldog fought in impossible fashion. He describes this huge wolf which kills all other wolves against which it is pitted and all other dogs — a wolf that can hamstring a horse or gut a steer — as ripping and slashing with long tearing strokes a score of times a bulldog a third its size without inflicting any serious injury upon the bulldog. Now this is simply nonsense. Two or three such bites would mean the death of the bulldog. I will make a comparison which will bring it home. It is possible, altho very improbable, that a feather-weight professional boxer, or say the champion heavyweight amateur boxer of a college or a theological institute, could knock out Jim Jeffries or John L. Sullivan when they were in full training. But it is not possible that the knockout could take place after Jeffries or Sullivan had a score of times knocked down said featherweight, or amateur heavyweight from a college or theological seminary, with blows striking them full on the point of the chin or over the heart. Such a description of a prize fight would be a purely fake description.

But this is small compared to Mr. London's second offense. He says that I claimed he was guilty of allowing a lynx to kill a wolf dog in a pitched battle, and that this was not true; that he never made such a statement in his story. Now turn to what I wrote on page 1325. What I say is that "London describes a great dog wolf being torn in pieces by a lucivee, a northern lynx." London denies this. Now turn to his book *White Fang*, page 83. He describes the she-wolf following a day-old trail of her mate, the great dog wolf. He goes on — "And she found him, or what remained of him, at the end of the trail. There were many signs of the battle that had been fought, and of the lynx's withdrawal to her lair after having won the victory." Mr. London should take the trouble to read what he himself has written before he again makes a denial of this type. A real nature observer, not a nature faker, James Sheldon, has just passed the winter in northern Alaska, and he caught or shot and weighed various lynxes, practically from the region London is supposed to discuss. The female lynx up there weighs barely twenty pounds; and London describes such an animal as tearing to pieces the huge fighting wolf six or seven times its weight. As a matter of fact, any capable fighting bull terrier would be an overmatch for such a lynx. I do not wonder that London did not like to admit having made such a statement, but

I am rather surprised at his having the effrontery to make such a denial in *Collier's*.

Now mind you, I have not the slightest intention of entering into any controversy on this subject with London. I would as soon think of discussing seriously with him any social or political reform. But it does seem to me that *Collier's* should be rather careful about admitting such an article into its columns, and of giving it such a headline as that I have above quoted. *Sincerely yours*

4884 · TO JAMES SCHOOLCRAFT SHERMAN   *Roosevelt Mss.*

Personal   Oyster Bay, September 9, 1908

My dear Sherman: Root wrote me making certain suggestions, which I thought admirable, in the way of enumerating some of the measures enacted by Congress during the last seven years. I think I was able thereby to strengthen what I said about Congress. I was not willing to say that I asked support for every nominal Republican Congressman, for there are three or four of them at least who, from the standpoint of the Republican party no less than of decent citizenship, are not entitled to any such support, men whose places it would have been a great advantage to us to have had filled by other people of almost any party during the last session of Congress. The people at National Headquarters felt very strongly that the letter should be split in two, and I split it accordingly.[1] I have adopted both of your suggestions — that of inserting "Republican" and that of striking out "disinterested public servants." I send you copy of the letter in its final form.

It is to me mere folly for our friends longer to oppose the renomination of Mr. Hughes. He must be renominated unless we are willing to face the possibility of grave disaster. *Sincerely yours*

4885 · TO A. H. FOX   *Roosevelt Mss.*

Oyster Bay, September 10, 1908

My dear Mr. Fox: When I wrote you I did not intend to take a shotgun to Africa. I find, however, that I would like to take such a gun, provided that at close quarters I could use it with ball also. In other words, I should like in case of an emergency to have it loaded with ball and use it as a spare gun for a lion. Now I have rather a pride in taking American rifles on this trip, and in the same way I should like to take an American gun; but of course you may have by this time decided that you do not care to repeat your very kind offer; in that event will you tell me what the cost of such a gun as I have described, twelve-bore and plain finish, would be? *Sincerely yours*

[1] See Numbers 4880, 4881.

[*Handwritten*] Of course the use with ball would be wholly exceptional; normally I should use it for geese, ducks, guinea fowl & etc.

4886 · TO HERBERT MYRICK

Roosevelt Mss.

Oyster Bay, September 10, 1908

My dear Mr. Myrick: [1] As unfortunately it is not in my power to be present at the dedication of your building at Springfield, I avail myself of this opportunity not only to wish you well on this occasion, but also to say a few words on the question of national co-operation in technical education, especially in agricultural education — a matter which I have so much at heart and for which your papers have so stoutly battled.

It is a matter of real gratification to all of us that you should be able now to dedicate your great building, for the Orange Judd agricultural papers have been managed so as to combine intelligent championship of the needs of the farm with successful handling of the enterprise itself as a business proposition. You have practically applied the principle of co-operation. Only once has your business been forced to reduce compensation — in the year 1894. I was both pleased and interested to know that on that occasion dividends were first reduced; then salaries, beginning with the head of the concern; and, finally, wages, but that the women were spared when the readjustment of wages began. Shortly after, wages were restored, then salaries, and finally, dividends. This recognizes the human element, the helpful idea, the principle of doing as one would be done by; the principle of genuine co-operation, a co-operation which in your case included agricultural labor, capital, and domestic economy. Such work can never be done in a merely sentimental spirit. It must represent sound, practical common sense, but it must also represent mutual confidence, helpfulness and service. I am glad to be told that in your case the result has proven profitable, alike to the coworker and the co-owner. It seems to me peculiarly valuable that a lesson like this should be taught by practical example to those engaged in farm work, as well as to those engaged in other occupations — and also to those whose work is in the homes. Self-help is the best help and makes the best citizenship; but the highest type of self-help is that which is combined with the right kind of helpfulness to others.

Now, in striving for co-operation between the National and State Governments and the farmers, for the uplifting of farm life, I am striving for exactly this principle, the principle of combining self-help with mutual helpfulness. Of course the prime thing to be done for the farmer, as for

[1] Herbert Myrick, president of the Orange Judd Company, versatile and energetic editor of several agricultural weeklies, editor also of *Good Housekeeping;* proponent of farmer co-operatives, subsidized agricultural education, and tariff protection for farm produce; author of *Co-operative Finance* (1912), *Rural Credits System for the United States* (1922), and, with his mother, of *Ode to the Organ, and Other Poems* (1926).

everyone else, is to help him to help himself. If he won't help himself, if he lies down on others and tries to make them carry him, we can rest assured that neither Nation, State, nor neighbors can permanently benefit him. Nevertheless, a helping hand is often of great service when extended even to those most capable of helping themselves. The individual, the community, the State, each must give an example of self-help; but groups of individuals and of States — and the largest group of all, the Nation — may all co-operate with advantage for their common interests. Perhaps this is especially true in trying to secure the conservation of our forests and waters, the protection of our streams from pollution, and the like. It is for this reason that I wish to see the Nation not only establish forest reserves wherever possible all thru the western States and Territories, but join in making the White Mountain region a forest reserve, just as it proposes to do with the Appalachian region.

We have been in the past, and we are yet, a people with whom agriculture has been the most important business. There never has been in history any movement comparable to the wonderful westward march of the hard-working American pioneer farmers, and of those who came after them, who have overspread this continent, who are now filling its remotest corners, and thanks to whom there are uninterrupted stretches of farm land from sea to sea, from the Gulf to the watershed of the Arctic Ocean. The rough wilderness has been subdued by those who in their veins blend in a common stream the blood of so many nations of the Old World. Thru that most wise economic statute, the homestead law, we have been enabled to develop the family farm, the most important and the most American of all our institutions; for our greatness as a people rests in no small degree upon the fact that instead of having here in the country districts a population of peasants on minute holdings, or else of tenants who work for large landowners, we have everywhere, as the typical American farm a medium-sized farm, tilled mainly or in large part by the owner himself and his sons.

But now that the more desirable areas of our public land have been settled, the homestead law does not meet the new conditions, and we adhere best to its spirit when we try to modify the system of landownership in such a way as to insure continuous progress and uplift so that the American farmer may not only obtain material prosperity, but on it build a high type of civilization. Important tho the city is, and fortunate tho it is that our cities have grown as they have done, it is still more important that the family farm, where the homemaking and the outdoor business are combined into a unit, should continue to grow. In every great crisis of our Government, and in all the slow, steady work between the crises which alone enables us to meet them when they do arise, it is the farming folk, the people of the country districts, who have shown themselves to be the backbone of the Nation.

Now, when I ask that the Nation co-operate with the States and with the farmers themselves for the steady growth and uplift of farm life, I am not so much asking that the State help the people as I am that it shall provide free opportunity for the people to continue their upward course thru self-help and associated effort.

The farms of America are worth some thirty billions of dollars, and their annual produce amounts to about eight billions. For this present year, 1908, the crops as a whole promise the largest aggregate in quantity, quality, and value ever produced in our history. This means that the six millions and over of farm families, more than thirty millions of farm people, are in a good position already; but I wish this position to be made sure and better.

The farm no longer produces the domestic manufactures of two generations ago, but merely the raw products of food and clothing; for the great improvements in agricultural production and in transportation have rendered it possible for one man on the farm now to produce food and clothing for three, whereas formerly it needed two to perform such a feat for themselves and a third. Thus with every improvement in crop and livestock production, an increased number of people are set free to work in other fashion for the building up of the permanent wealth of all of us, and for adding to the daily well-being, and meeting the intellectual and spiritual needs, of all of us.

It would be a very great wrong to allow our country people, who have prospered so much, whose welfare has meant so much for the Nation in the past, in any way to fall off from their former position. There is no need whatever for this happening. With wise care of our natural resources, our forests will grow better each year, our rivers more available for navigation, while the soil of our farms will improve with wise use instead of deteriorating. While as a Nation we are growing wealthier and wealthier, we should see that the schools and the roads — in short, all of what may be called the rural realty — should be improved. Here, as everywhere else, our prime object should be the development of the highest type of average citizen. Therefore, we should especially devote ourselves to the things that are of interest to the average citizen. The country school is therefore of even more importance than the higher college, thoroly alive tho we all should be to the vitalizing force which these higher colleges represent. There must be improvement in farm management; this is even now being brought about, partly by the work of the demonstration farmers, employed mostly at public expense, and partly by the joint action of the farmers themselves. So far as it is possible, we should strive for a common sense co-operation in institutions which shall do what the isolated farms cannot well do by themselves. As an example we can refer to the experiments recently carried on, by private individuals, and by the National Department of Agriculture, and by the State experiment stations, to show the extraordinary possibilities in improving the breeds of our food plants and of our animals.

In all of this we have to grapple with one fact which has made both the strength and the weakness of the American farmer, and that is, his isolation. This isolation implies a lack both of the pleasure and of the inspiration which come from closer contact between people, and from a well-developed organization for social pleasures, for religious life, for education. On the other hand, it is to this isolation more than to anything else that we owe the strength of character so typical of the American farmer, who lives under a peculiarly individualistic system in the management alike of the farm and of the farm home. The successfully managed family farm gives to the father, the mother, and the children better opportunities for useful work and for a happy life than any other occupation. Our object must be so far as practicable to do away with the disadvantages which are due to the isolation of the family farm, while conserving its many and great advantages. We wish to keep at its highest point the peculiarly American quality of individual efficiency, while at the same time bringing about that co-operation which indicates capacity in the mass. Both qualities can be used to increase the industrial and ethical proficiency of our people, for there is much the individual can only do for himself, and there is much also which must be done by all combined because the individual cannot do it. Our aim must be to supplement individualism on the farm and in the home with an associated effort in those country matters that require organized working together.

Moreover, we must not forget that there is a new phase of the matter of transportation, which is the problem of country homes for city workers. Cheap transportation, which has strengthened so much the tendency to city growth, is now helping to scatter the population of large cities for home purposes thru the adjacent country. As we come nearer the healthy ideal of a universal eight-hour day, and a closer association between employer and employee, there will be growth in the opportunity for city people to enjoy suburban homes.

Therefore we have to deal now, and will have to deal in the future, with a nation of families on the land; and our system of public education should be so broadened in its scope as to include not merely the traditional cultural studies, excellent and indispensable in their way, but also instruction relative to the farm, the trades, and the home. Our immediate purpose is to take the first steps in providing for the ninety-five per cent who are not now trained for a vocation, advantages corresponding to those enjoyed by the relatively few who are trained in the professional and technical schools. Industrial training, training which will fit a girl to do work in the home, which will fit a boy to work in the shop if in a city, to work on a farm if in the country, is the most important of all training aside from that which develops character; and it is a grave reproach to us as a nation that we have permitted our training to lead the children away from the farm and shop instead of toward them. We should try to provide the many with training in their professions, just as the few, the doctors, the ministers, the lawyers, are trained for their professions. In other words, the school system should be aimed primarily to fit the scholar for actual life rather than for a university. The exceptional individual, of the highest culture and most efficient training possible, is an important asset for the State. He should be encouraged and his development promoted; but this should not be done at the expense of all the other individuals who can do their work best on the farms and in the workshops; it is for the benefit of these individuals that our school system should be primarily shaped.

I thoroly believe that our people approve of the higher education; but I also believe that they are growing more and more to demand a reform in secondary schools which shall fit the ordinary scholar for the actual work of life. Therefore I believe that the National Government should take an active part in securing better educational methods in accordance with some such system as that outlined in the bill introduced in the last Congress by Mr. Davis.[2] It is not my place to speak of the details of such a bill, but in a general way I feel that the Nation should by making appropriations put a premium upon industrial, and especially agricultural, training in the State schools; the States themselves being required in these schools to contribute what is necessary for the ordinary training, and the expenditures for the National Government to be under the supervision of the Department of Agriculture. Teachers must be trained, or their teaching will not be adequate; and these teachers must then give vocational training to the scholars in the ordinary schools. The Nation would simply co-operate with the State or city or town, and what it thus gives would be applied to industrial, technical, agricultural training. The growth in the consolidated rural school which has in so many instances supplanted the old-time district school, offers the chance to do the best possible service by means of such a system as that outlined above. Where possible, the secondary agricultural schools should be in farm communities rather than in towns, and the training should be of the most practical character and such as will not only fit the scholars to do their part in farm work, but also fit them to enjoy in the fullest degree the pleasures and opportunities of country life. We should do everything that we can to give well-trained leaders to each country community. The United States Department of Agriculture would preserve an intimate relation to all these proposed agricultural high schools, as well as the branch stations connected with them, for the work that the Department does is steadily becoming of more and more consequence to the farmers.

All this simply means that the Nation ought to co-operate with the State to help the people help themselves thru better educational facilities, the schools being left wholly and directly under the control of the people thru their local authorities, but suggestion and general oversight as well as improvement being supplied by the experts employed by the nation, so that the children and the young men and girls in the smaller towns and in the country may have the educational facilities now only to be obtained in wealthier communities. This would merely be putting into effect that cardinal American doctrine of furnishing a reasonable equality of opportunity, of edu-

[2] Charles R. Davis.

cation and chance of development, to all our children, wherever they live and whatever may be their station in life. Such a federal co-operation in technical education will help in many ways. It will mean much for country life, for the life of the family farm, for the life of those city workers who seek landed homes in the country near the city in which they work. It will mean much along the lines of the great policy of the conservation of the natural resources of our land. Finally, it will mean much to the Nation of the future, because it will represent the effort to give exact justice, and an equal opportunity for development, to each of the boys and girls who in the future are to make up the Nation. *Sincerely yours*

4887 · TO GEORGE BRUCE CORTELYOU   *Roosevelt Mss.*

Oyster Bay, September 10, 1908

My dear Cortelyou: With all the latter part of your letter of the 8th I am in entire sympathy and will back up the service in every way in getting good men, and I will not permit red tape to interfere with it; but it is not possible to permit the regulations of the Commission to be evaded by having classified employees resign in order to do political work, and then be reinstated. When men are in the classified service they are supposed to be shielded because of its nonpartisan character, and they must not in their turn trespass on the domain of politics. Above all things I want to keep clear of hypocrisy in this matter. Cleveland was led into absolutely hypocritical professions and conduct both because he made sweeping promises and issued sweeping orders applying to everybody, classified and unclassified alike, and then did not live up to them even as regards the classified places. My order applies only to the classified places, but as regards those it will have to be carried out absolutely. *Sincerely yours*

4888 · TO JOSEPH BUCKLIN BISHOP   *Roosevelt Mss.*

Personal   Oyster Bay, September 10, 1908

My dear Bishop: I am glad you approve of the way I handled the Cleveland business.[1] Between ourselves, I haven't a doubt that under the pressure of the Constitution Club and similar outfits he did deviate from the truth in the matter, and then Nelson doubtless deviated still further on his own account. So far as I know, there hasn't a man peeped since the letters were published.

I look forward to seeing the Colonel.

With love to dear Mrs. Bishop, *Faithfully yours*

[1] By the publication of No. 4833 in the *Outlook*.

Oyster Bay, September 10, 1908

My dear White: Yes, I sincerely mourn Speck's loss, tho I cannot be sorry for the gallant little fellow himself, for life was one long torture for him. I have never met a man for whom I had a higher respect or regard. It is very hard on the Baroness.

Moreover, as you say, it is a real loss for the two countries. I shall keep Lancken in mind in the very improbable event I am given any chance to say anything in the matter.[1]

I intend to come out from East Africa by Khartoum, and have been in communication with Wingate,[2] who has been more than nice about everything. I only hope the British East Africa people will be as pleasant as he has been. Curzon has written me, on behalf of the authorities at Oxford, to ask me to deliver the Romanes lecture there and to get the same kind of degree, whatever it was, that they gave the Kaiser. I have accepted for sometime in May, 1910, which will be a month or six weeks after I have left Africa. When I am in England I suppose I shall be informally presented to the King. I shall be a private citizen then, and of course can only meet him as a private citizen — and in addition, I should greatly resent being treated as anything else, for I am no hanger-on to the shreds of departing greatness and when I leave the office I leave it completely and entirely. Now, I shall probably spend a few weeks in Europe before I reach England. I wish to travel as quietly as possible and simply see, for instance, the hill towns of Italy, certain country districts of France, and the like. If I could avoid seeing any sovereign I should like to do so, but if this would make me look churlish, or cause trouble in any way, why of course I shall be presented, trusting that the presentation will be informal and that under no circumstances will I be given a formal entertainment such as a dinner, &c. Now I have been much puzzled about the Kaiser — I have had a very pleasant correspondence with him at times, and there is much about him that I admire. On the other hand I would not of my own accord care to go to see him, for Berlin is out of my way and I will not put myself in an attitude of going to any place for the sake of being received by the man in authority. If he should wish to see me and should express that wish, I would go to Berlin and see him, but not otherwise; and the thing that puzzles me is how to avoid hurting his feelings by seeing the King of England and not him, and on the other hand not give him the erroneous impression that I would like to have him, as a favor to me, allow me to come to Berlin to pay him my respects. *Sincerely yours*

---

[1] The new German ambassador to the United States, selected without reference to Roosevelt's wishes, was Count Johann H. A. von Bernstorff.

[2] General Sir Francis Reginald Wingate, G.C.B., G.C.V.O., K.C.B., K.C.M.G., G.B.E., C.B., D.S.O., D.C.L., LL.D., Governor-General of the Sudan and Sirdar of Egypt, was, of all the European colonial officials in Africa, the most active in making arrangements for Roosevelt's trip.

Oyster Bay, September 11, 1908

Dear Will: Henry Beach Needham, who of course is now a wild supporter of yours, sends me some suggestions about your speech-making which I enclose to you. Hit them hard, old man! Why not call attention to Bryan's insincerity in saying he was my heir when without any protest he practically made as his own Clayton's speech at the Denver convention,[1] which was full of the foulest assault upon me. Let the audience see you smile *always*, because I feel that your nature shines out so transparently when you do smile — you big, generous, high-minded fellow. Moreover let them realize the truth, which is that for all your gentleness and kindliness and generous good nature, there never existed a man who was a better fighter when the need arose. The trouble is that you would always rather fight for a principle or for a friend then for yourself. Now hit at them; challenge Bryan on his record. Ask that you be judged by your record, and dare Bryan to stand on his.

Good luck to you, and love to dear Mrs. Taft. *Ever yours*

Personal   Oyster Bay, September 11, 1908

Dear Needham: I thank you for your letter of the 9th. I wish you would tell Taft just what you tell me. I have sent him your postscript, which seems to me to be admirable.

Now what I am about to say you must keep very quiet about. I have had in mind just exactly the considerations you mention. I did not include in my letter about Taft what I had to say about Congress, because I have thought the two campaigns should be kept distinct. I have positively refused to give a specific endorsement to the last Congress, or to say that all the Congressmen should be re-elected. I have simply said what I regard as the truth, that during the seven years as a whole the record was excellent, and that Taft could not do efficient work if a hostile — that is, a Democratic — Congress was elected. You know as well as I do that while I did not always get what I ought to have gotten from Cannon and his associates, I was always sure to get hostile action from Williams, Culberson, Tillman and that crowd. If a Democratic Congress is elected this time everything stops. Look at Clayton's address at the Denver

---

[1] Henry D. Clayton, Democratic congressman from Alabama, 1897–1914, sponsor of the Clayton Antitrust Act of 1914, in 1908 permanent chairman of the Democratic National Convention, had attacked Roosevelt in a speech filled with sentences such as this one: "The nomination of his would-be successor was largely accomplished by the use of official patronage and coarse machine methods and has delighted the chief apostle of strenuosity, and, at the same time, has not perturbed the conscience of the one-time civil service reformer, now the boss, an adept in the bestowal of public plunder and forgetful of all his resounding moral commonplaces."

convention if you desire to see how they will act the minute they get a chance. *Faithfully yours*

P.S. When I gave my approval to your writing the Panama articles for the magazines I assumed that you would confine them to conditions on the Isthmus. I am now informed that you intend to make an attack on the conditions on the Mesabi Range. I trust you will not do this without first having a full talk with me.

4892 · TO SAMUEL BALDWIN MARKS YOUNG *Roosevelt Mss.*

Oyster Bay, September 12, 1908

My dear General Young: I am interested and concerned with your letter and the enclosure.[1] I am sorry to say that it simply strengthens the impression that I had already gained. I fear that the only solution is to take the army out of the Park and have rangers of the McBride type do all the work. I shall take it up with Garfield.

With regards to Mrs. Young, believe me, *Faithfully yours*

4893 · TO GEORGE NATHANIEL CURZON *Roosevelt Mss.*

Oyster Bay, September 12, 1908

My dear Curzon: Surely no man was ever asked to do a pleasant thing in such a pleasant way as you have asked me! Indeed I hope I can visit you, as you so kindly suggest; but as yet I dare not make engagements, for I do not know enough of my plans. By the way, at Oxford I do hope I shall be able to see certain men with whose books I am familiar — Oman, who wrote the *Art of War;* Murray, whose History of the Greek Epic I have just finished; Ridgeway, the early Greek man;[1] and a number like them.

[1] Young had written about the sensational robbery of August 24 in Yellowstone Park which received nation-wide attention. In the authentic tradition of the Old West a single man had held up eight carriages and taken over $2000 from 125 park visitors. The victims, claiming that the army guards had been grossly negligent in their duty, had petitioned the government to redeem their losses. This incident underlined the inability of the army detachment at Yellowstone to police the park adequately.

In contrast with the Army's ineffectiveness the park's few civilian rangers, like the veteran scout, James McBride, had been doing excellent work in the prevention of poaching and forest fires and in the care of wild game. Roosevelt first planned to remove the soldiers and place a larger number of such rangers under Young's command. He found, however, that he did not have authority to issue such an order; see No. 4950. In his annual message to Congress, therefore, he urged the creation of a corps of civilian rangers to police and administer all national parks. Congress, though failing to act at this session, finally in 1915 adopted Roosevelt's suggestion.

[1] These Oxford scholars were Charles W. C. Oman, Gilbert Murray, and William Ridgeway.

Even Africa cannot supply anything better than *Ovis Poli,* rhinoceros, tiger, and bison, and I shall be glad indeed if I can get anything as good. I shall be very much interested in the reserve question, and I quite appreciate the two sides of it of which you speak. My feeling about those reserves is that we should not attempt too much, but that a reasonable number will be supported by popular opinion — even by the somewhat narrow and selfish judgment of the settler who is engaged in the very hard business of trying to make a living in a new country. The communities around the Yellowstone Park reserve, for instance, as a whole now take a real pride in the preservation of the game.

I think I am working out in my mind the kind of lecture I shall give. Would it be convenient if I made it about the middle of May?

Poor Speck! I could not be sorry for his death, because life had become one long torture to him, but I mourn his loss. He was, just as you say, a chivalric friend and a loyal and devoted public servant, and in addition, a gallant soldier. Have you ever read in Archibald Forbes' last book the chapter on "the pig-dog" in connection with the Franco-Prussian War? Speck is the hero of it. He was one of the best rifle shots and pistol shots I ever met. From the larger standpoint I sincerely regret his death, because he not only did all he could to promote good feeling between the United States and Germany, but he was one of the men who in every way deprecated and tried to prevent the growth in Germany of a feeling hostile to England. *Sincerely yours*

4894 · TO SAMUEL SCOTT SLATER   *Roosevelt Mss.*

Oyster Bay, September 12, 1908

My dear Senator Slater:[1] I shall have an investigation made of your charges; but let me relieve your mind on one point. You say that a certain engineer was given an opportunity to see "the errors and woeful extravagance practiced on the Isthmus." This is simple nonsense, and anyone who has told you so knows it. There have been no errors of consequence, and no woeful extravagance on the Isthmus, and any of the people you mention can go ahead and publish every magazine article they wish for all I care. It will reflect upon them, and not damage the administration or the Panama Canal people the least little particle. The work has been done extraordinarily well, as everyone who is both honest and competent and who knows anything whatever of the subject will gladly admit. I regret that you should embody a statement like this in your letter, which of course goes to the War Department for full action.[2] *Sincerely yours*

[1] A New York lawyer and businessman, Slater had been a Republican assemblyman during Roosevelt's governorship.
[2] The War Department found nothing to substantiate Slater's charges.

Oyster Bay, September 14, 1908

Dear Bonaparte: I have not the slightest question but that you are right about Judge Grosscup, and I hope that you will go ahead and prepare your brief to sustain the certiorari motion so that it will be an effective rejoinder.[1]

I have asked Cortelyou to allow Goldsborough[2] to do as you suggest unless there is serious objection. *Sincerely yours*

4896 · TO WILLIAM HOWARD TAFT   *Roosevelt Mss.*

Personal   Oyster Bay, September 14, 1908

Dear Will: I send you this article from Jermane,[1] a strong friend of yours, with some hesitation. The folly of mankind is difficult to fathom; it would seem incredible that anyone would care one way or the other about your playing golf, but do you know I have received literally hundreds of letters from the West protesting about it, some of them from men who themselves object, but more of them from men who do not object to it in the least, but who are convinced that it was having a bad effect. I think it will all vanish now, for I don't suppose you will have the chance to play until after election, and whether you have the chance or not, I hope you won't.* I am glad that Jones does not think you ought to speak on the religious business in the campaign at all. There I entirely agree with him. I also enclose a letter from Sleicher, with an article by Harvey which I think may help us among the Jews.[2]

In New York I think things are all right. Hughes will be nominated ⟨without any difficulty, probably without any opposition⟩ but only because we have forced his nomination. Indeed I think all the East is all right, altho I should not be in the least surprised if we had hard sledding in the State election in Maine tomorrow. I think we shall carry it, but by a small margin.

Lawrence Murray is taking up the guaranty of bank deposits business[3] and is to write a strong article about it. We have the railroad employees very much in our minds and I think we are handling them all right. I saw Medill McCormick and got him to go in and talk like a Dutch Uncle to Hitchcock about the need of putting the best men in charge of the Chicago headquarters.

---

[1] The Supreme Court, in November 1908, sustaining the government's application for a writ of certiorari, permitted a retrial of the Standard Oil of Indiana case; see No. 4819, note 2.

[2] Phillips L. Goldsborough, a Maryland delegate at the 1908 Republican convention.

---

[1] William Wallace Jermane, Cincinnati-born journalist, since 1889 chief of the Washington bureau of the Seattle *Daily News*.

[2] Charles M. Harvey, "What the Jew Owes to the Republican Party," *Leslie's Weekly*, 107:302 (September 24, 1908), one of a series of articles in which Harvey, obviously hoping that the party would collect, defined also the debt of farmers, labor, Negroes, and businessmen to the Republicans.

[3] Lawrence O. Murray had been Comptroller of the Currency since April 1908.

I do not think there is any danger, but I do not want to see any chances taken. *Ever yours*

* It is just like my tennis; I never let any ⟨people⟩ friends advertise my tennis, and never let a photo of me in tennis costume appear.

4897 · TO ELIHU ROOT   *Roosevelt Mss.*

Telegram   Oyster Bay, September 14, 1908

Your speech is really great[1] and ranks with your Canton speech eight years ago. I think it will fix Hughes' renomination all right; but let me know at once if you think there should be a message from me on the subject. I authorize you to quote me as being most strongly in favor of the renomination of Governor Hughes if you find it desirable to do so.

4898 · TO ELIHU ROOT   *Roosevelt Mss.*

Telegram   Oyster Bay, September 14, 1908

I do not think anything from Taft should be used. It might make the organization men turn against the Presidential ticket and let everything go by default. I hope you will make it clear to the organization leaders, on my behalf, and of course I am sure on your own also, that what we are doing is in no sense an attack on them and that we do not intend to sanction a general smash at them. Of course between ourselves you and I must freely admit that Hughes' attitude toward many of these organization men has been unwarranted and wanton. But the very fact that we do not sympathize with his attitude toward these men should make these men pay heed to us when we tell them that it is vital to their own interest, because it is vital to the interest of the republican party, that Hughes should be renominated. Say to them that no other nomination will meet the needs of the situation as it has developed in both the nation and the state.[1] If necessary to make any statement will you yourself publish

---

[1] In striking the keynote in the New York Republican convention at Saratoga on September 14, Root began with a tribute to Governor Hughes and his administration. His reference to Hughes provoked cheering from the gallery and the New York County delegates but left the upstate representatives unmoved. In most of his speech Root concentrated on national affairs, praising Roosevelt's policies and Taft's abilities, and attacking Bryan's record and platform.

---

[1] Root had wired Roosevelt from Saratoga that the anti-Hughes leaders were working aggressively to concentrate the feeling against Hughes in favor of some other candidate. This scheme had some chance for success; although Root had refused to run, Cortelyou, Butler, and David J. Hill were then under consideration. "I think," Root reported, "you better send a statement of your position framed with view to be given out if found advisable although I hate to have it done. I have a telegram from Taft intended to be used. Do you think it wise to bring him into the row?"

Taft was brought in indirectly. Hitchcock telegraphed Root that western Republican leaders felt that the failure to renominate Hughes would jeopardize the national ticket. Loeb from Oyster Bay released a similar statement from Roosevelt, thus obviating the need for Root to use the message the President had sent him.

the following, and if you think it wise you can of course publish it immediately:

I will of course gladly answer your request for my views. I most emphatically disclaim any desire to dictate the nomination of anyone; but I am a citizen of the State of New York, vitally interested in her welfare, and I am also a member of the republican party, anxious to see it succeed not only in the State but in the nation. I have for the last two months made diligent inquiry with an entirely unprejudiced mind to find out the views of her citizens generally as to the renomination of Mr. Hughes. As a result of painstaking and conscientious effort thus to find out the facts, I am convinced that a majority of the members of our party, and I believe a majority of the citizens of the state without regard to party, wish to see Mr. Hughes renominated, and I think it would be a grave mistake for the leaders of our party, now in convention assembled, to disregard this wish of the majority. I have freely expressed this view to any persons who have sought my advice.

4899 · TO KERMIT ROOSEVELT   *Roosevelt Mss.*

Oyster Bay, September 14, 1908

Dearest Kermit: I enclose you the letters of Selous and Buxton, and a copy of a letter from Sir Reginald Wingate. I am still inclined to agree with Selous that we ought to have a man to take care of the caravan, but I have not yet decided. Evidently we will have to go into Belgian territory after white rhinoceros. I am glad Selous has cut out the silly superfluities that were put in the list of our equipment. The Winchester rifles have come, and I shall practice with them tomorrow. Mr. Spring Rice has been writing some real Mrs. Gummidge letters to Mother about the trip, saying how much he disapproves of it, and expatiating upon the dangers from wild beasts, from sleeping sickness, the black fever, and the like. I was immensely amused the other day to see an article in the Philadelphia *Ledger* in which the writer stated that as I had had a very picturesque career, and as it was probably now at an end, it would really be a fitting, and on the whole a happy, conclusion if I came to my death in some striking way on the African trip! I do not think Mother thought it quite as humorous as I did.

Today we celebrated Ted's birthday by a picnic at Jaynes Hill. Mother and I rode over, Archie accompanying us on Betsey. Phil and Ethel rode together; Cornelia was driven by Ted in the East Williston cart; and the rest came in wagons. It was just like one of the old-time picnics and we all missed you.

I am very much pleased at the spirit in which Ted is approaching his work. He goes to the factory on October 1st,[1] and he has made up his mind to four

---

These pronouncements punctured the efforts of Hughes's opponents. The die-hards united on Speaker Wadsworth but on the first ballot Hughes won easily.

---

[1] Ted's first job was at the Hartford Carpet Corporation in Thompsonville, Connecticut.

years' steady grind, at least, and he is absorbed in the purpose to make good. I believe he will.

Mother went in town for a couple of days last week and Ted and I were alone. We played tennis and rode together, and I had some thoroly satisfactory talks with him. Of course it is never possible to be certain about success, but I think that Ted is starting with the right spirit anyhow.

Archie goes back to school tomorrow, and the house is already beginning to look very ghostly with all the heads and pictures and bookcases done up in white. Summer has gone, and there is something of the sharpness of fall in the weather already.

With love to Mr. Fergie, and whoever of my friends you are now with. *Your devoted father*

[*Handwritten*] P.S. Your letter has come just as I sign this; you must be having great fun.

4900 · TO VICTOR HOWARD METCALF   *Roosevelt Mss.*

Oyster Bay, September 15, 1908

My dear Metcalf: I should like to have tentative plans of new battleships mounting fourteen-inch guns prepared as soon as possible, unless they are already in course of preparation.[1] These plans I desire to have considered in conference by carefully selected officers, including some young officers of the stamp of those taking part in the conference at Newport. I think it desirable that soon after Congress meets we should be prepared to ask for an appropriation for battleships of a well-defined type, and that this type should be very superior to anything produced or contemplated abroad. *Faithfully yours*

4901 · TO LYMAN ABBOTT   *Roosevelt Mss.*

Oyster Bay, September 15, 1908

My dear Dr. Abbott: You should know for your own information, and if you deem it advisable, for whatever use you choose to make of it in *The Outlook*, of just the Hughes situation.[1] It gives an exact measure of the wisdom of the *Evening Post* style of mugwump and the *Sun* type of organ of the plutocracy. You will remember of course that these people started Hughes in as Governor with the idea that he should make a great show of absolute contrast to me, and that in particular he should not try in any way to interfere with or "dictate to" the Legislature. He assumed the latter position in various statements, and

[1] See Numbers 4865, 5022.

[1] Abbott chose to use very little of the information in this letter in the *Outlook*, but his editorial on Hughes's renomination advanced, in quieter tone, the President's view on Hughes's relations with the organization; *Outlook*, 90:137-138 (September 26, 1908).

also assumed that it was not his business to co-ordinate with anyone, that he would not try to work in conjunction with the President and did not wish to have the President work in conjunction with him; that he would not advise Parsons for or against an alliance with Hearst, &c., &c. There was an element of comedy in this in any event, because Hughes was nominated as Governor only because I, as President, insisted he should be. But there is a still further element of comedy in the fact that his whole campaign, the whole need of having him renominated, now rests upon his active effort to get the Legislature to pass certain laws. He has been obliged to come in this respect precisely to my position, a position to which he said he would not come. Of course only damage came from his shirking his duties as a party leader by refusing to tell Parsons that he ought not to go into the Hearst alliance. People have spoken of my being indignant because Hughes, when I sought to aid him in one of his gubernatorial fights rejected my aid, to the great delight of the *Evening Post*, *Sun*, Springfield *Republican*, and the like. I *was* indignant; but not in the least because of personal feeling. My indignation sprang from the fact that it was an evidence of just the kind of folly which I have so often seen mar the efforts of good people to accomplish political work worth doing. In politics wicked people are apt to accomplish so much because they work together; whereas, in too many cases, a good man will start in eager to be "independent," and stand alone with the firm determination primarily to save his own soul — to keep himself above criticism instead of bending his whole energy to serving the country, with the aid of anyone who will help, and not thinking of himself save in a wholly subordinate way. Mr. Hughes was very anxious that he should be regarded as immaculate by the *Evening Post* stamp of people, and to this end he entirely subordinated the question of how to accomplish most for the State. It of course stands to reason that a President and a Governor who are working for worthy ends, if they work together, receive each of them added strength. The proposition is so elementary that it ought not to be necessary to point it out. For the Governor to try to stand aloof can do nothing save please his vanity by making him think he is "independent."

Moreover, Mr. Hughes followed out the mugwump theory in other ways. He had been elected and could only have been elected by the sustained effort and hard work of the Republican party leaders. He was very glad to accept their aid before election. Now this aid entailed no obligation of any kind on the part of Mr. Hughes to do anything that was not for the interest of the public. «It was his» duty to refuse to listen to any man, no matter how useful that man had been, if he asked anything wrong; but according to my view it was no less his duty to refuse to jeopardize his power for good, and to jeopardize the cause of honest politics by wantonly insulting and wronging men who were active in politics merely because they *were* active in politics. Yet this course of wanton insult was the exact one he followed. He was just as wanton in insulting thoroly good fellows like Parsons, as when he had to deal with men whose motives he might legitimately suspect. In each case he was wrong. His aim should have been to guide Parsons, to prevent him from making mistakes like the alliance with Hearst, and to help him in every proper way, as being an honest man engaged in the incredibly difficult task of trying to make a big political organization in the greatest city in the country, both efficient and respectable. Hughes followed exactly the reverse course, and honest politicians, men who not only wanted nothing improper but wanted nothing at all, were just as much outraged by his conduct as the dishonest ones. He got of course the rather cheap satisfaction of being enthusiastically praised by the *Evening Post* whenever he committed a needless act of irritation in connection with some man who had been ⟨busy⟩ disinterestedly active in politics. But the damage he did far offset whatever good came from this gratification.

His more foolish adherents — men like Nicholas Murray Butler, for instance, not to speak of the New York *Evening Post* — were fatuously sure that this course rendered him impregnable, and especially rendered him impregnable as against me, for they hoped to build him up as my antitype. They were all certain that he could get every delegate from New York for the presidency and were very severe upon me because of my efforts on behalf of Taft; and they were afterwards certain that he could be renominated for Governor without any help from me, and rather hoped that I would be against him so as to emphasize his triumph.

Well, the result has been what you have seen. He had no strength at all for the Presidency. I did not think it wise from a political standpoint that his friends should feel that the New York candidate was slighted, and therefore I exerted myself, and had to exert myself hard, to prevent there being a great majority of the New York delegates against him out at Chicago. Even as it was I could not prevent his losing a dozen; but he would not have had much more than a dozen for him if I had not interfered to put a stop to the fight against him. Then we came to the gubernatorial campaign. I think Hughes has been guilty of grave errors, and errors of a kind that permanently hurt in the effort to achieve good government, but I believe that he has been an honest man and tho the evils he has fought have not been the greatest evils, nor needed the greatest courage to fight them, still he has done fairly good work and has been on the whole a good Governor; and after making the most careful investigation to find out about popular feeling both here and outside of the State, I came to the conclusion that on every account he ought to be renominated. I at first very sincerely hoped that I would not have to take a hand in the matter. It soon became evident, however, that unless I took an active and resolute part Hughes would be beaten in the State convention, overwhelmingly, and probably would not have over a quarter of the delegates. This I felt would be unfortunate from the public standpoint, and might prove a grave calamity from a party standpoint, and I was therefore forced to turn in and take an active hand in bringing about his renomination. I can more truthfully be said to have dictated his nomination as Governor than Taft's as President; and taking each nomination in its degree, I did not have to work as hard for Taft as for Hughes — and in Taft's case I was *obliged* to work, because the only way I could prevent my own nomination was by securing Taft's. Now I have secured Hughes' renomination. He would not have been renominated, and he would not have come anywhere near a re-nomination, if I had not taken this active part for him; in other words, if I had not possest the political power which the *Evening Post* has glorified Hughes for not possessing, Hughes would not now be the candidate, and he owes his candidacy purely to the fact that I had and exercised this power on his behalf. I did it at the cost of incurring much hostility from among the organization men who are my friends, and who have warned me that Hughes will do everything he can to upset me; all the more because he has a nature which resents the necessity of feeling gratitude. To this I have always answered that they could imagine nothing as to which I was more profoundly indifferent. I have not the slightest expectation of ever being a candidate for anything again. I shall certainly never request anything from Mr. Hughes; and while I shall keep in as close touch with the party organization of this State as possible, I shall do it merely as a part of the effort to keep things straight and decent and at the same time practical and efficient. But what a commentary the whole affair has been upon the *Evening Post* theory of politics.

I so enjoyed Lawrence's coming out here to lunch the other day, but I wish you could have come too. I have three or four articles which I am preparing for *The Outlook,* to be given to you before I get thru my Presidential term, altho to be used afterwards. In a couple of months I shall send them to you for any suggestions or corrections you would like. *Faithfully yours*

4902 · TO OSCAR SOLOMON STRAUS   *Roosevelt Mss.*

Oyster Bay, September 15, 1908

My dear Straus: Please show this letter to Neill. Senator Penrose may have gone thru the form of offering the position to Hayes, or Duncan, or Prester John if he can find him; and every other Senator, and every other Congressman, and all the potentates of Central Asia and Africa can likewise offer the position if they wish to amuse themselves; but no human being has had any authority from me to offer it, and it will be handled purely by me and by no one else. As a matter of fact my intention has been to give it to Keefe; and ordinarily I would be very glad to give another position to Duncan, such as one in connection with the Panama Commission, as I think him a square man. But of course if what I hear is correct, that Duncan has been backing up Gompers, he will have no position from me. Keefe is a man of unusual ability, and I will stand by him. This information can be given to both Mitchell and Keefe, but of course it must be understood that I do not promise anything and will reach no final decision until after the election.[1] *Sincerely yours*

4903 · TO SAMUEL BALDWIN MARKS YOUNG   *Roosevelt Mss.*

Oyster Bay, September 15, 1908

My dear General Young: I am informed that they have at Mammoth Hot Springs a fountain with a bronze cherub like the enclosed. A more ridiculous and incongruous thing cannot be imagined. Will you have it removed forthwith?

The inquiries I am making convince me that what we need in the Yellowstone Park is to have you as Superintendent with a purely civilian force composed of men like McBride. I am going over the whole matter with Garfield on my return to Washington next week. *Sincerely yours*

4904 · TO CECIL ARTHUR SPRING RICE   *Roosevelt Mss.*

Oyster Bay, September 17, 1908

Dear Cecil: Oh, you beloved Mrs. Gummidge! If you feel as melancholy over my trip in Africa as you do over the future of the race generally, at least you must not share the feeling too fully with Mrs. Roosevelt. I laughed until I almost cried over your sending her the pamphlet upon the "sleeping sickness," and explaining in your letter that it was perfectly possible that I would not die of that, because, (in the event of my not previously being eaten by a lion or crocodile, or killed by an infuriated elephant or buffalo) malarial fever or a tribe of enraged savages might take me off before the sleeping sickness got at me! I am bound to say, however, that the letter gave Mrs. Roosevelt a keen tho melancholy enjoyment, and she will now have the feeling that she is justified in a Roman-matron-like attitude of heroically bidding me to my death when I sail in a well-equipped steamer for an entirely comfortable and mild little hunting trip.

Seriously, both of us were really touched and pleased with your letters and with your thought of me. I feel excessively melancholy at being separated for so long from Mrs. Roosevelt, and I shall be so homesick, especially when, as I suppose will be the case, I have a slight attack of fever or something of

[1] In accordance with the partisan criterion here defined, Roosevelt in 1909 appointed Daniel J. Keefe Commissioner General of Immigration to replace Frank P. Sargent, who had died. Both Keefe and James Duncan had, with Gompers, presented labor's case to the Republican platform committee. Both were active members of the executive council of the A.F. of L., of the National Civic Federation, and of the Republican party. Duncan, however, because of the injunction issue, supported Bryan in 1908, while Keefe stood behind Taft. John William Hayes, editor of the *Journal of the Knights of Labor* and general master workman of that order, like Keefe both supported Taft and aspired to succeed Sargent, but the Knights were no longer significant enough to command recognition from the President. Neither Hayes nor Duncan received any appointment.

the kind, that I shall not know quite what to do with myself. But I am convinced that it is the wise thing for me to go; and also I freely admit that I am looking forward to the trip! I should like to have stayed on in the Presidency, and I make no pretense that I am glad to be relieved of my official duties. The only reason I did not stay on was because I felt that I ought not to; and I am exceedingly glad that I am to have the interest of this African trip before me. I think I wrote you that I am going for the National Museum. I shall take a couple of naturalists who are field taxidermists with me, and any specimens I shoot will be sent to the Museum. The Sirdar has been most kind, and he is going to give me a little boat which will enable me to get up the smaller tributaries of the Nile. Outside of this I do not believe I shall need any Government assistance; but a number of Englishmen, Selous, Buxton, Pease and others, have been too kind for anything in advising me and helping me secure my equipment.

I must see you when I am in England, which will be in May, 1910. Did I write you that I was to deliver the Romanes lecture at Oxford? Can't you get there then?

I am intensely interested in the liberal movement in the Moslem world. Of course it is very complicated. I earnestly hope that in Turkey the parliamentary talkers and the army fighters will be able to keep together and act not only in harmony but with moderation. Of course one of the things I fear is their being misled by false analogies. For instance, the fact that reform is necessary in Turkey does not in the least mean that it is now to the advantage of Egypt to have a parliament, and the fact that the Douma would do good in Persia does not mean that there ought to be a great legislative body at this time in Hindustan.

We are earnestly hoping for the best of news about your dear wife. *Ever yours*

[*Handwritten*] I wo'n't try to discuss the questions of European politics you raise, on paper; do come to England when I am there a year from next May.

4905 · TO ELIHU ROOT   *Roosevelt Mss.*

Oyster Bay, September 17, 1908

Dear Elihu: Your handling of the situation at Saratoga was masterly. It is a pleasure to feel how much you and I have had to do in shaping the course of politics in this State, and indeed in the Nation, since election of the Constitutional Convention in 1893. For fifteen years now you have been one of the great leading figures in our public life, and you have rendered service after service which I sincerely believe no one else could have rendered, certainly not in such effective fashion. I heartily congratulate you. *Ever yours*

Oyster Bay, September 19, 1908

Dear Will: I quite agree with you that I had better keep out of that Kentucky business.[1] It is not my funeral.

I do not see that we have to be bothered much about the Foraker-Standard Oil business.[2] On the contrary, I should suppose it was rather a clear-cut proof that you and I had been occupying a sound position in refusing to be guided by Mr. Foraker in corporation matters. It is possible, of course, that it will add a little to the distrust of the Republican party, but it is fortunate that the revelations should be made about the one man who is most openly hostile on this corporation issue to you and myself. As for Sibley's letter about myself, it is true to the extent that he has again and again spoken to me on behalf of the Standard Oil corporation, as have several score of other people, and I have given him the same polite attention as in the case of the others, and have disregarded what he said precisely as I disregarded what the others said.[3] *Faithfully yours*

P.S. I herewith return your enclosures.

[1] The Bradley and Yerkes factions of Kentucky Republicans were engaged in their usual difficulties.

[2] "Sentiment in favor of my re-election . . . . was strong enough to have overcome the combined opposition of both Roosevelt and Taft," Foraker recalled, ". . . . when, like a flash, the whole situation was changed by a speech made by Mr. William R. Hearst, at Columbus, Ohio, on the evening of September 17, 1908, in which, to make it appear that I had some kind of improper relations with the Standard Oil Company, he read a number of stolen letters to me from Mr. John D. Archbold of that company, showing payments to me at different times of various sums of money" (Foraker, *Notes of a Busy Life*, II, 328–329). Neither in 1908 nor later could Foraker convincingly demonstrate that those payments, retainers to a United States Senator from a corporation immediately concerned with national legislation, constituted anything but "improper relations." In 1908 Roosevelt seized on the letters which Hearst continued to publish, first to remove Foraker from the campaign and then to force him out of public life. In this policy Taft followed Roosevelt's leadership.

Stumping for the unknown who headed his Independence party ticket, Hearst, in his speeches of September 17 and 18, released equally damaging information about the treasurer of the Democratic party, Charles Nathaniel Haskell, incumbent Governor of Oklahoma. Again using Hearst's material, Roosevelt in a public statement of September 21 observed that whereas Foraker had been deprived of power in the Republican party, Haskell stood high in the councils of the Democrats. This attack, followed by public letters to Bryan (Numbers 4915, 4921), embarrassed the Democrats and forced Bryan to procure Haskell's resignation. These telling forays against the spectre of the Standard Oil Company and its influence in public life were probably the most effective contributions the President made to the campaign.

[3] The devoted sponsor of the interests of the Standard Oil Company to whom Roosevelt here referred was Joseph Crocker Sibley, Pennsylvania businessman, inventor, and politician; Democratic congressman, 1893–1895, 1899–1901; Republican congressman, 1901–1907; and chairman of the board of directors of the Galena-Signal Oil Company, a Standard Oil Company affiliate, 1905–1910. Hearst had made public some of Sibley's correspondence with Archbold.

Telegram: Confidential   Oyster Bay, September 19, 1908

Since writing, I have seen the further correspondence between Archbold and Foraker, published in the morning papers. Now, it is difficult for any man to advise another as to a given act in a campaign. Personally, if I were running for President, I should in view of these disclosures decline to appear upon the platform with Foraker, and I would have it understood in detail what is the exact fact, namely, that Mr. Foraker's separation from you and from me has been due not in the least to a difference of opinion on the negro question, which was merely a pretense, but to the fact that he was the attorney of the corporations, their hired representative in public life, and that therefore he naturally and inevitably opposed us in every way; that he opposed us when it came to appointments on the bench just as he opposed legislation that we asked for in Congress. I think it essential, if the bad effect upon the canvass of these disclosures is to be obviated, that we should show unmistakably how completely loose from us Mr. Foraker is. If this is not shown affirmatively, there is danger that the people will not see it and will simply think that all Republicans are tarred with the same brush. In other words there is need for aggressive action on our part. My own feeling is that nothing is gained by temporizing in a matter like this, or by paying heed to the ridiculous little politician who thinks it is a good thing to get harmony between you and creatures of the Foraker stamp. I would like to see you in the strongest and most emphatic way do what I should do in your place — make a fight openly on the ground that you stood in the Republican party and before the people for the triumph over the forces which were typified by the purchase of a United States Senator to do the will of the Standard Oil Company, and that you had been opposed by him because of this fundamental antagonism and that for the American people to beat you was to serve notice that they were willing to see a man punished because he declined to yield on such an issue.

Oyster Bay, September 21, 1908

Dear Nick: I think your speech is admirable in every way, and I think that on the third and fourth pages you have put a number of most telling points in exceedingly happy and epigrammatic form. I haven't a suggestion to make. I wish the widest publicity could be given to the speech.

I had to strip to the waist and fairly fight Hughes' nomination thru, but I am mighty glad that I succeeded.

I am not very much pleased with the way Taft's campaign is being handled. Whether it is Vorys, or Corbin, or Keifer,[1] or Charley Taft who is responsible for it, I cannot say. But I do wish that Taft would put more energy and fight into the matter. He ought to throw Foraker over with a bump. I have decided to put a little vim into the campaign by making a publication of my own.[2] I am anxious to do all I can. On the other hand I am no less anxious not to appear in such a way that it will look as if public attention was to be centered on me instead of where it should be centered, that is, on Taft. *Ever yours*

4909 · TO GEORGE RUMSEY SHELDON   *Roosevelt Mss.*

Oyster Bay, September 21, 1908

My dear Sheldon: I have been informed that you, or someone on behalf of the National Committee, have requested contributions both from Mr. Archbold and Mr. Harriman. If this is true I wish to enter a most earnest protest, and to say that in my judgment not only should such contributions not be solicited, but if tendered they should be refused; and if they have been accepted they should immediately be returned. I am not the candidate, but I am the head of the Republican Administration, which is an issue in this campaign, and I protest most earnestly against men whom we are prosecuting being asked to contribute to elect a President who will appoint an Attorney General to continue these prosecutions. Four years ago Mr. Cortelyou returned, as I am informed, any money forwarded by anyone who was being prosecuted or proceeded against by the National Government, or who had any personal interest whatever in any matter pending before the administration. At that time I was informed that money had been contributed to the national campaign by representatives of the Standard Oil Company, and I wrote the following letters:

October 26, 1904

My dear Mr. Cortelyou:

I have just been informed that the Standard Oil people have contributed one hundred thousand dollars to our campaign fund. This may be entirely untrue. But if true I must ask you to direct that the money be returned to them forthwith. I appreciate to the full the need of funds to pay the legitimate and necessarily great expenses of the campaign. I appreciate to the full the fact that under no circumstances will we receive half as much as was received by the National Committee in 1900 and 1896. Moreover, it is entirely legitimate to accept contributions, no matter how large they are, from individuals and corporations on the terms on which I happen to know that you have accepted them: that is, with the explicit understanding that they were given and received with no thought of any more obligation on the part of the National Committee or of the National administration than is implied in the statement that every man shall receive a square deal, no

---

[1] Lieutenant Governor Henry C. Corbin and Congressman J. Warren Keifer of Ohio, both in 1908 active in Taft's campaign, had attempted, before the publication of the Standard Oil Company correspondence, to enlist the support of Foraker.

[2] See Numbers 4906, note 2, and 4915, note 1.

more and no less, and that this I shall guarantee him in any event to the best of my ability. The big business corporations have a tremendous stake in the welfare of this country. They know that this welfare can only be secured thru the continuance in power of the Republican party; and if they subscribe for the purpose of securing such national welfare, and with no thought of personal favors to them, why they are acting as is entirely proper; but we cannot under any circumstances afford to take a contribution which can be even improperly construed as putting us under an improper obligation, and in view of my past relations[1] with the Standard Oil Company I fear that such a construction will be put upon receiving any aid from them. In returning the money to them I wish it made clear to them that there is not the slightest personal feeling against them, and that they can count upon being treated exactly as well by the Administration, exactly as fairly, as if we had accepted the contribution. They shall not suffer in any way because we refused it, just as they would not have gained in any way if we had accepted it. But I am not willing that it should be accepted, and must ask that you tell Mr. Bliss to return it.

Sincerely yours,
THEODORE ROOSEVELT

Hon. Geo. B. Cortelyou, Chairman,
Republican National Committee,
Manhattan Hotel,
New York, N. Y.

CONFIDENTIAL   October 27, 1904
My dear Mr. Cortelyou:

As supplemental to my letter of yesterday, containing my request that any contribution which the Standard Oil people may have made to the campaign be immediately returned, I wish to add that my judgment as to the propriety of this action is confirmed because of the fact brought into especial prominence by the Standard Oil Company's publication in the newspapers (which I saw after my letter was written and sent) that much importance seems to be attached to the political attitude of this company. Furthermore, in view of the open and pronounced opposition of the Standard Oil Company to the establishment of the Bureau of Corporations, one of the most important accomplishments of my administration, I do not feel willing to accept its aid. I request therefore that the contribution be returned without further delay.

Of course, I do not wish any public statement made about this matter, nor to take any step that will seem as if I were casting any reflection upon the Standard Oil people or their motives in making the contribution.

I greatly wish to see you in person. Please come on at the earliest opportunity; but have the contribution returned immediately.

Sincerely yours,
THEODORE ROOSEVELT

Hon. Geo. B. Cortelyou, Chairman,
Republican National Committee,
Manhattan Hotel,
New York, N. Y.

I hold that the reasons that then obtained are now far stronger. I would rather see us defeated than receive one dollar from the sources I have men-

---

[1] Explaining this reference, Roosevelt wrote in the margin of his letter to Sheldon: "That is, the trouble I had with them because of their determined fight against the establishment of the bureau of corporations."

tioned; and I regard it as an imperative duty, of the most binding kind, without an hour's delay, to retract any such request if it has been made, and to return any such contribution if it has been received. The acceptance of a dollar from such a source would do more to hurt Mr. Taft than all the money you could collect would help him. I shall of course send Mr. Taft a copy of this letter. *Sincerely yours*

4910 · TO WILLIAM HOWARD TAFT   *Roosevelt Mss.*

Personal   Oyster Bay, September 21, 1908

Dear Will: I enclose you a copy of a letter I have just sent Sheldon.[1] Kellogg called Loeb up and told him that Sheldon had solicited contributions from both Archbold and Harriman.

I suppose an outsider always gets nervous as he looks on at the game, and I thoroly understand that all kinds of disgruntled people send me protests; yet I do think there is urgent need that you should dominate more than you have yet done the National Committee; that it should be much more active than it has yet been, especially in the West; and that above all, you should take the most aggressive kind of attitude toward Bryan, hitting him hard. You will acquit me of any overfondness for Hughes, but his Youngstown speech was masterly, especially in its assault upon Bryan, and you could well afford to paraphrase or quote from that — I should prefer the former.

Kellogg says to me what dozens — indeed I may say hundreds — of men say, that the placing of du Pont in charge of the speaker's committee was a capital mistake. He should not have stayed on. Now, I know it is very difficult to advise an isolated act when a man must carry on the whole campaign on an organized plan. If I were in your place I would order Hitchcock to take du Pont off the committee; nevertheless I do not give this as advice, because you are at the center and have information which I do not have. But I do wish you to understand what a dreadful handicap du Pont's presence on the speaker's committee has been and now is.

Without asking your permission, and without giving Vorys' name, I have given to the press your letter to Vorys of July 20th a year ago,[2] because it seems to me that in this letter you show your stalwart independence, your fearlessness, your refusal for any consideration of personal gain, to be tainted

[1] Taft had already instructed Sheldon not "to take any money from either the trusts or the people closely identified with them." "If all these avenues are to be closed," Sheldon responded, ". . . . will you please tell me, Mr. Secretary, where I am going to get the money?" The treasurer did not believe that smaller businessmen could supply the sinews of political war. As Taft complained, it was difficult "to get it out of Sheldon's head that the place to get money is confined to a narrow strip of street in New York." Yet by October, Sheldon, reporting that contributions both large and small were satisfactory, stated that none were from "an improper source." – Pringle, *Taft*, I, 362–363.
[2] This was one of the letters in which Taft refused to make any compromise with Foraker, even for the sake of the Presidential nomination; see No. 4307, note 1.

in the slightest degree, and that you show this in such emphatic fashion that no statement from you now could make it as evident. It was a pity that Corbin and Keifer, who are very unsafe advisers, should have managed to make as much before the public of what they have been pleased to call a reconciliation between you and Foraker. Of course everyone on the inside knows that it was simply a case of Foraker tendering his support, which you of course accepted. This letter of yours makes clear your attitude.

Why don't you in your speech point out the fact that Haskell, whom Hearst has shown to be the tool and agent of the Standard Oil Company, is now the treasurer of the Democratic National Committee, and as soon as he was selected chairman Mack[3] announced that the Democratic campaign chest contained three hundred thousand dollars that was left over from the last campaign? Either this makes perfect nonsense of Parker's reiterated statements that they did not get much money in the last campaign, or, what is more probable, it shows that Mr. Haskell's appointment means Standard Oil money for Mr. Bryan. Bring this out, and smash and cut Bryan about it. *Ever yours*

[*Handwritten*] P.S If Sheldon has asked a contribution from Archbold or Harriman, I earnestly advise you *at once* to have him removed from his position as treasurer. Act *at once*. To let him stay on a day after he has made such a request might be ruinous.

4911 · TO VICTOR HOWARD METCALF   *Roosevelt Mss.*

Oyster Bay, September 21, 1908

My dear Secretary Metcalf: I thank you for your letter. Offhand, I am strongly inclined to favor the eight fourteen-inch rather than the ten fourteen-inch gun type of new battleship.[1] *Faithfully yours*

4912 · TO LYMAN ABBOTT   *Roosevelt Mss.*

Personal   Oyster Bay, September 22, 1908

My dear Abbott: That is a mighty good phrase of yours. We ought not to be aristocrats. I do not admire the aristocrat type, and even if I did it is hopelessly out of place in this country. But there is every reason why we should be gentleman democrats.

Oh Lord, I do get angry now and then over the campaign. Of course I suppose everyone always feels that he would manage things a little differently

[3] Norman Edward Mack, editor and publisher of the Buffalo *Times*, Democratic national committeeman from New York since 1900, in 1908 chairman of the national committee, an able political manager who every quadrennium adjusted his views on policy to conform with potentials for victory.

[1] The *Wyoming* and the *Arkansas*, authorized early in 1909, carried twelve 12-inch guns. The British battleships of the *Orion* class which were launched a year ahead of these two ships had main batteries of 13½-inch guns.

if he had the doing of them; but certainly I would like to put more snap into the business. In this Foraker affair I made up my mind that I would hit from the shoulder, inasmuch as Taft did not. Taft is quite right in saying that he does not wish to hit a man when he is down; but this is not a case of that kind. This is a case of a fight to a finish, and in such a fight (if you will pardon the simile by an old-time boxer) if a man wishes to win it is absolutely necessary that he shall knock out his opponent when he has the latter groggy.

For your private information I send you a letter which I have just written Sheldon. I have urged Taft all along to have du Pont taken off the speakers' committee, and I have also written him that in my judgment unless Sheldon retracts his extraordinary request of Archbold, he ought to be removed from the treasurership. Of course the request was perfectly honest, and Sheldon made it on the theory that he was asking everyone to contribute, not on personal grounds but on public grounds. Nevertheless it was a very stupid thing to do.

I return you the check, my dear fellow. We will count the China article simply as so much to the good for the first year of my agreement, when I will be able to do so little for you. *Faithfully yours*

4913 · TO WESLEY LIVSEY JONES   *Roosevelt Mss.*

Washington, September 23, 1908

My dear Congressman: I have received your letter of the 14th instant concerning the conduct of Internal Revenue Collector Crocker and United States Marshal Baker. They are of course bound to obey the exprest will of the people to work for you, and nothing else will be tolerated. I have sent them a letter of which the enclosed is a copy.[1]

With all good wishes, believe me, *Sincerely yours*

4914 · TO FRANK HARRIS HITCHCOCK   *Roosevelt Mss.*

Washington, September 23, 1908

My dear Mr. Hitchcock: Mr. du Pont is connected with a Trust which is being prosecuted by the Department of Justice. I have brought this matter several times to your attention. I think you agree with me that it was a very grave blunder to appoint him Chairman of the Speakers' Committee. The only question in your mind was whether it would not aggravate things to have him removed. In my judgment the time has come when no such consideration can longer be entertained. Mr. du Pont should resign at once. I

[1] Roosevelt directed George H. Baker, United States Marshal at Spokane, and Benjamin D. Crocker, collector of internal revenue at Tacoma, to refrain from opposing the candidacy for the United States Senate of Congressman Wesley Livsey Jones of Washington. Jones was elected. Similarly, the President interceded to protect the Republican senatorial candidate in California, George C. Perkins, who was also re-elected.

do not mean by that that he should resign next week, but I mean that his resignation should be in within an hour of your receiving this letter. I understand on first-class authority that du Pont is perfectly willing to get off and in that case it is perfectly inexcusable to keep him on. Great damage has already been done by his appointment and retention. It is impossible wholly to undo this damage, but it can be partially undone.[1] If Haskell should be asked to resign as Treasurer of the Democratic Committee and there is then a demand to take off du Pont most of the good will be lost. I earnestly hope you will act immediately. *Sincerely yours*

Washington, September 23, 1908

Dear Sir: In your telegram[1] you speak of so much of the charge against Governor Haskell as dealt with his relations, while in Ohio, with the Standard Oil Company. You omit the charge as to his relations with the Standard Oil interests, as shown by his action while Governor of Oklahoma, this very summer, this action being in part taken while he was at Denver, where, as you state, he was by your wish made chairman of the committee which drafted the platform upon which you are standing. In my statement I purposely made no specific allusion to the Ohio matter, and shall at this time make none, in spite of its significance, and in spite of the further fact that Governor Haskell's close relations with the Standard Oil interests while he was in Ohio was a matter of common notoriety. In Oklahoma it is a matter of court record. By this court record it appears that the Attorney General of the State, elected by the people, obtained an injunction to prevent the Prairie Oil and Gas Company from building a pipeline; and that Governor Haskell found this out while he was at Denver, as appears by the representation for the dissolution of the injunction made in his name on behalf of the State before a court of superior jurisdiction to that which had issued the injunction. In this the Governor states that the Acting Governor, in his absence, had asked that the hearing be postponed until he, the Governor, might return and have an opportunity to investigate the controversy. The Governor sets forth in his petition that he is the sole authority to determine such matters, and that the Attorney General and the judge of the lower court had no right in the matter, and that the action of the judge of the lower court represented

---

[1] Du Pont resigned September 25; see No. 4920.

[1] Replying to Roosevelt's public statement of September 21 on Haskell's dual connection with Standard Oil and the Democratic high command, Bryan, in a public telegram to the President, defended Haskell, asked for an investigation of Roosevelt's charges against Haskell, and asserted that "as the candidate of the democratic party," he would not "permit any responsible member of the republican organization to misrepresent the attitude of the democratic party in the present campaign." The Democrats, Bryan insisted, were "clear and specific" in their crusade against private monopoly; the Republicans, "uncertain and evasive."

"an encroachment by the judiciary." The Attorney General opposed the dissolution of the injunction, stating that the Prairie Oil and Gas Company was a foreign corporation which had not accepted the provisions of the constitution applicable to such corporations, and that without authority of law it was employing a great force of men and teams to dig up, across and into various highways of the State for the purpose of laying its pipelines. The Governor prevailed, the injunction was suspended, and the pipeline was permitted to continue its work, to use the words of the Attorney General, "without any color of law." I call your attention to the fact that the question is not whether or not the judge erred, of whether the injunction was proper. The point is that the Governor was alert to take out of the hands of the Attorney General what the Attorney General felt was his sworn duty to prevent, an alleged instance of the breaking of the laws by this particular great corporation.

As far as I have seen Governor Haskell has not even attempted anything which can be called a defense of this action of his. It thus appears that his action was as inexcusable as it was wanton, except on the theory that in defiance of the Attorney General of the State and at all hazards he intended for some reasons of his own to protect the interests of a great corporation against the law. It has been suggested on his behalf that, after all, he did not favor the Standard Oil Company, but merely the Prairie Oil and Gas Company. This claim is disposed of by the testimony of the Standard Oil Company itself taken in the latter part of 1907 in the suit now pending before the United States court at St. Louis against the Standard Oil Company. In this testimony the Standard Oil Company, upon being required by the Government to put in a list of all the companies in which it held stock, or in which its subsidiary companies held stock, reported among the others the Prairie Oil and Gas Company, total capital $10,000,000, of which the National Transit Company's proportion was $9,999,500; and furthermore it appears that the National Transit Company had a capital stock of $25,455,200, of which the Standard Oil Company owned $25,451,650. In other words, this Prairie Oil and Gas Company was owned, all except $500, by the National Transit Company, and this National Transit Company was owned, all except about $3,550, by the Standard Oil Company.

Now contrast your action in this case of Governor Haskell with Mr. Taft's action as regards Senator Foraker, as set forth in his letter of July 20, 1907, which I quoted in my statement. It was a matter of common notoriety about Senator Foraker, as it has long been a matter of common notoriety about Governor Haskell, that he was the defender and supporter of certain great corporate interests and therefore hostile to the policies for which this administration has stood. There was no such convincing proof against Senator Foraker at that time, however, as there was against Governor Haskell, when, as you say, he was with your approval made Treasurer of your campaign committee. But Mr. Taft refused to be a party to the renomination of Senator Foraker, even tho it was represented that only thus could he advance his own interests, showing by actual deeds that his words were true when he said, "I do not care for the Presidency if it has to come by compromise with anyone on a matter of principle." With a hundred-fold clearer evidence before you as to the connection of Governor Haskell with the Standard Oil than Mr. Taft then had as to the connection of Senator Foraker with any corporation, you nevertheless, having secured Governor Haskell as chairman of the committee to write the platform on which you stand, put him in as treasurer of your campaign committee.

Let me add that Governor Haskell's utter unfitness for any public position of trust, or for association with any man anxious to make an appeal on a moral issue to the American people, has been abundantly shown wholly irrespective of this action of his in connection with the Standard Oil interests. As an American citizen who prizes his Americanism and his citizenship far above any question of partisanship, I regard it as a scandal and a disgrace that Governor Haskell should be connected with the management of any national campaign. I have not the space in this letter to discuss Governor Haskell's conduct, for instance, in vetoing the child labor bill; or the fact that his name appears as one of the defendants in various suits brought by the Government to prevent the Creek Indians from having certain of their lands fraudulently taken;[2] or his connection with various other matters of the kind; but let me call your attention to his conduct in prostituting to base purposes the State University, as set forth in an article in *The Outlook* of September 5th last, under the heading of "Shall the People Rule — in Oklahoma?" In this article you will see that Governor Haskell was given full opportunity to make every explanation, and that he made none. After setting forth the facts as to Governor Haskell's conduct, *The Outlook* article concludes as follows:

"On this state of affairs we have two comments to make and two questions to ask.

"The people of Oklahoma are taxed to support their educational institutions, from the primary school to the university. They pay their money to

[2] The Bonaparte investigators in 1903 and William Dudley Foulke in 1906 had found and reported "overwhelming evidence of the dishonest scheduling of townsites" by federal and local officials and their friends throughout the lands of the Creek nation. Pursuant to a resolution of the Creek Council, and utilizing these findings, the attorney for the Creeks in 1907 brought civil suit to recover the town lots, particularly those containing oil lands, from a number of defendants of whom the most prominent politically was Governor Haskell. These suits were settled out of court in 1909. In that year the federal government instituted a criminal prosecution against virtually the same defendants, including Haskell, but in 1910 the court ruled that the statute of limitations protected them.

Angie Debo, who reported the story of the town lot frauds, observed caustically that "President Roosevelt used the fact that Governor Haskell was one of the defendants to good political advantage in the national campaign of 1908. His logic is not exactly clear, for his own administration was responsible for the frauds." This evaluation fails to include what Miss Debo elsewhere observed, that Roosevelt authorized the Bonaparte and Foulke investigations that revealed the unhealthy conditions in Oklahoma; see Debo, *And Still the Waters Run*, pp. 120–125, 203–205.

have their children educated. When the politicians use this money to promote the interests of a political machine or a Church sect, they are guilty of a breach of trust. What do the taxpayers of Oklahoma think of the use which their public servants are making of the public funds? What do they think about this financial policy — the taking of the money due their sons and daughters and diverting it for the benefit of politicians, ecclesiastical and civil?

"Governor Haskell was one of Mr. Bryan's right-hand men in the Democratic Convention, and, at Mr. Bryan's instance, has been made treasurer of the Democratic National Committee. It is appalling to think what would be the results in the educational systems of the Philippines and Porto Rico, in the digging of the Panama Canal, in the work of irrigation and reforestation, in the administration of the Post Office, the Interior and Agricultural Departments, in the appointments of foreign ministers and consuls, if the spirit which has actuated the Democratic authorities in the State of Oklahoma should be permitted to take control of the Federal Government at Washington. Governor Haskell, by actions which speak louder than words, has declared his disbelief in Grover Cleveland's motto, "A public office is a public trust." And Mr. Haskell is a representative leader in the Bryan Democracy. What does Mr. Bryan think of Mr. Cleveland's principle? What do the American people think of Mr. Haskell's contemptuous reversal of it?"

You close your telegram by saying that you expect and will demand fair and honorable treatment from those who are in charge of the Republican campaign. I am not in charge of the campaign, but am greatly interested in it. I have shown you above fairly and honorably that Governor Haskell is a man who, on every account I have named, is unworthy of any position in our public life. No further investigation of these facts is required. They are spread on the record before you, and they were available before Mr. Haskell was chosen for his position as treasurer. You also say that you will not permit any responsible member of the Republican organization to misrepresent the attitude of your party in the present campaign. You will have no difficulty in getting me to represent it aright, for my sole anxiety is that the people of the country shall understand this attitude clearly, and shall then condemn it as it should be condemned. You say that you have advocated more radical measures against private monopolies than either I or my party associates have been willing to undertake. You have indeed advocated measures that sound more radical, but they have the prime defect that in practice they would not work. I should not in this letter to you discuss your attitude on this question if you did not yourself bring it up; but as you have brought it up, I answer you that in my judgment the measures you advocate would be wholly ineffective in curing a single evil, and so far as they had any effect at all, would merely throw the entire business of the country into hopeless and utter confusion.

I put Mr. Taft's deeds against your words. I ask that Mr. Taft be judged by all his deeds, for he wishes none of them forgotten. I ask that you be judged both by the words you wish remembered, and by the words that seemingly you and your party now desire to have forgotten. I ask that your present plan for regulating the trusts be judged in connection with your past utterances that you did not believe in their regulation but in their destruction; and again in connection with your past utterances to the effect that only Government ownership by a complicated National and State system of railroads would avail; and again by your past utterances when you proposed to remedy all the sufferings of our people by a depreciated currency. For several years now I have been steadfastly fighting to secure thorogoing and far-reaching control in the interest of the public over the great business combinations which do an interstate business. In this effort I have been as much hampered by the extremists, well-meaning or otherwise, who demand visionary and impracticable radicalism, as by those other extremists, no less dangerous, who stand for the reactionary refusal to remedy any grievance. One side, the side on which I am obliged to say you have placed yourself, has shown itself to be just as much the enemy of progress as the other. I hold it entirely natural for any great law-defying corporation to wish to see you placed in the Presidency rather than Mr. Taft. Your plans to put a stop to the abuses of these corporations are wholly chimerical; how chimerical your last plan is you will yourself see if you read Governor Hughes' speech at Youngstown, Ohio. To recall to your mind what Governor Hughes said, I quote as follows: "When we consider these (proposed) remedies (of Mr. Bryan against the Trusts) x x x we find ourselves journeying in a land of dreams. Again the magician of 1896 waves his wand. At a stroke difficulties disappear and the complex problems of modern business are forgotten in the fascination of the simple panacea." The most important proposal of Mr. Bryan is "that any manufacturing or trading corporation engaged in interstate commerce shall be required to take out a Federal License before it shall be permitted to control as much as twenty-five per cent of the product in which it deals," and no corporation shall be permitted to control "more than fifty per cent of the total amount of any product consumed in the United States."

It might be interesting to inquire what is the meaning of "any product consumed in the United States." Does it refer to a class of commodities? And if so, how shall the classes be defined? Or does it refer to each separate article of commerce? And if so, what account does this proposal take of the skill and initiative of manufacturers who have built up a more or less exclusive trade in particular articles, often protected by trade-marks, although in most active competition with other articles designed for the same general purpose and seeking the same market? In a desire to correct the evils of business are we to place an embargo upon honest endeavor whose activities present none of the abuses requiring remedies? And, if not, what statutory definitions shall be found to be adequate and just if we lay down our prohibition in terms of volume or ratio of business and not in terms of right and wrong? If we adopt Mr. Bryan's proposal, to what period of production is the prohibition to apply? Is the excess for a day or for a month to be considered? Or is the average production for a year to be taken? And what system shall be devised by which suitable information may be furnished in the nature of danger signals along the routes of trade so that the manufacturer may know when he is about to exceed the prescribed ratio? He may justly be required to govern his own conduct, but how shall he be appraised of the conduct of others upon which is to depend his guilt or innocence?

Let me repeat that no law-defying corporation has anything to fear from you save what it will suffer in the general paralysis of business which any attempt on your part to reduce to practice what you have advocated would bring. This paralysis would affect the wageworker, the farmer, the small businessman, more than it would affect the great businessman. But it would affect the latter, too. Therefore I hope and believe that all farsighted citizens who wish to see this country prosper in material things will support Mr. Taft. But above all I ask for support for him because he stands for the moral uplift of the nation, because his deeds have made good his words, and because the policies to which he is committed are of immeasurable consequence alike to the honor and the interest of the whole American people. *Very truly yours*

4916 · TO WILLIAM HOWARD TAFT   *Roosevelt Mss.*

Washington, September 24, 1908

Dear Will: I think you are right on the tariff; but I think also that you want to move with great caution in the matter so as not to make the appearance of a conflict between you and the Congressional campaign committee. This would have very bad effects. Of course this is merely another way of saying that you will have to act with great caution in every such matter of policy now, just as I had to in 1904. Be careful what you commit yourself to; but when you do commit yourself, do it in your usual straightforward, fearless and direct manner. So with the Cox business; do not let them put you in any false position under any circumstances or make you take a single ground that is not right and proper. On the other hand, no good whatever comes from an open break with him. I am here again giving you merely the advice on which I myself act, and the advice I am sure that Root would give you. I do not wish you to do anything that would give the New York politicians, for instance, the feeling that your attitude toward party workers is that of Hughes. As far as I know I never either as Police Commissioner, Governor or President yielded improperly to Platt, Quigg, Lauterbach, or anyone else; but I resolutely refused to be drawn into a fight with them. I did what I thought was right, acted with them when I could, and when I could not I was perfectly definite, but also perfectly good-humored, over the refusal. Now and then the need comes for a smash, as in this case of Foraker. But the fight should never be gone into until it cannot possibly be avoided, and then it should be conducted without ruth.

Bryan gave me a bully chance to hit him and I think I have hit him to some purpose.

Good luck to you on your trip! *Ever yours*

[*Handwritten*] I am very glad you are doing such aggressive work in your speeches. Hit at Bryan & the Bryanites, not at Cox or other Republicans if it can possibly be avoided

4917 · TO ELIHU ROOT *Roosevelt Mss.*

Washington, September 25, 1908

Dear Elihu: This letter from Littauer explains itself. My judgment is very strong that we ought to refuse to deliver this man and that we ought to make announcement now.[1] We never should have had an extradition treaty with Russia. Its conduct toward so-called political criminals is so inconceivably brutal and foolish and it is so indifferent to the truth in demanding the reclamation of offenders such as this man that we have no business to treat it as we do the average civilized nation. Moreover, its consistent attitude in the matter of the passports is such as to justify us on that ground alone in refusing to perform such an act of mere international comity or courtesy as this. I find, by the way, that Adee has sent to the Attorney General a request of the Jewish Committee to know whether the action of the Russian Government in refusing passports to Jewish citizens has not worked an abrogation of the treaty. I have promptly directed the reference to be recalled as I think I know my Secretary of State and do not believe that he cares to have a question like this decided for him by even the best Department of Justice.

I wish you were here as a number of important matters have come up. Do go over the papers in this Pouren case carefully, and I will take it up with you as soon as you return. I feel that it would be a good thing from every standpoint if we could at once announce that we do not intend to permit the man to be extradited.

I am informed that under the uniform practice of the Department, the whole matter, both as to law and facts, as to extradition cases of this kind, is vested in the President. *Ever yours*

4918 · TO GEORGE RUMSEY SHELDON *Roosevelt Mss.*

Personal Washington, September 25, 1908

My dear Sheldon: There is one feature of your letter of the 22d which causes me much surprise. You say that in 1904 the contribution of the Standard Oil Company I spoke of was made under the authority of its executive committee. This is the first time I was aware that such a contribution was made. In response to my letters Mr. Cortelyou told me that no Standard Oil money

[1] Although Roosevelt was urging Root to announce that the government would not extradite Pouren, the Secretary of State, anxious to avoid a controversy with Russia, pursued a more cautious course; see Numbers 4874, 4934.

was received or would be received.[1] Later, after the campaign closed, I was informed from a different source that certain individuals who had contributed had Standard Oil as well as other interests. Mr. Cortelyou informed me that he made his statement on Mr. Bliss' authority, which he and I were of course warranted in accepting as final. *Sincerely yours*

4919 · TO HENRY CABOT LODGE   *Roosevelt Mss.*

Personal   Washington, September 25, 1908

Dear Cabot: I was glad to hear from you and I also heard from Sturgis.[1] I have been uneasy about you and am relieved that Tuckanuck did you the good it always does.

Since you wrote you have doubtless seen my statement about Foraker and my letter to Bryan, and you may have noticed how exactly I followed the lines indicated in your letter. As usual our minds worked in the same direction. You may have noticed particularly that I brought in the Brownsville matter. No one should feel a greater satisfaction than you over this vindication of your wisdom. Foraker is a brilliant man; he was a gallant soldier. I lament the fact that he was also a corrupt man and as this was so I am glad that he was exposed. I am all at sea about Hearst. No other public man has attacked him as roughly and as fearlessly as I have, and yet in this correspondence he takes pains to say that he believes in my honesty. As for our enemies, Cabot, the simple fact is that dishonest men are naturally opposed to us, and when they are exposed outside people say that we have had luck in having them as our enemies. I have been appalled recently by the many revelations of crookedness in high places. Ten years ago I did not believe there was anything like the amount of corruption high up in business and political circles that there actually is. It is a curious thing that I should have been instrumental in uncovering so much of it, for it was really not thru any conscious effort on my part, but rather because I took it for granted that corruption was to be assailed wherever it was found.

General Sam Young told me last night that a partner of Hanna's in September, 1896, before McKinley was elected, told him that Alger was to be made Secretary of War, altho McKinley at that time did not know it, because Huntington had fixt it up with Hanna as part of the deal in getting his railroad proper terminals. He also told me that John Kean's brother, I think probably Hamilton Kean, when in the Yellowstone Park this summer, told him (Young) that of course business interests were dissatisfied with me; that they had to furnish the money to carry any campaign, and that they had a right to be dissatisfied unless the President, and the Chairman of his Committee were such that the Chairman could go to the President about any leg-

---

[1] See No. 3307, note 1, and references therein.

[1] William Sturgis Bigelow.

islation that affected friendly interests and tell them that inasmuch as these interests had been friendly and had made big contributions, no action hostile to them could be allowed! Think of the sordid, squalid immorality of Kean and his brother, gentlemen by descent tho they are. Here again we have naturally earned the hostility of these men.[2]

Love to Nannie. *Ever yours*

4920 · TO FRANK HARRIS HITCHCOCK   *Roosevelt Mss.*

Personal   Washington, September 26, 1908

My dear Hitchcock: Nine tenths of wisdom is being wise in time. If du Pont's resignation had not come in yesterday the blunder would have been well-nigh fatal. If, on the other hand, it had come out even twenty-four hours before, above all if it had come out last week when I was insisting upon it, the gain to our cause would have been immeasurable. Mr. Taft had written me authorizing me to request you to come on here if there was any hesitancy on your part in removing du Pont. I know how hard your task is and how certain it is that any man doing such a task will be misjudged; but this makes it all the more necessary to avoid avoidable blunders. Both you and Sheldon will now have to exercise the most rigorous care to see that no chance is offered party opponents to score as they have in this case of du Pont. Of course there is no real parallelism between the cases of du Pont and Haskell. The latter is an unspeakable scoundrel, Bryan's personal choice for Treasurer. Du Pont, as far as I know, is simply a man of good character and reputation who, like many another businessman, has violated the antitrust law, and Taft knew nothing of his appointment. But while there is this immeasurable difference in the two cases, in reality in the popular mind, thanks to the misfortune of du Pont having stayed on so long, there is almost no difference whatever between the two cases. If he had been allowed to stay on another twenty-four hours the balance would have been heavily against us. If he had been removed a week ago, much less a month ago, it would not have counted against us at all.

Now, I am not altogether easy about what I hear as to New York State. The enclosed extract of a letter is but one of many such that I am receiving.

[2] The Keans were powerful figures in the financial and political life of New Jersey. Hamilton Fish Kean, a dealer in securities and chairman of the board of the Hackensack Water Company, was also a member of the Republican State Committee from 1905 to 1919, a member of the Republican National Committee from 1919 to 1928, and a United States Senator from 1929 to 1935. In 1908 his older brother John was far more prominent. Also a dealer in securities and director of many companies, he was likewise, while senator from 1899 to 1911, the president of the Elizabethtown Gaslight Company. Foraker called him "a watchdog" who lurked in the Senate to see that no "improper" legislation passed. From Roosevelt's point of view he watched the wrong bills, for he was ever allied with Aldrich, Hale, Gallinger, Platt, and Penrose. He provoked Roosevelt's special indignation by his obdurate opposition to all railroad rate legislation.

It was absolutely necessary to renominate Hughes; but we would be foolish to blind ourselves to the fact that to do so alienated many elements. I think that Taft should be brought to New York State; that Hughes must, if he is to carry the State, campaign from end to end; that Root should be put on the stump. Moreover, it is evident that the labor people are not satisfied. Far and away the best man to deal with it is James Bronson Reynolds; but whether you choose him or not, you should choose some person or persons who will go into the work at once. If it is not agreeable to have Reynolds in charge of labor matters put in Samuel B. Donnelly and Reynolds will work under him. Reynolds will work with or under any man. He merely wants to render the service without expectation of reward. *He ought to be put in charge.* Please see Congressman Bennet at once on these matters. He has a touch with the working people and the East Side people that renders his advice very important. Of course the New York State Committee should be able to handle New York; but if we lose it there will be small satisfaction indeed in saying that it was someone else's fault. We must make New York sure. *Sincerely yours*

4921 · TO WILLIAM JENNINGS BRYAN   *Roosevelt Mss.*

Washington, September 27, 1908

Dear Sir: I have seen your letter published in this morning's papers.[1] As to most of what you say about me personally I do not regard any answer as necessary. When you say that I am unfair to your platform you reiterate certain opinions as to which I had quoted with my hearty approval Governor Hughes in my first letter; and these, therefore, it is also unnecessary to answer. You have not answered the Hughes speech; and in my judgment you do well not to make the attempt. You say that your platform declares in favor of the vigorous enforcement of the law against guilty trust magnates and officials, and that the platform upon which Mr. Taft stands makes no such declaration. It was not necessary. That platform approved the policies of this administration and promised to continue them; and here, as usual, I have only to compare your words with the deeds of the administration and of Mr. Taft. You merely promise in your platform that you intend to do just what this administration has actually done and is doing.

To show the difference between deeds and words I will compare the record of this administration with the record of one of your most prominent supporters at the moment, Mr. Olney, Attorney General under the last Democratic administration. While Mr. Olney was Attorney General no cases whatever were brought, under the antitrust law, against combinations of capital, the only new cases which he brought being directed against combina-

[1] Bryan's letter, replying to Roosevelt's of September 23, followed by one day the announcement of Haskell's resignation. The content of the letter is adequately revealed in Roosevelt's reply.

tions of workingmen. During that entire administration the only cases brought against combinations of capital under the antitrust act were four in number, two of which were unsuccessful; one of the other two being the case which was decided by Judge Taft in favor of the Government.

Under this administration a mass of such cases has been brought, including the case against the Northern Securities Company;

> Against the beef packers;
> Against the Federal Salt Company;
> Against the General Paper Company;
> Against the Otis and other Elevator Companies;
> Against the American Tobacco Company;
> Against the Powder Trust;
> Against the Virginia Carolina Chemical Company;
> Against the Standard Oil Company, and others.

In a number of these cases the government has already succeeded by injunctions and otherwise. Some of the cases are now pending. In hardly any important case against great law-breaking corporations has the government yet suffered final defeat.

As regards suits to suppress railway abuses; under the last Democratic administration there were no indictments against shippers for receiving rebates or secret rates. Under my administrations there have been forty-nine indictments for secret rebates, resulting in eighteen convictions; and in only four cases have these indictments failed. The other twenty-seven cases are still pending. Among the railroads which have been convicted are Chicago and Alton; Chicago, Burlington and Quincy; The New York Central; the Chicago, Rock Island and Pacific, and the Chicago, Milwaukee and Saint Paul; while scores of cases are still pending against other leading railroads.

Among the shippers that have been convicted are some of the greatest corporations in the United States; as, for instance, the American Sugar Company, the aggregate fine actually paid being more than $150,000; Swift and Company; Armour Packing Company; the Cudahy Packing Company; Nelson, Morris and Company, each of whom was fined $15,000, and the cases have now been carried to the Supreme Court. The Standard Oil Case is still pending. This is a record of actual achievement, and beside it mere promises are empty indeed; and they would not be made now with any possibility of performance resulting, if it were not for the achievement above recited.

You state that the Steel Company, with my express consent, purchased one of its largest rivals, and thus obtained control of over fifty per cent of the total output. This action of the Steel Company (which increased its share of the total output by only about four per cent and in no way altered the standing of the Company under the law) may have been a violation of your plan, the absurdity of which has been exposed by Governor Hughes. But there was no violation of the law. I was cognizant of the entire transaction. It was not entered into by the Steel Corporation of its own desire, but solely at the urgent requests of the corporation purchased and of the big banks holding that corporation's securities, in order to enable them to prevent a crash which would have turned the panic of last fall into the most widespread disaster. I should indeed have been derelict in my duty if I had not so acted, and efficiently used all the power of the government, where it could be legally and properly used (as it was in this case) to see that the panic was kept within the smallest possible radius and the damage caused as slight as possible. You would better understand the principle on which I acted if you would rid yourself of the idea that I am trying to discriminate for or against any man or corporation because he or it is either wealthy or not wealthy. I regard such discrimination in either direction as utterly incompatible with a spirit of honesty and fair dealing. I base my distinctions on conduct, not on relative wealth. When the same men who were leaders in the Steel Corporation acted in connection with the Northern Securities suit in a manner which I regarded as contrary to the law, by my direction a successful suit was immediately undertaken against them. If they violate the law in connection with any act of the Steel Corporation I will immediately proceed against them. Until they do violate the law they will be treated precisely as any other corporation, great or small, which obeys the law, is treated.

I treat each man and each corporation with a view solely to whether he or it is acting rightly on a given occasion. Let me give you an example. I have proceeded against the corporations of which Mr. E. H. Harriman is the head on certain points where I believe they have violated the law. But when in connection with the breaking of the Salton Sea dam one of the Harriman corporations repaired the dam, I last winter did everything I could to have Congress reimburse Mr. Harriman for so much of the obligation as I felt ought to come upon the United States. I would hold myself unfit to be President if, because I prosecuted Mr. Harriman where I thought he had broken the law, I yet hesitated to do him justice where I thought the facts required that justice should be done him. In exactly the same way I have acted and shall act as regards the Steel Corporation.

You ask me to name a single official connected with a law-defying corporation who has declared or will declare that he is supporting you. In a St. Louis paper which reaches me at the same time that the papers containing this published letter of yours, I find a statement from Judge Henry S. Priest, Attorney for the Waters-Pierce Oil Company, the western subsidiary or representative of the Standard Oil Company, in which he announces that he is for Bryan and states that Wall Street believes that Bryan will be elected. In response to the question as to whether he could quote any of the Standard Oil magnates as feeling that way, he answered: "I did not say I saw any of the officials of the Standard Oil Company. I am giving you what I found was the drift of opinion among well-posted politicians as well as bankers. * * * I guess Governor Haskell is all right. They have not proved anything on him, have they?" The newspaper clipping goes on to say that "Judge

Priest was one of the lawyers who fought Attorney General Hadley in the State's ouster suit against the Waters-Pierce and Republic Oil Companies. His legal practice is chiefly with the big corporations and his firm is counsel for the United Railways Company and the North American interests in St. Louis. Judge Priest is credited with originating the phrase: 'Bribery is a conventional offense,' which he used in an argument at the trial of R. M. Snyder,[2] the Kansas City millionaire, now dead."

You say that the trust magnates know their own interests and are supporting Judge Taft. So far as their interests are simply the interests of the business community, and especially of the wageworkers, I believe they will support Judge Taft. So far as they have special interests which are to them more important than the general business welfare, I believe they will support you. I base this belief upon what happened in 1896. Your success then would, in my belief, have been a calamity for the country from the standpoint of the welfare of the businessmen, farmers, and workingmen, just as, in my belief, your success now would be a calamity to the country both from the standpoint of business (and especially of the interests of the wageworker) and from the standpoint of morals. One of your supporters, the New York *World*, in February last printed a list of contributions to your campaign funds of 1896, containing the names of individuals and corporations owning silver mines who made contributions to the aggregate amount of $288,000, one of these contributions being of $159,000 and another of $45,000, etc., etc. Now all the great financial magnates who then contributed to your campaign fund would have preferred business prosperity to business adversity, other things being equal; but they would rather have had the immense profit that would have accrued to them from the free coinage of the fifty-cent dollar than the smaller profit which would have accrued to them merely from the general industrial prosperity of the country. Because of their personal interests and against the interest of the community at large these "trust" magnates then supported you. My belief is, and the statement of Judge Priest quoted above, and the attitude of many men of large financial interest warrant me in expressing the belief, that those trust magnates whose fear of being prosecuted under the law by Mr. Taft, is greater than their fear of general business adversity under you, will support you and not Mr. Taft.

I now come to what you have to say as to contributions, and here you furnish your own answer. You state that it appears from the published statement of the contribution to Mr. Hughes' campaign for Governor two years ago that various men of wealth, some of them connected with big corporations, whom you name, to the number of nine, contributed from $20,000 to $500 apiece. You ask "Would the fact that these gentlemen contributed to his campaign fund strengthen or weaken his testimony against the reasonableness of our antitrust remedy?"; and later you continue by asking "Are you

<hr>

[2] Robert McClure Snyder, organizer of the natural gas pipeline system connecting the gas fields of southern Kansas and Oklahoma with Kansas City, Missouri.

willing to say that any public interest was served in 1904 by concealing until after election the contributions made to the Republican Campaign Committee by Mr. Harriman, and those collected by him for others? Are you willing to say that the publication before election of the contributions then made would have had no effect on the election?" You then propose to publish the names of contributors before election and ask us to do the same.

The amounts you mention as contributed to Mr. Hughes are utterly trivial compared to the amounts I have already mentioned as contributed to your campaign in 1896; but in my judgment the amount contributed has nothing whatever to do with the point at issue. The question was, for instance, whether Mr. Clark of Montana, when he contributed heavily to your campaign fund, had a proper motive, and whether your actions would or would not have been influenced properly or improperly by that contribution; and the same question applies to Mr. Hughes and to me. In the case of Mr. Hughes and myself the answer is fortunately easy. You have nothing to do but examine our records in the offices to which we were both elected. You either know or ought to have known before writing that in not one instance has Mr. Hughes, as Governor, done one thing of any kind, sort or description for any one of the contributors you mention, or for any other contributor to his fund, which ought not to have been done, and would not have been done if no contribution had been made. Yet you clearly imply that he is and has been improperly influenced by the fact of these contributions having been made. Do you consider such an implication either straightforward or sincere?

In a letter to the Chairman of my campaign committee on October 26, 1904, I specifically approved of the conditions under which the National Committee were accepting contributions, saying that their acceptance was to be "with the explicit understanding that they were given and received with no thought of any more obligation on the part of the National Committee or of the national administration than is implied in the statement that every man shall receive a square deal, no more and no less, and that this I shall guarantee him in any event to the best of my ability x x x If they subscribe for the purpose of securing such national welfare, and with no thought of personal favors to them, why they are acting as is entirely proper." I continued: "In returning the money to them (any contributors) I wish it made clear that there is not the slightest personal feeling against them, and that they can count upon being treated exactly as well by the administration, exactly as fairly, as if we had accepted the contributions. They shall not suffer in any way because we refused them, just as they would not have gained in any way if we had accepted them." No member of the National Committee has ever directly or indirectly suggested to me that I should either do or leave undone anything whatever because anyone had contributed or had failed to contribute.

These are the facts. Now for your proposal. You have yourself furnished its condemnation. You have quoted the subscriptions furnished to Governor Hughes as giving reason to distrust Governor Hughes' attitude toward corporations, and I am obliged to say that this cannot be sincere on your part for you know well what the Governor's attitude has been thruout his term. You quote the subscription of Mr. Harriman to my campaign, altho you know well that it did not interfere with any action taken by me as against Mr. Harriman, and ask if it would not have affected the campaign if known. Thereby you have furnished an excellent reason for refusing to meet your proposal; for you make it evident that to adopt your proposal would give to every man who cared merely for partisan success, the chance, by precisely the argument you have now made, to create to more purpose the false impression that you are now seeking to create. Mr. Taft's reputation, Mr. Taft's acts on the bench and in the executive service, show that he could not be swayed in any shape or way by any consideration save the public interest, and that the fact of any man's contributing or failing to contribute would in any way influence his action, any more than it has influenced my action or the action of Governor Hughes. I emphatically approve of the publication of campaign expenses after the election, whether provided for by law or not. You have shown by this letter of yours that if the contributions to Mr. Hughes' campaign fund had been made public before election you and those who act with you would have striven to give the false impression that Mr. Hughes was unfit to be entrusted with the position of Governor; and you have shown by this letter of yours that if Mr. Harriman's contribution to the campaign fund of 1904 (and incidentally, I may mention that I am informed that this particular contribution was not used for the National campaign at all, but in the New York State campaign) had been made known before the election, you and your supporters would have endeavored to use the fact of its having been made as an insincere and untruthful argument to show that I could not be trusted to deal out exact justice to Mr. Harriman. No stronger argument against your proposition has yet been advanced than this that you have thus unconsciously advanced.

I now come to the important part of your letter, your attitude toward Mr. Haskell. You state that Mr. Haskell has voluntarily resigned from the committee. You speak highly of the public service which he has rendered, and protest against any condemnation of him except such as may come in a court. Out of your own mouth you are condemned. You thereby set up that standard of "law honesty" which has been the bane of this people in endeavoring to get equity and fair dealing — as they should obtain among high-minded men — from great business corporations, and from individuals like Mr. Haskell. Apparently you disclaim even asking Mr. Haskell to retire from the position in which you placed him, so that he retires of his own free will; and you utter no word of condemnation of his gross offenses against public decency and honesty. On the contrary, you strive to make it appear that his misconduct in reference to the Standard Oil Company is all of which he is accused; whereas, shameless tho this particular act of his is, it is no worse than countless others in his career. I contrast your action in this case with that of Mr. Taft in reference to Senator Foraker. Mr. Taft's statement when the question of his nomination was at stake was that he would rather not accept it at the price of sacrificing principle by supporting Mr. Foraker for Senator. You do not venture in so much as the lightest possible manner even to censure Mr. Haskell for his manifold misdeeds; and you ask that he be held guiltless of them unless convicted in a court of law; altho you well know that as regards the worst of them no action in a court of law would lie. You say you were ignorant of Mr. Haskell's record. If so it was willful ignorance on your part. I call your attention to the letter of Mr. L. T. Russell, the editor of the *Morning Democrat* of Ardmore, Oklahoma, in which, writing to you on September 24, 1908, he states:

"If you were ignorant of such charges it is because you refused to read them when presented to you when you visited Oklahoma last fall in the interest of Candidate Haskell. At that time I personally presented to you ten typewritten pages of charges against Mr. Haskell, covering his operations in Ohio, New York, Arkansas, Texas, and Oklahoma. * * * The charges recently made by Mr. Hearst were all made by me at that time."

You ask that we leave the courts to deal with Mr. Haskell. As to some matters the courts have already dealt with him. As to others, various private individuals whom he has wronged, and the United States Government on behalf of helpless Indians whom he has wronged, are striving to have the courts so deal with him. Mr. M. L. Mott,[3] National Attorney for the Creek Nation, writes me as follows:

"In October, 1906, Mr. Foulke, of Richmond, Indiana, was sent to investigate the matter of the townsite frauds in the Creek Nation. Mr. Foulke's report is in the hands of the Secretary of the Interior. All parties connected with these townsite frauds have used the same means and methods. Upon the report filed by Mr. Foulke, I as attorney for the Creek Nation was directed by the Secretary of the Interior to file suits in equity for the cancellation of all deeds to town lots in the Creek Nation where the same had been secured by fraud. Proceeding upon instructions and after full investigation, I found that Governor C. N. Haskell, among others, had secured deeds to quite a number of lots in Muskogee by conspiracy and fraud; that he had had these lots scheduled in the name of 'dummies' or 'straw' men who lived in the State of Ohio and elsewhere, and then had them quit-claim back to him without consideration. By this dishonest means he succeeded in getting deeds to a large number of lots belonging to the Creek Indians at one half their appraised value. I have filed quite a number of suits against Governor Haskell in which conspiracy and fraud is charged and the manner of consummating

---

[3] M. L. Mott, national attorney for the Creek Nation, able and fearless protector of the interests of his charges, whose ability to understand business, he felt, was "utterly hopeless and impossible."

it is set out in detail. Haskell has not filed any answer in any of these cases. He has simply thru his attorney filed dilatory motions, such as demurrers, pleading to the jurisdiction, &c. He dare not answer and deny the allegations set up in our bill; such an answer would be a sworn lie and known to be by the large number of 'straw' men and 'dummies' he used in perfecting the fraud."

For this particular act of the man whose public record you endorse, you may rest assured that the Interior Department will endeavor to see that the courts do "justice" to him.

When Mr. Haskell was in New York various judgments were filed against him. I will not at the moment discuss the charges of perjury and fraud made against him by Attorney Albert H. Walker, of New York, in connection with the suit decided by Judge Lacombe in March, 1902. But the records of the County Clerk of New York County show that on February 21, 1900, a judgment for damages and costs amounting to $42,235.43, recovered in the Supreme Court of the County, was filed against Charles N. Haskell. On April 2, 1900, this judgment was returned on the Sheriff's execution satisfied to the extent of only $29.80, and the remainder of it remains still unsatisfied. In this instance your proposal that Mr. Haskell be left to the court does not seem to have produced thorogoing justice. Neither shall I touch upon the various suits of all kinds now pending against him for all kinds of reasons. Thus, it is reported in the press under date of September 19, 1908, that a $500 judgment had been obtained against Mr. Haskell by an attorney of Arkansas who was employed by him "to lobby before the city council of Muskogee to get through a franchise." The attorney's fee was never paid, but the franchise was granted. Nor again shall I touch upon the facsimile published in the press of September 25th last, showing Mr. Haskell's having three years ago joined an organization to prevent union labor from entering the city in which he lived. Indeed as regards this last statement I wish distinctly to acquit Mr. Haskell of being opposed on principle to either trade unions or corporations; for I wish to acquit him of being opposed on principle to anything.

Now as to Governor Haskell's connection with the Standard Oil Company in Oklahoma.

Governor Haskell advances the fact that the United States Government permitted the Standard Oil Company on the same terms as any and all other companies to enjoy the legal privileges to which it was entitled on the Indian reservations of Oklahoma, as his justification for having given it illegal privileges to which it was not entitled in the State of Oklahoma. The excuse furnishes the measure of Governor Haskell's moral quality. The Federal act of March 11, 1904, conferred upon the Secretary of the Interior the right to grant permits for oil and gas pipelines to cross Indian reservations. Regulations to carry out the law were drawn up by the Indian Office and approved by the Secretary of the Interior April 12, 1904. In compliance with the law and the regulations the Department of the Interior permitted the Standard

Oil pipeline company (the Prairie Oil and Gas Company) and the various rival pipeline companies (such as the Oklahoma Natural Gas Company, the Cary River Gas Company, the Denz Portland Cement Company, and others, including Texas and Gulf companies), all on the same terms and under the same conditions, the right of way across the Indian reservations. No preference or privilege was granted to any company that was not also granted to all the others. Any other action than that actually taken by the Interior Department would have been as grossly improper as the actions of Governor Haskell himself. The Government stood neither for nor against any company; but it required each to obey the law. Its action was precisely like the action which it took, for instance, in proceeding against the Standard Oil Company in the rebate matter; it did not thus proceed because the Standard Oil Company was involved, but because rebates had been granted; it would have proceeded just as quickly against the rivals of the Standard Oil as against the Standard Oil itself. Our only concern was to punish any guilty party. Our effort is to do equal justice to all, and to exact justice from all alike. We are no more to be swayed from this course by desire to punish a corporation than by desire to favor it, no matter whether it is the Standard Oil or any other. The permit of the National Government, as set forth in the telegram of the Secretary of the Interior to Governor Haskell of April 23, last, was merely to cross or use the restricted allotments and tribal property of the Indians; it had nothing to do with the question of compliance with the laws of the State of Oklahoma, and conferred no privilege to cross territory in Oklahoma outside of these reservations. Governor Haskell refuses to permit any proceedings to be taken against the Standard Oil Company altho this company declines to obey the law of Oklahoma. He claims that the Standard Oil's rights were superior to the requirements of the Oklahoma constitution, for which he was himself mainly responsible; he took the decision of this question away from the courts, and, against the opinion of his Attorney General, he decided it in favor of the Standard Oil Corporation. The Attorney General of Oklahoma has made the following statement in this matter:

The President's statement as to the Prairie Oil and Gas Company suit is less than the whole matter in its whole iniquity, because on the 23rd of April I had informed the Governor that the action taken by the Prairie Company was illegal and should be enjoined and that I had an open injunction suit. At that time, April 23rd, the Governor agreed with me as to the illegality of the action and approved the bringing of the injunction.

The same day the Governor left the State to go to Denver the Prairie Company started its trespass. This, I believe, was prearranged between the Governor and the Prairie Company, as the Prairie Company rushed the laying of its pipeline during the absence of the Governor from the State.

I wired the Governor on the first of July, asking whether he had given the Prairie Oil Company permission to build their line. His reply evaded my sole question, and instead of answering it, he said that he was satisfied that the Prairie Company would not violate the law.

Between the 22nd of April and the 2nd of July Governor Haskell received no advice from me, as his legal adviser, as to the matter, and if he had received advice from his assistant Attorney General he did not do me the honor of submitting the same to me.

When he heard of the bringing of the suit he directed the Acting Governor to order me to dismiss the suit and indulged in insolent language to the effect that he would not tolerate any proceedings by me except at his direction. The use of this insulting language regarding me, together with his sudden change of heart between April and July, evidences that some very deep and controlling motive of a personal nature was back of his action.

The only person that the prohibition could help was the Standard Oil Company, and that he hazarded as much as he did for them as he did after his sudden change of heart supplies the necessary factor for any intelligent man to reckon whether the Governor of Oklahoma has a leaning toward the Standard Oil Company; and therefore the President's statement seems to me a very mild rebuke.

Charles E. West,

Attorney General of
Oklahoma.

The National Government, obeying both the law and the principles of sound morality, discriminated neither for nor against either the Standard Oil Company or its rivals. Governor Haskell, against the law and against every principle of honesty and fair dealing, discriminated in favor of the Standard Oil Corporation. Failure to see the distinction between the two cases indicates moral obliquity rather than mental obtuseness.

I believe in radical reform; and the movement for such reform can be successful only if it frowns on the demagog as it does on the corruptionist; if it shows itself as far removed from government by a mob as from government by a plutocracy. Of all corruption, the most far-reaching for evil is that which hides itself behind the mask of furious demagogy, seeking to arouse and to pander to the basest passions of mankind. No better exemplification of this type of corruption could be found than in the case of Mr. Haskell.

You have uttered no word of condemnation of Haskellism, as we thus see it. That you have consciously sought to bring it about, I do not believe. That it was the natural result of the effort to apply in practice your teachings, I have no question. *Yours truly*

4922 · TO CHARLES DOOLITTLE WALCOTT   *Roosevelt Mss.*

Washington, September 28, 1908

My dear Mr. Walcott: The following plan for redistributing the bureaus of the Government which pertain to public health has been submitted to me by the Committee of One Hundred on National Health. I desire to make this plan, or a similar one, a part of my administration program, subject to the changes which your Commission[1] may find it necessary to make in order to co-ordinate it with the more general plan of redistributing the bureaus of all

---

[1] The Commission on Reorganization of Government Scientific Work.

kinds. I understand that the Committee of One Hundred prepared this plan in consultation with the members of your Commission who were available:

In brief the plan contemplates the ultimate conversion of the Department of the Interior into a Department of Health and Education, by:

Transferring out	The Land Office
	The Reclamation Service
	The Geological Survey
	The Patent Office
	The Pension Office
Transferring in	The Public Health and Marine Hospital Service from the Department of the Treasury.
	The Bureau of Chemistry from the Department of Agriculture, excepting the divisions which do not pertain to health.
	The Division of Vital Statistics from the Census Office — to be made a Bureau.
	The Department of Health of the District of Columbia.

By introducing new Bureaus:

A Children's Bureau, as advocated by the Child Labor Committee.

A Bureau of Medical Investigation and Publication, as advocated by the Committee of One Hundred.

Other bureaus possibly.

These new proposed bureaus do not especially concern your Commission except as they show the entire plan.

I expect to put in my message to Congress a recommendation for concentrating health bureaus into one department.[2] *Sincerely yours*

4923 · TO WILLIAM HOWARD TAFT   *Roosevelt Mss.*

Personal   Washington, September 28, 1908

Dear Will: The one man in New York who will be able (and has given assurance of it already) to handle things really well as regards getting the money necessary for the expenses of the campaign has been Bob Bacon. In the first place he is efficient & in the next he has as fine a point of honor as you yourself, so that you can rest certain that anything done by him or thru him is all right. If you want to write confidentially to any man or to have

[2] Roosevelt did not make such a recommendation in his annual message nor did Congress take any action to create a department of health and education.

anything confidential done in New York I very earnestly suggest that you write to Bacon.

I think I am thru with Mr. Bryan now,[1] and, to use the words of the last Democratic President, may lapse into a condition of innocuous desuetude. You seem to be getting along well on your trip. We look forward to seeing Mrs. Taft at dinner tomorrow night. *Ever yours*

4924 · TO WILLIAM KENT   *Roosevelt Mss.*

Personal   Washington, September 28, 1908

My dear Kent:[1] I have your letter of the 22d. I have directed that Mr. Devlin[2] be instructed by the Attorney General as you request and by wire.

Now, as to what you say about the campaign. I have been active this past week for exactly the reasons you suggest. I felt it was imperative to put aggressive life into the campaign. It seems to me incredible that people should fail to understand Taft's inherent worth. Of course I do not dare in public to express my real opinion of Bryan. He is a kindly man and well-meaning in a weak way; always provided that to mean well must not be translated by him into doing well if it would interfere with his personal prospects. But he is the cheapest faker we have ever had proposed for President. How any man of average intelligence can be taken in by the Prince of Peace speech and that speech of his at the dinner to the emissaries of the Russian revolution, of which you speak, I find it difficult to understand.[3]

With warm regards, believe me, *Sincerely yours*

4925 · TO JAMES SCHOOLCRAFT SHERMAN   *Roosevelt Mss.*

Washington, September 30, 1908

My dear Sherman: Of course all kinds of complaints come to me as to the management of the campaign by the National and State Committees. I cannot keep butting in and interfering and making a general nuisance of myself. How would it do hereafter for me to write to you when I have something to

---

[1] The President informed the press that he would not continue his public debate with Bryan.

[1] William Kent, successful Chicago businessman and civic reformer, had moved to California in 1907. Devoting himself to political reform there, he served as a Republican and Independent congressman, 1911–1917; a leader of the Progressive party in the state; and later, 1917–1920, a member of the United States Tariff Commission. In 1908 Kent, long a conservationist, gave the United States the Muir Woods.

[2] Robert Thomas Devlin, United States District Attorney at San Francisco, 1905–1912, one of the officeholders hostile to Senator Perkins whose re-election Heney and Kent favored.

[3] The Prince of Peace speech was a set lecture delivered throughout the country by Mr. Bryan to advance an understanding of Christianity. The speech contained the celebrated passage in which it was argued that "until you can explain a watermelon do not be too sure that you can set limits to the power of the Almighty."

suggest? And you could then exercise your own judgment in bringing it before the National and State Committees. Just at this moment, for instance, I am told that a Pittsburgh man who wanted to make a contribution to the National Committee came on to Philadelphia to complain that there was not a human being in Pittsburgh to whom he could make it; and wanted to know to whom it should be given. So I hear complaints about failure to attend to the labor people, the Grand Army, and the like. Wouldn't it be a good thing for you to be where you could exercise some aid and influence in the campaign with the two committees whenever you are not off on speaking trips yourself? *Faithfully yours*

4926 · TO FITZHUGH LEE   *Roosevelt Mss.*

Washington, September 30, 1908

Dear Fitz: We are all so interested to hear from you, and I must send you just a line myself to tell you how everything is getting on. Archie Butt is doing finely and we are devoted to him; but of course no one can quite take your place as Master of Horse and intimate friend of so many different members of the family!

Ted has now gone to work in a carpet mill up in Connecticut, and he will be kept close to the grindstone for the next few years. Kermit's embarkation on a career of hard labor is still a couple of years distant, and indeed, when he comes back from the African trip it is possible that he may decide to finish his course at Harvard. I shall always feel that you rendered an invaluable service to Kermit. It was thru you that he learned to ride, and to become fond of and at ease with horses. He hopes to do a little hunting in Geneseo this year. Archie is in Groton, and Quentin went to the Episcopal High School at Alexandria. He was hazed a good deal, which is all right; but unfortunately in the course of it they twice made him smoke until he was sick in the stomach and this completely upset his health so that he is now home and in bed; but I think he will soon be all right and back at school.

I look forward to hearing from you after the cavalry school has been open for a few weeks. I am sure I need not tell you, Fitz, how proud I am of you and how sure I am that you will do credit in all ways to yourself, to your family name, and to the United States Army. *Ever your attached friend*

P.S. If that war does ever come along I think we will have to take Archie Butt in some capacity with our cavalry brigade or division!

4927 · TO GEORGE BRUCE CORTELYOU   *Roosevelt Mss.*

Washington, October 1, 1908

To the Secretary of the Treasury: I hand you herewith the report of the Civil Service Commission and accompanying documents in the case of political assessments collected from the classified employees of the custom house at

Port Huron, Michigan. I desire that my action be given as wide publicity as possible. This so that all other Collectors and heads of bureaus or offices may be warned in the matter.

I regard the offense as very gross. The hardship and suffering entailed on people of small salary is set forth in touching manner in the letter of complaint. A Government employee in the classified service who is deprived by lawful authority of power to exercise political activity is entitled to absolute immunity for failure to pay assessments or perform political service. It appears from the report of the Commission that the present condition of affairs at Port Huron has lasted substantially ten years. I agree with the Commission that under the circumstances set forth in their letter either the Collector was ignorant of what he should have known for the protection of his force and for the proper discharge of the duties of his office — that is of things of public and general notoriety easily ascertained and established — or else that he knowingly and willfully permitted the evil practices to continue. In either case he is manifestly unfit to discharge the duties of his office and I shall forthwith remove him. He has already been heard at length by the Commission. I shall also remove Mr. Charles A. Bailey, the Special Treasury Agent, for the reasons set forth at length in the report of the Commission.[1]

4928 · TO JOHN S. LEECH *Roosevelt Mss.*

Washington, October 2, 1908

To the Public Printer: I send you herewith the Manual of Style, Government Printing Office, Secretary of State. This binding is absurd, and it is the kind of binding which I wish stopt everywhere in the Government service. A book like this is a purely routine and official matter. To put it in this kind of binding is ridiculous in point of taste and wholly unwarranted from the standpoint of economy. In not one instance hereafter is any Government volume of any kind to have any of these absurd bindings de luxe put upon them unless ordered by Congress or else specifically and in writing ordered by the President. I have called attention to this matter on various previous occasions. Now please see that no binding but cloths of the ordinary type is hereafter used on any Government publication. On January 1st you will report to me whether in any single instance this order has not been obeyed. I of course except any order specifically made by Congress.

4929 · TO KERMIT ROOSEVELT *Roosevelt Mss.*

Washington, October 3, 1908

Dear Kermit: This is such a nice letter that I thought I would send it to you. By the way, I wrote Wells that I hoped you would keep up on your own account your reading of Greek. I was extremely pleased to find you reading

[1] This letter was released for publication on October 4.

Homer last summer, just as I am glad that Ted reads Latin. I never got so that I could with any real pleasure read either Greek or Latin. It was a labor. You may be amused that both Mr. Loeb and I feel that you have chosen the exact six courses that we ourselves would have chosen! *Ever your loving father*

4930 · TO MAURICE FRANCIS EGAN   *Roosevelt Mss.*

Washington, October 5, 1908

My dear Egan: Butler wrote me enthusiastically about you and Hill as just the right types of American diplomats; and among the many reasons why I congratulate myself upon your appointment, as well as Hill's and Riddle's, is that it does serve as an offset to the tendency to put an exaggerated estimate on wealth here.

I look forward to seeing you to talk over the very interesting questions you touch upon as to conditions in Denmark. I am as much puzzled as you are by the fact that in a country of peasant farmers devoted to the soil, who live well and simply, there should be such a high rate of illegitimacy, such prevalence of suicide, and such growth of socialism, even tho the socialism is not of the worst type. If you see Mr. Gill [1] himself you might mention the fact that the most purely agricultural State we have is Mississippi, and tho there are many excellent points about the Mississippians, I do not think we could afford to have other Mississippis substituted for say Massachusetts and Iowa. I very emphatically believe in a big farming population as the basis for a country, and I am glad to see they have the larger share in the Government; but there must also be a big alloy of townfolk in order to get the best results. Vermont is a pretty good State, largely because there *is* this mixture. *Faithfully yours*

4931 · TO JONATHAN BOURNE, JUNIOR   *Roosevelt Mss.*

Washington, October 5, 1908

My dear Senator Bourne: I should greatly question the advisability of any public statement in the matter, and you are not to publish this letter without telegraphic authority from me. But, as I suppose I need hardly say, any statement that I, or anyone else with my knowledge, made any promise of any kind, sort or description to Senator Fulton or to anyone else for the purpose

[1] In all probability Wilson Lindsley Gill who in 1908 was president of the Children's International State which included representatives from European, Oriental, South American, and Scandinavian countries. Gill, as he was well aware, had an extraordinary career. He was a member of the first kindergarten class in this country and continued his education at Dartmouth, the Yale scientific school, and the Yale Law School. Thus prepared, he was, among other things, the general manager of a wheel and car works, a magazine editor, the engineer for the 42nd Street terminal under the East River, the supervisor of all United States Indian schools, the architect for the children's buildings at the expositions in 1893 and 1903. Primary concerns throughout his career were the education of children and democratic social organization.

of getting a delegation from Oregon or anywhere else is a simple falsehood. Moreover, any statement that the power of the administration is to be or may be used to break down the primary law or any other law in Oregon or any-where else, or to influence the legislature in Oregon or anywhere else to dis-regard any pledge they have given or instruction they have received, or to refuse to carry out the will of the people properly exprest in the constitu-tional and legal manner, is absolutely false.[1]

You say you are sure that I will feel indignant that any person should dare to suppose that I would quietly assent to, much less assist at, such an effort. You are quite right, and I am bound to say that I am inclined to be indignant that you should so much as think it necessary to get a denial from me. Your plain duty was, not to write to me a personal and confidential letter, but to state openly that you were confident that any such statements as those you say have been made were false, and that you challenged any man making them to dare to telegraph me to find out if they were true. *Yours truly*

4932 · TO ROBERT JACKSON GAMBLE   *Roosevelt Mss.*

Washington, October 5, 1908

My dear Senator Gamble: Your letter illustrates how very inadvisable it is that any of the executive work should be done save by purely executive bodies under the control of the President.[1] The legislative body from the very fact of its being fitted to do legislative work cannot perform executive functions well, and every effort to establish quasi-executive bodies which are composed of legislators or are responsible to the legislature rather than to the executive results in inferior service, and has as in this case produced com-plaints which it is difficult to meet and remedy. I will see if there is anything that the executive can do in the matter. *Sincerely yours*

4933 · TO LYMAN ABBOTT   *Roosevelt Mss.*

Washington, October 5, 1908

My dear Dr. Abbott: Now and then it is well to have certain things of record somewhere, and I write you this letter merely for the purpose of putting into

[1] Oregon had passed a law, effective for the first time in 1908, by which candidates for the state legislature were pledged to support for the United States Senate the candidate for that office who received the largest vote at the general election. This in effect established the popular election of senators. The law produced a curious situation, for the Republicans won a majority of the legislature but were forced, because of their pledge, to send to Washington the Democratic senatorial candidate, George E. Chamberlain, instead of Senator Fulton.

[1] Gamble was troubled by the inefficient and costly operation of the Battle Mountain sanitarium which had recently opened at Hot Springs, South Dakota. The sanitarium was a branch of the National Home for Disabled Volunteer Soldiers whose board of managers was responsible to Congress rather than the President.

convenient form certain facts in reference to the nomination of Mr. Taft. It has been violently asserted by various people, and notably among the press by the *Sun* and the *Evening Post*, that I dictated Mr. Taft's nomination by the use of the officeholders, especially in the Southern States; indeed, the charge is usually made only as regards the Southern States, because it is preposterous to suppose that it is true anywhere else.

There were in that convention six serious candidates: Taft, Fairbanks, Cannon, Knox, Hughes and La Follette. The States of Ohio, Indiana, Illinois, Pennsylvania, New York and Wisconsin stood *nearly* solidly each behind its respective candidate. Indiana alone was *absolutely* solid, however. In each of the other States Taft got one or more votes, and Foraker took away four from him in Ohio; Hughes losing votes in New York to both Taft and Cannon. In these six States the sentiment was undoubtedly in each case more or less warmly for the local candidate, and almost all the officeholders were also for that candidate except that in Ohio a considerable number of perhaps a majority of the officeholders went for Foraker, and in New York a much smaller proportion went against Hughes. But substantially in each of these cases except in Ohio the officeholders followed the wishes of the people of their districts.

Outside of these six States there were 27 northern, central and western States all of which had voted the Republican ticket at the previous election, and 12 southern States which had stood solidly for the Democratic ticket at the previous election. The former were of course totally uninfluenced by the officeholders, and could not have been influenced by the officeholders. They cast 379 votes for Taft and 13 for the other candidates. The 12 southern States, the only ones in which the officeholders could have counted, cast 247 for Taft and 18 for some of the other candidates. In other words, the proportion of votes against Taft was twice as great in the southern States, where alone the officeholders had influence and which are not expected to cast an electoral vote for the Republican candidate, as in the northern States (outside of the six favorite son States) in which officeholders had no influence. Moreover, if every vote from the Southern States (in which alone the officeholders had any influence) had been eliminated, Taft would still have been nominated by a nearly two-to-one vote.

Moreover, of the votes outside of the favorite son States which were given in the North against Taft, one came from Michigan, by Congressional influence for Cannon, and the others from New Jersey and New Hampshire, the two States in which the corporation influences had most to say.

In other words the vote shows that in the North, if the officeholders did anything they simply followed the general trend in their several districts, accordingly as it was for Taft, Hughes, Fairbanks, Cannon, Knox or La Follette. In the South there was a slightly greater percentage of opposition to Taft, due in part, I am convinced, to the absolute purchase of votes, in part to

1275

other causes; but the officeholders played no ponderable part. *Sincerely yours*

Roosevelt Mss.

Washington, October 6, 1908

To the Secretary of State: I enclose herewith a number of affidavits in the Pouren case. Unless controverted these affidavits seem to establish clearly the fact that Pouren was a revolutionist and took an active part in the revolutionary troubles in Livland Province, Russia, and that the crimes which he is alleged to have committed were acts committed by order of the revolutionary committees and which, whether defensible or indefensible in character, were parts of the revolutionary proceedings and therefore political crimes. It seems to me clear, therefore, that Pouren's case is one that comes directly under the clause of the treaty which forbids the extradition of political offenders.[1]

Roosevelt Mss.

Personal Washington, October 6, 1908

My dear Abbott: I have your letter of the 5th and return the enclosures herewith. As regards what Taft has said about the 13th, 14th and 15th amendments, he means nothing whatever except that he follows my position; in other words, that he takes the position of the *Outlook* in its capital editorial on Lunar Politics when it discust Messrs. Vardaman and Williams' efforts to reach the Senate from Mississippi by advocating, respectively, the abolition of the 14th and 15th amendments.

As to appointments, I suppose, without having any authority to speak, that he does mean that he would carry out the theory upon which I have acted. Thus I am the first President that has appointed colored men to responsible positions in the North, as in the case of Anderson in New York, Williams in Chicago, and Lewis in Boston. I could not give you the exact numbers of Negro appointments that I have made in the South; but I have decreased the total number of appointees and I think I have immeasurably raised their

[1] On October 11 Root ordered the reopening of the Pouren case (see Numbers 4874, 4917) to permit the introduction of new testimony based on these affidavits. The Russian government, contending that the extradition commissioner after six months of hearings had already decided that Pouren's offenses were common-law rather than political crimes, countered by bringing action in the circuit court to prevent the reopening of the case. Root then decided to dismiss the whole case "without prejudice to the right of the demanding Government [Russia] to initiate a new proceeding. . . ." This action, avoiding any decision on the legal technicalities of the extradition hearings, permitted the Administration to announce, shortly before election day as Roosevelt had desired, that Pouren's extradition had been refused. Russia immediately instituted a new proceeding, but on March 29, 1909, Pouren was finally discharged from the custody of the extradition commissioner. For details of the case see *Foreign Relations of the United States*, 1909 (Washington, 1914), pp. 513–523.

character. I enclose you a list of the principal Negro appointments, and you might ask Booker T. Washington as to their character. Most emphatically Taft will not make a Garrisonian issue of the question of Negro suffrage. I believe that his attitude is as nearly that of the *Outlook,* as nearly my attitude, as it could well be. *Faithfully yours*

4936 · TO WILLIAM ALLEN WHITE   *Roosevelt Mss.*

Personal   Washington, October 7, 1908

Dear White: The enclosed is of course funny; but do you think that it is right to make a jest which distinctly conveys the impression that I as well as Bryan, Haskell and Hearst, am lying and that all of us indiscriminately are rascals? Haskell lies, and is a rascal, why not say so? Personally I think that the amount of damage to the public conscience done by conscienceless and unscrupulous politicians and men of business is surpassed by that done by those newspapermen who are not only conscienceless and unscrupulous but are afflicted with an incurable levity and you ought never to be identified with such men. In New York State I think that Messrs. Hearst, Pulitzer, Laffan, Bennett, Villard and Ogden, according to their several degrees of noxiousness, represent a baser influence for evil than that of any corresponding number of the worst businessmen or politicians. Now you are one of the men in whom we who stand for decency believe, and I do not like to see you adopt the attitude, than which hardly any can be more mischievous — the attitude of teaching well-meaning but naturally puzzled private citizens that there is no difference between honest and dishonest men in public life; that an unspeakable scoundrel like Haskell — a man very much worse in kind than Tweed, altho not able to be worse in degree — is no more and no less a grafter and a liar than a man who is endeavoring with a measure of success to carry on the public business in a difficult and responsible office in accordance with proper ideals. There can be no worse service rendered to the public than is rendered by papers like the *Evening Post,* which endeavors to persuade the public that all the good and bad men in public life stand on the same level. When such belief is once adopted, every rascal profits and every honest man is hurt.

Now I hope you believe that I am not in the least concerned about myself in this matter. My work is done, or practically done. It is of very little consequence what is now said of me anyhow, and moreover, so far as it is of consequence, the ultimate judgment of me will be very little affected by what is now said of me. My concern is for the spirit of public decency; and therefore for the effect upon the average plain man, the man upon whom all our government rests, of articles teaching him what this clipping does. You may think that this is a rather serious letter to be drawn out by what was probably nothing more than a thoughtless kind of jest. But I do not like this kind of jest. There are some subjects, such as the character of a woman, as to which jesting is offensive. So I think is a jest of this kind. I have always regarded you as one of the potent influences for good in this country, and I do not want to see you do anything that tends for bad. *Faithfully yours*

4937 · TO VICTOR HOWARD METCALF   *Roosevelt Mss.*

Washington, October 8, 1908

To the Secretary of the Navy: I understand that the experiments with the torpedo invented by Lieutenant Commander Cleland Davis indicate that this torpedo may prove to be a very dangerous implement of warfare.[1] If this is true, then we should at once take measures in the design of our new ships as well as in those building to provide adequate protection, if possible, against attack from the Davis torpedo. I would like to know if this subject has received careful consideration, and also what steps have been taken to meet the situation.

4938 · TO JAMES SCHOOLCRAFT SHERMAN   *Roosevelt Mss.*

Washington, October 10, 1908

Dear Sherman: In regard to the matter of the circulation in the Catholic papers of Debs' ferocious assault on Taft in the *Appeal to Reason*,[1] I find that the National Committee has done nothing whatever about it. Apparently they do not see its value, or else do not know how to handle it. It is not a matter that needs money at all, or certainly a very insignificant amount. What is necessary is to get the Catholic layman to understand just the nature of the attack that has been made upon Taft, and that has been circulated extensively by a socialistic paper among Protestant clergymen and Masons. Doubtless it was paid for by some of the big people who hate Taft for the simple reason that he is honest. I think it is very important that steps should be taken not only in New York but in Indiana and Ohio, as well as Maryland, to see that this assault by the Debs socialists on Taft should be circulated in every Catholic paper; with, I suppose, the simple headline that it had been sent out to Masonic bodies, protestant clergymen and others, and was designed by misrepresentation to influence good citizens who do not know the facts against Taft simply because Taft had been absolutely upright and fair in his dealings with every church. *Sincerely yours*

[1] See No. 4863.

---

[1] Debs concentrated on Taft's Philippine policies, particularly in regard to the Catholic Church and the Church lands.

Washington, October 10, 1908

Dear Will: Of course I am importuned continually to give you advice on one point or another, and my answer usually is that I am enough of a nuisance as it is without deliberately and unnecessarily becoming such to a still greater extent. But Neill, the labor man, who has been doing good work, made a suggestion which I shall repeat to you. It is that hereafter, especially in the East, you do not attack Gompers by name.[1]

As a matter of fact I do not suppose you would think of doing so, but my own judgment would be in agreement with Neill's, that it would be better not to name him. Human nature is very queer, including labor human nature; and it has been an old experience of mine that friends or followers of a given opponent would often support me instead of that opponent, and yet become indignant and refuse to support me if I attacked the said opponent. Now and then it is necessary, but in this case I do not think that any advantage would be gained by it. All of which is doubtless entirely superfluous.

Keefe, of the Longshoremen's Union, has come out strongly in our favor. I have been in conference recently with Sherrill,[2] who has been doing first-class work among both businessmen and labor men. We have something on hand for New York which if it results rightly may help us a great deal with the labor people. Sherrill is a mighty good fellow and a mighty efficient fellow, and after election if you will permit me I am going to say something to you in his behalf. You will remember that he is a Yale man, the runner, and a very cultivated fellow.

Well, you only have three weeks more of your exhausting labor. I am perfectly clear that Bryan has lost ground during the last three weeks, and your speeches have grown stronger and stronger. You are making a great campaign. All I wanted to be sure of was that the people of this country should get really to see and know you. That once done, I had no fear of the result.

I am doing everything I can to bring about Hughes' election in New York, but unless you carry the State very handsomely, Hughes will have hard work defeating Chanler.[3] Won't you, while in New York, speak strongly

[1] This was also the view of other pro-Republican labor leaders. On October 16, however, Roosevelt wrote Taft that he had changed his mind "about leaving out Gompers' name" (Roosevelt Mss.). Gompers' aggressive stumping for Bryan doubtless provoked this reversal.

[2] Charles Hitchcock Sherrill, champion Yale sprinter who earned his "Y" in life as a New York attorney, Taft's minister to Argentina, a critic of Democratic foreign policy, and the author of "Stained Glass Tours" of the countries of western Europe.

[3] Lewis S. Chanler, Lieutenant Governor of New York, had won the Democratic gubernatorial nomination in spite of Tammany's reluctance to support him. He campaigned aggressively, but Hughes won the election with a plurality of almost 70,000, a larger margin than that of 1906. Chanler polled almost 70,000 votes more than did Bryan in New York.

for Hughes, pointing out his disinterestedness in making the campaign in the west, instead of purely keeping to New York? Hughes deserves credit for this; you would help him by speaking for him; it would do good from every standpoint. *Ever yours*

P.S. I see in the papers that you may be passing thru Washington. If so, of course make your headquarters with us. Let me know a little while in advance what your plans are.

4940 · TO WILLIAM HOWARD TAFT   *Roosevelt Mss.*

Personal   Washington, October 12, 1908

Dear Will: It did me good to get your letter of the 9th. I feel just as you do about Cannon. He is our burden in this campaign, and the ideal result would be to have a Republican Congress with a majority so small that neither Cannon nor Tawney can be made Speaker.

I am especially relieved at Cox's estimate about Ohio. I have lookt over the matter in New York as carefully as I know how and I am unable to figure out anything but a victory for you; and I am more and more inclined to believe that Hughes will pull thru, largely because of the admiration created by his stumping trip in the West.

I wish that the Catholic vote were better organized. The attacks upon you by a certain type of small Protestant bigots are so infamous as to make my blood boil. Van Cleave's support of the ticket has been a real injury. Morrissey,[1] by the way, told me emphatically that he was for you, and strongly for you, but he also told me that they were having great difficulty with many of their men.

My opinion of Burton is precisely yours.

I do not believe there will be a thing more for me to do in the campaign. The only possible contingency that I can see is if it should ever come when I could speak straightforwardly to the labor men and explain to them that they were cutting their own throats by voting for Bryan.[2] They seem to be most off in Pennsylvania, where they can do nothing but cut down the majority.

We shall expect you to stay at the White House while you are in Washington, unless you or your managers think you had better stay elsewhere. In that case, my dear Will, I need hardly say that I particularly want you to stay elsewhere; for the one thing is to make every move so that it will help in your campaign. I don't know whether your staying at the White House would hurt you; consult the managers, and then do just what you think will give least chance for trouble.

[1] P. H. Morrissey, head of the railway trainmen.
[2] The President spoke "straightforwardly" in his public letters to Dolan, Grace, and Knox; see Numbers 4945, 4956, 4959.

It was the greatest pleasure to see Mrs. Taft. *Ever yours*

[*Handwritten*] You have done magnificently on your trip; it has been the winning card.

4941 · TO JOHN RALEIGH MOTT   *Roosevelt Mss.*

Washington, October 12, 1908

My dear Mr. Mott: [1] Thru you I wish to send a word of special greeting to the young men of Russia. There is no nation in the world which, more than Russia, holds in its hands the fate of the coming years, and for this reason, not only should every young Russian feel a peculiar sense of responsibility, but all outsiders should likewise feel a special interest in the moral and ethical development of the mighty people which occupies so great and commanding a position alike in Europe and Asia.

Surely the lessons to be taught to young men are much the same everywhere; and for the matter of that so are the lessons that should be taught to all men. A high and fine patriotism, an intense devotion to one's own country, is not only not incompatible with, but on the contrary, is an aid to, a genuine love for and good feeling toward all mankind. He who helps to raise the national type of his own nation has helped all men in other nations. Material well-being is essential to a nation, and therefore there must be material efficiency in the individuals who make up the nation; to this end there is need of adequate physical as well as adequate mental development; and those who would be leaders in a reform movement must take care of both mind and body. But tho the body is important, and the mind still more important, what is most important of all is character, by which we mean the sum of those qualities which tell most in making a man both brave and tender, both generous and farsighted, both upright in his dealings with other men and insistent upon their showing a similar spirit to him in return.

To the young men of Russia, as to the young men of America, I would especially urge the need of combining a high ideal with practical efficiency in carrying it out. Scorn the base and sordid materialists who would teach that power in any form, whether of money or of political rule, justifies iniquity or is to be sought for at the expense of justice and fair dealing. Do not be misled by the so-called practical men who teach that success is all that counts, that the only kind of success worth having is that which brings money or power, and that the means of obtaining it are immaterial. Such success is found in the long run to be purchased

[1] John Raleigh Mott, chairman of the executive committee of the Student Volunteer Service since 1888; general secretary of the World's Student Christian Federation since 1895; foreign secretary of the international committee of the Y.M.C.A. since 1898; at this time about to leave on one of his many evangelical tours; later appointed by Wilson to the Mexican Commission, 1916, and the special mission to Russia, 1917.

at the cost of all that makes life really worth living. The only permanently happy life is that of the good man or good woman who does his or her duty earnestly and well.

But, while scorning the baseness of the mere materialists, shun also the visionary doctrinaire who bids you seek for an impossible, and I may incidentally add, a highly undesirable, Utopia. The idealist who refuses to make his ideals measurably practicable, and refuses to work for their achievement in measurably practical ways, is far more often a curse than a help both to his country and to mankind. Distrust the preacher whose life does not measurably correspond to his teaching. Distrust especially any scheme of life which cannot in practice be measurably realized, or which has to be realized by means of a violent cataclysm rather than by the sure steady growth which alone gives hope of retaining the benefits which are acquired by change.

The revolutionary and the reactionary play into one another's hands, for each in turn, by his foolish and blind violence, by the fury of his excesses, make good men turn in loathing from the side he champions. There are certain qualities, like honesty and justice, like fair treatment for all, which must be demanded absolutely; there are certain vices, such as cruelty, dishonesty and cowardice, with which there can be no compromise; but do not be misled by names into attacking a quality which is right and proper in itself, tho it may develop into an abuse. An unrighteous war is hideous; but it is hideous, not because it is war but because it is unrighteous; and the man who opposes all war, if his teachings were adopted by good people, might cause more far-reaching evil to mankind than any conqueror. Ignoble and unrighteous peace may be not only wrong in itself, but may breed every form of evil in the state where it obtains. Abuses spring up in family life; cut them out fearlessly; but never forget that the highest social relations of mankind are those which obtain in happy family life at its best, as we see it in the countries of christendom, where husband and wife live in love and honor, with many healthy children, doing their duty to each other, to their children, to their neighbors and to the state. Self-mastery, self-restraint moderation, common sense; these qualities are as vital as the most fervid zeal and love of righteousness.

Finally, aside from the duty of the man as an individual, I ask the young men of Russia to remember the duty that a great State owes in its international relations. Weakness is to be despised in the nation as in the individual. It is a shame to submit to wrong, as much in one case as in the other; and it is a shame to inflict wrong. Our aim in international affairs should be as our aim in private affairs. An upright man will not wrong his neighbor; and so all upright men should strive to see that the nation to which they belong refuses to wrong any neighbor, does justice to all within its gates as well as to the world outside, and makes the precepts of the golden rule its guide, exactly as it should be the guide of individuals in private life. The state must be practical and efficient; but the state should ever show its fealty to lofty ideals. *Yours truly*

4942 · TO JOHN RALEIGH MOTT   *Roosevelt Mss.*

Washington, October 12, 1908

My dear Mr. Mott: I very earnestly sympathize with the plea you make, in *The Future Leadership of the Church*,[1] for the strongest and best-trained young men to turn themselves more and more toward the leadership of the aggressive forces that make for christianity. It is a matter of grave concern that in the United States, especially, there should be a tendency in the number of students at the leading graduate theological schools to fall off at the very time that the communicant membership of the churches is markedly increasing. Indeed this question of recruiting the ranks of the christian ministry is one of world-wide interest and concern. But I do not speak only of ministers. I speak of all who take part in a broad and catholic spirit in work for the essentials of christianity, of all who without regard to differences of sect will join with one another, and indeed with all good men in whatever way they worship their Creator, to bring nearer the reign of righteousness and of brotherly kindness on this earth.

Small, narrow, one-sided men, no matter how earnest, cannot supply leadership for the moral and religious forces which alone can redeem nations. They can do good in their own way; but in addition to them, and especially for this particular work, the strongest are needed—men of marked personality who to tenderness add force and grasp, who show capacity for friendship, and who to a fine character unite an intense moral and spiritual enthusiasm.

Particularly do we need such forces in a nation like ours, which on the one hand in many places is only just emerging from the old pioneer conditions, and which on the other hand has developed to a peculiar degree the tense and highly complex industrialism which is characteristic of the present age of the world. In the growth of our people westward across this continent, a place the importance of which cannot be overestimated is filled by the heroic, self-denying, militant characters who constituted the pioneer christian ministry, who laid deep the foundations for the christian commonwealths which have grown up in the West, the Northwest and the Southwest. Our territories and our new states are still plastic; they are still near enough the pioneer days to be in the formative period; and it is of transcendent importance that the highest christian ideals shall dominate and determine their civilization.

But it is at least as important that this should be true also of the older states. Every great city calls with insistent longing for leaders able and willing to suffer and fight, to show fortitude and daring, to grapple with

[1] John R. Mott, *The Future Leadership of the Church* (New York, 1908).

iron will and undaunted front, the terrible evils that grow up where men are crowded together, where life is led under a constant and feverish strain, where great wealth and biting poverty jostle one another. The service can be rendered in the ministry, as I have known it to be rendered by Protestant clergyman and Catholic priest, aye, and by Jewish Rabbi, or it can be rendered by laymen, by such men as Jacob Riis, by many a man and woman whom I could name, who, with infinite self-devotion, with love for mankind, but with a wisdom which prevents this love from becoming hysterical or sentimental, work steadily for the uplifting of their kind.

The field for work is very broad and very diversified, and those who work in it are all too few. Immigrants come to our shores by the million to begin here a new life. They have been torn up by the roots from their ancient associations, and such uprooting gives peculiar opportunities to the powers of evil. Every possible effort should be made, for their sakes and for ours too, to supply new ties of morality, of religion, of honorable obligation as between man and man, to replace the old ties they have sundered. In the country districts, too, there is peculiar need for the church to serve as a revivifying ethical and social influence, and to do its part in giving broader opportunities for interest and usefulness in country life; and to do this will help to put a stop to the unhealthy drift toward the cities. We have a vast missionary responsibility, not only in the Philippines, but in Asia and Africa as well. Moreover, all clergymen, all laymen who thoroly believe that the tree is to be judged by its fruits, that religion and christianity cannot prosper unless they result in moral uplift and social betterment, are in honor bound to try to furnish leadership in every social movement for the self-mastery of the individual, for the uplifting of mankind. This means that ever before us there will be the problem of working, with fervor but with broad tolerance and charity, so that religion may find its expression in an upright and useful life. There must be union and co-operation among all good men who wish to see the spirit of true christianity given practical expression in accordance with the biblical precept that "by their fruits shall you know them." There are opportunities of note in the world for all such men, be they clergymen or laymen. Grave responsibilities rest upon them. Danger and work challenge them to action. Let the challenge be accepted. The work to be done is not easy. No work worth doing ever is easy. The fight for righteousness, the effort to realize the kingdom of God in this world, is fraught with infinite hardship and risk, with the certainty of wearisome labor and discouragement, with danger to all who are feeble and faint-hearted. It is because of this very fact that the best, the most resolute, and the most daring spirits, should listen to the summons which calls them to the life of effort and conflict. We ask that men of heroic temper undertake the great adventure. We ask it for the very reason that the work thus undertaken necessitates the sacrifice of self-interest. Heroic deeds are to be done in this struggle and we ask for heroic men to come forward and do them.

The trumpet call is the most inspiriting of all sounds, because it summons men to spurn ease and self-indulgence and timidity, and bids them forth to the field where they must dare and do and die at need. So now the call of duty to undertake this great spiritual adventure, this work for the betterment of mankind, should ring in the ears of young men who are high of heart and gallant of soul, as a challenge to turn to the hard life of labor and risk which is so infinitely well worth living.[2] *Sincerely yours*

4943 · TO RICHARD VICTOR OULAHAN   *Roosevelt Mss.*

Washington, October 12, 1908

Dear Dick: The enclosed is a sample of the kind of base work that is being done against Taft, and I suppose it is appealing to a small number of exceedingly foolish bigots. Now Taft is being attacked in reality because he has been square and fair toward Catholics. You, yourself a Catholic, know that both Taft and I would stand just as stiffly against anything wrong done by or for Catholics as against any wrong done to them. All that Taft has done is literally to give a square deal. It seems to me that special pains should be taken thru men like Ernest Harvier and Michael Walsh[1] to have the Catholic laymen of New York, the men who are good Americans and want no more than justice, understand the kind of assault that with the encouragement of Mr. Bryan's campaign management is being made upon Mr. Taft. It is made all thru the country. Sometimes it takes the form of attacking him because he is a Unitarian, but the underlying cause is because he acted fairly toward the Catholic church in Philippine matters. Please see Harvier and Michael Walsh and show them this letter as well as the one I am writing you, and get their advice as to how to handle the matter. *Sincerely yours*

4944 · TO CHARLES EVANS HUGHES   *Roosevelt Mss.*

Washington, October 14, 1908

My dear Governor: Permit me to congratulate you upon the admirable campaign work that you have been doing. I think it has been of the greatest service in the West; and what is more, I think it has been of great service in New York, not only to Taft but in the State campaign, to have had you do just what you did in the West. I have kept in the closest touch possible with the different organization men, and I believe now that you will have their hearty and undivided support. I was amused the other day

[2] This letter, in slightly revised form, was used as an introduction to *The Claims and Opportunities of the Christian Ministry* (New York, 1913), a series of essays compiled and edited by Mott. Among the other contributors to this volume was Woodrow Wilson.

[1] Michael J. Walsh, Irish-American publicist, member of the Catholic Club of New York City.

to find that one of the leaders, who had originally been very much opposed to your renomination, was now your enthusiastic backer, having been completely converted by your speeches in the West. Then again, my New York tailor happened to remark casually to me the other day that he had been intending to vote for Chanler, but your campaign in the West, the way you had handled Bryan, the aggressive fight you had made, and your disinterested willingness to help the entire Republican ticket even when it took you out of your own State, had converted him and he was heart and soul for you.

When you have handled things so admirably, it is needless for me to make *any* suggestions; and indeed, the only suggestions I would have to make are that you should continue precisely and exactly along the lines you have been following. In a fight like this, people do not want a mealy-mouthed man, and your aggressive hard-hitting against Bryan and Bryanism has been of enormous consequence. I believe the point you make about the judiciary is particularly good. Somebody suggested the other day that if Bryan came in he ought to make Gompers Chief Justice! I enclose a letter from Marcus Marks which I think contains a sound suggestion. It is good to show that Bryan is trying to excite class against class, and it is good also to dwell upon the fact that the success of Mr. Bryan means inevitably a period of very hard times indeed, and that the workingman who votes for him is voting against his own pocket as well as against all the principles of sound Americanism. Of course Bryan is not sincere in the panaceas he now advocates; but he is a specious creature, and men tend to forget the fact that the kindly, shallow, moderately well-meaning talker really has no sincerity of conviction.

I do not say anything about Chanler because you know how to handle that matter without any kind of a suggestion from me. What I have been drilling into our people is to make the fight perfectly straight for Taft and Hughes. You will gain some votes that Taft won't — that is, some negroes and some misled and rather bigoted evangelical Protestants who object to Taft either because he is too favorable to Catholics (which he is not) or because he is a Unitarian — as John Quincy Adams was (and while Lincoln was not, yet if Taft is to be opposed on religious grounds, then Lincoln ought never to have been elected). On the other hand, at present Taft will get some foreign votes that you won't, but I believe that this will be remedied by your campaign.

With all good wishes, believe me, *Sincerely yours*

4945 · TO THOMAS J. DOLAN   *Roosevelt Mss.*

Washington, October 15, 1908

My dear Mr. Dolan: I have your letter of the 13th instant and am much pleased with the copy of the article for your Journal which you enclose.

Indeed, you may rest assured that, if I did not believe that Taft would occupy just the position toward organized labor that I have tried to occupy, and in which you and I believe, then, fond tho I am of him, I would not back him. As you know, I have never for one moment hesitated to oppose organized labor on any point where I thought organized labor was wrong; but just as little do I hesitate to stand up for organized labor when I think it is right. The administration can well afford to stand on its record of positive achievement for organized labor; and as regards the Isthmus of Panama, where we have had most to do with organized labor, that record is Taft's. You yourself know well what the United States Government has done as regards the workingmen on the Isthmus; thanks to Mr. Taft the record of the Government at Panama is that of a model employer, both as regards wages and hours and as regards the housing and care of the employees. I do not believe that the laboring men of this country have ever had in office a stauncher friend than Mr. Taft. The attack upon him by certain self-constituted political leaders of organized labor if successful would in the long run gravely damage the cause of organized labor; for these men are trying to persuade the people of this country that organized labor has interests apart from, and hostile to, the interests of the great mass of the American people; and such an attitude if persisted in would inevitably in the end result disastrously to organized labor itself. I believe they will fail in this effort to misguide their followers, and to do wrong to the American people; and it is above all things for the interest of organized labor that they should fail. If Mr. Taft were not elected, the chief sufferers from the chaotic business conditions that would follow would be the workingmen; all of our citizens would benefit by Mr. Taft's election; but the workingmen most of all. *Sincerely yours*

4946 · TO HENRY CABOT LODGE   *Roosevelt Mss.*

Washington, October 15, 1908

Dear Cabot: Come now, when you yourself are being misrepresented by the newspapers why don't you feel it safe to assume, what as a matter of fact is the case, that Mr. Metcalf is being just as much misrepresented? The newspapers, in accordance with their habit, are sending broadcast over the country the statement that you in a speech declared that Japan would insult this country if it were not for the American navy. People have spoken to me about this speech of yours and editorials have appeared in the papers on the subject, as in the Washington *Post* of yesterday morning. I have always said I was sure you never said anything of the kind. Metcalf's only remark to the newspapermen was that he would not discuss the statement imputed to you because he did not believe you had made it and that if the Democratic party really wisht a navy adequate to protect our coast line we would need one greater than that of Great Britain. Metcalf says that he thinks, but cannot be sure, that he knows who Low is; but that he certainly never saw him or spoke to him on this subject.

Now, as to Murray, I will take the matter up with Cortelyou. I think his remarks were impolitic and I also think they were true.[1] Under Ridgely the conditions of the bank examiners had become very bad and there was real need of just such a statement as Murray made; but it was not wise to make it during the campaign, simply because it was certain to be misunderstood. *Always yours*

4947 · TO ISRAEL ZANGWILL   *Roosevelt Mss.*

Personal   Washington, October 15, 1908

My dear Mr. Zangwill:[1] Indeed I shall be very much pleased to have you dedicate the play to me when it comes out in book form. It was a very real pleasure to see Mrs. Zangwill and you, and I look forward to seeing you again when I reach England.

I am glad you made the change in your play.[2] I am very keenly sensible of the very many evils that exist in American life; I try to war on them, but I find that a sweeping overstatement in attacking them often does more damage than good. The New York *Herald* is one of a number of New York newspapers, including not merely the worst of the "yellow" press but organs of the capitalistic class like the New York *Sun* under Mr. Laffan,[3] and representatives of the so-called intellectuals like the *Evening Post* under Messrs. Ogden and Villard, which taken in the aggregate represent the worst and most depressing influence in our national life. It is to me hideous to see the brutal and insane levity of treatment of debasing crime such as you speak of as occurring in the editorial of the New York *Herald*. Perhaps one reason I felt so strongly about your sentence being cut out, in order not to mar your extraordinarily able and powerful play, was because I grow to feel such a sense of revolt and indignation when in the theater I listen to the audience laugh at a jest from the stage about universal corruption in

---

[1] Lawrence O. Murray had pointed out that national bank examiners had failed properly to discover or report the type of speculative investments which, weakening the credit structure, had underlain the panic of 1907 and impaired the confidence of potential depositors, particularly in the South and West. This observation reflected badly on William B. Ridgely, Murray's predecessor as Comptroller of the Currency.

---

[1] Israel Zangwill, British author, philanthropist, and prominent leader of the Zionist movement.

[2] Roosevelt, after seeing Zangwill's *Melting-Pot*, had asked him to change the lines in his play which stressed the prevalence of divorce and public corruption in America.

[3] William Mackay Laffan, an erratic man who achieved as an engraver and as a collector and connoisseur of Orientalia the distinction and proportion of judgment that his journalism lacked.

public life. It is the crackling of thorns under a pot. There was the same slight tendency to laugh, in the middle of the tragedy, on the part of the audience, when they heard this remark about divorce in your play, and it grated on me for the same reason. To attack all men as corrupt, all Americans as being given to divorce, mars the force of the relentless attack that ought to be made upon those Americans who *are* corrupt in public life, or who *do* treat the marriage bond with levity and immorality.

Let me again most heartily congratulate you upon your play. I do not know when I have seen a play that stirred me as much.

With warm regards to Mrs. Zangwill, believe me, *Sincerely yours*

4948 · TO STARR H. BEATTY *Roosevelt Mss.*

Washington, October 16, 1908

My dear Mr. Beatty: I thank you for your letter, but it seems to me that there could be no more severe blow struck at our institutions than to request a Presidential candidate thus to declare his religious beliefs as a prerequisite to receiving the votes of men who would otherwise not support him. It is a fundamental contradiction of one of the essentials of our American institutions. Those ministers who, for the reasons you mention, ⟨are going⟩ intend to vote against Mr. Taft ⟨are unfit to be citizens of this country⟩ are, doubtless unwittingly, wholly out of sympathy with the fundamental principles of American citizenship. On their own showing they would have had to vote against John Quincy Adams, for instance, who, like Taft, was a Unitarian and who while in Washington attended the same church which Mr. Taft now attends. Several times every winter the services in this church are performed by the Rev. Dr. Edward Everett Hale, the Chaplain of the United States Senate. These friends of yours surely cannot occupy an attitude of such spiritual arrogance and intolerance as to believe that Rev. Dr. Edward Everett Hale the Chaplain of the Senate, one of the most revered men in or out of the ministry in all the United States, can with propriety or wisdom be slighted or lookt down upon by any member of any Christian church. On the grounds that your friends profess they would have been an hundredfold more justified in voting against Abraham Lincoln than against Taft, and of this fact they either are or ought to be well aware.

If asked by Mr. Taft, I should most emphatically advise against his making any declaration as to his religious belief such as your friend ⟨advises and I am certain that on thinking it over you will see the gross impropriety, the gross offense against every principle of Americanism, that would be entailed by making any such request of him⟩ suggests. If there is one thing for which we stand in this country, it is for complete religious freedom and for the right of every man to worship his Creator as his conscience dictates. It is an emphatic negation of this right to cross-examine a man on his religious views before being willing to support him for office. Is he a good man, and is he fit for the office? These are the only questions which there is a right to ask, and to both of these in Mr. Taft's case, the answer ⟨is⟩ must be in the affirmative. In my own Cabinet ⟨I have now Catholic, Protestant and Jew⟩ there are at present Catholic, Protestant and Jew — the Protestants being of various denominations. I am incapable of discriminating between them, or of judging any one of them save as to the way in which he performs his public duty. ⟨I assume, of course, that each man's private life is upright and honorable.⟩ The rule of conduct applicable to Catholic, Protestant and Jew as regards lesser offices is just as applicable as regards the Presidency.[1] *Very truly yours*

4949 · TO STARR H. BEATTY   *Roosevelt Mss.*

Washington, October 16, 1908

My dear Mr. Beatty: I thank you for your letter of the 14th instant. If asked by Mr. Taft, I should most emphatically advise against his making any declaration as to his religious belief such as your friend suggests. If there is one thing for which we stand in this country, it is for complete religious freedom and for the right of every man to worship his Creator as his conscience dictates. It is an emphatic negation of this right to cross-examine a man on his religious views before being willing to support him for office. Is he a good man, and is he fit for the office? These are the only questions which there is a right to ask, and to both of these in Mr. Taft's case, the answer must be in the affirmative. In my own Cabinet there are at present Catholic, Protestant and Jew — the Protestants being of various denominations. I am incapable of discriminating between them, or of judging any one of them save as to the way in which he performs his public duty. The rule of conduct applicable to Catholic, Protestant and Jew as regards lesser offices is just as applicable as regards the Presidency. *Very truly yours*

4950 · TO SAMUEL BALDWIN MARKS YOUNG   *Roosevelt Mss.*

Washington, October 16, 1908

My dear General: I have heard from Dr. Lambert and the other men and have come to your conclusion in the matter. It is obvious that as the law is now nothing can be done by dividing authority. If I had the power I should insist upon your staying with the purely civilian force under you. As I have not the power, I reluctantly acquiesce in your request and hereby

[1] Roosevelt canceled this letter, substituting No. 4949, also to Starr H. Beatty of the Delavan, Illinois, *Times Press.*

accept your resignation.[1] I shall take out forthwith every soldier now in the Park. I shall appoint Major Benson[2] as superintendent, so that he will occupy both positions, and give him the choice of the soldiers that are to come in under him.

With regards to Mrs. Young, believe me, *Faithfully yours*

4951 · TO CHARLES NATHANIEL HASKELL   *Roosevelt Mss.*

Washington, October 16, 1908

Sir: I have received your letter of October 12th.[1] Your statements as to Messrs. Guffey, Barnsdall and Depew, including specifically your statement as to Senator Depew's having had any part in the granting of the Prairie Oil and Gas Company franchise, or as to its having been granted over Secretary Hitchcock's protest, are falsehoods which you either did know or should have known to be falsehoods when you wrote them. Your letter is accordingly returned. I shall answer any letter of yours in which you speak the truth and write in accordance with the rudimentary requirements of official propriety. The Government is at present suing you for your scandalous and criminal misconduct in defrauding the Creek Indians of their lands. Your public and private character is such that you are not entitled in your private capacity to an answer from any honest man or to associate with any honest man. As Governor of a State, however, you shall always receive in your official position proper consideration and proper treatment from the National Government provided that you yourself in your communications use language which permits such treatment to be accorded to you. Until you learn to respect in your official correspondence the ordinary decencies of public life you will have no further answer from the National Government. *Very truly*

[1] Young had resigned as superintendent of Yellowstone Park because of the recent widely publicized robbery; see No. 4892.
[2] Harry C. Benson.

[1] In a public letter printed throughout the nation on October 14, Haskell contended that "Messrs. Guffey, Barnsdall and Senator Depew, well-known Standard Oil representatives, with others of the same odor" had persuaded Roosevelt, who should have realized their purpose, to permit the leasing at low royalties of Indian oil lands to subsidiaries of the Standard Oil Company. "It was the same Senator Depew," Haskell asserted, "who induced you to grant the Prairie Oil and Gas Company franchise over the protest of Secretary Hitchcock," a transaction which "gave the Standard Oil Company a donation from the property of the Osage Indians of more than enough to pay the famous $29,000,000 fine." "Whether this gross injustice to our people," Haskell concluded, "was accomplished by your lack of consideration or in any other way the authorities of the State of Oklahoma will not rest until this lease has been canceled and justice done our people." Roosevelt's rebuttal is in No. 5000. For Hitchcock's views at the time of the lease see Numbers 4012, 4022.

Strictly confidential Washington, October 17, 1908

Dear White: The enclosed letter explains itself.[1] Of all the people in Europe you are the man in whom I have the most implicit trust, taking into consideration your experience, training, judgment, and good faith combined. Accordingly I ask you to read the enclosed. Then when you get the opportunity take it to London, give it to Arthur Lee, letting him read it as often as he likes, but yourself seeing that it is destroyed immediately thereafter and that no copy is kept of it. I have entire faith in Lee's honor, but it is well to run no risk about leaving such a letter where it could by any possibility be seen. When I come out of Africa in the spring of 1910 I shall stop in Paris to deliver a lecture at the Sorbonne as Jusserand has just delivered an invitation to me to do so. I think I wrote you that I was to deliver the Romanes Lecture at Oxford also.

With warm regards to Mrs. White, believe me, *Faithfully yours*

4953 · TO ARTHUR HAMILTON LEE *Roosevelt Mss.*

Washington, October 17, 1908

Dear Arthur: I hesitate to write about the matter I mentioned; but perhaps I had better tell you the facts. So I have asked a close and trusted friend in whose judgment and good faith you can place absolute dependence to hand this letter to you to read and then to destroy. I send it thru White because it can thereby be forwarded in our diplomatic pouch. Read it over and over as many times as you desire, but please destroy it before you let White get away.

The reason of my hesitation is that I do not like to be a Rancy Sniffle — you will not understand the allusion as you doubtless have never read *Georgia Scenes;*[1] he was a stirrer up of strife. On the other hand, as I have been persistently telling so many Englishmen that I thought their fears of Germany slightly absurd and did not believe that there was need of arming against Germany, I feel that perhaps it is incumbent upon me now to say that I am by no means as confident as I was in this position. As regards many points I have a real regard for the Emperor. I admire his energy, his ability, his activity, and what I believe to be his sincere purpose to do all that he can for the greatness of his country. He is, however, very jumpy; and more

---

[1] The letter dealt with William Bayard Hale's interview with the Kaiser; see No. 4838. Unlike Roosevelt, the Kaiser felt no need to keep secret his views on Great Britain. On October 28, with the Kaiser's permission, the London *Daily Telegraph* published an interview given to an anonymous Englishman whose report in many respects resembled that of Hale. This "calculated indiscretion" bred a storm both in England and in the Reichstag where the peace party was still strong.

---

[1] *Georgia Scenes,* a series of sketches — really a primitive and highly amusing sociological study — of the state, written in 1835 by A. B. Longstreet.

than once in the last seven years I have had to watch him hard and speak to him, with great politeness, but with equal decision, in order to prevent his doing things that I thought against the interests of this country. Last summer an American newspaperman named Hale, a very honorable fellow whom I know well, got an interview with the Kaiser. The Kaiser spoke to him with astounding frankness. The part of his conversation with which I am now concerned was that relating to England. He displayed great bitterness toward England. He said that England was a traitor to the white race because she had been encouraging the yellow peril by her alliance with Japan, and that Japan certainly intended to have war with the United States in a short time. Without any sense of inconsistency he then added that he was himself trying to give arms and organization to the Mussulmans, especially in Turkey, because they would in time be a bulwark against the yellow peril — a somewhat farfetched conclusion. He stated that he thought England was decadent; that India was seething with revolt which would probably find expression in open war before a year was over, and that the same was true of the Sudan and Egypt. Finally he remarked that he regarded war between England and Germany as inevitable and as likely soon to take place. He spoke very bitterly of the King, saying that he and all those immediately around him were sunk in ignoble greed and lookt at life from a purely stock market standpoint, and that he and they hated me virulently because they had money invested in America and attributed the loss of value in their investments to my action (parenthetically I think this was merely said to influence me; and I neither believed it, nor if I had believed it would I have cared).

Hale wrote this interview down and very honorably showed it both to the American Ambassador, Hill, and to the German Foreign Office. The Foreign Office nearly went thru the roof, and protested most emphatically that the utmost damage would result from its publication. Meanwhile he cabled his interview to the New York *Times*, who sent a representative out to me to ask my advice about printing the matter. I earnestly urged that it be not done, stating that it would undoubtedly create a general panic and would cause extraordinary bitterness between England and Germany; and adding, what I think was a much more effective argument with the *Times*, that while they would gain temporarily by the sensational nature of the interview, yet as the Emperor was absolutely certain to repudiate it and to insist that the correspondent had lied, that in the long run I did not think it would prove of credit to the *Times* itself. Which argument convinced them, or whether they were convinced by something wholly different, I do not know; but at any rate they have not printed the article, and Hale very honorably accepted the amendments of the Foreign Office and if he prints the article will print it as viséed by them.

Now, I do not for a moment believe that the utterances of the Emperor indicated a settled purpose; but they did make me feel that he indulged in red dreams of glory now and then, and that if he was indiscreet enough to talk to a strange newspaperman in such fashion it would be barely possible that sometime he would be indiscreet enough to act on impulse in a way that would jeopardize the peace. Therefore, as my advice to England of recent years has been in the direction of saying that there was nothing to apprehend from Germany, and as it is thru you that most of what I have said has been said (altho not all of it) I feel that you ought to know these facts. They should be told to no one save to Balfour and Grey, and to them only on the understanding that they are to go no further. I do not believe that the British Empire has any more intention of acting aggressively than has the United States, and I believe that in one case as in the other a powerful fleet is not only in the interest of the nation itself, but is in the interest of international peace, and therefore to be desired by all who wish to see the peace of the world preserved. I am now striving to have us build up our fleet because I think its mere existence will be the most potent factor in keeping the peace between Japan and ourselves and in preventing any possible outbreak thru disregard of the Monroe Doctrine in America. In exactly the same way I feel that Britain's great navy is a menace to no Power, but on the contrary is a distinct help in keeping the peace of the world, and I hope to see it maintained in full efficiency. *Ever yours*

4954 · TO KERMIT ROOSEVELT   *Roosevelt Mss.*

Washington, October 17, 1908

Dearest Kermit: The enclosed rather puzzling letter from the Kodak Company has come. Apparently we have paid for the kodak. Is it the kind you want, or is there some other kind that I should order?

I am glad you are still out for the freshman football eleven, and am glad you are going to try for the two-mile run. I haven't the least expectation that you can do anything in it, because I don't think you are good for less than ten miles, but it is a good thing for you to go out anyway. I am also glad you have joined the Republican Club.

Quentin performed a characteristic feat yesterday. He heard that Schmid, the animal man, wanted a small pig, and decided that he would turn an honest penny by supplying the want. So out in the neighborhood of his school he called on an elderly darkey who, he had seen, possest little pigs; bought one; popped it into a bag; astutely dodged the school — having a well-founded distrust of how the boys would feel toward his passage with the pig — and took the car for home. By that time the pig had freed itself from the bag, and, as he explained, he journeyed in with a "small squealish pig" under his arm; but as the conductor was a friend of his he was not put off. He bought it for a dollar and sold it to Schmid for a dollar and a quarter, and feels as if he had found a permanent line of business. Schmid then festooned it in red ribbons and sent it to parade the streets. I gather that

Quentin led it around for part of the parade, but he was somewhat vague on this point, evidently being a little uncertain as to our approval of the move.

We have had perfect weather this week and Mother and I have enjoyed our rides extremely, the coloring of the woods being beautiful beyond description and all the Rock Creek country at its loveliest. Yesterday the Ben Greet players[1] gave a couple of Hawthorne wonder plays in the afternoon on the White House grounds and it was really worth while seeing; the pretty costumes on the green knoll among the trees made a sight I know you would have enjoyed. This morning there is a similar performance for the schoolchildren. *Ever your father*

4955 · TO CHARLES JOSEPH BONAPARTE   *Roosevelt Mss.*

Washington, October 19, 1908

My dear Bonaparte: I enclose herewith the newspaper facsimiles of Grosscup's request for railroad passes, including especially his scandalous letter in which, while making the request, he points out that it is for the brother of the man who is a referee in a rate case in which the railroad is interested. I am told that if you will see Raymond Patterson, of the Chicago *Tribune* Bureau, he can give you much further information, and that George Wickersham,[1] of New York, can give you information about his action concerning the traction case. I hope action can be taken about Judge Grosscup. His presence on the bench is a disgrace, and it may be that there is material which will warrant our asking his impeachment.[2] *Sincerely yours*

4956 · TO P. H. GRACE   *Roosevelt Mss.*

Washington, October 19, 1908

My dear Mr. Grace: [1] I thank you for your letter. I need hardly say that I take a peculiar interest in the men who work on the railroads in this country, and I prize as one of the honors of which I am most proud the fact that I am an honorary member of the Brotherhood of Locomotive Firemen.

[1] An English theatrical group that tirelessly toured this country for forty years, bringing to the remotest corners safe and steady performances of the Bard.

[1] George Woodward Wickersham, general counsel for the Interborough Rapid Transit Company. A discerning and very able conservative, he served the state as Taft's Attorney General, as president of the International Arbitral Tribunal under the Young Plan, and as a member of the Commission on Reorganization of the New York State Government and of the Commission on the Enforcement of Prohibition. He was for years a figure of considerable influence in the politics of the city and state of New York.

[2] See No. 4744. Impeachment proceedings were not begun.

[1] P. H. Grace of Binghamton, New York, a local leader of the Brotherhood of Railroad Trainmen.

Thruout my whole term as President, now in its eighth year, I have devoted myself with especial interest to the questions affecting labor. The lasting prosperity of this country rests upon the welfare of the wageworker and the welfare of the tiller of the soil. My greatest aim and desire have been to do all that in me lies to advance their interest. I wish to help them to get the best out of their present positions; I wish to help them make those positions permanently better, of permanently greater importance and reward. No consideration of party fealty or personal friendship would induce me to advise either farmer or workingman to do anything that was not for his permanent benefit. With this fact keenly before me I earnestly advise all workingmen, in their own interest as workingmen, but above all as American citizens concerned in the honor and the prosperity of this great free Republic, to support Mr. Taft for President; just as I advise all farmers, businessmen, and men of the professions.

I do not believe the wageworkers of this country have ever had a better friend in the White House than Mr. Taft will prove himself to be. He has already shown his faith by his deeds. In the matter of the injunctions he issued he was absolutely right, and the principles he laid down in those injunctions have since then been accepted by every worthy leader of labor, and they are embodied in the principles and practices of all the railroad brotherhood at the present day. The abuses of injunction have been fearlessly exposed and attacked by Mr. Taft. He recognizes, as in my judgment all fair-minded men must recognize, that again and again in the past this process has been used to the detriment of wageworkers by certain judges. He is doing and will continue to do everything that can be done to do away with these abuses. He will not make vague promises impossible of fulfillment. He will actually and in good faith try to secure action. Let me give you an example of what he has just done. A year or so ago the editor of a paper especially devoted to the ironmolders' union called upon me to say that a decree had been entered in the United States Circuit Court at Milwaukee in the summer of 1906 which he regarded as grossly unjust and improper and as practically fatal to trades-unionism. The case was that of the ironmolders' union against the Allis-Chalmers Company of Milwaukee. The members of the union, having made certain demands for the betterment of their conditions of service which were refused, went on a strike, and an injunction suit followed in the United States Circuit Court. The late employees were enjoined from alleged illegal interference. The final decree was of the most drastic and far-reaching character, and besides enjoining the late employees from doing acts which were clearly illegal, it also enjoined them from any form of picketing, from inducing employees to leave the service of the Allis-Chalmers Company by persuasion or otherwise, and from any kind of interference with the company direct or indirect. So sweeping were the terms of this injunction that it practically forbade the union from making any effort, no matter how peaceful and proper, to maintain their position in this trade dispute. The editor of the *Iron Moulders'* *Journal*, Mr. J. P. Frey brought the case before me stating that the union did not know what to do; that its funds were limited; that he felt that they were suffering from a gross injustice which they were powerless to remedy. I called in Mr. Taft and asked Mr. Frey to lay the case before him, as of course Mr. Taft was far more competent than I was to express his judgment as to the legality and propriety of the action taken. Mr. Taft satisfied himself of the facts and at once became exceedingly indignant at such an injunction having issued. He stated that in his opinion the position taken by the court in issuing the injunction was clearly untenable, and that what was needed was that the union should get some first-class lawyer to represent them and should bring the case before the higher courts. He suggested, in response to Mr. Frey's request, that the union retain Mr. F. N. Judson, of St. Louis, who had represented the Brotherhood of Locomotive Firemen in the Wabash case in 1893, and who, by the way, is the author of the review of the labor decisions of Judge Taft published in the *Review of Reviews* in 1907. Mr. Taft explained that one of the troubles of the labor unions was that so often they did not get the best type of counsel, so that their cases were not properly presented, and that in his judgment Mr. Judson would be sure to present this case aright. He stated that the decision of the court ought certainly to be in their favor. The case was argued before the United States Circuit Court of Appeals by Mr. Judson and Mr. Rubin, of Milwaukee, for the union, and by Mr. James M. Beck, counsel for the National Manufacturers' Association, for the company. The decision of the court was handed down in Chicago on the 8th day of this month and it justifies Judge Taft's wisdom, for it sustains the most important contentions of the labor union. The court holds that while under the facts of the case the company was entitled to some injunction relief, the decree went far beyond the proper limits. It struck out of the decree all of the provisions which prevented peaceful picketing or the exercise of the right of persuasion in inducing employees to join the strike and also all reference to boycotting on the ground that there was no boycott, as the members of the union had a right to refuse to handle "struck" work — that is, the work from a factory where they were on a strike — wherever they found it. The opinion is important especially as showing that much can now be accomplished in getting the courts to correct abuses against employees in the exercise of the power of injunction, if such abuses are in effective form brought to their attention, as, thanks to the advice of Judge Taft, they were brought in this case. The right of peaceful picketing and persuasion so that employees may by peaceful means induce other employees to join them is forcibly set forth in this opinion, and it bases its decision largely upon Judge Taft's decision and upon the decision in the Wabash injunction case, which itself was largely based upon Judge Taft's decision; so that Judge Taft's decision is declared by the court to have settled the law as to the substantial rights of the parties, leaving only the application of the principles so declared as new cases arose. The great importance of this opinion is that it corrects abuses that have crept into injunctions and labor disputes in the Federal as well as the State courts. This decision goes far to protect the rights of workingmen, and it does so because it is explicitly based upon the labor decisions of Judge Taft; and this decision was secured only in consequence of following the advice given by Judge Taft as to the proper course of procedure. I speak from first-hand knowledge as I was personally cognizant of all the facts. A more striking instance could not be imagined of the zealous effort of a public servant, which Judge Taft then was, to secure justice for workingmen to whom he thought injustice had been done, altho the matter was not within his immediate control at the time. In this one instance Mr. Taft rendered to labor a great and signal service; a practical service, which shared the peculiarity of Mr. Taft's other services, for his services take the form of deeds rather than of mere words.

While on the bench Mr. Taft rendered a service to labor so great that it can hardly be overestimated. This was in the Narramore case against the C., C., C. & St. L. R.R. The plaintiff while working in the employ of the company had been hurt because the company had not provided the protection which the statute required it to furnish its employees. He got a verdict from the jury. The railroad appealed, and its counsel, Mr. Judson Harmon, argued that the verdict should be set aside because the employee had kept at work altho he knew the railroad had violated the law, and that therefore he had really contracted to take all the chances of being hurt. This conclusion, to my mind a cruelly iniquitous conclusion, had up to that time been sustained by most of the courts, including the New York State Court of Appeals. Nevertheless Judge Taft refused to follow the New York case, stating that the manifest legislative purpose was to protect the employee by positive law, for the very reason that it had proved impossible for him to protect himself by contract, and that the entire purpose of the law would be defeated if the employee was allowed by any form of contract to exempt the railroad company from the consequences of its failure to observe the law. This case has been cited all over the United States by counsel for workmen injured thru the failure of their employers to furnish the protection required by statute for their safety. Judge Taft's decision was that when a law is made applying to a dangerous business, in which four thousand men are killed and sixty-five thousand men are injured every year, the intention is that the railroads shall obey the law and that it shall not be nullified by judicial construction. Very many judges, unfortunately, have failed to follow his reasoning, but other judges, and the law-making bodies as well, have followed it, and this great decision marks one of the longest strides taken in the effort to secure for wageworkers full protection against, and full compensation for, injuries received by them in the line of their duty. Here again

Judge Taft rendered one of the greatest services that has ever been rendered to the cause of labor.

The two cases to which I have referred have a further importance when it is remembered that the President now to be chosen will probably himself choose a majority of the Justices of the Supreme Court during the next four years. It would be a dreadful calamity to have these justices chosen by a man of less than Mr. Taft's high purpose, great knowledge of the needs of the people, and firm resolution to do justice to every individual and every interest. This is one of the vital questions now before the American people.

Furthermore, I ask you to consider what Mr. Taft has actually done as an administrator. The Panama Canal has come specially under the direction and control of Mr. Taft as Secretary of War. He has taken a peculiar interest in the men who are digging that canal. He has made a special study of all that confronts them. He has made it his business to see that their interests are in every way amply protected; that they have an ample reward; that they are well housed, well fed, and so far as in his power lies that they receive compensation for injuries incurred in the line of their duty. A special committee which I have appointed to look into the conditions of labor on the Isthmus, which included upon it Mr. Samuel B. Donnelly, a labor representative, formerly the president of the International Typographical Union, has reported to me in effect that Uncle Sam has shown himself to be a model employer on the Isthmus, so that, thanks to Mr. Taft and the care and supervision which he has exercised, the men who work for the Government on the Isthmus are on the whole better paid, better protected, better cared for than in any private industrial enterprise in the United States. Mr. T. J. Dolan, the secretary-treasurer of the International Brotherhood of Steamshovel and Dredge men, who has most carefully investigated this subject because of the large number of the men of his organization employed on the Isthmus, has come to the same conclusion, and largely because of this fact he is ardently supporting Mr. Taft.

As opposed to the entire vagueness of Mr. Bryan's proposals, Mr. Taft stands pledged to continue the definite and constructive program of social reorganization outlined and already entered upon by the present administration, which has never hesitated in specific cases of sufficient importance to interfere for the purpose of securing an adjustment of labor troubles, at the same time conserving the rights of the wage earner. A conspicuous instance was the settlement of the anthracite coal strike. In April, 1907, when a strike was imminent on the western railroads which would have tied up forty-four lines with half a million employees and put half the country in a state of siege, negotiators were sent by the administration who demanded and secured in the name of the people a settlement of the difficulty by arbitration; and last Spring the administration by its vigorous action prevented a general reduction of wages on the railroads of the country which would have caused great suffering and far-reaching disturbance; but if Mr. Bryan was elected I have little doubt that the ensuing industrial chaos, necessitating great reduction of wages and widespread nonemployment, would be beyond the reach of such action as that which averted the threatened disaster last Spring. When the public coal lands were falling under monopolistic control the administration withdrew millions of acres from entry, insisting to the extent of its power that the coal and oil under these lands shall remain a Federal possession. For the first time in our history the administration has secured the enforcement of the eight-hour law in the Government departments and is trying to secure its extension by legislation. In the District of Columbia it has enacted a Federal child labor law which stands as a model law for State governments in their department of legislation.

Beyond these remedial enactments and arbitrations achieved by this administration stands a constructive and organic program of Federal activity in the way of social and industrial reform. Toward this end thru the years I have been in office I have consulted with all classes and conditions of men. We have been able on the whole to arrive at a remarkably close agreement among ourselves so long as all parties, representatives of labor and capital alike, kept in view their obligations to the commonwealth as joint workers toward this social reform. We are all agreed that free play shall be permitted only so long as it means fair play. We are endeavoring steadily to secure a more equitable adjustment of taxation toward the ideal of a distribution of the several costs of government in a ratio to the benefits derived. There is nothing in this of class or caste; from our program doctrinaires, individualist and socialist alike, are barred. Sociology comes not to breed a new class warfare; it knows man only as man. This administration has bent a large part of its efforts towards social advancement. The question has been asked, Why has not the National Government, thru its Bureau of Labor, done for the wage earner what, thru the Department of Agriculture, it has done for the farmer, by placing at his disposal thru Federal research the latest results of scientific discovery? My answer is, the time had not yet come when this was possible; we have advanced in each case just as fast and as far as was possible with the knowledge and means at our command. Between pure science or speculative theory and its practical application in the hands of a government lies of necessity a gap of years, years of patient investigation and experiment after truth. Ten years ago organic evolution in agriculture was still a speculative science. Today the farmer has only to specify that his wheat must ripen by such and such a date, stand up under a certain wind velocity, bear in its seed a certain percentage of starch, etc., and our Department can help build him a plant to order. The spineless cactus and the frostproof orange, soil chemistry, seed selection, and diversified farming have preceded in time of their discovery all those theories of social reconstruction upon which any Bureau of Labor could build. The task of helping to transform a population, with every advance of mechanical invention, it is no exaggeration to state, has awaited that precise knowledge which has come only within the last five years.

Given that knowledge, and given wisdom, self-restraint, and high purpose in applying it, and there is little this Nation cannot do for itself. With free scope for our Federal program, we will do much towards helping each member of the industrial army to get the chance to make everything possible out of himself. We can solve this problem of the unemployed best by having no more unemployable. Already our Bureau of Labor, for the past twenty years of necessity largely a statistical bureau, is practically a Department of Sociology, aiming not only to secure exact information about industrial conditions but to discover remedies for industrial evils. At this moment we are conducting investigations as to the labor of women and children, the disease and mortality rates of the various occupations, the problem of dealing with the unemployed, etc. The whole principle of material and social advancement has come to a quicker fruition in our Department of Agriculture for the reason that biology is more easily handled with reference to seeds and plants and cattle than as regards men. It is our confident claim, however, that applied science, if carried out according to our program, will succeed in achieving for humanity, above all for the city industrial worker, results even surpassing in value those today in effect on the farm. We believe that America should take the lead in this work. Much of it can begin now. All of it will have to be done at some time, and the first place in the world will come to that country which does it first and best. The work has already been begun under this administration. It will be continued and amplified under Mr. Taft. It will be brought to ruin if Mr. Bryan be elected. The National Government must help toward these great reforms by putting the results of its extended researches at the free disposal of all citizens. We believe not merely in retaining but developing to the utmost possible extent individual initiative, but we are not to be frightened by any outcry of paternalism or socialism from going into any experiment which promises to benefit either farmers or wage earners; for we regard a lawless and impracticable individualism as in itself quite as undesirable as the most deadening form of socialism.

It has been charged that Mr. Taft, and the administration in which he has borne so prominent a part, have not been sufficiently interested in economic and industrial questions. The above is, it seems to me, a sufficient answer to this charge. Mr. Taft's election should be advocated by all who believe in making a far-reaching effort towards the betterment of our scheme of social and industrial life. It should also be advocated by all who wish an immediate advance in these social and industrial conditions.

If Mr. Taft is not elected, a period of industrial chaos and business bad times will ensue in which the workingmen will suffer far more than any other class. They are the people who more than any other will pay the penalty. Because of their own material interests I believe that they should support Mr. Taft; and furthermore I believe that they should support him because he has by his actions over and over again proved himself to be a singularly fearless and effective champion of the rights of labor; and above all I feel that they should support him as good American citizens, because he embodies what is best and highest in our American citizenship.[2] *Sincerely yours*

4957 · TO CHARLES EVANS HUGHES   *Roosevelt Mss.*

Personal   Washington, October 20, 1908

My dear Governor: That is such an extremely nice letter of yours that I cannot forbear taking up your time by a line of acknowledgment. I have, naturally, the keenest sympathy for you in this campaign, because of the very fact you point out; that is, the twofold type of attack made upon you: the attack upon you because you stood for the corporations where they were right or where improper measures were aimed at them, and the attack upon you because you have declined to sanction abuses in their management or to refrain from trying to better their management. I am always astounded at the shortsightedness of the railroad corporations, for instance, in objecting to proper regulation. They seem to be unaware that only by regulating them in such effective fashion as to prevent abuses on their part will it be possible to prevent a general, a violent, and a very unfortunate, popular movement against them.

I believe that by your course since you have come from the West; that is, by your laying emphasis upon and bringing to a head the State issues in New York; you are helping the national ticket just as much as you helped it by your admirable fight on national grounds in the West. Taft, by the way, mentioned to me last Sunday that he regarded your Youngstown speech as far and away the most important utterance in this campaign.

Now one word. You say that your feeling is that "if the Republican support is energetic I shall unquestionably be elected." Is there any way that I can help in this matter of the Republican support? Pray let me know if you think that there is.

Taft, by the way, mentioned to me his great sense of obligation to you for your part in the campaign and his purpose to lay all possible emphasis upon the need of electing you, when he makes his speeches in New York.

I have been immensely amused by the attitude of the *Sun* and *Evening Post*. Apparently both of them have thought that I did not want you nominated, and accordingly howled for your nomination. When they found that I joined the general Republican feeling and felt that your nomination

[2] This letter was released for publication on October 26.

was indispensable, both of them cooled off. Apparently the *Sun* is supporting Chanler, so far as one can predicate any fixt policy from the maze of its tortuous mendacity. The *Evening Post* is supporting you still, but in such fashion that I think that its small influence is practically nil in any direction.

With all good wishes, believe me, *Sincerely yours*

4958 · TO KERMIT ROOSEVELT   *Roosevelt Mss.*

Washington, October 20, 1908

Dearest Kermit: It was good to hear from you and I enjoyed equally your letter to me and your letter to Mother and the scraps of your letter to Ethel which she read aloud. It seems to me that you have started very satisfactorily in college. Of course your work must be hard, but I think you are quite right to have gone into the football and running, both, even tho you did not expect to shine in either and tho it was pretty hard physical work; for it puts you in with the men of your class and gives you acquaintances that are peculiarly necessary if you decide to return to college after leaving Africa. I shall be greatly interested in your work among the sailors, and look forward to hearing from you about it. Tell me the details of the two-mile race, also. You must have had a really very pleasant time at Farmington and I am extremely pleased to hear about dear little Martha. I also think it was very nice of Edward Everett Hale to write you as he did.

We have been here a month now. It has been hot and dry, but beautiful, weather, and still is so Mother and I have had delightful rides. The grounds of the White House are now littered with dead leaves, but still very beautiful. When we came here the gardens were as luxuriant with flowers as in spring, but by this time most of the flowers have gone, altho in each garden there remains a couple of beds full of rather disheveled but lovely roses.

I have only taken one scramble walk, and have been very careful about jumping, because my leg still gives me trouble off and on. The bone is not right and I must keep it in trim that enables me to start off in fair shape to Africa. I believe that our first six months in Africa will be rather healthy than otherwise, and if we can only get thru that all right, then we can worry along in spite of troubles when we have gotten to the Nile, and are on the down grade of the trip so to speak. If we can once get a start in Africa under fairly good conditions I am confident we can make the trip all straight.

Taft spent Sunday here and was just a dear; he is a great big generous fellow. It seems to me impossible that the people of this country can prefer a cheap faker like Bryan to such a fine man. But one never can tell just what twist the folly of mankind will take. I am a good deal puzzled by the outlook. The surface indications are certainly our way and I am inclined to think that we shall carry the election with a big majority in the electoral college. But there are two or three influences at work against us the exact extent and power of which no one can tell, and they may upset us. There is first the defection in the Negro vote. This is real, but is only important if the election is very close. Second, there is the hostility of certain big corporation men to us. The Standard Oil and Harriman people, for instance, while they will hardly dare openly support Bryan, would undoubtedly much prefer seeing him elected to seeing Taft elected; because, altho they would dislike a period of business depression, they would dislike still more a continuance of the present policy of holding them to a rigid accountability before the law. Third, comes the labor vote. This is serious; the labor people have just cause of complaint with the Republican party taken as a whole, because Congress under the lead of Cannon treated them badly; and the courts, representing both the old school Republicans and the old school Democrats, have been curiously disregardful of their interests. They know me so well that I think they would support me without regard to their grievances real or imaginary against the courts and the Congress; but they do not know Taft; and under the lead of Gompers and the Democratic and labor demagogs generally they are demanding outrageous and impossible action both by the legislature and Executive, and are opposing Taft on grounds that are infamous. I am doing all I can to get them back to Taft. If they go sufficiently against him the results will be very serious. Fourth, comes the question of the unemployed; there are hundreds of thousands of these. Normally we should expect them almost all to vote against the party in power, and they may do that this year with disastrous effect. On the other hand we are endeavoring to show them that to elect Bryan means that they will continue unemployed, as will not be the case if they elect Taft. Finally, we have to do with the bigoted, narrow-minded, honest, evangelical Protestant feeling, especially among the Methodists, Lutherans, Baptists, and some Presbyterians, against Taft; this partly because small, insincere, narrow bigots hate him for doing justice to the Catholics, and partly because they are hostile to him on account of his being a Unitarian, objecting to him on grounds of pure dogmatic theology. I went to his church with him Sunday — the same church in which Edward Everett Hale sometimes preaches — and we listened to a sermon which, if we use the word Christian in a broad enough sense to make it of any value as a moral force, was as good, sound, Christian doctrine as could be preached anywhere. I did this hoping that it would attract the attention of sincere but rather ignorant Protestants who support me, and would make them tend to support Taft also.

With the above five elements against us, and inasmuch as we are ignorant as to how much each element will really amount to, it is out of the question to prophesy definitely as to the outcome. But Taft is so eminently the right man for President; his canvass is carried on along so high a plane; he represents so emphatically the forces of righteousness, of decency, of efficiency, of strength and honor, that I cannot help thinking he will pull thru. *Your loving father*

Washington, October 21, 1908

My dear Senator Knox: In your admirable speech of yesterday you speak of the action of Mr. Bryan and certain gentlemen claiming to be the special representatives of organized labor, foremost among them Mr. Gompers, to secure the support of laboring men for Mr. Bryan on consideration of his agreement to perform certain acts nominally in the interest of organized labor, which would really be either wholly ineffective or else of widespread injury not only to organized labor but to all decent citizens thruout this country. You have a peculiar right to speak on labor questions; for it was you, who, as Attorney General, first actively invoked the great power of the Federal Government on behalf of the rights of labor when, for the first time in the history of the Government, you, speaking for the Department of Justice, intervened in a private lawsuit which had gone against a locomotive fireman who had lost his arm in coupling cars, and by your intervention secured from the Supreme Court a construction of the safety appliance act which made it a vital remedial statute, and therefore has secured to hundreds of crippled employees and widows of crippled employees, compensation which they would not otherwise have obtained.[1]

The daily papers of October 13th contain an open letter from Mr. Samuel Gompers, President of the American Federation of Labor, appealing to workingmen to vote for Mr. Bryan.

In that letter are certain definite statements which interest the wider American public quite as much as those to whom Mr. Gompers makes his appeal. These statements warrant all you have said in your speech; and they would warrant you in asking Mr. Bryan to say publicly whether Mr. Gompers states correctly the attitude of his party and himself on a subject that is of vital concern to every citizen, including every businessman, as well as every farmer and every laboring man, who looks to the courts for the protection of his rights.

Mr. Gompers in his letter asserts that the judiciary of this country is destroying democratic government and substituting therefor an irresponsible and corrupt despotism in the interest of corporate power; and he further makes clear that the means by which he believes this alleged despotism has been set up in the place of democracy is by the process of injunction in the courts of equity.

[1] No case exactly fits the description in Roosevelt's letter, but *Johnson v. Southern Pacific Company*, 196 U. S. 1 (1903), involving a brakeman who had lost his arm in a coupling accident, was doubtless the case to which the President referred. It first came to Knox's attention in March 1903 when he was concerned with the act of that month that clarified the meaning of the safety appliances act of 1893. Knox had resigned, however, before the case was argued before the Supreme Court. The court's opinion gave to the safety appliances act a broad construction, permitting injured employees maximum latitude within the stipulations of the act for recovering damages against railroads that had failed to provide adequate safety appliances.

Mr. Gompers in his letter states that his appeal to the Republican convention at Chicago for remedy against the injunction was denied; and he then goes on to state not only that the Democratic party promised a remedy, but promised him the particular remedy that he had already asked of Congress.

His words are:

Labor's representatives then went to the Democratic party. That party made Labor's contentions its own. It pledged its candidates for every office to those remedies which Labor had already submitted to Congress.

The last sentence in this quotation indicates very definitely the specific remedies to which Mr. Gompers understands Mr. Bryan's party has pledged itself.

His statement now makes perfectly clear an important plank in the Bryanite platform which has heretofore seemed puzzling to a vast number of earnest-minded, thinking people, who are sincerely interested in the steady advance and the legitimate aspirations of labor, and who carefully read both platforms to know precisely what hope each held out for the improvement of the conditions of wage earners.

That plank reads as follows:

Questions of judicial practice have arisen especially in connection with industrial disputes. We deem that the parties to all judicial proceedings should be treated with rigid impartiality, and that injunctions should not be issued in any cases in which injunctions would not issue if no industrial dispute were involved.

This is the plank that promises the "remedy" against injunctions which Mr. Gompers asked of Mr. Bryan's party. It means absolutely nothing; no change of the law could be based on it; no man without inside knowledge could foretell what its meaning would turn out to be, for no man could foretell how any judge would decide in any given case, as the plank apparently leaves each judge free to say when he issues an injunction in a labor case whether or not it is a case in which an injunction would issue if labor were not involved. Yet this plank is apparently perfectly clear to Mr. Gompers, and in his letter to his followers he indicates beyond question just what he understands it to mean. He asserts that he has the requisite inside knowledge. His statement that Mr. Bryan's party (for it was Mr. Bryan who dictated the platform) pledged itself "to those remedies which labor had already submitted to Congress" is a perfectly clear and definite statement.

The "remedies" which Mr. Gompers has already submitted to Congress are matters of record, and the identification of his "remedy" against injunctions in labor disputes is easy and certain. This "remedy" is embodied in House Bill No. 94 of the first session of the Sixtieth Congress, the complete text of which is hereto appended.

The gist of the bill, as can be seen by referring to the complete text, is this:

1st. After forbidding any Federal Judge to issue a restraining order for an injunction in any labor dispute except to prevent irreparable injury to property or a property right, it specifically provides that "no right x x x to carry on business of any particular kind, or at any particular place, or at all, shall be construed, held, considered, or treated as property or as constituting a property right."

2nd. It provides that nothing agreed upon or done by two or more parties in connection with a labor dispute shall constitute a conspiracy or other criminal offense or be prosecuted as such unless the thing agreed upon or done would be unlawful if done by a single individual.

The bill here described is not only the "remedy" that Mr. Gompers has "already submitted to Congress," but it is the one and only "remedy" which he and those associated with him in his present movement have announced that they will accept in the matter of his grievance against the courts on the injunction issue.

The counsel for the American Federation of Labor, and Mr. Gompers, its President, are both on record to this effect.

At a hearing before the House Committee on Judiciary, the counsel for the American Federation of Labor, on February 5, 1908 (as appears from the printed hearings) stated:

The bill was considered by at least two sessions of the executive council of that organization, and unanimously approved. It was considered by two of its national conventions — the two latest — and by them unanimously endorsed. And in the face of many propositions to amend it, in the face of many proposed substitutes, in the face of pressure, from every direction, from high sources and sources not so exalted, the organization has stood by, and is today standing by, this bill without amendment.

Mr. Gompers himself in discussing this bill before the same Committee on February 28th, 1908 (as appears from the printed hearings) went on record as follows:

Events have demonstrated clearly to my mind that there is only one bill before the committee that can at all be effective to deal with this abuse, with this invasion of human rights, and that is the Pearre bill.

Further on in the same page of the hearings Mr. Gompers states:

I will say this, that I think I will try to make my position clear that the American Federation of Labor has so declared itself that it must insist upon the principles involved in the Pearre bill, and that I explained, as best I could, the position of labor — that we would rather be compelled to bear the wrongs which we have for a longer period than to give our assent to the establishment of a wrong principle, believing and knowing that time would give the justice and relief to which labor — the working people — are entitled.

This bill then, and none other, represents exactly the relief that Mr. Gompers demands in the way of anti-injunction legislation; and if the statement in his letter is correct, this bill represents what Mr. Bryan and his party are pledged to in the matter of anti-injunction legislation.

The injunction plank in the Bryanite platform may sound vague and hazy; but there is nothing vague or hazy about this bill.

It is more than a bill; it is a program of the most fixed and definite kind; and if Mr. Gompers is correct, this bill becomes, as it were an authorized appendix to Mr. Bryan's platform, or a footnote explaining in detail the briefer and vaguer injunction plank in that platform.

Does Mr. Bryan accept it as such?

Mr. Bryan should state publicly whether he in fact accepts the principle of this bill, which is the official program of Mr. Gompers and those who stand with him.

Mr. Gompers announces publicly that Mr. Bryan's party has made this program its own. Is Mr. Gompers correct in this statement?

Either Mr. Gompers is mistaken as to what Mr. Bryan's party has promised him in this matter of anti-injunction legislation, or those who drafted his party's platform, in their haste, failed to make the promise so clear that the general public would understand it precisely as Mr. Gompers understood it.

Mr. Bryan failed in his letter of acceptance to discuss this labor plank of his party's platform. So far as I am aware he has failed to discuss it since.

There should be such discussion as a matter of common fairness, not only to labor, but to all citizens alike. On a question of such grave consequence the people are entitled to know where Mr. Bryan stands.

Mr. Taft has repeatedly explained exactly where he stands in this matter of regulating injunctions.

Are we not entitled to know with equal clearness exactly where Mr. Bryan stands?

Mr. Gompers' public statements as to what his party has promised make it imperative that Mr. Bryan declare himself.

This bill, to the principle of which he says Mr. Bryan is pledged, declares that the right to carry on a lawful business in a lawful way shall not be regarded as a property right or entitled to the protection of a court of equity through the process of an injunction; and that the right to such protection which admittedly now exists under the law shall be taken away.

The counsel for the American Federation of Labor in his argument before the House Committee on February 5, at which Mr. Gompers himself was present, gave a very frank illustration of what he and Mr. Gompers perceived to be the consequences of that provision of this bill which says that the right to carry on business shall not be entitled to protection as a property right.

His words are: Suppose that workingman, by some operation or proceedings in the community (let us say by violence or persuasion or picketing away from the premises) reduce those works to a state of utter helplessness, and there was not a wheel moving, nor a process in operation, and this company had no help at all — that would be an interference with his right to do business; and for that I say he has no right to be protected by injunction.

Is Mr. Bryan in reality pledged to this point of view?

Will he definitely say either in writing or in a public address whether he believes with Mr. Gompers that the protection heretofore afforded by the courts of equity to the right to carry on a lawful business in a lawful way is despotic power, and that the judges who exercise that power are irresponsible despots?

So far as the second section of this bill is concerned, it is perfectly clear that it would legalize the black list and the sympathetic boycott carried to any extent. It would legalize acts which have time and again been declared oppressive, unjust, and immoral by the best and most eminent labor leaders themselves.

Does Mr. Bryan believe with Mr. Gompers that he and that part of the labor movement that agrees with him has the right morally, and should be given the right legally, to paralyze or to destroy with impunity the business of an innocent third person, against whom he or they have no direct grievance, simply because this third person refuses to join with them aggressively in a labor controversy with the real merits of which he may be utterly unacquainted, because he refuses to class as his enemy any and every other employer whom they point out as their enemy, because he refuses, merely upon their peremptory order, to excommunicate some other employer by ceasing all business relations with him? The black list and the secondary boycott are two of the most cruel forms of oppression ever devised by the wit of man for the infliction of suffering on his weaker fellows.

No court could possibly exercise any more brutal, unfeeling, or despotic power than Mr. Gompers claims for himself and his followers in this legislation, which would permit them without let or hindrance of any kind to carry on every form and degree of the secondary boycott.

The Anthracite Strike Commission, as fair-minded and distinguished a body of men as ever passed judgment on an industrial question, thus refers to the secondary form of boycott, that is, the boycott of innocent third persons for refusing to take an aggressive part in a controversy with which they have no concern:

To say this is not to deny the legal right of any man or set of men, voluntarily to refrain from social intercourse or business relations with any persons whom he or they, with or without good reason, dislike. This may sometimes be unchristian, but it is not illegal. But when it is a concerted purpose of a number of persons not only to abstain themselves from such intercourse, but to render the life of their victim miserable by persuading and intimidating others to refrain, such purpose is a malicious one, and the concerted attempt to accomplish it is a conspiracy at common law, and merits and should receive the punishment due to such a crime.

The Commission further states that this boycott can be carried to an extent "which was condemned by Mr. Mitchell, President of the United Mine Workers of America, in his testimony before the Commission, and which certainly deserves the reprobation of all thoughtful and law-abiding citizens."

Does Mr. Bryan agree with Mr. Gompers that all existing legal restraint on the enforcement of every degree of the boycott should be withdrawn; that the industrial excommunication of the innocent merchant who refuses to render unquestioned obedience to the orders of Mr. Gompers should be legalized and encouraged; or does he believe with us, and with Mr. Mitchell and other labor leaders who differ with Mr. Gompers in this matter, that this form of the boycott is morally wrong, that labor at war should fight with its enemies and respect the rights of neutrals, that innocent third parties should not be coerced into taking sides in industrial disputes to which they are in no sense parties, under penalty of having their business attacked and destroyed?

Mr. Taft is perfectly definite on this proposition.

Where does Mr. Bryan stand?

The citizen who votes for or against Mr. Taft on this proposition does so with his eyes open and with a clear understanding from Mr. Taft himself of his position. He has frankly discussed this subject time and again, with workingmen themselves, both in this campaign and prior to his nomination. He has been willing to express his position clearly and to assure workingmen that to protect them in their rights he is willing to go to the limits of what he considers justice, but that he will not go farther. His definition of justice to labor does not, as we understand it, include either of the principles contained in Mr. Gompers' program, as set forth officially in this bill.

Does Mr. Bryan disagree with Mr. Taft on these propositions?

Will he state publicly, definitely, categorically, whether he accepts the program outlined in this bill, as Mr. Gompers in his letters has assured the public that he does?

Mr. Bryan's party platform paid a high tribute to our courts of justice. It stated:

we resent the attempt of the Republican party to raise a false issue respecting the judiciary. It is an unjust reflection upon a great body of our citizens to assume that they lack respect for the courts.

The "great body of our citizens" to whom this platform refers is admittedly Mr. Gompers and his followers.

Mr. Gompers, now Mr. Bryan's open and avowed ally, has, in the letter here quoted, attacked the Federal courts in unmeasured terms of reproach because, by a long line of decisions, the equity courts have refused to make an outlaw of the businessman, because his right to carry on a lawful business under the peace of the law has been protected by the process of injunction, because in a word the most vital and most fundamental right of the business world, the right of a businessman to carry on his business, has been sustained and not denied by the processes of the courts of equity. This sweeping attack of Mr. Gompers upon the judiciary has been made in a frank and open effort to secure votes for Mr. Bryan.

Are these attacks made with Mr. Bryan's consent?

Do they meet with his approval?

Does he endorse them or does he repudiate them?

Mr. Bryan has frankly questioned Mr. Taft during the progress of this campaign, and very properly so, and has asked him to make clear his personal stand on public matters upon which the public were entitled to be enlightened.

In turn, with equal frankness and with equal propriety, Mr. Bryan should be asked to break a long-continued silence and make definite and certain his own position in regard to a matter which concerns not only businessmen and every decent, law-abiding citizen, whether a wageworker or not, just as much as it concerns Mr. Gompers and that part of organized labor that stands with him.

There is no need of generalities, of vague expressions of sympathy for labor. Let Mr. Bryan simply confine himself to the anti-injunction plank of his own platform and tell us publicly, definitely and clearly whether he accepts or rejects the statement of Mr. Gompers that this plank pledges him to the principles of the bill for which Mr. Gompers stands; and whether if elected he will endeavor to have this proposal enacted into law. This is asked honestly, in the interest of that large voting public which believes sincerely in the promotion of every legitimate right and interest of labor; but which believes also that, from the standpoint of the best interest of labor, it neither requires nor is entitled to more than justice, and that the right to destroy business should not be formally recognized in the law of the land.

I feel that I have the right to speak frankly in this matter because thruout my term as President it has been my constant object to do everything in my power, both by administrative action and by endeavoring to secure legislative action, to advance the cause of labor, protect it from unjust aggression, and secure to it its legitimate rights. I have accomplished something; I hope to accomplish something more before I leave office; and I have taken special and peculiar interest in Mr. Taft's candidacy because I believe that of all the men in this country he is the man best qualified for continuing the work of securing to the wageworkers of the country their full rights. I will do everything in my power for the wageworkers of the country *except to do what is wrong*. I will do wrong for no man; and with all the force in my power I solemnly warn the laboring men of this country that any public man who advocates doing wrong in their interest cannot be trusted by them; and this whether his promise to do wrong is given knowing that it is wrong, or because of a levity and lack of consideration which make him willing to promise anything without counting the cost if thereby support at the moment is to be purchased. Just as I have fought hard, and shall continue to fight hard, to bring about in the fullest way the recognition of the right of the employee to be amply compensated for injury received in the course of his duty, so I have fought hard and shall continue to fight hard to do away with all abuses in the use of the power of injunction. I will do everything I can to see that the power of injunction is not used to oppress laboring men. I will endeavor to secure them full and equal justice. Therefore, in the interest of all good citizens, be they laboring men, businessmen, professional men, farmers, or members of any other occupation, so long as they have in their souls the principles of sound American citizenship, I denounce as wicked the proposition to secure a law which, according to the explicit statement of Mr. Gompers, is to prevent the courts from effectively interfering with riotous violence when the object is to destroy a business, and which will legalize the black list and the secondary boycott, both of them the apt instruments of unmanly persecution.

But there is another account against Messrs. Bryan and Gompers in this matter. Ephraim feedeth on wind. Their proposed remedy is an empty sham. They are seeking to delude their followers by the promise of a law, which would damage this country solely because of the vicious moral purpose that would be shown by putting it upon the statute books, but which would be utterly worthless to accomplish its avowed purpose. I have not the slightest doubt that such a law as that proposed by Mr. Bryan would, if enacted by Congress, be declared unconstitutional by a unanimous Supreme Court — unless, indeed, Mr. Bryan were able to pack this court with men appointed for the special purpose of declaring such a law constitutional. I happen to know that certain great trust magnates have announced within the past few weeks, in answer to the question as to why they were openly or secretly favoring the election of Mr. Bryan, that the laws that Mr. Bryan proposed, including especially this law, would be wholly ineffective, because the court would undoubtedly throw them out, and that the promises to enact them could therefore be safely disregarded.

On July 2d last the special counsel to the Central Association of Building Trades of New York, Mr. Edward J. Gavegan, submitted to that association an opinion in the matter of injunctions; an opinion which was officially endorsed and approved the same day by the Central Association of Building Trades of New York. In this opinion in discussing proposals to do away with or modify the power of issuing injunctions in industrial disputes, Mr. Gavegan said that the proposal to favor defendants in industrial disputes above all others "would be class legislation and in the nature of special privilege. Special privilege is the bane of the workingman. Special privilege is what creates powerful special interests. What the wage earner wants, and all he wants, is 'equality before the law.' * * * It is playing into the hands of the 'special interests' to enact laws which are certain of annulment by the courts, even when they are intended in good faith for the betterment of the workingman. The special interests would rather see a thousand favorable but unenforcible new laws enacted for the wage earner than to have him learn the full power of a single existing remedy. The remedies so far suggested and made public cannot in the very nature of our system furnish any

"A household of children . . . makes all other forms of success and achievement lose their importance by comparison."

"You go home and stay there!"

"It won't fly."

needed relief. * * * Labor representatives should concentrate and use their influence for the enactment of general measures calculated to protect and not to destroy the remedy of injunction." This is admirably sound common sense, the opinion of the counsel to a great labor body, endorsed and adopted as its own by that labor body. It is a scathing condemnation of the proposals, both vicious and chimerical, to which Messrs. Bryan and Gompers are committed. They promise what would be in the highest degree detrimental to the interests of the general public if it could be performed, and what as a matter of fact could not be performed. I believe both in the patriotism and the intelligence of the workingmen, the laboring men, of America. Therefore I do not believe that they can be misled to their own deep hurt as Messrs. Bryan and Gompers seek to mislead them; I do not believe that they will permit Mr. Gompers to deliver them like chattels to Mr. Bryan in exchange for a sham.[2] *Sincerely yours*

4960 · TO HENRY CABOT LODGE   *Roosevelt Mss.*

Personal   Washington, October 21, 1908

Dear Cabot: I think we are all right: I believe that the situation is better than it was. Ohio I cannot be certain about. I have received the most conflicting accounts about the situation there. The ultratemperance people are inclined to go against Taft, and the ultraliquor people also. There is a real defection in the labor ranks. The more narrow-minded evangelical Protestants, especially the country clergymen of the Methodist, Lutheran, Baptist, and even Presbyterian creeds are showing a tendency to bolt him; some on the ground that he has behaved too well to the Catholics, but most of them on the ground that he is a Unitarian. I have received hundreds of letters chiefly from clergymen protesting against him on this ground. I enclose you a copy of the letter I have sent out in answer to same, and also a copy of one from the Methodist Bishop Hartzell,[1] which we think gives a good answer. All these hostile forces seem to be particularly strong in Ohio, where we are further complicated by the fact that some of the big capitalists like Ingalls[2] have a corporation lawyer, Cleveland's Attorney General, Judson Harmon, running for Governor, and are giving all the aid they can to the Bryanites. Nevertheless, I cannot help but feel that the drift our way in Ohio will save us. In New York every indication that we can get is that we are going to win handsomely, that we will pull Hughes thru, and knock out Chanler. Hughes has made an excellent fight. He has done excellently in the West and

[2] This letter was released for publication on October 22.

[1] Joseph Crane Hartzell, founder, 1875, of the *Southwestern Christian Advocate*, since 1896 Methodist missionary bishop to Africa.

[2] Melville Ezra Ingalls, railroad executive, chairman of the board of directors of the Cleveland, Cincinnati, Chicago and St. Louis Railroad; in 1903 unsuccessful Democratic candidate for mayor of Cincinnati; in 1905 president of the National Civic Association.

that fact has helped him in his own contest. I am trying to help him in every way. Up to a month ago things did not look well for us in the West; but Taft has made a great canvass and his work on the stump has told tremendously in our favor. Of course there are underground forces such as I have indicated above that are at work against us, and it may be that these may prove so powerful that we shall be beaten; but I do not think so. All the indications that I have are that we shall succeed. My own judgment is that we shall carry the country by nearly as large an electoral vote as four years ago. We shall probably lose Missouri and Nevada, tho we may carry both. Possibly we shall lose Nebraska, Colorado and Montana, but I think we shall carry all three. On the other hand I think we shall carry Maryland, and there is a chance of our carrying either Kentucky or Tennessee.

I am extremely glad that you are to be on the stump. The demand this year has been for Taft himself, Hughes, you, *and Beveridge!* — you must pardon my including Beveridge, but that is the fact, and the reason is the people feel that he is pecuniarily honest. Cannon has proved such a load that they have had to cancel his engagements in the very doubtful districts, the candidates being afraid to have him come into their districts. The people at large, whatever their own morals, are bound at this moment that they shall be led only by leaders who on the elementary questions of public morality are sound — and they don't think some of our leaders are. *Ever yours*

4961 · TO KENNETH GRAHAME   *Roosevelt Mss.*

Personal   Washington, October 22, 1908

My dear Mr. Grahame: The book hasn't come, but as I have never read anything of yours yet that I haven't enjoyed to the full, I am safe in thanking you heartily in advance. Of course it won't have "any problems, any sex, any second meaning" — that is why I shall like it. By the way, we have just been finishing *The Further Experiences of an Irish R.M.!* I hope you know them, and are as fond of them as we are.

Again heartily thanking you, and with real regret that you are not to come to this side while we are in the White House, believe me, *Sincerely yours*

4962 · TO JOHN ELLIOTT PILLSBURY   *Roosevelt Mss.*

Washington, October 23, 1908

My dear Admiral: I am really obliged to you for sending me the two letters from Admiral Sperry. I return them herewith. I am very glad our men did so well in the rifle shooting. How admirably Sperry has done his duty! Who do you think was responsible for those stories about the misconduct of the fleet?[1] I suppose the utmost care will be taken to see that coal is already at Colombo.[2] What was the hitch in New Zealand? *Sincerely yours*

4963 · TO WILLIAM DUDLEY FOULKE   *Roosevelt Mss.*

Washington, October 24, 1908

Dear Foulke: My view of the condition of politics in Indiana is of course worthless compared to yours, but so far as my information goes it exactly agrees with what you state.

Now about the articles in the *News*.[1] You ask me to call Hornaday[2] to

---

[1] Any stories of misconduct were completely overshadowed by the enthusiastic welcome the fleet received in both New Zealand and Australia; see Bailey, *Roosevelt and the Japanese-American Crises*, pp. 281–285.

[2] The coaling at Colombo, Ceylon, in December went off without a hitch.

---

[1] Foulke had written that charges made by the Indianapolis *News* against the President were damaging Republican prospects in the Indiana campaign. He therefore urged Roosevelt to answer them publicly. This request and Roosevelt's response ultimately led to the celebrated libel suit against the *News* and the New York *World*. Roosevelt's decision to institute this suit, however, was not, as has often been claimed (see Pringle, *Roosevelt*, p. 335), an immediate reaction to the articles printed in the two newspapers. During the month after he had received Foulke's letter, Roosevelt was merely contemplating the advisability of writing publicly what he was saying privately about the charges in the press and the men who were making them (see Numbers 4964, 4970). Partly because Foulke insisted on the political necessity of denying the *News's* accusations, partly because his own temper rose at the charges, Roosevelt late in November wrote Foulke a letter for publication. It was only after the *World* made a scathing attack on this published letter that Roosevelt contemplated a libel suit. Then, without adequately considering the implications of such an unprecedented action, the President announced to Congress that the government would start libel proceedings against the *News* and the *World;* see Numbers 5058, 5061, 5072.

Of the three broad accusations made by the *News* during October, the Harriman matter, already an old story (see No. 3286, note 1), received no attention after the fall campaign; the Tennessee Iron and Coal Company merger, investigated early in 1909 by a congressional committee, became a major political issue only after Roosevelt's break with the Taft Administration; but the charges concerning the Panama Canal syndicate were emphasized by the constant repetition of the *News* and ultimately dignified by Roosevelt's angry recourse to libel proceedings.

The *News*, like several other Democratic papers, based its information on Panama entirely upon stories printed by the New York *World*. On October 3, 1908, the *World* reported that W. J. Curtis of the firm of Sullivan and Cromwell had filed a complaint of blackmail with the District Attorney of New York City, William T. Jerome. The *World's* account read: "In brief, Mr. Curtis told Mr. Jerome it had been represented to Mr. Cromwell that the Democratic National Committee was considering the advisability of making public a statement that William Nelson Cromwell, in connection with M. Bunau-Varilla, a French speculator, had formed a syndicate at the time when it was quite evident that the United States would take over the rights of the French bondholders in the De Lesseps Canal, and that this syndicate included among others Charles P. Taft, brother of William H. Taft, and Douglas Robinson, brother-in-law of President Roosevelt. . . . It was further stated that the story as told against Mr. Cromwell fixed the profit of the syndicate at $36,500,000, this amount being divided among Government favorites in the world of politics and finance."

This story of Cromwell's blackmail complaint had no basis in fact. The district

some kind of account for his falsehoods. I never heard of Hornaday until I received your letter. (Loeb interjects here that I have heard of him a number of times from you, but the truth is that there are so many small moral vermin around that I continually forget their individual names.) The *News* is an infamous sheet. Its editor is a lying blackguard, and I have no doubt a corrupt crook. But it isn't a bit worse than the New York *Sun;* it couldn't be. It really is not any worse than the New York *Evening Post.* If I denied all the lies in these three papers, and say half the lies in the *World, Herald,* New York *Times,* Boston *Herald,* and so on ad infinitum, I would spend all of each day in pointing out the falsehoods that appeared in the editorials in those papers on that morning. Take the three editorials in the single issue of the Indianapolis *News* that you enclosed. The first one is on "The President's Machine." The first paragraph of this contains first the statement that I am utterly "demoralizing the country" by my Presidential influence, in asking people to see me at the White House! Surely you do not think that this is something that I need seriously deny. The paragraph goes on to say that "the work of raising money is being carried on by the President, and seemingly with brilliant success." This is of course an infamous falsehood. I have not taken any part whatever in raising money, unless you call it taking part to have written to Sheldon that under no circumstances should the Standard Oil people or Harriman be asked to contribute. I haven't an idea who has contributed and who has not, and know no more about this side of the campaign than you do — and not as much, if you know anything. The editorial says finally that there is no secrecy about the present performances, and that "the great office of President ought not to be available as an asset for either political party." Really, this does not rise to the dignity of being trivial. In 1864 do they suppose the great office of President under Lincoln was not the chief asset of the Republican party? The only way to answer an editorial like this would be to say that the writer was a malignant imbecile, and that Delavan Smith,[3] whether he wrote it or not, as he is

---

attorney's office, the *World* later admitted, had said nothing about the complaint and neither Jerome nor Curtis had been interviewed. The story came wholly from a statement made in the *World's* editorial office by Jonas Whitly, a former *World* reporter who, the paper claimed, was Cromwell's "press representative."

In spite of the origin of the story and of the protests by Cromwell and Taft, who branded the report "a fake," the *World* during October printed a series of articles on "Cromwell's Canal Syndicate Deal." These articles repeatedly mentioned Roosevelt, William H. Taft, J. P. Morgan, and Elihu Root as well as Charles P. Taft and Douglas Robinson. They further suggested that the Administration, to prevent embarrassing disclosures, had destroyed records recently received from the French canal company.

[2] James Parker Hornaday, since 1901 Washington correspondent for the Indianapolis *News.*

[3] Delavan Smith, a man of various interests, several talents, and independent views. A graduate of the Massachusetts Institute of Technology, he was the publisher of the Indianapolis *News* and vice-president of the Oliver Typewriter Company. To the paper he published he contributed, frequently, his own editorial opinions on current issues.

responsible for it, was a malignant imbecile. Now what would be the use in making such a declaration as that?

Now as to the second editorial. This is the kind of dishonest attack that I knew perfectly well would be made when I acted as I did as regards the Steel Corporation and the Tennessee Iron and Coal Company. To compare small things to great things, it was the kind of attack which Lincoln had to face again and again when Copperheads of the Delavan Smith type, and scoundrelly papers of the kind that the Indianapolis *News* is at present, were attacking him for trying to serve the people by saving the Union. We were in the midst of the most intense crisis of the panic. The Trust Company of North America was in imminent danger. If it had gone we should have seen such a crash as we saw in 1893. This trust company was loaded up with the Tennessee Coal and Iron stock, which was of little value, and the big brokerage house of Moore and Schley were involved in the same manner. The steel corporation did not particularly care to acquire the property, but the one way to give it value was for the Steel Corporation to acquire it and to put its solvency behind it. They were not willing to do so if they felt that action would be taken against them by the National Government for doing so. If I had possest a mean and timid soul; if my sole anxiety had been always to do away with the chance of scoundrels like the editor of this paper and the writer of this editorial attacking me, I would have followed the course they advocate and would have declined to express any opinion, but would have told them to consult their legal adviser. Instead of doing so I brought in the Attorney General, Mr. Bonaparte, a man of a standard of integrity so high that Delavan Smith and his associates cannot even understand it. We found that the purchase would only make a difference of about four per cent in the proportion of control of the steel business by the Steel Corporation, and stated, what was the obvious truth, that of course this acquisition would in no wise so alter the situation as to make it incumbent upon us to proceed against them.

Now as to the other editorial, that about the Panama Canal. The infamous creature who wrote this editorial asks that my brother-in-law, Douglas Robinson, deny that he made any money out of the deal or was concerned in it, because it says that his name has, "at least thru rumor, been connected with the transaction." Of course this is a lie, pure and simple. But why deny it? In the very next paragraph the editorial goes on to say that no matter how vehement the denial may be, it ought not to be accepted as conclusive, because all the records are in the possession and under the control of the Government! I hereby authorize you and Swift and any other honorable men (by which qualification I of course exclude scoundrels like Delavan Smith and his associates) to come on here, and you shall see every detail of the records in the Panama matter from top to bottom. As far as I know every important detail has already been made public, but I am delighted to have anything else in our possession made public at any time. Of course we have no possible means of knowing what went on in France among the people who finally sold their property to us for $40,000,000. Cromwell had nothing whatever to do with the revolution, so far as I am aware. He certainly had nothing whatever to do with my action, for he was greatly offended because I acted without consulting him. The action of the Government was just as straight as yours when you made your last purchase, whatever that may have been, or paid your last bill. I do not know whether it was to a tailor, or a butcher, or an art dealer, or a bookseller, but whatever that bill was I am sure that your conduct was honorable in paying it. But of course you cannot be sure that if it was a tailor or a butcher, he had paid his employees, or if it was a bookseller, that he was not in debt for the books, or if it was an art dealer that he had not hired someone to fake the picture. The odds are heavily against any of these things having been done; but if they had been done they would not have reflected upon you in any way.

Now Mr. Delavan Smith stands on a level with Mr. Laffan of the New York *Sun*, Mr. Harvey of *Harper's Weekly*, and Messrs. Ogden and Villard of the *Evening Post*. I cannot continually expose the purchased mendacity of the Indianapolis *News* and New York *Sun* any more than I can spend my time exposing the mendacity, purchased or unpurchased, of the *Evening Post*. I should not believe that this letter was worth publishing, but you are very welcome to show it to any of your friends, and to read any part of it to Mr. Delavan Smith or any of those concerned in writing the editorials in question. I hope you will show it to Swift. *Ever yours*

4964 · TO KERMIT ROOSEVELT   *Roosevelt Mss.*

Washington, October 24, 1908

Dearest Kermit: Since I wrote you about the political situation it seems to me to have changed materially for the better. I feel now that we are morally sure of enough votes to elect Taft; and in New York the conditions are so good that I expect a larger majority than we got four years ago. The one thing I cannot fathom is the A.P.A. movement among the ultra-Protestant bigots against Taft because he is a Unitarian and because he has acted squarely by the Catholics. In the East, except in Maryland, this movement does not seem to be very strong, altho we find it cropping up here and there both in New York and New England. But in the West it is very strong. It may cut down our vote everywhere and may even lose us Ohio and Indiana. It is an infamous movement.

Speaking of infamy, I don't think the worst politicians or the worst businessmen reach the level of infamy attained by so many newspapermen. Laffan, of the New York *Sun*; Ogden and Villard, of the *Evening Post*; Delavan Smith, of the Indianapolis *News*; the editors of *Harper's Weekly*, the *World*, *Herald*, *Times*, Boston *Herald*, and a multitude of other papers — I happen to have seen recently editorials from all of these papers which for malignant mendacity, whether purchased or unpurchased, come well up to anything I have ever known.[1] I do not think that there is any form of lying slander at which these men would stop.

I was much pleased with and interested in your letter to Mother. I think you very wise in the way you handled the Sailors Haven matter. I wish I could have been with you when you were there; and I also wish I could have been with you to see the prize fight! *Your loving father*

4965 · TO WILLIAM HOWARD TAFT   *Roosevelt Mss.*

Washington, October 24, 1908

Dear Will: I do not think you need to be put in good heart, but it won't do you any damage to have me write you that humanly speaking the result of the election is now absolutely assured. I won't pretend to say anything about Ohio. You are on the ground and know far more than I can about the State. My opinion is that things have greatly changed in our favor in Ohio and that the State will be all right. If so my original belief will come true and you will receive substantially my electoral vote, that is, somewhere between 300 and 350 votes in the electoral college. It may be a little over or a little under our vote of 1904. In New York State the tide is coming our way with a rush, and I believe you will get a larger majority than I got four years ago and that Hughes will be elected by a very handsome vote, also. *Ever yours*

4966 · TO LUKE EDWARD WRIGHT   *Roosevelt Mss.*

Washington, October 26, 1908

My dear Mr. Secretary: I have again read your letter of October 6th, concerning Captain Parker's report on machine-gun service, and have conferred on the matter with General Bell. In the main, I find myself quite in accord with your view, but one or two suggestions occur to me which I desire to submit to your consideration.

I am anxious to get some definite result in this connection as soon as possible. As Captain Parker's proposed regulations for machine-gun service are intended for provisional issue only, it would seem to be unnecessary to have them reviewed by both the General Staff and the Board of Officers of which General Wotherspoon is President. I would suggest that after it is gone over by the General Staff to detect manifest errors, and to make it accord with some tentative organization which you may approve, it had best be printed and issued at once, in order that it may be submitted to the test of practical use as soon as possible. This is the best and quickest way of determining such modifications as ought to be made.

[1] See No. 4963.

Having considered what is said in all the accompanying papers concerning the number of guns to a company, six guns for both peace and war seem to be a conservative mean of all the suggestions made. This number appeals to my judgment, as it would provide two guns for use with each battalion, should conditions of service ever render such use desirable, and because it is much easier to reduce each company by two guns and utilize them elsewhere, should six prove to be too many, than to add two more guns to each company, should four prove to be too few. Should war break out, it will always be necessary to equip volunteers and increase our machine-gun service. Should we find it desirable to reduce the companies by two guns, those withdrawn could be utilized to equip the organized militia; and when this is done, the surplus, if any, be stored for use in war. As soon as the organization, equipment, etc., are thoroly decided upon by experiment and use, a large supply of machine guns and materiel should be secured and stored to meet the necessities of possible war.

I fully concur in your suggestion that our next step in the matter should be to organize a machine-gun troop in some regiment of cavalry, for experimental purposes. I wish you would give orders to have this done without delay.

Finally, it is my judgment that little progress is to be expected in the perfection of machine-gun service in our army without the assistance of experts, whose special duty it is to supervise and work the companies up. Officers absorbed by routine duties of various kinds are too busy to concentrate upon the interests of this service that zeal and attention which is needed to push the undertaking to completion, and which is justified by its importance. Extra officers should be available in each branch of the service for this purpose, and a modification of the bill proposed by Captain Parker would seem to fit the necessities of both infantry and cavalry very well. Please, therefore, have submitted to the General Staff for report the attached modified copy of Captain Parker's proposed bill, with instructions to submit a proposition along the lines of the general discussion which will be applicable to both infantry and cavalry.[1] The necessities of seacoast artillery in the line of machine guns should also be studied and reported on.

I also see no objection to publishing an order such as outlined in Memorandum "A," attached hereto, as modified, should the extra-officers bill become a law.[2] I am informed that there are not enough officers now available for duty with troops to justify taking three more for duty with the machine-gun company at the present time. *Sincerely yours*

[1] The General Staff approved Captain John H. Parker's proposed bill creating a machine-gun company for each regiment of infantry and cavalry. Congress, however, took no action.
[2] Because the bill to increase the number of army officers was not enacted, even the provisional organization of the machine-gun service as outlined in this memorandum was not put into effect.

Washington, October 27, 1908

Dear Will: Bob Bacon has been in to see me after a conversation over the phone with Perkins. John Mitchell has come to Perkins and said he thinks it would be a very good thing if in this week you could outline your plans for the future as regards labor.[1] Now, I don't quite know how to advise you in this matter. What I should suggest is that you get Mitchell to see you in New York at as early an opportunity as possible; that you find out just what he desires done; and then so far as you feel you can that you use his suggestions as a basis for some remarks outlining what you intend your future policy to be. If you happened to see my letter # to the railroad trainmen you may have noticed that I had outlined loosely the policies that I believed you were going to stand for. It is possible that it would be worth your while to glance at them. I think I used rather overhead language, and you could put it into more homely and telling phraseology. But you might not want that matter at all, and this you could tell better after you had seen Mitchell.

I believe we have the election hands down, but of course it won't do to take any chances; and undoubtedly Gompers and his crowd intend to make a tremendous effort to rally and solidify the labor vote against you in the last two or three days of the campaign. If you can meet it by some such statement as this, in which, instead of being on the defensive as to your record, you will be affirmatively stating your policy as to the future, I think it would be well. At any rate, I put the matter before you for your consideration. *Ever yours*

copy enclosed

Washington, October 28, 1908

My dear Remington: It was good of you to write me and I appreciate it. You are one of the men whose friendship I value. Do you know I am rather ashamed to say that I cannot accept your condolence? I am still looking forward, and not back. I do not know any man who has had as happy a fifty years as I have had. I have had about as good a run for my money as any human being possibly could have; and whatever happens now I am ahead of the game. Besides, I hope still to be able to do some good work now and then; and I am looking forward to my African trip with just as much eagerness as if I was a boy; and when I come back there are lots of things

[1] On October 28, at Cooper Union in New York City, Taft stated his belief in the rights of labor to organize and to strike. "But they may not injure the property or unlawfully injure the business of their employers," "and they may not institute a secondary boycott in such a dispute."

in our social, industrial and political life in which I shall take an absorbed interest. I have never sympathized in the least with the kind of man who feels that because he has been fortunate enough to hold a big position, he cannot be expected to enjoy himself afterward in a less prominent position. In fact, I do not in the least care for a position because of its title, so to speak — I want to try to do good work wherever I am, and I am far more concerned with that than with the question of what position it is in which I am to do the good work. Cushing, who sunk the *Albemarle*, was only a lieutenant, but there are mighty few admirals with whom, if I had been in his shoes, I should have thought it worth while to change positions.

With warm regards to Mrs. Remington, believe me, *Faithfully yours*

4969 · TO ALICE ROOSEVELT LONGWORTH   *Roosevelt Mss.*

Washington, October 28, 1908

Darling Alice: I was so glad to hear from you. I would have entirely forgotten my own birthday if other people had not remembered it. I celebrated it by taking Roswell out in the afternoon and jumping him over all the hurdles. He is a fine old horse, and it is astonishing how well he jumps.

Well, the canvass is coming to a close and I am completely out in my calculations if we do not win a smashing victory. I still feel that Ohio is the most doubtful State, but I believe we shall carry it handsomely. In New York and New England I think there is at least an even chance that we shall beat our great majorities of four years ago. *Ever your father*

4970 · TO WILLIAM DUDLEY FOULKE   *Roosevelt Mss.*

Washington, October 30, 1908

My dear Foulke: I do not like Delavan Smith, but I like Pulitzer,[1] Laffan, Villard and Ogden still less, and I would not be willing to have anything published unless I included these men in what I said. But I am not sure that it is wise to publish anything at all. Skinning skunks is not a pleasant occupation, and tho I am glad to get rid of the skunks, it is at least an open question whether the game is worth the candle. The lies in the editorials of Delavan Smith which you sent me are as bad as they can be, but they neither are nor can be any worse than the lies appearing day by day or week by week in the editorial columns of the *Sun, World* and *Evening Post.* I hesitate to

---

[1] Joseph Pulitzer, the picturesque wizard who built the St. Louis *Post-Dispatch* and rebuilt the *World.* For the shoddy journalism of the latter in its struggle with Hearst's *Journal* for dominance in New York, Pulitzer must bear some responsibility. Though he retired in 1890, he remained an astute and energetic figure in the *World's* councils until his death in 1911. In the first decade of the century his New York paper, Democratic by persuasion, exerted a commanding influence upon public opinion.

gibbet the Indianapolis carrion without hanging the New Yorkers on the same gallows. They all deserve to stand on the same evil eminence of infamy.

These charges are all absurd; perhaps the most absurd being that in connection with the Panama canal. We paid the money to the liquidator appointed by the French Government. Not a cent was reserved or sent back for the use of anyone here; the $40,000,000 went to the French Government, whose business it was to see that it was distributed. The mere supposition that any American received from the French Government a rake-off is so ludicrous that it is difficult to discuss it with patience. Men capable of inventing such a lie would, as a matter of course, pay no heed whatever to any denial or any explanation. In the same editorial that they clamor for a denial they announce that they wouldn't accept it. Why don't you come on here immediately after the election? I will turn the whole business of the Panama deal over to you. The essential things have all been made public again and again. But you shall see the immense mass of documents for yourself and examine or have anyone else examine them. Not a document has been destroyed. Moreover the *News* utters a gratuitous falsehood when it says that the last documents were sent over to us in June of this year. As a matter of fact the last papers that we have received of any kind were sent over to us in May, 1904, and they have been accessible to every human being who cared to look at them ever since. I would be very glad if at the same time you took up some of the lies of the *Sun*, *World* and *Evening Post;* for instance, the Tennessee Coal and Iron Company business, and the assertions as to my having asked Harriman for contributions, and other matters. This Harriman matter illustrates to my mind the uselessness of denying a statement made by a scoundrel when the scoundrel knows it is false and has not the slightest intention of paying heed to the exposure of its falsehood. My last letter to Harriman explicitly stated that there was no need for his coming to see me until after the election as I had nothing to say to him that could not wait until then. Now of course this was incompatible with any theory that I wisht to ask him for money to carry the election. The letter on its face shows the falsity of the charge; but the *Sun*, *World*, *Post* and the rest of them, repeated it just as freely as ever.

They have stated that I "have raised a campaign fund." They lie. But what good does it do for me to say that they lie? Lying is defined as telling a falsehood deliberately and willfully, knowing that it is false. That is what Mr. Delavan Smith has done; that is what Messrs. Pulitzer, Laffan, Villard and Ogden continually and habitually do. What is the use of my answering them? If they were mistaken in the facts; if they had, any one of them, a shred of honesty; why, yes it would be worth my while to set them right. But it is a mere waste of time to correct any falsehood of theirs because they earn their livelihood by the constant, daily practice of mendacity, and it is out of the question for me to spend some part of each day reading and denying the falsehoods that they have concocted the day before. As a matter of fact I never read any of the four papers mentioned. I see their editorials only when someone sends them to me as you have sent these of Delavan Smith. Of course to you these seem peculiarly infamous. But to show you how difficult it would be to pick and choose among these men for offenses all of the same moral iniquity, I will speak of a letter I have just received from the United States District Attorney for the Eastern District of Louisiana, Mr. Rufus E. Foster. It appears that in an editorial in the *Sun* of last Friday it was asserted that Bonaparte and I sent injunctions to every District Attorney to suspend the operation of the Sherman antitrust law so far as labor organizations were concerned and that when the District Attorney in Louisiana began proceedings the actions were summarily halted by the Attorney General, the suspension of the law being by my direct order. Of course this is a falsehood; and the District Attorney writes to say that he had secured the indictment of some seventy-five members of a labor union for a violation of the law and never had a word of disapproval from the Attorney General or myself; and that on the contrary the Attorney General sent to Louisiana the leading criminal pleader of the Department to assist in carrying on the case; and that he (the District Attorney) during the past year has prosecuted two combinations of laborers and two corporations for violations of Federal laws, and that no one has ever sought to interfere with him in any way. In this case of the *Sun* the lie was just as flagrant as was the lie you quote from the *News*. Nor was it by any means the only lie in the editorial. I hardly ever see an editorial from either the *World*, *Sun*, *Evening Post* or Indianapolis *News* that I do not find it contains willful and deliberate perversions of the truth. Why should I single out one or two falsehoods for special mention? Above all why should I attack one paper?

I send you on herewith the rough draft of the letter I had thought of writing you if I wrote at all.[2] But my present inclination is not to write at all. The lies they uttered last year are now forgotten. They have probably forgotten them themselves. Of course now and then I have found, that it paid to denounce a lie, but as a rule my experience is that the best thing to do is simply to play the game; to go ahead, do the best possible, and let the Smiths and Laffans and the rest of them yell.

In any event before doing anything I wish you and Swift would come on here and let me talk it over with you. I doubt if I wish to make any denial. But if I do, I want to make it in solemn and serious form and put it out as applying to all of these people and as being written by me, not because they have any effect upon me personally, but because I wish to show the hideous damage they are doing to American institutions. *Sincerely yours*

P.S. Show this letter to Swift. If I write at all I should think it ought to be in answer to a letter from you alone or from you and Swift jointly, in which you take up specimen and outrageous charges of each of the four newspapers in question and perhaps of one or two others and ask me about

[2] This was a slightly revised copy of his letter of October 24; see No. 4963.

them.[3] Then in my answer I shall take, not the defensive about myself, but the offensive about these scoundrels, and point out that they neither have damaged nor can damage me; but they do damage to a certain extent the country as a whole. I feel such a profound contempt for them that I do not read their articles, and then when somebody sends me some peculiarly infamous lie which they have coined, just as you have sent me these lies of Delavan Smith, I feel angry for twenty-four hours but by the end of that time I have forgotten about them and am thinking only of the work that I am doing. But please come on here, bringing Swift if you can, and we will talk over the whole matter. It may be that I can take this opportunity of writing something that should be of some slight permanent use in calling a halt on such scoundrels. A peculiar feature of it is that inasmuch as they promulgate all these falsehoods about decent men all the time, they either have no time to waste upon attacks upon genuine scoundrels like Haskell, of Oklahoma, or, if they do attack him, what they say has no weight because they have used just as severe language in condemning honest men; and then after having practiced every conceivable form of slander, when some man does expose real iniquity, such as that of Haskell's, certain papers will turn virtuously around and say there ought not to be mudslinging! This last reflection is due to a cartoon which I have just seen reproduced from a blackmailing sheet, the *Saturday Globe*, of Utica, N. Y.

4971 · TO JOHN D. PRINGLE   *Roosevelt Mss.*

Washington, October 30, 1908

My dear Mr. Pringle: I thank you for your letter and for the very interesting copy of the *Labor World*. I am entirely confident of Mr. Taft's election; and what is more, I believe that he will show himself as staunch a friend of labor as ever has been in the White House. I hope much that you will be able to come to Washington shortly after election. I would like to talk over a number of things with you. *Sincerely yours*

4972 · TO CHARLES E. BODKIN   *Roosevelt Mss.*

Washington, November 1, 1908

Sir:[1] I did not answer your last letter, because the request you made was made in such a manner and at such a time as to be one of the grossest impropriety; and I deemed it best to leave it unanswered. But since you repeat it, I answer it.

[3] Roosevelt followed this procedure when he finally decided to make a public answer; see Numbers 5016, 5039, 5042.

[1] Charles E. Bodkin was on the staff of the Fordham University *Messenger of the Sacred Heart*.

You ask me to subscribe to the *Catholic Encyclopedia*. You say that the members of the Republican National Campaign Committee have not subscribed, and you ask me to "lend us your moral support" to aid you, as Mr. Norman E. Mack, the chairman of the National Democratic Campaign Committee, has aided you. In other words, at the close of this campaign you are deliberately trying to "strike" the managers of the two political parties, and other men prominent in them, and to make them subscribe to the *Catholic Encyclopedia* under duress. This is exactly and precisely what your request amounts to. It is the kind of strike that is attempted in hundreds of cases in all political campaigns. But there is a peculiar baseness about it, coming on behalf of a religious periodical; your letter (which as you rightly say is as explicit as possible) being written with the headline showing that it is from the office of the *Messenger,* of Fordham University, New York, the editors of which are John J. Wynne, S.J., Thomas J. Campbell, S.J., and Edward P. Spillane, S.J. I wish you would show this letter to Fathers Wynne, Campbell and Spillane. I believe they will reprobate your conduct as heartily as I do.[2] *Very truly yours*

4973 · TO RUSSELL BENJAMIN HARRISON   *Roosevelt Mss.*

Private   Washington, November 2, 1908

My dear Harrison:[1] Many thanks for your letter; and I am extremely glad to receive your opinion as to our chances in Indiana. As for the Indianapolis *News,* under Mr. Delavan Smith I have expected it to behave as it has behaved, because I know Mr. Delavan Smith to be a lying blackguard and believe him to be a mere tool of crooked financial interests. You are quite welcome to show him this letter if you wish. That he is a lying blackguard is shown by every issue of his paper. I cannot prove that he is a purchased crook, and therefore do not assert it; but I have no doubt that his mendacity is in one shape or another procured by and in the interest of Dan Reid [2] — and others associated with him — who represent the type of financier that sadly needs a corrupt paper for backing. The letters that Mr. Hearst has recently published show how the Standard Oil magnates seek to use or control certain papers and periodicals; and Mr. Delavan Smith seems to be

[2] The editor of the *Messenger,* divorcing the circulation of the *Catholic Encyclopedia* from politics, chastized Bodkin. Roosevelt then subscribed; see No. 4979.

[1] Russell B. Harrison, the son of Benjamin Harrison, was an Indianapolis lawyer.
[2] Daniel Gray Reid, Indiana banker, played a prominent part in the large-scale organization of the steel industry, first as president of the American Tin Plate Company, then as an organizer of the National Steel Company, the American Steel Hoop Company, and the American Sheet Steel Company, and finally as director and member of the executive committee of the United States Steel Corporation.

occupying toward Mr. Reid the position which Mr. Grasty[3] occupied or desired to occupy toward Mr. Archbold. *Sincerely yours*

4974 · TO CHARLES JOSEPH BONAPARTE   *Roosevelt Mss.*

Washington, November 2, 1908

To the Attorney General: I should like to have some man specially detailed to consult with the Interior Department and go down to Oklahoma and find out if there is not some way of bringing Governor Haskell to speedy justice. I think him one of the most corrupt blackguards that has ever drifted to the top in any place in our American political life. If he could be put in stripes it would be an admirable thing for the cause of decent government.[1]

4975 · TO WILLIAM HOWARD TAFT   *Roosevelt Mss.*

Washington, November 4, 1908

My dear Mr. Taft: This is to introduce to you Father Ketcham,[1] who has been the special representative of the interests of the Catholic Indians in connection with the Indian Bureau here at Washington. Father Ketcham has been a good friend of mine and one of your staunchest and most effective supporters. But I introduce him to you less because of these two facts than because he has been a high-minded, zealous and reasonable friend of the Indians. He has sought to secure in every way the rights of the Indians of his Church and of the representatives of his Church who are dealing with those Indians; but he has shown a peculiar open-mindedness in connection with all other creeds and an appreciation of the attitude of the Government toward all creeds; and what is very unusual, on the occasions when I have been obliged to differ from him in my view of Governmental policy he has not held the difference to indicate a criminal nature on my part. He is a very good fellow in every way, and I really wish you to see him and to know him. *Sincerely yours*

[3] Charles Henry Grasty, called, at his death, "the ablest all-around newspaperman in America." In his career he had reported for the Kansas City *Times,* published the St. Paul *Dispatch,* the *Pioneer Press,* and the Baltimore *Sun,* and served as treasurer of the New York *Times.* As an editor in Baltimore he fought the local machine and in 1912 helped to bring the Democratic convention to that city. As a reporter he was perceptive and accurate. His descriptions of men and action at the front (1917–1918), sent back to the New York *Times,* were remarkable journalistic achievements.

[1] The statute of limitations saved the "corrupt blackguard"; see No. 4921.

[1] Father William Henry Ketcham, a Catholic missionary in Indian Territory, 1891–1901; director of the Bureau of Catholic Indian Missions, 1901–1919; member of the Board of Indian Commissioners, 1912–1919.

Washington, November 4, 1908

To the Chairman of the Committee on Pensions, House of Representatives:
Is it not possible to report a bill granting a pension to Mrs. Cleveland such
as was granted to Mrs. Garfield and to Mrs. McKinley? [1] It is true that
Presidents Garfield and McKinley had served in the army; but the pensions
granted to their widows were really granted not because of their army
service, but because of their service as Presidents. It seems to me that on
every consideration of equity similar action should now be taken for Mrs.
Cleveland, and I earnestly hope that it will be. *Sincerely yours*

Washington, November 6, 1908

My dear Sir George: Well, the election is over and to say that I am pleased
with the result is to express it mildly.[1] I can hardly express my satisfaction. If
the result of my "renunciation" had been either the nomination of a reactionary in the place of Taft, or the turning over of the Government to Bryan, I
should have felt a very uncomfortable apprehension as to whether I did not
deserve a place beside Dante's pope who was guilty of *il gran refiuto.* Renunciation is so often the act of a weak nature, or the term by which a
weak nature seeks to cover up its lack of strength, that I suppose that every
man who feels that he ought to renounce something, also tends to feel a little
uncomfortable as to whether he is really acting in accordance with the
dictates of a sound morality or from weakness. Yet, feeling as I do about
this people and about the proper standard for its chosen leaders, I could
not have acted otherwise than as I did; and naturally the relief is very great
to have the event justify me. Taft will carry on the work substantially as
I have carried it on. His policies, principles, purposes and ideals are the
same as mine and he is a strong, forceful, efficient man, absolutely upright,
absolutely disinterested and fearless. In leaving I have the profound satisfaction of knowing that he will do all in his power to further every one of the
great causes for which I have fought and that he will persevere in every
one of the great governmental policies in which I most firmly believe. Therefore nothing whatever is lost by my having refused to run for a third term,
and much is gained. Washington and Lincoln set the standard of conduct
for the public servants of this people. They showed how men of the

---

[1] No pension bill for Mrs. Cleveland was reported during the following session of
Congress.

[1] Taft's overwhelming majority in the electoral college somewhat obscured the de-
crease of the Republican plurality, which in 1908 was only about half of Roosevelt's
margin in 1904. In Taft's wake the Republicans easily maintained their control of both
Houses of Congress.

strongest type could also possess all the disinterested, all the unselfish, devotion to duty and to the interests of their fellow countrymen that we have a right to expect, but can only hope to see in the very highest type of public servant. At however great a distance I have been anxious to follow in their footsteps, and anxious that, however great the difference in degree, my service to the Nation should be approximately the same *in kind* as theirs.

Of course if I had conscientiously felt at liberty to run again and try once more to hold this great office, I should greatly have liked to do so and to continue to keep my hands on the levers of this mighty machine. I do not believe that any President has ever had as thoroly good a time as I have had, or has ever enjoyed himself as much. Moreover I have achieved a far greater proportion than I had dared to think possible of the things I most desired to achieve. In fact I do not know any man of my age who has had as good a time as I have had during my life! Whatever comes hereafter I have had far more than the normal share of human happiness, far more happiness than any but a very, very few men ever have. But I am bound to say in addition that I cannot help looking forward to much enjoyment in the future. In fact, I am almost ashamed to say that while I would have been glad to remain as President, I am wholly unable to feel the slightest regret, the slightest sorrow, at leaving the office. I love the White House; I greatly enjoy the exercise of power; but I shall leave the White House without a pang, and, indeed, on the contrary, I am looking forward eagerly and keenly to being a private citizen again, without anybody being able to make a fuss over me or hamper my movements. I am as interested as I can be in the thought of getting back in my own home at Sagamore Hill, in the thought of the African trip, and of various things I intend to do when that is over. Indeed I have been, and am, very fortunate, and I trust I am duly thankful for it.

In May, 1910, after getting out of Africa I am to be in England to deliver the Romanes Lecture at Oxford. Will you be in England then, and if so where? I must see you if you are where it is possible for me to reach you.

Your new edition of the *Life of Macaulay* came and I have reread the whole volume with the delight it always gives me. But oh, my dear Sir George, why do you quote Rosebery's comment on Macaulay's marginal notes, to the effect that he was a "sublime guide to sublime things?" Don't you think that this is open to just the good-natured raillery with which Macaulay himself spoke of the "Yankee" who stated that to "see Macaulay at the grave of Wordsworth" would be a "sublime spectacle?" Rosebery has a slight tendency anyhow to overemphasis; as witness the way in which he speaks of Winston Churchill's clever, forceful, rather cheap and vulgar life of that clever, forceful, rather cheap and vulgar egoist, his father, as if it was one of the very greatest biographies in the world; instead of being one of the smart, bright, amusing books of a given season. "Sublime" is a word that should be reserved for certain things in nature, and for a very few of the loftiest feelings, emotions and actions of mankind. There is only an occasional cathedral, an occasional great poem, to which the word could rightly be applied; and not to marginal notes by anybody about anything.

I have made up my mind that I will have to take some books on my African trip,[2] and the special piece of resistance is to be Macaulay's complete works — to which I may have to add your *American Revolution*. My son Kermit, by the way, I was rather pleased to find, among his books for the voyage has included Homer in the original. He and my elder boy, Ted, have both rather chuckled over your inability to tell me the best translations of the Greek tragic poets on the ground that you were old-fashioned enough to read them in the original; for I am much pleased to find that Ted, for instance, who is now hard at work in a carpet factory, quite spontaneously reads Virgil and Horace for his own amusement before going to bed. I never got so that reading any Greek or Latin author in the original represented to me anything except dreary labor.

With regard, *Faithfully yours*

[*Handwritten*] I am extremely pleased at the way our battle fleet has done on its trip around the world; and at it's reception both in Australia and Japan.

4978 · TO CHARLES EVANS HUGHES   *Roosevelt Mss.*

Washington, November 6, 1908

My dear Governor: Now that it is all over I want to write you just a line of admiration for all that you accomplished during the campaign. We won out by such a sweep both for Taft and you that people now tend to forget that in the middle of September the outlook was anything but pleasant. Your stumping tour in the West was of great National importance, and then when you came back your stumping tour in New York was of both National and State importance. Let me repeat my hearty congratulations.

With regard to Mrs. Hughes, believe me, *Sincerely yours*

[2] Most of these books Roosevelt had bound in pigskin for protection against weather, dirt, and wear. During his African trip, he recalled, "I almost always had some volume with me, either in my saddle-pocket or in the cartridge-bag." The "Pigskin Library," Roosevelt explained, consisted of books of "unequal value," "chosen for various reasons, and for this particular trip." A few of the books and authors included may be of interest: Shakespeare, Milton, Emerson, Bacon, Poe, Crothers, Froissart, *Nibelungenlied*, Borrow, Euripides, *The Federalist*, Dante, Darwin. The amount of poetry is remarkable — much of it from the nineteenth century. For the complete list of titles in the "Pigskin Library" and Roosevelt's reflections on their merits, see *Literary Essays*, Nat. Ed. XII, 337–346.

The Final Legacies

November 1908–March 1909

Washington, November 6, 1908

My dear Father Corbett: [1] Your letter and action were just what I had expected.

Now, may I thru you subscribe to the *Catholic Encyclopedia?* Will it be too much trouble to you to send me on the subscription blank and tell me what the cost is?

With all good wishes, believe me, *Sincerely yours*

Washington, November 6, 1908

My dear Sir: [1] I have received your letter running in part as follows:

> While it is claimed almost universally that religion should not enter into politics, yet there is no denying that it does, and the mass of the voters that are not Catholics will not support a man for any office, especially for President of the United States, who is a Roman Catholic.
>
> Since Taft has been nominated for President by the Republican party, it is being circulated and is constantly urged as a reason for not voting for Taft that he is an infidel (Unitarian) and his wife and brother Roman Catholics. * * * If his feelings are in sympathy with the Roman Catholic church on account of his wife and brother being Catholics, that would be objectionable to a sufficient number of voters to defeat him. On the other hand if he is an infidel, that would be sure to mean defeat. * * * I am writing this letter for the sole purpose of giving Mr. Taft an opportunity to let the world know what his religious belief is.

I received many such letters as yours during the campaign, expressing dissatisfaction with Mr. Taft on religious grounds; some of them on the ground that he was a Unitarian, and others on the ground that he was suspected to be in sympathy with Catholics. I did not answer any of these letters during the campaign because I regarded it as an outrage even to agitate such a question as a man's religious convictions, with the purpose of influencing a political election. But now that the campaign is over, when there is opportunity for men calmly to consider whither such propositions as those you make in your letter would lead, I wish to invite them to consider them, and I have selected your letter to answer because you advance both the objections commonly urged against Mr. Taft, namely: that he is a Unitarian, and also that he is suspected of sympathy with the Catholics.

You ask that Mr. Taft shall "let the world know what his religious belief is." This is purely his own private concern; it is a matter between him and his Maker, a matter for his own conscience; and to require it to be made public under penalty of political discrimination is to negative the first princi-

[1] Reverend John Corbett, editor, the *Messenger.*

[1] J. C. Martin, a piano dealer of Dayton, Ohio.

ples of our Government, which guarantee complete religious liberty, and the right to each man to act in religious affairs as his own conscience dictates. Mr. Taft never asked my advice in the matter, but if he had asked it, I should have emphatically advised him against thus stating publicly his religious belief. The demand for a statement of a candidate's religious belief can have no meaning except that there may be discrimination for or against him because of that belief. Discrimination against the holder of one faith means retaliatory discrimination against men of other faiths. The inevitable result of entering upon such a practice would be an abandonment of our real freedom of conscience and a reversion to the dreadful conditions of religious dissension which in so many lands have proved fatal to true liberty, to true religion, and to all advance in civilization.

To discriminate against a thoroly upright citizen because he belongs to some particular church, or because, like Abraham Lincoln, he has not avowed his allegiance to any church, is an outrage against that liberty of conscience which is one of the foundations of American life. You are entitled to know whether a man seeking your suffrages is a man of clean and upright life, honorable in all his dealings with his fellows, and fit by qualification and purpose to do well in the great office for which he is a candidate; but you are not entitled to know matters which lie purely between himself and his Maker. If it is proper or legitimate to oppose a man for being a Unitarian, as was John Quincy Adams, for instance, as is the Rev. Edward Everett Hale, at the present moment Chaplain of the Senate, and an American of whose life all good Americans are proud — then it would be equally proper to support or oppose a man because of his views on justification by faith, or the method of administering the sacrament, or the gospel of salvation by works. If you once enter on such a career there is absolutely no limit at which you can legitimately stop.

So much for your objections to Mr. Taft because he is a Unitarian. Now, for your objections to him because you think his wife and brother to be Roman Catholics. As it happens, they are not; but if they were, or if he were a Roman Catholic himself, it ought not to affect in the slightest degree any man's supporting him for the position of President. You say that "the mass of the voters that are not Catholics will not support a man for any office, especially for President of the United States, who is a Roman Catholic." I believe that when you say this you foully slander your fellow countrymen. I do not for one moment believe that the mass of our fellow citizens, or that any considerable number of our fellow citizens, can be influenced by such narrow bigotry as to refuse to vote for any thoroly upright and fit man because he happens to have a particular religious creed. Such a consideration should never be treated as a reason for either supporting or opposing a candidate for political office. Are you aware that there are several States in this Union where the majority of the people are now Catholics? I should reprobate in the severest terms the Catholics who in those States (or in any other States) refused to vote for the most fit man because he happened to be a Protestant; and my condemnation would be exactly as severe for Protestants who, under reversed circumstances, refused to vote for a Catholic. In public life I am happy to say that I have known many men who were elected, and constantly re-elected, to office in districts where the great majority of their constituents were of a different religious belief. I know Catholics who have for many years represented constituencies mainly Protestant, and Protestants who have for many years represented constituencies mainly Catholic; and among the Congressmen whom I knew particularly well was one man of Jewish faith who represented a district in which there were hardly any Jews at all. All of these men by their very existence in political life refute the slander you have uttered against your fellow Americans.

I believe that this Republic will endure for many centuries. If so there will doubtless be among its Presidents Protestants and Catholics, and, very probably at some time, Jews. I have consistently tried while President to act in relation to my fellow Americans of Catholic faith as I hope that any future President who happens to be a Catholic will act towards his fellow Americans of Protestant faith. Had I followed any other course I should have felt that I was unfit to represent the American people.

In my Cabinet at the present moment there sit side by side Catholic and Protestant, Christian and Jew, each man chosen because in my belief he is peculiarly fit to exercise on behalf of all our people the duties of the office to which I have appointed him. In no case does the man's religious belief in any way influence his discharge of his duties, save as it makes him more eager to act justly and uprightly in his relations to all men. The same principles that have obtained in appointing the members of my Cabinet, the highest officials under me, the officials to whom is entrusted the work of carrying out all the important policies of my administration, are the principles upon which all good Americans should act in choosing, whether by election or appointment, the man to fill any office from the highest to the lowest in the land.[2] *Yours truly*

4981 · TO CHARLES HITCHCOCK SHERRILL   *Roosevelt Mss.*

Washington, November 7, 1908

My dear Sherrill: May I, thru you, present to my fellow D.K.E.'s on the occasion of their Sixty-second Annual Convention banquet, my hearty regards?

In the recent campaign the effort was made to array class against class. Should such an effort ever succeed it will represent the most damaging blow

[2] This letter elicited a mixed reception. For such newspapers as the Philadelphia *Public Ledger* and the Boston *Herald* it was a convincing rebuke to bigotry. To such as the *American Citizen,* it seemed a dangerous apology for Romanism.

that can ever be struck at what we think truest and finest in American life. Therefore I feel that peculiar good must come from an association such as that of D.K.E., an association which takes the form of a fraternity whose reason for existence is to be found in extending the bonds of good brotherhood. Of D.K.E. this is peculiarly true because of its great strength in the South, no less than in the North. Fraternity such as this should unite men without regard to section, creed or occupation, on the basis of the great qualities which they have in common — on the basis of virile strength and yet the determination to stand for what is right.

With all good wishes, believe me, *Sincerely yours*

4982 · TO HENRY LEWIS STIMSON *Roosevelt Mss.*

Washington, November 7, 1908

My dear Stimson: Let me most heartily congratulate you on the conviction of Morse.[1] It is a real and great triumph.

Now, I am going to give a dinner to a number of people interested in labor matters on Tuesday evening, November 17th, at 8:00 o'clock, and would greatly like you to be present.[2] Can you come? *Faithfully yours*

4983 · TO RUSSELL BENJAMIN HARRISON *Roosevelt Mss.*

Washington, November 7, 1908

My dear Harrison: In reference to my letter to Delavan Smith, I will ask you not to show it to anyone but Smith himself.[1] You are welcome to do that; but I do not want it to be made public or shown to anyone else, because vermin like Smith are really pleased if they are noticed. *Sincerely yours*

4984 · TO WILLIAM DUDLEY FOULKE *Roosevelt Mss.*

Washington, November 7, 1908

Dear Foulke: I suppose Swift has written to you that he does not believe I should say anything about Delavan Smith and those creatures.[1] I believe he is right. I do not believe we will hear another word about the Panama matter

[1] District Attorney Stimson had secured the conviction of Charles W. Morse, speculator, trust company promoter, and vice-president of the National Bank of North America, for fraudulent use of that bank's funds; see No. 4849.
[2] Stimson attended this dinner, which Roosevelt gave as a means to get suggestions about the labor sections of his annual message. Moody, Holmes, Neill, Straus, and Bacon were among the government officials present, while organized labor was represented by leading officers in the building trades and railroad brotherhoods and in the national organizations of glassworkers and steam-shovel men.

[1] See No. 4973.

[1] See Numbers 4963, 4973, 4983, 5039.

now. Smith knew he was lying and I do not believe he will think it worth while now to continue the lie. *Sincerely yours*

4985 · TO FREDERIC HARRISON   *Roosevelt Mss.*

Washington, November 8, 1908

My dear Mr. Harrison: It is most interesting that my birthday should be your wife's birthday too. I thank you for the card just received, and I thank you also for the *Realities and Ideals*.[1] Some of these essays I already know — all of them I shall read with the utmost interest. That I shall like the book, goes without saying. As I am dictating this I happen by pure accident to open the book at page 80 and find this phrase: "Women must choose to be either women or abortive men. They cannot be both women and men." What could be happier? I have always said that what we needed for women was equality of consideration, but recognition of the fact that there was complete difference of function. The family is the unit in the State. It is more important than the State, because it is on the family that the State rests; and in the family the woman is and ought to be supreme. *Faithfully yours*

4986 · TO ETHEL CAROW ROOSEVELT   *Roosevelt Mss.*

Washington, November 8, 1908

Darling Ethel: It was fine hearing from you. I enjoyed *my* letter; and both your letters to Mother, too. You had quite an adventure with your saddle pommel breaking, and I must confess that I shall be a little more easy when your hunting is thru. Kermit, by the way, is on here now, and was out jumping Roswell this afternoon. He is really a trump, and seems to be doing so well at Harvard. On election day we saw Ted, and it was delightful. He is absorbed in his business.

I chuckled over your letter to Mother in which you spoke of the way that the old bores *would* talk to you about your father's career, until you earnestly wisht that your father hadn't had any career. I remember the way that Gen. Sherman used to perfectly loathe hearing the band play "Marching Thru Georgia." He never went anywhere with anybody who could either sing or play that some idiot was not struck with the happy idea of starting up "Marching Thru Georgia" as a special and delicate compliment to the General; whereupon the latter, who had heard the tune on several million previous occasions, and was a straightforward old gentleman, used almost to jabber with rage.

Yesterday, to Mother's great amusement, I took the entire General Staff and War College — some fifty officers all told — on a scramble walk down Rock Creek. We did not go fast because of course with such a number we

[1] Frederic Harrison, *Realities and Ideals, Social, Political, Literary and Artistic* (New York, 1908).

had to wait for the tail-enders, and there were about a dozen who could not have gotten thru at all if we had kept at any gait. But they all climbed gallantly up the cliffs, waded the stream, (up to their chins) and wriggled along the hillsides. The younger men of course, and some of the older men like Duvall, were much better at it than I was; but it was an eye opener to those who had let themselves get out of condition.

This morning I cut church, and Mother and Kermit and I took a lovely ride. Kermit has, characteristically, brought as presents extremely nice books for us, chosen with the care that Kermit alone could show.

We have had a Sir Harry Johnston staying in the house — a funny little scrap of a man who has done all kinds of work for the British Government in African administration, and who is most interesting and helpful to me; and in addition has a large number of my fads, so that he has been a most congenial companion.[1] *Your loving father*

[*Handwritten*] Love to Mrs. Herbie & Mr. Herbie too.[2] But do'n't take too many chances! Ted has just been. . . .

4987 · TO EDWARD KENT   *Roosevelt Mss.*

Washington, November 9, 1908

My dear Mr. Chief Justice:[1] I have your letter of the 5th. That is really good business. I am delighted that Cameron[2] has been elected. I shall of course urge separate Statehood for Arizona and New Mexico in my message. If Governor Kibbey will come on here I will help him in every way in the preparation and urging of such a measure. *Faithfully yours*

4988 · TO HENRY WALLACE   *Roosevelt Mss.*

Washington, November 9, 1908

My dear Mr. Wallace: I wish at the outset cordially to thank you for the way in which you have taken hold of the work you are doing. No more valuable work for the people of this country can be done, because no more valuable work for the farmers of this country can be done.

Now of course the whole success of the work depends upon the attitude of the people in the open country, of the farming people of the United States.

[1] For Johnston's administrative experiences and abilities, see No. 4805, note 1.
[2] Ethel was then visiting Mr. and Mrs. Herbert Wadsworth of Avon, New York.

---

[1] Kent, who liked to recall that his father, a Governor of Maine, had been mentioned by name in the political song "Have you heard the news from Maine," was the Chief Justice of the Supreme Court of Arizona.
[2] Ralph Henry Cameron, miner of silver and copper, surveyor and constructor of the Bright Angel Trail into the Grand Canyon; Republican territorial delegate for Arizona, 1909–1912; United States Senator, 1921–1927.

If they feel an awakening interest in what you are doing, they should manifest it. Moreover, it is essential that the farmers, the men who actually live on the soil should feel a sense of ownership in this Commission, should feel that you gentlemen in very truth represent them and are responsive to their desires and wishes, no less than to their needs. It seems to me therefore that it would be wise to try to get into the closest possible touch with the farmers of the country and to find out from them, so far as you are able, just what they regard as being the subjects with which it is most important that you should deal. This you are already doing by sending out a circular of questions and by holding meetings in different parts of the United States. But perhaps something more can be done.

I accordingly suggest that you ask the farmers to come together in the several school districts of the country so that they may meet and consider these matters. I suggest the school districts because the schoolhouse would be the natural and proper place for such a meeting; or they could meet at other customary or convenient places. It would be well if the meetings could be held within the next three or four weeks; that is, before Congress adjourns prior to the Christmas holidays, so that at the time of the reassembling of Congress early in January you will have the reports of the meetings and so will be in position to advise definitely what should be done. I suggest that you ask them to meet not later than Saturday, December 5th; and you will of course use your own judgment whether to summon the meeting by circular or otherwise.

Thruout this letter where I use the word "farmers" I mean also to include all those who live in the open country and are intimately connected with those who do the farm work — ministers, schoolteachers, physicians, editors of country papers, in short all men and women whose life work is done either on the farm or in connection with the life work of those who are on the farm.

You know better than I what topics you will suggest. How would it do to include such topics as:

> The efficiency of the rural schools;
> Farmers' organizations;
> The question of farm labor;
> The need of good roads;
> Improved postal facilities;
> Sanitary conditions on the farm.

Your purpose is neither to investigate the farmer, nor to inquire into technical methods of farming. You are simply trying to ascertain what are the general, economic, social, educational, and sanitary conditions of the open country, and what, if anything, the farmers themselves can do to help themselves, and how the Government can help them. To this end your especial desire is to get in touch with and represent the farmers themselves.

The Commission now consists of five members. I shall ask two more gentle-men to serve upon it, so that the full membership will be as follows:

Prof. L. H. Bailey, New York State College of Agriculture, Ithaca, N. Y., Chairman;

Mr. Henry Wallace, *Wallace's Farmer*, Des Moines, Iowa;

Kenyon L. Butterfield, President Massachusetts Agricultural College, Amherst, Mass;

Gifford Pinchot, U. S. Forest Service, Washington, D. C.;

Walter H. Page, of North Carolina, Editor of the *World's Work*,

Charles S. Barrett, Union City, Ga., and

William A. Beard, Sacramento, Cal.

Again thanking you, and with all good wishes for your success in this great and important work, believe me,[1] *Very sincerely yours*

4989 · TO WILLIAM HOWARD TAFT · · · · · · · · · · · · · · · · *Roosevelt Mss.*

Personal · · · · · · · · · · · · · · · Washington, November 10, 1908

Dear Will: The returns of the election make it evident to me that you are the only man whom we could have nominated that could have been elected. Of course neither Cannon nor any other of the reactionaries would have stood a ghost of a chance. The only other man whom it would have been possible to carry was Hughes, and even Hughes I think would have been beaten. The sweep for you is so tremendous that people fail to remember what is meant by the election of the Democratic Governors in Minnesota, Indiana and Ohio, and the way the Republican Governors ran behind you in New York, Illinois and Michigan. In all six of these States I believe that the electoral vote would have been cast against any of your rivals for the nomination, even Hughes, and of course that would have meant the election of Bryan. You have won a great personal victory as well as a great victory for the party, and all those who love you, who admire and believe in you, and are proud of your great and fine qualities, must feel a thrill of exultation over the way in which the American people have shown their insight into character, their adherence to high principle.

By the way, Bryce is so overjoyed he can hardly contain himself and is utterly unable to resist telling me that he thinks this election speaks better for the American people than any other incident that has occurred within his knowledge.

I look forward eagerly to seeing you on Sunday, for I may not be up when you reach the White House Saturday night. Root will be in on Sunday and we will talk over together the Cannon business. It would of course be well if there was some first-class man to put in his place as Speaker;[1] but we

[1] Roosevelt sent identical letters to all the members of the Commission on Country Life.

cannot think of putting in some cater-cornered creature like Burton; and, moreover, if it is evident that four fifths of the Republicans want Cannon I do not believe it would be well to have him in the position of the sullen and hostile floor leader bound to bring your administration to grief, even tho you were able to put someone else in as Speaker.[1] Jim Sherman will loyally stand by you and do everything he can for you. Root will undoubtedly go to the Senate[2] and will be a tower of strength for your administration. *Ever yours*

4990 · TO HARRIET TAYLOR UPTON   *Roosevelt Mss.*

Private   Washington, November 10, 1908

My dear Madam:[1] I have your letter of the 9th instant. I will give you exactly my feeling about your request that I speak a word for woman suffrage in my annual message. I do not think it would be wise to do so; not in the least because of any consideration about myself, but because I think that it is not in any shape or way a live issue at this time, and because I do not see what good would come of my mentioning it.

Personally I believe in woman's suffrage, but I am not an enthusiastic advocate of it because I do not regard it as a very important matter. I am unable to see that there has been any special improvement in the position of women in those States in the West that have adopted woman suffrage, as compared with those States adjoining them that have not adopted it. I do not think that giving the women suffrage will produce any marked improvement in the condition of women. I do not believe that it will produce any of the evils feared, and I am very certain that when women as a whole take any

[1] The pat cynicism toward tariff revision expressed by the Speaker in an address at Cleveland shortly after the election had infuriated Taft, who throughout the campaign had recognized that Cannon was too often a political liability. Taft was ready to join the insurgents in a movement to unseat the "dirty old man." Roosevelt himself was approached by many of these insurgents who felt with William Kent that the President should "start a backfire against that miserable, antediluvian nuisance, the Honorable Joseph Cannon" (Kent to Roosevelt, November 4, 1908, Kent Mss.). Kent, with others, had even hoped for a Democratic House as a means to break the matchless parliamentarian's power. But Roosevelt and Root preferred caution; no strong alternative candidate seemed available, and a brief reconnaissance indicated that the insurgents had not yet developed enough strength to succeed, even with presidential aid. Taft therefore made peace; see Pringle, *Taft*, I, 402–407.
[2] The "Easy Boss," long since without real personal power, now feeling his age, had decided to retire from politics. For Platt's seat in the Senate there was only one logical candidate, Elihu Root, whose quiet boom State Senator Frederick M. Davenport had launched in September. When Root refused to continue as Secretary of State, Roosevelt and Taft joined those in New York supporting him. He had agreed to accept the office but declined to campaign for it. No campaign was necessary. Briefly and without enthusiasm the organization leaders backed Woodruff, but in late November Woodruff withdrew and all opposition to Root ceased. With the unanimous endorsement of the Republican caucus, Root was elected in January.

[1] Harriet Taylor (Mrs. George W.) Upton, active since 1890 in the suffrage movement; treasurer of the National American Woman Suffrage Association; author of *Our Early Presidents: Their Wives and Children* (1892).

special interest in the matter they will have the suffrage if they desire it. But at present I think most of them are lukewarm; I find some actively for it, and some actively against it. My two sisters are strongly against it; my wife favors it, but not very strongly. I am, for the reasons above given, rather what you would regard as lukewarm or tepid in my support of it because, while I believe in it, I do not regard it as of very much importance. I believe that man and woman should stand on an equality of right, but I do not believe that equality of right means identity of function; and I am more and more convinced that the great field, the indispensable field, for the usefulness of woman is as the mother of the family. It is her work in the household, in the home, her work in bearing and rearing the children, which is more important than any man's work, and it is that work which should be normally the woman's special work, just as normally the man's work should be that of the breadwinner, the supporter of the home, and if necessary the soldier who will fight for the home. There are exceptions as regards both man and woman; but the full and perfect life, the life of highest happiness and of highest usefulness to the State, is the life of the man and the woman who are husband and wife, who live in the partnership of love and duty, the one earning enough to keep the home, the other managing the home and the children.

I do not desire to go into a public discussion of this matter, so I will be obliged if you will treat this letter as private. *Sincerely yours*

4991 · TO JOHN CALLAN O'LAUGHLIN *Roosevelt Mss.*

Washington, November 13, 1908

Dear Cal: [1] Your letters I regard as very important, especially the one of October 11th. I have sent them both to Root. There are things I cannot put down in writing, which I shall tell you of in full when I see you. Let me reiterate that both about Hawaii and Japan your letters are of real value to me; but you know how impossible it is for me to get Congress to do what it ought to do. What it ought to do this year is to allow for building four battleships and also for naturalization of the Japanese.[2]

With warm regards and thanks, believe me, *Sincerely yours*

[1] John Callan O'Laughlin was at this time secretary of the United States Government Commission on the Tokyo Exposition.
[2] This familiar formula for Far Eastern policy continued to meet the resistance of the small navy group in Congress and the anti-Japanese of the West Coast. In 1908, strident nativism and a desire for economy in government placed an imposing obstacle in the way of sensible foreign policy. Doubtless blinded by his indignation at this shortsightedness, and doubtless also attempting by calculated exaggeration to facilitate his naval program, Roosevelt in the closing months of his administration discerned and defined a Japanese crisis that did not in fact exist. In January 1909 he magnified the importance of anti-Japanese agitation in California far beyond the dimensions of its diplomatic importance (see Bailey, *Roosevelt and the Japanese-American Crises*, ch. xiii). In November, perhaps to sustain his own convictions, he ignored in his correspondence the negotiations that resulted at the end of the month in the signifi-

Washington, November 13, 1908

My dear Mr. Brooks: [1] I have procured Stone's *Studies in the American Race Problem*[2] and Olivier's *White Capital and Coloured Labour.*[3] The latter is a suggestive book and I have no doubt that it has a real value as regards the West Indies. I think its value is small as regards the United States, and I should doubt if it was useful as regards Africa.

But I am more concerned with Mr. Stone. I never heard of him until you spoke of him and I got his volume, and I am interested in him only because he represents, not in his subject, but in his scandalous untruthfulness of treatment, so many of the men who try to combine the role of publicist and reformer. There are numbers of these men who write on subjects of the deepest interest where what they have to say would be of serious consequence *if true.*

I always try to test them by turning to some part of their books which touch on subjects that I know thoroly, and if I find them, not only false, but entirely indifferent to the truth, on these matters whereof I know, I do not waste a none-too-abundant leisure by reading what they say on matters whereof I do not know. I have for this reason given up reading Steffens and Jack London and Phillips. To illustrate what I mean, I will speak of a man named Russell,[4] who wrote a book the other day professing to describe how

cant exchange of notes between Root and Takahira. In this friendly exchange the United States and Japan announced their "common aim, policy, and intention" to encourage the peaceful development of their commerce on the Pacific Ocean, to maintain the *status quo* in the Pacific and respect the territorial possessions of each other there, to defend the principle of the Open Door in China and support "by all pacific means . . . . the independence and integrity of China," and to communicate with each other as to what measures to take should any of these principles be threatened; see Jessup, *Root,* II, 34–43; *Foreign Relations,* 1908, pp. 510–512.

[1] John Graham Brooks, after graduating from the Harvard Divinity School, was attracted, as so many of his contemporaries were, to the German universities. From 1875 to 1878 he studied at Berlin, Jena, and Freiburg. Upon his return he entered the field of economics and the allied subject of sociology. He taught for a time at Harvard, Chicago, and the University of California. In the two years he worked for the Department of Labor he made a report on workingmen's insurance in Germany. When not teaching or working in the government he produced books with such titles as *The Social Unrest* and *American Syndicalism.*

[2] *Studies in the American Race Problem* (New York, 1908), by Alfred Holt Stone, a cotton planter and banker, in 1912–1913 president of the Mississippi Historical Society; since 1932 chairman of the State Tax Commission of Mississippi. Mr. Stone has read this letter and has graciously consented that it should be published. He of course dissents vigorously from the implications by Roosevelt upon his character and maintains the truth of the statements in his book.

[3] *White Capital and Coloured Labour,* by Sydney Haldane Olivier, later Baron Olivier of Ramsden, at this time Governor of Jamaica. Olivier with British candor described his recreations as "the normal forms of loafing and dilettantism."

[4] Charles Edward Russell, city editor of the *World* for Joseph Pulitzer in the first years of the paper's circulation war with Hearst; later Hearst's editor on the Chicago *American.* A talented and lively author, he wrote in many fields: biography — Julia

a number of very rich financiers had made their money. I glanced at the book and was greatly interested in certain statements it contained, and sat down to read it. But very early I suddenly found Ryan described as owning the present Secretary of State, Mr. Root, and as controlling Panama contracts. Now here I was on ground I knew. To say that Ryan owned Root, because Root had once been the counsel of Whitney and Ryan, was a malevolent absurdity; and I knew all about the contracts in connection with the Panama Canal because, as a matter of fact, the work has hardly been done by contract at all, and I knew that Ryan had nothing of any kind, sort or description to do with any contracts concerning it. As soon as I found so colossal a falsehood, of so reckless a type, at the beginning of the book I tossed it aside.

So it is with Mr. Stone. I turned to his chapter on "Mr. Roosevelt and the Negro" because here I knew absolutely the facts — I don't refer to matters of opinion, to matters of judgment, but to matters of actual fact. Mr. Stone has deliberately, consistently and maliciously falsified the facts. He does it with the specious pretense of caring only for truth, which adds to his mendacity a peculiarly odious touch of hypocrisy. I do not know whether you are acquainted with Mr. Stone, but if so you are quite welcome to show him this letter.

I haven't the time to go thru the 109 pages of Mr. Stone's chapter. Let me turn to two or three of the most important points. First, as to what he calls "Mr. Roosevelt's Southern Referee System." He treats this "referee" system as an invention of mine. He is himself a native of Mississippi, and he must know perfectly well that his statement is false. When I became President I kept all the Cabinet officers of my predecessor, and consulted my predecessor's intimate friend and right-hand man and adviser, Senator Hanna, continually, because I was anxious to minimize the dislocation between the two administrations. From Senator Hanna, from the Postmaster General, from the Secretary of the Treasury, I speedily heard that such and such men were "referees" to whom questions of suggestion for appointments were referred in various Southern States. In the majority of cases I continued to consult the very men who were thus designated to me, and I made no change whatever in the system save as hereinafter mentioned; but I did change the name, calling the men "endorsers" instead of "referees," . . . . Mr. Stone's statement that I invented this system is simply false. It was in existence under McKinley to my personal knowledge. It was in existence under Harrison to my personal knowledge. Mr. Stone's further statement that it only applies to the

Marlowe and Theodore Thomas — social commentary, and American history. The book to which Roosevelt referred was *Lawless Wealth; the Origin of Some Great American Fortunes* (New York, 1908). In politics, as in journalism and literature, he was active as Socialist candidate for Governor of New York in 1910 and 1912, candidate for the same party for Mayor of the City of New York in 1913 and for United States Senator in 1914. In 1916 he declined the party nomination for President.

Roosevelt and Taft

"Of all men in the country, Taft is best fitted at this time to be President."

The Teddyfication of the White House

South is false. When I became President it applied to two or three of the Rocky Mountain States which did not have Republican congressmen or senators, just exactly as it applied to the Southern States. More than this it was precisely and exactly the system which under Cleveland was applied in the Republican States like Vermont and Maine, which had no democratic representatives or senators. All that it means is that where, under our system of party government, the President has no senators or congressmen of his own party from a given State he has to get outside advice from somewhere, and as there are a great multitude of appointments, chiefly postmasters, which have to be made, he has to devise some system of appointment, and select some men who will take the trouble to make recommendations to him. Where the civil service law is in existence all of this patronage business is done away with — thank Heaven — but where it does not exist, then Cleveland had to get some outsider to recommend to him whom to appoint as postmasters in Vermont and Maine, and McKinley had to get some outsider to make similar recommendations for Mississippi and South Carolina. I followed precisely the custom of Cleveland and McKinley and my various other predecessors in this matter, with the important modification, which Mr. Stone must know and which he would state if he had an ounce of honesty and truthfulness in his nature, that I made a far more resolute effort than any of my Republican predecessors had ever made to try to get the best possible quality of service and the highest possible character of men and women in the offices in the Southern States, and that I appointed to them a much greater proportion of men opposed to my own politics than any of my predecessors have done. As neither Mr. Stone nor anyone else can truthfully deny these statements it seems literally incredible that either he or anyone else should be willing to stoop to such base misrepresentation as that of which he is guilty in this article. He states on page 343 that my system consists in "appointing a southern white democrat to some Federal office and leaving to him all matters of Federal patronage in his State." Here again it is extraordinary to realize the baseness with which a man malevolently bent on perverting the truth will proceed to the extreme limit of falsification. In but one State, that of Mississippi, did I follow a course even remotely resembling that which Mr. Stone says, and there I did it for exactly opposite reasons to those which he gives. In Mississippi and South Carolina I found that there was no real Republican Party in existence, that is no party which cast any appreciable vote at the polls or had any appreciable weight in the community. But in South Carolina I found that the man whom Mr. Hanna called the "referee," who was already in power, was a National Committeeman, a gold democrat, a son of an Episcopalian bishop, had practically become a Republican, and I continued to take suggestions from him. He is now the Commissioner of Internal Revenue and an excellent Commissioner at that, and for the first time, at the last election, some thousands of white men in South Carolina voted the republican national ticket. In Mississippi there was no such man, and I found that the Republican leader was a man not of the best character who had been imported into the State from the north simply to give him an office. I regarded such a condition as scandalous. I found that the then Governor's brother-in-law, a man of excellent standing, had voted for Palmer and Buckner. Booker Washington recommended both him and the Governor to me as men who had endeavored to put a stop to lynching and to a division of the educational fund; and after some painful experiences with hopelessly corrupt and dishonest white and negro officeholders, who had been named thru the Republican machine, I decided I would have to give up all attempt at keeping in line with the politicians in Mississippi and would simply try to give a good service by getting some man I could trust to recommend to me good people for the offices. The Senators and Congressmen were for the most part of the type that one would naturally expect in active politics, where men like Mr. Stone are supposed to represent cultivated truthfulness and dispassionateness; that is, they were so violently partisan, so entirely unscrupulous in their actions, that it was out of the question for me to consult them. I accordingly made the brother of the Democratic Governor, a gold democrat, Marshal;[5] I made Cleveland's former District Attorney, a silver and Bryanite democrat, again District Attorney;[6] I consulted both of them, but especially Wilson, as to the different appointments; I appointed two or three colored men out of the hundreds of appointments I made and about 90 per cent of my appointees were Democrats and remained Democrats, voting, as far as I am informed, for Parker against me and for Bryan against Mr. Taft, and not being required to render a political service of any kind; the remaining 10 per cent were Republicans who acted just as Republicans in similar offices, north or south, usually act. By turning to the pages of the *Outlook* during the last few years you will see quotation after quotation from Mississippi papers, even those which violently condemned me, stating that the character of my appointees was higher than the character of the appointees of any previous President, in Mississippi. (This is true of all the Southern States, taken as a whole.) As a result of what I did I should have had the old Republican faction violently against me had there been the slightest chance of then making a successful war on me in the party, but as there was no chance there was of course no object in making the war. This system, a system of the broadest and most generous action on my part, made wholly without regard to politics, is that which Mr. Stone condemns, and apparently he refers to it as "bearing results as detestable as some features of reconstruction days." When he says this he says what is false. He cannot state to you or to anyone else anything that will bear out his assertion. Mind you, I am not talking of matters of opinion; I speak only of the facts which he has deliberately falsified.

Now for the Indianola incident. On page 309 Mr. Stone begins by the

[5] Edgar S. Wilson.
[6] Robert C. Lee.

gratuitous falsehood "that the Indianola affair would not have occurred but for (my) referee system." As a matter of fact I found the postmistress in the office serving her second term when I became President, and she had served six years steadily when the incident took place. She was appointed by McKinley; her nomination was approved by both the United States Senators from the State of Mississippi and they both approved her renomination. The State Senator from the district was on her bond, and his predecessor, an ex-State Senator and banker, was also on her bond. My referees had nothing whatever to do with the case and this Mr. Stone either did know or ought to have known when he penned the falsehood I have quoted above. Now what actually occurred was as follows. The postmistress was an intelligent, upright colored woman, the wife of a colored man of property, both were much liked by the respectable and law-abiding people of the community. Not a thought was entertained by any of the good people of the neighborhood of taking any action against either. But in a great many places, in all sections of our country, there are lawless and semicriminal characters who under certain circumstances will behave with great violence and injustice if they are certain that the respectable people will follow the example of Mr. Stone in this case and justify or condone their wrongdoing. There was such an element in Indianola. A colored doctor came to practice in the neighborhood of the town. He practiced only among negroes, but he thereby took away some of the practice of one or two of the lowest white doctors of the neighborhood. Instigated by these men or their friends a mob composed of turbulent and violent men and boys met one evening and past a resolution declaring that the colored doctor must leave town. The mayor, the sheriff, and other officials, and the representatives of the better element confined their action to "deploring" what had occurred; and the colored doctor abandoned his practice and fled — all of the Mr. Stones and their like who write these virtuous books keeping entire silence about the incident, as they do about all similar incidents, as they do about the crimes of peonage, and the other hideous abuses to which they shut their eyes. The mob then, having gotten its hand in, past a resolution directing the colored postmistress to resign her office or leave town before a given date. The mayor and sheriff told her they were sorry but they couldn't protect her. The decent citizens said they "deplored" what had happened; that they feared she would suffer unless she left; and she accordingly sent in her resignation. We knew nothing of the facts and couldn't understand what had happened. She was asked why she resigned, but would not answer. We sent a post-office inspector, a southern white man and democrat appointed to the service under Cleveland, who thoroly investigated the case and reported the facts as I have given them above. We asked the mayor and sheriff if they would furnish protection to the woman. They said that they could not, that they "deprecated" the action of the mob but that they could not do anything and that they could not be responsible for her life if she stayed. She left the office just before the appointed day, and she and her husband left town. I then, and this is the point which Mr. Stone omits, took precisely the action that in a similar case Cleveland had taken in Missouri, and as the least that I could do I did not fill her position for the remainder of her term. I then filled it by appointing the one man in the town who had openly and courageously upheld her and done what he could to arouse his fellow citizens to stand by her.

The above are the facts and neither Mr. Stone nor anyone else can controvert them. Mr. Stone is a Mississippian. The case attracted the widest attention and he and those like him, the so-called respectable people, with base cowardice stood by and made no effort to prevent the outrage; and now he strives to justify and conceal his cowardice by shameful mendacity, by misrepresenting and concealing the facts.

Where a man is guilty of such scandalous and shameless mendacity about the facts that I know, I shall not waste my time by trying to find out if he is telling the truth about the facts which I do not know. As I said, you are entirely welcome to show this letter to Mr. Stone himself, or to Mr. Willcox who wrote the introduction to his book, or to Mr. Garrott Brown, if you happen to see him. I do not, however, wish it made public because no possible object is to be attained by again going over the matter in public. Every fact I have stated has been stated again and again and has never been successfully controverted. All those facts were before Mr. Stone when he wrote. His misrepresentations are not due to ignorance but to willful and deliberate design and therefore nothing is to be gained by any controversy with him. *Sincerely yours*

[*Handwritten*] It is Mr. Stone, and those like him, who are more than any other men responsible for the peonage, the lynchings, and all that is worst in the negro situation; they lack the courage to protest against wrong, and they lack the honesty which would make them tell the truth.

4993 · TO JOSEPH HAMPTON MOORE   *Roosevelt Mss.*

Washington, November 13, 1908

My dear Mr. Moore: [1] Regretting my inability to attend the First Annual Convention of the Atlantic Deeper Waterways Association[2] at Baltimore, I extend to the assembled delegates my cordial greetings. The movement commends itself to all who desire to promote commerce between the States in an economical way and on terms of perfect equality between shippers. I wish it all success. *Sincerely yours*

[1] Joseph Hampton Moore, the president of the Atlantic Deeper Waterways Association, was a Philadelphia lawyer, banker, and politician who served as a Republican congressman from 1906 to 1920.
[2] For the significance of this type of organization in the development of Roosevelt's policies see No. 4741, note 1.

Washington, November 14, 1908

My dear Mr. Philbin: I should doubt the wisdom of doing that at this moment. You are probably aware that my published letter of last Monday[1] has caused very bitter comment among kindly, upright and well-meaning, but narrow-minded, people. I am certain that the letter was needed and that it will do good, but I think I would destroy its effect if on its heels I took the action you request which I presume to be unprecedented — though on this latter point I am not absolutely sure. It is a mere question of expediency in my mind. I believe I can do more good to the cause I had in mind when I wrote my letter of Monday last by not taking this action, than by taking it. I do not think you will find that any President has ever sent a message to a Pope on the occasion of an anniversary of his becoming a priest, and I do not think this would be a good time, either from my standpoint or from your standpoint, to make such a precedent. Even in congratulating people of prominence abroad on their birthday, sovereigns or others, I have only done it when they have already congratulated me; I doubt if any other course would be advisable. *Sincerely yours*

Telegram   Washington, November 14, 1908

Am inexpressibly shocked at the attempted assassination of Heney[1] and most earnestly hope he will recover. The infamous character of the would-be assassin, no less than the infamous character of the deed, call attention in a striking way to the true character of the forces against which Heney and you and your associates have been struggling. Every decent American who has the honor and interest of the country at heart should join, not only in putting a stop to the wave of violent crime of which this man's act is but one of the symptoms, but also in stamping out the hideous corruption in which men like this would-be assassin are bred and flourish; and that can only be done by warring, as Heney has warred, relentlessly against every man who is guilty of corrupt practices without any regard to his social standing, to his prominence in the world of politics or in the world of business. I earnestly hope that Heney will recover, and I give utterance to what I know would be Heney's wish when I say that I earnestly hope that, whether he recovers or not, there be no faltering in the work in which Heney has been so gallant and efficient a leader.

[1] No. 4980.

---

[1] In the late afternoon of November 13, Heney, who was then conducting the prosecution of Abe Ruef, was shot in the right side of the head by an ex-convict named Morris Haas. Happily "without a scar" Heney healed.

Washington, November 14, 1908

My dear Abbott: I have received your letter of the 13th instant. You need not be in the least sorry. I was not caused the slightest annoyance by the statement about the Standard Oil control of the paper. On the contrary, the only effect was to give the heartiest enjoyment to the entire Cabinet at the Cabinet meeting — and the Cabinet meetings are rarely melancholy anyhow. I wanted very much to issue a statement to the effect that if the Standard Oil really controlled *The Outlook*, I thought they must have experienced a change of heart when they hired me to write editorials for it! [1] But I thought it was not worth while. Last summer your father told me substantially what you tell me now, namely, that thirty years ago, when he bought *The Outlook* (then called *The Christian Union*) from Henry Ward Beecher and his friends, among the men who aided him was Mr. Stillman, who was an old friend and neighbor. He told me at the time that Mr. Stillman owned less than a tenth of the stock and never made any effort to influence the course of the paper. It was on the tip of my tongue to say that that was self-evident from all I had seen in the paper, but I did not say so because I was afraid your dear father might think that I was speaking a little harshly of Mr. Stillman. Let me say that I have never heard anything to Mr. Stillman's discredit.

As I understand, the story originated in the *Sun*. Mr. Laffan is by profession a liar and a blackguard. I think he is a purchased crook, but of this I have no proof and I should not say it in public. That he is a liar and a blackguard is proved by every issue of his paper, and if I ever get the chance to say it to him, especially if he is surrounded by the members of his staff who are younger and less experienced in mendacity, I shall do so. But I am not able to be angry with him for but a few minutes at a time; and really, on the whole I think the opposition of the *Sun* has been one of my valuable assets in the Presidency. It has been a guaranty of good faith, and I do not think that its purchased mendacity has caused me any real or serious damage. Now and then I have felt like attacking it, but on the whole I guess it is better to follow the old advice — "Don't complain; don't explain; do your work, and let them yell."

This affair did not cause me a moment's feeling of any kind beyond amusement. I am afraid you will have a number of such experiences now that you have entered upon the tempestuous career of association with me! *Always yours*

[1] In the previous week's issue of his magazine Abbott had announced that Roosevelt upon leaving office would join the *Outlook* staff as "a special contributing editor." Immediately several New York papers ran a story claiming that the *Outlook* was controlled by James Stillman. They also ingeniously claimed that since Stillman, the president of the National City Bank, was in some way an ally of Rockefeller, the President was, in effect, planning to work for the Standard Oil Company.

[*Handwritten*] Of course there is no "Standard Oil" money in the Outlook at all; thirty years ago Stillman may not have been in the Standard Oil, and, if he was, at that time the Standard Oil Company, even if in existence in its form (which I doubt) was not known to have done anything in any way wrong.

4997 · TO ALVIN HOWARD SANDERS   *Roosevelt Mss.*

Washington, November 15, 1908

My dear Mr. Sanders: [1] I have your letter of the 13th instant. I have not heard any serious proposal that the tariff bill be, as you say, "rushed thru at the short session of Congress." I entirely agree with you that such course would be improper and I would not consent to it. The new Congress, elected on that among other issues will, under the new administration, deal with the tariff question. If the present Congress at its final session can finish some of the work considered at the first session I shall of course be very much pleased. But I am sure that no one will seriously propose that it shall at its last session take up so totally new and complicated a problem as the revision of the tariff. *Sincerely yours*

P.S. Confidentially, you are entirely at liberty to make this public if you desire. [2]

4998 · TO FRANCIS LYNDE STETSON   *Roosevelt Mss.*

Washington, November 15, 1908

My dear Mr. Stetson: I have your letter of the 13th instant. All right, I have changed the sentence as you suggest and send you a new letter accordingly. [1] Please return the old one. I hardly think it is quite as strong in its changed form however, for I meant to refer not merely to the Bryanites but to the republicans as well, or at least to those many among the republicans whose criticism and abuse far surpast legitimate expression of legitimate party antagonism. I am very glad that you and Mrs. Cleveland liked what I said. *Sincerely yours*

4999 · TO FRANCIS LYNDE STETSON   *Roosevelt Mss.*

Washington, November 16, 1908

My dear Mr. Stetson: I regret that it is not possible for me to be present in person at the meeting held under the auspices of the Cleveland Memorial

[1] Alvin Howard Sanders, publisher of the *Breeders' Gazette,* chairman of the American Reciprocal Tariff League, 1905–1909; appointed by Taft to the United States Tariff Board in 1909.
[2] Loeb had already announced the views set forth in this letter, which Sanders made public on November 19.

[1] For the changed sentence see No. 4999.

Committee. I wish you all success in your efforts. I was a member of the Legislature when Mr. Cleveland became Governor of the State of New York at the beginning of the year 1883, and for the next twenty-five years on several different occasions I was brought into close contact with him. For two years during his second administration I served under him as Civil Service Commissioner. Like all others who were thrown closely with him I was much imprest by his high standard of official conduct and his rugged strength of character. Not only did I become intimately acquainted with the manner in which he upheld and enforced the civil service law, but I also saw at close quarters his successful fight against free silver, and the courage with which he, aided by men like the late Senator Cushman K. Davis of Minnesota, supported the judiciary at the time of the Chicago riot; and, finally, I happened to be in a position in which I knew intimately how he acted and the reasons why he acted in the Venezuelan matter. This knowledge gained at first hand enables me to bear testimony, which I am more than glad to bear, to the late President's earnest purpose to serve the whole country, and the high courage with which he encountered every species of opposition and attack. Owing to a peculiar combination of circumstances he went out of office assailed even more bitterly by his own party than by the opposing party, and shortsighted people thought that the great mass of American citizens had repudiated him and disbelieved in him. Six years later it happened that I was at St. Louis as President when Mr. Cleveland, then a plain private citizen, arose to make an address in the great hall of the Exposition; and no one who was there will ever forget the extraordinary reception given him by the scores of thousands present.[1] It was an extraordinary testimony to the esteem and regard in which he was held, an extraordinary testimony to the fact that the American people had not forgotten him, and, looking back, had recognized in him a man who with straightforward directness had sought to do all in his power to serve their interests.

Moreover, all Americans should pay honor to the memory of Mr. Cleveland because of the simplicity and dignity with which as ex-President he led his life in the beautiful college town wherein he elected to live. He had been true to the honorable tradition which has kept our Presidents from making money while in office. His life was therefore of necessity very simple; but it was the kind of life which it is a good thing to see led by any man who has held a position such as he held.

Again wishing you all good fortune, I am, *Sincerely yours*

[1] Roosevelt at Stetson's request had deleted from his first draft the final clause of this sentence. The original read "and no one there will ever forget the extraordinary reception given by scores of thousands present to the man who, six years before, had left the White House with seemingly hardly a handful of friends and supporters."

Washington, November 16, 1908

My dear Mr. Hitchcock: I send you for any changes you desire to make a copy of the statement dictated by me to Mr. Loeb this morning in your presence and that of Mr. W. Scott Smith, and containing our joint memory of what occurred in connection with the matter recited by the New York *Sun* of Sunday, November 15. Will you return it to me with such comment as you may care to make thereon? I had already written to the Departments of Justice and the Interior to find out if they had any material bearing upon the alleged report, or any document showing any difference of opinion between us as to the pipeline contract of the Prairie Oil and Gas Company, or as to the gas and oil leases. In view, however, of our conversation this morning, and of our recollections being absolutely the same that no such report or communication was ever submitted by you to me, and that in every case I ultimately followed your recommendations in regard to these oil and gas matters in Indian Territory and Oklahoma, I do not think I shall have the Departments hunt further thru their files for what is nonexistent and never has existed. I quite agree with you that there is nothing whatever to be gained by making this matter public at this time, but if Governor Haskell or anyone else starts an investigation by Congress it is as well to have the papers on hand.

It was a great pleasure to see you. *Faithfully yours*

November 15, 1908

Statement drawn up in the presence of ex-Secretary Hitchcock
and W. Scott Smith, formerly his Secretary.

In reference to the article appearing in the New York *Sun* of November 15, 1908. It opens with the allegation that an important report written by former Secretary Hitchcock was submitted by him to the President in 1904 setting forth his reasons for denying the application of the Prairie Oil and Gas Company for a pipeline permit; that the franchise was granted, nevertheless, but that this course was directed by President Roosevelt, who overruled the action of his Secretary of the Interior against Secretary Hitchcock's uncompromising resistance. The statement is false in every particular. No such report or communication was ever made to the President by Mr. Hitchcock. The franchise was not authorized by President Roosevelt against Mr. Hitchcock's protest, nor did he overrule the action of the Secretary of the Interior. This and similar franchises were not granted until Congress by law authorized them to be granted. The leases under which they were granted were already in existence, having originally been granted by order of former Secretary Hoke Smith. The latter had authorized these leases for a million and a half acres. Secretary Hitchcock deemed the amount of acreage improper and recommended that it be cut down to include between six thousand and eight thousand acres; suggesting the amount so as to protect the rights of the sublessees who had actually invested their money, made improvements, and paid royalties. Congress did this. The President signed the bill, on the advice of the Secretary, and granted the lease in question, embodying a decreased acreage, absolutely as he granted all other leases, the lease being approved and forwarded by Secretary Hitchcock and signed by the President.

The statement continues that this "adverse report" is in the Department of Justice and that nothing but a resolution of Congress will cause it to be made public because the President "dare not let its contents be known." As there is no such adverse report, and never has been, it is naturally neither in the Department of Justice nor anywhere else, and for the same reason, as its contents are imaginary they cannot be made known. No "politicians of national prominence" or otherwise ever, as the *Sun* alleges, spoke one word to the President about this Prairie Oil and Gas franchise; and neither did anyone else. The President knew nothing whatever about the matter save as Secretary Hitchcock told him about it and as it may have been alluded to in the correspondence between them. The President merely followed Secretary Hitchcock's advice at every stage of the matter.

As a matter of fact the President does not now recall, and Mr. Hitchcock tells him that he (Mr. Hitchcock) does not recall, one point in connection with any of these oil and gas franchises in the Indian Territory in which the President did not finally adopt the recommendation or approve the decision of Secretary Hitchcock. This was so in every case.

As regards "the letter written by Governor Higgins in the interest of Barnsdall," the statements in the *Sun* article are also direct falsehoods. The regulations proposed by Secretary Hitchcock were considered too drastic by the oil people. Governor Higgins and a number of others protested, and Mr. Barnsdall was brought to the President by ex-Senator Jones, and Governor Higgins and ex-Senator Jones wrote to the President a number of letters about the matter. The *Sun* article states that the President "ordered" Secretary Hitchcock to grant the permit and that the Secretary "yielded reluctantly." The President made no such request; the Secretary did not yield; on the contrary after the fullest investigation the President came to the conclusion that the Secretary's position was right, and the position of the men who had applied to the President wrong; and Secretary Hitchcock's successor, Secretary Garfield, after careful investigation also came to the conclusion that Secretary Hitchcock's position was right and his recommendations are those that were actually followed, and are now being followed in the regulations of the Department.

The statement that the Standard Oil contribution in 1904 was paid just after the President overruled Secretary Hitchcock and granted the Standard a pipeline is a lie. The President had not overruled Secretary Hitchcock in granting the Standard a pipeline. In every case he followed the Secretary's recommendation; and when it was reported to him that the Standard Oil had contributed to the campaign he wrote at once to Chairman Cortelyou that no such contribution should be received, and received from Mr. Cortelyou the statement that no Standard Oil money had been or would be received.

The *Sun* statement goes on to say that the regulations made by Secretary Hitchcock in December 1906 following the "favors" shown to the Standard Oil Company in 1904, were very drastic. As already pointed out above no favors were granted by the President to the Standard Oil Company in 1904 or any other year, and any statement to this effect is a willful and deliberate falsehood. The President simply followed the recommendations of the Secretary and, as a matter of fact, neither knew nor cared which of the different leases approved on the recommendation of the Secretary were Standard Oil and which were in the interest of independent operators. The statement that any promise was made to a western Senator or anyone else to remove Secretary Hitchcock is a lie, pure and simple.

5001 · TO WILLIAM HOWARD TAFT   *Roosevelt Mss.*

Washington, November 16, 1908

My dear Mr. Taft: Two committees, one from the National Service Reform Association and the other from the Fourth-class Postmasters' Association, will call upon you about something that I have very much at heart. I wish to classify the fourth-class postmasters, or rather, to make a beginning in classifying them. As you know, we have already broken ground in the direction of taking them out of politics by decreeing that their tenure shall be permanent unless good cause can be shown for the removal. There was great protest against this at first by Congressmen, politicians, and so forth, and now there is entire acquiescence in it. If we can take the appointments out of politics one of the greatest benefits will be conferred upon the politicians themselves. They do not know it and they will yell a little bit at first, but they will get over it. If Bryan had come in I would not have taken this move, because I am not very strong on the deathbed-repentance theory. But as it is, I very much want to do it; but before taking final action I would like to have these gentlemen put the matter before you. My intention is to classify certain States and districts first,[1] so that we will get the benefit of the actual working of the system in them before making it universal. There will be some objection in Congress, altho I do not think it will be as extensive

[1] Roosevelt on December 1 signed an executive order for the classification by competition of all fourth-class postmasters in fourteen states. These states, all in the area between the Atlantic Ocean and the Mississippi, contained more than half the total population of the United States and nearly one third of the fourth-class offices. The order was issued before Congress assembled, a "bold step" showing "the courage and conviction of the President" in "depriving the legislators of a large share of their patronage." — *Good Government*, 25:98 (December 1908).

as people believe. However, it is far better that I should bear the brunt of it, because I do not have to live very long with those people and you do! My purpose is to get the National Civil Service Reform Association, this Postmasters' Association, the Civil Service Commission, and the Post-Office Department, to join in getting out the regulations and the like, and I will promulgate the classification for the districts chosen sometime in December. Will you go over the matter with the joint committee, and greatly oblige *Very sincerely yours*

5002 · TO RICHARD WATSON GILDER   *Roosevelt Mss.*

Washington, November 16, 1908

My dear Gilder: I have received the slip from the *Evening Post* containing Mr. Garrott Brown's article. It is a little difficult to write of Mr. Brown's article with the courtesy that one desires to show toward an antagonist, because the article contains so many statements which are not matters of argument or conviction, but are simply plain misstatements of fact. If Mr. Brown were the character of man that Mr. Stone[1] apparently is — I enclose you a copy of a letter I have just written anent Mr. Stone — the glaring misstatements he makes would cause one to suspect his good faith. In view of his character, his mistakes must be ascribed to ignorance, and yet I am obliged to say that the ignorance is so great that it is not creditable for him to have displayed it in print. A man of repute and standing ought not to make statements about politics, and especially about public men of whom he disapproves, without knowing something of the facts that he states.

Mr. Brown opens by saying that Mr. Taft was nominated as he was because it was known "that he was the choice of President Roosevelt"; that my being for his nomination was of consequence chiefly because I had the control over the officeholders, and that any Republican President could within reasonable limits name his successor, provided of course the country stayed Republican. Now, as a matter of opinion, I think that no honest and competent man who had any right to express a judgment would fail to see that practically the entire strength that I contributed to Mr. Taft was strength arising from the fact that the great bulk of my party, (and the great bulk of the voters of the country), were in hearty accord with me and were very anxious, if I were not to be nominated, to see that my successor was a man who could be trusted implicitly to carry out the policies for which I stood, and to carry on the administration as I have been, and am, carrying it on. In the future a Republican President will be able to influence his successor's nomination precisely, and only, as I have done; that is, if he retains to the end of his term the leadership and confidence of his party, and the party's active and enthusiastic belief that the next President should be the same type of man that he, the existing President, is. There was

[1] See No. 4992.

loud opposition to my nomination among certain big politicians and certain big financiers in 1904; but they were not able to control a single delegate against me. In 1908 there was the same loud opposition from the same quarter, but my own strength was relatively much greater. Up to the time that the final roll call at Chicago began I would only have had to announce that I would abide by the choice of the convention if it chose to nominate me, and no human power could have stopped the nomination.

Now the above is a matter of opinion. What follows deals with matters of fact. Mr. Brown says that the patronage was all important in the South but not in the North. He says that "notwithstanding President Roosevelt's open support of Secretary Taft, his rivals did in fact make some headway in the North," and that had the contest been left to the North, Secretary Taft would not have won on the first ballot and might not have won at all. These statements are not in accordance with the facts, and Mr. Brown should not have made them without taking the trouble to at least look at the vote in the convention. There were in the North six States with favorite son candidates — Ohio, New York, Pennsylvania, Indiana, New York and Wisconsin. Each of these States supported its own candidate, but, with the exception of Indiana, lost some votes to other candidates. In each State the officeholders, the men holding my commissions, were rather more loyal than the rest of the population to the favorite sons, except in the State of Ohio, where a larger proportion were against Taft. Mr. Brown says that he would not have won his overwhelming lead over Governor Hughes, for instance, solely on his merits; that it was chiefly due to the officeholders. Mr. Brown by this time either does know or ought to know that Mr. Hughes was renominated for Governor only by an effort on my part far greater in proportion than the effort I made to nominate Mr. Taft, and that but for this earnest effort on my part he would not have had a fifth of the delegates, certainly not a fourth, in the Gubernatorial convention. As a matter of fact at the time of the Presidential nomination I had to do all I could with the Federal officeholders to keep them in line for Mr. Hughes in New York, it being in my judgment poor policy that Mr. Hughes' own State should not be for him; and if I had held my hands off the delegation would have been against Mr. Hughes by a large majority. Even as it was, a considerable number voted for Taft, and several for Cannon; the votes of the latter, of course, even Mr. Brown cannot believe were due to any dictation on my part.

Disregarding these favorite son States, there remained three hundred and ninety-two votes in the northern, Central and Western States, of which thirteen were against Mr. Taft and two hundred and sixty-five votes in the Southern States of which eighteen were against Mr. Taft. Now if Mr. Brown had taken the trouble to look at these votes, he would have seen that if not a Southern State had voted, Mr. Taft would have had a clear majority on the first ballot; and he would have seen, moreover, that in the Southern States, where he says the officeholders have power, the opponents of Mr.

Taft rallied proportionately twice as many votes as in the Northern States, where they have no power. The simple fact is, which Mr. Brown either did know or ought to have known, that the officeholders followed the drift of their several communities, save only that in the favorite son States they more or less unwillingly voted for the favorite son candidates. The only way in which I dictated to the officeholders was to dictate to them that they should not support me for a renomination. Literally this is the only piece of dictation, as far as the officeholders are concerned. As this was the most widely known and important fact connected with the campaign for the nomination, it would seem to me that it would have shown more frankness for Mr. Brown to have mentioned it.

Mr. Brown goes on to say that the Republican party could, if it would, strengthen itself in the South so as to contest with the Democrats the control of the State Governments, but that the northern managers of the Republican party have for years acted so as to prevent this, and that both these statements are "almost demonstrably true."

Mr. Brown begins by a statement of the Hayes-Tilden controversy, which I need not discuss; nor need I discuss what he further says up to where he speaks of my conduct; nor am I now expressing any opinion on the question of southern representation in the national convention. He says that McKinley got a hold upon the southern people such as no other President ever had. He says I completely lost this hold. This is not an important point. I shall simply mention that the figures of the elections do not in the least bear it out. In McKinley's second election the South voted far more strongly against him than when he was first a candidate, and but four Republican Congressmen were returned from the ex-Confederate States. In my election the vote against me in the South was almost the same as the vote against McKinley in his second election; the Republicans again carried four Congressmen, and in the ex-Confederate States I cut down the majorities in three cases and raised them, in some cases very slightly, in eight States, and in addition, gained the great State of Missouri, which is a Western rather than a Southern State. In the election which has just taken place, which indicates roughly the view in the South as to my second term, we made further gains, in both Congressmen and the popular voting, the fight being made straight out for Taft as representing my policies.

Mr. Brown speaks very kindly of my intentions. I shall not say anything as to his statement that I entertained two or three negroes at the White House, excepting to point out that there was only one, Booker Washington, as I should have supposed he would have known. But when he speaks of the Indianola post office case, I ask you to read over the enclosed letter about Mr. Stone, in which I discuss the incident. Not merely is it untrue that I acted either "precipitately or unjustly," but Mr. Brown's conduct in failing to condemn the iniquity of the deed instead of the very mild punishment for it, would itself deserve the very deepest condemnation if it were not that

Mr. Brown must be entirely ignorant of the facts. Mr. Stone is a Mississippian, and cannot be ignorant of them. Mr. Brown, I suppose, is ignorant of them. No man acquainted with the facts who fails heartily to condemn the action of those who were punished, and heartily to uphold the administration for its conduct, has any right to be considered an honorable and law-upholding citizen. There is no room for question on this point. There is plenty of room for question as to the wisdom of my having had Booker Washington to dinner, and however firmly convinced I may be that I was morally right, I will cheerfully admit that the matter is one for entirely legitimate difference of opinion. But in the Indianola case the issue is one of simple right and wrong in its plainest and simplest form. Any man who at the time knew the facts and failed to lift up his voice in support of what the administration did, was at best guilty of moral cowardice. Any man knowing the facts who now attempts to show that the administration acted otherwise than properly, grossly perverts the truth.

Mr. Brown goes on to say that the capital error of my policy lay in my failure to try to build up a reasonably strong opposition, that is, a reasonably strong Republican party, in the Southern States; and that I failed to make any real fight in any Southern State. This simply is not true. Mr. Brown complains that the Republican managers haven't spent time and money in contesting districts and States that were hopeless. Either Mr. Brown is absolutely ignorant of the rudiments of politics or he knows that the same thing is true of the Democratic managers. The Democratic National Committee when the November election comes around pays no more attention to Vermont, Michigan, or Maine, than the Republican managers do to Florida, Georgia or Alabama. The same is true, of course, of the Congressional districts. The Democrats don't try seriously to contest hopelessly Republican districts in New York or Massachusetts. The Republicans don't try seriously to contest hopelessly Democratic districts in Louisiana or Mississippi. But if Mr. Brown had taken the trouble to study the facts he would have known that the Republicans pay exactly as much attention to southern districts which there is a chance of carrying as to northern districts. The western North Carolina districts are helped much more than the Pennsylvania districts are helped, for example. So, when in the course of the last few years a Republican party gradually grew up in western Virginia, and we were able to carry one district and sometimes two, the result was that the Republican Congressional Committee lookt after these two districts exactly as they lookt after any two in Illinois or Wisconsin. Mr. Brown's complaint is in short that the Republican party, following precisely the course of the Democratic party, strives for victory, and therefore devotes its efforts to trying to carry the districts which there is a possibility of carrying, instead of deliberately wasting its efforts in hopeless districts. The complaint is a little absurd anyhow, but it is disingenuous in view of the fact that the conduct of the two parties is precisely alike; and yet Mr. Brown speaks as if only the Republicans refused to contest States and districts which there was not the slightest chance of carrying.

Mr. Brown goes on to say that there is "only too good reason to believe" that I have gone further than any of my predecessors in the abandonment of my party in the Southern States, because, practically ignoring the State committees, I have chosen a set of referees to pass on all appointments to office. Really, here it is very difficult for me to attribute Mr. Brown's statement merely to genuine ignorance and not to malevolence. Why, for years and years, as you Mr. Gilder, must be well aware, one of the loudest complaints of southerners and of independent and Democratic northerners, has been that the Federal appointees in the South were of a very low type, this being caused largely by the fact that we paid improper heed to the local Republican recommendations which it was alleged in no way represented the people of the States. I have felt that there was a great deal in this attack, and when I took office I made up my mind that I should strive to appoint as high a grade of men to office in the South as in the North, and that tho I would appoint but a limited number of colored men, yet that they should represent the very best type, the Booker Washington type, instead of the low colored politician type; and I therefore made up my mind that when I could not get a really good man who was a Republican I would unhesitatingly take a Democrat. It seems to me literally incredible that a man of honesty and intelligence, not blinded by the bitterest partisanship, can fail heartily to applaud such a course. This is the course I have carried out to the letter, with the result that my appointees in the South, taken as a whole, stand if anything even higher than the corresponding appointees in the North, because I have been able to act without having to pay anything like the same heed to political considerations as in dealing with States having Republican Senators; and moreover, my appointees in the South are on the whole of a higher grade than those of any previous President, Republican or Democratic, since the Civil War — and I make no exceptions. Absolutely the only reason why I have ever disregarded any local party organization has been because I have become convinced that that organization was not recommending to me thoroly good men. And yet Mr. Brown, this southerner, this nominal advocate of pure politics, condemns me because I have disregarded the political organizations in the South whenever, and only whenever, I believed that these political organizations in the recommendations that they made did not adequately represent the best interests of their State. It is difficult for me not to characterize as it deserves such an attitude on the part of Mr. Brown.

He goes on to say that I have appointed a set of "referees" to pass on all appointments to office. He adds that these men probably are in most cases worthier advisers than the party officials. Doesn't he see that this statement is itself a justification of my course? As a matter of fact, I have used these outside referees, as he calls them, where they have been created, only until I could make the local political organization understand that if it did not recommend good men for appointment to office it would not receive any offices. Mr. Brown is so ignorant of the facts of the political history concerning which he writes that he does not know that long before the contest for the Presidential nomination began, I had ceased using these referees (just as he says I ought to have ceased using them) in every Southern State save one, Mississippi. In Mississippi I was still largely guided by the advice of a Gold Democrat, the brother-in-law of the man who was Governor of the State when I became President. Everywhere else I was consulting the regular party authorities, altho in one or two instances I was still using certain Democrats of high character to whom I could apply if for any reason I doubted whether the man recommended to me was all that he should have been. In Louisiana, for instance, the Democrat whom I thus consulted was a man you know well — John McIlhenny, the Civil Service Commissioner — and your knowledge of him will show the wanton absurdity of Mr. Brown's accusation. In Louisiana I have a very exceptional set of public officials, so far as my own appointees are concerned, and the party leaders whom I recognize are of a very high type. But the national convention, as Mr. Brown either does know or ought to know, actually went back on me on the ground that I had adhered too much to the silk-stocking or "lily white" type, and split the representation between the party leaders I had recognized and their opponents, who represented what might be called the reconstruction era regime.

Mr. Brown then continues by stating that Mr. Chandler says that at a meeting of Republican leaders, the entire situation being before them, it was deliberately decided to keep the party as it was, and implies very plainly that I was present at the conference. This is a scandalous falsehood, and it is inexcusable of Mr. Brown to have given currency to such a falsehood. No such conference ever took place. I never heard that it was alleged to have taken place until I saw Mr. Brown's article. No such decision was ever reached by any body of Republican leaders so far as I am informed. A more outrageously untruthful accusation never was made. Mr. Brown goes on to say that I have purposely "devitalized my party in eleven States," and hints that it was done to give me advantage in the nominating conventions. Again, this is an outrageous falsehood — I am so indignant that I cannot use any word less strong. So far from purposely devitalizing the party, I have tried every conceivable means in different States in order to build it up. Where, as in Virginia, North Carolina, and Tennessee, I found a real Republican party, I have tried to strengthen it in every way. In Virginia, for instance, I have tried in the «most» part to strengthen it by the appointment of men like Henry Clay McDowell, at the suggestion of John Fox, whom you know; by the appointment of Judge Lewis[2] in Richmond, at the suggestion of Tom Page, whom you also know; by the appointment of Jeb Stuart,[3] the son of old Jeb Stuart,

[2] Lunsford Lomax Lewis, United States District Attorney in Richmond, Virginia.
[3] James Ewell Brown Stuart, collector of customs at Newport News, Virginia.

in eastern Virginia, hoping thus to show that I was trying to recognize and hold out my hand to the best old Confederate stock. For district attorney in western Virginia I put in Admiral Evans' nephew.[4] For postmaster at Richmond I put in one of the Cabells.[5] In short, I appointed the very best men I could find (almost all of them Republicans), and I have had the hearty support of some of the very best men in the State. If Mr. Garrott Brown would write to a man like Wyndham Meredith, of Richmond, or Joseph Wilmer, a brother of Willie Wilmer, of New York, whom you doubtless know, a son of Bishop Wilmer, he could have found out all these facts; and it was his business to try to find them out before he made such a scandalous accusation. I treated North Carolina, Tennessee and Virginia just exactly as I treated Vermont, Maine and Massachusetts. I tried to strengthen the organization by appointing the very best Republicans I could find, and also by recognizing certain Gold Democrats like Luke Wright and others. I did the same thing in Texas and Louisiana, where I found thoroly respectable white Republican parties. I did the same thing in Arkansas, getting, curiously enough, a recommendation from Octave Thanet (Miss French) as to the Republican leader whom I could thoroly trust. In Mississippi and South Carolina, where the Republican party was almost nonexistent, most of my appointments were of Democrats, and I tried in every way I could to strengthen the respectable Democrats who stood against Tillmanism in the one State and Vardamanism in the other. The present Governor of Mississippi Mr. Noel,[6] and ex-Governor Heyward [7] of South Carolina, have thanked me in the warmest way for what by this means I have done in each State. I did it knowing well that in each State I would probably have the Republican delegates against me if a chance to beat me or to beat my candidate in the national convention arose. But I did not anticipate the possibility of there being brought against me the accusation, at once so base and so foolish, that I had taken this course with the desire of getting control over delegates. If Mr. Brown knows anything he must know that if I had wanted to get control over the delegates of the two States, I would have given the offices to the old-style party leaders, and that by no possibility could my giving the offices to Democrats help me in getting delegates.

Mr. Brown then repeats the statement that I have dictated thru the office-holders what should be done in the matter of nominees in the South. The statement is not true. The officeholders followed in the South just the course that they did in the North, that is, they followed the general Republican drift. The leader in Texas, for instance, is Colonel Cecil Lyon; the leaders in

[4] Thomas L. Moore.
[5] Royal Eubank Cabell in 1909 became United States Commissioner of Internal Revenue.
[6] Edmund Favor Noel, Spanish War veteran; Democratic Governor of Mississippi, 1908-1912; first chairman of the first Conference of Governors, May 1908.
[7] Duncan Clinch Heyward, rice planter; banker; Democratic Governor of South Carolina, 1903-1907.

Louisiana, Messrs. Wight and Williams; the leader in Florida, Mr. Coombs. None of these four men are officeholders; they are all men of considerable fortune; they are all my personal friends; they were all wild to have me renominated — the coercion I had to exercise upon them was to get them to refrain from insisting on delegations to nominate me. They undoubtedly supported Taft chiefly because it was my wish, but they did it for precisely the same reason that made men like Guy Murchie and Louis Frothingham[8] in Massachusetts follow me in supporting Taft; and we carried Texas, Louisiana and Florida, just exactly as we carried Massachusetts. This was true in Tennessee, North Carolina & Virginia, also. In certain of the other Southern States the leaders were officeholders, just as is true in certain Northern States or in certain northern districts; but they went my way precisely as the non-officeholders whom I have mentioned went my way, and for the same reason.

Then Mr. Garrott Brown goes on to say that the South is eliminated from its share in the Government at Washington. It is eliminated solely because it is preposterous to expect political appointments to go in great mass to political opponents, and to States completely under the control of political opponents. At this moment in my Cabinet there sits an ex-Confederate from Tennessee at the head of the War Department, a position to which Mr. Cleveland would never have ventured to make such an appointment. The Commissioner of Internal Revenue is a South Carolinian, the head of the party organization there. Relatively to their numbers, southern Republicans have received more from me than northern Republicans.

With the rest of Mr. Garrott Brown's article I need hardly deal. I quite agree with the desirability of what he proposes. I was extremely glad that Mr. Taft was able to speak in the South, and have been almost equally glad to learn alike from Republicans and from Taft Democrats in the South, that the path had been made ready for Mr. Taft to speak by the course I have followed by my public acts, by my visits to the South, and the like.

Mr. Brown concludes his article by the rather grotesque statement that if Mr. Taft "could enfranchise the South he would destroy forever a system by which he has profited, and thereby ensure that no other Republican shall ever again be named for the Presidency as he himself has been." This is going back to his original statement, and is simply an untruth which the slightest attempt to find out the facts on his part would have shown him was an untruth. Let me repeat, that if not a Southern State had sent a delegate to the Republican convention, Mr. Taft would have been nominated on the first ballot, and that, whether the South is or is not changed as Mr. Brown hopes, other Republicans will always again be nominated for the Presidency just exactly as Mr. Taft has been when the conditions are the same; that is, when the Republican President in office is enthusiastically supported by the enormous majority of his party, who are firmly bent upon having his policies

[8] Louis Adams Frothingham, Spanish War veteran; Republican candidate for mayor of Boston, 1905; Lieutenant Governor of Massachusetts, 1908.

1363

continued, and when there is another man whom that President, and whom the bulk of the voters, recognize as being pre-eminently a man already identified with those policies and certain to continue to carry them out. *Sincerely yours*

P.S. I suppose that a man like Mr. Brown, who must be a good man with good intentions, is misled by reading papers like the *Evening Post* and *Sun*. Messrs. Laffan, Ogden and Villard, of those two papers, make their money by the practice of mendacity. Whether, as I suspect is the case with Mr. Laffan, their mendacity is purchased and they write what they know to be lies for hire, or whether they lie on their own account, to gratify their malevolence or to increase their circulation, does not in the least degree alter the profound immorality of their action. The three men I have named, taken with other editors like Pulitzer and Bennett, and the editors of papers like the Philadelphia *Record*, the Boston *Herald*, and the Indianapolis *News* represent a lower type than the worst and most corrupt politicians, or than the worst and most corrupt financiers, and on the whole do more evil.

The curious thing about this utterly untruthful attack of Mr. Brown is that it comes as the sequel to seven and a half years during which I have done exactly what all good people said ought to be done at the time I took office, and have lived up absolutely to the ideal I established for myself. When Vice-President, I used to talk over this matter with our beloved friend, John R. Proctor, the Civil Service Commissioner, a Kentucky Democrat and ex-Confederate; and I also talked of it with Booker Washington. With both of them I agreed that the thing to be done by any man who ever became President was, not to appoint many colored men in the South, but to appoint those few from the very best colored men there were to be found, and to accept, the recommendations, not of hack politicians, but of the best men of the colored race, like Booker Washington, in making the appointments. Mr. Proctor and the other southerners with whom I then consulted — men like General Basil Duke, for instance — kept saying that if only this could be done, no objection whatever would be made by the southern people, but on the contrary they would be glad to have a few reputable colored men of the best type put in office because that would place a premium upon cultivation, thrift, morality and good conduct in the colored race. They also agreed earnestly that in the appointment of whites the thing to do was to follow the Republican organizations so long as they recommended thoroly good men, but to get into touch with the best men of the community, who would be apt to be Democrats, and use them as advisers, and wherever I could not get a Republican or felt that the local Republican machine ought not to be trusted, that then I should appoint a thoroly good Democrat. Good Proctor, and Basil Duke, and the other men I consulted — including for instance General Buckner, of Kentucky, & ex-Governor Thompson, of South Carolina — all said that what they proposed represented probably an impossible idea, but that if it could be adopted all good southerners would feel the greatest relief, and even tho politically they might continue to differ from a Republican President who acted in such a way, they would heartily uphold him on the basis of their common citizenship. Well, I have acted in precisely and exactly this way. I have not deviated by a hair's breadth from the ideal thus set up by these ex-Confederates, these high-minded gentlemen, all of them southern Democrats; and the result of it is that a southerner of cultivation like Mr. Brown is willing to write such a letter as this to the *Evening Post!*

5003 · TO JOHN GRAHAM BROOKS   *Roosevelt Mss.*

Washington, November 16, 1908

My dear Brooks: It is a real pleasure to hear from you. I shall think over the matter; but it seems to me I can reach the end by emphasizing in my present article what is good in socialism. You say that Wells, for instance, does not believe in free love in any sense. On the contrary, at the end of that novel of his in which the world is changed by the comet (I have forgotten the title) he distinctly advocates what is in effect free love, altho he does not venture to do it frankly — and I should think better of him if he did it frankly.[1] I refer to where he describes how the woman the hero loved, who was married to another man, came back to live temporarily with the hero. Either this is free love or it is platonic mawkishness of a rather more unhealthy and revolting type.

It was a great pleasure to see you the other day. *Sincerely yours*

5004 · TO LUKE EDWARD WRIGHT   *Roosevelt Mss.*

Washington, November 18, 1908

To the Secretary of War: Wherever there is a vacancy for bandmaster in a white regiment, transfer a white bandmaster from a colored regiment to it and fill the place by the assignment of a colored man. This is to carry out the spirit of the order I have already issued. As soon as it can be done without injustice, I wish all the colored regiments supplied with colored bandmasters.

[1] *In the Days of the Comet* (1906), after the swish of a comet's tail had cooled and cleansed the human heart, mankind became "sane, understanding and infinitely tolerant." Jealousy, war, and poverty vanished from the earth. Not so sex. The *Spectator* and *The Times Literary Supplement* agreed that Wells's novel made "Free Love the dominant principle for the regulation of sexual ties" in the regenerated state. Wells, annoyed by this observation, later insisted that "personal sexual freedom and collective responsibility for the family" did not mean indiscriminate love, "polyandry or polygamy or anything of the sort."

Washington, November 19, 1908

Dear Gilder: I have your note of the 18th. Of course you are welcome to show the letter and enclosure to Brown. I have sincerely admired Brown and I was genuinely shocked when I saw what he had written.

One word of something entirely irrelevant. I was reading Trevelyan's *Macaulay* again last evening, and on page 298 of the new edition I came on his caustic comment on the people who think they can have a literature written to order. Don't you think that this applies to the excellent people who would try to get somebody to write a national anthem to order? Julia Ward Howe's "Battle Hymn of the Republic" is an inspiration of genius. No other nation has so fine a poem for its national anthem, and there is a first-class tune for it — a great popular tune. There really is not a word of sectionalism in the poem. We practically have "Dixie" as a national tune everywhere. There isn't the slightest reason why we should not have Julia Ward Howe's hymn as our national anthem. It is mere waste of time to get people of set purpose to write such an anthem. *Faithfully yours*

[*Handwritten*] My dear fellow, the volume of poems[1] has just come, as I was signing this. I am so touched and pleased at your sending it to me. I shall enjoy it all; the "Portrait of Senelus" is fine — fine; I have always liked The White Czar's People

Private   Washington, November 19, 1908

My dear Harrison: All right. Perhaps you are wise. So I ask you not to show the letter about Delavan Smith even to Smith himself, and keep it purely as a confidential communication for yourself.[1]

Now, my dear Colonel, I did not know that you ever wanted any position from me. I wish you had mentioned it sooner. Of course much would have depended upon what the position was. I have appreciated always your courtesy and kindness to me. *Faithfully yours*

Washington, November 19, 1908

My dear Mr. Rossiter: I have received those very interesting tables, and thank you for sending them to me. Upon my word, they are rather melancholy! By the middle of this century it looks as if all the civilized races would have stopt increasing. Of course, by that time, or before that time, it is perfectly possible that we may have gotten aroused to the moral side of the matter

[1] *The Poems of Richard Watson Gilder* (Boston, 1908).

[1] See Numbers 4973, 4983.

(when I say "we" I mean the civilized peoples) and the tendency may be changed; but it certainly is a very curious and lamentable tendency now. *Sincerely yours*

5008 · TO ALBERT JEREMIAH BEVERIDGE   *Roosevelt Mss.*

Washington, November 19, 1908

My dear Senator: I have your letter of the 16th instant.[1] It seems to me that it is mere folly to kick longer against the pricks. At the time of our conversation I urged you to let both States in at that time, and I think it would have been very much better to have done so; but I acquiesced of course in your decision, and stated to Senator Flint that tho I should personally prefer to have the States admitted at once, yet if you declined to do so I thought it was from every standpoint disadvantageous to undertake the fight and that the other leaders had better fall in with your views — which, as far as I am aware, Senator Flint did. But I do feel very strongly that no good whatever comes of any further delay. You will have to take them both in. You cannot take them both in together, and by keeping them out for a short time (which is all you can do) you merely irritate the people there against the Republican party. *Faithfully yours*

5009 · TO JOHN S. LEECH   *Roosevelt Mss.*

Washington, November 20, 1908

My dear Mr. Leech: I regret greatly to say that I feel that I must ask for your resignation. You have a very difficult task, a task needing exceptional abilities and exceptional qualities. I regard it as less your fault than your misfortune that you have not been able to rise to the needs of the task. The friction and complaint have been such that I feel it necessary to have a change. I believe there are other positions in the Government service which you could fill with advantage to the service. I believe that you would do well in control of a smaller office; but I do not believe that you are able to manage this particular office — one of peculiar difficulty and needing a peculiar combination of traits in the man who is to do the work successfully.[1] If the opportunity

[1] Beveridge was still advocating joint statehood for Arizona and New Mexico. A bill enabling each territory to become a state passed the House but failed to reach the Senate floor before the end of the session. It was, however, quickly passed at the following session. Both states were admitted in 1912.

[1] The Government Printing Office, like so many government offices and departments during the first decade of the twentieth century, was undergoing a drastic reorganization. Operating under archaic and often conflicting regulations, staffed to meet the printing needs of the Grant Administration, and under constant pressure of new work from both Congress and the executive departments, the Printing Office was running with a maximum of waste and expense. Congress, alarmed at the exceedingly rapid rise in government printing expenditures, in 1905 appointed an investigating committee and on the recommendations of this committee in 1907 passed most of the

comes I shall be glad to place you in some office commensurate with your abilities. *Sincerely yours*

Roosevelt Mss.

Washington, November 20, 1908

My dear Archbishop: I greatly appreciate your letter of the 17th instant. I wish I could see you so that we might congratulate each other on our victory, for most emphatically you are one of those who can feel an especial pride in it. At least give me the chance to see you at the White House if you return before the 4th of March.

I am particularly pleased that you liked that letter.[1] I am all the more convinced that it was wise to write it because of the attacks made upon me for having written it.

With all good wishes, my dear Archbishop, believe me, *Sincerely yours*

Roosevelt Mss.

Washington, November 20, 1908

My dear Mr. Brooks: [1] It was a pleasure to hear from you and I was greatly amused with parts of your letter. I enclose you a copy of a letter I sent Lodge a week before the election by which you will see that I expected just about the overwhelming victory that we won. I much enjoyed your account of the grave disapproval of the strict constitutionalists in England about my part in the contest. The entire Wall Street crowd felt the same way here. As a matter of fact by the end of September I saw clearly that it was an absolute necessity for me to go into the campaign just as hard as I knew how. We should have carried New York, New Jersey, New England and the like anyhow, but west of the Alleghenies, where the decisive battle was fought, it was absolutely essential that the voters should understand that Taft stood for the policies that I stand for and that his victory meant the continuance of those policies.

Personally I never am able so much as to consider a question of following a formal precedent in such a matter, and above all of being hypocritical about

---

necessary remedial legislation. The complex and trying work of putting this legislation into practice proved too much for Leech as it had for his two predecessors. His successor, Samuel B. Donnelly, however, was equal to the task and after a few false steps (see No. 5073) placed the Government Printing Office on a comparatively efficient administrative and financial basis.

---

[1] No. 4980.

---

[1] Sydney Brooks, editor of the *Saturday Review* and *Sperling's Journal.* Educated in England, he lived from 1896 to 1900 in the United States. Thereafter he frequently visited this country and contributed regularly to both American and British journals.

it. As President my position is more like that of the British Prime Minister than that of the President of the French Republic. My business is to govern. I am primarily the head of the nation, but I am the head of my party too, and I only belong to that party because with all my heart and strength I believe it best able to serve the nation. I wisht to see Taft elected as my successor so that my policies could be continued. I fought hard and openly for him. I did not use an office, or any underhand influence of any kind, in his behalf. I was able to be of help because the people at large stood behind me.

I am also much amused at what you tell me over the puzzled feeling about my use of the word "frazzle." [2] That bewilderment, much to my amusement, also existed in the northern states here. I am half southern, and "frazzle" has been a word I have always known. It is, as you say, a fine old English word which has persevered in the South, where it is unjustly lookt upon as a provincialism.

I appreciate what you say in compliment of the sturdy good sense of the American electorate in standing consistently for the last twelve years for one policy. Indeed, this is the eighth consecutive Congress which we have won for the Republican party. But do not forget that prior to 1896 it had lookt for years as if we were merely oscillating violently without much idea of whither we were drifting. I enclose you a copy of the letter Rhodes, the historian, recently wrote a friend who sent it to me. I do this because of your allusion to McKinley and Hanna. In 1896 and again in 1900 we won a victory which was really a victory for ultraconservatism against wild radicalism. If things had been allowed to continue in our party just as they were, we should have been upset with a smash soon afterwards. My business was to take hold of the conservative party and turn it into what it had been under Lincoln, that is, a party of *progressive* conservatism, or conservative radicalism; for of course wise radicalism and wise conservatism go hand in hand.

I also appreciate your kindly allusion to my joining the *Outlook*. The very fact that I so abhor the inanity and sensationalism of the yellow press, and the moral obliquity of the purchased press, not to speak of the odious hypocrisy of the professional mugwump press, makes me glad to be associated with a paper like the *Outlook*.

I cannot too warmly express my appreciation of what the Colonial Office and my English big game friends have done for me in the matter of the African trip. It has simply been fine. I look forward eagerly to coming to Oxford but I am a little uncertain as to making the address on "democracy" or the "problems of democracy" as you suggest. I had expected to make something that would be in part at least more academic. I shall take the liberty of speaking of your suggestion with Bryce who has himself delivered the Romanes lecture. I am also to speak at the Sorbonne in France. I am by

[2] The Democrats, Roosevelt had announced after the election, had been beaten to a "frazzle." For a time this choice of word provoked the kind of discussion that had previously attended the President's advocacy of simplified spelling.

no means sure that I could compress such a subject as democracy into any reasonable limits; and I would not like to speak on your democratic problems; it is the kind of subject upon which the most friendly foreigner might easily make mistakes.

Now as to what you say about India. I did not realize that any considerable number of our papers had been attacking England on the subject of India, and I am sorry to learn it. Taft in that matter feels precisely as I do, that English rule in India and Egypt like the rule of France in Algiers or of Russia in Turkestan means a great advance for humanity. English rule in India has been one of the mighty feats of civilization, one of the mighty feats to the credit of the white race during the past four centuries, the time of its extraordinary expansion and dominance. That you have committed faults I have not the slightest doubt, tho I do not know them — my business being to know the faults we have committed in the Philippines ourselves, of which I am well aware, and as to which I am steadily trying to advance and perfect remedies. I do not want to force speech on the subject, but if I get the chance I shall certainly speak very strongly.[3] I could not lay my hands on the allusions at the moment but I am certain that since I have been President I have, on several occasions, spoken with the heartiest praise of England's work in Egypt and I think in India. I happened to have my attention called chiefly to Egypt. Some of your writers, by the way, in *Blackwoods,* the *Saturday Review,* and the like, and in some books have been very foolish in the effort to be caustic about our work in the Philippines. With high regard, *Sincerely yours*

[*Handwritten*] This is the first time in our history that the Administration in power during a financial panic has been sustained at the following election.

5012 · TO THEODORE ROOSEVELT, JUNIOR   *Roosevelt Mss.*

Washington, November 20, 1908

Dear Ted: Ha ha! Don't jeer at your father about Standard Oil. *I* saw in yesterday's paper that the mills where you are working had just received a large Government contract, and it was evidently felt to be a most sinister coincidence. I guess we will both receive sentence together, and either Quentin or Archie will have to bail us out!

The misadventure of the Kaiser has been one of the most curious things

[3] Acting on the suggestion of several British friends, Roosevelt in a speech to the Methodist missionary workers on January 18 praised British rule in India. The London press considered his tribute an important rebuttal to the attacks of British "radicals" on their government's policy which, because of unrest in India, was then vulnerable; see Numbers 5026, note 1, 5096.

I have ever known.[1] It was utterly unexpected to me. I had known there was grumbling in Germany and a desire for a really representative government; but for the last fifteen or eighteen years (I have forgotten just how long his reign has been) the Kaiser has lorded it so over Germany, has been such a complete ruler, and his wishes have been met with such servility, that I did not for a moment believe the Germans would revolt; and the unanimity of the revolt no less than the suddenness was a complete surprise to me. Of course what happened was that for many years they had been storing up their wrath, and when the occasion came, when they finally gave vent to it, the pent-up body of anger simply broke thru the dams and swept everything with it. The conservatives, the members of the aristocrat party, upon which the Empire ought to count as its chief support, were at one with the socialists in the matter. I think it was one of these conservatives who quoted with hearty approval my remark that as an Ambassador I wisht to send a man and not a checkbook; the purport of the approval being of course to attack the Kaiser about his course in connection with Hill. Did I tell you of the Kaiser's interview with the American newspaperman Hale last summer, and of my part in helping to prevent the New York *Times* from publishing the interview? It was a far worse interview than the one that was actually published in the English paper, and the curious thing was that the things that he said were the direct reverse of those in the English paper. In the English interview he claimed to have been the great supporter of England, and to have refused the requests of Russia and France to form an alliance against her. In the interview with the American he was most bitter in his denunciation of England, and even in his denunciation of the King, and said that England was tottering to its fall, that there would soon be a Sepoy uprising in India, and that he expected very shortly that Germany would have to make war on England. If published as given that interview would have had far worse effects than the one that actually was published. The worst parts were struck out by Hale, and the remainder arranged as an article for the *Century* and actually printed in proof. The German Government then got this article itself supprest. I hardly know whether they were wise in doing so or not. I saw the article the other day. It contained a very bitter attack on the Roman Catholics which would have caused the Kaiser a great deal of trouble at home; but there was not much in the way of attacking foreign powers; and now that the article has been supprest of course everybody believes that it was full of all possible iniquity.

As you say, the movement in Germany is part of the general liberal movement. Moreover, as you say, it is a movement which at certain times and in

[1] Shocked by the publication of the Kaiser's views about England which had been cleared for release by the German chancellor, Prince von Bülow, and determined to oppose the Kaiser's personal and apparently warlike foreign policy, the National Liberals in an aggressive debate were demanding that the chancellor be made responsible to the Reichstag.

certain places has been pushed to hopeless extremes. I think that at the moment in England they have tended to go too far. There is a great deal of discontent and suffering and poverty in England, and the radical extremists are not helping matters by their actions. In France and in Germany, both, there has been a growth of the socialist party of recent years, and in Russia the movement for reform received a well-nigh fatal blow from the foolish conduct of the violent revolutionists, and of all of the silly visionary creatures who follow Tolstoi and his kind. If it had not been for these extremists I believe that at this moment Russia would be enjoying constitutional government; but the extremists went so far as to play right into the hands of the reactionaries, so that the Czar was enabled to re-establish the control of the bureaucratic despotism.

Here in this country I do not at present see any symptoms of our going too far. We are in just as much danger from the reactionaries and unscrupulous men of vast wealth as from the agitators; and, indeed, I think that the latter gain what strength they have only because of the intense indignation excited by the actions of the former. The overwhelming defeat of Bryan by Taft shows how completely unable as yet the agitators are to do any damage, even when the conditions favor them, provided only that we can oppose them with men whose honesty is above suspicion and who are known to be as sincerely opposed to wrongdoing by men of property as to wrongdoing by men of no property; men who really try to reform abuses and to bring about more equitable conditions, altho they set their faces like flint against all violence and against all attacks upon honest acquired and honestly used property.

Moreover, when we speak of the rising of the democratic tide and feel fear concerning the outcome, it is well to remember that again and again during the past century and a quarter the tide has been higher than at present. Of course the French Revolution was the greatest instance of this; but there the catastrophe was so wholly phenomenal that perhaps it can hardly be quoted. In the early 40's, in our own country, the ultrademocratic, the foolishly democratic, movement was at its zenith, and was much higher than it has ever been since. The excesses and follies of democracy were much greater a century ago, when Jefferson was the trusted leader of the people, than they are now. In Europe the foolish as distinguished from the wise side of democracy was most in prominence sixty years ago, in 1848. There has never been as much danger of the same kind since. In Germany the democratic movement was again very strong in the early 60's. It has lost ground, on the whole, during the past four years. The Democracy to which I pin my faith, in which I believe with all my heart, is the Lincoln democracy; the democracy of the plain people, who are honest and possess common sense.

I quite agree with you that our business should be to make the best use of what we have rather than to keep continually trying new experiments. On the other hand, there are certain new experiments which it is absolutely necessary to try in the interest of that wise conservatism which goes hand in hand with a wise radicalism. There must be far greater control over the giant corporations than our forefathers would have deemed wise or possible; if only for the reason that unless we establish such control we shall make it absolutely certain that the people will turn to violent leaders and follow violent counsels. The same holds true about labor. To reform real abuses is the best way to prevent a revolutionary movement which would derive its strength from the fact that the abuses were left unreformed, and which when started would work more evil than good.

As to what you say about female suffrage, I enclose you a copy of a letter I have just sent to some of the female suffragists.[2] Mother and I are rather lukewarmly inclined to favor female suffrage. Auntie Bye and Auntie Corinne are against it. I do not myself think it makes much difference one way or the other. They have it in Colorado and Wyoming, and I am unable to see that it has made much difference either for good or for evil when those two States are compared with neighboring States of similar conditions such as Montana and North Dakota. I should say that on the whole it may have worked a very, very little good — that is, that the balance would show that rather more good than harm had been done; but I do not think that either enough good or enough harm has been done to warrant much interest in the movement.

The other day I had Colonel Cecil Lyon, the Republican leader of Texas, at lunch, with Dr. Lyman Abbott and his two sons, and I wish you had seen their eyes start when he casually mentioned some homicidal incident that had varied the recent political life in the State. I heard him finally explain to the Doctor — "You see, Doctor, Texas is a revolver State, and that has got to be taken into account in handling any political movement there."

I am extremely pleased that you have gotten on so well in your work in that the time has passed so quickly. I think you are quite right in not trying to associate with the people round about you where it would be unnatural. It is possible, altho I suppose not probable, that there will come some occasion where you can naturally join with some of them in a common effort for some object. If so, do it, for the result will be good. But I quite agree with you that to do anything forced and unnatural would do damage, and mere social association, without any other object, would certainly come under this category. When I was ranching on the Little Missouri I got along excellently with everyone. I worked hard with them on the roundup; I participated with hearty interest in different political meetings; I took part in the work of the cattlemen's association, and, indeed, was its president. But I made no effort whatever for mere social association. When they had a formal ball ("formal" is an odd word, by the way, to use in describing a cowboy ball) I went to it because everyone did, and it would have lookt as if I was "putting on airs" if I had not gone; but I never visited the ranches for merely social purposes, or

[2] No. 4990.

1373

hung about town, or took part in any of the ordinary jollifications, or went into the saloons, which were the recognized clubhouses, so to speak. They all liked me, or at least most of them did, for they knew I liked and respected them; and when we were thrown together we worked on an absolute equality but we went our several ways without regard to one another, except where we had real interests in common, and where we naturally joined to work for those interests. *Your loving father*

5013 · TO SETH LOW

Roosevelt Mss.

Washington, November 21, 1908

Dear Seth: I have your letter of the 20th instant. My present feeling is that I should not support a measure simply inserting the word "unreasonable" and putting in an amnesty clause. The one point upon which I want to insist most urgently is that we shall not leave this law to be construed every which way by the courts, as they would construe the word "unreasonable." [1] What I want is more power for the Government to decide by executive action what is and what is not proper. My present judgment is that such a law as that proposed, which, your friends say, is all that could be obtained at the present session, would represent no real improvement and might represent a step backward. I would, however, cordially support a provision putting common carriers under the Interstate Commerce Commission, increasing the power of this commission over them, and allowing them to approve of traffic agreements and consolidations. My message has been printed, and I can only answer you tentatively and should like to consult with other people before giving you a final answer, but my present judgment is that the bill you propose might represent a step backward, and in any event would mean the abandonment of all effort to accomplish progress. You say that the lawyers present were opposed as a matter of principle to the establishment of Government control of private business. I gather from the context that this means that they are opposed to the effort to supervise and regulate interstate business by the National Government so as to prevent the gross abuses that have existed and that exist. I utterly disagree with them, and from what you say I am afraid my difference with these gentlemen is fundamental. I do not intend, as far as I am concerned, to take any backward step in the movement for supervision and control of these great corporations. I intend to fight any effort to take such a backward step. It may be that the proposition you make could be combined with other propositions in a way that would not make it a backward step. My present impression — subject of course to

[1] Low, for the Civic Federation, was again sponsoring proposals for a national incorporation law and the creation of a federal commission to regulate trusts. As was the case earlier in 1908 (see Numbers 4585, 4660), Roosevelt approved of this general plan but opposed permitting the judiciary to pass on the reasonableness of combinations (see also No. 5020). The issue remained academic, for Roosevelt's last Congress gave the matter no attention.

change if good reason can be shown me — is that it would be better to do nothing than merely to take the action proposed. *Faithfully yours*

Washington, November 22, 1908

Dearest Kermit: Three cheers for the football match! It must have been simply fine seeing it. How I wish I could have been there! I have never yet seen Harvard win against Yale at football, altho I saw one draw.

Col. Patterson, the man who killed the man-eating lions of Tsavo, spent Friday night with us, and was most interesting. Next day I had Carl Akeley,[1] the Chicago man who has also hunted elephant & rhino in Africa, at lunch, and it was interesting to hear the two. I think I got some valuable advice from both. There is no question that you and I must be extremely careful in dealing with lion, elephant, buffalo, and rhino; they are dangerous game. Both of us must be extremely cautious, and of course I shall want some first-class man with you until you grow accustomed to what is being done. All our arrangements are made; the stores have been sent to Africa, etc. etc. Both Patterson and Akeley were very much pleased at my having engaged Cuninghame,[2] and said that with a caravan the size of ours I would have been unable to have done much hunting if I had been obliged to manage the caravan myself.

It is not in the least like Buxton's trips, which are merely for a few days at a time away from the railroad. You and I want to go up into the really wild country such as Patterson described in that letter of his, if it is a possible thing.

The Kaiser has come an awful cropper. He has been a perfect fool, and the German people after standing his folly and bumptiousness for years finally exploded over something which was of course bad, but was no worse than scores of similar things he had done before.

I have finished both my Romanes lecture and my Sorbonne address. I wanted to get them off my hands before the Congress met, as I shall have in all probability a good deal of irritating work while Congress is in session, for the outgoing President hasn't very much power. They tell me Foraker is pre-

[1] Carl Ethan Akeley, naturalist, "in the very heart of Africa . . . . first came to know and love Theodore Roosevelt." Describing his hero in the preface to the National Edition of Roosevelt's *African Game Trails,* Akeley wrote: "Nothing that I know of Roosevelt better illustrates his habit of coming out in the open and going straight to the point than the way in which he approached his elephants." A collector of specimens of wild animals for the Field Museum and Museum of Natural History, Akeley was particularly fond of the elephant. His elephant group in the African hall of the American Museum is perhaps his most famous and stunning contribution. The inventor of the Akeley cement gun and the Akeley camera, he also wrote *In Brightest Africa* (1923). There, on safari, he died in 1926.
[2] R. J. Cuninghame.

paring a violent attack on me.[3] I can imagine nothing to which I should be more indifferent. *Your loving father*

[*Handwritten*] This morning when mother and I walked around the grounds as usual, she was still able to pick a rose for my buttonhole, from the rose beds in the garden. It was a misty morning; and the trees with their leafless branches, and the monument, were very beautiful.

5015 · TO CHARLES WILLIAM ELIOT   *Roosevelt Mss.*

Washington, November 23, 1908

My dear President Eliot: In all our history I do not know another university president, or another man connected with any institution of learning, who has played the great national part that you have played for the last thirty-five years;[1] and I can imagine nothing in which a man could feel greater or more legitimate satisfaction than to have worked with the fullest vigor right up to the end of an active career carried well past the allotted three score and ten years, and then to retire while every faculty is still unimpaired and every power still undimmed. Here I am leaving my task a quarter of a century earlier in life than you leave yours!

It has been a great career, my dear President Eliot, and as an American and as a Harvard man I congratulate you with all my heart. *Sincerely yours*

P.S. Cannot you and Mrs. Eliot come down to the Judiciary dinner on January 28th and spend the night with us? This dinner is one of the three big State dinners, and all the Justices of the Supreme Court will be present.

5016 · TO WILLIAM DUDLEY FOULKE   *Roosevelt Mss.*

Washington, November 23, 1908

Dear Foulke: If it were worth while feeling indignant with the Civil Service Reform Association over some of their acts I should do so. But they amuse me. If they make an attack in connection with the use of the offices to nominate Taft, all I wish is that you or Swift would give me the opportunity to furnish a few words, not in the way of answer but of comment on my accusers. The attack on Taft's nomination by the "allies" was corrupt and

[3] Renewing his attack on the Administration's handling of the Brownsville affair, Foraker in December introduced first a resolution directing Taft to produce all details on the employment of Browne and Baldwin, and then a bill establishing a board of inquiry to investigate the Brownsville matter. The bill failed but the resolution passed. After Taft submitted his report, the senator in January damned Roosevelt and Taft for the allegedly illegal methods of investigation which Browne and Baldwin had employed. Even a sympathetic biographer considered the tone of this speech "ill-advised"; see Walters, *Foraker*, p. 245.

[1] In the forty years during which Eliot had served in the presidency of Harvard University, from which he was then retiring, he had altered profoundly and beneficially the nature and tone of that institution and changed the face of privately endowed education in this country.

infamous; and it was backed up by most of the mugwumps. I dictated to the officeholders just one thing and that was that they should not be for my renomination. The only use I made of my position in my control over them was to prevent many of them doing what they earnestly desired to do, insisting upon my renomination. Outside of that they followed my lead simply as the great majority of the Republicans in their several communities; and literally the only difference was that in Ohio a good many of them went against Taft. In the "favorite son" States they reluctantly went for the favorite sons to much greater extent than the non-officeholding population did. I have seen Greene of the Civil Service Commission and he tells me the Commission investigated every instance of alleged political activity in the classified service. Outside of the classified service, from Cabinet officers to postmasters, the Civil Service law does not apply, save in certain narrowly limited cases, as to which it was strictly enforced. Never before in a political campaign has there been, as there has been in this campaign, a number of removals for violations of the Civil Service law during the heat of the campaign contest.

Do you want to write me a letter enclosing any statements made by the *News* about the Panama Canal since election, for me to write you a perfectly colorless statement of facts in return, which can be used or not at your discretion?[1] *Ever yours*

5017 · TO WILLIAM HOWARD TAFT   *Roosevelt Mss.*

Washington, November 23, 1908

Dear Will: We are in rather a scrape over those ships which Congress authorized to have purchased for the Panama Canal. The ship owners insist that the War Department approved the passage of the bill and the purchase of the ships with full knowledge that Goethals and the other officials protested against it, on the ground that the ships were not fitted for the work and were not needed. There is, however, nothing on record to show that this was the case, and Secretary Wright is properly reluctant to carry out, not a direction but a promise of Congress, by purchasing ships which Goethals and his people say are not needed and are unsuited for the work. Lodge says that these same statements were made by Goethals and his people before Congress and that Congress and the Department then disregarded the protests.

When you come to Washington will you see Wright, and if necessary me, about the matter and then give us some statement so we shall have on record just what you, when you were Secretary of War, did or how far you committed yourself?[1] I know you and I talked about it, but my recollection as to

[1] Foulke wrote such a letter on November 29. Roosevelt's answer, anything but colorless, was printed on December 7. It led to an attack on the author by the *World* on December 8 which in turn decided Roosevelt to bring a libel suit against the *World;* see Numbers 5039, 5042, 5058, 5064.

[1] For Taft's commitments see Numbers 4882, 5036.

the detail of the talk is hazy. Its general purport was that if the ships were fit for the purpose and if Congress gave the promise we would purchase them, because we all felt that any way we could we would help out American ship owners, who had actually been trying to keep American commerce on the high seas and had failed because of the inaction of Congress as regards a subsidy. *Ever yours*

5018 · TO LUKE EDWARD WRIGHT   *Roosevelt Mss.*

Washington, November 23, 1908

My dear Mr. Secretary: There is one matter as to which I am more interested in connection with this question of the ships than anything else. This man Archer, who is evidently an absolute scoundrel, is representing to outsiders that he and he alone can get ships taken. As it has turned out, it was most unfortunate that he was ever employed to purchase anything for the government, but no blame attaches to anyone for employing him when we were ignorant of his character. I wish orders publicly issued to the Commission and to all the subordinates of the War Department, that in view of the exposure of Archer's character, he is never again to be employed as principal or intermediary in any fashion, direct or indirect, by the War Department, the Isthmian Canal Commission, or any of their subordinates in connection with any purchase of any kind whatever. Moreover, I wish every member of the Commission and every important subordinate employee of the Commission and the Panama Railroad and Canal dealing with these matters in the War Department to be asked specifically if they are now in any communication with Archer, or if they have had any communication with him of any kind during the past nine months. Ask these questions before the order is issued, and require a detailed statement of all dealings by anyone with Archer, if such should prove to have existed.

Find out in connection with the investigation as to the alleged excessive price paid in 1905 for the two Cromwell ships and the failure to allow for depreciation; whether the members of the Commission and Mr. Rogers had any knowledge of the purchases at that time, and if so why they did not make a similar protest in that case to the protest they have made now; also whether Archer had anything to do with this purchase.[1] *Sincerely yours*

5019 · TO ARTHUR HAMILTON LEE   *Roosevelt Mss.*

Private   Washington, November 23, 1908

Dear Arthur: I had written you an exceedingly confidential letter which was to be put in your hands by Harry White and which you were then to destroy.[1] But recent publications have rendered it unnecessary for me to send

---
[1] See Numbers 4882, 5017, 5035, 5036.

---
[1] No. 4953.

you the letter, and I have directed White himself to destroy it. I had seen what has now been published, last August, and since then have been on the alert to find out if there was any need of warning you. But I found that there was no real need at the moment. I shall have some exceedingly amusing things to tell you when we meet. *Faithfully yours*

5020 · TO SETH LOW   *Roosevelt Mss.*

Washington, November 24, 1908

My dear Mr. Low: I have gone over with the Attorney General your letter and my answer thereto.[1] He feels at least as strongly as I do in the matter. I have now considered the matter carefully and I feel that I ought to tell you, and thru you the gentlemen whom you mention as having been present at the conference, that I could not sign such a bill as they advocate even if it were passed by Congress. I should consider it a retrograde action. The Department of Justice, I find, believe that the Standard Oil's fight for delay in these suits has been in the hope of getting thru some such measure as this. I have sent a copy of our correspondence to Mr. Taft, so that he shall have it before him to attach to it whatever weight he deems proper if the question comes up in his administration.

With regard, believe me, *Sincerely yours*

5021 · TO JOHN T. LOOMIS   *Roosevelt Mss.*

Washington, November 24, 1908

My dear Mr. Loomis:[1] I should prefer the pigskin if it does not weigh any more than the cloth, but I would make everything subordinate to weight. I return you the three volumes. I wonder if you could not get me a better set of selections from Poe. I do not care for the notes or the introduction; still less for the pictures. The poems are all right, but the choice of tales is not good.

I also return you the *La Chanson de Roland,* as you will want to bind that, and also the *Nibelungenlied.* Can't you get me the three Shakespeares such as I send you and have them bound in pigskin? Will you let me know the total weight? *Faithfully yours*

[*Handwritten*] Can't I get Browning's "Selections" instead of his "Men & Women"?

5022 · TO TRUMAN HANDY NEWBERRY   *Roosevelt Mss.*

Washington, November 25, 1908

My dear Mr. Newberry: I am puzzled what to do about the papers that you submit. I call your attention to the statement of Mr. Alger at the foot of page

[1] No. 5013.
_____
[1] John T. Loomis of W. H. Lowdermilk and Company, a Washington bookstore.

4 where he says "to go to a larger caliber now is therefore to acknowledge that our former action was an error." [1] This single sentence gives me a hearty distrust of Mr. Alger's whole judgment in this matter and of Admiral Mason's[2] judgment so far as it is based on Alger's. If there is one thing more than any other which our bureau chiefs and technical experts need to learn it is that they must never for a moment consider the question of acknowledgment of error in the past as a factor in doing what is best possible in the present. There is no habit of mind more destructive to efficiency in the navy than the habit of refusing to accept any new suggestion because to accept it may give rise to the belief that an error has been committed in the past. With such a development in naval matters as has occurred in the last fifty years, progress is conditioned upon a sufficient boldness to mean the occasional commission of errors and the frankest readiness to acknowledge that they have been committed. The same reason that is contained in this sentence would apply against our building a 20,000-ton battleship now because we have built 10,000-ton battleships in the past. To refuse to accept any change until its advantages have been demonstrated by actual experience means that we must always be behind the times.

Moreover, Mr. Alger's paper shows that he is content to follow the example of other nations. I want to see us lead other nations. Now this statement of mine has nothing whatever to do with the merits of the case, but it has to do with my willingness to accept the statements of Admiral Mason and of Mr. Alger as to the merits of the case.

The Newport Conference recommended that we should proceed with the development of the 14-inch gun. Every effort should be made to proceed with this development. I do not believe that the attitude of mind shown in the papers you have submitted to me is one that is conducive to the successful development of these guns. I should like to have you find out from these men, definitely, whether they can or cannot build these 14-inch guns. If they cannot then I shall want to consider their statement together with the statement of the Conference and see whether it is not to the advantage of the service that we shall make a change in the offices. I want you to find out at once from the Bethlehem people what they think as to their ability to build these guns.

I am not satisfied, as you know, as to the present bureau organization of the navy, but while it exists I intend that the bureaus shall do the best possible work, and if in any given bureau we cannot get the work done we will change the head and try and see if the new head cannot do it. *Sincerely yours*

[1] Professor Philip R. Alger, ballistics expert and member of the Board of Naval Ordnance, had led the opposition at the Newport Conference against placing 14-inch guns on the *Utah* and *Florida* (see No. 4900). He was now voicing similar objections to including such guns in the plans for the new ships which were soon to be voted on by Congress.
[2] Newton Eliphalet Mason, Chief of the Bureau of Ordnance.

Washington, November 25, 1908

My dear Nick: I want to write you personally about Mr. A. L. Faulkner, President of the National Window Glass Workers, of Cleveland, Ohio. You will recall the courage and disinterestedness with which, against great pressure, he came forward and stood for us in the last campaign. I regard him as a high-minded man of excellent judgment. He wishes to impress upon the committee the urgent need, from the standpoint of the workingman, of not reducing the tariff on window glass, ... section 101, so as to make any cut on the wages of our own people. As a matter of fact he says that the tariff should be increased in order to protect our own workingmen. Of course I should not for one moment venture to give any information on the matter, which is purely for the decision of the committee; but I wish to give to Mr. Faulkner privately this letter to you, so that you shall know who he is, his responsibility, and pay all attention you can to what he says. *Sincerely yours*

Washington, November 25, 1908

My dear Mr. Ambassador: Please treat this note as informal and unofficial. I greatly regret that your government thought that their Embassy in Washington ought to put forth such a statement as that which was put forth on behalf of the British officials in the Olympic Games. I should most emphatically have refused any request from the corresponding American officials to secure the publication of any similar statement in England thru the American Embassy. Absolutely no good whatever comes, or can come, from any action by any official of either the British or American Government in this matter. On the contrary, harm has come already from the publication made by the British Embassy, and further harm will come if either the American or the British Government takes any part whatsoever in this exceedingly unfortunate affair. Moreover, such action gives it an entirely unwarranted importance. I thoroly believe in athletics, but it is absurd to attach to them such portentous importance as would warrant the interference of the governments of the two countries to settle whether an American fouled an Englishman in the four hundred metre race, or whether the British officials behaved unfairly in the Marathon race. It is even more preposterous for the officials of the two governments to allow themselves to be made the solemn instruments of calling the attention of the public to a bitter controversy as to which given set of officials has or has not behaved badly; as to whether certain American or certain British papers have or have not published slanderous articles. The quarrel has been most regrettable, most unfortunate. Not the slightest good can come, in my judgment, from what would in any event be the rather absurd course of getting the two governments embroiled in the effort to nicely apportion the rights and wrongs of the various controversies. Such being the case, it seems to me exceedingly unwise to take any action which amounts to a provocation to continue the quarrel, and gives it an immense advertisement. We have received various inquiries from the American Amateur Athletic Union as to the action of the British Embassy, and I have just been informed that they intend to make an answer to this article because it comes from the British Embassy, altho they would not have done so under other circumstances. Some of their number are certain to ask, and, indeed, have already asked this government to take some action in response to what they regard as the official action of the British Embassy. My present intention is to positively refuse to be drawn in any way into the controversy or to say anything about it one way or the other, because I am convinced that the surest way to cause friction is to keep alive the discussion, and that from the point of view of international good relations the wisest possible thing to do for those in power in the two countries, is to say nothing whatever. For either government directly or indirectly to become responsible for anything said in the matter can by no possibility do any good, and may finally result in an amount of irritation and damage ludicrously disproportionate to the original cause.

I have seen these athletic rows again and again and when they have once started, time and silence are the only sure remedies. About the year 1895 I saw the Harvard-Yale football game which resulted in the complete breakup of all athletic relations between Harvard and Yale for two or three years. Each team firmly believed that its opponents had been guilty of every form of misdemeanor, including attempted mayhem. The graduates felt quite as violently as the undergraduates. I shall never forget my astonishment when I discovered that old and intimate Yale friends of mine believed that young fellows whom I knew on the Harvard team, young men of the highest stamp, were brutal creatures with a slightly homicidal cast of mind. Of course I am not writing quite seriously — but if you glance at the papers of that day you will see that there is very little exaggeration. In my turn I was equally astonished that certain Yale men who I quite sincerely thought bore characters of almost unblemished ruffianism were, according to my friends' view, singularly high-minded and blameless people — and since then by the way some of those same individuals have been among my most ardent political supporters. I found that any attempt to get Yale and Harvard men to agree as to what had been done merely resulted in an acrid discussion of the comparative iniquities of the teams. The two colleges never did get together until some time had elapsed and until there had been absolute silence and a refusal to reopen the discussion. Do let me point the moral by saying that any utterance of any kind by or on behalf of the Government of either country or by one of its officials, would simply lead to just such an acrid discussion of the iniquities committed on both sides and would leave each side as convinced as ever that the other was all wrong and would also have a very unhealthy public effect. The less there is said about the matter the better; and the most effective way to keep the subject alive would be to take any government action of any kind whatsoever. *Sincerely yours*

5025 · TO VICTOR HOWARD METCALF   *Roosevelt Mss.*

Washington, November 26, 1908

The Secretary of the Navy: Please issue an order specifically to every one of the members of the Newport Conference and to every other officer who you think stands in the slightest need thereof to the effect that under no circumstances is any officer to discuss before the public, or to give any information directly or indirectly concerning it, any question of naval policy without submitting what he wishes to say to the Secretary, or thru the Secretary, to the President. State in the order that this is issued by my direction, and that any officer disobeying it will be held to account.[1]

5026 · TO WHITELAW REID   *Roosevelt Mss.*

Personal   Washington, November 26, 1908

My dear Mr. Ambassador: I have just finished reading Winston Churchill's account of his white rhinoceros hunt, and this suggests to me that there is something very real in the way of aid which Lord Crewe and the Uganda authorities could do for me. The officials who were with Churchill were able to take him to a place where there were plenty of elephants and plenty of white rhinoceros. Now I should consider my entire African trip a success if I could get to that country and find the game as Churchill describes it. Would Lord Crewe specifically write to the Uganda people telling them that I will communicate with them, and that he would like me to be furnished with guides and information which would enable me to go to the same country as that in which Winston Churchill got his elephant and white rhinoceros, or to similar country? The white rhinoceros is the animal I care most to get — even more than the elephant. The Belgian authorities have promised me all the information and aid they can give, if I get into the Lado Enclave; but it is evident from Churchill's article that the Uganda people may themselves be able to put me on the path of obtaining what I desire.

I am concerned about what I see as to the unrest in India.[1] Have you

---

[1] The final report of the Newport conference was issued as a confidential order on November 18. Just before Roosevelt prohibited public discussion of the conference, Admiral Capps of the Bureau of Construction at a banquet in Chicago had read aloud letters from Dewey, Evans, Schley, and others "to prove that everything was as it should be and the so-called 'critics and insurgents' are persons of no consequence." — New York *Sun*, November 26, 1908.

[1] Not since the Mutiny had India witnessed the violence that broke out in the last months of 1908. Agitation for representative government reached its peak during the trial of Tilak, the most prominent native leader, who was sentenced to deporta-

much information about it? I think that for some time to come the Kaiser will not be a source of serious danger as regards international complications. But I do not like what I hear about India. It looks to me as if a very ugly feeling was growing up there. How do the British authorities feel about it? Are they confident that they can hold down any revolt?

Britain has anti-imperialists even more foolish than ours. I see Hall Caine[2] has started a novel in which the hero seems to be a new Mahdi who is to turn the English out of Egypt; and Caine, speaking thru the lips of the English subhero of the tale, is evidently inclined to believe that such a wild, unspeakably cruel fanatic, as a Mahdi must certainly be, would stand for moral uplift!

Here there isn't much that is exciting to tell you. Taft and Mrs. Taft will come to the White House on the 3d of March and spend the night, and this will save them the bother of moving in on Inauguration Day itself. I shall leave Taft at the Capitol and not drive back to the White House with him — which always struck me as a peculiarly senseless performance on the part of the man who had been President and was so no longer.

The British Embassy here, I am afraid by direction of the Government at home, did a very foolish thing in publishing, and getting the papers to circulate, the acrid protest of the British Olympic officials against the American officials and athletes. It of course immensely advertises the quarrel, and gives precisely the opportunity which I had hoped would not be given for the anti-British people to write bitter articles. It is utterly hopeless by any argument to try to bring the two sides of the quarrel into agreement. As a matter of fact there were features in the conduct of each side which were discreditable, and each side is blind to its own misdeeds and clamorously unjust about the misdeeds of the other. I saw Bryce and told him that I thought it was a mistake to have published the article; that we certainly would never have published such an article coming from the American athletes; and that you would never permit any such publication to come from your embassy; and that I thought far and away the best course to follow for the officials of both countries was not, directly or indirectly, to say anything further about the matter, and that the sooner the noise was allowed to die out, the better it would be all around. *Sincerely yours*

P.S. Since writing the above your letter has come, and I am amused to find

---

tion in December. While using severe repressive measures, it put down the agitation. Lord Morley at the same time recommended that Parliament broaden the basis of representation and increase the self-government of the local units.

[2] Sir Thomas Henry Hall Caine served his literary apprenticeship as a leader writer for the Liverpool *Mercury*. In 1881 he went to London, lived for a year with D. G. Rossetti, and worked as a journeyman in the pre-Raphaelite movement. Striking out on his own after Rossetti's death, he became a fabricator of novels in which practically everything happened. His stories had local as well as high color; many of them took place in the Isle of Man. Though in his genre he was extremely popular, he remained, for the judicious student of romance and sensation, a pale horse beneath the Haggard Rider.

how exactly your view of the course to follow in the matter of the athletic squabble coincides with what I had already written above. I saw Bryce last night and found that the Government had not communicated with the British Embassy, and I think the publication from it was due to a bit of slack management on their part. I was careful to impress upon him the fact that under no circumstances would you permit a similar protest from the American athletes here to receive what might be regarded as official sanction from your Embassy, and that what was most necessary was to keep just as quiet as possible about the matter. Of course when the British athletes sent over, as they did, a statement that they would forever hereafter disqualify Carpenter, they invited recriminations. As you say, I think both sides have been to blame, and it is a case for the application of one of my favorite anecdotes — that of the New Bedford whaling captain who told one of his men that all he wisht from him was "silence, and damn little of that."

In the same mail with your letter came an extremely nice letter from the Sirdar enclosing the article of Winston Churchill's, and saying that he would do everything in his power to get me a white rhinoceros; but it will do no harm for you to have Lord Crewe write the Uganda people anyhow, if I may bother you to take the trouble. The Sirdar tells me the King sent me his good wishes for the African trip. Would it be wise or proper for me to write him a personal note saying that I had heard of his kindly interest and wisht to thank him for it?

Would you be willing to find out from the British Museum people whether they would like a specimen of the white rhinoceros of Central Africa? I shall have, as you know, some field taxidermists with me. My first pair, male and female, would have to go to the National Museum here, but I should like to show my appreciation of the way the British authorities are treating me, and if they would care for a specimen, and *if I was able to secure a third specimen,* (which very probably will not be the case) I should be very glad to send it to them.

5027 · TO JOHN GRAHAM BROOKS   *Roosevelt Mss.*

Washington, November 26, 1908

My dear Mr. Brooks: I am sincerely obliged to you for the list of books and for your article. I was much imprest with your suggestions about my article and went over them with Dr. Abbott, and have recast it into two subarticles, the first with the heading, "Where we cannot work with the socialists," and the second with the heading, "Where we can work with the socialists." [1] Of course it is folly for us to be the slave of names, and when socialists abandon what is wicked and crazy in their old doctrines and turn the movement into one for social betterment both sane and fearless, I will heartily go with them

[1] These were published in the *Outlook,* 91:619–623, 662–664 (March 20 and 27, 1909).

without being in the least upset by their calling their movement "socialism."
Sincerely yours

[*Handwritten*] P.S I have read that article and like it immensely; I am especially imprest by the contrast you draw between Belgium & France.

5028 · TO FRANKLIN KNIGHT LANE   *Roosevelt Mss.*

Washington, November 27, 1908

My dear Lane: I have your letter of the 24th instant with enclosed clipping. I believe you should have absolute power over the railroads in raising and lowering rates; that it should be summary, and that no action should be taken without your prior consent. What I can do about it now I do not know.

I wish, by the way, that some case came up where your Commission would raise a rate. I have been told that this has never been done. Is this so? I should like to see you get absolute power to keep rates down and to lower them if necessary; but with as little hesitation you should raise them if necessary.

The Commission should also have the right to prescribe the method of co-operation between the railroads and the systems of waterways transportation.[1] *Sincerely yours*

5029 · TO LEONARD WOOD   *Roosevelt Mss.*

Private   Washington, November 27, 1908

My dear Leonard: While I cannot of course pretend to quote the exact words, the substance of Lord Cromer's statement was that he felt that your work in Cuba had been on the whole the most striking and most successful of all colonial administration of which he had knowledge during recent years, and this because you had to encounter not merely the ordinary difficulties of colonial administration, but the special difficulty attendant upon governing a people jealously on the lookout for any disposition to slight them or treat them as inferiors.[1]

Of course do not make this public. The statement was naturally entirely private.

It was delightful seeing Mrs. Wood and you here. *Ever yours*

[1] Although the railroads had long dominated both coastal and river transportation companies, neither the Hepburn Act nor the later Mann-Elkins Act gave the Interstate Commerce Commission jurisdiction over water carriers.

[1] Such a statement carried authority. Evelyn Baring, first Earl of Cromer, ruler of Egypt from 1883 to 1907, was one of the great nineteenth-century proconsuls.

Washington, November 27, 1908

Dear Ted: Your letter to Mother was fine, and I particularly enjoyed your description of the club. Perhaps Praed's vicar will prove a companion for you; you'll enjoy one cultivated friend.

Quentin is a funny mite. He takes with the utmost philosophy alternations of grandeur and of the life of a small street-mucker. Today he went to school in a carriage and pair. Yesterday it became his duty to provide a pig for Thanksgiving dinner; accordingly he started off early in the morning to the slaughter house, scraped an acquaintance with a negro who was driving a brick wagon, and rode over on the brick wagon, with two other negroes who were on their way to the station to beat a ride on a freight train to Richmond. He had a date with an elderly sporting friend — a funny old fellow who hunts rabbits, and fishes, with whom Quentin has an acquaintance. He got his pig all right and brought it home in triumph. The rest of the day he passed with various small boy friends, doing everything imaginable, and was so dirty by nightfall that good Ethel had herself to see that he was thoroly washt. When his head was washt she said that it yielded a thick stream of muddy water.

Bryce, the British Ambassador, was in last night, and he and I were speaking about sport, agreeing that it is a first-class thing as an amusement, but that it was simply dreadful when a young fellow made it the serious business of his life; and Bryce spoke with such admiration of the way you have gone in to work in the mill, and what a fine thing it was to have you doing that instead of leading a perfectly silly and vacuous life around the clubs or in sporting fields.

Every now and then solemn jacks come to me to tell me that our country must face the problem of "what it will do with its ex-Presidents"; and I always answer them that there will be one ex-President about whom they need not give themselves the slightest concern, for he will do for himself without any outside assistance; and I add that they need waste no sympathy on me — that I have had the best time of any man of my age in all the world, that I have enjoyed myself in the White House more than I have ever known any other President to enjoy himself, and that I am going to enjoy myself thoroly when I leave the White House, and what is more, continue just as long as I possibly can to do some kind of work that will count. *Ever your loving father*

Washington, November 28, 1908

My dear Strachey: I have your letter of the 17th instant. In the first place let me say how interested I was in your article on American ex-Presidents.[1] I am not sure, however, that I altogether agree with you. When people have spoken to me as to what America should do with its ex-Presidents, I have always answered that there was one ex-President as to whom they need not concern themselves in the least, because I would do for myself. It would be to me personally an unpleasant thing to be pensioned and given some honorary position. I emphatically do not desire to clutch at the fringe of departing greatness. Indeed, to me there is something rather attractive, something in the way of living up to a proper democratic ideal, in having a President go out of office just as I shall go, and become absolutely and without reservation a private man, and do any honorable work which he finds to do. My first work will be to go to Africa for the National Museum. I am fifty, I have led a very sedentary life for ten years, and I feel that this is my last chance for something in the nature of a "great adventure." If a war should occur while I am still physically fit, I should certainly try to raise a brigade, and if possible a division, of cavalry, mounted riflemen, such as those in my regiment ten years ago. But if, as I most earnestly hope, there is peace, then, after my return from Africa, and in view of the fact that I am not fit any longer for really arduous exploration, the work open to me which is best worth doing is fighting for political, social and industrial reform, just as I have been fighting for it for the twenty-eight years that I have been in politics. Now, the money consideration, except as an entirely subordinate way, does not enter into the matter at all. For my connection with *The Outlook* I will receive less than a fourth of what I have been offered to go on other publications, and less than an eighth of what I have been requested to consider if I would go into business. I feel very strongly that one great lesson to be taught here in America is that while the first duty of every man is to earn enough for his wife and children, that when once this has been accomplished no man should treat money as the primary consideration. He is very foolish unless he makes it the first consideration, up to the point of supporting his family; but normally, thereafter it should come secondary. Now, I feel that I can still for some years command a certain amount of attention from the American public, and during those years and before my influence totally vanishes I want to use it so far as possible to help onward certain movements for the betterment of our people. The character of the men associated with *The Outlook* makes *The Outlook* the best instrument with which I can work. My agreement is simply that whatever I have to say shall be said thru their columns. It may be a good deal and it may be a very little. In any event, it won't interfere

[1] "America and her Ex-Presidents," *Spectator*, 101:767–768 (November 14, 1908).

with anything else that I am doing, as is sufficiently shown by the fact that during my first year I go to Africa. All this is true; and yet I entirely agree with you that as regards the average President he should not be thrown out where he may have to earn his livelihood in ways not quite advisable for an ex-President. The subject is far from being without its difficulties.

Indeed I do hope we can see you and Mrs. Strachey. Aren't you near Selous? There is nothing I should like so much as to see Cromer, Selous and you all at the same time. But do not ask me to make a definite engagement now. I do not know enough of what my plans will be. But whoever else in England I see or do not see, Mrs. Strachey and you I certainly shall see. *Faithfully yours*

5032 · TO LEONARD WOOD   *Roosevelt Mss.*

Washington, November 28, 1908

Dear Leonard: I have your letter of the 26th. You are quite welcome to quote me publicly in that matter. I think the marines should be incorporated in the army. It is an excellent corps and it would be of great benefit to both services that the incorporation should take place.[1] *Sincerely yours*

5033 · TO WILLIAM HOWARD TAFT   *Roosevelt Mss.*

Washington, November 28, 1908

Dear Will: Tawney came in to see me today, very anxious to have an interview arranged between you and the Speaker. I think it extremely important that you should have this interview with him, but I won't bother you with the details on paper.[1] As soon as you get to Washington, however, I should like to have a chance to see you and give you a full statement of the facts as they seem to me; & also of the facts as Cannon and Tawney tell me *they* see them.

With love to Mrs. Taft, *Ever yours*

[*Handwritten*] Do'n't be led into bolstering up Woodruff for *any* position as a consolation prize.

---

[1] The incorporation did not take place; but in an order issued November 8, 1908, Roosevelt emphasized the increasing use of the Marines as a garrison and police force by relieving the Corps of all shipboard duties. In February 1909, Congress restored fleet duty for the Marines.

---

[1] Taft early in December "had a most satisfactory talk" with Cannon. The Speaker and also the Republican members of the Ways and Means Committee assured him that they would support his pledges and his program for a downward revision of the tariff. It later developed, of course, that in the mellowness of the postelection honeymoon neither the assurers nor the assured had understood the other.

Washington, November 28, 1908

Secretary of War: I understand that the Engineers are making a report upon the fourteen-foot deep-waterways project from St. Louis to the Gulf. As you know, I wish to concentrate all this work under the Waterways Commission.[1] Please direct the Engineers not to make any such report public until it has been submitted to the Waterways Commission, and then only upon my authorization.

5035 · TO LUKE EDWARD WRIGHT

Roosevelt Mss.

Washington, November 29, 1908

To the Secretary of War: In the matter of the purchase of those ships,[1] I have been shown the following letters written by the then Secretary of War on April 30th last:

My dear Senator:

I am just leaving for Panama and write this note to say that I approve of your amendment to the Sundry Civil Bill in regard to the purchase of two ships for the Panama trade and for the preference for American bottoms.

Very sincerely yours,
W. H. TAFT.

Hon. Henry Cabot Lodge.

My dear Senator Hale:

I am leaving tomorrow for the Isthmus to be gone for some days. I wish in my absence that there be no doubt as to my views on Senator Lodge's amendment to the Sundry Civil bill. Regarding the matter from all points of view I believe it to be good public policy and economy to purchase two large ships for the Isthmian Canal Commission and I favor the proposition to give preference to American ships.

Very truly yours,
W. H. TAFT.

Hon. Eugene Hale,
United States Senate.

I think this settles the question. It appears that all the objections that since the passage of the bill have been made to purchasing instead of hiring or building ships were made before the committees of Congress, and that after hearing them Congress disregarded them. The Secretary of War clearly

[1] In his annual message to Congress, Roosevelt asked that the control of the inland waterways be removed from the Army Engineer Corps and placed under "a permanent commission authorized to co-ordinate the work of all the government departments relating to waterways, and to frame and supervise the execution of a comprehensive plan" of waterway development (*State Papers*, Nat. Ed. XV, 525). A bill to create such a commission passed the House but died in the Senate.

[1] See Numbers 4882, 5017.

approved the policy on which the Senate acted, which policy was to purchase two American-built ships. All that there is to decide therefore is whether there is need of using ships, and whether the price of the ships offered is exorbitant. As I understand the naval and other boards have reported that the ships are suited for the purpose, and it appears that the Panama people must have ships to use as soon as possible. The question of policy — that is, as to whether ships shall be hired, built or purchased and as to whether they shall be American or foreign — was settled by Congress and is no longer debatable. The reports on file, as I am informed, show that the two ships for which negotiations have been going on are suitable. The question therefore simply is as to the price. Please have the negotiations closed at the earliest possible moment, as thru no fault of either yours or mine there has already been a much longer delay than there ought to have been.[2]

5036 · TO WILLIAM HOWARD TAFT   *Roosevelt Mss.*

Washington, November 29, 1908

Dear Will: Lodge showed me the two letters from you which I have quoted in the accompanying letter to Luke Wright.[1] Of course under the circumstances it is a matter of honorable obligation to follow out the course I have outlined in the letter to Luke Wright. I have told Lodge that my own feeling is, and I believe your feeling will be equally strongly, that hereafter there shall be no understanding by the Executive Department with Congress that in the event of merely permissive legislation we will purchase certain ships, or anything else. If Congress wishes us to follow a certain course, let it *direct* by law that this course be followed; but if it does not absolutely *direct* that this course shall be followed, I am clear that it is to the public interest that the Executive should have an absolutely free hand, should be unhampered by anything that can be even construed into a promise, and should consider nothing whatever but what is best for the Government within the limit set down by law, and without regard to anything but what the law on its face expressly sets forth.

I was cognizant of, and approved of, all you did in this matter, and what I am writing now represents no regret at what we did; for in view of all the circumstances, and of the advice of Chamberlain, the shipping commissioner, especially, we had every reason to believe that what we said and did was demanded by the public interest. But the experience I have had during the last six months has convinced me that this kind of an arrangement is not an advisable one to make. *Ever yours*

[2] The transaction was completed at once.

---

[1] See No. 5035.

Roosevelt Mss.

Washington, November 29, 1908

My dear Senator: I have offered the place of Assistant Secretary of the Navy to Herbert L. Satterlee, of New York, who has not yet notified me that he can accept; but he can only hold it until the 4th of March next in any event. It is a place for which I must have a man with peculiar qualifications, and of intimate association with and knowledge of the needs of the navy, so I cannot consider a man for the place from the ordinary standpoint. Herbert L. Satterlee fills these requirements, and I know of no other man in New York who does.[1] If he cannot take it I shall have to go out of the State.[2] *Sincerely yours*

Roosevelt Mss.

Personal   Washington, November 30, 1908

Dear White: I am really extremely pleased with your letter about my message.[1] I had originally written what I had to say about the judges in far stronger form. It is an outrage that a creature like Grosscup should be per-

[1] Satterlee, J. P. Morgan's son-in-law, was appointed Assistant Secretary on December 1, 1908, when Newberry, on Metcalf's resignation, became Secretary of the Navy. Owing to Metcalf's ill health, Newberry had been virtually in command of the department during the previous month. Satterlee, long active in the Naval Reserve, had served in the Navy during the war with Spain. In 1908 he was president of the Naval Reserve Association and general counsel for the Navy League.

[2] Roosevelt sent similar letters to Herbert Parsons and T. C. Platt.

[1] In his annual message Roosevelt stressed the need for a judiciary more responsive to social conditions. American judges, he contended, often "fail to understand and apply the needed remedies for the new wrongs produced by the new and highly complex social and industrial civilization which has grown up in the last half-century." Such judges must learn that these new conditions require a redefinition of legal concepts. They should also realize, Roosevelt continued, that "every time they interpret contract, property, vested rights, due process of law, liberty, they necessarily enact into law parts of a system of social philosophy; and as such interpretation is fundamental, they give direction to all lawmaking. The decisions of the courts on economic and social questions depend upon their economic and social philosophy; and for the peaceful progress of our people during the twentieth century we shall owe most to those judges who hold to a twentieth-century economic and social philosophy and not to a long outgrown philosophy, which was itself the product of primitive economic conditions. Of course a judge's views on progressive social philosophy are entirely second in importance to his possession of a high and fine character; which means the possession of such elementary virtues as honesty, courage, and fair-mindedness. The judge who owes his election to pandering to demagogic sentiments or class hatreds and prejudices, and the judge who owes either his election or his appointment to the money or the favor of a great corporation, are alike unworthy to sit on the bench, are alike traitors to the people; and no profundity of legal learning, or correctness of abstract conviction on questions of public policy, can serve as an offset to such shortcomings. But it is also true that judges, like executives and legislators, should hold sound views on the questions of public policy which are of vital interest to the people." — *State Papers,* Nat. Ed. XV, 508, 511.

mitted to stay on the bench. Of course there are very few judges that are actually corrupt, as I believe Grosscup to be; but there are many who are entirely unfit to occupy the positions they do, Brewer being a striking example of this kind. There is altogether too much power in the bench. I have taken the liberty of sending your letter to Mr. Justice Moody, who is entirely our kind of a judge. If they were all like him we would have no trouble. Meanwhile I do wish that you would write in the most emphatic manner to Taft. It could only do good. *Faithfully yours*

5039 · TO WILLIAM DUDLEY FOULKE   *Roosevelt Mss.*

Washington, December 1, 1908

My dear Mr. Foulke: I have received your letter of the 29th ultimo and have read it in connection with your previous letters enclosing quotations from the Indianapolis *News,* a paper edited by Mr. Delavan Smith.[1] As Mr. Smith certainly knew that all the statements he made were false, both as to this Panama matter and as to the other matters of which you enclosed me clippings, and inasmuch, therefore, as the exposure of the falsity will not affect his future statements, I am not very clear what good will result from such exposure. But inasmuch as you evidently earnestly desire some answer to be made, and inasmuch as you say that some reputable people appear to believe the falsehoods of the *News* and Mr. Smith, and inasmuch as you seem to think that his falsehoods as regards the Panama matter are the most prominent, I will answer them.

The *News* states in one of its issues that probably some of the documents dealing with the matter have been destroyed. This is false. Not one has been destroyed. It states that the last documents were sent over in June of this year, the object of this particular falsehood being, apparently, to connect the matter in some way with the nomination of Mr. Taft. As a matter of fact, the last papers that we have received of any kind were sent over to us in May, 1904, and they have been accessible to every human being who cared to look at them ever since, and are accessible now. Any reputable man within or without Congress, Republican or Democrat, has now and always has had the opportunity to examine any of these documents. You quote the *News* as stating that "the people have no official knowledge concerning the Panama Canal deal." The fact is that the people have had the most minute official knowledge; that every important step in the transaction and every important document have been made public in communications to Congress and thru the daily press, and the whole matter has been threshed over in all its details again and again and again. The *News* gives currency to the charge that "the United States bought from American citizens for forty million dollars property that cost these citizens only twelve million dollars." The statement is false. The United States did

[1] See Numbers 4963, 4984, 5042.

not pay a cent of the forty million dollars to any American citizen. The *News* says that there is no doubt that the Government paid forty million dollars for the property, and continues — "But who got the money? We are not to know. The administration and Mr. Taft do not think it right that the people should know." Really, this is so ludicrous as to make one feel a little impatient at having to answer it. The fact has been officially published again and again that the Government paid forty million dollars, and that it paid this forty million dollars direct to the French Government, getting the receipt of the liquidator appointed by the French Government to receive the same. The United States Government has not the slightest knowledge as to the particular individuals among whom the French Government distributed the sum. This was the business of the French Government. The mere supposition that any American received from the French Government a "rake-off" is too absurd to be discust. It is an abominable falsehood, and it is a slander not against the American Government but against the French Government. The *News* continues, saying that "The president's brother-in-law is involved in the scandal, but he has nothing to say." The President's brother-in-law was involved in no scandal. Mr. Delavan Smith and the other people who repeated this falsehood lied about the President's brother-in-law; but why the fact that Mr. Smith lied should be held to involve Mr. Robinson in a "scandal" is difficult to understand. The scandal affects no one but Mr. Smith; and his conduct has been not merely scandalous but infamous. Mr. Robinson had not the slightest connection of any kind, sort or description, at any time or under any circumstances, with the Panama matter. Neither did Mr. Charles Taft. The *News* says that Mr. Taft was a member of the "syndicate." So far as I know there was no syndicate; there certainly was no syndicate in the United States that to my knowledge had any dealings with the Government, directly or indirectly; and inasmuch as there was no syndicate, Mr. Taft naturally could not belong to it. The *News* demands that Mr. Taft "appeal to the evidence," by which it means what it calls "the records" — that is, the mass of papers, which are stored in the War Department, save such as, because of their technical character and their usefulness in the current work of the canal, it has been found advisable to send to the Isthmus. All of these documents that possess any importance as illustrating any feature of the transaction have already been made public. There remains a great mass of documents of little or no importance which the administration is entirely willing to have published, but which because of their mass and pointlessness, nobody has ever cared to publish. Any reputable man can have full access to these documents. If you or Mr. Swift, or Mr. Booth Tarkington, or Mr. George Ade[2] — in short, if any reputable man — will come on here,

---

[2] George Ade and Booth Tarkington around the turn of the century joined such men as Lew Wallace, Meredith Nicholson, Albert J. Beveridge, James Whitcomb Riley, and Benjamin Harrison to give a great deal of distinction to the intellectual life of

he shall have free access to the documents and can look over everything for himself. Congress can have them all printed if it wishes; but no Congressman has ever so far intimated any desire that this should be done; I suppose because to print such a mass of documents would be a great expense, and moreover, an entirely useless expense, unless, which is not the case, there was some object in printing them.

Now, my dear Mr. Foulke, I have answered in detail your questions and the statements of the *News*. You are quite welcome to print my answer; but I must frankly add that I don't think any good will come from doing so. Mr. Delavan Smith is a conspicuous offender against the laws of honesty and truthfulness; but he does not stand alone. He occupies, for instance, the same evil eminence with such men as Mr. Laffan of the New York *Sun*, editorials of whose paper you or others have from time to time called to my attention, just as you have called to my attention these editorials of the Indianapolis *News*. I never see an editorial in any one of these or similar papers unless for some reason it is sent to me by you or by someone else; and of the editorials thus sent me there is hardly one which does not contain some willful and deliberate perversion of the truth. For example, I have just made public the following statement concerning a tissue of utterly false statements which appeared in Mr. Laffan's paper, the *Sun:*

As the New York *Sun* story entitled "Roosevelt and Prairie Oil" has seemed to deceive a number of people, the following statement is made public about it:

As soon as the story was brought to President Roosevelt's attention he not only called for reports concerning the statements from the Department of Justice and the Department of the Interior, but also communicated with ex-Secretary Hitchcock so as to be sure that the President's recollection was not at fault. The story is false in every particular, from beginning to end. Not only is there no such report in the Department of Justice and never has been, but no such report was ever made. In granting the franchise of the Prairie Oil and Gas Company the President simply approved the recommendation of Secretary Hitchcock, submitted to him precisely as all other recommendations were submitted. Moreover, in every case referring to the granting of franchises or the adoption of regulations as regards oil and gas franchises in Oklahoma and the Indian Territory, the President approved the recommendation of Secretary Hitchcock, with the exception of one small and

---

Indianapolis. Ade, a newspaperman who took a serious and active interest in politics, was also the tireless author of stories, sketches, and novels, most of which described with pawky humor the vexations and customs of contemporary life. Booth Tarkington, also a native Hoosier, also a humorist, also interested seriously but not actively in politics, possessed a far larger talent. About the qualities of *Penrod, Penrod and Sam,* or *Seventeen* it is useless either to comment or argue; they are a part of the permanent baggage of our light literature. Tarkington's knowledge of and feeling for the mores of middle-class America, prominently displayed and gaily treated in the three books already mentioned, he projected into several other of his more impressive works. In *The Magnificent Ambersons,* with bitterness, and in *Alice Adams,* with almost a tragic sense, he dealt with the inequities and ambiguities of middle-class life in our towns and cities. On the whole, however, he shrank from the things he knew, or shrouded them in wit or sentimentality, perhaps because he felt this was what a gentleman from Indiana should do.

unimportant grant to a Delaware Indian to whom the Delaware Indians, in recognition of 8 years of service to the tribe, had voted in council a fee of $50,000, which he had declined to accept, and who was given twice the usual amount of land. The statement about the alleged promise to a western Senator is as ridiculous a falsehood as the rest of the story.

The fact is that these particular newspapers, habitually and continually and as a matter of business, practice every form of mendacity known to man, from the suppression of the truth and the suggestion of the false, to the lie direct. Those who write or procure others to write these articles are engaged in the practice of mendacity for hire; and surely there can be no lower form of gaining a livelihood. Whether they are paid by outsiders to say what is false, or whether their profit comes from the circulation of the falsehoods, is a matter of small consequence. It is utterly impossible to attempt to answer all of their falsehoods. When any given falsehood is exposed, they simply repeat it and circulate another. If they were mistaken in the facts, if they possess in their make-up any shred of honesty, it would be worth while to set them right. But there is no question at all as to any "mistake" or "misunderstanding" on their part. They state what they either know to be untrue, or could by the slightest inquiry find out to be untrue. I doubt if they themselves remember their own falsehoods for more than a very brief period; and I doubt still more whether anybody else does. Under these circumstances, it seems hardly worth while to single out for special mention one or two given falsehoods or one particular paper, the moral standard of which is as low as, but no lower than, that of certain other papers. Of course now and then I am willing to denounce a given falsehood, as, for instance, as regards this case of the Indianapolis *News*, or the case I have quoted of the New York *Sun*, simply because it appears that some worthy people are misled or puzzled by the direct shamelessness of the untruth. But ordinarily I do not and cannot pay heed to these falsehoods. If I did, I would not be able to do my work. My plan has been to go ahead, to do the work, and to let these people and those like them yell; and then to trust with abiding confidence to the good sense of the American people in the assured conviction that the yells will die out, the falsehoods be forgotten, and the work remain.

Therefore, as far as I am concerned I would rather make no answer whatever in this case. But I have much confidence in your judgment, and if you feel that these men ought to be exposed, why you are welcome to publish this letter. There is no higher and more honorable calling than that of the men connected with an upright, fearless, and truthful newspaper; no calling in which a man can render greater service to his fellow-countrymen. The best and ablest editors and writers in the daily press render a service to the community which can hardly be paralleled by the service rendered by the best and ablest of the men in public life, or of the men in business. But the converse of this proposition is also true. The most corrupt financiers, the most corrupt politicians, are no greater menace to this country than the newspapermen of the type I have above discust. Whether they belong to the yellow press or to the purchased press, whatever may be the stimulating cause of their slanderous mendacity, and whatever the cloak it may wear, matters but little. In any event they represent one of the potent forces for evil in the community. *Yours very truly*

5040 · TO GEORGE OTTO TREVELYAN *Roosevelt Mss.*

Washington, December 1, 1908

My dear Sir George: I send you a copy of my message to Congress; not to inflict on you the wanton outrage of asking you to read it, but to refer you to the point I have marked on page 2. I know that your legislative and administrative soul will go out in sympathy to me when I mention my pride in the fact that at the close of my administration, in spite of a panic, in spite of the purchase of Panama and of the beginning of the construction of the canal, in spite of having embarked on various schemes that need money, I yet leave the finances a good deal better off than when I found them. We have slightly reduced taxation. We have reduced the interest-bearing debt. We have reduced the amount of interest to be paid on the debt. We have a net surplus of ninety millions of receipts over expenditures for the seven and a half years. I am especially pleased, because the average reformer is apt to embark on all kinds of expenditures for all kinds of things, good in themselves, but which the nation simply cannot afford to pay for.

It was delightful to get your two letters. I congratulate your boy with all my heart. I look forward to seeing him and all of your family when I am in England; and we shall love to visit you at Stratford on Avon, tho I confess I should have particularly liked to see your Northumberland home in the fall, when there was some shooting.

The speech is simply delightful; so good that last night I took it to the Lodges, where we were dining, for I knew that both Senator and Mrs. Lodge would enjoy it as much as Mrs. Roosevelt and I did. Curiously enough, in my Romanes lecture (I have been unable to refrain from inserting therein two of my King Charles the First's heads), I have put in a paragraph or two emphatically insisting upon the duty of applying the moral test in our judgment of public men, and also insisting that no great history will ever be written unless it is a great piece of literature also. I quite agree with you about versified translations of a poet that one can't read in the original. Unless the new man is himself a real poet, and adapts rather than translates, as Fitzgerald did, the result is apt to be pretty poor. But I like Gilbert Murray's recent translations. Still, I prefer prose as a rule. I was interested to find that you loved Dante in Carlyle's prose translation as much as I do. It is one of the limited number of books which I shall take with me on my African trip. The prose translation can be read on one page, and then, even a very poor Italian scholar, as I am, can turn to the other page and get the sweep of the mighty original. In the same way I like the *Chanson de Roland* with the translations into modern French interleaved just as the Carlyle Dante. I have always felt that Scott's and Macaulay's poetry contained passages that gave one a better idea of Homer than any mere translation. The *Nibelungenlied* I am able to read without a translation simply because I am so familiar with it in modern German that I can guess at the archaic terms.

I was greatly interested to hear about Lady Trevelyan being a Unitarian.

The other day there were at lunch at the White House General and Mrs. Buckner of Kentucky. The General is a very fine old fellow; he was a gallant Confederate soldier. He was captured by Grant at Fort Donaldson, and Grant treated him very well; and when Grant, after leaving the Presidency, lost all his money at the hands of some Wall Street swindlers, Buckner instantly came forward and put his own small fortune at Grant's disposal. He is over eighty years old, and last summer there came to visit him a negro, also over eighty, who had been a slave on his father's plantation, and whom he had not seen for some fifty years; and the tottering ex-slave went back at once to the habit of his youth and spoke of the eighty-year-old ex-Confederate General as nothing but "young master" — this to distinguish him from the old master, who had been buried for half a century.

Buckner, by the way, rejoices in the given names, Simon Bolivar; he is of that generation which was named sometimes after the fathers of the Republic, sometimes after every imaginable foreign hero of contemporary or classical times. Cleveland's Minister of the Interior was Lucius Quintus Cincinnatus Lamar, and his Minister to Spain rejoiced in the name Jabez Mirabeau Lamar Curry.[1] They were both very good men, by the way. A noted Kentucky statesman was named Titus Pomponius Atticus Bibb; and a father and son who were big politicians in early Iowa showed great ingenuity in differentiating their names, the father being Caesar Augustus Dodge and the son Augustus Caesar Dodge. Tom Reed's predecessor in Congress was named Lorenzo De Medici Sweat — a name on which it is impossible to improve, so with it I shall close the list.

Mrs. Buckner, who is as delightful as her husband, has a descent that will appeal to you. She is not only a great granddaughter of Washington's sister, and of Mrs. Washington's sister too, but she is also descended from *the* Bishop Burnet — he whose History your uncle put so high. *Faithfully yours*

[1] Roosevelt understandably confused Mirabeau Buonaparte Lamar, second president of the Republic of Texas, with Jabez Lamar Monroe Curry, Cleveland's minister to Spain.

Washington, December 1, 1908

My dear Lord Morley: Last night I was reading the fourth volume of your Miscellanies — with the delight that whatever you write must of course always give. Two or three of the matters you deal with touch me rather closely. Take Comte's encyclopedia of great men. It always made me so indignant that I could not enjoy it. To exclude Calvin and Luther, while including Dominick and Loyola, is simply preposterous. To give Frederick the Great the rank he does for the reasons he assigns, is equally bad. Frederick was a great king and a great general; he comes among the greatest in history; he comes second to Napoleon, of course, and from my point of view he, like Napoleon, should be unsparingly condemned from the moral standpoint when compared with the Timoleon, Hampden, Washington type of public servant. I despise the virtue which springs simply from inefficiency and timidity; but I abhor as base the great powers which are used without reference to moral considerations, and this whether in public or private life.

The exclusion of the great men of the Byzantine Empire (Byzantine is a term that certainly ought to be used, if merely for the reason that only some clumsy paraphrase can replace it) reminds me of a curious slip of Frederic Harrison which I suppose proceeded from the same cause, an instinctive tendency to think of Europe merely as Latin Europe. In Harrison's essay on the Thirteenth Century, in which he sketches in outline the wonderful events of the century, he omits all reference to, and shows that he had no thought of, what was the most wonderful, and also the most harmful and terrible, event for almost the entire civilized world in that century, including the eastern half of Europe; namely, the rise of that fearsome and hideous phenomenon, the Mongol Empire. It was a phenomenon of mere destruction, for the Mongols made, so far as I know, not one single addition, moral or material, to the welfare of mankind. But they were the mightiest conquerors that the world had yet seen. They submerged Russia as a city is submerged by mud from a volcano. They struck Hungary and Poland prostrate. Europe was utterly helpless before them, the mail-clad chivalry of the age being impotent to make even a respectable fight against the Mongol armies. Yet there is not a hint of all this in Frederic Harrison's chapter.

I ought to be ashamed to mention this, by the way, for I have a profound admiration for Frederic Harrison, and admire him much, and such a slip is a mere matter of amusement.

I was delighted with your review of Lecky. It was Lecky's history of the Eighteenth Century which made me a Home-ruler. But he was one of that large class of men who can see things truly only in the far perspective; the "farsighted" man, as oculists would «say», who cannot read the clearest print close by; I think if Carlyle had been caught in the Commune of '71, his comments would have been in strong contrast to what he wrote about the revolution of 1789. As for Lecky, when he spoke of democracy his utterances did not arise to the level of a bad pamphlet. His comments on American affairs were ludicrous. This was partly because they were largely derived from Godkin and *The Nation;* and Godkin established his claims to mental superiority by as thoroly conscienceless and incessant exercise of slander and mendacity as any exemplar of the yellow press. I have been twenty-eight years more or less closely connected with American public life, and for all that time there is not one statement of *The Nation* or *The Evening Post,* under Godkin or Godkin's successors, which I would feel safe in accepting as even presumptively true unless corroborated by outside evidence. Godkin, like Lecky, became so embittered and sour that toward the last he regarded the nation as having insulted him by not going to the dogs. He could not bear to live here. It hurt him not to see disaster come upon the land of which he was an adopted citizen.

Macaulay's prophecy as to what would happen in the State of New York on some given occasion was in its essence curiously falsified by the great election thru which we have just passed. I am an immense admirer of Macaulay; but he was not interested in America, had no knowledge of it, and did not inform himself as to the facts before he wrote the letter in question. As a matter of fact, the American Constitution possesses any amount of anchor. In no other country have the courts such extraordinary power. I think they sometimes abuse their power, but it is always abused in the interest of conservatism and against radicalism — which, as I am personally a radical, may account for some of my feeling that the courts *do* abuse their power!

This last election took place very much under the conditions that Macaulay foretold. We had had a panic. There was great want and suffering among large masses of people. The Republican candidate had fifteen years before, during another panic, resolutely and fearlessly used his power as a judge to check, control, and severely punish workingmen, poor men suffering from hunger and feeling that they were wronged, who had most unwisely and improperly embarked on a career of violence against rich men. Many of these rich men had doubtless themselves been originally the chief offenders, and Taft, owing to the circumstances of the case, was obliged in most instances to use the powers of the courts against the poor man and for the rich man. Opposed to Taft was a kindly demagog who, together with his friends, made every kind of promise and appeal to the multitude; sought in every way to inflame them against Taft because of his labor decisions while on the bench; and appealed, just as Macaulay said they would appeal, to the people who were suffering, to vote "against the wealthy man who drank champagne and rode in a carriage." But we made the fight perfectly straight out, not making a promise we could not keep, flattering no man, apologizing for nothing we had done, and we won an overwhelming victory because we convinced the mass of the people, including the mass of the workingmen, of two things: first and most important, that what Bryan wisht them to do was morally wrong, and that justice and truth and righteousness were on the side of Taft; second, and almost equally important, we were able to appeal to the good sense and intelligence of the workingmen, and to show them that the effort to remedy their condition by bringing disaster upon men of means, was in the end certain to bring greater disaster to everybody. The result was a mighty satisfactory thing from the standpoint of those who believe in the perpetuity of free government, of democratic institutions. I have again and again seen State after State on some one issue follow a demagog, and even for some years act a little on the principle which Macaulay foretold. But in each case the democracy has finally righted itself, the people have come back to sober sense; and in no case has the infection spread over a sufficient area to endanger the nation as a whole.

I have scant sympathy with the people who talk about the failure of the Democratic movement to justify the rosy hopes of those who hailed its advent. In any movement of progress and reform there are always a large number of well-meaning enthusiasts who prophesy the impossible. To compare actual achievement with the impossible hopes of these visionaries, is not to act in good faith. There were a few people who firmly believed that when slavery was abolished the negro, the descendant of the savage who for untold generations had dwelt in African savagery, would in a few years become something between a Periclean Greek and an idealized New Englander. Inasmuch as such anticipations were not in the smallest degree realized, many of the men of little faith have ever since been muttering that no advance came from abolishing slavery — a position even more absurd and untruthful than that of the wildest abolitionist doctrinaires.

Foolish optimism is a stumbling block in the path of sane optimism. I firmly believe that we have good ground for hope for the future. I believe that we have gone forward and not back. This is certainly true of my own country during the last thirty-five years, and, as I believe, for the last hundred and thirty-five years. I think it is true of England. I think it is true of the world. Of course there are times when all humanity drops back, and there are places, at all times, in which humanity drops back. But I do not think that we are in one of the times of recession, and I know that the great progress of mankind has been made in and through countries like England and the United States, where the democratic movement of the kind that we believe in has been strongest, and not in countries like Russia and Spain, countries which really have escaped from the triumph of those forces which our critics assure us are so deleterious in our own cases.

I shall be in England in the spring of 1910, and I hope I shall then see you. I also want to see John Burns.

I grow concerned now and then at what I hear about the unrest in India. I know very little about it save that I realize the immensity of the burden which England has to bear in India; a burden that is now on your shoulders. I feel that on the whole the English rule in India has marked one of the signal triumphs of civilization. I do not suppose that there is any serious menace to it, and I am sure that you will be able gradually to work reform where reform is needed, without permitting yourselves to be overwhelmed by any reform movement gone crazy. If you feel at liberty, do tell me simply for my private information, what the situation in India really is. You will be telling it to a well-wisher. *Sincerely yours*

[*Handwritten*] As I am now ending ten years of much political activity, in which I have held high place, and have been treated with extraordinary confidence and support by the people, I take a satisfaction that you can readily understand in the feeling that during the whole time I have done nothing in which I did not heartily believe, and which, for instance, I would expect you to believe, as we talked things over; this is not especially important, as regards merely myself; but it is important, to us of the democracy, that throughout a decade this attitude should have been amply, and more than amply, rewarded by the mass of the people.

5042 · TO WILLIAM DUDLEY FOULKE   *Roosevelt Mss.*

Washington, December 2, 1908

My dear Foulke: I have received Goodwin's letter which you forwarded on to me. It is all right and I have nothing to suggest. I return it herewith. I have also just received Swift's letter. What a trump he is!

I have announced the classification of all the fourth-class post offices in the eastern and north central States from the Mississippi to the Atlantic coast. I thought that we had better get the thing done as soon as possible and then hurry up the rules.

I enclose the letter about Delavan Smith, and I think it is in pretty good shape now.[1] My addition of Laffan merely strengthens it. I would like, however, that you would either publish it Sunday or Monday morning, or else not until a day or two after my message has gone to Congress, which will be on the 8th of December. I made up my mind to hit the scoundrels, if I wrote at all. I guess you and Swift and . . . . *Faithfully yours*

[1] The letter (No. 5039) was made public on December 7.

Washington, December 2, 1908

My dear Mr. Stone: The other day I was concerned to find from one of the steamship lines, on which it was erroneously announced that I had taken my passage for Africa, that certain newspapermen, representatives of the press associations and individual newspapers, had also taken passage. Now, my trip is to be an entirely private trip, and I very earnestly hope, and shall very earnestly request, that the press associations and the newspapers of this country will under no circumstances send any representative with me, or try to see me or to have interviews with me or report my doings while I am on the trip. As you know, while I have been President I have done my best to give every proper and reasonable facility to every reputable newspaperman to know about all my public acts. Whenever I have gone on an expedition on the public business I have made every preparation for the newspapermen to accompany me, and have made provision for them on special trains if I was myself on one. Even when I went hunting I took the newspapermen with me, up to the point where I left the railroad for the hunt, doing this because they represented to me that inasmuch as I was President the mass of the people expected to follow what I was doing until I actually got into the woods.

But when I start on this African trip I shall have ceased to be President, and shall be simply a private citizen, like any other private citizen. Not only do I myself believe, but I am firmly convinced that the great mass of the American people believe, that when the President leaves public office he should become exactly like any other man in private life. He is entitled to no privileges; but on the other hand, he is also entitled to be treated no worse than anyone else. Now, it will be an indefensible wrong, a gross impropriety from every standpoint, for any newspaper to endeavor to have its representatives accompany me on this trip, or to fail to give me the complete privacy to which every citizen who acts decently and behaves himself is entitled. To send any reporters with me would really be a wanton outrage.[1] It would represent an effort to interfere as far as possible with my individual pleasure and profit in my trip; and moreover, it would result in gaining for the public nothing which would be of the slightest use or profit for the public to know. I have always, as I am sure you know, treated newspapermen with the heartiest good will and cordiality, and many of the friendships I most prize are those with representatives of the press, in all grades. But on this trip, from the time I leave America until the time I return, I shall not knowingly speak to any newspaperman.[2] If any men are sent along with

[1] Although Stone and Lawrence Abbott tried to persuade Roosevelt to modify his position on the reporting of the African trip (see No. 5146), the President continued to insist that his privacy was not to be violated. Consequently the only authentic account of his prolonged hunt is his own.

[2] Roosevelt explained this strong statement in No. 5049.

me I shall so far as possible avoid them, and I shall hold no conversation whatever with them that I can possibly avoid because I wish to have it understood in advance that any statement attributed to me during my absence is to be accepted as false on its face and as requiring no answer or denial from me. Any man who sends what purports to be any statement from me is to be considered as having sent it with full knowledge of the fact that I have already announced that I will not talk to any newspaperman on any subject if I know he is a newspaperman, and that any statement purporting to come from me is to be accepted as false without any need on my part to deny it. Until I actually come to the wilderness my trip will be precisely like any other conventional trip on a steamboat. It will afford nothing to write about, and will give no excuse or warrant for anyone's sending to any newspaper a line in reference thereto. After I reach the wilderness of course no one will be with me, and if anyone pretends to be with me or pretends to write concerning what I do, his statements shall be accepted as, on their face, not merely false but ludicrous. You doubtless remember the absurd falsehoods sent to various sensational newspapers in connection with my mountain lion hunt when I was Vice-President, and my bear hunts in Louisiana and Colorado, and my wolf hunt in Oklahoma, when I was President. In each and every instance the statements purporting to relate what I was doing on my trips were absolutely false. Nobody knew anything genuine until I came out, and prior thereto all statements made were ludicrous inventions. Any man pretending to send information of my trip from Africa will assuredly be a man of bad character who cares nothing for the truth, for no other man would undertake to perform the job, and no man, whether a bad character or not, will have any opportunity of knowing anything I have done. Have you seen the recent accounts in the newspapers of Mr. Bryan's supposed bear hunt in Mexico and his imaginary conflict with a bear? This account was a pure invention, for it now turns out that Mr. Bryan never went bear hunting and never was near a bear. In just the same way any statements made about my African hunt will have to be accepted as, on their face, sheer inventions.

Now it seems to me that I have the right to expect every honorable press association and every honorable newspaper to refuse to enter into any project of having any man accompany me or try to see me during any portion of my trip abroad. As I have said before, I shall then be a private citizen, entitled by every consideration of honorable and fair dealing to enjoy the privacy that should be a private citizen's right. My trip will have no public bearing of any kind, sort or description. It will be undertaken for the National Museum at Washington, and will be simply a collecting trip for the Museum, with nothing about it in the way of exploration or adventure. It will be inexpressibly distasteful to me, and of no possible benefit to any human being, to have any newspapers try to report or exploit the trip, or to send anyone with me, or to have anyone try to see me or meet me with a view to such reporting or exploitation.

Now don't you think that we can get the newspaper press of this country to acquiesce in this view and leave me alone when I am out of office and have left the country? Can't you make the request of the newspapers generally, by circular or otherwise? *Sincerely yours*

5044 · TO ROBERT JOSEPH COLLIER   *Roosevelt Mss.*

Personal   Washington, December 2, 1908

My dear Collier: I am very much obliged to you for your letter, and I shall be very glad to be your guest at the lunch you propose.[1] But please make it a lunch instead of a dinner. I shall be out in the country with Mrs. Roosevelt. It will be our last time together before I leave for the African trip, and I do not want to spend a night away from home. Could not we have it a lunch or breakfast at, say, 12:00 o'clock at the Harvard Club? There is one point only upon which I have any doubt and that is about having Harvey present. He has past the limit as far as I am concerned. I shall never personally have anything to do with him beyond exchanging entirely formal courtesies, because I know he is a liar and I firmly believe that he is a purchased crook. Still, it would be foolish for me to decline to meet him, or Croker, or anyone else, in ordinary, conventional, official intercourse; and as long as I am not in any way responsible for meeting him I do not care. *Sincerely yours*

5045 · TO THE DEPARTMENT OF STATE   *Roosevelt Mss.*

Washington, December 2, 1908

To the State Department: I enclose the draft of what I said so far as my memory serves me. It should be carefully gone over to see if anything ought to be left out.

I take this opportunity to point out two or three matters to which I think the Department should pay heed in the future.

In the first place, I wish to find out from the Department why it permitted the Chinese Ambassador today twice to use the phrase "Your Excellency" in addressing the President. Not only law but wise custom and propriety demand that the President shall be addrest only as "Mr. President" or as "The President." It is wholly improper to permit the use of a silly title like "Excellency" (and incidentally if titles were to be allowed at all, this title is entirely unworthy of the position of the President). Any title is silly when given the President. This title is rather unusually silly. But it is not only silly but inexcusable for the State Department, which ought above all other Departments to be correct in its usage, to permit foreign representa-

[1] A farewell party before the African trip.

tives to fall into the blunder of using this title. I would like an immediate explanation of why the blunder was permitted and a statement in detail as to what has been done by the Department to prevent the commission of any similar blunder in the future.

Now, as to the address itself. I did not deliver it as handed me because it was fatuous and absurd. I have already had to correct the ridiculous telegram that was drafted for me to send to China on the occasion of the death of the Emperor and the Empress Dowager. I do not object to the utter fatuity of the ordinary addresses made to me by, and by me to, the representatives of foreign governments when they come to me to deliver their credentials or to say good-by. The occasion is merely formal and the absurd speeches interchanged are simply rather elaborate ways of saying good morning and good-by. It would of course be better if they were less absurd and if we had a regular form to be used by the Minister and by the President on all such occasions, the form permitting of the slight variations which would be necessary in any particular case. It seems to me that some such form could be devised, just as we use special forms in the absurd and fatuous letters I write to Emperors, Apostolic Kings, Presidents, and the like — those in which I address them as "Great and Good Friend," and sign myself "Your good friend." These letters are meaningless; but perhaps on the whole not otherwise objectionable, when formally and conventionally announcing that I have sent a minister or ambassador or that I have received one. They strike me as absurd and fatuous, only when I congratulate the sovereigns on the birth of babies, with eighteen or twenty names, to people of whose very existence I have never heard; or condole with them on the deaths of unknown individuals. Still if trouble would be caused by abandoning this foolish custom, then it would be far more foolish to cause the trouble than it is to keep to the custom.

But on a serious occasion, as in the present instance where a statesman of rank has come here on a mission which may possess real importance, then there should be some kind of effort to write a speech that shall be simple, & that shall say something, or, if this is deemed inexpedient, that shall at least not be of a fatuity so great that it is humiliating to read it. It should be reasonably grammatical, and should not be wholly meaningless. In the draft of the letter handed me, for instance, I am made to say of the letter I receive: "I accept it with quite exceptional sentiments as a message of especial friendship." Of course any boy in school who wrote a sentence like that would be severely and properly disciplined. The next sentence goes on: "I receive it with the more profound sentiments in that you bring it now no less from the Emperor." What in Heaven's name did the composer of this epistle mean by "more profound sentiments" and "quite exceptional sentiments"? Cannot he write ordinary English? Continuing, at the end of the same sentence he speaks of the new Government and what he anticipates from it, in terms that would not be out of place in a prophecy about Alexander the Great on the occasion of his accession to the throne of Macedon. Politeness is necessary, but gushing and obviously insincere and untruthful compliments merely make both sides ridiculous; and are underbred in addition.[1]

5046 · TO WILLIAM BAYARD HALE   *Roosevelt Mss.*

Personal — Private: not for publication   Washington, December 3, 1908

My dear Dr. Hale: I have your letter of the 1st instant. One of the disadvantages of needed reforms is that together with the good they do they also now and then work an irritating limitation on the power to do some specific act which would be good in itself, but the performance of which is incompatible with the general scheme. All appointments in the consular service are now made to the lowest grade, and promotions are made on merit. Of this system I know you would approve, but it bars me out from making use

[1] Roosevelt prepared the following address as a substitute for the draft of the Department of State:

"Mr. Ambassador:

"It is a real pleasure to me to receive the letter you bear, and on behalf of the Government and people of the United States I accept it as a message of especial friendship from your August Sovereign, whose death, and the death of Her Imperial Majesty, the late Empress Dowager, have caused us grave concern and have aroused our sincere sympathy for your people.

"In receiving it under these circumstances I accept it also as coming from the Emperor whose accession to the throne is celebrated today and who has our most earnest good wishes for his future. It is our hope and belief, a hope and belief shared by the civilized nations of the world, that his reign will revive and perpetuate all that is best and greatest in the immemorial history of China.

"Therefore, Mr. Ambassador, I welcome you earnestly and cordially because of my feeling for the great country from which you come. I no less welcome you in your personal capacity. It is a pleasure to receive as His Imperial Majesty's Special Ambassador so distinguished a statesman as yourself, a man in whose integrity and capacity we have the highest confidence, a man whose reputation is such as to make his coming here a deeply appreciated compliment. I know you have been in the United States before and I hope your present sojourn will be most agreeable.

"I ask you to express to your August Sovereign and to the Chinese Government the appreciation of the Government and of the people of the United States of the sending of this special embassy. We accept it as a fresh manifestation of the confidence, good will and friendship existing between the United States and the Chinese Empire. We on our part will do all we can to foster this confidence, good will and friendship.

"I speak to you in no perfunctory manner. I feel it to be the duty of every powerful civilized nation to use its influence in securing justice and fair dealing for China. This Nation certainly intends to act justly itself, and it earnestly hopes that all other nations will show a like intention. Above all, our hope is, so far as the opportunity and the power permit, to aid those Chinese citizens who in working for the betterment of conditions in China, in working to bring China abreast of the general movement of civilized mankind, are showing themselves to be the truest friends and supporters of the ancient Chinese Empire. I believe that the world now realizes more than ever before that normally it is to the advantage, and not to the disadvantage, of other nations when any nation becomes stable and prosperous, able to keep the peace within its own borders, and strong enough not to invite aggression from without. We heartily hope for the progress of China, and so far as by peaceful and legitimate means we are able we will do our part toward furthering that progress."

1407

of you as I should otherwise be delighted to make use of you. It is possible, but not probable, that in some way we could use you as a special agent for Haiti.[1] The trouble as regards Haiti is not that the Government fails to understand the situation, but that the people, especially the educated people, refuse to understand it. The *Times* and *Evening Post*, for instance, represent a large constituency which was lukewarm or hostile to what I did about Santo Domingo — than which nothing so good for Santo Domingo has ever been done. I got it thru the Senate by two years' hard work, without a particle of aid from what likes to call itself the "educated conscience" of the people of the country. Now, in Haiti, what we need is something that will show our people that this Government, in the name of humanity, morality, and civilization, ought to exercise some kind of supervision over the island; but this should be done as a part of our general scheme of dealing with the countries around the Caribbean. In Cuba, Santo Domingo and Panama we have interfered in various different ways, and in each case for the immeasurable betterment of the people. I would have interfered in some similar fashion in Venezuela, in at least one Central American State, and in Haiti already, simply in the interest of civilization, if I could have waked up our people so that they would back a reasonable and intelligent foreign policy which should put a stop to crying disorders at our very doors. Such a policy would be a little in our own interest, but much more in the interest of the peoples in whose affairs we interfered. I think Mexico would have gone in with ⟨me⟩ us, on a rational policy. But in each case where I have actually interfered — Cuba, Santo Domingo, and Panama, for instance — I have had to exercise the greatest care in order to keep public opinion here with me so as to make my interference effective, and I have been able to lead it along as it ought to be led only by minimizing my interference and showing the clearest necessity for it. In the other cases I have mentioned, tho the need was great, it was not as great as those in which I did take action, and the need could not have been as clearly shown to our people. Our prime necessity is that public opinion should be properly educated.

Any time you are here, do not fail to let me see you. *Sincerely yours*

5047 · TO FRANK HARRIS HITCHCOCK   *Roosevelt Mss.*

Washington, December 3, 1908

My dear Mr. Hitchcock: Messrs. W. J. Massie and Clark Grier are to visit you soon. They represent the Taft clubs of Georgia, who were instrumental

[1] Haiti had been visited by another revolution, "one of the most orderly," the American minister reported, "that has occurred in Haiti for many years." It was the second revolt, the first to succeed, for the calendar year, 1908. Roosevelt sent no agent and took no other action.

in getting the remarkable vote we received in Georgia.[1] Every care should be taken to put Georgia on a good basis. I am confident that it would be a mistake to disturb the Taft organizations there, and above all, a mistake to have it supposed that they were upset merely by officeholders. We have a very fine set of men who have come to us in Georgia, and we should encourage and build them up just as we should encourage and build up our people in any part of the North.[2]

With hearty regard, believe me, *Sincerely yours*

5048 · TO CHARLES JOSEPH BONAPARTE   *Roosevelt Mss.*

Washington, December 3, 1908

The Attorney General: I think that Judge Gunnison ought to be reappointed.[1] Has the Department information that would make it feel the other way? I haven't a doubt that sometimes he is slow, but I also have no doubt that the real ground of opposition to him is that he has been closing the dance halls and gambling joints. Several years of experience of Alaskan officials makes me feel that if we get one who cannot be successfully accused of breaking say seven out of the ten commandments, we have done rather well, and if nothing but slowness is alleged against a man, and he is honest, I think we ought to stand by him.

5049 · TO MELVILLE ELIJAH STONE   *Roosevelt Mss.*

Washington, December 4, 1908

My dear Mr. Stone: I showed to Mr. Frank B. Noyes the letter I wrote you,[1] and on his suggestion, to prevent a possible misapprehension, I wish to explain that when I said I would not knowingly speak to a newspaperman I of course did not mean that I, who would then be a newspaperman myself in a sense, would not speak to my colleagues engaged in a similar business. Of course what I meant was that I would not knowingly speak to a newspaperman for publication or on any subject concerning which I had the slightest idea that he was talking with me with a view of publication. Of course I should treat any newspaperman with the civility with which I would treat anyone else, and naturally if I met friends who happened to be newspaper-

---

[1] The Democrats in 1908 carried Georgia by their smallest plurality in any national election between 1896 and the present. The unusual Republican strength rested in part on the organization of the Taft clubs which overcame the inertia of the Republican faction of Judson W. Lyons.

[2] Roosevelt sent a similar analysis to Taft.

---

[1] Roosevelt renominated Royal Arch Gunnison, United States District Judge at Juneau, Alaska. The Senate, however, did not confirm the nomination nor did Taft renew it.

---

[1] No. 5043.

men, I would greet them as I would friends in any other profession. *Sincerely yours*

5050 · TO WHITELAW REID

Roosevelt Mss.

Washington, December 4, 1908

My dear Mr. Ambassador: I was much interested in what you said, not only about plans for the reform of the House of Lords, but about the Kaiser. Literally I don't dare to put on paper all I know about these last interviews of the Kaiser and the light shed on his statements by what he had previously stated to me in connection with the Charlemagne Tower, Hill and Griscom imbroglio. I am amused by the statements made to you that the difference between the Kaiser and myself was "that I made good." That is literally true. I have never yet failed to do what I said I would do if called upon to do it! On this point also I wish someday to tell you for your own information the inside history of my relations with the Kaiser at the time of the Venezuela matter, of the message I finally felt obliged to send him, and of its instantaneous effect.[1] The recent voyage of the fleet around the world was not the first occasion in which I have used it to bring about prompt resumption of peaceful relations between this country and a foreign Power. But of course one of the conditions of such use is that it should be accompanied with every manifestation of politeness and friendship — manifestations which are sincere, by the way, for the foreign policy in which I believe is in very fact the policy of speaking softly and carrying a big stick. I want to make it evident to every foreign nation that I intend to do justice; and neither to wrong them nor to hurt their self-respect; but that on the other hand, I am both entirely ready and entirely able to see that our rights are maintained in their turn.

I wish I could see you and tell you all these things in person, but that looks unlikely at present.

On the way out to Mombasa I shall simply stop for the necessary day at Naples to change steamers, and I suppose for the two or three hours at Gibraltar and Suez that the steamers stop at those places. On these occasions I assume that I will be able to avoid all official functions whatever. I have an excellent reason for this course, because I particularly do not want to take any but the very simplest outfit of civilized clothing to Africa, and so I shall be in no condition either to receive or return visits of ceremony.

Do let the Foreign Office tell the British authorities in British East Africa and Uganda that, if I get into trouble with newspaper people trying to follow me, they will prevent their doing so away from the line of the railroad. Of

[1] Roosevelt had already described this episode to Reid (see No. 3691). The effect of the alleged ultimatum to the Kaiser on Venezuela had, as the years passed, become for Roosevelt "instantaneous." He was gradually building up to the celebrated account he gave to Thayer in 1916.

course I understand that in the big towns like Mombasa and Nairobi and on the railroad and on the steamboat lines alike I cannot expect to dodge reporters, but I do not want there to be any chance of their getting up a caravan and trying to follow me.

With warm regards, *Sincerely yours*

[*Handwritten*] P.S I really like, and in a way admire, him (the Kaiser), I wish he would not have brain storms.

5051 · TO WILLIAM GARROTT BROWN   *Roosevelt Mss.*

Washington, December 5, 1908

My dear Mr. Brown: Lodge has shown me your letter and I send you this thru him. I thank you sincerely for writing. You need not bother your head again about my letter to Gilder. Your letter makes it all right. I don't in the least mind people being mistaken about me. All I mind is willful and malicious misstatement; and now that your letter makes it clear that you had simply been led into error, why, my dear sir, don't think twice of the matter again.

You see, one reason why I felt indignant was that I had read your writings with great interest and admiration, and felt that you were exactly the southerner whom I was trying to represent, whose views I firmly believed I was meeting! If you had lived in Alabama, for instance, I would have certainly made you one of the much-talked-of "referees." Is there the slightest chance of your being in Washington? I should like to tell you in person the various struggles I made, and the misadventures I met with, in the painful endeavor to help build up a reputable Republican, or if not that, a reputable independent, organization in the different States in the South, trying one way in one State and one way in another. *Sincerely yours*

5052 · TO CHARLES STILLMAN SPERRY   *Roosevelt Mss.*

Washington, December 5, 1908

My dear Admiral: I am immensely interested and pleased with your letter of the 28th of October. I had already ordered the Department to arrange for painting the ships war color, and shall jog their memories again. My dear Admiral, I cannot overstate the pleasure and pride with which I have followed you. You have done your work in masterly manner. I look forward with the keenest interest to the 22d of February, when, off Hampton Roads, I shall see your fleet lift above the horizon.

I don't know whether I am most interested in what you say about the reception by Japan, or in what you say about the way in which the cruise has turned out a perpetual war game for the fleet. I am not only interested but amused and somewhat puzzled at the Emperor's being relieved by my taking the initiative and sending him a telegram first. It seemed to me perfectly natural in view of the way they were behaving. I anticipated good in every way from the voyage of the fleet; but it has far more than come up to my anticipations. *Sincerely yours*

5053 · TO GEORGE RUMSEY SHELDON   *Roosevelt Mss.*

Washington, December 5, 1908

Dear George: I enclose you an alleged report of your speech in which I have marked a paragraph. I am confident it is a misreport. Of course you know as well as I do that this is not the first time that a President of the United States goes into office without a single obligation being pledged to any man. No reputable man even among my opponents has ever dared to suggest that there was any pledge or obligation of any kind direct or indirect entered into by me or by my authorization before my election or at any other time. Doubtless you recall the public statement to this effect made by Chairman Cortelyou just before the close of my campaign.

Of course I should not write you this letter if I for one moment thought you had spoken as you are reported to have spoken. I merely call your attention to this misreport of what you said. *Sincerely yours*

5054 · TO RUSSELL BENJAMIN HARRISON   *Roosevelt Mss.*

Personal   Washington, December 7, 1908

My dear Harrison: I concluded to make public what I had to say about Delavan Smith in another way, and information I have now leads me to think that one sentence that I wrote you was not warranted, so I shall be much obliged, if you still have my letter,[1] if you will return it to me.

With regard, believe me, *Sincerely yours*

5055 · TO JOHN DALZELL   *Roosevelt Mss.*

Washington, December 7, 1908

My dear Mr. Dalzell: I see your comments as reported in the newspapers this morning upon the proposed hunting trip.[1] If you are correctly reported, I can only regret that you did not take the trouble to find out the facts before

---

[1] See No. 4973.

[1] Dalzell, a member of the board of regents of the Smithsonian Institution, had stated that the board had not and probably would not authorize any expenditures for Roosevelt's trip to Africa. With other opponents of Roosevelt Dalzell argued that Congress could not validly appropriate funds for such a purpose. As Roosevelt explained, however, the Smithsonian had granted a sum from a private donation over which the regents had no control. That money, furthermore, was to defray none of Roosevelt's personal expenses. Secretary Walcott, in a public statement, confirmed Roosevelt's rebuttal to Dalzell and added that the institution, in his opinion, would gain "much of value to the government" from the trip.

speaking. I am going on a scientific trip to Africa. I take my son with me. I pay every penny of my own expenses and those of my son. I have notified the Smithsonian that I will give it the specimens I collect. If I am successful this will mean a gift of a collection of very great value, pecuniary and otherwise. All the Smithsonian does is, by the use of funds provided especially for the purpose and no part of which is derived from any Government appropriation, to pay for three field naturalists and taxidermists who shall prepare and ship home the specimens. I do not receive anything whatever from the Government. I give the Government much of value. The Government is put to no expense, and its share in the transaction is limited to receiving a very valuable gift. Under such circumstances it seems to me ungracious to a degree for any representative of the Government to say anything that can be construed as finding fault with the arrangement. *Sincerely yours*

5056 · TO TRUMAN HANDY NEWBERRY   *Roosevelt Mss.*

Washington, December 7, 1908

To the Secretary of the Navy: Have regulations been issued providing that hereafter all our ships shall be painted war color? This should be done forthwith.

Moreover, what orders have been issued to permit the enlisted men to visit their homes soon after the ships return? For various reasons I think this most important.[1]

5057 · TO DENNIS JOSEPH O'CONNELL   *Roosevelt Mss.*

Washington, December 7, 1908

My dear Bishop O'Connell: I am glad you called about Marquise Wentworth.[1] I wish in the strongest manner to protest against her being given the chance to paint frightful daubs of prominent men because unwise friends of hers and of these prominent men ask that she be given sittings. I gave her a sitting purely because Father Doyle asked me to. The picture she painted was a travesty. She then called upon Ambassador White and insisted that he should force the French Academy to give it a good place and make an international issue of the refusal of the French Academy to place a wretched picture where it ought not to be put. Bishop O'Gorman took her to see Mr. Taft, just as Father Doyle took her to see me.

Now, my dear Bishop O'Connell, a good painter is a good painter, with-

[1] Newberry issued leave orders for enlisted personnel serving on the ships of the White Fleet.

---

[1] Cecile Smith de Wentworth while still Cecilia Smith studied in Paris in the studios of Cabanel and Detaille. For thirty years she exhibited portraits and paintings on religious themes in French galleries. The winner of many medals, a marquise by papal designation, she painted, among others, Presidents Roosevelt and Taft, Archbishop Corrigan, Cardinal Ferrata, Queen Alexandra, Pope Leo XIII, and General Pershing.

out regard to his or her creed. I feel that no Methodist bishop or Baptist or Presbyterian clergyman would have a right to request Taft or me or any other public man to be painted by some individual who cannot paint, because that individual happens to be a Baptist, a Methodist, or a Presbyterian. I have now and then been victimized by painters who had no business to be allowed to paint me, because I yielded to the request of some well-meaning friend. I shall do all I can to protect Taft from each of these same painters.

Do let me see you soon. *Sincerely yours*

5058 · TO PHILANDER CHASE KNOX   *Roosevelt Mss.*

Washington, December 8, 1908

My dear Senator: Mr. Oscar King Davis of the New York *Times* is trying to look into that Panama Canal transaction, and he has asked me for information that I am not able to furnish.[1] I do not know whether it can be furnished at all, but if it can be I suppose you would know more about it than anyone else.[2] He wants to get at the stock books of the Panama Canal Companies, old and new, if possible, to find out the votes by which the stockholders agreed to the various transactions with the United States Government. Did this Government obtain those stock books, or any records which would show who the stockholders were? If not, have you any idea where we could obtain any information about such records? *Sincerely yours*

[*Handwritten*] *Who* is to be investigated by congress in this matter? You? or are you & I both to appear before a Senate Committee? [3]

5059 · TO WILLIAM NELSON CROMWELL   *Roosevelt Mss.*

Washington, December 8, 1908

My dear Mr. Cromwell: A friend of mine has asked me for certain facts about the Panama Canal transaction as to which I should be obliged for any information you can give me.

Is there any way of getting at the stock books of the Panama Canal Companies, old and new, or any official record of the votes of the stockholders on the different proposals made to them for entering into agreement with the United States for the sale of their rights in Panama? [1]

[1] Davis had begun his investigation before the publication on December 7 of Roosevelt's letter to Foulke.
[2] Knox, as Attorney General in 1904, had handled the mechanics of the transactions. The stock books to which Roosevelt referred were still in France. Cromwell, however, at Roosevelt's request supplied some of the more significant of these records; see No. 5059.
[3] On December 7, Democratic Congressman Henry T. Rainey of Illinois had filed a resolution demanding a congressional investigation of the canal purchase. The resolution did not come to a vote.

[1] For the records of the old and new Panama Company which Cromwell sent Roosevelt, see No. 5061.

Did the United States Government ever get possession of any of these data? If not, can you tell me where they can be obtained, if in private possession here in America, or where they can be lookt up in France?

With regard, *Sincerely yours*

5060 · TO PHILANDER CHASE KNOX   *Roosevelt Mss.*

Washington, December 8, 1908

My dear Senator: I had Hoyt[1] in at once, as it was on his statement that I made my statement. It is after all a mere quibble over words. We paid the money to the liquidator in accordance with the decree of the Civil Tribunal of the Seine, and in accordance with this decree proportioned the amount between the old and new companies. There was a form of ministerial approval or acquiescence, as Mr. Hoyt informs me; but even if there was not, the act of the Civil Tribunal was of course the act of the French Government. By French Government I do not mean necessarily the French administration. The decree of the court here is a governmental act of the United States, even tho it is made by a judicial and not by an executive officer. I am greatly obliged to you for writing me. *Sincerely yours*

[*Handwritten*] Hoyt will issue a statement at once. I write you so quickly because I do'n't want the World quoting you as if I had made a misstatement.[2]

5061 · TO HENRY LEWIS STIMSON   *Roosevelt Mss.*

Washington, December 9, 1908

My dear Stimson: I do not know anything about the law of criminal libel, but I should dearly like to have it invoked about Pulitzer, of the *World*.[1]

[1] Henry Martyn Hoyt.

[2] The *World* on December 8 accused Roosevelt of making "deliberate misstatements of fact in his scandalous personal attack upon Delavan Smith" in his letter to Foulke which had been made public the previous day (see No. 5039). Payment was not made directly to the French government, the *World* asserted, but to J. P. Morgan and Company. The French government did not, as Roosevelt had stated, distribute the funds; they were divided between the old and new Panama Canal companies. Finally the *World* condemned as untrue the President's denial of the existence of a syndicate. The issue, the *World* concluded, was no longer the connection of Charles Taft or Douglas Robinson with the "Panama exploitation," it was now the veracity of the President of the United States. For Roosevelt's reactions to this editorial see No. 5061.

[1] Thoroughly aroused by the *World's* editorial of December 8 Roosevelt, after a brief consultation with Stimson and Bonaparte, decided to bring a libel suit. On December 15 the President sent a message to Congress which asserted that the stories about the Panama purchase in the *World* and the Indianapolis *News* "consist simply of a string of infamous libels, ... upon Mr. Taft and Mr. Robinson for instance. But they are in fact wholly, and in form partly, a libel upon the United States Government." Condemning the editor of the *World* as the "real offender," the President told Congress that "the Attorney-General has under consideration the form in which the proceedings against Mr. Pulitzer shall be brought."

Usually, papers in making charges do not ascribe improper motives of financial interest, but the *World* made the mistake of doing it in this instance. Pulitzer is one of these creatures of the gutter of such unspeakable degrada-

---

Roosevelt then gave a brief account of the purchase from the French company and described the numerous documents he was transmitting with the message. These documents, printed letters and records, also contained the information Cromwell had sent the President (see No. 5059), which included the following: a complete list of the stockholders of the Compagnie Nouvelle du Canal de Panama as of January 15, 1900; a list of all the stockholders present at the special meeting of that company held on February 28, 1902, to decide on the sale of their property to the United States government; and a certified copy of the final report of the liquidation of the Compagnie Universelle du Canal Interoceanique (the old Panama company), filed June 25, 1907, together with a summary account of the company's affairs written by the liquidator. Roosevelt also transmitted the two resolutions and the vote upon them made at the final meeting of the new company held April 24, 1904. Congress, after acknowledging receipt of the documents, forwarded them to the Committee on Interstate and Foreign Commerce of each House.

In considering Roosevelt's message and the resulting libel suit, two problems arise: first, the validity of the *World's* charges, and secondly, the advisability of bringing the suit. While there seems little doubt that the *World's* statements had no basis of truth and were, in fact, libelous, there is also little question that Roosevelt's action in having the government institute a libel suit because of these remarks was ill-advised. For the legal and constitutional aspects of the suit see No. 5072.

Roosevelt was quite correct when he wrote Knox that the *World's* charges concerning the President's "deliberate misstatements of fact" was "a mere quibble over words" (see No. 5060). The transaction was a perfectly routine one. J. P. Morgan and Company merely acted as fiscal agent to transfer the funds to the Bank of France. The funds were then apportioned to the creditors and stockholders of the old and new Panama companies in accordance with a decree of the French courts. The certified copy of the liquidator's report which Roosevelt sent to Congress described the transaction, while the list of stockholders at the new company's final meeting indicated who received that company's share of the funds.

The *World's* major accusation that a syndicate of financiers who were closely connected with the Administration had exploited the canal purchase remains completely unproved. An extended search by agents of the *World* in Paris, Bogotá, and Panama failed to disclose the existence of such a syndicate or to reveal evidence of fraud or corruption in the purchase of the properties of the French company. The *World's* representatives did claim that the French government prevented them from examining the records of the two canal companies. But by French law records of liquidation and receivership were placed on file in a depository selected by the government for reference if evidence of fraud should arise, and Pulitzer's agents had no such evidence. Moreover they refused the French government's offer to let them examine witnesses to create such evidence; see *The Roosevelt Panama Libel Case Against The New York "World"* (New York, 1911), pp. 20–21; J. M. Barrett, *Joseph Pulitzer and his "World"* (New York, 1941), p. 245.

The *World*, however, made much of the Panama Canal Company of America, a New Jersey corporation organized by Cromwell in 1899. This company was, as Roosevelt pointed out in his message and as the testimony in the Rainey Resolution hearings of 1912 also showed, a well-known project to "Americanize" the French canal company. In February 1899 Cromwell, to make the Panama route more acceptable to Congress, had suggested to the House Committee on Rivers and Harbors and to President McKinley that the French company be reorganized as an American corporation. Although the proposition had been unanimously approved in October 1899 by the directors in France, it was dropped shortly after the legal incorporation because of the strong opposition of the French stockholders. As Henry N. Hall, a representative of the *World*, later testified: "This company filed no report in Trenton, and, so far as the records show, did nothing." — *Hearings on the Rainey Resolution*, pp. 151–154.

tion that to him even eminence on a dunghill seems enviable, and he evidently hopes I will place him there beside Laffan and Delavan Smith. Heaven knows that they occupy a sufficiently low stratum of infamy, but Pulitzer has plumbed depths even lower and I do not wish to put him beside them unless it is necessary; this aside from the fact that when I was Police Commissioner I once for all summed him up by quoting the close of Macaulay's article about Barère as applying to him.[2] But if he can be reached by a proceeding on the part of the Government for criminal libel in connection with his assertions about the Panama Canal, I should like to do it. Would you have his various utterances for the last three or four months on this subject lookt up, and let me know? *Faithfully yours*

5062 · TO CHARLES JOSEPH BONAPARTE   *Roosevelt Mss.*

Washington, December 9, 1908

My dear Mr. Bonaparte: I have your letter of the 8th. My directions in connection with the Anaconda smelter matter are that we shall look carefully before we leap. No suit of this size and importance should be entered into by the Government until it has fully and carefully thought out what the consequences will be. The court must do its part, but the executive department must do its part also. The allegation is made that if this suit should be successful, not only Anaconda but Butte would be ruined, but practically the whole copper producing industry would be brought to a stop. Part of this allegation is that tens of thousands of workingmen would be completely thrown out of employment, and half the State of Montana suffer seriously. The Government is bringing the suit on the ground that the forests and grazing lands, and incidentally the waters, in the neighborhood of the smelters are destroyed. Before bringing the suit we should as a mere matter of common sense find out whether if successful we save some destruction at the cost of destroying twenty times as much property ourselves. The suit is especially important because of its relations to many other suits of the same kind that can be or should be carried on in other parts of the country. Such allegations as those made by seemingly responsible people, including the two Montana Senators, one Massachusetts Senator, and the leading business and labor associations of Butte and Anaconda should as a matter of course receive our careful consideration. I wish to know the facts before proceeding. I regard the fact of the damage to vegetation within a certain area of the smelter as established. I do not regard as established the allegation by the defendants that the smelters would have to stop completely if the suit was successful. I pay heed to the statement made on behalf of the Government that unless these parties are forced to by law, they will not stop their destructive proceedings, because expense will be involved in stopping them. But I wish to

[2] Macaulay's words were: "Renegade, traitor, slave, coward, liar, slanderer, murderer, hack writer, police-spy — the one small service which he could render to England, was to hate her: and such as he was may all who hate her be!"

know something about the expense, whether it really does represent prohibitive expense, which would mean the closing up of the works, or whether it merely represents a heavy necessary expense which can and should be borne and which will allow the work to be done, but only under conditions that prevent its being noxious to the vegetation round about.

The facts being as above, it seems to me imperative that there shall be a full and careful investigation before we go on with the suit.[1] To follow any other course would be, it seems to me, to act without regard to the interests of the people of Montana, and elsewhere. *Sincerely yours*

5063 · TO WILLIAM HOWARD TAFT   *Taft Mss.*

Memorandum   Washington, December 10, 1908

Men who have been staunch adherents of Mr. Taft under stress of adverse assault in positions not of the first rank:[1]

J. B. Bishop, Secretary Isthmian Canal Commission.
Joseph Murray, Deputy Commissioner of Immigration.
William W. Sewall, Collector of Customs in Maine.
Seth Bullock, Marshal, South Dakota.
Ben Daniels, Marshal, Arizona.
Miss Robertson, Postmaster at Muskogee.
   (Peculiarly high-minded and good woman.)
Charles W. Anderson, Collector of Internal Revenue, New York.
Maurice Francis Egan, Minister to Denmark.
Edgar S. Wilson, U. S. Marshal, Mississippi.
U. S. Marshal Tyree: ⎫
U. S. Marshal Elliott: ⎬ West Virginia
   Were original Taft men and instrumental in securing Taft delegation
      in that State.
[*Handwritten*] Jimmie Sloan, for Marshal in Ill.

5064 · TO PHILANDER CHASE KNOX   *Roosevelt Mss.*

Washington, December 10, 1908

My dear Senator Knox: Your letter in answer to mine about the Panama Canal stories gives all the facts so far as this Government is interested, but it

---

[1] After making a thorough investigation, Bonaparte late in January recommended bringing suit against the Anaconda and the Amalgamated Copper companies. Roosevelt then wrote Bonaparte that even though the evidence produced by the Justice Department warranted immediate proceedings, he thought it unwise to institute such an important suit in the last days of his term; see No. 5179.

---

[1] Although Roosevelt did not request Taft to give appointments to any of those he listed except Sewall (see No. 5079), he obviously considered them all deserving of appointments. His opinion influenced Taft, who arranged all but two assignments, those of Murray and Sloan, as Roosevelt suggested.

seems to me a least well worth considering whether it would not be wise once for all to nail the infamous and slanderous falsehoods of Mr. Pulitzer, published in his paper, the New York *World,* and of those who have taken their cue from the Pulitzer publications. Mr. Cromwell has sent on to me the complete lists of the stockholders of the Panama Canal Companies, the complete set of papers as to what those companies did in connection with our purchase of the canal, and a copy of a statement which he is about to make, together with the enclosed answer to a letter I sent him at the time I wrote to you a few days ago. Why would it not be a good thing for me to send all this matter in to the Senate or to the House, of my own motion?[1] Of course the whole attack in no shape or way touches any action of this Government. We had no more concern with who the stockholders of the Panama Company were, or what their relations to one another were, than a man has with the actions of the stockholders of a carriage-building company when he purchases a buggy. We had the same interest that the man who buys the buggy has; that is, we wished to be sure that the property was of value and that a clear title passed. But it might be well to make public these documents which Mr. Cromwell has sent me, entirely of his own accord and without my having the slightest right to ask for them. After the first falsehoods were published in the *World,* stating that Mr. Douglas Robinson, my brother-in-law, was implicated in the business, Mr. Cromwell directed Mr. Farnham, one of his partners, who was in Paris at the time, to secure copies of these papers and send them over to him. The originals are in Paris and can be examined by anyone who desires to do so. Mr. Cromwell notifies me thru Mr. Farnham that in case anybody in Congress desires to make an investigation, he will submit all these papers to him, and he will ask that both the Mr. Pulitzers, Mr. Alexander Bacon,[2] Mr. Van Hamm,[3] the editor of the *World,* and any other person connected with the circulation of these lying and slanderous statements, be brought before the committee and examined to see if they have any basis for their allegations. *Faithfully yours*

5065 · TO FRANCIS JOSEPH HENEY   *Roosevelt Mss.*

Washington, December 11, 1908

My dear Mr. Heney: I shall keep your letter always, and hand it on to my children. You are one of the Americans of whom I not merely feel proud, but whose deeds, whose high courage, high integrity, and entire disinterestedness of devotion to the country make me thrill with enthusiasm. When I learned of your assassination — for as such it was first reported to me — my

---

[1] This Roosevelt did on December 15.
[2] Colonel Alexander S. Bacon, a bitter opponent of Roosevelt in 1899 and 1900, had been quoted by the *World* in its first attack on Panama as saying "I tried to expose this syndicate as far back as 1904, when the United States bought the canal." Bacon on the following day denounced the story of the interview as a "fabrication."
[3] Caleb Marsh Van Hamm was editor of the *World* from 1903 to 1910.

grief was swallowed up in anger and eager desire to further the great work in which you had shown your entire willingness to sacrifice your own life. My sorrow for you was outweighed by my admiration for you, my pride in your life, and in the very fact that this life had been led so as to cause you nearly to be stricken to death. But for dear Mrs. Heney I felt the most abounding tenderness and sympathy. Give her my warmest and most affectionate regard. I am so pleased that you are almost recovered and without so much as a scar; but for Heaven's sake, don't take any chances. Follow your physicians' advice. Thank Heaven, you have convicted Ruef. Now I hope the others will be convicted in due time, from the big businessman straight thru to the corrupt public official. *Always yours*

5066 · TO THE DEPARTMENT OF STATE *Roosevelt Mss.*

Washington, December 12, 1908

To the State Department: I desire to make certain changes in the State Department. Mr. Wilson's name will be sent in at once for Roumania. Mr. Phillips will be appointed forthwith to Mr. Wilson's place. I have carefully considered this matter and direct that these instructions be carried out.[1]

5067 · TO WILLIAM BAYARD CUTTING *Roosevelt Mss.*

Washington, December 12, 1908

My dear Cutting: How could anyone be anything but complimented at what you said to me yesterday? Believe me, I was not only pleased, but touched. Why, of course the President of the United States or anyone else can well afford to take the mayoralty. I can afford to take *any* office in which I can do really good work for the people; but this is not the kind of job that I could do good work in. *Sincerely yours*

5068 · TO GEORGE WASHINGTON GOETHALS *Roosevelt Mss.*

Washington, December 13, 1908

My dear Colonel Goethals: I intend to send Mr. Taft down to the Isthmus in January, together with four or five of the best engineers in the country, for

---

[1] Roosevelt promoted William Phillips from Chief of the Division of Far Eastern Affairs to Third Assistant Secretary of State after consulting Root and Taft (see No. 5110). Phillips had performed well in his office, whereas Root had found Huntington Wilson his least congenial subordinate. Wilson, however, did not leave Washington. Appointed minister to Roumania in December and to Argentina in January, he took neither post. In March, Taft, to Root's dismay, made him First Assistant Secretary of State. Taft moved Phillips in October 1909 to London where he became secretary of the embassy.

a last and complete overhauling of the question in connection with the Gatun dam.[1] General Davis[2] and several others are convinced that the Gatun dam will be a failure, and all kinds of rumors come up here about it, while there is an evident movement in favor of a sea-level canal.

Now, my belief is, simply as a layman and judging from what I have heard, that the present plan is the right plan; that the Gatun dam can be built with entire safety, and that the sea-level canal is not advisable. But I don't care a rap about consistency in the matter, and you mustn't either. Nobody must care anything excepting to get the canal built according to the best and safest plans. The issue is altogether too big to be complicated in any way by any point of pride as to past recommendations by me or by anyone else. I want you therefore to approach the subject with an absolutely open mind, and to consult with Mr. Taft and the engineers he will bring with him, purely on the basis of finding out what the facts are and what is best to be done. Will you write me freely as to your judgment now and as to the reasons for your judgment?

I tell you it is a great comfort to feel that this thing is to be left in the hands of Taft. It would indeed have been a calamity if Bryan had come in.

There is a very good young fellow named William Stickney, a son of Albert Stickney of New York, a rather dreamy visionary but an honest and upright man. Young Stickney is left penniless by the death of his father, and is having the hard work that always comes to the man who is left penniless when he had expected to inherit a fortune. His record is as follows:

B.A. Harvard 1900; honorable mention in chemistry. Massachusetts Institute of Technology 3 years (2 in railway engineering; 1 in naval architecture). Glasgow University 1 year in naval architecture. Fore River Shipbuilding Company, Manager H. C. Smith, 3¼ years (¾ year work in yard on battleship *Vermont* as helper to shipfitter, 1½ years at steel foundries hurrying work, 1 year ordering castings for the company under the direction of the purchasing agent). Telluride, Colorado, ¾ year at Smuggler Mining

---

[1] Newspaper reports describing the "sinking" of Gatun Dam had revived demands for a sea-level canal. A reporter on November 21, observing that some of the preliminary fill for the dam had sunk several feet, had cabled that the dam was slowly dropping into an underground lake. Although such technical journals as the *Engineering News* and *Scientific American* labeled the report as an absurd product of sensational journalism, the story was widely accepted. In December the House Committee on Interstate and Foreign Commerce announced that it would make an investigation of the dam, but Roosevelt, acting at once, arranged for another expert examination of the whole lock question.

The engineering commission which late in January 1909 accompanied Taft to Panama reported that, as then planned, the Gatun Dam would be "safe, tight, and durable." More important, as Roosevelt stressed in his message forwarding its report to Congress, the commission's investigations showed "that it would be an inexcusable folly to change from the proposed lock canal to a sea-level canal." "In fact," the President continued, "this report not only determines definitely the type of canal, but makes it evident that hereafter attack on this type — the lock type — is in reality merely attack upon the policy of building any canal at all."

[2] George W. Davis, former canal commissioner and Governor of the Canal Zone.

Company's mill as roustabout, helper to batteryman, batteryman and vanner-man.

I am anxious to put him at work on the Isthmus. Is there not some position where he can be tried on his merits?[3]

Give my warm regards to Bishop. *Faithfully yours*

5069 · TO WILLIAM HOWARD TAFT   *Roosevelt Mss.*

Washington, December 13, 1908

Dear Will: We ought to get some of the very best engineers in the country to go down with you. How about Noble? Do you know of any better man? What do you say to taking down Parsons? He is disgruntled, and is hostile to us on the lock canal question, but for that very reason it is worth while considering whether he would not be a good man to take. Have you any man in mind who could suggest to me the names of the best engineers I could send?[1] I have written Goethals and Wright; I enclose you a copy of my letter to Goethals.

With love to Mrs. Taft, *Ever yours*

5070 · TO GILCHRIST STEWART   *Roosevelt Mss.*

Washington, December 15, 1908

My dear Mr. Stewart: I have your letter of the 13th instant.

I agree with you that probably not over thirty of those soldiers were implicated in the actual shooting at Brownsville. I think that most of Company B must have been accessory before the fact. But I think the great majority of Companies C and D were doubtless innocent of everything except failing to disclose afterwards all they knew of the facts, and as regards this I consider them less guilty than some of their advisers. The trouble about reinstating any of the men is that it cannot be done until we are able at the same time to identify at least approximately the really guilty, and until the men are willing frankly and honorably, as loyal soldiers, to tell the full and exact truth about what they knew. If they would approach the subject in this manner, I am confident that two thirds of them could be reinstated, and it is a bad thing for themselves as well as the service that they should perse-vere in a course of conduct which ⟨takes⟩ . . . it out of my power to do for them what they desire. Do you not yourself know some way by which they could be shown their duty to the nation, which is to tell the exact truth?

---

[3] Stickney did not take a position on the Isthmus.

---

[1] All but one of the seven engineers who sailed with Taft on January 13 for the Isthmus were suggested by Alfred Noble. These experts included John R. Freeman, Frederic P. Stearns, Isham Randolph, Allen Hazen, Arthur P. Davis, James Dix Schuyler, and Henry A. Allen.

Doubtless you saw the message I sent to the Senate on Monday.[1] *Sincerely yours*

5071 · TO WILLIAM HOWARD TAFT   *Roosevelt Mss.*

Washington, December 15, 1908

Dear Will: Cal. O'Laughlin came in today. He told me that Murray Crane had seen him and had said that he had called on you and that you had informed him that in pursuance of my conversation with you I would appoint (him) Cal. Assistant Secretary of State in Bacon's place.[1] He also told me that Mgr. Falconio had seen him and had informed him that he also had held an interview with you and that you had informed him that in pursuance of our conversation I was to appoint (him) Cal. Assistant Secretary of State and that when the 4th of March came you would "see what could be done" about retaining him. I told O'Laughlin that I was confident the Papal Delegate was mistaken; that you had told me that you would be glad to have me appoint him (O'Laughlin) in Bob Bacon's place, but that it must be with the distinct understanding that he retired on the 4th of March, because you believed that from geographical and other considerations it would be necessary to appoint someone else, and that while you had not made up your mind, I knew that you were considering someone else.

Knox called on me last night. I had a long talk over his accepting the position of Secretary of State and I am confident that he will do so. He had spoken with Root, and came and asked me to have Beekman Winthrop appointed instead of Cal. O'Laughlin, suggesting that I should send O'Laughlin

[1] This message transmitted the report of Browne and Baldwin, which, Roosevelt asserted, clearly established the fact that the soldiers of Company B had been actively concerned in the shooting. The C and D troops, he added, had deliberately concealed their knowledge of the affair, but they had done so, Roosevelt felt, in part because of threats from the guilty and in part because they "were encouraged by outsiders to persist in their course of concealment and denial." The President believed he could "afford to reinstate any of these men who now truthfully tell what has happened . . . . and show that they themselves . . . . were in no way implicated in the affair." He therefore recommended that a law be passed permitting the Secretary of War to reinstate any innocent soldiers who did all in their power to bring the guilty to justice. In the meantime the investigation was to continue; see *Congressional Record,* XLIII, 185–186.

Foraker attacked both this message and the proposed bill, but in February he accepted a compromise bill of Aldrich, which was passed. This measure provided for a court of high-ranking officers, to be appointed by the Secretary of War, who were to decide on eligibility for re-enlistment. The court ultimately heard the testimony of only eighty-two soldiers of whom only fourteen were found eligible for reinstatement, a record of such severity as to bear out Foraker's prediction that the court would be unfriendly to the troops.

[1] Bacon in January succeeded Root as Secretary of State; O'Laughlin became First Assistant Secretary. Beekman Winthrop, who was a candidate for the latter post, remained as Assistant Secretary of the Treasury, a position he had held since 1907. In March Taft made Winthrop Assistant Secretary of the Navy.

1423

temporarily to the Treasury. I told him that O'Laughlin was not fitted for the Treasury and that I happened to know that he would not accept the position, and that I had gone over the matter with you and had told you that if you desired to appoint Beekman Winthrop I would put him in Bacon's place; and added that I was very fond of Beekman Winthrop and had myself suggested his name for your consideration when you told me that you did not regard Cal. O'Laughlin as able to fill the place permanently. I continued, that you had answered saying that you would like to do something for Cal. O'Laughlin, altho you did not feel you could appoint him permanently and altho your present intention was to appoint Beekman Winthrop — an intention which you might change; that you told me you would be glad to have me appoint him, and asked me to tell him that it was done in accordance with your wishes, but that he must understand that he was to go out on the 4th of March.

I have just seen O'Laughlin and have told him the above, but have added that I should write to you so that there should be no misunderstanding in the matter. *Ever yours*

P.S. The rumor is going around that you intend to appoint Weeks instead of Meyer in your Cabinet.[2] Doubtless you remember that Weeks was one of the men whom Murray Crane and the rest of the extreme anti-Taft men used to antagonize your canvass for the nomination. He was very active against you and his appointment would in Massachusetts, I happen to know, be accepted as a slap in the face by the men who fought for you last spring and would be regarded as a personal humiliation of Lodge. I do not believe that you have the slightest idea of selecting him, but I thought I would write you this anyhow. Weeks is just now serving on the committee of reproof appointed by the House to bedevil me for expressing my views on the Secret Service. You will remember in the Cabinet last year the discussion we had on the Secret Service provision and how emphatically we told Cannon, Tawney, Smith, and others that it was crippling the Government and interfering with our getting at criminals to put the Secret Service paragraph in the form they did. They did this after the Senate had past it in satisfactory form.[3] To take

[2] The rumor was wrong. Taft made Meyer Secretary of the Navy; John Wingate Weeks remained in Congress.

[3] In his annual message Roosevelt had scolded Congress for amending the sundry civil bill of the previous session to confine the activities of the Secret Service to the suppression of counterfeiting and the protection of the President. The Secretary of the Treasury was prohibited from assigning any other details to the operatives. "This amendment," Roosevelt stated, "has been of benefit only, and could be of benefit only, to the criminal classes." It excluded those practices by which the executive departments had prevented lotteries, land frauds, and timber thefts and had convicted "formidable criminals," including violators of the antitrust laws. It kept the Secretary of the Treasury from properly policing customs service and mints. "The chief argument in favor of the provision," Roosevelt asserted crossly, "was that the congressmen did not themselves wish to be investigated." Although disagreeing with this argument, the President was willing to accept congressional immunity if the other restrictions were removed; see *State Papers*, Nat. Ed. XV, 527-528.

him after service on this committee would be accepted as an endorsement on your part of the position of the House.

5072 · TO LYMAN ABBOTT

Roosevelt Mss.

Personal

Washington, December 15, 1908

My dear Dr. Abbott: Here are two more articles, which I think will be the last ones.[1] Will you give me your candid judgment upon them, especially the Tolstoi piece? If you decide to use them I should of course want to see the proofs.

I shall do my best to have criminal libel suits brought against the New York *World* and the Indianapolis *News*. I hope you have read my message on Panama. More wanton lying has never been indulged in than that by the New York *World*, the Indianapolis *News* and company in this Panama matter. The *World* steered more clear of a libel suit than the Indianapolis *News*, simply because it was more experienced in wickedness. Of course either Charles P. Taft or Douglas Robinson has an absolute case for libel; but it is a thoroly unsatisfactory business for a private individual to go into a libel suit against a newspaper. It ought not to be asked of them. The Nation ought to undertake it. Unfortunately, the Nation has a very indirect jurisdiction in the matter.[2]

Roosevelt's Republican opponents in Congress, however, had no intention of changing the law. Cannon and his allies in particular objected to the use of secret-service men in antitrust investigations (see No. 4705, note 2), and delighted in opposing the nuisance in the White House who was, to their gratification, about to leave the seat of his power. They instituted a congressional investigation of the Secret Service which reported their view, and for the rest of Roosevelt's term they successfully fought his recommendation. The President responded in his correspondence of December through March and in special messages to Congress with vigorous but unproductive anger. See No. 5109.

---

[1] These articles were "National Character and the Characters of National Statesmen," *Outlook*, 91:190–193 (January 23, 1909), and "Tolstoy," *Outlook*, 92:103–105 (May 15, 1909).

[2] The nation's jurisdiction was indeed "indirect." By court decision and act of Congress federal courts had been given the power to punish as criminal offenses involving transgressions of federal statutes and certain other offenses not defined in federal statutes such as murder, rape, arson, and burglary if committed on federal property. Punishment of these latter offenses was to be made in accordance with the criminal law of the state in which the federal property lay.

The government in bringing criminal libel suit attempted to claim jurisdiction for itself on the grounds that the newspapers containing the alleged libel had been mailed in federal post offices and sold on federal lands. Acting on this claim Daniel W. Baker, the United States attorney in the District of Columbia, instituted proceedings for criminal libel against the editors and owners of the *World* and the *News*. On February 17, 1909, the grand jury returned indictments in the case (see Numbers 5121, 5142). In October 1910, however, Judge Anderson of the United States District Court in Indianapolis refused, on grounds of inadequate jurisdiction, the petition of the government for the extradition of Delavan Smith and Charles R. Williams. Since the defendants could not be brought to Washington the government dropped the indictments.

Also in 1909 District Attorney Henry Stimson filed suit for criminal libel against

It is the State authorities in the two States who ought to undertake the libel suits, and as they have no concern in the affair it is very difficult to get them to act. *Sincerely yours*

5073 · TO SAMUEL BRATTON DONNELLY   *Roosevelt Mss.*

Washington, December 15, 1908

To the Public Printer: I call your attention to my letter of October 2, 1908,[1] stating that hereafter no binding but cloths of the ordinary type should be used on Government publications. This direction of mine has been violated in connection with certain reports of Cabinet officers. What excuse is there for this violation? Moreover, I am informed that the President's message has been made needlessly expensive by the use of rough edges and gilt tops. What excuse was there for this? My desire is to have all of these Government publications put in the plainest and simplest kind of bindings. Please investigate this matter and send me a report as to the parties responsible for disobeying my orders.

5074 · TO THEODORE ROOSEVELT, JUNIOR   *Roosevelt Mss.*

Washington, December 16, 1908

Dear Ted: I completely forgot to speak to you about one matter while you were here, and now I have to write, which I do with the preface that I am not giving you any fixt opinion on my part, but merely suggesting something for you to consider. It might be well for you to talk over what I am about to say with Mr. Perkins.[1]

It is in reference to your going on the Governor's staff. You of course

the editors of the *World* in the federal district court in New York. Again the grand jury, in March 1909, returned the indictment (see Numbers 5141, 5142, 5164, 5166). Judge Hough in January 1910 decided, like his colleague in Indianapolis, that the federal courts could not claim jurisdiction in the case. There was, he said, a distinction between "that jurisdiction which grows out of the necessary exercise of national powers, and that which is based on the physical ownership of areas of land." The laws of Congress giving federal courts jurisdiction over certain specific crimes committed on federal land were never intended "to instruct the Federal Courts to take cognizance of any and every offense cognizable by local municipal law." On January 3, 1911, the Supreme Court sustained Hough's opinion.

A victory for the government in this case would have brought a great extension of the federal judicial power into an area from which by previous court decision and congressional legislation this judicial power had been withheld. It would also, in the opinion of many men at the time and since, have placed the freedom of the press in jeopardy for it would have established a precedent for future suits of criminal libel brought by the government itself. The question of jurisdiction in the case was therefore of transcendent importance.

[1] See Numbers 4928, 5009.

[1] R. P. Perkins was president of the Hartford Carpet Corporation where Ted was working.

know the facts and your needs at close hand, and there may be elements in the situation which render my judgment useless. But looking at it from a distance, I feel very strongly that it is unwise for you to accept, and that even now you can with entire propriety write to the Governor that on going over the matter with Mr. Perkins, or on examining your duties, you find that you will not be able to serve. I hate to have you go into anything unless you are really going to do the job up to the handle. Now, to my mind, a position on a Governor's staff is at best a rather comic position, and the only excuse for holding it is a determination to work so as to make it really amount to something. The appointment gives a man a certain unenviable notoriety — just the kind of notoriety that I should not think you would care to have. I understand the Governor said you need only be at his inauguration. After all, this would mean the expense for the uniform, and that your name would be in the papers, and very possibly comments made on the fact that you never appeared subsequently. Moreover, if the Governor came down to Taft's inauguration it might be absolutely necessary for you to come with him, and so you might find yourself forced to take part in other functions. It seems to me that it would be a waste of your time and to a certain extent a waste of money; and above all that it would put you into the very kind of prominence, a prominence with certain humorous associations, which you would not care for.

Now I may very well be completely mistaken in all this. I suggest that you show this letter to Mr. Perkins or talk over the matter with him, and of course follow his advice. There may be reasons which I do not know which would make it a good thing for you to accept the Governor's offer. But if you do not wish to, it is perfectly simple to write him and say that on thinking it over you feel that you would not have the time to do any real duty, and that you would not be willing to accept any office unless while filling it you were to fill it by doing your duty in thorogoing fashion.

It was delightful having you here. I am mighty glad we got that tennis. Yesterday George Meyer and I beat Jusserand and Archie Butt. Today Mother and I ride. Last evening I spoke at the Saint-Gaudens memorial meeting at the Corcoran Art Gallery. It was a very beautiful sight with the bright lights and the hundreds of pretty dresses among the columns and on the stairs, and there was a large audience present. *Your loving father*

P.S. If the Governor came down to the inauguration of Mr. Taft, with his staff, you would have to come no matter how much work you had at the mill, as your absence would cause comment.

5075 · TO ELIHU ROOT   *Roosevelt Mss.*

Washington, December 17, 1908

To the Secretary of State: Things are evidently on the verge of a complete upsetting in Venezuela. Surely this is a time to send a first-class man down there in order to be on the ground before the trouble takes place. He might go quietly to Curaçao, so that we could get him over at once to Venezuela, and then he could make such conditions before recognition as would insure us a living chance down there.[1]

5076 · TO ROBERT UNDERWOOD JOHNSON   *Roosevelt Mss.*

Private   Washington, December 17, 1908

My dear Johnson: I sincerely thank you for your letter and appreciate your having written. I shared your indignation at Columbia College having accepted such money for such a purpose from such a knave.[1]

As for the Hetch Hetchy matter, it was just one of those cases where I was extremely doubtful; but finally I came to the conclusion that I ought to stand by Garfield and Pinchot's judgment in the matter.[2] *Sincerely yours*

5077 · TO WILLIAM WOODVILLE ROCKHILL   *Roosevelt Mss.*

                                           Washington, December 17, 1908

My dear Mr. Rockhill: I am greatly obliged to you for your communication about the Dalai Lama.[1] It was just what I wanted. I am greatly interested in what you have written me. You have done exactly what I hoped you would in sending me the matter so at length.

Now, my dear Mr. Minister, about your request, I cannot ask Taft for any appointment. I will gladly tell him how highly I think of you, and of my

[1] General Gomez was about to complete his successful revolution in Venezuela. Immediately upon succeeding Castro, Gomez reversed the foreign policy of his difficult predecessor. Through the Brazilian government he expressed his desire to "settle satisfactorily all international questions." He also made it clear that he thought it would be "convenient" if an American warship were stationed at La Guaira. These welcome overtures Root at once accepted. On December 21 the Secretary of State sent William I. Buchanan, a veteran in Latin-American diplomacy, aboard the *North Carolina* as special commissioner to re-establish diplomatic relations between the United States and Venezuela. Buchanan's long instructions stipulated that as a condition of recognition he was to "complete definitively the signing and submission to arbitration of the pending claims." By mid-February 1909 he had achieved this end, accomplishing in two months' negotiations with the friendly Gomez what had been unattainable during the long term of the contentious Castro. The documents describing this mission are in *Foreign Relations*, 1909, pp. 609-622.

[1] Columbia had accepted a two million dollar endowment from Joseph Pulitzer to establish the School of Journalism.
[2] Garfield and Pinchot had approved a San Francisco petition to convert the beautiful Hetch Hetchy valley into a reservoir.

[1] The Dalai Lama, Rockhill reported, had been in Peking, where the Empress Dowager, while showering him with new titles and a larger pension, had resolutely persisted in her policy of reducing his temporal powers. She had even refused him an audience. Rockhill also observed that, notwithstanding the Dalai Lama's declining authority, the British had erred in failing to station an officer at Lhasa to deal directly with him while negotiating a trade treaty between India and Tibet; see Rockhill to Roosevelt, November 8, 1908, Rockhill Mss.

belief that you would do excellent work if continued in the service. But of course I should not be willing to speak of any particular place in which I thought you could do good work. I am not asking Taft for any appointment of any kind, and I am certain that you will appreciate the wisdom of this position of mine when you think over it. You see, if I ask for any man, I could not well avoid asking for a countless number whom I have appointed in the service.

With warm regards to Mrs. Rockhill, and heartiest good wishes for your continuance in the service, believe me, *Sincerely yours*

5078 · TO ANSLEY WILCOX   *Roosevelt Mss.*

Washington, December 17, 1908

My dear Wilcox: The enclosed copy of a letter from the Civil Service Commission explains itself. During the last fiscal year you will see that over 41,000 persons were appointed by means of competitive examination, and during the last year sixty-four special exceptions for appointment have been made. Probably sixty of these were absolutely demanded by the good of the service. I know that there were two, but there may possibly have been four or even six, where I appointed for reasons of sentiment — one of the men being a victor in the Olympic games. *Faithfully yours*

5079 · TO WILLIAM WINGATE SEWALL   *Roosevelt Mss.*

Washington, December 18, 1908

Friend William: Indeed I will accept those socks as a Christmas present from Mrs. Sewall and you with the greatest pleasure, and it is most kind of you to send them.[1] Will you thank Miss Kittie for her part in getting them from Sherman when she and Mrs. Sewall drove over there in the sleigh. I wrote Mrs. Caldwell at once as you suggested.

I am very glad you approve of what I said about the secret-service men. I think Congress is very foolish to have taken the action it did. I was careful never to condemn all Congressmen; but my business is to war against crookedness wherever I find it, and I am not going to let up as long as I continue to be President.

I spoke to Taft about you and gave him a memorandum and he said of course you would be all right, but I enclose you a letter[2] which you can send

[1] Roosevelt had asked Sewall to procure for him and Kermit a type of woolen sock he had earlier purchased through Sewall for hunting in Maine and in the West.
[2] The letter read: "This will be presented to you by, or on behalf of, Mr. W. W. Sewall, Collector of Customs for the Eastern District of Maine. You will remember that this is the case I spoke to you about and gave you a memorandum containing Sewall's name, and you said that as long as he did his duty and was a good officer he should be continued in office under you. He is an old personal friend of mine, with whom I have been thrown into long and intimate contact both in Maine and on my

him toward the end of your term if you find that there is any trouble; but I want you to be very careful that nobody sees it but Taft himself, for otherwise I should be deluged with requests for letters.

Again heartily thanking you and wishing you a merry Christmas and a happy New Year, and the same for all your family, I am, *Your friend*

[*Handwritten*] Have the socks been sent here?

5080 · TO WILLIAM MITCHELL KENDALL   *Roosevelt Mss.*

Washington, December 18, 1908

My dear Mr. Kendall: [1] I should like to have stone bison heads substituted for the stone lion heads under the mantelpiece in the State Dining Room. They make a much more characteristic and American decoration. It will have to be speedily done. Will you do me the kindness to consult Cass Gilbert [2] about it, as while he was here I showed to him and to Breck Trowbridge[3] just what I wanted and they cordially agreed with me.[4] *Sincerely yours*

5081 · TO TRUMAN HANDY NEWBERRY   *Roosevelt Mss.*

Washington, December 19, 1908

To the Secretary of the Navy: I am informed that the Curtis turbine, an American turbine, has really done excellently.[1] If such is the case I should emphatically advise against importing English turbines for use in the battleships building in the New York yard, and to use the Curtis turbine.

ranch on the Little Missouri, and a very good man in every way. Moreover he was a Taft man straight out long before the bread-and-butter brigade started to get aboard the bandwagon."

[1] William Mitchell Kendall, architect, member of the firm of McKim, Mead and White, member of the National Council of Fine Arts.

[2] Cass Gilbert, one of the great American architects. His best-known work, the Woolworth Building, remains one of the most majestic and lovely structures in the country. At this time he was president of both the American Institute of Architects and the American Academy of Arts and Letters.

[3] Samuel Breck Parkman Trowbridge, architect; incorporator, vice-president, and trustee of the American Academy in Rome; chairman of the National Council of Fine Arts.

[4] Stone bison heads, as Roosevelt requested, were installed in the state dining room.

[1] In 1907 the scout cruiser *Salem* and the battleship *North Dakota* had been equipped with the Curtis turbine. The *Salem*, commissioned in the fall of 1908, was then the first navy ship to operate with these engines, and her captain, Albert Key, had undoubtedly written Roosevelt of their excellent performance during the *Salem's* shakedown cruise in November. The Bureau of Steam Engineering, however, did not share Key's enthusiasm for the American engine. Both new battleships, the *Utah* and the *Florida*, carried British-made Parsons turbines.

Washington, December 19, 1908

My dear Mr. Gilbert: Now that I am about to leave office there is something I should like to say thru you to the American Institute of Architects. During my incumbency of the Presidency the White House, under Mr. McKim's direction, was restored to the beauty, dignity and simplicity of its original plan. It is now, without and within, literally the ideal house for the head of a great democratic republic. It should be a matter of pride and honorable obligation to the whole Nation to prevent its being in any way marred. If I had it in my power as I leave office, I should like to leave as a legacy to you, and to the American Institute of Architects, the duty of preserving a perpetual "eye of guardianship" over the White House to see that it is kept unchanged and unmarred from this time on. *Sincerely yours*

5083 · TO ALEXANDER JEFFREY MC KELWAY *Roosevelt Mss.*

Personal Washington, December 19, 1908

My dear Mr. McKelway: [1] I have your letter of the 17th instant. I would not like to write to any State Legislature or communicate directly or indirectly with any State Legislature on a matter pending before them. On thinking it over you will realize, I am sure, the accusations to which such a course would expose me.

As regards Governor Hoke Smith, I should be glad to have you state what I said, but do not try to put it in quotation marks or to quote me in the first person. It is impossible to recollect exactly what was said in a case like that, and sometimes trivial omissions will modify the meaning. For instance, the sentence as you quoted it puts the matter a little stronger than I stated it. My comparison was between Governor Smith and the Governors of the States in his neighborhood. As you will recall, the matter with which I had to deal, which concerned Governor Smith, referred purely to the Southern Railway.[2] So instead of putting it as you have, "that I got more practical common sense ideas from my discussion with him over railroad regulation than I have gotten from anyone else"; put it as I have put it, not in the comparative but in the positive form; that I wished to thank him heartily and openly for the good, practical common sense ideas that I had gained from my discussion with him about railroad regulation. I quite agree with you that the main work to be done in the control of railroads must be done by the Na-

[1] Alexander Jeffrey McKelway, relative of St. Clair McKelway, Presbyterian minister, newspaper editor, crusader for the prevention of child labor.
[2] In February 1908 Roosevelt and Smith had been in correspondence on wage reductions made by the Southern Railroad. Smith, who had won the governorship largely on the issue of railroad regulation, during his term transformed the Georgia commission into one of the country's most effective instruments of transportation control.

tional Government, but there must be important work also done by the State Governments and that much of the attitude of the National Government will be determined by the attitude of the State Governments. *Sincerely yours*

5084 · TO ARTHUR HAMILTON LEE   *Roosevelt Mss.*

Personal   Washington, December 20, 1908

Dear Arthur: Those pictures are simply fine. We are delighted, all the more so because the ordinary photographs of the picture have not been satisfactory. It is more than good of you to have sent them to us and to have taken such infinite pains to get them. As you say, they seem to preserve the spirit and technique of the original to a remarkable degree. For frames I shall adopt Laszló's suggestion and frame them like an Old English mezzotint in the regular 18th century pattern "ebony and gilt" frames.

I return to you the three, and as I was writing on them in pencil I did no more than put on my name and the date when Laszló was here last spring. I shall send to Root and Mrs. Lodge and my sisters and my daughter, copies, for Christmas. But I feel very selfish about the pictures and regard them as altogether too valuable to be distributed save in the most sparing and cautious way.

Indeed I did receive the long (and very wise) letter that you wrote me from Scotland in October. By this time you have doubtless received the note I sent you in answer, saying how I had sent a letter to Harry White to give you but later ordered it destroyed when the papers published broadcast the facts I wished to communicate to you. On account of the way that letters have been stolen I do not like to speak any more definitely. There is now no public need for me to write you, but I have many things to tell you when we meet.

I am glad indeed to hear from you that the British people are alive to the necessities of national defense. What you say as to the change in their attitude toward some form of compulsory service for home defense is simply astounding. Indeed the agreement with Japan is an admirable thing all around. As you say, it is a knockout for the mischief-makers on both sides of the Atlantic — and I may add on both sides of the Pacific. It is a good thing as keeping England and America closer together too; which, as you know, is something I always have peculiarly at heart. My policy of constant friendliness and courtesy toward Japan, *coupled with sending the fleet around the world*, has borne good results!

I am ending my career as President with just the same stiff fighting that has marked it ever since I took the office. But I am having a thoroly good time. I have achieved a large proportion of what I set out to achieve and I feel that I have measurably realized my ideals. Taft is as fine a fellow as ever sat in the President's chair and I cannot express the measureless content that comes over me as I think that the work in which I have so much believed will be carried on by him. Ordinarily I suppose I should be melancholy at leaving the Presidency and taking my hands off the levers of the great machine. But the trip I am to take in Africa represents to me the realization of a golden dream which I had never considered to be within the wildest circle of possibilities, and I look forward to it with such delight that it is quite impossible for me to regret even the Presidency.

Lord Warwick[1] was here the other day and seemed an uncommonly nice fellow. I took a great fancy to him. By the way, I have declined positively to make any set engagements, altho there are several things that I would like to do if I get the chance, when in England.

With warm regards to Mrs. Lee, and again most heartily thanking you, believe me, *Faithfully yours*

5085 · TO WILLIAM HOWARD TAFT   *Roosevelt Mss.*

Washington, December 21, 1908

Dear Will: I have given a line of introduction to you to an old personal friend of mine, Sir Horace Plunkett. He is an Irishman who has been one of the most useful men in the United Kingdom because of the work he has done for the agricultural betterment of Ireland; and the jacks there who do not stand much above us in farsighted intelligence have not always appreciated it.[1] In addition he has spent many years in America, has worked a farm here, and, with the exception of Gifford Pinchot, has done more for me in starting me right as regards the great problems of our agricultural life than any man in the United States. I know of no man anywhere who is as safe and wise a guide, no man who couples as he does an enthusiastic conviction with sanity as to the methods that ought to be pursued to turn that conviction into accomplished fact. Among the various legacies of trouble which I leave you there is none as to which I more earnestly hope for your thought and care than this. There are very big problems which we have to face in the United States. I do not know whether you yourself realize how rapid the decline in the birth rate is, how rapid the drift has been away from the country to the cities. In spite of our enormous immigration there is good reason to fear that unless the present tendencies are checked your children and mine will see the day when our population is stationary, and so far as the native stock is concerned is dying out, and when the people of the country regions will tend to be divided into absentee landlords, city summer residents, and a dispirited and dwindling farmer stock without the qualities on which this Nation has

[1] Leopold Guy Francis Maynard Greville, Earl of Warwick, veteran of the Boer War, Reuter's special correspondent during the Russo-Japanese War, in 1914-1915, A.D.C. to the Commander-in-chief, British Army in France.

[1] Failure to appreciate the talents of Sir Horace Plunkett as an agricultural reformer arose in large part from British regret that Sir Horace displayed equal talents as an advocate of Home Rule.

had to draw in order to meet every great crisis of the past. Now, I think all these tendencies for evil can be overcome. No one man and no two men can do very much, working alone, to overcome them. But, simply because of his position, the man who is President can do most, if he chooses to try to do it. Therefore I earnestly ask that you will give Sir Horace ample time to talk the matter over with you.

Will you please send me at once the date of your birth and any salient fact in your past career (of a noncriminal type!) with which I am not apt to be acquainted. I have promised to write an introduction of a thousand words to your inauguration book, this to be a sketch of your life.

With love to Mrs. Taft, *Faithfully yours*

P.S. I enclose you a copy of an Executive Order I am thinking of issuing.[2] What do you think of it?

5086 · TO HENRY FAIRFIELD OSBORN   *Roosevelt Mss.*

Washington, December 21, 1908

Dear Fair: I am very greatly obliged to you for the pains you took about the Romanes Lecture, and for your excellent suggestions. Those about South America I have practically adopted, excepting that I kept in the words "camels" and "big cats" instead of "llamas" and "pumas" because I wish to emphasize that the forms were of Old World type. Of course, as you say, the history of the South American fauna does not afford a complete analogy with any historical process. I introduce it merely to illustrate the necessity in our present stage of knowledge of our being willing to admit that many causes of tremendous changes are totally unknown to us.

I use "homology" in the ordinary literary, and not in the strict scientific sense.

As to Oklahoma, I do not think there are any statistics which would show the fertility of the crossbred marriages, but that they are fertile is patent to everyone. So far from being ashamed of Indian blood, the people of Oklahoma rather glory in it. Not only do the Senator and Representatives of whom I spoke speak proudly of it, but Senator Curtis of Kansas, who is one-quarter Kaw, is also proud of the fact. When the Oklahoma delegations present themselves, among the ladies there are generally sure to be two or three very evidently of Indian blood, just as well dressed and looking as nicely as the others; and if I speak to them about being of Indian blood I am almost certain to find that half a dozen others, apparently pure white, will eagerly step forward and state that they have some Indian blood in them also. In my

[2] Although it is not clear to which order Roosevelt referred, it may well have been that of January 19, 1909, appointing a Council of Fine Arts. The executive departments were to submit their building plans to this council for advice. This was the only executive order Roosevelt issued after December 21 of broad enough scope to affect the work of a succeeding Administration.

regiment there were about fifty men of Indian blood, almost all of them of mixt blood. They behaved exactly like the whites, and their careers since have been exactly like the white men's.

As to the statement of Anton Dohrn,[1] of Naples, I can only say that I think the chances are at least a million to one that neither in southern Italy nor in Sicily is there a single individual whose blood has come in anything like purity from the original Greek colonists, or from any other set of inhabitants of the land at the time say of the Pyrrhic Wars. From that day to this there has been a constant beating of ethnic waves over those lands. Sicily in particular was a vast slave farm under the rule of republican Rome, filled with people from Asia Minor, Africa, Spain, everywhere. It is a bare possibility that in some one nook a little Greek community has interbred with itself for a couple of thousand years without foreign admixture. But I do not think that even this much is more than a bare possibility. As you know, Greek entirely died out as the language in Sicily and southern Italy, and then was revived, for a time, several centuries later owing to the close Byzantine connection and the influx of Byzantine emigrants.

Ripley is an interesting writer, but I do not think that his conclusions are now generally accepted in their entirety, certainly not without great qualification. Ridgeway, for instance, has recently been upholding as his main thesis the idea that environment is in the long run the absolutely controlling influence on racial or physical form, features like hair color, eye color, etc. I do not think he is right, but I think he is as nearly right as Ripley.[2]

Now as to what you say as to the blending of long-skulled and short-skulled types. You say that they are stable in heredity; that if a brachycephalic weds a dolichocephalic, the offspring are either one or the other, but not necessarily mesaticephalic. Of course they are not necessarily so, but I firmly believe they are often so. On any other theory I do not know how to account for the fact that in any extensive collection of skulls from America and Europe it is absolutely impossible to draw the line separating one type from the other, the gradations being imperceptible from the brachycephalic to the dolichocephalic. Moreover, I think that the tendency you speak of in recent studies into heredity as to the belief that certain types persist and are not swamped by interbreeding but reappear in comparatively pure form in successive generations, is at best but a slight tendency, to be overborne by opposite tendencies. I suppose you refer to Mendel's law. Now we have

[1] Anton Dohrn, polylingual German zoologist, author of *Quaedam de Anatomia Hemipterorum* (1865), *Studien zur Embryologie der Arthropoden* (1868), *Die Pantopoden des Golfes von Neapel und der Angrenzenden Meeres-Abschnitte* (1881), *The Zoological Station at Naples, Italy* (1883).

[2] William Z. Ripley and William Ridgeway, the British classicist, took opposite sides on the problem of the relative influence of heredity and environment; compare Ripley, "Races in the United States," *Atlantic Monthly*, 102:745–759 (December 1908) and *The European Population of the United States* (London, 1908), with Ridgeway, "Application of Zoological Laws to Man," *Popular Science*, 73:500–522 (December 1908).

right before our eyes here in the United States an intermixture of two very divergent and persistent human types, which has gone on for a long period and on the largest scale. It is very difficult to make satisfactory studies on any extensive scale about breeding between brachycephalic and dolichocephalic types; but we can all of us see with the greatest ease what has happened in hundreds of thousands of cases in breeding between the black man and the white man. In the mulatto neither type ever persists in its purity; each type is invariably swamped by the interbreeding and does not reappear in comparatively pure form in any succeeding generation. When mulattoes interbreed the offspring may be darker or lighter, but is never either a negro or a white. Moreover, no one characteristic ever appears as purely white or purely negro; or if this is too extreme a statement, at least such appearance is so rare as to be negligible. In every mulatto of mulatto parents and grandparents, the hair and eye color, the skin tint, the shape of the skull, and in short all the other traits, represent something different from, but more or less like, the corresponding trait both in the white ancestor and in the black ancestor. Of course if the mulatto breeds either to the white or to the black, there will come in time a practically complete elimination of the traits of the single remote ancestor of the other blood.

I have profited by your advice to at once change what I said about the Dutch, Portuguese and Spanish, and I think I now have it so that no legitimate offense can be taken. But you rather frighten me by speaking of the importance which you say will be attached to my speech. I am speaking purely as a layman and as a private citizen, and when I accepted the invitation it never occurred to me that any more importance would be attached to what I said than, for instance, to what Curzon or Bryce said in their lectures.

Let me again thank you, my dear Fair, for your most useful kindness. *Faithfully yours*

5087 · TO CHARLES JOSEPH BONAPARTE *Roosevelt Mss.*

Washington, December 24, 1908

To the Attorney General: Why not appoint Mr. Dennis, of Indiana, at present Assistant Solicitor in the State Department, to the vacancy as Assistant Attorney General? Bacon says he is an excellent man, and Root is writing a letter to you to this effect.[1] I think Dennis has seen Hoyt. The sooner we act on this the better.

P.S. It seems to me that Spelling is of pretty small caliber to argue that

[1] William Cullen Dennis, Assistant Solicitor of the Department of State since 1906, remained in that office until 1910. Alford W. Cooley, who had earlier resigned because of bad health, was reappointed Assistant Attorney General.

important commodities case. Who is to take the laboring oar in that matter? We ought to have the very best man we can get for it.[2]

5088 · TO WILFRID LAURIER $\qquad$ *Roosevelt Mss.*

Washington, December 24, 1908

My dear Sir Wilfrid: In May of the present year the Governors of the several States and Territories of this Union met in the White House to confer with the President and with each other concerning the amount and condition of the natural resources of this country, and to consider the most effective means for conserving them. This conference included also the members of the Supreme Court, the Cabinet, and members of both Houses of Congress, together with representatives of the great associations of citizens concerned with natural resources. The conference was followed by the appointment of conservation commissions on the part of the Nation and of a majority of the States.

A second conference of the National Commission with the Governors, the State commissions, and the conservation committees of the great associations has recently been held in this city. It was called to consider an inventory of our natural resources prepared by the National Conservation Commission. Its most important result will doubtless appear in co-operation on the part of the Nation, the States, and the great associations of citizens for action upon this great question, upon which the progress of the people of the United States obviously depends.

It is evident that natural resources are not limited by the boundary lines which separate nations, and that the needs for conserving them upon this continent is as wide as the area upon which they exist. In view, therefore, of these considerations, and of the close bonds of friendship and mutual aims which exist between Canada and the United States, I take especial pleasure in inviting you to designate representatives of the Government of Canada to meet and consult with representatives of the State and other Departments of this Government, and the National Conservation Commission, in the City of Washington on February 18, 1909. The purpose of the conference I have the honor to propose is to consider mutual interests involved in the conservation of natural resources, and in this great field to

[2] The meaning and constitutionality of the commodities clause of the Hepburn Act were at issue in the case, to be argued before the Supreme Court in January. Thomas C. Spelling and L. Allison Wilmer, assisting the Attorney General and the Solicitor General, "were on the brief, for the United States." Together they apparently pulled a laboring oar that was stronger than Roosevelt expected. In May 1908, following their presentation of the government's case, the Supreme Court, reversing the decision of the circuit court, upheld the constitutionality of the disputed clause; see *The United States*, ex. rel. *the Attorney General of the United States* v. *Delaware and Hudson Company* et al., 213 U. S. 366–419 (1909); Jones, *Anthracite Coal Combination*, pp. 197–202.

deliberate upon the practicability of preparing a general plan adapted to promote the welfare of the nations concerned.

I have this day addressed a similar invitation to the President of Mexico, expressing my hope that representatives of that Government also will be present and participate in the proposed conference on the conservation of the natural resources of North America.

The conclusions of such a conference, while wholly advisory in character, could hardly fail to yield important beneficial results, both in a better knowledge of the natural resources of each Nation on the part of the others, and in suggestions for concurrent action for the protection of mutual interests related to conservation.

As my representative to convey to you this letter and invitation, and at your desire to consult with you concerning the proposed conference, I have selected an officer of this Government, Chief of the United States Forest Service and Chairman of the National Conservation Commission, whom I commend to your kind offices. *Sincerely yours*

5089 · TO EDWIN EMERSON, JUNIOR   *Roosevelt Mss.*

Personal   Washington, December 24, 1908

My dear Emerson: [1] I have seen a copy of your letter to Mr. Frank J. Dyer.[2] You say that a certain Guatemalan statesman "boldly makes the claim that he has bought the Republican administration of our country thru repeated campaign contributions at election times." Now such a statement is not merely an absurd falsehood, but it is also a scandalous falsehood. It is just as scandalous for you to repeat it or give any circulation to it of any kind, sort or description, as for the gossip-mongers in Guatemala to allege it. Apparently you are ignorant of the fact that well-nigh as heavy a responsibility rests upon any man who circulates directly or indirectly such an outrageous falsehood as upon the man who originated it. You are repeating mere gossip. I have told you once that the statement is an absolute falsehood. Your business is, if you follow up the matter at all, to find some responsible man who is willing to father the statement, and until you find such a responsible man you have no warrant of any kind for repeating it and you should be silent about it. Your information as regards this incident, on every point where I am able to check it, is wholly inaccurate, and your

[1] Edwin Emerson, Jr., a newspaperman, had been cited by Roosevelt for gallantry at San Juan, decorated by Castro of Venezuela, and captured by the Japanese during the Russo–Japanese War. By 1908 a free-lance author, he had written *Rough Rider Stories* (1900), *A History of the Nineteenth Century* (1902), and *The Monroe Doctrine in Venezuela* (1903). Among his later volumes are *Central American Dictators* (1911), *With the German Armies* (1917), and *Adventures of Theodore Roosevelt* (1928).
[2] Francis John Dyer, then Washington correspondent of the San Francisco *Chronicle*, already an authority on Latin American affairs; later author of a syndicated weekly "letter" and an American consul in Wales, Honduras, Mexico, and Germany.

statements without a shadow of foundation. For instance, you say that Señor Barrios has as his real object here to secure the recall of all the American diplomatic and consular representatives in Central America. Mr. Barrios has made no proposition of any kind or sort to us looking toward the recall of a single one of the men you name. As far as we know all of the men you mention are doing their duty, and if this is a fact that Government will of course stand by them. You continue and say that it is Señor Barrios' open boast that officials of our State Department have given him assurance that his wishes will be complied with, and that he has accomplished his ends by the liberal use of money distributed for him by a member of his suite. I do not know whether to be most surprised, amused, or indignant at your repeating a statement like that. Have you no sense of responsibility? Is it again necessary for me to tell you that to repeat such a ludicrous slander and falsehood is only one degree less culpable than originally to utter it! Are you ignorant that to accuse the highest officials among your own countrymen of being bribed is a piece of grave iniquity on your part? If any man has personal knowledge or proof of such a boast having been uttered, why does he not call upon the boaster to make good his statement? But to repeat injurious gossip without giving any authority for it is simply unpardonable on your part. *Very truly yours*

5090 · TO JACOB HENRY SCHIFF   *Roosevelt Mss.*

Washington, December 25, 1908

My dear Mr. Schiff: I have received a letter[1] of which I enclose a copy together with a statement of the official positions of the persons who signed

[1] The letter, from Homer Folks, Theodore Dreiser, James E. West, and others, written December 22, 1908, read as follows:

"In your message to Congress December 6, 1904, urging the establishment of a Juvenile Court for the District of Columbia, you said:

'No Christian and civilized community can afford to show a happy-go-lucky lack of concern for the youth of today; for, if so, the community will have to pay a terrible penalty of financial burden and social degradation in the to-morrow.'

"Congress promptly responded and enacted an excellent Juvenile Court Law. The wisdom of this step has already been proven by the work of the Court.

"Generally speaking, the cause of the delinquent child has been well advanced. Juvenile Courts have been established in many states; a considerable number of probation officers have been appointed; many of the Juvenile Reformatories are progressing along well-established lines of modern thought and are supported by generous appropriations from the public treasury; detention homes have been opened in many cities to keep children out of jail; parental schools are being established for the training of truants and unruly school children.

"The State has dealt generously with her troublesome children; but what is she doing for those who make no trouble but are simply unfortunate? There are a large number of these children for whom there is need of special activity and interest. Some are orphans or half-orphans; some are abandoned by heartless parents; some

it and a memorandum which is suggested for consideration and action if the conference which the letter suggests be held. I am confident that you will be imprest with the very great importance of the subject touched on in this letter, and the desirability that there should be the fullest discussion of the propositions, a memorandum of which I enclose.

Surely nothing ought to interest our people more than the care of the children who are destitute and neglected but not delinquent. Personally, I very earnestly believe that the best way in which to care for dependent children is in the family home. In Massachusetts many orphan asylums have been discontinued and thousands of the children who formerly have gone to the orphan asylums are now kept in private homes, either on board, with payment from public or private treasuries, or in adopted homes provided by the generosity of foster parents. Many religious bodies have within the past ten years organized effective child-placing agencies.

I am accordingly inviting a number of men and women, a list of whom

---

are victims of cruelty or neglect. They are not delinquents; they are accused of no fault; they are simply destitute or neglected.

"Destitute children certainly deserve as much consideration and help as those, who, by reason of some alleged delinquency, enforce the attention of the state and become objects of its care; but only a few states have defined responsibility for this class of children. Their care and protection is left in many localities to the fidelity of voluntary agencies without requiring proper standards of method or efficiency, and without definite responsibility to the state or the community.

"Unfortunately there has not been as frequent interchange of ideas and experiences among the officials of orphan asylums, with consequent progress, as among those who work for delinquents.

"These dependent children are cared for in different ways. According to a special bulletin of the United States Census there were in orphan asylums and kindred institutions on December 31st, 1904, not less than 92,887 children. In addition to these there were probably some 50,000 dependent children in family homes, under supervision.

"In many states, however, little or no child-saving work is done; and in many states the organizations are greatly handicapped by the lack of appreciation and of adequate support.

"It is of the highest importance to the welfare of this vast number of future citizens that all child-saving work shall be conducted on a high plane of efficiency; that in the placing of children in families the utmost care shall be taken to exclude all undesirable applicants; that every precaution shall be taken in the subsequent supervision of the children to prevent neglect, overwork, insufficient education or inadequate moral and religious training; and that institutions shall be so carried on as to secure the best physical, mental, moral and religious training of each individual child, and to fit it for active and creditable citizenship.

"The problem of the dependent child is acute; it is large, it is national. We believe that it is worthy of national consideration. We earnestly hope, therefore, that you will co-operate in an effort to get this problem before the American people.

"If a conference could be arranged, under your auspices, in Washington, some time in January, to which leaders of this particular phase of child-caring work could be invited, it would in our judgment greatly advance the cause of the dependent child. Such a conference could formulate a plan for your consideration, pointing out ways whereby you could specifically help by recommending to Congress certain legislation and in other ways.

"Hoping for your favorable consideration of this matter,"

I will announce to a conference to be held in Washington, January 25th and 26th. The conference will open by my receiving the members at the White House, January 25th at 2:30 p. m. Can you attend? Will you please communicate with Mr. James E. West, 1343 Clifton Street, N. W., Washington, D. C.? *Sincerely yours*

5091 · TO ELIHU ROOT   *Roosevelt Mss.*

Washington, December 26, 1908

Eminent Vocal: Before you lose your marked literary capacity by uninterrupted oratory in the Senate, won't you go over the draft of what I propose to say to the Methodists on January 18th? [1] I need not ask you for your frank comments; I will get 'em! At what hours of the day am I apt to find you in if I can stop at your house?

Give my love to dear Mrs. Root. I was so glad to catch a glimpse of her yesterday. *Ever yours*

5092 · TO WILLIAM II   *Roosevelt Mss.*

Washington, December 26, 1908

My dear Emperor William: A Happy New Year to Your Majesty! and may prosperity be yours, and your peoples'.

This is merely a letter of good will; now that I am about to leave office, I wish to assure you how much I have appreciated the unvarying friendship you have shown this country during the years that I have been President. The combination of your personality and your position render you the most influential and powerful of living men; and your hearty good will to America has been of real moment to my fellow countrymen.

Well, I should like to have continued as President, if I had felt it right, and in accordance with the best spirit of our traditions, so to do; and, had I wished it, I think I could have continued. But I shall leave the White House with entire satisfaction; for I have achieved more than a fair proportion of the things I set out to achieve; and I have many interests. I am looking forward with eagerness to my year in Africa; if I have fair luck it will be a great adventure. I shall spend a few weeks in Europe on my way back to America, in the spring of 1910. While in Africa I hope to cross the border into German East Africa; but I shall not make definite plans until I am actually on the ground, and can learn at first hand about the game, the character of the season, and the like.

It is very unlikely that I shall ever hold office again. But if — what I most earnestly hope may never occur — there should be a big war in which the United States was engaged, while I am still in bodily vigor, I should

[1] Roosevelt then spoke on British rule in India.

endeavor to get permission to raise a division of mounted rifles — cavalry, in our use of the word; that is, nine regiments such as the one I commanded in the war with Spain. I hope the chance may never come, however.

I mourned the death of Speck von Sternberg; you had no more loyal and devoted man under you. I have done what I could to make things easier for the poor Baroness. He and she made the German Embassy, in every relation, social and political, of the first importance, in Washington, and therefore in the whole country.

With all good wishes, and profound regard, I am, *Very faithfully yours*

5093 · TO ARTHUR B. FARQUHAR   *Roosevelt Mss.*

Private   Washington, December 26, 1908

My dear Mr. Farquhar:[1] I appreciate your letter of the 24th. I have not lookt into the matter, but my present feeling is that the error has been committed of imposing an excessive sentence upon Mr. Gompers,[2] just as an error was committed in imposing the excessive $29,000,000 fine on the Standard Oil Company. Any such excess of punishment defeats its own purposes. But of course at present there is no action I can take in either matter; and I am not giving you any deliberate or final judgment, for the facts may not be all before me. *Sincerely yours*

5094 · TO EUGENE FITCH WARE   *Roosevelt Mss.*

Washington, December 26, 1908

Dear Ware: I agree with you about those pension agencies but Congress has voted down the proposal and I have not been sure that it was worth while

[1] Arthur B. Farquhar began life on a farm before the Civil War, learned the machinist trade in York, Pennsylvania, as a youth, became an executive and investor in his twenties, and, in 1899, at fifty-one, president of his own firm manufacturing agricultural implements in York. In addition he was for several years the proprietor of the York *Gazette,* an active conservationist, and a prominent opponent of free silver and the protective tariff.

[2] Judge Wright, finding Gompers, Mitchell, and Morrison guilty of violating the injunction in the Bucks case (see No. 4859, note 4), had sentenced them respectively to one year, nine months, and six months in jail. The sentence was itself perhaps less controversial than Wright's characterization of their conduct as "utter, rampant, insolent defiance . . . .; unrefined insult, coarse affront, vulgar indignity." The defendants at once appealed the case, contesting both the validity of the original injunction and the penalty Wright had imposed. In November 1909 the court of appeals upheld the lower court, but in May 1911 the Supreme Court, while avoiding any ruling on the injunction, held that because the case was civil in nature, criminal penalties were not permissible. For a full account of this case from Gompers' point of view, see Gompers, *Seventy Years of Life and Labor,* II, 205–220.

making a fight about it.[1] I have to make so many fights on serious matters that I rather dislike going into one that is not vital.

Wishing you and yours a happy New Year, believe me, *Sincerely yours*

5095 · TO GEORGE CLEMENT PERKINS   *Roosevelt Mss.*

Washington, December 26, 1908

My dear Senator Perkins: Mr. Taft has written me urging very strongly that we make our legation in China an Embassy and I feel that this should be done, from every standpoint, and cordially agree with him. I think he has also written Mr. Root.

Don't you think we can do this on his suggestion?[1] *Sincerely yours*

5096 · TO SYDNEY BROOKS   *Roosevelt Mss.*

Washington, December 28, 1908

My dear Brooks: I like your article, and am pleased that you are to write another.[1] But first let me speak as to what you desire in connection with British rule in India. I was imprest by what you said as to Morley's evident desire that I should say something to put the British attitude in India in the proper light before the people of this country; and I also received a verbal message to the same effect thru an Englishman[2] who I think came to Washington for the purpose of giving it. I accordingly asked Bryce to come down, and found that he was very anxious that I should speak along the lines you mention, and that evidently there had been a good deal of discussion as to just how it would be possible to get published here what they wanted said. Bryce entirely agreed with me that it would not do to

---

[1] The Secretary of the Interior and the Commissioner of Pensions had recommended that the pension agencies throughout the country be discontinued and all pension matters be concentrated in one office in Washington. At the previous session of Congress the Senate had prevented such a consolidation but had agreed to a clause in the pension appropriation bill directing the Secretary of the Interior to report on its merits. Garfield's unequivocal report supported the consolidation as a means to permit a substantial economy without any sacrifice of efficiency or convenience. The G.A.R. disagreed, arguing that the change would make trouble for pensioners and deprive many veterans of their jobs in the existing agencies. Supported as it was by state legislatures and politicians, this argument again convinced the Senate. The House's version of the pension appropriation bill effected a consolidation by providing funds for only one agency. Contrary to Roosevelt's statement, this matter was still open in December. The President, however, gave it no attention, and in February the Senate restored appropriations for the agencies in the hinterland.

---

[1] The Senate did not follow this suggestion which had in the first instance been made to Taft by Roosevelt.

---

[1] "Fifty years of British Rule in India," *Harper's Weekly*, 52:22 (December 19, 1908); "Briton and Native in India," *Harper's Weekly*, 53:16 (January 16, 1909).
[2] Probably the Earl of Warwick; see No. 5084.

make a statement confined to India, and that it must come in in the course of some other speech. Accordingly I shall bring in the subject when I speak at a Methodist missionary meeting some three weeks hence.[3] I went over what I had written with Bryce, who had no suggestions to make and seemed pleased, so I trust it will be satisfactory. It certainly represents exactly what I believe.

Now, as to your very kind words about myself. You have interpreted exactly what I regard as my chief work. But will you permit me to say that I think you have not made quite the proper allowance for actual achievement both in the way of legislation and in the way of administration? You have put very clearly the difficulties in the way of securing legislation here. Probably it is better that legislation should be too hard to obtain than that it should be too easy; but the situation is a curious commentary upon Macaulay's statement in his famous letter fifty-one years ago, that our government was all sail and no anchor. Macaulay, whom I immensely admire, knew nothing about America, and he actually inverted our *governmental* dangers; as distinguished from those always inherent of course, in every government based on the extreme democratic principle (dangers very different from, but in my own judgment certainly no more serious than, those inherent in governments based on other principles; for as you probably realize, I am a pretty radical democrat in spite of the fact, or perhaps rather because of the fact, that I believe that wise radicalism must of necessity always go hand in hand with a wise conservatism).

During my term as President I have more than doubled the navy of the United States, and at this moment our battle fleet is doing what no other similar fleet of a like size has ever done — that is, circumnavigating the globe — and is also at this moment in far more efficient battle trim, from the standpoint of battle tactics, and even from the standpoint of gunnery, than when it started out a year ago; while the individual ships are each just a trifle more efficient.

Then take the Panama Canal. I do not think that any feat of quite such far-reaching importance has been to the credit of our country in recent years; and this I can say absolutely was my own work, and could not have been accomplished save by me or by some man of my temperament.

Again, I think the peace of Portsmouth was a substantial achievement. You probably know the part we played in the Algeciras conference.

Again, I believe what I did in settling the anthracite coal strike was a matter of very real moment from the standpoint not only of industrial but of social reform and progress.

Again, I have trebled or quadrupled the forest reserves of the country; have put thru the reorganization of the forest service, placing it under the Agricultural Department; and I may add as a small incident, have created

[3] For the British response to this speech see No. 5011, note 3.

a number of reservations for preserving the wild things of nature, the beasts and birds as well as the trees.

In legislation I succeeded in getting thru the national irrigation act. In the development of the semiarid States, of the great plains and Rockies, I think this achievement in importance comes second only to the creation of the homestead act; and indeed in those particular States it is more important than the homestead act.

During these eight sessions of Congress I have succeeded in getting the administration of the civil government in the Philippine Islands put upon a satisfactory basis; and I got Congress to approve of my action in interfering in Cuba — and here, by the way, let me interject that I think we have given a pretty fair example of international good faith of the kind I preach, for after having our army for the second time for several years in Cuba, we are now about to leave the island prosperous and thriving, and with a reasonable hope that it can achieve self-government for itself; at least, if it cannot, it is evident that we have done our best to put it on the road of stable and orderly independence. In Santo Domingo, after two years' delay I got the Senate to ratify the treaty I had made (and under which, incidentally, I had been acting for two years) and have now put the affairs of the island on a better basis than they have been for a century — indeed, I do not think it would be an overstatement to say on a better basis than they have ever been before. The Senate has ratified our actions with regard to South America, and in consequence our position in regard to the Latin American Republics is infinitely better than it ever has been before; and so, I may add, is the case with Japan, thanks to our demonstrating that we desire to act with fairness and courtesy, and in entire good faith, *and that we carry a big stick.*

We succeeded in passing a law improving the administration of the army, and also a law improving the administration of the national guard or militia. We got another law passed which established the Department of Commerce and Labor, with the Bureau of Corporations, and thereby enabled us to take the first really efficient step toward exercising proper national supervision and control over the great corporations.

Partly by law and partly by executive order we have completely reorganized the consular service of the United States. We passed a law giving vitality to the Interstate Commerce Commission, and for the first time providing some kind of efficient control by the National Government over the great railroads. We passed a law providing for Federal meat inspection of the packing houses, and also the pure food law, both of them of the utmost importance from the sanitary standpoint. In matters of social and industrial reform I got a law creating a juvenile court for the District of Columbia; another, providing for the investigation of the condition of women and child workers of the United States; an employers' liability law for corporations engaged in interstate commerce, and for the Government service itself, and for the District of Columbia; where we have also regulated child labor by law. This means, all told, a considerable sum of legislative achievement.

We settled the Alaskan boundary dispute; we have laid the Pacific cable. By the establishment of army and navy maneuvers I have, I think, much increased the efficiency of the army and doubled the efficiency of the navy. I have started the movement for the development of our inland waterways as part of the great movement for the conservation of our national resources. I also started the movement for the betterment of the conditions of country life. All these latter, however, have been done by me without the assistance of Congress. Furthermore, thru the Department of Justice we have brought big corporations and labor unions impartially before the courts, and have actually brought to justice and secured the punishment by fine and imprisonment of the most powerful wrongdoers in the land. So many successful suits, civil and criminal, have been undertaken by the Department of Justice that I would not even attempt to enumerate them. The anger of labor leaders like Gompers, and of the largest Wall Street magnates on the other side, is a sufficient guaranty of what we have done.

Inasmuch as you invite your fate I send you herewith the six volumes of my Presidential addresses and State papers. In the indexes you will find references to most of the matters of which I have above spoken.[4]

With all good wishes, believe me, *Sincerely yours*

5097 · TO THE NAVY DEPARTMENT   *Roosevelt Mss.*

Washington, December 29, 1908

Navy Department: In reference to the report of the General Board in favor of the 12-inch guns, I would like to know if you can make any specific report on the relative advantages of the 14-inch and 12-inch guns, the consideration of which I requested in my letter to you concerning the report made from the Chief of the Bureau of Ordnance. This matter is of such very great importance that I want to be certain that it has received the fullest consideration. I want the General Board's specific consideration of the views of the Bureau of Ordnance, the views of the Bethlehem Steel Work people and of the general proposition.[1] That is, I want a comparison of the advantages and disadvantages in detail of the two types.

[4] Brooks used Roosevelt's own assessment of his administration in "President Roosevelt's Record," *Living Age*, 261:259–266 (May 1, 1909).

---

[1] The Bureau of Ordnance had already completed its designs for the 14-inch gun which the Bethlehem Steel Company stated it could manufacture. Nevertheless, the ships authorized in 1909 carried 12-inch guns.

Washington, December 29, 1908

Dear Will: I shall not write you in detail what Loeb will say to you. He has been all over it with me. I need hardly say how earnestly I am concerned about him.[1] *Ever yours*

Washington, December 29, 1908

Dear Will: Hengelmüller, the Austrian Ambassador, called on me yesterday evidently a good deal concerned by the telegram of Mrs. Taft and you to the Serbians.[1] I know nothing about the incident, but I am glad to tell you what I think are undoubtedly the facts in the Balkans. No better bit of governmental work has been done in Europe than the work of the Austrians in governing Bosnia and Herzegovina. It is objected to by precisely the type of individual who objects to our having interfered in the Philippines, Santo Domingo, and Panama. I need hardly tell you that while Serbia has done better as an independent power than she did under Turkey, she has done hideously, nevertheless. The present King is the beneficiary of an assassination of the most atrocious kind, and the real authors of the assassination have never been punished. I hope and believe that the Southern Slavs will ultimately grow able to stand by themselves and do as well as the Bulgarians and Roumanians have done; but at present independence or annexation to Serbia would work for Bosnia and Herzegovina very much as Bryan's theory of immediate independence would work for the Philippines.

I am going to give the English a good word for their work in India when I make a missionary address soon. This I know will meet your hearty approval. *Ever yours*

[1] Both Roosevelt and Loeb were concerned about the latter's future. There was some hope that Taft might appoint the private secretary to a Cabinet post. When this was not forthcoming. Loeb accepted the collectorship of the port of New York. He later became associated with the American Smelting and Refining Company.

[1] The Tafts, according to an erroneous newspaper report, had sent expressions of sympathy to an association of Serbian women which was one of many organizations then propagandizing for Serbian independence.

Washington, December 29, 1908

Gentlemen: [1] Thru Senator Lodge I have received your letter of December 16th. As I understand the circumstances of the case, the Indians in whose behalf this appeal is made were a group of notorious outlaws, led by a medicine man named By-a-lil-le, an Indian of the type of Geronimo in earlier days. They made their home in an inaccessible part of the Navajo Reservation, whence they were accustomed to descend upon their industrious and peaceable fellow tribesmen, ravage their little home places, destroy or steal their livestock and crops, carry off their women, and generally exercise a rule of terror over them. Some of the more daring of the band tried also to bully the scattered whites on the border of the reservation by threats of violence; and had this sort of thing been much longer continued there is little doubt that a few hotheads on one side or the other would have started a fight which would have led to a great deal of bloodshed before it was finished.

When some of the Indians opened fire upon a troop of soldiers who had penetrated their country on a lawful errand, they were fired upon in return, and the ringleaders of the band were taken prisoners and carried to Fort Huachuca, just as twenty-odd years ago Geronimo and his band were captured and carried to a military post for discipline. The only point at which the Commissioner of Indian Affairs took a hand in the matter was in recommending to his superiors in office that, instead of the sentence of ten years at hard labor which had been suggested as appropriate, it would be wiser to give them a sentence of indeterminate length, as is now done in most civilized communities with offenders as to whom the hope is for their reform rather than for their mere punishment, so that when they can satisfy their custodians that they have learned their lesson and are ready to lead a better life, they may be restored to freedom. For his share in the matter the Commissioner has always claimed full responsibility.

The alternative courses open to him were to recommend that these men be set free, or that they be sent where they could learn to do perhaps the only honest work they had ever done in their lives. There was no middle course. Grand juries in a thinly settled frontier country, as everyone knows who is familiar with conditions there, have scant time to give to troubles between Indians still in a wild state who pay no share of the taxes; and the particular troubles which the Commissioner was aiming to suppress were the hostilities practiced by By-a-lil-le and his outlaws upon other Indians who were trying to do right and respond to the Government's efforts

[1] John D. Long, Edward Henry Clement, retired editor in chief of the Boston *Transcript,* and John S. Lockwood, Boston bibliophile, had written Roosevelt for the Boston Indian Citizenship Committee.

in behalf of their civilization. That was his duty, and the conditions made it an extremely difficult duty to perform.

What the Commissioner "is reported to have said at the recent Mohonk Conference," according to your resolutions, could be read with a better understanding if you had not stripped it bare of its context. I prefer to judge it in the light of what went with it, whatever that may have been. The little hint you give of the purport of the rest of the speech, in the closing sentence which follows the asterisks, shows that Mr. Leupp in this case, as in every other in which I have seen him tried, wisht only to know what the law was. If the law, as set forth by Congress or the court of last appeal, forbids such a course as he took, that ends his responsibility; but where the law is uncertain — as it is in a matter of this sort, for which there are no actual precedents — it is his duty to do that which is right according to his best lights, instead of waiting to quibble over questions which could not possibly be settled, as to the technical construction of phrases in the Constitution or the statutes. I may add that any other rule of conduct would have paralyzed his work — the good results of which no one can question — in fighting the illicit liquor traffic in the Indian country, for the decisions of the lower courts on that subject have been almost as multifarious as the devices of the offenders.

The demand of the moment in the By-a-lil-le case was that this gang of marauders, whose actions he had already investigated through the best machinery available to him, should be taught that there was a Government in Washington powerful enough to protect their victims of their own race as well as the white people in their country. I am sure that if the worthy people who, in their ignorance of every essential fact in the case, complain of him were as well acquainted with the Indian race as he is, they would understand that it is both foolish and mischievous to try to make one rule fit all cases. The stage of development reached by any group of Indians, their attitude toward the Government, and the nearness of their contact with civilization, must always be studied before deciding what practice shall be followed in dealing with their offences. Devoutly as all of us may look forward to the day when the most backward Indian shall have been brought to the point where he can be governed just as the ignorant white man is governed in one of our civilized communities, that day has not yet arrived. The surest way to delay its coming is to obstruct the efforts of the Government to deal with Indians who are still, like the outlaw Navajos, in a wild state, in the only manner which will command their respect and thus bring them to a better realization of their obligation to their neighbors.

If there is any statute which forbids the course taken in circumstances corresponding to those which surround this case, or any decision of the Supreme Court of the United States which covers it, I wish you had cited it, for I am sure that no one would be more thankful for such assistance than the very Commissioner of Indian Affairs whose conduct you assail.

I have seen a good many Commissioners of Indian Affairs. I do not believe that we have had any man who has accomplished as much for the good of the Indians as has Mr. Leupp. I appointed him wholly without regard to politics, because of his intimate knowledge of the needs of the Indians and of work among the Indians. He has more than made good, and I cannot speak too strongly of his courage and efficiency, and utter disregard of everything except the interests of the Indians. The reason we have a Commissioner of Indian Affairs is because the Indians of the wilder tribes are not in the status of white men. My own belief is that no more mischievous action could be taken against the Indians than that which would result from the position which you seek to establish in this case being established. It can only be established if the Indian is practically turned loose to hold his own as best he can in the communities where the reservations are now placed. Surely you must realize the very evil effect this would have upon the Indian himself. If you are correct in your position, the effort by the Commissioner to prevent the sale of liquor to Indians would hereafter be practically nullified.

In this particular case I have investigated the matter very carefully and sent out as a personal representative Colonel Hugh L. Scott of the regular army. I found that Mr. Leupp's action had been just in every particular. The Indians killed were lawless criminals who had been committing unspeakable outrages against peaceable and well-disposed Indians. The charges made against Mr. Leupp had been made by a so-called missionary, who to Colonel Scott withdrew them in the most complete, and, indeed, abject manner; and the other information I have received as to this so-called missionary, including, for instance, the statement of General Constant Williams, satisfies me that he is not to be believed on oath in any matter wherein he has any interest whatever; this being General Williams' statement about him, in which I cordially agree.

I enclose you a copy of a communication on this subject which I have sent to Mrs. Francis H. Lee, of Salem, Massachusetts.[2] *Very truly yours*

5101 · TO MRS. FRANCIS HENRY LEE   *Roosevelt Mss.*

Washington, December 29, 1908

My dear Mrs. Lee: [1] It is always a pleasure to hear from you. I know all about the action of Commissioner Leupp in the case referred to, but of course my attention had not previously been called to what you say regarding the families of the two Navajo Indians who were killed in the engagement with the troops on the east end of their reservation last fall. The two letters from the Rev. Howard R. Antes to Agent Brosius of the Indian

[2] No. 5101.

---

[1] Mrs. Francis Henry Lee, aunt by marriage of Alice Hathaway Lee Roosevelt.

Rights Association I have turned over to Commissioner Leupp, for such inquiry into the cases as may be advisable. I may say, however, that the fact that these men were killed in the course of an affray with the military does not seem, at first blush, to entitle their families to more especial consideration than the families of Indians who die in other ways. The Navajos have thus far been kept as far as possible from the evil pauperizing influences which have been the ruin of so many other tribes, and unless there is something out of the common in these cases, it is possible that it may not be thought wise to make them especial objects of charity. You may depend upon Mr. Leupp's handling of the matter as being humane and considerate, irrespective of anything which has happened hitherto, as he never allows his judgment to be influenced by any irrelevancies.

Last winter Mr. Antes flooded the country with long and fierce denunciations of Superintendent Shelton, and the United States troop whom he had used to shoot down in cold blood two poor inoffensive Indians, and more of the same sensational character. Substantially identical letters were sent to me, to various benevolent associations interested in Indians, to leading Senators and Representatives, and to individual citizens of prominence thruout the country, and to such newspapers as he evidently believed would print such stuff without inquiry. In these letters, moreover, were serious reflections against the fair dealing of the Indian Office. This led Commissioner Leupp to make a point of requesting an investigation by some person entirely outside of the Indian Service, and, if possible, outside of the Department of the Interior; also, that the investigator be a person who knew Indians, and who had, or could soon gain, their confidence, so that they would pour forth their grievances freely to him; and, finally, that it be one whose name would stand before the country as of itself a sufficient guaranty of the fairness and thoroness of his investigation and the candor of his report. Mr. Leupp absolutely refused to have anything to do with the selection of this special emissary.

I chose Colonel Hugh L. Scott of the regular army, Superintendent of the United States Military Academy at West Point. The Interior Department turned over to him every letter, memorandum, or scrap of evidence of any sort, it had on its files about the matter in question, and Commissioner Leupp scrupulously avoided seeing Colonel Scott except on one occasion when the Colonel called at his office to interrogate the Commissioner on one or two points in the testimony.

Colonel Scott is a master of the Indian sign language, and took with him two Indians who had formerly served with him. He was able thus to check up, thru the use of the sign language, the work of the interpreters, and to make sure that he procured all the testimony the Indian witnesses had to offer.

Colonel Scott's report was a complete exoneration of the Government officers and employees concerned in the business of which complaint had been made. He also brought back the letter of retraction and apology, dated at Aneth, Utah, April 23, 1908, of which a copy is enclosed. The original, which is on file as a part of the report, is in Antes' own handwriting.

After a number of the letters of accusation first sent out by Antes had come into the Indian Office by reference, the Commissioner recalled the man's name, and believed that he remembered having heard it mentioned by Brigadier General Constant Williams of the United States Army, who in the 'nineties, while still a captain, was Acting Indian Agent for the Navajos for some years. As Mr. Leupp could not remember in what connection the name had been mentioned, he wrote General Williams the inquiry of which a copy is enclosed, and received the answer which accompanies it.

Antes was requested to leave the Navajo reservation, some years ago, for reasons which, as the Department believed, amply justified such a measure. From that time to this, Antes has lost no opportunity of trying to harm Superintendent Shelton, whom he regarded as primarily responsible for his being *persona non grata*. The history of his relations with the Indian establishment is now in process of being dug out of the official files for submission to me. Superintendent Shelton is a man of very positive characteristics — the kind of man who always may depend upon having plenty of enemies. For years the Indian Rights Association, thru its Washington agent, Mr. Brosius, has maintained an attitude of hostility toward Mr. Shelton, the value of which may be judged by the fact that last year, when this business was at its thickest, Mr. Leupp asked Mr. Brosius what he thought of certain improvements Shelton had made at his school, and the admission came out that altho Mr. Brosius had been within thirty-five miles of Shelton's headquarters — where one of Shelton's most persistent enemies was living — he had never visited Mr. Shelton or seen the school or the agency with his own eyes.

On the other hand, all unprejudiced persons who have visited Mr. Shelton's place, including experts from the Department of Agriculture, and others competent to judge, are compelled to yield him the largest praise for the way he is handling things there and the success he has achieved, under great difficulties, in turning a piece of desert into a garden.

Indeed, when Commissioner Leupp came into office, he found that an inspecting officer who had been sent to Shelton's agency to compose conflict of authority which had arisen between Shelton and two other Government employees there, had reported in Shelton's favor; but Colonel J. S. Lockwood of Boston and a few other persons interested in Indians, but living at a like distance from them, had complained that this decision was unjust, and that the inspecting officer was prejudiced. The Commissioner at once took measures to find out what other inspecting officer would be satisfactory to the complainants. They agreed with practical unanimity on Mr. Frank Mead, then a special supervisor of the Indian Office. The Commissioner ordered Mr. Mead at once to the spot, instructing him to disregard anything that had gone before, but to investigate and report upon the merits of the case as an original proposition. The report upheld Superintendent Shelton unequivocally, and was accompanied by the resignations of the two employees who were fighting him.

I call your particular attention to the abject apology made on April 23d last by Mr. Antes to Colonel Scott, copy of which is enclosed; and to General Williams' opinion of Mr. Antes, which is also enclosed.

No statement that Mr. Antes makes in this matter is entitled to one moment's consideration; nor, indeed, is any statement he makes on any matter entitled to any consideration. Commissioner Leupp is one of the best and most efficient and high-minded public servants to be found anywhere in the Government. Colonel Scott is one of the best officers in the army, and probably the officer best fitted from his experience to pass judgment on such a case as this.

With great regard, believe me, *Sincerely yours*

5102 · TO TRUMAN HANDY NEWBERRY   *Roosevelt Mss.*

Washington, December 29, 1908

The Secretary of the Navy: My attention has been called to the language in the annual report of the Chief Constructor concerning the criticisms made by Commander Key on the features of the design of the *North Dakota*.[1] Commander Key is not named in the report, but he might as well have been; and, indeed, it would have been more frank and straightforward to have

[1] Capps's report revealed the bitterness created during the previous year by the determined effort of the reformers to reorganize the naval administration. In his report, which mentioned no names, Capps savagely attacked the officer whose critical official statements about the design of the *North Dakota* had led to the Newport conference. The Chief Constructor pointed out that although this officer had been in Washington while the *North Dakota* plans were being drawn up, he had withheld any comment until the battleship's construction was eighteen months under way. Therefore, Capps implied, this criticism, like that made earlier in the Reuterdahl article, was not intended to improve the fighting qualities of American ships but solely to discredit the Bureau of Construction and Repair.

Such attacks on his bureau had, Capps maintained, been proved completely unwarranted. At the Senate hearings on the charges made in the Reuterdahl article, the Chief Constructor claimed that the only "serious criticism" made of the *North Dakota's* design concerned the location of the armor belt. Without any reference to the convincing testimony of Key on the validity of the charge, Capps wrote that such criticism "was shown to be without proper foundation in fact, and was . . . . definitely and finally disposed of by a very decisive majority of the officers assembled at the Newport conference." That conference, Capps was certain, had completely vindicated the work of his bureau. Saying nothing about the resolution passed at Newport sustaining Key's major charges, Capps reported: "the fact that the Newport conference . . . . should, after mature deliberation have expressed itself so positively concerning the merits of the *North Dakota* design as a whole is in itself a complete refutation of the ill-considered adverse criticisms." Key, furious at these statements, demanded an official investigation of the remarks in the Chief Constructor's report. Roosevelt, thoroughly annoyed by this public display of controversy within the Navy, found Capps's explanation for his action unsatisfactory; see No. 5105.

named him. The statements in this official report are the most flagrant possible violation of my directions as to avoiding public recrimination between officers in this matter. If the Chief Constructor has any explanation to make, I should be glad to hear it.

5103 · TO WILLIAM HOWARD TAFT   *Roosevelt Mss.*

Washington, December 31, 1908

Dear Will: I will see the Austrian Ambassador at once and tell him. It was stated in the papers that you and Mrs. Taft had sent some dispatch to a Serbian women's association or something of the kind, the dispatch being apparently rather vague but expressing sympathy with the purposes of the association. I had seen the statement in the papers but it had made no impression upon me; however, evidently it had given anxiety to the great and good statesmen of the dual Empire. The fact that I saw the dispatch and statement in the papers did not create in my mind even a presumption that you had sent it; but as long as the Austrian Ambassador came around and called upon me I thought I had better write you, as he hoped I would and asked me to; because I was not prepared to say anything about whether you had sent it or not.

Cabot, who is going to see you, bears a message from me.[1]

Ha ha! *you* are making up your Cabinet. *I* in a lighthearted way have spent the morning testing the rifles for my African trip. Life has compensations! *Ever yours*

[*Handwritten*] Spencer Eddy is a poor stick; we have demoted him to Roumania, at his earnest request, as he loves even a third rate European court; but he is a good man to let stay demoted.[2]

5104 · TO WILLIAM HOWARD TAFT   *Roosevelt Mss.*

Personal   Washington, January 1, 1909

Dear Will: I would like you to know from me just what I did in connection with the Ohio senatorship;[1] and this letter is to be shown no one excepting

[1] About Loeb; see No. 5107.
[2] Spencer Eddy began his diplomatic career as private secretary to John Hay. He then served eight years as an embassy secretary successively in London, Paris, Constantinople, St. Petersburg, and Berlin. After a year's service as minister to Argentina, Eddy welcomed the opportunity to trade assignments with Huntington Wilson, who had been scheduled to go, as minister, to Roumania, Servia, and Bulgaria. In September 1909 Eddy resigned from the diplomatic service.

[1] Roosevelt had intervened to frustrate Foraker's quest for the Ohio senatorship. Until the end of December, Foraker, Burton, and Charles P. Taft had struggled for that office. Although the President-elect, embarrassed by his half-brother's candidacy, wisely refused to intercede, Charles Taft counted on Boss Cox to deliver the Republican caucus. Fearing just that, Foraker and Burton opposed selection by caucus. Foraker wanted to throw the contest directly into the legislature, where he

of course Mrs. Taft. After you left here the last time, Charlie came in to see me and I was rendered very uncomfortable by our conversation. He was very bitter against Burton and stated that he had begun to believe that it would be worse to have Burton as Senator than to have Foraker. I at once answered him that he must not say that to anyone, not even to me; that Foraker's daring, his ability and his unscrupulousness, as well as his prominent position before the country and the perfectly frank confession of infamy on his part in connection with the Standard Oil people, rendered it vital from the standpoint of your success and of the success of your administration and from the standpoint of the welfare of the Republican party and of the honor of the country that he should be defeated; and that compared to the importance of defeating Foraker it was of no consequence at all what particular man was chosen to succeed him; that while I was sorry he (Charlie) had gone into the race, yet that inasmuch as he had gone in, I of course hoped he would be elected, but that this was of entirely secondary importance to defeating Foraker. A few days ago Gus Karger[2] came in with a message from Charlie saying in effect that the situation had developed so that there was grave danger of Foraker being elected; that Burton's conduct had been very bad, and so forth, and so forth. Karger also said that Charlie thought if the fight became purely between Burton and Foraker, Foraker might win. I told Karger that my information was different on this last point; that I thought Charlie had grown weaker and Burton stronger, but that I could not advise about details; that my whole concern was not to see such a calamity before your administration, at the very outset, as would be implied in the election of Foraker, and that I regarded it as outrageous, from your standpoint and from the public standpoint alike, to consider any personal question whatever as of weight compared with the one vital question of putting in for Senator any decent man who could be elected as against Foraker; that I did not presume to say what particular step should be taken

hoped to arrange for the support of the Democrats as well as that of his faithful personal guard. Burton, relying upon nonorganization Republicans and independents, also preferred a decision in the legislature. On December 29, Roosevelt announced that "to support Foraker in his attempt to prevent a caucus would be an act of treason against the Republican party" (Walters, *Foraker*, p. 283). It would, Roosevelt explained, set the stage for a Foraker-Democratic bargain by which Foraker would be elected in 1909 and a Democrat would be chosen to replace Dick in 1911. The President also, as the letter above indicates, made it clear that he considered Burton a stronger candidate than Charles Taft. If Roosevelt intended these statements not only to stop Foraker but also to elect Burton, he had his way. On December 31 Taft withdrew. The party, he declared, was more important than personal ambition; a prolonged contest in the legislature was at all costs to be avoided. His withdrawal assured Burton of Cox's support. On January 1, Foraker, recognizing that re-election had become "impossible," also dropped out. Burton then easily carried both caucus and legislature.

[2] Gustav J. Karger, since 1906 Washington correspondent of the Cincinnati *Times-Star*, in 1908 Taft's personal press representative, in 1912 director of the bureau of organization of the Republican National Committee, a journalist-politician who tried to play for Taft the kind of part O. K. Davis had tried to play for Roosevelt.

in order to accomplish this purpose, but that I did emphatically feel that it was the one purpose which should be held chiefly in mind by all concerned. I asked Karger when he sent this on to ask Charlie to repeat it to you. *Ever yours*

5105 · TO TRUMAN HANDY NEWBERRY   *Roosevelt Mss.*

Washington, January 2, 1909

To the Secretary of the Navy: I have received your report, with the endorsement of the Chief Constructor.[1] The closing paragraph (6) of the Chief Constructor's remarks states that he regrets "that an evident misapprehension as to the facts has caused the propriety of his official conduct to be questioned." So far from agreeing with his view, I regard his conduct as gravely reprehensible. To publish in his official report reflections upon a brother officer, which had not even the merit of being frank, as the brother officer tho clearly indicated was not named, amounts to grave misconduct. I thoroly reprobate the action; and to show my disapproval I direct that the order conferring the duties of Chief Engineer upon him be forthwith revoked.[2] What action I shall subsequently take I have not yet decided.

5106 · TO TRUMAN HANDY NEWBERRY   *Roosevelt Mss.*

Washington, January 4, 1909

My dear Mr. Secretary: On mentioning the matter of the physical test to Dr. Rixey I found that I had evidently misunderstood the situation and that he did not approve of the way the test had finally been ordered. I have accordingly prepared the enclosed general order and approved it. Will you please have it issued?

I have thought more and more over the Capps matter and it made me look into the scheme upon which we are now proceeding.[1] I am not satisfied with

[1] See No. 5102.
[2] Capps had been appointed Acting Chief of the Bureau of Steam Engineering in December as a preliminary step in the amalgamation of that bureau with the Bureau of Construction and Repair (see No. 5106, note 1). Lieutenant Commander Hutchinson I. Cone now replaced Capps as head of the Bureau of Steam Engineering. Capps, however, remained Chief Constructor.

[1] Letters from Sims as well as the Capps report caused Roosevelt to reconsider the current plans for naval administrative reorganization. At the time of the Newport conference, Sims, following Admiral Luce's suggestion, had written Roosevelt recommending the appointment of a commission to investigate the organization of the Navy Department. Although the President had enthusiastically endorsed this recommendation, he had made no effort to act upon it during the fall of 1908.

When Newberry became Secretary on December 1, he immediately put forward his own plan for reform. The new Secretary proposed the enlargement of the General Board to include representatives from all the bureaus, the amalgamation of the Bureau of Construction and Repair and the Bureau of Steam Engineering, and the inclusion in the new bureau of several line officers. Although the advocates of

it. We have two points to meet in connection with the navy: first, business efficiency, and second, the preparation of the navy as a fighting machine. I think the proposed reorganization would help on the first point, but I am by no means sure that it would not be a detriment as regards the second matter. I shall accordingly have a number of line officers and ex-line officers, and perhaps one or two other men, together here for their advice. I will speak to you about the details after Cabinet tomorrow. *Sincerely yours*

5107 · TO WILLIAM HOWARD TAFT   *Roosevelt Mss.*

Washington, January 4, 1909

Dear Will: Lodge has just arrived and has told me about his interview with you. I want to thank you most heartily for what you are to do for Loeb. As you know, he has been very near my heart; and this not because of his relations with me, but because of his extreme staunchness to you, so that I wisht to see no injury befall him. The collectorship of the port of New York

reform both in the Navy and in the press protested that Newberry's plan failed to meet any real needs, Roosevelt, primarily because the plan could be instituted without congressional action, gave it his approval.

Sims then wrote the President two letters which expressed fully the insurgents' view. The enlarged board, Sims told Roosevelt, was in no sense the general staff for which the President had asked in his annual message to Congress. Newberry's board had no real power over the bureaus and, in fact, thanks to the large representation of bureau men would probably become an instrument by which the bureaus could even more effectively dominate the Navy. "Secretary Newberry is doubtless in favor of reform," Sims wrote Roosevelt, "but he confuses successful (harmonious) administration with successful preparation for war." "If we don't act," he concluded, "Congress (Senator Hale) will doubtless put through a reorganization that will have the effect of strengthening the power of the bureau system." — Morison, *Sims*, pp. 222–223.

Sims's letters and Capps's report, because they impressed the President with the explosiveness of the reform issue, help account for Roosevelt's complicated maneuverings during January 1909 on the question of naval administrative reform. Roosevelt wanted to avoid at all costs open controversy until Congress had provided for two new battleships. For this reason the group of experts called to Washington by the President to advise him on reform was asked to meet on January 16, the same day the navy bill was reported out of committee. Although this impressive group of ex-Secretaries and officers active and retired ultimately did nothing more than approve Newberry's plan, its presence in Washington throughout the debate on the navy bill was a master stroke. By its very presence it silenced those who claimed nothing was being done to improve the naval organization and, at the same time, presented a threat to those who claimed that nothing needed to be done. It therefore neutralized the reorganization issue during debate on naval appropriations.

On January 22 the House, where the opposition to naval expansion was stronger than in the Senate, passed the navy bill by the surprising vote of 150 to 60. The victory, caused in part by the President's handling of the anti-Japanese agitation in California, ended Roosevelt's worries about getting "the two battleships on which I had set my heart" (see No. 5131). The President was, therefore, willing to consider seriously again the problem of administrative reform and on January 27 he finally carried out Sims's suggestion of the previous August by appointing a commission to examine the defects in the organization of the Navy Department; see Numbers 4844, 5140.

is a very important office which he can fill with the utmost credit to himself and the utmost advantage to the public and to your administration. I had been sure from what I had heard, both from the business and the political standpoint, that it would not be possible for you to keep the present incumbent. Root heartily approves of Loeb's appointment and will write you; and the Congressmen from New York had already offered to do anything they could for Loeb in any position. I entirely agree with you that not a word should be said about it now, and that the appointment should be made immediately after your inauguration. I should suggest that it be made the next day, as your Cabinet will then be coming in and as it will be a great advantage to anticipate any trouble from New York in the way of pressure by conflicting factions for the place.

Cabot also told me that you wisht me to know that you did not intend to reappoint either Garfield or Straus. I have already known that you did not intend to reappoint Newberry, Cortelyou, or Bonaparte, and after our last conversation had concluded that you probably would not appoint Garfield or Straus. Now I think it would be well for you to write them all at once that you do not intend to reappoint them. They will be making their plans, and less than two months remain, and I do not think they ought to be left in doubt. Cortelyou and Bonaparte, I am sure, have no expectation of staying. I do not think the other three have, but I think it would be well to assure them immediately. Of course I am perfectly willing to tell them if you will write to me to do so, but I do not think I ought to tell them unless I have some direct communication from you. You are quite right in thinking that Garfield ought not to take, and would not desire to take, any foreign mission. Whether Straus would or not I cannot say. I will say to either whatever you authorize me to say.

I am exceedingly pleased at the good news about Meyer. As I never wisht to ask you for any appointment, I had been scrupulously careful not to ask you for Meyer's appointment, altho from what I said you of course saw how admirably I felt he would fill either the secretaryship of the treasury or the secretaryship of the navy. In neither position would it be possible for you to get a better man, and he was one of the men who from the beginning stood side by side with Lodge in the fight for you, when it was an even thing whether New England would be turned for Hughes against you or not. You will find him an exceptionally competent and faithful public servant and the most loyal and staunch of supporters. From the standpoint of Massachusetts politics I have grown to feel during the last two or three weeks that it was of the utmost importance to Lodge that Meyer's appointment should be made, and that it would be a most serious blow to him if the appointment were not made. I cannot say how pleased I am that the matter is settled.

There is now no need of Loeb's going down to see you.

Give my love to Mrs. Taft, and my regards to Henry if he is still with you. *Ever yours*

5108 · TO JOSEPH GURNEY CANNON · *Roosevelt Mss.*

Washington, January 4, 1909

My dear Mr. Speaker: Since seeing you I have had a long consultation with Secretary Root and we have heard repeatedly from Ambassador Griscom. The calamity in Italy is appalling; the need for funds *at once* very great; and I do not think it would be safe for us to appropriate less than half a million in addition to the rations on the two supply ships. It is possible that when the two ships arrive there the money we have already appropriated will make it unnecessary to use the rations, altho about this it is of course difficult now to be sure.[1] *Sincerely yours*

5109 · TO EUGENE HALE · *Roosevelt Mss.*

Washington, January 5, 1909

My dear Senator Hale: I have requested the different Departments of the Government, not only those to whom you sent requests but those to whom you did not, to give me all the information about the use of special attorneys, special agents, inspectors, &c., in their departments which will enable me to put before you all the facts which, as I understand it, your Committee[1] desire to have. I transmit these reports herewith. I call especial attention to the reports of the Secretary of State, the Secretary of the Treasury, and the Attorney General.

Let me at the outset earnestly express my cordial agreement with the view that it is not only the right but the duty of Congress to investigate the workings of the secret service or detective agents by which alone the Government can effectually safeguard itself against wrongdoing, punish crime, and bring to justice criminals. I am well aware of the liability to abuse inherent in any effective detective system or secret-service system; for the measure of the efficiency of the system is also the measure of the

---

[1] In Sicily and Calabria, in the vicinity of the historic towns of Messina and Reggio, an earthquake without parallel in its destructive force had within three minutes leveled the buildings within an area of 150,000 square miles and taken over 100,000 lives. "Instantly and with a gratifying absence of red tape," Roosevelt ordered two naval supply ships, the *Celtic* and the *Culgoa*, to the scene of the disaster. There they were to dispense food, clothing, and other supplies to the value of $300,000. In a special message to Congress on January 4 the President requested both approval of this order and an appropriation of $500,000 more for relief. Congress at once enacted a satisfactory law. With the consent of Speaker Cannon, Roosevelt and Root then gave to the Italian government complete discretion in the use of the relief funds.

[1] The Senate Committee on Appropriations, then preoccupied with the secret-service issue.

seriousness of the abuses of the system if it be applied to wrong purposes or directed in an improper manner. It is eminently to the public interest that there should be vigilant inquiry into the working of this agency both by the heads of the executive departments and by Congress.

It nevertheless remains true that this system is absolutely indispensable if the popular interest is to be adequately safeguarded and wrongdoers taught to fear the law. To show how indispensable detectives are when important work of a confidential character must be done, I refer you to the experience of the Immigration Commission appointed by Congress and largely composed of Senators and Representatives, which has found it absolutely necessary to employ detectives in order to achieve the best results. In my communication of the 4th instant to the Lower House I have set forth at length the reasons why, in my judgment, it is eminently desirable that, in addition to the special detectives or inspection service of each department, there should be in some one department, preferably the Department of Justice, a service which can be used at need in any department in order to achieve the ends I have described.[2] I would like to state here that very frequently accusations have been made to me privately by members of the two Houses to the effect that the secret service has been used as a "police of morals" or to shadow Senators, Congressmen, and other public officials. Hitherto the effort to discover the basis for such allegations has always been fruitless. I should be greatly obliged if any information could be furnished me tending to show any instance where this has been done in times past.

Certain of the special agents, inspectors, and the like, in the several departments have a highly specialized work to perform. In the Treasury Department the secret service is especially trained to deal with counterfeiters and the special agents with customs frauds. In the Post-Office Department the corps of inspectors is especially trained and peculiarly fitted to detect criminality or abuses or fraudulent use of the mails in connection with the

---

[2] Offended by the references in the President's annual message to the relations of congressmen with the secret service (see No. 5071, note 3), the House had passed a resolution declaring that Roosevelt's "plain meaning" was that "the majority of the Congressmen were in fear of being investigated by secret service men." This resolution asked the President "to transmit to the House any evidence connecting any Member of the House of Representatives of the Sixtieth Congress with corrupt action in his official capacity." Replying in a message of January 4, Roosevelt disavowed the meaning attributed to his words. "I have made no charges of corruption against Congress nor against any Member of the present House," he explained. Had he had any proof of corruption, he declared, he would of course have brought legal action long since. The committee to consider this reply reported that the House "must insist on its own capacity to understand the import of the President's language." It recommended that the portion of the annual message referring to the secret service and the whole of the special message of January 4 be laid on the table, and that the latter be regarded as an invasion of the privileges of the House. A resolution incorporating these recommendations passed by the spanking vote of 211 to 36. Overjoyed by the outcome, Speaker Cannon considered it the greatest triumph of the legislative over the executive since Henry Clay had fathered the resolution censuring Jackson's bank policy.

postal service. In the Interior Department the special agents of the land office and the inspectors of the Indian bureau are trained in similar fashion to meet special needs. In addition, it is urgently necessary, as set forth in Mr. Root's accompanying report, that there shall be a central force of secret-service men who can be detailed for work anywhere in the Government service.

Of course, in the investigation of specific frauds we sometimes come across wholly unexpected phases of misconduct. The frauds in the postal department which were unearthed some six years ago, for instance, offer a case in point. My suspicions were first aroused by a report made as to the very extravagant and debauched manner of life of a certain postal employee, this report being made by an official of the secret service in connection with another transaction on which he was at work. So with cases of the abuse of the franking privilege. The post office never of set purpose inspects any package sent through the mails by a Senator or Congressman, but sometimes through the accidental breaking of such package the contents are exposed, and if they are of a character which makes their transmission by franking privilege illegal, steps are taken by the post-office authorities to collect the full postage. Some of these instances represent real abuses, but in other cases they are due to carelessness or ignorance, and very often doubtless are entirely unknown to the Congressmen themselves and no good purpose would be served by any publicity in the matter.

But a case has just arisen of a different kind which it seems to me I should put before you as illustrating in striking fashion the way in which investigations begun by any of these various agents in the strict line of their duty may develop facts of high importance, which the investigators would not in the first instance have sought to discover, which when discovered ought not to be hidden or suppressed, but the development of which may tend to create an erroneous impression that the agents in question were being used for purposes not within the line of their lawful duty.

On the 19th of February, 1908, (see Exhibit A) Senator Tillman called the attention of the Senate to a circular of a syndicate firm for the sale of lands in Oregon, particularly in Coos and Douglas counties, which had been granted to corporations by the Government, the circular stating that the company in possession of the lands was bound to sell them for $2.50 an acre or upon their refusal would be prosecuted by the Government, and that "among those who have spoken for a part of this land is Senator Tillman of South Carolina, the leader of the Democratic party in the Senate, a man who usually gets what he goes after." Senator Tillman denied the statement of this circular and expressed a wish for an investigation, and upon his request the Post-Office Department, through its inspectors, made such an investigation. He stated in reference to this circular, "I have not bought any land anywhere in the West nor undertaken to buy any. I have made some inquiries, as one naturally would, in roaming through the West. I simply want the people of the country to be put on notice that this swindler at Portland has no warrant whatever for endeavoring to inveigle others into his game." I enclose the circular referred to, as Exhibit B; the report of the post-office inspectors, under date of July 27, 1908, as Exhibit C. This is a confidential report of a type usually not furnished, but in this case the matter is so serious that I feel I should put it before you. I enclose you also, as Exhibits D 1, D 2, D 3, D 4, and D 5, photographic facsimiles of letters and envelopes and telegram from Senator Tillman and his agent, William E. Lee. It appears that on October 20, 1907, Senator Tillman wrote a letter (Exhibit D 3) to Messrs. Reeder and Watkins, of Marshfield, Oregon, who were attorneys representing people who were applicants for the purchase of certain wagon road land-grant land; Dorr was a land agent making his filings through Reeder and Watkins. Senator Tillman's letter runs in part as follows:

I wired you from (Wausau, Wisconsin) as follows, and write to confirm it. "Wm. E. Lee, my agent, will see you about land. I want nine quarters reserved. Will forward signed applications and money at once. Members of my family are entrymen. Letter follows. (Signed) B.R.T." I write now to say I wired Mr. Lee, who resides at Moscow, Idaho, to go at once to Marshfield and see you about the land, to locate Qrs for the seven members of my family who are of age & one for my private secy. J. B. Knight, whom I desire to let in to the deal & of course he wants a Qr for himself.

The letter continued, stating in detail what was to be done in order to enable the Senator to get the land. The William E. Lee to whom Senator Tillman thus referred as his agent, wrote to Reeder & Watkins, under date of December 7th, a letter, photographic copy of which is herewith submitted, marked Exhibit D 4. In this letter Mr. Lee explains that he had written Senator Tillman fully as to the status of the land matter, advising him that it was "a good gamble," but that the Senator was lecturing, so that he did not get Mr. Lee's letter until a week and a half previously. The letter continues:

In case Senator Tillman gets in on this deal with some good land in the eight quarters we want, I am satisfied that he can be of great help in getting matters started from Washington, and cause the Government to get busy and do something along the line you desire. He will set up such a howl that it will be impossible to do otherwise. This will be very important for your whole scheme to have a man of his influence here to aid you at this end of the line. By all means save a lot of good land for us, as we intend to be of more value than any one of the others in this matter

On the 31st of January, 1908, Senator Tillman introduced in the Senate the following resolution:

Whereas at divers times various railroads and other corporations have received large grants of public lands of the United States, under and by virtue of acts of the Congress, containing conditions to the effect that such lands should be sold to actual settlers only, or in quantities not exceeding for any one purchaser a limit fixed by the act relating thereto, or at a price per acre not greater than an amount mentioned in the act authorizing such grant, to the end that such lands might promptly become the homes of citizens of the United States; and

Whereas it is currently reported and widely believed that the Department of Justice has information to the effect that certain of the corporations aforesaid, or their alleged successors in title, having obtained colorable title to large tracts of land within a State or State of the Pacific slope by virtue of the grants above mentioned, and still holding considerable portions thereof, have violated or evaded the equitable and salutary conditions so as aforesaid imposed by the Congress upon such grants for the public good; yet the Senate is not advised that any action has been taken by the Department of Justice to enforce the said conditions or restore the said lands to the public domain: Now therefore be it

Resolved, etc., That the President be requested, if not incompatible with the public interest, to inform the Senate what information, if any, has been received, and what action, if any, has been taken by the Department of Justice with respect to the matters and things in the preamble to this resolution set forth.

and pressed vigorously for immediate action. The resolution being laid over, Senator Tillman introduced the same day a further and joint resolution containing the same recitals but concluding as follows:

Resolved, etc., That the Attorney General be, and he is hereby, directed, authorized, and empowered to take such proceedings or institute such suit or suits on behalf of the United States as may be necessary, appropriate, or expedient to insure a compliance with the above-mentioned conditions or to restore the said lands to the public domain, or to report to the Congress why such action as aforesaid has not been or should not be taken.

On February 15th Senator Tillman wrote to Messrs. Reeder and Watkins. A photograph of this letter is also attached as Exhibit D 5. In it I call your attention to the fact that he speaks again of Mr. Lee as his agent and of the correspondence carried on through Mr. Lee. He states that what he has done in stirring up the question of the Oregon land grants to railroads has been done entirely apart from any personal interest he has in the matter, and adds, "although I never would have had my attention called to it but for the investigation as set on foot in connection with the proposed purchase by me of some of the timber land in question. Of course, if I decide to make the tender and go into the lawsuit, I will bear your proposition in mind, but I would have you understand that nothing I do here in the Senate will be done because of any personal purchase of any of the land. If I can succeed in causing the Government to institute suit for the recovery of the land and make it easier for others *as well as myself* (the italics are mine) to obtain some of it, I shall do it without any regard to the dealings with your firm. I still want to get some of the timber land, if it is possible, and as it is probable that Mr. Lee or some other representative of mine will be in your country in the next two months we will leave the matter of payment for the initiatory steps and subsequent proceedings in abeyance for the present. Any contract we might make will be entirely apart from, and independent of, my work here in the Senate. I will be glad for you to hold in reserve eight of the best quarter sections of which you have definite information and I will in the meantime press the investigation and other work here which will facilitate the final purchase, and in effect obviate the necessity of your making any case in the courts at all."

This letter in which Senator Tillman requested that eight of the best quarter sections be held in reserve for him was written just four days before he announced in the Senate that he had not undertaken to buy any land in the West. It is unnecessary to comment upon his proposal, made in this letter, to use his influence as Senator to force the Government to institute a suit which would make it easy for him personally to obtain some of the land. This letter, purely pertaining to Mr. Tillman's personal and private business, was sent in a franked envelope, of which I attach photographic copy marked Exhibit D 5.

The assault by Senator Tillman upon Mr. Dorr was, according to the report of the inspectors, a wanton assault made to cover up Senator Tillman's own transactions.

I call your attention to the letter of Mr. Dorr to the Postmaster General under date of November 22, 1908, (Exhibit E) in which he asks for relief from the cases which Senator Tillman had brought against him, saying that he had no knowledge that Senator Tillman desired his operations to be kept hidden and secret from general public knowledge. The report of the inspectors seems to indicate that this young man, Mr. Dorr, acted in good faith, but that he used Senator Tillman's application for land as an advertisement.[3] *Very truly yours*

[3] This letter and the exhibits that accompanied it were released for publication on January 9 in spite of Hale's preference that they remain confidential (see No. 5115). They were then, on January 11, at the request of Senator Tillman, printed in full in the *Congressional Record*, XLIII, 719-739. Although Tillman challenged Roosevelt's interpretation of his conduct, he did not deny the accuracy of the facts the President had compiled. Admitting that he had been interested in the Oregon lands, Tillman explained that he had not purchased any and had violated no law. He continued to insist, as he had earlier charged, that Bryan R. Dorr, president of the St. Paul and Pacific Timber Syndicate, was, contrary to the report of the postal inspector, guilty of using the mails to defraud. "I have not attempted to deceive anybody; I have not told any falsehoods; I have not broken any law; I have not been guilty of any immoral conduct," the senator declaimed. ". . . . I declare most emphatically I have never concealed my efforts to buy land." Roosevelt, Tillman contended, had sought only to buttress his own views on the secret service by defaming an able opponent. "He has prepared his indictment with consummate ability and skill. He is even cunning in the apparently innocent pretense that in making a search through the Secret Service for one kind of malefactor he had run down another. . . . [Yet] he has been in the possession of all the facts in this case since July last, and men will be curious to know why, if his zeal was honest, he did not make them known then. . . . The eagerness and intensity with which he has presented his case against me, ... his taking from the committee to which he had forwarded them the papers and giving them to the press before that committee had considered them, indicate that Theodore Roosevelt enjoys to the limit the feeling of getting even with Ben. Tillman and lays on the big stick with the keenest relish, doubtless believing that the pitchfork has gone out of business." — *Congressional Record*, XLIII, 740-743.

Tillman's candor and oratory won the laughter and applause of the gallery in

Washington, January 6, 1909

Dear Will: Root, Cabot, and Bacon have all spoken to me about the case of young Phillips, and want me to call your attention to it. I do so with the distinct understanding that I merely recite the facts to you. You probably remember that when you and I and Root talked over the State Department it was agreed that I should appoint Phillips as Third Secretary because of his acquaintance with Eastern affairs, and because to appoint him now would result in establishing a certain continuity of the office. I accordingly sent in his nomination. It has been held up by Senator Hale, not that he objects to Phillips, whom on the contrary he would like to see get any other place, but because he wishes to keep this place open for his son, Chandler Hale, whom he intends to ask you to appoint. Chandler Hale is a good young fellow and there are minor positions in which he could do well. I appointed him Secretary to The Hague conference, and the job was too big for him. It is the opinion of Root, Bacon, and, I may add, of myself, that he is not fit to be a good Third Secretary of the State Department;[1] certainly that he is not in the same class with Phillips in any way. You may or may not wish to mention this to Knox. I merely stated that I would put the facts before you. *Always yours*

Confidential Washington, January 6, 1909

My dear Mr. Ambassador: I do not like Winston Churchill but I suppose I ought to write him. Will you send him the enclosed letter[1] if it is all right?

You gave me exactly what I wished to know about the British rule in India. Bryce had spoken to me, giving me to understand that the people at home would be very much obliged if I would say something to correct the tendency here among well-meaning but foolish people to feel that the English rule in India is an iniquity. I shall do so in a speech a fortnight hence.

I think that the Olympic game squabble is dying a natural death. What you wrote me at the very outset has been shown more and more by events to have been absolutely true. I entirely agree with you that the recent experiences of the pastry cook, the floorwalker, and the Indian have tended to make the thing a screaming farce. The fact is that the three men are all exceptionally good long-distance runners and exceptionally close together, so

---

the Senate and of his Democratic colleagues. Yet when the senator finished, the impression firmly remained that his conduct, while well within the letter of the law, had been at least disingenuous.

[1] In October 1909, Chandler Hale succeeded Phillips as Third Assistant Secretary of State.

[1] No. 5112.

that one might win at one time and the other at another, and no one could be sure of the result on a given occasion, any more than when two crack baseball nines get together. Probably the Indian, Longboat, is normally better than either; but they were both better than he was at the Olympic game. Dorando fell and did not finish when he ran against Longboat, just as was the case when he ran against Hayes in London. They are all three of the professional type pure and simple, and to have had all the yell and trouble concerning them as amateurs at the Olympic games does seem a little absurd.

You make me very melancholy as to what you say about my clothes in Africa; but I suppose I shall have to carry all that you suggest, excepting that I think I shall take in place of the regular frock coat a black cutaway coat, so that on emergencies I can wear this without that atrocity and horror — a top hat.

Now as for what you say about The Kaiser. There is no reason why I should not tell you what happened. In the first place, as to Hale; he is of entirely good character, but of course it is nonsense to represent him as my "friend," save as any reputable newspaperman whom I know can be called such; and as for being my "guest at The White House for a week," as far as I know he has never set foot in The White House. He spent about four days, a year or so ago, in Washington, and he spent all of each morning in the anteroom where my callers congregate; where at this moment, for instance, there are twenty or thirty people and where newspapermen go continually. This was literally all. He wrote on the whole accurately, and obviously with an entirely truthful purpose.

He asked us to get him admission to the Kaiser, which we promptly refused, and how he got admitted to him I have not the slightest idea. I believe that every word he reported about the Kaiser was true. I first heard of it last July or August, when O. K. Davis of the New York *Times* came out to see me with the full and exceedingly unexpurgated interview. He had wired it over after his interview with the Kaiser, but had since telegraphed to the *Times* that the Foreign Office objected greatly to its publication; and the *Times* had sent out to inquire what I thought they ought to do. The interview contained not only the *Century* matter[2] (which, altho foolish, was not very harmful excepting for two pages of attack on the Catholic Church) but in addition statements from the Kaiser to the effect that King Edward was a poor creature, given over to the worship of money in a sordid form; that he was surrounded by people who cared for nothing except the profits of the stock market; that England was decadent; that there would be a revolt in India this winter, and that in any event he believed the Germans would soon have to go to war with England, and that Japan and the United States would also soon have a war; and that he was arranging for an alliance between China, Germany and the United States against Japan, and that it would be

[2] Roosevelt's reference was to a recapitulation and analysis of the Kaiser's interview in *Nineteenth Century*, 64:908-923 (December 1908).

very shortly announced. I told Davis that the interview lookt like a pipe dream; that I had not the slightest hesitation in believing that it was absolutely accurate; but I also had not any hesitation in advising the *Times* not to print it; that the Emperor would certainly repudiate it; and while many people would believe it to be true, many people would also believe that the *Times* had faked it, and they could not afford to be caught in such a transaction. This was aside from the fact that the publication of the interview would really jeopardize the peace of the world.

I need hardly say that you must use the greatest care in letting anyone know what I have told you.

I am greatly obliged to you for sending me over the rifle. *Faithfully yours*

5 1 1 2 · TO WINSTON LEONARD SPENCER CHURCHILL   *Roosevelt Mss.*

Washington, January 6, 1909

My dear Mr. Churchill: Thru Mr. Reid I have just received the beautiful copy of your book,[1] and I wish to thank you for it. I had read all the chapters as they came out, with a great deal of interest; not only the chapters upon the very important and difficult problems of the Government itself, but also the hunting chapters and especially the one describing how you got that rare and valuable trophy, a white rhinoceros head. Everyone has been most kind to me about my proposed trip to Africa. I trust I shall have as good luck as you had.

Again thanking you, believe me, *Sincerely yours*

5 1 1 3 · TO HENRY HURD RUSBY   *Roosevelt Mss.*

Personal   Washington, January 7, 1909

My dear Sir: [1] I have your letter of the 6th instant. I entirely agree with your point of view, and that is the point of view of the integrity of the pure food act. Moreover, I feel that Dr. Wiley was of the utmost service in creating sentiment that secured the passage of the act. The trouble with Dr. Wiley is, that to my personal knowledge, he has been guilty of such grave errors of judgment in matters of such great importance as to make it quite impossible to accept his say-so in a matter without a very uneasy feeling that I may be doing far-reaching harm to worse than no purpose.[2] I tested him personally

[1] Winston Spencer Churchill, *My African Journey* (London, 1908).

[1] Dr. Henry Hurd Rusby, physician and botanist; since 1888 a professor at the Columbia University College of Pharmacy; expert in drug products in the Bureau of Chemistry of the Department of Agriculture, 1907-1909; pharmacognosist in that bureau, 1912.

[2] Roosevelt and Wiley had had a major disagreement over the administration of the Pure Food Law. In a bulletin issued in the summer of 1908, Wiley had prohibited the use of benzoate of soda as a food preservative. Packing houses and manufacturers of various foodstuffs, including catchup, pickles, canned fruits,

in reference to corn syrup, the use of saccharine, and the importation of French vinegar. In each case he had made a ruling which was nonsensical, the kind of ruling which, if we allowed it to stand and to be followed by similar rulings, would certainly have meant the upsetting of the whole pure food law. These instances gave me a great distrust of Wiley's good judgment. On the other hand, I have such confidence in his integrity and zeal that I am anxious to back him up to the limit of my power wherever I can be sure that doing so won't do damage instead of good. I have entire confidence in his colleague, Professor Dunlap. Would you be willing to have me show your letter to Professor Dunlap, or write me such a letter as I could show him?

Thanking you for your letter, I am, *Sincerely yours*

5114 · TO TRUMAN HANDY NEWBERRY   *Roosevelt Mss.*

Personal   Washington, January 7, 1909

My dear Mr. Secretary: I have your letter of the 6th.[1] I quite agree with you as to the two questions you ask. The great reason why I wish to have the gentlemen you name, however, brought together is that I want to secure from them a plan for putting the organization of the Department on the highest plane of efficiency from the standpoint of making ready the navy for war in time of peace, and of utilizing the navy in war should one occur. I would like to suggest that you have Assistant Secretary Satterlee with you at the meeting. Will you not all of you lunch with me on January 15th? *Sincerely yours*

5115 · TO EUGENE HALE   *Roosevelt Mss.*

Washington, January 7, 1909

My dear Senator Hale: I started to rewrite my letter in accordance with our conversation of this morning, and as soon as I tried to do it it became evident to me that the task was one of extreme difficulty. I should of course have to begin by saying something that would show that the report was put in this form in accordance with your request to me. As soon as that is done it will create a clamor to have my original letter made public. Indeed, I think that from the standpoint of what you desire to attain, it would merely make mat-

---

baked beans, and soups, protested this ruling. At Roosevelt's direction the question was then referred to the expert consulting group of which Ira Remsen was president. Before the experts reported, however, and without Wiley's consent, the Board of Food and Drug Inspectors on December 28 in a new bulletin reversed Wiley's ruling on benzoate of soda. This reversal had the support of George P. McCabe, solicitor of the Department of Agriculture, and Professor F. L. Dunlap, a chemist, who with Wiley made up the board.

---

[1] Newberry had written about the naval experts whom Roosevelt had ordered to Washington for a conference beginning January 16 on administrative reform; see No. 5106.

ters worse. I am of course very desirous of meeting your wishes in any way I possibly can; and I am always anxious, my dear Senator, to defer to your judgment when I can with propriety do so. No harm will come from a few days' delay, and so I will gladly in accordance with your request refrain from giving out the letter for publication. But do let me say that I think it a mistake not to lay before your committee my letter which is now in your possession. As I told you, I am not willing to withdraw it, and sooner or later it must come out; and if I now write you another letter containing but part of my first letter and stating that this letter is written in consequence of our conversation of this morning, the only effect will be to confuse men's minds without any real permanent benefit to anyone. The longer I have thought over our conversation of this morning, the more I have become convinced that the wise action is to treat my letter now in your possession as it must sooner or later be treated, that is, as the one to be laid before the committee. I do not see what advantage is gained by not laying it before the committee now, when it certainly must be laid before it within a few days.

The enclosed correspondence between the postmaster at Washington and Senator Tillman has just been brought to my attention. He is one of the public men to whom I alluded as getting into trouble over this franking matter.

By the way, I keep my judgment in suspense as to so much of the report of the special investigators as concerns giving Dorr a complete bill of health.

May I hear from you soon? I am, of course, in accordance with your request, keeping the printed copies of my letter to you in the office, and not giving them to the press. But surely it can be but a short time before they will have to be given to the press. *Sincerely yours*

5116 · TO ALBERT LENOIR KEY

Roosevelt Mss.

Washington, January 8, 1909

My dear Commander Key: I have received your letter. I am a little puzzled what to make of it. On the first page you say that you intend to take an "active and aggressive interest" in two matters essential to the navy; that it will be "a great temptation" whenever you see "false or misleading public statements official or otherwise to establish the facts and the truth." You preface these remarks by stating that you are going to speak quite frankly; but as a matter of fact you do not speak quite frankly, for apparently your remarks refer to my caution to you against furnishing information to the press in a way that would foment the row going on about the navy. In this voluntary statement on your part you leave me in doubt as to whether you do or do not intend to obey my caution. I am not competent to speak on certain questions of naval construction, but I am entirely competent to say that the backbiting, and attacks, and counterattacks in connection with the Newport matters and the navy generally, including equally those of the champions of the side you champion and those who are against you, are to the last degree detrimental to the public service, and cause more detriment than can be offset by any good obtained by either style of attack. I cautioned you and Sims because I am attached to you both; but I need hardly say to you that if you or anyone else disobeys the order I have issued I shall take the action I deem necessary as Commander in Chief, without any regard to questions of personal friendship.

As for what you say about the eight 14-inch gun ships, I had a number of the very sea-going captains of whom you speak in here the other day and went into the question of the new type of ship. I became convinced that we should work toward not a four-turret but a five-turret ship — that is, a ten 14-inch gun ship — but that our present knowledge of the 14-inch gun was not such as to warrant our putting in these 14-inch guns. They have not been tried. I went into the matter most carefully and there was not the slightest room for doubt that the proper course was to follow that upon which the General Board agree as to the ships to be provided this year.

To recur for a moment to your statement that I have been "misinformed or misled" as to the Newport conference. I do not understand you; but I do know one thing, and that is that in the past I have found the opinions of those with whom you are identified almost as often wrong as those whose opinions you protest. Very much of what appeared in the Reuterdahl article, for instance, was simple nonsense, and many of the claims advanced against the *North Dakota* style of ship were absurdly exaggerated — and this is not open to discussion, for I listened carefully to the trying out of some of these claims by both sides. Again, the men who are responsible for much of these criticisms were for the most part against the cruise of the battle fleet around the world; and it was impossible to demonstrate by a more striking instance their bad judgment, for nothing that has happened in recent years has been better for the navy in every way than this cruise.

If your letter were not personal I should officially forward to the Navy Department the part in which you speak of Capps and Alger. As it is, I shall make an immediate private inquiry. I wish to point out, however, that I regard the concluding paragraphs of your letter as not being in entire accord with the opening paragraphs. I quite agree with you that the discipline and integrity of the commissioned personnel of the navy is hurt by such statements as those to which you object, but you apparently do not realize that in the opening paragraphs of your letter you seem to be championing practices which are also demoralizing to the discipline and integrity of the personnel, for much the same reasons as those you assign in the latter part of your letter. Whether there should be a court-martial on you or either Alger or Capps, I am not prepared to say. Such a court-martial may be necessary in order to avert harm. But you are apparently ignorant of the fact that it would also inevitably do harm. The enemies of the navy welcome every squabble and fight in the navy, and every court-martial dealing with a case of this kind. I shall make an immediate inquiry, however.[1] *Sincerely yours*

5 1 1 7 · TO TRUMAN HANDY NEWBERRY   *Roosevelt Mss.*

Personal   Washington, January 8, 1909

My dear Mr. Secretary: I have received from Commander Key in a letter marked "Personal" a complaint running as follows:

I have not yet heard anything from the Department concerning my official report of Capps, but have received a very unsatisfactory reply to my report of Alger. If a decent standard of discipline is to be maintained among commissioned officers, either they or I must be court-martialed, for I have officially reported the first named for making an untruthful statement, in an official report, calculated to discredit and injure my reputation in the estimation of my official superiors and my brother officers. I have officially reported Capps for a deliberate and specific violation of the Navy Regulations and for making official and public statements calculated to wrongfully and unjustly injure me, and I have also formally invited the attention of the Department to the plainly evident fact that either Capps or I gave false and misleading official testimony as to material facts before

---

[1] Though obviously sympathetic to Key, Roosevelt in this letter carefully hid that fact from his former naval aide. He made no mention of his own anger at the Capps report (see Numbers 5102, 5105, 5117). His letter of December 29 (No. 5097) shows that, contrary to what he told Key, he was not absolutely satisfied with the General Board's decision on the 14-inch guns for the new ships. Moreover, in spite of what he wrote here, Roosevelt had been impressed by Key's criticism of the *North Dakota's* design; see Numbers 4782, 4847, 4865.

Roosevelt's handling of this officer is indicative of his treatment of the whole insurgent element in the Navy. His personal contacts with the Navy were primarily with officers of this group. Almost all of his personal correspondence with naval officers is with them. Their leaders he picked for naval aides. Roosevelt fully appreciated the insurgents' talents and he was well aware of the need for imagination, courage, and creative ability in an institution which by its very nature tended to repress such talents.

Yet the President kept a tight rein on these officers. Given their heads, he justifiably feared, they could cause much damage. Their aggressive methods of bringing about change and their inability to understand their opponents' point of view had already created intense bitterness within the service. Moreover, these enthusiastic younger officers were oversanguine about their ability to mobilize public opinion behind their reforms. In an era when the muckrakers were making sensational charges about crimes of big business and the shame of municipal politics, it was difficult to arouse public opinion to the need of naval administrative reorganization. Nevertheless, an aroused public opinion was necessary to force Congress to change the bureau system which gave it such an effective control over the politically useful naval appropriations.

Roosevelt was acutely aware of both the strength of the conservatives in the Navy and Congress' vested interest in the bureau system. Therefore, although as his messages to Congress attest, he agreed completely with the insurgents on the need for revising the system of promotion, for reforming the bureau system, and so forth, he never actually attempted to force Congress or the department to make such desirable changes. Nor would he ever permit demands for reform to jeopardize his basic naval policy of maintaining a fleet second only to that of Great Britain. And if he failed to create a modern administrative organization for the Navy, he did succeed in giving the nation a modern fleet; see No. 5163.

the Congressional Naval Committees: If the Navy has reached that stage of discipline and tone that commissioned officers are permitted to indulge in the practices, of which I have officially accused Alger and Capps, or if a commissioned officer is permitted to indulge in such official accusations as I have made against them, unless well founded, without drastic action, or rigid investigation by the Department, then it must be conceded that the Navy is in a demoralized state with respect to the discipline and integrity of its commissioned personnel.

I do not wish this letter of mine to be filed; but I do feel that action of a drastic kind should be taken as regards Capps, Alger, and possibly Key himself.[1] Whether a court-martial is called for I do not know; but it is simply out of the question if any discipline is to be observed, to pass by such conduct as that of which Capps is guilty; and I gravely doubt whether it is possible to pass by conduct like that of Alger. I am inclined to ask Key a categorical question as to any information he furnished to any newspaper. Please report to me specifically on these accusations against Capps. I should like the full opinion of the Judge Advocate General. *Sincerely yours*

5 1 1 8 · TO KERMIT ROOSEVELT   *Roosevelt Mss.*

Washington, January 10, 1909

Dearest Kermit: Since you left, Ethel has continued in the whirl. On Friday night we had a dinner and dance for her; but there were also many older people present. The Speaker, for instance, was at the dinner; and all the Ambassadors and their wives came to the dance. I think it was one of the very pleasantest dances that has ever taken place in The White House. I danced myself two or three times, and persuaded Mother to dance with me. She lookt so pretty and shy, tho she finally accepted; and evidently had much the same feeling that she would have had if we had been secretly engaged and she was afraid that such a public attention might compromise her! Poor, blessed Mother; the dance coming on top of the rest of the week's activities was the final straw, and tho she thoroly enjoyed it, the next morning she had one of her worst headaches and it is only now, twenty-fours later, that she has recovered. I have gotten her to promise that she will now try taking breakfast in bed and I will have my breakfast up in the room with her.

Congress has been having a brainstorm — a brainstorm in its belly, so to speak; both Houses have held a can-can over the secret service. Personally I doubt if they have gained very much. I think I have knocked the paint off of Tillman, who is one of the foulest and rottenest demagogs in the whole country; and I do not see how the House can get away from what I have said about it.*

John Jay White, that African hunter who struck us as being a little nerv-

---

[1] No action was taken against these officers, except for the removal of Capps as Acting Chief of the Bureau of Steam Engineering.

ous,[1] to judge by his letters, was on here to lunch. He was very interesting and gave me one or two points. He was also very kind; he has left his double-barreled .450 cordite in Nairobi. He says it is in fine trim and that he will give it to us. Accordingly I wrote to Newland, Tarlton & Company, our agents in Nairobi, who have the gun, to get it all ready and get cartridges for it. If necessary either you or I can take this gun and the other take the double-barreled Holland, and therefore we now have each a type of the hard-hitting double-barreled English gun which they say is necessary. Personally I cannot help feeling that the Winchester will be our ordinary weapon, but of course I may be utterly mistaken. Moreover, nice George Meyer has given me his little Manlicher rifle, which has a telescopic sight. The weapon is a perfect beauty; and with the telescopic sight one certainly does see marvelously up to say 300 yards. I have made up my mind not to take out my 45.70 rifle, and shall take this little Manlicher in place of it. The more I have thought over the matter the more convinced I have become that I would prefer the .405 Winchester for any purpose for which I desired to take the 45.70, and as long as I now have an extra .405 it is not worth while taking the 45.70 at all. My Holland double barrel is on the way here for me to try.

Give my regards to Randy and to all the other boys, including Charlie Emory. I hope he goes to the sailors' union with you. I felt that we had just about the most satisfactory Christmas and Christmas holiday from the stand-point of the entire family as it was possible to have.

Taft told me with a chuckle, when he was last here, that one of his friends in New York had said to him that he supposed that between the election and his inauguration there would be a period of stagnation at Washington. I have felt like wiring him that the period of stagnation continues to rage with uninterrupted violence. *Your loving father*

[*Handwritten*] I enclose the list of the English donors of my rifle.

Quentin has left school without permission, and told untruths about it; I had to give him a severe whipping. Mother and I are worried about him.

* [*Handwritten*] Still, it won't hurt the House, and this they know. Election is over 18 months off; this will be forgotten then; I will no longer count, appreciably, for Taft will be President, and the fight will have to be, and ought to be, on Tafts record only.

5119 · TO CHARLES JOSEPH BONAPARTE   *Roosevelt Mss.*

Washington, January 11, 1909

My dear Mr. Attorney General: I have received your letters of the 7th and 8th. I am inclined to agree with you that it is doubtful whether a good pur-pose would be served by putting the matter before Congress. In the present

---

[1] John Jay White, Jr., capitalized on his own adventures and Roosevelt's coming experiences in a series of articles entitled "Hunting Ahead of Roosevelt in Africa," *Harper's Weekly* (March 13–April 3, 1909).

temper of Congress it seems to me that we must take account of the fact that a considerable number of people will probably be glad to find in favor of the two judges, simply because the administration thinks that they have not acted well. Moreover, all experience shows that impeachments succeed only in the clearest possible cases, and as long as there is no better and easier remedy for getting rid of an incompetent or improper occupant of a judicial office, more harm than good may result from an attempt to impeach him. In the case of Grosscup, to my mind much the worst count against him is his use of an officer of his court to extort a pass from a railroad by serving notice on the railroad that a relative of the man for whom the pass is asked is himself about to give judgment upon the conduct of the railroad in proceedings against it.[1] This seems to me to be right up to the verge of blackmail, a blackmail of a peculiarly discreditable kind, and to stand entirely aside from any ordinary request for a pass. But I am not at all sure, in view of the action of Congress about the secret service, that Congress will take this view; and inasmuch as it is doubtful whether it is our duty to lay the matter before Congress I wish . . . . to go carefully over the whole affair with you prior to doing so. *Sincerely yours*

5120 · TO LYMAN ABBOTT

Roosevelt Mss.

Washington, January 11, 1909

My dear Dr. Abbott: It is curious how our minds work together. No wonder I joined the *Outlook*! I have been feeling just as you have been feeling over the question of direct nominations. I was originally in favor of it. I can see strong reasons in favor of it now; but its actual working in certain Western States has given me such serious doubt that I would want to go carefully into the matter before finally committing myself. I can see, for instance, in New York how Tammany could nominate a Republican Senator if it chose to go into the Republican primaries on the year when it thought Democratic defeat imminent, or did not care for Democratic victory. For this reason I shall not express myself publicly until I knew better exactly the proposal we shall have to face in New York, and until I got clearer in my mind.[1] *Faithfully yours*

[1] See Numbers 4744, 4955. Roosevelt and Bonaparte did not institute impeachment proceedings.

[1] Governor Hughes in his annual message had proposed that New York establish a system of direct nominations for all elective offices other than those of Presidential electors. Long an opponent of the Republican bosses, Hughes hoped to "promote true party leadership by making it less susceptible to misuse." His careful program to accomplish this included recommendations for an official primary ballot, for extending the enrollment system, for limiting primary elections to enrolled party voters, for public financing of primary election expenses, and for the limitation and publication of the campaign expenditures of all primary candidates. Although these suggestions incorporated the best of the tested experiments in such states as Oregon and Wisconsin, Abbott, while applauding them, urged that New York delay and investigate before acting (*Outlook*, 91:91–92, January 16, 1909). Roosevelt,

Washington, January 12, 1909

Dear Douglas: The District of Columbia authorities are prepared to proceed criminally against the New York *World* and the Indianapolis *News,* and the grand jury will have their first hearing on Monday, the 18th instant.[1] For this purpose it will be necessary to have you as a witness and they will summon you. Of course you will stay at the White House while you are here. There will not be much for you to testify to, because I see that even the *World* has abandoned the lie against you; but the little you do show will be of vital consequence. *Ever yours*

5122 · TO KERMIT ROOSEVELT *Roosevelt Mss.*

Washington, January 14, 1909

Dearest Kermit: There has been a good deal of talk in Congress and in the papers and among the grumblers in the army and navy about my physical exercise order, which as a matter of fact was very moderate. So I concluded, on the suggestion of Dr. Rixey, to ride ninety miles in one day myself, which would put a stop to any grumbling because I required other people to ride ninety miles in three days. Accordingly yesterday Dr. Rixey, Dr. Grayson,[1] Archie Butt and I rode out to Warrenton and back from and to the White House. It was just ninety-eight miles, altho the people at Warrenton claim it was 104. We left the White House a few minutes after half past three in the morning and got back there a few minutes after half past eight in the evening, lunching at Warrenton, where I had to shake hands with prominent citizens, say a word to the school children, &c. We had sent out relays of horses, and each rode four horses, riding each horse twice as the journey back was over the same ground. I began and ended the day on old Roswell, who is really a perfect trump. The last fifteen miles in were done in pitch darkness and with a blizzard of sleet blowing in our faces. But we got thru safely, and altho we are a little stiff and tired nobody is laid up.

Congress of course feels that I will never again have to be reckoned with and that it is safe to be ugly with me. Accordingly, in one way I am not having an easy time, and I shall have additional fights over certain veto messages

---

in foreseeing the possibility of new Tammany tactics, either failed to understand or chose to ignore Hughes's plans for enrollment. Until he returned from Africa the President did not support the governor on the primary question.

---

[1] The grand jury returned indictments against the editors and owners of the *World* and *News* on February 17, 1909; see No. 5142.

---

[1] Cary Travers Grayson, naval doctor, surgeon on the *Mayflower,* and consulting physician at the Washington dispensary, 1907–1913; physician to, and confidant of, Woodrow Wilson, 1913–1921; chairman of the American Red Cross, 1935–1938; a quiet little man with a talent for winning the confidence of the powerful.

I shall send.[2] But I am pretty philosophical about it. I did not expect any legislation this winter, and I don't see that Congress can really do very much to harm me. I have gotten the men I went after, Foraker and Tillman, and I shall soon start the libel suits against the *World* and the Indianapolis *News*.

I have had a great run for my money, and I should have liked to stay in as President if I had felt it was right for me to do so; but there are many compensations about going, and Mother and I are in the curious and very pleasant position of having enjoyed the White House more than any other President and his wife whom I recall, and yet being entirely willing to leave it, and looking forward to a life of interest and happiness after we leave.

I enclose a copy of the list of the men who have given me my gun, with annotations put on by E. N. Buxton. Will you send it back to me? *Your loving father*

5 1 2 3 · TO WILLIAM HOWARD TAFT   *Roosevelt Mss.*

Washington, January 16, 1909

Dear Will: I have your letter of the 13th instant. All right, I will wait until the Census Bureau bill comes to me, and see what to do about it, in view of its then exact form. I am exceedingly glad that you so heartily favor a veto if a veto shall be necessary to prevent the Census Office being subjected to the spoils system.[1] I entirely agree with you.

As for Foraker and his resolution about the Emergency Fund matter, you need not be under the least anxiety.[2] I will see that the matter is put in such shape that no possible difficulty arises from the disclosure of matters which ought to be kept confidential. I knew in a general way of all that you did,

---

[2] The two vetoes to provoke a fight were those of the census bill and of a water-power bill; see Numbers 5123, 5156.

---

[1] The Census Bill provided for the appointment of 4000 clerks in the Census Bureau by noncompetitive examinations to be prescribed by the Director of the Census. During debates on the bill the House and Senate made no secret of their intention to distribute these appointments. Swift, Foulke, and Richard H. Dana, among others, therefore urged Roosevelt to veto the bill. The President briefly considered classifying the 4000 offices in spite of the provision in the bill, rejected this plan as "tricky" and probably illegal, and then, when the offensive provision was not deleted by the Congress, on February 5 vetoed the measure. His veto message asserted that because it was "of high consequence to the country that the statistical work of the census . . . be conducted with entire accuracy, ... appointees should be chosen by competitive examination from the lists provided by the Civil Service Commission," not, as the act stipulated, "under the spoils system." — *Congressional Record*, XLIII, 1965–1966.

[2] The resolution, which the Senate agreed to on January 12, directed the Secretary of the Treasury to report in detail the purposes and amounts of all payments made out of the President's "emergency fund to meet unforeseen contingencies," a fund of $3,000,000 appropriated in 1899. Foraker's hope was that this report would reveal some appalling impropriety in the hiring of Browne and Baldwin. In fact it disclosed only that they had been paid $15,000, a disbursement previously reported by the War Department.

just as I knew in a general way of all that Root did while he was your predecessor; and I heartily approved, and accept full responsibility for, the acts of both of you. *Ever yours*

5124 · TO JAMES NORRIS GILLETT   *Roosevelt Mss.*

Telegram   Washington, January 16, 1909

We are greatly concerned at newspaper reports of anti-Japanese legislation in California legislature.[1] Have written you at length on subject. Earnestly hope that no progress will be made on bills until you have chance to receive my letter, and if necessary to discuss its contents with leaders of two houses. My knowledge of the international situation, particularly with reference to emigration of Japanese laborers from United States, satisfies me that passage of proposed legislation would be of incalculable damage to State of California as well as to whole Union.

5125 · TO JAMES NORRIS GILLETT   *Roosevelt Mss.*

Washington, January 16, 1909

My dear Governor: I am greatly concerned over the anti-Japanese bills which are apparently going thru or are on their way thru the California legislature. They are in every sense most unfortunate. At last we have in first-class working order the arrangement which with such difficulty we succeeded in getting thru two years ago. The Japanese Government are obviously acting in entire good faith. During the six months ending October 31, last, the total

---

[1] In a recrudescence of anti-Japanese feeling, members of the California Legislature had proposed a number of discriminatory bills. Of these only three, dealing with landholding and with segregation in the schools (all fully analyzed in No. 5136), received serious attention. The Assembly judiciary committee on January 15 reported favorably the first of the three. This bill, providing that aliens acquiring title to land in California had to become citizens within five years or dispose of their holdings, was clearly intended to penalize the Japanese who were ineligible for citizenship.

To block this measure and the even more controversial school segregation bill, Roosevelt on January 16 began an important correspondence with Governor Gillett and Speaker Philip A. Stanton of the California Assembly (Numbers 5125, 5135, 5136, 5137, 5150, 5153, 5154, 5160, 5165). Their effective co-operation ultimately assured the defeat of the anti-Japanese bills. Roosevelt designed his telegrams and letters as much for the mobilization of public opinion as for the direction of his California allies. The publication of his correspondence and the section of his speech of January 19 to the Methodists on a square deal for the Japanese made a national issue of the California crisis. This doubtless helped persuade the California Legislature to exercise restraint and the United States Senate to support the President's naval program. Yet, as Professor Bailey's excellent chapter on the whole episode ably demonstrates, in pursuing these ends Roosevelt attached more importance to the anti-Japanese agitation than did the Japanese government or the Japanese press (Bailey, *Roosevelt and the Japanese-American Crises,* ch. xiii). For Roosevelt's views on the crisis and on its relation to the naval program, besides the correspondence cited above, see Numbers 5127, 5129, 5151, 5161.

number of Japanese who have come to the mainland of the United States has been 2,074, and the total number who have left has been 3,181. In other words, the whole object nominally desired by those who wish to prevent the incoming of Japanese laborers has been achieved. More Japanese are leaving the country than are coming in, and by present indications in a very few years the number of Japanese here will be no greater than the number of Americans in Japan; that is, the movement will be as normal in one case as in the other, which is just what we desire. There is, therefore, no shadow of excuse for action which will simply produce great irritation and may result in upsetting the present agreement and throwing open the whole situation again. These agitators have themselves to thank if trouble comes from what they do, if there is a fresh influx of Japanese hither. They hamper the National Government in what it has now so efficiently accomplished — the agreement by peaceful means, and thru the friendly initiative of the Japanese Government, to keep Japanese immigrants out of the United States save as Americans themselves visit Japan. Is it not possible to get the legislature to realize the great unwisdom from the standpoint of the country at large, and above all from the standpoint of California, of what is being done?[1] *Sincerely yours*

5126 · TO JAMES BRYCE   *Roosevelt Mss.*

Washington, January 21, 1909

My dear Mr. Bryce: Many thanks for your note. I am very glad that Grey and Morley liked what I said. But, my dear Mr. Ambassador, nobody owes me any credit or appreciation in the matter. I felt that it ought to be said, and particularly at this time, when there was the agitation in India, and when there were foolish people here, and worse than foolish people in other countries, who lookt with mischievous pleasure on that agitation. If I have been of the least use in the matter, I am more than pleased. *Sincerely yours*

5127 · TO WILLIAM KENT   *Roosevelt Mss.*

Washington, January 22, 1909

My dear Kent: That is a very nice letter of yours and I sincerely thank you for it. By George! I wish I could get California to call a halt in its proposed Japanese action. The whole business has been most unfortunate, and I am

---

[1] It was possible. Roosevelt and Gillett arranged for the preparation and publication of the President's letter of January 26, No. 5136. Furthermore, Gillett on January 25 sent a special message urging the legislature to do nothing that might disturb American-Japanese relations. The "evident disposition . . . . of the governor to veto undesirable measures . . . . did much to improve the complexion of affairs." — Bailey, *Roosevelt and the Japanese-American Crises*, p. 307.

more concerned over it than over any of the other rather stormy incidents during my career as President.

With heartiest good wishes, believe me, *Faithfully yours*

5128 · TO ROBERT SIMPSON WOODWARD   *Roosevelt Mss.*

Washington, January 22, 1909

My dear President Woodward: [1] Professor Barrett Wendell has called my attention to the remarkable work in the collection of frontier ballads of Professor John A. Lomax, of the University of Texas. He is making a very original and instructive study into a phase of native American literary and intellectual growth which of course has been totally neglected, and it seems to me that it would be a great advantage to real scholarship if his studies could be facilitated. One thousand dollars a year for three years would enable him to carry them to a successful conclusion. He has no means of his own. I believe that the Carnegie Institution might with great advantage take up this case. [2]

With great respect, believe me, *Sincerely yours*

5129 · TO ANDREW CARNEGIE   *Roosevelt Mss.*

Washington, January 22, 1909

My dear Mr. Carnegie: I have your letter of the 21st instant. I think you are right about "waiting for further developments before adding to the flames." Could you not get the influential men in the peace societies to communicate with people in California so as to have the good people of California take the initiative? [1] That would avoid the objections which you so properly and clearly see. *Faithfully yours*

5130 · TO WILLIAM HOWARD TAFT   *Roosevelt Mss.*

Washington, January 22, 1909

Dear Will: Your letters of the 17th and 20th about the North Carolina judgeship have been received. What made me change my mind about Timberlake[1]

[1] Robert Simpson Woodward, astronomer and geographer; dean of the College of Pure Science at Columbia, 1895–1905. As president of the Carnegie Institution of Washington, 1905–1920, he guided that institution through its early difficult years, and by his virtually unfailing judgment between the worthy and the worthless project, placed it upon a sound foundation.
[2] John Avery Lomax, the first serious and sensitive scholar in the field of American folk song and balladry, completed his *Cowboy Songs and Other Frontier Ballads*, dedicated to Roosevelt and published in 1910, with the aid not of the Carnegie Institution but of a Sheldon fellowship from Harvard University.

[1] Carnegie could not. To Roosevelt's disgust, the peace societies did nothing about anti-Japanese sentiment in California; see No. 5161.

[1] John E. Timberlake, formerly postmaster at Raynor, North Carolina.

was its being called to my attention that after he left the bench he was content not to pursue the practice of the law, but to settle down as postmaster in a small town; and I found that there was a very general feeling that this showed that he was not the character of man who really ought to be made judge. Then Silas McBee's brother-in-law, Judge Hoke,[2] of the highest North Carolina court, a man whom I have good reason to believe represents all that is best at the North Carolina bar and among North Carolina people, entirely of his own accord, unless possibly it was suggested to him by Jimmie Williams,[3] wrote saying that Seawell was the best man.[4] I was a little wary of the very influences of which you speak and cross-examined Seawell closely as to his corporate connections. He has had none either with the Southern Railway or Seaboard Railway or the Tobacco Trust, and indeed the only railway he has ever been connected with at all is a little line thirty-four miles long, the name of which I forget. After seeing all three I was inclined to put him first, Hicks second, and Timberlake third. Timberlake struck me about the size of a justice of the peace up in our country, and I doubted if he was ahead of Skinner; all are good men in their ways.

Give my love to Mrs. Taft. I hope you will have a most delightful trip to Panama. *Ever yours*

5131 · TO KERMIT ROOSEVELT   *Roosevelt Mss.*

Washington, January 23, 1909

Dearest Kermit: Your hockey must really be interesting and it must be a great relief to the monotony of constant long-distance running. I suppose you are about as busy as can be with your studies just at present. If the Sphinx does not hold its election until early in March I suppose they will bar you out of consideration.

Here I am in the thick of the fight as usual. I have finished my Berlin address, or rather the rough draft, and hope early next week to have it definitely off my mind; then I have nothing to do further in the way of elaborate literary preparation either for a speech or a message to Congress or an address, and can turn my attention purely to the instant need of things.

[2] William Alexander Hoke, Justice of the Supreme Court of North Carolina, 1904–1925.
[3] James Thomas Williams, Jr., North Carolina-born newspaperman; an Associated Press representative at the Portsmouth Conference, 1905; Washington correspondent of the Boston *Evening Transcript,* 1906–1908; appointed United States Civil Service Commissioner by Taft in 1909; later editor of the *Transcript* and in 1912 a Massachusetts delegate-at-large to the Republican National Convention.
[4] Herbert Floyd Seawell was nominated by Roosevelt as United States Judge for the Eastern District of North Carolina. The Senate, however, did not confirm the appointment. Taft appointed Seawell United States attorney for that district and gave the judgeship to H. G. Connor.

I am also getting everything in pretty good shape for the African trip. You and I must be vaccinated when you come down here. Have you had your teeth attended to? I am having mine done now. As soon as I get my Winchester rifle I will make my last trial of the rifles. We have a first-class target-practice rifle arrangement, such as they use in the Navy, in the top hall, in the attic, where I shall soon begin to practice, and you can practice at it when you come down here.

There are plenty of people in Congress who would like to cause me trouble but so far they have not quite ventured, and it really looks as if I shall get the two battleships on which I had set my heart.[1] I am having hard work in connection with the California matters in the effort to keep things so that Japan will not be outraged. I think I shall succeed but it has been rather ticklish and as usual I had to refuse to accept the strict and limited constitutional, or President Buchanan, view. If I had not gone outside of my duty and appealed to the Californians we should have had trouble. Then the jacks in the Senate started to insist upon my giving them information which it was improper for me to give them. The Judiciary Committee had Herbert Knox Smith before them to force him to divulge confidential information about the Steel Corporation.[2] I, however, promptly ordered him to put all the papers in my possession, and I then saw Clark, the Chairman of the Judiciary Committee, and told him they would not be given to the Senate, that I could not be forced to give them, and I did not see why they should make any effort to get them unless they were prepared to go to the length of trying to have me impeached. This called for a showdown and I rather doubt if they press their point, altho they are so foolish that I am not certain on the subject. *Ever your loving father*

[1] On January 22 the House had passed the navy bill authorizing the two new battleships by a vote of 150 to 60; see No. 5106.

[2] A subcommittee of the Senate Judiciary Committee was seeking information about the Tennessee Coal and Iron properties purchased by the United States Steel Corporation during the panic of 1907. The committee had been directed by a resolution introduced by Senator Culberson to report whether the President by authorizing the purchase had violated the Sherman Antitrust Law.

The committee asked Smith to produce confidential business information which the steel corporation had voluntarily given the Bureau of Corporations for its study of the steel industry. Roosevelt then ordered Smith to send all his data on United States Steel to the White House. According to the law creating the Bureau of Corporations, Roosevelt pointed out, such information could be made public only by the President. Roosevelt after examining these papers turned a portion of them over to the committee, claiming that "no part of any such confidential information hereby withheld had any bearing whatever upon the subject matter of the Senate resolution referred to."

The committee, unable to reach an agreement, made no report. Three Democratic and one of the Republican members officially stated to Congress that in their opinion the President had no authority to permit the absorption of the Tennessee company. Republicans in the committee and in Congress argued that the question was irrelevant, since Roosevelt did not authorize the purchase but merely said he would not "interpose any objection."

Washington, January 23, 1909

Dear Bay: It is rather absurd to ask you — author of *Cain* and *Herakles* — to turn in as the corrector of an ephemeral copy. But your good nature has led you into the scrape. I enclose you the rough draft of the Berlin University address and the finished drafts of the Oxford and Sorbonne addresses. The last are merely for you to glance at, so that you may see whether I have been guilty of improper repetition, or have plagiarized from myself, so to speak. Would you be willing to come around tomorrow (Sunday) evening at 8:30 with the three infernal documents and give me your criticisms? *Ever yours*

Washington, January 26, 1909

My dear Senator Aldrich: I re-enclose the bill.[1] I have made one pencil suggestion, approved by Lodge, which I think makes it better. Outside of this the only thing I have to suggest is that instead of saying "five general officers" you say "five officers not below the rank of colonel." It might be a serious interruption to the work of the War Department to have to take five general officers on this business, whereas, say with three colonels and two generals, the objection would be obviated. Outside of this I entirely approve of the bill. *Sincerely yours*

Washington, January 26, 1909

My dear Mr. Secretary: I have once had to accept your resignation as Secretary of War. Now I have to accept it as Secretary of State. On the former occasion you retired from a great office where you had done work which no other man could have done as well, and after a few months you came back to fill a still higher office. In this higher office you have again done work which no other man could have done as well. I do not suppose that this letter can be made public, for some foolish people would think I was speaking hyperbolically, whereas I am speaking what I believe to be the literal truth, when I say that in my judgment you will be regarded as the greatest and ablest man who has ever filled the position of Secretary of State.

You leave the office to go into the Senate. I do not see how you can possibly do better work in the Senate than you have done in the Cabinet, but I am sure you will do as good work. *Ever faithfully yours*

---

[1] Aldrich was then framing the Administration's bill on the reinstatement of the Negro troops involved in the Brownsville shooting (see No. 5070, note 1). He incorporated the suggestions Roosevelt made in this letter and in Numbers 5138, 5148.

5135 · TO JAMES NORRIS GILLETT   *Roosevelt Mss.*

Telegram   Washington, January 26, 1909

Will mail you full letter on legislation[1] matter tomorrow. This letter will set forth why we think that the only bill that is proper is that relating to the ownership of real property by aliens, with the amendment suggested by Secretary Root. I most cordially thank you for your attitude and for the service you are thereby rendering not only to California but to the entire Union.

5136 · TO JAMES NORRIS GILLETT   *Roosevelt Mss.*

Washington, January 26, 1909

My dear Governor: Prior to receiving your letter and the accompanying copies of bills you had sent identical telegrams to the Secretary of State and myself, and to this the Secretary of State answered as follows:

January 25, 1909.

Honorable J. N. Gillett,
    Governor of California,
      Sacramento, California.

    I see no objection to the passage of a law which treats all aliens alike in acquiring and transferring real property. To avoid conflict with the Constitution of the United States, however, such statute should contain an express provision excepting from its operation any rights secured by treaty between the United States and foreign nations. See decisions of the Supreme Court of the United States in the cases of *Chirac v. Chirac,* two Wheaton two fifty-nine, *Hughes v. Edwards* nine Wheaton four eighty-nine, *Hauenstein v. Lynham* one hundred U. S. Reports four eighty-three, *Geoffrey v. Riggs* one thirty-three U. S. Reports two fifty-eight, and a long line of similar decisions by the Supreme Court.

ELIHU ROOT.

    I have now received your letter and the copies of the bills. One of these, in reference to the Board of Railroad Commissioners, is, I think, enclosed by mistake. As to the others, the Secretary of State has submitted to me the following memorandum, which has my cordial approval;

    Memorandum for the President on bills in the California Legislature relating, or supposed to relate, to Japanese:

    I have only been able to make a very cursory examination of these bills and can only give you first impressions. It is quite possible that upon careful consideration other ideas might present themselves.

    1. Senate Bill No. 71, entitled "An Act to prohibit alien ownership of lands in the State of California.

    This appears to apply to aliens generally and in that view is free from specific objection, except in this. The Act provides that aliens shall have such rights as to personal property as are accorded to citizens of the United States under the

[1] No. 5136.

1483

law of the nation to which such alien belongs, *or by treaties with the United States, except as the same may be affected by the provisions of this Act or the Constitution of this State.* This inverts the order of authority. It is settled beyond any possibility of doubt or question by repeated decisions of the Supreme Court of the United States that a treaty made in pursuance of the Constitution is controlling as against inconsistent provisions of either the Statutes or the Constitution of any State. That is the expressed provision of the Constitution of the United States under which the State of California was admitted to Union. Treaties between the United States and a considerable number of foreign nations have reciprocal provisions for reciprocal rights of citizens as to holding both real and personal property. It is perfectly well settled that the making of such reciprocal provisions is within the treaty-making power, and instead of aliens having in the State of California such rights as are accorded to them by these treaties except as they may be affected by the provisions of the Act or of the Constitution of California, the precise reverse is necessarily true. The proper statement would be that their rights are prescribed and limited in the Act except as they are conferred and declared by treaty. This general statement is true as to all aliens, the citizens or subjects of nations which have such treaties as I have described with the United States.

In the particular case of Japan the second article of the treaty of November 22, 1894, provides that the citizens of each in the other country "may trade in any part of the territories of the other by wholesale or retail, in all kinds of produce, manufactures, and merchandise of lawful commerce, either in person or by agents, singly or in partnership with foreigners or native citizens or subjects; and they may there own or hire and occupy houses, manufactories, warehouses, shops, and premises which may be necessary for them, and lease land for residential and commercial purposes, conforming themselves to the laws, police and customs regulations of the country like native citizens or subjects."

In my opinion this provision does not confer rights to either own or hire agricultural lands, but is limited to owning and hiring lands and the structures thereon for residential and commercial purposes, including within commercial purposes both manufacture and trade. To the extent that these rights go, that is to say, as to residential and commercial purposes, it is not competent for the Legislature of California to change in any way the provisions of the treaty or to impose any limitations inconsistent therewith. To the extent of owning or hiring lands for agricultural purposes, so far as Japan is concerned it is clearly competent for the State of California to enact its own laws, and it is gratifying to observe that it is the purpose of this bill to make those laws general as to aliens.

2. Assembly bill No. 78, entitled "An Act to regulate the ownership or possession of land by aliens."

The observations which I have made regarding Senate Bill No. 71 apply in substance to this Act. As bearing upon both Acts I transmit herewith copy of a telegraphic correspondence had between the Governor of California and myself consisting of a telegram from the Governor dated Saturday last and my reply of this morning. In my reply you will perceive that I suggest the insertion of a clause in any legislation regarding the holding of lands by aliens which will save their treaty rights, and that I also refer to some of the decisions of the Supreme Court on the subject.

3. Assembly Bill No. 14, entitled "An Act to amend 1662 of the political code."

This bill aims to reproduce in the form which created so much natural resentment on the part of Japan two years ago the specific discrimination against Japanese in the schools. It was by securing the abandonment of this discrimination on the part of the San Francisco School Board that the National Government was enabled to bring about the informal agreement or arrangement with Japan under which the two countries are now harmoniously and successfully preventing the coming of Japanese laborers to this country. The essential feature of this arrangement is the adoption by Japan of a series of strict and effective regulations determined upon after full consultation and discussion with the Government of the United States, preventing the issue of passports for the United States to Japanese laborers. At the same time the President, in the exercise of powers specially conferred upon him by Congress, as a part of the arrangement, prevents the indirect immigration of Japanese who do not carry passports for the United States from the Japanese Government. If this bill were to be passed that arrangement with the Japanese Government would necessarily come to an immediate end. The people of the State of California have to consider, not the question whether they will have the present arrangement through which Japanese are now being excluded plus such legislation as this, but whether they will substitute this legislation for the exclusion of Japanese laborers. I can see no doubt that what the people of California would sacrifice by the enactment of this Act would, considering their own interests alone, be of far greater value and importance than the legislation itself. The exclusion of Asiatic laborers through the co-operation of their own government has, in the case of China, proved to be far more successful and satisfactory than would the exclusion without the aid of the Government by the simple enforcement of a statute on this side of the Pacific. The same would inevitably be the case with Japan. No exclusion act passed by Congress would be so efficient as the present arrangement, and it would be accompanied inevitably by ill-feeling and resentment, the consequences of which would be of the most serious character. I may observe that the experience of the San Francisco School Board indicates there is no occasion whatever for any such legislation, for the regulation which they adopted as a substitute for the discriminating regulation, as I am informed by them, proved entirely satisfactory and effective to accomplish all that they wished to accomplish by the discriminatory regulation.

Viewing in a larger aspect the relations of California to the rest of the Union, it is difficult to find words strong enough to characterize the violation of patriotic duty which would be involved in a causeless and objectless enactment constituting a serious affront to a friendly nation and certain to plunge the entire Union into the doubtful conditions of enmity to a great and hitherto most friendly power which is our neighbor upon the Pacific.

4. Among the bills handed to me by you is Assembly Bill No. 71, relating to transportation by the State of California.

On such examination as I have been able to give I find in it no provision affecting the Japanese or any other aliens as distinguished from the general traveling and shipping public.

ELIHU ROOT.

To this memorandum I have but little to add. The United States Government has no objection to the enactment of a law in California as regards the right of aliens to hold real estate provided that the suggestions of the Secretary of State are complied with as contained in the above memorandum. Such a law would not be in any substantial respect different from similar laws that have been passed in other states. Many foreign countries, including Japan itself, have similar laws.

But for the reasons set forth in Mr. Root's memorandum the Federal

Government would most emphatically object to the passage of the proposed school legislation, and would also object to legislation such as the newspapers describe as having been proposed to force the Japanese to live in separate residential quarters. No copy, however, of any such bill has been sent me.

I most earnestly trust that for the reasons set forth in Mr. Root's memorandum, and for the reasons set forth in my previous telegrams and letter, none of the objectionable proposed legislation will be enacted into law.

With high appreciation of your courtesy, believe me, *Sincerely yours*

5137 · TO JAMES NORRIS GILLETT   *Roosevelt Mss.*

Telegram   Washington, January 27, 1909

I must again express from the standpoint of all our people my appreciation of the great services that you are rendering.[1] I have absolute and entire faith in the judgment and patriotism of the people of the great State of California, and I know that they will support you. My letter is already on its way to you and you may make it public whenever you desire.

5138 · TO NELSON WILMARTH ALDRICH   *Roosevelt Mss.*

Washington, January 27, 1909

My dear Senator: I am entirely indifferent to the exact terminology used in the bill, provided it is made clear that the language is permissive and not mandatory and that the board of officers is to be allowed to make eligible for reinstatement, and nothing more than eligible, those men whom the board may feel have been guiltless of the assault itself and of such criminal knowledge of the assault as would make it improper to put them back in the army.

My personal views have been exprest in my last message to Congress. I have no question, personally, that the bulk of Company B, including especially Mingo Saunders,[1] are guilty to a degree that would rightly bar them from ever again re-entering the American army. I am strongly inclined to believe, however, that the bulk of the members of Companies C and D had no such guilty knowledge as would make it necessary permanently to debar them from re-entry to the service. But there must be absolutely nothing in the bill which could be interpreted as compelling the Executive to put any man back.

I have talked this over with Senator Lodge and should be delighted to

[1] Gillett's special message (see No. 5125, note 1) had just been published in the Eastern papers.

[1] First Sergeant Mingo Saunders, recipient of the Medal of Honor, of all the soldiers in Troop B was Foraker's favorite. In his bitter exchange with Roosevelt at the Gridiron dinner, the senator had spoken of Saunders, "who had twenty-six years of service to his credit, and a record of honor for bravery in battle, being turned out, when he was nearing the time when he would have a right to retire on pay, without honor, ... left dependent and disgraced." — Foraker, *Notes of a Busy Life,* II, 251.

have you show this letter to him and Senators Warren and Warner, and for the matter of that to Senator Foraker and the Democratic members of the Committee if you deem it wise. *Sincerely yours*

5139 · TO WILLIAM HOWARD TAFT   *Roosevelt Mss.*

Washington, January 27, 1909

Dear Will: From two or three different sources I have heard that messages have been sent to certain members of the Cabinet (whether or not purporting to come from you I cannot say) to the effect that they are not to be retained because I have made some request for some other member of the Cabinet to be retained or even to be put in the place of the man to whom the message was given. Twice inquiries have been made of me on the subject. In each case I answered that you had never said anything of the kind and that whoever purported to represent you as having said it told what was an untruth.

I added that I had not asked you to retain a single member of the Cabinet; that at one period you had exprest to me the intention to retain the majority of the members; that since then you had exprest your intention to retain either none or only one or two;[1] that I had given you full information about every member of the Cabinet in any case where I had information that you did not already possess; that I had made no request for the retention of any man, and least of all any request to have one member of my present Cabinet kept at the expense of, or in substitution for, any other man. *Ever yours*

5140 · TO ALFRED THAYER MAHAN   *Roosevelt Mss.*

Washington, January 27, 1909

My dear Sir: I have appointed you as a member of a commission to consider certain needs of the navy.[1] The organization of the Department is now not

[1] Taft retained Meyer and, oddly enough, Wilson. On January 22, he informed the rest of Roosevelt's Cabinet that he would not need them, for "the task which confronted him was different from that of the Roosevelt years and a 'somewhat different personnel in the Cabinet' seemed necessary" (Pringle, *Taft*, I, 386). This decision, while it doubtless disappointed Roosevelt and his colleagues, violated no pledge.

[1] This commission, which in addition to Mahan included ex-Secretaries Moody and Morton, Admirals Luce, Folger, Cowles, and Evans, and Judge Alston G. Dayton, submitted two reports to the President late in February. These were remarkable both in general concept and specific recommendation. Basing its suggestions on a cardinal principle of naval organization "that success in war and victory in battle can be assured only by that constant preparedness and that superior fighting efficiency which logically result from placing the control and responsibility in time of peace upon the same individuals and the same agencies that must control in time of war," the commission in its first report stated that a board of line officers must be created to advise the Secretary and to co-ordinate the work of the bureaus.

Its second report, which provided a specific plan of reorganization, divided the

such as to bring the best results, and there is a failure to co-ordinate the work of the Bureaus and to make the Department serve the one end for which it was created, that is, the development and handling of a first-class fighting fleet. With this proposition in view I will ask you to consider:

1. All defects in the law under which the Navy Department is now organized, including especially the defects by which the authority of Chiefs of Bureaus is made in certain respects practically equal to that of the Secretary or the President.

2. The division of responsibility and consequent lack of co-ordination in the preparations for war and conduct of war.

3. The functions of certain Bureaus, so as to see whether it is not possible to consolidate them.

4. The necessity of providing the Secretary of the Navy with military advisers, who are responsible to him for co-ordinating the work of the Bureaus and for preparation for war.

5. The necessity for economical allotment and disbursement of appropriations and for a system which will secure strict accountability.

6. Finally, I want your views as to how best to recognize and emphasize the strictly military character of the navy, so that preparation for war shall be controlled under the Secretary by the military branch of the navy, which bears the responsibility for the successful conduct of war operations.

I wish to have the above subjects considered under two general heads:

First, as to the fundamental principles of an organization that will insure an efficient preparation for war in time of peace, a separate report under this head to be submitted at the earliest practicable date.

Second, specific recommendations as to the changes in the present organization that will accomplish this result, the report under this head to be submitted later.

In addition to the above reports I desire your recommendation as to the number, location and general facilities of the navy yards which are required by strategic considerations in time of war and for maintaining the fleet in constant readiness for war in time of peace. *Sincerely yours*

Navy Department into five great divisions: the Office of the Assistant Secretary, and the Divisions of Naval Operations, of Personnel, of Material, and of Inspection. The men in charge of these divisions, all line officers, made up two councils to advise the Secretary. The General Council included all five men with the chief of the Division of Naval Operations as its responsible head, while the Military Council included only the chiefs of Naval Operations, Personnel, and Inspection.

Although realizing that no action would be taken on the reports, Roosevelt forwarded them to Congress during the last week of February. Apparently the President was anxious before leaving office to place on record a document which not only clearly demonstrated the need to eliminate the defects in the independent bureau system but also set forth a plan for making the necessary changes. Perhaps Roosevelt thought that such a document might serve as a guide for reform in the Taft administration. Taft's naval secretary did, in fact, follow the suggestion of the Moody-Mahan commission and in the fall of 1909, by administrative order, created the four grand divisions of operations, personnel, material, and inspection.

Telegram   Washington, January 27, 1909

Do if you can act as complaining witness and give Jerome a chance to bring the libel suit.[1]

5142 · TO HENRY LEWIS STIMSON *Roosevelt Mss.*

Telegram   Washington, January 28, 1909

Referring to your telegram to Secretary Loeb, when the District Attorney of Washington feels just as emphatically as you do and in directly the opposite sense, it is a simple impossibility to overrule without a chance to hear both you and District Attorney Baker in person. The Attorney General notifies the President that the District Attorney here says he will not be responsible for trying to obtain an indictment if your suggestions are carried out.[1] Moreover, I do not understand why the declaration from you is not sufficient. Of course if action here can be obtained in day or two what harm can delay do? Why cannot you come on here Sunday and on that day meet the Attorney General and District Attorney Baker at the White House? Unless there is grave reason to the contrary I wish you would do this. Please answer.

5143 · TO HENRY CABOT LODGE *Roosevelt Mss.*

Personal   Washington, January 28, 1909

Dear Cabot: I have been reading the letters of John Hay.[1] There are three or four of the statements he makes which I think will be so understood as to cause a serious misapprehension of the facts, and therefore I write you about them.

Hay was a man of remarkable ability. I think he was the most delightful man to talk to I ever met, for in his conversation he continually made out of hand those delightful epigrammatic remarks which we would all like to make, and which in books many people appear as making, but which in

---

[1] Jerome, district attorney for New York City, had written Stimson that he planned to institute a suit against the *World* for criminal libel on behalf of Douglas Robinson in connection with the charges regarding the Panama Canal purchase (see Numbers 4963, 5072, 5121, 5142). Jerome, however, did not file such a suit.

[1] District Attorney Daniel W. Baker was opposing Stimson's suggestion to drop Pulitzer's name from the list of indictments in the *World* libel case. Baker, supported by Roosevelt and Bonaparte, continued the hearing which led to the indictment on February 17 of Pulitzer and his editors, Van Hamm and Lyman, by the grand jury of the District of Columbia. Stimson, however, asked the New York jury for indictments only against Van Hamm and the Press Publishing Company. These were returned March 4, 1909; see Numbers 5072, 5164, 5166.

[1] Henry Adams had selected and Clara Louisa Stone (Mrs. John Hay) had edited, for private distribution, the *Letters of John Hay and Extracts from Diary*. Printed in Washington in 1908, these three volumes were the major source for Thayer's *Hay*.

actual life hardly anyone ever does more than think about when it is too late to say them. He was moreover, I think without exception, the best letter-writer of his age; altho the present volume does not give this impression, as it is atrociously edited. His dignity, his remarkable literary ability, his personal charm, and the respect his high character and long service commanded thruout the country, together with his wide acquaintance with foreign statesmen and foreign capitals, made him one of the public servants of real value to the United States. But he was not a great Secretary of State. For instance, he was not to be mentioned in the same breath with Root. He was no administrator. He had a very ease-loving nature and a moral timidity which made him shrink from all that was rough in life, and therefore from practical affairs. He was at his best at a dinner table or in a drawing room, and in neither place have I ever seen anyone's best that was better than his; but his temptation was to associate as far as possible only with men of refined and cultivated tastes, who lived apart from the world of affairs, and who, if Americans, were wholly lacking in robustness of fiber. His close intimacy with Henry James and Henry Adams — charming men, but exceedingly undesirable companions for any man not of strong nature — and the tone of satirical cynicism which they admired, and which he always affected in writing them, marked that phase of his character which so impaired his usefulness as a public man. In public life during the time he was Secretary of State under me he accomplished little. I was personally extremely fond of him. I had a great admiration for his fastidious literary skill, and liked to listen to him; I saw much of him, and found his company a relaxation; but in the Department of State his usefulness to me was almost exclusively the usefulness of a fine figurehead. He never initiated a policy or was of real assistance in carrying thru a policy; but he sometimes phrased what I desired said in a way that was of real service; and the general respect for him was such that his presence in the Cabinet was a strength to the administration. He was always afraid of Senators and Congressmen who possess any power or robustness, this fear being due in part to timidity and nervousness, and in part to a sheer fastidiousness which made him unwilling to face the rather intimate association which is implied in a fight. Accordingly, in actual practice he hardly ever opposed a Senator or Congressman, especially in the matter of patronage, and almost always did, especially in the matter of appointment or promotion, whatever any one of them, even the worst, asked, no matter how bad it might be. The result was thoroly bad for the Department and the service, and it had the further and rather unexpected effect of making Hay himself talk against Senators and Congressmen with extraordinary violence, the Senators being the especial object of his wrath. The very fact that in action in the presence of a Senator he was always feeble, made him try to atone to his own self-respect by being very forcible about him afterwards in speech. He would urge me to make any kind of improper appointment which a Senator desired, and then would relieve his feelings by railing in very bitter and very amusing and well-chosen language against the Senator and all his colleagues; and later still, to outsiders, would wail over, and lament, the appointment, if it happened that I had been misled by him into making it. Of course, much of his attack on the Senate was simply foolish. When he became Secretary of State the Senate contained among its leaders Republicans like Cushman K. Davis, Orville H. Platt, Allison, and Hoar, and Democrats like Cockrell. In character and intellect, these men stood at least level with all but the foremost of the men who have held the Presidency. Cockrell was a Missouri ex-Confederate, entirely fearless, as straight as a string, and a man of single-minded devotion for the public good; he and Allison rendered unwearied and invaluable service in the actual, and indispensable, working out of legislative business. Hoar was a scholar of the loftiest ideals, and ignorant of the meaning of the word fear. Davis was one of the most brilliantly able men I have ever met in public life, and the embodiment of courage and farsighted patriotism; old Orville H. Platt was not as brilliant a man, but he was of fine ability, of entire fearlessness, and of a transparently upright and honorable nature; we should have been fortunate to have either one as President or as Secretary of State. I saw much of all these men. It was a pleasure to work with them, and my association with them always left me with a higher sense of duty and a stronger feeling about my obligations as a public servant. Only the best Presidents, the best Cabinet officers, the highest judges, could be compared with them from the standpoint of service rendered to the public, and of credit and honor conferred by such service upon our public life. To villify in unmeasured terms, utterly without discrimination, a Senate which held these men and which acknowledged them as standing among its leaders, was to occupy a position both foolish and mischievous.

It is distressing to read the letters in which Hay harps on how tired he is of the "sordid wrangles" he lives among; they are not the letters of a strong or brave man. He was dealing with great affairs, he was backed by me in every way. In the Panama business, after the revolution, he did good work, but not as good as Knox and Root. The vital work, getting Panama as an independent Republic, on which all else hinged, was done by me without the aid or advice of anyone, save in so far as they carried out my instructions; and without the knowledge of anyone. But, when once it was done, Hay and Root were invaluable in finishing the business, and Knox also, tho at first he was a little sulky at not having known anything.

I think the most notable error into which an outsider would be led by these letters is concerning the Alaskan Treaty. Hay speaks of this as being in effect purely his own thought and his own work, and claims the result as his. As a matter of fact he had nothing to do with the treaty in any vital matter, his function being simply to phrase the statements which he was told to make; every original proposal he made as regards the treaty was rejected by me, and he in turn made futile objections, which I disregarded, to those things the doing of which brought about the actual result. His original proposal to me was for an arbitration treaty of the usual sort, one or more arbitrators being chosen by each country, and there being an outsider with a casting vote. To this I would not consent; and if I had consented, it would not have obtained a half-dozen votes in the Senate. There was not the slightest justification for the Canadian position, which England had been reluctantly and against her real convictions driven to champion. No American worthy of respect would for one moment have entertained the thought of giving up the territory which the Canadians claimed as being in dispute. To Sir Julian Pauncefote and to Michael Herbert I explained this repeatedly, when they pressed me to go into a treaty in the matter, saying to them not once but again and again that our position was impregnable and that we would no more consent to arbitrate (using the word "arbitrate" in the ordinary accepted sense) than the English would consent to arbitrate the possession of the Orkneys or the Hebrides, and that the utmost I would do would be to agree that representatives of both sides should come together and see if they could not themselves agree on the boundary line. I added that before doing this they must understand how serious the result would be if there was a failure among the men thus appointed to agree, because it would render it necessary for me to reduce to possession the territory in dispute; and as the time for making the agreement approached I actually moved troops up into Alaska so as to be able immediately to take possession of the important disputed points and hold them against small bodies of Canadians in the event that the effort to come to an agreement resulted in nothing. At first Pauncefote and Herbert said that in view of my statement they did not see how we could enter on negotiations. I was much hampered by the fact that Hay had previously and wholly without warrant consented to a *modus vivendi* with Great Britain under which American territory, afterwards admitted to be American territory and at this present moment held as such, was temporarily and improperly put under the British flag. After I had definitely told Hay that there would be no arbitration but simply an agreement of the kind indicated, he at first said, as did the two British Ambassadors, that there was no possibility of getting England to go into such an agreement. Afterwards he came to me and told me that he believed England would consent after all, as she was extremely anxious to have the matter settled. I told him at once to go ahead, and to be sure that Choate, who was then Ambassador, understood my attitude, and realized fully, and made the English realize, that I was simply going into the arrangement so as to let them have an easy way out of an otherwise impossible position, that the men I appointed would never consent to abandon American territory, and that if no agreement were reached I should have to reduce the territory to possession and would under no circumstances consent to an arbitration. When Choate came over in the spring I found that Hay had never made any such statement to him, and, when sitting with me and Hay on the rear portico of the White House, he solemnly told me that in case the two parties failed to agree there would have to be an arbitration. I answered him that he had evidently failed to receive or understand my directions; that he was now to understand absolutely that there would be no arbitration under any circumstances, &c., &c., as I have above stated. Choate immediately veered around, and said he clearly understood my position and would act accordingly. The Senate was extremely reluctant to ratify any treaty which even seemed to admit that there was anything to arbitrate in connection with the Alaskan boundary. The one chance of getting it thru the Senate was to convince the Senators that the men I appointed were men who would at all costs sustain the American contention; while nevertheless it was absolutely necessary to have these men of such high character that their actions could not be doubted nor their motives misconstrued. After a good deal of thought I announced that I should name Root, with you (a Republican Senator), and Turner (a Democratic Senator). The Senate would not have passed the treaty had I not let my intentions be known, or had I not intended to put on you and Turner. Hay strongly objected to both you and Turner, and at first was not satisfied with Root, altho he afterwards became so.

Thus up to this point there was nothing whatever which tended to make the negotiations successful for which he had been responsible. After this point he did nothing at all. The whole work was done by the three commissioners, save that I not only kept Choate up to the mark but also, as you know, wrote to Judge Holmes and to Harry White letters to be shown Chamberlain and Balfour — and which were shown to them — which I think were instrumental in making the British understand that there had to be an agreement with us, that I was not bluffing, and that the consequences would be very serious for them if there was a failure to adopt what was practically our position — for by no possibility could any just judge take any other position. Hay's part in the Alaskan boundary dispute from beginning to end was of far less consequence than that of Root, you and Turner. The letters to Holmes and White run as follows:

Oyster Bay, N. Y.,
July 25, 1903.

My dear Judge Holmes:

I thank you very much for your letter, which I thoroughly enjoyed. There is one point on which I think I ought to give you full information, in view of Chamberlain's remark to you. This is about the Alaska Boundary matter and if you happen to meet Chamberlain again you are entirely at liberty to tell him what I say, although of course it must be privately and unofficially. Nothing but my very earnest desire to get on well with England and my reluctance to come to a break made me consent to the appointment of a Joint Commission in this case; for I regard the attitude of Canada, which England has backed, as having the scantest possible warrant in justice. However, there were but two alternatives. Either I could appoint a commission and give a chance for agreement; or I could do as I shall of course do in case this commission fails, and request Congress to make an appropriation which will enable me to run the boundary on my own hook. As regards most of Great Britain's claim, there is not, in my judgment, enough to warrant so much as a consideration by the United States; and if it were not that there are two or three lesser points on which there is doubt, I could not, even for the object I have mentioned, have consented to appoint a commission. The claim of the Canadians for access to deep water along any part of the Canadian coast is just exactly as indefensible as if they should now suddenly claim the island of Nantucket. There is not a man fit to go on the commission in all the United States who would treat this claim any more respectfully than he would treat a claim to Nantucket. In the same way the preposterous claim once advanced, but I think now abandoned by the Canadians, that the Portland Channel was not the Portland Channel but something else unknown, is no more worth discussing than the claim that the 49th Parallel meant the 50th Parallel or else the 48th.

But there are points which the commission can genuinely consider. There is room for argument about the islands in the mouth of the Portland Channel. I think on this the American case much the stronger of the two. Still, the British have a case. Again, it may well be that there are places in which there is room for doubt as to whether there actually is a chain of mountains parallel to the coast within the ten-league limit. Here again there is a chance for honest difference and honest final agreement. I believe that no three men in the United States could be found who would be more anxious than our own delegates to do justice to the British claim on all points where there is even a color of right on the British side. But the objection raised by certain Canadian authorities to Lodge, Root and Turner, and especially to Lodge and Root, was that they had committed themselves on the general proposition. No man in public life in any position of prominence could have possibly avoided committing himself on the proposition, any more than Mr. Chamberlain could avoid committing himself on the question of the ownership of the Orkneys if some Scandinavian country suddenly claimed them. If this claim embodied other points as to which there was legitimate doubt, I believe Mr. Chamberlain would act fairly and squarely in deciding the matter; but if he appointed a commission to settle up all these questions, I certainly should not expect him to appoint three men, if he could find them, who believed that as to the Orkneys the question was an open one. Similarly, I wish to repeat that no three men fit for the position could be found in all the United States who would not already have come to some conclusion as to certain features of the Canadian claim — not as to all of them.

Let me add that I earnestly hope the English understand my purpose. I wish to make one last effort to bring about an agreement through the commission, which will enable the people of both countries to say that the result represents the feeling of the representatives of both countries. But if there is a disagreement I wish it distinctly understood, not only that there will be no arbitration of the matter, but that in my message to Congress I shall take a position which will prevent any possibility of arbitration hereafter; a position, I am inclined to believe, which will render it necessary for Congress to give me the authority to run the line as we claim it, by our own people, without any further regard to the attitude of England and Canada. If I paid attention to mere abstract right, that is the position I ought to take anyhow. I have not taken it because I wish to exhaust every effort to have the affair settled peacefully and with due regard to England's dignity.

Faithfully yours,
THEODORE ROOSEVELT.

Hon. O. W. Holmes,
  Care J. S. Morgan & Co.,
    London, England.

My dear White:

Many thanks for your very interesting letter. I was particularly delighted with what you say about the Alaska business. I most earnestly hope that your forecast is true. The Canadians have had some very ugly articles published, which I was afraid might influence English opinion. This would be unfortunate. It would be a bad thing for us if there was a deadlock in the present Commission; but it would be a very much worse thing for the Canadians and English; because it would leave me no alternative but to declare as courteously, but as strongly, as possible that the effort to reach an agreement having failed, I should be obliged to treat the territory as ours, as being for the most part in our possession, and the remainder to be reduced to possession as soon as in our judgment it was advisable — and to declare furthermore that no additional negotiations of any kind would be entered into.

* * * *

Faithfully yours,
THEODORE ROOSEVELT.

Mr. Henry White,
  6 Whitehall Gardens, S.W.,
    London, England.

So in what Hay says of appointments to office. He is continually howling and moaning and complaining about bad men being forced upon him by the Senators, and continually saying that he cannot help himself, that these appointments are made in spite of him. On page 234, writing on October 1, 1901, about an interview with me, he says: "It is also evident I shall have no voice in appointments. The sordid 'necessities of the situation' will control, as heretofore. H(errick) is to have R(ome) when M(eyer) resigns. S(torer) is to go to P(aris), if P(orter) gives up." The inference is that these appointments were unfit appointments of the old style. This is not ingenuous on his part, for at the time I explained to him at length what, as a matter of fact, I found he already knew, that I was simply carrying out McKinley's explicit promises in these two cases. Hanna told me when I came in that there were two or three promises that McKinley had made which he must ask me to carry out because McKinley's honor and his were involved in keeping them. They included the promise to Thompson that he should go as Ambassador to Brazil or Mexico, and to Herrick that he should go to Rome (altho Herrick in the end declined the office); and I had also personally promised, on behalf of McKinley and at his explicit direction, both Archbishop Ireland and Storer that Storer should have an embassy as soon as possible, this promise having been made by McKinley, in writing, thru me a few months previously while I was Vice-President. In these matters I simply carried out in good faith McKinley's positive pledges. I never said a word to Hay that would warrant his sneer about the "sordid necessities of the situation." On the contrary, I again and again, and always in vain, asked him to tell me of the fitness or unfitness of any men, for that I would not on any account appoint or retain an unfit man. But he was continually complaining of the bad character of the men put in, and at the same time positively and unequivocally declining, in response to my requests, to put in writing anything against them which would warrant my turning them out. Not only this, but he always deprecated, and strove to prevent my making any move to turn anyone out, no matter how unfit, or refusing to appoint any man, no matter how bad, if backed by strong influence. Here again the trouble was fundamental. Hay would never stand up against any strong man, whether Senator or other politician. No matter how bad a man was, he would appoint or retain him if a big politician, coarse, robust and powerful, insisted upon it. He would then revenge himself to himself by violently denouncing the Senator and the appointee in private. As I have always endeavored to translate words into action, this conduct on his part very nearly got me into serious scrapes, for again and again, acting on what he said, I would either attack a given Senator or start to turn out a given man, only to find that Hay would not stand to what he said when the pressure came, so that I would be left without justification for my action. I suppose fifty times, when I heard that something was wrong in the consular service, I asked him if certain men were bad; and he always replied that they were. I would then propose to turn them out and he would at once positively refuse to make any complaint against them, leaving me, of course, unable to act, for he was the immediate head, who alone could speak with authority. In excuse, he used always to say that just as bad men would be appointed in their places. I would answer that if so it would be his own fault, as I should absolutely follow his advice. But nothing could be done with him; he would never venture to attack any abuse. Finally I took the matter into my own hands. The situation in China grew intolerable, and as Hay would not act I acted over his head. I sent out Peirce[2] to China, and, paying no heed whatever to Hay, after investigation I removed Williams, McWade and Goodnow,[3] three thoroly bad men who had brought great discredit upon the service, who were backed respectively by the entire Republican organization of New York, Pennsylvania and Minnesota. There was a yell which frightened Hay white. After a short while it died out. I put first-class men in the places of the delinquents, and then proceeded to try to clean out the rest of the service. It would have been quite impossible for me to have done this in really thorogoing and satisfactory fashion while Hay was in, because it was so exceedingly cumbersome to be running the office over his head — which I had to do not only as regards the consular service, but as regards everything else during the last year and a half of his incumbency. But I made a first-class beginning, by curing the evil where it was

[2] Herbert Henry Davis Peirce.
[3] John Goodnow, consul general at Shanghai, Robert M. McWade, consul general at Canton, and William Martin, consul at Nanking, were the officers removed. They were replaced respectively by James L. Rodgers, Julius G. Lay, and Thornwell Haynes.

worst, and at the same time most difficult to cure. As soon as Root came in the situation changed as if by magic. All friction with the Senate ceased, and yet Root never yielded to the improper demands of any Senator, whereas Hay almost always did. Root proceeded immediately to reorganize the consular service, and by a system of investigations, and by securing some legislation and where he could not secure legislation supplying its lack by executive action, in the shape of regulations, he completely eliminated all questions of politics in the appointment of consuls to any but the very lowest grades, and in these grades strictly subordinated favoritism to merit; while in the higher grades nothing but merit was or is considered. I never saw a more remarkable instance of a strong man working a great reform in the presence of the need of which a weaker man had been wholly helpless.

It is pathetic to read Hay's ceaseless jeremiads about the way Senators forced bad appointments, and then to realize that under the same President and the same Senate all the difficulties ceased as soon as Root took charge. As I have said, the abuses became so very bad that before Root took charge I had been myself obliged to go over Hay's head, take the situation in the Far East into my own hands, and weed out the worst offenders.

It is curious also to read what Hay says about certain of the treaties. The first canal treaty was a simple atrocity as he drew it up. It prevented our fortifying the Isthmus, gave us no real control over it, and actually invited the powers of continental Europe to interfere in the matter. The Senate acted with the highest wisdom and patriotism in amending this treaty. The British Government rejected the treaty on account of the amendments. But when I came in the new treaty was promptly ratified by both Governments, and was practically and essentially, altho not altogether in form, what the old treaty had been after the Senate amendments had been adopted.

The fact was that Hay could not be trusted where England was concerned. His letter to Balfour on page 254 shows this. He had been the intimate companion of Lincoln. He was at the time Secretary of State, and had held that position under two Presidents; yet he wrote to Balfour congratulating him upon having become Prime Minister in a letter in which he stated that the position of Prime Minister was "the most important official post known to modern history." If he really thought the position of Prime Minister more important than that of President, he was foolish; but to give expression to the thought in writing to the English Prime Minister while he was the American Secretary of State was worse than foolish. On the other hand, he was foolishly distrustful of the Germans. Comparatively early in the Russian-Japanese war the Kaiser wrote us proposing a declaration by the powers in favor of the neutrality and integrity of China. This declaration we were extremely anxious to have made. The Kaiser's proposal was in poor form; it was drawn so as to interfere with any possible action by England or France, but not with action by Russia. The obvious thing was to put it in right form and agree to it. Hay actually proposed to reject it, and brought me around a draft of a note rejecting it. I told him that of course we could never justify ourselves in such a position, but on the contrary we must accept the proposal at once, and in our acceptance ignore the limitations the Kaiser set and announce our cordial adherence to his proposal in words that would commit him to a guarantee of the neutrality and integrity of the entire Chinese Empire. This was accordingly done, and the result was of far-reaching importance. Poor Hay was a sick man, however, by the time the Russian-Japanese war began, and I had ceased being able to pass matters to him. I did not consult him at all in any of the movements that led to the peace of Portsmouth; everything about this was concluded between the time that Hay died and that Root took office; while Taft was in the Philippines. In most matters I have always consulted Root and Taft if I could get at them; rarely did I consult Hay. The biggest matters however, such as the Portsmouth peace, the acquisition of Panama, and sending the fleet round the world, I managed without consultation with anyone; for when a matter is of capital importance, it is well to have it handled by one man only. In dealing with the Japanese situation at every stage I outlined and directed what was to be done; Root however rendered me thruout literally invaluable service, of a kind Hay would have been utterly helpless to render.[4] *Ever yours*

5144 · TO THEODORE ROOSEVELT, JUNIOR *Roosevelt Mss.*

Washington, January 31, 1909

Dear Ted: I have entered on the last month of my Presidency and I think I can hold Congress down so that no disastrous breakup can occur during that period. But they have been anxious to see if they could not do me up this winter. I have a very strong feeling that it is a President's duty to get on with Congress if he possibly can, and that it is a reflection upon him if he and Congress come to a complete break. For seven sessions I was able to prevent such a break. This session, however, they felt that it was safe utterly to disregard me because I was going out and my successor had been elected; and I made up my mind that it was just a case where the exception to the rule applied and that if I did not fight, and fight hard, I should be put in a contemptible position; while inasmuch as I was going out on the 4th of

[4] Unhappily there are things in this letter that are not true. As anyone who wishes to consult Dennet, *Hay,* chapter xxix, can discover, the account of the Alaskan boundary settlement contains errors of fact and distortions of emphasis. Wittingly or unwittingly, Roosevelt in the interest of his own argument did not state exactly what happened. In such a situation each observer must obviously decide for himself the general question of what this means about Theodore Roosevelt and the specific one of whether or not the inaccuracy of the supporting evidence warrants the destruction of the principal conclusion; in this instance whether the distorted account of a diplomatic negotiation renders unacceptable a conclusion about the response of a certain kind of temperament to power and responsibility.

March I did not have to pay heed to our ability to co-operate in the future. The result has, I think, justified my wisdom. I have come out ahead so far, and I have been full President right up to the end — which hardly any other President ever has been.

I am so glad to have had nice Mr. Bob Bacon made Secretary of State before I went out. ⟨*Faithfully yours*⟩ *Your loving father*

5145 · TO WHITELAW REID   *Roosevelt Mss.*

Personal   Washington, January 31, 1909

My dear Mr. Ambassador: I have just received your letter. I thank you for the clippings and for what you say about me.

Now for the important part; that relating to yourself. Naturally, from selfish reasons it would be extremely pleasant to me to have you in London when I reach there. But I have not asked Mr. Taft to retain a single man, no Cabinet officer, nobody in any position. In the cases of a very few small men in different States who had been devoted adherents of his for the nomination I have informed him of the fact, and I have given him full information about a number of the men in office concerning whom he asked me; and as to one or two, in response to questions of his have told him positions in which I thought they would do well or which I thought they would like. But I have volunteered no information and said nothing to him unless he has asked me to say it; except that as regards one representative at a foreign court whom I had appointed I told him certain facts which I felt I ought to, as they were not to the representative's credit. Now, Taft will be at the White House on the 3rd of March. If he gives me the opportunity and puts any question to me I will gladly speak to him along the line you indicate. But I cannot do it unasked. If I did it in one case I should be expected to do it in countless others. I can, however, call his attention to the services that you rendered to him concerning which you speak, as I have not hesitated to call his attention in certain cases to such services. But I cannot ask for any man's retention or appointment, or put anything on the ground of personal favor to me, and this I am sure you will understand.[1] *Sincerely yours*

5146 · TO MELVILLE ELIJAH STONE   *Roosevelt Mss.*

Telegram   Washington, January 31, 1909

The more I have thought over your suggestion of last night the more confident I am that I don't wish to be responsible for any newspaperman going with me, not even for Lawrence Abbott. My earnest desire is that no representative of any paper shall go with me on that trip. I shall ask the steamer people not to send out wireless messages referring to me from the steamer, and on the steamer excepting to exchange the ordinary greetings demanded

[1] Reid remained ambassador to the Court of St. James's until his death in 1912.

by courtesy, I shall have no communication with any newspaperman. I still feel exactly as I exprest myself in all my letters to you on the subject.[1]

5147 · TO CASPAR WHITNEY   *Roosevelt Mss.*

Washington, January 31, 1909

My dear Whitney: I have rewritten that letter to Needham in the form of a statement [1] as you request. I wish, however, that you would give the date

---

[1] Numbers 5043, 5049.

[1] The statement follows:

"February 1, 1909.

"You ask me to speak about vigor of body. I believe in it for its own sake; I believe in it still more as an aid to vigor of mind, and above all, to vigor of character. But I do not believe in it at all if it is made an end instead of a means, and especially if play is permitted to become the serious business of life.

"High proficiency in sport is not necessary in order to get good out of it; altho of course it is in every way bad to show a slipshod indifference to high proficiency, an unwillingness or inability to put one's whole heart into the contest. Personally, as you know, I am not really good at any games. Perhaps in my time I came nearer to being fairly good as a walker, rider, and rifle-shot than in any other way; but I was simply an average good man even in these three respects.

"Whatever success I have had in game hunting — and it has been by no means noteworthy — has been due, as well as I can make it out, to three causes: first, common sense and good judgment; second, perseverance, which is the only way of allowing one to make good one's own blunders; third the fact that I shot as well at game as at a target. This did not make me hit difficult shots, but it prevented my missing easy shots, which a good target shot will often do in the field. Most of my bears, for instance, were killed close up, and the shots were not difficult so long as one did not get rattled. Now of course the possession and practice of these three qualities did not make me by any means as successful a hunter as the men who in addition to possessing them were also better shots than I was, or who had greater power of endurance, or who were more skilled in plainscraft and woodcraft. But they did enable me to kill a reasonable quantity of big game and to do it in ways that have made my observations of real value to the faunal or outdoor naturalist. Besides, I knew what I wanted, and was willing to work hard to get it.

"In short, I am not an athlete; I am simply a good, ordinary, out-of-doors man. The other day I rode one hundred and four miles. Now this was no feat for any young man in condition to regard as worth speaking about; twice out in the cattle country, on the round-up, when I was young. I have myself spent thirty-six hours in the saddle, merely dismounting to eat, or change horses; the hundred-mile ride represented what any elderly man in fair trim can do if he chooses. In the summer I often take the smaller boys for what they call a night picnic on the Sound; we row off eight or ten miles, camp out, and row back in the morning. Each of us had a light blanket to sleep in, and the boys are sufficiently deluded to believe that the chicken or beefsteak I fry in bacon fat on these expeditions has a flavor impossible elsewhere to be obtained. Now these expeditions represent just about the kind of things I do. Instead of rowing it may be riding, or chopping, or walking, or playing tennis, or shooting at a target. But is always a pastime which any healthy middle-aged man fond of outdoors life, but not in the least an athlete, can indulge in if he chooses.

"I think my last sentence covers the whole case — that is, when I say 'if he chooses.' It has always seemed to me that in life there are two ways of achieving

which I have put on, and also make a brief introductory remark stating that this was orginally in the form of a letter written to Needham four years ago, and that in response to the request of yourself I have put in so much of the letter as referred to vigor of body. *Sincerely yours*

P.S. I want the date I have put kept on this because, while I have been more than delighted to do anything I could for *Collier's*, I don't want, after I leave the White House, to get into the position where I am writing articles for one periodical at the same time I am refusing large monied offers to write for other magazines.

5148 · TO NELSON WILMARTH ALDRICH

Washington, February 2, 1909

My dear Senator Aldrich: Since writing you my note of this morning I have seen the Secretary of War. He informs me that in his judgment the fact that the man is rendered eligible for re-enlistment leaves the President at complete liberty to exercise his judgment as to whether or not the man should be allowed to re-enlist.[1] This being so, I do not think that the objections of the gentleman[2] to whom I alluded this morning were good. I think it very desirable, however, that you should state this to be the construction of the proposed act, so that no question of doubt could arise hereafter as to what the National Legislature intended. I have no question that the President would follow the advice of the board, but it is of course wrong from every standpoint to have it understood that he is *compelled* to follow the advice of the board. *Sincerely yours*

———

success, or, for the matter of that, of achieving what is commonly called greatness. One is to do that which can only be done by the man of exceptional and extraordinary abilities. Of course this means that only this one man can do it, and it is a very rare kind of success or of greatness. The other is to do that which many men could do, but which as a matter of fact none of them actually does. This is the ordinary kind of success or kind of greatness. Nobody but one of the world's rare geniuses could have written the Gettysburg speech, or the second inaugural, or met as Lincoln met the awful crises of the Civil War. But most of us *can* do the ordinary things, which, however, most of us do *not* do. My own successes have come within this second category. Any fairly hardy and healthy man can do what I have done in hunting and ranching if he only really wishes to, and will take the pains and trouble, and at the same time use common sense.

"Anyone that chose could lead the kind of life I have led, and anyone who had led that life could if he chose — and by 'choosing,' I of course mean choosing to exercise in advance the requisite industry, judgment and foresight, none of them to an extraordinary degree — have raised my regiment or served in positions analogous to those in which I have served in civil life."

———

[1] Aldrich was then completing the Brownsville bill.
[2] Senator Borah.

Washington, February 2, 1909

My dear Dr. Shaw: Senator Burton has phoned me; and Congressman Mouser[1] and Thomas J. Maxwell, member of the State Committee from Fremont, Ohio, have just been in to see me about the postmaster at Fremont whose name at your request I directed to be sent in for reappointment. They tell me that Gessner was most active in trying to get Foraker delegates from his district and that to appoint him is to endorse the Foraker wing and will be a blow to the Taft people. I have told them that I have given you my word and that I cannot go back on it, in view of the postmaster's record; but that I should lay the facts before you. What do you desire? The man has been a good postmaster but he has evidently been an active Foraker man whose appointment will be felt as a blow by Taft people. I shall do whatever your feeling is in the matter.[2]

I need not say how I enjoyed catching a glimpse of you the other evening. *Sincerely yours*

Telegram Washington, February 4, 1909

Your kind letter just received. What is the rumor that California legislature has past bill excluding Japanese children from public schools? [1] This is the most offensive bill of all and in my judgment is clearly unconstitutional and we should at once have to test it in the courts. Can it not be stopt in the legislature or by veto?

---

[1] Grant Earl Mouser, Republican congressman from Ohio, 1905–1909.
[2] Roosevelt did not withdraw the appointment of Gustavus A. Gessner as postmaster at Fremont.

---

[1] The rumor was correct. The temporary calm that followed Gillett's special message of January 25 had suddenly evaporated. On January 30, a Japanese university graduate was attacked by a gang in Berkeley. On February 4, by a vote of 45 to 29, the California Assembly passed the anti-Japanese school bill.

Governor Gillett the next day sent another message to the legislature. Repeating Roosevelt's argument that the bill, a violation of the Japanese-American treaty, was unconstitutional, he condemned the measure as also impolitic. This message was strong, but only the intercession of Speaker Stanton saved the situation. With ominous restraint the speaker warned his colleagues that they were "treading upon very dangerous ground." Stanton pleaded with the Assembly to let the bill "go over" for reconsideration "until the governor will be in a position to explain more fully the reasons for the Federal government's request for delay" (Washington *Post,* February 6, 1909). His counsel prevailed. Not the governor alone, but also the President himself in two public telegrams to Stanton (Numbers 5154, 5160), explained the reasons for delay.

My dear Kent: I have your letter of the 29th and enclosure, and entirely agree with you. Our line of policy must be adopted holding ever in view the fact that this is a race question, and that race questions stand by themselves. I did not clearly see this at the outset; but for nearly three years I have seen it, and thruout my treatment of the question have shaped my course accordingly. The one important point is that the Japanese should, as a race, be excluded from becoming permanent inhabitants of our territory, they in return excluding us from becoming permanent inhabitants of their territory. In other words, let the arrangement between Japan and the United States be entirely reciprocal. Let the Japanese and Americans visit one another's countries with entire freedom as tourists, scholars, professors, sojourners for study or pleasure or for purposes of international business; but keep out laborers, including agricultural laborers, men who want to take up farms, men who want to go into the small trades or even in the professions where the work is of a noninternational character: that is, keep out of Japan those Americans who wish to settle and become part of the resident working population, and keep out of America those Japanese who wish to adopt a similar attitude. This is the wise and proper policy. It is the policy we already pursue as regards the Chinese. In the case of Japan it is certainly compatible with mutual respect, and, indeed, mutual admiration as between the two peoples. It is merely a recognition of the fact that in the present stages of social advancement of the two peoples, whatever may be the case in the future, it is not only undesirable but impossible that there should be racial intermingling, and the effort is sure to bring disaster.

Yet, while this is the wise view, and while it is the view that the Japanese would undoubtedly take in regard to American emigration to Japan if it began on a scale like the recent Japanese emigration to America, it may be phrased in very offensive terms, and is peculiarly apt to be misunderstood and to cause intense humiliation and bitterness and arouse intense resentment; especially in the case of a people very sensitive and at the same time very self-confident in their warlike strength, as is true with the Japanese. In such circumstances the wise policy is to insist on keeping out Japanese immigration; but at the same time to behave with scrupulous courtesy to Japan as a nation and to the Japanese who are here; and also to continue to build up and maintain at the highest point of efficiency our navy. This three-fold policy is precisely the policy of the administration for the past two years. We are building up the navy in spite of the opposition of men like Senator Hale, Senator Perkins of California, and those who follow them. We have actually succeeded in coming to an agreement with the Japanese Government under which the number of Japanese immigrants has so decreased that during the last six months more Japanese have left the United States than have come into them. The total number of Japanese in this country is actually less than it was six months ago. Yet at the same time we are endeavoring to treat the Japanese with studied politeness and to show that we respect and admire them; to make ample appropriations for their Exposition, &c. &c.

Now the wickedness and folly of the few demagogs in California and Nevada[1] who try to pass or succeed in passing laws to prevent the Japanese from attending the public schools and the like, must be evident to anyone who really thinks out the question. These laws do not prevent the Japanese from coming in, and so they totally fail in accomplishing anything that goes to the root of the difficulty; but they irritate profoundly all the Japanese who are here, and they give great offense in Japan itself. In other words, they accomplish nothing whatever of the object really desirable to attain, and at the same time they jeopardize the public peace. My object is to show the maximum efficiency in doing away with the race problem by excluding immigration, and at the same time cause the minimum of disturbance in the relations between the United States and Japan. These people of whom I complain combine the minimum of efficiency as regards attaining their object and the maximum of insult. The same Legislature that re-elects the foe of the navy — so far as a man like Perkins, who has no more backbone than a sea anemone, can be said to be the foe of anything — yet takes steps which tend to put us in a situation from which nothing but the strongest kind of a navy can extricate us without war, or bring us thru if there is war.

I entirely agree with what you say about Hawaii. For years I have been opposing the policy of the sugar planters. I would rather see the sugar plantations fail than see them a success at the cost of being tilled by coolie labor. As regards these islands I would like to see the immigration laws amended so that we could bring in tens of thousands of Spaniards, Portuguese, or Italians, or of any of the other European races that could make a living off the land in Hawaii. I am for the small settler, the small homemaker, whom we can assimilate. *Sincerely yours*

5152 · TO WILLIAM EMLEN ROOSEVELT   *Roosevelt Mss.*

Washington, February 4, 1909

Dear Emlen: No kinder offer was ever made, my dear fellow, than that you have made. But surely you and your family will not be going down on the

[1] The Nevada Assembly had passed a resolution addressed to the California Legislature in support of the anti-Japanese measures pending there. This offensively worded document described the Japanese as the parasite race of the world and a menace to civilization, and urged the Californians to ignore the coercion and interference of the President. Roosevelt, reminding the press of the impotence of the State of Nevada during the Goldfield episode, at first dismissed the resolution as ridiculous. When it received increasing publicity, however, he persuaded Nevada Senators Newlands and Nixon to intercede. Their admonitions for caution influenced the state Senate to table the resolution.

train which we will probably take on March 4th, which will be at 10:00 o'clock at night, and I think it would really be better to have Edith and myself simply take our places in that train. It is perfectly comfortable, and I should rather like from the outset to make it evident that we are not doing anything unusual or in a swell way.[1] My dear Emlen, I cannot say how touched both Edith and I are by your thoughtfulness and kindness.

With love to all, believe me, *Ever yours*

5153 · TO JAMES NORRIS GILLETT   *Roosevelt Mss.*

Telegram   Washington, February 6, 1909

I saw Flint as soon as your message came. He has been helping me in every way, and after consultation with him I wired the Speaker a message[1] which he can make public if he thinks best. Please see him. I am astounded at Perkins' conduct. He has for the last seven years done what he could to hamper us in building up the navy and has always acted against the real advocates of the navy, and yet now he advises a policy of wanton insult.[2] I have nothing to advise at the moment, for I cannot speak too highly in praise of the course you have followed. I suppose my telegram to the Speaker is the best way I can render assistance. Please wire me if you think there is anything more I can do.[3] Again let me thank you heartily.

5154 · TO PHILIP ACKLEY STANTON   *Roosevelt Mss.*

Telegram   Washington, February 6, 1909

Pray accept the expression of my profound obligation on behalf of the American people as a whole for the high and patriotic service you are rendering. I have unlimited confidence in the sane good sense and right-mindedness of the people of the State of California. I know that they appreciate that the National Government is at this moment engaged in doing everything it can to achieve the ends that California has in view while at the same time preserving unbroken the relations of respect and good will with a great and friendly nation; and therefore I am sure that the people of California will support you in taking the position you have taken, which is so eminently in

[1] On March 4 the ex-President and his wife in an "ordinary Pullman car" "travelled in a most democratic manner" from Washington to New York City. From New York to Oyster Bay he traveled by private car.

---

[1] No. 5154.
[2] Senator Perkins of California, unlike Senator Flint who had supported Roosevelt's arguments, had expressed sympathy for anti-Japanese legislation. Before the reconsideration of the school bill, however, Perkins advised his friends in the Assembly to heed the advice of Governor Gillett; see Washington *Post*, February 7, 11, 1909.
[3] The governor suggested that Roosevelt wire Stanton a more complete statement of his views. This the President did on February 8; see No. 5160.

the interest not only of the American people as a whole but especially of the State of California itself.

5155 · TO THEODORE ROOSEVELT, JUNIOR

Roosevelt Mss.

Washington, February 6, 1909

Dear Ted: At Ethel's dance on Friday night I, for the first time, made the acquaintance of Mrs. Munn and liked her very much. It was funny realizing that I had never seen her before when I knew the rest of the Munn family quite intimately. The dance was a great success with just the right mixture of social and political people. All the regular social set was there having a splendid time, the Ambassadors and everybody of that kind, and in addition numbers of Congressmen and Senators and their daughters, and I believe they all had a very good time indeed, and to many of them I am sure the dance in the White House meant a good deal. I had a first-class dance with Ethel and was much flattered because she really seemed to think that I danced well.

I have spent my usual lively week; but the troubles I have with Congress don't count at all when compared with the trouble I am having with California over Japan. I have been vigorously holding the lid down for the last three weeks, with varying success. I think I shall succeed but I cannot be sure. One of the Senators, Flint, has stood by me like a trump. I would like to break the neck of the feebly malicious angleworm who occupies the other seat as California's Senator; he is a milk-faced grub named Perkins.

I send you herewith my Lincoln speech which I deliver next Friday. Be careful it does not get out until then. Lincoln is my great hero, as you know, and I have put my heart into this speech.[1] *Your loving father*

5156 · TO ELBERT FRANCIS BALDWIN

Roosevelt Mss.

Washington, February 6, 1909

My dear Mr. Baldwin: I have your letter of the 5th about the Census bill. I do not think this is my most important veto.[1] I think my veto of that water-power bill [2] was even more important. But I regard this as important. You

[1] For Roosevelt's speech in Hodgenville, Kentucky, at the celebration of the 100th anniversary of Lincoln's birth, see *Men of Action* (New York, 1926), Nat. Ed. XI, 210–214.

[1] For Roosevelt's veto see No. 5123, note 1.
[2] On January 15, Roosevelt had vetoed a bill authorizing William H. Standish "to construct a dam across James River, in Stone County, Mo., and divert a portion of its waters . . . . to create electric power." "The bill," Roosevelt declared, "gives to the grantee a valuable privilege, which by its very nature is monopolistic, and does not contain the conditions essential to protect the public interest." Haphazard policy in the disposition of power sites, Roosevelt warned, was no longer tolerable. Grants should be made only if subject to continuing official inspection, to adjustable license fees, to renewal or forfeiture at a reasonable terminal date, and to restrictions preventing hydro-electric combinations in restraint of trade; see *Congressional Record,* XLIII, 978–980.

have doubtless seen my reasons in full. I am inclined to think that I might have met the difficulty by classifying the offices anyhow; but I thought that this might be regarded as tricky, and I preferred to meet the issue in straightforward manner. *Sincerely yours*

5157 · TO LUKE EDWARD WRIGHT   *Roosevelt Mss.*

Washington, February 7, 1909

To the Secretary of War: I have received your letter of February 6th and the accompanying report of Mr. Browne on the Brownsville raid. I agree with you that it is not necessary to send this report to Congress. Mr. Browne clearly establishes, however, by the testimony of the colored men themselves that the shooting was done by colored soldiers and in all human probability by the men he mentions. He also shows clearly that First Sergeant Mingo Saunders, in spite of his reputation for personal courage, was as thoroly dangerous, unprincipled and unworthy a soldier as ever wore the United States uniform, and that under no conceivable circumstances should he ever be allowed again in the army. The testimony is clear as to the part of Holloman also. If the Senate legislation passes, this letter of mine and the accompanying documents will be put before the board of officers who are to consider the question of what men, if any, are to be reinstated; and they will also be put before the President if the board decides that any of the men shall be made eligible for reinstatement.

5158 · TO ARTHUR HAMILTON LEE   *Roosevelt Mss.*

Personal   Washington, February 7, 1909

Dear Arthur: I am glad you like what I said about India. I have had it in mind to say ever since Bryan made his silly and hysterical pronunciamento which, so far as by flattery one can say it meant anything, meant that he thought there should be a kind of Indian republic established out of hand. Keir Hardie's coming over here,[1] and the knowledge I had of the unrest in India, and my further knowledge of the fact that agitators in England and agitators in India both sometimes traded on supposed American support of the Indian agitation, made me feel that it was a good time to speak. If I did any good, I am pleased.

Yes, I have followed the line of argument — in the form of questions — which you have been making about the two-power navy policy, and I entirely agree with you. I do not believe this country can possibly take any offense at your argument if you make it as you outline it in your letter to me; and most emphatically there will be no justification for taking offense. Your

---

[1] James Keir Hardie, British Fabian, a founder of the Labour party and its first leader in Parliament, 1906–1907, during his inspection of the American labor movement convincingly voiced the anti-imperialist views of his political associates.

stand should be that you are urging a permanent policy; that it is not a policy aimed at any nation; that it is not meant to bring on war, but to avoid war, and that it is consistent with the most genuine feeling of friendship for, and desire to keep on friendly terms with, all other nations; that in particular you have the very heartiest feeling of friendship for the United States, and would laugh at any thought of trouble between the two great English-speaking peoples; but that if England discriminates in favor of any one nation, she can do it only by giving offense to other nations, and thereby transforming into a just objection to the policy what is now an objection without any real merit whatever; that if you in parliament specifically except America you will rightly be asked why you do not specifically except any one of several other powers, with all of which England is and hopes to remain on the friendliest terms, and that then you would be asked why you regard any power as possibly hostile; in short, that this is simply a policy for the preservation and defense of the Empire, entirely impersonal, and that for the very reason that it is not aimed at any nation, you think it would be grossly improper specifically to name any nation either as excepted or included; for if you named any given nation as excepted from the policy, it would be equivalent to stating that other friendly nations were really those against which the policy was directed. To name one as excepted, is equivalent to stating that each and every other is included.

I am having a lively time at the finish of my term as President, but so far I am well ahead of the game. The thing that gives me serious uneasiness is the friction with Japan. I have been reluctantly forced to the conclusion that it is indispensable for the Japanese to be kept from coming in any numbers as settlers to the United States, the feeling in our western States on this point being as strong as it is in Australia and British Columbia. In the first place, this feeling is so strong that it ought not to be disregarded. In the next place, it simply could not be disregarded. If London and Washington should to-morrow unite in saying that the Japanese should be admitted wholesale to all countries under the British and American flags, we should the following week see our Pacific States and British Columbia declare their independence as a separate republic, in close alliance with Australia. Under such circumstances, every wise and patriotic man, whether in public or private life, must face facts. My policy therefore is threefold:

(1) To keep out the Japanese.
(2) To do it with the minimum of friction and the maximum of courtesy.
(3) To build up the navy.

But our Keir Hardies, our labor agitators generally, the demagogs among certain of our politicians, and large numbers of fatuous and shortsighted people in peace societies and the like, wish the country to amble along with inane complacency, committed to a policy which shall combine insult and helplessness, and which could only end in disaster.

Give our love to Mrs. Lee. We look forward eagerly to seeing you, and I hope I shall have a good time in Africa. Bar accidents, I feel that I am fairly certain to do so. *Always yours*

5159 · TO THE UNITED STATES ARMY WAR COLLEGE   *Roosevelt Mss.*

Washington, February 8, 1909

To the War College: I believe there is now a committee at work on the revision of the field service regulations. Won't you take up the matter of pack trains? I feel there should be at least a full pack train with every squadron of cavalry, as much a part of it as its own horses. Won't you look up the organization and training laid down by the orders of General Wood for pack trains in the Philippine Islands, and also what General Barry has done for those in Cuba? If I remember rightly, in the Philippines Scott and Daly had much to do with the matter. I feel that we ought to provide for this in the regulations; that we certainly need a better organization and training of the army pack trains, which are, in my judgment, the only proper transportation for cavalry. We must not allow packing to become a lost art in the army. The old timers in the Rocky Mountains are passing away and we must look to the army to keep up the knowledge of this essential and invaluable service art.

5160 · TO PHILIP ACKLEY STANTON   *Roosevelt Mss.*

Telegram   Washington, February 8, 1909

I trust there will be no misunderstanding of the Federal Government's attitude. We are jealously endeavoring to guard the interest of California and of the entire West in accordance with the desires of our western people. By friendly agreement with Japan we are now carrying out a policy which while meeting the interests and desires of the Pacific slope, is yet compatible not merely with mutual self-respect, but with mutual esteem and admiration between the Americans and Japanese. The Japanese Government is loyally and in good faith doing its part to carry out this policy, precisely as the American Government is doing. The policy aims at mutuality of obligation and behavior. In accordance with it the purpose is that the Japanese shall come here exactly as Americans go to Japan, which is in effect that travelers, students, persons engaged in international business, men who sojourn for pleasure or study, and the like, shall have the freest access from one country to the other, and shall be sure of the best treatment, but that there shall be no settlement in mass by the people of either country in the other. During the last six months under this policy more Japanese have left the country than have come in, and the total number in the United States has diminished by over two thousand. These figures are absolutely accurate and cannot be impeached. In other words, if the present policy is consistently followed and works as well in the future as it is now working, all difficulties and causes of friction will disappear, while at the same time each nation will retain its self-respect and the good will of the other. But such a bill as this school bill accomplishes literally nothing whatever in the line of the object aimed at and gives just and grave cause for irritation; while in addition the United States Government would be obliged immediately to take action in the Federal courts to test such legislation, as we hold it to be clearly a violation of the treaty. On this point I refer you to the numerous decisions of the United States Supreme Court in regard to State laws which violate treaty obligations of the United States. The legislation would accomplish nothing beneficial and would certainly cause some mischief, and might cause very grave mischief. In short, the policy of the administration is to combine the maximum of efficiency in achieving the real object which the people of the Pacific Slope have at heart, with the minimum of friction and trouble, while the misguided men who advocate such action as this against which I protest are following a policy which combines the very minimum of efficiency with the maximum of insult, and which, while totally failing to achieve any real result for good, yet might accomplish an infinity of harm. If in the next year or two the action of the Federal Government fails to achieve what it is now achieving, then thru the further action of the President and Congress it can be made entirely efficient. I am sure that the sound judgment of the people of California will support you, Mr. Speaker, in your effort. Let me repeat that at present we are actually doing the very thing which the people of California wish to be done, and to upset the arrangement under which this is being done cannot do good and may do great harm. If in the next year or two the figures of immigration prove that the arrangement which has worked successfully during the last six months is no longer working successfully, then there would be ground for grievance, and for the reversal by the National Government of its present policy. But at present the policy is working well and until it works badly it would be a grave misfortune to change it, and when changed it can only be changed effectively by the national Government.[1]

5161 · TO PHILANDER CHASE KNOX   *Roosevelt Mss.*

Washington, February 8, 1909

My dear Senator Knox: You are soon to become Secretary of State under Mr. Taft. At the outset both he and you will be overwhelmed with every kind of work; but there is one matter of foreign policy of such great and permanent importance that I wish to lay it before the President-to-be and yourself. I speak of the relations of the United States and Japan.

It is utterly impossible to foretell as regards either foreign or domestic policy what particular questions may appear as at the moment of most engrossing interest. It may be that there will be no ripple of trouble between Japan and the United States during your term of service. It may very well be that

[1] Roosevelt prepared this telegram with the assistance of Senator Flint and Franklin K. Lane.

you will have acute trouble about Cuba, or with Venezuela or in Central America, or with some European power; but it is not likely that grave international complications — that is, complications which can possibly lead to serious war — can come from any such troubles. If we have to interfere again in Cuba, or take possession of the Island, it will be exasperating, and we may in consequence have to repeat our Philippine experiences by putting down an annoying but unimportant guerrilla outbreak. But this would represent merely annoyance. The same would be true of anything in Central America or Venezuela. I do not believe that Germany has any designs that would bring her in conflict with the Monroe Doctrine. The last seven years have tended steadily toward a better understanding of Germany on our part, and a more thoro understanding on the part of Germany that she must not expect colonial expansion in South America. As for England, I cannot imagine serious trouble with her. The settlement of the Alaskan boundary removed the one grave danger. The treaties now before the Senate are excellent, and all we have to fear is some annoying, but hardly grave, friction, in the event of the failure of the Senate to ratify them.

But with Japan the case is different. She is a most formidable military power. Her people have peculiar fighting capacity. They are very proud, very warlike, very sensitive, and are influenced by two contradictory feelings, namely, a great self-confidence, both ferocious and conceited, due to their victory over the mighty empire of Russia; and a great touchiness because they would like to be considered as on a full equality with, as one of the brotherhood of, Occidental nations, and have been bitterly humiliated to find that even their allies, the English, and their friends, the Americans, won't admit them to association and citizenship, as they admit the least advanced or most decadent European peoples. Moreover, Japan's population is increasing rapidly and demands an outlet, and the Japanese laborers, small farmers, and petty traders would, if permitted, flock by the hundred thousand into the United States, Canada, and Australia.

Now for our side. The events of the last three years have forced me to the clear understanding that our people will not permit the Japanese to come in large numbers among them; will not accept them as citizens; will not tolerate their presence as large bodies of permanent settlers. This is just as true in Australia and Columbia as in our Rocky Mountain and Pacific States; but at present the problem is more acute with us because the desire of the Japanese to come here has grown. The opposition to the presence of the Japanese, I have reluctantly come to feel, is entirely warranted, and not only must be, but ought to be, heeded by the national Government in the interest of our people and our civilization; and this in spite of the fact that many of the manifestations of the opposition are unwise and improper to the highest degree. To permit the Japanese to come in large numbers into this country would be to cause a race problem and invite and insure a race contest. It is necessary to keep them out. But it is almost equally necessary that we should both show all possible courtesy and consideration in carrying out this necessarily disagreeable policy of exclusion,* and that we should be thoroly armed, so as to prevent the Japanese from feeling safe in attacking us. Unfortunately, great masses of our people show a foolish indifference to arming, and at the same time a foolish willingness to be offensive to the Japanese. Labor unions pass violent resolutions against the Japanese and almost at the same moment protest against strengthening our military resources on land or sea. Big corporations seek to introduce Japanese coolies, so as to get cheap labor, and thereby invite agitation which they are powerless to quell. The peace societies, and Senators and Congressmen like Burton of Ohio, Perkins of California, Perkins of New York,[1] Tawney of Minnesota, McCall of Massachusetts, and Bartholdt of Missouri, blatantly or furtively oppose the navy and hamper its upbuilding, while doing nothing whatever to prevent insult to Japan. The California Legislature is threatening to pass the most offensive kind of legislation aimed at the Japanese, and yet it re-elects a wretched creature like Perkins to the Senate altho he has opposed, with his usual feeble timidity and so far as he dared, the upbuilding of the navy, following Hale's lead.

We are therefore faced by the fact that our people will not tolerate and ought not to tolerate, the presence among them of large bodies of Japanese and that so long as they are here in large bodies there is always chance either of violence on the part of mobs or of indiscreet and improper action by the legislative bodies of the Western States under demagogic influence. Furthermore, in Hawaii the Japanese already many times outnumber the whites, and have shown on more than one recent occasion a spirit both truculent and insolent.

In Hawaii the trouble is primarily due to the shortsighted greed of the sugar planters and of the great employers generally, who showed themselves incapable of thinking of the future of their children and anxious only to make fortunes from estates tilled by coolie labor. Accordingly they imported, first masses of Chinese laborers, and then masses of Japanese laborers. Thruout my term as President I have so far as possible conducted our policy against this desire of the sugar planters, against the theory of turning Hawaii into an island of coolie-tilled plantations, and in favor of making it so far as possible the abode of small settlers. With this purpose, I have done everything I could to encourage the immigration of Southern Europeans to the islands, and have endeavored so far as I could in the absence of legislation to restrict the entrance of Asiatic coolies. So far as possible our aim should be to diminish the number of Japanese in the islands without any regard to the fortunes of the sugar planters, and to bring in Europeans, no matter of what ancestry, in

---

[1] James Breck Perkins had abandoned a Rochester law practice to write French history. After five years in Paris he returned to Rochester and New York politics, serving as a Republican congressman from 1901 until his death in 1910.

order that the islands may be filled with a white population of our general civilization and culture.

As regards the mainland, our policy should have three sides, and should be shaped not to meet the exigencies of this year or next, but to meet what may occur for the next few decades. Japan is poor and is therefore reluctant to go to war. Moreover, Japan is vitally interested in China and on the Asiatic mainland and her wiser statesmen will if possible prevent her getting entangled in a war with us, because whatever its result it would hamper and possibly ruin Japan when she came to deal again with affairs in China. But with so proud and sensitive a people neither lack of money nor possible future complications will prevent a war if once they get sufficiently hurt and angry; and there is always danger of a mob outbreak there just as there is danger of a mob outbreak here. Our task therefore is on the one hand to meet the demands which our own people make and which cannot permanently be resisted and on the other to treat Japan so courteously that she will not be offended more than is necessary; and at the same time to prepare our fleet in such shape that she will feel very cautious about attacking us. Disturbances like those going on at present are certain to occur unless the Japanese immigration, so far as it is an immigration for settlement, stops. For the last six months under our agreement with Japan it has been stopped to the extent that more Japanese have left the country than have come into it. But the Japanese should be made clearly to understand that this process must continue and if there is relaxation it will be impossible to prevent our people from enacting drastic exclusion laws; and that in such case all of us would favor such drastic legislation. Hand in hand with insistence on the stopping of Japanese immigration should go insistence as regards our own people that they be courteous and considerate, that they treat the Japanese who are here well; and above all that they go on with the building of the navy, keep it at the highest point of efficiency, securing not merely battleships but an ample supply of colliers and other auxiliary vessels of every kind. Much of the necessary expense would be met by closing the useless navy yards. By the way, the fighting navy should not be divided; it should be kept either in the Pacific or in the Atlantic, merely a squadron being left in the other ocean and this in such shape that in the event of war it could avoid attack and at once join the main body of fighting ships.

All this is so obvious that it ought not to be necessary to dwell upon it. But our people are shortsighted and have short memories — I suppose all peoples are shortsighted and have short memories. The minute we arrange matters so that for the moment everything is smooth and pleasant, the more foolish peace societies, led by men like ex-Secretary of State Foster and ex-Secretary of the Navy Long, clamor for a stoppage in the building up of the navy. On the other hand, at the very moment when we are actually keeping out the Japanese and reducing the number of Japanese here, demagogs and agitators like those who have recently appeared in the California and Nevada Legislatures work for the passage of laws which are humiliating and irritating to the Japanese and yet of no avail so far as keeping out immigrants is concerned; for this can be done effectively only by the National Government. The defenselessness of the coast, the fact that we have no army to hold or reconquer the Philippines and Hawaii, the fact that we have not enough battleships nor enough auxiliaries in the navy — all these facts are ignored and forgotten. On the other hand, the Japanese, if we do not keep pressure upon them will let up in their effort to control the emigration from Japan to this country, and they must be continually reminded that unless they themselves stop it, in the end this country is certain to stop it, and ought to stop it, no matter what the consequences may be.

There is no more important continuing feature of our foreign policy than this in reference to our dealing with Japan; the whole question of our dealings with the Orient is certain to grow in importance. I do not believe that there will be war, but there is always the chance that war will come, and if it did come, the calamity would be very great, and while I believe we would win, there is at least a chance of disaster. We should therefore do everything in our power to guard against the possibility of war by preventing the occurrence of conditions which would invite war and by keeping our navy so strong that war may not come or that we may be successful if it does come. *Sincerely yours*

[*Handwritten*] P.S. I enclose a copy of my telegram to the Speaker of the California Lower House; this was really meant almost as much for Japan as for California, and sets forth, seemingly as incidental, what our future policy must be.

* [*Handwritten*] If possible, the Japanese should be shown, what is the truth, that our keeping them out means not that they are inferior to us — in some ways they are superior — but that they are *different;* so different that, whatever the future may hold, at present the two races ought not to come together in masses.

5162 · TO ROBERT LATHAM OWEN   *Roosevelt Mss.*

Washington, February 9, 1909

My dear Senator Owen: [1] I have your letter of the 8th. I thoroly agree with you that the Indians should bear as rapidly as possible their share of the burden of taxation. Secretary Garfield has just had a long interview with me on the point you raise. He insists that at the conference you and I and he

[1] Robert Latham Owen, Democratic senator from Oklahoma, 1907–1925; originally a Virginian of Cherokee descent, "handsome, dominating, one of the ablest men ever produced by . . . Oklahoma."

held, the agreement reached was embodied in the bill for the removal of restrictions which was passed last year.[2] My memory does not coincide with his as to what it was that we agreed upon, but I do not remember with sufficient clearness to be certain in my statements. As late in the session as this, with everything crowding upon me, it is a simple physical impossibility for me to take up the whole matter again with the thought of overruling the decision of the Secretary of the Interior, who has made a peculiarly close study of the question and is infinitely more familiar with it than I am. It is out of the question for me, I am sorry to say, to do this. *Sincerely yours*

5163 · TO GEORGE KIBBE TURNER   *Roosevelt Mss.*

Personal   Washington, February 10, 1909

My dear Mr. Turner: I shall take the liberty of showing your letter to Mr. Newberry. I had not seen the statement of his to which you refer. I think your figures will be of real use to me. I believe that I have forced Messrs. Hale, Perkins, Tillman, and the rest of the Naval Committee up to the two-battleship point. Of course they ought to provide for four battleships and make up for the extra expense by closing a third of the navy yards. But I cannot expect too much. When I became President they had stopt building up the navy. I can look back with profound gratification to what we have accomplished in the last eight years.[1] It is not nearly as much as we should have accomplished, but it marks a very great advance indeed. *Sincerely yours*

[2] The law of 1908 defined which of the lands of the Five Civilized Tribes could be offered for sale. Indians of three-fourths or more Indian blood were restricted in all their holdings; those whose blood was between one-half and three-fourths Indian could sell their surplus land but not their homesteads; all others were released from all restrictions. This act also declared all unrestricted land subject to taxation. Restricted lands, in accordance with treaties between the federal government and the tribes, were tax free. Before and after the law was passed, Senator Owen attempted unsuccessfully to increase the amount of unrestricted land and thereby the tax potential of the State of Oklahoma. As an alternative he suggested, also without success, that the federal government reimburse the state for taxes lost because of restrictions. For a full discussion of this issue see Debo, *And Still the Waters Run*, pp. 174–180.

[1] Such gratification was justified. The eight years had seen the creation of a modern American navy which ranked second only to that of Great Britain. The ships authorized during Roosevelt's administration constituted almost half the American fleet, excluding the obsolete scout and armored cruisers, that saw service in the First World War.

During his administration Roosevelt also established the general precedent of adding capital ships to the fleet every year. However, because of congressional opposition at home in 1912 and 1913 and expanded building programs abroad, the United States on the eve of the World War was behind both England and Germany in naval strength. The following chart gives a summary of naval building programs, 1902–1915:

Private · Washington, February 10, 1909

Dear Harry: Bonaparte showed me your letter yesterday telling me that he did not agree with it; that he thought it was peculiarly important to indict the Pulitzers, and that the major part of the lesson that we were trying to teach and the service that we were trying to render was lost without their indictment. I am speaking only as a layman. But from the standpoint of the

NAVAL BUILDING PROGRAMS 1902–1915

A. SHIPS AUTHORIZED UNDER ROOSEVELT

1. 1902–1905 Pre-dreadnought

1902	2 battleships	2 cruisers	
1903	5 battleships		
1904	1 battleship	4 cruisers	4 submarines
1905	2 battleships		
TOTAL	10 battleships	6 cruisers	4 submarines

2. 1906–1909 Post-dreadnought

1906	1 battleship		8 submarines	3 destroyers
1907	1 battleship			2 destroyers
1908	2 battleships		8 submarines	10 destroyers
1909	2 battleships		4 submarines	5 destroyers
TOTAL	6 battleships		20 submarines	20 destroyers
TOTAL UNDER TR	16 battleships	6 cruisers	24 submarines	20 destroyers
ACTIVE FLEET 1909	25 battleships	36 cruisers	12 submarines	16 destroyers

B. SHIPS AUTHORIZED UNDER TAFT

1910	2 battleships	4 submarines	6 destroyers
1911	2 battleships	4 submarines	8 destroyers
1912	1 battleship	8 submarines	6 destroyers
1913	1 battleship	4 submarines	6 destroyers
TOTAL	6 battleships	20 submarines	26 destroyers

C. SHIPS AUTHORIZED UNDER WILSON PRIOR TO EXPANSION OF 1916

1914	3 battleships	8 submarines	6 destroyers
1915	2 battleships	18 submarines (16 small non-seagoing)	6 destroyers
TOTAL	5 battleships	26 submarines	12 destroyers

D. U. S. ACTIVE FLEET, JANUARY 1917

	Total	Authorized under TR
BB 1st line	12	6
BB 2nd line	25	10
C	35	6
DD	49	20
S	42	24

public good I emphatically agree with him. I have tried so far as possible in every case, whether the offender was a big financier, a big politician, or a big newspaperman, to reach the head man rather than a subordinate. A wealthy man who deliberately chooses to play the part of a scoundrel is enormously encouraged thereto if he thinks he can himself escape with a trivial financial fine and can let the real penalty be paid by subordinates. I regard the public service rendered as immeasurably greater if in three suits we can once convict personally the real offender, even if twice he is acquitted, rather than win all three against subordinates. I think that much more service would be rendered by indicting the two Pulitzers with only one chance in three of convicting them, than by indicting their subordinates with three chances out of four of convicting them.

I am not a lawyer, but I am a public man and I know what public policy means, and I am sure that this is right from the standpoint of public policy.

This letter is purely private and is merely to explain why I agree with Bonaparte that no effort should be made to get the District Attorney here to abandon his position, as you suggest. *Sincerely yours*

5165 · TO JAMES NORRIS GILLETT   *Roosevelt Mss.*

Telegram   Washington, February 10, 1909

Accept my heartiest congratulations.[1] All good Americans appreciate what you have done. Pray extend my congratulations individually to all who have aided you. I feel that the way in which California has done what was right for the Nation makes it more than ever obligatory on the Nation in every way to safeguard the interests of California. All that I personally can do towards this end, whether in public or in private life, shall most certainly be done.[2]

5166 · TO HENRY LEWIS STIMSON   *Roosevelt Mss.*

Washington, February 13, 1909

Dear Harry: All right, I will tell Bonaparte the substance of your letter. The District Attorney here says that in his belief if he declined to present Pulitzer for indictment, the grand jury would positively refuse to indict anyone at all.[1] It is a curious instance of the different way different grand juries look at

[1] The California Assembly on February 10 reconsidered and rejected the school bill by a vote of 41 to 37. A motion to reconsider this vote then failed. For the remainder of the session the anti-Japanese proposals were dead.
[2] Roosevelt sent a similar telegram to Stanton.

[1] See No. 5142.

matters. I will have a word or two with you about it when you come on here for lunch. *Faithfully yours*

5167 · TO WILLIAM NELSON CROMWELL   *Roosevelt Mss.*

Private   Washington, February 13, 1909

My dear Mr. Cromwell: I am in receipt of your letter of the 13th, with enclosure. I am glad you sent that letter to Representative Olcott. Rainey is evidently a scoundrel or he would never have made his charges, in the first place, or even granted that he was misled into making them, he would have given a full and complete retraction of them by this time. I think you used him up in great shape.[1] *Sincerely yours*

5168 · TO WILLIAM HOWARD TAFT   *Roosevelt Mss.*

Washington, February 13, 1909

Dear Will: (In less than three weeks the way we address one another will be reversed.) Your two letters have come and naturally I was immensely interested in them. I look forward to seeing you on the 24th, and of course any advice or counsel that can be given by me will be entirely at your service. I am delighted, altho not in the least surprised, at what you say about the Canal work. As for Goethals, my judgment is that he will break down unless he is forced to take a holiday; but I think there are one or two men under him who can, if need should arise, be substituted for him without any serious impairment in the efficiency of the work. After all, one particular man is no more indispensable in the office of Canal Commissioner than in the office of President!

I was immensely amused with peppery little Sir Harry Johnston's correspondence with you.[1] I admire immensely the good temper and thoroness with which you answered him.* I also admire the draft of your letter to the President of Panama about the timber contract.[2] I am glad to learn, by the

---

[1] Henry T. Rainey, Democratic congressman from Illinois, 1903–1921, 1923–1927, had made on the floor of the House sensational charges concerning Panama. He told of waste, mismanagement, and corruption in the construction of the canal, citing as an example the purchase by the canal commission of two useless ships (see No. 4882). He repeated the New York *World's* charges of the profiteering of an American syndicate from the sale of the canal. Finally he accused Cromwell and José Domingo de Obaldía, the President of Panama, of conniving to exploit Panamanian timber lands (see No. 5168). Cromwell sent Olcott documents and other information which the New York congressman used in making a detailed reply to Rainey on February 12. Rainey's repetition of these charges at subsequent sessions of Congress led to the congressional hearing on Panama in January–February 1912.

[1] For Johnston's correspondence see No. 5173.
[2] Roosevelt referred to a proposition made by a New York corporation to the government of Panama to build a railroad from Panama City to the town of David near the Costa Rican border in return for a grant of timber land amounting

way, that the Panama Assembly has postponed the consideration of the matter.

Since you have been away I have had a very serious time over the Japanese business in the California Legislature. The Republican machine finally came to my help in fine shape and we got the thing all right; but I hope you will read a letter I have sent to Knox as your future Secretary of State in which I dealt with this Japanese business. I think it has more pre-eminently serious features about it than any other phase of our foreign policy.

Rainey is of the ordinary cur and blackguard type.

With love to Mrs. Taft, believe me, *Faithfully yours*

* [*Handwritten*] He has just written me to express the nervous hope that you didn't mind his letter.

5169 · TO TRUMAN HANDY NEWBERRY   *Roosevelt Mss.*

Washington, February 13, 1909

My dear Mr. Secretary: The enclosed order issued by Mr. Taft, regarding the establishment of a Department of Hygiene at the Military Academy, seems to me to be based on the right idea, and I believe that a similar practice should be established at the Naval Academy, where the importance of instruction in this subject and in that of physical training is equally great. It is apparent that all young line officers should be efficiently schooled in matters of sanitation and hygiene, and that the medical officer selected as instructor should have special qualifications and special knowledge on the subjects concerned and that representation on the Academic Board commensurate with the importance of his position there should be accorded him.

I desire, therefore, that the following order be issued to the naval service for the information and guidance of all concerned:

A Department of Naval Hygiene and Physiology is hereby established at the United States Naval Academy. The Senior medical officer at the Academy shall be the head of the Department and shall act as a member of the Academic Board.

Very truly yours

5170 · TO A. HOWARD HOPPING   *Roosevelt Mss.*

Washington, February 13, 1909

My dear Mr. Hopping: I thank you for your letter and enclosures. Your letter to Willett was admirable. In view of your courtesy I desire to give you in full a statement of what actually occurred in the case referred to by the man named Hazard. Senator Lodge and I were riding, followed by my orderly, a

---

to 1,000 hectares of timber land for each kilometer built. It was this plan which Congressman Rainey denounced as a plot conceived by Cromwell and President Obaldía to despoil Panama of its most valuable natural resources; see No. 5167, note 1.

sergeant in the regular army. A girl, seemingly about sixteen years old, riding astride, joined the orderly and entered into a conversation with him. This was foolish and unseemly, but I paid no attention to it. She continued for some four miles riding with the orderly just behind us, and continually talking to him, the orderly, much embarrassed, either not answering at all or occasionally answering with a monosyllable. When we reached the ford of Rock Creek it had grown dark and I did not think it wise, or proper on any account, that this totally unknown young girl should continue riding with three strange men after dark. Accordingly, I halted and told her that I did not think she ought to ride along with the party and that I would be obliged if she would continue along the highroad, and that we would turn up into the woods along what is called the Blagden road. She murmured something in the way of objection and I then repeated that she must not continue with us, and on this occasion asked her to take whichever road she chose and we would take the other. She accordingly went along the highroad by the side of Rock Creek and we turned up the Blagden Road. As I say, I thought it, both from her standpoint and ours, very inadvisable that she should go up the wood road with three men whom she had never seen before, and who knew nothing about her, and this after dark.

With regard and renewed thanks for your courtesy, believe me *Sincerely yours*

P.S. While I do not wish this letter made public, if you ever happen to meet Mr. Hazard you are entirely at liberty to show it to him.

5171 · TO THEODORE ROOSEVELT, JUNIOR   *Roosevelt Mss.*

Washington, February 13, 1909

Dear Ted: It was good to get your letter, but I don't want you to feel that you must answer me. I shall write you pretty regularly until I go to Africa, because after I am in Africa I shall most of the time have to send family letters, so to speak, to Mother, and trust to her circulating them among all of you.

Bob Perkins has accepted for the 18th, and I am looking forward to seeing him. General and Mrs. Wood are coming also.

I think I have won out as regards the Japanese-California trouble. One of my services, incidentally, was persuading Baron Takahira to make an address on Lincoln's birthday, for I knew that with our queer, sentimental people this would have a good effect. The Californians are, I am reluctantly but firmly convinced, right in their contention that the Japanese, as settlers in mass, must be kept out. In the first place I think it undesirable that we should have settlements in mass by the Japanese in our Western States, for I think it would certainly bring about the gravest kind of race trouble. But aside from this being my personal conviction, there is the further fact that the people of the Rocky Mountain and Pacific Coast States simply won't allow the Japanese to settle among them, and if they come in in large numbers trouble is absolutely certain to ensue and the movement for exclusion by law to grow overwhelming. I wish to give the Japanese Government a chance to restrain emigration of its own initiative, but if it does not take advantage of the chance, then whether we will or not we shall be forced to pass exclusion laws. But in such event I earnestly desire to see this country, when doing a disagreeable thing, do it with as much courtesy and consideration as possible; and most of all, when we take action which may result in war, I wish to see us face the possibility of war and take such ample measures of precaution as will either prevent war coming or give us victory if it does come. The Californian demagogs united needless insult with utter inefficiency. *Your loving father*

P.S. I am very glad you like my Lincoln speech.

5172 · TO CORNELIUS J. TON   *Roosevelt Mss.*

Private   Washington, February 15, 1909

My dear Mr. Ton: [1] This letter must be treated as confidential, as it is not my business to interfere in a State Senatorial fight. But there is no reason why I should not confidentially answer your private question. My understanding is that the popular vote at the primaries declared in favor of Senator Hopkins. That being the case it seems to me that it is not good faith to fail to support him. My personal views about Senator Hopkins are of no consequence, but as you ask for them I will say that he has been one of the constant and loyal supporters of the great majority of the policies with which this administration has been identified, and that personally I earnestly hope for his re-election.[2] *Sincerely yours*

5173 · TO HARRY HAMILTON JOHNSTON   *Roosevelt Mss.*

Washington, February 15, 1909

My dear Sir Harry: I have your letter of the 3rd instant.

Taft was not in the least angry about your letter. He wrote me and enclosed a copy of the letter which he sent you.[1] We have the utmost difficulty in meeting the susceptibilities of the Panamans. The breakwater of which you

---

[1] Cornelius J. Ton, Republican member of the Illinois House of Representatives.
[2] In large part because Hopkins had been a "constant and loyal supporter" of Roosevelt, the Republican organization in Illinois opposed his re-election to the Senate. Until May 26, in ninety-four ballots, the Republican vote in the Illinois Legislature remained divided, preventing the election of anyone. On the ninety-fifth ballot fifty-five organization Republicans and fifty-three Democrats combined to elect an inveterate agent of the Old Guard, Congressman William Lorimer. This election the Senate later invalidated because of the corrupt methods used to engineer it.

---

[1] See No. 5168.

speak will soon be started and it is evident that we will have to just disregard the Panamans' susceptibilities and build a good hotel ourselves in Colón.

I could not take my *Wanderjahr* in Central America and the Caribbean because the one essential was that I should keep clear of anything like politics this year when I have just left office and my successor has come in. I could not go to Central America without appearing as an envoy from this country. *Sincerely yours*

Washington, February 16, 1909

Dear Jim: I send you a copy of the foreword I was to have written for the book by Gifford and you. I quite agree that it would be inadvisable to have it appear in that particular book, but I wished you to have a copy for yourself anyhow.[1]

With love to your dear wife, *Faithfully yours*

[1] In his last month in office Roosevelt was effusive in his praise of the work of both Garfield and Pinchot; see Numbers 5186, 5196, his foreword to their book, *The Fight for Conservation* (1910), included here as No. 5198; and the following original foreword which was enclosed in the above letter:

FOREWORD.

Thruout my term as President no two men have been more intimately associated with all phases of my work than James R. Garfield and Gifford Pinchot. No two men have been as closely indentified with so many of the policies for which this administration has stood. I am sincerely glad that they are to write in brief form just what has been meant by these various policies, just what has been accomplished in the way of putting them into effect.

Mr. Pinchot has been in a peculiar sense responsible for all that the administration has done in connection with the conservation of natural resources and the development of a healthy country life. His has been peculiarly the responsibility for what has been accomplished in working for the preservation of the forests, for National aid to irrigation, for striving to secure the utilization of our navigable waters, for the betterment of social conditions in the country.

Mr. Garfield has successively held under me the positions of Civil Service Commissioner, Commissioner of Corporations, and Secretary of the Interior. It has been in large part thru him that I have dealt with the problems of securing adequate control and supervision over the great corporations engaged in interstate commerce, for securing the administrative betterment of the public service and keeping it at a high plane of honor and efficiency, for dealing with the great questions affecting the public lands and preventing fraud and dishonesty in connection therewith. But both have aided me in many more lines than these with which they are peculiarly identified. They have stood foremost among that group of public servants to whose uprightness, courage, keen sense of honor, and great efficiency in doing the public work, so very much of whatever the administration has achieved has been due.

Messrs. Pinchot and Garfield — and the other men, public servants of the same stamp, so numerous that I regret to say it would be idle to attempt to give their names — have realized to the full the need of a many-sided efficiency in doing the work of the public. Both have stood for absolute honesty, for absolute devotion to the needs of the public. Both have stood no less for entire sanity and for far-sighted understanding of the many diverse needs of the Nation. They have been

Washington, February 16, 1909

Dear Gifford: Here is a copy of the foreword I had intended to write, and while I agree that it is not well for me to write it, I want you and Jim to have a copy of it, because it expresses my deep conviction about you both.

And now, my dear Gifford, I want to thank you personally for the things that you said in the conversation between you and Mott and McBee. I am very well aware that I do not deserve them, but I am glad that you believe them. *Faithfully yours*

5176 · TO CAMERON MC REA WINSLOW *Roosevelt Mss.*

Washington, February 16, 1909

My dear Captain Winslow: I am pleased to receive your letter of the 10th and am glad that you approve of my putting Sims in command of a battleship.[1] I felt that he had earned it.

I am particularly interested in what you say about the way you have got your ammunition hoists in good shape.

Now that I am ending my term as President, my dear Captain, I wish you to know how much I appreciate the invaluable aid you have given me. I am greatly indebted to you. *Faithfully yours*

---

fearless in opposing wrong, whether by a great corporation or by a mob; by a wealthy financier, or by a demagog. They have understood clearly that a high and fine standard of family life represented the foundation of national well-being, and therefore they have sympathized with and aided every movement which it was possible for the Federal Government to undertake for the betterment of social conditions in town or country, for securing to wageworkers their rights, for bringing nearer the day when equity shall be done as between man and man and between man and woman; when there shall be no shirking of duties and no abandonment of rights. But this devotion to social and industrial reform from within has not, as is so often the case, meant a failure on their part to understand that the Nation must retain the stern and hardy virtues which are necessary in national life as in individual life. They understand that it is just as complete a dereliction of duty to fail to build up the navy and army, to fail to hold ourselves ready to resist aggression from without, as it is a dereliction of duty to fail to reform abuses that exist within our own borders. They scorn the baseness that would advocate this country's going into an unjust war; and they also scorn the baseness, as wicked as it is foolish, which in the name of peace would render this people powerless to defend itself against aggression. They believe that the foreign policy of the Government should be conducted on the same high level of honorable obligation, alike to others and to our own self, which we accept as natural on the part of an honorable man in dealing with his fellows. It is because they sympathize with, and have had intimate knowledge of, the policies for which this administration has stood in so many different fields at home and abroad and the reasons why these policies have been upheld, that I am glad to have Mr. Garfield and Mr. Pinchot write of them.

---

[1] Sims took command of the U.S.S. *Minnesota* on March 1, 1909. This was his first command and first sea duty in seven years; it was also the first time an officer with the rank of commander had been given a battleship, a break in naval precedent that irritated a great many men in the service.

Washington, February 16, 1909

To the Secretary of the Navy: As I have followed somewhat closely the Navy's progress in gunnery, ordnance, etc., at least since about 1897, particularly in connection with the development of the elements of our battle efficiency, and as I note that the official record of Commander Sims, who has been Inspector of Target Practice since 1902, contains practically no account of the influence of his work upon this development, I deem it desirable to state the following facts in connection therewith.

In a general way I am acquainted with the reports on construction, ordnance, gunnery, etc., made by Commander Sims from Paris in 1897–1900, from the China station in 1900–02, and those made since that time, and I have been imprest not only by the professional ability and energy therein displayed, but have noted with satisfaction that many of the recommendations they contain have proved of benefit to the service.

Among others I may mention those reports which set forth the military advantages of the all-big-gun type of battleship, and which were evidently a determining factor in convincing those who had been opposed to such ships.

But I would also invite special attention to the numerous reports upon gunnery training and ordnance, beginning in 1897 and continued since that time, which have been the principal means of bringing about the remarkable improvements of the last few years in the Navy's efficiency in target practice, in which respect it has long been, and still is, my conviction that Commander Sims has done more than any other man in the United States, and that it is chiefly due to him that we shoot as well as we now do.

The above facts are those only which came within my personal knowledge; but as it would seem fitting that an officer's record should contain all of the essential facts concerning the value of his services, it is directed that you cause to be compiled and attached to Commander Sims' record a full statement thereof, including those recommendations or suggestions that have proved of value in gunnery, ordnance, construction, etc.

You will also please attach this letter to the above indicated statement, and send a copy of the latter to me.[1]

Washington, February 18, 1909

Sir: I desire to call your attention to certain provisions in the naval bill as it passed the Senate which should have your serious consideration.

[1] This letter was written after Roosevelt discovered that no statement of Sims's achievements as inspector of target practice appeared in the officer's official record. Because there were indications that, as soon as Roosevelt left office, enemies of the insurgents within the service would take reprisals against Sims, Roosevelt wished, by his own stated approval to put the officer beyond the reach of hostile action.

As to the matter of the marines, I wish merely to point out that the statement that under the present arrangement the marines could not be used as they actually were used at the time of the trouble between Colombia and Panama and on all similar occasions in the past, is without the slightest warrant in fact and is the direct reverse of the fact. On the contrary, the present arrangement was made with the explicit object of retaining the marines for the purposes of an expeditionary force so that they could be utilized for every service in any way akin to the services of value which they have repeatedly rendered during the past decade. Their presence as part of a fighting ship's complement at sea is not necessary, and is, on the whole, rather detrimental. But the damage is not serious, and tho the bill as it passed the Senate will, as regards this point, do a little damage, it does not do very much, and this damage will be limited chiefly to creating the belief that the marines are kept aboard ship for nonmilitary reasons.[1]

There are certain other matters connected with the naval bill in its present shape, however, which really are serious. I call your attention to the enclosed memorandum from the Chief of the Bureau of Ordnance submitted to me by the Secretary of the Navy, and ask careful consideration of what is therein set forth. I entirely concur in the statement of the Chief of the Bureau of Ordnance. Great loss of life may at any moment come from the failure to provide for improving the turret ammunition hoists on the vessels now in commission. The curious provision preventing the purchase of torpedoes if lawsuits are brought concerning them, may hopelessly hamper the navy in getting the torpedoes which it urgently needs. The provision as to the purchase of powder may not only seriously hamper the work of the navy, but in the event of war may prove literally ruinous — indeed, instead of saying that it may prove literally ruinous, it is probably more correct that I should say that it undoubtedly would prove literally ruinous.

I also call your attention to the memorandum from the General Board to the Secretary of the Navy on these points, for I concur in the opinion of the General Board that these provisions would dangerously hamper the Navy Department in its preparations for war, and might be the cause of disaster and defeat.[2]

[1] The bill provided for a marine detachment on every naval vessel. This provision annulled the President's executive order relieving the Marine Corps from shipboard duty; see No. 5032.

[2] The conference committee on the naval bill only partly changed the provisions which Roosevelt considered so damaging to the Navy. It made no attempt to provide for the improvement of the ammunition hoists, nor did the committee pay heed to the President's request to raise the limit on the cost of the Pearl Harbor dry dock. It did limit the prohibition on the purchase of torpedoes only to those against which suits were pending. It also modified the amendment prohibiting the purchase of powder from any trust or combination in restraint of trade to permit such purchases "in an extraordinary emergency." Finally the committee agreed to drop what Roosevelt considered the most dangerous provision in the act: "That there shall be kept, in the discretion of the President, as far as practicable one-half of the Navy of the United States on the Pacific at all times."

As regards the dry dock at Pearl Harbor, I wish to call the attention of the Committee to the fact that at present it is not possible to keep the fleet as a whole permanently in the Pacific, because of inadequate docking facilities. The dry dock at Mare Island is in a bad place. It should be in the neighborhood of where the commercial dry docks are, and it is a matter of note that the fleet now returning from its voyage round the world had to use the commercial dry docks when in San Francisco, these docks being the only docks available. The limit of cost of the Pearl Harbor dock should be $3,500,-000 rather than $2,000,000, otherwise the starting of the construction of the dock may be delayed for some months and possibly a year, and it ought not to be delayed a day beyond what is absolutely necessary. The dock should be made of the largest size, in view of the opening of the Panama Canal, which we have a right to believe will take place within about six years. I do not admit that the Senators and Representatives from the Pacific Coast States have any greater interest than the Senators and Representatives from any other part of the Union in the defense of the Pacific Coast States and the maintenance of American rights in the Pacific; because I hold that every American citizen is vitally interested in every foot of American soil, wherever it is, and is equally concerned in the honor of the American flag, wherever that flag may float. But the Pacific Coast Representatives in the Senate and the House ought to be peculiarly alive to the needs of the Pacific. I have urged as strongly as I know how the immediate building of impregnable fortifications to protect Pearl Harbor and the adjacent region from any possible land attack. I urge that at the same time this great dry dock be provided.

It ought not to be necessary to point out that any plan looking to a division of our fleet between the Atlantic and the Pacific prior to the establishment of the Panama Canal is so foolish as to verge on that kind of folly which must be condemned as criminal folly. The history of all wars up to and including the very latest has shown that in over half the cases one or both of the combatants endeavor to strike a crippling blow before the actual declaration of war. In the event of the United States at any time being menaced by war with an antagonist of approximately even strength, to divide the fleet between the two oceans would be to invite attack, and if attack were made, to insure disaster. There is one principle of naval strategy so elemental, so sound, and yet so simple that even an intelligent child ought to appreciate it, and that is, never to divide, save purely temporarily, the battle fleet. If in one ocean, of course it need not be permanently kept together in all its parts, because it could be reassembled within a short time. But if separated in two oceans, there would always be the chance of serious disaster in the event of some sudden international complication. *Very respectfully*

Washington, February 18, 1909

My dear Mr. Attorney General: In reference to the reports of the Solicitor General as to the lawsuit against the Anaconda people, I have to say that after carefully reading over the correspondence, my judgment is the same as the Solicitor General's as to the course of the Anaconda Company and the Amalgamated Company in this matter.[1] If my administration were to continue I should direct that the suit against these companies be immediately prosecuted. But as less than a fortnight of my term remains, and inasmuch as the suit would have to be carried on under my successor, it does not seem to me wise to begin it at this time. I return the memoranda submitted to me and request that they, together with this letter, be filed with the case, so that the attention of your successor on his taking office may be called to the matter, that he may take what action he desires.[2] *Sincerely yours*

Washington, February 19, 1909

My dear White: I must reply just to say that I think you have struck it exactly right as regards Jeffersonianism and Hamiltonianism. I have no use for the Hamiltonian who is aristocratic, or for the Jeffersonian who is a demagog. Let us trust the people as Jefferson did, but not flatter them; and let us try to have our administration as effective as Hamilton taught us to have it. Lincoln, and Washington, struck the right average.

By George! I wish you were on here to advise and help me as to some of the things that are going on, as I am at my wits' end just how far to go in some of the fights at present, for Congress feels that it is getting safer and safer to attack me. But I have battled to the end, at any rate. *Faithfully yours*

Washington, February 19, 1909

Sir: I have seen the report presented by Senator Hemenway on behalf of your Committee in reference to the secret-service matter.[1] The report is

---

[1] See No. 5062.
[2] There is nothing in the Justice Department annual reports, in the annual reports of the two copper companies, or in the files of the *Commercial and Financial Chronicle* to show that Taft's Attorney General instituted a suit.

---

[1] The important contentions in Hemenway's report are dealt with in this letter which Roosevelt made public. Although the report marked the end of the Senate's consideration of Roosevelt's recommendations for an adequate secret-service appropriation, the President, using his executive authority, accomplished his purpose by creating an investigatory agency within the Department of Justice.

certain corrections in reference to statements which appear therein, and in inaccurate and misleading in various important respects, and I desire to make the subsequent debate.

Until last year the secret service, a small body of sixty or seventy men in the Treasury Department under Chief Wilkie, was practically the only body of public servants engaged almost purely in criminal investigation. The secret-service men were assigned at different times to different Departments to investigate crime and criminals. They were thus assigned on different occasions, for instance to the State and Navy Departments; but above all to the Interior Department and the Department of Justice. During the seven years of my administration they were instrumental in bringing to justice great numbers of criminals. I append herewith the occasions on which they were furnished by the request of the Attorney General to the Department of Justice during the year 1907 and the first six months of 1908. They rendered invaluable assistance in securing the conviction of many criminals of desperate character, and of many other offenders of great wealth and of social and political prominence. In not one single instance during these seven years has it been shown that their action jeopardized any man who was not connected with illegal transactions. In not a single instance has it been shown that they took any but proper steps against a criminal. No pretense has been made that they did not do their work against criminals efficiently. I desire to put on record my emphatic belief that the secret service under Chief Wilkie has been composed of men of an exceptionally high grade of character and capacity, who have rendered exceptional service to the public, and that Chief Wilkie himself, in a very trying and responsible position, has shown qualities of the highest kind, and has been one of the main stand-bys of the Government. No other man in the Government employ is so dreaded and hated by lawbreakers, and they especially desire to see his activities, and those of the men under him, restricted in every way.

Congress last year forbade by law the use of the secret-service men to put a stop to crime aside from counterfeiting; and thereby not only hampered justice in other Departments, but deprived the Secretary of the Treasury, the official guardian of a billion and a half of the Nation's actual money, of the power effectively to exercise that guardianship. Moreover, the Congress provided no substitute whatever for the secret service. In consequence, the Department of Justice was obliged to develop as speedily as possible its own corps of special detectives to take the place of the secret-service agents which it had previously used; and the nucleus of this force was made up of officers formerly connected with the secret service and trained in its methods. I call your especial attention to the fact that if the Department of Justice had not taken this action there would have been a complete failure to enforce the law against many types of criminals; and as it was, in the early months of the present fiscal year, during the Morse prosecution in New York, and in connection with certain other important cases, serious inconvenience and anxiety were caused to the prosecuting officers by this action of Congress in depriving them of the aid of the experienced operatives of the secret service on whom they had been accustomed to rely. I call your attention to the further fact that the Department of Justice had never taken any steps to organize this force so long as it could get men detailed to it from the secret service. In other words, the action of the Congress in reference to the secret service would have caused the grossest miscarriage of justice had it not been in large part nullified by the prompt action of the Department of Justice, on its own initiative, and without any further legislation of any kind by the Congress, in providing a species of secret service within the Department of Justice itself.

Your Committee in its report states that it has never been the intention of the Congress to build up a "spy" system. The next sentence, however, advocates the building up of precisely this "spy" system in the Department of Justice. Not only have I again and again requested that the secret service be placed under the Department of Justice, but the chief of the secret service has himself specifically requested on different occasions that the same course be followed. As regards the general policy which should be followed, therefore, your Committee has declared for the policy the adoption of which I have urged, and all the difficulties would be met by providing specifically and amply for carrying out that policy. Chief Wilkie should be transferred to the Department of Justice, and put at the head of the force therein organized.

But in your report, and the subsequent debate, direct and indirect attacks are made upon the secret service, with a curious persistency, and a curious indifference to the fact that your Committee recommends that a precisely similar secret service to the one attacked be now established in the Department of Justice; and be it observed that no limitation is proposed for the new secret service; so that the limitation is only imposed upon the secret service which has already shown its efficiency and has already become an object of terror to criminals. Senator Hemenway states that "there are more than three thousand men now in the secret service and inspection work of the Government"; and that in the last few years the number has trebled; and that if they were to march through the streets of Washington they would make an "army"; while it was also stated in the same debate that at the close of President McKinley's administration there were only "167" such men on the payroll, whereas it was alleged that we now have "over 3000," and that the appropriations on that account for last year amounted to "about $10,000,000." These statements are not in accordance with the facts. I submit to you herewith a substantially, although not entirely, accurate statement of the number of men employed on "secret-service work" or "criminal investigation" work during the year that has just passed, as compared with the years 1901–1902. Owing to the very brief period which I have had to get at these figures, it was impossible to get them with entire accuracy, but they are not out of the way more than a score or so in either direction. According to these figures it appears that in the neighborhood of 1200 men of this type were employed seven years ago, and somewhat over 1900 now; that is, instead of having trebled in number in accordance with one of the statements made above, instead of having increased nearly twenty-fold in accordance with the other statement, they have increased but a little over one half, a little over fifty per cent. Moreover, of this increase considerably over half was in the number of men used in securing the punishment of violators of the internal revenue laws, a matter wholly outside of that discussed by any of the gentlemen who have objected to the use of the secret service. The remaining increase is due to such causes as the natural growth of the Post-Office Department, the appointment of individuals to enforce the pure food and the meat inspection laws, the more rigorous enforcement of the safety appliance act, the suppression of the liquor traffic among the Indians, the protection of the public lands and timber, and the like. I call your especial attention to the fact that the great majority of these men are not primarily or mainly or indeed ordinarily engaged on secret-service or criminal investigation or inspection work at all; I have employed these terms merely because they were so employed by members of your committee and others in the course of the debates in the House and Senate; but they are entirely misleading in so far as they give an impression that the chief work of the men mentioned was of the character assigned it by Senator Hemenway and others in the quotations given above and in similar statements. As regards nineteen twentieths of these men, the proportion of their time given to secret-service work or criminal investigation is altogether insignificant and is only an occasional incident of their ordinary duties. To speak of these men as having become an "army" or as "3000 men engaged in secret-service" and similar work is comically out of accord with the actual facts. The increase was 700 men, of whom but a score or two are habitually engaged in "secret-service work." As for the account expended the statements in the debate in both houses are so exaggerated as to bear no reference whatever to the actual figures. Thus it was stated that two thirds of the money appropriated for the Department of Justice was spent in criminal investigation. As a matter of fact, the Attorney General reports to me that the appropriation so spent, construed on the most liberal possible basis, was in reality one and seven-tenths per cent, so that the statement in question was a thirty-fold exaggeration. In the same way it was stated that $10,000,000 (or as one gentleman put it, that $20,000,000) represented the amount expended for this secret-service work, while the totals of another set of figures amount to $32,000,000 as money which could have been expended for such work. A table carefully compiled covering all the departments shows the amount actually expended during the first six months of the present fiscal year, in all work that can by any possibility be considered to come under this heading, as a little less than $764,000, — an estimated total for the entire fiscal year of approximately $1,500,000; — which goes to show that the statements referred to contain only from five to seventeen per cent of warrant in fact.

Senator Hemenway quoted the Secretary of the Interior as the authority for the statement that but one secret-service man was ever detailed to the Interior Department. This statement of Senator Hemenway is completely misleading. The secret-service men were used in the Interior Department cases at the request of the Secretary of the Interior, but for convenience in operation they were assigned to and paid by the Department of Justice. This has been set forth with the utmost clearness again and again in the reports of the Interior Department. As the prosecutions had to be carried on by the Department of Justice, it was desirable that the secret-service men should work with and under the Department of Justice officials. By turning to the list to which I have already alluded, you will see, for example, that in the year 1907 the Department of Justice, on January 5th, asked for one man in a land fraud case; that on January 25th it asked five men to be detailed for timber entry frauds; on January 30th four additional men to assist in land fraud investigations; on February 27th six more men; on March 4th two more men; on April 2d three more men; on April 10th six more men; on May 28th and June 10th one additional man; on August 22d three additional men. These men were not assigned to the Interior Department, but they were used for the Interior Department cases under the Department of Justice. How much officers discharged their duties in a previous case of which I happen to have personal knowledge, is shown by the following letter:

DEPARTMENT OF JUSTICE,
December 28, 1906.

The Chief of the United States Secret Service,
  Washington, D. C.
Sir:
    The Department is in receipt of a letter dated the 21st instant from the United States Attorney for the District of Nebraska, reporting the trial and conviction of Bartlett Richards and other defendants on the charge of conspiring to defraud the United States of public lands. This is one of the cases in which several operatives of your office have been employed under Operative Lucien C. Wheeler, and the United States Attorney takes occasion, in making his report, to commend most highly "the very able service of the operative in charge, Mr. Lucien C. Wheeler, and his secret-service agents."
    The Department is also in receipt of a letter from the Secretary of the Interior, dated the 22nd instant, expressing his "appreciation of the splendid work done by" the United States Attorney, his Special Assistant, and Mr. Wheeler; and transmitting a copy of a telegram which he sent to Mr. Wheeler on the 21st instant, as follows:
    "I congratulate you most heartily on the splendid work you have done in connection with the verdict, which must give renewed confidence to all those who believe that the law must be obeyed."
    I desire to add to what has been quoted above the appreciation of the Department here of the work done by Mr. Wheeler, who had shown himself to be a

conscientious and highly efficient instrumentality in bringing about much desired results in Nebraska.

Very respectfully,
ALFORD W. COOLEY
Acting Attorney General.

The limitation of the use of the secret service was not in the least degree technical; it was real and actual. If such a condition as arose in the Interior Department some four years ago again arises in that Department, with this limitation we should be prevented from employing the secret service, and the result would be harmful to the Government and of benefit only to the criminals; unless, of course, we are able to build up a precisely similar secret service in the Department of Justice — in which case the action of the Congress would have been effective only as showing its disapproval of the admirable work done by Chief Wilkie and his division. Unless the new secret service in the Department of Justice does its work in precisely similar fashion to Chief Wilkie's secret service, it will not do good and effective work, and I call your attention to the fact that the result of the action of Congress has hitherto been, by the creation of two secret services, markedly to increase the total cost of this class of work.

The facts in reference to the detection and suppression of the land frauds and the punishment of criminals engaged in them, have been made public again and again; but in view of the report of your Committee, it is as well to refer to them once more. Secretary Hitchcock became convinced that there were widespread frauds in his Department, and that his own force was unable to deal with them. Through the Department of Justice he had a number of secret-service operatives assigned to work on the Interior Department cases, together with one secret-service operative who was assigned direct to the Interior Department. Mr. Hemenway speaks as if the Attorney General and the Secretary of the Interior had not known of such assignments; as a matter of fact every such assignment was made on the written request of the head of the Department. The first result of the work in question was to find that various departmental officials had failed in their duty; and none of them were accordingly dismissed.

The results of the assignment of the secret-service men — taken of course in connection with the activity of the representatives of the Department of Justice itself, and of the activity of the reorganized force of special agents of the Interior Department — are found in the conviction of many defendants, some of them being among the wealthiest and most influential people in their communities; others standing high in the political world, one of them being a Senator and another a Representative in Congress, while a second Representative in Congress was indicted. If the limitation of the use of the secret service which your Committee upholds had been in force at the time of which I speak, the Senator, the Representative, and the various men of wealth and high political influence who were convicted, would all have escaped punishment. I hold that such an outcome would have been in the interest of the criminals only.

Once the emergency had passed the need for the detail of the secret-service men no longer existed, and they were accordingly withdrawn. But the history of these land frauds shows conclusively the need of having some secret-service body subject to emergency detail to departments in which it is not ordinarily employed.

Before the secret service was used in the Interior Department as I have above outlined, the prosecutions for land frauds were insignificant in their results. At that time there was no effective desire shown to limit the use of the secret service. Then the secret-service agents were used in connection with those land frauds; and they secured the prosecution and conviction of many men, influential because of their wealth or their social or political prominence. Forthwith there began that active agitation against the use of the secret service which continued until the action of the Congress last spring. *Very respectfully*

P.S. This letter is in part based on statements furnished by the Attorney General and the Secretary of the Interior. It has been carefully read over by them and the statements of fact which it contains, so far as they refer to the Department of Justice and the Department of the Interior, have been checked and approved by them.

I enclose various documents as follows:

Statement showing requests of Department of Justice for the assignment of secret-service operatives during the year 1907 and the first six months of 1908.

Statement of number of men employed on secret-service or criminal investigation work during the year just passed as compared with the year 1901–2.

5182 · TO DOUGLAS ROBINSON AND CORINNE ROOSEVELT ROBINSON   *Roosevelt Mss.*

Telegram   Washington, February 21, 1909

I am heartbroken at the dreadful news[1] and at the hideous necessity that makes me unable at once to come to you. There is nothing I can say to comfort you, but I feel infinite love and sorrow. I cannot fail, as President, to greet the fleet, or else I would come to you this very hour.

5183 · TO LAWRENCE FRASER ABBOTT   *Roosevelt Mss.*

Washington, February 23, 1909

Dear Lawrence: I send you the editorial on the Japanese question, and the change rendered necessary thereby in the Tolstoi article. Will you please have the Japanese article printed in one number and the Tolstoi in the

[1] Stewart Douglas Robinson had been killed by a fall from a sixth-floor window in Hampden Hall, a Harvard dormitory.

number immediately succeeding it? I think it would be well to have them appear a month or six weeks after I have left the Presidency.[1] *Faithfully yours*

5184 · TO WILLIAM HOWARD TAFT   *Roosevelt Mss.*

Personal   Washington, February 23, 1909

Dear Will: The perfectly easy way to meet the situation aroused by the telegram of the Merchants' Association[1] is to make the change on the 5th of March. Every particle of trouble will have disappeared by the 7th in that case, and by the 8th all memory of it will have vanished. The only way to insure trouble is to defer action. Of course these letters are entirely fictitious and the agitation is entirely fictitious. If at the time of your incoming, when you are announcing your Cabinet, you make the change, not a ripple of trouble will be caused. But of course an agitation allowed to gather head often does cause trouble. Fowler is at present at work among the steamship people, and you will hear from them next. Different leaders from up the State have been in to see me. All were a unit in saying that Fowler should be changed; and several of them have mentioned to me that in his opposition to you Fowler had gone beyond all reasonable lengths, stating that he should oppose you if nominated, that he would use his influence among labor leaders to have your labor record attacked. Not the slightest difficulty will be caused if quick action is taken. On the 5th of March request Fowler's resignation by telegraph. If he does not send it in at once, remove him and make a recess appointment of Loeb. *Faithfully yours*

5185 · TO JAMES JOSEPH WALSH   *Roosevelt Mss.*

Personal   Washington, February 23, 1909

My dear Dr. Walsh:[1] I have your letter of the 20th. Indeed I should be flattered to have you dedicate your book to me; but, my dear Doctor, I have had to make an invariable rule not to give my permission for books to be dedicated to me. I have deviated from that rule, so far as I can remember, in but two cases, and those two deviations cost me an infinity of trouble. Many books have been dedicated to me — as, for example, Buell's Life of Andrew Jackson[2] — which I was very deeply pleased to have dedicated to me; but it was done by the author on his own responsibility.

[1] They did; see Theodore Roosevelt, "The Japanese Question," *Outlook*, 92:61–62 (May 8, 1909) and "Tolstoy," *Outlook*, 92:103–105 (May 15, 1909).

[1] The Merchants' Association had requested Taft to retain Colonel Edward S. Fowler as collector of the port of New York.

[1] James Joseph Walsh, professor of "physiological psychology" at Cathedral College, New York, had requested permission to dedicate the second series of his *Catholic Churchmen in Science* to Roosevelt.
[2] *History of Andrew Jackson* (New York, 1904), by Augustus C. Buell, secretary to Charles H. Cramp; author of biographies of John Paul Jones, Sir William Johnson and William Penn.

I need hardly say how I enjoyed having you at lunch the other day. I think the trouble about Darwinism is that people confound it with evolution. I suppose that all scientific students now accept evolution, just as they accept the theory of gravitation, or the general astronomical scheme of the solar system and the stellar system as a whole; but natural selection, in the Darwinian sense, as a theory, evidently does not stand on the same basis. It must be tested, as the atomic system is tested, for instance. I shall be much interested in seeing Driesch's Gifford Lectures,[3] and shall look them up at once.

With hearty regard, believe me, *Sincerely yours*

5186 · TO GIFFORD PINCHOT   *Roosevelt Mss.*

Personal   Washington, February 24, 1909

Dear Gifford: There has been a peculiar intimacy between you and Jim and me, because all three of us have worked for the same causes, have dreamed the same dreams, have felt a substantial identity of purpose as regards many of what we three deemed the most vital problems of today. The first piece of real work I undertook as President was with you, for before I moved into the White House, after returning from Canton, you called to see me and we went into the irrigation fight heart and soul from that moment.

But this letter is not written about you. It is written about Jim. Jim has made a sacrifice in entering public life that you and I have not made. It is just about seven years ago that I got him to come to Washington; and since then you and he and I have worked shoulder to shoulder together in many different matters, and in a way such as I think has been very rare with any three men in any administration. I tried him first as Civil Service Commissioner, being moved thereto by knowledge I had gained of him half incidentally while I was Police Commissioner, and afterwards while I was Governor of New York. As I had expected, he did very well; so well, that when the Bureau of Corporations was created and I felt that I needed a man of high and peculiar qualifications to fill a position at once so responsible and so difficult and delicate, I named him. Here again he did so well that two years ago I made him Secretary of the Interior. Because of my interest in the affairs of the West, I have long been familiar with the work of our Secretaries of the Interior; that is, I can speak with reasonable knowledge of the performance of all of them since and including Carl Schurz. Some of them have been very good and able men; but in administrative efficiency, in ability to get good results, in power to get on with men, in entire disinterestedness, courage and loyalty to a high ideal — in all these qualities, and the many others that go to make up the highest type of Cabinet officer, *taken together*, I verily believe that Jim has stood above everyone. Doubtless there have been Secretaries who on some one point were ahead of him; but on the whole I think that he has

[3] Hans Driesch, Heidelberg professor, published the lectures he had given as Gifford Lecturer at the University of Aberdeen, 1907-1908, under the title, *The Science and Philosophy of the Organism.*

been the best Secretary we have ever had in the Interior Department. For seven years in every position, he has been a literally invaluable public servant; and his best service has been rendered in the highest position.

In a sense I did Jim a personal injury by getting him to take office seven years ago. He was then thirty-seven years old, and after years of hard labor had just begun to make a fine position for himself in his profession. His law practice has of course gone to the winds, and his work for the Government has not been such as to make it easy for him to resume this practice with profit to himself. He has sacrificed much for the privilege of doing as good work for the public as any man of our acquaintance has done. *Faithfully yours*

5187 · TO RICHARD WAINWRIGHT

Roosevelt Mss.

Washington, February 25, 1909

Sir: I desire to appoint you as a member of a Commission[1] for the purposes indicated in my message to Congress of which I send you herewith a copy.

I also send you herewith a copy of a memorandum prepared for me by a naval officer of high rank, to which I invite your attention in connection with your work. *Sincerely yours*

5188 · TO JOSEPH GURNEY CANNON

Roosevelt Mss.

Washington, February 25, 1909

My dear Mr. Speaker: In reference to the clause in the sundry civil bill doing away with the longevity arrangement on the Isthmus, permit me to say that I hope the section will not be kept in the bill. If nothing else can be done, would it not be possible to keep the longevity clause as regards those employees whose chances of promotion are practically nil? I can understand that something may be said against the clause as regards those who are promoted and who get the increase of wages thereby; but is it not possible to have the measure continue as regards those who are not promoted?[1] *Sincerely yours*

---

[1] Roosevelt had appointed this commission to determine the distribution and number of the navy yards required by the Navy. Since the Army was involved in protecting these yards, the commission included Generals Bell, Wotherspoon, and W. L. Marshall as well as Admirals Mahan, Sperry, and Wainwright. Despite the earnest recommendations of this commission and the persistent efforts of Secretary Meyer, political pressures prevented any reduction of navy yards during Taft's administration.

---

[1] The President's request went unheeded. After July 1, 1909, no increase of pay was granted on the Isthmus for length of service.

Personal   Washington, February 25, 1909

My dear Mr. Raines: [1] I have your letter of the 23rd. Stories like those you mention are circulated about me as I suppose they are circulated about all public men. I do not see that there is anything I can do about them. You say that on this particular occasion they were put in circulation by an Episcopal clergyman of New York and by a schoolteacher. I wish you would see them and put this letter before them. I do not think from what you say of them that they would knowingly do wrong, but I do think they did their part in circulating as infamous and base a lie as has ever been put in circulation. It happens that in the matter of drinking I am an extremely abstemious man; I suppose that no man not a total abstainer could well drink less than I do; and whisky and brandy I practically never touch. The accusation that I ever have been addicted in the slightest degree to drinking to excess, or to drinking even wine — and liquor, as I say, I practically never touch — in any but the most moderate way, is not only the blackest falsehood but an utterly ridiculous falsehood; it does not represent any distortion or exaggeration; it has no slightest base in fact; it is simply malignant invention — just as sheer an invention as if they had said that at the age of five I had poisoned my grandmother or had been mixt up in the assassination of Lincoln by Wilkes Booth. One accusation would be exactly as infamous and exactly as ludicrous as the other.

This letter is not to be made public, because no man will venture to make such an accusation public; and where there is no public statement there should be no public denial. But I should be glad to have you show it to the clergyman and teacher in question, and say to them from me, in all kindness, that hereafter they would do well to think twice before assisting in the work of spreading baseless slanders. *Sincerely yours*

Washington, February 25, 1909

My dear Mr. Jusserand: A Texas professor[1] is doing some really good work in collecting frontier ballads in the cow-country of Texas. They are of course for the most part mere doggerel, (as I believe to be true with the majority of all ballads as they were originally written); but these are interesting because they are genuine. The deification of Jesse James is precisely like the deification of Robin Hood; and the cowboy is a hero exactly as the hunter of the greenwood was a hero. Also, the view taken of women seems to be much the

[1] William Guy Raines was a New York lawyer and brother of John Raines.

[1] John A. Lomax.

same as that taken in many of the medieval ballads! I will talk to you about them when I see you. *Faithfully yours*

5191 · TO WILLIAM HOWARD TAFT   *Roosevelt Mss.*

Washington, February 26, 1909

Dear Will: Your letter of February 25th is so very nice — nice isn't anything like a strong enough word, but at the moment to use words as strong as I feel would look sloppy — that I must send you this line of warm personal thanks and acknowledgment. I am really delighted about Booker Washington's attitude and what he says Crum will do.[1] That is first-rate.

How could I but be delighted with your Inaugural? It is simply fine in every way. I cannot imagine a better Inaugural, and it marks just exactly what your administration will be. I have carefully reread the addition to your message and I think it is all right in every way. I did not wish unreservedly to praise it until I had carefully gone thru it. Now I have gone thru it carefully and I have no suggestions to make.

As for Fowler, my judgment is that once he is out you will find no difficulty whatever. That is why I so strongly feel it wise to give Loeb the recess appointment, so that when the Senate convenes, Loeb will be in office and Fowler will have no object in defeating him; because to defeat him would not reinstate Fowler. I shall see Depew tomorrow. He has already promised to do everything, and I heard Aldrich promise Loeb that he would do everything, to help the matter thru. Let Fowler go out at once; then the difficulty is solved.

Thank you again, my dear fellow, for your letter. *Ever yours*

[*Handwritten*] You put in the right way to address me, at the end![2]

5192 · TO ANDREW CARNEGIE   *Roosevelt Mss.*

Washington, February 26, 1909

My dear Mr. Carnegie: To deny Root credit for what the Department of State has done because it has been done under me as President is a good deal like denying credit to Sherman and Sheridan because they were under Grant. The President is of course responsible for the general policy of the administration in foreign as in domestic affairs, and here and there or now and then he must himself work out some given problem; for example, the Portsmouth peace, the Panama business, the sending of the fleet around the world, the earliest and most important part of the Algeciras business, were all worked

[1] The controversial Dr. Crum had been persuaded to resign his post as collector of customs at Charleston. This step, which Booker T. Washington had reported Crum would take in "good spirit," facilitated Taft's intention of avoiding appointments of Negroes to prominent positions in the South; see Pringle, *Taft,* I, 390.
[2] The last words of Taft's letter to the President were "with love and affection, my dear Theodore."

out by me personally. But in most things done by the State Department it is the Secretary of State, if he is a man like Root, who does practically all of the work. For instance, during the last three years the bulk of the most important work we have done has been in connection with the South and Central American States. We have done more as regards these States than ever before in the history of the State Department. This work has been entirely Root's. My part in it has been little beyond cordially backing him up. It was he who thought of making that extraordinary trip around South America which did more than has ever been done previously to bring the South American States into close touch with us. It was he who made the Pan-American Congress a matter of real and great importance for the Commonwealths of the Western Hemisphere. It was he who gave life to the Bureau of American Republics. It was he who brought about the formation of the international court for the Central American States. It was he who finally got the Senate to accept the Santo Domingo treaty, which secured an extraordinary increase in peace and prosperity in Santo Domingo and may prove literally invaluable in pointing out the way for introducing peace and order in the Caribbean and around its borders. No European statesman of whom I have heard has done as much for peace in any quarter of the world as Elihu Root has done in the Western Hemisphere during the last three years. No other American has rendered services to the cause of peace in any way comparable to his.

I very profoundly appreciate the honor done me by giving me the Nobel prize. As you know, I took the money which was given me and put it into the hands of Mr. Straus to form the basis of a foundation for industrial peace. Surely in no other way could I have so thoroly shown my appreciation of the honor conferred upon me. It was far more than I could do by making a speech in Norway. I should much have liked to go to Norway and to make this speech, but as you know I had accepted three invitations to speak, namely: at Paris, Berlin, and Oxford before I received the invitation from Norway, and I had refused a score or two of other invitations, including for example, invitations from the University of Cambridge in England, from the University of Geneva, representing the church of my fathers, from the University of Dordrecht,[1] representing the country from which my fathers came, and so on and so on. I could not accept another invitation after refusing these; and in any event my time was so limited as to forbid my venturing on another engagement. *Faithfully yours*

5193 · TO CARL ETHAN AKELEY   *Roosevelt Mss.*

Washington, February 27, 1909

My dear Mr. Akeley: I am greatly indebted to you for that plaster cast of the elephant's head. It was just what I wisht. It seems to me that in a side shot

[1] There is not, and never was, a university at Dordrecht.

at an elephant's head I ought to shoot forward of the hole in the ear — that is, about one-third way toward the eye. In a front shot I should be very much puzzled.

With hearty regard, believe me, *Faithfully yours*

5194 · TO JOHN B. TIVNAN

Roosevelt Mss.

Washington, March 1, 1909

My dear Sir:[1] Congressman Gardner has shown me your letter of February 20, 1909, in which you make the request that I should send you a "big stick" to be competed for at the next lawn party held for the benefit of the City Orphan Asylum, of Salem, Massachusetts.

Inasmuch as I am very glad indeed to take advantage of an opportunity to assist you in your efforts in behalf of the orphans, I have entrusted to Mr. Gardner's care a "big stick" which I trust will serve your purpose.

With best wishes for the success of your undertaking, I am, *Sincerely yours*

5195 · TO FREDERIC CHARLES WINKLER

Roosevelt Mss.

Washington, March 1, 1909

My dear General Winkler:[1] I genuinely prize your letter. You know, I trust, that I am not given to insincere compliment, and therefore you will accept at its face value what I say when I tell you that ever since I met you at the convention twenty-five years ago and found out just the type of man you were and the high reputation you bore, I have been strengthened and helped by your influence.

Now I wonder if you will feel offended if I speak of one little instance which much imprest me. When Prince Henry was here, among the various eminent Americans of German birth whom I had to meet him was yourself; I had asked you to come the long distance because I was proud of you and wisht to have you appear as a representative of what I thought best in American citizenship, entirely irrespective of birthplace. All, or almost all, of the other men when they met Prince Henry showed just a trifle of overappreciation of the fact that he was of royal birth; they all spoke to him in German, for instance, and bowed a little lower than they would to a distinguished American. This was true of Carl Schurz, and, indeed, of almost all who were there. You greeted him with all possible respect and courtesy, but you spoke to him in English and treated him in every way as you would have treated

---

[1] John B. Tivnan, president of the Aid Society of the City Orphan Asylum of Salem, Massachusetts.

---

[1] Frederic Charles Winkler, German-born Union general of volunteers; Milwaukee lawyer, businessman, and Republican; president of the Wisconsin Bar Association, 1902–1903.

any distinguished outsider whom we had gathered to honor; and at the time I turned to the Secretary to the President, Mr. Loeb, himself of German parentage, and said that you were showing yourself, as always, an example to Americans of every kind.

I hope you won't mind my repeating this anecdote to you. *Faithfully yours*

5196 · TO GIFFORD PINCHOT   *Roosevelt Mss.*

Washington, March 2, 1909

Dear Gifford: I have written you about others; I have written you about many public matters; now, just a line about yourself. As long as I live I shall feel for you a mixture of respect and admiration and of affectionate regard. I am a better man for having known you. I feel that to have been with you will make my children better men and women in after life; and I cannot think of a man in the country whose loss would be a more real misfortune to the Nation than yours would be. For seven and a half years we have worked together, and now and then played together — and have been altogether better able to work because we have played; and I owe to you a peculiar debt of obligation for a very large part of the achievement of this administration.

With love to your dear mother, I am, *Ever faithfully your friend*

5197 · TO PAUL MORTON   *Roosevelt Mss.*

Washington, March 2, 1909

Dear Paul: It was characteristic of you to write me as you have written me. Indeed, my dear fellow, I do not mind in the least the general cry that you quote — the old, old cry of "The King is dead! Long live the King!" I have done my work; I am perfectly content; I have nothing to ask; and I am very grateful to the American people for what they have done for me. Above all, I am grateful to the friends like you, to whom I owe the opportunity to do whatever I have done. But my dear fellow, for Heaven's sake don't talk about my having a future. My future is in the past, save as I may do the decent work that every private citizen can do.

Indeed Mrs. Roosevelt *is* the very best mistress of the White House that there ever has been therein! Love to dear Mrs. Morton. *Faithfully yours*

5198 · TO GIFFORD PINCHOT AND JAMES RUDOLPH GARFIELD   *Roosevelt Mss.*

Washington, March 3, 1909

Gentlemen: Thruout my term as President no two men have been more intimately associated with all phases of my work than you two. No two men have been so closely identified with so many of the policies for which this

1541

administration has stood. I am sincerely glad that you are to write in brief form just what has been meant by these various policies, just what has been accomplished in the way of putting them into effect. No two men are better fitted to do so. *Faithfully yours*

Washington, March 3, 1909

To the Secretary of War: I wish the following memorandum filed in the record of Captain Butt.

Captain Archibald W. Butt has been for eleven months with me as chief aide. In addition to our purely personal association and the performance of his duties in connection with the White House proper, I have treated him thruout that time as a general in the field would treat a staff officer of unusual ability, because I have found that from him I was able to get information of real consequence to me in planning and working for the betterment of the army conditions. He has been an exceptionally tactful and diplomatic aide-de-camp; he is an exceptionally able and efficient officer; and if ever again it should befall me to command troops I should desire him to serve under me.

Washington, March 3, 1909

My dear Mr. Shaffer: No human being could write a kinder and pleasanter letter than yours which I have just received; and no President has received or ever will receive a letter that will touch him more.[1] I thank you for it. *Faithfully yours*

[1] Shaffer's letter, characteristic of many Roosevelt was then receiving, read: "I have felt in the last few days a mental depression at your leaving the White House. I feel like one who might be a passenger on an ocean steamer and who had been acquainted with the captain of the steamer and permitted to walk the deck with him now and then. The storms and ice-bergs and the rainy days brought him into closer communion with the captain until he began to feel as if he were a part of the crew. But suddenly his buoyancy of spirit is changed. The Captain meets him and says: 'I am going to turn over the ship to one of my other officers and I will not be on the bridge as before.' A keen sense of the loss of friendship and the loss of interest in the navigating of the ship settles down into his heart and mind. He does not want to leave the ship but he does not want to walk on the bridge the first day the new officer takes charge. He feels too keenly and too deeply the loss of his former captain.

"I am not going to the inauguration. Judge Taft has been kind enough to send me a special card and asked me to be on the President's reviewing stand. I was there four years ago. I cannot go this time. My feelings are too intense. A little later on if the captain invites me to walk the bridge with him, at morning, noon, or night, I will respond for I believe he is a capable captain and I shall be glad to be a part of his crew, but I am indulging the hope that my favorite captain will again some time walk the bridge and permit me occasionally to walk with him." — Shaffer to Roosevelt; March 1, 1909, R. M. A. Mss.

Washington, March 3, 1909

My dear Admiral: I had already warned Mr. Taft on the subject of dividing the battle fleet, and had shown him my letter to Mr. Foss of the House Naval Committee, the paragraph of which that deals with the subject I enclose for your information. I shall send him in writing one final protest. I am sure that the fleet will never be divided. We got the mischievous proposition struck out of the bill. *Faithfully yours*

P.S. I enclose you a copy of my final letter to Taft.

Washington, March 3, 1909

Dear Will: One closing legacy. Under no circumstances divide the battleship fleet between the Atlantic and Pacific Oceans prior to the finishing of the Panama Canal.[1] Malevolent enemies of the navy, like Hale; timid fools, like Perkins; and conscienceless scoundrels, like Tillman, will try to lead public opinion in a matter like this without regard to the dreadful harm they may do the country; and good, but entirely ignorant, men may be thus misled. I should obey no direction of Congress and pay heed to no popular sentiment, no matter how strong, if it went wrong in such a vital matter as this. When I sent the fleet around the world there was a wild clamor that some of it should be sent to the Pacific, and an equally mad clamor that some of it should be left in the Atlantic. I disregarded both. At first it seemed as if popular feeling was nearly a unit against me. It is now nearly a unit in favor of what I did.

It is now nearly four years since the close of the Russian-Japanese war. There were various factors that brought about Russia's defeat; but most important by all odds was her having divided her fleet between the Baltic and the Pacific, and, furthermore, splitting up her Pacific fleet into three utterly unequal divisions. The entire Japanese force was always used to smash some fraction of the Russian force. The knaves and fools who advise the separation of our fleet nowadays and the honest, misguided creatures who think so little that they are misled by such advice, ought to take into account this striking lesson furnished by actual experience in a great war but four years ago. Keep the battle fleet either in one ocean or the other and have the armed cruisers always in trim, as they are now, so that they can be at once sent to join the battle fleet if the need should arise. *Faithfully yours*

[1] The legacy was honored; Taft did not divide the fleet.

Appendix

THEODORE ROOSEVELT AND THE PANAMA CANAL: A STUDY IN ADMINISTRATION [1]

By Alfred D. Chandler, Jr.

To the historian, the study of the American Presidency is a tale of politics and policy but rarely a study in administration. Yet the primary duties of the chief executive, as the Constitution stresses, are administrative. Thus the story of Panama, which for the historian of the Roosevelt administration usually ends in 1904 when the diplomatic and political narrative closes, was in that year only beginning for the President. The history of the canal after 1904 provides one of the most illuminating examples of Theodore Roosevelt as an administrator.

Roosevelt's executive abilities lay less in the realm of theory than in the field of practice. To him the concepts of a Hobbes, a Montesquieu, a John C. Calhoun, or even a Woodrow Wilson were mere metaphysical subtleties with little meaning in the actual ruling of men. Nor was he much more interested in the creation of institutional forms to meet specific but broad administrative needs. There is nothing in his work comparable to Elihu Root's reorganization of the army, to Alexander Hamilton's organization of the administrative framework of the American government, or to John D. Rockefeller's creation of the Standard Oil Company. Instead of originating plans, as these men did, to anticipate administrative difficulties, Roosevelt usually waited until his management problems were fully upon him before taking positive action.

As a practical executive, Roosevelt's talents were threefold. First, he made decisions rapidly. He tried to obtain the best advice available, but he was not afraid to act when such advice and information proved inadequate. Second, Roosevelt understood the need to choose capable men for important administrative posts, to give such men his fullest support, and, most sig-

---

[1] The data for this study come almost wholly from the Theodore Roosevelt Collection in the Library of Congress. Especially useful were three boxes which include correspondence between the canal's administrators as well as letters from these men to Roosevelt. The information for the charts was taken from the *Annual Reports of the Isthmian Canal Commission*. The most satisfactory secondary works on the construction of the canal are Gerstle Mack, *The Land Divided*, and Miles P. DuVal, Jr., *And the Mountains Will Move*.

nificant, to convince his subordinates of the value of their work. Finally, from his experience as Civil Service Commissioner, Police Commissioner, Assistant Secretary of the Navy, and Governor of New York, he learned not only that authority and responsibility must be centralized but that authority to act must be commensurate with the responsibility exacted.

The insufficiencies as well as the sufficiencies of these administrative characteristics were fully revealed in Panama. There the President was faced with as difficult a task as an administrator can be asked to do. He had to create and staff an entirely new administrative organization which had to perform an unprecedented job. This organization had to be responsible for digging, dredging, and constructing locks and dams on a huge scale. It had to provide for a regular and systematic flow of supplies and materials from the United States over 2,000 miles of water to the Isthmus. It had to recruit a laboring force of skilled and unskilled labor, to transport the force to Panama, and then to house and feed these men. The care of their health required a large medical staff to fight yellow fever and other tropical diseases. Furthermore, this administrative unit had to govern the Canal Zone and handle relations between the Americans and the Panamanians. Finally, the organization had to operate under pressures from Congress, labor officials, the press, and the American public.

II

In supervising the construction of the canal, Roosevelt was required by the Spooner Act to work through a seven-man Isthmian Canal Commission. Congress, by providing in this act that four of the commissioners were to be trained engineers, reflected its failure to understand the administrative task facing the commission. Roosevelt, by appointing able engineers but no competent administrators, indicated that he, like Congress, looked on the commission as an advisory rather than an administrative body. Even the commissioners were confused about their functions. "The Commission," reads its first annual report, "holds a relation to the canal construction work similar to that of a board of directors to a great railway enterprise, except that the Commissioners are in closer touch with their work and the majority being civil engineers, stand in the relation of consulting and designing engineers to the canal work."

If the commission had acted as a consulting board of engineers, it might have been able to make recommendations for the proper design of the canal. If it had operated as a board of directors, it might have been able to begin work on the Isthmus. By attempting to act as both, it was unable to do either. As a board of directors it courted even more certain failure by endeavoring to operate without a centralized administrative organization and by failing to provide for interdepartmental communication on the Isthmus (see Chart 1). All requests for men, money, and materials, all proposals and recommendations for action at Panama had to be approved by the seven-man board which remained in Washington. Working within this defective administrative organization, such able men as Chief Engineer John G. Wallace, Doctor William C. Gorgas, Governor George W. Davis, and Paymaster Eugene C. Tobey were soon in constant conflict with each other and with the commission in Washington. By the end of 1904 the work on the Isthmus was almost at a standstill.

By this time Roosevelt had become fully aware of the administrative difficulties in Panama. In January 1905 he asked Congress to reorganize the commission so that it would be "used only as an executive instrument for the executive and administrative work." The Senate, however, refused to approve the House bill granting the President full power to create the administrative staff to build the canal. The opponents of the bill, although admitting the need to increase efficiency, were reluctant to grant the concentration of executive power necessary to achieve this end.

When Congress failed to act, Roosevelt, with little hesitation, made the desired change through an executive order. By appointing a special board of engineers to recommend the type of canal to be built, he terminated the advisory duties of the commission. Then, following the advice of Wallace and his own administrative precepts, Roosevelt placed the major administrative functions of the commission under three departments (see Chart 2). The heads of the departments — the chairman, the chief engineer, and Governor of the Zone — formed an executive committee which administered the business of the commission, the whole body meeting only four times a year. The chairman, residing in Washington, handled the purchasing of supplies of materials and also acted as liaison officer between the commission and the executive and legislative branches of the government. The chief engineer, for the first time a member of the commission, was given sole charge of all the work on the Isthmus directly connected with the construction of the canal. The governor was made responsible for the health conditions as well as the political administration of the Zone. He also acted as the American minister to Panama.

With administrative authority and responsibility concentrated in three offices, Roosevelt searched carefully for competent men to fill these posts. After Root and Henry C. Frick had refused appointments, he found two admirable administrators in Theodore Perry Shonts and John Frank Stevens. He made the first of these two veteran railroad builders and operators the chairman of the commission; the other he appointed as chief engineer on Wallace's resignation in June 1905. In the hope of encouraging these men to do the best work possible, he promised both Shonts and Stevens an absolutely free hand in carrying out their respective tasks.

These were, Roosevelt soon learned, impossible promises. He had given the best available appointees full responsibility and authority, but this was not enough. In the late fall of 1905 Shonts surprised Roosevelt by protesting against interference from the Secretary of War. The President, he claimed, was not standing by his promise to allow him a free hand. Even more disturbing, Roosevelt wrote to one correspondent, was the fact that "Stevens has just the same feeling about not being interfered with by Shonts that Shonts has about Taft." On the Isthmus Stevens and Gorgas began to take sides against Shonts and Charles E. Magoon, the expert on colonial affairs whom Roosevelt had appointed Governor of the Zone to replace Davis. Stevens, too, resented the credit Shonts was getting for the work for which he, as chief engineer, was wholly responsible. Despite the increasing friction, much was accomplished on the Isthmus. By the summer of 1906, however, Shonts wrote that the canal's management could no longer hope to steer "clear of open ruptures by sweet oil methods, and promises of remedies later on."

Roosevelt readily agreed. Fully cognizant of the growing conflicts within the commission, he had blamed them on individual personalities rather than organizational maladjustment. By the middle of 1906 he had come to appreciate two facts which he failed to understand in 1905. First, in a multifunctional organization like the canal commission the duties, powers, and responsibilities of each major division must be clearly defined and carefully integrated into the larger administrative structure. Second, authority and responsibility for the unit as a whole must be centralized in one office.

After consultations with Shonts, Stevens, and Taft, Roosevelt during his visit to Panama in November 1906 issued the executive order which systematically departmentalized function and centralized authority and responsibility (see Chart 3). The three-man executive committee was abolished. A single man, the chairman, was given supreme authority. Seven departments were created whose heads were directly responsible to the chairman. They in turn were given complete authority to appoint and remove their subordinates. In January the President completed the centralizing process by combining the offices of chairman and chief engineer and divided the chief engineer's department into functionally separate departments. Roosevelt then appointed the heads of the four major departments — excavating and dredging, locks and dams, motive power and machinery, and labor and quarters — and of the departments of sanitation and political administration as members of the commission. With these appointments the metamorphosis of the Isthmian Canal Commission from an advisory body to a streamlined administrative unit was complete.

III

Late in February 1907, three months after he had completed the canal's administrative organization, Roosevelt announced that the government would build the canal under army supervision. In 1904 Roosevelt, Congress, and the American people expected the major construction work on the canal to be done by private contractors under the direction of civilian administrators. By 1907 the President had become aware of the difficulties of selecting competent private contractors for such a vital government work. At the same time he had discovered that civilian administrators were ill-equipped to handle the broader management problems involved in operating a large national project.

The canal's railroad-trained administrators, Roosevelt complained to Taft in the summer of 1906, "do not even yet understand this is not like a private work." Shonts and Stevens were, he told the Secretary of War:

the very best men we could get for actually digging the canal, but their phenomenal administrative and engineering qualities are not accompanied by any appreciation of the exact qualities necessary in dealing . . . . with a small Spanish-American power, or with Congress or with the labor situation. . . . Shonts and Stevens must keep in mind the fact that they are not now working for Hill on the Great Northern but for the United States Government, and that this means they will have to take into account, so far as with propriety it is possible, the more deep seated convictions and prejudices of the American people.

If Shonts and Stevens were unaware of the differences between government and private work, Roosevelt was partly to blame. Not only did he fail to warn his administrators of the glaring and constant publicity under which they must work, but he actually promised them freedom from outside interference.

Accustomed to the comparative privacy and independence of railroad management, Shonts and Stevens found the publicity and external pressures of their new task extremely uncomfortable. They disliked being called from their work to talk to congressmen, newspaper reporters, and representatives of civic, business, and labor organizations. They were annoyed at having to answer what they considered absurd charges of mismanagement and corruption at Panama. They saw no reasons why social and diplomatic amenities should interfere with their efforts to clean up Colón and Panama City. Finally, they resented not having a free hand in their relations with labor.

Stevens, especially, had looked on the canal's labor force as his own. During 1905 he had transformed a demoralized agglomeration of laborers into a loyal and efficient force with a remarkable *esprit de corps*. Though popular, Stevens was a strict master. When a worker disapproved too vocally of the chief engineer's labor policies, he was unceremoniously shipped off the Isthmus. Stevens paid little attention to the eight-hour day and other requirements of government work, and even less to the demands of organized labor. When the steam-shovel operators threatened to strike unless their wages were made equal to those of the locomotive engineers, Stevens reportedly told them: "You all know damn well that strikes do not get you anywhere. Now, get the hell out of this office and back to work on those shovels." The operators went back to work. They also sent back angry protests to their national union officials who immediately took the matter to their congressmen and to Roosevelt.

The President, understanding fully the need for good relations with labor and the public, was troubled by the limitations of his managers. Such limitations, however, did not in his opinion warrant a change in command. Instead he began to handle the commission's labor and public relations himself. During the fall and winter of 1906 Roosevelt studied the demands of organized labor and held conferences with labor officials on working conditions in Panama. At the same time he discussed canal matters with many congressmen and encouraged congressional junkets to the Isthmus. By arranging for Root's visit to Panama in September and by making a trip of his own in November, . he was able to soothe the feelings of the Panamanians who had been upset by Stevens' direct and abrupt methods. Since he and Taft could handle these broader administrative matters, Roosevelt was perfectly content to have Stevens, after the resignation of Shonts in January 1907, take complete charge of the work which he had so auspiciously begun.

Under this *modus operandi* Stevens and his railroad-trained staff might well have brought the work to a successful conclusion. This arrangement, however, was broken up almost as soon as it was instituted by an unforeseen circumstance — the difficulties attendant upon the letting of contracts to private firms. Because these difficulties proved so great, Roosevelt became convinced that the government must build the canal and that construction must be supervised by army engineers.

The history of this episode is, briefly, as follows. In July 1906, at Roosevelt's request, Stevens and Walston H. Brown, of Brown Brothers and Company, presented separate proposals for the letting of contracts. Both men recommended a scheme that would enable the government to select the most competent contractors in the country to work on the several different kinds of construction required at the Isthmus. The principle of both plans was that an association of the selected contractors, through negotiation with a committee of men representing both the government and the construction association, would agree on an estimated cost for the canal, an approximate date of completion, and on goods and services to be supplied by the association. The contractors would receive a percentage, to be arranged by the committee, of the total cost.

To this proposal the Secretary of War objected, largely on the grounds that the selection of contractors, precluding as it did competitive bidding, would stir up unpleasant political reactions. With this objection such skilled politicians as Spooner and Cannon agreed. Stevens, in reply, pointed out that, with competitive bidding, price rather than competence had to be the criterion for selection. Under a bid contract, he was quite certain, the government would get second-rate contractors who, lacking ability and experience, were willing to sell their services more cheaply than the more reputable firms.

Roosevelt, after consulting with Shonts, Cabinet members, and contractors, accepted Taft's view. On October 9, 1906, the commission issued an invitation for bids. Because of the difficulty of framing a satisfactory invitation for such an unprecedented task and because of the impressive financial qualifications required of the contractors, the responses were something less than satisfactory. Only two companies presented bids "worthy of consideration" and neither of these bids could be accepted by the government without further negotiations. With cooling enthusiasm for the whole project, Roosevelt arranged a series of conferences with the two firms to decide which should receive the contract.

On February 12, 1907, three days before the first conference, Roosevelt received a letter from Stevens which precipitated his decision to have the canal built by the government under supervision of army engineers. Since the opening of the bids on January 12, Stevens had sent cables to Washington repeating his objections to competitive bidding and criticizing the firm most likely to receive the contract. Distressed by the outcome of the contract plan, he now gave vent to his rising irritations with the pressures under which he was working. He had erred, he told Roosevelt, in assuming that "this enterprise was to be a purely business proposition." Instead of being permitted to concentrate on building the canal, he had been forced to "fight a continuous battle with enemies in the rear" and had been "continually subject to attack by a lot of people, and they are not all in private life, that I would not wipe my boots on in the United States." Stevens closed by asking the President to relieve him in two or three months if it did not "embarrass in any way, your plans."

Roosevelt was thoroughly exasperated by Stevens' letter. Although the President realized it was not a formal letter of resignation, he told Taft that the chief engineer must be immediately relieved. The truculent tone of the letter was not only annoying in itself, but it demonstrated that Stevens was not adapting himself to the pressures of public work. In fact, he actually appeared to be breaking under these strains. Moreover, he was threatening to quit his post at a critical moment in the canal's history — just after Shonts had resigned to become president of the Interborough Metropolitan Company and just before the decision on the contracts was to be made. On the 14th Roosevelt wrote Stevens that he would be relieved at the earliest possible moment, probably by an army engineer. On the 18th the President called Major George W. Goethals to the White House, informed him that he would replace Stevens, and asked him to suggest army officers to fill the major administrative positions in Panama.

One basic reason for turning to the army, Roosevelt told Goethals, was to assure a continuity of command. He could not afford to have his principal administrators leave or threaten to leave in time of trouble as Stevens and Wallace had done, or, like Shonts, to quit when another position was offered. In the second place, Roosevelt believed that army officers were more accustomed than civilian administrators to the publicity and the irritations involved in government work. Finally, since Shonts and Stevens had admirably solved the transportation problems of the construction, army engineers with their training in the building of locks and dams were technically able to carry out the task in Panama.

During the same week that Roosevelt wrote Stevens and talked with Goethals, he conferred with the two contracting syndicates. Even before the last of these conferences he had become thoroughly convinced that Stevens had been right about bid contracts. Only by negotiating a contract could the government obtain the best contractors at a price equitable to both government and contractors. On the other hand, the President still agreed with Taft that an arranged contract was a political liability. The answer to this dilemma, it was now clear, was to have the army build the canal. This solution was more obvious in February 1907 than in the spring of 1906, for thanks to Stevens' brilliant work in preparing the physical plant and organizing the labor force on the Isthmus, there was no longer a real need for the specialized skills of expert contractors.

On February 26 the President simultaneously announced that the bids of the private contractors had been rejected and that army officers would take charge of the canal construction. With this announcement, Roosevelt's major administrative concerns in Panama were over. Goethals and his army engineers took over the administrative machinery Roosevelt had completed in November 1906. With only a few minor alterations these were the men and this was the organization that completed the canal in 1914. The canal commission under Goethals proved to be one of the most successful administrative bodies the government has established. Thanks to its managerial competence, Americans learned for almost the first time that the government could carry out a huge economic enterprise in an efficient manner.

The effectiveness of the canal commission, once its administrative and personnel problems were solved, was a tribute to Roosevelt's administrative ability. The delay in solving these problems revealed his limitations. Roosevelt met his administrative crises successfully, but he failed to anticipate them. On the other hand, these crises were not anticipated by Shonts, Stevens, Wallace, Taft, or anyone else connected with the construction of the canal. Although Roosevelt, like most trained administrators, lacked administrative imagination, he showed himself in Panama a competent, pragmatic executive. There he met the problems caused by the unprecedented nature of his task by applying the principles he had learned from experience. He centralized authority and responsibility, he chose able men as managers, and he did not procrastinate in reaching decisions. When these principles proved inadequate, the President learned quickly. He re-examined his problems, found where he had erred, and again with little hesitation made the needed changes. In this way Roosevelt in a comparatively short time perfected, despite the restrictions placed on him by Congress, the admirable organization and staff which built the Panama Canal.

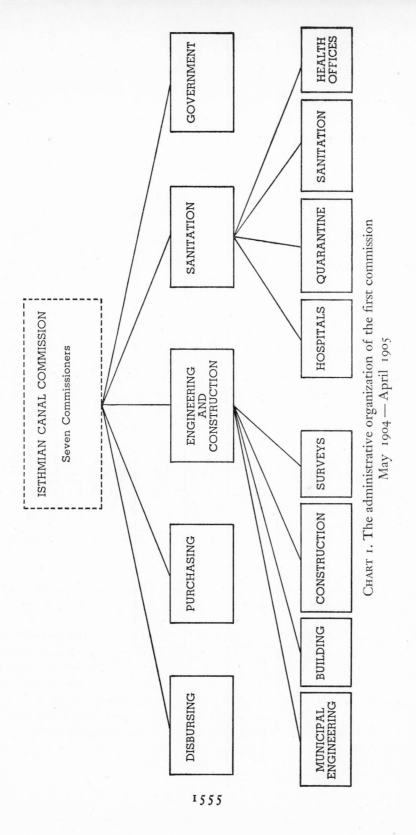

CHART 1. The administrative organization of the first commission
May 1904 — April 1905

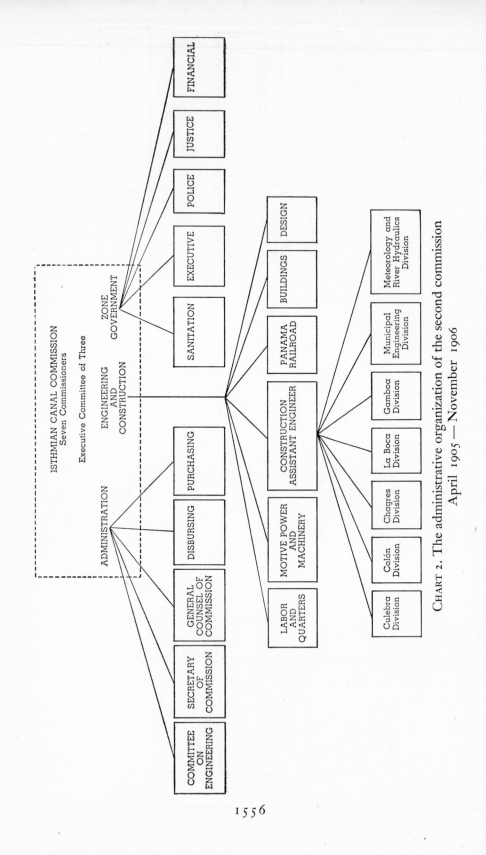

CHART 2. The administrative organization of the second commission
April 1905 — November 1906

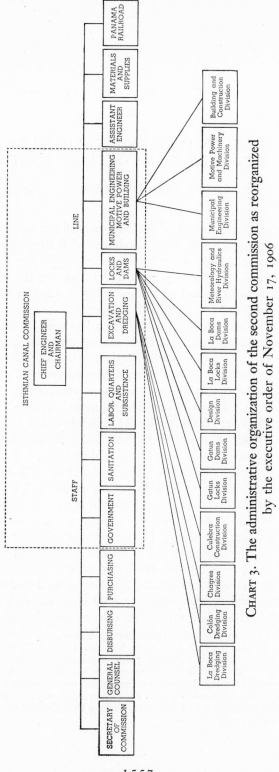

CHART 3. The administrative organization of the second commission as reorganized by the executive order of November 17, 1906

THEODORE ROOSEVELT AND THE HEPBURN ACT: TOWARD AN ORDERLY SYSTEM OF CONTROL[1]

By JOHN M. BLUM

Behind all the political manipulation, beneath all the legalistic forensics, the issue was control. Theodore Roosevelt intended that an administrative agency should have the authority to rectify the inequities in the business of transportation. Nelson Aldrich, the resourceful leader of the President's opposition, intended that it should not. Roosevelt demanded that the Interstate Commerce Commission be invested with power to revise railroad rates. Here, he felt, lay the key to control. Aldrich, when he drew his lines, sought to transfer the final decision on rates from the commission to the courts, to leave the judiciary in its traditional, ineffectual, disorderly role of monitor of the price of transportation. President and senator, sensitive always to each other's strength, delighting in the test, came slowly to a crisis.

"I am well aware," Roosevelt stated in his annual message to Congress of 1905, "of the difficulties of the [railroad] legislation that I am suggesting, and of the need of temperate and cautious action in securing it. I should emphatically protest against improperly radical or hasty action. . . . [But] the question of transportation lies at the root of all industrial success, and the revolution in transportation which has taken place during the last half-century has been the most important factor in the growth of the new industrial conditions. . . . At present the railway is [the highway of commerce] . . . . and we must do our best to see that it is kept open to all on equal terms. . . . It is far better that it should be managed by private individuals than by the government. But it can only be so managed on condition that justice is done the public. . . . What we need to do is to develop an orderly system, and such a system can only come through the gradually increased exercise of the right of efficient government control."

[1] This essay is based on Roosevelt's large correspondence about railroad regulations from November 1904 through June 1906, Volumes IV and V, this work; on his speeches on the same topic, particularly his messages to Congress; on the large newspaper record contained in the scrapbooks in the Theodore Roosevelt Collection in the Harvard College Library; on the debates and hearings on the Hepburn Act in the *Congressional Record* and its accompanying documents; and on the bibliography cited in connection with No. 3348, Volume IV, this work; see also Appendix I, Volume IV, this work.

A year earlier Roosevelt had sent Congress only a paragraph on railroad legislation. Now he spelled out the elements of what he considered an orderly system of control. These he had derived from the accumulated findings of the Bureau of Corporations and the Interstate Commerce Commission and from the expert advice of the lawyers and railroad men in his Cabinet: Paul Morton, a former Santa Fe executive; Attorney General William Moody; Elihu Root, wisest counselor of his time; and William Howard Taft. Their recommendations, embodied in the Hepburn Bill with Administration guidance, substantially as Roosevelt had announced them, covered every aspect of the railroad problem then recognized by William Z. Ripley, the foremost authority on railroad economics in the United States. Grounded as it was on thorough study by essentially conservative men, much of Roosevelt's program provoked little congressional dissent.

The area of agreement was large. The Elkins Antirebate Act of 1903 had failed utterly to prevent the discriminations it explicitly forbade. Alive to this, and to the public's growing displeasure over the outrageous practices of Armour and Standard Oil, practices as harmful to the railroads as to the competitors of the favored, Congress shared the President's opinion that "all private-car lines, industrial roads, refrigerator charges, and the like should be expressly put under the supervision of the Interstate Commerce Commission . . . . so far as rates, and agreements practically affecting rates, are concerned . . . . [for] a rebate in icing charges, or in mileage, or in a division of the rate for refrigerating charges is just as pernicious as a rebate in any other way." Conscious of the experience of the government in investigating both railways and industrial concerns, Congress, like Roosevelt, had reached the common-sense conclusion that standardized records open to official inspection were a prerequisite for the determination of adequate policies of regulation as well as for the prevention of familiar abuses in corporation management. Congress was also willing, by providing for expeditious action in cases arising under the commerce act, to destroy "the weapon of delay, almost the most formidable weapon in the hands of those whose purpose is to violate the law." [2]

Had Roosevelt recommended and Congress agreed to nothing else, these provisions would in themselves have been worth-while but inadequate achievements. They did not fundamentally alter the existing relationship between the federal government and the railroads. They established no new device of regulation. The prevention of rebates, now strengthened, had earlier existed; the inspection of records, now facilitated, had long since begun; the expedition of trial for suits involving infractions of the Interstate Commerce Act had already been provided for suits arising under the Antitrust Act. Roose-

[2] Without presidential prodding, the Senate added to the Hepburn Bill two important clauses, one imposing criminal penalties for certain violations, another, more significant, forbidding corporations producing such commodities as coal from owning the railroads that transported them.

velt's orderly system of efficient government control depended not on these precedents but on an innovation to which many in Congress were still openly hostile. The President proposed that the I.C.C. be given limited authority to make rates. As he carefully defined it, this was his central objective.

Roosevelt, contrary to the acid assertion in Robert La Follette's messianic autobiography, took his first and final position on rates in his annual message of 1904. He there considered it "undesirable . . . . finally to clothe the commission with general authority to fix railroad rates." "As a fair security to shippers," however, he insisted that "the commission should be vested with the power, where a given rate has been challenged and after full hearing found to be unreasonable, to decide, subject to judicial review, what shall be a reasonable rate to take its place; the ruling of the commission to take effect immediately." The "reasonable rate," Roosevelt implied by his reference to the Supreme Court's interpretation of the Reagan-Cullom Act, was to be only a maximum rate. This meaning he made explicit in 1905 when he requested that the commission receive power "to prescribe the limit of rate beyond which it shall not be lawful to go — the maximum reasonable rate, as it is commonly called."

To Senator Robert La Follette, to John Sharp Williams, the Democratic leader of the House, to Ray Stannard Baker, then at the height of his popularity as a muckraker, Roosevelt's proposal seemed to provide an insufficient curb on the powers of the railroads. The President disagreed. Since Congress simply would not then consider legalized pooling, "the best possible regulation of rates," he preferred his maximum rate plan to any alternative. His Attorney General had advised that legislation empowering the commission to set definite rate schedules — the objective of La Follette, Williams, and Baker — might be declared unconstitutional. "The one thing I do not want," Roosevelt explained to Baker, "is to have a law passed and then declared unconstitutional." Furthermore, he argued, the authority to prescribe a maximum rate, while perhaps short of the ultimate ideal, promised immediate, substantial improvement in existing conditions. "Surely you must see," he wrote Baker, "that if the Commission has the power to make the maximum rate that which the railroad gives to the most favored shipper, it will speedily become impossible thus to favor any shipper." If, after a test, it proved inadequate, he would then be willing to try to secure a definite rate proposition. "I believe," he explained to the impatient, "in men who take the next step; not those who theorize about the two-hundredth step."

Roosevelt intended primarily to protect individual shippers from excessive or discriminatory rates. He agreed with Baker that the maximum rate provision would afford little remedy for discrimination between commodities or between localities, but such discriminations seemed to him relatively impersonal. He cared less about freight classification and long and short haul differentials because he could not readily associate those matters with a doer of evil and a victim. Discriminations against a small shipper or exorbitant rates the President understood and despised. They were, he was sure, immoral. His interest had also political meaning, for the spokesmen of the shippers' organizations concentrated on the problems that a maximum rate provision could begin to resolve. They neglected to mention, and Roosevelt did not apparently recognize, that no recommendation in the annual messages or provision in the Hepburn Bill prevented shippers or their consignees from passing on rate burdens originating in any discriminatory device to the still unorganized, essentially undiscerning consumers.

The maximum rate proposal, in many respects inadequate, properly labeled so by liberals of the time, nevertheless earned for Roosevelt the opprobrious criticism of a large part of the business community and the tenacious opposition of a near majority of the United States Senate. Modest as the proposal was, it challenged the most cherished prerogative of private management, the most hoary tenet of free private enterprise — the ability freely to make prices. This threat gave Roosevelt a reputation, persisting still among railway executives, of being a scandalous advocate of something closely akin to socialism. A more radical proposition, the President well knew, would have had no chance for success.

Roosevelt had constructed the Hepburn Bill with practiced care. "If I were merely anxious for temporary ease and temporary credit, and desired to stand forth for the moment as 'the friend of the people,' " he explained to Brooks Adams during the final stage of the struggle over railroad regulation, "I should be glad to see the Hepburn bill beaten . . . . ; for I fully appreciate that any such measure is sure to cause trouble by the disappointment certain to be felt over its workings even among men of sense; while the extremists after a short while are sure to say that it has accomplished nothing. But as a matter of fact the bill accomplishes a real step forward in that movement of reform which will be effective only if it is not made too violent." Including as it did just enough to satisfy his purpose, it contained nothing that would alarm the marginal supporters without whom it could not survive. This was the last in a series of calculated tactics by which, since November 1904, Roosevelt had prepared the parliamentary environment for his railroad program. "I have a very strong feeling," he acknowledged, "that it is a President's duty to get on with Congress if he possibly can, and that it is a reflection upon him if he and Congress come to a complete break." He permitted no break. Understanding his situation, he made the powers of his office and the talents of his person the instruments of viable leadership.

Immediately after the election of 1904, at the height of his popularity, Roosevelt first proposed that the I.C.C. be given authority to set rates. He had already won surely to his side, for this and other policies, those Republican legislators who shared his purpose of meliorative reform. He could rely less surely upon those who, less purposeful, had shared the political favors that lay within his power to dispose. At once he also recruited a host of the Old Guard in the House. At his contrivance, they grudgingly accepted his railroad program in return for his willingness to leave intact the tariff structure they revered.[3] During the lame-duck session of the Fifty-ninth Congress his tripartite coalition, joined by the Democrats, put through the House by an overwhelming vote the Esch-Townsend Bill, a tentative embodiment of Roosevelt's program. But this measure, fiercely resisted by the railroads, by the organized spokesmen of big business and finance, and by their political associates in the Senate, died in the upper chamber.

Roosevelt had expected little better of the outgoing Congress. Welcoming the issue now clearly drawn, he went with gusto to the people. In Texas and Colorado, at Chautauqua and Chicago, along the southeastern seaboard, he spoke to adulating audiences the righteousness, and yet the reasonableness, of his cause. If, in part, the prestige of his office drew them to hear him, the fervor in his falsetto persuaded them to listen. The overdrawn counterpropaganda of the railroads, whatever its merit in logic, could scarcely compete in a society primed by the muckrakers with the explosive personality of the President. Assertively he equated his view of rate making with his then regnant dictum of a square deal for every man. He would restrain the perverters of privilege who by their manipulations of rates and rebates purloined the just profits of their honest competitors and threatened to provoke by their excesses the menace of socialism. This was a crisis (Theodore Roosevelt coped constantly with crises),[4] but he would shackle greed and, routing the proponents of nationalization, save the railroads from themselves. Roosevelt's demands were not new. Indeed, he added nothing to the principles or to the histrionics of the Granger and Populist railroad regulators of years gone by. But he did bring to their long-rejected national program a new respectability, an incomparable personal vitality, and assurances, impressive to thoughtful conservatives, that he, unlike his predecessors, would direct regulation to constructive ends.

The last was particularly important. By the fall of 1905 such reliable Republican senators from the West as Allison of Iowa and Spooner of Wisconsin, traditionally conservators of the status quo, now sensitive to the growing complaints of the farmers and shippers whose protests had preceded and exceeded Roosevelt's, realized that their political life rested upon an unprecedented capitulation to their constituents. In the President they recognized a safe sponsor for reform. If his language seemed at times extravagant, if his central purpose was a genuine departure from the past, he nevertheless, they knew from experience, guarded their party and, in the largest sense, their principles. This knowledge may also have comforted others who deeply distrusted the emotions Roosevelt evoked. Before the Sixtieth Congress con-

[3] For a full account of the tariff-railroad understanding, see Appendix I, Volume IV, this work. During a later session of Congress, on that occasion in behalf of his naval program, Roosevelt again won a round with the leaders of the House partly by a calculated feint on the tariff; see No. 4648.
[4] To enhance his naval program in 1908, Roosevelt, with timely conviction, conjured up a crisis with Japan; see No. 4991.

vened, the roar of the President's crowds penetrated, perhaps, the cold quiet where Nelson Aldrich, by preference undisturbed, made policy. That master of the Senate, in any case, unlike the tone-deaf Foraker, was thereafter willing to make a conciliatory gesture toward Roosevelt and his allies.

The President had set his stage. Reminded of the arrangements by which the tariff remained inviolate, the new House in February 1906, with only seven adverse votes, passed the Hepburn Bill. It provided for every objective of the Administration. The most thoughtful member of the I.C.C., Commissioner Prouty, told Roosevelt that it represented "an advance so extraordinary that he had never dared to suppose it would be possible to pass it." The President judged that it was "as far as we could with wisdom go at this time." Politically he was surely correct. Although an aroused constituency cheered the champions of the bill in the Senate, Nelson Aldrich, as debate began, had yet to surrender command of the chamber he had so long dominated. Roosevelt, until this time the aggressor, had now to adjust to the strength and the tactics of a talented oppositionist.

How unlike the President in many ways his adversary was: so urbane, so controlled, so indifferent to manifestations of approval, so patently disdainful of the string-tie statesmanship surrounding him; but, like Roosevelt, so bemused by the endless adventure of governing men. Did his friend Allison have, of a summer, to explain himself in ponderous periods from a rural podium? How dreary for Allison. Aldrich preferred the politics that the caucus controlled, the constituents one met graciously over liqueurs, the measured exchanges between mutually respectful equals who understood the manners and the meaning of their power. For all that, Aldrich was not the less discerning, not the less tenacious. Many of the dreadful things that Theodore did, the senator knew, he had to do. The people, after all, could vote. The railroads were unpopular. Roosevelt could have his bill, but not the way he wanted it. A gesture now, a delaying action — then, perhaps, the worst would pass. Perhaps, again, it would not pass; the comfortable world was changing. In that case, delay had of itself some value. And the means to resist were familiar and strong.

Aldrich had a corps of allies: first, among the Republicans, the intractables, such as Crane of Massachusetts, Hale of Maine, Foraker of Ohio, Hemenway of Indiana, Knox of Pennsylvania, Kean of New Jersey, Depew of New York, Elkins of West Virginia. There were others, all reliable — some, like Knox, outstanding men; some, like Hale, expert parliamentarians. There were also among the Democrats those who regularly resisted any reform and others, bound by quixotic tradition confounded with visions of miscegenation, who could be made to shy at any extension of the federal executive power. These were less reliable. Yet Aldrich in the past by prestige and by persuasion had combined these parts into a solid phalanx to front, unbudging, the bills that carried change.

Aldrich, disingenuous, moved quietly to bring the Hepburn Bill with its objectionable clause on rates into the arena where he and his allies had long had their way. While the measure lay before the Committee on Interstate and Foreign Commerce he labored at a disadvantage. There, with few exceptions, his trusted assistants had no seat. There Roosevelt's friends, making the President's moderation their own, seemed capable by co-operation with the Democratic committeemen of carrying crucial votes. There Jonathan Dolliver, the junior senator from Iowa, then beginning the progressive period of his career, ably pleaded the case of the Administration. Dolliver's continuing intimacy with Roosevelt and Moody made him as informed as he was ardent. If Dolliver could with the Democrats model the bill to Roosevelt's satisfaction and then bring it out of committee as a party measure, he would have thereafter a tactical advantage. In these parts, Aldrich did not try to shape the bill in committee. He could not have persuaded a majority to go his way, but he could and did persuade a majority to ease his way. Seeming to yield, disarming Dolliver, Aldrich permitted the Hepburn Bill to be reported unamended. Then, supported by Democratic votes on which Dolliver had counted, he secured a motion reserving to each committee member the right to propose amendments from the floor. The issue, still unresolved, was now before the whole Senate.

The same Democratic votes sustained Aldrich's next move. Had Dolliver, as he expected, been designated to guide the measure on the floor, he would still have been an asset to the President and the bill might still have been presented as the party's. Almost the senator from Iowa could see the "Hepburn-Dolliver Act" engraved in history. The Democrats, however, desiring some credit for regulating railroads, preferred that half that title belong to them. This preference Aldrich exploited. He had won the Democrats in the committee to reporting the bill for amendment from the floor by arranging to name as its floor leader one of their party, Benjamin Tillman of South Carolina. With that serpent-tongued agrarian as its guide, the bill could not be labeled "Republican." For Dolliver this was a staggering personal blow; for Aldrich, a beguiling triumph; for Roosevelt, an embarrassing problem in communication. The President and Tillman had long loathed each other. Only recently the senator had made one of his calculated, insulting attacks on Roosevelt's character. For years they had not spoken. Now Aldrich had forced them either to co-operate or to endanger the policy they both espoused. Whatever their course, furthermore, Aldrich had moved the bill into a position where he and his collaborators had an excellent chance of neutralizing it by amendment. "Aldrich," Roosevelt concluded irritably, had "completely lost both his head and his temper." The President had lost the first round.

Well before the Hepburn Bill reached the Senate, Aldrich and his associates had determined on the nature of their attack. Perhaps out of deference to the electorate, they refrained from a direct assault on the maximum rate clause. Instead, they concentrated on amendments by which they intended to endow the judiciary, the least mobile of the branches of government, with the authority to nullify and to delay the rate rulings of the I.C.C. In behalf of these amendments they debated not the economics of rate making or the proprieties of privilege, but the constitutionality of the regulatory process, the orderly system that the President proposed to create.

Roosevelt had noted with care that the I.C.C. or a substitute commission "should be made unequivocally administrative." To an administrative body as opposed to an executive department, Congress could, he believed, within the meaning of the Constitution on the separation of powers, delegate the authority to fix maximum rates. This has become a commonplace assumption, the basis of a proliferation of alphabet agencies, but in 1906 men of disinterested conviction as well as those who were sheer obstructionists questioned the legality of combining in one body the quasi-legislative power of determining rates, even maximum rates, the quasi-judicial authority of deciding upon the validity of rates, and the quasi-executive function of investigation and enforcement. The unsuccessful Esch-Townsend Bill of 1905, attempting to resolve this constitutional difficulty, had included a clause, briefly resuscitated in 1910 by the Mann-Elkins Act, establishing a special court of commerce to review the rate decisions of the I.C.C. The Hepburn Bill as it emerged from the House, however, made no similar provision. Dodging the whole issue of judicial review, it said nothing at all about jurisdiction in cases arising under it.

On the question of judicial review, the proponents and the opponents of Roosevelt's program drew their lines. Contrasted to the large and varied significance of the whole railroad measure, this deployment seems at first almost chicane. Yet since the debates on Hamilton's reports, American legislators had persisted in clothing their differences in constitutional terms. Nor, in the case of the Hepburn Bill, was this lawyers' legacy meaningless. Roosevelt envisioned a new kind of federal executive power to control the complex processes of an industrialized state. He anticipated the methods of the future. His opponents in the Senate, seeking to perpetuate the method or lack of method of the past, relied upon the prevailing dicta of the American courts to prevent the executive from interfering in the day-by-day operations of American business. In government based on law, this was in 1906 still a legal as well as an economic issue. Both sides assiduously spoke the Constitution fair.

The President by no means denied the right of judicial review. He did not believe that any legislation could "prevent . . . . an appeal" from a ruling of the I.C.C. "The courts will retain, and should retain, no matter what the Legislature does," he had asserted, "the power to interfere and upset any action that is confiscatory in its nature." Yet Roosevelt also preferred that judicial review should be limited essentially to procedural questions — to a determination, in any mooted case, of whether the commission's method of reaching the decision had been fair to the carrier. His opponents, on the other hand, hoped to emasculate his program by providing explicitly for broad judicial reinterpretation of the facts of each case. This, as Jonathan Dolliver pointed out, would have given the courts, considered friendly by the railroads, rather than the commission, which the railroads feared, the real authority over rates.

By its reticence on the matter, the House's version of the Hepburn Bill left to the courts themselves the determination of the scope of review. Roosevelt expressed his satisfaction with this evasion. Attorney General Moody, however, advised him that the measure, in order to pass the test of constitutionality, needed an amendment affirming the right of the railroads to have the courts review the commission's decisions. Roosevelt then considered it only desirable but not essential that the bill provide narrow review. As he began negotiations with the leaders of the Senate, he sought not a limitation to procedural review but only an ambiguous declaration, consonant with the evasion in the unamended version, of the right of review.

Inherent in, but in Roosevelt's opinion subordinate to, the problem of the scope of judicial review was the question of the time at which the rate decisions of the I.C.C. should become effective. Roosevelt had asked that they take effect "immediately," a stipulation the Hepburn Bill fulfilled to his satisfaction by making them effective in thirty days. But if the railroads took to court a decision of the commission, the long process of litigation would postpone indefinitely the application of the revised maximum rate. The House had avoided this problem. In the Senate, while the friends of the railroads wanted just such a delay, the advocates of regulation endeavored to construct some amendment that would prevent the use of injunctions to suspend, pending the outcome of litigation, the rulings of the commission. Roosevelt when debate began preferred, but, as on the question of narrow review, did not insist, that the use of injunctions be restricted.

Against the President's moderate, almost uncertain, position the prorailroad senators launched an offensive. Philander Chase Knox, who had while Attorney General seemed to endorse Roosevelt's program, refused in a conference with Moody to reach an agreement on an amendment pertaining to judicial review. Moody's draft, supported by the President, protected the constitutionality of the Hepburn Bill without increasing the appellate jurisdiction of the courts. This was not enough for Knox. In conference he stated that he preferred the House's bill to Moody's amendment. To the Senate he proposed in February that the courts pass on the "lawfulness" of the commission's orders — a term Moody considered so vague as to invite continuing litigation on the economic details of each rate order and their constitutional implications. Knox's broad definition of review, carrying as it did the prestige of its author, provided in compelling form precisely the objective of Aldrich and his allies. To graft upon the Hepburn Bill Knox's amendment or one just like it, Aldrich had maneuvered the measure out of committee and onto the floor.

Roosevelt, while Aldrich deployed, had not been idle. From the time the Hepburn Bill reached the Senate, even as it lay in committee, the President had begun to confer with his Republican associates about amendments. Like Aldrich, he had able collaborators. Most helpful of these were William B. Allison of Iowa and John C. Spooner of Wisconsin who, in other years, had with Aldrich and the now deceased O. H. Platt composed the Senate's inner council of control. Allison, of that Four the most sensitive to the tolerances of public opinion and the most skillful negotiator, "rendered," Roosevelt later recalled, "unwearied and invaluable service in the actual, and indispensable, working out of legislative business. . . . It was a pleasure to work with [him]." Spooner, scarcely less gifted, had a large personal stake in the satisfactory resolution of the problem of regulation, for his home bastion rattled before the guerrillas of the insurgent La Follette. Allison and Spooner brought with them a loyal corps — Nelson of Minnesota, Long of Kansas, Dolliver, and lesser western Republican veterans for whom freight rates had assumed pressing political importance. The President could also rely upon, though he would not confide in, La Follette, Beveridge, Borah, Clapp, Bourne — the intense Republican left. Could these men clearly demonstrate their strength, others in the party, like Henry Cabot Lodge, would reluctantly go their way. Finally, there were the Bryan Democrats, Tillman, Bailey of Texas, and a few more cautious in thought and less erratic in deportment who would probably, as Williams had in the House, damn Roosevelt's bill but give it their votes.

So positioned, Roosevelt planned at first to carry the bill by sponsoring amendments which would attract the Republican center without alienating the bipartisan left. Throughout February and much of March, while the bill lay in committee, he sought only to perpetuate explicitly the ambiguities implicit in the House's version. The plan seemed feasible so long as the committee might fashion a party measure. But Aldrich's coup, preventing this, also permitted the senator to vitiate Roosevelt's influence with the uncertain. Naturally, like Aldrich, disposed to trust the judiciary to brake change, the Republican center, relieved of party discipline, now looked more favorably on broad review. Tillman as floor leader for the bill was scarcely fit by temperament or inclination to dissuade them. The President, consequently, had to adjust his strategy to Aldrich's *démarche*.

Roosevelt acted at once. As his personal, unofficial representative in the Senate he selected Allison, who could reach and convince a larger number of Republicans than could have any other possible agent. He arranged also to communicate with Tillman through ex-Senator William E. Chandler, a mutual friend and advocate of regulation. By this clumsy device, with Tillman's help and through Allison's negotiations, Roosevelt then set out to construct a new coalition. "Inasmuch as the Republican leaders have tried to betray me . . . . ," he explained, "I am now trying to see if I cannot get . . . [the bill] through in the form I want by the aid of some fifteen or twenty

Republicans added to most of the Democrats." For this purpose, involving as it did both the enthusiasm of Tillman and the loyalty of Allison, Roosevelt had to move cautiously but clearly to the left of his original position.

Largely to Allison fell the difficult task of seeking a formula which would solve the problems of judicial review and the use of injunctions to the satisfaction of the divers partners to the potential coalition. Aldrich, if not surprised, must have been a little hurt to find his friend working the other side of the aisle. The work was tedious. Senator after senator contributed to the dozens of amendments under consideration. Three of these sufficiently reveal the nature of Allison's predicament. That of Senator Long, the well-advertised product of a White House conference held just at the time Roosevelt decided to rely upon a coalition, prevented, according to the consensus of the Senate, judicial reconsideration of the facts of a case. In endorsing it, the President, no longer equivocal, won the favor of the coalition's Republicans and populist Democrats. Yet this was not enough. Senator Bailey of Texas, Tillman's closest associate, and other persistent Jeffersonians opposed the amendment, as Aldrich expected they would, because it seemed to them an unwarranted extension of executive power. Both Tillman and Bailey, moreover, considered the injunction issue more important than judicial review. The Texan had introduced an amendment, endorsed by most Democrats, which deprived the courts of authority to issue temporary writs suspending rate orders. Although this proposal effectively prevented delay in the application of rate rulings, it seemed to Roosevelt and his harassed lieutenants to be clearly unconstitutional. As negotiations proceeded, the President feared that Aldrich might adopt Bailey's plan or any of several like it in order with Democratic support to write a law that the courts would promptly nullify. Roosevelt and Allison therefore sponsored as an alternative an amendment drafted by Spooner. It provided that whenever a court suspended a rate order the amount in dispute between the carrier and the commission should be placed in escrow pending the outcome of litigation. Spooner's plan at once prevented confiscation of railroad property without due process of law, protected the shippers, and eliminated any advantage for the railroad in seeking litigation simply to cause delay.

Had Roosevelt and Allison been dealing only with resilient men, such ingenuity as Spooner's might, in time, have permitted them to devise a winning compromise. Bailey, for one, began to trim toward Allison. But a few Republicans and Tillman Democrats remained so adamantly for narrow review, many other Democrats so firmly for broad review, that Spooner's promising solution for injunctions never commanded the serious attention of either extreme. Before Allison had a chance to homogenize these stubborn parts, Aldrich precipitated crisis. He, too, had been active across the aisle. On April 18, as he predicted, the Democratic caucus refused to follow Tillman and Bailey. Roosevelt's attempt at coalition had failed.

Aldrich, the second round his, doubtless hoped that Roosevelt would either capitulate or, as he had a few weeks earlier, move further left. The President could have consolidated a noisy defense by throwing in his lot with the La Follette Republicans and Tillman Democrats. He could with them have swelled the rising voices of protest. He might, by such a move, have earned a popularity beyond even that already his. But he would have lost his bill. Seeing this as clearly as did Aldrich, Roosevelt had already prepared once more to redeploy.

Six days earlier, sensing defeat, the President had begun to hedge. If he could not win with Tillman, he might still win on his own original terms without the Democrats. "I am not at all sure," he then wrote Allison, "but that the easy way will be to come right back to the bill as it passed the House, and with very few unimportant amendments to pass it as it stands." On April 22 Roosevelt told Knox, again his confidant, that this opinion was "evidently gaining ground." Indeed it was, for Nelson Aldrich turned toward Roosevelt after the Democrats turned away. Aldrich, Knox, and Hale — the leaders of the President's Republican opposition — by early May ceased to insist on an explicit statement for broad review. Perhaps Aldrich became impatient with the continuing delay in the work of the Senate brought about by the ever-lasting debate on regulation. Perhaps he decided that Republican solidarity was more important than Roosevelt's purpose was dangerous. Probably, however, he saw that he had miscalculated. When Roosevelt, refusing to list with the left, reverted doggedly to the ambiguous center where he had first stood, he impelled Tillman, La Follette, and their likes, his erstwhile allies, into embittered opposition. Their protestations, couched in their inevitable vocabulary of revolt, attested to the safe reasonableness Roosevelt had ever claimed as his own. The uncertain minds of the wavering Republican center might now hear Allison out — might now, as Allison and Spooner had, see in Roosevelt safety. By some new alignment, like that he had hoped Dolliver would muster, with time the President in *Thermidor* might triumph. At least, so Aldrich may have reasoned. In any case he retreated.

Aldrich's friendly biographer, overlooking this retreat, has maintained that the senator won his fight. He drafted, it is alleged, the amendment which, introduced by Allison, won a majority vote and thereby secured the enactment of the Hepburn Bill. Whether or not Aldrich drafted it, Allison's amendment, leaving the bill in effect as the House had written it, gave Roosevelt what he had started out to get. The authorship of the amendment, like the working of Aldrich's mind, remains obscure. Whoever wrote it, Allison guided it. His activities in the two weeks following the Democratic caucus may be accurately surmised. Leaving no records, the "unwearied and invaluable" senator from Iowa, camped in the cloakroom where he excelled, had fashioned for the President a compromise that satisfied enough Republicans to save the bill.

The Allison amendment covered both judicial review and the use of injunctions. With purposeful obscurity, it granted jurisdiction in cases arising under the Hepburn Act to the circuit courts but left the definition of the scope of review to the courts. In a flood of oratory over the meaning of the amendment, each senator interpreted it to suit himself and his constituents. Both sides claimed victory. In so far as the amendment was described as a victory for either narrow or broad review, the claims were nonsense. The question of review remained in May as unsettled as it had been in February. Roosevelt had then asked for no more. Ultimately the Supreme Court, which he trusted so little, in the first decision involving rate rulings made his preference law by refusing to review the facts of the case.

The Allison amendment did affirmatively settle the matter of injunctions by empowering the courts to "enjoin, set aside, annul, or suspend any order" of the I.C.C. It also prescribed that no injunction restraining such orders should be granted without five days' notice to the commission, and that appeals from the orders of the I.C.C. were to go directly to the Supreme Court with the calendar priorities of antitrust cases. The amendment did not, however, specify the grounds for suspension or establish an escrow scheme such as that Spooner had proposed. There remained, consequently, the possibility of considerable delay before rate rulings took effect. Roosevelt had constantly expressed his preference for an arrangement less favorable to the railroads, but he had also continually indicated that he would accept a solution like that of the Allison amendment. On this matter Tillman and Bailey, but neither Aldrich nor Roosevelt, had been defeated.

Roosevelt was "entirely satisfied" with the Allison amendment, he pointed out, because he was "entirely satisfied with the Hepburn bill." The amendment, he informed a less satisfied representative of midwestern shippers, was "only declaratory of what the Hepburn bill must mean, supposing it to be constitutional. . . . I should be glad to get certain [other] amendments . . . . ; but they are not vital, and even without them the Hepburn bill with the Allison amendment contains practically exactly what I have both originally and always since asked for."

Characteristically, Roosevelt overstated his case. "Always since" did not apply, for in his maneuvers of late March and April, although only at that time, the President had asked for more. Tillman and Bailey, who had joined him then, with rankling disappointment attacked him for returning to what he had originally requested. Their attacks, repeated by Chandler and La Follette, have persuaded two generations that Roosevelt, irresolute and insincere, deserting his friends, yielding to Aldrich, lost the battle for regulation. Surely his detractors felt this, but they erred. Roosevelt had made overtures to Tillman and Bailey only for tactical reasons. He had, temporarily and for parliamentary support, enlarged his earlier demands. When this did not produce sufficient support, he reverted for tactical reasons to his first position. In so doing he deserted his temporary allies, but he did not compromise his policy. Tillman and Bailey, proud veterans of the Senate, perhaps resented most the knowledge that they had been used. Doubtless their pain gave Aldrich, who had made Roosevelt woo them and leave them, some amused satisfaction.

His objective attained, Roosevelt exulted. "No given measure and no given set of measures," he believed, "will work a perfect cure for any serious evil; and the insistence upon having only the perfect cure often results in securing no betterment whatever." The Hepburn Act was not perfect. But, Roosevelt maintained, it represented "the longest step ever yet taken in the direction of solving the railway rate problem." This was a fair assessment. With his clear perception of political situations, Roosevelt had set the highest practicable goal. By his mastery of political devices, in contest with another master, he had reached it. The Senate, in the end, supplied the federal executive with authority beyond any antecedent definition to mitigate the maladjustments of a growing industrial society.

The Hepburn Act endowed the Interstate Commerce Commission with power commensurate with its task. By informed, expert decisions, it could at last alter the artificial configurations of a market that had long since ceased, in the classic sense, to be free. The courts inexpertly had judged transportation by criteria which, however precious in jurisprudence, bore little relation to the economics of the process. Released from the inhibition of judicial reinterpretations (the bond that Aldrich had sought to supply), endowed with weapons the carriers respected, the I.C.C. began to develop after 1906 the techniques of effective supervision. The need for further change of course remained. But the Hepburn Act provided the precedent, accepted by the courts and enlarged by later Congresses, by which federal regulatory agencies have promoted the national welfare. Now vastly ramified, government by administrative commission remains, though somewhat shabby, a useful part of American political arrangements.

For a troubled people in a complex time perhaps only the executive could have become steward. Aldrich, in that case, fought history and Roosevelt only accelerated what no man could have prevented. But Roosevelt's reputation rests securely even in acceleration, for the inevitable sometimes takes too long, and he knew just what he did. For an orderly administrative system, for the right of efficient federal controls, for, in short, the positive government for the general good of an industrial society, he mobilized in a crucial first skirmish the full powers of his office. And he won.

APPENDIX III

SPECIAL MESSAGE OF THE PRESIDENT OF THE UNITED STATES

Communicated to the Two Houses of Congress on January 31, 1908

(First Session of the Sixtieth Congress)[1]

To the Senate and House of Representatives:

The recent decision of the Supreme Court in regard to the employers' liability act, the experience of the Interstate Commerce Commission and of the Department of Justice in enforcing the interstate commerce and antitrust laws, and the gravely significant attitude toward the law and its administration recently adopted by certain heads of great corporations, render it desirable that there should be additional legislation as regards certain of the relations between labor and capital, and between the great corporations and the public.

The Supreme Court has decided the employers' liability law to be unconstitutional because its terms apply to employees engaged wholly in intrastate commerce as well as to employees engaged in interstate commerce. By a substantial majority the Court holds that the Congress has power to deal with the question in so far as interstate commerce is concerned.

As regards the employers' liability law, I advocate its immediate reenactment, limiting its scope so that it shall apply only to the class of cases as to which the Court says it can constitutionally apply, but strengthening its provisions within this scope. Interstate employment being thus covered by an adequate national law, the field of intrastate employment will be left to the action of the several States. With this clear definition of responsibility the States will undoubtedly give to the performance of their duty within their field the consideration the importance of the subject demands.

I also very urgently advise that a comprehensive act be passed providing for compensation by the Government to all employees injured in the Government service. Under the present law an injured workman in the employment of the Government has no remedy, and the entire burden of the accident falls on the helpless man, his wife, and his young children. This is an outrage. It is a matter of humiliation to the Nation that there should not be on our statute books provision to meet and partially to atone for cruel mis-

[1] This message was published with appendices under the above title by the Government Printing Office in 1908. For its significance, see No. 4579, note 1.

1572

fortune when it comes upon a man through no fault of his own while faithfully serving the public. In no other prominent industrial country in the world could such gross injustice occur; for almost all civilized nations have enacted legislation embodying the complete recognition of the principle which places the entire trade risk for industrial accidents (excluding, of course, accidents due to willful misconduct by the employee) on the industry as represented by the employer, which in this case is the Government. In all these countries the principle applies to the Government just as much as to the private employer. Under no circumstances should the injured employee or his surviving dependents be required to bring suit against the Government, nor should there be the requirement that in order to insure recovery negligence in some form on the part of the Government should be shown. Our proposition is not to confer a right of action upon the Government employee, but to secure him suitable provision against injuries received in the course of his employment. The burden of the trade risk should be placed upon the Government. Exactly as the workingman is entitled to his wages, so he should be entitled to indemnity for the injuries sustained in the natural course of his labor. The rates of compensation and the regulations for its payment should be specified in the law, and the machinery for determining the amount to be paid should in each case be provided in such manner that the employee is properly represented without expense to him. In other words, the compensation should be paid automatically, while the application of the law in the first instance should be vested in the Department of Commerce and Labor. The law should apply to all laborers, mechanics, and other civilian employees of the Government of the United States, including those in the service of the Panama Canal Commission and of the insular governments.

The same broad principle which should apply to the Government should ultimately be made applicable to all private employers. Where the Nation has the power it should enact laws to this effect. Where the States alone have the power they should enact the laws. It is to be observed that an employers' liability law does not really mean mulcting employers in damages. It merely throws upon the employer the burden of accident insurance against injuries which are sure to occur. It requires him either to bear or to distribute through insurance the loss which can readily be borne when distributed, but which, if undistributed, bears with frightful hardship upon the unfortunate victim of accident. In theory, if wages were always freely and fairly adjusted, they would always include an allowance as against the risk of injury, just as certainly as the rate of interest for money includes an allowance for insurance against the risk of loss. In theory, if employees were all experienced business men, they would employ that part of their wages which is received because of the risk of injury to secure accident insurance. But as a matter of fact, it is not practical to expect that this will be done by the great body of employees. An employers' liability law makes it certain that it will be done, in effect, by the employer, and it will ultimately impose no real additional burden upon him.

There is a special bill to which I call your attention. Secretary Taft has urgently recommended the immediate passage of a law providing for compensation to employees of the Government injured in the work of the Isthmian Canal, and that $100,000 be appropriated for this purpose each year. I earnestly hope this will be done; and that a special bill be passed covering the case of Yardmaster Banton, who was injured nearly two years ago while doing his duty. He is now helpless to support his wife and his three little boys.

I again call your attention to the need of some action in connection with the abuse of injunctions in labor cases. As regards the rights and wrongs of labor and capital, from blacklisting to boycotting, the whole subject is covered in admirable fashion by the report of the Anthracite Coal Strike Commission, which report should serve as a chart for the guidance of both legislative and executive officers. As regards injunctions, I can do little but repeat what I have said in my last message to the Congress. Even though it were possible, I should consider it most unwise to abolish the use of the process of injunction. It is necessary in order that the courts may maintain their own dignity and in order that they may in effective manner check disorder and violence. The judge who uses it cautiously and conservatively, but who, when the need arises, uses it fearlessly, confers the greatest service upon our people, and his preeminent usefulness as a public servant should be heartily recognized. But there is no question in my mind that it has sometimes been used heedlessly and unjustly, and that some of the injunctions issued inflict grave and occasionally irreparable wrong upon those enjoined.

It is all wrong to use the injunction to prevent the entirely proper and legitimate actions of labor organizations in their struggle for industrial betterment, or under the guise of protecting property rights unwarrantably to invade the fundamental rights of the individual. It is futile to concede, as we all do, the right and the necessity of organized effort on the part of wage-earners and yet by injunctive process to forbid peaceable action to accomplish the lawful objects for which they are organized and upon which their success depends. The fact that the punishment for the violation of an injunction must, to make the order effective, necessarily be summary and without the intervention of a jury makes its issuance in doubtful cases a dangerous practice, and in itself furnishes a reason why the process should be surrounded with safeguards to protect individuals against being enjoined from exercising their proper rights. Reasonable notice should be given the adverse party.

This matter is daily becoming of graver importance and I can not too urgently recommend that the Congress give careful consideration to the subject. If some way of remedying the abuses is not found the feeling of indignation against them among large numbers of our citizens will tend to grow so extreme as to produce a revolt against the whole use of the process of injunction. The ultra-conservatives who object to cutting out the abuses will do well to remember that if the popular feeling does become strong many of those upon whom they rely to defend them will be the first to turn against them. Men of property can not afford to trust to anything save the spirit of justice and fair play; for those very public men who, while it is to their interest, defend all the abuses committed by capital and pose as the champions of conservatism, will, the moment they think their interest changes, take the lead in just such a matter as this and pander to what they esteem popular feeling by endeavoring, for instance, effectively to destroy the power of the courts in matters of injunction; and will even seek to render nugatory the power to punish for contempt, upon which power the very existence of the orderly administration of justice depends.

It is my purpose as soon as may be to submit some further recommendations in reference to our laws regulating labor conditions within the sphere of Federal authority. A very recent decision of the Supreme Court of the United States rendered since this message was written, in the case of Adair v. United States, seemingly of far-reaching import and of very serious probable consequences, has modified the previously entertained views on the powers of the Congress in the premises to such a degree as to make necessary careful consideration of the opinions therein filed before it is possible definitely to decide in what way to call the matter to your attention.

Not only should there be action on certain laws affecting wage-earners; there should also be such action on laws better to secure control over the great business concerns engaged in interstate commerce, and especially over the great common carriers. The Interstate Commerce Commission should be empowered to pass upon any rate or practice on its own initiative. Moreover, it should be provided that whenever the Commission has reason to believe that a proposed advance in a rate ought not to be made without investigation, it should have authority to issue an order prohibiting the advance pending examination by the Commission.

I would not be understood as expressing an opinion that any or even a majority of these advances are improper. Many of the rates in this country have been abnormally low. The operating expenses of our railroads, notably the wages paid railroad employees, have greatly increased. These and other causes may in any given case justify an advance in rates, and if so the advance should be permitted and approved. But there may be, and doubtless are, cases where this is not true; and our law should be so framed that the Government, as the representative of the whole people, can protect the individual against unlawful exaction for the use of these public highways. The Interstate Commerce Commission should be provided with the means to make a physical valuation of any road as to which it deems this valuation necessary. In some form the Federal Government should exercise supervision over the financial operations of our interstate railroads. In no other way can justice be done between the private owners of those properties and the public which pay their charges. When once an inflated capitalization has gone upon the market and has become fixed in value, its existence must be recognized. As a practical matter it is then often absolutely necessary to take account of the thousands of innocent stockholders who have purchased their stock in good faith. The usual result of such inflation is therefore to impose upon the public an unnecessary but everlasting tax, while the innocent purchasers of the stock are also harmed and only a few speculators are benefited. Such wrongs when once accomplished can with difficulty be undone; but they can be prevented with safety and with justice. When combinations of interstate railways must obtain Government sanction; when it is no longer possible for an interstate railway to issue stock or bonds, save in the manner approved by the Federal Government; when that Government makes sure that the proceeds of every stock and bond issue go into the improvement of the property and not the enrichment of some individual or syndicate; when, whenever it becomes material for guidance in the regulative action of the Government, the physical value of one of these properties is determined and made known—there will be eliminated from railroad securities that element of uncertainty which lends to them their speculative quality and which has contributed much to the financial stress of the recent past.

I think that the Federal Government must also assume a certain measure of control over the physical operation of railways in the handling of interstate traffic. The Commission now has authority to establish through routes and joint rates. In order to make this provision effective and in order to promote in times of necessity the proper movement of traffic, I think it must also have authority to determine the conditions upon which cars shall be interchanged between different interstate railways. It is also probable that the Commission should have authority, in particular instances, to determine the schedule upon which perishable commodities shall be moved.

In this connection I desire to repeat my recommendation that railways be permitted to form traffic associations for the purpose of conferring about and agreeing upon rates, regulations, and practices affecting interstate business in which the members of the association are mutually interested. This does not mean that they should be given the right to pool their earnings or their traffic. The law requires that rates shall be so adjusted as not to discriminate between individuals, localities, or different species of traffic. Ordinarily, rates by all competing lines must be the same. As applied to practical conditions, the railway operations of this country can not be conducted according to law without what is equivalent to conference and agreement. The articles under which such associations operate should be approved by the Commission; all their operations should be open to public inspection; and the rates, regulations, and practices upon which they agree should be subject to disapproval by the Commission.

I urge this last provision with the same earnestness that I do the others.

This country provides its railway facilities by private capital. Those facilities will not be adequate unless the capital employed is assured of just treatment and an adequate return. In fixing the charges of our railroads, I believe that, considering the interests of the public alone, it is better to allow too liberal rather than too scanty earnings, for, otherwise, there is grave danger that our railway development may not keep pace with the demand for transportation. But the fundamental idea that these railways are public highways must be recognized, and they must be open to the whole public upon equal terms and upon reasonable terms.

In reference to the Sherman antitrust law, I repeat the recommendations made in my message at the opening of the present Congress, as well as in my message to the previous Congress. The attempt in this law to provide in sweeping terms against all combinations of whatever character, if technically in restraint of trade as such restraint has been defined by the courts, must necessarily be either futile or mischievous, and sometimes both. The present law makes some combinations illegal, although they may be useful to the country. On the other hand, as to some huge combinations which are both noxious and illegal, even if the action undertaken against them under the law by the Government is successful, the result may be to work but a minimum benefit to the public. Even though the combination be broken up and a small measure of reform thereby produced, the real good aimed at can not be obtained, for such real good can come only by a thorough and continuing supervision over the acts of the combination in all its parts, so as to prevent stock watering, improper forms of competition, and, in short, wrongdoing generally. The law should correct that portion of the Sherman Act which prohibits all combinations of the character above described, whether they be reasonable or unreasonable; but this should be done only as part of a general scheme to provide for this effective and thoroughgoing supervision by the National Government of all the operations of the big interstate business concerns. Judge Hough, of New York, in his recent decision in the Harriman case, states that the Congress possesses the power to limit the interstate operations of corporations not complying with Federal safeguards against the recurrence of obnoxious practices, and to license those which afford the public adequate security against methods calculated to diminish solvency, and therefore efficiency and economy in interstate transportation. The judge adds that in these matters "the power of Congress is ample, though as yet not fruitful in results." It is very earnestly to be desired that either along the lines the judge indicates, or in some other way equally efficacious, the Congress may exercise the power which he holds it possesses.

Superficially it may seem that the laws, the passage of which I herein again advocate — for I have repeatedly advocated them before — are not connected. But in reality they are connected. Each and every one of these laws, if enacted, would represent part of the campaign against privilege, part of the campaign to make the class of great property holders realize that property has its duties no less than its rights. When the courts guarantee to the employer, as they should, the rights of the employer, and to property the rights of property, they should no less emphatically make it evident that they will exact from property and from the employer the duties which should necessarily accompany these rights; and hitherto our laws have failed in precisely this point of enforcing the performance of duty by the man of property toward the man who works for him, by the man of great wealth, especially if he uses that wealth in corporate form, toward the investor, the wageworker, and the general public. The permanent failure of the man of property to fulfill his obligations would ultimately assure the wresting from him of the privileges which he is entitled to enjoy only if he recognizes the obligations accompanying them. Those who assume or share the responsibility for this failure are rendering but a poor service to the cause which they believe they champion.

I do not know whether it is possible, but if possible, it is certainly desirable, that in connection with measures to restrain stock watering and overcapitalization there should be measures taken to prevent at least the grosser forms of gambling in securities and commodities, such as making large sales of what men do not possess and "cornering" the market. Legitimate purchases of commodities and of stocks and securities for investment have no connection whatever with purchases of stocks or other securities or commodities on a margin for speculative and gambling purposes. There is no moral difference between gambling at cards or in lotteries or on the race track and gambling in the stock market. One method is just as pernicious to the body politic as the other in kind, and in degree the evil worked is far greater. But it is a far more difficult subject with which to deal. The great bulk of the business transacted on the exchanges is not only legitimate, but is necessary to the working of our modern industrial system, and extreme care would have to be taken not to interfere with this business in doing away with the "bucket shop" type of operation. We should study both the successes and the failures of foreign legislators who, notably in Germany, have worked along this line, so as not to do anything harmful. Moreover, there is a special difficulty in dealing with this matter by the Federal Government in a Federal Republic like ours. But if it is possible to devise a way to deal with it the effort should be made, even if only in a cautious and tentative way. It would seem that the Federal Government could at least act by forbidding the use of the mails, telegraph and telephone wires for mere gambling in stocks and futures, just as it does in lottery transactions.

I inclose herewith a statement issued by the Chief of the Bureau of Corporations (Appendix 1) in answer to certain statements (which I also inclose) made by and on behalf of the agents of the Standard Oil Corporation (Appendix 2) and a letter of the Attorney-General (Appendix 3) containing an answer to certain statements, also inclosed, made by the president of the Santa Fe Railway Company (Appendix 4). The Standard Oil Corporation and the railway company have both been found guilty by the courts of criminal misconduct; both have been sentenced to pay heavy fines; and each has issued and published broadcast these statements, asserting their innocence and denouncing as improper the action of the courts and juries in convicting them of guilt. These statements are very elaborate, are very ingenious, and are untruthful in important particulars. The following letter and inclosure from Mr. Heney sufficiently illustrate the methods of the high officials of the Santa Fe and show the utter falsity of their plea of ignorance, the similar plea of the Standard Oil being equally without foundation:

DEPARTMENT OF JUSTICE,
OFFICE OF THE UNITED STATES ATTORNEY,
DISTRICT OF OREGON,
Portland, January 11, 1908.

THE PRESIDENT,
Washington, D. C.

DEAR MR. PRESIDENT: I understand that Mr. Ripley, of the Atchison, Topeka and Santa Fe Railway system, has commented with some severity upon your attitude toward the payment of rebates by certain transcontinental railroads and that he has declared that he personally never knew anything about any rebates being granted by his road. * * * I inclose you herewith copy of a letter from Edward Chambers, general freight traffic manager of the Atchison, Topeka and Santa Fe Railway system, to Mr. G. A. Davidson, auditor of the same company, dated February 27, 1907. * * *

This letter does not deal with interstate shipments, but the constitution of the State of California makes the payment of rebates by railroads a felony, and Mr. Ripley has apparently not been above the commission of crime to secure business. You are at liberty to use this inclosure in any way that you think it can be of service to yourself or the public. * * *

Sincerely, yours,

FRANCIS J. HENEY.

SAN FRANCISCO, *February 27, 1907.*

DEAR SIR: I hand you herewith a file of papers covering the movement of fuel oil shipped by the Associated Oil Company over our line from January 1, 1906, up to and including November 15, 1906.

We agreed with the Associated Oil Co.'s negotiations with Mr. Ripley, Mr. Wells, and myself, that in consideration of their making us a special price on oil for company use, which is covered by a contract, and the further consideration that we would take a certain quantity, they would in turn ship from Bakersfield over our line to San Francisco Bay points a certain minimum number of barrels of fuel oil at rate of 25 cents per barrel from Bakersfield, exclusive of the switching charge.

These statements cover the movement, except that they have included Stockton, which is not correct, as it is not a bay point and could not be reached as conveniently by water. We have paid them on account of this movement $7,239 which should be deducted from the total of movement shown in the attached papers.

I wish you would arrange to make up a statement, check the same, and refund to the Associated Oil Company down to the basis of 25 cents per barrel from Bakersfield where they are the shippers, regardless of who is consignee, as all their fuel oil is sold delivered. The reason for making this deal in addition to what I have stated, is that the Associated Oil Company have their own boats and carry oil from fields controlled by themselves along the coast near San Luis Obispo to San Francisco at a much lower cost than the special rate we have made them and in competition with the Union Oil Company and the Standard Oil Company, it was necessary for them to sell at the San Francisco Bay points on the basis of the cost of water transportation from the coast fields. They figured they could only afford to pay us the 25 cents per barrel if by doing this they sold our company a certain amount of fuel oil, otherwise the business covered by the attached papers would have come in by boat from the coast fields.

I am writing this up completely so that there may be in the papers a history of the reasons why this arrangement was made. I wish you would go ahead and make the adjustment as soon as possible, as the Associated Oil Company are very anxious to have the matter closed up. The arrangement was canceled on November 15th at a conference between Mr. Ripley, Mr. Wells, Mr. Porter, and myself.

> Yours, truly,   EDWARD CHAMBERS.

SHIPMENTS-ASSOCIATED OIL COMPANY,
   Mr. G. A. DAVIDSON,
     Auditor, Los Angeles.

The attacks by these great corporations on the Administration's actions have been given a wide circulation throughout the country, in the newspapers and otherwise, by those writers and speakers who, consciously or unconsciously, act as the representatives of predatory wealth — of the wealth accumulated on a giant scale by all forms of iniquity, ranging from the oppression of wageworkers to unfair and unwholesome methods of crushing out competition, and to defrauding the public by stock jobbing and the manipulation of securities. Certain wealthy men of this stamp, whose conduct should be abhorrent to every man of ordinarily decent conscience, and who commit the hideous wrong of teaching our young men that phenomenal business success must ordinarily be based on dishonesty, have during the last few months made it apparent that they have banded together to work for a reaction. Their endeavor is to overthrow and discredit all who honestly administer the law, to prevent any additional legislation which would check and restrain them, and to secure if possible a freedom from all restraint which will permit every unscrupulous wrongdoer to do what he wishes unchecked provided he has enough money. The only way to counteract the movement in which these men are engaged is to make clear to the public just what they have done in the past and just what they are seeking to accomplish in the present.

The Administration and those who support its views are not only not engaged in an assault on property, but are strenuous upholders of the rights of property. The wise attitude to take is admirably stated by Governor Fort, of New Jersey, in his recent inaugural address; the principles which he upholds as regards the State being of course identical with those which should obtain as regards the Nation.

"Just and fair regulation can only be objected to by those misconceiving the rights of the State. The State grants all corporate powers to its railways and other public utility corporations, and may not only modify, but repeal all charters and charter privileges it confers. It may, therefore, impose conditions upon their operation at its pleasure. Of course in the doing of these things, it should act wisely and with conservatism, protecting all vested rights of property and the interests of the innocent holders of the securities of existing *quasi*-public corporations. Regulation, therefore, upon a wise basis, of the operation of these public utilities companies, including the fixing of rates and public charges, upon complaint and subject to court review, should be intrusted to a proper board, as well as the right to regulate the output of stock and the bonded issues of such corporations. If this were done, it would inure to the benefit of the people and the companies, for it would fix the value of such securities, and act as a guaranty against their depreciation. Under such a law, the holders of existing securities would find them protected, and new securities offered would have the confidence of the people, because of the guaranty of the State that they were only issued for extensions or betterments and upon some basis of the cost of such extensions or betterments. It is difficult to suggest any legislation that would give greater confidence to the public and investors than a wise public utilities bill; and the mere suggestion of its enactment should cause this class of security holders to feel that their holdings were strengthened, and that the State was about to aid the managers of its public utility corporations to conserve their corporate property for the public benefit and for the protection of invested capital. * * *

"The time has come for the strict supervision of these great corporations and the limitation of their stock and bond issues under some proper public official. It will make for conservatism, and strengthen the companies doing a legitimate business, and eliminate, let us hope, those which are merely speculative in character and organized simply to catch the unsuspecting or credulous investor. Corporations have come in our business world to remain for all time. Corporate methods are the most satisfactory for business purposes in many cases. Every business or enterprise honestly incorporated should be protected, and the public made to feel confidence in its corporate organization. Capital invested in corporations must be as free from wrongful attack as that invested by individuals, and the State should do everything to foster and protect invested corporate capital and encourage the public in giving to it support and confidence. Nothing will do so much to achieve this desirable result as proper supervision and reasonable control over stock and bond issues, so that overcapitalization will be prevented and the people may know when they buy a share of stock or a bond * * * that the name of the State upon it stands as a guaranty that there is value behind it and reasonable safety in its purchase. The act must make it clear that the intent of the supervision by the Commissioner is not for the purpose of striking at corporate organizations or invested corporate capital, but rather to recognize and protect existing conditions and insure greater safeguards for the future. * * *

"Capital does not go into a State where reprisals are taken or vested interests are injured; it comes only where wise, conservative, safe treatment is assured, and it should be our policy to encourage and secure corporate rights and the best interests of stock and bond holders committed to our legal care."

Under no circumstances would we countenance attacks upon law-abiding property, or do aught but condemn those who hold up rich men as being evil men because of their riches. On the contrary, our whole effort is to insist upon conduct, and neither wealth nor property nor any other class distinction, as being the proper standard by which to judge the actions of men. For the honest man of great wealth we have a hearty regard, just as we have a hearty regard for the honest politician and honest newspaper. But part of the movement to uphold honesty must be a movement to frown on dishonesty. We attack only the corrupt men of wealth, who find in the purchased politician the most efficient instrument of corruption and in the purchased newspaper the most efficient defender of corruption. Our main quarrel is not with these agents and representatives of the interests. They derive their chief power from the great sinister offenders who stand behind them. They are but puppets who move as the strings are pulled. It is not the puppets, but the strong cunning men and the mighty forces working for evil behind and through the puppets, with whom we have to deal. We seek to control law-defying wealth; in the first place to prevent its doing dire evil to the Republic, and in the next place to avoid the vindictive and dreadful radicalism which, if left uncontrolled, it is certain in the end to arouse. Sweeping attacks upon all property, upon all men of means, without regard to whether they do well or ill, would sound the death-knell of the Republic; and such attacks become inevitable if decent citizens permit those rich men whose lives are corrupt and evil to domineer in swollen pride, unchecked and unhindered, over the destinies of this country. We act in no vindictive spirit, and we are no respecters of persons. If a labor union does wrong, we oppose it as firmly as we oppose a corporation which does wrong; and we stand equally stoutly for the rights of the man of wealth and for the rights of the wageworker. We seek to protect the property of every man who acts honestly, of every corporation that represents wealth honestly accumulated and honestly used. We seek to stop wrongdoing, and we desire to punish the wrongdoers only so far as is necessary to achieve this end.

There are ample material rewards for those who serve with fidelity the mammon of unrighteousness; but they are dearly paid for by the people who permit their representatives, whether in public life, in the press, or in the colleges where their young men are taught, to preach and to practice that there is one law for the rich and another for the poor. The amount of money the representatives of certain great moneyed interests are willing to spend can be gauged by their recent publication broadcast throughout the papers of this country, from the Atlantic to the Pacific, of huge advertisements attacking with envenomed bitterness the Administration's policy of warring against successful dishonesty, and by their circulation of pamphlets and books prepared with the same object; while they likewise push the circulation of the writings and speeches of men who, whether because they are misled, or because, seeing the light, they yet are willing to sin against the light, serve these their masters of great wealth to the cost of the plain people. The books and pamphlets, the controlled newspapers, the speeches by public or private men to which I refer, are usually and especially in the interest of the Standard Oil Trust and of certain notorious railroad combinations, but they also defend other individuals and corporations of great wealth that have been guilty of wrongdoing. It is only rarely that the men responsible for the wrongdoing themselves speak or write. Normally they hire others to do their bidding, or find others who will do it without hire. From the railroad-rate law to the pure-food law, every measure for honesty in business that has been passed during the last six years has been opposed by these men on its passage and in its administration with every resource that bitter and unscrupulous craft could suggest and the command of almost unlimited money secure. But for the last year the attack has been made with most bitterness upon the actual administration of the law, especially through the Department of Justice, but also through the Interstate Commerce Commission and the Bureau of Corporations. The extraordinary violence of the assaults upon our policy contained in these speeches, editorials, articles, advertisements, and pamphlets, and the enormous sums of money spent in these various ways, give a fairly accurate measure of the anger and terror which our public actions have caused the corrupt men of vast wealth to feel in the very marrow of their being. The attack is sometimes made openly against us for enforcing the law, and sometimes with a certain cunning, for not trying to enforce it in some other way than that which experience shows to be practical. One of the favorite methods of the latter class of assailant is to attack the Administration for not procuring the imprisonment instead of the fine of offenders under these antitrust laws. The man making this assault is usually either a prominent lawyer or an editor who takes his policy from the financiers and his arguments from their attorneys. If the former, he has defended and advised many wealthy malefactors, and he knows well that, thanks to the advice of lawyers like himself, a certain kind of modern corporation has been turned into an admirable instrument by which to render it well-nigh impossible to get at the head of the corporation, at the man who is really most guilty. When we are able to put the real wrongdoer in prison, this is what we strive to do; this is what we have actually done with some very wealthy criminals, who, moreover, represented that most baneful of all alliances, the alliance between the corruption of organized politics and the corruption of high finance. This is what we have done in the Gaynor and Greene case, in the case of the misapplication of funds in connection with certain great banks in Chicago, in the land-fraud cases, where, as in other cases likewise, neither the highest political position nor the possession of great wealth, has availed to save the offenders from prison. The Federal Government does scourge sin; it does bid sinners fear; for it has put behind the bars with impartial severity, the powerful financier, the powerful politician, the rich land thief, the rich contractor — all, no matter how high their station, against whom criminal misdeeds can be proved. All their wealth and power can not protect them. But it often happens that the effort to imprison a given defendant is certain to be futile, while it is possible to fine him or to fine the corporation of which he is head; so that, in other words, the only way of punishing the wrong is by fining the corporation, unless we are content to proceed personally against the minor agents. The corporation lawyers to whom I refer and their employers are the men mainly responsible for this state of things, and their responsibility is shared with all who ingeniously oppose the passing of just and effective laws, or who fail to execute them when they have been put on the statute books.

Much is said, in these attacks upon the policy of the present Administration, about the rights of "innocent stockholders." That stockholder is not innocent who voluntarily purchases stock in a corporation whose methods and management he knows to be corrupt; and stockholders are bound to try to secure honest management, or else are estopped from complaining about the proceedings the Government finds necessary in order to compel the corporation to obey the law. There has been in the past grave wrong done innocent stockholders by overcapitalization, stock-watering, stock jobbing, stock-manipulation. This we have sought to prevent, first, by exposing the thing done and punishing the offender when any existing law had been violated; second, by recommending the passage of laws which would make unlawful similar practices for the future. The public men, lawyers, and editors who loudly proclaim their sympathy for the "innocent stockholders" when a great law-defying corporation is punished, are the first to protest with frantic vehemence against all efforts by law to put a stop to the practices which are the real and ultimate sources of the damage alike to the stockholders and the public. The apologists of successful dishonesty always declaim against any effort to punish or prevent it, on the ground that any such effort will "unsettle business." It is they who by their acts have unsettled business; and the very men raising this cry spend hundreds of thousands of dollars in securing, by speech, editorial, book, or pamphlet, the defense by misstatements of what they have done; and yet when public servants correct their misstatements by telling the truth they declaim against them for breaking silence, lest "values be depreciated." They have hurt honest business men, honest workingmen, honest farmers; and now they clamor against the truth being told.

The keynote of all these attacks upon the effort to secure honesty in business and in politics is well expressed in brazen protests against any effort for the moral regeneration of the business world, on the ground that it is unnatural, unwarranted, and injurious, and that business panic is the necessary penalty for such effort to secure business honesty. The morality of such a plea is precisely as great as if made on behalf of the men caught in a gambling establishment when that gambling establishment is raided by the police. If such words mean anything they mean that those whose sentiments they represent stand against the effort to bring about a moral regeneration of business which will prevent a repetition of the insurance banking, and street railroad scandals in New York; a repetition of the Chicago and Alton deal; a repetition of the combination between certain professional politicians, certain professional labor leaders, and certain big financiers, from the disgrace of which San Francisco has just been rescued; a repetition of the successful effort by the Standard Oil people to crush out every competitor, to overawe the common carriers, and to establish a monopoly which treats the public with a contempt which the public deserves so long as it permits men of such principles and such sentiments to avow and act on them with impunity. The outcry against stopping dishonest practices among wrongdoers who happen to be wealthy is precisely similar to the outcry raised against every effort for cleanliness and decency in city government, because, forsooth, it will "hurt business." The same outcry is made against the Department of Justice for prosecuting the heads of colossal corporations that has been made against the men who in San Francisco have prosecuted with impartial severity the wrongdoers among business men, public officials, and labor leaders alike. The principle is the same in the two cases. Just as the blackmailer and bribe giver stand on the same evil eminence of infamy, so the man who makes an enormous fortune by corrupting legislatures and municipalities and fleecing his stockholders and the public, stands on the same moral level with the creature who fattens on the blood money of the gambling house and the saloon. Moreover, in the last analysis, both kinds of corruption are far more intimately connected than would at first sight appear; the wrongdoing is at bottom the same. Corrupt business and corrupt politics act and react with ever increasing debasement, one on the other; the corrupt head of a corporation and the corrupt labor leader are both in the same degree the enemies of honest corporations and honest labor unions; the rebate taker, the franchise trafficker, the manipulator of securities, the purveyor and protector of vice, the blackmailing ward boss, the ballot-box stuffer, the demagogue, the mob leader, the hired bully, and mankiller — all alike work at the same web of corruption, and all alike should be abhorred by honest men.

The "business" which is hurt by the movement for honesty is the kind of business which, in the long run, it pays the country to have hurt. It is the kind of business which has tended to make the very name "high finance" a term of scandal to which all honest American men of business should join in putting an end. The special pleaders for business dishonesty, in denouncing the present Administration for enforcing the law against the huge and corrupt corporations which have defied the law, also denounce it for endeavoring to secure sadly needed labor legislation, such as a far-reaching law making employers liable for injuries to their employees. It is meet and fit that the apologists for corrupt wealth should oppose every effort to relieve weak and helpless people from crushing misfortune brought upon them by injury in the business from which they gain a bare livelihood. The burden should be distributed. It is hypocritical baseness to speak of a girl who works in a factory where the dangerous machinery is unprotected as having the "right" freely to contract to expose herself to dangers to life and limb. She has no alternative but to suffer want or else to expose herself to such dangers, and when she loses a hand or is otherwise maimed or disfigured for life, it is a moral wrong that the whole burden of the risk necessarily incidental to the business should be placed with crushing weight upon her weak shoulders, and all who profit by her work escape scot-free. This is what opponents of a just employers' liability law advocate; and it is consistent that they should usually also advocate immunity for those most dangerous members of the criminal class — the criminals of great wealth.

Our opponents have recently been bitterly criticising the two judges referred to in the accompanying communications from the Standard Oil Company and the Santa Fe Railroad for having imposed heavy fines on these two corporations; and yet these same critics of these two judges exhaust themselves in denouncing the most respectful and cautious discussion of the official action of a judge which results in immunity to wealthy and powerful wrongdoers or which renders nugatory a temperate effort to better the conditions of life and work among those of our fellow countrymen whose need is greatest. Most certainly it behooves us all to treat with the utmost respect the high office of judge; and our judges, as a whole, are brave and upright men. Respect for the law must go hand in hand with respect for the judges; and, as a whole, it is true now as in the past that the judges stand in character and service above all other men among their fellow-servants of the public. There is all the greater need that the few who fail in this great office, who fall below this high standard of integrity, of wisdom, of sympathetic understanding and of courage, should have their eyes opened to the needs of their countrymen. A judge who on the bench either truckles to the mob and shrinks from sternly repressing violence and disorder, or bows down before a corporation; who fails to stand up valiantly for the rights of property on the one hand, or on the other by misuse of the process of injunction or by his attitude toward all measures for the betterment of the conditions of labor, makes the wageworker feel with bitterness that the courts are hostile to him; or who fails to realize that all public servants in their several stations must strive to stop the abuses of the criminal rich — such a man performs an even worse service to the body politic than the legislator or executive who goes wrong. The judge who does his full duty well stands higher, and renders a better service to the people, than any other public servant; he is entitled to greater respect; and if he is a true servant of the people, if he is upright, wise and fearless, he will unhesitatingly disregard even the wishes of the people if they conflict with the eternal principles of right as against wrong. He must serve the people; but he must serve his own conscience first. All honor to such a judge; and all honor can not be rendered him if it is rendered equally to his brethren who fall immeasurably below the high ideals for which he stands. Untruthful criticism is wicked at all times, and whoever may be the object; but it is a peculiarly flagrant iniquity when a judge is the object. No man should lightly criticise a judge; no man should, even in his own mind, condemn a judge unless he is sure of the facts. If a judge is assailed for standing against popular folly, and above all for standing against mob violence, all honorable men should rally instantly to his support. Nevertheless if he clearly fails to do his duty by the public in dealing with lawbreaking corporations, lawbreaking men of wealth, he must expect to feel the weight of public opinion; and this is but right, for except in extreme cases this is the only way in which he can be reached at all. No servant of the people has a right to expect to be free from just and honest criticism.

The opponents of the measures we champion single out now one and now another measure for especial attack, and speak as if the movement in which we are engaged was purely economic. It has a large economic side, but it is fundamentally an ethical movement. It is not a movement to be completed in one year, or two or three years; it is a movement which must be persevered in until the spirit which lies behind it sinks deep into the heart and the conscience of the whole people. It is always important to choose the right means to achieve our purpose, but it is even more important to keep this purpose clearly before us; and this purpose is to secure national honesty in business and in politics. We do not subscribe to the cynical belief that dishonesty and unfair dealing are essential to business success, and are to be condoned when the success is moderate and applauded when the success is great. The methods by which the Standard Oil people and those engaged in the other combinations of which I have spoken above have achieved great fortunes can only be justified by the advocacy of a system of morality which would also justify every form of criminality on the part of a labor union, and every form of violence, corruption, and fraud, from murder to bribery and ballot-box stuffing in politics. We are trying to secure equality of opportunity for all; and the struggle for honesty is the same whether it is made on behalf of one set of men or of another. In the interest of the small settlers and landowners, and against the embittered opposition of wealthy owners of huge wandering flocks of sheep, or of corporations desiring to rob the people of coal and timber, we strive to put an end to the theft of public land in the West. When we do this, and protest against the action of all men, whether in public life or in private life, who either take part in or refuse to try to stop such theft, we are really engaged in the same policy as when we endeavor to put a stop to rebates or to prevent the upgrowth of uncontrolled monopolies. Our effort is simply to enforce the principles of common honesty and common sense. It would indeed be ill for the country should there be any halt in our work.

The laws must in the future be administered as they are now being administered, so that the Department of Justice may continue to be, what it now is, in very fact the Department of Justice, where so far as our ability permits justice is meted out with an even hand to great and small, rich and poor, weak and strong. Moreover, there should be no delay in supplementing the laws now on the statute books by the enactment of further legislation as outlined in the message I sent to the Congress on its assembling. Under the existing laws much, very much, has been actually accomplished during the past six years, and it has been shown by actual experience that they can be enforced against the wealthiest corporation and the richest and most power-ful manager or manipulator of that corporation, as rigorously and fearlessly as against the humblest offender. Above all, they have been enforced against the very wrongdoers and agents of wrongdoers who have for so many years gone scot-free and flouted the laws with impunity, against great law-defying corporations of immense wealth, which, until within the last half dozen years, have treated themselves and have expected others to treat them as be-ing beyond and above all possible check from law.

It is especially necessary to secure to the representatives of the National Government full power to deal with the great corporations engaged in inter-state commerce, and above all, with the great interstate common carriers. Our people should clearly recognize that while there are difficulties in any course of conduct to be followed in dealing with these great corporations, these difficulties must be faced, and one of three courses followed.

The first course is to abandon all effort to oversee and control their actions in the interest of the general public and to permit a return to the utter lack of control which would obtain if they were left to the common law. I do not for one moment believe that our people would tolerate this position. The extraordinary growth of modern industrialism has rendered the common law, which grew up under and was adapted to deal with totally different condi-tions, in many respects inadequate to deal with the new conditions. These new conditions make it necessary to shackle cunning as in the past we have shackled force. The vast individual and corporate fortunes, the vast com-binations of capital, which have marked the development of our industrial system, create new conditions, and necessitate a change from the old attitude of the State and the Nation toward the rules regulating the acquisition and untrammeled business use of property, in order both that property may be adequately protected, and that at the same time those who hold it may be prevented from wrongdoing.

The second and third courses are to have the regulation undertaken either by the Nation or by the States. Of course in any event both the National Government and the several State governments must do each its part, and each can do a certain amount that the other can not do, while the only really satisfactory results must be obtained by the representatives of the National and State governments working heartily together within their respective spheres. But in my judgment thoroughgoing and satisfactory control can in the end only be obtained by the action of the National Government, for almost all the corporations of enormous wealth — that is, the corporations which it is especially desirable to control — are engaged in interstate com-merce, and derive their power and their importance not from that portion of their business which is intrastate, but from the interstate business. It is not easy always to decide just where the line of demarcation between the two kinds of business falls. This line must ultimately be drawn by the Federal courts. Much of the effort to secure adequate control of the great corporations by State action has been wise and effective, but much of it has been neither; for when the effort is made to accomplish by the action of the State what can only be accomplished by the action of the Nation, the result can only be disappointment, and in the end the law will probably be declared unconstitutional. So likewise in the national arena, we who believe in the measures herein advocated are hampered and not aided by the extremists who advocate action so violent that it would either be useless or else would cause more mischief than it would remedy.

In a recent letter from a learned judge of the supreme court of one of the Gulf States, the writer speaks as follows:

"In all matters pertaining to interstate commerce the authority of the National Government already exists and does not have to be acquired, and the exercise of this existing authority can be in no sense a usurpation of, or infringement upon, the rights of the States. On the contrary, had the Federal Government given this question more attention in the past and applied a vigorous check to corporate abuses, conditions would now be better, because the States would have had fewer real or imaginary grievances and have had less cause not only to attempt the exercise of the authority reserved to the National Government, but to act without proper moderation in matters peculiarly within their own provinces. The National Government has been remiss in the past, but even at this late day it can solve this problem, and the sooner the National authority is exercised the less apt are the States to take action which will represent encroachment upon the National domain. There is a field of operations for both powers, and plenty alike for National and State governments to do in order to protect both the people and the public utilities. The line of demarcation between Federal and State authority can and should be speedily settled by the Federal courts. The fact that the National Government has omitted to exercise the authority conferred upon it by the interstate commerce clause of the Constitution has made the States restive under what they deem corporate abuses, and in some cases has probably stimulated them to go too far in the attempt to correct these abuses, with the result that all measures which they passed, good or bad, have been held up by the Federal Courts. The necessary equitable and uniform regulation can not be obtained by the separate action of the States, but only by the affirmative action of the National Government."

This is an appeal by a high State judge, alarmed, as good citizens should be alarmed, by conflicts over the matter of jurisdiction, and by the radical action advocated by honest people smarting from a sense of injury received from corporations; which injury the Federal courts forbid the States to try to remedy, while the Federal Government nevertheless refrains from itself taking adequate measures to provide a remedy. It can not too strongly be insisted that the defenders and apologists of the great corporations, who have sought in the past and still seek to prevent adequate action by the Federal Government to control these great corporations, are not only proving false to the people, but are laying up a day of wrath for the great corporations themselves. The Nation will not tolerate an utter lack of control over very wealthy men of enormous power in the industrial, and therefore in the social, lives of all our people, some of whom have shown themselves cynically and brutally indifferent to the interests of the people; and if the Congress does not act, with good tempered and sensible but resolute thoroughness, in cutting out the evils and in providing an effective supervision, the result is certain to be action on the part of the separate States, sometimes wise, sometimes ill-judged and extreme, sometimes unjust and damaging to the railroads or other corporations, more often ineffective from every standpoint, because the Federal courts declare it unconstitutional.

We have just passed through two months of acute financial stress. At any such time it is a sad fact that entirely innocent people suffer from no fault of their own; and everyone must feel the keenest sympathy for the large body of honest business men, of honest investors, of honest wageworkers, who suffer because involved in a crash for which they are in no way responsible. At such a time there is a natural tendency on the part of many men to feel gloomy and frightened at the outlook; but there is no justification for this feeling. There is no nation so absolutely sure of ultimate success as ours. Of course we shall succeed. Our's is a nation of masterful energy, with a continent for its domain, and it feels within its veins the thrill which comes to those who know that they possess the future. We are not cast down by the fear of failure. We are upheld by the confident hope of ultimate triumph. The wrongs that exist are to be corrected; but they in no way justify doubt as to the final outcome, doubt as to the great material prosperity of the future, or of the lofty spiritual life which is to be built upon that prosperity as a foundation. No misdeeds done in the present must be permitted to shroud from our eyes the glorious future of the Nation; but because of this very fact it behooves us never to swerve from our resolute purpose to cut out wrong-doing and uphold what is right.

I do not for a moment believe that the actions of this Administration have brought on business distress; so far as this is due to local and not world-wide causes, and to the actions of any particular individuals, it is due to the specu-lative folly and flagrant dishonesty of a few men of great wealth, who seek to shield themselves from the effects of their own wrongdoing by ascribing its results to the actions of those who have sought to put a stop to the wrong-doing. But if it were true that to cut out rottenness from the body politic meant a momentary check to an unhealthy seeming prosperity, I should not for one moment hesitate to put the knife to the corruption. On behalf of all our people, on behalf no less of the honest man of means than of the honest man who earns each day's livelihood by that day's sweat of his brow, it is necessary to insist upon honesty in business and politics alike, in all walks of life, in big things and in little things; upon just and fair dealing as between man and man. Those who demand this are striving for the right in the spirit of Abraham Lincoln when he said:

"Fondly do we hope, fervently do we pray, that this mighty scourge may speedily pass away. Yet, if God wills that it continue until all the wealth piled by the bondsmen's two hundred and fifty years of unrequited toil shall be sunk, and until every drop of blood drawn with the lash shall be paid by another drawn with the sword, as was said three thousand years ago, so still it must be said, 'The judgments of the Lord are true and righteous altogether.'

"With malice toward none; with charity for all; with firmness in the right, as God gives us to see the right, let us strive on to finish the work we are in."

In the work we of this generation are in, there is, thanks be to the Almighty, no danger of bloodshed and no use for the sword; but there is grave need of those stern qualities shown alike by the men of the North and the men of the South in the dark days when each valiantly battled for the light as it was given each to see the light. Their spirit should be our spirit, as we strive to bring nearer the day when greed and trickery and cunning shall be trampled under feet by those who fight for the righteousness that exalteth a nation.

CHRONOLOGY

September 1, 1905 – March 4, 1909

1905

SEPTEMBER

1 Oyster Bay. Conference with Loomis, Sen. Burnham. Armistice signed by Russia and Japan
2 Oyster Bay
3 Oyster Bay. J. W. Wadsworth at Sagamore Hill
4 Oyster Bay. Callers include Cortelyou, Beveridge, Penfield. Conference with Cooley on civil service regulations in Panama
5 Oyster Bay. Portsmouth Treaty signed. Appointment of Robert Bacon as Assistant Secretary of State
6 Oyster Bay
7 Oyster Bay
8 Oyster Bay. Fairbanks at Sagamore Hill
9 Oyster Bay. Lunch with Takahira, Komura. Dinner with Witte, Baron Rosen
10 Oyster Bay
11 Oyster Bay. Lunch with Panama Canal board of consulting engineers. Callers include L. M. Shaw, John Barrett
12 Oyster Bay
13 Oyster Bay. Lunch with Rosen
14 Oyster Bay
15 Oyster Bay
16 Oyster Bay
17 Oyster Bay
18 Oyster Bay. Conference with members of Chinese Embassy on Chinese boycott. Dinner with Bonapartes
19 Oyster Bay
20 Oyster Bay. Conference with Root, Lodge, Choate
21 Oyster Bay
22 Oyster Bay
23 Oyster Bay
24 Oyster Bay
25 Oyster Bay
26 Oyster Bay. Callers include Gen. Porter, Shonts
27 Oyster Bay
28 Oyster Bay
29 Oyster Bay
30 Morning departure for Washington

OCTOBER

1 Washington. Dinner with Jusserand
2 Washington. Conference on Keep Commission investigations with Pinchot, Garfield, Hitchcock. Conference with Foraker on railroad rebates. Conference with Sen. Burkett on railroad legislation. Callers include Hemenway, Fulton, McCumber, Dick. Dinner with Taft, Root, Garfield
3 Washington. Cabinet meeting on Chinese boycott and beef trust cases. Conference with Cortelyou on postal appointments. Discussion of railroad rate legislation with Rep. Hull. Conference with John Mitchell on coal situation
4 Washington. Conference with Townsend on railroad rate legislation. Conference with Hemenway and Landis on consular appointments. Discussion of naval legislation with Rep. T. S. Butler. Lunch with Meyer. Conference with Dick on Ohio state campaign. Callers include G. M. Bowers, O. J. Ricketts
5 Washington. Railroad rate conference with Townsend. Conferences with Moody, Taft. Lunch with Drs. Rixey, Stokes
6 Washington. Cabinet meeting on Chinese exclusion, meat packing legislation, second Hague conference, and Panama Canal administration. Conference with Townsend. Callers include Rep. Burton
7 Washington. Conference with Bartholdt on Brussels interparliamentary conference. Conference with Rep. Slemp on Virginia politics
8 Washington
9 Washington. Conference on collegiate football with Root and representatives from Yale, Harvard, Princeton. Callers include Aldrich, Heyburn, Bartholdt,

Landis. Reception for Supreme Court Justices

10 Washington. Cabinet meeting on participation of Cabinet members in local campaigns. Conference with Cullom and Rodenburg on tariff revision and railroad rate legislation. Conference with Moody. Lunch with W. J. Calhoun and conference on Venezuela. Callers include L. M. Shaw

11 Washington. Conference with Rep. Hill on Philippines. Callers include Greene, Cooley, delegation of lumbermen

12 Washington. Conference with Rep. Campbell on railroad rate legislation. Conference with Long on Philippines. Conference with Metcalf, Garfield on annual message. Lunch with Knox and Root. Callers include Sen. Proctor

13 Washington. Cabinet meeting on Venezuela. Callers include Boutell, Cooley, Jusserand

14 Washington. Conference with Rep. Curtis on Philippines. Conference with Root, Bacon, Taft. Callers include Reps. Hopkins, Dalzell; Pinchot and Garfield

15 Washington

16 Washington. Conference with Grosvenor on financial legislation. Callers include ex-Sen. McLaurin, Baron Rosen

17 Washington. Conference with S. E. Payne on Philippines. Callers include L. M. Shaw. Executive order giving departmental heads authority to dismiss employees

18 Departure for southern trip with J. C. Greenway, Latta, Rixey and others. Stops at Fredericksburg, Ashland, Va. Speech at Richmond. Evening departure for Raleigh, N. C.

19 Raleigh. Speech on railroads, forestry. Departure for Charlotte, N. C., with stops at Durham, Greensboro, High Point, Salisbury

20 Roswell, Ga. Visit to Bulloch home and breakfast with Sen. Clay. Speech at Atlanta

21 Jacksonville, Fla. Speech on Panama Canal. Evening arrival at St. Augustine

22 St. Augustine. Evening departure for Mobile, Ala.

23 Mobile

24 Tuskegee. Speech at Tuskegee Institute on citizenship. Speeches at Montgomery and Birmingham

25 Little Rock, Ark. Speech on lynching

26 New Orleans, La. Speech and reception. Afternoon departure for Washington on USS *West Virginia*

27 En route Washington

28 En route Washington

29 En route Washington

30 En route Washington

31 Arrival at Washington. Callers include Hitchcock, Cortelyou, Root. Evening conference with Jusserand

NOVEMBER

"Wolf Hunt in Oklahoma" published in *Scribner's Magazine*

1 Washington. Conference with Root. Conference with Takahira. Railroad rate conference with Tawney. Lunch with Jusserand. Callers include C. A. Stillings, Cullom, Knox, Clapp, Leupp, Hitchcock

2 Washington. Conference on railroad rate legislation with Cullom, Dolliver. Callers include Elmer Dover, C. G. Bennett, Bonaparte, Moody, L. M. Shaw, New York Hungarian Club delegation

3 Washington. Cabinet meeting. Railroad rate conference with Fairbanks. Callers include Redfield Proctor. Reception for Prince Louis of Battenberg

4 Washington. Conferences with Adm. Dewey, Depew. Lunch with von Sternberg. Callers include H. S. Tucker. State dinner for Prince Louis of Battenberg

5 Washington. Evening conference with Morton on Equitable Life Assurance Society investigation

6 Washington. Conference with Cullom on Cuban sanitary conditions. Discussion of Russian atrocities with Root, Oscar Straus. Callers include Redfield Proctor. Lunch with Prince Louis of Battenberg. Midnight departure for Oyster Bay to vote

7 Oyster Bay

8 Washington. Conference on Oklahoma statehood with Del. McGuire, C. M. Cade. Discussion of Panama conditions with Rep. Wanger

9 Washington. Conference on Delaware politics with Allee. Callers include Elkins, Spooner, W. D. Bynum

10 Washington. Conference with J. L. McLaurin, Judge Speer on southern politics

11 Washington. Callers include B. T. Washington

12 Washington
13 Washington. Conferences with Knox, Hemenway. Conference with Lauterbach on New York politics. Lunch with B. I. Wheeler, Bonaparte
14 Washington. Cabinet meeting. Callers include Taft, W. A. Smith, Jusserand, L. O. Murray
15 Washington. Conference with T. C. Platt, Barnes on N. Y. appointments. Tariff revision conference with Gov. Douglas and delegation of Massachusetts shoe manufacturers. Callers include Cannon, Susan B. Anthony, Cullom, Curtis.
16 Washington. Conference with Mellen on railroad legislation. Conference with McCumber on pure food legislation. Discussion of life insurance investigation with Dryden. Callers include Hale, Burrows, Cannon, Proctor. James Ford Rhodes, P. B. Stewart at White House
17 Washington. Cabinet meeting. Conference with W. A. Smith on tariff revision. Conference with Taft on railroad legislation. White House dinner including Baron Rosen, Lt. Com. W. S. Sims, Justice Brewer
18 Washington. Callers include Hepburn, Hopkins, Cullom, Cannon
19 Washington
20 Washington. Railroad rate conference with Root, Knox, Cullom, Moody, Hepburn, Prouty, Mann. Conference with Moody, Knox on Pennsylvania politics. Dinner and conference on New York politics with Root, Cortelyou, Gov. Higgins
21 Washington. Discussion of railroad rate and Panama legislation with Kean, Millard, Foster. Callers include Heney. Wedding of Lt. Com. W. S. Sims and Anne Hitchcock
22 Washington. Conference with Heyburn on Idaho appointments. Callers include Foraker, W. Willcox
23 Washington. Conference with Frantz and Leupp on Osage Indian affairs. Callers include M. P. Kinkaid, Curtis
24 Washington. Cabinet meeting. Callers include H. J. Hagerman. Diplomatic reception
25 Washington. Railroad rate conference with Millard. Lunch with Taft, Hitchcock, Moody. Callers include Mayor Walbridge and delegation of St. Louis businessmen. Evening conference with Cockrell on railroads
26 Washington

27 Washington. Conference on New York politics with Root, Olcott. Conference with Curtis on statehood bill. Lunch including Mark Twain, von Sternberg, Moody, Bonaparte. Callers include R. J. Wynne, L. M. Shaw, Cannon. Night conference with Root, Taft, Knox, Garfield
28 Washington. Cabinet meeting. Conference with Dolliver on railroad legislation. Callers include Hinshaw, Millard, Root, Fairbanks, Fulton
29 Washington. Callers include Beveridge, Lacey, Foraker, Root, Bonaparte
30 Morning departure for Albemarle County, Va. Thanksgiving Day with family at Plain Dealing

DECEMBER

1 Albemarle County. Evening return to Washington
2 Princeton, N. J. Army-Navy football game
3 Washington
4 Washington. 59th Congress convenes. Conference on New York politics with Olcott
5 Washington. Cabinet meeting. Annual message to Congress. Conference with Hemenway. Callers include Sens. Morgan, Long, Allison, Pettus; Rep. Williams. N. M. Butler at White House
6 Washington. Conference on Brooklyn appointments with Woodruff, S. E. Payne. Conference with Gorgas on Philippine health conditions. Lunch with Takahira. Callers include Smoot, Crumpacker, Frye, Clapp, Spooner, Flint. Dinner including Baron Hengelmuller, Hale, Lodge, Longworth, Wetmore
7 Washington. Conference with T. C. Platt, R. C. Morris on New York appointments. Callers include Fairbanks, Foraker, Teller, Gallinger, Cockran
8 Washington. Cabinet meeting. Tariff discussion with Dingley. Callers include Foraker, Fulton
9 Washington. Conference with Beveridge on statehood bill. Lunch with Gen. Thomas, Seth Bullock, W. H. H. Llewellyn, Longworth. Callers include E. P. Bacon, Felix Adler
10 Washington
11 Washington. Conference on Chicago appointments with C. E. Smith. Conference on Chinese exclusion with

Mitchell, Gompers, R. M. Easley and others

12 Washington. Cabinet meeting. Conference with Rep. Landis on insurance legislation. Conference with Sulzer and Marcus Braun. Callers include Crane, Dolliver, ex-Gov. Yates, Carnegie

13 Washington. Discussion of irrigation problems with Smoot, Sutherland. Conference with Bishop on canal matters. Callers include Penrose, Long, Aldrich, Cannon, Wetmore, Heyburn

14 Washington. Conference with W. F. Wakeman on Philippine tariff bill. Callers include Fairbanks

15 Washington. Cabinet meeting. Conference with G. C. Perkins, Flint on California appointments. Conference with R. L. Cox, Rep. Alexander on insurance investigation

16 Washington. Conference with Spooner on Santo Domingo. Discussion of Panama Canal legislation with Hepburn, Hale. Conference on appointments with Hemenway, Beveridge. Callers include Bartholdt, Hopkins. "Federal Social Legislation" published in *Charities and the Commons*

17 Washington

18 Washington. Conference with Taft, Moody, Shonts, Sen. Kittredge on canal salaries. Conferences with Gallinger, Proctor, Dillingham on pension agent appointment. Lunch with R. W. Gilder, G. W. Dunn, F. H. Scott

19 Washington. Conference with Moody, Millard, Long. Callers include W. W. Cocks, Seth Bullock, Landis. J. B. Bishop appointed to canal commission

20 Washington. Conferences with Kittredge, Aldrich on canal legislation. Discussion of Delaware politics with Allee

21 Washington. Discussion of Panama Canal affairs with Millard. Congressional recess. State dinner

22 Washington. Discussion of Wyoming forest reserves with Warren. Callers include Whitelaw Reid, G. C. Perkins, Flint. Dinner at Fairbanks'

23 Washington. Conference with M. J. Dady on Brooklyn appointments. Conferences with J. B. Bishop, Hepburn. Dinner with J. W. Riley, Fairbanks

24 Washington. Evening conference on New York politics with J. W. Wadsworth, Jr.

25 Washington

26 Washington

27 Washington. Departure for Albemarle County, Va. with family

28–31 Albemarle County

1906

1 Washington. White House reception

2 Washington. Cabinet meeting. Conference with Hale. Callers include Sens. Carter, Proctor, Long, Fulton, Warner, Burrows

3 Washington. Conference with Grosvenor. Conference with Beveridge on statehood bill. Callers include Hepburn, Spooner, Cannon, Burkett, Lacey, Hinshaw. Lunch and conference on New York politics with J. R. Sheffield. Cabinet dinner at Root's

4 Washington. Congress reconvenes. Hepburn Bill introduced in House. Diplomatic reception. Lunch with von Sternberg, W. Reid

5 Washington. Cabinet meeting. Conference with Beveridge, Overstreet on Indianapolis appointment. Evening conference with Root, Taft, Bonaparte, Moody on naval personnel bill

6 Washington. Conference on canal labor with Shonts, J. B. Harris. Discussion of Negro appointments with C. W. Anderson. Callers include B. F. Tracy

7 Washington

8 Washington. Conference with Hemenway on Indiana politics. Reception for American Bar Assoc. comm. Callers include Root, Taft, Hitchcock, Cortelyou, Sens. Warner, Gamble, Reps. Watson and Weems. Message to Congress on Panama Canal

9 Washington. Cabinet meeting. Conference on land fraud cases with Heney. Callers include Sens. Alger, Long, Fulton, Warner

10 Washington. Conference with Denby on Detroit postmastership. Callers include Beveridge, Aldrich, Dolliver, Crane, Alger, Taft, Root, Cortelyou. Appointment of H. L. Stimson as U. S. attorney for southern district of New York. Address before American Medical Association

11 Washington. Discussion of Santo Domingo treaty with Dominican property owners. Conference with E. J. Hill on Philippine tariff bill. Callers include Spooner, Long, Rep. Bell. Diplomatic dinner at White House

12 Washington. Conference with Rep. Watson on Philippine tariff bill. Callers include Crumpacker. Cabinet meeting

13 Washington. Conference with Stevens and Bishop. Conference on Hepburn Bill with Esch and Hepburn. Callers include Root, Fairbanks, Millard, Beveridge

14 Washington

15 Washington. Conference with Herbert Parsons on New York politics. Conference with Kittredge on canal investigation. Callers include Shonts, Cortelyou, Taft, Whitelaw Reid, Aldrich, Fulton, Millard, C. D. Edwards

16 Washington. Cabinet meeting. Conference including Lodge, Allison, Piles, R. S. Ryan, ex-Gov. Swineford on Alaskan governorship. Callers include Gen. Chaffee, Cannon, Watson. Algeciras Conference convenes. Philippine tariff bill passed in House

17 Washington. Conference with Lodge, Piles on Alaska. Conference with Elkins on railroad rate legislation. Conference with Bartholdt on Hague conference. Lunch including Taft, Herbert Parsons. Callers include Cannon, Brandegee, Burrows, Dalzell, Gardner, Watson

18 Washington. Conference with Spooner on Santo Domingo treaty. Conference with Porto Rican delegation. Callers include L. E. Wright, Allee, Alger, Clarke, Hepburn, Olcott, Taft, Wilson, Moody. Reception for judiciary. La Farge and J. E. Roosevelt at White House

19 Washington. Cabinet meeting. L. E. Wright appointed ambassador to Japan. Douglas Robinson at White House

20 Washington. Conference with Elkins on railroad rate legislation. Conference with Adm. Dewey, Frye, Spooner, McCall. Callers include Root, Hitchcock, Alger

21 Washington. Conference on Brooklyn appointments with Woodruff. Callers include Lincoln Steffens

22 Washington. Conference with A. L. Atkinson on Portuguese labor for Hawaii. Discussion of New Jersey post-office reform with Mayor Fagan. Conference with Watson on statehood bill. Dinner with Lodge. Conference with Black on New York politics

23 Washington. Cabinet meeting. Conference with Cannon, Humphrey. Callers include Sulzer, Allee, Crane, Alger

24 Washington. Conference with Morton on Far Eastern matters. Callers include Foster, Overman, L. M. Shaw. Reception for Imperial Chinese commissioners

25 Washington. Discussion of statehood bill with numerous congressmen. Lunch with W. D. Hyde. Dinner for Supreme Court Justices.

26 Washington. Cabinet meeting. Conference with Metcalf, McLaurin, Overman on Oriental commerce

27 Washington. Lunch with Dryden, Gov. Stokes. Gridiron Club dinner. Callers include C. E. Smith, Overstreet

28 Washington

29 Washington. Conference with Rep. Keifer. Funeral of Gen. Wheeler. Evening musicale. Callers include L. E. Wright

30 Washington. Cabinet meeting. Conference on Panama with Gov. Magoon. Dinner at Cortelyou's

31 Washington. Conference on Porto Rico with Larrinaga, R. H. Todd. Lunch with Root, Bonaparte, Riis. Callers include Cannon, Beveridge, Alger, Penrose

FEBRUARY

1 Washington. Conference with Dolliver, Clapp on railroad rate legislation. Conference with La Follette, Spooner on Wisconsin appointments. Callers include Dick, Allison, Beveridge, Fulton, Burton

2 Washington. Discussion of government printing office affairs with Landis. White House musicale. Robinsons at White House

3 Washington. Conference with Foss on naval expansion. Dinner for Harvard class of 1880. Callers include Taft, Hull

4 Washington

5 Washington. ICC report on alleged Pennsylvania RR violations of antitrust law sent to House. Callers include Allison, Hansbrough, Fulton, Cannon, Taft

6 Washington. Cabinet meeting. Publication of letter to Congress on Annapolis hazing laws. Lunch with John Burroughs, Maj. Pitcher. Callers include Warner, Penrose, Littauer. Dinner on *Mayflower*

7 Washington. Callers include Fairbanks, Spooner. Dinner with Wynne
8 Washington. Conference with House naval affairs committee on Annapolis hazing. Conference with Hepburn. House passes Hepburn Bill. Army-Navy reception
9 Washington. Cabinet meeting. Conference with T. C. Platt, Depew, E. H. Butler on Buffalo appointments. Conference with Elkins on railroad rate legislation. Callers include Spooner, Judge Magoon, W. H. H. Llewellyn. Dinner for members of Republican National Executive Comm.
10 Washington. Conference with National Businessmen's League delegation. Callers include Beveridge, Dolliver, Cowles
11 Washington
12 Washington. Conference with Lodge on Chinese exclusion. Callers include Beveridge, Hull, Root
13 Washington. Cabinet meeting. Conference on naval expansion with Foss. Callers include von Sternberg, Penrose
14 Washington. Conference with Bonaparte. Callers include members of Dawes Commission, Cannon, Littauer, L. M. Shaw, Root, Dolliver, La Follette, Brandegee
15 Washington. Callers include Aldrich, Allison, Cannon, Beveridge, Root, L. M. Shaw, B. T. Washington
16 Washington. Cabinet meeting. Conference with Root, L. M. Shaw on German tariff. Conference on pure food legislation with Massachusetts delegation
17 Washington. Wedding of Alice Roosevelt and Nicholas Longworth
18 Washington. Evening conference with Stillings, Pinchot. Robinsons at White House
19 Washington. Conferences with Mellen, Knox, Moody, Knapp, Prouty on railroad legislation. Callers include Hemenway, Landis, Gallinger, Curtis. Message to Congress on lock-type canal
20 Washington. Cabinet meeting. Conference with Knox, Spooner on railroad legislation
21 Washington. Conferences with Moody, Dolliver, Clapp, Cannon, Hepburn, Crane. Conference on German tariff with Root, L. M. Shaw
22 Washington. Conferences with Dolliver, Crane, Moody
23 Washington. Cabinet meeting. Conference with Fulton. Callers include Beveridge
24 Washington. Conference with Moody, Root on German tariff. Conference with Humphrey on ship subsidy bill. Callers include Allison, Burrows, Clapp, Dolliver, Burkett, Cannon, Hepburn
25 Washington
26 Washington. Conference with Elkins on railroad bill. Discussion of Philippine tariff and statehood bills with Lodge. Callers include Fairbanks, Fulton, Parsons, Root, Taft
27 Washington. Cabinet meeting
28 Washington. Callers include Spooner, Crane, Heyburn, Long, Beveridge, Alger, Burton

MARCH

"Factory Laws for Women and Children" published in *Ladies' Home Journal*
1 Washington. Conference on railroad legislation with Crane, Spooner. Callers include Jusserand, Root, Gamble, Ankeny, Beveridge
2 Washington. Conference with Spooner. Callers include Flint, Fulton, Warner
3 Washington. Conferences with Lodge, Allison, Warren, Cannon, Millard, Taft, Hitchcock. "City of Washington an Example" published in *Charities and the Commons*
4 Washington
5 Washington. Conferences on Alaskan governorship with Hemenway, Flint, Hitchcock. Conference on railroads with Clapp, Crane. Callers include Moody, Root, H. S. Tucker
6 Washington. Cabinet meeting. Lunch including Root, Taft, Elkins, Hemenway, Piles
7 Washington. Conference with Larrinaga on Porto Rico. Railroad conferences with Knox, Moody, Bonaparte
8 Washington. Speech to delegation of National Lumber Dealers' Association. Conference with Rep. Vreeland. Callers include members of Supreme Court. Evening conference including Loeb on Tillman-Gillespie resolution
9 Washington. Cabinet meeting. Conference with Knox. Conference with Hopkins on canal affairs. Callers include Marcus Braun, Pinchot
10 Washington. Discussion of Panama Canal progress with Sen. Dryden, An-

keny. Conference with Beveridge on statehood bill. Callers include Cullom, Cannon, Long, Burkett, Hemenway, Justice Brewer

11 Washington

12 Washington. Conference with Root, Taft on Supreme Court appointment. Conference on statehood bill with Cannon, Watson. Callers include Grosvenor

13 Washington. Cabinet meeting. Conference with Spooner on Tillman-Gillespie resolution

14 Washington. Speech before delegates to Consular Reform Convention. Lunch with Longworths. Callers include Kittredge, Littauer

15 Washington. Callers include Fulton, Clapp, Dolliver, Foster, Root, Chandler. Dinner at Longworths'

16 Washington. Cabinet meeting. Conference with Cannon on statehood bill. Callers include Spooner, Penrose, Fulton, Taft, Gardner

17 Washington. Conference with Adm. Dewey. Conference with Hepburn on the canal. Gridiron Club dinner

18 Washington

19 Washington. Conference with Dryden on canal

20 Washington. Cabinet meeting. Conference with Elkins. Callers include Jusserand. Evening conference with Keep Commission at Pinchot's

21 Washington. Conference with Gompers on labor legislation

22 Washington. Conference with Moody, Taft, Garfield. Callers include Knox, Fulton

23 Washington. Cabinet meeting. Conference on railroad rate legislation. Conference with Taft, Leupp, Lacey on Oklahoma public lands

24 Washington. Conference with Moody, Heney on Bristol case. Callers include Olcott, Lacey, Campbell

25 Washington

26 Washington. Conference with Neill on eight-hour law violations. Callers include W. B. Hoggatt, Larrinaga

27 Washington. Cabinet meeting. Conference with Taft, Knox, Heney, Bonaparte, Metcalf, Moody on Bristol appointment. Conference with Rep. Cooper on Porto Rico

28 Washington. Callers include Spooner, Bartholdt, Foss

29 Washington

30 Washington. Cabinet meeting on coal strike. Conference with Dolliver on railroad legislation

31 Washington. Railroad conference with Allison, Dolliver, Clapp, Cullom, Long, Moody, Knapp, Prouty. Conference with Wadsworth on New York state appointments. Conference with La Follette on Five Civilized Tribes bill. Callers include L. M. Shaw, W. B. Cockran, Cortelyou, Overman

APRIL

1 Washington

2 Washington. Conference with Elkins on court review amendment to Hepburn Bill. Conference on Porto Rico with Winthrop

3 Washington. Cabinet meeting. Lunch with Mellen, T. E. Byrnes. Dinner for Gov. Grey of Canada

4 Washington. Railroad conference with Hepburn. Conference with Burnham, Pyles, Kinkaid, Ankeny, Tawney on Alaskan railroads

5 Washington. Callers include Overman, Dillingham

6 Washington. Cabinet meeting. Conference with Allison, Long, Rayner on railroad legislation. Callers include Proctor, Dryden, W. A. Smith

7 Washington. Conference with Lacey on public lands. Lunch with Moody, Spooner. Conference with Rosen. Boone and Crockett Club dinner

8 Washington

9 Washington. Railroad conference with Knox. Discussion of ship subsidies with Grosvenor. Callers include Cannon, J. S. Sherman, Taft

10 Washington. Cabinet meeting. Railroad conference with Clapp, Nelson, Spooner. Conference with Burton on preservation of Niagara Falls. Callers include Littauer, Spooner, Fowler

11 Washington. Conference with Allee, Bonaparte

12 Washington. Callers include Taft, Bonaparte, Allee, Cannon, Penrose, von Sternberg, Wadsworth

13 Washington. Cabinet meeting. Conferences on railroad legislation with Crane, Overman, Nelson. Conference with Fulton on Interior Department affairs. Callers include Burton, H. S. Tucker

14 Washington. Conference with Hemenway on Indiana politics. Conference with Taft, Humphrey on ship sub-

sidies. Address at cornerstone laying of House of Representatives — "The Man with the Muck-Rake"

15 Washington
16 Washington. Conferences with Moody, Taft. Callers include Metcalf, Cortelyou, Burrows, Hepburn, Warren
17 Washington. Cabinet meeting. Conference on railroad legislation with Spooner, Simmons. Callers include F. V. Greene, Alger, Burkett
18 Washington. Conference with L. M. Shaw. Railroad rate conference with Elkins, Hepburn, Lodge. Callers include Beveridge, Bartholdt, Gardner, Burrows. Special message to Congress on beef packers trial. San Francisco earthquake
19 Washington. Public appeal for aid to San Francisco. Conference with Scott on West Virginia appointments. Callers include L. M. Shaw, Moody, Root, Foraker, Fulton, Crane, von Sternberg, Rep. Cocks. Reception for DAR
20 Washington. Cabinet meeting on San Francisco disaster. Conference with Spooner. Callers include Heney, Ankeny
21 Washington. Railroad conference with Allison, Crane, Long, Hopkins. Conference with Moody. Callers include Root, Taft, Albert Shaw, Gen. Corbin, Loomis. "The Man with the Muck-Rake" published in the *Outlook*
22 Washington
23 Washington. Callers include Piles, Grosvenor, von Sternberg, Quesada, Larrinaga. Reception and dinner for Adm. Campion and French officers
24 Washington. Departure for John Paul Jones exercises at Annapolis. Speech
25 Washington. Conference on San Francisco with Flint. Callers include Piles, Ankeny, Dalzell, Littauer, Bonaparte, Garfield, C. N. Bliss
26 Washington. Railroad conference with Knapp, Prouty. Callers include Smoot, Taft, Walcott, Dubois
27 Washington. Cabinet meeting. Railroad conference with Allison, Cullom. Callers include Piles, Cocks, Meyer, Calder, Grosvenor
28 Washington. Conference with Allison on court review amendment to Hepburn Bill. Callers include Sulzer, J. D. Long. Afternoon departure for trip on *Sylph*
29 On board *Sylph*
30 Washington. Conference with Sen. Flint. Callers include Hepburn, Fairbanks, Wilson, Gen. Corbin

MAY

1 Washington. Cabinet meeting. Conference with Moody, Cannon. Callers include Beveridge, Lodge, A. W. Merrifield
2 Washington. Callers include Beveridge, Hopkins, Moody, Larrinaga. Dinner with Cowles'
3 Washington. Conference on railroad legislation with Crane. Callers include Sulloway, Bartholdt, Taft, Hopkins, Carter, Flint. Reception for Ambassador Aoki
4 Washington. Cabinet meeting. Conference with Newlands on federal aid for San Francisco. Callers include Long, Crane. N. M. Butler, W. S. Bigelow at White House
5 Washington. Public statement supporting Hepburn Bill and Allison amendment. Trip to Mount Vernon on *Sylph* with N. M. Butler. Dinner with Higgins and conference on New York politics. Callers include Carnegie, Neill, Root, Cullom
6 Washington
7 Washington. Railroad conferences with Crane, Carter, Dolliver, Beveridge, Burnham, Warner, Proctor, Flint, Perkins, Hemenway, Ankeny, Clapp, Burkett. Callers include Kohlsaat, Bartholdt, Sherman, Hepburn, Parsons, F. Hendricks
8 Washington. Cabinet meeting on California disaster and Metcalf's trip. Conference on Standard Oil prosecutions with Atty. Gen. Davidson of Kansas. Callers include Marion Butler, Judge T. A. Jones, Col. Mosby
9 Washington. Railroad conference with Dolliver. Callers include Beveridge, Proctor, Flint, Garfield, Cannon
10 Washington. Conference with Wadsworth, J. M. Wainwright, Cocks on New York politics. Callers include Dick, Beveridge, Carter, Crane, Elkins, H. S. Tucker, G. C. Perkins
11 Washington. Cabinet meeting. Conference with Hitchcock, Leupp on Indian affairs. Senate approves of 4 of Allison amendments
12 Washington. Conference with Gompers, Morrison on eight-hour law violations, anti-injunction bill. Callers

include Dolliver, Root, Flint, Neill, Underwood, J. W. Gaines

13 Washington. Dinner with Lodge. Conference with Root, Taft, Lodge

14 Washington. Rate bill conferences with Clapp, Moody, Allison, Long. Callers include Reps. Kahn, Mudd, Dixon. Death of Carl Schurz

15 Washington. Cabinet meeting. Reception for delegates of National Civil Service Reform League convention. Callers include Harlan, Piles, Beveridge, Bacon

16 Washington. Naval affairs conference with Reps. Sherman, Cocks. Conference with Moody, Cortelyou. Callers include Millard, Piles, Penrose, Spooner, Rodenberg

17 Washington. Callers include Dolliver, Cullom, Moody, Alger, Hemenway, W. H. H. Llewellyn

18 Washington. Cabinet meeting. Conference with Sherman on New York politics. Callers include Lodge, Pinchot, Bacon, Foss. Railroad rate bill passed by Senate

19 Washington. Callers include H. S. Tucker, Beveridge, Bacon, Wadsworth, Hopkins, Cannon, Hepburn

20 Washington

21 Washington. Callers include Fairbanks, Hopkins, Warner, Fulton, Aiken, Kinkaid, Carter

22 Washington. Cabinet meeting. Callers include Kahn, Warner, Shonts, Fulton, Cannon

23 Washington. Conference with Aldrich. Callers include Elkins, Crane, Dolliver, Mann, Cocks, Hepburn, Wachter, Wynne

24 Washington. Conference with Allee on Delaware politics. Discussion of Chicago stockyards with Reps. Brooks, Cocks; W. L. Carlisle, W. E. Skinner. Callers include Elkins, Allison, Proctor, Taft, L. M. Shaw, Tawney. Dinner for Ambassador Aoki including Forakers, Hales, Lodges, H. E. Pellews

25 Washington. Cabinet meeting. Conference on Panama and railroads with Allison, Knox, Hepburn. Callers include P. B. Stewart, Jusserand, Bacon, Fairbanks, Nelson

26 Washington. Conferences on Beveridge's meat inspection amendment with Cullom, Cannon, Lorimer, Beveridge, J. B. Reynolds, Neill. Callers include Flint, Proctor, Cortelyou, Slemp, Adams, Allen

27 Washington

28 Washington. Conferences on beef inspection bill with Beveridge, Carter, Neill. Callers include Marcus Braun

29 Washington. Cabinet meeting. Afternoon departure for Norfolk on *Mayflower*

30 Portsmouth, Va. Address at unveiling of Army and Navy Union monument. Speech at Hampton Institute on Negro education

31 Washington. Conference with Carter, Beveridge, Cannon, Wadsworth on beef inspection amendment. Dinner for Justice Brown at New Willard

JUNE

1 Washington. Cabinet meeting. Conferences with Wadsworth, Crumpacker, Reynolds on meat inspection amendment. Speech before graduating class of Howard University

2 Washington. Receives Neill-Reynolds report on Chicago stockyards. Callers include Keifer, Watson, Grosvenor, Dalzell, Moody

3 Washington

4 Washington. Special message to Congress on federal inspection of packing industry. Callers include Cannon, Hull, La Follette, Taft, F. P. Spooner, Shonts, Stevens

5 Washington. Cabinet meeting. Reception for Assoc. of Railway Special Agents. Callers include Dryden, Dolliver, Parsons, Olcott, Black

6 Washington. Commencement address at National Cathedral School

7 Washington. Conference with Cannon. Reception for Cooper Union delegation. Callers include Allison, Flint, La Follette, Dolliver, Perkins, Taft, Moody. Evening conference with Reynolds and Neill

8 Washington. Cabinet meeting. Conference with Neill on beef trust investigation. Agriculture Department report sent to Congress

9 Washington. Callers include Spooner, Taft, Rosen, La Follette, Lodge, Long, Robert **Bacon**

10 Washington

11 Washington. Canal conference with Knox. Conference on meat inspection legislation with Cannon, Beveridge, Hopkins, Rep. Henry. Callers include Needham, Marcus Braun, Ansley Wilcox

12 Washington. Cabinet meeting. Conference with California delegation on rebuilding of San Francisco. Conference with Missouri delegation on packing house conditions

13 Washington. Canal conference with Hepburn. Callers include Parsons, Payne, Dalzell, Quesada, Taft

14 Washington. Conference with Allee on Delaware politics. Immigration conference with members of Immigration Protective League. Commencement address at Georgetown University. Callers include Beveridge, Reynolds, Fulton, Fairbanks

15 Washington. Cabinet meeting. Conferences with Cannon, Hopkins, Reynolds on meat inspection legislation. Callers include B. I. Wheeler, Allee, Fulton, Burton

16 Washington. Canal conference with Hopkins. Conference with Flint, Perkins on San Francisco rebuilding. Discussion of Chicago stockyards report with Beveridge, Reynolds. Approval of statehood bill. Callers include Warren, Allee, Hemenway, Gallinger, Clapp, Taft

17 Washington. Evening conference with Cannon

18 Washington. Conference with Allison. Discussion of beef legislation with Rep. Humphrey. Callers include Clapp, Warner, Ankeny, Parsons, Landis, Taft, L. M. Shaw, Hitchcock, Moody

19 Washington. Cabinet meeting. Conferences with Beveridge, Judge S. M. Cowan on meat inspection bill. Conference with Bonaparte on Maryland patronage

20 Washington. Conference with Kittredge on South Dakota appointments. Conference with Simon Wolf on Jewish massacres. Discussion of Oklahoma politics with Oklahoma delegation. Callers include Fairbanks, Dick, Spooner, La Follette, Heyburn, Dixon, Butler, Root, Taft, Moody

21 Washington. Conference with Boutell on building of Great Lakes training ship. Approval of lock-type canal by Senate

22 Washington. Cabinet meeting on Standard Oil prosecutions. Callers include Beveridge, Hopkins, Overstreet, Lacey, Crane, Spooner

23 Washington. Conference with Martin, Burke on South Dakota patronage. Conference on Standard Oil proceed-

ings with Moody. Callers include Grosvenor, H. D. Peirce, Overman, Merriam

24 Washington

25 Washington. Conference with Cannon and Hepburn. Conference with Taft on Panama trip. Callers include Allison, Spooner, Beveridge, Warren, Penrose, L. M. Shaw, Moody, Abner McKinley

26 Washington. Cabinet meeting. Conference with Carter and Dixon on Montana appointments. Callers include Gamble, Elkins, Proctor, Crane, Olcott, Calder

27 Washington. Discussion of Indian appropriations with L. M. Shaw, Dolliver, Lacey. Callers include Flint, Penrose, Larrinaga, Moody, Fulton, W. H. H. Llewellyn

28 Washington. Reviews National Guard parade. Callers include La Follette, Heyburn, Fairbanks, Neill, Dixon, Crumpacker, F. P. Sargent, F. B. Kellogg, C. B. Morrison

29 Washington. Cabinet meeting. Callers include Elkins, Spooner, La Follette, Dryden, Flint, Warren, Fulton, Humphrey. Approval of Panama Canal Act, Pure Food Act, Agricultural Appropriation Act

30 Washington. Adjournment of Congress. Conference with Cannon. Midnight departure for Oyster Bay

JULY

1 Oyster Bay
2 Oyster Bay
3 Oyster Bay
4 Oyster Bay. Independence Day speech
5 Oyster Bay
6 Oyster Bay. Lunch with Premier Ward of New Zealand
7 Oyster Bay. Conference with Taft on Army matters
8 Oyster Bay
9 Oyster Bay
10 Oyster Bay
11 Oyster Bay
12 Oyster Bay
13 Oyster Bay
14 Oyster Bay
15 Oyster Bay
16 Oyster Bay. Conference with Taft and Robert Bacon on Central American affairs. Lunch with Taft, Bacon, F. W. Whitridge, F. P. Dunne, Col. T. A. Bingham
17 Oyster Bay

18 Oyster Bay
19 Oyster Bay
20 Oyster Bay
21 Oyster Bay
22 Oyster Bay
23 Oyster Bay. Lunch with Cannon, Sherman, Abner McKinley, Loudenslager. Conference on congressional campaign
24 Oyster Bay
25 Oyster Bay
26 Oyster Bay
27 Oyster Bay. Conference with E. E. Clark on ICC work. Callers include Gen. T. H. Barry, Robert Bacon
28 Oyster Bay. Conference with C. E. Smith on Pennsylvania politics
29 Oyster Bay
30 Oyster Bay
31 Oyster Bay. Lunch and conference with Dick, Elmer Dover on Ohio and Middle Western politics

AUGUST

1 Oyster Bay
2 Oyster Bay
3 Oyster Bay
4 Oyster Bay
5 Oyster Bay
6 Oyster Bay. Lunch with W. J. Youngs, C. J. Smiths, W. W. Cocks, H. L. Stimson, J. A. Sleicher. Conference with Penrose
7 Oyster Bay
8 Oyster Bay
9 Oyster Bay. Conference with ex-Sen. Jones, Barnsdall on Standard Oil investigation
10 Oyster Bay
11 Oyster Bay
12 Oyster Bay
13 Oyster Bay. Conference with J. S. Sherman and Longworth on congressional campaign. Conference on Panama Canal with Shonts and Bishop
14 Oyster Bay
15 Oyster Bay
16 Oyster Bay. Conference with Moody
17 Oyster Bay. J. S. Harlan appointed to ICC
18 Oyster Bay
19 Oyster Bay
20 Oyster Bay
21 Oyster Bay
22 Oyster Bay
23 Oyster Bay. Conference with Cortelyou on campaign. Conference with Gen. J. F. Bell on Brownsville affair
24 Oyster Bay

25 Oyster Bay. Conference on Chile with Robert Bacon
26 Oyster Bay
27 Oyster Bay
28 Oyster Bay
29 Oyster Bay
30 Oyster Bay
31 Oyster Bay. Lunch with Parsons and conference on New York politics. Callers include Brander Matthews, Leupp, Leigh Hunt, Lyman Abbott, Silas McBee, Count Gleichen

SEPTEMBER

1 Oyster Bay
2 Oyster Bay. Von Sternberg and Rixey at Sagamore Hill
3 Oyster Bay. Reviews North Atlantic fleet from the *Mayflower*
4 Oyster Bay
5 Oyster Bay. Lunch and conference on New York politics with Cortelyou and Littauer
6 Oyster Bay. Lunch with W. H. H. Llewellyn. Longworths at Sagamore Hill. Callers include Raymond Patterson
7 Oyster Bay. Conference with A. R. Page
8 Oyster Bay. Speech at Christ Church
9 Oyster Bay
10 Oyster Bay. Conference on New York politics with Gov. Higgins. Callers include Morton
11 Oyster Bay
12 Oyster Bay. At work on annual message
13 Oyster Bay
14 Oyster Bay. Conference on Cuban insurrection with Taft, Bonaparte, Bacon
15 Oyster Bay. Callers include Woodruff, J. S. Sherman, Albert Shaw
16 Oyster Bay
17 Oyster Bay
18 Oyster Bay
19 Oyster Bay. Proclamation opening acreage in Oklahoma to homesteaders. Order extending eight-hour law to government work
20 Oyster Bay
21 Oyster Bay
22 Oyster Bay
23 Oyster Bay
24 Oyster Bay
25 Oyster Bay
26 Oyster Bay
27 Oyster Bay
28 Departure on *Mayflower* for Province-

town, Mass. to review North Atlantic fleet

29 On board *Missouri* for target practice and lunch. Afternoon departure for Oyster Bay on *Mayflower*
30 Oyster Bay

1 Departure for Washington. Conference on train with C. E. Hughes. Evening conference with Moody and Root
2 Washington. Cabinet meeting on Cuban affairs. Callers include Knox, Foraker, Frank Sargent, Reps. Kennedy, Sparkman, Gaines
3 Washington. Appointment of C. E. Magoon as Provisional Gov. of Cuba. Callers include Root, Metcalf, Payne, Cocks, F. K. Lane. Dinner with Roots and Magoons
4 Departure for Harrisburg and York, Pa., with Knox, Penrose, Latta, Dr. Rixey. Speeches at Pennsylvania State Capitol and York Fair. Return to Washington
5 Washington. Cabinet meeting. Appointment of C. H. Robb as associate justice of District Court of Appeals. Callers include Warren, Lane
6 Washington. Conference with Magoon and Gen. Bell. Callers include C. H. Robb, A. W. Cooley, Warren, J. M. Wright
7 Washington. Political conference with Sherman and Penrose
8 Washington. Conference with Sherman on New York congressional campaign. Conference on Indiana politics with Overstreet. Canal conference with Shonts. Callers include C. H. Schwab. Reception for Supreme Court Justices
9 Washington. Cabinet meeting. Conference on Illinois politics with Hopkins. Conference with Tawney. Conference on antitrust legislation with Root and Bonaparte
10 Washington. Callers include Metcalf, Bonaparte, Moody, Father A. P. Doyle, H. W. Taft, Rep. Burton, Major J. M. Burke. Reception for Spanish War veterans
11 Washington. Conference with Spooner on Cuban affairs. Conference with W. J. Youngs on New York politics. Conference with J. S. Harlan and F. K. Lane. Callers include M. F. Egan, Pinchot
12 Washington. Conference with J. M.

Wainwright, W. L. Ward on New York politics. Lunch with Arthur Lee, Morton
13 Washington. Conference with Beveridge on Cuban annexation and the annual message to Congress. Callers include Herbert Putnam
14 Washington. Evening conference with Cannon and Watson
15 Washington. Conference with Allee, du Pont, Ball on Delaware politics. Conference on Ohio politics with Grosvenor. Callers include Hitchcock, Wilson
16 Washington. Cabinet meeting. Conference with Root, Cortelyou. Lunch including Gov. Montague
17 Washington. Conference with Knox on Pennsylvania politics. Conference with Root on Root's campaign speech for Hughes. Conference with Cortelyou
18 Washington. Conference with Knox on annual message. Callers include Col. McCook
19 Washington. Cabinet meeting. Conference with Moody on trust prosecutions
20 Washington. Conference with Harlan, White, Day on Supreme Court vacancy. Conference with Taft, Root, Bishop, Ropes on Panama Canal bids
21 Washington. Evening conference with L. M. Shaw on national finances
22 Washington. Conferences with Taft, Root on their campaign tours. Conference with Shonts, Taft, Root on canal contracts. Conference with Moody, J. J. Sullivan on Standard Oil case
23 Washington. Cabinet meeting. Conference with Bacon and Loomis
24 Washington. Conference with Metcalf on conditions at Ellis Island. Callers include Taft, Hitchcock, Moody, Cortelyou, H. L. Higginson, H. Ridder
25 Washington. Conference with Wilson. Lunch with Jusserand, Root, Taft, Cowles. Conference with J. D. Terrill on Cuban finances. Callers include Moody, C. H. Darling
26 Washington. Cabinet meeting. Conference with Root. Appointment of A. W. Cooley as Asst. Atty. Gen.
27 Washington. 48th birthday. Conference with Metcalf on Japanese school question in California. Conference with Shonts. Lunch including Root, Munsterberg, Metcalf
28 Washington
29 Washington. Conference on New York

politics with Root, Cortelyou. Callers include Judge Wilfley

30 Washington. Conference on New York politics with Root, Cortelyou
31 Washington. Conference with Acting Gov. Atkinson on Hawaiian labor conditions. Afternoon departure for Pine Knot, Va.

NOVEMBER

1 Pine Knot
2 Pine Knot
3 Richmond, Va.
4 Departure for Washington
5 Washington. Conference with Sen. Penrose. Callers include W. M. Collier, Hitchcock, Bonaparte, C. H. Davis. Midnight departure for Oyster Bay
6 Oyster Bay. Votes. Return to Washington
7 Washington. Conference with labor leaders including Gompers on Pearre anti-injunction bill. Callers include Root, Hitchcock, Moody, Cortelyou, Brewer, A. L. C. Atkinson
8 Washington. Callers include Hitchcock, Ambassador Aoki, H. W. Taft, Marcus Braun, James O'Connell. Afternoon departure for trip to Panama on U.S.S. *Louisiana*
9 On board *Louisiana*. Off Cape Hatteras
10 On board *Louisiana*. Near Savannah, Ga.
11 On board *Louisiana*. Near Jacksonville, Fla.
12 On board *Louisiana*. Off Cuba
13 On board *Louisiana*. Near Colón
14 Afternoon arrival at Colón
15 Trip from Colón to Panama City with Shonts, Stevens, President Amador and others
16 Panama City. Trip to Culebra cut
17 Afternoon arrival at Cristobal. Dinner at Gen. Manager Biers'. Reception and ball. Evening departure for Porto Rico on *Louisiana*
18 En route Porto Rico
19 En route Porto Rico
20 Near Ponce, P.R.
21 Arrival at Ponce. Speech at City Hall. Morning departure for San Juan with lunch at Cayey and stop at Rio Piedras. Evening reception given by Gov. Winthrop. Night in San Juan
22 Return to Ponce with stop at Arecibo. Afternoon departure on *Louisiana*
23 On board *Louisiana*
24 On board *Louisiana*. Off Cape Hatteras

25 On board *Louisiana*
26 Evening arrival at Washington
27 Washington. Cabinet meeting. Conference with C. W. Anderson, E. J. Scott on dismissal of Negro soldiers. Callers include Fairbanks, Cullom, Cooley, Col. Bromwell, Seth Bullock, Cannon. Lunch with Root, Taft, Bacon, John LaFarge, Longworth
28 Washington. Conferences with Sens. Penrose, Scott, Burkett. Callers include Fulton, Hale, Burrows, Alger, Taft, Hitchcock, Cannon, Bonaparte, B. I. Wheeler, Shallenberger
29 Washington. Thanksgiving Day
30 Washington. Conference with B. I. Wheeler, Metcalf on Japanese school question in California. Cabinet meeting. Callers include Gompers, Dalzell, Loudenslager, Overstreet, Cannon, Gen. Black, Cooley, Bullock

DECEMBER

1 Washington. Conference with Hepburn on interstate commerce legislation. Conference with Beveridge on child labor bill. Conference with Warren and Hull on army appropriation bill. Callers include R. E. Peary, Flint, Keifer, Foraker, McCumber, Garfield, Taft, L. M. Shaw, Hitchcock
2 Washington
3 Washington. Congress reconvenes. Callers include Kean, Depew, Millard, Burrows, Wetmore, Dryden, Gamble, Grosvenor, Kahn, Cocks, Littlefield
4 Washington. Message to Congress
5 Washington. Conference with C. P. Neill, E. A. Moffett on Canal Zone labor conditions. Callers include Hopkins, Piles, Ankeny, Allee, Underwood
6 Washington. Callers include Baron Rosen, W. Barnes, Jr., Depew, Olcott, Parsons, Cocks, Calder, Root, Spooner, Gallinger, Warren, Dick, Hemenway, La Follette, Cullom, Kinkaid, Sutherland, du Pont
7 Washington. Cabinet meeting. Conference with Bacon. Callers include Flint, Spooner, Piles, Larrinaga, Shonts. Speech to delegates of Rivers and Harbors Congress. Dinner at Lodge's
8 Washington. Conference on N.Y. politics with Platt, Woodruff. Callers include Taft, L. M. Shaw, Fairbanks, Mondell, Mark Twain, J. P. Sousa, Adm. Dewey, Rep. Foss, Jusserand, Payne, Spooner

9 Washington. Publication of correspondence with the Bellamy Storers
10 Washington. Official presentation of Nobel Prize in Christiania, Norway. Callers include Norwegian Minister Hauge, Bacon, Sulloway, C. P. Neill, John Barrett, Cannon, Root, Crumpacker, Hale, Alger, Jane Addams
11 Washington. Cabinet meeting. Conference with Hughes on New York politics. Callers include Millard, Patterson, Fulton, Hopkins, Bartholdt, Mark Twain. Dinner with Republican campaign committee, Hughes, Taft, Cortelyou, Lodge, Loeb, Cannon, Bacon, Keep
12 Washington. Callers include Penrose, Warner, Gamble, Kittredge, Spooner, Aldrich, Long, Garfield, Curtis
13 Washington. Callers include Moody, Root, Bonaparte, Flint, Allee, Spooner, Parsons. Morton, B. Winthrop at White House. Cabinet dinner
14 Washington. Cabinet meeting. Callers include Spooner, Cullom, Overman, Watson, Dixon, Bacon, Sherman
15 Washington. Conference with Rep. Townsend on freight car shortage. Conference with "Buffalo Bill" on western irrigation. Callers include Burrows, La Follette, Simmons, Cocks, Watson, Lacey, Hale, Gaines, Landis, Grosvenor, Humphrey, F. K. Lane. Dinner at Fairbanks'. Douglas Robinson at White House
16 Washington
17 Washington. Special messages to Congress on Panama Canal, Navy personnel bill, public land laws. Conference with Metcalf, Bonaparte, Moody, Foss on naval appropriations bill. Lunch with Lt. Wright. Callers include Hale, Warner, Piles, Smoot, Hemenway, Humphrey, Overstreet, Littlefield, Scott, Gardner, Clarkson, Justice Fuller
18 Washington. Conference with Littauer on government salaries. Conference with Clapp on freight car shortage. Conference on Indian affairs with Sherman. Conference on loan for Jamestown Exposition with H. S. Tucker. Cabinet meeting
19 Washington. Conference on freight car shortage with Hansbrough, McCumber, Clapp, Nelson, Gov. Cummins. Callers include Carter, Allee, du Pont, Pettus, Flint, Fulton, Burton, Grosvenor, Tawney, Scott, Burke, H. Fish, M. Butler

20 Washington. Conference with Flint, Walcott, F. H. Newell on Colorado River break. Conference with C. P. Neill on child labor legislation. Callers include Fulton, Lodge, Warner, Long, Burkett, Lacey, Hitchcock, Bacon, Leupp, Pinchot. Dinner at Roots'. N. M. Butler at White House
21 Washington. Cabinet meeting. Lunch with Durand, Whitelaw Reid. Callers include Carter
22 Washington. Callers include Newberry, Root, Taft, Fairbanks, Burrows, Grosvenor, Warner
23 Washington
24 Washington. Immigration conference with Sargent. Canal conference with Taft. Conference with Warren, Long, Cullom on Brownsville incident. Callers include Mann, Parsons, Straus, Garfield
25 Washington
26 Pine Knot, Virginia
27 Pine Knot
28 Pine Knot
29 Pine Knot
30 Pine Knot
31 Departure for Washington

1907

1 Washington. New Year's reception
2 Washington. Conference with Cannon and Longworth. Callers include Root, Taft, Hitchcock, Bonaparte, Depew, Fulton, Piles
3 Washington. Conference with Walcott, F. H. Newell on flood control of Colorado River. Callers include Taft, Lodge, Crane, Scott, Allee, Grosvenor, Parsons, Curtis, W. Willcox
4 Washington. Cabinet meeting. Continued conference with Walcott on Colorado River control. Callers include Carnegie, Crane, Beveridge. Dinner with Cannon, Aldrich, J. A. McIlhenny, Grosvenor, J. W. Pinchot, Lt. Douglas MacArthur. Evening musicale
5 Washington. Conference with Sen. Perkins and Dist. Atty. Devlin on Japanese school question in San Francisco. Callers include Beveridge, Humphrey, Olcott, Parsons, Hull, H. W. Taft
6 Washington
7 Washington. Conference with Hemenway, Hopkins, Burkett, Hansbrough on Brownsville affair. Callers include

Clapp, Reps. Lacey, Mann, Scott, Landis, Gov. Hoggatt

8 Washington. Cabinet meeting. Legislative conference with Lodge, Knox, Nelson. Callers include Jusserand, Reps. Wiley, Loudenslager, Gardner

9 Washington. Callers include J. S. Williams, Humphrey, Overstreet, Beveridge, Alger, Fairbanks, Hitchcock, Bonaparte

10 Washington. Conference with Rep. Burton on rivers and harbors bill. Callers include Crane, Allison, Dolliver, Overman, Warner, Hale, Watson. Diplomatic dinner

11 Washington. Conference on Brownsville affair with M. D. Purdy. Callers include Lodge, Spooner, Clapp, Teller, Grosvenor. Dinner with Straus, Oliver, Longworth, Robert Grant. Evening musicale

12 Washington. Special message to Congress on appropriations for repair of Colorado River breaks. Conference on Panama Canal with Sen. Hopkins. Callers include Burrows, Piles, Alger, Blackburn, Cannon, C. P. Neill

13 Washington. Evening conference with J. W. Wadsworth, on New York politics. Evening conference with Garfield

14 Washington. Special message to Congress on Brownsville affair. Conference with Littauer on ship subsidies. Callers include Leupp, Piles, Hale, Hansbrough, Allee, Taft, J. B. Bishop

15 Washington. Cabinet meeting. Conference with Bonaparte on case of Judge Wickersham. Callers include Lodge, Crane, Boutell. Reception for executive comm. of Republican clubs. Dinner at Taft's

16 Washington. Conference on Wyoming land fraud cases with Hitchcock, Garfield, Cooley, Purdy, Warren. Conference on ship subsidy bill with Grosvenor, Humphrey. Lunch with Root, C. N. Bliss, Cortelyou. Callers include La Follette, Burrows, Piles, Heyburn, Warner, Beveridge, Reps. McKinley, Calder, Landis, Gardner, Gaines, Watson

17 Washington. Railroad conference with Knapp, Harlan, Clark, Clements. Callers include Dick, Allee, Littauer, Calder, Root, Taft, Bacon, Metcalf. Reception for judiciary. Emlen Roosevelt at White House

18 Washington. Cabinet meeting. Conference with Beveridge on child labor bill. Conference on Panama labor conditions with G. W. Dunn. Callers include Lodge, Littauer, Humphrey

19 Washington. Conference with Gov. Glenn on North Carolina cotton mill affairs. Callers include Fairbanks, Lodge, Hansbrough, La Follette, Warren, Piles, Burrows, Elkins, Bonaparte, Metcalf, Hull, Littlefield

20 Washington. Conference on Brownsville affair at Lodge's home

21 Washington. Conferences on Foraker resolution on Brownsville affair with Spooner, Crane, Knox, Clapp, Warner, Warren, Hansbrough, Alger, Piles, Carter, du Pont. Callers include L. M. Shaw. Conference with Tawney on pending financial legislation. Conference on ship subsidy bill with Grosvenor. Reclamation conference with Lacey. Conference with Bacon and Taft on Swettenham incident. Sloan Simpson at White House

22 Washington. Conference with Lodge on Swettenham incident and Brownsville affair. Cabinet meeting on canal construction contracts. Conference with Purdy on coal land frauds. Conference with La Follette on bill for leasing of coal and oil lands

23 Washington. Message to Congress for ship subsidy legislation. Callers include Knox, delegation of independent smokeless powder companies. Conference with Rep. Davis on government salaries

24 Washington. Canal conference with Millard. Dinner for Supreme Court

25 Washington. Cabinet meeting on contract for canal construction. Conference with Sen. Fulton on Oregon appointments. Conference with Hopkins on canal legislation. Conference with du Pont on smokeless powder companies' accusations

26 Washington. Conference with Rep. Davis on government salaries increase. Conference with Lodge, Taft, Spooner on canal contracts. Conference with Sen. Sutherland on Smoot case. Funeral of Sen. Alger. Gridiron Club dinner

27 Washington

28 Washington. Discussion of New Hampshire politics with Winston Churchill. Conference on land legislation with Heyburn. Conference with Pinchot on livestock conventions at

Salt Lake City and Denver. Conferences with Bonaparte and Hull. Callers include Longworth, Gov. Hoggatt

29 Washington. Cabinet meeting. Canal conference with Shonts. Conference with Mondell on Wyoming affairs. Conference with R. M. Easley on civic improvements in Washington

30 Washington. Conference on Japanese school question with California congressional delegation. Callers include Metcalf, Underwood

31 Washington. Callers include Taft, Metcalf, L. M. Shaw, Lodge, Fulton, Ankeny, Burrows, Piles, Sherman, Calder. Congressional reception

1 Washington. Cabinet meeting. Conference with B. S. McGuire on Oklahoma railroad laws. Conferences with Warren, Clark, Mondell on state appointments. White House musicale

2 Washington. Callers include Reps. Hill, Marshall; Sen. Guggenheim

3 Washington

4 Washington. Conference with Bonaparte, Garfield, Dist. Atty. Sims on Standard Oil cases. Callers include Reps. Kahn, Hayes. Evening conference with Hansbrough, Nelson, Carter, Newlands, McLaurin, Pinchot, Walcott, Garfield, G. K. Holmes on legislation for the withdrawal of coal lands

5 Washington. Conference with T. F. Ryan on canal construction. Cabinet meeting. Conference with Littauer. Conference with Burton on rivers and harbors legislation. Callers include Fairbanks, Spooner. Dinner at Hitchcock's

6 Washington. Conference with Rep. Perkins on Chinese exclusion laws

7 Washington. Conference with Taft on canal contract bids. Conference with Heyburn on public land legislation. Conference with Dick, Reps. Southard, Burton on Ohio appointments. Army-Navy reception

8 Washington. Cabinet meeting. Conference with Taft on Cuba. Conference with Payne on appropriation bills. Callers include Clark, Hopkins, Kahn

9 Washington. Conference with Root, Mayor Schmitz, Kahn, Hayes, delegation from San Francisco Board of Education on Japanese school question.

Conference with McCumber on western land laws

10 Washington

11 Washington. Second conference with Schmitz. Conference with Reps. Lacey, Martin on coal lands legislation. Conference with Garfield, Pinchot on western land leases. Conference with Rep. Bennet on immigration legislation. Visit with Smoot

12 Washington. Cabinet meeting on Japanese school question. Callers include Spooner, Hansbrough, Pinchot. Dinner at Wilson's

13 Washington. Conference with Root, Cannon, Taft, Schmitz on Japanese school question. Conference with Sargent on immigration. Callers include Gamble, Heyburn, Beveridge, Lodge, Mann, Weeks, Hale. Message to Congress for leasing of western coal lands. Conference with R. S. Oliver on canal contracts

14 Washington. Conference with Reps. Bartholdt, Williams on second Hague conference

15 Washington. Conference with Root, Schmitz. Cabinet meeting

16 Washington. Conference with Garfield, Sen. Curtis on sale of Indian lands. Callers include Longworth, Gamble, A. H. Tanner, Neill

17 Washington

18 Washington. Conference with Sen. Flint on Japanese school question. Discussion of Idaho judgeship with Heyburn

19 Washington. Cabinet meeting. Conference with Cannon, Watson, Hinshaw, Gallinger on ship subsidies. Appointment of W. C. Bristol as U. S. district attorney for Oregon. Conference on canal contracts with Shonts, Taft, Oliver. Callers include W. A. Smith. Dinner with Straus

20 Washington. Conference with R. A. Ballinger. Conference with Rep. Wanger on railroad legislation. Approval of immigration bill

21 Washington. Conference with Flint on Colorado River break. Conference on naval strength with Metcalf, Adm. Dewey. Callers include Fairbanks, Dick, Longworth, Jusserand

22 Washington. Conferences with Warner, Heyburn, Bankhead on state judgeships. Departure for Boston

23 Boston. Breakfast at Dr. W. S. Bigelow's with Arlo Bates, L. R. Briggs,

Rev. Samuel Crothers. Speech on athletics at Harvard Union reception. Meeting with Porcellian Club

24 Boston. Breakfast including Gov. Guild, G. H. Lyman, Austin Wadsworth. Trip to Groton for day at W. A. Gardner's. Return to Boston and departure for Washington

25 Washington

26 Washington. Conference with Pettus, Underwood on Alabama judgeship. Conference with Beveridge on child labor bill. Callers include W. A. Smith, Gardner

27 Washington. Conference with Pettus, Clayton on Alabama appointments. Conference with Rep. Sherman on labor laws. Conference with Board of Indian Commissioners on leasing of coal lands. Callers include La Follette

28 Washington. Conference with Sen. Clark on Wyoming judgeship. Conference with Reps. Dawes and Heyburn on Ohio and Idaho judgeships. Callers include Lodge, Spooner, Hopkins, Patterson, Dryden, Cocks, Kahn, Olmstead, Burton

MARCH

1 Washington. Resignation of Hitchcock and L. M. Shaw. Conference with Watson on ship subsidies. Callers include Keifer, Calder, Weeks, Hull

2 Washington. Conference with Cannon, Hemenway, Watson on Indiana appointments. Conference with Meyer, Overstreet on postal affairs. Conference with Smoot on Utah coal lands. Conference with Elkins on canal construction. Evening conference with Root and Meyer

3 Washington

4 Washington. Adjournment of 59th Congress. J. B. Bishop succeeds Shonts on canal commission

5 Washington. Cabinet meeting. Callers include Dillingham, Gamble, Reginald Post, Grosvenor

6 Washington. Immigration conference with Lodge, Latimer, Dillingham, Burkett. Conference with Beveridge and Hemenway on Indiana patronage. Conference with Humphrey on ship subsidy bill. Conference with Heyburn on Idaho judgeship

7 Washington. Railroad conference with Hepburn and Neill. Callers include Dolliver, Allison, Hemenway

8 Washington. Cabinet meeting on Japanese immigration questions. Conference with Larrinaga on Philippine appointments

9 Washington. Conference with Foss on naval personnel bill. Callers include Reynolds, Hemenway, Beveridge, Flint, Allison, Clark, Elkins, Scott, H. S. Tucker

10 Washington

11 Washington. Immigration conference with Bonaparte, Straus, Sargent. Conference with McCumber and Bartholdt. Conference with Flint on Los Angeles water supply

12 Washington. Cabinet meeting. Conference with J. P. Morgan. Conference on postal appointments with Beveridge and Hemenway. Callers include Larrinaga

13 Washington. Conference with Taft on enforcement of eight-hour law. Immigration conference with Flint, Dixon, Lodge, Beveridge. Callers include Lacey, Gamble

14 Washington. Panic on New York Stock Exchange. Conference with A. B. Stickney on federal control of railroads. Conference with J. D. Crimmins

15 Washington. Cabinet meeting on Wall Street panic. Conference with Harlan and Prouty. Interstate commerce conference with Hemenway. Conference on panic with Cortelyou

16 Washington. Conferences with J. S. Speyer, Beveridge, Crane, Heyburn on financial situation. Conference with Gov. Deneen and Atty. Gen. Stead of Illinois on Harriman and Illinois railroad

17 Washington. Publication of appointments to Inland Waterways Commission

18 Washington. Opening of Louisville Exposition. Conference with Gamble on South Dakota patronage. Callers include Reps. Gaines and Porter

19 Washington. Cabinet meeting. Political conference with Hansbrough. Railroad conference with C. S. Mellen. Conference with Franklin Lane. Callers include Hitchcock, Heyburn, Jusserand, Garfield, Bacon

20 Washington

21 Washington. Conference with Overman. Callers include Jusserand

22 Washington. Cabinet meeting. Conference with Burton and Inland Waterways Commission. Callers include Kittredge

23 Washington. Conference with Garfield and Leupp on Indian matters. Conference with F. H. Levy on tobacco trusts. Conference with J. C. Blackburn on canal commission

24 Washington

25 Washington. Conference with Beveridge on statehood for New Mexico and Arizona. Callers include Fairbanks, Del. Andrews, Ben Daniels, "Bat" Masterson

26 Washington. Railroad conference with Cortelyou, Root, Lane, Clark. Immigration conference with Neill, Jenks, Dillingham, Lodge, Latimer, Burnett. Conference with Rep. Kennedy on canal. Conference with Dalzell, Scott on state appointments. Callers include R. S. McCormick

27 Washington. Lunch with Carnegie, Fairbanks, Cortelyou, Bacon, McCormick

28 Washington. Callers include Dick, Fairbanks

29 Washington. Cabinet meeting. Railroad conference with Neill, Knapp, Cullom. Callers include Meyer, J. W. Gerard, Gov. Davidson of Wisconsin

30 Washington. Canal conference with Rep. Marshall. Railroad conference with August Belmont, J. M. Levy, F. B. Kellogg. Callers include R. H. Post

31 Washington

APRIL

1 Washington. Callers include Burrows, McCall, Bishop

2 Washington. Publication of correspondence about Harriman and 1904 campaign fund. Callers include Commissioner Lane, Sen. Flint. Cabinet meeting

3 Washington. Callers include Harlan, Cullom, Flint, Satterlee, Rep. Kennedy

4 Washington. Callers include Garfield, Metcalf, Hull, Foss, Burrows, Hale

5 Washington. Cabinet meeting

6 Washington. Conference with Sens. Bourne, Hansbrough

7 Washington

8 Washington. Canal conference with Cannon. Discussion of U. S. interests in Honduras with Rep. W. S. Smith. Callers include Jacob Riis, Judge Morrow, Sen. Flint

9 Washington. Dinner for Baron de Constant including Jusserand, Bonaparte, Meyer, Bacon, Pinchot, Longworth, Abbott

10 Washington. Conference with ex-Del. Flynn on Oklahoma appointments. Canal conference with Sen. Curtis. Callers include H. B. MacFarland

11 Washington. Canal conference with Tawney and Olcott

12 Washington. Cabinet meeting. Conference with Root, Cortelyou. Conference with Gamble on South Dakota appointments

13 Washington. Callers include Cannon, Abp. Ireland, Rep. Humphrey

14 Washington. Dinner for C. W. Eliot including Meyer, Garfield, Bonaparte, O. W. Holmes, Moody, Leupp, Pinchot

15 Washington. Conference with Rep. Alexander on New York politics. Callers include H. W. Taft, Elkins, Ballinger

16 Washington. Cabinet meeting on Borah indictment

17 Washington. Railroad conference with ex-Gov. Larrabee of Iowa

18 Washington. Callers include S. H. Cowan, Adm. Evans, Clark, Mondell, Elkins, Hull

19 Washington. Cabinet meeting. Callers include Allee, Bartholdt, Meyer, Foraker, W. J. Coombs

20 Washington. Conference with Stevens on canal affairs. Conference with L. M. Shaw. Callers include W. R. Wheeler, Sen. Carter

21 Washington

22 Washington. Conference with Rep. Parsons on New York politics. Callers include James Bryce, Warren

23 Washington. Cabinet meeting. Conference with Borah. Callers include Rep. Gaines. White House musicale

24 Washington. Conference on New York politics with Vreeland, Sherman, Littauer. Conference with Borah on indictment. Callers include W. R. Willcox. Dinner including Cowles, Meyer, Garfield, Jusserand, Justice Day, Gen. Crozier, Capt. McCoy, Herbert Wadsworth

25 Washington. Conference with Sens. Penrose and Bourne. Conference with New. Conference with Rep. Burton on Inland Waterways Comm. Departure for Jamestown, Va.

26 Jamestown. Opening of Exposition. Speech, reception

27 Jamestown. Afternoon departure for Washington
28 Washington
29 Washington. Callers include ex-Gov. Durbin, A. J. Miller, Foraker, G. F. Dunn, Cannon
30 Washington. Conference on naval matters with Foss and Meyer

MAY

1 Washington. Conferences with Knox, Taft, Hemenway. Railroad conference with C. S. Mellen and T. F. Byrnes. Conference with J. B. Reynolds
2 Washington. Conference on Moyer-Haywood case with Reynolds. Callers include Hansbrough. J. W. Roosevelt at White House
3 Washington. Cabinet meeting
4 Washington. Conference with Lodge, Wilson, Rep. Gill on provisions of Pure Food and Drug Act. Conference with Taft on Gatun Dam. Lunch with Gov. Deneen and members of Inland Waterways Comm.
5 Washington
6 Washington. Conference with Rep. Parsons on New York politics
7 Washington. Cabinet meeting. Conference with Elkins on Internal Revenue Bureau appointments. Lunch with Riis. Conference with Bonaparte. Reception for members of American Medical Congress
8 Washington. Conference with ex-Del. Flynn on Oklahoma statehood. Callers include Newlands, Sherman
9 Washington. Conference with Pinchot on Mississippi River trip. Callers include Bonaparte, Ballinger, Warner
10 Washington
11 Washington. Cabinet meeting. Conference with Secy. Taft and H. W. Taft on Ohio politics. Callers include Cullom, W. I. Buchanan. Dinner including Cabinet members, Kuroki, Duke of Abruzzi, Gen. Bell, Adm. Davis, Capt. McCoy
12 Washington
13 Washington. Conference on New York appointments with Loeb, Cortelyou
14 Washington. Callers include Gaines, Hull
15 Washington. Cabinet meeting. Conference with Sen. Curtis on Kansas and Oklahoma politics. Conference with Canal Commissioner Smith. Callers include Cannon, Judge Gray

16 Washington. Conference with Cullom, Burton, Burrows, Martin. Lunch including Root, John Barrett
17 Departure for Pine Knot, Va.
18 Pine Knot
19 Pine Knot
20 Pine Knot
21 Pine Knot
22 Departure for Washington
23 Washington. Conference with Cocks on New York politics. Conference with Cannon. Callers include Longworth, Taft, Cullom
24 Washington. Cabinet meeting. Conference with Pettus on Senate military affairs committee meeting. Callers include John Barrett
25 Washington. Conference with Frank Hitchcock on postal inspection trip. Callers include Warren, Bourne, Garfield, Hemenway, Bryce
26 Washington
27 Washington. Trip to Mount Vernon
28 Washington. Conference with Bonaparte on Japanese exclusion. Conference with Hemenway. Callers include F. H. Hitchcock, Bourne, Bartholdt. Evening departure for Canton, Ohio
29 Canton, Ohio. Mrs. McKinley's funeral. Dinner at Justice Day's
30 Arrival at Indianapolis, Ind., with stops at Sidney, Ohio, Union City and Muncie, Ind. Lunch including Fairbanks, Beveridge, Hemenway, Overstreet, New, Thomas Taggart, James Whitcomb Riley. Visit with L. B. Swift, W. D. Foulke
31 Lansing, Mich. Speech at Michigan Agricultural College. Speech at State Capitol. Visit with B. I. Wheeler

JUNE

"Railroad Investments" published in *Review of Reviews*
1 Arrival in Washington with stop in Pittsburgh
2 Washington
3 Washington. Conference with Metcalf and Adm. Brownson. Callers include Cullom, C. D. Walcott
4 Washington. Cabinet meeting. Conference with Root, Metcalf, Adm. Brownson. Callers include Rep. Calder, Lummis, Elkins, Jusserand
5 Washington. Conference with Bonaparte on mine railroads. Conference with F. K. Lane on Harriman case.

Callers include Root, Taft, F. B. Kellogg

6 Washington. Callers include George Shiras

7 Washington. Conference on trusts with M. D. Purdy. Conference with Burton on Inland Waterways Comm. work. Cabinet meeting

8 Washington. Conference with Bonaparte, Ballinger on land laws. Callers include Cullom, John Barrett, G. C. Carter, Garfield, Wilson, James Bryce, Larrinaga, Hemenway, Wetmore, J. S. Sherman

9 Departure for Jamestown on *Mayflower*

10 Jamestown. Speech at Exposition. Return to Washington

11 Washington. Cabinet meeting. Conference with Sen. Carter on federal land policy. Conference with F. K. Lane on Harriman case

12 Departure for Oyster Bay

13 Oyster Bay

14 Oyster Bay

15 Oyster Bay. Callers include John Temple Graves

16 Oyster Bay. Callers include Beveridge

17 Oyster Bay

18 Oyster Bay

19 Oyster Bay

20 Oyster Bay

21 Oyster Bay

22 Oyster Bay

23 Oyster Bay

24 Oyster Bay. Approval of Dominican customs treaty

25 Oyster Bay

26 Oyster Bay

27 Oyster Bay. Callers include Metcalf, Capt. Wainwright, Ernest Ingersoll

28 Oyster Bay

29 Oyster Bay

30 Oyster Bay

JULY

1 Oyster Bay

2 Oyster Bay

3 Oyster Bay

4 Oyster Bay

5 Oyster Bay

6 Oyster Bay

7 Oyster Bay

8 Oyster Bay

9 Oyster Bay

10 Oyster Bay. Hepburn at Sagamore Hill

11 Oyster Bay

12 Oyster Bay. Lunch with Adm. Yamamoto, Aoki, Bacon, E. D. Morgan, Julius and Max Fleischmann

13 Oyster Bay. Conference with Neill and telephone companies' delegates. Conference with Bonaparte

14 Oyster Bay

15 Oyster Bay

16 Oyster Bay. All-night camping trip

17 Oyster Bay. Lunch with Hopkins, H. E. Miles

18 Oyster Bay

19 Oyster Bay

20 Oyster Bay

21 Oyster Bay

22 Oyster Bay

23 Oyster Bay. Callers include William Willcox

24 Oyster Bay

25 Oyster Bay

26 Oyster Bay

27 Oyster Bay

28 Oyster Bay

29 Oyster Bay. Lunch with Gov. Guild, T. Newberry

30 Oyster Bay. Naval conference with Newberry

31 Oyster Bay

AUGUST

1 Oyster Bay

2 Oyster Bay. Callers include Bacon, A. W. Cooley, Peter Jay

3 Oyster Bay

4 Oyster Bay. Death of Saint-Gaudens

5 Oyster Bay

6 Oyster Bay

7 Oyster Bay

8 Oyster Bay

9 Oyster Bay

10 Oyster Bay

11 Oyster Bay

12 Oyster Bay

13 Oyster Bay. Callers include Taft, Root, Meyer

14 Oyster Bay. Callers include Root

15 Oyster Bay

16 Oyster Bay

17 Oyster Bay. Conference with E. S. Sims on Standard Oil of Indiana rebate case

18 Oyster Bay

19 Oyster Bay

20 Speech at Provincetown, Mass.

21 Oyster Bay

22 Oyster Bay. G. W. Perkins at Sagamore Hill

23 Oyster Bay. Callers include Newberry,

Adms. Evans, Brownson; Lincoln Steffens, Leupp
24 Oyster Bay
25 Oyster Bay
26 Oyster Bay
27 Oyster Bay
28 Oyster Bay
29 Oyster Bay
30 Oyster Bay. Callers include Garfield, McEnery, Foster
31 Oyster Bay

SEPTEMBER

"Nature Fakers" published in *Everybody's*
1 Oyster Bay
2 Oyster Bay
3 Oyster Bay
4 Oyster Bay
5 Oyster Bay
6 Oyster Bay. Lunch with Judge Landis
7 Oyster Bay
8 Oyster Bay
9 Oyster Bay
10 Oyster Bay
11 Oyster Bay
12 Oyster Bay
13 Oyster Bay
14 Oyster Bay
15 Oyster Bay
16 Oyster Bay
17 Oyster Bay
18 Oyster Bay
19 Oyster Bay
20 Oyster Bay
21 Oyster Bay
22 Oyster Bay
23 Oyster Bay
24 Oyster Bay
25 Departure for Washington
26 Washington. Conference with Bonaparte on trusts. Naval conference with Metcalf. Discussion of presidential nomination with McCumber and Curtis. Lunch with Loeb, W. L. Ward. Callers include Garfield, Bacon, Oliver, Cooley, W. A. Smith
27 Washington. Callers include Cullom, Cooley, Warner, Hyatt
28 Washington. Conference with Meyer on railroad mail rates. Conference with Metcalf, Adms. Cowles, Brownson on coaling stations for Pacific fleet. Callers include Bishop, Curtis, Silas McBee
29 Washington. Evening departure for the West
30 Canton, Ohio. Parade and dedication of McKinley memorial

OCTOBER

"Small Country Neighbors" published in *Scribner's*
1 Speeches at Meridosia, Ill. and Keokuk, Iowa
2 Speech on the navy at St. Louis. Departure on steamer *Mississippi* for Cairo, Ill.
3 Speech at Cairo. Departure for Memphis, Tenn.
4 Speech at Memphis. Departure for Lake Providence, La.
5 Lake Providence and Stamboul, La.
6-19 Bear hunt near Stamboul
20 Return to Stamboul
21 Departure for Vicksburg, Miss. Speech and reception
22 Speeches at Nashville, Chattanooga, Tenn.
23 Stops at Roanoke, Lynchburg, Va. Arrival in Washington. Evening conference with Bacon
24 Washington. Financial conferences with Root, Knox, Metcalf, Asst. Secy. Edwards, Garfield, McCumber. Callers include Warner, Capt. McCoy, Justice Harlan
25 Washington. Cabinet meeting on naval affairs. Financial conference with Elkins. Callers include Hemenway, Long, Rep. Watson, Bacon, F. K. Lane
26 Washington. Naval conference with Metcalf, Adms. Evans, Brownson. Callers include Straus, Garfield, Flint, Long, Dalzell, Del. Andrews
27 Washington. Birthday. Reception for Hungarian Club of New York
28 Washington. Conference with Tawney on canal appropriations. Conferences on Oklahoma constitution with Gov. Frantz, Rep. McGuire, Sens. McCumber, Long, Carter
29 Washington. Cabinet meeting on finances. Financial conference with Cortelyou. Conference with Frantz, Sen. Warner. Reception for delegation of Spanish War veterans
30 Washington. Conferences with Hepburn and Mann
31 Washington. Political conference with Sen. Scott

NOVEMBER

"Roosevelt, by Himself" published in *Cosmopolitan*
1 Washington. Cabinet meeting. Conference with Paul Morton. Evening con-

ference with Garfield and Leupp on Ute reservation

2 Washington. Conference on Oklahoma appointments with Garfield, Bonaparte, Frank Frantz

3 Washington

4 Washington. Conference with Cortelyou on national finances. Conference with E. H. Gary, H. C. Frick, Root. Conference with Cummins on Iowa appointments. Callers include Fairbanks, Sen. Scott. Evening conference with Sen. Nelson, Cortelyou, delegation of bankers on government financial aid in moving grain crops. Midnight departure for Oyster Bay to vote

5 Oyster Bay. Return to Washington

6 Washington. Conference with C. S. Mellen on investigation of NY, NH&H railroad. Conference with Bonaparte, Garfield, Frantz, C. H. Hunter on Oklahoma appointments. Callers include Moody, Burrows, Long, Warner, Rep. Fowler

7 Washington. Callers include Gallinger, Herbert Parsons, Heyburn

8 Washington. Cabinet meeting. Conference on New York politics with J. B. Reynolds, J. A. Stewart

9 Washington. Conference with Dillingham, J. W. Jenks, W. R. Wheeler on immigration commission work. Conference with AF of L officials including Gompers, Morrison. Callers include Rep. Clark, P. B. Stewart

10 Washington

11 Washington. Conference on prohibition with ex-Rep. Babcock. Callers include Sen. Bourne, Larrinaga, L. C. Griscom

12 Washington. Cabinet meeting. Conference with Rep. Vreeland on New York politics and Indian oil leases. Callers include Baron Rosen, Allee, Clark

13 Washington. Conference with Meyer on government postal savings banks. Lunch for delegates to Central American peace conference

14 Washington. Conference with Meyer, Rep. Campbell on government aid to banks. Lunch with Arthur Train, Herbert Parsons, J. R. Sheffield. Callers include D. J. Hill, Burkett, Long, Flint, Burrows

15 Washington. Cabinet meeting. Visit with Abp. Ireland

16 Washington. Callers include W. H. H. Llewellyn, Foraker, McCumber

17 Washington

18 Washington. Conference with Bartholdt on waterways commission work. Dinner with Joel Chandler Harris

19 Washington. Cabinet meeting. Conference with Root, Cortelyou, Meyer. Lunch and conference with Delegate Cade of Alaska. Callers include Scott, Elkins, B. I. Wheeler. Paderewski recital

20 Washington. Financial conference with Lodge. Callers include Meyer, Garfield. Hemenway, Flint, Needham, Cowles. J. G. Leishman

21 Washington. Canal conference with Rep. Taylor. Callers include T. N. Page, G. F. Adams, H. St. G. Tucker. Sulzer, C. P. Neill, Fulton, Bourne. Langley, Lowden

22 Washington. Cabinet meeting. Evening conference on financial situation with J. P. Morgan, G. F. Baker, Bacon. Cortelyou

23 Washington. Tariff conference with Payne, Dalzell. Conference on Porto Rico with R. H. Post, Beekman Winthrop. Callers include W. J. Bryan, J. B. Reynolds

24 Washington

25 Washington. Tariff conference with Rep. Hull. Conference with Gamble, Kittredge on South Dakota appointments. Callers include C. D. Wright, C. D. Walcott, Cowles, Hansbrough

26 Washington. Cabinet meeting. Conference on South Dakota appointments with Gamble. Conference with Loudenslager on work of Republican congressional committee. Callers include Hale, Long, A. W. Cooley. Reception for International YMCA

27 Washington. Callers include Borah, Gore, Piles, Tawney, Overman, Sutherland. Wedding of Edith Root and U. S. Grant. J. C. Greenway, Longworths at White House

28 Thanksgiving Day visit to Montpelier, Va.

29 Washington. Cabinet meeting. Callers include Dillingham, Latimer, Needham, Curtis. Dinner including Pres. Amador, Adm. Evans, Root, Oliver, Tawney, Longworth, W. B. McKinley, Bacon, Gen. Bell, Col. Howze, Lt. Com. Sims, Pinchot

30 Washington. Callers include Gompers, Allison, Gamble, Hansbrough, Overman, Depew, Smoot, McCumber, Davis, Beveridge, Cocks, Humphrey, Hayes

1 Washington
2 Washington. 60th Congress convenes. Conference with Hansbrough on currency legislation. Conference with Cooper on Interstate Commerce Act amendment. Callers include Aldrich, Crane, Beveridge, La Follette, Culberson, Ankeny, Dick, Cockran, Littlefield, Hinshaw. Conference with Ambassador Aoki
3 Washington. Annual message to Congress. Cabinet meeting. Evening conference with Aldrich, Crane on financial legislation
4 Washington. Callers include R. H. Post, Lodge, G. C. Perkins, Warner, Gaines, Overstreet, Weeks, Gen. Clayton
5 Washington. Lunch with Gov. Cummins, H. S. New, W. M. Bullitt, C. H. Merriam, Dr. Rixey. Callers include Underwood, Bede, T. E. Byrnes, Wm. Barnes, Jr. Brander Matthews, Lounsbury at White House
6 Washington. Cabinet meeting. Callers include F. B. Kellogg, Frye, Clapp, McLaurin, Bede, Campbell, Davenport. Visit to Corcoran Art Gallery with Brander Matthews. Dinner with members of Louisiana hunting party, Meyer, Bacon, Loeb, Pinchot, J. M. Dickinson, Cecil Lyon, Fitzhugh Lee
7 Washington. Callers include Townsend, Gaines, Gardner, McGuire, Gov. Smith, Metcalf, Cockrell. Mrs. J. West Roosevelt at White House
8 Washington
9 Washington. Callers include Warren, Long, Clapp, Bourne, Perkins, Fairbanks, Hepburn, Kahn, Fassett, Gompers, C. P. Neill. Lunch with Thomas Watson
10 Washington. Cabinet meeting. Callers include Overstreet, Bede, Humphrey
11 Washington. Callers include J. S. Williams, Bede, Sutherland, Bonaparte, Meyer, Hitchcock
12 Washington. Conference with Thomas Watson. Conference with Flint, G. C. Perkins, Knowland on appointments. Lunch with Hoke Smith. Callers include Long, Warner, Burton, Fassett, Jusserand, Cooley
13 Washington. Cabinet meeting. Callers include Newberry, Curtis, Warren, Hopkins, Hepburn, Fassett
14 Washington. Conference on postal affairs with Meyer. Conference with Fairbanks
15 Departure on *Mayflower* for Hampton Roads, Va.
16 Speech at departure of fleet on world cruise. Return to Washington
17 Washington. Cabinet meeting. Conference with Bartholdt on Missouri appointments. Callers include T. W. Lawson, Warner
18 Washington. Callers include Fulton, Lodge, Proctor, Dixon, Dillingham, Gamble, Bede, Underwood, Calder
19 Washington. Callers include Warren, Hopkins, Lorimer, Woodruff, J. A. Stewart, Cullom, Hale, Gov. Hoggatt, Sherman. Cabinet dinner
20 Washington. Cabinet meeting. Callers include Piles, von Sternberg, Woodruff, Cullom
21 Washington. Conference with Parsons, Olcott, J. A. Merritt on New York politics. Callers include Taft, Cannon, Burrows, Allison, Fulton, Bourne, Warner, Longworth, Gov. Hoggatt. Reception for delegates of Central American peace conference
22 Washington
23 Washington. Callers include Long, Burkett, Bede, Bowers, Garfield. Conference with Flint, Humphrey on fortification of Pacific Coast. Conference with Sen. Nixon. Lunch with L. S. Rowe
24 Washington. Cabinet meeting. Conference with Hansbrough on financial situation. Conferences with Heney, Gov. Hoggatt. Callers include Bourne, Longworth, Beekman Winthrop
25 Washington
26 Washington. Afternoon departure for Pine Knot, Va., with stop at Charlottesville
27 Pine Knot
28 Pine Knot
29 Pine Knot
30 Afternoon departure for Washington
31 Washington

1908

JANUARY

"In the Louisiana Canebrakes" published in *Scribner's*
"Our National Inland Waterways Policy" published in *Annals of the American Academy*

1 Washington. New Year's Day reception
2 Washington. Appointment of J. E.

Pillsbury as Chief of the Bureau of Navigation. Conference with Taft. Callers include Sens. McCreary, Nelson, Secy. Metcalf, Seth Bullock

3 Washington. Cabinet meeting. Callers include Sen. Bourne, S. N. D. North, Asst. Postmaster General De Graw. Dinner including Beveridge, Whitelaw Reid, Rockhill, Goethals

4 Washington. Conference on Nevada labor conditions with C. P. Neill, L. O. Murray. Conference with Rep. Humphrey on Puget Sound coast defences. Callers include Root, Metcalf, Sens. Brown, Curtis, Perkins, Warner, Reps. Dalzell, Kahn. Lunch with F. S. Butterworth

5 Washington

6 Washington. Congress reconvenes. Conference with Reps. Parsons, Olcott, Bennet on NYC appointment. Callers include Taft, Meyer, Hansbrough, Warren, Beveridge, Murray, C. H. Treat

7 Washington. Cabinet meeting. Callers include Sens. Carter, Clapp, Hemenway, Rep. Gaines, Robert Bacon, C. A. Prouty

8 Washington. Conference with Payne, Dalzell. Callers include Root, Clapp, Overman, Johnston, Col. J. J. McCook, Townsend

9 Washington. Callers include Taft, Wilson, La Follette, Bourne, Butler, Hopkins

10 Washington. Cabinet meeting. Conference with Sens. Burkett, Brown on Nebraska postal appointments. Callers include Taft, Cooley, Harlan, McEnery. Dinner including Cannon, Borah, J. S. Williams, Herbert Putnam, S. E. Payne

11 Washington. Conference with Reps. Kahn, Hayes on fortification of Pearl Harbor. Tariff conference with Heyburn. Conference with Knox on employers' liability bill. Callers include L. M. Shaw, H. K. Smith, Seth Bullock, F. V. Greene, J. G. Capers, Taliaferro

12 Washington

13 Washington. Conference with Garfield, Ballinger on land fraud prosecutions. Conference with Bonaparte. Conference with Sen. Burkett on Nebraska appointments. Callers include J. F. Vivian, Gov. Buchtel, Proctor

14 Washington. Cabinet meeting. Conference with Dist. Atty. Sims on Standard Oil cases. Dinner at Root's

15 Washington. Conference on battleship construction with R. P. Hobson. Callers include Payn, Crumpacker

16 Washington. Dinner for diplomatic corps

17 Washington. Cabinet meeting. Callers include Sens. Smoot, Brown

18 Washington. Conferences with Sens. Burkett, Brown. Callers include C. H. Treat

19 Washington

20 Washington

21 Washington. Cabinet meeting. Callers include Proctor, Grosvenor, Elmer Dover. Dinner at Cortelyou's

22 Washington. Conference with Rep. Bennet, Fassett on candidacy of Hughes for President. Death of M. K. Jesup.

23 Washington. Conference with Sen. McLaurin on army matters. Reception for judiciary

24 Washington. Cabinet meeting on postal appointments. Dinner including Warren, Depew, Sens. Frazier, Briggs, Bankhead, Reps. Dalzell, Sherman

25 Washington. Conference with Rep. Parsons on New York politics. Lunch with E. H. Gary. Callers include Fairbanks, Cannon, John Barrett. Gridiron Club dinner

26 Washington

27 Washington. Reception for members of National Editorial Association

28 Washington. Cabinet meeting. Conference with Rep. Campbell on candidacy of Taft for President. Conference with Seth Low, Gompers on trust legislation. Dinner at Bonaparte's

29 Washington. Conference on Kentucky appointments with Langley, Edwards, J. B. Bennett, James. Callers include Overman, Piles, Hopkins, Clapp, Dixon, Kahn

30 Washington. Callers include Gov. Floyd, J. W. Noble, Dolliver, Flint. Dinner for Supreme Court

31 Washington. Message to Congress urging legislation for workers' injury compensation, increased federal control of railroads, corporations. Cabinet meeting. Conference on canal affairs with Goethals. Callers include Bacon, Clay, Borah, Clapp, Hinshaw

FEBRUARY

1 Washington. Conference with Rep. Landis on Govt. Printing Office affairs

1615

2 Washington
3 Washington. Conference with Woodruff on New York politics. Callers include Fairbanks, La Follette, Capt. Peary
4 Washington. Cabinet meeting. Dinner at Meyer's
5 Washington. Suspension of Public Printer Stillings. Conference with Taft and Gen. Bell. Conference with delegation of National Assoc. of Manufacturers on appointment of permanent tariff commission
6 Washington. Conference with House naval affairs committee. Callers include Sens. Borah, Nelson, Heyburn, Burrows. Congressional reception
7 Washington. Cabinet meeting. Conference with Taft, Root, Magoon on Cuban affairs. Callers include Warren, Gardner, Overstreet, Foster, Smoot. Endicott Peabody and Jacob Riis at White House
8 Washington. Callers include L. M. Shaw, Allison
9 Washington
10 Washington. Conference with Rep. Hull on balloon experiments. Conference with Longworth on Ohio politics
11 Washington. Cabinet meeting. Callers include Ballinger, Sen. Ankeny. Dinner at Metcalf's
12 Washington. Conference with Aldrich
13 Washington. Conference with F. H. Hitchcock on Taft campaign in the South. Conference with Bonaparte on Alaskan miners' strike
14 Washington. Cabinet meeting. Callers include Frantz, Cecil Lyon, Dillingham. Evening reception at National Society of Fine Arts
15 Washington
16 Washington. Conference with W. S. Rossiter
17 Washington. Conferences with Sen. Nixon, F. H. Hitchcock. Douglas Robinsons at White House
18 Washington. Cabinet meeting on immigration. Callers include Curtis Guild. Dinner including Jusserand, Justice Day, Meyer, Lodge, Whitelaw Reid, Longworth, Robinson. Dinner at Garfields'
19 Washington. Conferences with Sherman and Knox on antitrust laws. Conference with Meyer on postal appointments. Callers include F. H. Hitchcock. Dinner including Crane, Lodge, von Sternberg, Gov. Fort, Rep. Cockran, N. M. Butler, ex-Gov. Bates
20 Washington. Conference with Rep. Hobson on battleship appropriations. Conference with James Speyer. Conference with Smoot. Army-Navy reception
21 Washington. Conference with Rep. Waldo on impeachment of Judge Wilfley. Conference with Rep. Davis on industrial school bill. Conference with Rep. Hobson. Financial conference with Aldrich. Conference with Taft, Goethals on Panama labor conditions. Callers include F. B. Kellogg, Hemenway, J. A. Stewart
22 Washington. Conference with Rep. Miller on Southern Pacific claim for repair of Colorado River bank. Conference with Rep. Hull on military appropriations bill. Conference on Mass. politics with Rep. Gardner, J. C. Cobb. Conference with Rep. Sherman on alleged submarine lobby
23 Washington
24 Washington. Conference with McCumber, Rep. Gronna on La Follette campaign. Canal conference with Goethals. Lunch with H. S. New, Taft, Root. Callers include G. C. Perkins, Flint, delegation of Nat. Education Assoc.
25 Washington. Cabinet meeting. Conference with Rep. Landis on Govt. Printing Office affairs. Callers include F. B. Loomis, Sen. Carter, Reps. Madden, Burton. Funeral of Bishop Satterlee. Cabinet dinner given by Secy. Wilson
26 Washington. Report of Inland Waterways Comm. sent to Congress. Callers include Sens. Cockran, du Pont, Cullom, Borah
27 Washington. Conference with Board of Indian Commissioners. Conference with Taft. Conference on nomination of public printer with Rep. Langley. Callers include Judge Wilfley, Rep. Gardner
28 Washington. Cabinet meeting. Discussion of Wilfley case. Conference with Reps. Cockran, Driscoll on Wilfley case. Conference on tariff commission bill with Beveridge
29 Washington. Conference with H. Ridder on paper trust. Callers include Fairbanks, Carter, C. P. Neill. Evening conference with Commander Sims on battleship construction

1 Washington
2 Washington. Conferences with Hepburn and Crane
3 Washington. Cabinet meeting. Dinner at Straus'
4 Washington. Evening conference with H. H. Kohlsaat. Death of Senator Proctor
5 Washington. Conference with Sen. Burkett, Rep. Hinshaw
6 Washington. Cabinet meeting on postal treaties with France and Italy. Conference with Adm. Dewey on warship construction. Callers include Lodge, Aldrich
7 Washington. Conference with Beveridge on tariff commission bill. Endorsement of Hughes by N. Y. Republican State Committee
8 Washington
9 Washington. Naval conferences with Reps. Hobson, Foss. Callers include Taft
10 Washington. Cabinet meeting. Conference with Aldrich. Speech and reception for National Congress of Mothers
11 Washington. Conference with Sen. Long on Taft campaign. Conference with Montana delegation on alleged illegal holdings of Northern Pacific R.R. Evening conference on Colorado River break restitution with Garfield, Maxwell Evarts
12 Washington. Conference with Frantz on Oklahoma politics. Lunch with Stuyvesant Fish. Callers include L. A. Coolidge, Rep. Kennedy
13 Washington. Cabinet meeting. Conference with Reps. Parsons, Langley. Callers include Sen. Hopkins
14 Washington. Conferences with Sen. Gamble, Reps. Perkins, Tirrell on Taft campaign. Conference with Sen. Bourne on third term. Conference with Sen. Overman on Brownsville affair. Callers include Jusserand
15 Washington
16 Washington. Legislative conference with Aldrich. Conference with Rep. Hale on Tennessee politics
17 Washington. Cabinet meeting. Conference and lunch with Carnegie. Callers include Cullom, Rep. McKinley
18 Washington. Conference with Sen. Taylor on Tennessee judgeship. Conference with Sen. Simmons on ship subsidy bill. Conference with Rep. Hill on Aldrich currency bill. Conference and lunch with William Barnes and Longworth
19 Washington. Conference on Phillippine affairs with Taft, E. A. Philbin. Callers include Rep. Cockran, delegation of Spanish War veterans
20 Washington. Conference with Sen. Carter on appointment of solicitor of internal revenue. Conference with Judge Wilfley. Evening conference with western businessmen on tariff revision
21 Washington. Legislative conference with Aldrich, Payne, Dalzell. Tariff revision conferences with Crane, Beveridge
22 Washington
23 Washington. Conference on New York politics with Woodruff. Callers include Taft
24 Washington. Cabinet meeting. Discussion of postal service salary increase. Conference on battleship appropriations with Rep. Hobson. Conference with Borah on Brownsville affair. Conference with Flint on battleship cruise
25 Washington. Special message to Congress on antitrust, interstate commerce and financial legislation, child labor laws. Conference with Bartholdt on public buildings bill. Conference with delegation of Nebraska cattlemen on government land grants. Conference with pure food advisory board. Callers include Hemenway, Burkett, Gov. Sheldon, Sen. Taylor
26 Washington. Conference with Hepburn on antitrust legislation. Callers include Beveridge, Overstreet, M. D. Purdy, Wilson, Sen. Stephenson
27 Washington. Cabinet meeting on Alaskan strikes and Venezuelan dispute. Conference with Sen. Frazier and Tennessee delegation on judgeship
28 Washington. Conference with Borah on Foraker's employers' liability bill. Conference with Knox on Knox's liability bill. Conference with Rep. Weeks on currency legislation. Boone and Crockett dinner
29 Washington
30 Washington. Conference with Root on Venezuela. Conference with Taft on yellow fever quarantine in Cuba. Conference with Knapp, Lane and Clark.

Evening conference with Root, Bacon, von Sternberg

31 Washington. Nomination of D. J. Hill as ambassador to Germany, S. F. Eddy as minister to Argentina. Conference with Rep. Tirrell on Massachusetts politics. Callers include J. G. Carlisle

APRIL

1 Washington. Conference with Rep. Gardner on Massachusetts primaries. Conference on Indian affairs with Sen. Owen. Conference on battleship construction with Rep. Hobson. Callers include Cannon, Sen. Bourne. Lunch with G. C. Ward

2 Washington. Conference with Rep. Parsons on New York politics

3 Washington. Cabinet meeting. Conference with John Mitchell on investigation of Isthmian labor conditions. Conference with Sen. Curtis. Military drill at Fort Myer in afternoon

4 Washington. Appointment of J. S. Leech as public printer. Conference with Beveridge on Indiana state convention. Conference with Hobson on battleship construction. Callers include Henry Watterson

5 Washington

6 Washington. Conferences with Reps. Hill and Weeks

7 Washington. Cabinet meeting. Conference with H. Ridder on paper trust. Callers include Heyburn

8 Washington. Conference with Heyburn on Snake River irrigation dam. Conference with Reps. Moore, Small, Goulden, Wanger, Capron, Burton on inland waterways project from Boston to Key West

9 Washington. Statement to Congress urging legislation against anarchy. Conference on New York politics with Reps. Fassett and Cocks

10 Washington. Cabinet meeting. Callers include Reps. Humphreys, Jones, Porter

11 Washington. Conference with Sen. Cullom. Conference with Larrinaga on Porto Rico. Dinner with Bacons, Longworths, Cowles', Humphrey Wards, Austin Wadsworths, Mrs. Whitelaw Reid

12 Washington

13 Washington. Conferences with Parsons, Calder, Cocks on New York politics. Conference with Garfield on Alaskan coal lands. Dinner at Moody's

14 Washington. Cabinet meeting. Evening conference with Rep. Watson on adjournment of Congress. Conference with Rep. Vreeland on currency bill

15 Washington. Lunch including Bryce

16 Washington. Conference with Crane and Lodge on Massachusetts patronage. Conference with Vreeland on currency bill. Conference with delegation of American Bankers' Assoc. on currency legislation. Conference with advisory committee of National Gallery of Art. Conference with Taft

17 Washington. Cabinet meeting. Conference with Rep. McKinley on Japanese immigration. Callers include Michael Dady, Rep. Calder

18 Washington. Conference with R. M. Easley on amendment of Sherman Act. Callers include Taft

19 Washington

20 Washington. Conference with Rep. Hill on currency legislation. Conference with Emerson Hough and Hart Merriam on Alaskan game preserves. Callers include E. A. Hitchcock, Dolliver

21 Washington. Cabinet meeting. Conference with Clapp on Minnesota judgeship. Callers include Dolliver

22 Washington. Conference with Pacific Coast senators on battleship program. Callers include Surgeon General Wyman, Overstreet. "Grover Cleveland and the Coal Strike" published in the *Outlook*

23 Washington. Callers include Cooley, C. M. Pepper, Overman

24 Washington. Cabinet meeting

25 Washington. Conference on Tennessee judgeship with Rep. Gaines

26 Washington

27 Washington. Conferences with Sens. Allison, Nixon, Piles on battleship issue. Callers include Sen. Cullom. Special message to Congress on injunctions and national control of corporations

28 Washington. Cabinet meeting

29 Washington. Conferences with Sens. Ankeny, Piles, on Indian claims to land. Callers include W. R. Wheeler, F. K. Lane, Clapp, McCreary, Lodge, Watson, Foster, Hull, Underwood, Overstreet

30 Washington. Conference with Rep. Hull on western political conditions. Conference with Sen. Piles, Rep. Jones on Snake River dam bill. Conference with Reps. Hepburn, Townsend,

Campbell, Sulzer on appropriation bill for enforcement of Hepburn Act

1 Washington. Cabinet meeting. Callers include Parsons, Piles, Long
2 Washington. Callers include Elkins, Rayner
3 Washington
4 Washington. Conference with F. H. Hitchcock on Taft campaign. Conference with Reps. Watson, Alexander on current legislation. Callers include Hopkins, Rep. Pearre
5 Washington. Cabinet meeting. Conference with Carter on postal savings bank bill. Conference with Borah on Brownsville affair. Conference with Cannon on current legislation
6 Washington. Conference with Rep. Gaines, Alexander on Tennessee judgeship. Conference with C. M. Cade, C. E. Hunter on Oklahoma patronage. Conference with Rep. Humphrey on Alaskan game preserve bill. Conference with Smoot on Utah forest reserve. Lunch including Cardinal Gibbons
7 Washington
8 Departure for Pine Knot, Va., with Mrs. Roosevelt and Burroughs
9 Pine Knot
10 Pine Knot. Return to Washington
11 Washington. Callers include Smoot, Lodge. Lunch with Carnegie, Root, Abp. Ireland, R. C. Kerens. Laying of cornerstone of Bureau of American Republics
12 Washington. Cabinet meeting. Conference with Rep. Watson. Dinner with members of conservation conference, Supreme Court Justices, Wilson, Garfield
13 Washington. Conference with Rep. Watson on currency. Conference with Sen. Warren on Stewart case. Callers include Jusserand, Sen. Burkett, Hale, Rep. Bede. Governors' conference on conservation
14 Washington. Governors' conference on conservation. Conference with Reps. Townsend, Sterling on anti-injunction bill. Conference with Rep. Maynard on contract for Norfolk, Va., navy yard
15 Washington. Governors' conference on conservation. Reception for members of conservation conference
16 Washington. Conference with Rep.

Richardson on Rainy River dam bill. Callers include John Mitchell, Borah, Hepburn, Rep. Watson, Gov. Sheldon. Conference with Peary on planned Arctic trip. Speech and reception at Methodist convention at American University near Tenleytown, D. C.
17 Washington. Evening conference on New York politics with Woodruff
18 Washington. Conference with Taft on canal affairs. Conference on Kentucky patronage with Rep. Langley
19 Washington. Cabinet meeting on Panama election frauds. Conference on inland waterways bill with Reps. Moore, Capron, Goulden, Wanger, Burton, Small. Callers include Rep. Sherman
20 Washington. Conference with Cannon. Conference with Rep. Townsend on anti-injunction legislation. Conference with Dillingham on amendments to Sherman Act. Conference with Meyer, Littauer on ship subsidy provision in post-office appropriation bill. Callers include Knox, F. H. Hitchcock, Rep. Campbell
21 Washington. Conference on Venezuela with Cullom. Conference on Rainy River dam project with Rep. Bede, Hepburn, Garfield, Stevens. Conference with Burrows. Conference with delegation urging battleship construction at Norfolk navy yard. Callers include Lodge, Allison
22 Washington. Cabinet meeting. Callers include Rep. Langley, Adm. Evans. Conference with Wadsworth on New York politics
23 Washington
24 Washington
25 Washington. Conference with Garfield on Indian Territory affairs. Callers include Sens. Kean, Warren, Sutherland, Rep. Sulzer
26 Washington. Conferences with Bonaparte, Root, Garfield, Metcalf. Attends wedding of Elizabeth Oliver and Francis R. Stevens. Conference with Depew on government liability bill. Conference with Rep. Fassett on J. S. Sherman as vice-presidential candidate. Conference with Allison, Hepburn. Lunch with Col. H. L. Scott
27 Washington. Conference with Taft
28 Washington
29 Washington. Cabinet meeting. Callers include Cannon, Flint, Underwood, H. L. Satterlee, D. S. Barry
30 Washington. Signs remaining bills at

Capitol in evening. Adjournment of Congress
31 Washington

JUNE

"Successful Mother" published in the *Ladies' Home Journal*
1 Washington. Conference with Rep. Alexander on workers' compensation bill. Conference on paper trust with Rep. Mann. Callers include Hepburn. Evening conference with Taft, F. H. Hitchcock, Garfield, Sen. Hopkins, W. H. Ellis, Frank Kellogg on Republican campaign
2 Washington. Cabinet meeting. Callers include A. B. Hart, Warren, Dick, Borah, Vreeland, Sulzer
3 Washington. Callers include Taft, Capt. J. G. Capers, Heyburn, Humphrey
4 Washington. Conference with Sen. Cullom on Republican tariff platform. Campaign conference with Sen. Long. Conference with Secy. Wilson, Dr. Wiley. Callers include ex-Rep. Sibley
5 Washington. Cabinet meeting. Callers include C. A. Moore
6 Washington. Conference on Canal Zone affairs with Taft. Callers include Carter, Piles, Borah, Beveridge. Evening conference on campaign with Taft, Root, Burkett
7 Washington. Conference with Taft
8 Washington. Conference with Metcalf on naval affairs. Conference with Taft. Callers include Hepburn, Spencer Eddy
9 Washington. Cabinet meeting. Conference with Cortelyou on currency legislation. Callers include Sens. Warren, Clark. Lunch with Curtis Guild, Jr.
10 Washington. Callers include L. A. Coolidge, Borah, B. T. Washington. Evening conference with delegation from Liberia
11 Washington. Conference with F. B. Loomis on Tokyo Exposition. Callers include Dalzell, E. A. Philbin, Col. Symons
12 Washington. Cabinet meeting. Callers include Hepburn, Burkett, members of Spanish Treaty Claims Commission
13 Washington
14 Washington
15 Washington. Conference with Taft. Conference with Commissioner Macfarland on prison reform in Washington. Callers include Metcalf

16 Washington. Cabinet meeting. Campaign conference with Stewart. Conference with Taft
17 Washington
18 Washington. Callers include L. M. Shaw, Bacon, "Billie Sunday"
19 Washington. Cabinet meeting. Conference with Taft
20 Departure for Oyster Bay
21 Oyster Bay
22 Oyster Bay
23 Oyster Bay
24 Oyster Bay
25 Oyster Bay
26 Oyster Bay. Funeral of Grover Cleveland in Princeton, N. J.
27 Oyster Bay. Conference on War Dept. affairs with Taft and L. E. Wright. Political conference with F. B. Kellogg, W. L. Ward. Callers include Robert Bridges, Lincoln Steffens
28 Oyster Bay
29 Oyster Bay. Conference with Caspar Whitney on plans for African trip
30 Oyster Bay

JULY

1 Oyster Bay. Lunch with S. S. McClure, Caspar Whitney
2 Oyster Bay
3 Oyster Bay
4 Oyster Bay
5 Oyster Bay
6 Oyster Bay
7 Oyster Bay. Conference with Robert Bridges on plans for African trip. Conference with J. S. Leech on Government Printing Office. Lunch with Robert Peary
8 Oyster Bay
9 Oyster Bay
10 Oyster Bay
11 Oyster Bay. Speech at unveiling of John Underhill monument at Matinecock, L.I. Dr. Lambert at Sagamore Hill
12 Oyster Bay
13 Oyster Bay
14 Oyster Bay
15 Oyster Bay. Lunch including H. F. Osborn, F. D. Millet, Charles Scribner, C. A. Moore. Callers include John Williams
16 Oyster Bay
17 Oyster Bay
18 Oyster Bay. Conference with Bonaparte. Conference on Central American affairs with Bacon

19 Oyster Bay
20 Oyster Bay
21 Oyster Bay. Evening departure for Newport on *Mayflower*
22 Arrival at Newport. Speech at Naval War College conference
23 Return to Oyster Bay
24 Oyster Bay. Conference with Taft
25 Oyster Bay. Lunch including Lawrence Abbott, W. B. Howland, Leigh Hunt, Beekman Winthrop
26 Oyster Bay
27 Oyster Bay
28 Oyster Bay
29 Oyster Bay
30 Oyster Bay
31 Oyster Bay. Callers include L. E. Wright, Pinchot, J. B. Bishop

AUGUST

1 Oyster Bay. Conference with L. E. Wright, Bacon on dismissals at West Point. Conference on canal affairs with Bishop
2 Oyster Bay
3 Oyster Bay
4 Oyster Bay
5 Oyster Bay. Death of Senator Allison
6 Oyster Bay
7 Oyster Bay. Campaign conference with F. H. Hitchcock. Conference on West Point dismissals with Wright. Callers include H. L. Higginson, F. M. Chapman
8 Oyster Bay
9 Oyster Bay
10 Oyster Bay
11 Oyster Bay
12 Oyster Bay
13 Oyster Bay
14 Oyster Bay
15 Oyster Bay
16 Oyster Bay
17 Oyster Bay
18 Oyster Bay
19 Oyster Bay
20 Oyster Bay. Conferences with J. S. Sherman, W. S. Bennet, C. J. Smith, M. J. Dady, Cocks, F. H. Hitchcock, Bacon, Capt. Winslow on renomination of Gov. Hughes
21 Oyster Bay
22 Oyster Bay
23 Oyster Bay
24 Oyster Bay. Death of von Sternberg
25 Oyster Bay. Lunch with Gov. Magoon. Evening departure for Jordanville, N. Y.

26 Jordanville, N.Y. Dedication of library given by Douglas Robinson
27 Oyster Bay. Lunch with Cornelius Vanderbilt
28 Oyster Bay. Callers include Sherman, Gen. Bell, Capt. Winslow, McKinley, Loudenslager
29 Oyster Bay. Ambassador Takahira at Sagamore Hill
30 Oyster Bay
31 Oyster Bay. Reception for members of American Olympic Team

SEPTEMBER

1 Oyster Bay. Conference with W. L. Ward
2 Oyster Bay. Silas McBee at Sagamore Hill
3 Oyster Bay
4 Oyster Bay. Death of F. P. Sargent
5 Oyster Bay. W. A. Wadsworth at Sagamore Hill
6 Oyster Bay
7 Oyster Bay
8 Oyster Bay
9 Oyster Bay
10 Oyster Bay
11 Oyster Bay
12 Oyster Bay
13 Oyster Bay
14 Oyster Bay. Conference with Root, Cocks
15 Oyster Bay. Nomination of C. E. Hughes for governor
16 Oyster Bay
17 Oyster Bay. Lunch with Mark Sullivan, Norman Hapgood. Reception for Oyster Bay townspeople
18 Oyster Bay
19 Oyster Bay. "Candidacy of Taft" published in the *Outlook*
20 Oyster Bay
21 Oyster Bay. Conference with Woodruff, A. P. Gardner
22 Departure for Washington
23 Washington. Political conference with Ballinger. Conference with Bonaparte, Gov. Haskell. Callers include Overman, Simmons, John Barrett. Reception for members of international fishery congress
24 Washington. Conference with Scott on West Virginia politics. Conference with Gen. Corbin on Ohio politics. Callers include Gen. Young
25 Washington. Cabinet meeting. Conference with Hopkins and Graff on Illinois politics

26 Washington. Conference with Rep. Bennet on New York politics. Conference on international immigration congress with W. R. Wheeler, Straus. Callers include Adm. Dewey, Rep. Moore, L. F. Abbott

27 Washington

28 Washington. Conference with Burrows on tariff legislation. Callers include Bacon, Pinchot, Wilson

29 Washington. Cabinet meeting on Standard Oil cases. Callers include Rep. Pearre

30 Washington. Callers include Fletcher Maddox, J. H. Hammond, E. A. Mosley, Rep. Porter, E. C. O'Brien

OCTOBER

1 Washington. Conference on Negro affairs with R. S. Baker. Conference on New York politics with Olcott, Calder, Dady. Conference with Scott. Canal conference with Goethals

2 Washington. Cabinet meeting on New York politics. Conference with ex-Sen. Dietrich on Nebraska politics. Evening campaign conference with Root. Callers include Overman

3 Washington. Labor conference with Morrissey, W. S. Stone. Speech at International Congress on Tuberculosis

4 Washington

5 Washington. Conference with Bonaparte and Gov. Comer on Alaskan railroad injunctions. Callers include Mudd, J. G. Capers, Root, Allee

6 Washington. Cabinet meeting. Callers include J. A. Stewart, G. M. Bowers, Warner. Lunch with G. R. Sheldon, C. S. Francis. Evening conference on New York politics with Root, Cortelyou, Bacon, W. L. Ward, Meyer, Loeb

7 Washington. Conference with Hemenway on Indiana politics. Conference on New York politics with W. L. Ward. Lunch with Zangwill. Dinner at Straus'

8 Washington. Conference on New York politics with W. R. Willcox

9 Washington. Cabinet meeting on fleet travels, army appointments. Conference with J. B. Reynolds on labor vote

10 Washington. Conference on labor vote with Willis Moore. Conference with Elmer Dover. Conference on New York politics with Rep. Perkins

11 Washington

12 Washington. Reception for Supreme Court

13 Washington. Cabinet meeting. Conference with Kohlsaat. Callers include Warren, Gen. Corbin, C. C. Glover

14 Washington. Conference on New York politics with Mark Sullivan. Callers include Meyer

15 Washington. Conferences with Garfield, Pinchot, Straus, Loudenslager. Callers include H. B. F. Macfarland, Cyrus Adler. Lunch with Lord Northcliffe

16 Washington. Cabinet meeting

17 Washington

18 Washington. Breakfast, conference, lunch, dinner with Taft

19 Washington. Conference with Taft. Callers include Meyer, Gen. Powell Clayton, Sen. Scott

20 Washington. Cabinet meeting. Cabinet dinner

21 Washington. Conference with Sen. Dixon on Montana politics. Conference with J. B. Reynolds on labor vote

22 Washington. Conference on Indiana politics with Lt. Gov. Miller

23 Washington. Cabinet meeting on Ohio politics. Conference with Root

24 Washington. Discussion of African trip plans with Bishop J. C. Hartsell. "American Attitude toward the Philippines" published in the *Outlook*

25 Washington

26 Washington. Conference with Rep. Parker on New Jersey politics. Conference with Gen. Bell on army machine gun service. Callers include Gipsy Smith

27 Washington. 50th birthday. Reception for delegation from Hungarian Republican Club. Cabinet meeting

28 Washington

29 Washington. Conference with Meyer on Ohio politics. Conference with Bonaparte, Rep. Dwight on New York politics. Callers include F. V. Greene, McIlhenny, R. J. Wynne, Black

30 Washington. Cabinet meeting

31 Washington. Conference with F. B. Kellogg on Standard Oil cases

NOVEMBER

1 Washington

2 Washington. At work on annual message. Midnight departure for Oyster Bay to vote

3 Oyster Bay. Election of Taft and Sherman. Return to Washington

4 Washington. Callers include Wright

5 Washington. Conference on trusts with Bonaparte
6 Washington. Cabinet meeting. Tariff conference with Aldrich. Canal conference with Goethals. Evening discussion of African trip with Sir Harry Johnston
7 Washington. Tariff conference with Payne. Conference on civil service appointments with Black, Greene, McIlhenny. Conference on Philippines with W. C. Forbes. Callers include Meyer, Wilson, Bacon, Garfield
8 Washington. Dinner including Pinchot, J. G. Brooks, Winthrop, Chairman Bailey of Country Life Comm.
9 Washington. Callers include Scott, Meyer, Dalzell, E. A. Hitchcock, Minister Quesada, Garfield, Rep. Hull
10 Washington. Cabinet meeting. Tariff conference with Cullom. Callers include Count Moltke, Wanamaker, Olcott, Cockran, Wade Ellis
11 Washington. Lunch with F. H. Hitchcock, Sherman, R. J. Wynne, W. L. Ward, T. L. Woodruff, Seth Low, Howard Pyle, Albert Shaw. Callers include Root, J. H. Moore, Rep. Burton
12 Washington. Tariff conference with Rep. Weeks. Callers include Wilson, Henry White, Justice McKenna, L. A. Frothingham
13 Washington. Cabinet meeting. Callers include Adm. Evans, Rep. Perkins
14 Washington. Speech at Episcopal High School in Alexandria, Va. Dinner with Maj. E. A. Mearns, Percy Madeira and discussion of African trip. Newberry appointed Secy. of the Navy
15 Washington. Conference with Root. Taft at White House
16 Washington. Callers include Depew, W. R. Hearst
17 Washington. Cabinet meeting. Tariff conference with McCumber. Dinner for labor men including Morrissey, D. MacKay, T. V. Powderly, W. S. Stone, O. W. Holmes, Moody, Straus, H. Parsons, Gen. Wood, C. P. Neill, Pinchot, Lyman Abbott, L. F. Abbott
18 Washington. Conference with Sen. Carter on postal savings bank bill. Conference with C. P. Neill. Callers include McCumber, Heyburn, H. H. D. Peirce. Evening discussion of African trip with C. A. Lyon
19 Washington. Callers include Abp. Ryan, Hepburn, Lovering

20 Washington. Cabinet meeting. Conference with Straus on Ellis Island immigration service. Discussion of African trip with Carl Akeley
21 Washington. Callers include J. B. Reynolds, Fulton, W. D. Foulke, Jusserand, Garfield, Bacon. Evening conference with Lodge
22 Washington
23 Washington. Tariff conference with Tawney. Callers include Fairbanks, Hoggatt, Lodge
24 Washington. Cabinet meeting. Callers include Straus, Metcalf, Calderhead, Kennedy
25 Washington. Conference with Tawney. Conference with B. T. Washington. Callers include Cannon, Aldrich, Burkett, Delegate Andrews. Unveiling of Gen. Sheridan statue
26 Washington. Laying of YMCA cornerstone
27 Washington. Cabinet meeting. Conference with Gardner on Massachusetts patronage. Conference with Tawney. Reception for diplomatic corps
28 Washington. Conference with Littauer on New York senatorship. Callers include C. P. Taft, Penrose. "The Awakening of China" published in the *Outlook*
29 Washington
30 Washington. Conference with Root. Tariff conference with Piles. Conference with J. C. Shaeffer on Indiana politics. Callers include Cullom, Dixon, Rep. Pearre, Larrinaga

DECEMBER

"Getting Christmas Dinner on a Ranch" published in *Everybody's*

1 Washington. Cabinet meeing. Appointment of Satterlee as Asst. Secy. of the Navy. Appointment of D. J. Keefe as Commissioner Gen. of Immigration
2 Washington. Conferences with Hepburn, Root, Woodruff
3 Washington. Conference with Dalzell, Burke on Ohio politics. Conference including Bonaparte, Dixon on investigation of Anaconda Copper Co. Callers include Gov. Hoggatt, Satterlee
4 Washington. Cabinet meeting
5 Washington. Conference on Anaconda Copper Co. dispute including Solicitor Gen. Hoyt, Pinchot, Carter, Dixon, Lodge, John Ryan. Callers include Lord Northcote, James Bryce, Smoot,

Warren, Kean, Overman, Hepburn, Nixon
6 Washington
7 Washington. 60th Congress, 2nd Session, convenes. Conference with Garfield, Bonaparte, Vespasian Warner on Oklahoma land fraud cases. Conference with Civil Service Commissioners. Callers include John Dos Passos, Dr. Lambert, A. L. Lowell. Evening reception at Corcoran Art Gallery
8 Washington. Annual message to Congress. Speech at conservation meeting. Dinner including Moody, Newberry, Longworth, Gen. Young, Carnegie, H. K. Smith, Commander Sims
9 Washington
10 Washington. Canal conference with H. W. Farnham. Conference on appointments with Scott, Elkins. Callers include Sherman
11 Washington. Cabinet meeting. Dinner with the Earl of Warwick. Evening conference with Taft
12 Washington. Conferences on appointments with Keifer, Landis, Smoot, Hepburn, Cummins. Callers include F. H. Hitchcock, Wright, Magoon, Hemenway. Conference and lunch with Taft, Root. Boone and Crockett, Gridiron Club dinners
13 Washington
14 Washington. Report on Brownsville affair sent to Congress
15 Washington. Cabinet meeting. Message to Congress on Panama Canal contracts
16 Washington. Discussion of African trip with C. D. Walcott. Conferences with Hemenway, Watson, Hopkins on appointments
17 Washington. Message to Congress on administration of District of Columbia. Conference with Wright on Foraker resolution for inquiry into secret service. Conference with W. H. and C. P. Taft. Callers include F. B. Kellogg. Cabinet dinner
18 Washington. Cabinet meeting on Foraker resolution. Callers include G. W. Perkins, Beveridge, F. Kellogg, Townsend, Gaines, Parsons, Maxwell Evarts, Flint. Paul Morton at White House. "Lessons from China" published in *Science*
19 Washington. Callers include W. R. Wheeler, Gov. Kibbey, Depew, Parsons
20 Washington

21 Washington. Callers include Sir Horace Plunkett, Rep. Bates
22 Washington
23 Washington. Meeting of Country Life Commission. Conference with Knox. Callers include Heney
24 Washington. Discussion of African trip with Maj. Mearns. Callers include Aldrich, Perkins
25 Washington. Christmas dinner at the Cowles'
26 Washington. Conference on Indian land frauds with Garfield, Bonaparte. Conference on Immigration Comm. work with Rep. Bennet. Callers include Hepburn, Burkett, Heney, Wadsworth
27 Washington
28 Washington. Conference with Hoggatt on Alaskan legislation. Reception for delegation of N. Y. musicians' union. Callers include F. H. Hitchcock, Gamble, McCumber, Dixon. Ethel Roosevelt's debut
29 Washington. Cabinet meeting
30 Washington. Conference with Carter, Burkett on postal savings bank bill. Tariff conference with Underwood. Conference with Jusserand. Reception for Count von Bernstorff. Visit to Newberry at Navy Department
31 Washington. Afternoon trip to Dr. Rixey's farm near Cherrydale, Va.

1909
JANUARY

1 Washington. New Year's reception
2 Washington. Conference with Cabinet members and congressmen on aid to Italy in earthquake disaster. Callers include Maj. Mearns, Wright, Newberry, Meyer, Bourne, Cockran, Gen. Crozier, P. A. Jay, Gen. Young
3 Washington
4 Washington. Special message to Congress on the secret service. Message to Congress for aid to Italy. Callers include Newberry, Meyer, Bacon, Lodge, Piles, Borah, Overman, Kahn, Underwood, Keifer, Bennet, Cocks, J. B. Reynolds, G. R. Sheldon
5 Washington. Cabinet meeting. Conference with Meyer. Callers include Cullom, J. B. Reynolds, Gov. Hoggatt, Capt. Sims, Reps. Beale, Gaines. Dinner at Root's
6 Washington. Message to Congress on Tennessee Coal and Iron Co. Callers include Root, Bonaparte, Meyer,

Bacon, Lodge, Overman, W. D. Foulke, J. A. Stewart

7 Washington. Publication of land fraud charges against Sen. Tillman. Callers include Fairbanks, Meyer, L. M. Shaw, Fulton, Hale, McEnery, Gardner, F. B. Kellogg, McIlhenny. Diplomatic reception. Franklin D. Roosevelts at White House

8 Washington. Cabinet meeting. Callers include Bacon, Bryce, Overman, Fulton, Commissioners Black, Greene, McIlhenny. Dinner including Cannon, Herbert Parsons

9 Washington. Callers include Meyer, Straus, Depew, Overman, Lodge, A. Wilcox, W. D. Foulke, Warner

10 Washington

11 Washington. Message to Congress for civic improvements in the District of Columbia. Callers include Cortelyou, Garfield, Lodge, Warren, Curtis, Straus, R. M. Easley, Hopkins. Attends reception for Senate members at Fairbanks'

12 Washington. Cabinet meeting. Callers include Fairbanks, Borah, Cullom, H. K. Smith, Gen. Young, Reps. Bede, Vreeland, Martin. Dinner at Wright's

13 Washington. Horseback ride to Warrenton, Va.

14 Washington. Naval conference with Newberry. Conference with AF of L executive council. Conference with Knox. Callers include F. K. Bowers, Capt. Butt, Beveridge, Lodge, Gamble, Vreeland, Parsons. Diplomatic dinner

15 Washington. Lunch and conference on Navy Dept. reorganization with Morton, Moody, H. L. Satterlee, Adms. Luce, Mahan, Folger, Evans, Cowles, Judge Dayton, Capt. Sims, Newberry. Callers include Depew, Nixon, Dixon, Cullom, Elmer Dover

16 Washington. Naval conference with Hale. Callers include Root, Harlan, Bennet, du Pont, Hepburn, Humphrey, E. A. Hitchcock, Frank Butterworth, J. G. Coolidge

17 Washington

18 Washington. Callers include Newberry, Clarke, Dolliver, Crane, McEnery, Hull, Littauer, C. P. Taft. Evening speech to Methodists

19 Washington. Cabinet meeting. Callers include W. H. Phipps, Rep. Davidson. Attends Cabinet dinner at Bonaparte's

20 Washington. Executive order appointing a National Council of Fine Arts.

Callers include Knox, Curtis, Cockran, Langley, Cocks, Mark Sullivan

21 Washington. Conference with Flint, Fulton on Japanese school question. Callers include Gen. Young, J. J. McClure, Root, Borah, Beveridge, Garfield, Gen. Corbin, Townsend. Reception for judiciary

22 Washington. Cabinet meeting. Report of National Conservation Comm. sent to Congress. Conference on Japanese school question with J. D. Phelan, Gen. Young, Lodge, Parsons, Cocks, Hull. Dinner including J. C. O'Laughlin, Warren, von Bernstorff, Satterlee, William Phillips

23 Washington. Conference on appointments with Aldrich. Conference with California congressional delegation on Japanese school question. Callers include Wilson, Garfield, Straus, Bacon, Beveridge, Warren, Burkett. Dinner for J. S. Sherman

24 Washington

25 Washington. Callers include Fairbanks, Root, Bonaparte, Wright, Garfield, Cockran, Cocks, Nixon, Smoot, Beveridge, Kerens. Reception for committee of state food and dairy commissioners

26 Washington. Cabinet meeting. Callers include Bankhead, Cummins, Dolliver, Lodge, Depew, H. K. Smith, J. D. Phelan, Bennet, Cooper, Foster, Bacon, Beveridge. Afternoon ride to Warrenton, Va. Speech at dinner of conference on care of dependent children

27 Washington. Appointment of Bacon to succeed Root. Appointment of J. C. O'Laughlin to succeed Bacon. Appointment of commission for Navy Dept. reorganization. Callers include Newberry, Lodge, Gamble, Needham, Flint, E. G. Buckland, Beveridge, Bankhead, Stephenson, Aldrich, Slemp, Landis, Calder, Larrinaga

28 Washington. Callers include Bacon, Straus, Sherman, Ball, Sulloway, Dolliver, Smoot, Borah, Austin, Judge Wilfley, F. B. Kellogg, J. J. McReynolds, Clarkson. Dinner for Supreme Court Justices

29 Washington. Cabinet meeting. Callers include La Follette, Borah, Parsons, Winthrop, Albert Shaw, Gov. Hoggatt

30 Washington. Callers include T. L. Woodruff, Newberry, Cortelyou, Bacon, Dolliver, G. R. Sheldon, Pin-

chot, C. Whitney. Gridiron Club dinner

31 Washington

"Tribute to Lincoln" published in *Review of Reviews*

1 Washington. Callers include Bacon, Cullom, Wright, Warren, Beveridge, Gamble, Pinchot, Gov. Kibbey, Curtis. Visit to Holy Cross Academy. Dinner at Lodge's

2 Washington. Dinner at Newberry's

3 Washington. Callers include Bacon, Bonaparte, Borah, Harlan, Clapp, Nixon, Newlands, La Follette, Stevens, Gaines, Driscoll, Cocks, J. C. O'Laughlin, Gov. Magoon, F. K. Lane, McIlhenny, W. H. Page, Albert Halstead

4 Washington. Callers include Newberry, Garfield, Nixon, Flint, Beveridge, Burrows, Stephenson, Bartholdt, Landis, Esch, H. K. Smith, Neill, Gardner, Bowers

5 Washington. Callers include Leupp, Pinchot, Sulzer, Loeb, Satterlee. Dinner including Bacon, Bourne, Cummins, E. Peabody, Miss Eleanora Sears

6 Washington. Callers include Newberry, Cortelyou, Flint, Nixon, Depew, Moody, Sulloway, Cooper, Hawley, Gillett, F. K. Lane, Major Slocum

7 Washington

8 Washington. Conference on Japanese school question with Bacon, O'Laughlin, Kahn, Flint, F. K. Lane. Lunch with Henry Adams. Callers include Bacon, Cullom, La Follette, Elkins, Kahn, Flint, Parsons, Sloan Simpson, Winthrop

9 Washington. Cabinet meeting. Country Life Commission report sent to Congress. Callers include Cannon, Nye, John Barrett, McCreary, Pinchot, Lodge. Dinner at Garfield's

10 Washington. Reception for members of Council of Labor. Callers include Bacon, O'Laughlin, Calder, Gardner, E. F. Acheson, Cocks, Powell Clayton

11 Washington. Conference on New Mexico statehood with Gov. Curry. Departure for Hodgenville, Ky., for Lincoln anniversary celebration. Stops at Baltimore, Harrisburg, Altoona, Pa.

12 Hodgenville. Speech and laying of cornerstone at birthplace memorial. Departure for Washington

13 Washington

14 Washington

15 Washington. Callers include Bacon, Knox, Aldrich, Flint, Smoot, Clapp, Kinkaid, Gen. Edwards. Reception at Grace Reformed Church

16 Washington. Cabinet meeting. Conference with Taft on Panama trip. Callers include O. W. Holmes, Aldrich, Dixon, McCumber, Kahn, Sulzer, Borah, Hamlin Garland, A. Lewisohn. Dinner at Wilson's

17 Washington. Conference with Taft. Report of Panama inspection tour sent to Congress. Callers include Newberry, Wright, Piles, Clapp, Burkett, Littauer, Goethals, F. K. Lane, F. B. Kellogg, Grosvenor

18 Washington. Callers include Lodge, Bacon, Cummins, Foss, Cocks, O'Laughlin, Pinchot, E. J. Baldwin, W. Willcox, R. Watchorn, Delegate Andrews. Speech to delegation of North American Conservation Conf. Army-Navy dinner. Gen. Wood, W. A. Wadsworth at White House

19 Washington. Lunch including Cullom, Bacon, Pinchot, Wadsworth, de Quevado, H. S. Beland. Issuance of invitations to an international conservation congress at The Hague. Callers include Paul Morton, M. Gates, Abp. Ryan

20 Washington. Lunch with Wright, Newberry. Callers include H. K. Smith, F. Steinhart, E. A. Moseley, Knapp, Aldrich, Cummins, Lodge, Smoot, Hepburn, Gardner, Newlands

21 Washington. Departure for Hampton Roads, Va., to review Atlantic fleet

22 Hampton Roads, Va.

23 Washington. Cabinet meeting. Callers include J. W. Jenks, Curtis, Stephenson, Flint, McLaughlin, Calder, Foster. Evening departure for NYC

24 NYC. Funeral of Stewart D. Robinson. Return to Washington

25 Washington. Report of naval commission sent to Congress. Callers include Bonaparte, Wright, Moody, Goethals, Black, Dryden, Guggenheim

26 Washington. Report of North American Conservation Conference sent to Congress. Lunch with Adm. Sperry. Callers include Gen. Crozier, W. I. Buchanan, Morton, Cockran, Coudrey, Flint, Knox

27 Washington. Lunch with Gen. Crozier, Adms. Sperry, Wainwright. Callers include Seth Bullock, Garfield, Wright, Harlan, Pinchot, Clapp, De-

pew, La Follette, Hepburn, Bede, Crane, Bourne, Parsons

28 Washington

MARCH

1 Washington. Lunch including Moody, Bacon, Newberry, Loeb, Satterlee, Leupp, Neill, J. C. Rose, H. L. Stimson, Pinchot, O'Laughlin, Woodruff, J. B. Reynolds, Jusserand, W. W. Sewall, H. S. Pritchett, Capt. Butt, John Abernathy. Congressional farewells. Tea at Garfield's. Dinner at Bacon's

2 Washington. Final Cabinet meeting. Numerous callers. Dinner at Straus's

3 Washington. Numerous callers. Taft at White House

4 Washington. Attends Taft-Sherman inaugural ceremonies. Departure for NYC and Oyster Bay

INDEX

regulation in, 754, 764, 767, 772, 815, 878, 1175; segregation in, 1003. *See also* Republican party

Alabama Claims Commission: 219

Alaska: boundary dispute, 63, 319, 320, 732, 1446, 1491–95, 1498, 1511; consolidation of coal holdings in, 1044; dance and gambling halls in, 1409; development of, 1219; game-shooting in, 204; Japan and, 724–26, 730; payment for, 6, 62; and Republican nomination (1908), 847; withdrawal of coal lands in, 526. *See also* Patronage

Albemarle: 1322

Albert, Prince Consort: 32

Alberta: Japanese exclusion and, 919

Albuquerque: 1098

Alcohol tax: 377

Alderman, Edwin: id., iv, 857; and Pure Food Act, 908; m., 553

Aldrich, Nelson W.: id., iii, 199; and banking and currency legislation, 559, 883, 894; and Brownsville affair, 1423; and Compensation Act, 1038; and National Monetary Commission, 908; and patronage, 1538; and railroad rate regulation, 158, 170, 174, 201, 209, 215, 273, 341; R on, 266; and ship subsidy bill, 556; and statehood, 301; and tariff, 15, 27, 41, 136; m., 503, 1053, 1258; letters to, 141, 1482, 1486, 1501

Aldrich Bill: opposition to, from South and West, 904; m., 621, 908, 949. *See also* Currency

Aldrich-Vreeland Act: 559, 908, 1044, 1046. *See also* Currency

Aldridge, George W.: id., i, 558; and N.Y.S. politics, 120, 153; supports Hughes for president (1908), 926

Aleshire, James B.: appointed Quartermaster General, 685, 697, 699, 705

Alexander, DeAlva S.: id., ii, 1376; and government employee compensation act, 1031; letter to, 1031

Alexander the Great: 19, 961, 1114

Alexander, Prince: *see* Battenberg

Alexander Bill: 1031–32

Alexandrine, Princess: 108

Alfred the Great: 339

Algeciras Conference: account of, 230–52; estimate of R's role at, 319, 358; Jusserand and, 220–21; R discouraged about, 169; m., 26, 145, 342, 349, 458. *See also* Morocco

Algeciras Convention: Senate ratification of, 317–18

Alger, George W.: id., 188; article of, circulated by R, 188; pamphlet cited, 714,

903; on Taft and labor, 1202; letter to, 188

Alger, Philip R.: id., 1380; and battleship gunnery, 1379–80; criticized by Key, 1470–72; and ship design, 1174

Alger, Russell A.: id., i, 653; and patronage under McKinley, 1257; letter to, 306

Algiers: French rule in, 1370; m., 16

Alien Property Holding: 1477, 1483, 1484, 1485. *See also* Japan

Aliens: *see* Contract Labor; Immigration

Allee, J. F.: 27

Allen, Henry A.: 1422

Allen, William: 697

Allis-Chalmers Company: strike against, 485, 1296

Allison, John: id., 80; recommended for federal judgeship, 1007; letter to, 80

Allison, William B.: id., iii, 62; appointed to Inland Waterways Commission, 1055, 1056; and battleship appropriation, 1018; and Iowa senatorship, 1074; member National Conservation Commission, 1066; and railroad rate regulation, 204, 209, 210, 215, 274, 275; R on, 1491; and tariff negotiations, 27; m., 318, 489, 503; letters to, 41, 72, 210, 258, 261, 270, 600, 851, 1074

Allison Amendment: 210, 215, 258–60. *See also* Hepburn Act; Railroads, rate regulation

Altenberg, G. P.: 746

Altgeld, John P.: 219

Amador, Manuel: 1029

Amalgamated Copper Company: suit against, 1417–18

Ambassadors: R's evaluation of, 265. *See also* Diplomatic Service

American Academy of Arts and Letters: 1430

American Academy in Rome: 1430

American Agriculturist: 845

American Amateur Athletic Union: 1382

American Association for the Advancement of Science: 664

American Bankers' Association: and currency legislation, 510, 825, 1046; and petition for Curtis, 1177

American Car and Foundry Company: 117

American Chamber of Commerce: 281

American Federation of Catholic Societies: 973, 974

American Federation of Labor: active in Maine politics, 350; and Chinese exclusion, 191; in congressional election (1906), 413, 455; and federal eight-hour law, 191; and Haywood trial, 653; lobby in Washington, 504; in N.Y.S. campaign (1906), 442, 457; opposes labor injunction, 190, 191, 1195, 1307-13; and presidential campaigns, 1077; m., 1241. *See also* Gompers, Samuel; Labor; Unions

American Flint Glass Workers' Union: 198

American History: lectures on, in Europe, 644, 645. *See also* American Revolution

American Institute of Architects: 1430-31

American Jewish Committee: protests Russian refusal of passports to Jews, 1256

American Magazine: on Negroes in politics, 1046-47

American Malting Company: 1128

American Monthly Review of Reviews: 584, 636-38, 1297

American Museum of Natural History: 708, 1093-94, 1375

American National Livestock Association: 707

American National Red Cross Association: *see* Red Cross

American Newspaper Publishers' Association: 467

American Paper and Pulp Association: 838

American Protective Association: opposes Taft's candidacy, 1318

American Railway Union: 1059

American Reciprocal Tariff League: 1351

American Red Cross: *see* Red Cross

American Revolution: 223, 225, 351, 410, 773, 880-81

American Sheet Steel Company: 1326

American Smelting and Refining Company: 1447

American Society of Civil Engineers: 1067

American Steel Hoop Company: 1326

American Sugar Refining Company: prosecution and conviction of, 127, 1260

American Tin Plate Company: 1326

American Tobacco Company: and licorice price rebates, 752; suit against, 692-93, 1261

Americanism: R on, 637-38, 1042-43

Ames, Matthew H.: 579

Amesbury, Mass.: 708

Amidon, Charles F.: 801-02

Anaconda, Montana: 1417

Anaconda Copper Company: 1417-18, 1527

Anarchists: publications excluded from mail, 977; in Russia, 23, 61; State Department, fear of, 1019

Anderson, Albert B.: appointed judge, 667; and Standard Oil retrial, 1141; and *World* libel suit, 1425

Anderson, Charles W.: Negro officeholder, 1276; recommended to Taft, 1418

Anderson, John C.: id., 877; letter to, 877

Andrews, Charles M.: 1050

Andrews, William H.: id., iii, 330; and New Mexico land frauds, 177, 649, 739, 757

Angell, James B.: 678

Anglo-American Fisheries Agreement: 462. *See also* Fisheries; Newfoundland

Anglo-Japanese Alliance: 18, 29, 61

Anglo-Saxon Race: *see* English-Speaking People

Anglophilia: 1497

Anglophobia: 602

Animal Industry Bureau: 176-77, 295, 299

Ankeny, Levi: 937

Annapolis: 779. *See also* United States Naval Academy

Antes, Howard R.: 1450-53

Anthracite Coal Strike: 427, 1299, 1444

Anthracite Strike Commission: 1309

Anti-Imperialists: in Great Britain, 253, 254, 1384; and Japanese exclusion, 1512, 1513; and N.Y.S. campaign (1906), 456; and Philippine independence, 774, 775, 782; and Republican nomination (1908), 796; R on, 351, 411, 1447, 1507-08; in U.S., 253-55; m., 19, 20, 112, 533, 542, 779. *See also* Imperialism; Pacifism

Anti-Injunction Law: demand for, 190-91. *See also* American Federation of Labor; Injunctions; Labor; Unions

Antitrust Movement: *see* Corporations; Trusts

Aoki, Viscount Siuzo: appointed ambassador to U.S., 129; lunches with R, 713; protests discrimination against Japanese, 717, 718; R on, 597; m., 656

A.P.A.: see American Protective Association

Appalachian Forest Reserve: 29, 605, 1225

Appalachian National Forest Association: 902-03

Appeal to Reason: angers R, 186; attacks Taft's Philippine policy, 1278

Appleton, William, Jr.: 522

Apponyi, Count Albert: id., 312; 312-15

Arabi Pasha, Ahmed: 253

Arbitration: in international disputes, 346, 640-41, 1023; in mine labor disputes, 202, 203. *See also* Hague Tribunal

Archbold, John D.: contribution requested by Republican National Committee, 1245, 1247-49; and Foraker correspondence, 1244; and Standard Oil payments, 1243; and Standard Oil suit, 1097, 1107; m., 955, 1327

Archer, Mr.: and Panama Canal ship purchase, 1378

Life Commission, 1169, 1340; letter to, 1167

Bailey Amendment: 173–74, 209, 274–75

Baker, Daniel W.: and *World* libel suit, 1425, 1489

Baker, Francis E.: 666, 1142

Baker, George F.: 854

Baker, George H.: 1249

Baker, Ray S.: id., ii, 1160; on Brownsville affair, 1422; on railroads, 25; m., 46, 68; letters to, 25, 76, 83, 88, 100, 634, 1046, 1094

Baker, Sir Samuel W.: id., 116

Balboa, Vasco Núñez de: 496

Baldwin, Elbert F.: id., iii, 113; letters to, 1032, 1506

Baldwin, W. G.: and Brownsville affair, 1105, 1376, 1476

Balearic Islands: 941

Balfe matter: 1109, 1113

Balfour, Arthur J.: advised of Hale interview, 1294; and Alaska boundary dispute, 1493; compared with R, 32; distrust of, 366, 400; Hay's letter to, 1497; resigns as Prime Minister, 151; and Russian imperialism, 23; and Russo-Japanese peace, 8; m., 12, 921, 965; letter to, 959

Balkans: 344; R on, 1447

Ballard, Charles L.: 741

Ballinger, Richard A.: appointed Land Office Commissioner, 533, 549, 606; and forest reserves, 606; on McHarg, 765; and public opinion on conservation, 681; letter to, 555

Baltimore *American:* 1194

Baltimore *Sun:* and R's Mississippi trip, 816; supports Taft (1908), 1194–95; m., 1327

Bampard, Maurice: French ambassador, 61

Bangor and Aroostook Railroad: 573

Bangs, Anson M.: 598

Bangs, Mr.: 561

Bank deposits: government guarantee of, as campaign issue (1908), 1128, 1131–33, 1139, 1202–03; 1234

Bank of England: and 1907 panic, 848

Bank Examiners: inefficiency of, as campaign issue (1908), 1288

Bank of Mound Bayou: 310

Bankers: and Currency legislation, 485. *See also* American Bankers' Association

Bankers' Magazine: attack on Aldrich-Vreeland Bill, 1046

Bankhead, John H.: member Inland Waterways Commission, 619; member National Conservation Commission, 1067

Banking: government regulation of, 858; in Mississippi, 310; national legislation on, 636; in Pennsylvania, 148; R on, 949;

Schiff on, 131. *See also* American Bankers' Association; Bank Deposits; Bank examiners; Bankers; Currency; Panic of 1907

Bannon, Henry T.: 1128

Banton, Pembroke B.: 949–50

Baptist Church: and Hughes nomination, 833

Barbados: 499, 504

Barber, Charles E.: 406

Barber, Harry A.: 1103

Barber Lumber Company: 662, 736, 767

Baring, Evelyn: *see* Cromer, Lord

Barnes, Benjamin F.: id., iii, 1061; 205

Barnes, William, Jr.: id., ii, 923; and Hughes nomination (1908), 1192, 1198; m., 94, 153; letters to, 1193, 1196

Barney, Charles A.: 822, 845, 859

Barnsdall, Theodore N.: and oil and gas leases, 369–72, 387, 482, 1291, 1354

Barrett, Charles S.: 1340

Barrett, John: id., iii, 393; 396

Barrios, Señor: 1439

Barry, John: 685

Barry, Thomas H.: 1509

Bartholdt, Richard: id., ii, 1378; and navy expansion, 201, 1008, 1512; letters to, 35, 557

Bartlesville *Daily Enterprise:* 388

Bartlett, Charles L.: 557

Bartlett, Mr. (of Cheyenne): 564

Bartlett, Willard: 904

Barton: and Florida judgeship, 716

Bates, John L.: 452

Bates, Lindon W.: id., iv, 1137; 789

Battenberg, Prince Alexander Albert of: 69

Battenberg, Prince Louis of: id., iv, 1206; 69

Battle Hymn of the Republic: 1076, 1366

Battle Mountain Sanitarium: 1274

Battleships: *see* United States Navy

Baxter, Irving F.: Nebraska District Attorney, 481

Bay: *see* Lodge, George C.

Bay of Fundy: and fisheries dispute, 1205

Bay State: see United States Navy, *Ships*

Beach, John K.: id., 698; and judicial appointment, 698, 712, 719, 778

Beaconsfield, Benjamin Disraeli, Earl of: 859

Bean, Robert S.: id., 21; and judgeship, 21, 86

Bear Lodge Forest Reserve: 603

Beard, William A.: appointed to Commission on Country Life, 1340

Beatty, Starr H.: id., 1290; letters to, 1289, 1290

884; and N.Y.S. politics, 429; and patronage, 180; m., 437, 451, 925
Black Canyon: 279
Black list: 192, 1008, 1309
Blackburn, Edmond S.: id., 309
Blackburn, Joseph C. S.: and Brownsville affair, 560; and Panama Canal, 560, 794, 857
Blackmore, R. D.: 137
Blackwood's: anti-American sentiment in, 499; on U.S. in Philippines, 1369
Blagden, Arthur C.: 214
Blaine, James G.: 935
Blanchard, Newton C.: 1067
Bliss, Cornelius N.: id. i, 507; and campaign funds, 91, 193–96, 642, 794, 1246, 1257; defends federal courts, 1065; and patronage, 455; treasurer Republican campaign committee, 38, 196, 267, 1117; letter to, 193
Bliss, Tasker H.: id., 128
Blocksom, Augustus P.: 521, 558
"Bloody shirt": 226
Blount, James H.: 470
Blount, James H., Jr.: 470
Blue Book: Algeciras Conference, 250
Blue Mountain Forest Reserve: 603
Bluffton, Ohio: 930
Blun, Henry: 934
Board of Education (San Francisco): 510
Board of Mediation and Conciliation; 947, 948
Boardman, Mabel T.: id., 216; letter to, 216
Bodkin, Charles E.: id., 1325; requests R subscribe to Catholic Encyclopedia, 1325–26; letter to, 1325
Boer War: 223, 225, 529
Boise, Idaho: cavalry stabled at, 363; irrigation congress convened at, 381; m., 198, 771
Boise, Idaho, *Statesman:* 302
Bonaparte, Charles J.: id., i, 151; appointment of, and Catholics, 1042–43; attacks on, 715–16, 782; as Attorney General, 461; and campaign manager (1908), 1099; and Catholic Church in Philippines, 171; Chicago speech, 883; and corporation licensing proposal, 1379; and Cuban crisis, 409; and destruction of the *Constitution,* 362; genealogy of, 1043; and Harriman merger, 710; and Japanese problem, 700, 729; and judicial appointments, 665, 927; and judo, 155; and land frauds, 570, 571, 662, 673, 714, 736, 737, 1252; and liquor labeling law, 804; and mail exclusion, 978; and Maryland election (1905), 70; and Mexican revolutionaries, 1099,

1100; and navy hospital ships, 876; at navy review, 353; and Oklahoma constitution, 673; and patronage, 716, 719, 915; and Post's indiscretions, 827; and Pulitzer libel suit, 1415, 1489, 1516–18; and railroads, 685–86; and right of appeal in criminal cases, 593; R on, 362; and secret service, 1533; and Sherman Act amendment, 997; and Standard Oil, 758, 1107, 1141, 1143, 1145; and steel merger, 1317; and Storers, 101, 181, 200; and Supreme Court, 570–71; and Taft, 1485; at White House, 69; m., 486, 740, 750, 1040; letters to, 10, 77, 121, 149, 155, 159, 324, 333, 343, 353, 361, 399, 496, 511, 673, 685, 692, 710, 715, 741, 752, 763, 764, 766, 779, 830, 873, 883, 977, 981, 983, 987, 1010, 1059, 1097, 1099, 1141, 1143, 1174, 1234, 1295, 1327, 1409, 1417, 1436, 1473, 1527
Bonaparte, Mrs. Charles J.: 333, 558, 1142
Bonapartists: 182
Bond, Robert: id., iv, 1031; 790
Bonynge, Robert W.: id., iv, 1082; 278
Bookwalter, Charles A.: elected mayor, Indianapolis (1905), 70
Borah, William E.: id., 413; and Brownsville affair, 1501; elected to Senate, 413; and Idaho land frauds, 662–63, 714, 736–37, 983; prosecution of, 722–23, 742, 753, 765, 767–71
Borrow, George: 1330
Bosnia: 1447
Bossism: as issue (1905), 71; N.Y.S., 96–99, 120; and officeholding, 829; R on, 119, 125, 163, 264, 266. *See also* Republican Party; Patronage; Tammany
Boston: appraiser's store site, 408; opinion of R in, 409–10
Boston *Evening Transcript:* on Brownson resignation, 911; on 1908 convention, 998; on Taft nomination, 723; m., 212, 1448, 1480
Boston *Herald:* on Lodge, 727; and Gardner candidacy (1906), 486; on Post, 827; on Taft-Foraker deal, 970; on Taft nomination, 723–24; R on, 390, 729, 1316, 1318–19, 1364; m., 212
Boston Indian Citizenship Committee: 1448
Boston *Journal:* 811
Boston and Maine Railroad: and New York, New Haven and Hartford railroad, 686, 705, 1011; and patronage, 1011; prosecution of, 1011; and Republican nomination (1908), 914
Boston Old Home Week: 723
Boston Steamship Company: and sale of ships to War Department, 1220
Bosworth, C. A.: 596

Bourne, Jonathan, Jr.: id., 780–81; and federal incorporation bill, 1114–15; R on, 975; and Standard Oil suit, 1097, 1107, 1175; letters to, 955, 1107, 1114, 1273

Bourne, Mrs. Jonathan, Jr.: 1115

Boutell, Henry S.: id., 590; and playgrounds, 590

Bowdoin College: 71

Bowen, Herbert W.: id., iv, 1164; and Venezuela crisis, 132; indiscretions of, 579, 602

Bowker, Richard R.: on Stevens, 629; letter to, 629

Boxer Rebellion: indemnity scholarships, 206; indemnity returned by U.S., 1044; m., 809

Boycotts: Anthracite Strike Commission on, 1309–10; unions enjoined, 873, 1195–96; Taft on, 1297, 1321

Boyle, John J.: id., 685; sculpture of, 684–85

Brackett, Edgar T.: 926

Bradford, Gamaliel: id., 1073

Bradford, Royal B.: id., iii, 441; and Santo Domingo, 10

Bradford, Rhode Island: 513

Bradley, Edward: 1123

Bradley, William O'C.: id., iv, 798; and anti-Taft delegation, 1064

Brainerd, Frank: id., 92

Brandegee, Edward D.: letter to, 172

Brandegee, Frank B.: 206

Brandeis, Louis D.: and New York, New Haven and Hartford railroad, 686, 1040; letter to, 551

Bratton, Ulysses S.: id., 711; 716

Braun, Marcus: id., 43; report on immigration, 43–4; and Storer, 314; letter to, 43

Brazil: U.S. Diplomatic Service in, 396; as representative of American interests in Venezuela, 957; R misquoted on, 119; and ship building, 945

Breeders' Gazette: 1351

Brennan, Patrick J.: 581

Brent, Bishop Charles H.: id., iv, 975; attacks American government of Philippines, 772–775, 782; letter to, 1100

Brewer, David J.: id., 397; attacks R, 855–57; decisions of, 188–89; and pacifism, 943; R on, 397, 1393

Bricklayer and Mason: 188

Bridges, Robert: id., ii, 933; letters to, 75, 355, 1105, 1172

Bristol, William C.: 348, 830

Bristow, Joseph L., id., iii, 444; 541

British Columbia: hostility to Japanese in, 786, 851, 869, 875, 1508; and Japanese exclusion, 919, 921

British East Africa: and R's African trip, 1206–07, 1230

British Grocers' Federation: and meat inspection, 333, 338

British Museum: 1385

Brodie, Alexander O.: id., ii, 833; letter from, cited, 104–05

Bronx Zoo: 703

Brooke, George D.: id., 504; 504–06

Brooker, Charles F.: id., iv, 964; 936, 1210

Brooklyn Eagle: attacks R, 741; disavows Bryan (1906), 395; m., 307

Brooklyn, New York: 453

Brooks, Franklin E.: id., iv, 655; 277

Brooks, John G.: id., iv, 838; id., 1343; article by, m., 1386; letters to, 1343, 1365, 1385

Brooks, Phillips: 110

Brooks, Sydney: id., 1368; on R's record, 1446; letters to, 1368, 1443

Brosius, Samuel M.: 1450, 1452

Brotherhood of Locomotive Firemen: and Wabash case, 1297

Brotherhood of Railroad Trainmen: 1280, 1295, 1321

Broward, N. B.: 1067

Brown, George H.: id., 308; letter to, 308

Brown, George W.: 140, 141

Brown, Henry A.: former Rough Rider chaplain, 476

Brown, Henry B.: id., iii, 400; and labor legislation decisions, 188, 189; resigns from Supreme Court, 186

Brown, Walston H.: and Panama Canal construction, 356–57, 363

Brown, Walter F.: 670, 727

Brown, William C.: id., 1140; and railroad rate raises, 1140; letter to, 1151

Brown, William G.: R criticizes, 1356–65; m., 1201, 1348, 1366; letter to, 1411

Brown Brothers and Company: 356

Browne, Herbert J.: id., 1105; and Brownsville affair investigation, 1105, 1376, 1423, 1476, 1507

Brownell, George C.: id., 85

Brownell, William C.: 573

Browning, Robert: 263, 590

Brownfield, Texas: and statue of R, 1179

Brownson, Willard H.: appointed chief, Bureau of Navigation, 723; and fleet's Pacific cruise, 744–45, 759; and Navy reform, 1000; resignation of, 876–77, 891–92, 911; letter to, 730

Brownsville Affair: affidavits on, 517; Browne report, 1507; examination of bullets, 865–66; campaign (1908) and, 999, 1163; dishonorable discharge for, 489–90, 498, 509; Gridiron dinner exchange on,

571, 596; investigating expenses, 1476; investigation requested, 521, 524–25, 557–58; and Negro delegates to Republican National Convention, 1012; and Negro solidarity, 634–35; and nomination (1908), 934; and N.Y. politics, 999; and Ohio politics, 695–96; and reinstatement legislation, 965–66, 968, 1016–17, 1024–26, 1482, 1486, 1501; reinvestigation of, 1105; renewed attacks on R for, 1376; Republican Club condemnation of, 789; R on, 534, 559–60, 1163; R message to Congress on, 968; Taft attacked for, 705, 712–13, 1376; Senate investigation of, 690–91; Senate report on, 695, 966–67; m., 1004. *See also* Negroes

Bruce, M. Linn: and N.Y.S. gubernatorial nomination, 429, 437; and N.Y.S. Republican convention chairmanship, 369

Brundage, Andrew J.: 393

Brundidge, Stephen, Jr.: 304

Bryan, William J.: alleged bear hunt in Mexico, 1404; approves R message (1908), 922–23; articles by, 662, 664; on bank deposits, 1202; on Britain in India, 1507; criticizes R annual message (1906), 533; on Cuba, 414, 428; on federal licensing of corporations, 847; on government ownership, 460; in England, 338; N.Y. *Times* evaluates, 1117; and (1907) panic, 849; on Philippine independence, 1447; and plain people, 875; Prince of Peace speech, 1270; radicalism of, 1128; R on, 328, 338–40, 347, 397, 469, 1270, 1303; R letter to, m., 1257; silver policy of, 218; and Standard Oil, 453, 1243; statue of, 1179–80; m., 329, 348, 349, 467, 482, 803, 954, 1194, 1277, 1340, 1346, 1421; letters to, 923, 1250, 1259

CAMPAIGN OF 1896: contributions to, 38, 1262, 1263; platform, 697; and McKinley, 675; m., 667

CAMPAIGN OF 1906: campaign committee, 482; Madison Square Garden speech, 394–95; m., 467

CAMPAIGN OF 1908: acceptance speech, 1178; attacks Republican conservatives, 1209; attacks Taft's Philippine policy, 1285; contributions, 1170, 1248; and church vote, 1179; defeat of, 1328; and labor, 1241, 1279, 1280, 1305–11; nomination, 1096, 1105; platform, 1132; R attacks, 1251–55, 1259–68, 1270; R estimate of campaign, 1124; R estimate of strength of, 1202; R on implications of defeat of, 1372, 1400; R on labor promises of, 1299–1302; and Standard Oil payments, 1243;

strategy against, 1204, 1231, 1247, 1286; m., 1304

Bryce, James: appointed British ambassador to U.S., 488; and M. King's U.S. visit, 917, 921; letter from, m., 1208; and Olympics dispute, 1384–85; overjoyed at 1908 election returns, 1340; Pilgrims' dinner for, 552; Provincetown speech, 760; as Romanes lecturer, 1180; and R's Romanes lecture, 1369; and R's speech on India, 1443–44, 1465; on sports, 1387; m., 600, 644, 699, 1436; letters to, 1147, 1210, 1381, 1478

Bryce, Mrs. James: m., 1147, 1210

Bryn Mawr College: 754

Buchanan, James: and limited executive powers, 428, 430, 1481; R on, 803

Buchanan, William I.: 1428

Buchtel, Henry A.: 413

Bucket shop bill: 959

Buckner, Simon B.: id., iii, 601; and patronage, 1364; m., 1346, 1398

Buckner, Mrs. Simon B.: 1398

Bucks Stove and Range Company: injunction issued in strike against, 1195, 1442

Bucks Stove and Range Co. v. *A.F. of L.*: 873, 1442

Budapest: 312

Buddhism: 698

Buell, Augustus C.: 1534

Buell, George C.: letter to, 1181

Buffalo Bill: *see* Cody, William F.

Buffalo *Times*: 1248

Bulgaria: and Russian imperialism, 23; R on, 1447

Bulkeley, Morgan G.: id., 50

Bullock, Seth: meets R on Mississippi trip, 813–15; on Republican National Convention, 1041, 1060; R recommends to Taft, 1418; m., 267, 589

Bulmer, Mr.: 589

Bülow, Prince Bernhard von: id., iv, 1288; 1371

Bunau-Varilla, Philippe J.: 1315

Bunyan, John: 953

Burch, Marsden C.: 771

Burgess, John W.: appointed appraiser in New York Customs House, 27

Burgess, John William: id., 644; lectures at Berlin, 644–45

Burke, Edmund: 375–76

Burke, Timothy F.: and Wyoming land frauds, 445, 519, 570, 680

Burkett, Elmer J.: id., 810; 1204

Burma: British administration in, 16, 20

Burnet, Bishop Gilbert: 1398

Burnett, Henry L., id., iii, 428; 47–49

torial campaign, 1262, 1263; as issue in elections, 193, 791, 1170, 1263, 1323; and patronage, 194; and political favors, 1257; and Republican party, 794, 1157, 1158, 1209, 1210; publicity on, 1117, 1158; R on improper, 1256, 1257; silver miners and (1896), 1262, 1263; Standard Oil and, 791, 804, 1354, 1355; tobacco industry and, 194; m., 196. *See also* Democratic Party; Republican Party

Campbell, James U.: id., 85

Campbell, John A. L.: 784

Campbell, Philip P.: 540, 1045

Campbell, Thomas J.: 1326

Campbell-Bannerman, Sir Henry: 1017

Camplin: candidate for office, 680

Canada: and Alaska boundary, 320, 1492–95; anti-Japanese sentiment in, 787, 788, 917–21; co-operation with United States on conservation, 1437, 1438; and Great Britain, 1104, 1159; immigrants from, 637, 1104; Japanese immigrants in, 609, 612, 858, 921; King's visit to United States, 985; population increase, 869; proposals to annex to United States, 644; railroad securities of, 746, 750, 755; U.S. and, 154, 1159; and wood pulp tariff, 918. *See also* French Canadians; Newfoundland Fisheries Dispute

Canal Record, The: R on, 789

Canal Zone: government of, 355, 794; governor appointed, 560; living conditions in, 1009; sale of liquor in, 1082; railroads in, 497–98. *See also* Isthmian Canal Commission; Panama; Panama Canal

Canary Islands: 941

Cannon, Joseph G.: id., iii, 603; and campaign (1906), 397, 403, 404, 413, 415, 454–57, 470, 489; and currency legislation, 559; at Ethel R's dinner, 1472; and Italian earthquake relief, 1459; and labor, 367, 397, 1304; on legislative supremacy, 1460; a liability in 1908 campaign, 1280, 1314, 1340; and Maine politics, 350; and navy building program, 892, 956; and New Mexico land frauds, 757; and Newlands Bill, 956; and postal savings, 1077; and presidential nomination (1908), 339, 781, 796, 915, 937, 969, 1275, 1357; and pure food legislation, 292, 299; and railroad regulation, 136; relations with R, 145, 1231, 1340, 1341; revolt against, 1095; and secret service, 1019, 1424; and ship subsidy bill, 555, 556; and tariff, 32, 350, 361, 367, 397, 405, 806, 1341, 1380; m., 41, 158; letters to, 157, 167, 168, 285, 301, 317, 322, 359, 413, 526, 555, 557, 581, 604, 956, 980, 1019, 1020, 1030, 1459, 1536

Canterbury, Archbishop of: 108

Canton: *see* China

Canton, Ohio: R at, 675–76; 812

Cape Colony: 775

Cape May Warbler: 258

Capers, John G.: id., iii, 176; and patronage, 784, 878, 879, 901; and Republican National Convention, 936

Capitalism: 199, 229. *See also* Business

Capitalization: limits on, 212

Capitol: commission to complete, 684

Capps, Washington L.: and battleship construction, 970, 1102, 1174; Key criticizes, 1470–72; and naval design, 1453, 1456, 1457; and Newport Conference, 1383

Capron, Adin B.: id., 561; letter to, 561

Caribbean: defenses of, 951, 952; Germans in, 359; and Monroe Doctrine, 63; U.S. policy in, 640. *See also* Cuba; Monroe Doctrine; Porto Rico; West Indies

Carlyle, Thomas: on democracy, 1400; prose translation of Dante, 1397–98; m. 359

Carmack, Edward W.: 112

Carnegie, Andrew: and anti-Japanese movement, 1479; and banking reforms, 949; and campaign funds, 50; and German war preparations, 542–44; intimacy with Earl Grey, 348; member National Conservation Commission, 1068; and naval limitation, 398–99; and peace movement, 638, 639, 651, 699, 700; and railroad rate regulation, 201; letters to, 345, 398, 592, 638, 1479, 1538

Carnegie, Mrs. Andrew: 346, 592

Carnegie Institution, Washington: 1093, and Lomax's frontier ballad collection, 1479

Carow, Emily T.: 891, 972; letter to, 792

Carpenter, J. C.: and Olympics dispute, 1181–85, 1190, 1385

Carroll, Lewis: 910

Carson, John M.: 544

Cartagena, Pact of: 941

Carter, George R.: letter to, 309

Carter, John R.: 921

Cary River Gas Company: 1267

Cascade Forest Reserve: 603

Cassatt, Alexander J.: id., iii, 141; letter to, 162

Cassini, Arturo P.: 238

Caster, Curran, and Bullet: 513

Castle, William R., Jr.: id., 164

Castro, Cipriano: American opinion on, 984, 1148; military preparations of, 132; treatment of American interests in Venezuela, 761, 957; revolution against, 1428

Cathedral: *see* Washington Cathedral

Cathedral College, New York: 1534
Catholic Church, Roman: American, and
Shanghai controversy, 973–74; American
religious freedom and, 259; and appointment of American cardinals, 107–11; attacks on, 1371, 1466; communicants of,
in cabinet, 1042, 1043, 1290, 1335; communicants of, as officeholders in Philippines, 976; communicants of, and patronage, 123, 1423; communicants of, in public
office, 342; communicants of, in railroad
industry, 281; factionalism in, 213; in
France, 597; on immigration, 393; as issue in 1908 campaign, 1179, 1278, 1285–
86, 1304, 1318, 1333–34, 1368; and Italians,
393; missions to Indians, 1327; in Philippines, 46, 171, 976, 977, 1179; in politics,
442–43, 467, 1178, 1335; requests R to
favor Wentworth, 1414; requests R to
greet Pope, 1349; requests R to influence
Vatican, 108–110; R on doctrines of,
1200; R on organization of, 1280; in
Shanghai, 972–73; and Storer, 161, 180–
82, 200, 538–39; William II on, 1164
Catholic Encyclopedia: R subscription to,
1325–26, 1333
Catholic Indian Missions, Bureau of: 1327
Catholic University, Washington: 140
Catron, Thomas B.: 739
Cattlemen: *see* Stockmen
Cavalry: *see* United States Army, Cavalry
Cavour, Camillo B. di: 252
Cawein, Madison J.: id., 69; lunches with
R, 69
Cease, D. L.: id., 1197; and Taft's labor
decisions, 1197
Census of 1910: and statehood, 822
Census, Oklahoma: 692, 784
Census Bill: R veto, 1476, 1506
Census Bureau: changes in organization
proposed, 1269; and women's and chil-
dren's labor, 269, 594–95; m., 13, 1219
Central America: international court for,
1539; laborers from, 337; R on future re-
lations with, 1511; R misquoted on, 119;
R on presidents of, 1150; U.S. and
Mexico avert war in, 640, 772. *See also*
Caribbean; South America; *and by in-
dividual countries*
Central American Peace Conference: 334,
772
Central Association of Building Trades of
New York: 1312
Central and South American Telegraph
Company: 874
Century Light and Power Company: *see*
New Century Light and Power Com-
pany

Century Magazine: on Egypt, 252; and
Hale's interview with Kaiser, 1371; R's
article in, 272; R's commitments to, 1108;
R's friendliness toward, 786
Cervera, Pascual: 1103
Chadwick, French E.: id., i, 632; letters to,
142, 1103, 1113
Chagres River: 496
Chamber of Commerce, New York State:
170
Chamber of Commerce, Pittsburgh: 939
Chamberlain, C. J.: 1067
Chamberlain, Eugene T.: 1391
Chamberlain, George E.: id., iii, 477;
elected to U.S. Senate from Oregon,
1274; letter to, 21
Chamberlain, Joseph: and Alaska dispute,
1493–94; retirement of, 859
Champlain, N.Y.: 1050
Champlin, Edgar R.: id., 670
Champlin, Mr.: 1154
Chandler, William E.: id., i, 521; and rail-
road rate legislation, 174, 258, 269, 273–
75; and Republican party in South, 1361;
resigns from Spanish Treaty Claims Com-
mission, 804
Chanler, Laura: 312
Chanler, Lewis S.: Democratic guberna-
torial nominee (1908), 1279, 1302; m.,
1286
Chanler, Winthrop: id., i, 352; letter to, 311
Channing, William E.: 783
Chapman, Frank M.: id., ii, 948; 704;
letters to, 1028, 1061
Charity Organization Society, N.Y.C.: 216
Charlemagne: 39
Charles II: 500
Charleston, S.C.: aristocracy of, 224–28,
310; exposition at, 227
Chase's Theater, Washington: 435
Chatfield, Thomas I.: 304, 306, 668
Chatham, William Pitt, Earl of: 351, 773
Chautauqua: 457
Chemistry, Bureau of: 1269, 1467
Cherokee Indians: *see* Indian Affairs; In-
dian Territory; Oklahoma
Chicago: insurance convention in, 201, 202;
labor in, 229; and (1907) panic, 849; play-
grounds in, 591; public schools, 140;
Pullman strike, 1352; silver convention
(1893), 697; teamsters' strike (1905), 714;
m., 393. *See also* Beef trust; Insurance;
Meat Packing
Chicago and Alton Railroad Co.: finances
of, 630; investigation of, 779; suit against,
746, 757, 758, 764, 785, 1260; m., 887
Chicago *American:* 1343
Chicago Board of Trade: 302, 307

Chicago Bureau of Charities: 1051
Chicago, Burlington and Quincy Railroad: fined, 215; rate discrimination by, 464; suit against, 1260; m., 489
Chicago *City Press:* 140
Chicago Civic Federation: 165. *See also* National Civic Federation
Chicago Clearing House Committee: 825
Chicago *Inter Ocean:* 140, 175
Chicago, Milwaukee and Saint Paul Railroad: suit against, 1260
Chicago, Rock Island and Pacific Railroad: finances of, 617; suit against, 1260
Chicago *Tribune:* on meat investigation, 208–09; on Republican 1908 nomination, 806; m., 1295
Chicago Union Traction Company: 1059
Chicago, University of: economics and sociology at, 1343; m., 1067
Chickasaw Tribe: 138. *See also* Indians
Child labor: in District of Columbia, 1219, 1300, 1446; legislation on, 435, 557, 985, 986, 1019, 1020, 1038; N.A.M. opposes legislation on, 1203; regulation of, 844; R on, 957, 958, 1446; m., 1078. *See also* New York State
Child Labor Committee: 1269
Children: care of dependent, 1439–40; rights of, 259. *See also* Women and Children
Children's Bureau: establishment of proposed, 1269
Chile: and panic (1907), 747; revolution (1891), 337; m., 119
China: American court in, 409; American missionaries in, 1201; American troops in, 432; army of, 132–33, 809; art of, 117; and balance of power in Orient, 1164; and Boxer indemnity, 206, 1044; boycott by, of U.S., 90–91, 132, 165, 809; character of people of, 29; coalition of European powers against, 231–32; conditions in coastal cities of, 138; death of emperor of, 1407; diplomacy of, 853; diplomatic information on, 1210–11; foreign interests in, 15; and Great Britain, 15; Hankow railway in, 29–30; immigrants from, excluded by U.S., 135, 963, 1485, 1503; immigrants from, in British colonies, 254, 775; immigrants from, in Hawaii, 775, 933, 1512; immigrants from, in Japan, 657, 920; immigrants from, in U.S., 90, 91, 132, 135, 138, 165, 190–91, 266, 776, 933; Kaiser on foreign policy of, 1466, 1497–98; and Japan, 18, 232, 946; Japanese-American statement on open door in, 1343; labor standards in, 138; laborers from, on Panama Canal, 337–38, 368, 499, 504; minister

to U.S., 809; open door in, 993, 1343; and Russo-Japanese treaty, 17, 18; R on Hay's policy in, 1496–97; R on Japan and, 1513; R on legation in, 1443; segregation of children from, 473; special ambassador from, 1405–07; students from, 206; Taft visit, 149; and Tibet, 1428; and U.S., 15, 77, 91, 205, 973; m., 344, 359, 458. *See also* Diplomatic Service
Chinese Exclusion: *see* China, immigrants from; Immigration; Immigration Restriction
Chirac v. *Chirac:* 1483
Chiriqui, Pennsylvania: 513
Chittenden, Russell H.: 909
Choate, Joseph H.: id., i, 34; and Alaska boundary dispute, 1492, 1493; definition of contraband by, 732; and election of N.Y.S. judges, 442; and federal courts, 1065; requested as minister by Japan, 26; m., 12
Choctaw Tribe: 138. *See also* Indians
Christian Socialism: R on, 1079–81
Christian Union: 1350
Churches: R on role of, 1283–85; separation from state, 107–11. *See also* Catholic Church
Churchill, Randolph H. S.: R on, 468, 597, 1034, 1329
Churchill, Winston: id., 378; and New Hampshire patronage, 914; letters to, 378, 586
Churchill, Winston L. S.: gift to R, 1467; R on, 408, 468, 1034, 1329, 1465; and white rhinoceros hunt, 1383–85; letter to, 1467
Churchman: 472
Cienfuegos: 399. *See also* Cuba
Cincinnati, Ohio: and election (1905), 70; Longworth visit to, 312; patronage in, 596, 878–79; reform in, 837; Roosevelt Club in, 487, 837
Cincinnati *Times-Star:* 1455
Circuit Court: *see* Judiciary; Patronage
City Forum of New York: 856
City Orphan Asylum: 1540
Civil Service: and compensation for injuries, 1219, 1232; and fourth-class postmasters, 1355–56, 1402; and Indian agents, 52; and Interior Department, 52–54; and meat inspection, 300; and naturalization inspectors, 705, 709; salaries of, 568; Schurz and reform of, 287; R on qualities of public servant, 124–25; m., 461. *See also* Consular Service; Isthmian Canal Commission; Officeholders; Patronage
Civil Service Commission: and census clerks, 1476; exceptions to appointment

by examination, 1429; and political activity of classified service, 827–29, 931–33, 1229, 1337; and political assessments, 11, 1271–72; Taft and, 1480

Civil Service Law: Cleveland and, 1352; McKinley and, 1352; R on, and patronage, 1345; R charged with violation of, 915

Civil Service Reform Association: attacks on political activity, 827–29, 1355–56, 1376–77; Bonaparte as president of, 362

Civil War: *Albemarle*, 1322; hospital ships in, 894; military history of, 553–54; political issues of, 539–40; records of, 632; Vicksburg campaign, 195; m., 224, 225, 346, 352, 466, 721, 881. *See also* Veterans

Clapp, Moses E.: id., 148; 158, 174

Clark, Clarence D.: id., 104; m., 1481; letter to, 104, 680

Clark, Edgar E.: id., 397; letter to, 397

Clark, Edward B.: 617, 786

Clark, Edward E.: 413, 1208–09

Clark, George R.: 880

Clark, James B. (Champ): id., iv, 853; 1067

Clark, Walton: 188

Clark, William A.: id., iv, 1009; 1263

Clark, William J.: 188

Clarkson, James S.: id., i, 241, iii, 256–57; letter to, 43

Claverly Hall: 42, 164

Clay, Alexander S.: on Atlanta riot, 635; and Commerce and Labor Department, 324; R on, 487

Clay, Henry: descendants of, 668; and Jackson, 1460; politics of, 163; m., 184

Clayton, Henry D.: attacks R, 1231–32

Clayton, Powell: id., iii, 701; 767; 936

Clearing House Association: 747

Clearing House certificates: and panic (1907), 822

Clemenceau, Georges E. B., 365, 1187

Clemens, Samuel L.: 137, 267, 590, 813

Clement, Edward H.: id., 1448; letter to, 1448

Clements, Judson C.: id., 461; on Interstate Commerce Commission, 461, 754, 1004; letters to, 461, 815

Cleveland, Frances F.: 1328, 1351

Cleveland, Grover: and anthracite coal strike, 1152–57, 1229; and 1892 campaign, 34, 38, 194, 195; at Chamber of Commerce ceremony, 1155; and civil service, 829, 1229; as governor, 1352; and immigration, 294; judicial appointments of, 666; and patronage, 929, 1345, 1346, 1348, 1363; and Pullman strike, 1059; and railroad regulation, 1260; R on, 735, 1352; St. Louis speech, 1352; secretary of, 212;

and tariff, 72, 806; and tenement cigar law, 189; on trusts, 328, 1259–60; at Wilson's Princeton inauguration, 1155; m., 264, 470

Cleveland (Ohio): election (1905) in, 70; traction interests in, 777; water works, 188

Cleveland, Cincinnati, Chicago & St. Louis Railroad, 188, 1299, 1313

Cleveland Memorial Committee: 1351, 1352

Cleveland *Plain Dealer:* 157

Clothing Trades Bulletin: 188

Clowes' Pocketbook: 970

Clubs: *see* A.D. Club; Arion Singing Society; Army and Navy Union; Constitution Club; D.K.E.; Dory Club; Economics Club of N.Y.; Gridiron Club; Hamilton Club; Harvard Club; Hasty Pudding; Hungarian Republican Club of N.Y.; Iroquois Club; Japan Society; Memorial Society; Metropolitan Club; Porcellian; Reform Club of New York; Republican Club of New York; Roosevelt Club, Cincinnati; Roosevelt Home Club; Seawanhaka-Corinthian Yacht Club; Sphinx; United States Medal of Honor Club

Coal Industry: investigation of, 187; and land frauds, 525–26; monopoly in, 291; strikes in, 166, 1152–57, 1229; wage dispute in, 202–03. *See also* Strikes

Coal Lands: Colorado, 276; consolidation of Alaska holdings, 1044; entry rights, 525–26, 568–69; public rights in, 1300; and railroads, 461; withdrawal order, 324, 446, 568, 594, 616, 681–82. *See also* Hitchcock, Ethan A.; Indians; Railroads

Cobb, Calvin: id., 302; letter to, 302

Cobb, Frank I.: id., 328

Cochran: and patronage, 134

Cockran, William B.: id., i, 399; and Catholic Church, 171; and travel expenses, 304; letter to, 972

Cockrell, Francis M.: id., i, 374; 1491

Cocks, William W.: id., 1193; 429, 1193, 1196

Cody, William F.: 267

Coeur d'Alene Riots: 196. *See also* Debs, Eugene V.; Haywood, William D.; Idaho; Moyer, Charles H.

Coffey, James V.: id., 631

Cohen, Walter L.: 1071

Cohen, William N.: id., ii, 937; and N.Y. politics, 87, 92, 95, 97

Coinage: design of, 842–43; *see also* Currency; Mint

Colby, Everett: 70

Cole, Ralph D.: 930

service and, 828; confidential shipping report, 544–45; in Germany, 89; and immigration, 285; in Mexico, 28; reform of, 377, 1219, 1445, 1497; right of asylum in legations, 337; rumors of corruption in, 1439; at Sierra Leone, 101. See also Diplomatic Service; State Department

Continental Congress: 223, 773

Contract Labor: in Hawaii, 933; in Panama, 337; in South Carolina, 556; law against, 191, 285. See also Immigration

Contracts, Government: for battleships, 1015; for drydocks, 1001, 1005–06; illegality in, 13; importance of, 1378; Navy Yard supplies, 362; for Panama Canal, 823, 996; and reclamation service, 380; for shells, 986. See also Isthmian Canal Commission

Converse, George A.: id., iv, 1006; and defects in battleship construction, 892; and fleet concentration, 77; fleet review, 343; naval reforms, 1000; position in Navy, 982; m., 121; letter to, 403

Cook County, Illinois: 393

Cook's Tourist Agency: 441

Cooley, Alford W.: id., ii, 1096; advises R on speech, 750; and Idaho land frauds, 771; letter by, quoted, 1531–32; and naturalization inspectors, 709; and New Haven railroad prosecution, 693; and New Mexico land frauds, 649–50, 659–60, 752–53, 765; and patronage, 1097; resignation and reappointment, 1436; and southern delegates, 712; and tennis, 922; and Wyoming district attorney, 564–65; m., 328, 742, 860, 1176

Cooley, Thomas M.: id., 54

Coolidge: with R at Harvard, 944

Coolidge, Archibald C.: 645

Coolidge, Thomas J.: 750

Coolidge, Thomas J., Jr.: id., 933; letter to, 933

Coolie labor: 138. See also Japan; Immigration; Labor

Coombs, James N.: 928, 936, 1363

Cooper, James F.: 813

Cooper Union: 1321

Co-operatives: 303

Coos Bay: 1069

Copper industry: litigation in, 797–98, 1417–18, 1527

Copperheads: 540

Coquille Forest Reserve: 603

Corbett, James J.: 1103

Corbett, Rev. John, id., 1333; letter to, 1333

Corbin, Henry C.: id., ii, 893; recalled

from Philippines, 128; and Taft campaign, 1163, 1245, 1248

Corcoran Art Gallery: 1427

Cornell University: College of Agriculture, 845; represented at Olympics, 1181, 1184; m., 94, 845

Corporations: and campaign funds, 35–8, 344, 452–53; as election issue, 376, 458–60, 465, 470, 1128–29, 1253–54; favors to, 453; influence in Republican convention, 1275; licensing of, 847, 1254; prosecutions of, 906–07; regulation of, 34, 54, 83–4, 218, 374, 536, 801–02, 875, 877–78, 884–90, 922, 1007, 1129; responsibility of officers, 906–07; in Rocky Mountain states, 303; R on, 328, 366, 1114–15; Sherman Act and, 997; state regulation of, 878; Supreme Court and, 368, 396; m., 407. See also Corporations, Bureau of; National Civic Federation; Railroads; Trusts; and by name

Corporations, Bureau of: and confidential business information, 1481; and harvester trust, 763–65; investigation of beef trust, 190; investigation of coal industry, 187; investigation of oil industry, 293; powers of, 334–35; and railroad stock issues, 923; report on oil freight rates, 291; report on Standard Oil, 409; R on, 1219, 1445; Standard Oil opposition to, 1246; m., 352, 375, 450, 1067. See also Commerce and Labor, Department of; Corporations

Corrigan, Michael A.: 213

Corruption: beef packers' bribes and, 140–41; charges of, in government, 54–56; of Republican leaders, 78–79; R on, 45, 100, 1257; in San Francisco, 148–49, 219; of Southern Senators, 112; of Tammany, 156. See also Land Frauds; Patronage; Tammany Hall; and by states

Cortelyou, George B.: id., iii, 57; and cabinet changes, 461; and campaign funds, 37–8, 73, 91, 194–95, 267, 642–43, 791, 1245–46, 1256–57, 1412; charged with corruption in Indian affairs, 1127; and Hughes, 429, 483; and inefficiency of bank examiners, 1288; and Knickerbocker Trust Co., 914; manages R's campaign, 1112; and N.Y.S. gubernatorial nomination, 1235; and N.Y.S. politics, 87, 447, 457, 460, 466–67; and panic (1907), 633, 748, 822, 830, 833, 847–48, 851, 854, 865; and patronage, 12, 205, 325–26, 455, 596, 625, 827, 883; and presidential nomination (1908), 781, 784, 796, 837, 847, 865; and railroad postal charges, 607; and Republican National Committee, 1207;

rumors about, 764; and stock market, 621; Taft fails to reappoint, 1458; m., 328, 461, 825, 1234; letters to, 362, 822, 823, 848, 854, 904, 1013, 1229, 1271

Cortez, Enrique: 756

Coryell, John R.: 1080

Cosgrave, John O'H.: id., iii, 46; 1050, 1051

Cosmopolitan: on corruption, 156–57; and railroad mail rates, 362; R on, 184, 189, 307, 362, 363

Council of Fine Arts: 1434

Counterfeiting: 528, 910

Country Life Commission: duties of, 1338–40; organization of, 1167–70; R on, 1446

Court Martial: 143–45, 515, 911. *See also* Brownsville Affair; United States Army; United States Navy

Cowan: and meat inspection, 300

Cowles, Anna R.: R picture to, 1432; on woman suffrage, 1342, 1373; m., 688

Cowles, David S.: letter to, 837

Cowles, William H.: id., 974; letter to, 974

Cowles, William S.: appointed to Navy Commission, 1487; and battleship design, 1197; to Jamestown with R, 688; on intrigue against Evans, 646; on fleet coaling, 759; on naval reform, 980; at Quebec tercentenary, 1159; letters to, 726, 1197

Cox, George B.: and Ohio senatorship, 1454–55; and Ohio vote, 1280; opposes R's railroad program, 27; and Taft, 652, 727, 837, 1255; m., 70, 833, 970

Cox, W. W.: 309–10

Cramp, Charles H.: 1534

Crandall, Rev. L. D.: 186

Crane, Morton: 783

Crane, Winthrop M.: id., i, 676; and campaign (1908), 1113; and Hepburn Act, 273–74; offered Treasury secretaryship, 936; and patronage, 1423; and Philippine tariff, 141; at Republican National Convention, 1064, 1095; and statehood, 301; and Taft nomination, 723–24, 727, 998; m., 68, 158

Crank, Clyde M.: 511–12

Cranston, Earl: id., 1056; letter to, 1056

Creasy, Edward S.: 1035

Creek Indians: *See* Indians

Creelman, James: id., 963; article of, 1203; letter to, 963

Crest, Raymond F.: 544

Crocker, Benjamin D.: 1249

Croker, Richard: id., i, 297; 1405

Croly, Herbert: 922

Cromer, Evelyn Baring, Earl of: career in Egypt, 138, 253–56, 352, 605, 775; quoted

on colonialism, 773; R on, 254; on Wood in Cuba, 1386

Cromer, George W.: 300

Cromwell, Oliver: 1087

Cromwell, William N.: and campaign (1908), 1157, 1158; and Panama boundary settlement, 756, 759; and Panama Canal charges, 1315–16, 1318; and Panama Canal documents, 1414–16, 1419; and Panama timber lands, 1518–19; R's doubts about, 714; Taft's doubts about, 342; m., 121; letters to, 211, 1414, 1518

Cronin, John J.: 636–38

Cross, Joseph: 668

Crothers, Samuel McC.: id., 72; 223, 954, 1330

Crouse: and Panama labor, 508

Crow King: 283

Crowder, Enoch H.: 1018

Crozier, William: id., ii, 1085; 865

Cruikshank, George: 137

Crum, William D., id., iii, 376; 227, 1538

Crumpacker, Edgar D.: id., iv, 982; and merchant marine, 136; opposes R on labor investigation, 269; and tariff, 359; letter to, 339

Cuba: advisory law commission in, 1018; American administration in, 1386; American evacuation of, 1105; American imperialism in, 955; American intervention in, 69, 391, 399–402, 408–09, 418, 420, 430–32; American navy in, 399; American opinion on, 444, 761–62; American plans for government of, 993–94; American provisional government of, 454; American troops in, 434–35, 440, 640, 1018; and cable rights, 1105; campaign in, 322; claim to Isle of Pines, 69; defenses in, 951–52, 1137; discrimination against American business, 68–9; fever epidemics in, 69; Germany and, 69; indemnities, 446–47; provisional government of, 355; request for American ammunition, 386; revolution in, 391, 407, 410–14, 418–20, 422–29, 430–37, 602; R compares with Porto Rico, 501; R on government of, 1206; R on U.S. relations with, 255–56, 410, 414, 444, 648, 1087, 1408, 1445, 1511; R on view of, 495; resumption of independence, 907, 1137–38; Spanish administration in, 993; Spanish-American war and, 16; Sternberg on, 993; treaty with U.S., 69, 412, 414, 454; m., 253, 644, 775. *See also* Caribbean; Diplomatic Service

Cudahy Packing Company: 1260

Culberson, Charles A.: hostility of, to R, 1231; and investigation of U.S. Steel,

1481; member, National Conservation Commission, 1067; and patronage, 860, 1111; and railroad rate raise, 1175–76; m., 112; letter to, 1134

Culebra Cut: *see* Panama Canal

Cullom, Shelby M.: id., i, 374; and Algeciras treaty, 318; and Cuba, 68–9; and railroad rate bill, 271; m., 503; letter to, 317

Cummins, Albert B.: id., iii, 137; and (1908) campaign, 1204; and Iowa senatorship, 1074–75; and Republican factionalism, 27; and tariff, 297; and vice-presidency, 1077, 1083, 1094; letter to, 657

Cunard Line: 43–4, 512, 628

Cuninghame, R. J.: 1146, 1375

Currency: American Banker's Association and, 825, 1046; bank deposits and, 1203; demands for asset banking, 558–59; inability of authorities to agree on, 1046; inelasticity of, 131, 133; as issue in 1908 campaign, 1254; National Monetary Commission and, 908; national reserve association advocated, 825; panic of 1907 and, 833, 836–37, 846, 848–50; R on, 450, 485, 510, 585, 805, 872, 883, 1202–03, 1219; Schurz and, 287; tax on, 904; western views on, 908; m., 608. *See also* Aldrich Bill; Aldrich-Vreeland Act; Fowler Bill; Vreeland Bill

Curry, E.: visits R on Mississippi boat, 814

Curry, George: id., 650; appointed New Mexico governor, 649–50, 659, 661–62; charges against, 753; and New Mexico Republicans, 739–40, 864; R on, 731; threatens to resign, 765–66; m., 734; letters to, 757, 821

Curry, Jabez L. M.: id., iii, 217; 1398

Curtin, Jeremiah: 868, 1136

Curtis, Alfred H.: 1176–77

Curtis, Charles: id., iv, 1061; 735, 1434

Curtis, Charles L.: 670

Curtis, Edward S.: id., 994; letter to, 994

Curtis, W. J.: 1315

Curtis, William E.: id., iv, 1146; letter to, 276

Curtis Turbine: *see* United States Navy

Curzon, George N.: invites R to lecture at Oxford, 1180, 1186, 1205, 1230; m., 1436; letters to, 1177, 1232

Cushing: with R at Harvard, 944

Cushing, Grafton D.: id., 954; letter to, 954

Cushing, William B.: 1322

Custer, George A.: 283, 994

Customs Administrative Act: 700

Cutler, Johnny: 860

Cutting, William B.: letter to, 1420

Czar: *see* Nicholas II

Czermak, Mrs. Frederick: letter to, 296

Czolgosz, Leon: 676, 1017

Dady, Michael J.: id., 1193; and Hughes renomination (1908), 1193, 1194, 1196

Dagos: R on, 465. *See also* Cuba; Italy

Daily Consular and Trade Reports: 544

Daily Mirror (London): 1181

Dalai Lama: *see* Tibet

Dallas, Texas: 860–61

Dalny: 4, 15, 18

Daly, Mr.: 1509

Dalzell, John: id., iii, 433; and German tariff negotiations, 32, 41; and immigration legislation, 285; member national conservation commission, 1067–68; and ship subsidies, 556; letter to, 1412

Dan: *see* Wister, Owen

Dana, Paul: id., i, 652; letter to, 704

Dana, Richard H.: id., i, 151; and census bill veto, 1476; letter to, 827

Daniels, Benjamin F.: and appointment as U.S. marshal, 104–07; R recommends to Taft, 1418; m., 267, 328

Dante: 1330, 1397

Danton, Georges J.: 345

Darling, Charles H.: id., iii, 446; 10, 690

Darwin, Charles R.: 290, 1330

Darwinism: R on, 1535

Daugherty, Harry K.: 804, 1176

Davenport, Frederick M.: id., 714; and Root boom for Senate, 1341; letter to, 714

Davenport, Iowa: 297

Davidson, John O.: id., 142–43

Davis, Arthur P.: 1422

Davis, Charles H.: id., i, 221; charges against, 646; Lee commends, 644; retires, 646, 801; R meets at target practice, 437; and troop landing in Jamaica, 579

Davis, Charles R.: id., 568; and bill to increase government employee salaries, 568; and vocational training, 1228; letter to, 568

Davis, Charles S.: 945

Davis, Cleland: torpedo experiments, 1197, 1278

Davis, Cushman K.: id., i, 379; 1352, 1491

Davis, G. H.: id., 957; letter to, 957

Davis, George W.: id., iii, 487; 1421

Davis, Gherardi: 95

Davis, Jefferson (of Arkansas): 1046–47

Davis, Jefferson (of Mississippi): 225, 500

Davis, McLain W.: id., 537

Davis, Oscar K.: id., 722; and Hale interview with Kaiser, 1163–64, 1466–67; and Panama investigation, 1414; m., 736, 1455; letter to, 722

Davis torpedo: 1197, 1278. *See also* United States Navy

Dawes Commission (1902): 138

Dawson, William M. O.: id., 1039

Day, James R.: attacks R, 297, 884; m., 925

Day, William R.: id., i, 638; iii, 347; advises R on judicial appointments, 368–69, 408, 668; dissent in *Lochner* v. *New York*, 189; holds federal employers' liability law unconstitutional, 903; on Moody, 527; R on, 666; m., 675; letter to, 903

Dayton, Alston G.: id., 1039; on injunction, 873; on Navy Commission, 1487; and Republican politics, 1083; R on, 668; letters to, 1039, 1040

Deakin, Alfred: id., 966

Dean Brothers: and cattle investments, 192

De Bell, E. J.: id., 1127; 1127–28

Debs, Eugene V.: attacks R, 186; attacks Taft's Philippine policies, 1278; and Christian socialism, 1079–1081; and Idaho riots, 197–99; and Pullman strike, 1059; R on, 219, 653, 714, 737, 1151; m., 266, 452, 954, 1135

De Kay, Charles: id., 272

Delano, Frederick: id., 54; letter to, 54

De La Rey, J. H.: 225

Delavan, Illinois, *Times Press:* 1290

Delaware: *see* Patronage; Republican Party

Delaware: see United States Navy, *Ships*

Delaware Indians: 1396. *See also* Indians

Delcassé, Théophile: id., iv, 1190; colonial policy of, 241; and Russo-Japanese peace, 63; m., 235, 236

De Lesseps Canal: 1315–18. *See also* Panama Canal

Delta Penny Savings Bank: 310

Democracy: see Adams, Henry

Democratic Party: and Catholic vote, 442, 1326; and colonialism, 256; and corporations, 453; and direct nominations, 1474–75; and election (1904), 27; and election (1905), 27, 70; and election (1906), 347, 350, 360, 369, 386–87, 393–95, 413, 421, 439, 447, 452, 456, 467–68, 489; and election (1907), 833; and election (1912), 1327; and labor demands, 1304; and land frauds, 372; and lock canal issue, 306; in New Mexico, 739; and Ohio senatorship, 1455; in Oklahoma, 673; and Panama Canal charges, 1315; patronage to, 368, 666–69, 712; and President's travel expenses, 304; and prohibition, 1207; and railroad rate legislation, 270–71, 273–75; and Republican strongholds, 1359–60;

Senate caucus, 147; and Southern senators, 111–12; and Southern suffrage, 226–27, 265, 1275; and Standard Oil payments, 1243, 1248

  Election (1908): Bryan nomination, 338–39, 1096; national convention, 1116, 1231; platform, 1127–29, 1131–32, 1178, 1306–13; state victories, 1340; strategy, 1124, 1250, 1259

  See also Bryan, William J.; Tillman, Benjamin

Denatured alcohol law: 1219

Denby, Charles: 724–25

Deneen, Charles S.: 630

Denison, Arthur C.: 392

Denison, Lindsay: id., 200

Denmark: immigrants from, to U.S., 1104; internal conditions in, 19; old age pension in, 787; socialist movement in, 1151. *See also* Diplomatic Service

Dennis, William C.: id., 1436

Dennison: 930

Denver: university in, 413; U.S. gold deposits in, 1013

Denver *News:* on statehood, 480

Denver, Northwestern and Pacific Railway: 276–78

Denver and Rio Grande Railway: 276–78

Denz Portland Cement Company: 1267

Departmental Methods Committee: 99, 1050

De Pauw University: 571

Depew, Chauncey M.: id., i, 480; and French ambassadorship, 447–48; 451; and government employee compensation act, 1037–38; and Indian oil land leases, 1291; and N.Y. Republican party factionalism, 87; and patronage, 180, 642, 1049–50, 1392, 1538; letters to, 1049, 1392

Derby, Richard, Jr.: 214

Desborough, William H. G.: id., 1190

Desert Land Act: 1069. *See also* National Conservation Commission

Des Moines *Register and Leader:* on Iowa politics, 297

Detaille, Jean B. E.: 1413

Devine, Edward T., id., 216; 216, 220

Devlin, Robert T.: 729, 1270

Devol, Carroll: 1009–10

De Wet, Christian R.: 225

Dewey, George: id., i, 632; and charges against Evans, 646; and fleet review, 353; and Newport Conference, 1383; and Pacific cruise, 952; and report on Manila defense, 937; and Venezuela crisis, 319, 358

Diaz, Porfirio: article on, 963; and Mexican revolutionaries, 1100; Root proposes to visit, 785; and U.S. in Central America, 772; m., 809

Dicey, Edward: 1073

Dick, Charles W. F.: id., ii, 1055; and 1908 nomination, 652, 670, 872; opposes R's railroad program, 27; and patronage, 595, 878, 930; R on, 347; and tariff, 359; m., 1455

Dick, James J.: 484

Dickens, Charles: bitterness in Cairo, Illinois, about, 815; R compares with Thackeray, 953; m., 137, 145–46, 175, 229, 263–64, 339, 590, 958, 959

Dickerson, Joseph T.: 516

Dickey: see D.K.E.

Dickinson, Goldsworthy L.: 549

Dickson, Harris: id., 1084; letter to, 1084

Diego, Mr.: 863

Diesel engine: 850

Dietrich, Frank S.: 662

Dill, James B.: id., ii, 1106; 68

Dill, Samuel: 500

Dillingham, William P.: id., iv, 775; 550

Dillingham Commission: See Immigration Commission

Dillingham family (Hawaii): 933

Dingley Tariff Bill: 102, 297, 392. See also Tariff

Diplomacy: see Colonialism; Imperialism; Investments; and by individual countries

Diplomatic Service: appointments of personnel to, 129–30, 451–52, 455, 698, 844–45, 1454; in Argentina, 845, 1420; in Austria-Hungary, 107–11, 171–72, 180–81, 183, 579; in Brazil, 396; and Catholic Church, 107–11, 161, 538; in China, 1443, 1496–97; in Cuba, 402, 411, 426, 435, 440–41; in Denmark, 713, 1151, 1418; in Ecuador, 28; in Ethiopia, 713; in France, 109; in Germany, 109, 845, 989–92, 1002; in Great Britain, 150, 1210–11; in Greece, 698; in Italy, 335; in Japan, 26, 128–29, 713; in Liberia, 102; McKinley commitments and, 1495; in Morocco, 252; in the Netherlands, 845; in Paraguay, 441; and patronage, 447–48, 1428–29, 1499; in Persia, 698; R on, 532, 644, 927, 1273, 1499; in Roumania, 1420, 1454; rumors of corruption in, 1439; in Russia, 177, 658, 731; in Santo Domingo, 470; in Shanghai, 724; in Spain, 161, 183; training and qualifications for, 129–30; wealth and, 1002, 1371; in Uruguay, 441; in Venezuela, 579, 602; wives of ambassadors, 108–09. See also Consular Service; State Department

Disarmament: naval, 6, 17, 19, 35, 348–49, 366, 398–400, 462–64, 475, 529, 542, 546, 597, 601, 641, 700; R on, 16, 17, 19, 63, 357–59, 366, 463, 601, 639–41, 1159; m., 30. See also Hague Conference; Pacifism

Disraeli, Benjamin: see Beaconsfield, Earl of

District of Columbia: amusement licenses in, 435; board of commissioners of, 589; child labor law in, 958, 985–86, 1020, 1038, 1446; health department of, 1269; housing conditions in, 1211–12; insurance regulation in, 91, 201–02, 551; juvenile court in, 1439–40, 1445; playgrounds in, 590–91; prosecution of ice dealers in, 409; schools of, 589; World libel suit in, 1475, 1489

"Dixie": 1076, 1366

Dixon, Joseph M.: id., iv, 757; member of National Conservation Commission, 1067

D.K.E.: (Harvard undergraduate club), R message to, on sixty-second annual convention, 1335, 1336; m., 465, 561

Dodd, William E.: 575

Dodge, Augustus C.: 1398

Dodge, Caesar A.: 1398

Dodge, Cleveland H.: id., i, 28; iii, 654; 216

Dodge, F. J.: 105

Dodge, Frederic: 667

Dodge, Grenville M.: id., iii, 466; 911

Dodge City, Kansas: 104–05, 731

Dodgson, Charles L.: see Carroll, Lewis

Dohrn, Anton: 1435

Dolan, Patrick: 166

Dolan, T. J.: and Panama labor investigation, 1299; m., 415, 1281; letter to, 1286

Dolan's Journal: see Steam Shovel and Dredge Magazine

Dolliver, Jonathan P.: id., i, 393; candidate for vice-presidency, 1077, 1083, 1094; and child labor legislation, 986; and Philippine tariff, 141; and railroad labor hours, 555; and railroad rates, 142, 174, 258; and railroad stock issues, 923; and Republican campaign (1908), 1124; and Republican national convention, 1032; m., 148, 158, 1075, 1204

Dolphin: see United States Navy, Ships

Donnelly, Samuel B.: and Government Printing Office, 1367; investigates labor conditions in Panama, 1009, 1299; and labor in 1908 campaign, 1258–59; letters to, 1191, 1426

Donovan: of St. Joseph, 1173

Dooley, Mr.: see Dunne, Finley P.

Dorando: see Pietri, Dorando

Dorchester House: 150, 503

Dordrecht, University of: R's erroneous reference to, 1539

Dorr, Bryan R.: 1462, 1463, 1469

Dory Club: 800

Dostoevsky, Feodor: 23

Ferriss, Franklin: 1097
Field Museum: 1375
Fields, Andrew C.: 103, 116
Fifteenth Amendment: 540, 1276. *See also*
Negroes
Filipinos: *see* Philippines
Finkelnburg, Gustavus A.: 668
Finland: Russian persecution of, 207
Finlayson, Frank G.: 118
Finley, William W.: 741
Finot, Jean: 637
First National Bank of Chicago: 825
First National Bank of Cincinnati: 878
First National Bank of New York: 854
Firth-Sterling Company: 986
Fish: conservation of, 104
Fish, Hamilton: id., i, 520; telegram to,
cited, 123, 124; m., 79, 87
Fish, Sidney W.: 1117–1123
Fisher, Irving: id., 664
Fisheries: Newfoundland dispute, 320, 400–
01, 1205–06; provisional agreement on,
462; treaty, 401
Fisk, James: 224
Fitzgerald, Edward: 402, 1397
Five Civilized Tribes: emancipation of,
576–77; sale of lands of, 311, 1514–15.
See also Indians
Flammer, Charles A.: 73
Flanigan, Patrick L.: 937
Fleischmann, Julius: id., 696
Fleischmann, Max C.: id., 696
Fleming, William H.: id., 343; 386, 472, 488
Flint, Frank P.: id., iv, 1105; and anti-
Japanese legislation, 610, 1505–06, 1510;
and Arizona statehood, 1367; and battle-
ships, 1016; and Gore canyon, 280; and
Los Angeles water supply, 315–16; mem-
ber, National Conservation Commission,
1067; and Yosemite Park, 294; letter to,
1016
Flood control: in Imperial Valley, 526–27,
530–31; Inland Waterways Commission
and, 619–20, 1031; reforestation and, 902
Florida: 928. *See also* Patronage; Repub-
lican Party
Florida: see United States Navy, *Ships*
Flotow, Hans von: German chargé, 235
Flower, Roswell P.: 439
Flynn, Dennis T.: id., 284; 284, 416, 471–72
Folger, William M.: id., iv, 729; appointed
to navy commission, 1487
Folks, Homer: letter from, to R, cited,
1439
Football: 46, 76, 93, 94, 172, 227, 341, 836,
853
Foraker, Joseph B.: id., i, 709; and Arizona
mining interests, 71; and Brownsville af-

fair, 385, 524, 534, 558, 560, 571–72, 634,
695–96, 705, 865–66, 966–68, 999, 1017,
1024–26, 1376, 1423, 1476, 1486–87; and
campaign (1908), 1195; and candidacy
for presidential nomination, 596, 646,
652, 695–97, 712, 726–27, 742, 784, 872, 914,
1275; and Cuba, 436; and election (1906),
489; and Ohio factionalism, 70, 347; and
Ohio senatorship, 1454–55; and patronage, 595–96, 670, 878–79, 929–30; and railroad regulation, 27, 261, 265, 274; and
Republican national convention, 1033,
1502; R on, 427–29, 1257, 1476; and
Standard Oil, 1166, 1243–45, 1251–52,
1455; and statehood bill, 71, 301; and
Taft, 647, 723, 934, 969–70, 1247–49, 1265;
m., 265, 925, 1128, 1255, 1258; letters to,
429, 595
Forbes, Archibald: 1233
Force School: 261
Ford, Henry: 10
Ford, John: 156
Ford, John F.: 832
Ford, Worthington C.: 1050
Fordham University: 1325–26
Fore River yards: 750
Foreign Policy: *see* United States Foreign
Policy; *and by individual countries*
Foreign Trade: *see* Exports; Merchant
Marine
Forest reserves: coal in, 568–69; creation
of, 603–04; exploitation by timber com-
panies, 604–05; government purchase of,
28, 29; grazing permits in, 122; R on,
902–03, 1444–45; settlement in, 682–84;
and water supply, 99; m., 809, 1169,
1225
Forest Service: achievements of, 382–83;
m., 315–16, 686–87, 845, 1067, 1219, 1340
Forestry Bureau: *see* Forest Service
Forests: *see* Conservation; Forest Reserves;
Forest Service
Forgan, James B.: id., 825
Formosa: 920
Fort Riley: curriculum in school at, 903.
See also United States Army
Fort Wayne: 677
Foss, George E.: id., iv, 1097; and naval
building program, 892, 1006, 1008, 1543;
R on, 437; m., 956; letters to, 143, 201,
529, 1524
Foster, John W.: id., i, 610; and disarma-
ment, 366; on naval power, 1513
Foster, Rufus E.: m., 1324
Foulke, William D.: id., i, 152; and census
bill veto, 1476; and Creek land frauds,
1252, 1265; and Panama Canal, 1414–15;
and patronage, 914–15; m., 677, 1149; let-

ters to, 538, 846, 914, 927, 969, 1315, 1322, 1336, 1376, 1393, 1402
Foulke, Mrs. William D.: 540, 849
Fourteenth Amendment: 585, 1276
Fourth-class Postmasters' Association: 1355–56
Fowler, Charles N.: id., iii, 571; and currency reform, 558–59, 908; letter to, 558
Fowler, Edward S.: 1534, 1538
Fowler Bill: 908, 1046. *See also* Currency
Fox, A. H.: letter to, 1223
Fox, Austen G.: 73
Fox, Gustavus V.: 982, 1000
Fox, John W., Jr.: id., i, 384; 668, 1361
France: and Algiers, 345, 1370; alleged alliance with Germany, 1371; American arbitration treaty with, 1023; American diplomatic service in, 109; and Anglo-Japanese alliance, 61; army of, 237, 1021; banking interests in, 247; and Canary and Balearic Islands, 941; and China, 1497; and Cuba, 430; and disarmament, 475; financial panic in, 746–47, 749–50, 755; foreign policy of, 19, 345–46; and Germany, 145, 169, 220–21; government steamship subsidies in, 626, 628; history of, 954; imperialism of, 16, 359; internal problems of, 19, 365; and Japan, 135; liberalism in, 1372; and Morocco crisis, 168–69, 230–42, 252; navy of, 234, 463; opinion in, of American strength, 724–25, 730; and Panama Canal, 1394, 1414–15; people of, 102; politics in, 182; railroads in, 1072; R on, 320, 359, 1138; and Russia, 145; and Russo-Japanese Peace, 9, 63; and second Hague Conference, 31; and Venezuela, 132; m., 16, 824
Francis, Charles S.: id., iv, 796; as ambassador to Hungary, 180; and torpedoes, 658; m., 312; letter to, 314
Francis, Mrs. Charles S.: m., 315
Franco-Prussian War: 130, 1233
Frankfort, Treaty of: 230
Franklin, Benjamin: 224, 517, 637
Franks, Herbert M.: id., 784
Frantz, Frank: id., 284; charges against, 284, 415–17; exonerated, 471–72; investigated, 386, 438; and Oklahoma statehood bill, 477, 479–80; visits R, 814; m., 446
Frantz, Mont: 416, 438
Frantz, Orville: 76, 438
Frear, Walter F.: letter to, 933
Fred Hartweg: 816
Frederick the Great: 1399
Free Silver: Cleveland's fight against, 1352. *See also* Currency
Freeman, John R.: 1422
Freeman, Mary E. W.: letter to, 681

Freer, Charles L.: id., 117–18
Freetown, Sierra Leone: 101
Freight cars: shortage of, 565–67. *See also* Interstate Commerce Commission; Railroads
French, Alice: *see* Thanet, Octave
French, Asa P.: advises R, 750; and New Haven Railroad, 686, 693
French, Daniel C.: 223
French Academy: 1413
French Canadians: 637, 1104. *See also* Canada
French Parliamentary Group of International Arbitration and Conciliation: 103
French Revolution: R on excesses of, 45, 94, 337, 345, 469, 802, 1048–49, 1372
Frenssen, Gustav: author of *Jörn Uhl,* 495
Frey, John P.: id., 192; and labor injunctions, 191–92, 484–85, 1297
Frick, Henry C.: id., i, 526; campaign contributions, 34, 195; and Harriman suit, 1103; and panic (1907), 830–31; and patronage, 1102; and Standard Oil case, 862; letter to, 862
Friedlander, T. C.: id., 90; letter to, 90
Friedrich Wilhelms University: 644
Frizell, Dr.: 1128
Frobisher, Sir Martin: 497
Froissart, Jean: 1330
Frothingham, Louis: 214, 665, 1363
Frye, William P.: id., ii, 806; letter to, 975
Frye Act: 136. *See also* Merchant Marine
Fuel shortage: 688, 811–12
Fuller, Melville W.: id., iii, 314; and Smithsonian Museum, 118; and judicial decisions, 188–89; letter to, 117
Fulton, Charles W.: id., iii, 572; defeated in senatorial election, 1274; and forest reserves, 604; and land frauds, 348; and patronage, 20–21, 85–86; and Taft nomination, 797; letters to, 20, 85
Fulton, Elmer L.: 386
Funston, Frederick: id., ii, 1014; and Cuban revolution, 434–35; and Goldfield strike, 863

Gabbert, W. H.: 413
Gabriel: 714
Gabriels, Bishop Henry: id., 342
Gage, Lyman: 1344
Gaillard, David D.: 599
Gaines, John W.: 339, 1007
Galena, Illinois: 662
Galena-Signal Oil Company: 1243
Galey, John H.: 369–70; 372
Gallinger, Jacob H.: id., iii, 296; and currency legislation, 1044; at Republican national convention (1908), 1095; m., 1258

944; R on, 1540–41; singing societies among, 1076; views on prohibition, 1128; m., 287, 541

See also Wilhelm II

Geronimo: 1448

Gerrish, John H.: 582

Gessner, Gustavus A.: 1502

Gibbon, Edward: 290

Gifford lectures: 1535

Gilbert, Cass: id., 1430; 1430; letter to, 1431

Gilder, Richard W.: id., i, 101; poetry of, 1366; R letter to, m., 1411; m., 223; letters to, 207, 272, 316, 934, 1366

Giles, William B.: 349

Gill, Wilson L.: id., 1273

Gillett, James N.: id., 608; and anti-Japanese agitation: 618–19, 1477–78, 1483, 1505; and Japanese war scare, 725; letters to, 608, 610, 614, 618, 1477, 1483, 1486, 1502, 1505, 1517

Gilman, Daniel C.: 908

Gissing, George R.: 549

Gladstone, William E.: as Romanes lecturer, 1180; R on, 400, 707, 859

Gleaves, Albert: id., 658; 658, 853

Gleeson, Father Matthew C.: 579

Gleichen, Lord Edward: id., 169

Glenn, Robert B.: 741

Glenwood Springs, Colorado: 232

Gloucester, Mass., *Times:* 670

Godfrey, Edward S.: 790

Godkin, Edwin L.: id., i, 74; R on, 1400; m., 10, 26, 724

Goethals, George W.: id., iv, 1260; appointed to fuel board, 687; attacks on canal management of, 697, 857–58; and cable rights, 874; and construction contracts, 599, 996; and excavation statistics, 776; protests ship purchase, 1220, 1377, 1518; and Reynolds canal report, 1171, 1191; R on, 1192; and Smith resignation, 789; succeeds Stevens, 587–88; and Zone governorship, 793–94; m., 744, 823; letters to, 686, 1009, 1420

Goff, John B.: id., iii, 1; 128

Gold imports: and 1907 panic, 849–50

Goldfield, Nevada: strike in, 863, 866, 868, 1504; troops in, 877

Goldsborough, Phillips L.: id., iii, 46; 1234

Gomez, Juan V.: 1428

Gompers, Samuel: and campaign (1906), 350, 393, 403, 413–14, 454, 457, 488; and 1908 campaign, 1077, 1304–13, 1321; and child labor, 844; and Chinese canal labor, 368; and Chinese exclusion, 190; and Coeur d'Alene riots, 198; confers with R, 451, 714, 843; and eight-hour law, 190,

555; and labor injunction, 190, 476, 581, 1077, 1195–96, 1442; and patronage, 1240–41; and railroad wage dispute, 948; R on, 1203, 1446; sentenced in Bucks case, 1442; and Taft, 1279; m., 459, 714, 1286; letter to, 476

Gooding, Frank R.: id., 302; and Borah indictment, 742; and Coeur d'Alene riots, 302, 491; and gubernatorial campaign, 413, 415, 488–89, 537–38; m., 737. *See also* Idaho

Goodnow, Frank J.: 188

Goodnow, John: id., iii, 901; 1496

Goodrich, Caspar F.: 646

Goodrich, David M.: id., ii, 833; 824

Goodwin, Elliot H.: id., iii, 596; 1402

Gordon, Peyton: 673, 753, 864

Gordon, William A.: 553

Gore, Thomas P.: 1044

Gore Canyon: 276–280

Gorgas, William C.: and Panama sanitation, 364, 507, 1192; R on, 499; Stevens and, 630; m., 200, 355

Gorham Company: and coinage, 406

Gorki, Maxim: 179

Gorman, Arthur P.: id., i, 153; 27, 70

Goudy, Frank C.: 1067

Gould, Ashley M.: and labor injunctions, 873, 1195

Gould, Jay: 224, 267, 277, 746

Government ownership: as campaign issue (1906), 460; and railroads, 395; R on, 536, 1072; m., 187

Government Printing Office: extravagance of, 1272, 1426; dissension in, 12–13; investigation of, 924; labor problem in, 380, 714; and spelling reform, 378, 390; reorganization of, 1367–68

Governors' conference: 1030–31; 1437. *See also* Conservation

Grace, P. H.: id., 1295; m., 1280; letter to, 1295

Grahame, Kenneth: id., 693; letters to, 693, 1314

Grahame, Laurance H.: 501

Grand Army of the Republic: and pensions, 580, 1443

Grand Canyon: 278–79, 1338

Grand River, Colorado: 279

Grand Valley Project: 51

Grandfield, Charles P.: 1111

Grant, Ulysses S.: financial troubles of, 1398; indiscretions of, 1045; m., 170, 410, 540, 553

Grant, Ulysses S., III: 725

Grass, John: 283

Grasty, Charles H.: id., 1327

Graves, Henry S.: 1067

Gray, David: id., 1035; visits R, 1035; letter to, 1130
Gray, George: id., iii, 352; letter to, 46
Gray, John H.: 188
Grayson, Cary T.: id., 1475
Grayson, David: 1094
Grazing: conservation and, 707; and fee payments, 122–23; and illegal fencing, 192–93, 583–84; and railroads, 276. *See also* Conservation; Public Lands
Great Britain: and Alaska boundary dispute, 319–20, 733, 1492–94; and Algeciras conference, 242, 246–48, 250–51; alleged alliances against, 1371; American friendship for, 63, 875; and American Revolution, 410; Americans in, 320, 732; anti-American sentiment in, 499, 602, 1181–85, 1190; anti-German movement in, 231–32; army of, 169–170; athletics in, 591; and Canada, 790; and Canary and Balearic islands, 941; chauvinism in, 529; and China, 15, 1210–11, 1497; colonial administration of, 20, 135, 138, 253–56, 605, 773, 775; and Cuba, 430; diplomatic service of, 32, 169, 318, 579; and disarmament, 348, 357, 398–400, 463, 475, 601, 700; in Egypt, 253–56, 345, 1293; election expenditures, 194; exports, 747; and France, 528; foreign policy, 19, 318, 401, 871; and Germany, 32, 63, 169, 357, 596, 1164, 1292–94, 1371, 1466; House of Lords reform, 1410; immigrants from, 541, 944; imperialism, 16, 18, 20, 29, 135, 138, 359; income tax in, 261; internal problems, 19; and India, 1147, 1206, 1210–11, 1293, 1370, 1383–84, 1402, 1441, 1443, 1447, 1465, 1478, 1507; investments of, in the United States, 1293; Irish-American hostility to, 10, 1011, 1104; and Jamaica, 579; and Japan, 29, 61, 135, 528, 670–71, 790; labor injunctions in, 485; labor movement in, 368; liberal party in, 348; and Malaya, 16; and Mediterranean shipping, 545; and Morocco crisis, 230–39; and Newfoundland fisheries, 13, 320, 400–01, 718–19, 732–33, 785, 1205–06; and Niagara Falls treaty, 154; and Olympic games dispute, 1381–82, 1384–85; and Panama treaty, 1497; and panic (1907), 746, 750, 755; opinion in, of U.S., 725, 730, 790; Parliament, 149, 152, 365; public sentiment on defense, 1432; railroads in, 634, 674, 746, 750, 777, 1072; restriction of Oriental immigration, 786, 919–21, 940–41, 963, 985; R on, 319, 875, 1372, 1401, 1432, 1497, 1511; and Russo-Japanese peace, 9, 18; shipbuilding in, 945; socialists in, 971; and South Africa, 544; steamship subsidies, 626, 628; and

Sudan, 1293; and tariff, 151–52; and Tibet, 1147, 1210–11; treaty of arbitration with, 1023; U.S. and, in Far East, 49, 1147, 1210–11; and Venezuela, 319; m., 345
    Navy of: and Australia, 869; compared with American, 1008, 1515; gunnery in, 1248; hospital ships, 894; proposed battleship program, 549, 601; R on, 1159, 1294; strength of, 16, 161, 169, 234, 324, 334, 348–49, 366, 1018; target practice, 455; visits U.S., 10, 69; m., 398, 762
    See also Bryce, James; Diplomatic Service; Durand, Henry M.; English-speaking People
Great Northern Railway Co.: 356, 464
Great Plains: R on, 322
Great White Fleet: *see* United States Navy
Greece: immigrants from, to U.S., 718, 1104; laborers from on Panama Canal, 337, 339; U.S. diplomats in, 698
Greek civilization: 961
Greely, Adolphus W.: 220
Green: of Interior Department, 192–93
Green River Reservoir: 279
Greenbacks: 849
Greene, Francis V.: id., i, 512; 467, 1377; letter to, 11
Greene, Mrs. Francis V.: 12
Greene, J. D.: 1118
Greene, J. M.: 936
Greene, Warwick: 12
Greenville: 930
Greenway, John C., id., ii, 1009; offered land office appointment, 533; relations with R, 60, 799, 860; visited by Theodore R, Jr., 793
Greville, Leopold G. F. M.: *see* Warwick, Lord
Grey, Sir Edward: advised of Hale interview, 1294; and Carnegie rumor, 348; and Durand's inefficiency, 488; on India, 1478; and report on Jamaica, 579; R plans to visit, 1187; Strachey on, 152; m., 169, 318, 359, 921; letters to, 462, 527, 600
Gridiron Club: dinner and Brownsville affair, 1486, m., 157, 503, 571, 596
Grier, Clark: 1408–09
Griffith, Mr.: (of Yuma), 105
Griggs, John W.: 265
Grilk, Charles: 297
Griscom, Lloyd C.: id., iii, 393; and German embassy, 990–92, 1410; hospitality of, 2; minister to Japan, 15, 46; reports on Italian earthquake, 1459; and Russian embassy, 396; m., 130
Griscom, Mrs. Lloyd C.: 2

Hammond, John H.: id., 1163; 1068; letter to, 1163
Hampden, John: R on, 773, 1087, 1399
Hampden Hall: 1533. *See also* Harvard University
Hankow Railroad: 15, 29, 30
Hanks, Charles S.: and investigation of railroad accounts, 552, 574-75; and college boxing, 944-45; letter to, 574
Hanna Marcus A.: and Commerce and Labor Department, 334; and patronage, 1257, 1344-45, 1495; R on, 265; and Storers, 110; m., 420, 1112, 1369
Hansbrough, Henry C.: id., iii, 424; 763
Hapgood, Norman: id., iv, 814; on Attorney General, 541; and Coeur d'Alene riots, 491; R on, 303, 307, 340, 480, 1220; m., 1116
Harbin: 7, 296
Hardie, James K.: id., 1507; visit to U.S., 1507, 1508
Harkins, Herschel S.: 308
Harlan, James S.: 363, 397
Harlan, John M.: id., iv, 722; 189, 923
Harmon, Judson: id., iv, 1210; 114, 1298, 1313
Harper, Samuel A.: id., 407; letter to, 407
Harper's Monthly: on wealth and democracy in American colleges, 341
Harper's Weekly: and anthracite coal strike, 1152-53; on hunting, 1473; on India, 1443; on presidential nomination, 735; R on, 307, 798, 835-36, 847, 857, 875, 1318-19
Harriman, Edward H.: id., iii, 285; and Alaska, 994; and Alton road securities, 630; attacks R, 885; campaign contributions, 452-53, 642-43, 647, 1245-48, 1264, 1304, 1316, 1323; and Colorado River break, 526, 530, 531; connection with Brandeis, 1040; I.C.C. report on, 716; and insurance investigation, 50, 78-79; investigation of, 535-36, 563; as issue (1908), 1315; and panic (1907), 822, 856; and patronage, 447-52; at Republican National Convention, 631-32; requests to see R, 607-08; R on, 1261; suit against, 462, 1103; m., 276, 465, 617, 653, 654, 674, 772, 797, 845, 859, 925; letters to, 526, 530
Harriman, George W. R.: and I.C.C. statistics, 552-53, 574-75
Harrington, John L.: id., 713; letter to, 713
Harris, Abram W.: 908
Harris, Andrew L.: id., 1013; letter to, 1013
Harris, Joel C.: R eulogy of, 1108-10; letter to, 1075

Harris, Julian: and *Uncle Remus's Home Magazine*, 1108-10; letters to, 1108, 1109
Harrison, Benjamin: and appointments, 1025-26, 1344; campaign costs of, 38; monument of, 648-49, 677; m., 34, 264, 1394
Harrison, Frederic: id., ii, 914; R on, 1337, 1399; m., 1180; letters to, 866, 1337
Harrison, Russell B.: id., 1326; and canal charges, 1326, 1336, 1366, 1412; letters to, 1326, 1336, 1366, 1412
Hart, Albert B.: id., iii, 594; 1050; letter to, 905
Hart, Mrs. Albert B.: 905
Hart, Ernest E.: 936
Hartford Carpet Corporation: 1236, 1426
Hartzell, Joseph C.: 1313
Hartzfeldt-Wildenburg, Hermann von: id., 1196; letter to, 1196
Harvard Club of New York: 1405
Harvard Graduates' Magazine: 694
Harvard University: athletics at, 1119-21, 1183-84, 1190, 1382; and Boxer indemnity, 206; classmates of R at, 805, 944; crew, 665, 1184; discipline at, 1117-23; divinity school, 1343; dormitories, 42, 1533; economics at, 1343; Eliot and, 1376; faculty of, 645; football at, 46, 93, 94, 172, 227, 821, 853, 1375; graduates of, 267, 352, 420, 597, 732; Kermit at, 146, 1271; museum at, 289; R declines to speak at, 410; R as possibility for president of, 172; Sheldon fellowship, 1479; sociology at, 1343; Theodore R, Jr., at, 522; visit to, 608; Wister speech at, 880; m., 149, 164, 214, 361, 562, 669, 836-37, 861
Harvey, Charles M.: id., 1203; 1234; letter to, 1203
Harvey, George B. M., id., iii, 673; and anthracite mine story, 1152; article by, 170; compares R to Jackson, 697; R on, 1318, 1405
Harvey, William S.: letter to, 28
Harvier, Ernest: id., 213; 1178, 1285; letter to, 213
Harwood, Henry: 599
Haskell, Charles N.: and oil land leases, 1291, 1353; resigns from Democratic National Committee, 1259; R on, 1258, 1277; and Standard Oil, 1243, 1250-52, 1264-68; suits against, 1266, 1327; Taft attacks, 1248; m., 1261, 1325; letter to, 1291
Hasler: and beef trust bribes, 140-41
Hasty Pudding: 562, 1122-23
Hauenstein v. *Lynham:* 1483
Havana: 399. *See also* Cuba; Moro Castle
Havenner, George C.: 924
Haverty, Frank: 454

Hawaii: fleet visit to, 745; fortifications of, 912–14, 937–39, 956; immigration to, 473, 510, 580, 609, 612, 720, 858, 933, 1022, 1504, 1512; Japan and, 724–26, 730, 853, 870; R on, 309, 1504, 1512; shipping to, 628; special commissioner in, 470

Hawaiian Commercial and Sugar Company: 1062

Hawthorne, Nathaniel: 137, 1295

Hay, John: and Hague Conference, 30–31; letters of, 1489; negotiates Niagara Falls treaty, 154; R guest of, 675; R on, 24, 1489–98; ultimatum to Venezuela, 132; m., 232, 1074, 1158, 1454, 1495

Hay, Clara L. S.: and Hay letters, 1489

Hay-Bond treaty: 462

Hay-Bunau-Varilla treaty: 874

Hayes, John J.: 1465–66

Hayes, John W.: 1240–41

Hayes-Tilden controversy: 1358

Haymarket affair: 199, 219

Haynes, Thornwell: 1496

Haywood, William D.: acquittal of, 733; armed forces for trial of, 196–99; connection with Borah indictment, 722–23, 737, 767–68, 770; defenders of, 302, 459, 714; indictment of, 189; trial of, 653–55; m., 219, 266, 307, 452, 863, 1080–81

Hazard, Frederick R.: 1006

Hazard, Mr.: 1519–20

Hazen, Allen: 1422

Health: 664, 1269. See also Public Health

Health and Education: proposed department of, 1269–70

Healy, Timothy: 188

Hearst, William R.: alliance with Parsons, 832–33; 1238–39; attacks Haskell, 1265; attacks Taft, 791; belief in R's honesty, 1257; competition with Pulitzer, 1322; criticizes courts, 212; and Jewish vote, 453–54; journalism of, 156, 266, 268; and N.Y.C. election (1905), 50, 70–71, 73, 156; and N.Y. Press, 491, 715; and N.Y.S. election (1906), 156, 347, 369, 395–96, 429, 437, 439, 441–43, 447, 452, 456–7, 460, 465, 467, 470, 486, 488, 1192; and public opinion, 875; reveals Standard Oil payments to Foraker, 1243, 1248, 1326; R on, 307, 459–60, 468–69, 1277; and Vermont politics, 1204; western opinion of, 444; m., 350, 458, 1343

Hearst Municipal Ownership League: 50

Heath, Frank: 865

Hébert, Jacques R.: 345

Hedges, Job E.: id., 87

Heid, John J.: 937

Heinze, F. Auguste: and copper corner, 747, 798, 822; m., 198, 845, 859

Hellenistic civilization: R on, 19

Heller, Edmund: 1146

Helm, James M.: 999

Helm, Major: 1084

Hemenway, James A.: id., iv, 899; and Brownsville affair, 1026; and Republican campaign (1908), 1124; and secret service, 1527–33; letter to, 690

Hemenway Gymnasium: 562

Hemphill, James C.: id., 751

Hendrick, Bishop Thomas A.: 976

Hendricks, Francis J.: id., ii, 891; and Hughes gubernatorial nomination (1908), 1193, 1198

Hendricks, Thomas A.: 540

Heney, Francis J.: id., iv, 1127; attempt to assassinate, 1349, 1419–20; and California senatorship, 1270; investigates San Francisco corruption, 219; investigates timber frauds, 148; and land fraud prosecutions, 481, 483, 770–71; and patronage, 85–6, 668, 788, 829–30; m., 1062; letters to, 148, 1419

Heney, Mrs. Francis J.: 1420

Hengelmüller von Hengelvar, L.: 558, 1447, 1454

Henry of Prussia, Prince: 990, 1540

Henry Sidgwick Memorial Lecture: 959

Hepburn, William P.: id., iii, 420; and Commerce and Labor Department, 334–35; and corporate registration, 926; and immigration legislation, 285; and railroad rate bill amendments, 157–58; and stock transaction regulation, 959; m., 711; letters to, 291, 320

Hepburn Act: administrative remedies in, 567; bookkeeping procedures under, 1020; congressional alliance for, 204, 258–59, 270–75; constitutionality of, 76–77, 1436–47; debate on, 142–43; N.Y. Times on, 167; penalties under, 215; right of appeal under, 157–59, 162; R on, 257; and tariff, 136, 206; Tillman and, 170; m., 148, 172, 177, 292, 328–29, 341, 536, 643, 885, 1386. See also Aldrich, Nelson W.; Allison Amendment; Bailey Amendment; Interstate Commerce Commission; Knox Amendment; Long Amendment; Mallory Amendment; Railroads; Spooner Amendment; Appendix II

Hepburn-Dolliver Bill: see Hepburn Act

Herbert, Hilary A.: 1171; letter to, 553

Herbert, Michael H.: id., i, 167; and Alaska dispute, 1492; R on, 579, 602; m., 503

Hermann, Binger: id., ii, 976; 481

Herrick, Myron T.: id., iii, 152; Hay on, 1495; and Ohio election (1905), 70; and

1659

and, 583–84; policy on, 122. *See also* Homestead Law

Honduras: American intervention in, 432; relations with neighbors, 592, 772

Honolulu: *see* Hawaii

Hooker, Samuel P.: id., 120

Hoover, Irwin H.: id., 83

Hopewell, W. S.: and New Mexico land frauds, 649, 659–60, 731, 733

Hopkins, Albert J.: id., i, 281; and nomination (1908), 796, 1045; and senatorial election, 1521; m., 1078; letter to, 722

Hopping, A. Howard: letter to, 1519

Hornaday, James P.: id., 1316; 1315–16

Hornaday, William T.: 703–04

"Horse Order" (Cuba): 446–47

Horses: Achilles, 1043; Audrey, 313, 860, 1035, 1043; Betsey, 1236; Georgia, 1075; Mollie, 520, 860; Nicoletta, 1005; Roswell, 635, 665, 860, 1005, 1035, 1043, 1322, 1337, 1475; Sagamore, 1035

Hospital Ships: *see* United States Navy

Hot Springs, Arkansas: 471

Hough, Charles M.: 304, 668, 1426

Hough, Emerson: id., 1022; letter to, 1022

Hours of Labor: on railroads, 373, 555, 581, 1152, 1219. *See also* Eight-Hour Day

House Office Building: 157

Housing: R on, 1211–12

Houston, Andrew J.: 1134

Houston, General Sam: 1134

Houtin, Abbé Albert: 597

Howard, Clifford: id., 55; 54–6

Howard, Henry F.: 1159

Howe, Julia W.: 1076, 1366

Howell, Clark: id., iii, 430; 635; letters to, 472, 487

Howells, William D.: id., i, 173; 276

Howland, William B.: id., iii, 564; letter to, 1144

Howry, Charles B.: 553

Hoyt, Henry M.: id., iv, 1015; and New Mexico land frauds, 864; and Panama Canal transaction, 1415; and patronage, 1436; m., 328

Hubbell, Frank A.: 739

Hughes, Charles E.: and antigambling bill, 1192; compared with R, 856; and direct nominations, 1474–75; campaign contributions to, 1262–64; and gubernatorial election (1906), 388–89, 393, 395–96, 429, 435–37, 440–41, 447, 454, 456–57, 459–60, 465–67, 470, 483, 1192; and gubernatorial election (1908), 833, 847, 1144–46, 1149–50, 1160, 1165, 1170, 1172–73, 1178, 1180, 1192–94, 1196–99, 1202, 1207–10, 1223, 1234–39, 1244, 1255, 1259, 1279–80, 1286, 1313–14, 1319, 1330; and insurance investigation,

50, 103; and N.Y.C. mayoralty, 49–50; orders election recount, 156; and patronage, 828; and presidential nomination (1908), 486, 742, 780–82, 784, 796–97, 828, 837, 865, 916, 926, 1005, 1161, 1275, 1340, 1357, 1458; R on, 469, 490–91, 735–36, 1160–61, 1172–73, 1302; statement of national principles, 922; and tariff, 806; and Taft campaign, 1285; and vice-presidency, 926, 1077, 1082–83; Youngstown speech, 1247, 1254–55, 1259, 1261, 1302; m., 369, 456, 1117; letters to, 116, 438, 442, 443, 490, 1285, 1302, 1330

Hughes, Mrs. Charles E.: m., 1330

Hughes, Thomas: 1123

Hughes v. Edwards: 1483

Hughes League: 926

Hughett, Marvin: id., iii, 347; 617, 808

Huguenots: 671

Hulbert, Homer B.: id., 96

Hull, John A. T.: id., iv, 877; letters to, 154, 1039

Hull House: 140, 491, 942

Humphrey, Andrew B.: 999

Humphrey, George S.: 789

Humphrey, J. Otis: and beef packers' suit, 190, 212, 335

Humphrey, William E.: and dreadnought program, 1008; and drydocks, 1005–06; letter to, 1005

Humphreys, Andrew A.: 620

Hundley, Oscar R.: 667

Hungarian Republican Club of New York: 44

Hungary: *see* Austria-Hungary

Hunt, Leigh S. J.: id., iv, 725; 978

Hunt, William H.: id., iii, 151; 668

Hunter, Wiles R.: id., 1051; R on, 1051, 1079, 1080

Hunting: 40–41; R on, 1125. *See also* Roosevelt, Theodore, Biography

Huntington, Collis P.: 224, 266, 1257

Hurley, Augustus W.: 416

Hurst, Carlton B.: id., iii, 684; 110

Huxley, Thomas H.: as Romanes lecturer, 1180

Hyde, James H.: and French ambassadorship, 78–79, 447–48, 451–52, 445, 642, 1102

Hyde, William De W.: id., 71; 223

Idaho: Democratic party in, 537; election of 1906 in, 413, 415, 471, 491–92; and forest reserves, 604; irrigation congress in, 381–82; labor riots in, 196–200, 266; land frauds in, 662–63, 714, 723–24, 736–37, 753, 765, 767–71, 983; Mormons in, 259–60, 491, 537, 538; patronage in, 53; riots in, 214; stabling cavalry in, 363;

statehood of, 477; syndicalism in, 413, 415, 537; m., 459. *See also* Gooding, Frank R.; Haywood, William D.; Patronage; Republican Party

Idaho: see United States Navy, *Ships*

Ide, Henry C.: id., iii, 382; and Philippines, 129, 341, 605

Ijuin, Admiral: 663, 671

Ikoma: 970

Illinois: election (1905), 70; and railroads, 630; R on, 813–14. *See also* Patronage; Republican Party

Illinois Central Car Supply Case: 215

Illinois Manufacturers' Association: 1140, 1208

Immigration: of anarchists, 978; Austrian government and, 314; in Australia, 787; and birth rate, 19, 1433; to British colonies, 254; and contract labor law, 191, 556; and Cunard line, 43–4; hostility to, 71, 401; inspection of, 43–4, 162–63, 285, 1096, 1160; investigation of, 322–23; labor and, 191, 537; mine owners and, 285; and naturalization, 705, 709; newspapers, 287; and politics, 457, 1286; and resettlement, 285; R on, 19, 44, 296–97, 1042–43, 1284; sociologists and, 524; South Carolina and, 556; and standard of living, 286; steamship companies and, 285, 550; of transients, 776. *See also* Immigration Bureau; Immigration Commission; Immigration Restriction; *and by country of origin*

Immigration Bureau: annual report of commissioner, 323; appointment of commissioner, 1241; Chinese boycott and, 165; improper acts of officials of, 162; and proposed investigation, 322–23; R on, 90

Immigration Commission: and complaints of P. F. Hall, 1097; created, 322–23, 550; funds for, 557; and secret service, 1460; m., 140, 783

Immigration Restriction: under Cleveland, 294; labor and, 191, 537; Oriental, 788, 963; as political issue, 285, 360; R on, 393, 940. *See also* China; English-Speaking Peoples; Japan

Immunity: Congressional definition of, 190

"Immunity Bath" decision: 190, 212

Imnaha Forest Reserve: 603

Imperial Order of the Rising Sun: 656

Imperial Valley: 526–27, 530–31

Imperialism: and American administrative problems, 773–76; and defense problems, 726, 761–62, 1108; and Far East interests, 15, 29, 30, 912–13, 963–65; R justifies American, 16, 26, 253–57, 345, 602, 640, 955, 1206. *See also* Colonialism; Investments; *and by countries*

Inauguration: of Taft, 1542

Income tax: as campaign issue (1908), 1128; in Great Britain, 261; R on, 217, 344, 366

Indemnities: in Russo-Japanese Peace Treaty, 2–9, 18, 22, 57–9

Independence Party: 1204, 1243

Independent: on insurance, 551; on Negroes, 343; on Panama, 321; m., 56

India: administration of, 20, 253; diplomatic information on, 1210–11; Japan and, 29; Kaiser on, 1293, 1371, 1466; reports on, 1147; R on British in, 1370, 1441, 1443, 1447, 1465, 1478, 1507; R on problems of, 1206; and Tibet, 1428; unrest in, 1383–84, 1402

Indian Appropriation Act (1906): 386

Indian Rights Association: 1450–52. *See also* Indians

Indian Territory: judges in, 516; discontent in, and Republican party, 386; oil leases in, 369–70, 372, 386–87, 476, 482, 1353–55, 1395; R on, 333; Standard Oil in, 369; and statehood, 71, 137, 322. *See also* Oklahoma

Indian Territory Illuminating Oil Company: 417

Indiana: A.P.A. movement in, 1318; and election (1905), 70–71; and election (1908), 914, 1326, 1357; renaissance in, 1394

Indianapolis: election (1905), 70; intellectual life in, 1394–95; manufacturers' bureau in, 957; memorial exercises in, 684; patronage in, 123; R visits, 676

Indianapolis *News:* libel action against, 1315–19, 1425, 1475–76; and Panama Canal charges, 1323–24, 1377, 1393–95, 1415; on patronage, 969; on presidential nomination (1908), 847; R on, 1322–24, 1326, 1364, 1396

Indianapolis *Star:* on Knickerbocker Trust Co., 914; on patronage, 914–15

Indianola, Mississippi: post office in, 309–10, 1346–48, 1358–59

Indians: administration of Indian affairs, 283, 534, 927, 1448–53, 1461; agents, 52, 829; allotments, 578; Cherokee claims, 386–87; and coal and asphalt lands, 138, 577; Creek land alienation, 370, 1252, 1265–68, 1291; corruption and, 1127; and Custer, 994; disposition of holdings of, 138, 311; intermarriage with, 1434–35, 1514; investigations of officials of, 415–17, 438, 471–72; and land frauds, 1327; and land policy, 311, 577–78; legislation for,

576–77, 1266–67; liquor traffic and, 809, 1530; missionaries and, 1327, 1450–51; and oil and gas leases, 104, 283–84, 369–72, 416, 577–78, 1291, 1353–55, 1395–96; Osage frauds, 284, 370–71, 417; reservations, 471, 682; R on, 1448–50; soldiers attacked by, 1448–53; superintendent of warehouse, 379; taxation of land sales by, 1514–15; tribal funds, 141; wardship of, 576–77; m., 407

Indo-China: 231

Industrial Commission: 68

Industrial Peace Committee: 521, 524

Industrial training: see Education, Industrial

Ingalls, Melville E.: id., 1313; 188

Ingersoll, Ernest: 704

Ingram, Arthur F. W.: Bishop of London, 732

Inheritance Tax: R on, 212, 216–17, 261, 344, 366, 1013

Initiative and Referendum: 809, 1052

Injunctions: and boycotts, 873; and election (1906), 395, 460; and election (1908), 1065, 1077–78, 1140, 1179, 1195–96, 1216–17, 1241, 1296–98, 1305–09, 1324; labor unions and, 191–92, 476, 484–85, 1442; Oklahoma constitution and, 809; proposed constitutional amendment on, 810; and railroad rates, 815, 878, 1174–75; R on, 581, 922, 983, 1022, 1076–78, 1081, 1216–17

Inland Waterways Commission: appropriation for, 1030–31; creation of, 619–21, 1066; and Newlands Bill, 956; preliminary report of, 1054–55; and St. Louis-Gulf deep waterways project, 1390; suggests governors' conference, 839; m., 1072

Insurance: campaign funds and, 35–38; in District of Columbia, 93, 201–02, 551; federal control of, 50; investigation of, 50, 103, 119, 622, 706; reform of, 201–02; R on, 34, 93, 518

Interborough Metropolitan Company: 561, 747, 797–98

Interborough Railroad: see Interborough Metropolitan Company

Interborough Rapid Transit Company: 581, 902, 1295

Interior, Department of the: attacks on, 476; and coal fields, 324, 568; and Colorado River, 974; and conservation, 277–80; and illegal fencing, 192; and forest service, 382; and Indians, 138, 284, 370–72, 386, 576–78, 1448–53, 1514–15; and inland waterways, 621; and land frauds, 415–16, 445–46, 483, 564–65, 570–71, 659–

61, 673, 1265–66, 1327; and Moffatt railroad, 51; and oil leases, 482, 1266–68, 1353–55, 1395; and Oklahoma statehood, 476–81; patronage in, 52, 53; and pensions, 534, 1443; and public lands, 518–20; publications of, 276; publicity by, 476–82; reorganization of, 276, 1269; R on, 533–34, 570, 1535–36; and secret service, 1461, 1528, 1531–33; and water power, 975; and Wyoming investigation, 481. See also Forest Service; Garfield, James R.; General Land Office; Hitchcock, Ethan A.

International Association of Machinists: 504

International Brotherhood of Electrical Workers: 188

International Brotherhood of Stationary Firemen: 188

International Brotherhood of Steam Shovel and Dredge Men: 415, 1299

International Bureau of American Republics: 1539

International Conference: see Hague Conference

International Dredging Company: 581

International Harvester Company: annual report of, 1071; suit against, 763–65, 1094

International Institute of Agriculture, Rome: 329

International police force: 345, 359

International Quarterly: 123

International Typographical Union: 380, 1299

International Waterways Commission: 154

Interparliamentary Peace Congress: 315

Interstate Commerce Act: amendment of, 1218; m., 293, 375, 397. See also Hepburn Act; Railroads

Interstate Commerce Commission: and accounts, 574–75; appointments to, 111, 363, 397; appropriation for, 1020; and demurrage, 566–67; enlargement of, 397; and fuel storage, 688; and International Harvester Co., 763; investigations by, 461–62, 552–53, 622, 630; and labor disputes, 946–48, 952–53, 974; and licensing, 622; and mergers, 622, 711; and monopolies, 187; and Negro accommodations, 987–88, 1003–04; as political issue, 449–52; and pressures from localities, 100–01; prosecutions by, 115, 462, 593; and railroad accidents, 600; and rate discrimination, 187; and rate regulation, 76–7, 83–4, 88, 142, 157–59, 162, 173–75, 204, 210, 215, 270–71, 274, 291, 464–65, 844, 1140–41, 1175, 1386; report on Harriman, 710, 715; R on, 144, 987, 1374; and securities, 622, 711, 923; and state regulation, 754; and valuations, 272, 622, 636, 650, 664; and waterways, 1054, 1386; m., 54; letters to, 272, 464, 622, 946. *See also* Hepburn Act; Railroads

Investments, American: in China, 15, 29, 30, 49, 90–1; in Cuba, 69; in Japan, 670; shipping and, 626–29; in South Africa, 544; in Venezuela, 957. *See also* Imperialism

Iowa: election (1905), 27; election (1906), 403, 466, 471, 489; Labor Bureau, 504; and tariff, 27, 297; m., 814. *See also* Republican Party

Ireland: agricultural reforms in, 1433; attitudes of immigrants from, on foreign affairs, 1104; societies of immigrants from, 1011

Ireland, Archbishop John: id., ii, 954; calls on Ambassador White, 335; and cardinalate, 108–09, 181; Kaiser's hostility to, 1164; and Storers, 181–82, 200, 1495; letters to, 161, 1368

Iron Moulders' Journal: 191, 1297

Iron Moulders' Union: injunctions against, 484–85, 1296; suit by, 191

Iroquois Club: 162

Irrigation: and Colorado River break, 526–27, 530–31; congress on, 381; dams for, 276–78; Grand Valley project, 51; and Los Angeles, 315–16; and power companies, 316; R on, 381–82, 1219, 1445; sectional opposition to, 626; and water use, 684. *See also* Reclamation Service

Irvine, William: 1067

Irving, G. A.: 538

Irving, Washington: 813

Irwin, Wallace: 75

Isle of Pines Treaty: 69

Isthmian Canal Commission: administrative organization of, 78, 125–27, 168–69, 776, 1009–10, *see also* Bishop, Joseph B.; Goethals, George W.; Gorgas, William C.; Shonts, Theodore P.; Smith, Jackson; Stevens, John F.; Taft, William H.; Appendix I; chairmanship, *see* Goethals, George W.; Shonts, Theodore P.; Stevens, John F.; compensation to employees, 1032; and construction bids, 572–73, 598–600, 996; duties of employees, 125–27; investigation of, 321; and lock canal, 306, 1418, 1421–22; and patronage, 28, 1240; represented on fuel board, 687; R on, 789; salaries under, 126–27, 487, 1536; and ship purchase, 1095, 1220, 1377–78, 1390–91, 1518; and Y.M.C.A., 281. *See also* Canal Zone; Panama Canal; Taft, William H.

Italy: arbitration treaty with, 1023; birth rate in, 19; civilization of, 961; compared with Porto Rico, 501; conversion of debt of, 336; and disarmament, 463, 475; earthquake relief for, 1459; immigrants from, 393, 401, 439, 473, 541, 978, 1104, 1504; and International Institute of Agriculture, 329; laborers from, on Panama Canal, 338; and Morocco crisis, 231, 234–35, 243, 252; nationalism in, 252; navy, 894; U.S. diplomats in, 335

Ito, Marquis: 178

Ivins, William: and N.Y.C. election (1905), 50, 70, 73

Izvolsky, Count Alexander: id., 336

Jackson, Andrew: bank policy, 1460; R on, 148, 697, 810

Jackson, John B.: id., iii, 183; 698

Jackson, William H.: 1175

Jackson, William P.: 1175

Jacobs, William W.: 500

Jamaica: earthquake, 579, 674; laborers from, on canal, 364, 499, 504, 602; senators' visit to, 644

James, Elizabeth C. L.: 1040

James, Henry: 1490

James, Jesse: 1537

James, William: 944

Jameson, John F.: id., 1050; letter to, 1050

Jamestown Exposition: 262

Jamestown and Southern R.R. Co. v. *Jones:* 279

Japan: arbitration treaty with, 1023; army of, 5, 56, 58, 140, 474, 528, 724; art of, 117; and balance of power, 1164; battle in sea of, 403; bonds of, 670; characteristics of people of, 1, 2, 22, 23, 62, 528, 663; and China, 18, 231, 946; conceit of, 1511; diplomatic service of, 656; and disarmament, 358, 359, 463; evaluation of R in, 19; fleet visit to, 709–10, 952, 979, 996, 1330, 1411, 1432; and France, 135; and Germany, 135, 528; governing class of, 15; and Great Britain, 18, 29, 135, 670, 790, 1432; hostility to America in, 473, 699, 705, 717, 720, 727–29, 738, 1511; hostility to foreigners in, 965; immigration to, 656–57, 718; immigration to, restricted, 920; imperialism of, 22, 869–70, 919, 946; industrialism in, 1139; internal affairs of, 13, 15, 18, 58, 59, 62, 589; and international agreements, 17, 59; Kaiser on, 1164, 1293, 1466; and Korea, 29, 96, 135, 160, 853; and Kuriles, 161; laborers from, on canal, 337; Lodge on, 1287; and Manchuria, 135, 474, 528, 853; militarism in, 16, 140, 1010; navy, 4, 22, 121, 159–61, 334, 348–49, 403, 427, 455, 474, 529, 549,

601, 730, 743, 892, 894, 945, 967, 970, 1008, 1018, 1294, 1543; and open door, 1343; opinion in, of Russo-Japanese peace, 58, 59; opinion in, of U.S., 473, 530, 532; and panic (1907), 747; and Philippines, 49, 135, 528, 762; population of, 1511; and prisoners of war, 140; and race, 1503–04; R on, 824, 1533–34; R's interview with diplomats from, 713; and Russia, 17, 18, 135, 528, 895; and Sakhalin, 161; seal poachers, 353, 473, 542, 551, 941; statesmen of, 15; steamship lines of, 626, 628; Taft's visit to, 149, 742; and U.S. role in Russian peace, 6, 19, 22, 26, 49, 59, 63, 128, 135, 160, 177, 178; and U.S. foreign policy, 875, 1445; and U.S. war scare, 688, 720–25, 727–30, 941, 1012–13, 1116–42; war plans of, 945–46, 1513

Immigrants from: in Australia, 597, 786, 875, 1511; and British empire, 941; and Canada, 786, 788, 790, 875, 917–21, 1010, 1511; compared with Greeks, 718; competition for employment, 995; coolies excluded, 550; and corporations, 1512; English-speaking people and, 963, 965, 966, 985; and election (1908), 1127; failure of efforts for treaty on, 851–52; fear of sexual misconduct by, 995; Gentlemen's Agreement and, 473–75, 510–11, 521, 528–33, 536–37, 541–42, 589, 596–98, 600, 608–15, 618–19, 656, 671–72, 699–700, 709–10, 717–18, 725, 728–29, 786, 1126, 1150, 1342–43, 1477–79, 1481, 1483–86, 1502, 1504–06, 1508–14, 1517–21, *see also* California, San Francisco; in Hawaii, 726, 933, 1022, 1504, 1512; Hawaiian, to mainland, 510–11, 580, 858; hostility to, justifies increased naval appropriations, 869–70, 1457; joint Canadian action on, 919–21; in Latin America, 724, 726, 940–41; naturalization of, 1342; number of, 984, 995, 1022, 1477–78, 1509–10, 1513; and population increase, 1511; relationships to general immigration law, 532–33, 556; rights of, 484; R on, 602, 761–62, 809, 1022, 1503–04, 1508, 1520–21; violations of Gentlemen's Agreement, 919; and war plans, 717–20, 741, 776

See also Diplomatic Service; Russo-Japanese Peace Treaty; Tokyo Exposition

Japan *Daily Mail:* 670
Japan Society: 713
Japanese Chamber of Commerce: 738
Japanese Sufferers Fund: 195
Java: 253
Jaxon, Honoré: id., 653; letter to, 653
Jayne's Hill: 793

Jefferson, Thomas: and excesses of democracy, 1372; political philosophy of, 1527; religion of, 1200; R on, 224, 304, 347–49, 351, 407, 410, 469, 801–04
Jeffries, James: 1222
Jenkins, John J.: id., iii, 299; letter to, 593
Jenks, Jeremiah W.: id., iii, 68, iv, 1038; 68, 550; letter to, 165
Jermane, William W.: id., 1234
Jerome, King of Westphalia: 69
Jerome, William T.: dinner for, 73; N.Y.S. election (1906), 369, 395, 396; R on, 388–89, 396; and *World* libel suit, 1315, 1489; m., 1161, 1165
Jews: American intercession on behalf of, 536; anniversary of settlement in U.S., 113; attitudes of, 1104; in cabinet, 129, 1042–43, 1335; condition of, in Russia, 23, 112, 113, 207, 336, 345; in England, 250; and extradition of Russian political prisoners, 1207, 1256; immigration of, 1096; and patronage, 123, 461, 878; in politics, 439, 443, 453, 461, 1234, 1335; religious freedom of, 259; Russia refuses passports to, 1256
Johannesburg: 544
Johns Hopkins University, The: 175, 908
Johnson, Andrew: 170, 585
Johnson, B. B.: 847
Johnson, Hiram: and Schmitz removal, 219, 1064
Johnson, John A.: 202
Johnson, Ligon: id., 902; letter to, 902
Johnson, Robert U.: id., i, 770; letter to, 1428
Johnson, Samuel: 786
Johnson, Tom L.: id., iii, 326; 27, 777, 832
Johnson, Willis G.: id., 845; letter to, 845
Johnson v. Southern Pacific Company: 1305
Johnston, Gordon: id., 175; letter to, 175
Johnston, Sir Harry H.: id., 1125; at White House, 1338; m., 1180, 1518, 1519; letters to, 1125, 1521
Joint Board of Army and Navy: 952, 984. *See also* United States Army; United States Navy
Jones, James K.: and oil leases, 369–73, 482, 1354
Jones, Mr.: and 1908 campaign, 1234
Jones, Thomas G.: id., iii, 161; and Alabama railroad regulation, 754, 767, 772, 815, 878; appointed, 667; m., 488
Jones, Bishop W. A.: 862
Jones, Wesley L.: 1249; letter to, 1249
Jordan, David S.: id., iii, 180; letter to, 104
Jordan, Mr.: 853
Journal of Commerce: see New York *Journal of Commerce*

naval administration, 891, 982, 1000, 1469–72; m., 980; letters to, 534, 982, 999, 1469
Keys, John B.: 836–37
Kiaochow: 253
Kibbey, Joseph H.: id., 417; and Arizona statehood, 417, 822, 1338; letter from, cited, 106; letters to, 417, 778, 872
Kildea, Henry F.: 508
King, Horatio C.: id., ii, 1158; 925
King, John R.: 101
King, W. L. Mackenzie: on Japanese war plans, 1010; visits U.S., 917–21, 985, 995; m., 966, 1159
Kipling, Rudyard: R on, 39, 41, 522, 812
Kirke, Edmund: 701
Kittredge, Alfred B.: id., iv, 758; 736
Knapp, Martin A.: id., 157; and Harriman merger, 710; and I.C.C., 600; and security issues, 621, 711; and railroad regulation, 565–66; and railroad wages, 948; letters to, 186, 565
Knapp, Seaman A.: id., 1167
Knappen, Loyal E.: 667
Knickerbocker Trust Company: 748, 822, 914
Knight, George A.: 937
Knight, J. B.: 1462
Knights of Labor: and 1908 campaign, 1241
Knoblauch, Charles E.: id., 959; letter to, 959
Knoeler, Edward: 442
Knott, Richard W.: letter to, 833
Knowland, Joseph R.: 788–89
Knox, Philander C.: id., iii, 94; advises R on speech, 458; and antitrust suits, 328; and Brownsville affair, 558; and campaign contributions, 11; and confederate notes, 910; and election (1906), 419; and employer's liability, 1305; and insurance regulation, 93; Kalamazoo speech, 939; Memorial Day address, 1045; and Panama Canal, 306, 414–15; and patronage, 665–69, 803–04, 927, 1465; and Pennsylvania politics, 647; Pittsburgh speech, 77, 939; powers of corporation bureau, 334; and presidential nomination (1908), 736, 781–82, 796, 847, 915, 1275; and prosecution of senators, 481, 483; and railroad regulation, 77, 158, 162, 259, 274; and right of appeal, 593; and Standard Oil, 862; and Supreme Court judgeship, 185; Taft's Secretary of State, 1423, 1510, 1519; and tariff, 806; visits R, 429; m., 88, 450, 794, 1280; letters to, 11, 148, 215, 418, 939, 1305, 1414, 1415, 1418
Knox, Mrs. Philander C.: 429
Knox Amendment: 174, 274. See also Railroads

Kohlsaat, Hermann H.: id., ii, 1045; 666, 1059; letters to, 908, 1082
Kohrs, Conrad: id., 1212; 1124; letter to, 1212
Komura, Jutaro: appointed Privy Councillor, 178; note to U.S., 59; and peace negotiations, 177; and postponement of exposition, 1188; and San Francisco question, 473; m., 13
Korea: and Anglo-Japanese alliance, 61; Japan in, 4, 15, 49, 96; and Russo-Japanese peace, 22, 61; and U.S., 49, 96
Korean Review: 96
Kremmling Reservoir: 279–80
Kuang Sü: letter to, 17
Kuhn, Loeb & Co.: 1040
Kunz, Mr.: and coinage design, 406
Kurama: 970
Kuroki, Tamesada: 663, 671

La Boca Dam: 497. See also Panama Canal
Labor: and anti-Oriental agitation, 190–91, 473–74, 1512; in Chicago, 1059; and child labor regulation, 844; and compensation for government employees, 1038; and election (1906), 350, 365, 367–68, 376, 403, 415, 438–40, 454–55, 457, 460, 488; and election (1908), 1197, 1208–09, 1216, 1259, 1279–80, 1287, 1296, 1304; and employer's liability, 376, 888–89; and experience of British, in politics, 368; hours of, 190–91, 379; and immigration, 556–57, 611; and industrial education, 907; and injunctions, 190–92, 395, 484, 485, 873; investigation of conditions of, 594–95; mediation of disputes, 947–48; N.A.M. opposition to legislation on, 1203; in N.Y.S. bakeries, 188; organization of, 544; and Panama Canal, 338, 356, 364, 368, 415, 505, 508–09; as political force, 152, 413–14; R on, 327, 350, 366, 1336; riots, 197–99; in San Francisco, 266, 486; and Sherman Act, 997; standards of, 138; strikes by government employees, 380; and Supreme Court, 368, 396, 923; unions, 166, 189; in Utah mines, 188–89; wages of, 946–48; m., 407, 889. See also American Federation of Labor; Gompers, Samuel; Haywood, William D.; Hours of Labor; Injunctions; Mitchell, John; Strikes; Unions
Labor, Bureau of: investigates immigration, 322–23; investigates meat packing industry, 177, 282; investigates women and children workers, 269, 594–95, 1301; lack of accomplishments, 1300–01; and strikes, 396, 948; m., 140, 191. See also Commerce and Labor, Department of

Lee, George C., Jr.: id., 906; letter to, 906
Lee, Henry (Light-Horse Harry): 554
Lee, Robert C.: 1346
Lee, Robert E.: 553–54
Lee, Stephen: 882
Lee, William E.: 1462
Lee, Higginson & Co.: 705, 906
Leech, John: 24
Leech, John S.: 924, 1367; letters to, 1272, 1367
Legislation: see Adams Act; Agricultural Appropriations Bill; Aldrich Bill; Aldrich-Vreeland Act; Alexander Bill; Allison Amendment; Bacon Amendment; Bailey Amendment; Beveridge Amendment; Bucket Shop Bill; Commodity Clause Amendment; Compensation Act; Consular Reorganization Bill; Customs Administrative Act; Denatured Alcohol Law; Desert Land Act; Dingley Tariff Bill; Fowler Bill; Frye Act; Gallinger Ship Subsidy Bill; Hepburn Act; Indian Appropriation Act; Interstate Commerce Act; Juvenile Court law; Knox Amendment; Long Amendment; McCumber Act; Mallory Amendment; Mann-Elkins Act; Newlands Bill; Overman Amendment; Pearre Bill; Platt Amendment; Pure Food and Drug Act; Reclamation Act; River and Harbor Act; Safety Appliance Act; Sherman Antitrust Act; Spooner Amendment; Sterling-Beveridge Bill; Sundry Civil Bill; Tillman-Gillespie Resolution; Timber and Stone Act; Valuation Act (1912); Vreeland Bill; Warren Amendment
Leib, William R.: id., 11
Leipsic, Ohio: 930
Leipzig: 70, 355
Lenox, Mass.: 765
Leonard, Henry: 809
Leopold, King: 439
Leslie's Weekly: 1234
Le Temps: 178
Leupp, Francis E.: id., i, 269; charged with corruption, 1127–1128; and Indian land allotments, 138, 141, 577; and lawless Indians, 1448–50, 1451–53; and Oklahoma investigation, 417, 471; and patronage, 52, 379; R on, 438, 534; letters to, 138, 146, 415, 438
Levy, Jefferson: 745
Lewis, Alfred H.: id., i, 718; m., 267; letters to, 156, 731
Lewis, Lunsford L.: 1361
Lewis, Robert E.: 667
Lewis, Thomas: 166

Lewis, William H.: 227, 1276
Lewis and Clark Forest Reserve: 603
Libby's Company: 295
Liberia: 102, 1048
Liberty Hall Academy: 554
Licorice Trust Case: 752
Lincoln Trust Company: 822
Lincoln, Abraham: and abolition, 101, 329, 1053; attacks on religion of, 1200; birthday banquet, 526; democracy of, 1372; Hay's intimacy with, 1497; negro policy of, 1026; political philosophy of, 1527; quoted, 890; and Republican party, 1369; R on, 341, 351, 375, 410, 444, 466, 469, 517, 539, 573–74, 773, 798, 802, 810, 826, 1087, 1136, 1328–29, 1506
Lincoln Memorial Commission: 684
Lincoln State Journal: 158
Lindsey, Ben B.: 413
Linevitch, Nicolas P.: 57
Lingenfelter, C. H.: 1097
Linnen, Edward B.: and Wyoming and Colorado land frauds, 53–54, 445–46, 564, 570–71
Liquor: labeling of, 624–25, 645, 804; restrictions on sale of, 797, 809, 1082, 1530. See also Prohibition
Lissa, battle of: 173
Literacy test: 285. See also Immigration
Littauer, Lucius N.: id., ii, 967; 784, 1256
Little, Arthur W.: 571
Little Bighorn Battle: 283
Little Rockies Forest Reserve: 603
Littlefield, Charles E.: id., iii, 429; on labor injunctions, 1021; and election (1906), 350, 360, 365, 367–68, 403, 408; and election (1908), 1179; and Philippine shipping, 136; R on, 147, 361; m., 148; letter to, 1021
Liverpool Mercury: 1384
Living Age: on Panama Canal, 364; on R record, 1446
Livy: 738
Llewellyn, Morgan O.: 649, 673; letter to, 864
Llewellyn, William H. H.: id., ii, 902; and New Mexico Republican factionalism, 649–50, 739–40; resignation as district attorney, 766, 864; m., 267; letter to, 733
Lloyd's Neck, N.Y.: 350, 805
Lobbies: for A.F. of L., 504; for corporations, 151; for Indians, 1452; for meat packers, 292; for railroads, 607; for power companies, 277; m., 119
Lochner v. New York: 188–89, 904
Locke, George H.: id., 39; letter to, 39
Lockouts: 192. See also Labor; Strikes; Unions

Lockwood, John S.: id., 1448; 1452; letter to, 1448

Lodge, Anna C. M. D.: id., i, 75; dines with R, 176, 1397; R gift to, 1432; m., 4, 13, 71, 347, 350, 437, 440, 486, 692, 696, 710, 833, 995, 1040, 1096, 1136, 1160, 1163, 1180, 1258; letters to, 176, 549, 798, 1083

Lodge, George C.: id., i, 164; m., 176

Lodge, Henry C.: and Alaska dispute, 1493-94; attacks on, 163, 727; as author, 437; and battleship appropriation, 1014; and Boston Indian Citizenship Committee, 1448; and Boyle, 685; and Brownsville affair, 558, 705, 966, 1482, 1486-87; and child labor, 557, 986; and contract labor, 556; on Dickens, 958-59; and election (1906), 350, 439, 452; and election (1907), 803; and election (1908), 1314, 1368; and immigration, 360, 1096-97; and labor, 1077; letter by cited, 3; and Loeb's future, 1454, 1457; and Maine politics, 350; Malden speech, 803; McKinley visit, 675; and merchant marine, 136; and New Haven merger, 706; and oil industry, 291; *Outlook* criticizes, 118; and Panama ship purchase, 1220, 1377, 1390-91; and patronage, 1423, 1458, 1465; and Philippine tariff, 206; Provincetown speech, 760; and railroad regulation, 118-19, 258, 272; reads classics, 500; relations with R, 141, 163, 176, 312, 439, 470, 664-65, 860, 935, 1397, 1482; and Republican National Convention (1908), 998, 1045, 1060, 1083, 1095, 1134-35; R on, 152; and Russo-Japanese peace, 59; and Storers, 538; and Supreme Court appointment, 396; and Taft nomination, 723; and tariff, 359-60; at Tuckanuck, 1257; m., 145, 299, 352, 503, 736, 749, 784, 801, 1071, 1411, 1519; letters to, 2, 12, 67, 70, 206, 252, 273, 327, 346, 349, 361, 396, 407, 427, 436, 439, 458, 460, 465, 470, 485, 503, 645, 651, 670, 691, 696, 705, 709, 723, 750, 779, 783, 790, 803, 832, 997, 1014, 1040, 1045, 1061, 1064, 1077, 1078, 1083, 1095, 1134, 1160, 1179, 1220, 1257, 1287, 1313, 1482, 1489

Lodge, John E.: 696

Lodge, Matilda E. F. D.: 176

Loeb, William: id., ii, 1061; accused of corruption, 55, 1127; appointment as secretary, 1112, 1113; and bank deposit guaranty, 1202; and campaign funds, 36, 1247; and election (1904), 449; and election (1908), 697, 1127; German ancestry of, 1541; and Hughes, 50, 1235; and Indian Bill, 311; and Iowa factionalism, 297; and liquor labeling law, 804; and Mormons, 491; Moffatt railroad, 276;

and Panama syndicate, 1316; and Panama trip, 392; and patronage, 305-06, 720; and Penrose, 647; and publication of Eliot correspondence, 1118; and railroad legislation, 274-75; and Republican National Convention, 712, 797, 807, 1095; and R children, 204, 808, 1273; and R's publishing negotiations, 1115; R on future of, 1447, 1454, 1457-58, 1538; and *Smart Set*, 732; and Standard Oil, 1141; and tariff, 1351; and third term, 1041; trip with R, 61; and *World* libel suit, 1489; m., 60, 126, 741, 749, 777, 784, 786, 911, 988, 1060, 1107, 1353

Loeffler, Charles D. A.: 1045

Lomax, John A.: id., 1479; 1537-38

Lombos, Philip A. L. de: id., 875; paints R portrait, 875, 919, 995, 1037; m., 1432

Lombos, Mrs. Philip A. L. de: 995

London: 312, 320

London, Jack: R gives up reading, 1343; R on, 41, 617, 1081, 1221-23

London *Daily Telegraph*: 503, 1292

London *Morning Post*: on Newfoundland fisheries, 462, 1205; on Olympics, 1183; R on, 250; and third term, 918

London *Spectator*: 918-19

London *Standard*: 545

London *Times*: diplomatic information to, 344; R on, 875; m., 995

Long, Chester I.: id., 142; and senatorial re-election, 541; and Taft nomination, 735; m., 736; letter to, 142. See also Long Amendment

Long, John D.: id., i, 72, 603; and Boston Indian Citizenship Committee, 1148; and naval power, 1513; and Taft nomination, 998; letter to, 1448

Long, John H.: 909

Long, John L.: 289

Long, William J.: id., iii, 468; R on, as "nature faker," 39, 40-41, 289-90, 617, 679, 700-04, 708, 786

Long Amendment: 174, 204, 215, 258-60, 271, 274. See also Railroads, rate regulation

Longboat, Thomas: 1465-66

Longfellow, Henry W.: 137

Longino, Andrew H.: id., iii, 419; 1346, 1361

Longshoremen's Union: 1279

Longstreet, A. B.: 1292

Longworth, Alice R.: absence from Washington, 1104; and Archbishop Aglipay, 46; engagement of, 149; health of, 841; and presidential nomination (1908), 652; relations to R, 149, 488, 1432; trips, 1; wedding of, 134, 141, 146, 181; m., 339,

695, 696, 860; letters to, 1, 312, 488, 836, 1322

Longworth, Nicholas: and Cincinnati politics, 837; and liquor labeling law, 804; and naval construction, 1008; and patronage, 669-70; and presidential nomination, 646-47; R on, 149-50, 488; and Storers, 181; travel plans, 312; wedding, 134, 149, 181; m., 489; letters to, 646, 652, 669, 695, 841, 1244, 1381

Longworth, Nicholas, Sr.: 181

Longworth, Susan W.: 181, 836

Loomis, Francis B.: id., iii, 508; 356, 1074

Loomis, John T.: id., 1379

Loose, C. E.: 936

Lord, Arthur: 705

Lorimer, George H.: id., 262; 571; letter to, 262

Lorimer, William: id., iii, 139; 292, 1521

Loring, J. Alden: 1146

Los Angeles, California: 315-16

Los Angeles Chamber of Commerce: 51

Los Angeles *Times-Mirror:* 541

Loudenslager, Henry C.: 1201

Louis Napoleon: 1087

Louisiana: 803

Louisville and Nashville Railroad: and wage reductions, 946-49

Louvre: 1090

Love, Alfred H.: id., 346

Lovely, Mr.: 1097

Lövland, J.: id., 524; letter to, 524

Low, Maurice: id., iv, 1316; R on, 250, 462, 918-19; m., 1288

Low, Seth: id., i, 136; 925-26, 1006; letters to, 530, 824, 925, 983, 986, 997, 1374, 1379

Lowden, Frank O.: 937

Lowdermilk, W. H., and Company: 1379

Lowell, Francis C.: id., i, 489; 935-36, 953; letter to, 129

Lowell, Mrs. Francis C.: 130

Lowell, James R.: 573

Lowther, Gerald: 488

Loyola, Ignatius: 1399

Lubin, David: id., 329

Luce, Mrs. John D. H.: 646

Luce, Stephen B.: 1171, 1487

Lucretius: 290

Lukesh, George M.: 362

Luna, Solomon: 936

Lurton, Horace H.: id., 338; considered for Supreme Court appointment, 338, 363, 368, 408; R on, 343

Luther, Martin: 696, 1399

Lyman, George H.: id., i, 489; 935-36

Lyman, Hart: id., 876; 1489; letter to, 876

Lynching: and patronage, 1346; proposed commission to investigate, 487-88; R on, 509, 1348; Russians refer to, 336; threat of, 1347-48; of white immigrants, 401; m., 130. *See also* Negroes

Lyon, Cecil A.: id., iv, 1140; and patronage, 928, 1111, 1362; and Republican National Convention, 936; on Texas politics, 1373; m., 138; letter to, 989

Lyons, Judson W.: id., iii, 206; and presidential nomination (1908), 934; m., 130, 937, 1409

Lyric Hall: 1080

MacAndrews and Forbes Company: 752

MacArthur, Arthur: 415

MacArthur, Arthur F.: 598, 600

MacArthur-Gillespie Contracting Syndicate: 357, 572, 598, 600

Macaulay, Thomas B.: on America, 1400; on American government, 1444; cited in attack on Pulitzer, 1417; poetry of, 1398; R on, 24, 137, 290, 840-41; R takes works to Africa, 1330

McBee, Silas: id., ii, 268; approves annual message, 472; impressed by royalty, 339; and patronage, 1479; m., 1204, 1523; letters to, 509, 772

McBlair, A. McDonald: 711

McBride, James: 1232, 1241

McBride, Thomas A.: id., 20; and Oregon judgeship, 20-21, 86

McCabe, George P.: id., 299; and meat packing legislation, 300-01; and pure food law, 1468

McCall, John A.: id., 34; and campaign funds, 34, 37

McCall, Samuel W.: attacks R, 766; and immigration legislation, 580; and naval power, 597, 1012, 1512; on railroad legislation, 147; R on, 408; m., 350, 421, 429

McClellan, George B.: and N.Y.C. mayoralty, 10, 70, 73, 156

McClellan, Robert: 678

McClelland, Charles P.: id., iii, 526; and insurance investigation, 116-17; and patronage, 103; letter to, 103

McClernand, John A.: 995

McClintock: Yale coach, 93

McClure, Samuel S.: id., 45; letter to, 45

McClure's Magazine: and African trip articles, 1106; on naval reform, 891; on railroads, 25; R on, 184, 517; on Taft, 1202; m., 45

McConnell, William J.: id., 146; letter to, 146

Magoon, Charles E.: id., 355; as Cuban provisional governor, 355, 391, 454, 994, 1018, 1137; and Cuban cable rights, 1105; and election (1908), 1105; and Isthmian Canal Commission, 126, 355; R on, 127; m., 169, 704; letter to, 873, 993

Mahan, Alfred T.: member, Departmental Methods Commission, 1050; member, Navy Yards Commission, 1536; on mixed-caliber battleship, 403, 427; m., 1073; letters to, 550, 1487, 1542

Mahdists: 17

Mahon, W. D.: 188

Mail rates: 607

Maine: election in (1906), 350, 360, 403, 408; election in (1908), 1207; prohibition issue in, 403; tariff issue in, 75–6, 392; Spanish-American War, fear of attack in, 1011. *See also* Patronage; Republican Party

Malaya: British imperialism in, 16, 20, 128, 253–55, 775; people of, in Philippines, 774

Malby, George R.: 1049

Mallory Amendment: 210–11. *See also* Railroads, rate regulation

Malthie, Milo R.: 188

Mammoth Hot Springs: 1241

Manchuria: and balance of power in Asia, 474; Japanese foreign policy and, 135, 528; Japanese soldiers returned from, 941; railroad of, 4, 7; and Russo-Japanese peace, 15, 17, 22

Manila: fleet visit to, 745; R on defensibility of, 738; U.S. shipping to, 628; m., 12, 731. *See also* Philippines

Mann, James R.: id., iii, 399; and Commerce and Labor Department bill, 334–35; and Panama Commission reorganization, 168; and railroad legislation, 1386

Mann-Elkins Act: 1386

Manney, Henry N.: and fleet cruise, 725–26

Manufacturers' Association of New York: 1140

Manufacturers' Bureau: 544

Manufacturers' Bureau, Indianapolis: 957

Marat, Jean P.: 345

Marco Polo: 677

Mare Island: 220, 955. *See also* United States Navy

Marinette, Wisconsin: post office in, 324–26

Marion, Francis: 225

Mariposa Big Tree Grove: *see* Yosemite National Park

Mark Twain: *see* Clemens, Samuel L.

Marks, Marcus: id., iv, 1015; and election (1908), 1286

Marlborough, Duchess of: *see* Vanderbilt, Consuelo

Marlborough, Duke of: *see* Spencer-Churchill, C. R. J.

Marshall, John: R on, 407, 469, 802

Marshall, William L.: appointed Chief of Engineers, Army, 1070; on Navy Yards commission, 1536

Martin, Alvah H.: 936

Martin, J. C.: id., 1333; letter to, 1333

Martin, James L.: 668

Martin, William: recalled from China, 1496

Marvin, Winthrop L.: id., 811; letter to, 811

Maryland: A.P.A. movement in, 1318; election (1905), 27, 70; election (1908), 1194, 1196, 1205, 1314. *See also* Patronage; Republican Party

Marx, Karl: 1022

Mason, Newton E.: id., 1380; and gunnery, 1380

Masons: 1278

Massachusetts: care of dependent children in, 1440; election (1904), 27; election (1905), 27, 70, 118–19; election (1906), 350, 393, 455, 460–61, 466–67, 470; and New Haven merger, 686, 691–93, 705; railroad regulation in, 634; and tariff, 118, 349, 405, 593–94. *See also* Lodge, Henry C.; Patronage; Republican Party

Massachusetts Agricultural College: 1169, 1340

Massachusetts Federation of Labor: and 1906 election, 455

Massachusetts Institute of Technology: 1055, 1067

Massie, W. J.: 1408–09

Masterson, Bat: 104, 267, 731

Mather, Robert: 844

Matre, Anthony: 972–74

Matthews, Franklin: 745

Matthews, James B.: id., i, 147; and spelling reform, 378; letters to, 86, 527, 723

Maumee, Ohio: 930

Maxwell, Thomas J.: 1502

Mayer, Julius H.: id., iv, 971; and N.Y.C. elections, 156, 439; letter to, 156

Mayflower: see United States Navy, *Ships*

Mazzini, Giuseppe: 1002

Mead, Albert E.: id., 605; letter to, 605

Mead, Frank: 1452

Mearns, Edgar A.: id., 1146; letters to, 1146, 1191

Meat Packing: defense of practices in, 302, 307; investigation of, 140, 176–77, 190, 208–09, 282, 287–89, 294–96, 302, 307–08, 340–41, 403; legislation on, 282–83, 291–92, 300–01, 317, 365, 406–07, 643, 1218;

R on, 180, 287, 1445; secret service and law on, 1530; m., 297. *See also* Beef Trust

Medal of Honor: *see* United States Medal of Honor Club

Medical Investigation and Publication Bureau: establishment proposed, 1269

Medicine Bow Forest Reserve: 603

Mediterranean: 544–45

Mediterranean Expeditionary Force: World War 1, 139

Medora: 1072

Mellen, Charles S.: id., iii, 481; and New Haven Railroad merger, 685–86, 907, 1011; and New Haven Railroad steamboat holdings, 1040; and R interview, 617, 625; letter to, 778

Melville, Whyte: 137

Memorial Hall: 562

Memphis, Tenn.: R speech at, 815; m., 816

Mendel's Law: R on, 1023, 1435–36

Menocal, Anicito G.: 434, 573

Merchant Marine: and coastal shipping, 792, 1040; commission for, 811; encouragement of, 1378; and Hawaii, 913; Mediterranean, 544–45; and navy fueling, 811–12; and Philippines, 136; R on, 485; subsidies to, 167–68, 555–56, 625–29. *See also* Isthmian Canal Commission

Merchants' Association, New York: and patronage, 1534

Meredith, George: id., 901; letter to, 901

Meredith, Wyndham: 1362

Mergenthaler Company: 13

Mérou, Garcia: 119

Merrell, Mrs. E. H.: id., 576; letter to, 576

Merrell, John P.: id., 1108; letter to, 1108

Merriam, Clinton H.: and biological survey, 578; quoted on mammals, 702–03; R on, 880; letters to, 971, 1023

Merrifield, Arthur W.: 267

Merrill, Clarence S.: 788–89

Merritt, Edwin A.: 120

Merritt, John A.: 205

Merry del Val, Raphael Cardinal: 107–08, 597

Merrymount Press: 737

Mesabi Range: 1232

Messenger of the Sacred Heart: 1325–26, 1333

Messina: 1459

Metcalf, Victor H.: id., iv, 794; and anti-Japanese agitation, 474, 510, 532, 610, 612; and battleship appropriations, 1014–16; and cabinet changes, 461; and Chinese exclusion, 90; and judicial appointments, 667; reports to, on Japanese policy, 853; resignation of, 1392; and statement on

Japan, 1287; and submarines, 749–50; m., 979; letters to, 162, 269, 510, 572, 891, 893, 937, 952, 955, 967, 970, 980, 997, 1101, 1237, 1248, 1278, 1383

Methodists: and election (1908), 1313; R speech to, on India, 1370, 1441, 1444, 1447, 1477; m., 1056

Metropolitan Club, Washington: 250, 918

Mexican War: 580

Mexico: Colorado River flood and, 530, 531, 974; conquest of, 407; Creelman's article on, 963–64; and conservation, 1438; and inter-American affairs, 334, 592, 640, 772, 1408; Japanese in, 609, 612, 720; immigrants from, 71; revolutionaries from, 1099–1100

Meyer, George von L.: id., i, 489; and African trip equipment, 1473; and anti-semitism in Russia, 207; appointed to cabinet, 935–36; and cabinet changes, 461; and Czar, 15; genealogy of, 1043; and guaranty of bank deposits, 1131–32; informed of Algeciras negotiations, 250, 252, 359; letters by, cited, 5, 6, 8, 336; letters to, cited, 4, 6; and New Haven Railroad investigation, 750; and panic (1907), 822, 848; and patronage, 596, 625, 720, 1128; and presidential nomination (1908), 780; relations with R, 664–65, 922, 1427; and Republican National Convention, 712; R on, 8, 675; and Russian Revolution, 71; and Taft, 1458, 1487; urges R to visit Kaiser, 1187; m., 62, 130, 182, 852, 1035, 1097, 1495; letters to, 145, 625, 688, 1102, 1103, 1111

Michigan: and conservation, 684; R visit to, 677–78; university of, 678. *See also* Patronage; Republican Party

Michigan: see United States Navy, *Ships*

Michigan Car Company: 117

Michigan State College of Agriculture: 678

Midshipmen: *see* United States Naval Academy

Mikado: *see* Mutsu Hito

Miles, Herbert E.: id., 722; and tariff, 722, 981; m., 361; letter to, 731

Miles, Nelson A.: id., ii, 840; 420

Milholland, John E.: 999

Militarism: R on, 17, 19, 942. *See also* Disarmament

Militia: 154. *See also* National Guard; United States Army

Millard, Joseph H.: id., iv, 1200; 355, 385

Millard, R.: 416–17

Miller, James M.: id., 949; letters to, 949, 974

Miller, John P.: 143–44

Miller, William A.: 714
Millet, Frank D.: 1074
Milner, Alfred, Viscount: 775
Milton, John: R on, 390, 495, 500; in pig-skin library, 1330
Milwaukee, Wisconsin: 485
Minear, A. Bruce: 281
Mineral Lands: claims to, 477. *See also* Warren Amendment
Mining and Scientific Press: on San Francisco labor and politics, 1055-56
Minnesota: 27, 793, 799. *See also* Patronage; Republican Party
Minneapolis, Minn.: 849
Miraflores: 320
Miscegenation: 227, 310. *See also* Negroes; Race
Missionaries: among Indians, 1450, 1451; Methodists, 1370
Mississippi: aristocracy in, 225; R visits, 821. *See also* Indianola, Mississippi; Patronage; Republican Party; Williams, John S.
Mississippi River: commercial importance of, 802; R trip on, 813-14, 816
Mississippi Valley: and demands for waterways improvement, 619; and railroads, 620; and shipping legislation, 628-29
Missouri: description of, 813-14; election (1904), 27; election (1906), 466; election (1908), 1205, 1314
Missouri: see United States Navy, *Ships*
Mitchell, Edward P.: id., 180; 182
Mitchell, John: id., iii, 323; and boycott, 1309; and Bucks case, 1442; and coal strike, 166, 1154; and Idaho riots, 198; and labor injunctions, 1195-96; and National Conservation Commission, 1068; prosecution of, 483; and Taft campaign, 1321; and United Mine Workers, 202-03; m., 267, 413, 530, 1240
Mitchell, John H.: id., iii, 207; 85, 481-82
Moffat, David H.: id., 276
Moffat Railroad Company: 51, 278
Moffat, Yard & Co.: 75
Moffett, Edward A.: 188
Mohammedans: liberal movements among, 698, 1242; and yellow peril, 1164, 1293; m., 774
Mohler, John R.: 299
Mohonk Conference: 346, 1449
Mollie: *see* Horses
Molly McGuires: 327
Mondell, Frank W.: 569, 680, 707
Monfort, E. R.: 596
Mongolians: 226, 610
Moniteur de la Flotte: 403
Monitors: *see* United States Navy

Monroe, James: 475
Monroe Doctrine: interpretations of, 645; as election issue (1906), 374; Germany and, 63, 1511; justifies large navy, 546, 1008, 1108, 1294; public opinion on, 761; R on, 1511. *See also* Caribbean; Central America; South America
Montague, Andrew J.: id., iv, 1155; 472, 487
Montana: and copper suit, 1417-18, 1527; election (1906), 466; election (1908), 1314; forest reserves in, 603-04; patronage in, 53
Montana Stock Growers' Association: 1212
Montant, Augustus P.: 442-43
Montezuma Forest Reserve: 603
Moody, William H.: id., i, 489; appointed to navy commission, 1487; attends R labor dinner, 1336; and beef trust, 140-41, 176; and cabinet changes, 390, 935-36; and conservation, 280; and corporations, 54; and election (1906), 439, 461, 467, 470-71, 483, 486; and employer's liability, 888; and insurance regulation, 93; and International Harvester, 763; and Interstate Commerce Commission, 363; and judicial appointments, 665, 1202; and land frauds, 446, 476-7, 481, 520; and Lurton, 396; and meat packing legislation, 300; and N.Y. District Attorney appointment, 127; and patronage, 47, 117; and Philippine tariff, 141; and railroad regulation, 76-7, 83, 88, 100, 157-58, 162, 215, 270-72, 274-75, 450, 464; R on, 328, 438, 517, 1393; and R's speeches, 458, 801, 804; and Steffens, 829; and Supreme Court appointment, 338, 390, 397, 527, 666; m., 229, 953; letters to, 50, 102, 114, 134, 140, 186, 191, 196, 215, 347, 390, 527, 801
Moody-Mahan Commission: *see* Navy, Department of the
Moore, Alfred S.: 669
Moore, John H.: letter to, 816
Moore, Joseph H.: id., 1348; letter to, 1348
Moore, Thomas L.: 1362
Moore, Willis: 56
Moore and Schley: 830, 1317
Moors: 243. *See also* Morocco
Moran, John B.: id., 350; and election (1906), 437, 460-61, 467; Lodge on, 458; R on, 350, 452, 459-60
Morawetz, Victor: recommended as Attorney General, 541; and Sherman Act amendment, 986-87, 997
More, Thomas: 695
Moreland, Sherman: id., 120; 120, 125
Morgan, Charles: 1117-1123

Morgan, Edward M.: 704

Morgan, Edwin V.: id., iv, 719; lack of intelligence by, on Cuban crisis, 440–41; m., 402, 1018

Morgan, Sir Henry: 497

Morgan, J. Pierpont: confers with R, 617, 625, 674, 843, 854; and Hankow railway, 15, 29, 30; and Massachusetts railroads, 686; and North American Indian Incorporated, 994; and Panama Canal syndicate, 1316, 1415–16; and panic (1907), 748, 822, 830; and railroad regulation, 88, 451; and tariff, 217–18; m., 267, 631, 706, 1002, 1040, 1392

Morgan, John T.: id., i, 414; 112, 261

Morley, John: on India, 1206, 1384, 1443, 1478; informed on Tibet, 1210–11; as Romanes lecturer, 1180; m., 729; letter to, 1399

Mormon Church: attacks on, 259, 260; and Idaho politics, 491, 537–38

Morning Democrat (Ardmore, Oklahoma): 1265

Moro Castle: 433, 542

Morocco: American treaty with, 317–18; convention of Madrid, 232, 237, 317; open door in, 318; R on, 1148; R on American role in, 1444, 1538–39; Schurz proposal on, 168; State Bank of, 243–44. *See also* Abdul-Aziz; Algeciras Conference

Moros: 175, 256. *See also* Philippines

Morrill, Charles H.: 937

Morris, Gouverneur: 337

Morris, Page: 668

Morris, Robert C.: 47–49; 87

Morris, William: 23

Morris and Company: 406

Morrison, Charles B.: id., 140; and beef packers' suit, 140–41, 189–90; consults R, 451; and Standard Oil, 409, 757–58, 785; m., 328; letter to, 189

Morrison, Daniel T.: and labor injunction, 1195

Morrison, Frank: id., 190; sentenced in Bucks case, 1442; letter to, 190

Morrissey, P. H.: 451, 1280

Morrow, Mary: postmistress at Abilene, Texas, 1111, 1134

Morrow, William W.: id., 219

Morse, Charles W.: and coastal shipping, 1040; conviction of, 1336; copper corner, 747, 822; indictment of, 1176; and secret service, 1528–29; m., 845, 859

Mortimer, Sir: *see* Durand, Henry M.

Morton, Oliver P.: 539–40, 677, 1053

Morton, Paul: id., ii, 1019; appointed to Navy Commission, 1487; and insurance regulation, 518; proceedings against, 114–

15; and railroad regulation, 450–51; m., 739; letters to, 74, 77, 535, 563, 1541

Morton, Pauline: 536, 1541

Moseley, Edward A.: 593

Moseley, L. B.: 936

Moser, E. H.: 930

Mott, John R.: id., 1281; m., 1523; letters to, 1281, 1283

Mott, John T.: id., 153; 154

Mott, M. L.: id., 1265

Mount Hope Reservoir: 363–64. *See also* Panama Canal

Mouser, Grant E.: 1502

Moyer, Charles H.: id., 189; and Borah charges, 662–63; 723, 737, 768; defenders of, 302, 307, 653–55; trial of, 189, 196–99; R on, 219, 452, 459, 714; m., 266, 1080–81

Muck-rake Speech: 157, 217

Mugwumps: election (1906) and, 456; nomination (1908) and, 796; R attacked for appointing, 112; and R campaign letter, 349; R on forces producing, 408; R on press of, 1073, 1160–61; R on Hughes as, 1238; R on McCall as, 766; R on Rhodes as, 540; R on Schurz followers as, 724. *See also* Anti-imperialists; *Nation;* New York *Evening Post*

Muir, John: id., iii, 447; and Hetch Hetchy valley, 793; m., 701; letter to, 793

Mukden: 57, 139, 296

Mullen, W. E.: Attorney-General of Wyoming, 680

Müller, Admiral George von: 990

Mulvane, David W.: 936

Munger, Thomas C.: 668

Municipal Affairs: 188

Munn, Mrs.: 1506

Munsey, Frank A.: id., iv, 971; letter to, 1011

Munsey's Magazine: on business situation, 1012

Münsterberg, Hugo: id., iii, 71; 141

Murch, Mr.: 261

Murchie, Guy: 1363

Murdock, Victor: 607

Murphy, Charles F.: 156

Murphy, William D.: letter to, 60

Murray, George G. A.: id., 398; R on, 398, 1084; m., 1136, 1232, 1397

Murray, James A. H.: id., 404

Murray, Joseph: id., i, 246; 1418

Murray, Lawrence O.: id., iv, 723; and bank deposit guarantee, 1234; criticizes national bank examiners, 1288; and Goldfield strike, 863, 896; m., 328, 1179; letters to, 719, 724

Museum of Natural History: *see* American Museum of Natural History

Muskogee: 1418
Mussulmans: *see* Mohammedans
Mutsu Hito: and Russo-Japanese peace, 2-3, 9, 12, 19. *See also* Japan; Russo-Japanese peace
Mutual Life Insurance Company: 103
Myer, A. L.: 1100
Myrick, Herbert: id., 1224; letter to, 1224
Myton, H. P.: 105

Nannie: *see* Lodge, Anna C. M. D.
Napier, Charles: 840
Napoleon: R on, 69-70, 172, 1399
Narramore case: 1298
Nashville, Chattanooga and St. Louis Railway Company: 987-88
Nation: R on, 352, 540, 721, 724, 729, 1048, 1073, 1400
National Academy, London: 1159
National Advisory Board on Fuels and Structural Materials: 687
National American Woman Suffrage Association: 1341
National Arbitration and Peace Conference: 639
National Association of Audubon Societies: 578
National Association of Insurance Commissioners: 551
National Association of Manufacturers: and injunctions, 1077, 1179, 1297; and labor legislation, 1078-79, 1203; and meat packing investigation, 307; and politics, 350
National Association of Wool Manufacturers: 811
National Bank of North America: misuse of funds of, 1176, 1336
National Banks: and shortage of call money, 81; and panic (1907), 833, 849; supervision of, by federal government, 824-25; Treasury deposits in, 621
National Character: 528. *See also* English-Speaking Peoples; *and by countries*
National City Bank: 1350
National Civic Federation: committee to investigate municipal ownership, 187-88; conference on trusts and combinations, 825, 844; proposals to regulate corporations, 926, 983-84, 1115, 1374, 1379; report on living conditions in Panama, 744; m., 165, 166, 530, 1241, 1313
National Conference on Trusts and Combinations: 825, 844
National Congress of Mothers: 259
National Conservation Commission: appointments to, and duties of, 1066-69; governors' conference and, 839; and

neighboring countries, 1437-38; President's power to appoint, questioned, 1071; report of, 1069; m., 213
National Council of Commerce: 1067
National Council of Fine Arts: 1430
National Defense Board: 950
National Founders' Association: 192
National Guard: R on law improving administration of, 1445
National Home for Disabled Volunteer Soldiers: 1274
National Hughes League: 1209
National Irrigation Congress: 1098
National Monetary Commission: 908
National Museum: and R's African trip, 1089, 1093-94, 1096, 1136, 1146-48, 1161, 1172, 1186, 1207, 1242, 1385, 1388, 1404. *See also* Smithsonian Institution
National Parks: policing of, 1232, 1241. *See also individual parks by name*
National Public Ownership League: 188
National Republican Progressive League: 781
National Rivers and Harbors Congress: 1055
National Steel Company: 1326
National Transit Company: 1251
National Waterways Commission: 1031. *See also* Inland Waterways Commission
National Window Glass Workers: 1381
Naturalization: appointment of inspectors for, 705, 709; bureau of, created, 286; as issue in 1906 election, 360; R on, 1219. *See also* Immigration
Nature fakers: R on, 289-90, 700-04, 707-08, 1220. *See also* Burroughs, John; London, Jack; Long, William J.
Navajo Reservation: disturbances in, 1448-53
Naval limitation: *see* Disarmament
Naval Reserve Association: 1392
Naval War College: *see* United States Navy
Navy, The: 706
Navy, Department of the: administrative organization of, 563, 891-92, 967-68, 980, 982-83, 999-1001, 1171, 1199, 1453, 1456-57, 1468-72, 1487-88; and defense estimates, 951-52; dissension in, 1453-56, 1470-72, 1524; and eight-hour law, 379-80; and fleet disposition, 1525-26; and National Defense Board, 950; and Panama ship purchase, 1220; and secret service, 1528; Secretary of, 17, 69, 1392; letter to, 1446. *See also* Bonaparte, Charles J.; Disarmament; Metcalf, Victor H.; Newberry, Truman H.; United States Navy
Navy League: 706, 1392

Near East: 230

Nebraska: election of 1908 in, 1314; land frauds in, 481, 1531–32; m., 809. *See also* Patronage; Republican Party

Needham, Henry B.: id., iv, 1280; and liquor labeling law, 804; and Panama Canal investigation, 1009, 1191; and railroad rate regulation, 273, 275; R on, 1112; R statement to, on outdoor life, 1500–01; letter to, 1231

Needham, William H.: 523

Negroes: banks of, 309–10; characteristics of, 509, 1125–26; civil rights of, 343, 368, 396, 1276–77; disenfranchisement of, 70; education of, 1346; European interest in, 336, 1125–26; and intermarriage, 1436; labor of, on Panama Canal, 364, 368, 499, 504; and patronage, 101–02, 988, 1276–77, 1346–48, 1356–65, 1538; as physicians, 1347; in politics, 489, 509, 695–96, 1026, 1046, 1140, 1163, 1286, 1304; and Republican National Convention (1908), 934, 999, 1012, 1070–71; religion and, 228; R on, 1047–48, 1126, 1343–48, 1401; segregation on railroads, 987–88, 1003–04; in South, 226–28, 310, 472; in U.S. Army, 1365; at White House, 1358; m., 1398. *See also* Atlanta race riots; Brownsville Affair; Indianola, Mississippi; Lynching; Race; Washington, Booker T.

Neill, Charles P.: id., 140; attends R labor dinner, 1336; and child labor investigation, 557, 595; and Immigration Commissioner, 1240; and immigration investigation, 322–323, 550, 556; and eight-hour law, 379; and election (1908), 1279; and employer's liability bill, 1010; and Goldfield strike, 396, 863; and government employee compensation act, 1031–32, 1037–38; and Interstate Commerce Commission statistics investigation, 574–75; and meat packing investigation, 177, 190, 208–09, 282–83, 286, 291–92, 294–95; and navy yard layoffs, 986; and railroad wage dispute, 948; R on, 269; letters to, 323, 379, 552

Nelson, Henry L.: id., ii, 1083; 1152–53, 1229

Nelson, Admiral Horatio: 1113–1114

Nelson, Knute: id., iii, 424; member National Conservation Commission, 1067, 1068; letters to, 209, 334, 1007

Nelson, William R.: id., iii, 204; 864

Nelson, Morris and Company: conviction of, 1260; investigation of, 295

Nesbit, Evelyn: 1025

Netherlands: *see* Holland

Nettleton, Alfred B.: 521

Nevada: and anti-Japanese agitation, 1504, 1514; and election (1906), 466; and election (1908), 1205, 1314; forest reserve in, 603; strike and federal troops in, 863, 866, 868–69, 877, 895–96, 923, 927

New, Harry S.: id., ii, 1435; and campaign (1908), 937, 1032, 1104; letter to, 963

New Century Light and Power Company: 277–78

New England: A.P.A. in, 1318; politics in, 1322. *See also by states*

New Hampshire: *see* Churchill, Winston; Patronage; Republican Party

New Hampshire: see United States Navy, *Ships*

"New Idea" Republicans: 70

New Jersey: elections (1905), 70; naval militia, 343. *See also* Republican Party

New Mexico: corruption of officials in, 177; forest reserves in, 603; land frauds in, 177, 649–50, 658–62, 673, 731, 733–34, 752–53, 757, 765–66, 864, 909, 946; political situation in, 177, 739, 757, 765–66; statehood of, 71, 135, 322, 417, 778, 816, 822, 1338, 1367. *See also* Democratic Party; Republican Party

New Orleans: lynching at (1891), 401; and panic (1907), 849

New Panama Canal Company: 211

New River Coal: 513

New Testament: 773

New York Board of Trade and Transportation: 1007

New York Central and Hudson River Railroad Company: and rate increases, 1140, 1152; suit against, 127, 1260

New York Chamber of Commerce: 131, 875

New York City: coal supply in, 513; election (1905), 49–50, 70–71, 73, 156, harbor, 343; panic of 1907 in, 747, 849; playgrounds in, 592; politics of, 119–20, 124–25; reform in, 1052, 1474; and West, 199; and *World* libel suit, 1489. *See also* New York State

New York Clearing House: 849

New York *Evening Post*: on Bonaparte, 764–65; on Hughes nomination (1906), 369, 460, 1192; on Hughes renomination (1908), 1202, 1238–40, 1302–03; on Lodge, 727; on naval expenditures, 706; on presidential nomination (1908), 735, 742, 781, 769, 914, 1275, 1356; and Republican Party in South, 1201; and Riordan, 33; R on, 701, 721, 724, 751, 753, 798, 835, 847, 857, 875, 1048, 1073, 1081, 1160, 1179, 1277, 1288, 1316, 1318–19, 1322–24, 1364–65, 1400, 1408; on R's Provincetown

and Panama ship purchase, 1220; and Republican national convention (1908), 936; and Taft, 1458; m., 328, 1515; letter to, 725, 734, 743, 749, 759, 986, 989, 1029, 1082, 1102, 1107, 1165, 1174, 1199, 1379, 1413, 1430, 1453, 1456, 1468, 1471, 1519, 1524

Newell, F. H.: and Colorado River break, 974; and conservation, 681; and reclamation, 1098; member, Inland Waterways Commission, 619; member, National Conservation Commission, 1067

Newfoundland Fisheries Dispute: English-speaking people and, 529; and Hague Arbitration, 640, 718–19, 1205–06; Newfoundland opinion on, 400–01, 790; provisional agreement on, 462; R considers sending warship, 13, 320; Root and, 13, 785; U.S. policy concerning, 732–33; and U.S. Senate, 644; m., 458

Newlands, Francis G.: and anti-Japanese agitation, 1504; and conservation, 1067; and waterways, 619, 956, 1031

Newlands, Tarlton & Company: 1473

Newlands Bill: 956

Newman, William H.: 617

Newport Conference: and battleship design, 1101, 1107, 1166, 1174, 1199, 1453; and gunnery, 1380; and navy schism, 1470–71, 1204; R limits publicity on, 1383; m., 1237, 1456. See also Key, Albert L.; Newberry, Truman H.; Sims, William S.; United States Navy

Newport, R.I.: R on, 223–25

Newport News, Va.: 513

Newspaper Publishers' Association: 1129

Newspapermen: and African trip, 1404–05, 1409–10; and navy cruise, 745, 759; R on, 307

Newspapers: censorship of, 1164; leaks by, 607; R on, 468–69, 491. See also Appeal to Reason; Associated Press; Baltimore American; Baltimore Sun; Bartlesville Daily Enterprise; Boise, Idaho, Statesman; Boston Evening Transcript; Boston Herald; Boston Journal; Brooklyn Eagle; Buffalo Times; Chicago American; Chicago City Press; Chicago Inter Ocean; Chicago Tribune; Cincinnati Times-Star; Cleveland Plain Dealer; Daily Mirror; Delavan, Illinois, Times Press; Denver News; Des Moines Register and Leader; Erie Herald; Fall River Evening News; Gloucester Times; Home Herald; Indianapolis News; Indianapolis Star; Japan Daily Mail; Kansas City Star; Kansas City Times; La Lucha; Leaven-worth Times; Le Temps; Lincoln State Journal; Liverpool Mercury; London Daily Telegraph; London Morning Post; London Spectator; London Standard; London Times; Los Angeles Times-Mirror; Morning Democrat; New York Evening Post; New York Herald; New York Journal; New York Journal of Commerce; New York Press; New York Staats-Zeitung; New York Sun; New York Times; New York Tribune; New York World; Orange, New Jersey, Journal; Philadelphia Ledger; Philadelphia Record; Providence Journal; St. Louis Globe-Democrat; St. Louis Post-Dispatch; St. Paul Dispatch; St. Paul Pioneer Press; San Francisco Chronicle; Seattle Daily News; Springfield Republican; Sunday Democrat; Toledo Blade; Vincennes Sun; Wall Street Journal; Washington Post; Washington Star; Washington Times; York Gazette

Newsprint Industry: 838

Niagara Falls: treaty for preservation of, 154

Nicaragua: canal in, 573; and U.S. intervention in foreign affairs of, 592, 772

Nicholas II: and Hague conference, 25–26, 30–31, 464; and International Peace Conference (1899), 25; and Russo-Japanese peace, 1–9, 12, 15, 26, 58, 62, 177–78

Nichols, Mr.: 873

Nicholson, Meredith: 1394

Nicoletta: see Horses

Nicolson, Sir Arthur: and Algeciras Conference, 246–47, 251

Nile: and African trip, 1161; battle of, 161

Niles, Henry C.: 668

Nineteenth Century: on Kaiser's interview, 1466

Nixon, George S.: 1504

Nixon, S. Fred: id., ii, 959; 120

Nobel Peace Prize: R and, 520–21, 524, 530, 1539

Noble, Alfred: 1422

Noble, Mr.: 1175–76

Noel, Edmund F.: 1362

Norfolk, Duke of: see Howard, Henry F.

Norfolk, Va.: 513

Norfolk Navy Yard: see United States Navy

Norman, Captain: 800

North, Frederick, Lord: 773

North, Samuel N. D.: 594, 595

North American Company: 1262

North American Review: compares R with Andrew Jackson, 697

Oliver, Frederick S.: id., 347; R on, 368, 693; m., 349, 645, 785; letter to, 350

Oliver, Robert S.: and army chaplain examinations, 958; and army maneuvers, 154; and rotation of army officers, 1006; letter to, 863

Oliver, William J.: and Panama Canal construction bids, 357, 572–73, 581–82, 598–600

Oliver Typewriter Company: 1316

Olivette: see United States Navy, *Ships*

Olivier, Sydney H.: 1343

Olney, Richard: id. i, 333; as Attorney General, 1260; and Gentlemen's Agreement, 580; R on, 265

Olympic Forest Reserve: 603, 605

Olympic games: and civil service exceptions, 1429; disqualification of American at, 1181–85, 1190, 1465–66; m., 394

Oman, Charles W. C.: 1187, 1232

O'Meara, Stephen: id., 439

O'Neil, William T.: id., i, 58; 456; letter to, 456

Opdycke, Leonard: 805

Opdycke, Leonard E. O.: 805

Open door policy: in China, 993, 1343; in Morocco, 232, 243, 247–48, 318; and sea power, 1008

Open Shop: 459, 714. *See also* Labor; Strikes; Unions

Orange Judd Company: 1224

Orange, New Jersey, *Journal:* 754

Orchard, Harry: and Idaho riots, 189, 197

Oregon: anti-Japanese sentiment in, 917, 919–21; defense of, 913; election reform in, 1274, 1474; forest reserves in, 603–04; judiciary in, 20; land frauds in, 20, 21, 148, 348, 481, 520, 1461–64, 1469. *See also* Patronage; Republican Party

Orient: *see* Far East

Orientals: proposed legislation against, 809. *See also* China; California, Japan; Immigration, San Francisco

Orion: 1248

Osage Tribe: 284, 370–71, 416–17, 471–72; 1291. *See also* Indians; Oklahoma

Osborn, Henry F.: id., i, 612; 786; letters to, 1150, 1434

Otero, Miguel A.: id., 673; and New Mexico politics, 673, 739–40, 864

Otis, Harrison G.: id., 541

Otis Elevator Company: 1260

Ottawa: 920

Otter Forest Reserve: 603

Oulahan, Richard V.: id., i, 652; and fleet cruise, 759; and Storers, 180, 182; letter to, 1285

Outlook: on Brownson's resignation, 911–

12; on Christian socialism, 1079; on direct nominations, 1474; on government graft, 54–6; on Hughes renomination, 1327; on Idaho riots, 377; on immigration, 1042; on Knox's speeches, 939; on Lodge, 118; on Mississippi patronage, 1346; on Mormons, 537–38; on muckraking, 219; on nature fakers, 700–704; on Oklahoma, 1252; on Olympics, 1181; on politics, 1276–77; on R and court decisions, 714; R on Cleveland and anthracite strike, 1153, 1229; R on China, 1201; R on Japanese, 1533–34; R on national character, 1425; R on Tolstoi, 1425, 1533–34; R on E. A. Robinson, 707; R on socialists, 1385; R friendliness to, 307, 701, 704, 786, 843–44; R remuneration by, 1388; R as special contributing editor to, 344; 1350, 1369; R writing commitments to, 1106, 1108, 1116, 1144, 1162–63, 1172, 1240, 1249; and Russian extradition cases, 1207; on Taft, 969; and Wister's Harvard speech, 880; m., 344

Overman, Lee S.: and conservation, 1068; and railroad rate legislation, 258–260, 271, 274

Overman Amendment: 258–260, 271, 274. *See also* Railroads, rate regulation

Overstreet, James: id., iv, 877; 123

Owen, Robert L.: id., 1514; letter to, 1514

Owens Valley, California: 315–16

Oyama, Marshal Iwao: 57, 296

Oyster Bay: 82, 223–24, 312–13, 343, 392, 765, 779, 793, 798–99, 1061, 1072

Oxford University: R as Romanes lecturer at, 1186–87, 1369, 1482, 1539

Pacific cable: 1446

Pacific Lumbermen's Association: 566

Pacifism: and arbitration treaties, 346; and armaments, 345; conference on (1907), 638–41, 651, 699–700; growth of, 596–97; and Japanese exclusion, 1479, 1512–13; and naval power, 201; R on, 348–49, 366, 533, 871, 942–44. *See also* Anti-Imperialism; Disarmament

Pack, Charles L.: 1067

Packing Industry: *see* Beef Trust; Meat Packing Investigation

Page, Thomas N.: 553, 1361; letter to, 625

Page, Walter H.: 1169, 1340

Paine, Ralph D.: letter to, 853

Palma, Tomas E.: and Cuban revolution, 391, 399, 402, 409–11, 413, 418–19, 422–25, 428, 430–34, 436

Palmer, Frank W.: 12, 13

Palmer, John McA.: 1346

Palmer, William: 1146

1684

elections, 1473; on conservation, 604, 681, 684; on currency and finance, 754, 772, 845-46, 848-51, 856-58, 908; on foreign affairs and imperialism, 1, 3, 57, 151-53, 245, 249, 256, 358-59, 401, 419, 424, 432, 454, 529, 717, 761-62, 774-75, 782, 1408; on Germany, 541-42, 989-92; on government control of business, 1374; on Great Britain, 1370, 1443-44, 1465, 1495; on meat packing investigation, 286, 308; on Monroe Doctrine, 645; on national honor, 159; on naval cruise, 709, 720-21, 738, 745, 747, 779; on navy, 394, 1471, 1543; on Negro problem, 487, 489, 509, 534, 560; on Panama Canal, 356, 364; on plutocracy, 887; on preparedness, 149, 151-52, 159; on preservation of game, 578, 1283; pressure groups and, 307-08; and railroad regulation, 152-53, 617; R on, 100, 140-41, 148, 651, 1537; on secret service, 1530; on Taft's golf-playing, 1234; on tariff, 405, 427, 798; and third term, 874, 1041-42; on trusts, 390; on whisky labeling, 645. *See also* Magazines; Newspapers; *and by country and topic*
Public School Athletic League of New York: 591
Public Schools: 140
Public Service Commission of New York: 581, 798
Public Works: 687
Puget Sound: 745, 759
Pulitzer, Joseph: competition with Hearst, 1322; endows Columbia journalism school, 1428; libel suit against, 1415-17, 1419, 1489, 1516-17; R on, 1277, 1323, 1364; m., 1343
Pullman strike of 1894: 1059, 1352
Punch: 24
Purcell: affidavit on Frantz brothers, 416
Purdy, Milton D.: id., 409; and Brownsville investigation, 558; and land frauds, 564-65, 570-71; and Sherman Act, 692-93; letter to, 923
Pure Food and Drug Act: administration of, 1467-68; amendments to, on inspection clause, 291-92, 298-300, 326; dating of canned food, 317; referee board under, 908-09; R on, 624, 1445; and whisky, 645; m., 286, 328, 333, 365, 885, 1218
Putnam, George H.: letters to, 1123, 1138
Putnam's, G. P., Sons: 350, 1123

Quackenboss, Mrs.: 905
Quakers: 175, 346
Quarles, Joseph V.: appointed judge, 1007;

and labor injunction, 484-85; and patronage, 325; letter to, 484
Quarles, Mrs. Joseph V.: 484
Quartermasters Corps: *see* United States Army
Quay, Matthew S.: id., i, 148; 649, 739
Quebec: tercentenary celebration, 1159
Quesada, Don Gonzalo de: letter to, 411
Quigg, Lemuel E.: id., i, 354; and N.Y. Republican party factionalism, 87, 97-98, 429; relations with R, 1255
Quito: 28

Rabelais, François, 1030
Race: and civilization, 960-63; economic factors and, 528, 612, 718, 940-41, 995; and English-speaking people, 529; and immigration restriction, 532; and Indian intermarriage, 1434-35; and Indian status, 1515; and Japanese immigration, 610, 869-71, 1511-12, 1520; Kaiser on, 1164; Negroes and, 1026; race suicide, 636-38; R on Aryans, 723; R on differences of, 774, 1503-04, 1512-14; R on theory of, 1048-49, 1126, 1435; and southern representation, 226; in Vancouver, 787-88, 790. *See also* Immigration, Intermarriage, Japan, Negroes
Radcliffe, Wallace: 981
Radicals: R on, 196-200, 366, 375
Radolin, Prince Hugo von: id., 237; German ambassador at Paris, 241
Rae, Charles W.: 511-12
Railroads: accidents on, 600, 622; capital invested in, 621; in China, 15; and coal lands, 461; coal roads, 29; conferences on, 607-08, 617, 625, 630-31; courts and, 100-01, 173-75, 215; employers' liability and, 888-89, 1445-46; in England, 634; freight car shortages, 565-67; in Germany, 101; and grain elevators, 461; hours of labor on, 555, 581; increase in rates of, 1140-41, 1144, 1151-52, 1174-76; and Indian reservations, 276-80; inefficiency of, 584-85, 620; investigations of, 461-62, 535, 563, 622; investors in, 633; land grants to, 1462-63; and mail rates, 83-4, 362-63; passes and favors by, 1474; and patronage under McKinley, 1257; as political issues, 447, 449-52; and politics, 363; and post office, 607; preferential rates of, 292-93; proposed regulation of, 825, 877-78; and rate reductions, 1300; rate regulation, 76-7, 83-4, 88-9, 111, 118, 136-37, 142-43, 147-48, 157-59, 167, 170, 172, 206, 209-11, 258-60, 270-71, 292, 328-29, 341, 461-62, 464, 535-36, 617, 643, 844, 1258; rebates, *see* American Sugar Refin-

ing Company, Hepburn Act, Standard Oil Company; receivership and, 692, 761; R on government and, 25, 27, 54, 1216; R on shortsightedness of, 617, 633–34, 1258, 1302; R's record on, 1214–16, 1260; securities of, 677, 711, 923; state regulation of, 634, 674, 815, 1431; suits against, 114–15, 462, 634, 685–86, 693; threatened strike on, 1299; traffic agreements of, 674; valuation of, 636, 648, 650, 664, 946–48. *See also* Hepburn Act; Interstate Commerce Commission; *and railroads by name*

Railway Trainmen's Journal: 1197

Rain-in-the-Face: 283

Raines, John: id., i, 283; and Hughes nomination (1908), 1193; m., 1537

Raines, William G.: id., 1537; letter to, 1537

Rainey, Henry T.: and Panama corruption, 1414, 1416, 1518–19

Rainier Forest Reserve: 603

Rainsford, William S.: id., i, 577; 942

Rand, William, Jr.: 1473

Randall Company: 435

Randolph, Isham: 1422

Randolph-Macon College: 575

Ranlett, Frederick J.: letter to, 694

Ransdell, Joseph E.: appointed to Inland Waterways Commission, 1055; member National Conservation Commission, 1067

Rathbone, Estes G.: id., iii, 264; 420

Rathom, John R.: id., 467; letter to, 467

Ratibor, Princess: 15

Rawlinson, Father Bernard S.: 976

Ray, Major Beecher B.: 1128

Ray, George W.: 668–69

Rayner, Isidor: 1024–27

Raynolds, J. Wallace: and New Mexico land frauds, 649, 673, 733–34, 739, 864

Reade, Philip: 804

Reader Magazine: Beveridge-Bryan debate, 662, 664

Rebates: *see* Interstate Commerce Commission; Railroads

Reber, Samuel: 705

Reciprocal Demurrage Association: 566

Reciprocal Trade Agreements: 33, 67–8, 79. *See also* Tariff

Reclamation Act: 279, 381, 682

Reclamation Service: accomplishments of, 381, 1098; allotment of funds to, 280; and bids for government contracts, 380; and Colorado River, 276–78, 530–31; government investments in, 381–82; and government land irrigation, 1098; and Moffatt railroad, 51; proposed transfer, 1269; and settlement, 381–382; m., 1067. *See also*

Conservation; Inland Waterways Commission; Irrigation

Reconstruction: 225, 366, 540

Record, George L.: 70

Red Bank Cattle Company: 445

Red Cloud: 283

Red Cross: and earthquake relief, 216, 219–20; fund of, 195; and hospital ships, 894

Reed, Henry T.: 667

Reed, Thomas B.: id., i, 150–51; and tariff, 405; m., 184, 1398

Reed, Walter: 410

Reed, Mrs. Walter: 410

Reeder, Mr.: 1462

Referee System: *see* Patronage

Referendum: 809

Reform Club of New York: 1175

Reggio: 1459

Reid, Daniel G.: id., 1326; 1327

Reid, Jean: 1035

Reid, Ogden M.: 1206

Reid, Silas H.: New Mexico attorney-general, 660

Reid, Whitelaw: id., i, 136; and Alice R, 320; and Churchill gift, 1467; and Newfoundland matter, 718–19; social demands on, 312; Taft retains, 1499; m., 182, 252, 441, 503; letters to, 18, 29, 32, 137, 169, 187, 230, 318, 333, 338, 348, 488, 543, 552, 656, 732, 785, 985, 1011, 1035, 1073, 1186, 1205, 1383, 1410, 1465, 1499

Reid, Mrs. Whitelaw: m., 20, 108, 138, 170, 320, 339, 349, 488, 544, 552, 733, 1011, 1035, 1206

Relief: see United States Navy, *Ships*

Religion: government and, 107–11; as issue in 1908 election, 1179, 1200, 1204, 1234, 1289–90, 1304, 1318, 1333–35; and politics, 442–43; R on, 107–11, 772–73, 1042, 1283–84. *See also by denominations*

Remington, Frederic: letter to, 1321

Remmel, Harmon L.: 716

Remsen, Ira: id., 908; 1468; letter to, 908

Reno, Nevada: 994–95

Republic Oil Co.: 1262

Republic Steel Co.: 287

Republican Club of N.Y.: 526, 789

Republican Party: in Alabama, 712, 936; in Arizona, 937, 1367; in Arkansas, 767, 1362; border states and, 832; bossism and, 71, 78–9; in California, 466, 471, 486, 631, 788–89, 1249; campaign books, 414, 459–60; campaign funds, 33–38, 50, 79, 447, 449, 451–53, 486, 490; and colonialism, 256; in Colorado, 413, 466, 471, 780; conservatism of, 429, 1082, 1369; and corporations, 453; corruption rumors, 1438;

and Cuba as issue, 427–29, 436; in Delaware, 27, 1170; and Democratic strongholds, 1359–60; 1896 and 1900 elections, 1369; 1904 election, 1358; 1906 election, 336, 361, 365, 367, 372–78, 394–95, 397, 403, 408, 413–15, 419, 427–29, 435–39, 441–43, 447–60, 465–67, 470–71, 483, 486, 488–92; 1908 election, 936, 986, 1026, 1054, 1096, 1124, 1129, 1131–33, 1145, 1149, 1195–96, 1201–04, 1207, 1218–20, 1223, 1231, 1234, 1243–45, 1255, 1259, 1280, 1286, 1300–04, 1313–16, 1319, 1321–22, 1328, 1340, 1381; and ethnic groups, 45, 73, 101–02, 441–43, 461, 489, 1207, 1234, 1304; in Florida, 752, 928, 1061, 1362; in Georgia, 712, 934, 1408–09; in Idaho, 413, 415, 471, 483, 488–89, 491–92, 537–38, 662, 767–71; in Illinois, 402, 483, 1045, 1201, 1208, 1275, 1521; in Indian Territory, 386; in Indiana, 914, 963, 1202, 1275, 1315–16; and Interstate Commerce Commission, 111; in Iowa, 27, 146, 297, 403, 466, 471, 1074–75, 1077, 1094; and judicial appointments, 666–69; in Kansas, 142, 540–41, 735, 1045; in Kentucky, 486–87, 832, 841–42, 1064, 1243; and labor, 413–14, 443, 455, 1076–77, 1195–97, 1234, 1241, 1280, 1300–01, 1304, 1306–13, 1381; in Louisiana, 1062, 1070–71, 1361–63; in Maine, 113, 350, 408, 413, 441; in Maryland, 1175, 1234; in Massachusetts, 27, 67, 73, 439, 466–67, 470, 483, 486, 712, 803, 832, 998–99, 1005, 1041, 1363; in Michigan, 781, 1275; in Minnesota, 712; in Mississippi, 712, 1346, 1362; in Missouri, 466; in Montana, 466; national convention (1884), 675; national convention (1904), 448; in North Carolina, 130, 308–09, 1359, 1361–63; in Ohio, 27, 70, 347, 403, 483, 487, 646–47, 652, 670, 695–96, 712, 720, 742, 777, 781, 837, 878–79, 914, 1149, 1166, 1275, 1280, 1313, 1377, 1454–56; in Oklahoma, 284, 416, 472, 673, 969; in Oregon, 780–81, 797, 1273–74; and patronage to nonparty members, 1344–48, 1360–65; in Pennsylvania, 70, 347, 403, 459, 466–67, 471, 647, 1275, 1280; and postal savings, 1076–77; and prohibition, 403, 1207; and railroads, 170, 204, 273–75, 451–52; and reform, 657; in Rhode Island, 467; R on factionalism in, 349; R on local organization of, 92, 1270–71; R on speaker, 1280; and sectional politics, 167–68; in South, 933–34, 999, 1201, 1357–66, 1411; in South Carolina, 712, 784, 1362; and square deal, 71; and tariff, 27, 349–50, 353–54, 377, 392, 405, 427, 806; in Tennessee, 1361–63; in Texas, 989, 1041, 1111, 1362–63, 1373;

in Vermont, 1041; in Virginia, 1359, 1361–63; in Washington, 780, 1249; in West Virginia, 781, 1039, 1041, 1045; as a white party, 130, 1362; in Wisconsin, 142, 326, 1275; in Wyoming, 680

National Committee: and campaign contributions, 1245–49, 1256–58, 1263, 1271; and *Catholic Encyclopedia,* 1326; chairmanship of, 1099; and Chicago headquarters, 1234; committeemen, 1170, 1175, 1208; and contesting delegations, 1062, 1064–65; and du Pont, 1249–50, 1258; and labor, 1195–97; and Philippine policy, 1278; and postal savings, 1102; and presidential nomination, 872; R criticisms of, 1033, 1207–10, 1244–45, 1247–49, 1258–59; treasurer of, 1123–24; m., 195, 267, 386, 460, 963, 1219, 1455

National Convention (1908): Lodge's speech at, 1083; Negroes at, 1012, 1070–71; platform, 999, 1065, 1076–77, 1097, 1127–28, 1241, 1306–13; panic of 1907 and nomination at, 748; patronage and nomination at, 596, 784, 797, 1502; presidential possibilities at, 329, 339, 525, 705, 726–27, 797, 803, 929, 1357–66; R on, 1082; sectional and state alignments at, 647, 670, 695–96, 712, 720, 735–36, 742, 780–81, 784, 788, 796–97, 833, 837, 841–42, 865, 914, 926, 934, 936–37, 989, 998, 1005–07, 1039, 1041, 1045, 1061–62, 1064, 1070–71, 1234, 1239, 1273–75, 1357, 1362–63, 1377, 1458; South and, 933–34, 937, 1275, 1358, 1362–63; Taft nomination by, 697, 796, 1040, 1060, 1073; temporary chairmanship of, 963, 1032; third term sentiment at, 1041, 1045, 1083; vice-presidency at, 1077, 1083, 1094; m., 1033, 1085, 1480

National Convention (1912), 284, 1094; in Nebraska, 735, 810; in New Hampshire, 712, 914, 1275; in New Jersey, 70, 832, 1041, 1201, 1258, 1275; in New Mexico, 649–50, 659, 661, 739–40, 757, 765–66, 864, 1367; in Nevada, 466

In N.Y.S.: and direct nominations, 1474–75; and election (1906), 395, 403, 435–39, 441–43, 447–52, 454–60, 465–67, 470, 483, 486, 488–92; and election (1908), 736, 781, 796–97, 837, 926, 1005–07, 1145, 1207, 1239, 1275, 1280, 1357; factionalism, 47, 50, 70, 73, 85–86, 95–9, 102, 120, 124, 347, 368–69, 388–89, 429, 448–49, 453, 455, 789, 833; and Hughes nomination (1908), 1180, 1197–99, 1208, 1235–40, 1258–59; N.Y.C. convention, 50; N.Y.C. organization, 92, 833; N.Y. County committee, 87, 92, 95–98, 393, 865; and patronage,

447–48, 451–52, 455, 704; R on, 440; state committee, 153, 369, 1259; state convention, 999, 1041, 1208, 1235–36, 1242; state organization, 1192–93; m., 102, 461, 526
See also Campaign Funds; Elections; Patronage

Reuterdahl, Henry: and naval reform, 891–92, 1470; m., 980, 1453

Reuters: 1433

Review of Reviews: see American Monthly Review of Reviews

Révoil, Amédée J. P.: 242

Revolutionary War: *see* American Revolution

Reyburn, Robert: 937

Reyes, Rafael: 756

Reynolds, James B.: id., i, 697; and housing reform, 1212; and meat packing investigation, 140, 208–09, 282, 291, 294–95, 299–301; and N.Y. election (1906), 466; and Panama Canal investigation, 1009, 1191; recommended by R, 1259; R on, 317, 1112; m., 267; letters to, 165, 1170, 1191

Rhode Island: election (1905), 70; election (1906), 467. *See also* Republican Party

Rhodes, James F.: id., iv, 1049; 540, 585, 1002, 1369

Richards, Bartlett: 1531

Richards, Howard, Jr.: id., 1201

Richards, John K.: 666

Richards, Laura E.: 267

Richards, William A.: id., iii, 477; 445, 519, 564

Ricketts, Oscar J.: 12, 13

Ridder, Herman: 467, 1128–29

Riddle, John W.: id., ii, 1366; 130, 1273

Ridgely, William B.: 692, 1288

Ridgeway, William: 1232, 1435

Riis, Jacob A.: id., i, 278; advises R, 1100; on election apathy, 1195; R on, 317, 1284; supports Hughes, 1160–61; m., 267; letter to, 212

Riley, James W.: 1394

Riner, John A.: federal judge, Wyoming, 680

Rio de Janeiro: 333

Riordon, William L.: id., 33; letter to, 33

Riots: *see* Atlanta; Idaho; Japan

Ripley, Edward P.: 535

Ripley, Joseph: 588, 599

Ripley, William Z.: id., 68; R on theories of, 1435; letters to, 68, 158

River View: 435

Rivers and Harbors Act: 1031

Rivers, Improvement of: 619–21. *See also* Inland Waterways Commission

Rixey, Presley M.: attends Archibald R,

606; and physical exercise order, 1475; travels with R, 61, 385, 495, 860

Roadstrum, Victor N.: 417, 471

Roanoke College: 228

Robb, Charles H.: id., iii, 496; appointed judge, 689–90; investigates miner's union, 302–03; Justice Department investigation, 830

Robbins, Francis L.: id., 166; and bituminous coal dispute, 202–03; letter to, 166

Robertson, A. G. M.: 937

Robertson, Alice M.: 1418

Robespierre, Maximilien: 345

Robinson, Corinne R.: Jamestown trip, 688; R picture to, 1432; and woman's suffrage, 1342, 1373; m., 902; letters to, 966, 1533

Robinson, Douglas: Jamestown trip, 688; and Panama transaction, 1315–17, 1394, 1415, 1419, 1425; receiver for N.Y. Railway Co., 902; and *World* libel suit, 1475, 1489; letters to, 845, 901, 1475, 1489, 1533

Robinson, Edwin A.: id., iv, 1145; 69, 86, 521, 647, 707

Robinson, Joseph T.: 518

Robinson, Stewart D.: id., i, 375; death of, 1533

Robinson, John K.: 511–12

Roche, James J.: id., iii, 693; letter to, 173

Roche, Mrs. James J.: 173

Rochester, New York: 828–29

Rock Creek Park: 1520

Rock Island Company: 844

Rockefeller, John D.: and election (1908), 647; and panic (1907), 755, 822, 856; and Standard Oil suit, 1107; m., 772, 797, 845, 859, 886, 906, 925, 1350

Rockhill, William W.: id., i, 343; on Tibet, 1147, 1210; letters to, 18, 344, 1428

Rockhill, Mrs. William W.: 345, 1211, 1429

Rodd, James R.: 527–28, 1151

Rodey, Bernard S.: 739–40

Rodgers, James L.: 1496

Rodgers, Mark A.: id., 321

Rogers, James T.: id., 125

Rogers, Richard R.: and canal ships purchase, 573, 582, 1378; resigns as canal counsel, 857

Roloff, Carlos: 704

Roman Catholic Church: *see* Catholic Church

Roman Empire: 14, 19, 35, 960–61

Romanes Lecture, Oxford: contents of, 1397, 1434; invitation to deliver, 1172, 1177–78, 1180, 1186–87, 1205–06, 1230; plans for, 1232–33; writing of, 1375; m., 1242, 1292, 1329

Rome: 107–10. *See also* Vatican

Roosevelt, Alice H. L.: 906, 1450

Roosevelt, Alice L.: *see* Longworth, Alice

Roosevelt, Archibald B.: on attacks on R, 655; career plans, 800; on crew, 1030, 1184; difficulties in studies, 647, 1043–44, 1060; gifts to, 675; at Groton, 793, 807, 859–60, 1237, 1271; health of, 606–07, 617, 635, 644, 671, 859–60, 915; pets of, 465, 558, 665; at picnic, 1236; plans for Annapolis, 1060; play of, 43; plays football, 475; reading, 175, 520; R on, 175–76, 972; sails, 347, 422; studies of, 61, 589; vacation of, 800; m., 813, 1370; letters to, 805, 811, 890, 915, 1004

Roosevelt, Christine K.: 803, 953

Roosevelt, Edith C.: activities during R's absence, 800–01; and African trip, 1089, 1162, 1178, 1236, 1241; decorated by Sultan, 1104; dines with Lodge, 1397; family life, 671, 696, 860; gifts by, 1035; gifts to, 733, 873; homes of, 60, 688–89, 799, 1030; on leaving White House, 1476; love of animals, 890–91; and N.Y.S. Assembly of Mothers, 576; picnics, 350, 1236; on politics, 781; in Porto Rico, 502; post-presidential plans, 24–25; presentation to European sovereigns planned, 1187; reading tastes, 69, 71, 136, 221–22, 340, 378, 681, 693, 800, 1151; relations with children, 76, 175–76, 261, 313, 422, 436, 606, 608, 1387; relations with R, 2, 60–61, 82, 107, 134, 146, 313, 347, 421–22, 465, 520–21, 635, 647, 675, 805, 891, 922, 1043, 1059, 1084, 1160, 1295, 1338, 1376, 1405; riding, 1012; sketched, 995; and Spring Rice, 698; and Storers, 181; trips, 385, 392, 475, 495, 500, 589, 972, 1031, 1035, 1044, 1504–05; visit to Groton, 579; and White House social life, 1472; wine cellar of, 783; on woman's suffrage, 1342, 1373; m., 251, 311, 349, 394, 527, 558, 705, 716, 807, 836, 869, 995, 1002, 1148, 1159, 1237, 1303, 1319, 1337, 1541

Roosevelt, Ethel C.: and African trip, 1089, 1178; and animals, 1004; family life, 860; interest in football, 82; and other children, 313–14, 1236, 1387; relations with R, 696; riding of, 520, 1005; R on, 800; at Sagamore, 688–89; social life of, 2, 1472, 1506; teaches Sunday school, 422; trips of, 475, 606, 675, 759, 1044; m., 589, 1303; letters to, 60, 313, 812, 1337

Roosevelt, George: 422, 608, 1183

Roosevelt, James A.: 2, 1030

Roosevelt, John K.: 315

Roosevelt, Kermit: and African trip, 1034, 1060–61, 1089, 1096, 1136, 1146, 1236, 1330, 1375, 1413, 1481; and athletics, 654, 1294, 1303, 1480; confirmation of, 176; Christmas celebration, 1472–73; and Groton, 296, 314, 562, 654, 688, 793, 1184; and Harvard, 146, 808, 815, 1271, 1303, 1337; hunting and shooting, 679, 759; joins Republican club, 1294; outdoor life, 793; photographed, 635; on picnic, 350; reading of, 175, 204, 1272–73, 1330; relations with Archibald R, 807, 1044; riding of, 635, 1130, 1338; R on, 799; and Sailors Haven, 1319; with Thirteenth Cavalry, 799; vacation plans, 800; visits Cowles, 1303; m., 1030; letters to, 69, 134, 145, 175, 204, 296, 421, 465, 475, 495, 496, 501, 520, 557, 589, 606, 635, 646, 655, 675, 688, 759, 807, 813, 859, 916, 922, 953, 958, 971, 1005, 1012, 1043, 1059, 1236, 1272, 1294, 1303, 1318, 1375, 1472, 1475

Roosevelt, Philip J.: expelled from St. Mark's, 313–14; poetry of, 953, 1013; at picnic, 1236

Roosevelt, Quentin: antics of, 261, 606, 635, 860, 1387; and baseball, 971, 1004, 1030; character of, 916; and church, 476; and exercise, 916; and friends, 890; on leaving White House, 1084; letter writing of, 798–99; reading of, 175; R on, 61, 175–76, 261, 520, 800, 1473; and sale of pig, 1294–95; schooling of, 422, 589, 1271; snake collection, 811–12; m., 1370; letter to, 203

ROOSEVELT, THEODORE, BIOGRAPHY:

Before 1900: as Civil Service Commissioner, 675, 1352; genealogy and ancestry, 350–51, 751, 1075, 1109, 1539; at Harvard, 214, 539–40, 694–95, 943–44; at Harvard-Yale football game (1895), 1382; hunting trips, 113, 1191, 1404; as N.Y.C. police commissioner, 264, 783, 1019, 1072, 1100, 1417, 1535; as N.Y.S. governor, 34, 36, 353, 387, 1535; as N.Y.S. legislator, 264, 600, 1352; opposes Blaine nomination, 935; outdoor life in youth, 1500–01; ranching, 678, 1212, 1373–74, 1429–30; relations with McKinley, 675; resigns from Reform Club, 1175; in Spanish-American War, 495, 695, 731; as vice-president, 963, 1364, 1404; youth, 113

President: birthday celebration, 1322; cabinet appointments, 1344; diplomatic activities, 1–8, 25–30, 32, 62, 231–51, 358; election (1904), 36, 1112, 1195, 1356–57; election (1906), 399, 456–58; election (1908), 354, 387, 503, 1212–20; in Fort Wayne, 677; gifts to, 102–03, 134, 873, 940, 1429–30; Harriman correspondence, 791; holiday celebrations, 1387, 1472–3; honorary membership, Locomotive Fire-

American intervention on behalf of minorities, 207–08; American economy, 365; American principles, 314; American Revolution, 224; Americans and European royalty, 339, 1035–36, 1089, 1187; ancient Greek character, 549; Anglo-Japanese Alliance, 18, 61, 670–71; animal stories, 39–41, 290, 701–02; anti-imperialism, 253–55, 924, 959; arbitration, 733; armaments, 333, 358; Armenians, 16; armies, 17, 123; art, 117–18, 684–85; Aryan race, 723; athletics, 341, 1500–01; attacks on himself, 764, 797, 856, 884–90, 948, 1323–25; automobiles, 812–13; balance of power, 169, 474; battleship size, 201; birth control, 638; birth rate, 19, 35; Boer War, 225; bossism, 119, 120, 125, 163, 264, 266; British intellect, 232; British naval history, 1113–14; British parliamentary politics, 785; Brownsville affair, 560; Bryan, 338–39; Burma, 16; cabinet, 297, 387, 467–68, 476–78; campaign funds, 34–38, 50, 91, 194–95, 1246–48; canal opposition, 321; capitalism, 180; central bank, 858; China, 17, 29, 30, 77, 90, 91, 132–33; Chinese exclusion, 190; civil service, 829; Civil War, 225; class consciousness, 152, 219, 302, 307, 452, 795, 1049, 1056–58, 1063, 1177, 1335–36; colonial administration, 20; Colorado politics, 303; competition, 388, 763, 939–40, 949, 987; Congress, 145, 147, 150–51, 365–66, 372–73, 1044, 1218–20; conservation, 28, 104, 122, 151, 279–80; conservatism, 395, 1282, 1369, 1444; conspiracies against government, 20; consular service, 130; coolie labor, 138; corporal punishment, 261; corporations, 34, 100, 147, 151, 167, 201, 268–69, 293, 303, 327, 458–60, 490–91; corruption, 11, 20, 23, 45, 55, 56, 78, 79, 100, 112, 119–21, 173, 177, 307–08, 378, 400, 452, 490–91, 661, 829, 874–75, 1062–64, 1072, 1192, 1288; cowboys, 1537; critics of government, 253; Cuba, 16; currency, 131, 133, 559, 836; death, 676; Debs, 186, 197–98; decline of civilizations, 19, 870, 960; dedication of books to himself, 1534; democracy, 70, 352, 573–74; Democratic party, 147, 338; demagogues, 100, 147, 327, 378, 400, 453; desperadoes, 104; despotism, 345, 874–75, 1047; difficulties of presidency, 589–90; diplomacy, 1–3, 7, 8, 12, 22, 31–2, 151–53, 252, 345, 728, 871, 1108; diplomatic service, 129–30; direct nomination, 1474–75; disarmament, 16, 17, 19, 30, 345, 358–59, 398–400, 600, 639–41, 651; discipline, 143–45; distribution of wealth, 955; divorce. 1288–80; dreadnoughts, 427;

Egypt, 16, 17; eight-hour law, 190; eighteenth-century philosophy, 352; election (1906), 365, 386–89, 394, 454, 471, 488–89, 491; election (1908), 651, 1328–29; election frauds, 156; enduring quality of his policies, 798, 855–56, 879; English-speaking people, 22, 63; European military history, 1113; European tensions, 233; expansion, 69; expatriates, 251, 312–13, 320, 488; extremists, 178, 1255; family antecedents, 783–84; Far East, 135; fatherhood, 576; favoritism, 262, 267; fighting qualities, 22, 139, 159–61; fine printing, 737–38; football, 46; foreign news, 344; foreign policy, 63, 64, 151, 244, 320, 346; Forty-Eighters, 168; France, 16, 19, 102; free love, 1365; French character, 954; French Revolution, 94, 269; friendship and politics, 118, 267; gentlemen, 528; George, Henry, 218; German designs on South America, 63; German foreign policy, 233; German help in Russo-Japanese peace, 251; German-Americans, 249–50; gossip, 542–44, 803, 1537; government administrative problems, 30, 74, 78, 192–93, 269, 328, 417, 445–46, 533–34, 569, 664; government finances, 123, 400; government historical research, 632–33; government ownership, 54, 460; government regulation, 54, 187, 288–89, 295, 298–99, 328; great speeches, 1135; Hanna, 184; happy medium, 308; hazing, 143–45; Hearst, 156; his own political position, 216–17, 875; his role as peacemaker, 345–46, 474; history, 290, 407, 961–62, 1397; Holland, 150; home and family, 60, 707, 1337; honesty in government, 78–9; human nature, 307; humanitarianism, 224, 871; humor, 31; hunting, 40, 41, 815; ideal public servant, 124, 221; immigration, 19, 45, 90, 91, 296–97, 360, 393, 550; immigration restriction, 285–86, 327, 361, 532, 541, 557, 598; imperialism, 16–20, 26, 30, 69, 138, 232, 345; importance of college training, 799, 808; income tax, 217, 261, 344; indemnities, 57; independence in politics, 183, 1238; inheritance tax, 216, 217, 261, 344, 458; insurance regulation, 50, 201–02; intellectuals, 352, 400, 420, 540, 597, 798, 801, 871, 884; international agreements, 17; international athletics, 1181–85, 1190, 1381–85; international law, 16, 17; interstate jealousies, 279–80; Isle of Pines, 69; Japan, 1–4, 13, 15–19, 22, 23, 59, 62, 135; Japan, possibility of war with, 725, 824; Japanese character, 140, 474, 549, 663, 729; Japanese-Americans, hostility to, 473, 475, 541, 608–09, 613; Jews,

13, 718–19, 785; and New York politics, 87, 98, 102; opinion of Durand, 251; opinion of Sternberg, 242; and Pacific cruise of fleet, 952; and Pan-Americanism, 346; and Panama, 361, 385, 1029, 1082; and Panama Canal, 78, 572, 582, 588, 630, 1316; and panic (1907), 822, 848; and patronage, 47, 49, 117, 668, 697, 927, 1202, 1436; and Peru telegram, 958; and Philadelphia election (1905), 70; and presidential nomination (1908), 339, 651, 735; and Quartermaster General, 705; and railroad rate bill, 272; relations with R, 141, 450, 655, 664–65, 750, 1432; at Republican convention (1904), 1032; resigns as Secretary of State, 1423, 1482; R on, 438, 517, 1538; rumors of hostility to Bonaparte, 764; and Russo-Japanese peace, 59, 1498; San Francisco visit, 396; and Shanghai controversy, 972–73; and shipping, 626–28; on Sherman, 1194; and State Department appointments, 1420, 1465, 1497; and stock market, 621; and Storer affair, 109, 181; and Supreme Court judgeship, 185; and U.S. foreign policy, 282; Utica speech, 535; and Venezuela, 132, 957, 984; and Whitney and Ryan, 1344; m., 12, 24, 74, 112, 229, 252, 289, 328, 409, 452, 458, 692, 726, 736, 743, 807, 824, 904–05, 917–21, 980; letters to, 25, 49, 68, 96, 101, 119, 132, 154, 180, 367, 394, 440, 521, 610, 717, 724, 738, 756, 808, 851, 858, 874, 945, 946, 957, 984, 1010, 1018, 1022, 1104, 1137, 1149, 1163, 1207, 1235, 1242, 1256, 1427, 1441, 1482

Root, Mrs. Elihu: South American tour, 367; m., 26, 396, 719, 809, 1138, 1165, 1441

Root, Elihu, Jr.: 367

Root-Takahira agreement: 1342–43

Rosalsky, Otto A.: 442, 443

Rose, John C.: id., i, 283; 1097; letter to, 984

Rosebery, Archibald P., Lord Primrose: 1187, 1329

Rosen, Baron Roman: id., iv, 1311; and antisemitism in Russia, 207; and Hague Conference, 25–6, 30–1

Ross, David W.: id., 127; 169

Ross, Edward A.: id., 794; letters to, 794, 795

Ross, Herbert: 392

Rossetti, Dante G.: 1384

Rossiter, William S.: 12, 13, 924; letter to, 1366

Roswell: see Horses

Rothschild, Leopold G.: 123

Rothschild family: 217

Rough Riders: appointments of, 650, 661, 740–41, 766, 861; chaplain of, 476; comparisons with, 881; m., 60, 61, 175, 284, 959, 1438

Roulhac, Thomas R.: 712

Roumania: American minister to, 1420, 1454; R on, 1447

Rouvier, Maurice: id., iv, 1256; and Morocco crisis, 235; and Russo-Japanese peace, 12; telegram by, cited, 239; m., 241

Rowe, Leo S.: id., 879; letter to, 879

Rowe, Thomas W.: 198

Rubens, Harry: id., 287

Rubin, W. B.: 485, 1297

Rudolph, Cuno H.: 590

Ruef, Abraham: conviction of, 1420: prosecution of, 1349; and San Francisco corruption, 219

Ruick, Norman M.: and Idaho land frauds, 662, 723, 736–37, 742, 753, 765, 767–71; and Idaho politics, 1097

Rural free delivery: 568

Rural New Yorker: 1145

Rusby, Henry H.: id., 1467; letter to, 1467

Russell, Charles E.: 1343–44

Russell, Gordon: 422

Russell, Robert: 582

Russell, William W.: 984

Russia: anarchists in, 23, 61; and Anglo-Japanese alliance, 61; army of, 557; and Bulgaria, 62; characteristics of people, 22, 23, 62; and China, 1497; diplomacy of, 1, 17, 19, 62, 1371; and disarmament, 464; and European balance of power, 169; and extradition of political refugees, 1207, 1256, 1276; and France, 145; and Hague Conference, 30; imperialism of, 16, 23, 359; internal conditions in, 15, 31, 112, 145, 474, 528, 943, 1139; Japan and, 135, 528; Jewish problem in, 112, 207, 336, 345; and Manchuria, 474; and Morocco crisis, 231, 235, 238, 242; navy of, 5, 22, 121, 403, 549, 601, 743, 895, 1543; passports of Jews from, 1256; prisoners of war of, 3, 5–7; progress in, 1401; proposed coalition against, 112–13; reform in, 1372; revolution in, 61, 71, 145, 179; revolutionaries from, in U.S., 1270; R on, 344, 346, 871, 1281–82; and Turkestan, 345, 1370; and Turkey, 62; and U.S., 112–13, 177–78, 344, 658, 731; and yellow peril, 1164

Russo-Japanese peace: and balance of power in Asia, 61–2, 474; criticism of R and, 296; gifts to R for part in, 103; Hay not consulted on, 1498; negotiation of, 1–9, 13–15, 17, 18, 22, 25, 31, 57–60; role of R in, 178, 1444, 1498, 1538–39; m., 177, 458

Russo-Japanese war: Hamilton, I. S. M., on, 139; hospital ships in, 895; naval battles, 159, 403; neutrality of China, 1497–98; and panic (1907), 747–48; R on, 1543; m., 26, 135

Ryan, Thomas: id., 479; 479, 569

Ryan, Thomas F.: attacks on, 1344; and campaign contributions, 195; and Interborough company, 798; and N.Y.S. election (1906), 453; m., 845

Sabatier, Paul: 597

Safety Appliance Act: and secret service, 1530; and Supreme Court, 1305; m., 1219

Sagamore: see Horses

Sagamore Hill: R's attachment to, 43, 688, 1139, 1320; sparrows at, 971; m., 655, 676, 681

Sage, Russell: 224

St. Augustine, Florida: 60

Saint-Gaudens, Augustus: and coinage design, 405–06, 574, 842; memorial meeting for, 1427; m., 223, 267

St. John, Mr.: 199

St. John, Spenser B.: 1125

St. Joseph Military Tournament: 1173

St. Lawrence County: 457

St. Louis, Missouri: and deeper waterways project, 1390; exposition in, 1074, 1352; as market for natural gas, 371–72; R in, 814–15

St. Louis Globe-Democrat: 1203

St. Louis Post-Dispatch: 1322

St. Mark's School: 314, 953

St. Paul Dispatch: 1327

St. Paul Island: 353

St. Paul and Pacific Timber Syndicate: 1464

St. Paul Pioneer Press: 1327

St. Paul's School: 591

St. Petersburg: 71, 344, 824

Sakhalin: Japanese history in, 161; Russo-Japanese peace and, 3–8, 15, 22, 58, 60, 62; m., 235, 656, 920

Salem, Mass.: 765, 1540

Salt Lake City, Utah: 276

Salton Sea: 279, 1261

Salvador: 334, 495, 772

Samar: 731

Samoan Islands: 989

Sampson, Archibald J.: id., 28; letter to, 28

San Antonio, Texas: 384–85

San Francisco: anti-Japanese agitation in, 608–13, 656, 671, 699–700, 710, 720, 725, 728–29, 787–88, 790; corruption in, 219;

earthquake in, 213, 216, 219–20, 747–48; and navy cruise, 745, 759, 791; and Japanese employment agency licensing, 700, 717, 729, 738; and Japanese school children segregation, 473, 510–11, 521, 530, 533, 541, 609–12, 614, 618–19, 632, 1484–86; labor movement in, 266; panic of 1907 in, 747–48; patronage in, 1027; politics in, 1056–57; prosecution of businessmen in, 885, 887; prosecution of graft in, 1062–64; U.S. gold deposits in, 1013; water supply of, 793, 1428

San Francisco Chronicle: 1438

San Francisco Gas Company: 1062

San Francisco Merchants' Exchange: 90

San Juan: battle at, 1103; R's visit to, 501; m., 391

San Juan Forest Reserve: 603

San Salvador: see Salvador

Sanders, Alvin H.: id., 1351; letter to, 1351

Sanders, Archie D.: 828–29

Sanders, Billy: 1075

Sanderson, Mrs.: 957

Sands, James H.: id., 155

Sands, William F.: 355

Sandwich Islands: 135

Santa Fe Central Railroad, 739–40, 948

Santiago: campaign of, 695; R's nostalgia for, 265; Wood at, 420; m., 501

Santo Domingo: as campaign issue (1906), 365, 374; revolutions in, 10, 470; R on U.S. relations with, 1087; treaty with, 10, 111, 137, 147, 151–52, 170, 346, 602, 640, 761, 1408, 1445, 1539; U.S. intervention in, 10, 253, 255–57, 432, 775, 1408, 1447; m., 1, 26, 232, 233, 234

Sargent, Frank P.: and alien contract labor law violations, 191; and campaign (1906), 413; death of, 1241; and immigration investigation, 322–24; and immigration legislation, 285; report of, on Japanese, 776; letter to, 776

Sater, John E.: 668

Satsuma: 529, 970

Satterlee, Henry Y.: 110, 536, 1100

Satterlee, Herbert L.: id., 706; and Assistant Secretaryship of Navy, 1392; and naval reform, 1468; letter to, 706

Saturday Evening Post: 262

Saturday Review: anti-American opinion in, 499; on U.S. in Philippines, 1369

Saunders, Eugene D.: 667

Saunders, Mingo: 1486, 1507

Saunderstown, Rhode Island: 223

Savannah, Georgia: 227

Savings bank insurance: 551. See also Insurance

Sayre, William H.: 581

Scandinavia: immigrants from, 285; internal problems of, 19

Schiff, Jacob H.: id., ii, 885; on American banking, 131, 133; and antisemitism in Russia, 207; and San Francisco earthquake relief, 216; letters to, 112, 336, 631, 1439

Schiff, Mortimer L.: 337

Schley, Grant B.: 830

Schley, Winfield S.: id., ii, 1016; and Newport conference, 1383; R on, 420

Schmid, Edward S.: 811, 1294–95

Schmitz, Eugene E.: and anti-Japanese agitation, 610–12; reversal of conviction of, 1064; and San Francisco earthquake relief, 219–220; letters to, 219, 614

Schoff, Hannah K.: id., 259; letter to, 259

Schofield, George A.: id., 393

Schools: California segregation legislation for, 1477, 1486; in District of Columbia, 589; Indian, 141; R on, 1226–29. *See also* San Francisco

Schurman, Jacob G.: id., ii, 138; letter to, 393

Schurz, Carl: death of, 287; and Moroccan crisis, 168; R on, 540, 1540; m., 26, 724, 1535; letters to, 16, 30

Schuylkill County: 11

Schuyler, James D.: 1422

Schuyler, Louisa L.: 352

Schwab, Gustav H.: 1067

Scientific American: on Gatun Dam, 1420

Scott, Alexander: 695

Scott, Charles F.: id., ii, 1060; 540, 1067

Scott, Charles H.: 936

Scott, Charles P. G.: id., 390; letter to, 390

Scott, Hugh L.: id., iii, 312; and investigation of Navajo Indians, 1450–53; and Philippines, 1509

Scott, Sir Walter: 137, 175, 1398

Scribner, Charles: 1105

Scribner's Magazine: Brownell on Lowell, 573; and R's African trip articles, 1106, 1115–16, 1136, 1162; R's articles in, 826, 831–32; R on, 786; m., 1108, 1172

Scribner's Sons, Charles: 86

Scripps-McRea Press Association: 450

Scull, David: id., 754; letter to, 754

Sea of Japan Battle: 121, 403, 427

Seaboard Air Line Railway: 552, 1480

Seal fisheries: 353, 458, 542

Seaman, Mr.: 800

Seaman, Louis L.: id., 56; 56, 60

Seaman, William H.: 1142

Sears, Clinton B.: 816

Seattle, Washington: 1070

Seattle *Daily News:* 1234

Seawanhaka-Corinthian Yacht Club: 353

Seawell, Herbert F.: 1480

Secret Service: Congress and, 1424, 1472, 1474; expenditures for, 1530–31; investigatory agency established, 1527; and land frauds, 1531–32; and McKinley, 1529; number employed in, 1529–30; R on, 82, 347, 1019, 1021, 1429, 1459–64, 1527–33

Securities Issues: 922

Segregation: *see* Japan; Negroes; San Francisco

Selous, Frederick C.: id., i, 577; on J. H. Patterson, 824; and R's African trip, 1005, 1060, 1089, 1236, 1242; m., 978, 1002, 1090, 1389; letter to, 115

Serbia: 1447, 1454

Settsu: 970

Severn, Mr.: 505

Sewall, William W.: id., i, 40; and appointment as customs collector, 113–14, 1418; m., 267; letter to, 1429

Sewall, Mrs. William W.: 1429

Sewanee University: 751

Seward, William H.: 225

Seymour, Horatio: 466, 540

Shaffer, John C.: id., iii, 263; 71; letter to, 1542

Shakespeare, William: 390, 1330

Shaler, Nathaniel S.: 694

Shallenberger, William S.: id., 363; 362–63

Shanghai: 409, 724

Sharon, Frederic W.: 944

Shaw, Albert: id., i, 565; as adviser to R, 196; letters to, 636, 1033, 1502

Shaw, Leslie M.: id., ii, 1432; and coinage mottoes, 94; financial policy of, 80–81, 133, 559; and N.Y. campaign (1906), 456; and Republican party factionalism, 27; and tariff, 41, 297; m., 11, 408; letters to, 26, 31, 89, 297, 405, 522

Shawmut: 1220

Shea, Cornelius T.: 714

Sheffield, James R.: id., ii, 1039; m., 87, 92, 99; letter to, 47

Sheldon, George R.: and campaign contributions, 1245, 1247–49, 1316; and du Pont, 1258; as Republican National Committee treasurer, 1117, 1123–24; letters to, 1245, 1256, 1412

Shelton, William T.: 1451–52

Shepard, Edward: 833–35

Shepherd, Seth: 553

Sheppard, William B.: 716, 752, 767

Sheridan, Mrs.: 427

Sherley, Swager: 1067

Sherman, James S.: and campaign (1906), 336, 372, 413, 419, 456, 460–61; and campaign (1908), 1129, 1203; and campaign contributions, 452; and Hughes renomi-

Smith, Samuel W.: id., 1208; 1424

Smith, W. Scott: id., 471; 471–72, 1353

Smith, William A.: id., 1016; 1024, 1025; letter to, 1016

Smith, Mackenzie & Co.: 1147

Smithsonian Institution: and African trip expenditures, 1412–13; and Freer art collection, 117–18; and preservation of North American birds, 578; m., 1093

Smokeless powder: 149

Smoot, Reed: and Mormons, 537; member, National Conservation Commission, 1067–68

Smyser, Martin L.: 930

Snyder, Robert McC.: id., 1262

Socialists: attack Taft's Philippine policies, 1278; in France, 365; as issue in election (1906), 489; in N.Y. elections, 1344; R on, 184, 229

Society for the Promotion of Industrial Education: 907

Sociology: and anthracite strike, 1156; on race suicide, 636–38; and social service, 466, 523, 1051, 1198, 1211–12; R on, 1300–01; at colleges, 794, 1343

Soils Bureau: 1067

Solace: see United States Navy, *Ships*

Somerville, Edith O.: 1314

Song of Roland: 39

Sorbonne: R's lecture at, 1177, 1292, 1369, 1375, 1482, 1539

Sornborger, Charles B.: 134

Sosa: 320

South: characteristics of people, 224–28. *See also* Democratic Party; Negroes; Patronage; Republican Party; *and individual states by name*

South Africa: American businessmen in, 544; Boer War, 223; and federation, 347

South America: and canal labor supply, 337; and good neighbor policy, 879; and navy cruise, 791; R on U.S. policy to, 1445; Root's good will tour of, 333; U.S. trade with, 556, 626–28. *See also* Central America; *and individual countries by name*

South Carolina: R family antecedents in, 225; history of, 225–26; and immigration, 556. *See also* Patronage; Republican Party

South Carolina: see United States Navy, *Ships*

South Dakota: *see* Patronage

South Norwalk Electric Works: 188

Southeastern Freight Association: 1140, 1175

Southern Appalachian Forest Reserve: 29, 684, 902–03

Southern Pacific Railroad Company: and Colorado River, 527, 974; investigation of, 461, 622; prosecution of, 767; and Union Pacific, 710

Southern Railroad Company: and rate reductions, 1431; and state rate regulation, 741, 754; and wage dispute, 948; m., 88, 1480

Southey, Robert: 677

Southwestern Railroad Association: and railroad rate raise, 1140, 1175

Spain: arbitration treaty with, 1023; birth rate of, 19; and Canary and Balearic islands, 941; decline of, 960, 1113; and France, 230; immigrants from, in Hawaii, 1504; laborers from, on Panama Canal, 337–38; and Morocco crisis, 230, 243–49; navy of, 894; R on progress in, 1401; U.S. diplomats in, 161, 183

Spalding, John L.: letter to, 1056

Spanish-American War: and American imperialism, 16, 255; fear of Spanish attack, 1011; hospital ships, 894–95; public opinion on, 148, 346, 529, 761; Santiago campaign, 106; veterans of, 56, 105, 394, 648–49; m., 475, 1103, 1392, 1442

Spanish Treaty Claims Commission: 347, 803–04

Sparks, John: 863; letters to, 866, 868, 877, 895, 923, 927

Speck: *see* Sternberg, Hermann S. von

Spectator: on ex-presidents, 1388; on R's speeches, 532, 786; m., 597

Speculation: regulation of, 904–05; R on, 80–1, 133–34. *See also* Panic of 1907

Speer, Emory: and railroad rate raise, 1174–76

Speer, Robert W.: 413

Spelling, Thomas C.: 1436, 1437

Spelling Reform: 378, 386, 389–90, 404, 409–10, 527

Spencer, Samuel: id., 88; and railroad regulation, 88

Spencer-Churchill, C. R. J.: 488

Spenser, Edmund: 917

Sperling's Journal: 1368

Sperry, Charles S.: and naval reform, 1000; and navy yards commission, 1536; R commends for fleet cruise, 1314; m., 996; letters to, 979, 1411

Speyer, James: id., iii, 525; founds R chair at Berlin, 644; on Schiff's speech, 131; m., 924; letters to, 510, 621, 777

Sphinx (Harvard club): 522, 1480

Spies: 542. *See also* Secret Service

Spillane, Edward P.: 1326

Spinney, George F.: 559

Spooner, John C.: id., iii, 121; attacks R,

856–57; and Brownsville affair, 558; and lock canal, 306; and patronage, 324–26, 668–69; m., 299; letter to, 379

Spooner Amendment: 173–75, 210, 258–59, 271, 274

Sportsman: on Olympics, 1181–85

Spreckels, Rudolph: id., 1062; and San Francisco graft prosecutions, 1062–1064; letters to, 1062, 1349

Springfield *Republican:* 729, 1238

Spring Rice, Cecil A.: id., i, 118; advises R of dangers of African trip, 1236; on Gleichen, 169; and Jewish question in Russia, 336; R desires appointment as ambassador to U.S., 488; R letter to, m., 4; R on, 251, 318; m., 458, 503; letters to, 61, 698, 869, 1002, 1138, 1241

Spring Rice, Mrs. Cecil A.: 699, 872, 1003, 1139

Square Deal: 71, 883–84

Squiers, Herbert G.: id., iii, 367; and Cuban revolution, 426; minister to Panama, 355

Stadler, Charles A.: id., 1128

Stafford, Wendell P.: 690

Stamboul, Louisiana: 816

Standard Oil Company: and campaign (1908), 1248, 1250–52, 1264–65, 1304; and campaign contributions, 791, 804, 1245–46, 1256–57, 1316, 1354–55; discriminatory practices of, 76, 291–93, 409; and Foraker, 1243–45; and Hearst, 1326; and Hepburn Bill, 275; as monopoly, 887; and naval oil, 512; and New York *Press,* 715; and oil land leases, 372, 388, 1291; and *Outlook,* 1350–51; and panic (1907), 885; and pipe line permits, 1266–67; R attacks, 297; R on fine as excessive, 1442; R misunderstands decision against, 1175; stock ownership of, 906; subsidiaries of, 369–70, 1261; suits against, 453, 535–36, 643, 746, 757–58, 764, 766–67, 779, 785, 862, 1094, 1097, 1107, 1141–43, 1145, 1175, 1234, 1260, 1379; and Republican National Convention (1908), 1039; m., 833, 948, 1370, 1454. *See also* Chicago and Alton Railroad

Standish, William H.: 1506–07

Stanton, Philip A.: and anti-Japanese agitation, 1502; m., 1477; letter to, m., 1517; letters to, 1505, 1509

Starek, Charles: 552, 574–75

State Attorneys General: conference of, 825

State, Department of: appointments in, 164, 1420, 1423, 1465; Hay and patronage in, 1490, 1495–97; and immigration inspectors, 44; and Jusserand on Morocco, 243;

and navy review, 353; R on, 1405–07, 1538; and Russian extradition cases, 1207; and secret service, 1019, 1459, 1528; and Storer removal, 200; and Venezuela revolution, 1428; m., 1; letters to, 1405, 1420. *See also* Consular Service; Diplomatic Service; Hay, John; Patronage; Root, Elihu; Taft, William H.

State Street: 803

Statehood: amendments to bill, 476–81; and judiciary, 516; and Oklahoma constitution, 673; opposition to, 71, 135, 321, 417, 778, 816, 821–22; relation to other legislation, 137, 172, 301; m., 299. *See also* Arizona; Indian Territory; New Mexico; Oklahoma

States' Rights: and railroad regulation, 815, 877–78; R on, 797, 810

Statute of limitations: 767, 906, 1327

Stead, William H.: id., 630; letter to, 630

Steam Shovel and Dredge Magazine: 1286

Stearns, Frederic P.: 1422

Steddon, Rice P.: 299

Steerage: 285–86

Steffens, Joseph L.: id., i, 472; attacks campaign contributions, 34–37; attacks corruption, 146–47; compares R with Taft and La Follette, 1051–52; and election (1906), 491; R on, 340, 1343; letters to, 35, 146, 615, 649, 829, 1050, 1072

Steiner, Edward A.: id., 1042; 1042–43

Steinhart, Frank M.: id., iii, 271; iv, 758; and Cuban revolution, 399, 402, 408, 1105

Stephenson, Isaac: 326

Sterling, John A.: 1032

Sterling-Beveridge Bill: 1032

Sternberg, Hermann S. von: id., i, 209; on army maneuvers, 1021; death of, 1196, 1210, 1230, 1442; on Durand, 251; and Carnegie, 544; on Cuba, 993; on Far East, 946; and Franco-Prussian War, 1233; and naval gunnery, 403; health of, 721–22; on Japanese aspirations, 724, 1010; and Morocco crisis, 230–242, 244–46, 248–50; R on, 318–19, 542–43; R's relations with, 476; letters to, 14, 33, 720, 726

Sternberg, Baroness Hermann S. von: 15, 722, 726, 1230

Stetson, Francis L.: id., i, 373; and Cleveland Memorial Committee, 1351; and Sherman Act amendment, 987, 997; letter to, 1351

Steunenberg, Frank: assassination of, 189, 196–98, 219, 302, 307, 413, 415, 537, 653, 767, 1080. *See also* Haywood, William D.; Moyer, Charles H.

Stevens, John F.: appointment as chairman, Isthmian Canal Commission, announced,

Sullivan, Mark: id., 665; and African trip articles, 1115–16; R on, 1220; m., 1220; letters to, 665, 1220
Sullivan, Mrs. Mark: 1116
Sullivan and Cromwell: 1315
Sulloway, Cyrus A.: id., 580; letters to, 580, 1328
Sully, Maximilien de B.: 102–03
Sumner, Charles: 163, 225, 540
Sumner, Samuel S.: id., ii, 836; 1103
Sumner, William G.: 352, 880
Sumter, Thomas: 225
Sunday Work: 981–82
Sunday Creek Coal Company: 202
Sunday Democrat: 213
Sundry Civil Bill: 304, 1019, 1020, 1220
Surtees, Robert S.: id., 136; 170
Survey: 216
Sutherland, Alexander: 35
Sutro, Mr.: 95
Swain, George F.: 1055, 1067
Swayne, Harald G. C.: 115
Swayne, Wager: id., i, 698; 47
Sweat, Lorenzo De M.: 1398
Sweatshop laws: 435
Sweden: immigrants from, in U.S., 1104; socialist movement in, 1151
Sweet, Mr.: 862
Swettenham, Alexander: and American troops at Jamaica, 499, 579, 601–02, 644
Swettenham, Frank A.: 20
Swift, Louis: 283
Swift, Lucius B.: id., i, 154; and census bill veto, 1476; and civil service reform, 1376; and Panama Canal charges, 1317–18; m., 677, 1324, 1325, 1336, 1394, 1402; letters to, 123, 836
Swift and Company: conviction of, 1260; and meat investigation, 295
Swinburne, Algernon C.: 785
Switzerland: civilization in, 961; internal affairs of, 943; and Morocco crisis, 243, 248
Sylph: see United States Navy, *Ships*
Symons, Thomas W.: id., iii, 547; improper actions of, 1069, 1070; letter to, 1069
Syndicalism: *see* Debs, Eugene V.; Haywood, William D.; Moyer, Charles H.
Syracuse University: 297

Tacitus: R on, 290, 495, 500, 738
Tacoma, Washington: 1249
Taft, Charles Phelps: alleged Catholicism of, 1333–34; and campaign (1908), 652, 791, 878–79, 1105, 1170, 1245; and Ohio senatorship, 1454–56; and Panama Canal transaction, 1315–16, 1394, 1415, 1425; and patronage, 929

Taft, Charles Phelps, II: 1004
Taft, Henry W.: id., ii, 937, 1482; and licorice trust case, 752; and N.Y. politics, 87, 92, 99; m., 1459
Taft, William H.: absence of, 1; acceptance speech, 1127, 1139–40, 1144; acting Secretary of State, 232; advises R, 450; Akron speech, 70; and Anglo-Japanese alliance, 61; appointments by, 1420, 1480; appointments in War Department, 155; attacks on, 791; Bath speech, 1078; and Brownsville affair, 525, 695–96, 966, 1105, 1163, 1376, 1477–78; and cabinet changes, 461; and campaign contributions, 1170, 1247; and Caribbean trip, 655; and Catholic Cardinals, 107–08; and Catholics in Philippines, 171; on China legation, 1443; and Cleveland politics, 777; and colonial administration, 256; compared with Bryan, 1253–55; compared with R, 1051; continuity of policies of R, 1089, 1328, 1368–69, 1433; Cooper Union speech, 1321; and corporation regulation, 1379; and Cuba, 391, 410, 412, 422, 428–29, 431–36, 446, 454, 465, 994; and division of fleet, 1543; and du Pont resignation, 1258; and election (1905), 70; and election (1906), 350, 360, 367–68, 394, 413, 415, 460, 467, 470–71, 483, 487, 737; and election (1908), 1124, 1128, 1151, 1195, 1197, 1203, 1209–10, 1212–19, 1234, 1314, 1328, 1330, 1340; and election (1912), 326, 763; entertained at Oyster Bay, 1095; and Foraker affair, 724, 969, 1243–44, 1251–52; and foreign policy, 875; and golf, 1234; and government guarantee of bank deposits, 1131; honesty of, 1264–65; and Hughes campaign (1908), 1172–73, 1180, 1198, 1235, 1259, 1285, 1302; and immigrant vote, 1286; inauguration of, 1384, 1427, 1434; and judicial appointments, 668, 927, 1202, 1393; Kaiser's hostility to, 1164; and labor, 796, 1202, 1241, 1287, 1296–1302, 1304, 1321, 1400–01; and labor injunctions, 1078, 1216, 1308–13; letter to Hill, 1179; and liquor labeling, 804; and Lodge, 784; Memorial Day address, 1045; and Military Academy, 1519; and movement to unseat Cannon, 1341; and naval reorganization, 1488; and Negro vote, 1276–77, 1286; and newspapers, 1117, 1144, 1356–66; and Oklahoma constitution, 673; and Panama Canal, 79, 211, 306, 317, 320–21, 342–43, 356–57, 372, 582, 588, 602, 630, 1009–10, 1220, 1316, 1377, 1390–91, 1393, 1420–22; and Panama elections, 1082; Panama trip of, 385, 392, 585, 1480; and Panama wages, 1019;

Toiyabe Forest Reserve: 603
Tokugawa, Keiki: 160
Tokyo: exposition in, 964–65, 1073–74, 1189–90, 1342, 1504; riots in, 15, 58–9. See also Japan
Toledo *Blade:* 670
Tolstoi, Leo: novels of, 179; pacifism of, 870; R on, 23, 942–43, 1081, 1372, 1533–34
Ton, Cornelius J.: id., 1521; letter to, 1521
Tories: 410
Toronto, Canada: 39
Tower, Charlemagne: id., iii, 310; and appointment of ambassador to Germany, 844–45, 989–92, 1018, 1410; and German tariff negotiations, 33, 41; and torpedo factory inspection, 658; m., 1002; letters to, 853, 941, 989, 991
Tower, Mrs. Charlemagne: 108
Town Topics: R on, 732; m., 1135
Townley, Lady Susan: on canal conditions, 364
Townsend, Hosea: 516
Townsend, William K.: id., iv, 1064; 47, 667
Tracey, James F.: id., iii, 393; 976, 1043
Trachoma: 162
Trade, Foreign: R on, 806
Trade-Unions: *see* Unions
Trafalgar: 161, 1113–14
Train, Arthur: id., 783; letter to, 783
Train, Mrs. Arthur: 783
Training Camp Activities Commission: 93
Transit Companies: 777, 797–98. *See also by name*
Trans-Mississippi Commercial Congress: 627–29
Transvaal: 544
Travers, Vincent: 442–43
Treasury Department: and Brownsville investigation payments, 1476; and business conditions, 621; customs house employees' political assessments, 1271–72; and gold deposits, 1013; and panic (1907), 522, 748, 822, 848–49; and patronage, 878–79; reorganization proposed, 1269; and secret service, 1019, 1424, 1459–60, 1528; special agents in Germany, 89; and speculation, 80–1, 621; and Western money demands, 81. *See also* Cortelyou, George B.
Treat, Charles H.: 87
Treat, Charles P.: 573
Treaties: presidential powers in negotiation of, 30, 151. *See also by name*
Treaty of Paris: 69
Treaty of Portsmouth: *see* Russo-Japanese peace
Tremont: 1220
Trent, William P.: id., i, 370; 1123

Trevelyan, George M.: 696, 785, 1397
Trevelyan, George O.: gift to, 880; invited to White House, 25; life of Macaulay, 1329; R on, 840, 1330; m., 1017, 1090, 1366; letters to, 22, 71, 136, 365, 399, 498, 579, 840, 880, 1085, 1328, 1397
Trevelyan, Lady: 1398
Trial by Jury: as issue in 1908 campaign, 1127
Trinity College, North Carolina: 228
Trollope, Anthony: 204, 400
Trowbridge, Samuel B. P.: id., 1430
Trunk Line Association: 1140
Trust Company of North America: and panic of (1907), 822, 830, 1317
Trusts: Bryan and, 395; as campaign issue (1906), 377, 458–60; as campaign issue (1908), 1128; Cleveland and, 328, 1259–60; conference on, 926; and harvester investigation, 763–65; and panic (1907), 750, 755; prosecution of, 27, 692–93, 751–52, 1260–61; public opinion and, 390; R on, 622, 1129; Standard Oil and, 293; m., 407
Tsushima: 427. *See also* Sea of Japan Battle
Tuckanuck, Massachusetts: 9, 1257
Tuckerman, Emily: letter to, 917
Turkestan: 16, 1370
Turkey: and Armenians, 113, 337, 345; army of, 17; in Balkans, 23; decorates Mrs. R, 1104; and German arms, 1293; internal affairs of, 1242; problem of, 1148; and Russian imperialism, 23; and Serbia, 1447; m., 359
Turner, Frederick J.: 1050
Turner, George K.: and Alaska treaty, 1493–94; letter to, 1515
Tuskegee Institute: 228. *See also* Washington, Booker T.
Twain, Mark: *see* Clemens, Samuel L.
Tweed, William M.: 1080, 1277
Twitchell, Ralph E.: id., 1098; 739; letter to, 1098
Tyler, John: 170
Tyree, Frank H.: 1418

Uganda: 1180, 1206, 1383–85
Uhrichsville, Ohio: 930
Umpqua Forest Reserve: 603
Uncle Remus's Home Magazine: 1108–11. *See also* Harris, Joel C.
Uncompahgre Forest Reserve: 603
Underwood, Herbert S.: 945
Unemployment: 971, 1300–01, 1304
Union Metallic Cartridge Company: 865
Union Pacific Railway Company: investigation of, 461, 622; and Moffat railroad,

277; prosecution of, 766–67; securities of, 710

Unions: as election issue, 376, 489; R on Cleveland's suits against, 1259–60; R on tyranny of, 366; strikes for eight-hour day, 380. *See also* American Federation of Labor; American Flint Glass Workers' Union; American Railway Union; Association of Street Railway Employees; Brotherhood of Locomotive Firemen; Brotherhood of Railroad Trainmen; Central Association of Building Trades of New York; International Association of Machinists; International Brotherhood of Electrical Workers; International Brotherhood of Steam Shovel and Dredge Men; International Brotherhood of Stationary Firemen; International Typographical Union; Iron Moulders' Union; Knights of Labor; Labor; Longshoremen's Union; Massachusetts Federation of Labor; National Window Glass Workers; Strikes; United Mine Workers; Western Federation of Miners

Unitarianism: as campaign issue (1908), 1179, 1200, 1285–86, 1289, 1304, 1313, 1318, 1333–34; m., 1398

United Breweries: 287

United Gas Improvement Company: 188

United Mine Workers: and bituminous wage agreement, 202–03; strikes by, 166, 1195; m., 1309

United Press Association: 450

United Railroads: 219

United Railways Company: 1262

United States v. *Armour and Company:* 195, 298

United States v. *MacAndrews and Forbes Co.:* 752

United States Army: administrative organization in, 980, 1445; appropriations for, 123; and Atlantic defense, 951; bandmasters in, 1365; and Brownsville affair, 384–85, 521; and Catholic property in Philippines, 171; cavalry in, 105, 363; chaplains in, 958; China hostilities, preparations for, 133; commissioned officers in, 514, 1016–17, 1320; compared with European, 600–01; and conservation, 816, 1067; and Cuba, 391, 414–15, 454, 474–75; desertions from, 205, 997; discipline in, 489–90, 498, 509, 965–66, 968, 1423; enlisted men in, 435, 715, 1016–17; field regulations, 1509; horsemanship, 897; and Indian attacks, 1448, 1450–51; machine-gun companies, 1319; maneuvers, 1446; and Mare Island Board, 955; and marine corps, 1389; marksmanship, 760; medical

services, 56, 893–95; and Mexican revolutionaries, 1100; Mounted Service School, 790; and national parks police, 1232, 1291; Negroes in, 385, 691, 1365; and Pacific defense, 937–39, 950–52; pack trains in, 1509; and Panama Canal, 587, 599; pensions, 1328; in Philippines, 127–28, 499; preparedness of, 725; presidential powers over, 1016–17, 1024–27; prisoners in, 384–85; promotions in, 123, 685, 804, 1000–01, 1024–27, 1039; Quartermasters Corps, 685, 697, 705; retirement in, 301; rotation of officers in, 905–06, 1006; salaries in, 1044; size of, 17, 358, 463, 641; and strikes, 214, 863, 866, 868–69, 895–96, 923, 927; training of, 139, 205, 651–52, 1475; and Venezuela campaign plans, 135; Y.M.C.A. in, 281. *See also* War Department

United States Army War College: 715; letter to, 1509

United States Express Conference: 1054

United States Foreign Policy: and balance of power in Asia, 474, 640, 912–13, 1514; complications for Taft administration, 1510–11; and Europe, 640; and Japanese war scare, 941, 946, 1342–43; and Latin America, 346, 626–29, 772, 879, 1408, 1445, 1539; minority rights, 207–08; and naval power, 398–99, 1432, 1503, 1507–08; as political issue, 265; and public opinion, 281–82, 344–45, 1408; R on, 420–21; R's big stick policy, 1410, 1445; state action and, 400–01; treaty making power and, 618–19, 1484, 1510–13. *See also* Colonialism; Disarmament; Imperialism; Investments; Merchant Marine; Open Door; *and by countries*

United States Government: employees of, 376, 950, 1446; historical research in, 632–33; publications of, 276, 1050; scientific work, 1268; supremacy over state, 365. *See also* Civil Service; Contracts; Legislation; Patronage; United States Supreme Court

Congress: achievements of, 365–67; cloture in, 150; conservatism of Senate, 151; and control of industry, 292; immunity of, 1424; and impeachment, 1474–81; investigations by, 34, 114–15, 187, 321–23, 445, 924, 1453, 1481; need for legislative compromises in, 147–48; and outgoing presidents, 1475–76, 1498–99; and patronage, 52–3, 304–05, 1111–12; popular election of Senators, 1274; relations with executive, 145, 1460, 1481; R on strength of Senate, 150–53; and secret service, 1424–25, 1459–60; Senate power to confirm appointments, 830; and spelling reform, 378; subservience to great corporations, 147; and tariff negotiations, 33; treaty powers of Senate, 33, 111, 147, 151, 281, 317–18, 346, 463, 644. *See also by subject of legislation*

Executive: administrative control within, 1274; Cannon on triumph of Congress over, 1460; and libel suits, 1416–17, 1419, 1425; nonpartisanship in administration, 111–12; powers in foreign affairs, 414, 1445; relations to Congress, 1481; R on powers of, 428, 430, 580, 1374, 1481, 1498, 1538–39; salaries of, 112; and secret service, 1527. *See also* Cabinet; *and agencies and executive departments by name*

United States Marine Corps: and Cuban revolution, 408–09; integration in Navy proposed, 563–64; and shipboard duty, 1389, 1525-26; and Panama election, 1082; and Venezuela, 984

United States Medal of Honor Club: 695

United States Military Academy: 123, 903, 1451, 1519

United States Mint: 213, 405–06

United States Naval Academy: Archibald R's plan to enter, 800; curriculum at, 903; hazing at, 143–45; judo at, 155; R recommends department of hygiene at, 1519; teaching personnel in, 734

United States Navy: administrative reform of, 1380, 1475, 1478–88; see Brownson, Willard H.; Capps, Washington L.; Key, Albert L.; Metcalf, Victor H.; Newberry, Truman H.; Newport Conference; Sims, William S.; Winslow, Cameron McR.; ammunition for, 149, 582–83; appropriations, *see* United States Navy, *Size of;* Asiatic Fleet, 77, 353; and Atlantic defense, 951; Atlantic Fleet, 343; battleship design, 706, 1108, 1237; Bureau of Construction and Repair, 121; Bureau of Medicine and Surgery, 56; Bureau of Navigation, 155, 876, 891–92; Bureau of Ordnance, 1446; and China, 77; coaling problems, 496, 512–13, 811–12, 1315; coastal defense, 148–49; colliers, 1220; collisions, 342, 362; contracts for battleships, 1015; and Cuban revolution, 391, 399, 408–09, 431, 474–75; defects in construction, 980, 1000, 1101–02, 1174, 1453–56, 1470–72; division of fleet, 1513, 1543; drydocks, 1525–26; efficiency of, 374, 1524; engineering equipment of, 511, 759; engineers in, 324; General Board, 353, 403, 645–46, 743, 745, 823, 982–83, 1108; German respect for, 168; Guam and, 989;

gun factory, 1015–16; in Hawaii, 912–13, 937–39, 1525; hospital ships, 876, 891, 893–95, 911–12; hygiene, 1519; and Jamaica earthquake, 579, 601–02; lubricants, 511–12; maneuvers of, 1446; and Mare Island Board, 955; meat purchases, 362; medical corps, 56, 534–35; monitors, 1011; and Monroe Doctrine, 1294; and Moody-Mahan Commission, 1487–88; and New York Yard, 362; and Newport Conference, 1101, 1107, 1166, 1174, 1199, 1204, 1383; and Norfolk Navy Yard, 362; and Pacific Coast dry dock, 955, and Pacific defenses, 912–14, 950–52, 956, 1001, 1006, 1008–09; and patriotic celebrations, 723; submarines, 10, 15, 749–50; Surgeon General, 56; turbines, 324, 1430; and Venezuela, 319, 358, 948, 1428; War College, 1101, 1107–08; war plans, 551; in West Indies, 319; William II on, 1164; yards, 220, 362, 986, 1001, 1032, 1488, 1536; Y.M.C.A. work in, 281

Armament of: and ammunition hoists, 1525; for battleships, 121, 545–49, 1200; compared with Japanese, 970; evaluation of gun sizes, 496, 970, 1446; five- and six-inch guns, 403; fourteen-inch guns, 1237, 1380, 1470–71; Mahan on, 427; on new ships, 166; problems of, 970; R on, 455, 475, 1166, 1174, 1248; six-inch guns, 334; torpedoes, 121, 658, 1197, 1278, 1525

Armor: battleship, 1200; on new ships, 980, 1166, 1453

Fleet Cruise: to Australia, 966, 979, 1159, 1188, 1210; criticism of, 1470; helps preserve peace, 1410; itinerary, 744–45, 791–92, 985, 993; to Japan, 979, 996; leaves for men on, 1412–13; misconduct on, 1314–15; to Peru, 958; prolonged, 952; return, 1411–12; R greets fleet, 1533; R on, 1087, 1498, 1538–39; m., 709, 717, 718, 720, 721, 725, 726, 734, 738, 759, 762, 779, 784, 797, 853, 940, 979, 1073, 1330

Gunnery: marksmanship, 760; Inspector of Target Practice, 333, 760; report on, 821; and Sea of Japan battle, 121; target practice, 333, 433, 437, 515, 663, 745, 791, 821, 993

Personnel: amusement of enlisted men, 435; bill on, 563, 572; board, 534–35; desertions, 997; diet, 515–16; discipline, 514–15, 911–12, 1470–72; education, 903; enlisted men, 301, 515–16; officers, 514, 534–35; physical exercise for, 861–62, 1475; promotions, 534–35, 563, 645–46, 1000–01, 1029, 1165, 1199; requirements for ship commanders, 905; reserve, 1392; retirements, 301, 1029; salaries, 561, 1044; in

Vatican: American diplomatic relations with, 335; diplomats of, 538–39; and France, 597; R on, 696; and Storer affair, 107–110. *See also* Pius X; Roman Catholic Church

Velvin, Ellen: 75

Venezuela: American claims against, 957; Cleveland and, 1352; Colombia and, 132; compared with Turkey, 1148; crisis in, 132; France and, 132; future relations with, 1511; Germany and, 358–59; Hague arbitration and, 319, 640; indiscretions of American minister in, 579, 602; military preparations by, 132; planned campaign against, 135, 984; public opinion on, 761, 1408; revolution in, 1427–28; R on, 119; ultimatum to Germany on, 1410; United States breaks relations with, 957; m., 1, 26, 234, 458

Venosta, Marquis: id., 252; and Algeciras conference, 252

Vermont: 277, 361. *See also* Patronage; Republican Party

Vermont: see United States Navy, *Ships*

Vernon, William T.: 130

Veterans: cabinet appointment of, 1043, 1363; Civil War, 154, 541, 882; Confederate, 368; and election (1908), 1195; Mexican War, 580; and patronage, 105, 1007; pensions to, 580; rivalry of Civil and Spanish-American War, 648–49; Taft's speech to, 1045; m., 391, 541. *See also* Rough Riders

Victor, Samuel G.: 969

Victor Emmanuel III: 1187

Victoria, Queen: 32

Vienna: 312

Vigilancia: see United States Navy, *Ships*

Vikings: 104

Villard, Oswald G.: id., ii, 1184; R on, 307, 420, 701, 1277, 1288, 1318–19, 1322–23, 1364; m., 1073

Vilter Manufacturing Company: 484

Vincennes *Sun:* 480

Vinght, Mr.: 746

Virginia: legislature endorses third term, 130; R consults president of university of, 908. *See also* Patronage; Republican Party

Virginia Carolina Chemical Co.: 1260

Vital Statistics Division: 1269

Vivian, John F.: 53, 54

Vladivostok: 5, 7, 296, 824

Vocational Education: 1227–29

Vorys, Arthur I: id., 720; and election campaign (1908), 720, 1042, 1099, 1104, 1113, 1149, 1245; and presidential nomination (1908), 727, 837; and patronage, 878; Taft letter to, 1247

Vreeland, Edward B.: 145, 153

Vreeland Bill: 908

Wabash case: 1297

Wadsworth, Elizabeth G. P.: 12, 799

Wadsworth, Herbert: 1338

Wadsworth, Mrs. Herbert: 1338

Wadsworth, James W.: id., i, 72; and Biological Survey, 578; and Hughes nomination, 828; and meat packing legislation, 292, 298–300; and patronage, 205; R on, 389; letters to, 282, 291, 294, 298

Wadsworth, James W., Jr.: id., iv, 850; elected speaker, N.Y. Assembly, 119–20, 124, 153; and N.Y. gubernatorial nomination, 1236; and patronage, 389; letter to, 124

Wadsworth, William A.: id., i, 131; 12, 799, 1035

Wagner, L. H.: 11

Wainwright, J. Mayhew: id., 120; 124

Wainwright, Richard: and navy yard commission, 1536; letter to, 1536

Waite, John D.: 936

Walcott, Charles D.: id., ii, 806; iii, 443; and African trip, 1412; and coal lands, 526; and Colorado River break, 974; and Geological Survey, 315–16; and Interior Department publications, 276; letters to, 531, 1093, 1268

Wales, Prince of: 1159

Walker, Albert H.: 1266

Walker, George R.: id., 134

Walker, James E.: 1165

Walker, John G.: id., i, 629; 74

Walker, Mr. (of Wyoming): 477–78

Walker Board (1896): 1101, 1102

Wall Street: attitude to R, 631, 706, 803, 885; and Brownsville affair, 534; and depression, 846; and election (1906), 460; and election (1908), 1368; and Grant, 1398; and immigration, 285; and New Mexico politics, 739; newspapers and, 753, 765, 777, 782, 798, 875; and panic (1907), 535, 621, 746–48, 822, 849; and politics, 264, 453; and premature release of message, 854; and presidential nomination (1908), 796; and railroads, 585; and Republican party, 429; R on, 266, 1012, 1446; and R's Provincetown speech, 760; and Schiff's speech, 131; and speculation, 81; symbol of privilege, 1049; and treasurer, Republican National Committee, 1117, 1123; views Cleveland as ideal president, 735; and West, 199

ruption, 944; R on, 311; speech at Harvard, 880; letters to, 221, 309, 880

Wister, Mrs. Owen: 229

Witherbee, Frank S.: id., i, 572; 944

Witherbee, Mrs. Frank S.: 944

Witherbee, John: 944

Witherbee, Walter: 929

Witte, Count Serge: id, iv, 1276; and anti-semitism in Russia, 207; and Russo-Japanese peace, 8, 22–23, 177–78; on U.S. and Anglo-Japanese alliance, 61; on Russian internal affairs, 62

Wolverton, Charles E.: 668; letter to, 85

Woman's Suffrage: 1341–42, 1373

Women and children: investigation of conditions of, 269, 594–95, 1301, 1445

Wood, Charles E. S.: id., ii, 1087; 21

Wood, Fremont: 189

Wood, James P.: id., 804; and Spanish Treaty Claims Commission, 803–04

Wood, Leonard: id., i, 690; and African trip, 1191; attacks on, 354; Cuban administration commended, 1386; and Cuban crisis, 419–20; compared with Cromer, 773; at French and German army maneuvers, 1021; health of, 127–28; and immigration, 294; and pack trains, 1509; and Philippines, 20, 138, 253–54, 256; m., 420, 774, 1000, 1520; letters to, 127, 135, 205, 294, 1386, 1389

Wood, Mrs. Leonard: m., 128, 1386, 1520

Woodford, Stewart L.: 1006

Woodruff, George W.: 1067

Woodruff, Timothy L.: id., ii, 908; and Hughes renomination (1908), 1193; and N.Y.S. election (1906), 439, 442–43, 453; as N.Y.S. gubernatorial possibility, 429, 437; and N.Y.S. Republican Committee Chairmanship, 153; and Senate candidacy, 1341; and Taft appointments, 1389; letters to, 454, 456, 461

Woodward, Mr.: 461

Woodward, Robert S.: id., 1479; letter to, 1479

Woods, William A.: 1059

Woods Hole Oceanographic Institution: 289

Woodstock, Vermont: 361

Workingmen's Party, California: 266

Workmen's Compensation: see Employer's Liability

World's Student Christian Federation: 1281

World's Work: 1169, 1340

Wotherspoon, William W.: id., 715; and brigadier generalship, 715; and machine guns, 1319; and Navy Yard Commission, 1526

Wrest Park: 503

Wright, Carroll D.: id., i, 449; and anthracite strike, 1155

Wright, Francis M.: and Bucks case, 1196, 1442; R on appointment of, 667

Wright, J. G.: 372

Wright, Luke E.: id., iii, 269; appointed ambassador to Japan, 128–29; appointed Secretary of War, 1095; and Cuban cable rights, 1105; and Gentlemen's Agreement, 589; as Gold Democrat, 1362; and lock canal question, 1422; and Panama Canal ship purchase, 1220, 1377–78, 1391; as representative of South, 1043; R satisfaction with, 1099; m., 773, 1128, 1138; letters to, 128, 1319, 1365, 1378, 1390, 1507, 1520

Wright, Mrs. Luke E.: 129

Wright, Marcus J.: 553

Wu Ting-fang: Chinese minister to U.S., 809

Wyckoff, Walter A.: id., iii, 91; 179

Wynne, John J.: 1326

Wynne, Robert J.: id., iii, 461; Consul General, 732; m., 1043

Wyoming: forest reserves in, 603–04; land frauds in, 445, 481, 519–20, 564, 570–71; and statehood, 477; woman's suffrage in, 1373. See also Republican Party

Wyoming: see United States Navy, Ships

Yale University: athletics at, 46, 76, 82, 93–4, 853, 1183, 1190, 1375, 1382; and Boxer Indemnity, 206; forest school, 1067; law school, 47; president of, consulted by R, 908; R on graduates of, 732; Root lectures at, 728–29; m., 134, 267, 664, 929, 1068, 1279. See also Hadley, Arthur T.

Yamamoto, Tatsuo: 713, 718

Yancy, William L.: 225

Yard, Robert S.: id., 75

Ybarra, Alejandro: 132

Ybeni, General: see Ybarra, Alejandro

Yellow Fever: 410

Yellow Peril: 787, 1164, 1293. See also William II

Yellow Sea, Battle of: 121

Yellowstone Forest Reserve: 603

Yellowstone National Park: robbery in, 1232, 1290–91; policing of, 1241; and preservation of game, 1233

Yerby, William J.: 101

Yi Hiung: 96

Y.M.C.A.: see Young Men's Christian Association

Yoakum, B. F.: 617

York Gazette: 1442

Yosemite National Park: 293–94

Yosemite Valley: 793
Young, J. S., Company: 752
Young, James A.: 304, 306
Young, Miss: 891
Young, Samuel B. M.: on McKinley appointments, 1257; resigns as superintendent, Yellowstone Park, 1290–91; letters to, 1232, 1241, 1290
Young, Mrs. Samuel B. M.: 1232, 1291
Young Men's Christian Association: Quentin and. 016: work of. 281; m., 443, 1281

Younghusband, George J.: id., iii, 83; 499
Youngman, Elmer H.: id., 1046; letter to, 1046
Youngs, William J.: id., ii, 909; letter to, 807
Youngs, Mrs. William J.: 807
Yuma, Arizona: 526

Zangwill, Israel: id., 1288; letter to, 1288
Zangwill, Mrs. Israel: 1288, 1289
Zola, Émile: R on, 179, 264